Introductory Financial Accounting for Business

Second Edition

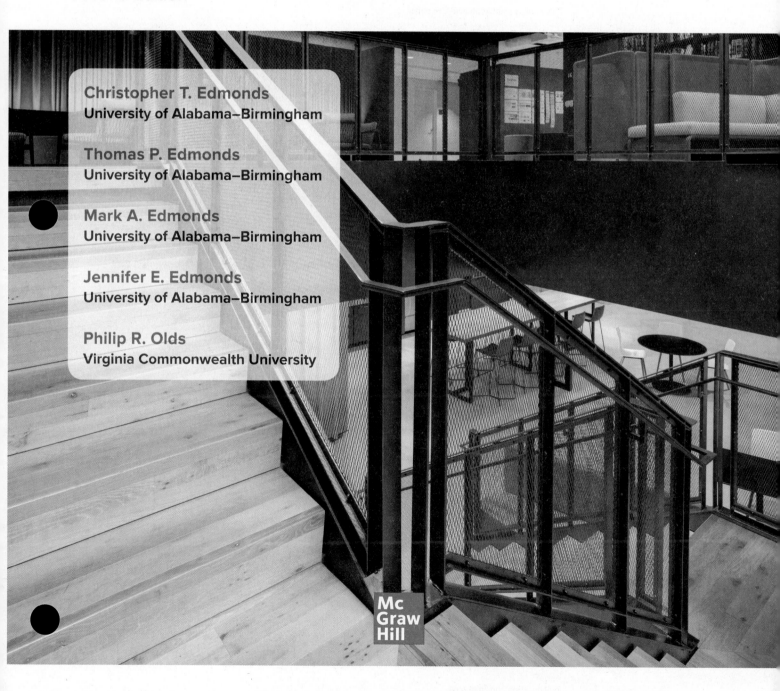

Christopher T. Edmonds
University of Alabama–Birmingham

Thomas P. Edmonds
University of Alabama–Birmingham

Mark A. Edmonds
University of Alabama–Birmingham

Jennifer E. Edmonds
University of Alabama–Birmingham

Philip R. Olds
Virginia Commonwealth University

Mc
Graw
Hill

INTRODUCTORY FINANCIAL ACCOUNTING FOR BUSINESS, SECOND EDITION

Published by McGraw-Hill Education, 2 Penn Plaza, New York, NY 10121. Copyright © 2021 by McGraw-Hill Education. All rights reserved. Printed in the United States of America. No part of this publication may be reproduced or distributed in any form or by any means, or stored in a database or retrieval system, without the prior written consent of McGraw-Hill Education, including, but not limited to, in any network or other electronic storage or transmission, or broadcast for distance learning.

Some ancillaries, including electronic and print components, may not be available to customers outside the United States.

This book is printed on acid-free paper.

1 2 3 4 5 6 7 8 9 LWI 21 20

ISBN   978-1-260-81444-6 (bound edition)
MHID 1-260-81444-0 (bound edition)
ISBN   978-1-264-09693-0 (loose leaf edition)
MHID 1-264-09693-3 (loose leaf edition)

Accounting Director: *Rebecca Olson*
Product Developers: *Erin Quinones / Danielle McLimore*
Marketing Manager: *Zachary Rudin*
Lead Content Project Managers: *Jill Eccher / Brian Nacik*
Senior Buyer: *Susan K. Culbertson*
Senior Designer: *Matt Diamond*
Content Licensing Specialist: *Melissa Homer*
Cover Image: *©McGraw-Hill Education*
Compositor: *Aptara®, Inc.*

All credits appearing on page or at the end of the book are considered to be an extension of the copyright page.

Library of Congress Cataloging-in-Publication Data

Names: Edmonds, Christopher T., author.
Title: Introductory financial accounting for business / Christopher T.
   Edmonds [and three others].
Description: Second edition. | New York, NY : McGraw-Hill Education, [2021]
   | Includes index.
Identifiers: LCCN 2019030798 | ISBN 9781260814446 (hardcover ; alk. paper)
   | ISBN 1260814440 (hardcover ; alk. paper) | ISBN 9781264096930 (spiral bound)
Subjects: LCSH: Accounting.
Classification: LCC HF5636 .E363 2021 | DDC 657–dc23
LC record available at https://lccn.loc.gov/2019030798

The Internet addresses listed in the text were accurate at the time of publication. The inclusion of a website does not indicate an endorsement by the authors or McGraw-Hill Education, and McGraw-Hill Education does not guarantee the accuracy of the information presented at these sites.

This book is dedicated to our students, whose questions have so frequently caused us to reevaluate our method of presentation that the students themselves have become major contributors to the development of this text.

Christopher T. Edmonds

Courtesy of
Christopher Edmonds

Christopher T. Edmonds, PhD, is an Associate Professor in the Department of Accounting and Finance at the UAB Collat School of Business. He is the course coordinator for the face-to-face and online principles of accounting courses. Dr. Edmonds specializes in teaching and developing engaging face-to-face and online introductory accounting courses. He is a frequent speaker at conferences and universities on best teaching practices and has delivered over 30 professional teaching workshops. His passion for helping students learn inspired him to create hundreds of short videos teaching the fundamental concepts of accounting. This work led to the publication of the first interactive video textbook for introductory accounting. Dr. Edmonds has received numerous prestigious teaching awards, including the UAB President's Award for Excellence in Teaching, UAB Faculty Student Success Award, UAB Transformative Online Course Award, UAB Loudell Ellis Robinson Classroom Teaching Award, UAB Disability Support Recognition Award, and the Virginia Tech Favorite Faculty Award. He has published four textbooks and has written numerous articles that have appeared in publications, including *The Accounting Review, Auditing: A Journal of Practice & Theory, Journal of Accounting and Public Policy, Issues in Accounting Education, Advances in Accounting Education, Advances in Accounting,* and *Review of Quantitative Finance and Accounting.* Dr. Edmonds started his career as a web application developer creating software solutions to put newspapers online. He began his academic training at Colorado State University. He obtained an MBA from UAB. His PhD with a major in accounting was awarded by Virginia Polytechnic Institute and State University. Check out his blog at **www.accountingstepbystep.com**.

Thomas P. Edmonds

Courtesy of
Thomas Edmonds

Thomas P. Edmonds, PhD, is Professor Emeritus in the Department of Accounting at the University of Alabama at Birmingham (UAB). He has been actively involved in teaching accounting principles throughout his academic career. Dr. Edmonds has coordinated the accounting principles courses at the University of Houston and UAB. He has taught introductory accounting in mass sections and in distance learning programs. He has received several prestigious teaching awards, including the Alabama Society of CPAs Outstanding Educator Award, the UAB President's Excellence in Teaching Award, and the distinguished Ellen Gregg Ingalls Award for excellence in classroom teaching. He has written numerous articles that have appeared in many publications, including *Issues in Accounting,* the *Journal of Accounting Education, Advances in Accounting Education, Accounting Education: A Journal of Theory, Practice and Research, The Accounting Review, Advances in Accounting,* the *Journal of Accountancy, Management Accounting,* the *Journal of Commercial Bank Lending,* the *Banker's Magazine,* and the *Journal of Accounting, Auditing, and Finance.* Dr. Edmonds has served as a member of the editorial board for *Advances in Accounting: Teaching and Curriculum Innovations* and *Issues in Accounting Education.* He has published five textbooks, five practice problems (including two computerized problems), and a variety of supplemental materials including study guides, work papers, and solutions manuals. Dr. Edmonds's writing is influenced by a wide range of business experience. He is a successful entrepreneur. He has worked as a management accountant for Refrigerated Transport, a trucking company. Dr. Edmonds also worked in the not-for-profit sector as a commercial lending officer for the Federal Home Loan Bank. In addition, he has acted as a consultant to major corporations, including First City Bank of Houston (now Citi Bank), AmSouth Bank in Birmingham (now Regions Bank), Texaco, and Cortland Chemicals. Dr. Edmonds began his academic training at Young Harris Community College in Young Harris, Georgia. He received a BBA degree with a major in finance from Georgia State University in Atlanta, Georgia. He obtained an MBA with a concentration in finance from St. Mary's University in San Antonio, Texas. His PhD with a major in accounting was awarded by Georgia State University. Dr. Edmonds's work experience and academic training have enabled him to bring a unique user perspective to this textbook.

Mark A. Edmonds

Mark A. Edmonds, PhD, CPA, is an Assistant Professor in the Department of Accounting and Finance at the University of Alabama at Birmingham. He has taught principles and advanced accounting classes in face-to-face, flipped, and online formats. He is the recipient of the Loudell Ellis Robinson excellence in teaching award. Dr. Edmonds began his career providing assurance services for the internationally recognized accounting firm Ernst & Young. At the conclusion of his professional service, he obtained his PhD from Southern Illinois University Carbondale. He serves as the education adviser on the board of the Institute of Internal Auditors Birmingham Chapter. Dr. Edmonds's research focuses on alternative learning strategies and auditor decision making.

Courtesy of
Mark Edmonds

Jennifer E. Edmonds

Jennifer Echols Edmonds, PhD, is an Associate Professor at the University of Alabama at Birmingham (UAB) Collat School of Business. Her primary teaching areas are financial and managerial accounting. She has experience teaching in the undergraduate, MAC, and MBA programs and currently serves as the course coordinator for the managerial accounting sequence at UAB. She has received the UAB Loudell Ellis Robinson Classroom Teaching Award, as well as teaching grants from Deloitte, UAB, and Virginia Tech. She created teaching resources for incorporating International Financial Reporting Standards into Intermediate Accounting that were published online at the American Accounting Association. Dr. Edmonds is also active in the research community. She has published articles in prominent journals such as *Journal of Accounting and Public Policy, Advances in Accounting, Research in Accounting Regulation*, and *The CPA Journal*. Dr. Edmonds received a bachelor's degree in accounting from Birmingham-Southern College and completed her master's and PhD degrees in accounting at Virginia Polytechnic Institute and State University.

Courtesy of
Jennifer Edmonds

Philip R. Olds

Professor Olds is Associate Professor of Accounting at Virginia Commonwealth University (VCU). He serves as the coordinator of the introduction to accounting courses at VCU. Professor Olds received his AS degree from Brunswick Junior College in Brunswick, Georgia (now College of Coastal Georgia). He received a BBA in accounting from Georgia Southern College (now Georgia Southern University), and his MPA and PhD are from Georgia State University. After graduating from Georgia Southern, he worked as an auditor with the U.S. Department of Labor in Atlanta, Georgia. A former CPA in Virginia, Professor Olds has published articles in various professional journals and presented papers at national and regional conferences. He also served as the faculty adviser to the VCU chapter of Beta Alpha Psi for five years. In 1989, he was recognized with an Outstanding Faculty Vice-President Award by the national Beta Alpha Psi organization. Professor Olds has received both the Distinguished Teaching Award and the Distinguished Service Award from the VCU School of Business. Most recently, he received the university's award for maintaining High Ethical and Academic Standards While Advocating for Student-Athletes and Their Quest Towards a Degree.

Courtesy of Philip Olds

AUTHORS' VIEW OF

● PREPARING ACCOUNTING STUDENTS FOR A CHANGING BUSINESS ENVIRONMENT

Automated data capture, data analytics, and artificial intelligence are transforming the business environment. Technology has greatly reduced or, in some cases, eliminated the need for humans to be involved in recording and reporting procedures. Rather than gathering information, today's students will be required to analyze and interpret information. They will have to make decisions early and often. In summary, instead of memorizing recording procedures, today's students must learn to think like business professionals.

Business professionals tend to think about bottom-line consequences: If I do this or that, how will it affect my company's net income, total assets, cash flow, and so on? We use a financial statements model to teach students how to mimic this thought process. The model arranges the balance sheet, income statement, and statement of cash flows horizontally across a single line of text, as shown here:

Balance Sheet					Income Statement					Statement of Cash Flows
Assets	=	Liab.	+	Equity	Rev.	–	Exp.	=	Net Inc.	

Throughout the text, students are taught to show how accounting events affect the statements represented in the model. For example, an $8,400 cash payment to settle an interest payable liability would require the student to show the effects as follows:

Balance Sheet					Income Statement					Statement of Cash Flows	
Assets	=	Liab.	+	Equity	Rev.	–	Exp.	=	Net Inc.		
(8,400)		(8,400)		NA	NA		NA		NA	(8,400)	OA

In the statement of cash flows, the student is required not only to identify the item as an inflow or outflow, but also to classify the item as an operating activity (OA), investing activity (IA), or financing activity (FA).

● WITHOUT DEBITS AND CREDITS, IMPLEMENTATION AND LEARNING ARE EASY

Instructors have little difficulty implementing the statements model approach. Indeed, it is easier to show students how a single event affects financial statements than it is to show them how a series of events are recorded and then summarized in financial statements. Instead of using confusing debit/credit terminology, common increase/decrease terminology is all that is necessary to explain the interrelationships between business events and how they affect financial statements. This is analogous to skipping the middleman: instead of going from events to financial statements through a set of recording procedures, you skip the recording procedures and focus on a direct link between events and statement effects. Accounting comes alive with purpose, rather than being reduced to a boring memorization task. Student comprehension and motivation increase, with virtually no learning curve for instructors.

The business-oriented statements model approach does not require knowledge of debit and credit terminology. Indeed, early exposure to debit and credit terminology can hinder learning. After all, a debit or a credit is just a confusing way of saying an increase or a decrease. We believe that students should learn the essential relationships between events and statements before technical jargon is used to describe those relationships. The appropriate place to introduce debits and credits is at the end, rather than the beginning, of the text.

Some worry that accounting majors will not get enough exposure to recording procedures to prepare them for intermediate accounting. We provide a solution to this dilemma. Specifically, we offer two capstone course projects. These projects are designed to be covered during the last two weeks of class. By this time, students will have enough exposure to accounting to classify themselves as accounting majors or general business students. Those who consider themselves accounting majors should be assigned the General Ledger Capstone Project, while other students should be assigned the Financial Statement Analysis Capstone Project. The General Ledger Capstone Project provides instructors with a mechanism to drill students about debits and credits, while the Financial Statement Analysis Capstone Project teaches students how to use financial information to make management and investment decisions. These projects let instructors solve the age-old problem of accommodating the differing needs of accounting majors versus general business students. You can find a detailed discussion of these capstone course projects in the "How Are Chapter Concepts Reinforced?" section of this book's front matter.

This text includes all topics that are normally covered in a traditional introductory financial accounting book, including debits, credits, and all of the typical recording procedures associated with double-entry accounting. As a result, any questions that might be raised regarding accreditation and transfer credit can be easily answered.

"Sequential approach evident throughout the chapters. Building . . . building . . . building. . . . done!"

—NANCY SNOW
UNIVERSITY OF TOLEDO

EMPIRICAL EVIDENCE SUPPORTING A DELAYED DEBITS/CREDITS APPROACH FOR ACCOUNTING MAJORS

Shifting the focus from debits and credits to financial statement impacts does not mean that accounting majors will be ill-prepared for intermediate. We compared student performance under the "traditional" approach of introducing debits and credits early in the course (Chapter 3) to the "delayed" approach of introducing debits and credits at the end of the course (Chapter 13). Across a sample of 773 introductory students, we compared students' ability to 1) recognize financial statement impacts and 2) record journal entries at the end of the introductory accounting course. We found that students in the "delayed" group did significantly better in their ability to recognize the impact of accounting events on financial statements. Interestingly, we found no difference in their ability to record journal entries even though the "delayed" group was only exposed to this material briefly at the end of the course. In fact, students in the "delayed" group actually scored higher on the journal entry assessment, although the difference was not statistically significant.

A firm understanding of the relationship between accounting events and the accounting equation facilitates the process of learning debits/credits. Since students in the delayed group had more exposure to these relationships, they were able to grasp debit/credit terminology quickly. This conclusion is consistent with the education literature that shows knowledge retention improves when material is introduced in a sequential fashion. For more information on this study contact Chris Edmonds, cedmonds@gmail.com.

EXPOSURE TO DATA ANALYTICS

Beyond learning to think like business professionals, students need exposure to data analytics software. Just as spreadsheet software transformed accounting practice, data analytics is likely to have a similar impact. While there is general agreement that introductory accounting students need exposure to data analytics, agreement regarding the level and type of exposure is evolving. Do students need to know how to use the software or will the ability to interpret the output of the software be sufficient? We offer opportunities for you to expose your students to either or both options.

For those looking to give their students a deeper dive into data analytics, we offer an in-depth project, Applying Tableau, where students get hands-on operational experience with the software to answer a variety of business type questions. The answers to Applying Tableau are auto-gradable in *Connect*, saving you valuable time. Applying Tableau includes a tutorial video that walks students through the Tableau software and demonstrates the basic skills students need to get started using the software. A thorough description of this project is located in Appendix H at the end of the text.

For those who prefer to focus their students on understanding outputs rather than learning software, we have included short exercises, called Tableau Dashboard Activities, at the end of each chapter requiring students to make decisions using Tableau dashboards. These Tableau Dashboard Activities do not require students to learn Tableau. Instead, the Tableau dashboards are served up directly within *Connect* and accompanied by auto-gradable questions that students must answer based on the visualizations. The use of these Tableau Dashboard Activities creates a streamlined, integrated experience and allows students to focus on interpreting the outputs rather than creating them.

Having multiple options for teaching data analytics to your students gives you flexibility in how you want to incorporate these resources into your classroom. As data analytics trends continue to evolve, these resources should keep your curriculum current and your students up to date.

USING ANALYTICS TO IMPROVE VIDEO QUALITY

We know that there are a lot of videos out there, but all videos are not equal. In order for a video to be successful, students must watch it. If students stop watching in the early stages of a video, you know that they are not getting the content exposure they need and you can rest assured that failure is just around the corner. Based on this rationale, we have implemented a continuous quality improvement program for the videos that accompany our texts. Specifically, we analyze drop and finish rates to determine which videos are working and which ones are not. A typical analytical report is shown here:

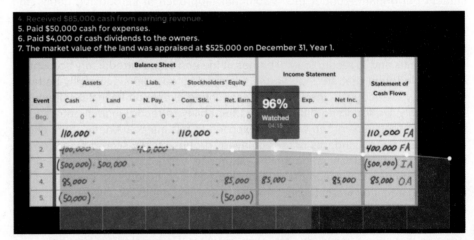

This report shows that the video kept 96 percent of students tuned-in at the half-way point and 85 percent of students completed the entire video. While there is always room for improvement, this video produced a high-quality result. We completed an extensive analysis of all first edition videos and replaced select videos that had a finish rate of less than 80 percent. The results of this analysis lead us to create new and/or improved videos for learning objectives 1-1, 4-1, 4-7, 7-1, 7-2, 7-3, 8-2, 8-5, and 8-8.

If you have questions or comments regarding the lecture videos, please contact Chris Edmonds at cedmonds@gmail.com.

STEP-BY-STEP LEARNING APPROACH

The order in which material is presented can strongly influence what is learned, how fast it is learned, and even whether the material is learned at all. (1) Traditionally, teaching the first course in accounting starts with an overview of a full set of financial statements. However, many introductory students are not equipped to comprehend the items shown in the financial statements. Since terms such as *accounts receivable, accumulated depreciation, prepaid expenses,* etc. are not easily explained to a beginner, students are forced to memorize. Confusion and boredom follow in quick pursuit.

In contrast, this text employs a sequential, or step-by-step, learning approach. The text begins with the events rather than the statements that result from the events. Each time a new event is introduced, the terms presented in the event are defined and the effects of the event on the accounting equation are explained. Finally, students are shown how the information in the accounting equation is used to prepare financial statements. At no time are students exposed to terms that have not been fully explained. In other words, information is presented in a step-wise fashion with each new step following logically from the previous one. This sequential approach is used throughout the text. For example, cash transactions are introduced in Chapter 1, accrual events in Chapter 2, and deferral transactions in Chapter 3. Other texts traditionally tend to introduce these events simultaneously, which can result in information overload and lead to memorization. In contrast, our step-by-step approach gradually introduces concepts in a logical sequence that promotes understanding and stimulates interest while increasing motivation and engagement.

STATEMENT OF CASH FLOWS COVERED THROUGHOUT THE TEXT

The transaction-by-transaction analysis we use in the financial statements model enables an early introduction to the statement of cash flows. While the statement of cash flows is critically important in the real world, coverage of this statement in traditional textbooks is usually slighted and relegated to the last chapter of the text. The usual justification for this treatment is that teaching students to convert accrual accounting data into cash flow is complicated. In fact, it does not have to be this way. We removed the complexity by implementing a more direct method: a transaction-by-transaction teaching strategy.

We begin by defining the terms *operating*, *investing*, and *financing activities*. Thereafter, students are required to classify individual cash events as belonging to one of the three categories. As shown earlier, we implement this strategy via the financial statements model. The last column of the statements model represents the statement of cash flows. In this column, students distinguish between cash inflows and outflows and classify each cash flow as being an operating activity (OA), an investing activity (IA), or a financing activity (FA). See the entry for the $8,400 cash payment to settle an interest payable liability that was shown in the statements model earlier as an example.

This teaching strategy is applied consistently through the first 11 chapters. As a result, students develop the ability to distinguish between operating, investing, and financing activities and to prepare a statement of cash flows. This knowledge base provides the foundation for grasping the more complicated process of converting accrual accounting numbers to their cash flow equivalents, which is presented in Chapter 12.

● FINANCIAL STATEMENT ANALYSIS

The text provides extensive coverage of financial statement analysis. A separate section titled "The Financial Analyst" is included in each chapter. This section covers the financial ratios related to the topics covered in the chapter. For example, the *accounts receivable turnover ratio* and *number of days to collect receivables* are covered in the receivables chapter. Likewise, *inventory turnover* and *number of days to sell inventory* are covered in the merchandise inventory chapter. We not only provide coverage of how to calculate the ratios but also provide real-world industry data to help students identify benchmarks and learn how to make meaningful comparisons of financial performance. In other words, the text shows students how to interpret ratios, as well as how to calculate them.

In addition, the text includes a separate chapter, Chapter 14, which provides in-depth coverage of the analysis of financial statements. This chapter includes two full sets of exercises, problems, and test bank material, along with all the *Connect* features. Finally, the appendices of the text include two comprehensive financial statement analysis projects. One pertains to Target's 10K annual report, which is included in the text. The other is an open-ended project that allows the instructor or the student to choose the company to be analyzed.

Once students understand how events affect financial statements, the next step is understanding how to analyze statements. The choice to cover financial statement analysis (FSA) at the introductory level really depends on the level of your students. We provide thorough coverage of FSA for the introductory level, but we separate it in such a way that covering this topic is left to the discretion of the professor.

(1) Frank E. Ritter; et al., eds. (2007). *In order to learn: How the sequence of topics influences learning*. Oxford series on cognitive models and architectures. Oxford/ New York: Oxford University Press.

WHAT WE DID TO MAKE IT BETTER

We profoundly appreciate the comments and suggestions provided by so many of the first edition adopters and reviewers of *Introductory Financial Accounting for Business*. In response, we made the following three major enhancements to the text and supporting materials.

Response to Adopter/Reviewer Suggestions

Data Analytics

Until recently data analytics, business intelligence, and big data were only buzz words that have now become essential components of the accounting curriculum at virtually all forward-thinking business schools. This edition offers a convenient way to address this subject matter in your introductory accounting course. Specifically, we offer a data analytics project that requires students to create data visualizations from a large data set in Tableau. Tableau is widely recognized as one of the leading business intelligence software packages in practice today. The details of this project can be found in Appendix H located in the end-of-text materials. Instructors can find more information in the Instructor Resource Center.

Test bank enhancements

Many of our adopters and reviewers recommended that we expand the test bank to include questions that specifically address the horizontal financial statements model. In response, we have added multiple-choice questions in each chapter that directly relate to this model. Here is an example:

Jantzen Company recorded employee salaries earned but not yet paid. Which of the following represents the effect of this transaction on the financial statements?

	Balance Sheet			Income Statement			Statement of Cash Flows
	Assets	= Liab.	+ Stk. Equity	Rev.	− Exp.	= Net Inc.	
a.	+	+	n/a	+	n/a	+	OA
b.	n/a	+	−	n/a	+	−	IA
c.	−	n/a	−	n/a	+	−	n/a
d.	n/a	+	−	n/a	+	−	n/a

The correct answer is "d". Liabilities (Salaries Payable) increase. Expenses (Salaries Expense) increase thereby decreasing net income and retained earnings. Cash flow is not affected. Overall, the test bank revision includes more than 50 new questions. We have also worked to make sure that consistent terminology is used across the text and test bank. We understand that assessment is an important part of teaching and hope that these changes will improve teaching and learning with the text.

Student Active Learning Worksheets

An increasing number of students are choosing to adopt the electronic version of textbooks. Since many students do not bring computers to class, working a particular exercise or problem in class is frustrated by the fact that students may not have access to the exercise or problem being worked. To resolve this issue, we provided a set of Active Learning Worksheets that included copies of the Set B exercises and problems. The blank forms include guidance and check figures designed to facilitate student engagement in the classroom. These Active Learning Worksheets are available as downloadable Word documents via McGraw-Hill *Connect*. An example is shown next.

Exercise 2-1B, Requirement a, Appears as Follows:

Exercise 2-1B *Recording events in a horizontal financial statements model*

The Bruce Spruce Co. experienced the following events during its first year of operations, Year 1:

1. Acquired $75,000 cash by issuing common stock.
2. Earned $48,000 cash revenue.
3. Paid $34,000 cash for operating expenses.
4. Borrowed $20,000 cash from a bank.
5. Paid $38,000 cash to purchase land.
6. Paid a $2,000 cash dividend.

Required

a. Use a horizontal financial statements model to show how each event affects the balance sheet, income statement, and statement of cash flows. More specifically, record the amounts of the events into the model. Also, in the Statement of Cash Flows column, classify the cash flows as operating activities (OA), investing activities (IA), or financing activities (FA). The first transaction is shown as an example.

	Balance Sheet									Income Statement					Statement of Cash Flows
	Assets			=	Liab.	+	Stk. Equity								
					Notes		Com.		Ret.						
Event	Cash	+	Land	=	Pay.	+	Stk.	+	Earn.	Rev.	−	Exp.	=	Net Inc.	
1.	75,000	+	NA	=	NA	+	75,000	+	NA	NA	−	NA	=	NA	75,000 FA

Student Active Learning Worksheet for Exercise 2-1B, Requirement a, Appears as Follows:

Exercise 2-1B *Requirement An Active Learning Worksheet*

The Bruce Spruce Co.
Horizontal Statements Model for Year 1

	Balance Sheet									Income Statement					Statement of Cash Flows
	Assets			=	Liab.	+	Stockholders' Equity								
					Notes		Common		Retained					Net	
Event	Cash	+	Land	=	Payable	+	Stock	+	Earnings	Rev.	−	Exp.	=	Inc.	
1.	75,000	+	NA	=	NA	+	75,000	+	NA	NA	−	NA	=	NA	75,000 FA
2.															
3.															
4.															
5.															
6.															
	69,000	+ 38,000	=	20,000	+	75,000	+	12,000		48,000	−	34,000	=	14,000	69,000 NC

Instructor Active Learning Worksheets

We also provide an instructor version of the Active Learning Worksheets. The instructor version shows exercises and problems along with the corresponding solution. Matching the exercises and problems with solutions avoids the necessity of flipping back and forth between the textbook and the solutions manual. It is now possible to display both the exercise or problem and the corresponding solution simultaneously. An example of the solution for Exercise 2-1B instructor version appears next. Although a copy of the exercise also appears in the instructor version, we do not show that here due to space limitations.

Instructor Active Learning Worksheet (Solution)

		The Bruce Spruce Co.										
		Horizontal Statements Model for Year 1										

	Balance Sheet							Income Statement				Statement of Cash Flows
	Assets			= Liab.	+	Stockholders' Equity						
Event	Cash	+	Land	= Notes Payable	+	Common Stock	+ Retained Earnings	Rev.	−	Exp.	= Net Inc.	
1.	75,000	+	NA	= NA	+	75,000	+ NA	NA	−	NA	= NA	75,000 FA
2.	48,000	+	NA	= NA	+	NA	+ 48,000	48,000	−	NA	= 48,000	48,000 OA
3.	(34,000)	+	NA	= NA	+	NA	+ (34,000)	NA	−	34,000	= (34,000)	(34,000) OA
4.	20,000	+	NA	= 20,000	+	NA	+ NA	NA	−	NA	= NA	20,000 FA
5.	(38,000)	+	38,000	= NA	+	NA	+ NA	NA	−	NA	= NA	(38,000) IA
6.	(2,000)	+	NA	= NA	+	NA	+ (2,000)	NA	−	NA	= NA	(2,000) FA
	69,000	+	38,000	= 20,000	+	75,000	+ 12,000	48,000	−	34,000	= 14,000	69,000 NC

The instructor version of the Active Learning Worksheets is provided in an electronic format using Microsoft Word documents. The Active Learning Worksheets provide innovative opportunities to improve classroom presentations. Just open a Word document and display any Set B exercise or problem along with the corresponding solutions. With a couple of keystrokes, you can hide any portion of a solution. The hidden data can be made to reappear as the instructor discusses the solution. Not only will you avoid the annoying chalk dust, but your students will appreciate a presentation that perfectly matches their working paper forms. A short video that shows you how to implement this very attractive feature is available in the instructor resources section of *Connect*.

Other Improvements

In addition to the three major enhancements described above we made several other changes as described below:

Improved Readability — Improved readability through the use of more consistent terminology and the reduction of duplicate terminology. In Chapters 1 through 12 we removed all references to terms such as ledger, journals, and entries. This allowed us to improve our focus on conceptual issues prior to the introduction of recording procedures. Procedural issues including debit/credit terminology, journals, ledgers, closing, and other recording practices are introduced in Chapter 13.

Reorganized Coverage of Business Liquidations — To reduce the possibility of information overload in Chapter 1, we moved the coverage of business liquidations to Chapter 11.

Debit/Credit Decision Aid — Employed a three-step decision aid to teach students to use debit/credit terminology to describe increases and decreases in account balances.

Added content related to end-of-period adjustments — In Chapter 2, relabeled "Event 6" and "Adj. 1" and added a discussion of the adjusting process. All other events related to adjustments were labeled with the "Adj." prefix. The goal here was to explain the need for end-of-period adjustments and to label events so as to distinguish between those occurring during an accounting period from the adjustments required at the end of an accounting period.

Redesigned Exhibits 3.2 and 3.7 — Replaced the display containing ledger accounts with a display that shows data in an accounting equation. The change results in consistency in the way content is shown across Chapters 1, 2, and 3.

Improved coverage of freight terms — In Chapter 5 we added content (text and new Exhibits 4-3 and 4-4) to better explain freight terms (FOB Shipping Point and FOB Destination).

Uncollectible accounts expense versus bad debts expense — While the account title **bad debts expense** is frequently used in practice, the term is a misnomer because it is a receivable rather than a debt that has turned bad. To avoid confusion in the early stages of the learning process the author team has chosen to use the term uncollectible accounts expense, which provides an accurate description of the actual expense. Even so, we have added a footnote in Chapter 7 that alerts instructors to the term and provides an explanation as to why we use uncollectible accounts expense rather than bad debts expense.

Double taxation — In Chapter 11 we revised the discussion regarding double taxation to reflect the new 21% corporate rates.

Maintaining Currency

As with all new editions, we conducted a thorough review of all features and made extensive changes to ensure that all content is current and relevant. The specific changes we made are highlighted here.

Chapter 1 An Introduction to Accounting

• Revised *The Curious Accountant* 1 & 2 content
• Revised *Focus on International Issues* text box that includes IFRS coverage
• Updated Exhibit 1.18 with new real-world data
• Updated exercises, problems, and cases

Chapter 2 Accounting for Accruals

• Updated *The Curious Accountant* content
• Added new International Issues feature
• Updated exercises, problems, and cases

Chapter 3 Accounting for Deferrals

• Updated *The Curious Accountant* content
• Revised *Reality Bytes* feature
• Updated Exhibit 3.6 with new real-world data
• Updated Exhibit 3.10 with new real-world data
• Updated exercises, problems, and cases

Chapter 4 Accounting for Merchandising Businesses

• Updated *The Curious Accountant* content.
• Updated Exhibit 4.1 with new real-world data
• Updated Exhibit 4.11 with new real-world data
• Updated exercises, problems, and cases

Chapter 5 Accounting for Inventories

• Revised *The Curious Accountant* content
• Updated the *Focus on International Issues* feature
• Revised *Reality Bytes* feature
• Updated Exhibit 5.6 with new real-world data
• Updated exercises, problems, and cases

Chapter 6 Internal Control and Accounting for Cash

• Updated *The Curious Accountant* content
• Updated exercises, problems, and cases

Chapter 7 Accounting for Receivables

- Revised *The Curious Accountant* content
- Updated *Reality Bytes* feature.
- Updated Exhibit 7.7 with new real-world data
- Updated Exhibit 7.8 with new real-world data
- Updated exercises, problems, and cases

Chapter 8 Accounting for Long-Term Operational Assets

- Updated *The Curious Accountant* content
- Updated Exhibit 8.8 with new real-world data
- Updated exercises, problems, and cases

Chapter 9 Accounting for Current Liabilities and Payroll

- Revised *The Curious Accountant* content
- Updated *Reality Bytes* feature
- Updated Exhibit 9.6 with new real-world data
- Updated exercises, problems, and cases

Chapter 10 Accounting for Long-Term Debt

- Revised *The Curious Accountant* content
- Updated *Reality Bytes* feature
- Updated the new real-world data in *The Financial Analysis*
- Updated exercises, problems, and cases

Chapter 11 Proprietorships, Partnerships, and Corporations

- Updated *The Curious Accountant* content
- Updated two *Reality Bytes* features
- Updated exercises, problems, and cases

Chapter 12 Statement of Cash Flows

- Revised *The Curious Accountant* content
- Updated *Reality Bytes* feature
- Updated Exhibit 12.16 with new real-world data
- Updated exercises, problems, and cases

Chapter 13 The Double-Entry Accounting System

- Revised *The Curious Accountant* content
- Added a new decision aid to assist students with debits/credits
- Updated exercises, problems, and cases

Chapter 14 Financial Statement Analysis

- Revised *The Curious Accountant* content
- Updated all real-world ratio data
- Updated exercises, problems, and cases

New Appendix H

- New Data Analytics Project

HOW DOES THE BOOK

Sergey Tikhomirov/123RF

● REAL-WORLD EXAMPLES

The text provides a variety of real-world examples of financial accounting as an essential part of the management process. There are descriptions of accounting practices from real organizations such as **Coca-Cola**, **Enron**, **General Motors**, and **Amazon.com**. These companies are highlighted in blue in the text.

"Relating this material to real life is key to get the students interested and make it applicable regardless of the major. This does a great job."

—ROB STUSSIE, UNIVERSITY OF ARIZONA

● THE CURIOUS ACCOUNTANT

Each chapter opens with a short vignette. These pose a question about a real-world accounting issue related to the topic of the chapter. The answer to the question appears in a separate sidebar a few pages farther into the chapter.

Corbis/Getty Images

● FOCUS ON INTERNATIONAL ISSUES

These boxed inserts expose students to IFRS and other international issues in accounting.

● THE FINANCIAL ANALYST

Financial statement analysis is highlighted in each chapter under this heading.

● CHECK YOURSELF

These short question/answer features occur at the end of each main topic and ask students to stop and think about the material just covered. The answer follows to provide immediate feedback before students go on to a new topic.

©Paul Sakuma/AP Images

● REALITY BYTES

This feature expands on the topics by showing how companies use the concepts discussed in the chapter to make real-world business decisions.

MOTIVATE STUDENTS?

● ANNUAL REPORTS

Excerpts from the 2018 annual report for Target Corporation are shown in Appendix B.

Business Applications Cases related to the annual report are included at the end of each chapter.

A Capstone Financial Statement Analysis Project for the annual report is located in Appendix E. Also, a general purpose annual report project is included for instructors to assign for any company.

> "I like the way the book stresses real world applications and makes the transactions and discussions meaningful and engaging."
>
> —STACY KLINE,
> DREXEL UNIVERSITY

Source: U.S. Securities and Exchange Commission

● A LOOK BACK/A LOOK FORWARD

Students need a roadmap to make sense of where the chapter topics fit into the "whole" picture. A Look Back reviews the chapter materials and a Look Forward introduces students to what is to come.

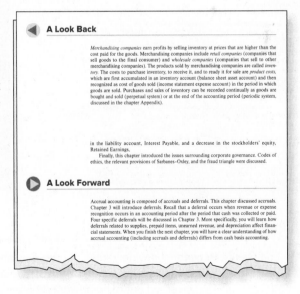

A Look Back

Merchandising companies earn profits by selling inventory at prices that are higher than the cost paid for the goods. Merchandising companies include *retail companies* (companies that sell goods to the final consumer) and *wholesale companies* (companies that sell to other merchandising companies). The products sold by merchandising companies are called *inventory*. The costs to purchase inventory, to receive it, and to ready it for sale are *product costs*, which are first accumulated in an inventory account (balance sheet asset account) and then recognized as cost of goods sold (income statement expense account) in the period in which goods are sold. Purchases and sales of inventory can be recorded continually as goods are bought and sold (perpetual system) or at the end of the accounting period (periodic system, discussed in the chapter Appendix).

in the liability account, Interest Payable, and a decrease in the stockholders' equity, Retained Earnings.

Finally, this chapter introduced the issues surrounding corporate governance. Codes of ethics, the relevant provisions of Sarbanes-Oxley, and the fraud triangle were discussed.

A Look Forward

Accrual accounting is composed of accruals and deferrals. This chapter discussed accruals. Chapter 3 will introduce deferrals. Recall that a deferral occurs when revenue or expense recognition occurs in an accounting period after the period that cash was collected or paid. Four specific deferrals will be discussed in Chapter 3. More specifically, you will learn how deferrals related to supplies, prepaid items, unearned revenue, and depreciation affect financial statements. When you finish the next chapter, you will have a clear understanding of how accrual accounting (including accruals and deferrals) differs from cash basis accounting.

Regardless of the instructional approach, there is no shortcut to learning accounting. Students must practice to master basic accounting concepts. The text includes a prodigious supply of practice materials and exercises and problems.

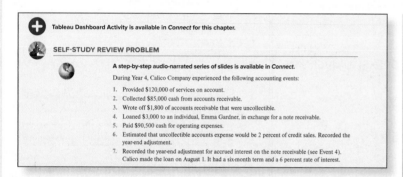

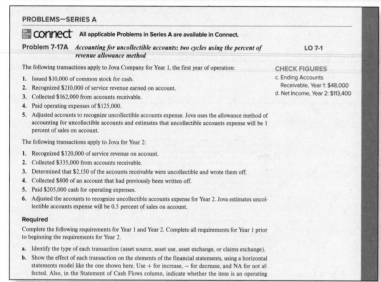

● SELF-STUDY REVIEW PROBLEM

These example problems include a detailed, worked-out solution and provide support for students before they work problems on their own. These review problems are included in an animated audio presentation in the *Connect* Library.

● EXERCISE SERIES A & B AND PROBLEM SERIES A & B

There are two sets of problems and exercises: Series A and B. Instructors can assign one set for homework and another set for classwork.

• Check Figures

The figures provide key answers for selected problems.

• Excel

Many problems can be solved using the Excel™ templates available in the *Connect* Library. A logo appears in the margins next to these problems.

"There is a rich variety of material of all levels of complexity. Between the wide variety of problems and the algorithmic versions in *Connect*, I doubt I would ever run out of homework problems."

—EDWARD R. WALKER,
UNIVERSITY OF CENTRAL OKLAHOMA

REINFORCED?

ANALYZE, THINK, COMMUNICATE (ATC)

Each chapter includes an innovative section titled Analyze, Think, Communicate (ATC). This section offers Business Applications Cases, Group Assignments, Real-World Cases, Writing Assignments, Ethical Dilemmas, Research Assignments, and Spreadsheet Assignments.

We use icons to help students identify the type of question being asked.

  • Writing assignments

 • Internet assignments

 • Group exercises

• Real company examples

 • Ethics cases

©McGraw-Hill Education

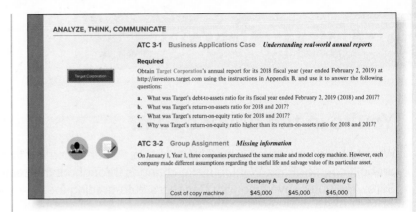

ANALYZE, THINK, COMMUNICATE

ATC 3-1 Business Applications Case *Understanding real-world annual reports*

Required
Obtain Target Corporation's annual report for its 2018 fiscal year (year ended February 2, 2019) at http://investors.target.com using the instructions in Appendix B, and use it to answer the following questions:

a. What was Target's debt-to-assets ratio for its fiscal year ended February 2, 2019 (2018) and 2017?
b. What was Target's return-on-assets ratio for 2018 and 2017?
c. What was Target's return-on-equity ratio for 2018 and 2017?
d. Why was Target's return-on-equity ratio higher than its return-on-assets ratio for 2018 and 2017?

ATC 3-2 Group Assignment *Missing information*

On January 1, Year 1, three companies purchased the same make and model copy machine. However, each company made different assumptions regarding the useful life and salvage value of its particular asset.

	Company A	Company B	Company C
Cost of copy machine	$45,000	$45,000	$45,000

"The strong Analyze, Think, Communicate section promotes judgment, decision making, and critical thinking."

—ANGELA WOODLAND
MONTANA STATE UNIVERSITY

"The number and coverage of the end of chapter material is one of the strong selling points of the text."

—WENDY POTRATZ
UNIVERSITY OF WISCONSIN—OSHKOSH

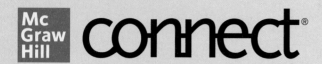

You're in the driver's seat.

Want to build your own course? No problem. Prefer to use our turnkey, prebuilt course? Easy. Want to make changes throughout the semester? Sure. And you'll save time with *Connect's* auto-grading too.

65%
Less Time Grading

Laptop: McGraw-Hill; Woman/dog: George Doyle/Getty Images

They'll thank you for it.

Adaptive study resources like SmartBook® 2.0 help your students be better prepared in less time. You can transform your class time from dull definitions to dynamic debates. Find out more about the powerful personalized learning experience available in SmartBook 2.0 at **www.mheducation.com/highered/connect/smartbook**

Make it simple, make it affordable.

Connect makes it easy with seamless integration using any of the major Learning Management Systems—Blackboard®, Canvas, and D2L, among others—to let you organize your course in one convenient location. Give your students access to digital materials at a discount with our inclusive access program. Ask your McGraw-Hill representative for more information.

Padlock: Jobalou/Getty Images

Solutions for your challenges.

A product isn't a solution. Real solutions are affordable, reliable, and come with training and ongoing support when you need it and how you want it. Our Customer Experience Group can also help you troubleshoot tech problems—although *Connect's* 99% uptime means you might not need to call them. See for yourself at **status.mheducation.com**

Checkmark: Jobalou/Getty Images

FOR STUDENTS

Effective, efficient studying.

Connect helps you be more productive with your study time and get better grades using tools like SmartBook 2.0, which highlights key concepts and creates a personalized study plan. *Connect* sets you up for success, so you walk into class with confidence and walk out with better grades.

Study anytime, anywhere.

Download the free ReadAnywhere app and access your online eBook or SmartBook 2.0 assignments when it's convenient, even if you're offline. And since the app automatically syncs with your eBook and SmartBook 2.0 assignments in *Connect*, all of your work is available every time you open it. Find out more at **www.mheducation.com/readanywhere**

> *"I really liked this app—it made it easy to study when you don't have your textbook in front of you."*
>
> - Jordan Cunningham, Eastern Washington University

No surprises.

The Connect Calendar and Reports tools keep you on track with the work you need to get done and your assignment scores. Life gets busy; *Connect* tools help you keep learning through it all.

Calendar: owattaphotos/Getty Images

Learning for everyone.

McGraw-Hill works directly with Accessibility Services Departments and faculty to meet the learning needs of all students. Please contact your Accessibility Services office and ask them to email accessibility@mheducation.com, or visit **www.mheducation.com/about/accessibility** for more information.

Top: Jenner Images/Getty Images, Left: Hero Images/Getty Images, Right: Hero Images/Getty Images

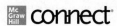

● MCGRAW-HILL *CONNECT*

McGraw-Hill *Connect* is a digital teaching and learning environment that gives students the means to better connect with their coursework, their instructors, and the important concepts they will need to know for success both now and in the future. With *Connect*, instructors can deliver assignments, quizzes, and tests easily online. Students can review course material and practice important skills. *Connect* provides the following features:

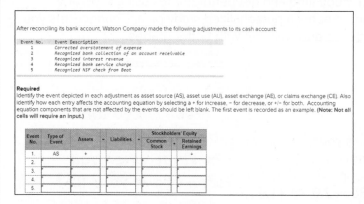

- SmartBook 2.0
- Auto-graded Online Homework.
- Using McGraw-Hill's free ReadAnywhere App, access your media-rich eBook anywhere, even offline.
- Dynamic links between the problems or questions you assign to your students and the location in the eBook where that concept is covered.
- A powerful search function to pinpoint and connect key concepts to review.

In short, *Connect* offers students powerful tools and features that optimize their time and energy, enabling them to focus on learning.

For more information about *Connect*, go to www.mheducation.com/highered/connect, or contact your local McGraw-Hill Higher Education representative.

• SmartBook

Within *Connect*, Smartbook brings these features to life by interleaving reading with active practice. As students read, Smartbook encourages them to answer questions to demonstrate their knowledge—then, based on their answers, highlights those areas where students need more practice.

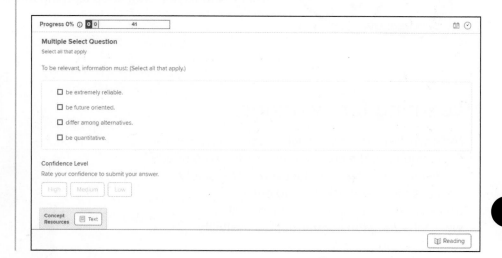

IMPROVE STUDENT SUCCESS?

• Online assignments

Connect helps students learn more efficiently by providing feedback and practice material when they need it, where they need it. *Connect* grades homework automatically and gives immediate feedback on any questions students may have missed. Our assignable, gradable end-of-chapter content includes a general journal application that looks and feels like what you would find in a general ledger software package. Also, select questions have been redesigned to test students' knowledge more fully. They now include tables for students to work through rather than requiring that all calculations be done offline.

End-of-chapter content in *Connect* includes:

• Quizzes (multiple-choice questions)
• Exercises
• Problems
• Analyze, Think, Communicate Cases
• Comprehensive Problems

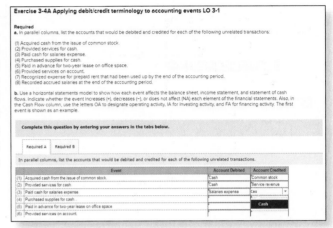

• Lecture videos

One or more lecture videos are available for every learning objective introduced throughout the text. The videos have been developed by a member of the author team and have the touch and feel of a live lecture. The videos are accompanied by a set of self-assessment quizzes. Students can watch the videos and then test themselves to determine if they understand the material presented in the video. Students can repeat the process, switching back and forth between the video and self-assessment quizzes, until they are satisfied that they understand the material.

> "Using the Lecture Videos would allow me to delve deeper into the subject in class."
>
> —LINDA TARRAGO,
> HILLSBOROUGH
> COMMUNITY COLLEGE

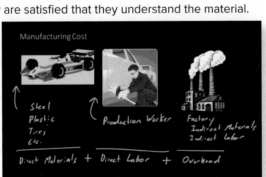

McGraw-Hill Global Education Holdings, LLC

• Excel simulations

Simulated Excel questions, assignable within *Connect,* allow students to practice their Excel skills—such as basic formulas and formatting—within the content of financial accounting. These questions feature animated, narrated Help and Show Me tutorials (when enabled), as well as automatic feedback and grading for both students and professors.

• Guided Examples/Hint Videos

The Guided Examples/Hints videos in *Connect* provide a video-based, step-by-step walkthrough of select exercises similar to those assigned. These short videos can be made available to students as hints by instructors and provide reinforcement when students need it most.

Microsoft Corporation

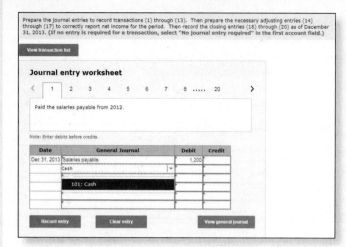

• Capstone General Ledger Project

General Ledger Problems provide a much-improved student experience when working with accounting cycle questions, offering improved navigation and less scrolling. Students can audit their mistakes by easily linking back to their original entries and can see how the numbers flow through the various financial statements. Many General Ledger Problems include an analysis tab that allows students to demonstrate their critical thinking skills and a deeper understanding of accounting concepts.

• Instructor Resources

The *Connect* Instructor Resources is your repository for additional resources to improve student engagement in and out of class. You can select and use any asset that enhances your lecture. The *Connect* Instructor Library includes access to:

- Solutions Manual
- Instructor's Manual
- Test Bank
- Instructor PowerPoint® slides
- Media-rich eBook

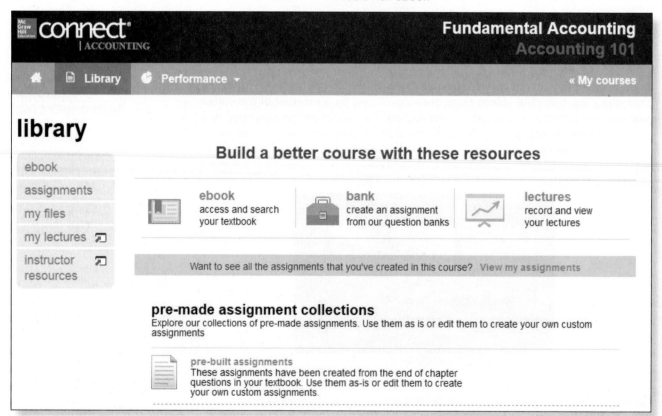

● TEGRITY: LECTURES 24/7

 Tegrity in Connect is a tool that makes class time available 24/7 by automatically capturing every lecture. With a simple one-click start-and-stop process, you capture all computer screens and corresponding audio in a format that is easy to search, frame by frame. Students can replay any part of any class with easy-to-use, browser-based viewing on a PC, Mac, iPod, or other mobile device.

Educators know that the more students can see, hear, and experience class resources, the better they learn. In fact, studies prove it. Tegrity's unique search feature helps students efficiently find what they need, when they need it, across an entire semester of class recordings. Help turn your students' study time into learning moments immediately supported by your lecture. With Tegrity, you also increase intent listening and class participation by easing students' concerns about note-taking. Using Tegrity in *Connect* will make it more likely you will see students' faces, not the tops of their heads.

• Custom Publishing through Create

 McGraw-Hill Create™ is a new, self-service website that allows instructors to create custom course materials by drawing upon McGraw-Hill's comprehensive, cross-disciplinary content. Instructors can add their own content quickly and easily and tap into other rights-secured third-party sources as well, then arrange the content in a way that makes the most sense for their course. Instructors can even personalize their book with the course name and information and choose the best format for their students: color print, black-and-white print, or an eBook.

Through Create, instructors can

• Select and arrange the content in a way that makes the most sense for their course.
• Combine material from different sources and even upload their own content.
• Choose the best format for their students: print or eBook.
• Edit and update their course materials as often as they like.

Begin creating now at www.mcgrawhillcreate.com.

• McGraw-Hill Customer Experience Group Contact Information

At McGraw-Hill, we understand that getting the most from new technology can be challenging. That's why our services don't stop after you purchase our products. You can contact our Product Specialists 24 hours a day to get product training online. Or you can search the knowledge bank of Frequently Asked Questions on our support website. For Customer Support, call **800-331-5094,** or visit www.mhhe.com/support. One of our Technical Support Analysts will be able to assist you in a timely fashion.

Assurance of Learning Ready

Many educational institutions today are focused on the notion of *assurance of learning*, an important element of many accreditation standards. *Introductory Financial Accounting for Business 2e* is designed specifically to support your assurance of learning initiatives with a simple, yet powerful, solution.

Each chapter in the book begins with a list of numbered learning objectives, which appear throughout the chapter, as well as in the end-of-chapter assignments. Every Test Bank question for *Introductory Financial Accounting for Business* maps to a specific chapter learning objective in the textbook. Each Test Bank question also identifies topic area, level of difficulty, Bloom's Taxonomy level, and AICPA and AACSB skill area. You can use *Connect* to easily search for learning objectives that directly relate to the learning objectives for your course.

AACSB Statement

McGraw-Hill Education is a proud corporate member of AACSB International. Understanding the importance and value of AACSB accreditation, *Introductory Financial Accounting for Business 2e* recognizes the curricula guidelines detailed in the AACSB standards for business accreditation by connecting selected questions in the text and the Test Bank to the general knowledge and skill guidelines in the revised AACSB standards.

The statements contained in *Introductory Financial Accounting for Business 2e* are provided only as a guide for the users of this textbook. The AACSB leaves content coverage and assessment within the purview of individual schools, the mission of the school, and the faculty. While *Introductory Financial Accounting for Business 2e* and the teaching package make no claim of any specific AACSB qualification or evaluation, we have, within the text and test bank, labeled selected questions according to the eight general knowledge and skill areas.

McGraw-Hill's *Connect*

Connect offers a number of powerful tools and features to make managing your classroom easier. *Connect* with Edmonds 2e offers enhanced features and technology to help both you and your students make the most of your time inside and outside the classroom.

ACKNOWLEDGMENTS

Our grateful appreciation is extended to those who helped to make this second edition possible.

We would like to give special thanks here to the talented people who prepared the supplements. These take a great deal of time and effort to write, and we appreciate their efforts. Thank you to Helen Roybark and Beth Kobylarz for reviewing the text. Thank you to Ann Brooks for authoring LearnSmart. Jack Terry developed the Excel Templates. Thank you to LuAnn Bean for preparing the PowerPoints and Instructor's Manual and Helen Roybark for accuracy checking the PowerPoints and Instructor's Manuals. We are grateful for to Jean Bissell for her work as the Lead Subject Matter Expert, and to Patricia Lopez and Beth Kobylarz for reviewing *Connect* content.

We extend our sincere appreciation to Tim Vertovec, Rebecca Olson, Jill Eccher, Brian Nacik, Danielle McLimore, Erin Quinones, Zachary Rudin, Matt Diamond, and Susan Culbertson. We deeply appreciate the long hours you committed to the formation of a high-quality text.

- **Christopher T. Edmonds** • **Thomas P. Edmonds** • **Mark Edmonds**
- **Jennifer Edmonds** • **Philip R. Olds**

We would like to express our gratitude and appreciation to those who have provided reviews for our second edition of *Introductory Financial Accounting for Business:*

Arek Arekelian, California State University, Dominguez Hills

Margaret Atkinson, Stark State College

Robyn Barrett, St. Louis Community College–Meramec

Marcia Behrens, Nichols College

Jaclyn Boichat, Johnson & Wales University

Robbie Coleman, Northeast Mississippi Community College

Rachel Cox, Oklahoma State University

Caroline Falconetti, Nassau Community College

Corinne Frad, Eastern Iowa Community Colleges

Ann Henderson, Georgia Southern University

Bambi Hora, University of Central Oklahoma

Kevin Jones, University of California, Santa Cruz

Pamela Jones, William Carey University

Sara Kern, Gonzaga University

Stacy Kline, Drexel University

Jeffrey Lark, University of Georgia

Mark Lawrence, University of North Alabama

Tara Maciel, Mesa College

Theresa Meza, James Sprunt Community College

Stephanie Morris, Mercer University

Rania Mousa, University of Evansville

Sia Nassiripour, William Paterson University

Leslie Oakes, University of New Mexico

Roshelle Overton, Central New Mexico Community College

Scott Paxton, Valencia College

Diep Phan, Beloit College

Wendy Potratz, University of Wisconsin–Oshkosh

Barbara Rice, Kentucky Community and Technical College System

Pinky Rusli, Montana State University

Melissa Schulte, University of Missouri–Kansas City

Tracy Sewell, Gulf Coast State College

Vincent Shea, St. John's University

Sherrie Slom, Hillsborough Community College

Nancy Snow, University of Toledo

George Starbuck, McMurry University

Sean Stein Smith, Lehman College, City University of New York

Gloria Stuart, Georgia Southern University

Rob Stussie, University of Arizona

Linda Tarrago, Hillsborough Community College

Mary Teal, University of Central Oklahoma

David Waite, Brigham Young University–Hawaii

Edward R. Walker, University of Central Oklahoma

Angela Woodland, Montana State University

Jennifer Wright, Drexel University

Jill Zietz, Concordia College

BRIEF CONTENTS

CONTENTS

Roman Tiraspolsky/
Shutterstock

Tracy Fox/123RF

Kristoffer Tripplaar/Alamy Stock Photo

Sergey Tikhomirov/123RF

Ken Wolter/123RF

Chapter 6 Internal Control and Accounting for Cash 280

jvdwolf/123RF

Super Nova Images/Alamy Stock Photo

Brad Sauter/Shutterstock

Chapter 9 Accounting for Current Liabilities and Payroll   432

Komenton/Shutterstock

Chapter 10 Accounting for Long-Term Debt   484

Lukmanazis/Shutterstock

Stockbyte/Getty Images

Chapter 11 Proprietorships, Partnerships, and Corporations 536

Chapter 12 Statement of Cash Flows 586

Wirul Kengthankan/123RF

Tea/123RF

Chapter 13 The Double-Entry Accounting System   640

Yooran Park/123RF

Chapter 14 Financial Statement Analysis
(Available online in *Connect*)   14-0

Introductory Financial Accounting for Business

Second Edition

CHAPTER 1

An Introduction to Accounting

LEARNING OBJECTIVES

After you have mastered the material in this chapter, you will be able to:

SECTION 1: COLLECTING AND ORGANIZING INFORMATION

LO 1-1   Identify the ways accounting benefits society.

LO 1-2   Identify reporting entities.

LO 1-3   Identify the components of the accounting equation.

LO 1-4   Classify business events as asset source, asset use, asset exchange, or claims exchange transactions.

LO 1-5   Show how business events affect the accounting equation.

LO 1-6   Prepare and interpret balance sheets for multiple accounting cycles.

SECTION 2: REPORTING INFORMATION

LO 1-7   Prepare and interpret information shown in an income statement.

LO 1-8   Prepare and interpret a statement of changes in stockholders' equity.

LO 1-9   Prepare and interpret a statement of cash flows.

LO 1-10 Identify the ways financial statements interrelate.

Video lectures and accompanying self-assessment quizzes are available in *Connect* for all learning objectives.

Tableau Dashboard Activity is available in *Connect* for this chapter.

The Curious Accountant

Roman Tiraspolsky/Shutterstock

Who owns **Apple, Inc.**? Who owns the **American Cancer Society** (ACS)? Many people and organizations other than owners are interested in the operations of Apple and the ACS. These parties are called *stakeholders*. Among others, they include lenders, employees, suppliers, customers, benefactors, research institutions, local governments, cancer patients, lawyers, bankers, financial analysts, and government agencies such as the Internal Revenue Service and the Securities and Exchange Commission. Organizations communicate information to stakeholders through *financial reports*.

How do you think the financial reports of Apple differ from those of the ACS? (Answer on page 10.)

SECTION 1:

COLLECTING AND ORGANIZING INFORMATION

Why should you study accounting? You should study accounting because it can help you succeed in business. Businesses use accounting to keep score. Imagine trying to play football without knowing how many points a touchdown is worth. Like sports, business is competitive. If you do not know how to keep score, you are not likely to succeed.

Accounting is an information system that reports on the economic activities and financial condition of a business or other organization. Do not underestimate the importance of accounting information. If you had information that enabled you to predict business success, you could become a very wealthy Wall Street investor. Indeed, communicating economic information is so important that accounting is frequently called the *language of business*.

ROLE OF ACCOUNTING IN SOCIETY

LO 1-1

Identify the ways accounting benefits society.

How should society allocate its resources? Should we spend more to harvest food or cure disease? Should we build computers or cars? Should we invest money in IBM or General Motors? Accounting provides information that helps answer such questions.

Using Free Markets to Set Resource Priorities

Suppose you want to start a business. You may have heard "you have to have money to make money." In fact, you will need more than just money to start and operate a business. You will likely need such resources as equipment, land, materials, and employees. If you do not have these resources, how can you get them? In the United States, you compete for resources in open markets.

A **market** is a group of people or entities organized to exchange items of value. The market for business resources involves three distinct participants: consumers, businesses, and resource owners. *Consumers* use resources. Resources are frequently not in a form consumers want. For example, nature provides trees but consumers want houses. Businesses transform resources such as trees into desirable products such as houses. *Resource owners* control the distribution of resources to businesses. Thus, resource owners provide resources (inputs) to businesses that provide goods and services (outputs) to consumers.

For example, a home builder (a business) transforms labor and materials (inputs) into houses (output) that consumers use. The transformation adds value to the inputs, creating outputs worth more than the sum of the inputs. Suppose a house that required $220,000 of materials and labor to build could have a market value of $250,000.

Common terms for the added value created in the transformation process include **profit, income**, or **earnings.** Accountants measure the added value as the difference between the cost of a product or service and the selling price of that product or service. The profit on the house described earlier is $30,000, the difference between its $220,000 cost and $250,000 market value.

Businesses that successfully and efficiently (at low cost) satisfy consumer preferences are rewarded with high earnings. These earnings are shared with resource owners, so businesses that exhibit high earnings potential are more likely to compete successfully for resources.

David Buffington/Photodisc/Getty Images

Return to the original question. How can you get the resources you need to start a business? You must go to open markets and convince resource owners that you can produce profits. Exhibit 1.1 illustrates the market trilogy involved in resource allocation.

The specific resources businesses commonly use to satisfy consumer demand are financial resources, physical resources, and labor resources.

Financial Resources

Businesses need **financial resources** (money) to get started and to operate. *Investors* and *creditors* provide financial resources.

- **Investors** provide financial resources in exchange for ownership interests in businesses. Owners expect businesses to return to them a share of the business, including a portion of earned income.

- **Creditors** lend financial resources to businesses. Instead of a share of the business, creditors expect the businesses to repay borrowed resources plus a specified fee called **interest.**

Investors and creditors prefer to provide financial resources to businesses with high earnings potential because such companies are better able to share profits and make interest payments. Profitable businesses are also less likely to experience bankruptcy.

Physical Resources

In their most primitive form, **physical resources** are natural resources. Physical resources often move through numerous stages of transformation. For example, standing timber may be successively transformed into harvested logs, raw lumber, and finished houses. Owners of physical resources seek to sell those resources to businesses with high earnings

EXHIBIT 1.1

Market Trilogy in Resource Allocation

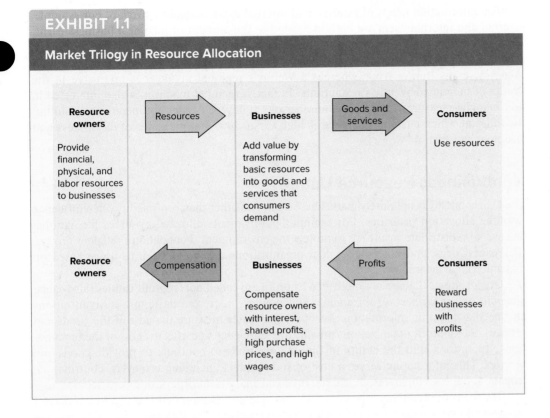

potential because profitable businesses are able to pay higher prices and make repeat purchases.

Labor Resources

Labor resources include both intellectual and physical labor. Like other resource providers, workers prefer businesses that have high income potential because these businesses are able to pay higher wages and offer continued employment.

Accounting Provides Information

How do providers of financial, physical, and labor resources identify businesses with high profit potential? Investors, creditors, and workers rely heavily on accounting information to evaluate which businesses are worthy of receiving resources. In addition, other people and organizations have an interest in accounting information about businesses. The many **users** of accounting information are commonly called **stakeholders.** Stakeholders include resource providers, financial analysts, brokers, attorneys, government regulators, and news reporters.

The link between businesses and those stakeholders who provide resources is direct: businesses pay resource providers. Resource providers use accounting information to identify companies with high earnings potential because those companies are more likely to return higher profits, make interest payments, repay debt, pay higher prices, and provide stable, high-paying employment.

The link between businesses and other stakeholders is indirect. Financial analysts, brokers, and attorneys may use accounting information when advising their clients. Government agencies may use accounting information to assess companies' compliance with income tax laws and other regulations. Reporters may use accounting information in news reports.

Types of Accounting Information

Stakeholders such as investors, creditors, lawyers, and financial analysts exist outside of and separate from the businesses in which they are interested. The accounting information these *external users* need is provided by **financial accounting.** In contrast, the accounting information needed by *internal users,* stakeholders such as managers and employees who work within a business, is provided by **managerial accounting.**

The information needs of external and internal users frequently overlap. For example, external and internal users are both interested in the amount of income a business earns. Managerial accounting information, however, is usually more detailed than financial accounting reports. For example, investors are concerned about the overall profitability of Wendy's versus Burger King; whereas a Wendy's regional manager is interested in the profits of individual Wendy's restaurants. In fact, a regional manager is also interested in nonfinancial measures, such as the number of employees needed to operate a restaurant, the times at which customer demand is high versus low, and measures of cleanliness and customer satisfaction.

Nonbusiness Resource Usage

The U.S. economy is not purely market-based. Factors other than profitability often influence resource allocation priorities. For example, governments allocate resources for national defense, to redistribute wealth, or to protect the environment. Foundations, religious groups, the Peace Corps, and other benevolent organizations prioritize resource usage based on humanitarian concerns.

Organizations that are not motivated by profit are called **not-for-profit entities** (also called *nonprofit* or *nonbusiness organizations*). Stakeholders interested in nonprofit organizations also need accounting information. Accounting systems measure the cost of the goods and services not-for-profit organizations provide, the efficiency and effectiveness of the organizations' operations, and the ability of the organizations to continue to provide goods and services. This information serves a host of stakeholders, including taxpayers, contributors, lenders, suppliers, employees, managers, financial analysts, attorneys, and beneficiaries.

The focus of accounting, therefore, is to provide information that is useful to a variety of business and nonbusiness user groups for decision making. The different types of accounting information and the stakeholders that commonly use the information are summarized in Exhibit 1.2.

EXHIBIT 1.2

Accounting as Information Provider

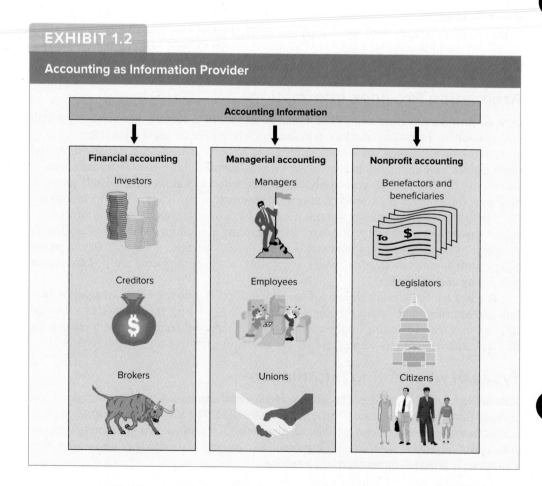

Careers in Accounting

What do accountants do? Accountants identify, record, analyze, and communicate information about the economic events that affect organizations. They may work in either public accounting or private accounting.

Public Accounting

You are probably familiar with the acronym CPA. CPA stands for *certified public accountant*. Public accountants provide services to various clients. They are usually paid a fee that varies depending on the service provided. Services typically offered by public accountants include (1) audit services, (2) tax services, and (3) consulting services.

- *Audit services* involve examining a company's accounting records in order to issue an opinion about whether the company's financial statements conform to generally accepted accounting principles. The auditor's opinion adds credibility to the statements, which are prepared by the company's management.
- *Tax services* include both determining the amount of tax due and tax planning to help companies minimize tax expense.
- *Consulting services* cover a wide range of activities that include everything from installing sophisticated computerized accounting systems to providing personal financial advice.

All public accountants are not certified. Each state government, as well as Washington, DC, and four U.S. territories, establish certification requirements applicable in that jurisdiction. Although the requirements vary from jurisdiction to jurisdiction, CPA candidates normally must have a college education, pass a demanding technical examination, and obtain work experience relevant to practicing public accounting.

Private Accounting

Accountants employed in the private sector usually work for a specific company or nonprofit organization. Private sector accountants perform a wide variety of functions for their employers. Their duties include classifying and recording transactions, billing customers and collecting amounts due, ordering merchandise, paying suppliers, preparing and analyzing financial statements, developing budgets, measuring costs, assessing performance, and making decisions.

Private accountants may earn any of several professional certifications. For example, the Institute of Management Accountants issues the *Certified Management Accounting (CMA)* designation. The Institute of Internal Auditors issues the *Certified Internal Auditor (CIA)* designation. These designations are widely recognized indicators of technical competence and integrity on the part of individuals who hold them. All professional accounting certifications call for meeting education requirements, passing a technical examination, and obtaining relevant work experience.

Measurement Rules

Suppose a store sells an MP3 player in December to a customer who agrees to pay for it in January. Should the business *recognize* (report) the sale as a December transaction or as a January transaction? It really does not matter as long as the storeowner discloses the rule the decision is based on and applies it consistently to other transactions. Because businesses may use different reporting rules, however, clear communication also requires full and fair disclosure of the accounting rules chosen.

Communicating business results would be simpler if each type of business activity were reported using only one measurement method. World economies and financial reporting practices, however, have not evolved uniformly. Even in highly sophisticated countries such as the United States, companies exhibit significant diversity in reporting methods. Providers of financial reports assume that users are educated about accounting practices.

The **Financial Accounting Standards Board (FASB)**[1] is a privately funded organization with the primary authority for establishing accounting standards in the

Lars A. Niki

[1]The FASB consists of seven full-time members appointed by the supporting organization, the Financial Accounting Foundation (FAF). The FAF membership is intended to represent the broad spectrum of individuals and institutions that have an interest in accounting and financial reporting. FAF members include representatives of the accounting profession, industry, financial institutions, the government, and the investing public.

United States. The measurement rules established by the FASB are called **generally accepted accounting principles (GAAP).** Financial reports issued to the public must follow GAAP. This textbook introduces these principles so you will be able to understand business activity reported by companies in the United States.

Companies are not required to follow GAAP when preparing *management accounting* reports. Although there is considerable overlap between financial and managerial accounting, managers are free to construct internal reports in whatever fashion best suits the effective operation of their companies.

REPORTING ENTITIES

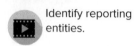

Identify reporting entities.

Think of accountants in the same way you would think of news reporters. A news reporter gathers and discloses information about some person, place, or thing. Likewise, an accountant gathers and discloses financial information about specific people or businesses. The people or businesses accountants report on are called **reporting entities.** When studying accounting, you should think of yourself as the accountant. Your first step is to identify the person or business on which you are reporting. This is not always as easy as it may seem. To illustrate, consider the following scenario.

Jason Winston recently started a business. During the first few days of operation, Mr. Winston transferred cash from his personal account into a business account for a company he named Winston Enterprises. Mr. Winston's brother, George, invested cash in Winston Enterprises for which he received an ownership interest in the company. Winston Enterprises borrowed cash from First Federal Bank. Winston Enterprises paid cash to purchase a building from Commercial Properties, Inc. Winston Enterprises earned cash revenues from its customers and paid its employees cash for salaries expense.

How many reporting entities are described in this scenario? Assuming all of the customers are counted as a single entity and all of the employees are counted as a single entity, there are a total of seven entities named in the scenario. These entities include: (1) Jason Winston, (2) Winston Enterprises, (3) George Winston, (4) First Federal Bank, (5) Commercial Properties, Inc., (6) the customers, and (7) the employees. A separate set of accounting records would be maintained for each entity.

Your ability to learn accounting will be greatly influenced by how you approach the entity concept. Based on your everyday experiences you likely think from the perspective of a customer. In contrast, this text is written from the perspective of a business entity. These opposing perspectives dramatically affect how you view business events. For example, as a customer, you consider a sales discount a great bargain. The view is different from the perspective of the business granting the discount. A sales discount means an item did not sell at the expected price. To move the item, the business had to accept less money than it originally planned to receive. From this perspective, a sales discount is not a good thing. To understand accounting, train yourself to interpret transactions from the perspective of a business rather than a consumer. Each time you encounter an accounting event, ask yourself: How does this affect the business?

CHECK YOURSELF 1.1

In a recent business transaction, land was exchanged for cash. Did the amount of cash increase or decrease?

Answer The answer depends on the reporting entity to which the question pertains. One entity sold land. The other entity bought land. For the entity that sold land, cash increased. For the entity that bought land, cash decreased.

FOCUS ON INTERNATIONAL ISSUES

IS THERE GLOBAL GAAP?

As explained in this chapter, accounting is a measurement and communication discipline based on rules referred to as *generally accepted accounting principles (GAAP)*. The rules described in this text are based on GAAP used in the United States, but what rules do the rest of the world use? Is there a global GAAP, or does each country establish its own unique GAAP?

Until recently, each country developed its own unique GAAP. Global companies were required to prepare multiple sets of financial statements to satisfy each country's GAAP. The use of multiple accounting standards across the globe made comparing company performance difficult and expensive. To address the need for a common set of financial standards, the International Accounting Standards Committee was formed in 1973. The committee was reorganized as the **International Accounting Standards Board (IASB)** in 2001. The IASB issues **International Financial Reporting Standards (IFRS),** which are rapidly gaining support worldwide. In 2005, companies in the countries who were members of the European Union were required to use the IFRS as established by the IASB, which is headquartered in London. Today, over 100 countries require or permit companies to prepare their financial statements using IFRS.

Kristi Blokhin/Kevin Roche John Dinkeloo and Associates/Shutterstock

As of 2019, most of the major economic countries had switched from their local GAAP to IFRS. One notable exception is the United States, but even here, there is an active process in place to reduce the differences between IFRS and U.S. GAAP.

There are many similarities between the IASB and the FASB. Both the FASB and the IASB are required to include members with a variety of backgrounds, including auditors, users of financial information, academics, and so forth. Also, both groups primarily require that their members work full-time for their respective boards; they cannot serve on the board while being compensated by another organization. (The IASB does allow up to three of its members to be part-time.) Members of each board serve five-year terms and can be reappointed once. The funds to support both boards, and the large organizations that support them, are obtained from a variety of sources, including selling publications and private contributions. To help maintain independence of the board's members, fund-raising is performed by separate sets of trustees.

Despite their similarities, there are significant differences between the IASB and the FASB. One of these relates to size and geographic diversity. The FASB has only seven members, all from the United States. The IASB has 16 members, and these must include at least 4 from Asia, 4 from Europe, 4 from North America, 1 from Africa, and 1 from South America.

Not only is the structure of the standards-setting boards different, but the standards and principles they establish may also differ significantly. In this chapter, you will learn that GAAP employs the *historical cost concept.* This means that the assets of most U.S. companies are shown on the balance sheet at the amount for which they were purchased. For example, land that has a market value of millions of dollars may be shown on Ford's financial statements with a value of only a few hundred thousand dollars. This occurs because GAAP requires Ford to show the land at its cost rather than its market value. In contrast, IFRS permits companies to show market values on their financial statements. This means that the exact same assets may show radically different values if the statements are prepared under IFRS rather than GAAP.

Throughout this text, where appropriate, we will note the differences between U.S. GAAP and IFRS. However, by the time you graduate, it is likely that among the major industrialized nations, there will be a global GAAP.

CREATING AN ACCOUNTING EQUATION

The Accounting Equation is composed of three **elements** called assets, liabilities, and stockholders' equity. Stockholders' equity may be subdivided into two additional elements called common stock and retained earnings. Each of these elements is discussed in this section of the chapter.

Businesses use resources to conduct their operations. For example, Carmike Cinemas, Inc. uses buildings, seating, screens, projection equipment, vending machines, cash registers, and so on in order to make money from ticket sales. The resources a business uses to make money are called **assets.** So, where do businesses get assets? There are three distinct sources:

LO 1-3

Identify the components of the accounting equation.

1. *A business can borrow assets from creditors.* Usually a business acquires cash from creditors and then uses the cash to purchase the assets it needs to conduct its operations.

Answers to The Curious Accountant

Anyone who owns stock in **Apple** owns a part of the company. Apple has many owners. In contrast, nobody actually owns the **American Cancer Society** (ACS). The ACS has a board of directors that is responsible for overseeing its operations, but the board is not its owner.

Ultimately, the purpose of a business entity is to increase the wealth of its owners. To this end, it "spends money to make money." The expense that Apple incurs for research is a cost incurred in the hope that it will generate revenues when it sells smartphones and tablets. The financial statements of a business show, among other things, whether and how the company made a profit during the current year. For example, Apple's income statements show that in 2018 it spent $14.2 billion on research and development, and generated $265.6 billion in revenues.

The ACS is a not-for-profit entity. It operates to provide services to society at large, not to make a profit. It cannot increase the wealth of its owners, because it has no owners. When the ACS spends money to assist cancer patients, it does not spend this money in the expectation that it will generate revenues. The revenues of the ACS come from contributors who wish to support efforts related to fighting cancer. Because the ACS does not spend money to make money, it has no reason to prepare an *income statement* like that of Apple. The ACS's statement of activities shows how much revenue was received from contributions versus from "investment income."

Not-for-profit entities do prepare financial statements that are similar in appearance to those of commercial enterprises. The financial statements of not-for-profit entities are called the *statement of financial position*, the *statement of activities*, and the *cash flow statement*.

When a business receives cash from creditors it accepts an obligation to return the cash to the creditors at some future date. In accounting terms, the obligations a business has to its creditors are called **liabilities.**

2. *A business can acquire assets from investors.* When a business acquires assets from investors, it commits to keep the assets safe and to use the assets in a manner that benefits the investors. The business also grants the investor an ownership interest in the business, thereby allowing the investor (owner) to share in the profits generated by the business. The specific commitments made to the investors are described in certificates called **common stock**. In accounting terms investors are called **stockholders**. Further, the business's commitment to the stockholders is called **stockholders' equity**.

3. *A business can acquire assets from operations.* Businesses use assets in order to produce higher amounts of other assets. For example, **Best Buy** may sell a TV that cost the company $500 for $600. The $100 difference between the sales price and the cost of the TV results in an increase in Best Buy's total assets. This explains how operations can be a source of assets. Of course operations may also result in a decrease in assets. If Best Buy has to discount the sales price of the TV to $450 in order to sell it, the company's total assets decrease by $50.

The purpose of a for-profit business is to acquire assets through operations (Source 3). Net increases in assets generated from operations are commonly called *earnings* or *income*. Net decreases in assets caused by operations are called *losses*. As a result of their ownership status, the stockholders reap the benefits and suffer the sacrifices that a business experiences from its operations. A business may distribute all or part of the assets generated through operations to the shareholders. The distribution of assets generated through earnings is called a *dividend*.

Notice that paying dividends is an option—not a legal requirement. Instead of paying dividends, a business may retain the assets it generates through operations. If a business retains the assets, it commits to use those assets for the benefit of the stockholders. This increase in the business's commitments to its stockholders is normally called **retained earnings.** Also, note that earnings that have been retained in the past can be used to pay dividends in the future. However, a company that does not have current or prior retained earnings cannot pay dividends.

As a result of providing assets to a business, the creditors and investors are entitled to make potential **claims**[2] on the assets owned by the business. The relationship between a business's assets and the claims on its assets is frequently expressed in an equality called the **accounting equation.** Based on the relationships described above, the accounting equation can be developed as follows:

$$\text{Assets} = \qquad\qquad \text{Claims}$$

$$\text{Assets} = \overbrace{\text{Liabilities} + \text{Stockholders' equity}}$$

$$\text{Assets} = \text{Liabilities} + \overbrace{\text{Common stock} + \text{Retained earnings}}$$

✓ CHECK YOURSELF 1.2

Gupta Company has $250,000 of assets, $60,000 of liabilities, and $90,000 of common stock. What percentage of the assets was provided by retained earnings?

Answer   First, determine the dollar amount of retained earnings:

Assets = Liabilities + Common stock + Retained earnings
Retained earnings = Assets − Liabilities − Common stock
Retained earnings = $250,000 − $60,000 − $90,000
Retained earnings = $100,000

Second, determine the percentage:

Percentage of assets provided by retained earnings = Retained earnings/Total assets
Percentage of assets provided by retained earnings = $100,000/$250,000 = 40%

TYPES OF TRANSACTIONS

An **accounting event** is an economic occurrence that changes an enterprise's assets, liabilities, or stockholders' equity. A **transaction** is a particular kind of event that involves transferring something of value between two entities. Examples of transactions include acquiring assets from owners, borrowing money from creditors, and purchasing or selling goods and services. The following section of the text explains how several different types of accounting events affect a company's accounting equation. There are four types of transactions that can affect the accounting equation:

LO 1-4

 Classify business events as asset source, asset use, asset exchange, or claims exchange transactions.

1. *Asset source transactions* increase the total amount of assets and increase the total amount of claims.

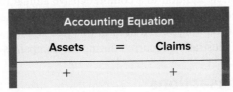

Accounting Equation		
Assets	**=**	**Claims**
+		+

2. *Asset exchange transactions* increase one asset and decrease another asset. The total amount of assets is not affected.

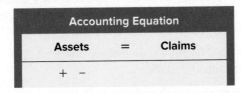

Accounting Equation		
Assets	**=**	**Claims**
+ −		

---

[2]A claim is a legal action to obtain money, property, or the enforcement of a right against another party.

3. *Asset use transactions* decrease the total amount of assets and the total amount of claims.

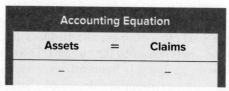

4. *Claims exchange transactions* increase in one claim and decrease in another claim. The total amount of claims is not affected.

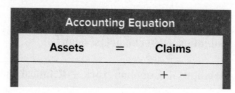

As you proceed through this text, practice classifying transactions into one of the four categories. Businesses engage in thousands of transactions every day. It is far more effective to learn how to classify the transactions into meaningful categories than to attempt to memorize the effects of thousands of transactions. The following section of the text will introduce asset source, asset exchange, and asset use transactions. Examples of the fourth type, claims exchange transactions, will be introduced in Chapter 2.

RECORDING BUSINESS EVENTS UNDER THE ACCOUNTING EQUATION

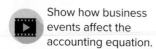

LO 1-5

Show how business events affect the accounting equation.

Detailed information about the accounting equation is maintained in records commonly called **accounts.** For example, information regarding *assets* may be organized in separate accounts for cash, equipment, buildings, land, and so forth. The types and number of accounts used by a business depend on the information needs of its stakeholders. Some businesses provide very detailed information; others report highly summarized information. The more detail desired, the greater number of accounts needed. Think of accounts like the notebooks students keep for their classes. Some students keep detailed notes about every class they take in a separate notebook. Other students keep only the key points for all of their classes in a single notebook. Similarly, some businesses use more accounts than other businesses.

Diversity also exists regarding the names used for various accounts. For example, employee pay may be called salaries, wages, commissions, and so forth. Do not become frustrated with the diversity of terms used in accounting. Remember, accounting is a language. The same word can have different meanings. Similarly, different words can be used to describe the same phenomenon. The more you study and use accounting, the more familiar it will become to you.

Companies typically report about events occurring over a span of time called an **accounting period**. The typical accounting period for a complete set of financial statements and disclosures is one year. However, in addition to a comprehensive annual report, the Securities and Exchange Commission requires public companies to issue abbreviated reports on a quarterly basis. The length of the accounting period used in this text is normally one year. The events described in the following illustration occurred during the company's first accounting period.

Asset Source Transactions

Asset source transactions increase total assets and total claims. As previously mentioned, businesses obtain assets (resources) from three sources. They acquire assets from owners (stockholders); they borrow assets from creditors; and they earn assets through profitable operations. Let's look at a few asset source transactions and see how they affect the accounting equation.

EVENT 1   Rustic Camp Sites (RCS) was formed on January 1, Year 1, when it acquired $120,000 cash from issuing common stock.

When RCS issued stock, it received cash and gave each investor (owner) a stock certificate as a receipt. Because this transaction provided $120,000 of assets (cash) to the business, it is an

asset source transaction. It increases the business's assets (cash) and its stockholders' equity (common stock).

Accounting Equation								
Assets			=	Liab.	+	Stockholders' Equity		
Cash	+	Land	=	Notes Pay.	+	Com. Stk.	+	Ret. Earn.
120,000	+	NA	=	NA	+	120,000	+	NA

Notice the major components of the accounting equation have been divided into accounts. For example, *assets* are divided into a Cash account and a Land account. Do not be concerned if some of the other account titles shown in the accounting equation are unfamiliar. They will be explained as new transactions are presented. Recall that the number of accounts a company uses depends on the nature of its business and the level of detail management needs to operate the business. For example, Amazon would have an account called Inventory, although GEICO Insurance would not. Why? Because Amazon sells goods (inventory) but GEICO does not.

Also, notice that a stock issue transaction affects the accounting equation in two places, both under an asset (cash) and also under the source of that asset (common stock). All transactions affect the accounting equation in at least two places. It is from this practice that the **double-entry bookkeeping** system derives its name.

EVENT 2 RCS acquired an additional $400,000 of cash by borrowing from a creditor.

This transaction is also an *asset source transaction.* It increases assets (cash) and liabilities (notes payable). The account title Notes Payable is used because the borrower (RCS) is required to issue a promissory note to the creditor (a bank). A promissory note describes, among other things, the amount of interest RCS will pay and for how long it will borrow the money.[3] The effect of the borrowing transaction on the accounting equation is indicated next.

Accounting Equation								
Assets			=	Liab.	+	Stockholders' Equity		
Cash	+	Land	=	Notes Pay.	+	Com. Stk.	+	Ret. Earn.
400,000	+	NA	+	400,000	+	NA	+	NA

Asset Exchange Transactions

Businesses frequently trade one asset for another asset. In such cases, the amount of one asset decreases and the amount of the other asset increases. Total assets are unaffected by asset exchange transactions. Event 3 is an asset exchange transaction.

EVENT 3 RCS paid $500,000 cash to purchase land.

This asset exchange transaction reduces the asset account Cash and increases the asset account Land. The amount of total assets is not affected. An **asset exchange transaction** simply reflects changes in the composition of assets. In this case, the company traded cash for land. The amount of cash decreased by $500,000 and the amount of land increased by the same amount.

Accounting Equation								
Assets			=	Liab.	+	Stockholders' Equity		
Cash	+	Land	=	Notes Pay.	+	Com. Stk.	+	Ret. Earn.
(500,000)	+	500,000	=	NA	+	NA	+	NA

[3]For simplicity, the computation of interest is ignored in this chapter. Interest computation is discussed in Chapter 2 and in subsequent chapters.

Another Asset Source Transaction

EVENT 4   RCS obtained $85,000 cash by leasing camp sites to customers.

The *economic benefit* a company derives from providing goods and services to its customers is called **revenue**. In this example, the economic benefit is an increase in the asset Cash. Businesses may receive other benefits that will be discussed later. However, at this point we will limit our definition of revenue to being *an increase in assets* that results from providing goods and services to customers. Since the stockholders reap the rewards of operating the business, revenue increases the stockholders' claim on the company's assets. The increase in claims is shown in the stockholders' equity account, Retained Earnings. For this event, the increase in the asset account Cash is balanced by an increase in the amount of stockholders' equity (Retained Earnings). The effects on the accounting equation are as follows.

Accounting Equation								
Assets			=	Liab.	+	Stockholders' Equity		
Cash	+	Land	=	Notes Pay.	+	Com. Stk. +	Ret. Earn.	Acct. Title
85,000	+	NA	=	NA	+	NA +	85,000	Revenue

Asset Use Transactions

Businesses use assets for a variety of purposes. For example, assets may be used to pay off liabilities or they may be transferred to owners. Assets may also be used in the process of generating earnings. All **asset use transactions** decrease the total amount of assets and the total amount of claims on assets (liabilities or stockholders' equity).

EVENT 5   RCS paid $50,000 cash for operating expenses such as salaries, rent, and interest.

An economic sacrifice a business incurs in the process of generating revenue is called an **expense**. In this example, the economic sacrifice is a decrease in the asset Cash. While expenses may result in other types of sacrifice, at this point we will limit our definition of expense to being a *use of assets* that is necessary to generate revenue. Since the stockholders suffer the sacrifices of operating the business, expenses decrease the stockholders' claim on the company's assets. The decrease in claims is shown in the stockholders' equity account, Retained Earnings. For this event, the decrease in the asset account Cash is balanced by a decrease in the amount of stockholders' equity (Retained Earnings). The effects on the accounting equation are as follows:

Accounting Equation								
Assets			=	Liab.	+	Stockholders' Equity		
Cash	+	Land	=	Notes Pay.	+	Com. Stk. +	Ret. Earn.	Acct. Title
(50,000)	+	NA	=	NA	+	NA +	(50,000)	Expense

Note that RCS could have recognized each type of expense separately. However, the management team does not currently desire this level of detail. Remember, the number of accounts a business uses depends on the level of information managers need for decision making.

EVENT 6   RCS paid $4,000 in cash dividends to its owners.

To this point, operating RCS has caused the amount of total assets to increase by $35,000 ($85,000 of revenue − $50,000 of operating expenses). Because the owners bear the risk and reap the rewards of operating the business, the $35,000 increase in assets benefits them. RCS can use the additional assets to grow the business, or the company can transfer the earned assets to the owners. If a business transfers some or all of its earned assets to owners, the transfer is called a **dividend**. The $4,000 dividend paid by RCS reduces the asset account Cash and the amount of stockholders' equity (Retained Earnings). The effects on the accounting equation are as follows.

Accounting Equation								
Assets		=	Liab.	+	Stockholders' Equity			
Cash	+ Land	=	Notes Pay.	+	Com. Stk.	+	Ret. Earn.	Acct. Title
(4,000)	+ NA	=	NA	+	NA	+	(4,000)	Dividends

Like expenses, dividends can be viewed as a sacrifice in that paying dividends causes a decrease in a company's assets. However, the purpose of the sacrifice is different. Expenses are incurred for the purpose of generating revenue, while dividends are paid for the purpose of rewarding the stockholders.

EVENT 7   The land that RCS paid $500,000 to purchase had an appraised market value of $525,000 on December 31, Year 1.

Although the appraised value of the land is higher than the original cost, RCS will not increase the amount recorded in its accounting records above the land's $500,000 historical cost. In general, accountants do not recognize changes in market value. The **historical cost concept** requires that most assets be reported at the amount paid for them (their historical cost) regardless of increases in market value.

Surely investors would rather know what an asset is worth instead of how much it originally cost. So why do accountants maintain records and report financial information based on historical cost? Accountants rely heavily on verification. Information is considered to be more useful if it can be independently verified. For example, two people looking at the legal documents associated with RCS's land purchase will both conclude that RCS paid $500,000 for the land. That historical cost is a verifiable fact. The appraised value, in contrast, is an opinion. Even two persons who are experienced appraisers are not likely to come up with the same amount for the land's market value. Accountants do not report market values in financial statements because such values are not reliable.

There are exceptions to the application of the historical cost rule. When market value can be clearly established, GAAP not only permits but requires its use. For example, securities that are traded on the New York Stock Exchange must be shown at market value rather than historical cost. We will discuss other notable exceptions to the historical cost principle later in the text. However, as a general rule you should assume that assets shown in a company's financial statements are valued at historical cost.

Summary of Transactions

A summary of the accounting events and the effects on the accounting equation are shown in Exhibit 1.3. The Revenue, Expense, and Dividend account data appear in the retained earnings column. These account titles are shown immediately to the right of the dollar amounts listed in the retained earnings column.

PREPARING A BALANCE SHEET

As previously discussed, stakeholders use accounting information for a variety of reasons. Creditors and investors need information to identify the best business prospects. Workers want information that enables them to pick the best employer. Regulators use the information to determine whether businesses are complying with laws and paying taxes. Journalists and correspondents use accounting information to prepare news stories. Accountants provide information to satisfy these and other stakeholder needs.

Many real-world businesses experience millions of transactions each year. Assessing business performance by analyzing an accounting equation containing millions of transactions would be too burdensome for most stakeholders. To improve the usefulness of the information, the transaction data contained in an accounting equation are organized into formal reports called **financial statements.** One of those statements is a balance sheet.

The **balance sheet** draws its name from the accounting equation. Indeed, the statement shows the equality (the balance) between the assets and the sources of those assets. It is based on the balances in the accounts included in an accounting equation at the end of an

LO 1-6

Prepare and interpret balance sheets for multiple accounting cycles.

EXHIBIT 1.3

Accounting Events

1.	RCS issued common stock, acquiring $120,000 cash from its owners.
2.	RCS borrowed $400,000 cash.
3.	RCS paid $500,000 cash to purchase land.
4.	RCS received $85,000 cash from earning revenue.
5.	RCS paid $50,000 cash for expenses.
6.	RCS paid dividends of $4,000 cash to the owners.
7.	The land that RCS paid $500,000 to purchase had an appraised market value of $525,000 on December 31, Year 1.

Effects on the Accounting Equation

Event No.	Cash	+	Land	=	Notes Payable	+	Common Stock	+	Retained Earnings	Other Account Titles
	Assets			**= Liabilities**		**+**	**Stockholders' Equity**			
Beg. Bal.	0		0		0		0		0	
1.	120,000						120,000			
2.	400,000				400,000					
3.	(500,000)		500,000							
4.	85,000								85,000	Revenue
5.	(50,000)								(50,000)	Expense
6.	(4,000)								(4,000)	Dividend
7.	NA		NA		NA		NA		NA	
End Bal.	51,000	+	500,000	=	400,000	+	120,000	+	31,000	

accounting period. To illustrate, we return to the accounting equation for Rustic Camp Sites (RCS) shown in Exhibit 1.3.

The Year 1 balance sheet for RCS is shown in Exhibit 1.4. Notice that the information in the balance sheet mirrors the year-end information in the accounting equation. Specifically, total assets is equal to total liabilities plus total stockholders' equity ($551,000 = $400,000 + $151,000). The difference between the ending balances in the accounting equation and the balance sheet is simply a matter of format. For example, the accounting equation displays the information horizontally, while the balance sheet shows the information vertically. Even so, the format issue is important. The accounting equation format is useful for gathering information, while the balance sheet is designed for analyzing information. While the differences may seem insignificant at this point, their importance will become more apparent as different types of accounting events are introduced.

The order in which assets are shown in the balance sheet is important. Assets are displayed in the balance sheet based on their level of liquidity. Financial **liquidity** is measured by how fast an asset can be converted to cash. Because land has to be sold to obtain cash, it is less liquid than cash. Indeed, cash is the most liquid asset and is therefore listed first on the balance sheet. The remaining assets are listed in the order of how rapidly they are normally converted into cash. This explains why cash is listed before land on RCS's balance sheet.

Observe carefully that the balance sheet is dated with the phrase *As of December 31, Year 1*, indicating that it describes the company's financial position at a specific *point in time*. The balance sheet does not attempt to explain the transactions that caused the ending account balances. It only defines the financial position that exists *at the end* of the accounting period. While this text focuses on annual reports, be aware that a balance sheet could be prepared as of any specific point in time.

Second Accounting Cycle

Financial reporting occurs in cycles. There is a starting point with beginning account balances, a series of accounting events that occur over a span of time, and a stopping point with

EXHIBIT 1.4

RUSTIC CAMP SITES
Balance Sheet
As of December 31, Year 1

Assets		
Cash	$ 51,000	
Land	500,000	
Total Assets		$551,000
Liabilities		
Notes Payable		$400,000
Stockholders' Equity		
Common Stock	$120,000	
Retained Earnings	31,000	
Total Stockholders' Equity		151,000
Total Liabilities and Stockholders' Equity		$551,000

ending account balances. The span of time used in this text is normally one year. The ending account balances of the first cycle become the beginning account balances for the second cycle. Think of it this way. If you have $51,000 of cash at the very end of Year 1, you would have the same amount of cash at the very beginning of Year 2.

To show how multiple accounting cycles affect the balance sheet, we return to the Rustic Camp Sites (RCS) example. Based on the balance sheet shown in Exhibit 1.4, RCS ended its first accounting cycle on December 31, Year 1, with the following account balances:

	Accounting Equation						
	Assets			**+**	**Liabilities**	**Stockholders' Equity**	
Event No.	**Cash**	**+**	**Land**	**=**	**Notes Payable**	**+ Common Stock +**	**Retained Earnings**
Beg. Bal.	51,000	+	500,000	=	400,000	+ 120,000 +	31,000

The Year 1 ending balances become the Year 2 beginning balances. RCS experienced the following transactions during its Year 2 accounting cycle:

1. Acquired $32,000 cash by issuing common stock.
2. Received $116,000 cash for providing services to customers (leasing camp sites).
3. Paid $62,000 cash for operating expense.
4. Paid a $9,000 cash dividend to the owners.
5. Sold land that had cost $200,000 for $200,000 cash.
6. Paid $300,000 cash to pay off a portion of its notes payable.

The effects of these events are shown in an accounting equation shown in Exhibit 1.5. You should be comfortable with recording Events 1 through 4 as they are similar to events that occurred in Year 1. In Event 5, RCS sold $200,000 of the land it purchased in Year 1. This is an asset exchange transaction because the Cash account increases and the Land account decreases. In Event 6, RCS paid off $300,000 of the notes payable. This asset use transaction decreases the asset account, Cash, and decreases the liability account, Notes Payable.

Note that to calculate ending balances for Year 2, we must consider the beginning account balances. For example, the $28,000 ending cash balance is calculated as the beginning balance of $51,000 + changes in cash that occurred during Year 2 of $32,000 + $116,000 − $62,000 − $9,000 + $200,000 − $300,000. The same process is used to calculate the ending balances in the other accounts in Exhibit 1.5.

The balance sheet is prepared by using the account balances at the end of the accounting period on December 31, Year 2. These balances are shown on the bottom row of the accounting equation in Exhibit 1.5. The Year 2 balance sheet is shown in the second column of Exhibit 1.6. Once again, the balance sheet information is consistent with the information in the accounting equation. Specifically, total assets ($328,000) is equal to total liabilities plus total stockholders' equity ($100,000 + $228,000 = $328,000).

EXHIBIT 1.5

	Accounting Events Year 2 Effects on the Accounting Equation									
	Assets			**Liabilities**		**Stockholders' Equity**				
Event No.	**Cash**	**+**	**Land**	**=**	**Notes Pay.**	**+**	**Com. Stk.**	**+**	**Ret. Earn.**	**Other Account Titles**
Beg. Bal	51,000	+	500,000	=	400,000	+	120,000	+	31,000	
1.	32,000	+	NA	=	NA	+	32,000	+	NA	
2.	116,000	+	NA	=	NA	+	NA	+	116,000	Revenue
3.	(62,000)	+	NA	=	NA	+	NA	+	(62,000)	Expenses
4.	(9,000)	+	NA	=	NA	+	NA	+	(9,000)	Dividend
5.	200,000	+	(200,000)	=	NA	+	NA	+	NA	
6.	(300,000)	+	NA	=	(300,000)	+	NA	+		
End Bal.	28,000	+	300,000	=	100,000	+	152,000	+	76,000	

EXHIBIT 1.6

RUSTIC CAMP SITES
Balance Sheets
As of December 31

	Year 1	Year 2
Assets		
Cash	$ 51,000	$ 28,000
Land	500,000	300,000
Total Assets	$551,000	$328,000
Liabilities		
Notes Payable	$400,000	$100,000
Stockholders' Equity		
Common Stock	120,000	152,000
Retained Earnings	31,000	76,000
Total Stockholders' Equity	151,000	228,000
Total Liabilities and Stockholders' Equity	$551,000	$328,000

As indicated earlier, one difference between an accounting equation and a balance sheet is that the equation is shown horizontally while the balance sheet is shown vertically. The vertical format is used for the balance sheet because that format is more conducive for presenting information covering multiple accounting cycles. Specifically, the account titles and balances are shown vertically with the accounting periods (Year 1, Year 2, and so on) shown horizontally. Exhibit 1.6 provides an example of two balance sheets presented in a vertical format.

Interpreting Information Shown in a Balance Sheet

It is important to notice that while the amounts in liabilities, common stock, and retained earnings are measured in dollars, they do not represent cash. In other words, there is no cash in the liability, common stock, or retained earning accounts. You can see this clearly by analyzing RCS's Year 2 balance sheet in Exhibit 1.6. Given that the balance sheet shows $76,000 in retained earnings at the end of Year 2, can the company pay a $50,000 cash dividend? The answer is no. Remember, there is no cash in retained earnings. The only cash the company has is listed in the asset section of the balance sheet. In this case, the maximum cash dividend that can be paid is $28,000, because that is all the cash the company has available.

Even though the retained earnings balance does not represent an amount of cash held by a company, it does limit the amount of cash that can be used to pay dividends. To illustrate,

EXHIBIT 1.7

RUSTIC CAMP SITES
Balance Sheets
As of December 31

	Year 2	
Assets		
Cash	$ 28,000	
Land	300,000	
Total Assets	$328,000	
		As a Percent
Liabilities and Stockholders' Equity	In dollars	of Total Assets
Notes Payable	$100,000	30.49%
Stockholders' Equity		
Common Stock	152,000	46.34%
Retained Earnings	76,000	23.17%
Total Liabilities and Stockholders' Equity	$328,000	100%

look at RCS Year 1 balance sheet (Column 1 in Exhibit 1.6). Given that RCS has $51,000 in cash at the end of Year 1, can the company pay a $50,000 dividend? The answer is no. Based on the information in the balance sheet, RCS has only $31,000 of retained earnings at the end of Year 1. Because dividends are a distribution of assets that were generated through earnings, the maximum dividend RCS can distribute at this time is $31,000. In summary, the payment of dividends is limited by both the amount of cash and the amount of retained earnings.

A good way to think about the liability and stockholders' equity sections of the balance sheet is to think of them as percentages of assets instead of dollars. To illustrate, Exhibit 1.7 shows RCS's December 31, Year 2, balance sheet in two different formats. Specifically, Column 1 shows the liability, common stock, and retained earnings account balances using dollar amounts (same as Column 2 in Exhibit 1.6), while Column 2 shows the same account balances expressed as a percentage of total assets. Reading Column 2, we would say that 30.49 percent of RCS's assets came from creditors, 46.34 percent came from owners, and 23.17 percent from earnings. The actual composition of assets is shown in the asset section of the balance sheet. In this case, the asset section is composed of Cash and Land. The company has no other assets.

Real-world financial statements do not show percentages in the liability and stockholders' equity accounts. Even so, it is insightful to realize that the balances in the liability and stockholders' equity accounts represent the portion of total assets that was provided by creditors, investors, and earnings. These account balances are not directly related to the amount of cash held by the company.

Two Views of the Liabilities and Stockholders' Equity Sections of the Balance Sheet

Another important point to recognize is that there are two views of the liabilities and stockholders' equity section of the balance sheet. One view is that this section shows the sources of assets. Clearly, when a company borrows money from a bank, the business receives an asset: cash. Therefore, we say creditors are a source of assets. However, borrowing money creates an obligation for the business to return the amount borrowed to creditors. Thus, we can view the liabilities of a company as its obligations to return assets to its creditors. In summary, liabilities can be viewed as sources of assets or, alternatively, as obligations of the business.

Similarly, a business may acquire assets from its owners by issuing stock or it may earn assets through its operations. Therefore, common stock and retained earnings can be viewed as sources of assets. However, the business has a **stewardship** responsibility, which means it has a duty to protect and use the assets for the benefit of the owners. As a result, common stock and retained earnings can be viewed as sources of assets or, alternatively, as commitments to the investors. In summary, liabilities and stockholders' equity can be viewed either as sources of assets or as the obligations and commitments of the business.

SECTION 2:

REPORTING INFORMATION

The Curious Accountant

The RCS case includes only seven business events, one of which is not recognized in the accounting equation. These events are assumed to have taken place over the course of a year. In contrast, real-world companies engage in thousands, even millions, of transactions in a single day. For example, think of the number of sales events **Ebay** processes in a day,

LightField Studios/Shutterstock

or how many tickets **Priceline.com** sells. Presenting this many events in accounting equation format would produce such a volume of data that users would be overwhelmed with details. To facilitate communication, accountants summarize and organize the transaction data into reports called *financial statements*. This section discusses the information contained in financial statements and explains how they are prepared. While the RCS illustration contains only a few transactions, the financial statements prepared for this company contain the same basic content as those of much larger companies.

Recall that the balance sheet shows a company's financial condition at a specific point in time. For example, RCS's balance sheet in Exhibit 1.6 shows the financial position as of December 31, Year 1 and Year 2, which is the end of the company's first and second accounting periods. In other words, the balances for the Year 1 balance sheet summarize the final results stemming from all the transactions that occurred during the first

EXHIBIT 1.8

Time Line for Reporting Financial Statements

	Dec. 31, Year 1		Dec. 31, Year 2
	Balance Sheet	Income statement Statement of Changes in Stk. Equity Statement of Cash Flows	Balance Sheet
	Shows the financial condition as of the end of Year 1	Each statement summarizes particular events that occurred *during* Year 2	Shows the financial condition **as of the end** of Year 2

accounting period, while balances for the Year 2 balance sheet summarize the final results stemming from all the transactions that occurred during the first and second accounting periods.

While the year-end balance sheet information is useful, additional insight can be gained by examining information about the transactions that lead to the ending account balances. Indeed, the Financial Accounting Standards Board (FASB) requires companies to issue three financial statements that provide information about events occurring during an accounting period. These statements include the income statement, the statement of changes in stockholders' equity, and the statement of cash flows. While the balance sheet shows the company's financial condition at the end of each accounting cycle, the other statements report on the events that occur during an accounting cycle. Exhibit 1.8 shows the time line for financial reporting over two accounting cycles.

While FASB requires the preparation of these statements for every accounting period (Year 1 and Year 2), for illustration purposes we are going to prepare an income statement, statement of changes in stockholders' equity, and statement of cash flows for only the Year 2 accounting period. To illustrate the preparation and use of these statements, we return to the Rustic Camp Sites example.

PREPARING AN INCOME STATEMENT

As previously stated, the balance sheet provides information about a company's financial position *as of the end* of an accounting period. This section of the text focuses on the income statement and the statement of changes in stockholders' equity which explain what caused certain balance sheet accounts to change from one period to the next.

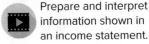

LO 1-7

Prepare and interpret information shown in an income statement.

Examining the balance sheets shown in Exhibit 1.6 reveals that total stockholders' equity increased from $151,000 at the end of Year 1 to $228,000 at the end of Year 2. This is great for the stockholders, but what events during Year 2 caused this increase? The Year 2 income statement along with the Year 2 statement of changes in stockholders' equity explain the increase. One important factor causing stockholders' equity to increase is the amount of net income earned during Year 2.

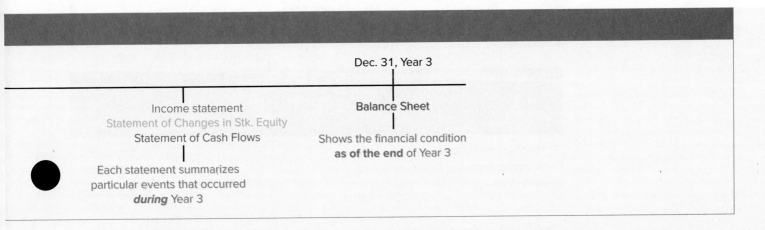

Dec. 31, Year 3

Income statement
Statement of Changes in Stk. Equity
Statement of Cash Flows

Balance Sheet

Shows the financial condition
as of the end of Year 3

Each statement summarizes
particular events that occurred
during Year 3

Income Statement and the Matching Concept

The **income statement** reports on how the business performed *during* a specific accounting period—in this case, Year 2. Business performance is measured as the benefits earned from customers (revenue) minus the sacrifices that were incurred (expenses) to earn those benefits (revenues). If revenues exceed expenses, the difference is called **net income**. If expenses are greater than revenues, the difference is called **net loss**. The practice of pairing revenues with expenses on the income statement is called the **matching concept**. The primary components of the income statement including revenue, expense, and net income are sometimes called the elements of the income statement.

The purpose of a business is to produce net income, and one method of evaluating the performance of a business is to look at the amount of net income it produced. Exhibit 1.9 shows how revenue and expenses that we previously recorded under the accounting equation can be formally presented on an income statement. Reviewing the accounting equation, we recorded revenue (Event 2) as increases to retained earnings, and expenses (Event 3) as decreases to retained earnings. The income statement presented at the bottom of Exhibit 1.9 shows that RCS earned $116,000 of revenue and incurred $62,000 of expenses, resulting in net income of $54,000. Using our definition of revenue as increases in assets, and expenses as decreases in assets, we can conclude that the net income figure of $54,000 represents an increase in the total amount of RCS's assets.[4]

EXHIBIT 1.9

Accounting Events Year 2

1.	Acquired $32,000 cash by issuing common stock.
2.	Received $116,000 cash for providing services to customers (leasing camp sites).
3.	Paid $62,000 cash for operating expense.
4.	Paid a $9,000 cash dividend to the owners.
5.	Sold land that had cost $200,000 for $200,000 cash.
6.	Paid $300,000 cash to pay off a portion of its notes payable.

Effects on the Accounting Equation

	Assets			=	Liabilities	+	Stockholders' Equity			
Event No.	Cash	+	Land	=	Notes Pay.	+	Com. Stk.	+	Ret. Earn.	Other Account Titles
Beg. Bal	51,000	+	500,000	=	400,000	+	120,000	+	31,000	
1.	32,000	+	NA	=	NA	+	32,000	+	NA	
2.	116,000	+	NA	=	NA	+	NA	+	116,000	Revenue
3.	(62,000)	+	NA	=	NA	+	NA	+	(62,000)	Expenses
4.	(9,000)	+	NA	=	NA	+	NA	+	(9,000)	Dividend
5.	200,000	+	(200,000)	=	NA	+	NA	+	NA	
6.	(300,000)	+	NA	=	(300,000)	+	NA	+		
End Bal.	28,000	+	300,000	=	100,000	+	152,000	+	76,000	

RUSTIC CAMP SITES
Income Statement
For the Year Ended December 31, Year 2

Revenue (asset increases)	$116,000
Operating Expenses (asset decreases)	(62,000)
Net Income	$ 54,000

[4]The definitions for revenue and expense are expanded in subsequent chapters as additional relationships among the elements of financial statements are introduced.

Observe the phrase *For the Year Ended December 31, Year 2*, in the heading of the income statement. This income statement is a report about matching the revenues occurring in Year 2 with the expenses that occurred in Year 2. Income can be measured weekly, monthly, quarterly, semiannually, or using any other desired time period. Accordingly, the terminology used to describe the date should clearly indicate the time period covered by the statement. This text normally assumes an annual reporting period and therefore uses the terminology "For the Year Ended . . . ."

Notice that the cash RCS paid to its stockholders (Event 4 in Exhibit 1.9) is not reported as an expense on the income statement because the dividends were not incurred for the purpose of generating revenue. For example, a company pays employees so that they will work to produce revenue. Because the salary payment was made for the purpose of producing revenue, it is called an expense. In contrast, a business pays dividends to reward stockholders for the investment they made in the business. The stockholders are not being paid to produce revenue. A business first determines how much income it has earned and then decides how much of that income it will distribute to reward stockholders. The portion of earnings (income) distributed to owners is called a dividend. In summary, dividends are paid after the amount of income is determined. Therefore, dividends are not included on the income statement.

 CHECK YOURSELF 1.3

Mahoney, Inc. was started when it issued common stock to its owners for $300,000. During its first year of operation, Mahoney received $523,000 cash for services provided to customers. Mahoney paid employees $233,000 cash. Advertising costs paid in cash amounted to $102,000. Other cash operating expenses amounted to $124,000. Finally, Mahoney paid a $25,000 cash dividend to its stockholders. What amount of net income would Mahoney report on its earnings statement?

Answer The amount of net income is $64,000 ($523,000 Revenue − $233,000 Salary Expense − $102,000 Advertising Expense − $124,000 Other Operating Expenses). The cash received from issuing stock is not revenue because it was not acquired from earnings activities. In other words, Mahoney did not work (perform services) for this money; it was contributed by owners of the business. The dividends are not expenses because the decrease in cash was not incurred for the purpose of generating revenue. Instead, the dividends represent a transfer of wealth to the owners.

STATEMENT OF CHANGES IN STOCKHOLDERS' EQUITY

The **statement of changes in stockholders' equity** shown at the bottom of Exhibit 1.10 explains the effects of transactions on stockholders' equity during the accounting period. The accounting equation in Exhibit 1.10 shows the events that affected stockholders' equity during Year 2. Looking at the Common Stock account, you can see that we started the year with a beginning balance of $120,000. During the year, RCS raised an additional $32,000 by issuing additional common stock (Event 1). After the stock issuance, common stock had an ending balance of $152,000. These changes are presented formally to stakeholders on the Statement of Changes in Stockholders' Equity.

In addition to reporting the changes in common stock, the statement describes the changes in retained earnings for the accounting period. Refer back to the accounting equation to see the changes in the Retained Earnings account. RCS had a beginning balance in retained earnings of $31,000. During the period, the company earned $54,000 in net income (revenue of $116,000 in Event 2 less expenses of $62,000 in Event 3) and paid $9,000 in dividends to the stockholders (Event 4), producing an ending retained earnings balance of $76,000 ($31,000 + $54,000 − $9,000). These changes are also presented formally on the Statement of Changes in Stockholders' Equity shown at the bottom of Exhibit 1.10. Because equity

LO 1-8

 Prepare and interpret a statement of changes in stockholders' equity.

EXHIBIT 1.10

Accounting Events Year 2

1.	Acquired $32,000 cash by issuing common stock.
2.	Received $116,000 cash for providing services to customers (leasing camp sites).
3.	Paid $62,000 cash for operating expense.
4.	Paid a $9,000 cash dividend to the owners.
5.	Sold land that had cost $200,000 for $200,000 cash.
6.	Paid $300,000 cash to pay off a portion of its notes payable.

Effects on the Accounting Equation

	Assets			=	Liabilities	+	Stockholders' Equity			Other
Event No.	Cash	+	Land	=	Notes Pay.	+	Com. Stk.	+	Ret. Earn.	Account Titles
Beg. Bal	51,000	+	500,000	=	400,000	+	120,000	+	31,000	
1.	32,000	+	NA	=	NA	+	32,000	+	NA	
2.	116,000	+	NA	=	NA	+	NA	+	116,000	Revenue
3.	(62,000)	+	NA	=	NA	+	NA	+	(62,000)	Expenses
4.	(9,000)	+	NA	=	NA	+	NA	+	(9,000)	Dividend
5.	200,000	+	(200,000)	=	NA	+	NA	+	NA	
6.	(300,000)	+	NA	=	(300,000)	+	NA	+		
End Bal.	28,000	+	300,000	=	100,000	+	152,000	+	76,000	

RUSTIC CAMP SITES
Statement of Changes in Stockholders' Equity
For the Year Ended December 31, Year 2

Beginning Common Stock	$120,000	
Plus: Stock Issued	32,000	
Ending Common Stock		$ 152,000
Beginning Retained Earnings	$ 31,000	
Plus: Net Income	54,000	
Minus: Dividend	(9,000)	
Ending Retained Earnings		76,000
Total Stockholders' Equity		$228,000

consists of common stock and retained earnings, the ending total equity balance is $228,000 ($152,000 + $76,000). This statement is also dated with the phrase *For the Year Ended December 31, Year 2,* because it describes what happened to stockholders' equity during the Year 2 accounting period.

Do not be confused by the formal format of the statement of changes in stockholders' equity shown at the bottom of Exhibit 1.10. Recall that the purpose of the statement is to explain the differences between the beginning and ending balances in the stockholders' equity account. The key components causing the Year 2 increase in stockholders' equity from a beginning balance of $151,000 to an ending balance of $228,000 are summarized in Exhibit 1.11. We recommend you strive to understand the causes of change in beginning and ending account balances outlined in the exhibit. The comprehension of casual factors is far more important than the memorization of the reporting format.

EXHIBIT 1.11

Key Components of Change in Stockholders' Equity

	Year 2
Beginning Stockholders' Equity	$151,000
Plus: Stock Issued	32,000
Plus: Net Income	54,000
Minus: Dividends	(9,000)
Total Stockholders' Equity	$228,000

PREPARING A STATEMENT OF CASH FLOWS

The accounting equation in Exhibit 1.13 shows that during the Year 2 accounting period the balance in RCS's cash account decreased from a beginning balance of $51,000 to an ending balance of $28,000. What caused this change? The **statement of cash flows** answers this question. The statement identifies the cash receipts and payments that caused the balance of the cash account to change during an accounting period. Receipts of cash are called cash inflows, and payments are cash outflows. The statement classifies cash inflows and outflows into three categories:

LO 1-9

Prepare and interpret a statement of cash flows.

1. **Financing activities** include obtaining cash from owners by issuing stock (cash inflow) or paying dividends to owners (cash outflow). Financing activities also include borrowing cash from creditors (cash inflow) and spending cash to repay a principal balance to creditors (cash outflow). Businesses normally start with an idea. Implementing the idea usually requires cash. For example, RCS needed cash to purchase the land used to operate its camp site rental business. Acquiring cash to start a business is a financing activity.

2. **Investing activities** involve paying cash (outflow) to purchase long-term assets or receiving cash (inflow) from selling long-term assets. Long-term assets are normally used for more than one year. Cash outflows to purchase land or cash inflows from selling a building are examples of investing activities. After obtaining cash from financing activities, RCS used some of the cash to purchase land. The purchase of the land is an investing activity.

3. **Operating activities** involve receiving cash (inflow) from revenue and paying cash (outflow) for expenses. Note that cash spent to purchase short-term assets such as office supplies is reported in the operating activities section because the office supplies would likely be used (expensed) within a single accounting period. After investing in the land, RCS started renting camp sites to customers. The activities associated with conducting a business are called operating activities.

The amount of time the asset is held determines whether it is classified as an investing or operating activity. Purchases of long-term assets (used more than a year) are classified as investing activities, while purchases of short-term assets (used less than a year) are classified as operating activities.

As indicated earlier, borrowing money is classified as a financing activity. Even so, interest paid on borrowed money is classified as an expense. Consistent with other expenses, cash paid for interest is reported in the operating activities section of the statement of cash flows.

The primary cash inflows and outflows related to the types of business activity introduced in this chapter are summarized in Exhibit 1.12. The exhibit will be expanded as additional types of events are introduced in subsequent chapters.

To prepare the statement of cash flows, let's refer to the accounting equation in Exhibit 1.13 and classify the cash transactions as either operating, investing, or financing

EXHIBIT 1.12

Classification Scheme for Statement of Cash Flows

Cash flows from operating activities:
Cash receipts (inflows) from customers
Cash payments (outflows) to suppliers

Cash flows from investing activities:
Cash receipts (inflows) from the sale of long-term assets
Cash payments (outflows) for the purchase of long-term assets

Cash flows from financing activities:
Cash receipts (inflows) from borrowing funds
Cash receipts (inflows) from issuing common stock
Cash payments (outflows) to repay borrowed funds
Cash payments (outflows) for dividends

activities. The Cash column starts with a beginning balance of $51,000. During Year 2, six events affected Cash and would be classified on the Statement of Cash Flows as follows:

- *Operating Activities*: Events 2 and 3 are operating activities. Event 2 is a $116,000 operating cash inflow from customers and Event 3 is a $62,000 operating cash outflow for payment of expenses. The net affect of these two events is a $54,000 increase in cash from operating activities. These events and the $54,000 net effect are presented formally in the operating activities section of the statement of cash flows below the accounting equation.

- *Investing Activities*: The sale of the land in Event 5 is the only investing activity in Year 2. This $200,000 cash inflow is presented formally in the investing activities section of the statement of cash flows.

- *Financing Activities*: Events 1, 4, and 6 are financing activities. Event 1 is a $32,000 financing cash inflow from issuing common stock, Event 4 is a $9,000 financing cash outflow for paying dividends, and Event 6 is a $300,000 financing cash outflow for payment to repay the note payable. The net effect of these three events is a $277,000 cash outflow from financing activities. All three of these events and the $277,000 net effect are presented formally in the financing activities section of the statement of cash flows.

Summing the three sections, $54,000 operating + $200,000 investing + ($277,000) financing, nets a decrease in cash for Year 2 of $23,000 which is also presented on the statement of cash in flows in Exhibit 1.13. Notice that the reconciliation from the beginning to the ending balance in cash occurs at the bottom of the statement. The beginning balance in the Cash account was $51,000; subtracting the $23,000 decrease to the beginning balance results in a $28,000 ending balance. Notice that the $28,000 ending cash balance on the statement of cash flows is the same as the amount of cash reported in the asset section on the December 31, Year 2, balance sheet (Exhibit 1.6).

The statement of cash flows in Exhibit 1.13 is dated with the phrase *For the Year Ended December 31, Year 2*. Specifically, this statement of cash flows explains what caused the balance in the Cash account to decrease by $23,000 during the Year 2 accounting period. The next statement of cash flows will explain what happens to the Cash account during the Year 3 accounting period and so on with subsequent accounting periods.

Again, do not be confused by the format of the statement. The purpose of the statement is to explain the differences between the beginning and ending balances in the cash account. The key components causing the Year 2 decrease from a beginning balance of $51,000 to an ending balance of $28,000 are summarized in Exhibit 1.14. Here also you should strive to understand the reasons for the change rather than memorizing the format of the statement.

EXHIBIT 1.13

Accounting Events Year 2

1.	Acquired $32,000 cash by issuing common stock.
2.	Received $116,000 cash for providing services to customers (leasing camp sites).
3.	Paid $62,000 cash for operating expense.
4.	Paid a $9,000 cash dividend to the owners.
5.	Sold land that had cost $200,000 for $200,000 cash.
6.	Paid $300,000 cash to pay off a portion of its notes payable.

Effects on the Accounting Equation

	Assets			=	Liabilities	+	Stockholders' Equity			
Event No.	Cash	+	Land	=	Notes Pay.	+	Com. Stk.	+	Ret. Earn.	Other Account Titles
Beg. Bal	51,000	+	500,000	=	400,000	+	120,000	+	31,000	
1.	32,000	+	NA	=	NA	+	32,000	+	NA	
2.	116,000	+	NA	=	NA	+	NA	+	116,000	Revenue
3.	(62,000)	+	NA	=	NA	+	NA	+	(62,000)	Expenses
4.	(9,000)	+	NA	=	NA	+	NA	+	(9,000)	Dividend
5.	200,000	+	(200,000)	=	NA	+	NA	+	NA	
6.	(300,000)	+	NA	=	(300,000)	+	NA	+		
End Bal.	**28,000**	+	**300,000**	=	**100,000**	+	**152,000**	+	**76,000**	

RUSTIC CAMP SITES
Statement of Cash Flows
For the Year Ended December 31, Year 2

Cash Flows from Operating Activities:		
Cash Receipts from Customers	$116,000	
Cash Payments for Operating Expenses	(62,000)	
Net Cash Flow from Operating Activities		$ 54,000
Net Cash Flow from Investing Activities		
Cash Receipts from the Sale of Land		200,000
Net Cash Flow from Financing Activities		
Cash Receipt from Stock Issue	32,000	
Cash Payment for Dividends	(9,000)	
Cash Payment to Repay Note Payable	(300,000)	
Net Cash Flow from Financing Activities		(277,000)
Net Decrease in Cash		(23,000)
Plus: Beginning Cash Balance		51,000
Ending Cash Balance		$ 28,000

EXHIBIT 1.14

Key Components of Change in Cash Flow

Beginning Cash Balance	$ 51,000
Net Cash Flow from Operating Activities	54,000
Net Cash Flow from Investing Activities	200,000
Net Cash Flow from Financing Activities	(277,000)
Ending Cash Balance	$ 28,000

CHECK YOURSELF 1.4

Classify each of the following cash flows as an operating activity, investing activity, or financing activity.

1. Acquired cash from owners.
2. Borrowed cash from creditors.
3. Paid cash to purchase land.
4. Earned cash revenue.
5. Paid cash for salary expenses.
6. Paid cash dividend.

Answer (1) financing activity; (2) financing activity; (3) investing activity; (4) operating activity; (5) operating activity; (6) financing activity.

FINANCIAL STATEMENT ARTICULATION

LO 1-10

Identify the ways financial statements interrelate.

Take note that the same information may appear on more than one financial statement. For example, the amount of net income reported on the income statement also appears on the statement of changes in stockholders' equity. Likewise, the ending cash balance appears on the balance sheet as well as the statement of cash flows. Accountants use the term **articulation** to describe the interrelationships among the various components of the financial statements. The articulated relationships in RCS's financial statements are shown in Exhibit 1.15. The key relationships are highlighted with the arrows.

The diagram shows two balance sheets that present RCS's financial condition at specific points in time. The financial condition shown in the December 31, Year 1, balance sheet is different from the condition shown in the December 31, Year 2, balance sheet. What caused the changes in these balance sheets? The income statement, statement of changes in stockholders' equity, and statement of cash flows provide partial explanations. For example, the contributed capital section of the statement of changes in stockholders' equity explains that the balance in the common stock account increased from $120,000 to $152,000 because the company issued $32,000 common stock during Year 2. Similarly, the retained earnings section shows that the $45,000 change in retained earnings ($76,000 Ending balance − $31,000 Beginning balance) was caused by a $54,000 increase from net income less a $9,000 dividend payment.

The statement of cash flows identifies the financing, investing, and operating activities occurring during Year 2 that caused the balance in the cash account to change from $51,000 on December 31, Year 1, to $28,000 on December 31, Year 2. Specifically, the statement shows that the company experienced a $54,000 net cash inflow from operations, a $200,000 net cash inflow from investing activities, and a $277,000 net cash outflow from financing activities, resulting in a negative $23,000 net change in cash during Year 2. Subtracting this $23,000 decrease from the $51,000 beginning cash balance yields the $28,000 December 31, Year 2, ending cash balance.

You may have wondered why some of the other changes in the two balance sheets are not explained by other financial statements. For example, why is there no *statement of changes in liabilities* to explain the changes in the notes payable account balances? Indeed, there could be different statements that would explain all of the differences in the Year 1 versus Year 2 balance sheet account balances. However, the demand for information that would be provided by additional statements has not been sufficient to merit the creation of such statements.

The four financial statements currently recognized by generally accepted accounting principles (GAAP) have evolved slowly. Indeed, the first mention of an income account appeared in a treatise written by Luca Pacioli in 1494. Even so, it was not until the early 1930s, with the establishment of the Securities and Exchange Commission, that contemporary forms of income statements and balance sheets were required in annual reports. Further, it was 1987 when the FASB mandated that a *statement of cash flows* be included in annual

EXHIBIT 1.15   Articulation Diagram

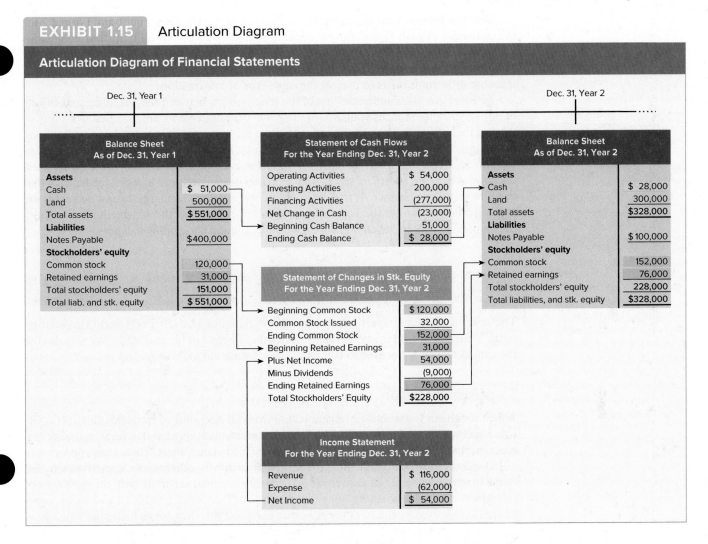

reports as the fourth financial statement. In summary, the current set of financial statements are designed to satisfy the most pressing needs of today's stakeholders. Other statements may be developed if the benefits of providing additional information justify the cost that would be incurred to produce and distribute that information.

An examination of Exhibit 1.16 reveals a pattern used in financial statements to explain changes in account balances from one accounting period to the next. Specifically, the beginning balance plus increases and minus decreases equals the ending balance. This pattern is presented as Format 1 in Exhibit 1.16. While the logic behind this pattern is intuitive, it is not used in the statement of cash flows. Instead, the cash statement uses an alternative format where the increases and decreases to the cash account are shown first. The increases and decreases are totaled, resulting in a line item titled *net change in cash*. The beginning cash balance is then added to the net change in cash, resulting in the ending cash balance. The differences in the two formats are summarized in Exhibit 1.16.

EXHIBIT 1.16

Format 1	Format 2
Beginning balance	Plus: Increases
Plus: Increases	Minus: Decreases
Minus: Decreases	Yields: Net change
Yields: Ending balance	Plus: Beginning balance
	Yields: Ending balance

Why use Format 1 for the statement of changes in stockholders' equity and Format 2 for the statement of cash flows? GAAP permits some degree of flexibility in how companies present information in their financial statements. Remember that accounting is a language. Different people use different words to describe the same event. Likewise, different accountants use different formats to present the same type of information.

To develop a clear understanding of the relationships between the beginning and ending balances, you should focus your attention on what the statements are designed to convey to the stakeholders, rather than trying to memorize the various presentation formats that companies may use. Regardless of the particular format used, both the statement of changes in stockholders' equity and the statement of cash flows can be understood by focusing on intuitive logic. There are always increases and decreases associated with a beginning balance that result in an ending balance. It makes no difference whether the increases and decreases are presented before or after the beginning balance; the purpose of the statements is to identify the events that caused the changes between the beginning and ending balances.

The Financial Analyst

This section of each chapter introduces topics related to analyzing real-world financial reports. We focus first on the types of businesses that operate in the real world. We also discuss the annual report that is used to communicate information to stakeholders.

Reporting Order

Which statement is shown first? There is no Financial Accounting Standards Board (FASB) rule regarding the order in which financial statements are reported. However, most companies report the income statement first, followed by the balance sheet. There is an approximate 50/50 split as to which statement is the third and fourth. In other words, approximately half of the time the statement of cash flows is the third statement reported, with the statement of changes in stockholders' equity being reported last, or vice versa. Exhibit 1.17 shows the order of appearance used by the 30 companies that comprise the Dow Jones Industrial Average.

EXHIBIT 1.17

Order of Appearance of Financial Statements for Companies in the Dow Jones Industrials Index

	PERCENTAGES			
Position of Statement	Income Statement	Balance Sheet	Stmt. of Cash Flows	Changes in Equity
First	83%	17%		
Second	17%	80%		3%
Third		3%	50%	47%
Fourth			50%	50%

Real-World Financial Reports

As previously indicated, organizations exist in many different forms, including *business* entities and *not-for-profit* entities. Business entities are typically service, merchandising, or manufacturing companies. **Service businesses,** which include doctors, attorneys, accountants, dry cleaners, and housekeepers, provide services to their customers. **Merchandising businesses,** sometimes called *retail* or *wholesale companies,* sell goods to customers that other entities make. **Manufacturing businesses** make the goods that they sell to their customers.

Some business operations include combinations of these three categories. For example, an automotive repair shop might change oil (service function), sell parts such as oil filters (retail function), and rebuild engines (manufacturing function). The nature of the reporting entity affects the form and content of the information reported in an entity's financial statements. For example, governmental entities provide statements of activities while business entities provide income statements. Similarly, income statements of retail companies show an expense item called *cost of goods sold,* but service companies that do not sell goods have no such item in their income statements. You should expect some diversity when reviewing real-world financial statements.

Throughout this book we usually present income statements that end with "Net income." Due to an accounting rule that became effective at the end of 2009, income statements of large, real-world companies often appear to have three lines for net income. The partial income statements for Merck & Company, a large pharmaceutical company, shown in Exhibit 1.18, illustrate this issue. Notice that the third line from the bottom of the statement is called "Net income." However, "Net income attributable to noncontrolling interests" is subtracted from this first net income to arrive at "Net income attributable to Merck & Co., Inc." The illustrations in this text always assume that there is no net income attributable to noncontrolling interests; therefore, our examples simply end with the term "Net income."

Some real-world companies with complex operations report information related to *comprehensive income.* Comprehensive income is determined by adding or subtracting certain items to or from net income. A description of the items used to determine comprehensive income is complex and beyond the scope of this course. Even so, the reader should be aware that, as of 2011, companies that must report comprehensive income may do so in one of two ways. First, comprehensive income items can be added to the bottom of the primary statement of earnings. Alternatively, a separate statement showing the determination of comprehensive income can be presented immediately following the primary statement of earnings. If a company chooses to report comprehensive income in a separate statement, the company's annual report will contain five financial statements. This text limits coverage to the four major financial statements that appear in real-world annual reports. The statement of comprehensive income is not covered.

EXHIBIT 1.18 Real-World Financial Reporting

MERCK & CO., INC. AND SUBSIDIARIES
Consolidated Statement of Income (partial)
Years Ended December 31
($ in millions except per share amounts)

	2017	2016	2015
Sales	$40,122	$39,807	$39,498
Costs, expenses, and other			
Materials and production	12,775	13,891	14,934
Marketing and administrative	9,830	9,762	10,313
Research and development	10,208	10,124	6,704
Restructuring costs	776	651	619
Other (income) expense, net	12	720	1,527
	33,601	35,148	34,097
Income before taxes	6,521	4,659	5,401
Taxes on income	4,103	718	942
Net income	2,418	3,941	4,459
Less: Net income attributable to noncontrolling interests	24	21	17
Net income attributable to Merck & Co., Inc.	$ 2,394	$ 3,920	$ 4,442

Annual Report for Target Corporation

Organizations normally provide information, including financial statements, to *stakeholders* yearly in a document known as an **annual report.** The annual report for Target Corporation is referred to in some of the end-of-chapter assignments, and it is worth your while to review it as an example of a real-world annual report. This report can be found online at http://investors.target.com. On the web page that appears, under the "Investors" link at the top of the page, click on "sec filings." Next, under "filter by form type," select "Annual filings" and then select the most recent "10-K" form from the list that appears. The pdf format is the easiest to work with. This report includes the company's financial statements (see pages 35–39 of the 2017 annual report). Immediately following the statements are a set of notes that provide additional details about the items described in the statements (see pages 40–62 of the 2017 annual report). The annual report contains the *auditors' report,* which is discussed in Chapter 6. Annual reports also include written commentary describing management's assessment of significant events that affected the company during the reporting period. This commentary is called *management's discussion and analysis (MD&A).*

The U.S. Securities and Exchange Commission (SEC) requires public companies to file an annual report in a document known as a 10-K. The SEC is discussed in more detail later. Even though the annual report is usually flashier (contains more color and pictures) than the 10-K, the 10-K is normally more comprehensive with respect to content. As a result, the 10-K report frequently substitutes for the annual report, but the annual report cannot substitute for the 10-K. In an effort to reduce costs, many companies now use the 10-K report as their annual report.

Todd Pearson/Digital Vision/PunchStock

McGraw-Hill Education/Andrew Resek

Monty Rakusen/Cultura/Getty Images

Special Terms in Real-World Reports

The financial statements of real-world companies include numerous items relating to advanced topics that are not covered in introductory accounting textbooks, especially the first chapter of an introductory accounting textbook. Do not, however, be discouraged from browsing through real-world annual reports. You will significantly enhance your learning if you look at many annual reports and attempt to identify as many items as you can. As your accounting knowledge grows, you will likely experience increased interest in real-world financial reports and the businesses they describe.

We encourage you to look for annual reports in the library or ask your employer for a copy of your company's report. The Internet is another excellent source for obtaining annual reports. Most companies provide links to their annual reports on their home pages. Look for links labeled "About the Company" or "Investor Relations" or other phrases that logically lead to the company's financial reports. The best way to learn accounting is to use it. Accounting is the language of business. Learning this language will serve you well in almost any area of business you pursue.

REALITY BYTES

The **Snapchat** application for smartphones was launched in 2011, and was being used widely by 2012. On February 2, 2017, the parent company of Snapchat, **Snap, Inc.**, announced formally that it planned to become a public company through an initial public offering of its stock, commonly referred to as an "IPO."

The company's IPO in 2017 was one of the most highly anticipated new stock offerings of the past several years. However, the documents filed by the company with the Securities and Exchange Commission showed that while its revenues were growing rapidly, its net losses were also growing. In fact, the company had never made a profit, and its cumulative losses through 2017 were $4.7 billion. Even so, *The Wall Street Journal* reported that the price of the company's stock at its IPO was expected to indicate that the value of the company was

James D. Morgan/Getty Images

around $25 billion. Clearly, investors' primary focus was not on past earnings.

Investors frequently use more information than just what is reported in a company's annual report. The annual report focuses on historical data, but investors are more interested in the future than the past. The historical information contained in the annual report is important because the past is frequently a strong predictor of what will occur in the future, but it does not provide a complete picture of a company's prospects.

A new company that has never earned a profit, like Snap, may have an idea that is so innovative that investors rush to buy its stock, even though they believe it will be a few years before the company has positive earnings. Although Snap has consistently reported losses in the past, it has become one of the leading providers of social media technology. Investors and creditors may also be motivated by nonfinancial considerations such as social consciousness, humanitarian concerns, or personal preferences. For example, people who buy stock in the **Green Bay Packers**, the only publicly traded NFL team, are motivated by team spirit, not profit.

While accounting information is very important, it is only part of the information pool that investors and creditors use to make decisions.

A Look Back

This chapter introduced the role of accounting in society and business: to provide information helpful to operating and evaluating the performance of organizations. Accounting is a measurement discipline. To communicate effectively, users of accounting must agree on the rules of measurement. *Generally accepted accounting principles (GAAP)* constitute the rules used by the accounting profession in the United States to govern financial reporting. GAAP is a work in progress that continues to evolve.

This chapter showed how basic business events affect the components of the accounting equation: *assets, liabilities, common stock, and retained earnings.* The accounting cycle was introduced by recording events for two accounting periods. From the ending balances in the accounting equation, a *balance sheet* was prepared for each accounting period. Three other financial statements were prepared for the second accounting period: the *income statement,* the *statement of changes in stockholders' equity,* and the *statement of cash flows.* The chapter discussed the form and content of each statement, as well as the interrelationships among the statements.

The concepts covered in this chapter are foundational, and it is extremely important that you fully understand this chapter before proceeding to Chapter 2.

A Look Forward

To keep matters as simple as possible and to focus on the interrelationships among financial statements, this chapter considered only cash events. Obviously, many real-world events do not involve an immediate exchange of cash. For example, customers use telephone service throughout the month without paying for it until the next month. Such phone usage represents an expense in one month with a cash exchange in the following month. Events such as this are called *accruals*. Understanding the effects that accrual events have on the financial statements is a primary focus of Chapter 2.

Video lectures and accompanying self-assessment quizzes are available in *Connect* for all learning objectives.

Tableau Dashboard Activity is available in *Connect* for this chapter.

SELF-STUDY REVIEW PROBLEM

Carrington Company (CC) started its fourth year of operations with account balances shown in the accounting equation presented in Requirement *a*. During Year 4, the company experienced the following transactions.

1. CC acquired $28,000 cash by issuing common stock.
2. CC received $96,000 cash for providing services to customers.
3. CC paid $57,000 cash for operating expenses.
4. CC paid an $11,000 cash dividend to the owners.
5. CC paid $80,000 cash to purchase land.
6. CC paid $20,000 cash in a partial settlement of its note payable.

Required

a. Record the transaction data in an accounting equation like the one shown next. When recording revenue, expense, and dividend transactions, provide the title of the equity account affected by the transaction in the Account Titles column. Otherwise, write NA in the Account Titles column to indicate that the transaction does not affect revenue, expense, or dividend accounts. The first transaction is shown as an example.

			Accounting Equation							
	Assets				Liabilities		Stockholders' Equity			
Event No.	Cash	+	Land	=	Notes Pay.	+	Com. Stk.	+	Ret. Earn.	Account Titles
Beg. Bal.	69,000	+	90,000	=	50,000	+	65,000	+	44,000	
1.	28,000	+	NA	=	NA	+	28,000	+	NA	NA

b. Identify each event as an asset source, use, or exchange transaction.
c. Use the information in the accounting equation to prepare an income statement, a statement of changes in stockholders' equity, and a balance sheet.
d. Create a statement of cash flows. (*Hint:* It may be helpful to review each of the six transactions and classify the impact on cash flow as being an operating, investing, or financing activity before attempting to create the statement.)
e. As of December 31, Year 4, can CC pay an $80,000 cash dividend? What is the maximum dividend the company can pay?
f. As of December 31, Year 2, what percentage of total assets were acquired from the owners of the business?
g. Could CC be forced into bankruptcy if the note payable is due on January 1, Year 5?

Solution

a.

							Accounting Equation				
		Assets			**Liabilities**		**Stockholders' Equity**				**Account**
Event No.	**Cash**	+	**Land**	=	**Notes Pay.**	+	**Com. Stk.**	+	**Ret. Earn.**		
Beg. Bal.	69,000	+	90,000	=	50,000	+	65,000	+	44,000		
1.	28,000	+	NA	=	NA	+	28,000	+	NA		NA
2.	96,000	+	NA	=	NA	+	NA	+	96,000		Revenue
3.	(57,000)	+	NA	=	NA	+	NA	+	(57,000)		Operating Expenses
4.	(11,000)	+	NA	=	NA	+	NA	+	(11,000)		Dividend
5.	(80,000)	+	80,000	=	NA	+	NA	+	NA		NA
6.	(20,000)		NA		(20,000)		NA		NA		NA
End Bal.	25,000	+	170,000	=	30,000	+	93,000	+	72,000		

b.

1. CC acquired $28,000 cash by issuing common stock. — ASSET SOURCE
2. CC received $96,000 cash for providing services to customers. — ASSET SOURCE
3. CC paid $57,000 cash for operating expenses. — ASSET USE
4. CC paid an $11,000 cash dividend to the owners. — ASSET USE
5. CC paid $80,000 to purchase land. — ASSET EXCHANGE
6. CC paid $20,000 cash as a partial settlement of its note payable. — ASSET USE

c.

Carrington Company
Income Statement
For the Year Ended December 31, Year 4

Revenue	$96,000
Operating Expenses	(57,000)
Net Income	$39,000

Carrington Company
Statement of Changes in Stockholders' Equity
For the Year Ended December 31, Year 4

Beginning Common Stock	$ 65,000	
Plus: Stock Issued	28,000	
Ending Common Stock		$ 93,000
Beginning Retained Earnings	44,000	
Plus: Net Income	39,000	
Minus: Dividend	(11,000)	
Ending Retained Earnings		72,000
Total Stockholders' Equity		$165,000

Carrington Company
Balance Sheet
As of December 31, Year 4

Assets		
Cash	$ 25,000	
Land	170,000	
Total Assets		$195,000
Liabilities		
Notes Payable	$ 30,000	
Total Liabilities		$30,000
Stockholders' Equity		
Common Stock	93,000	
Retained Earnings	72,000	
Total Stockholders' Equity		165,000
Total Liabilities and Stockholders' Equity		$195,000

d.

1. CC acquired $28,000 cash by issuing common stock. — FINANCING ACTIVITY
2. CC received $96,000 cash for providing services to customers. — OPERATING ACTIVITY
3. CC paid $57,000 cash for operating expenses. — OPERATING ACTIVITY
4. CC paid an $11,000 cash dividend to the owners. — FINANCING ACTIVITY
5. CC paid $80,000 to purchase land. — INVESTING ACTIVITY
6. CC paid $20,000 cash as a partial settlement of its note payable. — FINANCING ACTIVITY

Carrington Company
Statement of Cash Flows
For the Year Ended December 31, Year 4

Cash Flows from Operating Activities:		
Cash Receipts from Customers	$96,000	
Cash Payments for Other Expenses	(57,000)	
Net Cash Flow from Operating Activities		$39,000
Net Cash Flow from Investing Activities		
Cash Payment to Purchase Land	(80,000)	
Net Cash Flow from Investing Activities		(80,000)
Net Cash Flow from Financing Activities		
Cash Receipt from Stock Issue	28,000	
Cash Payment to Repay Liability	(20,000)	
Cash Payment for Dividend	(11,000)	
Net Cash Flow from Financing Activities		(3,000)
Net Change in Cash		(44,000)
Plus: Beginning Cash Balance		69,000
Ending Cash Balance		$25,000

e. CC cannot pay an $80,000 cash dividend as of December 31, Year 4. CC is restricted by both retained earnings and the amount of cash. The company has only $72,000 of retained earnings, so it does not have sufficient retained earnings to pay the $80,000 dividend. Further, the Company has only $25,000 cash, so it does not have the cash to pay an $80,000 dividend. The maximum dividend the company can pay on this date is $25,000 because that is all of the cash the company has.

f. CC acquired $93,000 of assets from the owners ($65,000 ending balance for Year 3 plus $28,000 stock issue in Year 4). Total assets as of December 31, Year 4, amount to $195,000 ($25,000 cash + $170,000 land). Accordingly, 47.69 percent of assets ($93,000 common stock ÷ $195,000 total assets) were acquired from the owners.

g. CC could be forced into bankruptcy on January 1, Year 5. On that date, the note payable is $30,000, while the company has only $25,000 of cash available to repay the debt. In practice, most companies do not carry sufficient cash to repay all of their liabilities. Most debt is simply refinanced. In other words, the existing debt is repaid by acquiring funds through new borrowing.

KEY TERMS

Account 12
Accounting 3
Accounting equation 11
Accounting event 11
Accounting period 12
Annual report 32
Articulation 28
Asset 9
Asset exchange transaction 13
Asset source transaction 13
Asset use transaction 14
Balance sheet 15
Claims 11
Common stock 10
Creditor 4
Dividend 14
Double-entry bookkeeping 13

Earnings 4
Elements 9
Expenses 14
Financial accounting 5
Financial Accounting Standards Board (FASB) 7
Financial resources 4
Financial statements 15
Financing activities 25
Generally accepted accounting principles (GAAP) 8
Historical cost concept 15
Income 4
Income statement 22
Interest 4

International Accounting Standards Board (IASB) 9
International Financial Reporting Standards (IFRS) 9
Investing activities 25
Investor 4
Labor resources 5
Liabilities 10
Liquidity 16
Managerial accounting 5
Manufacturing businesses 30
Market 4
Matching concept 22
Merchandising businesses 30
Net income 22

Net loss 22
Not-for-profit entities 6
Operating activities 25
Physical resources 4
Profit 4
Reporting entities 8
Retained earnings 11
Revenue 14
Service businesses 30
Stakeholders 5
Statement of cash flows 25
Statement of changes in stockholders' equity 23
Stewardship 19
Stockholders 10
Stockholders' equity 10
Transaction 11
Users 5

QUESTIONS

1. Explain the term *stakeholder*. Distinguish between stakeholders with a direct versus an indirect interest in the companies that issue financial reports.

2. Why is accounting called the *language of business*?

3. What is the primary mechanism used to allocate resources in the United States?

4. In a business context, what does the term *market* mean?

5. What market trilogy components are involved in the process of transforming resources into finished products?

6. Give an example of a financial resource, a physical resource, and a labor resource.

7. What type of income or profit does an investor expect to receive in exchange for providing financial resources to a business? What type of income does a creditor expect from providing financial resources to an organization or business?

8. How do financial and managerial accounting differ?

9. Describe a not-for-profit or nonprofit enterprise. What is the motivation for this type of entity?

10. What are the U.S. rules of accounting information measurement called?

11. Explain how a career in public accounting differs from a career in private accounting.

12. Distinguish between financial statements and accounts.

13. What role do assets play in business profitability?

14. To whom do the assets of a business belong?

15. Describe the differences between creditors and investors.

16. Name the accounting term used to describe a business's obligations to creditors.

17. What is the accounting equation? Describe each of its three components.

18. Who ultimately bears the risk and collects the rewards associated with operating a business?

19. Discuss the two views of the right side of the accounting equation.

20. If a company has $2,000 cash, $1,200 liabilities, and $800 retained earnings, can it pay a dividend of $1,000?

21. How does acquiring capital from owners affect the accounting equation?

22. What is the difference between assets that are acquired by issuing common stock and those that are acquired using retained earnings?

23. How does earning revenue affect the accounting equation?

24. What are the three primary sources of assets?

25. What is the source of retained earnings?

26. How does distributing assets (paying dividends) to owners affect the accounting equation?

27. What are the similarities and differences between dividends and expenses?

28. What four general-purpose financial statements do business enterprises use?

29. Which of the general-purpose financial statements provides information about the enterprise at a specific designated date?

30. What causes a net loss?

31. Explain the matching concept.

32. What three categories of cash receipts and cash payments do businesses report on the statement of cash flows? Explain the types of cash flows reported in each category.

33. How are asset accounts usually arranged in the balance sheet?

34. Discuss the term *articulation* as it relates to financial statements.

35. What is the historical cost concept and how does it relate to verifiability?

36. Identify the three types of accounting transactions discussed in this chapter. Provide an example of each type of transaction, and explain how it affects the accounting equation.

37. What type of information does a business typically include in its annual report?

38. What is U.S. GAAP? What is IFRS?

EXERCISES—SERIES A

 All applicable Exercises in Series A are available in *Connect*.

LO 1-1

Exercise 1-1A   *The role of accounting in society*

Free economies use open markets to allocate resources.

Required

Identify the three participants in a free business market. Write a brief memo explaining how these participants interact to ensure that goods and services are distributed in a manner that satisfies consumers. Your memo should include answers to the following questions: If you work as a public accountant, what role would you play in the allocation of resources? Which professional certification would be most appropriate to your career?

LO 1-1

Exercise 1-2A   *Careers in accounting*

While public and private accounting overlap, various professional certifications are designed to attest to competency for specific areas of interest.

Required

a. Name the most common professional certification held by public accountants. Describe the general requirements for attaining this certification.

b. Name two types of professional certification, other than CPA, held by private accountants. Describe the general requirements for attaining these certifications.

LO 1-2

Exercise 1-3A   *Identifying reporting entities*

Karen White helped organize a charity fund to help cover the medical expenses of her friend, Vicky Hill, who was seriously injured in a bicycle accident. The fund was named the Vicky Hill Recovery Fund (VHRF). Karen contributed $1,000 of her own money to the fund. The $1,000 was paid to WKUX, a local radio station that designed and played an advertising campaign to educate the public about Vicky's predicament. The campaign resulted in the collection of $20,000 cash, and VHRF paid $12,000 to Mercy Hospital to cover Vicky's outstanding hospital cost. The remaining $8,000 was donated to the National Cyclist Fund.

Required

Identify the entities mentioned in the scenario and explain what happened to the cash accounts of each entity you identify.

Exercise 1-4A   *Define the components of financial statements*

Required

Match the terms (identified as a through g) with the definitions and phrases (marked 1 through 7). For example the term "a. Assets" matches with definition 7. Economic resources that will be used by a business to produce revenue.

a. Assets
b. Common Stock
c. Creditors
d. Liability
e. Retained Earnings
f. Stockholders
g. Stockholders' Equity

1. Individuals or institutions that have contributed assets or services to a business in exchange for an ownership interest in the business.
2. Common Stock + Retained Earnings.
3. Certificates that evidence ownership in a company.
4. Assets − Liabilities − Common Stock.
5. An obligation to pay cash in the future.
6. Individuals or institutions that have loaned goods or services to a business.
7. Economic resources that will be used by a business to produce revenue.

Exercise 1-5A   *Identify missing information in the accounting equation*

Required

Calculate the missing amounts in the following table:

Accounting Equation							
					Stockholders' Equity		
Company	Assets	=	Liabilities	+	Common Stock	+	Retained Earnings
A	$?		$25,000		$48,000		$50,000
B	40,000		?		7,000		30,000
C	75,000		15,000		?		42,000
D	125,000		45,000		60,000		?

Exercise 1-6A   *Account titles and the accounting equation*

The following account titles were drawn from Food Supplies, Incorporated (HFSI): Computers, Operating Expenses, Rent Revenue, Building, Cash, Land, Trucks, Gasoline Expense, Retained Earnings, Supplies, Accounts Payable, Office Furniture, Salaries Expense, Common Stock, Service Revenue, Dividends.

Required

a. Create an accounting equation using assets, liabilities, and stockholders' equity. Use the accounting equation to classify each account title under the element of the accounting equation to which it belongs.
b. Will all businesses have the same number of accounts? Explain your answer.

Exercise 1-7A   *Missing information and recording events*

As of December 31, Year 1, Moss Company had total cash of $195,000, notes payable of $90,500, and common stock of $84,500. During Year 2, Moss earned $42,000 of cash revenue, paid $24,000 for cash expenses, and paid a $3,000 cash dividend to the stockholders.

Required

a. Determine the amount of retained earnings as of December 31, Year 1.
b. Create an accounting equation and record the beginning account balances.
c. Record the revenue, expense, and dividend events under the accounting equation created in Requirement *b*.
d. Prove the equality of the accounting equation as of December 31, Year 2.
e. Identify the beginning and ending balances in the Cash and Common Stock accounts. Explain why the beginning and ending balances in the Cash account are different but the beginning and ending balances in the Common Stock account remain the same.

LO 1-4

Exercise 1-8A *Classifying events as asset source, use, or exchange*

Nevada Company experienced the following events during its first year of operations:

1. Acquired an additional $1,000 cash from the issue of common stock.
2. Paid $2,400 cash for utilities expense.
3. Paid a $1,500 cash dividend to the stockholders.
4. Provided additional services for $6,000 cash.
5. Purchased additional land for $2,500 cash.
6. The market value of the land was determined to be $24,000 at the end of the accounting period.
7. Acquired $16,000 cash from the issue of common stock.
8. Paid $3,500 cash for salary expense.
9. Borrowed $10,000 cash from New South Bank.
10. Paid $6,000 cash to purchase land.
11. Provided boarding services for $10,500 cash.

Required

Classify each event as an asset source, use, or exchange transaction or as not applicable.

LO 1-2, 1-4

Exercise 1-9A *Identifying reporting entities and transaction types*

Riley Company paid $60,000 cash to purchase land from Clay Company. Clay originally paid $60,000 for the land.

Required

a. Did this event cause the balance in Riley's cash account to increase, decrease, or remain unchanged?
b. Did this event cause the balance in Clay's cash account to increase, decrease, or remain unchanged?
c. Did this event cause the balance in Riley's land account to increase, decrease, or remain unchanged?
d. Did this event cause the balance in Clay's land account to increase, decrease, or remain unchanged?
e. Was this event an asset source, use, or exchange transaction for Riley Company?
f. Was this event an asset source, use, or exchange transaction for Clay Company?

LO 1-5

Exercise 1-10A *Effect of events on the accounting equation*

Olive Enterprises experienced the following events during Year 1:

1. Acquired cash from the issue of common stock.
2. Paid cash to reduce the principal on a bank note.
3. Sold land for cash at an amount equal to its cost.
4. Provided services to clients for cash.
5. Paid utilities expenses with cash.
6. Paid a cash dividend to the stockholders.

Required

Explain how each of the events would affect the accounting equation by writing the letter I for increase, the letter D for decrease, and NA for does not affect under each of the components of the accounting equation. The first event is shown as an example.

	Accounting Equation				
				Stockholders' Equity	
Event No.	Assets	= Liabilities	+	Common Stock	+ Retained Earnings
1	I	NA		I	NA

Exercise 1-11A   *Prepare a balance sheet after recording transactions in an accounting equation*   LO 1-5, 1-6

Better Corp. (BC) began operations on January 1, Year 1. During Year 1, BC experienced the following accounting events:

1. Acquired $7,000 cash from the issue of common stock.
2. Borrowed $12,000 cash from the State Bank.
3. Collected $47,000 cash as a result of providing services to customers.
4. Paid $30,000 for operating expenses.
5. Paid an $8,000 cash dividend to the stockholders.
6. Paid $20,000 cash to purchase land.

Required

a. Record the events in an accounting equation like the one shown next. Record the amounts of revenue, expense, and dividends in the Retained Earnings column. Provide the appropriate titles for these accounts in the last column of the table.

BETTER CORP.
Accounting Equation

Event No.	Assets		=	Liabilities	+	Stockholders' Equity		Acct. Titles for RE
	Cash	Land		Notes Payable		Common Stock	Retained Earnings	
Beg. Bal.	0	0		0		0	0	

b. As of December 31, Year 1, determine the total amount of assets, liabilities, and stockholders' equity and prepare a balance sheet.

c. What is the amount of total assets, liabilities, and stockholders' equity as of January 1, Year 2?

d. Assume that the land has a market value of $22,000 as of December 31, Year 1. At what amount will the land be shown on the December 31, Year 1, balance sheet? Why is this amount used in the balance sheet?

Exercise 1-12A   *Prepare balance sheets for two accounting periods using a vertical format*   LO 1-5, 1-6

This exercise continues the scenario described in Exercise 1-11A shown earlier. Specifically, the Better Corp. Year 1 ending balances become the Year 2 beginning balances. These balances are shown in the following accounting equation.

BETTER CORP.
Accounting Equation Year 2

Event No.	Assets		=	Liabilities	+	Stockholders' Equity		Acct. Titles for RE
	Cash	Land		Notes Payable		Common Stock	Retained Earnings	
Beg. Bal.	8,000	20,000		12,000		7,000	9,000	

Better Corp. completed the following transactions during Year 2:

1. Purchased land for $5,000 cash.
2. Acquired $25,000 cash from the issue of common stock.
3. Received $75,000 cash for providing services to customers.

4. Paid cash operating expenses of $42,000.
5. Borrowed $10,000 cash from the bank.
6. Paid a $5,000 cash dividend to the stockholders.
7. Determined that the market value of the land on December 31, Year 2, is $35,000.

Required

a. Record the transactions in the appropriate accounts under an accounting equation. Record the amounts of revenue, expense, and dividends in the Retained Earnings column. Provide the appropriate titles for these accounts in the last column of the table.

b. Prepare balance sheets for Year 1 and Year 2. These statements should be presented in the vertical format with Year 1 and Year 2 shown in side-by-side columns. Recall that the Year 1 ending balances become the Year 2 beginning balances. These ending/beginning balances can be found on the first row of the table shown earlier. More specifically, the Year 1 ending balances include $8,000 cash, $20,000 land, $12,000 notes payable, $7,000 common stock, and $9,000 retained earnings.

c. How much cash is in the notes payable account?

d. How much cash is in the common stock account?

e. How much cash is in the retained earnings account? What is the balance of the cash account? Explain why the balances in the cash and retained earnings accounts are the same or different.

f. What is the amount of the land shown on the December 31, Year 2, balance sheet? Why is it shown at this amount?

LO 1-5, 1-6

Exercise 1-13A   *Interpreting information shown in a balance sheet*

Jones Enterprises was started on January 1, Year 1, when it acquired $6,000 cash from creditors and $10,000 from owners. The company immediately purchased land that cost $12,000. The land purchase was the only transaction occurring during Year 1.

Required

a. Create an accounting equation and record the events under the equation.

b. As of December 31, Year 1, Jones's obligations to creditors represent what percentage of total assets?

c. As of December 31, Year 1, Jones's stockholders' equity represents what percentage of total assets?

d. What is the maximum cash dividend Jones can pay on December 31, Year 1?

e. Assume the debt is due December 31, Year 1. Given that Jones has $10,000 in stockholders' equity, can the company repay the creditors at this point? Why or why not?

LO 1-6

Exercise 1-14A   *Interpreting information shown in a balance sheet*

Both balance sheets shown in the following table were dated as of December 31, Year 3.

Balance Sheets for	Allen Co.	White Co.
Assets		
Cash	$10,000	$ 0
Land	0	12,000
Total Assets	$10,000	$12,000
Liabilities	$ 7,500	$ 3,000
Common Stock	2,000	7,200
Retained Earnings	500	1,800
Total Liab. and Stk. Equity	$10,000	$12,000

Required

a. Based only on the information shown in the balance sheets, can Allen Co. pay a $2,000 cash dividend?

b. Based only on the information shown in the balance sheets, can White Co. pay a $1,000 cash dividend?

c. Reconstruct the balance sheets for each company using percentages for the liabilities and stock-holders' equity sections of the statements instead of dollar values.

d. Define the right side of an accounting equation without using the terms *liabilities* or *stockholders' equity*.

Exercise 1-15A   *Calculate missing amounts and interpret results*   LO 1-3, 1-5, 1-6

The following table shows the transactions experienced by J G Gutter Works (JGGW) during Year 7. The table contains missing data which are labeled with alphabetic characters (a) through (j). Assume all transactions shown in the accounting equation are cash transactions.

| | Accounting Equation | | | | | | | | |
| | Assets | | | Liabilities | | Stockholders' Equity | | | |
Event No.	Cash	+	Land	=	Notes Pay.	+	Com. Stk.	+	Ret. Earn.	Account
Beg. Bal.	(a)	+	90,000	=	(b)	+	(c)	+	25,000	
1.	(d)	+	NA	=	NA	+	68,000	+	NA	NA
2.	(e)	+	NA	=	NA	+	NA	+	(f)	Revenue
3.	(57,000)	+	NA	=	NA	+	NA	+	(57,000)	Expenses
4.	(14,000)	+	NA	=	NA	+	NA	+	(g)	Dividend
5.	(50,000)	+	(h)	=	NA	+	NA	+	NA	NA
6.	(10,000)	+	NA	=	(10,000)	+	NA	+	NA	NA
End Bal.	69,000	+	(i)	=	40,000	+	123,000	+	(j)	

Required

a. Determine the correct amount represented by each character (a) through (j).

b. Is there sufficient cash available to repay the debt on January 1, Year 8?

c. Based on the information in the table, what is the maximum cash dividend JGGW could pay on January 1, Year 8?

EXERCISES—SERIES A

Exercise 1-16A   *Prepare an income statement*   LO 1-7

Ollie Company experienced the following events during its first-year operations:

1. Acquired $72,000 cash from the issue of common stock.
2. Borrowed $26,000 from the First City Bank.
3. Earned $59,000 of cash revenue.
4. Incurred $43,000 of cash expenses.
5. Paid a $7,000 cash dividend.
6. Paid $43,000 to purchase land.

Required

a. Identify the events that will affect the income statement.

b. Prepare an income statement that shows the results of Year 1 operations.

Exercise 1-17A   *Preparing and interpreting information in an income statement and two*   LO 1-6, 1-7
balance sheets

At the end of Year 1, Emma, Inc. had $600 of cash, $400 of liabilities, $200 of common stock, and zero in retained earnings. During Year 2, the company generated $560 of cash revenue and incurred $900 of cash expenses.

SECTION 2

Required

Based on this information, prepare balance sheets for Year 1 and Year 2. Also, prepare a Year 2 income statement.

LO 1-8

Exercise 1-18A   *Prepare a statement of changes in stockholders' equity*

Ollie Company experienced the following events during its first-year operations:

1. Acquired $72,000 cash from the issue of common stock.
2. Borrowed $26,000 from the First City Bank.
3. Earned $59,000 of cash revenue.
4. Incurred $43,000 of cash expenses.
5. Paid a $7,000 cash dividend.
6. Paid $43,000 to purchase land.

Required

Prepare a statement of changes in stockholders' equity.

LO 1-5, 1-6, 1-7, 1-8

Exercise 1-19A   *Preparing an income statement, statement of changes in stockholders' equity, and a balance sheet*

Majka Company was started on January 1, Year 1 when it acquired $50,000 from the sale of common stock. During Year 1, the company experienced the following three accounting events: (1) earned cash revenues of $28,600, (2) paid cash expenses of $13,200, and (3) paid a $1,500 cash dividend to its stockholders. These were the only events that affected the company during Year 1.

Required

a. Create an accounting equation and record the effects of each accounting event under the appropriate account headings.
b. Prepare an income statement, statement of changes in stockholders' equity, and a balance sheet dated December 31, Year 1, for Majka Company.
c. Explain why different terminology is used to date the income statement than is used to date the balance sheet.

LO 1-7, 1-8

Exercise 1-20A   *Analyzing retained earnings to determine net income*

The December 31, Year 1, balance sheet for Deen Company showed total stockholders' equity of $156,000. Total stockholders' equity increased by $65,000 between December 31, Year 1, and December 31, Year 2. During Year 2, Deen Company acquired $20,000 cash from the issue of common stock. Deen Company paid a $5,000 cash dividend to the stockholders during Year 2.

Required

Determine the amount of net income or loss Deen reported on its Year 2 income statement. (*Hint:* Remember that stock issues, net income, and dividends all change total stockholders' equity.)

LO 1-9

Exercise 1-21A   *Statement of cash flows*

On January 1, Year 1, Moore, a fast-food company, had a balance in its Cash account of $45,800. During the Year 1 accounting period, the company had (1) net cash inflow from operating activities of $24,800, (2) net cash outflow for investing activities of $16,000, and (3) net cash outflow from financing activities of $6,800.

Required

a. Prepare a statement of cash flows.
b. Provide a reasonable explanation as to what may have caused the net cash inflow from operating activities.
c. Provide a reasonable explanation as to what may have caused the net cash outflow from investing activities.
d. Provide a reasonable explanation as to what may have caused the net cash outflow from financing activities.

Exercise 1-22A   *Prepare a statement of cash flows*

All-Star Automotive Company experienced the following accounting events during Year 1:

1. Performed services for $25,000 cash.
2. Purchased land for $6,000 cash.
3. Hired an accountant to keep the books.
4. Received $50,000 cash from the issue of common stock.
5. Borrowed $5,000 cash from State Bank.
6. Paid $14,000 cash for salary expense.
7. Sold land for $9,000 cash.
8. Paid $10,000 cash on the loan from State Bank.
9. Paid $2,800 cash for utilities expense.
10. Paid a cash dividend of $5,000 to the stockholders.

Required

a. Indicate how each of the events would be classified on the statement of cash flows as operating activities (OA), investing activities (IA), financing activities (FA), or not applicable (NA).
b. Prepare a statement of cash flows. Assume All-Star Automotive had a beginning cash balance of $9,000.

Exercise 1-23A   *Preparing financial statements*

Dakota Company experienced the following events during Year 2:

1. Acquired $30,000 cash from the issue of common stock.
2. Paid $12,000 cash to purchase land.
3. Borrowed $10,000 cash.
4. Provided services for $20,000 cash.
5. Paid $1,000 cash for utilities expense.
6. Paid $15,000 cash for other operating expenses.
7. Paid a $2,000 cash dividend to the stockholders.
8. Determined that the market value of the land purchased in Event 2 is now $12,700.

Required

a. The January 1, Year 2, account balances are shown in the following accounting equation. Record the eight events in the appropriate accounts under an accounting equation. Record the amounts of revenue, expense, and dividends in the Retained Earnings column. Provide the appropriate titles for these accounts in the last column of the table. The first event is shown as an example.

DAKOTA COMPANY
Accounting Equation

Event No.	Assets		=	Liabilities	+	Stockholders' Equity		Acct. Titles for RE
	Cash	Land		Notes Payable		Common Stock	Retained Earnings	
Beg. Bal.	2,000	12,000		–0–		6,000	8,000	
1.	30,000					30,000		

b. Prepare an income statement, statement of changes in stockholders' equity, year-end balance sheet, and statement of cash flows for the Year 2 accounting period.
c. Determine the percentage of assets that were provided by retained earnings. How much cash is in the retained earnings account?
d. Based on the December 31, Year 2, balance sheet, what is the largest cash dividend Dakota could pay?

LO 1-5, 1-6, 1-7, 1-8, 1-9

Exercise 1-24A   *Preparing financial statements and interpreting the information in those statements*

On January 1, Year 2, the following information was drawn from the accounting records of Carter Company: cash of $800; land of $3,500; notes payable of $600; and common stock of $1,000.

Required

a. Determine the amount of retained earnings as of January 1, Year 2.

b. After looking at the amount of retained earnings, the chief executive officer (CEO) wants to pay a $1,000 cash dividend to the stockholders. Can the company pay this dividend? Why or why not?

c. As of January 1, Year 2, what percentage of the assets were acquired from creditors?

d. As of January 1, Year 2, what percentage of the assets were acquired from investors?

e. As of January 1, Year 2, what percentage of the assets were acquired from retained earnings?

f. Create an accounting equation using percentages instead of dollar amounts on the right side of the equation.

g. During Year 2, Carter Company earned cash revenue of $1,800, paid cash expenses of $1,200, and paid a cash dividend of $500. Prepare an income statement, statement of changes in stockholders' equity, a balance sheet, and a statement of cash flows dated December 31, Year 2. (*Hint:* It is helpful to record these events under an accounting equation before preparing the statements.)

h. Comment on the terminology used to date each statement.

i. What is the largest cash dividend that Carter could pay on December 31, Year 2?

LO 1-6, 1-7, 1-8, 1-9

Exercise 1-25A   *Preparing financial statements—cash flow emphasis*

As of January 1, Year 2, Room Designs Inc. had a balance of $9,900 in Cash, $3,500 in Common Stock, and $6,400 in Retained Earnings. These were the only accounts with balances on January 1, Year 2. During the Year 2 accounting period, the company had (1) revenue of $18,100, (2) expenses of $8,300, and (3) dividends of $2,000. Assume that all transactions are cash transactions. The following accounts and balances represent the financial condition of Room Designs Inc. as of December 31, Year 2.

ROOM DESIGNS INC.								
December 31, Year 2								
	Assets		=	Liabilities	+	Stockholders' Equity		Acct. Titles for RE
	Cash	Land		Notes Payable		Common Stock	Retained Earnings	
Ending Bal.	14,200	16,500		9,000		7,500	14,200	

Required

a. Determine the amount of net cash flow from operating activities.

b. What did the company purchase that resulted in the cash outflow from investing activities?

c. Assume that the net cash inflow from financing activities of $11,000 was caused by three events. Based on the earlier information, identify these events and determine the cash flow associated with each event.

d. Prepare a statement of cash flows.

e. Prepare an income statement, statement of changes in stockholders' equity, and a balance sheet.

LO 1-5, 1-6, 1-7, 1-8, 1-9, 1-10

Exercise 1-26A   *Prepare financial statements covering two accounting cycles*

Ortho Company experienced the following events during its first- and second-year operations:

Year 1 Transactions:

1. Acquired $68,000 cash from the issue of common stock.

2. Borrowed $36,000 cash from the National Credit Union.

3. Earned $59,000 of cash revenue.
4. Incurred $43,000 of cash expenses.
5. Paid a $7,000 cash dividend.
6. Paid $37,000 cash to purchase land.

Year 2 Transactions:

1. Acquired $50,000 cash from the issue of common stock.
2. Borrowed $20,000 cash from the National Credit Union.
3. Earned $85,000 of cash revenue.
4. Incurred $62,000 of cash expenses.
5. Paid a $2,000 cash dividend.
6. Paid $25,000 cash to purchase land.

Required

a. Record the transactions in an accounting equation like the equation shown next. Record the amounts of revenue, expense, and dividends in the Retained Earnings column. Provide the appropriate titles for these accounts in the last column of the table. Show the totals at the end of Year 1 and use these totals as the beginning balances for the second accounting cycle.

ORTHO COMPANY
Accounting Equation

Event No.	Assets		=	Liabilities	+	Stockholders' Equity		Acct. Titles for RE
	Cash	Land		Notes Payable		Common Stock	Retained Earnings	
Beg. Bal.	–0–	–0–		–0–		–0–	–0–	

b. Prepare an income statement, a statement of changes in stockholders' equity, a balance sheet, and a statement of cash flows for Year 1 and Year 2. Use a multicycle format that shows Year 1 and Year 2 information in side-by-side columns.

Exercise 1-27A   *Relationships between financial statements*

LO 1-10

Match the financial statements with the appropriate statement to describe them.

Financial Statements	Descriptions
1. Balance Sheet	A. Summarizes the activity under the cash account within the accounting equation. Explains the activities that caused the cash balance to change from the beginning of the year to the end of the year.
2. Income Statement	B. Summarizes all the activity under the equity section of the accounting equation. This statement generally shows how common stock and retained earnings changed from the beginning of the year to the end of the year.
3. Statement of Cash Flows	C. Summarizes all the company's accounts under the accounting equation as of a point in time. All other financial statements can be created from activity included in this statement.
4. Statement of Stockholders' Equity	D. Summarizes the revenues and expenses recorded under the retained earnings column of the accounting equation. This statement focuses on company performance over a fixed period of time.

IFRS

Exercise 1-28A *International Financial Reporting Standards*

Composite Fabricators, Inc. is a U.S.-based company that develops its financial statements under GAAP. The total amount of the company's assets shown on its balance sheet for the current year was approximately $370 million. The president of Composite Fabricators is considering the possibility of relocating the company to a country that practices accounting under IFRS. The president has hired an international accounting firm to determine what the company's statements would look like if they were prepared under IFRS. One striking difference is that under IFRS the assets shown on the balance sheet would be valued at approximately $430 million.

Required

a. Would Composite Fabricators' assets really be worth $60 million more if it moves its headquarters?

b. Discuss the underlying conceptual differences between U.S. GAAP and IFRS that cause the difference in the reported asset values.

PROBLEMS—SERIES A

All applicable Problems in Series A are available in *Connect*.

LO 1-1

Problem 1-29A *Accounting's role in not-for-profits*

Beverly Moore is struggling to pass her introductory accounting course. Beverly is intelligent but she likes to party. Studying is a low priority for Beverly. When one of her friends tells her that she is going to have trouble in business if she doesn't learn accounting, Beverly responds that she doesn't plan to go into business. She says that she is arts-oriented and plans someday to be a director of a museum. She is in the school of business to develop her social skills, not her quantitative skills. Beverly says she won't have to worry about accounting, because museums are not intended to make a profit.

Required

a. Write a brief memo explaining whether you agree or disagree with Beverly's position regarding accounting and not-for-profit organizations.

b. Distinguish between financial accounting and managerial accounting.

c. Identify some of the stakeholders of not-for-profit institutions that would expect to receive financial accounting reports.

d. Identify some of the stakeholders of not-for-profit institutions that would expect to receive managerial accounting reports.

LO 1-2

CHECK FIGURE
1. Entities mentioned:
   Bob Wilder and Wilder Co.

Problem 1-30A *Accounting entities*

The following business scenarios are independent from one another:

1. Bob Wilder starts a business by transferring $10,000 from his personal checking account into a checking account for his business, Wilder Co.

2. A business that Sam Pace owns earns $4,600 of cash revenue from customers.

3. Jim Sneed borrows $30,000 from the National Bank and uses the money to purchase a car from Iuka Ford.

4. OZ Company pays its five employees $2,500 each to cover their salaries.

5. Gil Roberts loans his son Jim $5,000 cash.

6. Gane, Inc. paid $100,000 cash to purchase land from Atlanta Land Co.

7. Rob Moore and Gil Thomas form the MT partnership by contributing $20,000 each from their personal bank accounts to a partnership bank account.

8. Stephen Woo pays cash to purchase $5,000 of common stock that is issued by Izzard, Inc.

9. Natural Stone pays a $5,000 cash dividend to each of its seven shareholders.

10. Billows, Inc. borrowed $5,000,000 from the National Bank.

Required

a. For each scenario, create a list of all of the entities mentioned in the description.

b. Describe what happens to the cash account of each entity that you identified in Requirement *a.*

Problem 1-31A   *Classifying events as asset source, use, or exchange*   **LO 1-3, 1-4**

The following unrelated events are typical of those experienced by business entities:

1. Acquire cash by issuing common stock.

2. Pay other operating supplies expense.

3. Agree to represent a client in an IRS audit and to receive payment when the audit is complete.

4. Receive cash from customers for services rendered.

5. Pay employee salaries with cash.

6. Pay back a bank loan with cash.

7. Pay interest to a bank with cash.

8. Transfer cash from a checking account to a money market account.

9. Sell land for cash at its original cost.

10. Pay a cash dividend to stockholders.

11. Learn that a financial analyst determined the company's price-earnings ratio to be 26.

12. Borrow cash from the local bank.

13. Pay office supplies expense.

14. Make plans to purchase office equipment.

15. Trade a used car for a computer with the same value.

Required

Identify each of the events as an asset source, use, or exchange transaction. If an event would not be recorded under generally accepted accounting principles, identify it as not applicable (NA). Also indicate for each event whether total assets would increase, decrease, or remain unchanged. Organize your answer according to the following table. The first event is shown in the table as an example.

Event No.	Type of Event	Effect on Total Assets
1	Asset source	Increase

Problem 1-32A   *Relating titles and accounts to financial statements*   **LO 1-6, 1-7, 1-8, 1-9**

Required

Identify the financial statements on which each of the following items (titles, date descriptions, and accounts) appears by placing a check mark in the appropriate column. If an item appears on more than one statement, place a check mark in every applicable column.

Item	Income Statement	Statement of Changes in Stockholders' Equity	Balance Sheet	Statement of Cash Flows
Financing activities				
Ending common stock				
Interest expense				
As of (date)				
Land				
Beginning cash balance				
Notes payable				
Beginning common stock				
Service revenue				
Utility expense				
Stock issue				
Operating activities				
For the period ended (date)				
Net income				
Investing activities				
Net loss				
Ending cash balance				
Salary expense				
Consulting revenue				
Dividends				

LO 1-6, 1-7, 1-8, 1-9

Problem 1-33A   *Interrelationships among financial statements*

Pratt Corp. started the Year 2 accounting period with total assets of $30,000 cash, $12,000 of liabilities, and $5,000 of retained earnings. During the Year 2 accounting period, the Retained Earnings account increased by $7,550. The bookkeeper reported that Pratt paid cash expenses of $26,000 and paid a $2,000 cash dividend to stockholders, but she could not find a record of the amount of cash revenue that Pratt received for performing services. Pratt also paid $3,000 cash to reduce the liability owed to a bank, and the business acquired $4,000 of additional cash from the issue of common stock. Assume all transactions are cash transactions.

Required

a. Prepare the Year 2 income statement.

b. Prepare the Year 2 statement of changes in stockholders' equity.

c. Prepare the Year 2 balance sheet.

d. Prepare the Year 2 statement of cash flows.

e. Determine the percentage of total assets provided by creditors, investors, and earnings.

Problem 1-34A *Preparing financial statements for two complete accounting cycles*

LO 1-5, 1-6, 1-7, 1-8, 1-9, 1-10

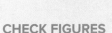

Mark's Consulting experienced the following transactions for Year 1, its first year of operations, and Year 2. Assume that all transactions involve the receipt or payment of cash.

Transactions for Year 1

1. Acquired $20,000 by issuing common stock.

2. Received $35,000 for providing services to customers.

3. Borrowed $25,000 cash from creditors.

4. Paid expenses amounting to $22,000.

5. Purchased land for $30,000 cash.

Transactions for Year 2

Beginning account balances for Year 2 are:

Cash	$28,000
Land	30,000
Notes payable	25,000
Common stock	20,000
Retained earnings	13,000

1. Acquired an additional $24,000 from the issue of common stock.

2. Received $95,000 for providing services in Year 2.

3. Paid $15,000 to reduce notes payable.

4. Paid expenses amounting to $71,500.

5. Paid a $3,000 dividend to the stockholders.

6. Determined that the market value of the land is $47,000.

Required

a. Write an accounting equation, and record the effects of each accounting event under the appropriate headings for each year. Record the amounts of revenue, expense, and dividends in the Retained Earnings column. Provide appropriate titles for these accounts in the last column of the table. Total the amounts in the accounts as of December 31, Year 1, and December 31, Year 2.

b. Prepare an income statement, statement of changes in stockholders' equity, year-end balance sheet, and statement of cash flows for Year 1 and Year 2. Use a multicycle format with Year 1 and Year 2 information shown in side-by-side columns.

c. Determine the amount of cash in the Retained Earnings account at the end of Year 1 and Year 2.

d. Compare the information provided by the income statement with the information provided by the statement of cash flows. Point out similarities and differences.

LO 1-6, 1-7, 1-8, 1-9, 1-10

Problem 1-35A *Missing information in financial statements*

Required

Fill in the blanks (indicated by the alphabetic letters in parentheses) in the following financial statements. Assume the company started operations January 1, Year 1, and all transactions involve cash. Note there is no letter "o" due to the similar appearance to 0.

	For the Years		
	Year 1	Year 2	Year 3
Income Statements			
Revenue	$ 900	$ 1,800	$ 2,500
Expense	(a)	(600)	(1,200)
Net income	$ 300	$ (m)	$ 1,300
Statements of Changes in Stockholders' Equity			
Beginning common stock	$ 0	$ (n)	$ 7,000
Plus: Common stock issued	6,000	1,000	3,000
Ending common stock	6,000	7,000	(t)
Beginning retained earnings	0	200	1,100
Plus: Net income	(b)	1,200	1,300
Less: Dividends	(c)	(300)	(500)
Ending retained earnings	200	(p)	1,900
Total stockholders' equity	$ (d)	$ 8,100	$11,900
Balance Sheets			
Assets			
Cash	$ (e)	$ (q)	$ (u)
Land	0	(r)	5,000
Total assets	$ (f)	$14,000	$16,800
Liabilities	$ (g)	$ 5,900	$ 4,900
Stockholders' equity			
Common stock	(h)	(s)	10,000
Retained earnings	(i)	1,100	1,900
Total stockholders' equity	(j)	8,100	11,900
Total liabilities and stockholders' equity	$8,100	$14,000	$16,800
Statements of Cash Flows			
Cash flows from operating activities			
Cash receipts from customers	$ (k)	$ 1,800	$ (v)
Cash payments for expenses	(l)	(600)	(w)
Net cash flows from operating activities	300	1,200	1,300
Cash flows from investing activities			
Cash payments for land	0	(5,000)	0
Net cash flows from investing activities	0	(5,000)	0
Cash flows from investing activities			
Cash receipts from loan	1,900	6,000	0
Cash payments to reduce debt	0	(2,000)	(x)
Cash receipts from stock issue	6,000	1,000	(y)
Cash payments for dividends	(100)	(300)	(z)
Net cash flows from financing activities	7,800	4,700	(1,500)
Net change in cash	8,100	900	2,800
Plus: Beginning cash balance	0	8,100	9,000
Ending cash balance	$8,100	$ 9,000	$11,800

EXERCISES—SERIES B

Exercise 1-1B *The role of accounting in society*

LO 1-1

Resource owners provide three types of resources to businesses that transform the resources into products or services that satisfy consumer demands.

Required

Identify the three types of resources. Write a brief memo explaining how resource owners select the particular businesses to which they will provide resources. Your memo should include answers to the following questions: If you work as a private accountant, what role would you play in the allocation of resources? Which professional certification would be most appropriate for your career?

Exercise 1-2B *Careers in accounting*

LO 1-1

Accounting is commonly divided into two sectors. One sector is called public accounting. The other sector is called private accounting.

Required

a. Identify three areas of service provided by public accountants.

b. Describe the common duties performed by private accountants.

Exercise 1-3B *Identifying the reporting entities*

LO 1-2

Ray Steen recently started a business. During the first few days of operation, Mr. Steen transferred $100,000 from his personal account into a business account for a company he named Steen Enterprises. Steen Enterprises borrowed $60,000 from First Bank. Mr. Steen's father-in-law, Stan Rhoades, invested $75,000 into the business for which he received a 25 percent ownership interest. Steen Enterprises purchased a building from Zoro Realty Company. The building cost $150,000 cash. Steen Enterprises earned $56,000 in revenue from the company's customers and paid its employees $31,000 for salaries expense.

Required

Identify the entities that were mentioned in the scenario and explain what happened to the cash accounts of each entity you identify.

Exercise 1-4B *Define the components of financial statements*

LO 1-3

Required

a. Match the terms (identified as a through g) with the definitions and phrases (marked 1 through 7). For example, the term "g. Assets" matches with definition 7. Economic resources that will be used by a business to produce revenue.

a. Stockholders' Equity

b. Liability

c. Stockholders

d. Common Stock

e. Retained Earnings

f. Creditors

g. Assets

1. Individuals or institutions that have contributed assets or services to a business in exchange for an ownership interest in the business.

2. Common Stock + Retained Earnings.

3. Certificates that evidence ownership in a company.

4. Assets − Liabilities − Common Stock.

5. An obligation to pay cash in the future.

6. Individuals or institutions that have loaned goods or services to a business.

7. Economic resources that will be used by a business to produce revenue.

LO 1-3

Exercise 1-5B   *Identify missing information in the accounting equation*

Required

Calculate the missing amounts in the following table:

Accounting Equation						
					Stockholders' Equity	
Company	Assets	=	Liabilities	+	Common Stock	+	Retained Earnings
A	$?		$30,000		$ 50,000		$62,000
B	50,000		?		10,000		25,000
C	85,000		20,000		?		40,000
D	215,000		60,000		100,000		?

LO 1-3

Exercise 1-6B   *Account titles and the accounting equation*

The following account titles were drawn from Pest Control, Incorporated (PCI): Cash, Land, Accounts Payable, Office Furniture, Salaries Expense, Common Stock, Service Revenue, Trucks, Supplies, Operating Expenses, Rent Revenue, Computers, Building, Gasoline Expense, Retained Earnings, Dividends.

Required

a. Create an accounting equation using assets, liabilities, and stockholders' equity. Use the accounting equation to classify each account title under the element of the accounting equation to which it belongs.

b. Will all businesses have the same number of accounts? Explain your answer.

LO 1-3

Exercise 1-7B   *Missing information and recording events*

As of December 31, Year 1, Dunn Company had total cash of $156,000, notes payable of $85,600, and common stock of $52,400. During Year 2, Dunn earned $36,000 of cash revenue, paid $20,000 for cash expenses, and paid a $3,000 cash dividend to the stockholders.

Required

a. Determine the amount of retained earnings as of December 31, Year 1.

b. Create an accounting equation and record the beginning account balances.

c. Record the revenue, expense, and dividend events under the accounting equation created in Requirement *b*.

d. Prove the equality of the accounting equation as of December 31, Year 2.

e. Identify the beginning and ending balances in the Cash and Common Stock accounts. Explain why the beginning and ending balances in the Cash account are different, but the beginning and ending balances in the Common Stock account remain the same.

LO 1-4

Exercise 1-8B   *Classifying events as asset source, use, or exchange*

Trip's Business Services experienced the following events during its first year of operations:

1. Acquired $20,000 cash from the issue of common stock.
2. Borrowed $12,000 cash from First Bank.
3. Paid $5,000 cash to purchase land.
4. Received $25,000 cash for providing boarding services.
5. Acquired an additional $5,000 cash from the issue of common stock.
6. Purchased additional land for $4,000 cash.
7. Paid $10,000 cash for salary expense.
8. Signed a contract to provide additional services in the future.

9. Paid $1,200 cash for rent expense.

10. Paid a $1,000 cash dividend to the stockholders.

11. Determined the market value of the land to be $18,000 at the end of the accounting period.

Required

Classify each event as an asset source, use, or exchange transaction or as not applicable (NA).

Exercise 1-9B   *Identifying reporting entities and transaction types*

LO 1-2, 1-4

Middleton Co. paid $80,000 cash to purchase land from Saws Lumber Company. Saws originally paid $80,000 for the land.

Required

a. Did this event cause the balance in Middleton's cash account to increase, decrease, or remain unchanged?

b. Did this event cause the balance in Saw's cash account to increase, decrease, or remain unchanged?

c. Did this event cause the balance in Middleton's land account to increase, decrease, or remain unchanged?

d. Did this event cause the balance in Saw's land account to increase, decrease, or remain unchanged?

e. Was this event an asset source, use, or exchange transaction for Middleton Co.?

f. Was this event an asset source, use, or exchange transaction for Saws Company?

Exercise 1-10B   *Effect of events on the accounting equation*

LO 1-5

Morrison Co. experienced the following events during Year 1:

1. Acquired cash from the issue of common stock.

2. Borrowed cash.

3. Collected cash from providing services.

4. Purchased land with cash.

5. Paid operating expenses with cash.

6. Paid a cash dividend to the stockholders.

Required

Explain how each of these events affect the accounting equation by writing the letter I for increase, the letter D for decrease, and NA for does not affect under each of the components of the accounting equation. The first event is shown as an example.

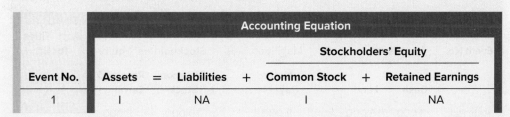

		Accounting Equation				
				Stockholders' Equity		
Event No.	**Assets**	**=**	**Liabilities**	**+**	**Common Stock**	**+**	**Retained Earnings**
1	I		NA		I		NA

Exercise 1-11B   *Prepare a balance sheet after recording transactions in an accounting equation*

LO 1-5, 1-6

Green Gardens, Inc. began operations on January 1, Year 1. During Year 1, Green Gardens experienced the following accounting events.

1. Acquired $20,000 cash from the issue of common stock.

2. Borrowed $8,000 cash from the State Bank.

3. Collected $38,000 cash as a result of providing services to customers.

4. Paid $15,000 for operating expenses.

5. Paid a $5,000 cash dividend to the stockholders.

6. Paid $18,000 cash to purchase land.

Required

a. Record the events in an accounting equation like the equation shown next. Record the amounts of revenue, expense, and dividends in the Retained Earnings column. Provide the appropriate titles for these accounts in the last column of the table.

	Green Gardens, Inc.						
	Accounting Equation						
Event No.	Assets		=	Liabilities	+	Stockholders' Equity		Acct. Titles for RE
	Cash	Land		Notes Payable		Common Stock	Retained Earnings	
Beg. Bal.	0	0		0		0	0	

b. As of December 31, Year 1, determine the total amount of assets, liabilities, and stockholders' equity and prepare a balance sheet.

c. What is the amount of total assets, liabilities, and stockholders' equity as of January 1, Year 2?

d. Assume that the land has a market value of $22,000 as of December 31, Year 1. At what amount will the land be shown on the December 31, Year 1, balance sheet? Why is this amount used in the balance sheet?

LO 1-5, 1-6

Exercise 1-12B *Prepare balance sheets for two accounting periods using a vertical format*

This exercise continues the scenario described in Exercise 1-11B shown earlier. Specifically, Green Gardens's Year 1 ending balances become the Year 2 beginning balances. At the beginning of Year 2, Green Gardens's accounting records had the following accounts and balances:

	Green Gardens, Inc.						
	Accounting Equation						
Event No.	Assets		=	Liabilities	+	Stockholders' Equity		Acct. Titles for RE
	Cash	Land		Notes Payable		Common Stock	Retained Earnings	
Beg. Bal.	28,000	18,000		8,000		20,000	18,000	

Green Gardens completed the following transactions during Year 2:

1. Purchased land for $12,000 cash.
2. Acquired $20,000 cash from the issue of common stock.
3. Received $50,000 cash for providing services to customers.
4. Paid cash operating expenses of $42,000.
5. Borrowed $20,000 cash from the bank.
6. Paid a $2,000 cash dividend to the stockholders.
7. Determined that the market value of the land purchased in event 1 is $70,000.

Required

a. Record the transactions in the appropriate accounts under an accounting equation. Record the amounts of revenue, expense, and dividends in the Retained Earnings column. Provide the appropriate titles for these accounts in the last column of the table.

b. Prepare balance sheets for Year 1 and Year 2. These statements should be presented in the vertical format with Year 1 and Year 2 shown in side-by-side columns. Recall that the Year 1 ending balances become the Year 2 beginning balances. These ending/beginning balances can be found on the first row of the table shown earlier. More specifically, the Year 1 ending balances include $28,000 cash, $18,000 land, $8,000 notes payable, $20,000 common stock, and $18,000 retained earnings.

c. How much cash is in the notes payable account?

d. How much cash is in the common stock account?

e. How much cash is in the retained earnings account? What is the balance of the cash account? Explain why the balances in the cash and retained earnings accounts are the same or different.

f. What is the amount of the land shown on the December 31, Year 2, balance sheet? Why is it shown at this amount?

Exercise 1-13B   *Interpreting information shown in a balance sheet*

LO 1-5, 1-6

Lewis Enterprises was started on January 1, Year 1 when it acquired $4,000 cash from creditors and $6,000 from owners. The company immediately purchased land that cost $9,000. The land purchase was the only transaction occurring during Year 1.

Required

a. Create an accounting equation and record the events under the equation.

b. As of December 31, Year 1, Lewis's obligations to creditors represent what percentage of total assets?

c. As of December 31, Year 1, Lewis's stockholders' equity represents what percentage of total assets?

d. What is the maximum cash dividend Lewis can pay on December 31, Year 1?

e. Assume the debt is due December 31, Year 1. Given that Lewis has $10,000 in stockholders' equity, can the company repay the creditors at this point? Why or why not?

Exercise 1-14B   *Interpreting information shown in a balance sheet*

LO 1-6

Both balance sheets shown in the following table were dated as of December 31, Year 3:

Balance Sheets for	Smith Co.	James Co.
Assets		
Cash	$15,000	0
Land	0	$20,000
Total Assets	$15,000	$20,000
Liabilities	$10,000	$ 6,000
Common Stock	4,000	12,000
Retained Earnings	1,000	2,000
Total Liab. and Stk. Equity	$15,000	$20,000

Required

a. Based only on the information shown in the balance sheets, can Smith Co. pay a $2,000 cash dividend?

b. Based only on the information shown in the balance sheets, can James Co. pay a $1,000 cash dividend?

c. Reconstruct the balance sheets for each company using percentages for the liabilities and stockholders' equity sections of the statements instead of dollar values.

d. Define the right side of an accounting equation without using the terms *liabilities* or *stockholders' equity*.

LO 1-3, 1-5, 1-6

Exercise 1-15B   *Calculate missing amounts and interpret results*

The following table shows the transactions experienced by Walter Enterprises during Year 7. The table contains missing data which are labeled with alphabetic characters (a) through (j). Assume all transactions shown in the accounting equation are cash transactions.

	Assets			Liabilities		Stockholders' Equity			
Event No.	Cash	+ Land	=	Notes Pay.	+ Com. Stk.	+ Ret. Earn.	Account
Beg. Bal.	(a)	+ 70,000	=	(b)	+ (c)	+ 20,000	
1.	(d)	+ NA	=	NA	+ 50,000	+ NA	NA
2.	(e)	+ NA	=	NA	+ NA	+ (f)	Revenue
3.	(30,000)	+ NA	=	NA	+ NA	+ (30,000)	Expenses
4.	(18,000)	+ NA	=	NA	+ NA	+ (g)	Dividend
5.	(65,000)	+ (h)	=	NA	+ NA	+ NA	NA
6.	(5,000)	+ NA	=	(5,000)	+ NA	+ NA	NA
End Bal.	90,000	+ (i)	=	35,000	+ 130,000	+ (j)	

Required

a. Determine the correct amount represented by each character (a) through (j).

b. Is there sufficient cash available to repay the debt on January 1, Year 8?

c. Based on the information in the table, what is the maximum cash dividend Walter could pay on January 1, Year 8?

EXERCISES—SERIES B

LO 1-7

Exercise 1-16B   *Prepare an income statement*

Leaf Company experienced the following events during its first-year operations:

1. Acquired $65,000 cash from the issue of common stock.
2. Borrowed $18,000 from the First City Bank.
3. Earned $48,000 of cash revenue.
4. Incurred $34,000 of cash expenses.
5. Paid a $5,000 cash dividend.
6. Paid $40,000 to purchase land.

Required

a. Identify the events that will affect the income statement.

b. Prepare an income statement that shows the results of Year 1 operations.

LO 1-6, 1-7

Exercise 1-17B   *Preparing and interpreting information in an income statement and two balance sheets*

At the end of Year 1, Jameson Co. had $800 of cash, $500 of liabilities, $300 of common stock, and zero in retained earnings. During Year 2, the company generated $650 of cash revenue and incurred $950 of cash expenses.

Required

Based on this information, prepare balance sheets for Year 1 and Year 2. Also prepare a Year 2 income statement.

Exercise 1-18B *Preparing a statement of changes in stockholders' equity*

LO 1-8

Forrest Inc. experienced the following events during its first-year operations:

1. Acquired $65,000 cash from the issue of common stock.
2. Borrowed $20,000 from the First City Bank.
3. Earned $65,000 of cash revenue.
4. Incurred $52,000 of cash expenses.
5. Paid a $5,000 cash dividend.
6. Paid $35,000 to purchase land.

Required

Prepare a statement of changes in stockholders' equity.

Exercise 1-19B *Preparing an income statement, statement of changes in stockholders' equity, and a balance sheet*

LO 1-5, 1-6, 1-7, 1-8

Petre Company was started on January 1, Year 1 when it acquired $30,000 from the sale of common stock. During Year 1, the company experienced the following three accounting events: (1) earned cash revenues of $14,500, (2) paid cash expenses of $9,200, and (3) paid a $500 cash dividend to its stockholders. These were the only events that affected the company during Year 1.

Required

a. Create an accounting equation and record the effects of each accounting event under the appropriate account headings.
b. Prepare an income statement, statement of changes in stockholders' equity, and a balance sheet dated December 31, Year 1, for Petre Company.
c. Explain why the income statement uses different terminology to date the income statement than is used to date the balance sheet.

Exercise 1-20B *Analyzing retained earnings to determine net income*

LO 1-7, 1-8

The December 31, Year 1, balance sheet for James Company showed total stockholders' equity of $156,000. Total stockholders' equity increased by $65,000 between December 31, Year 1, and December 31, Year 2. During Year 2, James Company acquired $20,000 cash from the issue of common stock. James Company paid a $5,000 cash dividend to the stockholders during Year 2.

Required

Determine the amount of net income or loss James Company reported on its Year 2 income statement. (*Hint:* Remember that stock issues, net income, and dividends all change total stockholders' equity.)

Exercise 1-21B *Statement of cash flows*

LO 1-9

On January 1, Year 1, Palmer, a fast-food company, had a balance in its Cash account of $32,000. During the Year 1 accounting period, the company had (1) net cash inflow from operating activities of $15,600, (2) net cash outflow for investing activities of $23,000, and (3) net cash outflow from financing activities of $4,500.

Required

a. Prepare a statement of cash flows.
b. Provide a reasonable explanation as to what may have caused the net cash inflow from operating activities.
c. Provide a reasonable explanation as to what may have caused the net cash outflow from investing activities.
d. Provide a reasonable explanation as to what may have caused the net cash outflow from financing activities.

LO 1-9

Exercise 1-22B   *Preparing a statement of cash flows*

National Service Company experienced the following accounting events during Year 1:

1. Paid $4,000 cash for salary expense.
2. Borrowed $8,000 cash from State Bank.
3. Received $30,000 cash from the issue of common stock.
4. Purchased land for $8,000 cash.
5. Performed services for $14,000 cash.
6. Paid $4,200 cash for utilities expense.
7. Sold land for $7,000 cash.
8. Paid a cash dividend of $1,000 to the stockholders.
9. Hired an accountant to keep the books.
10. Paid $3,000 cash on the loan from State Bank.

Required

a. Indicate how each of the events would be classified on the statement of cash flows as operating activities (OA), investing activities (IA), financing activities (FA), or not applicable (NA).

b. Prepare a statement of cash flows for Year 1. Assume National Service had a beginning cash balance of $9,000 on January 1, Year 1.

LO 1-5, 1-6, 1-7, 1-8, 1-9

Exercise 1-23B   *Preparing financial statements*

Tennessee Company experienced the following events during Year 2:

1. Acquired $50,000 cash from the issue of common stock.
2. Paid $15,000 cash to purchase land.
3. Borrowed $25,000 cash.
4. Provided services for $60,000 cash.
5. Paid $12,000 cash for rent expense.
6. Paid $22,000 cash for other operating expenses.
7. Paid a $5,000 cash dividend to the stockholders.
8. Determined that the market value of the land purchased in Event 2 is now $16,500.

Required

a. The January 1, Year 2, account balances are shown in the following accounting equation. Record the eight events in the appropriate accounts under accounting equation. Record the amounts of revenue, expense, and dividends in the Retained Earnings column. Provide the appropriate titles for these accounts in the last column of the table. The first event is shown as an example.

TENNESSEE COMPANY								
Accounting Equation								
Event No.	Assets		=	Liabilities	+	Stockholders' Equity		Acct. Titles for RE
	Cash	Land		Notes Payable		Common Stock	Retained Earnings	
Beg. Bal.	15,000	10,000		–0–		20,000	5,000	
1.	50,000					50,000		

b. Prepare an income statement, statement of changes in equity, year-end balance sheet, and statement of cash flows for the Year 2 accounting period.

c. Determine the percentage of assets that were provided by retained earnings. How much cash is in the retained earnings account?

d. Based on the December 31, Year 2, balance sheet, what is the largest cash dividend Tennessee Company could pay?

Exercise 1-24B *Preparing financial statements and interpreting the information in those statements*

On January 1, Year 2, the following information was drawn from the accounting records of Zeke Company: cash of $200; land of $1,800; notes payable of $600; and common stock of $1,000.

Required

a. Determine the amount of retained earnings as of January 1, Year 2.

b. After looking at the amount of retained earnings, the chief executive officer (CEO) wants to pay a $300 cash dividend to the stockholders. Can the company pay this dividend? Why or why not?

c. As of January 1, Year 2, what percentage of the assets were acquired from creditors?

d. As of January 1, Year 2, what percentage of the assets were acquired from investors?

e. As of January 1, Year 2, what percentage of the assets were acquired from retained earnings?

f. Create an accounting equation using percentages instead of dollar amounts on the right side of the equation.

g. During Year 2, Zeke Company earned cash revenue of $500, paid cash expenses of $300, and paid a cash dividend of $50. Prepare an income statement, statement of changes in stockholders' equity, a balance sheet, and a statement of cash flows dated December 31, Year 2. (*Hint:* It is helpful to record these events under an accounting equation before preparing the statements.)

h. Comment on the terminology used to date each statement.

i. What is the largest cash dividend that Zeke could pay on December 31, Year 2?

j. If on December 31, Year 2, the land had an appraised value of $2,200, how would this affect the financial statements?

Exercise 1-25B *Preparing financial statements–cash flow emphasis*

As of January 1, Year 2, Shundra Inc. had a balance of $4,500 in Cash, $2,500 in Common Stock, and $2,000 in Retained Earnings. These were the only accounts with balances on January 1, Year 2. During Year 2, the company had (1) revenue of $9,900, (2) expenses of $4,800, and (3) dividends of $900. Assume that all transactions are cash transactions. The following accounts and balances represent the financial condition of Shundra Inc. as of December 31, Year 2.

SHUNDRA INC. December 31, Year 2								
Event No.	Assets		=	Liabilities	+	Stockholders' Equity		Acct. Titles for RE
	Cash	Land		Notes Payable		Common Stock	Retained Earnings	
Ending Bal.	4,200	13,000		3,000		8,000	6,200	

Required

a. Determine the amount of net cash flow from operating activities.

b. What did the company purchase that resulted in the cash outflow from investing activities?

c. Assume that the net cash inflow from financing activities of $7,600 was caused by three events. Based on the information presented, identify these events and determine the cash flow associated with each event.

d. Prepare a statement of cash flows.

e. Prepare an income statement, statement of changes in stockholders' equity, and balance sheet.

Exercise 1-26B *Prepare financial statements covering two accounting cycles*

Amelia Company experienced the following events during its first- and second-year operations:

Year 1 Transactions:

1. Acquired $75,000 cash from the issue of common stock.

2. Borrowed $28,000 cash from the National Credit Union.

3. Earned $72,000 of cash revenue.

4. Incurred $55,000 of cash expenses.
5. Paid a $5,000 cash dividend.
6. Paid $34,000 cash to purchase land.

Year 2 Transactions:

1. Acquired $45,000 cash from the issue of common stock.
2. Borrowed $15,000 cash from the National Credit Union.
3. Earned $90,000 of cash revenue.
4. Incurred $55,000 of cash expenses.
5. Paid a $7,000 cash dividend.
6. Paid $22,000 cash to purchase land.

Required

a. Record the transactions in an accounting equation like the equation shown next. Record the amounts of revenue, expense, and dividends in the Retained Earnings column. Provide the appropriate titles for these accounts in the last column of the table. Show the totals at the end of Year 1 and use these totals as the beginning balances for the second accounting cycle.

Amelia Company **Accounting Equation**								
Event No.	Assets		=	Liabilities	+	Stockholders' Equity		Acct. Titles for RE
	Cash	Land		Notes Payable		Common Stock	Retained Earnings	
Beg. Bal.	–0–	–0–		–0–		–0–	–0–	

b. Prepare an income statement, a statement of changes in stockholders' equity, a balance sheet, and a statement of cash flows for Year 1 and Year 2. Use a multicycle format that shows Year 1 and Year 2 information in side-by-side columns.

LO 1-10

Exercise 1-27B *Relationships between financial statements*

Match the financial statements with the appropriate statement to describe them.

Financial Statements	Descriptions
1. Statement of Cash Flows	A. Summarizes the activity under the cash account within the accounting equation. Explains the activities that caused the cash balance to change from the beginning of the year to the end of the year.
2. Balance Sheet	B. Summarizes all the activity under the equity section of the accounting equation. This statement generally shows how common stock and retained earnings changed from the beginning of the year to the end of the year.
3. Statement of Stockholders' Equity	C. Summarizes all the company's accounts under the accounting equation as of a point in time. All other financial statements can be created from activity included in this statement.
4. Income Statement	D. Summarizes the revenues and expenses recorded under the retained earnings column of the accounting equation. This statement focuses on company performance over a fixed period of time.

IFRS

Exercise 1-28B *International Financial Reporting Standards*

Corrugated Boxes Inc. is a U.S.-based company that develops its financial statements under GAAP. The total amount of the company's assets shown on its balance sheet for the current year was approximately $305 million. The president of Corrugated is considering the possibility of relocating the company to a country that practices accounting under IFRS. The president has hired an international accounting firm to determine what the company's statements would look like if they were prepared under IFRS. One striking difference is that, under IFRS, the assets shown on the balance sheet would be valued at approximately $345 million.

Required

a. Would Corrugated Boxes's assets really be worth $40 million more if it moves its headquarters?

b. Discuss the underlying conceptual differences between U.S. GAAP and IFRS that cause the difference in the reported asset values.

PROBLEMS—SERIES B

Problem 1-29B   *Applying GAAP to financial reporting*

LO 1-1

Jan Perkins is a business consultant. She analyzed the business processes of one of her clients, Diamond Companies, in November, Year 1. She prepared a report containing her recommendation for changes in some of the company's business practices and presented Diamond with the report in December, Year 1. Jan guarantees that her clients will save money by following her advice. She does not collect for the services she provides until the client is satisfied with the results of her work. In this case, she received a cash payment from Diamond in February, Year 2.

Required

a. Define the acronym GAAP.

b. Assume that Jan's accountant tells her that GAAP permits Jan to recognize the revenue from Diamond in either Year 1 or Year 2. What GAAP rule would justify reporting the same event in two different ways? Write a brief memo explaining the logic behind this rule.

c. If Jan were keeping records for managerial reporting purposes, would she be bound by GAAP rules? Write a brief memo to explain how GAAP applies to financial versus managerial reporting.

Problem 1-30B   *Accounting entities*

LO 1-2

The following business scenarios are independent from one another:

1. Chris Hann purchased an automobile from Classic Auto Sales for $10,000.

2. Sal Pearl loaned $15,000 to the business in which he is a stockholder.

3. First State Bank paid interest to Strong Co. on a certificate of deposit that Strong Co. has invested at First State Bank.

4. Cindy's Restaurant paid the current utility bill of $135 to Midwest Utilities.

5. Sun Corp. borrowed $50,000 from City National Bank and used the funds to purchase land from Carriage Realty.

6. Sue Wang purchased $10,000 of common stock of International Sales Corporation from the corporation.

7. Chris Gordon loaned $6,000 cash to his daughter.

8. Motor Service Co. earned $20,000 in cash revenue.

9. Poy Imports paid $4,000 for salaries to each of its four employees.

10. Borg Inc. paid a cash dividend of $4,000 to its sole shareholder, Mark Borg.

Required

a. For each scenario, create a list of all the entities mentioned in the description.

b. Describe what happens to the cash account of each entity you identified in Requirement *a*.

Problem 1-31B   *Classifying events as asset source, use, or exchange*

LO 1-3, 1-4

The following unrelated events are typical of those experienced by business entities:

1. Pay cash for operating expenses.

2. Pay an office manager's salary with cash.

3. Receive cash for services that have been performed.

4. Pay cash for utilities expense.

5. Acquire land by accepting a liability (financing the purchase).

6. Pay cash to purchase a new office building.

7. Discuss plans for a new office building with an architect.

8. Repay part of a bank loan.
9. Acquire cash by issuing common stock.
10. Purchase land with cash.
11. Purchase equipment with cash.
12. Pay monthly rent on an office building.
13. Hire a new office manager.
14. Borrow cash from a bank.
15. Pay a cash dividend to stockholders.

Required

Identify each of the events as an asset source, use, or exchange transaction. If an event would not be recorded under generally accepted accounting principles, identify it as not applicable (NA). Also indicate for each event whether total assets would increase, decrease, or remain unchanged. Organize your answer according to the following table. The first event is shown in the table as an example.

Event No.	Type of Event	Effect on Total Assets
1	Asset use	Decrease

LO 1-6, 1-7, 1-8, 1-9

Problem 1-32B *Relating titles and accounts to financial statements*

Required

Identify the financial statements on which each of the following items (titles, date descriptions, and accounts) appears by placing a check mark in the appropriate column. If an item appears on more than one statement, place a check mark in every applicable column.

Item	Income Statement	Statement of Changes in Stockholders' Equity	Balance Sheet	Statement of Cash Flows
For the period ended (date)				
Net income				
Investing activities				
Net loss				
Ending cash balance				
Salary expense				
Consulting revenue				
Dividends				
Financing activities				
Ending common stock				
Interest expense				
As of (date)				
Land				
Beginning cash balance				
Notes payable				
Beginning common stock				
Service revenue				
Utility expense				
Stock issue				
Operating activities				

Problem 1-33B   *Interrelationships among financial statements*

LO 1-6, 1-7, 1-8, 1-9

Blix Corp. started the Year 2 accounting period with total assets of $50,000 cash, $20,000 of liabilities, and $20,000 of retained earnings. During the Year 2 accounting period, the Retained Earnings account increased by $8,500. The bookkeeper reported that Blix Corp. paid cash expenses of $15,000 and paid a $4,000 cash dividend to stockholders, but she could not find a record of the amount of cash revenue that Blix Corp. received for performing services. Blix Corp. also paid $2,000 cash to reduce the liability owed to a bank, and the business acquired $8,000 of additional cash from the issue of common stock. Assume all transactions are cash transactions.

CHECK FIGURES
a. Net Income: $12,500
c. Total Assets: $64,500

Required

a. Prepare the Year 2 income statement.
b. Prepare the Year 2 statement of changes in stockholders' equity.
c. Prepare the Year 2 balance sheet.
d. Prepare the Year 2 statement of cash flows.
e. Determine the percentage of total assets that were provided by creditors, investors, and earnings.

Problem 1-34B   *Preparing financial statements for two complete accounting cycles*

LO 1-5, 1-6, 1-7, 1-8, 1-9, 1-10

Marco's Consulting experienced the following transactions for Year 1, its first year of operations, and Year 2. *Assume that all transactions involve the receipt or payment of cash.*

Transactions for Year 1

1. Acquired $50,000 by issuing common stock.
2. Received $100,000 cash for providing services to customers.
3. Borrowed $15,000 cash from creditors.
4. Paid expenses amounting to $60,000.
5. Purchased land for $40,000 cash.

Transactions for Year 2

Beginning account balances for Year 2 are:

Cash	$65,000
Land	40,000
Notes payable	15,000
Common stock	50,000
Retained earnings	40,000

1. Acquired an additional $20,000 from the issue of common stock.
2. Received $130,000 for providing services.
3. Paid $10,000 to creditors to reduce loan.
4. Paid expenses amounting to $75,000.
5. Paid a $15,000 dividend to the stockholders.
6. Determined that the market value of the land is $50,000.

Required

a. Write an accounting equation and record the effects of each accounting event under the appropriate headings for each year. Record the amounts of revenue, expense, and dividends in the Retained Earnings column. Provide appropriate titles for these accounts in the last column of the table. Total the amounts in the accounts as of December 31, Year 1, and December 31, Year 2.

b. Prepare an income statement, statement of changes in stockholders' equity, year-end balance sheet, and statement of cash flows for Year 1 and Year 2. Use a multicycle format with Year 1 and Year 2 information shown in side-by-side columns.

c. Determine the amount of cash that is in the Retained Earnings account at the end of Year 1 and Year 2.

d. Compare the information provided by the income statement with the information provided by the statement of cash flows. Point out similarities and differences.

LO 1-6, 1-7, 1-8, 1-9, 1-10

Problem 1-35B   *Missing information in financial statements*

Required

Fill in the blanks (indicated by the alphabetic letters in parentheses) in the following financial statements. Assume the company started operations January 1, Year 1, and all transactions involve cash.

	For the Years		
	Year 1	Year 2	Year 3
Income Statements			
Revenue	$ 700	$ 1,300	$ 2,000
Expense	(a)	(700)	(1,300)
Net income	$ 200	$ (m)	$ 700
Statements of Changes in Stockholders' Equity			
Beginning common stock	$ 0	$ (n)	$ 6,000
Plus: Common stock issued	5,000	1,000	2,000
Ending common stock	5,000	6,000	(t)
Beginning retained earnings	0	100	200
Plus: Net income	(b)	(o)	700
Less: Dividends	(c)	(500)	(300)
Ending retained earnings	100	(p)	600
Total stockholders' equity	$ (d)	$ 6,200	$ 8,600
Balance Sheets			
Assets			
Cash	$ (e)	$ (q)	$ (u)
Land	0	(r)	8,000
Total assets	$ (f)	$11,200	$10,600
Liabilities	$ (g)	$ 5,000	$ 2,000
Stockholders' equity			
Common stock	(h)	(s)	8,000
Retained earnings	(i)	200	600
Total stockholders' equity	(j)	6,200	8,600
Total liabilities and stockholders' equity	$8,100	$11,200	$10,600
Statements of Cash Flows			
Cash flows from operating activities			
Cash receipts from customers	$ (k)	$ 1,300	$ (v)
Cash payments for expenses	(l)	(700)	(w)
Net cash flows from operating activities	200	600	700
Cash flows from investing activities			
Cash payments for land	0	(8,000)	0
Net cash from investing activities	0	(8,000)	0
Cash flows from investing activities			
Cash receipts from loan	3,000	$ 2,000	0
Cash payments to reduce debt	0	(0)	(x)
Cash receipts from stock issue	5,000	1,000	(y)
Cash payments for dividends	(100)	(500)	(z)
Net cash flows from financing activities	7,900	2,500	(1,300)
Net change in cash	8,100	(4,900)	(600)
Plus: Beginning cash balance	0	8,100	3,200
Ending cash balance	$8,100	$ 3,200	$ 2,600

ANALYZE, THINK, COMMUNICATE

ATC 1-1 Business Applications Case *Understanding real-world annual reports*

Required

Obtain Target Corporation's annual report for its 2018 fiscal year (year ended February 2, 2019) at http://investors.target.com using the instructions in Appendix B, and use it to answer the following questions:

a. What was Target's net income for 2018 (the year ended February 2, 2019)?

b. Did Target's net income increase or decrease from 2017 to 2018? By how much?

c. What was Target's accounting equation for 2018?

d. Which of the following had the largest percentage change from 2017 to 2018: sales, cost of sales, or selling, general, and administrative expenses? Show all computations.

Target Corporation

ATC 1-2 Group Assignment *Missing information*

The following selected financial information is available for Best, Inc. Amounts are in millions of dollars.

Income Statements	Year 1	Year 2	Year 3	Year 4
Revenue	$ 860	$1,695	(a)	$2,900
Expenses	(a)	(1,070)	(2,400)	(2,600)
Net Income	$ 20	(a)	$ 175	(a)

Balance Sheets	Year 1	Year 2	Year 3	Year 4
Cash	(b)	$2,520	(b)	$1,860
Other Assets	1,900	(b)	2,500	(b)
Total Assets	$2,250	$3,700	(c)	$4,420
Liabilities	(c)	(c)	$1,000	(c)
Stockholders' Equity				
Common Stock	$1,500	$1,500	(d)	$2,000
Retained Earnings	(d)	645	820	(d)
Total Stockholders' Equity	1,520	(d)	2,320	3,120
Total Liab. and Stk. Equity	$2,250	$3,700	$3,320	$4,420

Required

a. Divide the class into groups of four or five students each. Organize the groups into four sections. Assign Task 1 to the first section of groups, Task 2 to the second section, Task 3 to the third section, and Task 4 to the fourth section.

Group Tasks

  (1) Fill in the missing information for Year 1.

  (2) Fill in the missing information for Year 2.

  (3) Fill in the missing information for Year 3.

  (4) Fill in the missing information for Year 4.

b. Each section should select two representatives. One representative is to put the financial statements assigned to that section on the board, underlining the missing amounts. The second representative is to explain to the class how the missing amounts were determined.

c. Each section should list events that could have caused the unusual items category on the income statement.

ATC 1-3   Real-World Case   *Classifying cash flow activities at six companies*

The following cash transactions occurred in six real-world companies:

1. In January, 2018 Ford Motor Company announced that it was acquiring Autonomic and TransLoc to enhance its development of driverless automobiles. No price was given. Assume this was a cash purchase.

2. During the third quarter of 2018 (July 1 through September 30), Facebook, Inc. paid approximately $5.8 billion for expenses.

3. During the third quarter of 2018 (July 1 through September 30), General Electric Company sold some of its business units, including its Value-Based Care Division. These sales generated cash inflows of $5.6 billion.

4. During the third quarter of 2018 (July 1 through September 30), General Motors Company borrowed $32.8 billion using notes payable.

5. During the third quarter of 2018 (July 1 through September 30), International Business Machines (IBM), Inc. collected approximately $19.1 billion in cash from revenue related to the products and services it sold.

6. During the third quarter of 2018 (July 1 through September 30), McDonald's, Inc. paid $780 million of dividends.

Required

Determine if each of the preceding transactions should be classified as an *operating, investing,* or *financing* activity. Also, identify the amount of each cash flow and whether it was an *inflow* or an *outflow*.

ATC 1-4   Business Applications Case   *Forecasting from financial reports*

The following information was drawn from the annual report of Machine Imports Company (MIC):

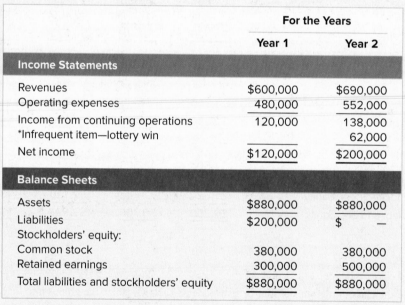

	For the Years	
	Year 1	Year 2
Income Statements		
Revenues	$600,000	$690,000
Operating expenses	480,000	552,000
Income from continuing operations	120,000	138,000
*Infrequent item—lottery win		62,000
Net income	$120,000	$200,000
Balance Sheets		
Assets	$880,000	$880,000
Liabilities	$200,000	$ —
Stockholders' equity:		
Common stock	380,000	380,000
Retained earnings	300,000	500,000
Total liabilities and stockholders' equity	$880,000	$880,000

*By definition, infrequent items are not likely to recur in the future.

Required

a. Compute the percentage of growth in net income from Year 1 to Year 2. Can stockholders expect a similar increase between Year 2 and Year 3?

b. Assuming that MIC collected $200,000 cash from earnings (i.e., net income), explain how this money was spent in Year 2.

c. Assuming that MIC experiences the same percentage of growth from Year 2 to Year 3 as it did from Year 1 to Year 2, determine the amount of income from continuing operations that the owners can expect to see on the Year 3 income statement.

d. During Year 3, MIC experienced a $40,000 loss due to storm damage. Liabilities and common stock were unchanged from Year 2 to Year 3. Use the information that you computed in Requirement *c* plus the additional information provided in the previous two sentences to prepare an income statement and balance sheet as of December 31, Year 3.

ATC 1-5 Writing Assignment   *Components of financial statements defined*

Sam and his sister Blair both attend the state university. As a reward for their successful completion of the past year (Sam had a 3.2 GPA in business, and Blair had a 3.7 GPA in art), their father gave each of them 100 shares of The Walt Disney Company stock. They have just received their first annual report. Blair does not understand what the information means and has asked Sam to explain it to her.

Required

Assume you are Sam. Write Blair a memo explaining the following financial statement items to her. In your explanation, describe each of the two financial statements and explain the financial information each contains. Also define each of the items listed for each financial statement and explain what it means.

Balance Sheet
Assets
Liabilities
Stockholders' equity
Income Statement
Revenue
Expense
Net income

ATC 1-6 Ethical Dilemma   *Loyalty versus the bottom line*

Assume that Kevin has been working for you for five years. He has had an excellent work history and has received generous pay raises in response. The raises have been so generous that Kevin is quite overpaid for the job he is required to perform. Unfortunately, he is not qualified to take on other, more responsible jobs available within the company. A recent job applicant is willing to accept a salary $5,000 per year less than the amount currently being paid to Kevin. The applicant is well qualified to take over Kevin's duties and has a very positive attitude. The following financial statements were reported by your company at the end of its most recent accounting period:

Required

a. Reconstruct the financial statements (shown below), assuming that Kevin was replaced at the beginning of the most recent accounting period. Both Kevin and his replacement are paid in cash. No other changes are to be considered.

b. Discuss the short- and long-term ramifications of replacing Kevin. There are no right answers. However, assume you are required to make a decision. Use your judgment and common sense to support your choice.

Financial Statements		
Income Statement		
Revenue		$ 57,000
Expense		(45,000)
Net income		$ 12,000
Statement of Changes in Stockholders' Equity		
Beginning common stock	$20,000	
Plus: stock issued	5,000	
Ending common stock		$25,000
Beginning retained earnings	50,000	
Net income	12,000	
Dividends	(2,000)	
Ending retained earnings		60,000
Total stockholders' equity		$85,000

continued

Balance Sheet	
Assets	
Cash	$85,000
Equity	
Common stock	$25,000
Retained earnings	60,000
Total stockholders' equity	$85,000

Statement of Cash Flows		
Operating activities		
Inflow from customers	$57,000	
Outflow to suppliers expenses	(45,000)	
Net inflow from operations		$12,000
Investing activities		0
Financing activities		
Inflow from stock issue	5,000	
Outflow for dividends	(2,000)	
Net inflow from financing activities		3,000
Net change in cash		15,000
Plus: beginning cash balance		70,000
Ending cash balance		$85,000

ATC 1-7   Research Assignment   *Finding real-world accounting information*

This chapter introduced the basic four financial statements companies use annually to keep their stakeholders informed of their accomplishments and financial situation. Complete the following requirements using the most recent (20xx) financial statements available on McDonald's website. Obtain the statements on the Internet using the following steps. (The formatting of the company's website may have changed since these instructions were written.)

1. Go to corporate.mcdonalds.com.
2. Click on the "Investors" link at the top of the page.
3. Click on the "Financial Information" link at the upper left side of the page.
4. Click on the "Annual Reports, LEARN MORE" link.
5. Click on the "*20xx Annual Report*" pdf link.
6. Go to the company's financial statements that begin around page 30 of the annual report.

Required

a. What was the company's *net income* in each of the last two years?

b. What amount of total *assets* did the company have at the end of the most recent year?

c. How much *total shareholders' equity (deficit)* did the company have at the end of the most recent year?

d. For the most recent year, what was the company's *cash flow from operating activities, cash flow from investing activities*, and *cash flow from financing activities*?

CHAPTER 2

Accounting for Accruals

Video lectures and accompanying self-assessment quizzes are available in *Connect* for all learning objectives.

Tableau Dashboard Activity is available in *Connect* for this chapter.

LEARNING OBJECTIVES

After you have mastered the material in this chapter, you will be able to:

LO 2-1	Use a horizontal financial statements model to show how accounting events affect financial statements.
LO 2-2	Show how receivables affect financial statements.
LO 2-3	Show how payables affect financial statements.
LO 2-4	Prepare financial statements that include accruals.
LO 2-5	Show how accrued interest expense affects financial statements.
LO 2-6	Identify the causes for changes in beginning and ending account balances.
LO 2-7	Identify the primary components of corporate governance.

CHAPTER OPENING

Suppose a painting company signs a contract to paint a house. Two weeks after signing the contract a painter starts the job. The job is completed in one week. The company sends the client a bill a few days after the job is complete. The company receives payment from the client 10 days after the bill was sent. Should the paint company recognize revenue on the day the contract was signed, when the work started, when the work was finished, when the bill was sent, or when the cash was collected? To provide guidance in answering such questions, the Financial Accounting Standards Board (FASB) issued Accounting Standards Codification 606, which provides the following core principal:

[A]n entity should recognize revenue to depict the transfer of promised goods or services to customers in an amount that reflects the consideration to which the entity expects to be entitled for those goods or services.[1]

In lay terms, this means that revenue should be recognized in the period in which the service is provided, regardless of whether cash has or has not been collected. More specifically, companies may recognize revenue on the income statement in a different accounting period than the period in which they collect the related cash. Furthermore, companies frequently make cash payments for expenses in accounting periods other than the periods in which the expenses are recognized in the income statement. Recognizing revenue when it is earned and expenses when they are incurred, regardless of when cash changes hands, is commonly called **accrual accounting.**

To illustrate, assume Johnson Company provides services to customers in Year 1 but collects cash for those services in Year 2. When should Johnson recognize the services revenue? The answer depends on whether a company is using cash basis or accrual-based accounting methods.

Many small private companies use cash basis accounting. Users of *cash basis* accounting recognize (report) revenues and expenses in the period in which cash is collected or paid. Under cash basis accounting, Johnson would recognize the revenue in Year 2 when it collects the cash. In contrast, users of accrual accounting recognize revenues and expenses in the period in which they occur, regardless of when cash is collected or paid. Under accrual accounting, Johnson would recognize the revenue in Year 1 (the period in which it performed the services) even though it does not collect the cash until Year 2.

Accrual accounting is required by generally accepted accounting principles (GAAP). Virtually all major companies operating in the United States use it. Its two distinguishing features are called *accruals* and *deferrals.*

- The term **accrual** describes a revenue or an expense event that is recognized *before* cash is exchanged. Johnson's recognition of revenue in Year 1 that is related to cash collected in Year 2 is an example of an accrual.

[1]2016. Revenue from Contracts with Customers (Topic 606). Financial Accounting Standard Board.

The term **deferral** describes a revenue or an expense event that is recognized *after* cash has been exchanged. Suppose Johnson pays cash in Year 1 to purchase office supplies it uses in Year 2. In this case, the cash payment occurs in Year 1 although supplies expense is recognized in Year 2. This example is a deferral.

Chapter 2 focuses on accounting for accruals, while Chapter 3 focuses on deferrals.

The Curious Accountant

Suppose a company located in St. Louis, Missouri, needs to ship goods to a customer located 2,000 miles away in Portland, Oregon. The company arranges to have **Union Pacific Corporation**, a large transportation company, ship the goods to Portland by rail. Union Pacific will be paid $2,000 for shipping the goods, but payment will not be made until after the goods have been delivered.

When should Union Pacific report it has earned the revenue for shipping the goods? (Answer on page 77.)

Tracy Fox/123RF

THE HORIZONTAL FINANCIAL STATEMENTS MODEL

LO 2-1

Use a horizontal financial statements model to show how accounting events affect financial statements.

Before delving into the specifics of accrual accounting, we will introduce a model that will teach you how to think like a business professional. Business professionals tend to think about bottom-line consequences. If I do this or that, how will it affect my company's net income, total assets, cash flow, and so on. This type of thinking occurs whether you work in accounting, management, marketing, finance, insurance, real estate, or virtually any other area of business. Accordingly, learning to mimic this thinking approach will benefit all business students regardless of your major.

This text uses a **horizontal financial statements model** to help you understand how business events affect financial statements. This model shows a set of financial statements horizontally across a single page of paper. The balance sheet is displayed first, adjacent to the income statement, and then the statement of cash flows. Due to space limitations, the statement of changes in stockholders' equity is not shown in the horizontal statements model.

The model frequently uses abbreviations. For example, activity classifications in the statement of cash flows are identified using OA for operating activities, IA for investing activities, and FA for financing activities. NC designates the net change in cash. The horizontal financial statements model uses NA when an account is not affected by an event. The background of the *balance sheet* is red, the *income statement* is blue, and the *statement of cash flows* is green. To illustrate, we use it to display the seven accounting events that Master Builders experienced during its Year 1 operations.

1. Acquired $110,000 cash from the issuance of common stock.
2. Borrowed $400,000 cash.

3. Paid $500,000 cash to purchase land.
4. Received $85,000 cash from earning revenue.
5. Paid $50,000 cash for expenses.
6. Paid $4,000 of cash dividends to the owners.
7. The market value of the land was appraised at $525,000 on December 31, Year 1.

Event No.	\multicolumn{3}{Balance Sheet}								Income Statement				Statement of Cash Flows
	\multicolumn{3}{Assets}	=	Liab.	+	\multicolumn{2}{Stockholders' Equity}			\multicolumn{3}{ }		
	Cash	+	Land	=	Notes Pay.	+	Com. Stk.	+	Ret. Earn.		Rev.	−	Exp.	=	Net Inc.	
Beg.	0 +		0 =		0 +		0 +		0		0 −		0 =	0	NA
1.	110,000 +		NA	=	NA	+	110,000 +		NA		NA −	NA =	NA	110,000 FA
2.	400,000 +		NA	=	400,000 +		NA	+	NA		NA −	NA =	NA	400,000 FA
3.	(500,000) +	500,000 =		NA	+	NA	+	NA		NA −	NA =	NA	(500,000) IA
4.	85,000 +		NA	=	NA	+	NA	+	85,000		85,000 −	NA =	85,000	85,000 OA
5.	(50,000) +		NA	=	NA	+	NA	+	(50,000)		NA −	50,000 =	(50,000)	(50,000) OA
6.	(4,000) +		NA	=	NA	+	NA	+	(4,000)		NA −	NA =	NA	(4,000) FA
7.	NA +		NA	=	NA	+	NA	+	NA		NA −	NA =	NA	NA
End	41,000 +	500,000 =	400,000 +	110,000 +	31,000					85,000 −	50,000 =	35,000	41,000 NC

Recognize that horizontal financial statements models are learning tools. Because they are helpful in understanding how accounting events affect financial statements, they are used extensively in this book. However, the models omit many of the details used in published financial statements. For example, the horizontal model shows only a partial set of statements. Also, because the statements are presented in aggregate, the description of dates (i.e., "as of" versus "for the period ended") does not distinguish end of period data from during the period data.

ACCOUNTING FOR RECEIVABLES

Recall that accruals occur when revenue or expense is recognized before cash is collected or paid. To examine the effects of accrual accounting on financial statements, we will analyze seven events experienced by Cato Consultants, a training services company that begins operations on January 1, Year 1.

EVENT 1 Cato Consultants was started on January 1, Year 1, when it acquired $5,000 cash by issuing common stock.

Acquiring cash from the issue of common stock is an asset source transaction. The event causes increases in an asset account (Cash) and a stockholders' equity account (Retained Earnings). The transaction does not affect the income statement. Because the company is being financed by acquiring cash from the owners, the cash inflow is classified as a financing activity (FA). The effects on the financial statements are shown next:

\multicolumn{3}{Balance Sheet}				\multicolumn{3}{Income Statement}			Statement of Cash Flows
Assets	=	Liab.	+	Stk. Equity						
Cash	=		+	Com. Stk.	Rev.	−	Exp.	=	Net Inc.	
5,000	=	NA	+	5,000	NA	−	NA	=	NA	5,000 FA

Accounting for Accounts Receivable

EVENT 2   During Year 1, Cato Consultants provided $84,000 of consulting services to its clients. Cato has completed the work and sent bills to the clients, but has not yet collected any cash. This type of transaction is frequently described as providing services *on account*.

Accrual accounting requires companies to recognize revenue in the period in which the work is done regardless of when cash is collected. In this case, revenue is recognized in Year 1 even though cash has not been collected. Recall that revenue is an economic benefit (an increase in assets) that results from providing goods and services to customers. The specific asset that increases is called **Accounts Receivable**. The balance in Accounts Receivable represents the amount of cash the company expects to collect in the future.

Because the revenue recognition causes assets (Accounts Receivable) to increase, it is classified as an asset source transaction. On the balance sheet, assets (Accounts Receivable) and stockholders' equity (Retained Earnings) increase. On the income statement the increase in revenue increases net income. The collection of cash will occur in the future. Because cash was not collected or paid, the statement of cash flows is not affected for this event. The effects on the financial statements are shown next:

Balance Sheet									Income Statement						Statement of Cash Flows
Assets			=	Liab.	+	Stk. Equity									
Cash	+	Accts. Rec.	=			Com. Stk.	+	Ret. Earn.	Rev.	−	Exp.	=	Net Inc.		
NA	+	84,000	=	NA	+	NA	+	84,000	84,000	−	NA	=	84,000		NA

EVENT 3   Cato collected $60,000 cash from customers in partial settlement of its accounts receivable.

The collection of an account receivable is an asset exchange transaction. The event causes one asset account (Cash) to increase and another asset account (Accounts Receivable) to decrease. The amount of total assets is not affected. Notice that the company does not recognize revenue when the cash is collected. Remember that the revenue was recognized back when the work was completed (see Event 2). Revenue would be double counted if it were recognized again when the cash is collected. Accordingly, this event does not affect the income statement. Because the cash collection was derived from normal business operations, it is classified as an operating activity (OA). The effects on the financial statements are shown next:

Balance Sheet									Income Statement						Statement of Cash Flows
Assets			=	Liab.	+	Stk. Equity									
Cash	+	Accts. Rec.	=			Com. Stk.	+	Ret. Earn.	Rev.	−	Exp.	=	Net Inc.		
60,000	+	(60,000)	=	NA	+	NA	+	NA	NA	−	NA	=	NA		60,000 OA

Other Events

EVENT 4   Cato paid an instructor a $10,000 cash salary for teaching courses.

Cash payment for salary expense is an asset use transaction. On the balance sheet, assets (Cash) and stockholders' equity (Retained Earnings) decrease. Recognizing the expense decreases net income on the income statement. Because Cato paid cash for a normal operating expense, the statement of cash flows reflects a cash outflow from operating activities (OA). The effects on the financial statements are shown next:

Balance Sheet							Income Statement			Statement of Cash Flows
Assets			= Liab. +		Stk. Equity					
Cash	+ Accts. Rec.	=			Com. Stk.	+ Ret. Earn.	Rev. −	Exp.	= Net Inc.	
(10,000) +	NA	=	NA +		NA	+ (10,000)	NA −	10,000	= (10,000)	(10,000) OA

EVENT 5 Cato paid $2,000 cash for advertising costs. The advertisements appeared in Year 1.

The cash payment for advertising expense is an asset use transaction. On the balance sheet, assets (Cash) and stockholders' equity (Retained Earnings) decrease. Recognizing the expense decreases net income on the income statement. Because Cato paid cash for a normal operating expense, the statement of cash flows reflects a cash outflow from operating activities. The effects on the financial statements are shown next:

Balance Sheet							Income Statement			Statement of Cash Flows
Assets			= Liab. +		Stk. Equity					
Cash	+ Accts. Rec.	=			Com. Stk.	+ Ret. Earn.	Rev. −	Exp.	= Net Inc.	
(2,000) +	NA	=	NA +		NA	+ (2,000)	NA −	2,000	= (2,000)	(2,000) OA

ACCOUNTING FOR PAYABLES

Accrual accounting requires that companies recognize expenses in the period in which they are incurred regardless of when cash is paid. As a result, expenses may be recognized before cash is paid. For example, Cato must recognize an expense for all of the work its employees performed in Year 1 even if the employees are not paid until Year 2. Expenses that are recognized before cash is paid are called **accrued expenses**.

Recognizing accrued expense is a **claims exchange transaction**. The claims of creditors increase and the claims of stockholders decrease. Total claims remain unchanged. To illustrate, return to Cato, who has an employee who worked during Year 1 but will not be paid

LO 2-3

Show how payables affect financial statements.

until sometime in Year 2. At the end of Year 1, Cato would need to adjust its records for the following:

EVENT 6   At the end of Year 1, Cato owed an instructor $6,000 for courses the instructor taught in Year 1. Cato will not pay the instructor for these courses until Year 2. To account for this liability, Cato adjusts its records to recognize $6,000 of accrued salary expense.

The effects of recording $6,000 of accrued salary expense on the financial statements are shown below.

Balance Sheet								Income Statement				Statement of Cash Flows
Assets			=	Liab.	+	Stk. Equity						
Cash	+	Accts. Rec.	=	Sal. Pay.	+	Com. Stk.	+	Ret. Earn.	Rev.	−	Exp.	=	Net Inc.	
NA	+	NA	=	6,000	+	NA	+	(6,000)	NA	−	6,000	=	(6,000)	NA

On the balance sheet the liability account (**Salaries Payable**) increases and the stockholders' equity account (Retained Earnings) decreases. The balance in the Salaries Payable account represents the amount of cash the company is obligated to pay the instructor in the future. The decrease in Retained Earnings is reported as salary expense on the income statement and therefore decreases net income for Year 1. Because cash was not paid or collected, there is no impact on the statement of cash flows.

Expenses were previously defined as assets consumed in the process of generating revenue. However, in this case Cato's adjustment to recognize accrued salaries expense resulted from an increase in liabilities (i.e., Salaries Payable). Expenses that result from an increase in liabilities are called accrued expenses as the expense is recognized before the cash is paid. *An expense can therefore be more broadly defined as an economic sacrifice (a decrease in assets or an increase in liabilities) resulting from operating activities undertaken to generate revenue.*

Be careful not to confuse liabilities with expenses. Although liabilities may increase when a company recognizes expenses, liabilities are *not* expenses. Liabilities are obligations. They can arise from acquiring assets as well as recognizing expenses. For example, when a business borrows money from a bank, it recognizes an increase in assets (Cash) and liabilities (Notes Payable). In this case the increase in liabilities is not related to the recognition of expenses.

End-of-Period Adjustments

All business events that we have examined up to Event 6 occurred *during* an accounting period. Personnel in the accounting department are normally alerted to a business event by some source document such as an invoice, a receipt, or an electronic message. However, when an accounting period ends there may be some transaction data that has not been captured through the normal recording process. If these data are omitted from the accounting system, the financial statements will contain inaccuracies. To properly identify missing information and avoid inaccuracies, the accounting records must be scrutinized at the end of each accounting period. Any missing or inaccurate information must be identified and corrected before the financial statements are prepared. The end-of-period process of identifying and correcting discrepancies is called *adjusting the records*. Recording accrued salary expense in Event 6 is our first example of an **end-of-period adjustment**. We will see many more examples of end-of-period adjustments throughout the text.

EVENT 7   Cato signed contracts for $42,000 of consulting services to be performed in Year 2.

The $42,000 for consulting services to be performed in Year 2 is not recognized in the Year 1 financial statements. Revenue is recognized for work actually completed, not work expected to be completed. This event does not affect any of the financial statements.

Summary of Events and Their Effects on the Accounting Equation

The previous section of this chapter described seven events Cato Consultants experienced during the Year 1 accounting period. These events and their effects on the accounting equation are summarized in Exhibit 2.1. The information in the accounting equation is used to prepare the financial statements.

CHECK YOURSELF 2.1

During Year 1, Anwar Company earned $345,000 of revenue on account and collected $320,000 cash from accounts receivable. Anwar paid cash expenses of $300,000 and cash dividends of $12,000. Determine the amount of net income Anwar should report on the Year 1 income statement and the amount of cash flow from operating activities Anwar should report on the Year 1 statement of cash flows.

Answer Net income is $45,000 ($345,000 revenue − $300,000 expenses). The cash flow from operating activities is $20,000, the amount of revenue collected in cash from customers (Accounts Receivable) minus the cash paid for expenses ($320,000 − $300,000). Dividend payments are classified as financing activities and do not affect the determination of either net income or cash flow from operating activities.

EXHIBIT 2.1

Cato Consultants Events and Effects on the Accounting Equation

Accounting Events for Year 1

1.	Cato Consultants acquired $5,000 cash by issuing common stock.
2.	Cato provided $84,000 of consulting services on account.
3.	Cato collected $60,000 cash from customers in partial settlement of its accounts receivable.
4.	Cato paid $10,000 cash for salary expense.
5.	Cato paid $2,000 cash for Year 1 advertising costs.
6.	Cato recognized $6,000 of accrued salary expense.
7.	Cato signed contracts for $42,000 of consulting services to be performed in Year 2.

Effects on the Accounting Equation

Event	Cash	+	Accounts Receivable	=	Salaries Payable	+	Common Stock	+	Retained Earnings	Other Account Titles
Beg.	0	+	0	=	0	+	0	+	0	
1.	5,000	+	NA	=	NA	+	5,000	+	NA	
2.	NA	+	84,000	=	NA	+	NA	+	84,000	Consulting revenue
3.	60,000	+	(60,000)	=	NA	+	NA	+	NA	
4.	(10,000)	+	NA	=	NA	+	NA	+	(10,000)	Salary expense
5.	(2,000)	+	NA	=	NA	+	NA	+	(2,000)	Advertising expense
6.	NA	+	NA	=	6,000	+	NA	+	(6,000)	Salary expense
7.	NA	+	NA	=	NA	+	NA	+	NA	
End	53,000	+	24,000	=	6,000	+	5,000	+	66,000	

(Assets = Liabilities + Stockholders' Equity)

PREPARING FINANCIAL STATEMENTS

The financial statements for Cato Consultants's Year 1 accounting period are shown in Exhibit 2.2. The information in the accounting equation in Exhibit 2.1 has been color coded to facilitate your understanding of the source of the information contained in the financial statements. The items colored red appear on the balance sheet. The items colored in blue appear on the income statement. The items colored green are used on the statement of cash flows. As you read the following explanations of each financial statement, trace the color-coded financial data from Exhibit 2.1 to Exhibit 2.2.

LO 2-4

Prepare financial statements that include accruals.

EXHIBIT 2.2   Financial Statements

Balance Sheet
As of December 31, Year 1

Assets		
Cash	$53,000	
Accounts receivable	24,000	
Total assets		$77,000
Liabilities		
Salaries payable		$ 6,000
Stockholders' equity		
Common stock	$ 5,000	
Retained earnings	66,000	
Total stockholders' equity		71,000
Total liabilities and stockholders' equity		$77,000

CATO CONSULTANTS
Financial Statements
Income Statement
For the Year Ended December 31, Year 1

Consulting revenue	$84,000
Salary expense	(16,000)
Advertising expense	(2,000)
Net income	$66,000

Statement of Changes in Stockholders' Equity
For the Year Ended December 31, Year 1

Beginning common stock	$ 0	
Plus: Common stock issued	5,000	
Ending common stock		$ 5,000
Beginning retained earnings	0	
Plus: Net income	66,000	
Less: Dividends	0	
Ending retained earnings		66,000
Total stockholders' equity		$71,000

Statement of Cash Flows
For the Year Ended December 31, Year 1

Cash flows from operating activities		
Cash receipts from customers	$60,000	
Cash payment for salary expense	(10,000)	
Cash payment for advertising expense	(2,000)	
Net cash flows from operating activities		$48,000
Cash flows from investing activities		0
Cash flows from financing activities		
Cash receipt from issuing common stock	5,000	
Net cash flow from financing activities		5,000
Net change in cash		53,000
Plus: Beginning cash balance		0
Ending cash balance		$53,000

Balance Sheet

The balance sheet discloses an entity's assets, liabilities, and stockholders' equity at a particular point in time. As of December 31, Year 1, Cato Consultants had total assets of $77,000 ($53,000 cash + $24,000 accounts receivable). These assets are equal to the obligations and commitments Cato has to its creditors and stockholders. Specifically, Cato has a $6,000 obligation (liability) to creditors, with the remaining $71,000 of assets available to support commitments (stockholders' equity) to stockholders.

Income Statement

Notice that the amount of net income ($66,000) is different from the amount of cash flow from operating activities ($48,000). The income statement reflects accrual accounting. Recall that accrual accounting recognizes revenue in the accounting period in which it is earned even when the associated cash is collected in a subsequent accounting period. This is because the income statement shows the total benefits received from operating the business. Benefits include items in addition to cash. In this case, Cato obtained a $24,000 increase in accounts receivable, as well as a $60,000 collection of cash. Accordingly, the total $84,000 of benefits (cash + increase in receivables) is reported as revenue on the income statement. In contrast, only the $60,000 of cash collected from customers is reported on the statement of cash flows.

Similarly, expenses include all sacrifices incurred to produce revenue regardless of whether cash has been paid. In this case, the Year 1 income statement includes $6,000 of salary expense even though Cato will not pay cash for these expenses until Year 2. These accrual reporting practices will cause differences between the amount of *net income* shown on the income statement and the amount of *cash flow from operating activities* shown on the statement of cash flows. Detailed comparisons are shown later.

Statement of Changes in Stockholders' Equity

The statement of changes in stockholders' equity explains the change in the amount of stockholders' equity that occurred during the Year 1 accounting period. In this case, total stockholders' equity increased from a beginning balance of zero to an ending balance of $71,000. The issue of stock explains $5,000 of the increase. The remaining $66,000 was caused by earnings.

Statement of Cash Flows

The statement of cash flows explains the change in cash from the beginning to the end of the accounting period. It can be prepared by analyzing the Cash account. Since Cato Consultants was established in Year 1, its beginning cash balance was zero. By the end of the year, the cash balance was $53,000. The statement of cash flows explains this increase. The Cash account increased because Cato collected $60,000 from customers and decreased because Cato paid $12,000 for expenses. As a result, Cato's net cash inflow from operating activities was $48,000. Also, the business acquired $5,000 cash through the financing activity of issuing common stock, for a cumulative cash increase of $53,000 ($48,000 + $5,000) during Year 1.

Comparing Cash Flow from Operating Activities with Net Income

The amount of net income measured using accrual accounting differs from the amount of cash flow from operating activities. For Cato Consulting in Year 1, the differences are summarized as follows:

	Accrual Accounting	Cash Flow
Consulting revenue	$84,000	$60,000
Salary expense	(16,000)	(10,000)
Advertising expense	(2,000)	(2,000)
Net income	$66,000	$48,000

Many students begin their first accounting class with the misconception that revenue and expense items are cash equivalents. The Cato illustration demonstrates that a company may recognize a revenue or expense without a corresponding cash collection or payment occurring in the same accounting period.

The Matching Concept

Cash basis accounting can distort reported net income because it sometimes fails to match expenses with the revenues they produce. To illustrate, consider the $6,000 of accrued salary expense that Cato Consultants recognized at the end of Year 1 (Event 6). The instructor's teaching produced revenue in Year 1. If Cato waited until Year 2 (when it paid the instructor) to recognize $6,000, then the expense would not be matched with the revenue generated. By using accrual accounting, Cato recognized all the salary expense in the same accounting period in which the consulting revenue was recognized. A primary goal of accrual accounting is to appropriately match expenses with revenues, known as the **matching concept**.

Appropriately matching expenses with revenues can be difficult even when using accrual accounting. For example, consider Cato's advertising expense. Money spent on advertising may generate revenue in future accounting periods as well as in the current period. A prospective customer could save an advertising brochure for several years before calling Cato for training services. It is difficult to know when and to what extent advertising produces revenue. When the connection between an expense and the corresponding revenue is vague, accountants commonly match the expense with the period in which it is paid. Cato matched the entire $2,000 of advertising cost with the Year 1 accounting period even though some of that cost might generate revenue in future accounting periods. Costs that cannot be matched with revenue are typically expensed in the period in which they are paid. These costs are called **period costs**.

Matching is not perfect. Although it would be more accurate to match expenses with revenues, there is sometimes no obvious direct connection between expenses and revenue. Accountants must exercise good judgment to select the accounting period in which to recognize revenues and expenses.

Stockbyte/Getty Images

FOCUS ON INTERNATIONAL ISSUES

As explained in Chapter 1, companies in the United States must follow GAAP, as established by the Financial Accounting Standards Board (FASB), while most of the remainder of the world follows International Financial Reporting Standards (IFRS), which are established by the International Accounting Standards Board (IASB). Although there are some significant differences between GAAP and IFRS, it is the goal of the two rule-making bodies to have as much uniformity as possible. The process of trying to achieve this goal is often referred to as "convergence."

One very clear example of the attempt at convergence relates to revenue recognition. On May 28, 2014, both boards issued a converged standard related to how companies should recognize revenue earned from contract agreements. The FASB issued ASU 2014-09 (Topic 606) and the IASB issued IFRS 15. Both statements were titled "Revenue from Contracts with Customers." Although the wording of the two pronouncements was not exactly the same, the requirements were. For example, both statements list the same five-step process to be used to determine when revenue should be recognized:

1. Identify the contract(s) with a customer.
2. Identify the performance obligations in the contract.
3. Determine the transaction price.
4. Allocate the transaction price to the performance obligations in the contract.
5. Recognize revenue when (or as) the entity satisfies a performance obligation.[2]

Although the five steps are worded exactly the same in the two pronouncements, the wording that explains each of these steps is a bit different. Keep in mind that while differences between U.S. GAAP and IFRS exist, the two rule-making bodies are working diligently to keep these differences to a minimum. Therefore, the accounting you learn in the United States is very relevant to the financial reporting of companies throughout the world.

[2]2016. Revenue from Contracts with Customers (Topic 606). Financial Accounting Standard Board.

ACCOUNTING FOR NOTES PAYABLE

Cato's Year 1 ending account balances become Year 2's beginning account balances. As a result, Cato begins Year 2 with $53,000 cash, $24,000 accounts receivable, $6,000 accrued salaries payable, $5,000 common stock, and $66,000 of retained earnings. During Year 2, Cato experiences the following accounting events.

LO 2-5

Show how accrued interest expense affects financial statements.

EVENT 1 Cato paid cash to its employees to settle the $6,000 of salaries payable that was accrued in Year 1.

This event reduces assets (Cash) and liabilities (Salaries Payable) on the balance sheet. It does not affect the income statement because the expense associated with the salaries payable was recognized in Year 1. Recognizing these expenses again in Year 2 would result in double counting and therefore would overstate expenses. The statement of cash flows shows a $6,000 cash outflow. This outflow is classified as an operating activity because it is associated with expense recognition. The effects on the financial statements are shown next:

Balance Sheet						Income Statement					Statement of Cash Flows
Assets	=	Liab.	+	Stk. Equity							
Cash		Sal. Pay.				Rev.	−	Exp.	=	Net Inc.	
(6,000)	=	(6,000)	+	NA		NA	−	NA	=	NA	(6,000) OA

EVENT 2 Cato acquired $3,000 cash by issuing common stock.

This event type has been discussed previously. Its effects on the financial statements are shown in the following horizontal financial statements model. If you are having trouble understanding these effects, you should return to Chapter 1.

Balance Sheet						Income Statement					Statement of Cash Flows
Assets	=	Liab.	+	Stk. Equity							
Cash				Com. Stk.		Rev.	−	Exp.	=	Net Inc.	
3,000	=	NA	+	3,000		NA	−	NA	=	NA	3,000 FA

EVENT 3 Cato incurred $4,000 of utility expense on account.

Recognizing an accrued expense is a claims exchange transaction. The claims of creditors increase and the claims of stockholders decrease. Total claims remain unchanged. On the balance sheet the liability account (**Accounts Payable**) increases and the stockholders' equity account (Retained Earnings) decreases. The balance in the Accounts Payable account represents the amount of cash the company is obligated to pay the utility supplier in the future. Also, recognizing the utility expense decreases net income. Because cash was not paid or collected, there is no impact on the statement of cash flows. The effects on the financial statements are shown next:

Balance Sheet						Income Statement					Statement of Cash Flows
Assets	=	Liab.	+	Stk. Equity							
		Accts. Pay.		Ret. Earn.		Rev.	−	Exp.	=	Net Inc.	
NA	=	4,000	+	(4,000)		NA	−	4,000	=	(4,000)	NA

EVENT 4   Cato paid $3,500 cash in partial settlement of its accounts payable.

This event reduces assets (Cash) and liabilities (Accounts Payable) on the balance sheet. It does not affect the income statement because the expense associated with the accounts payable was recognized in Event 3. Recognizing utility expenses again when the cash is paid would result in double counting and therefore would overstate expenses. The statement of cash flows shows a $3,500 cash outflow. This outflow is classified as an operating activity because it is associated with expense recognition. The effects on the financial statements are shown next:

Balance Sheet						Income Statement					Statement of Cash Flows
Assets	=	Liab.		+	Stk. Equity						
Cash		Accts. Pay.				Rev.	−	Exp.	=	Net Inc.	
(3,500)	=	(3,500)		+	NA	NA	−	NA	=	NA	(3,500) OA

EVENT 5   On February 1, Year 2, Cato borrowed $5,000 cash from the State Bank.

As evidence of the debt, Cato issues a promissory note that describes the company's obligations to the bank. The primary difference between *notes payable* and *accounts payable* is that notes generally have longer terms and usually require interest charges. In this case, the note stipulates a one-year term and an annual interest rate of 6 percent.

Issuing the note is an asset source transaction. The asset account Cash increases and a new liability account called Notes Payable increases. The income statement is not affected. The statement of cash flows shows a $5,000 cash inflow from financing activities. The effects on the financial statements are shown next:

Balance Sheet						Income Statement					Statement of Cash Flows
Assets	=	Liab.		+	Stk. Equity						
Cash		Notes Pay.				Rev.	−	Exp.	=	Net Inc.	
5,000	=	5,000		+	NA	NA	−	NA	=	NA	5,000 FA

Notice that interest is not recognized on the day the money is borrowed. Interest expense is recognized after Cato has had access to the borrowed money. While interest accrues continuously, we will recognize it at the end of the accounting period.

EVENT 6   During Year 2, Cato Consultants provided $89,000 of consulting services on account.

This event type was discussed previously. Its effects on the financial statements are shown in the following horizontal financial statements model:

Balance Sheet						Income Statement					Statement of Cash Flows
Assets	=	Liab.		+	Stk. Equity						
Accts. Rec.					Ret. Earn.	Rev.	−	Exp.	=	Net Inc.	
89,000	=	NA		+	89,000	89,000	−	NA	=	89,000	NA

Be careful not to confuse the terminology "provided service *on account*" in Event 6 with the terminology "incurred expense *on account*" in Event 3. The meaning of "*on account*" terminology depends on the business event. In Event 6, Cato provided services so Cato expected to *receive* money from its customers in the future. Therefore, Cato recorded Accounts Receivable and increased Retained Earnings. The increase in assets was an economic benefit and reported as revenue on the income statement. In Event 3, utility services were provided to Cato so Cato expected to *pay* money to the utility supplier in the future. Therefore, Cato increased Accounts Payable and decreased Retained Earnings. The increase in liabilities was an economic sacrifice and was reported as an expense on the Income Statement.

EVENT 7   Cato collected $95,000 cash from customers in a partial settlement of its accounts receivable.

How could Cato collect $95,000 when the company earned only $89,000 on account during Year 2? Recall that at the end of Year 1 (beginning of Year 2) Cato had a $24,000 balance in its Account Receivables account. Cato is able to collect more cash in Year 2 than the amount of revenue earned on account in Year 2 because the company is collecting the $24,000 of Year 1 receivables, as well as part of the $89,000 of receivables generated in Year 2.

The collection of an account receivable is an asset exchange transaction. Cash increases, while another asset, Accounts Receivable, decreases. The effects on the financial statements are shown next:

Balance Sheet							Income Statement					Statement of Cash Flows
Assets			=	Liab.	+	Stk. Equity						
Cash	+	Accts. Rec.					Rev.	−	Exp.	=	Net Inc.	
95,000	+	(95,000)		NA	+	NA	NA	−	NA	=	NA	95,000 OA

EVENT 8   Cato paid $11,000 for salary expense during Year 2.

Cash expenses have been discussed previously. The effects of this event on the financial statements are shown in the following horizontal financial statements model:

Balance Sheet					Income Statement					Statement of Cash Flows
Assets	=	Liab.	+	Stk. Equity						
Cash				Ret. Earn.	Rev.	−	Exp.	=	Net Inc.	
(11,000)	=	NA	+	(11,000)	NA	−	11,000	=	(11,000)	(11,000) OA

EVENT 9   Cato paid $10,000 cash dividend.

The payment of cash dividends has been discussed previously. Its effects on the financial statements are shown in the following horizontal financial statements model:

Balance Sheet					Income Statement					Statement of Cash Flows
Assets	=	Liab.	+	Stk. Equity						
Cash				Ret. Earn.	Rev.	−	Exp.	=	Net Inc.	
(10,000)	=	NA	+	(10,000)	NA	−	NA	=	NA	(10,000) FA

ADJ. 1   On December 31, Year 2, Cato adjusts its books to recognize the amount of interest expense incurred during Year 2.

Recall that Cato borrowed $5,000 on February 1, Year 2. As a result, Cato owes the bank interest for the 11 months the loan was outstanding during the year. The amount of accrued interest is computed as follows:

1. First, determine the amount of annual interest. The interest rate is normally stated in annual terms. In this case, the bank is charging Cato 6 percent of the amount borrowed ($5,000 principal balance) per year. Accordingly, Cato is required to pay the bank $300 ($5,000 × .06) interest per year.

2. Second, determine the amount of interest per month. This is simply the annual interest divided by 12. Specifically, $300 annual interest divided by 12 months equals $25 per month

3. Third, multiply the amount of the monthly interest times the number of months that the loan was outstanding during the accounting period. In this case, the amount of interest is $275 ($25 per month × 11 months).

These steps can be summarized in a simple formula as follows:

$$\text{Principal} \times \text{Annual interest rate} \times \text{Time outstanding} = \text{Interest revenue}$$
$$\$5,000 \ \times \qquad\qquad 0.06 \qquad\quad \times \qquad (11/12) \qquad = \qquad \$275$$

The recognition of interest expense is a claims exchange event. On the balance sheet the liability account (Interest Payable) increases, and the stockholders' equity account (Retained Earnings) decreases. The income statement would report an increase in interest expense, which decreases net income. However, there is no effect on cash flow because the actual cash payment for interest will be made on the maturity date in Year 3. The effects on the financial statements are shown next:

Balance Sheet						Income Statement					Statement of Cash Flows
Assets	=	Liab.	+	Stk. Equity		Rev.	−	Exp.	=	Net Inc.	
		Int. Pay.		Ret. Earn.							
NA	=	275	+	(275)		NA	−	275	=	(275)	NA

ADJ. 2   At the end of Year 2, Cato recorded an accrued salary expense of $5,500. The salary expense is for courses the instructor taught in Year 2. However, Cato will not pay the instructor cash until Year 3.

This is a claims exchange transaction that has been discussed previously. Its effects on the financial statements are shown in the following horizontal financial statements model:

Balance Sheet						Income Statement					Statement of Cash Flows
Assets	=	Liab.	+	Stk. Equity		Rev.	−	Exp.	=	Net Inc.	
		Sal. Pay.		Ret. Earn.							
NA	=	5,500	+	(5,500)		NA	−	5,500	=	(5,500)	NA

EXHIBIT 2.3

Accounting Events for Year 2

1. Paid $6,000 cash for salaries that were accrued in Year 1.
2. Acquired $3,000 by issuing common stock.
3. Incurred $4,000 of utility expense on account.
4. Paid $3,500 cash in partial settlement of accounts payable.
5. On February 1, Year 2, borrowed $5,000 cash from the State Bank.
6. Recognized $89,000 of revenue on account.
7. Collected $95,000 cash from customers in partial settlement of its accounts receivables.
8. Paid $11,000 for salary expense.
9. Paid a $10,000 cash dividend.
Adj. 1. Adjusted records to recognize $275 of interest expense incurred during Year 2.
Adj. 2. Recognized $5,500 of accrued salary expense.

Effects of Year 2 Events Shown Under an Accounting Equation

Event No.	Cash	+	Acc. Rec.	=	Acc. Pay.	+	Sal. Pay.	+	Int. Pay.	+	Note Pay.	+	Com. Stock	+	Ret. Earn.	Other Account Titles
Beg.	53,000	+	24,000	=	NA	+	6,000	+	NA	+	NA	+	5,000	+	66,000	
1.	(6,000)	+	NA	=	NA	+	(6,000)	+	NA	+	NA	+	NA	+	NA	
2.	3,000	+	NA	=	NA	+	NA	+	NA	+	NA	+	3,000	+	NA	
3.	NA	+	NA	=	4,000	+	NA	+	NA	+	NA	+	NA	+	(4,000)	Utility Exp.
4.	(3,500)	+	NA	=	(3,500)	+	NA	+	NA	+	NA	+	NA	+	NA	
5.	5,000	+	NA	=	NA	+	NA	+	NA	+	5,000	+	NA	+	NA	
6.	NA	+	89,000	=	NA	+	NA	+	NA	+	NA	+	NA	+	89,000	Revenue
7.	95,000	+	(95,000)	=	NA	+	NA	+	NA	+	NA	+	NA	+	NA	
8.	(11,000)	+	NA	=	NA	+	NA	+	NA	+	NA	+	NA	+	(11,000)	Salary Exp.
9.	(10,000)	+	NA	=	NA	+	NA	+	NA	+	NA	+	NA	+	(10,000)	Dividend
Adj. 1	NA	+	NA	=	NA	+	NA	+	275	+	NA	+	NA	+	(275)	Interest Exp.
Adj. 2	NA	+	NA	=	NA	+	5,500	+	NA	+	NA	+	NA	+	(5,500)	Salary Exp.
End	125,500	+	18,000	=	500	+	5,500	+	275	+	5,000	+	8,000	+	124,225	

Assets $143,500	=	Liabilities $11,275	+	Stk. Equity $132,225

The events experienced by Cato during Year 2 are summarized in Panel 1 of Exhibit 2.3. The impacts of the events on the accounting equation are summarized in Panel 2 of the exhibit.

The financial statements for Cato Consultants' Year 2 accounting period are represented in the financial statements in Exhibit 2.4.

Accounting Events for Notes Payable at Maturity Date

The Year 2 ending balances become the Year 3 beginning balances. Cato engaged in numerous transactions during Year 3. However, only three of these transactions offer insight on new topics. These three events are discussed next.

EVENT 1 On maturity date, January 31, Year 3, Cato adjusts its books to recognize the amount of interest expense incurred during Year 3.

The amount of interest recognized in Year 3 is calculated as follows:

Principal × Annual interest rate × Time outstanding = Interest revenue
$5,000 × 0.06 × (1/12) = $25

EXHIBIT 2.4   Financial Statements

Balance Sheets
As of December 31

	Year 1	Year 2
Assets		
Cash	$ 53,000	125,500
Accounts receivable	24,000	18,000
Total assets	$ 77,000	143,500
Liabilities		
Salaries Payable	$ 6,000	$ 5,500
Accounts Payable	0	500
Interest Payable	0	275
Note payable	0	5,000
Total Liabilities	6,000	11,275
Stockholders' equity		
Common stock	5,000	8,000
Retained earnings	66,000	124,225
Total stockholders' equity	71,000	132,225
Total liabilities and stockholders' equity	$ 77,000	$143,500

CATO CONSULTANTS
Financial Statements
Income Statements
For the Year Ended December 31

	Year 1	Year 2
Consulting revenue	$ 84,000	$ 89,000
Salary expense	(16,000)	(16,500)
Advertising expense	(2,000)	0
Utility expense	0	(4,000)
Interest expense	0	(275)
Net income	$ 66,000	$ 68,225

Statements of Changes in Stockholders' Equity
For the Year Ended December 31

	Year 1	Year 2
Beginning common stock	$ 0	$ 5,000
Plus: Common stock issued	5,000	3,000
Ending common stock	5,000	8,000
Beginning retained earnings	0	66,000
Plus: Net income	66,000	68,225
Less: Dividends	0	(10,000)
Ending retained earnings	66,000	124,225
Total stockholders' equity	$ 71,000	$132,225

continued

| EXHIBIT 2.4 | *Concluded* |

Statements of Cash Flows
For the Year Ended December 31

	Year 1	Year 2
Cash flows from operating activities		
Cash receipts from customers	$60,000	$ 95,000
Cash payment for salary expense	(10,000)	(17,000)
Cash payment for advertising	(2,000)	0
Cash payment for utilities	0	(3,500)
Net cash flows from operating activities	48,000	74,500
Cash flows from investing activities	0	0
Cash flows from financing activities		
Cash receipt from issuing common stock	5,000	3,000
Cash receipt from borrowing		5,000
Cash paid for dividends	0	(10,000)
Net cash flow from financing activities	5,000	(2,000)
Net change in cash	53,000	72,500
Plus: Beginning cash balance	0	53,000
Ending cash balance	$53,000	$125,500

The effects on the financial statements are shown next:

Balance Sheet					Income Statement						Statement of Cash Flows
Assets	=	Liab.	+	Stk. Equity							
		Int. Pay.		Ret. Earn.	Rev.	−	Exp.	=	Net Inc.		
NA	=	25	+	(25)	NA	−	25	=	(25)		NA

EVENT 2 On maturity date, January 31, Year 3, Cato pays cash to pay off the amount of interest payable.

The second entry records Cato's cash payment for interest payable. This entry is an asset use transaction that reduces both the Cash and Interest Payable accounts for the total amount of interest due: $300. The interest payment includes the 11 months interest accrued in Year 2 and 1 month accrued in Year 3 ($275 + $25 = $300). There is no effect on the income statement because Cato recognized the interest expense previously. The statement of cash flows would report a $300 cash outflow from operating activities. The effects on the financial statements are shown next:

Balance Sheet					Income Statement						Statement of Cash Flows
Assets	=	Liab.	+	Stk. Equity							
Cash		Int. Pay.			Rev.	−	Exp.	=	Net Inc.		
(300)	=	(300)	+	NA	NA	−	NA	=	NA		(300) OA

EVENT 3 On maturity date, January 31, Year 3, Cato pays cash to pay off the notes payable.

The third entry on January 31, Year 3, reflects repaying the principal. This entry is an asset use transaction. The Cash account and the Notes Payable account each decrease by $5,000.

There is no effect on the income statement. The statement of cash flows would show a $5,000 cash outflow from financing activities. The effects on the financial statements are shown next:

Balance Sheet						Income Statement					Statement of Cash Flows	
Assets	=	Liab.	+	Stk. Equity		Rev.	−	Exp.	=	Net Inc.		
Cash		Notes Pay.										
(5,000)	=	(5,000)	+	NA		NA	−	NA	=	NA		(5,000) FA

After these events, there will be a zero balance in the interest and notes payable accounts. Exhibit 2.5 provides a summary of how the Year 3 events affected these accounts.

EXHIBIT 2.5

Year 3 Changes in Interest Payable		Year 3 Changes in Notes Payable	
Beginning interest payable balance	$275	Beginning notes payables balance	$5,000
Plus: Interest accrued during Year 3	25	Plus: Additional borrowing during Year 3	0
Minus: Payments to settle the liability	(300)	Minus: Payments to settle the liability	(5,000)
Yields: Ending interest payable balance	$ 0	Yields: Ending notes payables balance	$ 0

 CHECK YOURSELF 2.2

On September 1, Year 1, Jordan Company borrowed $9,000 cash. The loan had a one-year term and a 7 percent annual interest rate. Based on this information alone, answer the following questions.

a. What is the amount of interest expense to recognize on the December 31, Year 1, income statement?

b. What is the amount of total liabilities as of December 31, Year 1?

c. What is the amount of cash paid for interest during Year 2?

d. What is the amount of total liabilities as of December 31, Year 2?

Answer

a. Interest Expense:

   Year 1: $9,000 principal × .07 × 4/12 = $210
   Year 2: $9,000 principal × .07 × 8/12 = $420

b. Total liabilities = $9,000 principal balance + $210 accrued interest = $9,210

c. The total amount of interest ($9,000 × .07 = $630) is paid in Year 2.

d. Both the interest payable and the notes payable account balances are paid off in full on the maturity date on August 31, Year 2. As a result, there will be zero liabilities on December 31, Year 2.

CAUSAL FACTORS FOR CHANGES IN ACCOUNT BALANCES

As explained in the previous chapter, GAAP does not require specific financial statements to explain all transactions that occur during an accounting period. For example, there is no statement of changes in accounts receivable. Likewise, there is no statement of changes in accounts payable. Even so, it is insightful to apply the logic used in the statement of changes in stockholders' equity to other balance sheet accounts. For example, the effects of the Year 2 relationships between the beginning and payable are shown in Exhibit 2.6.

LO 2-6

Identify the causes for changes in beginning and ending account balances.

EXHIBIT 2.6

Year 2 Changes in Accounts Receivable	
Beginning accounts receivable balance	$24,000
Plus: Increases due to sales on account	89,000
Minus: Decreases due to receivables collections	(95,000)
Yields: Ending accounts receivable balance	$18,000

Year 2 Changes in Accounts Payable	
Beginning accounts payable balance	$ 0
Plus: Increases due to expenses incurred on account	4,000
Minus: Decreases due to payment of accounts payable	(3,500)
Yields: Ending accounts payable balance	$ 500

✓ CHECK YOURSELF 2.3

During Year 2, Be Bold, Inc. (BBI) earned $34,000 of revenue on account. The beginning balance in accounts receivable was $3,000, and the ending balance was $5,000. Also, the Year 2 ending balance in accounts payable was $2,400. Further, during Year 2 the company incurred $25,000 of operating expenses on account and paid $27,000 cash to settle accounts payable. Determine the amount of cash collected from accounts receivable. Also, determine the beginning balance in accounts payable.

Answer

Year 2 Changes in Accounts Receivable	
Beginning accounts receivable balance	$ 3,000
Plus: Increases due to sales on account	34,000
Minus: Decreases due to receivables collections	X = (32,000)
Yields: Ending accounts receivable balance	$ 5,000

Year 2 Changes in Accounts Payable	
Beginning accounts payable balance	X = $ 4,400
Plus: Increases due to expenses incurred on account	25,000
Minus: Decreases due to payment of accounts payable	(27,000)
Yields: Ending accounts payable balance	$ 2,400

LO 2-7

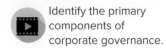

Identify the primary components of corporate governance.

The Financial Analyst

Corporate governance is the set of relationships between the board of directors, management, shareholders, auditors, and other stakeholders that determine how a company is operated. Clearly, financial analysts are keenly interested in these relationships. This section discusses the key components of corporate governance.

CORPORATE GOVERNANCE

Importance of Ethics

The accountant's role in society requires trust and credibility. Accounting information is worthless if the accountant is not trustworthy. Similarly, tax and consulting advice is useless if it comes from an incompetent person. The high ethical standards required by the profession state "a certified public accountant assumes an obligation of self-discipline above and beyond requirements of laws and regulations." The **American Institute of Certified Public Accountants (AICPA)** requires its members to comply with the **Code of Professional Conduct**. The preface of the Code includes six Principles of Professional Conduct that are summarized in Exhibit 2.7. The importance of ethical conduct is universally recognized across a broad spectrum of accounting organizations. The Institute of Management Accountants requires its members to follow a set of Standards of Ethical Conduct. The Institute of Internal Auditors also requires its members to subscribe to the organization's Code of Ethics.

EXHIBIT 2.7

Principles of Professional Conduct: AICPA Code of Professional Conduct

Responsibilities Principle
In carrying out their responsibilities as professionals, members should exercise sensitive professional and moral judgments in all their activities.

The Public Interest Principle
Members should accept the obligation to act in a way that will serve the public interest, honor the public trust, and demonstrate commitment to professionalism.

Integrity Principle
To maintain and broaden public confidence, members should perform all professional responsibilities with the highest sense of integrity.

Objectivity and Independence Principle
A member should maintain objectivity and be free of conflicts of interest in discharging professional responsibilities. A member in public practice should be independent in fact and appearance when providing auditing and other attestation services.

Due Care Principle
A member should observe the profession's technical and ethical standards, strive continually to improve competence and the quality of services, and discharge professional responsibility to the best of the member's ability.

Scope and Nature of Services Principle
A member in public practice should observe the Principles of the Code of Professional Conduct in determining the scope and nature of services to be provided.

The Sarbanes–Oxley Act

Credible financial reporting relies on a system of checks and balances. Corporate management is responsible for preparing financial reports while outside, independent accountants (CPAs) audit the reports. The massive surprise bankruptcies of Enron in late 2001 and WorldCom several months later suggested major audit failures on the part of the independent auditors. An audit failure means a company's auditor does not detect, or fails to report, that the company's financial reports are not in compliance with GAAP. The audit failures at Enron, WorldCom, and others prompted Congress to pass the Sarbanes–Oxley Act (SOX).

Prior to SOX, independent auditors often provided nonaudit services, such as installing computer systems, for their audit clients. The fees they earned for these services sometimes greatly exceeded the fees charged for the audit itself. This practice had been questioned prior to the audit failures at Enron and WorldCom. Critics felt the independent audit firm was subject to pressure from the company to conduct a less rigorous audit or risk losing lucrative nonaudit work. To strengthen the audit function, SOX included the following provisions:

- Prior to the enactment of SOX, independent auditors were self-regulated by the membership of the American Institute of Certified Public Accountants and by state boards of accountancy. Beyond self-regulation, SOX established the Public Company Accounting Oversight Board (PCAOB) to regulate accounting professionals that audit the financial statements of public companies.

- Independent auditors must register with the PCAOB or cease all participation in public company audits and abide by the board's pronouncements.

- The PCAOB has the responsibility to conduct inspections of registered firms. To ensure enforcement, the board has a full range of sanctions at its disposal, including suspension or revocation of registration, censure, and significant fines.

- To reduce the likelihood of conflicts of interest, SOX prohibits all registered public accounting firms from providing audit clients, contemporaneously with the audit, certain nonaudit services, including internal audit outsourcing, financial-information-system design and implementation services, and expert services.

- SOX provides significant corporate governance reforms regarding audit committees and their relationship to the auditor, making the audit committee responsible for the appointment, compensation, and oversight of the issuer's auditor.

Other provisions of SOX clarify the legal responsibility that company management has for a company's financial reports. The company's chief executive officer (CEO) and chief financial officer (CFO) must certify in writing that they have reviewed the financial reports being issued and that the reports present fairly the company's financial status. An executive who falsely certifies the company's financial reports is subject to a fine up to $5 million and imprisonment up to 20 years.

Common Features of Criminal and Ethical Misconduct

Unfortunately, it takes more than a code of conduct to stop fraud. People frequently engage in activities that they know are unethical or even criminal. The auditing profession has identified three elements that are typically present when fraud occurs, including:

1. The availability of an opportunity.
2. The existence of some form of pressure leading to an incentive.
3. The capacity to rationalize.

The three elements are frequently arranged in the shape of a triangle, as shown in Exhibit 2.8.

Opportunity is shown at the top of the triangle because without opportunity fraud could not exist. The most effective way to reduce opportunities for ethical or criminal misconduct is to implement an effective set of internal controls. **Internal controls** are policies and procedures that a business implements to reduce opportunities for fraud and to ensure that its objectives will be accomplished. Specific controls are tailored to meet the individual needs of particular businesses. For example, banks use elaborate vaults to protect cash and safety deposit boxes, but universities have little use for this type of equipment. Even so, many of the same procedures are used by a wide variety of businesses. The internal control policies and procedures that have gained widespread acceptance are discussed in a subsequent chapter.

EXHIBIT 2.8

The Fraud Triangle

OPPORTUNITY

PRESSURE   RATIONALIZATION

Only a few employees turn to the dark side even when internal control is weak and opportunities abound. So, what causes one person to commit fraud and another to remain honest? The second element of the fraud triangle recognizes **pressure** as a key ingredient of misconduct. A manager who is told "either make the numbers or you are fired" is more likely to cheat than one who is told to "tell it like it is." Pressure can come from a variety of sources, including:

- Personal vices such as drug addiction, gambling, and promiscuity.
- Intimidation from superiors.
- Personal debt from credit cards, consumer and mortgage loans, or poor investments.
- Family expectations to provide a standard of living that is beyond one's capabilities.
- Business failure caused by poor decision making or temporary factors such as a poor economy.
- Loyalty or trying to be agreeable.

The third and final element of the fraud triangle is **rationalization**. Few individuals think of themselves as evil. They develop rationalizations to justify their misconduct. Common rationalizations include the following:

- Everybody does it.
- The company is not paying me enough. I'm only taking what I deserve.
- I'm only borrowing the money. I'll pay it back.
- The company can afford it. Look what it is paying the officers.
- I'm taking what my family needs to live like everyone else.

Most people are able to resist pressure and the tendency to rationalize ethical or legal misconduct. However, some people will yield to temptation. What can accountants do to protect themselves and their companies from unscrupulous characters? The answer lies in personal integrity. The best indicator of personal integrity is past performance. Accordingly, companies must exercise due care in performing appropriate background investigations before hiring people to fill positions of trust.

Ethical misconduct is a serious offense in the accounting profession. A single mistake can destroy an accounting career. If you commit a white-collar crime, you normally lose the opportunity to hold a white-collar job. Second chances are rarely granted; it is extremely important that you learn how to recognize and avoid the common features of ethical misconduct. To help you prepare for the real-world situations you are likely to encounter, we include ethical dilemmas in the end-of-chapter materials. When working with these dilemmas, try to identify the (1) opportunity, (2) pressure, and (3) rationalization associated with the particular ethical situation described. If you are not an ethical person, accounting is not the career for you.

A Look Back

This chapter introduced the *accrual accounting* concept. Accrual accounting causes the amount of revenues and expenses reported on the income statement to differ significantly from the amount of cash flow from operating activities reported on the statement of cash flows because of timing differences. These differences are readily apparent when relevant events are recorded in a horizontal financial statements model. To review, study the following transactions and the corresponding horizontal financial statements model. Set up a horizontal financial statements model on a piece of paper and try to record the effects of each event before reading the explanation.

Events

1. Provided $600 of services on account.
2. Collected $400 cash from accounts receivable.
3. Accrued $350 of salary expense.
4. Paid $225 cash in partial settlement of salaries payable.

	Balance Sheet							Income Statement					Statement of Cash Flows
	Assets			=	Liab.	+	Stk. Equity						
Event	Cash	+	Accts. Rec.	=	Sal. Pay.	+	Ret. Earn.	Rev.	−	Exp.	=	Net Inc.	
1.	NA	+	600	=	NA	+	600	600	−	NA	=	600	NA
2.	400	+	(400)	=	NA	+	NA	NA	−	NA	=	NA	400 OA
3.	NA	+	NA	=	350	+	(350)	NA	−	350	=	(350)	NA
4.	(225)	+	NA	=	(225)	+	NA	NA	−	NA	=	NA	(225) OA
End	175	+	200	=	125	+	250	600	−	350	=	250	175 NC

Notice the $250 of net income differs from the $175 cash flow from operating activities. The entries in the horizontal financial statements model demonstrate the reasons for the difference. Although $600 of revenue is recognized, only $400 of cash was collected. The remaining $200 will be collected in the future and is currently shown on the balance sheet as Accounts Receivable. Also, although $350 of salary expense is recognized, only $225 was paid in cash. The remaining $125 will be paid in the future. This obligation is shown as Salaries Payable on the balance sheet. Study these relationships carefully to develop a clear understanding of how accrual accounting affects financial reporting.

Also, the definition of an expense has been expanded. The expanded definition of an expense is an *economic sacrifice* incurred in the process of generating revenue. More specifically, an expense is a decrease in assets or an *increase in liabilities* that is incurred to produce revenue. For example, recognizing accrued interest expense results in an increase in the liability account, Interest Payable, and a decrease in the stockholders' equity, Retained Earnings,

Finally, this chapter introduced the issues surrounding corporate governance. Codes of ethics, the relevant provisions of Sarbanes–Oxley, and the fraud triangle were discussed.

A Look Forward

Accrual accounting is composed of accruals and deferrals. This chapter discussed accruals. Chapter 3 will introduce deferrals. Recall that a deferral occurs when revenue or expense recognition occurs in an accounting period after the period that cash was collected or paid. Four specific deferrals will be discussed in Chapter 3. More specifically, you will learn how deferrals related to supplies, prepaid items, unearned revenue, and depreciation affect financial statements. When you finish the next chapter, you will have a clear understanding of how accrual accounting (including accruals and deferrals) differs from cash basis accounting.

 Video lectures and accompanying self-assessment quizzes are available in *Connect* for all learning objectives.

 Tableau Dashboard Activity is available in *Connect* for this chapter.

 SELF-STUDY REVIEW PROBLEM

Gifford Company experienced the following accounting events during Year 1:

1. Started operations on January 1 when it acquired $20,000 cash by issuing common stock.
2. Earned $27,000 of revenue on account.
3. Borrowed $10,000 cash from the City Bank on May 1, Year 1. The note carried a 9 percent annual interest rate and a one-year term.
4. Incurred operating expenses of $17,000 on account.
5. Paid a $2,700 cash dividend to stockholders.
6. Collected $25,000 cash from accounts receivable.

Adj. 1   Recognized accrued interest expense on December 31, Year 1.

Gifford Company experienced the following accounting events during Year 2:

1. Recognized $28,000 of revenue on account.
2. Paid $15,000 cash in partial settlement of accounts payable.
3. Collected $21,000 cash from accounts receivable.
4. Incurred $22,000 of operating expenses on account.
5. Paid a $5,000 cash dividend to stockholders.
6. Accrued interest expense on the note payable described in Year 1, Event 3.
7. Paid cash to settle accrued interest expense.
8. Paid $10,000 cash to pay off the note payable described in Year 1, Event 3.

Required

a. Record the events in a horizontal financial statements model like the following one. In the cash flow column show not only the amount but also indicate whether the event represents a financing activity (FA), investing activity (IA), or operating activity (OA). The first event is recorded as an example.

	Balance Sheet							Income Statement			Statement of Cash Flows
	Assets	=	Liabilities		+	Stk. Equity					
Event	Cash + Accts. Rec.	= Accts. Pay.	+ Int. Pay. +	Notes Pay. +	Com. Stk. +	Ret. Earn.		Rev. −	Exp. =	Net Inc.	
1.	20,000 + NA	= NA	+ NA +	NA	+ 20,000 +	NA		NA −	NA =	NA	20,000 FA

b. What amount of revenue would Gifford report on the Year 1 income statement?

c. What amount of net cash flow from customers would Gifford report on the Year 1 statement of cash flows? Explain any difference between the amounts calculated in Requirements b and c.

d. What is the amount of total liabilities as of December 31, Year 1?

e. What is the net cash flow from operating activities shown on the Year 2 statement of cash flows?

f. What amount of total assets would Gifford report on the December 31, Year 2, balance sheet?

g. What obligations and commitments would Gifford report on the December 31, Year 2, balance sheet?

Solution to Requirement a

Event	Cash +	Accts. Rec. =	Accts. Pay. +	Int. Pay. +	Notes Pay. +	Com. Stk. +	Ret. Earn.	Rev. −	Exp. =	Net Inc.	Statement of Cash Flows
1.	20,000 +	NA =	NA +	NA +	NA +	20,000 +	NA	NA −	NA =	NA	20,000 FA
2.	NA +	27,000 =	NA +	NA +	NA +	NA +	27,000	27,000 −	NA =	27,000	NA
3.	10,000 +	NA =	NA +	NA +	10,000 +	NA +	NA	NA −	NA =	NA	10,000 FA
4.	NA +	NA =	17,000 +	NA +	NA +	NA +	(17,000)	NA −	17,000 =	(17,000)	NA
5.	(2,700) +	NA =	NA +	NA +	NA +	NA +	(2,700)	NA −	NA =	NA	(2,700) FA
6.	25,000 +	(25,000) =	NA +	NA +	NA +	NA +	NA	NA −	NA =	NA	25,000 OA
Adj.	NA +	NA =	NA +	600 +	NA +	NA +	(600)	NA −	600 =	(600)	NA
End	52,300 +	2,000 =	17,000 +	600 +	10,000 +	20,000 +	6,700	27,000	17,600	9,400	52,300 NC

Balance sheet account balances carry forward from Year 1 to Year 2

Income accounts show data for only one year—no carry forward.

Event	Cash +	Accts. Rec. =	Accts. Pay. +	Int. Pay. +	Notes Pay. +	Com. Stk. +	Ret. Earn.	Rev. −	Exp. =	Net Inc.	Statement of Cash Flows
Beg. Bal.	52,300 +	2,000 +	17,000 +	600 +	10,000 +	20,000 +	6,700	NA −	NA =	NA	NA
1.	NA +	28,000 =	NA +	NA +	NA +	NA +	28,000	28,000 −	NA =	28,000	NA
2.	(15,000) +	NA =	(15,000) +	NA +	NA +	NA +	NA	NA −	NA =	NA	(15,000) OA
3.	21,000 +	(21,000) =	NA +	NA +	NA +	NA +	NA	NA −	NA =	NA	21,000 OA
4.	NA +	NA =	22,000 +	NA +	NA +	NA +	(22,000)	NA −	22,000 =	(22,000)	NA
5.	(5,000) +	NA =	NA +	NA +	NA +	NA +	(5,000)	NA −	NA =	NA	(5,000) FA
6.	NA +	NA =	NA +	300 +	NA +	NA +	(300)	NA −	300 =	(300)	NA
7.	(900) +	NA =	NA +	(900) +	NA +	NA +	NA	NA −	NA =	NA	(900) OA
8.	(10,000) +	NA =	NA +	NA +	(10,000) +	NA +	NA	NA −	NA =	NA	(10,000) FA
End	42,400 +	9,000 =	24,000 +	0 +	0 +	20,000 +	7,400	28,000 −	22,300 =	5,700	9,900 NC

Solutions to Requirements *b–g*

b. Gifford would report $27,000 of revenue earned on account in Year 1.

c. The cash inflow from customers in Year 1 is $25,000. The $27,000 of revenue calculated in Requirement *b* represents the amount of work Gifford completed during Year 1, while the $25,000 is the amount of cash collected for the work performed. Note that the $2,000 difference between these two amounts is equal to the ending balance in accounts receivable. The accounts receivable balance represents the amount of cash the company expects to collect in the future. In summary, Gifford earned $27,000 of income and collected $25,000 of cash in Year 1 and expects to collect $2,000 of additional cash in Year 2.

d. The December 31, Year 1, balance sheet will report total liabilities of $27,600 ($17,000 accounts payable + $600 interest payable + $10,000 notes payable).

e. Net cash flow from operating activities in Year 2 is a $5,100 inflow ($21,000 inflow from customers minus $15,000 out flow to reduce accounts payable minus $900 outflow to reduce interest payable).

f. Assets on the December 31, Year 2, balance sheet are $51,400 ($42,400 cash + $9,000 accounts receivable).

g. Obligations of the business are its liabilities. Commitments to investors is measured by the amount of stockholders' equity. Accordingly, total obligations plus commitments is $51,400 ($24,000 accounts payable + $20,000 common stock + $7,400 retained earnings). Note that the amount of total assets computed in Requirement *f* is equal to the total amount of obligations and commitments ($51,400 total assets = $24,000 liabilities + $20,000 common stock + $7,400 retained earnings).

KEY TERMS

Accounts Payable 83
Accounts Receivable 76
Accrual 73
Accrual accounting 73
Accrued expenses 77
American Institute of Certified Public Accountants (AICPA) 92

Claims exchange transaction 77
Code of Professional Conduct 92
Deferral 74
End-of-period Adjustment 78

Expenses 78
Horizontal financial statements model 74
Internal controls 93
Matching concept 82
Opportunity 93

Period costs 82
Pressure 94
Rationalization 94
Salaries Payable 78

QUESTIONS

1. What does accrual accounting attempt to accomplish?

2. Define *recognition*. How is it independent of collecting or paying cash?

3. If cash is collected in advance of performing services, when is the associated revenue recognized?

4. What effect does the issue of common stock have on the accounting equation?

5. How does the recognition of revenue earned on account affect the income

statement compared to its effect on the statement of cash flows?

6. When is revenue recognized under accrual accounting?

7. What effect does expense recognition have on the accounting equation?

8. What does the term *claims exchange transaction* mean?

9. When are expenses recognized under accrual accounting?

10. Why may net cash flow from operating activities on

the cash flow statement be different from the amount of net income reported on the income statement?

11. How does net income affect the stockholders' claims on the business's assets?

12. What does the term *expense* mean?

13. What is the purpose of the statement of changes in stockholders' equity?

14. What is the main purpose of the balance sheet?

15. Why is the balance sheet dated *as of* a specific date

when the income statement, statement of changes in stockholders' equity, and statement of cash flows are dated with the phrase *for the period ended*?

16. What does the statement of cash flows explain?

17. Give several examples of period costs.

18. Give an example of a cost that can be directly matched with the revenue produced by an accounting firm from preparing a tax return.

EXERCISES—SERIES A

Mc Graw Hill **connect** **All applicable Exercises in Series A are available in *Connect*.**

Where applicable in all exercises, round computations to the nearest dollar.

Exercise 2-1A   *Recording events in a horizontal financial statements model*

LO 2-1

The Ramires, Incorporated experienced the following events during its first year of operations, Year 1:

1. Acquired $56,000 cash by issuing common stock.
2. Earned $52,000 cash revenue.
3. Paid $27,000 cash for operating expenses.
4. Borrowed $15,000 cash from a bank.
5. Paid $40,000 cash to purchase land.
6. Paid a $1,000 cash dividend.

Required

a. Use a horizontal financial statements model to show how each event affects the balance sheet, income statement, and statement of cash flows. More specifically, record the amounts of the events into the model. Also, in the Statement of Cash Flows column, classify the cash flows as operating activities (OA), investing activities (IA), or financing activities (FA). The first transaction is shown as an example.

	Balance Sheet								Income Statement					Statement of Cash Flows
	Assets		=	Liab.	+	Stk. Equity								
Event	Cash	+ Land	=	Notes Pay.	+	Com. Stk.	+ Ret. Earn.		Rev.	− Exp.	=	Net Inc.		
1.	56,000	+ NA	=	NA	+	56,000	+ NA		NA	− NA	=	NA		56,000 FA

b. Prepare a formal income statement, statement of changes in stockholders' equity, balance sheet, and statement of cash flows.

Exercise 2-2A   *Showing how accounting events affect a horizontal financial statements model*

LO 2-1

The Candle Shop experienced the following events during its first year of operations, Year 1:

1. Acquired cash by issuing common stock.
2. Paid a cash dividend to the stockholders.
3. Paid cash for operating expenses.
4. Borrowed cash from a bank.
5. Provided services and collected cash.
6. Purchased land with cash.
7. Determined that the market value of the land is higher than the historical cost.

Required

Use a horizontal financial statements model to show how each event affects the balance sheet, income statement, and statement of cash flows. Indicate whether the event increases (I), decreases (D), or does not affect (NA) each part of the financial statements model. Also, in the Statement of Cash Flows column, classify the cash flows as operating activities (OA), investing activities (IA), or financing activities (FA). The first transaction is shown as an example.

Event	Balance Sheet						Income Statement					Statement of Cash Flows
	Assets		=	Liab.	+	Stk. Equity						
	Cash	+ Land	=	Notes Pay.	+ Com. Stk.	+ Ret. Earn.	Rev.	−	Exp.	=	Net Inc.	
1.	I	+ NA	=	NA	+ I	+ NA	NA	−	NA	=	NA	I FA

LO 2-1

Exercise 2-3A *Calculate missing amounts and interpret results*

The following horizontal financial statements model shows the transactions experienced by The Frame Shop (TFS) during Year 1. The table contains missing data that are labeled with alphabetic characters (a) through (n). Assume all transactions shown in the accounting equation are cash transactions.

Event	Balance Sheet						Income Statement					Statement of Cash Flows	
	Assets		=	Liabilities	+	Stk. Equity							
	Cash	+ Land	=	Notes Pay.	+ Com. Stk.	+ Ret. Earn.	Rev.	−	Exp.	=	Net Inc.		
Beg.	0 +	0	=	0 +	0	+ 0	0	−	0	=	0	NA	
1.	200,000 +	NA	=	NA +	(a)	+ NA	(b)	−	NA	=	(c)	200,000	FA
2.	350,000 +	NA	=	350,000 +	NA	+ NA	NA	−	NA	=	(d)	350,000	(e)
3.	(500,000) +	(f)	=	NA +	NA	+ NA	NA	−	NA	=	NA	(500,000)	(g)
4.	(h) +	NA	=	NA +	NA	+ (i)	95,000	−	NA	=	95,000	95,000	OA
5.	(65,000) +	NA	=	NA +	NA	+ (j)	NA	−	(k)	=	(65,000)	(65,000)	OA
6.	(12,000) +	NA	=	NA +	NA	+ (12,000)	NA	−	NA	=	NA	(12,000)	(l)
End	(m) +	500,000	=	350,000 +	200,000	+ 18,000	(n)	−	65,000	=	30,000	68,000	NC

Required

a. Use amounts or alphabetic letters to fill in the blanks highlighted by each character (a) through (n). Use the letters NA to indicate that no amount is related to the alpha character shown in the model. Use the letters FA to represent financing activity, IA to represent investing activities, OA to represent operating activities, and NC to represent net change.

b. Determine the total amount of assets that will appear on the December 31, Year 1, balance sheet.

c. Determine the total amount of net income that will appear on the income statement.

d. Determine the amount of cash flow from financing activities that will appear on the statement of cash flows.

LO 2-2, 2-4

Exercise 2-4A *Effect of collecting accounts receivable on the accounting equation*

Holloway Company started operations on January 1, Year 1. During Year 1, Holloway earned $18,000 of service revenue and collected $14,000 cash from accounts receivable.

Required

Based on this information alone, determine the following for Holloway Company. (*Hint:* Record the events in a horizontal financial statements model before satisfying the requirements.)

a. The balance of the accounts receivable that would be reported on the December 31, Year 1, balance sheet.

b. The amount of net income that would be reported on the Year 1 income statement.

c. The amount of net cash flow from operating activities that would be reported on the Year 1 statement of cash flows.

d. The amount of retained earnings that would be reported on the Year 1 balance sheet.

e. Why are the answers to Requirements *b* and *c* different?

Exercise 2-5A *Recording accounts receivable and other events in a horizontal financial statements model*   LO 2-1, 2-2, 2-4

The Containers Inc. experienced the following events during its first year of operations, Year 1:

1. Acquired $42,000 cash by issuing common stock.
2. Earned $25,000 revenue on account.
3. Paid $18,000 cash for operating expenses.
4. Borrowed $10,000 cash from a bank.
5. Collected $22,000 of the balance in accounts receivable.
6. Paid a $1,000 cash dividend.

Required

Use a horizontal financial statements model to show how each event affects the balance sheet, income statement, and statement of cash flows. More specifically, record the amounts of the events into the model. Also, in the Statement of Cash Flows column, classify the cash flows as operating activities (OA), investing activities (IA), or financing activities (FA). The first transaction is shown as an example.

	Balance Sheet									Income Statement					Statement of Cash Flows
	Assets		=	Liab.	+	Stk. Equity									
Event	Cash	+	Accts. Rec.	=	Notes Pay.	+	Com. Stk.	+	Ret. Earn.	Rev.	−	Exp.	=	Net Inc.	
1.	42,000	+	NA	=	NA	+	42,000	+	NA	NA	−	NA	=	NA	42,000 FA

a. Would the accounts receivable account appear in the assets, liabilities, or stockholders' equity section of the December 31, Year 1, balance sheet?

b. Determine the balance of the accounts receivable account that would appear on the December 31, Year 1, balance sheet.

c. Determine the amount of net income that would appear in the Year 1 income statement.

d. Determine the amount of the cash flow from operating activities that would appear in the Year 1 statement of cash flows.

e. Explain why the amount determined in Requirement *c* differs from the amount determined in Requirement *d*.

Exercise 2-6A *Effect of settling accounts payable on financial statements*   LO 2-1, 2-3, 2-4

Troy Company earned $15,000 of cash revenue. Troy incurred $12,000 of utility expense on account during Year 1. The company made cash payments of $8,000 to reduce its accounts payable during Year 1.

Required

Based on this information alone, determine the following for Troy Company. (*Hint:* Record the events in a horizontal financial statements model before satisfying the requirements.)

a. The balance of the accounts payable that would be reported on the December 31, Year 1, balance sheet.

b. The amount of expenses that would be reported on the Year 1 income statement.

c. The amount of net cash flow from operating activities that would be reported on the Year 1 statement of cash flows.

d. The amount of retained earnings that would be reported on the Year 1 balance sheet.

e. Why are the answers to Requirements *b* and *c* different?

Exercise 2-7A *Effect of accrued expenses on the accounting equation and financial statements*

During Year 1, Chung Corporation earned $8,000 of cash revenue and accrued $5,000 of salaries expense.

Required

(*Hint:* Record the events in accounts under an accounting equation before satisfying the requirements.) Based on this information alone:

a. Prepare the December 31, Year 1, balance sheet.
b. Determine the amount of net income that Chung would report on the Year 1 income statement.
c. Determine the amount of net cash flow from operating activities that Chung would report on the Year 1 statement of cash flows.
d. Why are the answers to Requirements *b* and *c* different?

Exercise 2-8A *Effect of accruals on the financial statements*

Milea Inc. experienced the following events in Year 1, its first year of operations:

1. Received $20,000 cash from the issue of common stock.
2. Performed services on account for $56,000.
3. Paid the utility expense of $2,500.
4. Collected $48,000 of the accounts receivable.
5. Recorded $10,000 of accrued salaries at the end of the year.
6. Paid a $2,000 cash dividend to the stockholders.

Required

a. Record the events in accounts under an accounting equation. In the last column of the table, provide appropriate account titles for the Retained Earnings amounts. The first transaction has been recorded as an example.

MILEA INC.							
Accounting Equation							
Event No.	Assets		= Liabilities	+	Stockholders' Equity		Acct. Titles for Ret. Earn.
	Cash	Accounts Receivable	= Salaries Payable	+	Common Stock	Retained Earnings	
1.	20,000	NA	= NA	+	20,000	NA	

b. Prepare the income statement, statement of changes in stockholders' equity, balance sheet, and statement of cash flows for the Year 1 accounting period.
c. Why is the amount of net income different from the amount of net cash flow from operating activities?

Exercise 2-9A *Effect of accounts receivable and accounts payable transactions on financial statements*

The following events apply to Lewis and Harper, a public accounting firm, for the Year 1 accounting period:

1. Performed $70,000 of services for clients on account.
2. Performed $40,000 of services for cash.

3. Incurred $36,000 of other operating expenses on account.
4. Paid $10,000 cash to an employee for salary.
5. Collected $47,000 cash from accounts receivable.
6. Paid $16,000 cash on accounts payable.
7. Paid an $8,000 cash dividend to the stockholders.
8. Accrued salaries were $2,000 at the end of Year 1.

Required

a. Show the effects of the events on the horizontal financial statements model like the following one. In the Statement of Cash Flows column, use OA to designate operating activity, IA for investment activity, FA for financing activity, and NC for net change in cash. Use NA to indicate the account is not affected by the event. The first event is shown as an example.

Event No.	Cash	+	Accts. Rec.	=	Accts. Pay.	+	Sal. Pay.	+	Ret. Earn.	Rev.	–	Exp.	=	Net Inc.	Statement of Cash Flows
1.	NA	+	70,000	=	NA	+	NA	+	70,000	70,000	–	NA	=	70,000	NA

b. What is the amount of total assets at the end of Year 1?
c. What is the balance of accounts receivable at the end of Year 1?
d. What is the balance of accounts payable at the end of Year 1?
e. What is the difference between accounts receivable and accounts payable?
f. What is net income for Year 1?
g. What is the amount of net cash flow from operating activities for Year 1?

Exercise 2-10A   *Effect of accruals on the financial statements*   LO 2-2, 2-3, 2-4

Cordell Inc. experienced the following events in Year 1, its first year of operation:

1. Received $40,000 cash from the issue of common stock.
2. Performed services on account for $82,000.
3. Paid a $6,000 cash dividend to the stockholders.
4. Collected $76,000 of the accounts receivable.
5. Paid $53,000 cash for other operating expenses.
6. Performed services for $19,000 cash.
7. Recognized $3,500 of accrued utilities expense at the end of the year.

Required

a. Identify the events that result in revenue or expense recognition.
b. Based on your response to Requirement a, determine the amount of net income reported on the Year 1 income statement.
c. Identify the events that affect the statement of cash flows.
d. Based on your response to Requirement c, determine the amount of cash flow from operating activities reported on the Year 1 statement of cash flows.
e. What is the balance of the Retained Earnings account that appears on the Year 1 balance sheet?

LO 2-2, 2-3, 2-4

Exercise 2-11A   *Net income versus changes in cash*

In Year 1, Lee Inc. billed its customers $62,000 for services performed. The company collected $51,000 of the amount billed. Lee incurred $39,000 of other operating expenses on account, and paid $31,000 of the accounts payable. It acquired $40,000 cash from the issue of common stock and invested $21,000 cash in the purchase of land.

Required

(*Hint:* Identify the six events described in the paragraph and record them in accounts under an accounting equation before attempting to answer the questions.) Use the preceding information to answer the following questions:

a.   What amount of revenue will Lee report on the Year 1 income statement?

b.   What amount of cash flow from revenue will be reported on the statement of cash flows?

c.   What is the net income for the period?

d.   What is the net cash flow from operating activities for the period?

e.   Why is the amount of net income different from the net cash flow from operating activities for the period?

f.   What is the amount of net cash flow from investing activities?

g.   What is the amount of net cash flow from financing activities?

h.   What amounts of total assets, liabilities, and stockholders' equity will be reported on the year-end balance sheet?

LO 2-4

Exercise 2-12A   *Matching concept*

Companies make sacrifices known as *expenses* to obtain benefits called *revenues.* The accurate measurement of net income requires that expenses be matched with revenues. In some circumstances, matching a particular expense directly with revenue is difficult or impossible. In these circumstances, the expense is matched with the period in which it is incurred.

Required

a.   Identify an expense that could be matched directly with revenue.

b.   Identify a period expense that would be difficult to match with revenue. Explain why.

LO 2-5

Exercise 2-13A   *Effects of recognizing accrued interest on financial statements*

Ben Bradley started Bradley Company on January 1, Year 1. The company experienced the following events during its first year of operation:

1.   Earned $2,000 of cash revenue for performing services.

2.   Borrowed $8,000 cash from the bank.

3.   Adjusted the accounting records to recognize accrued interest expense on the bank note. The note, issued on August 1, Year 1, had a one-year term and a 6 percent annual interest rate.

Required

a.   What is the amount of interest expense in Year 1?

b.   What amount of cash was paid for interest in Year 1?

c.   Use a horizontal financial statements model to show how each event affects the balance sheet, income statement, and statement of cash flows. Indicate whether the event increases (I), decreases (D), or does not affect (NA) each part of the financial statements model. Also, in the Statement of Cash Flows column, designate the cash flows as operating activities (OA), investing activities (IA), or financing activities (FA). The first transaction has been recorded as an example.

	Balance Sheet									Income Statement			Statement of Cash Flows
	Assets	=	Liab.	+			Stk. Equity						
Event	Cash	=	Notes Pay.	+	Int. Pay.	+	Com. Stk.	+	Ret. Earn.	Rev.	− Exp.	= Net Inc.	
1.	I	=	NA	+	NA	+	NA	+	I	I	− NA	= I	I OA

Exercise 2-14A *Recognizing accrued interest expense*

Leach Company borrowed $80,000 cash by issuing a note payable on June 1, Year 1. The note had an 8 percent annual rate of interest and a one-year term to maturity.

Required

a. What amount of interest expense will Leach recognize for the year ending December 31, Year 1?

b. Show how the recognition of interest on December 31, Year 1, affects the accounting equation.

c. What amount of cash will Leach pay for interest expense in Year 1?

d. What is the amount of interest payable as of December 31, Year 1?

e. What amount of cash will Leach pay for interest expense in Year 2?

f. What amount of interest expense will Leach recognize in Year 2?

g. What is the amount of interest payable as of December 31, Year 2?

Exercise 2-15A *Determine missing amounts in the accounts receivable account*

Required

Determine the missing amounts in each of the following four independent scenarios:

a. X Co. had a $4,500 beginning balance in accounts receivable on January 1, Year 4. During Year 4, the company earned $69,400 of revenue on account and collected $68,200 cash from accounts receivable. Based on this information alone, determine the amount of the ending balance in accounts receivable.

b. X Co. had a $3,400 ending balance in accounts receivable on December 31, Year 4. During Year 4, the company earned $62,200 of revenue on account and collected $63,100 cash from accounts receivable. Based on this information alone, determine the amount of the beginning balance in accounts receivable.

c. X Co. had a $9,700 beginning balance in accounts receivable on January 1, Year 4. During Year 4, the company earned $99,700 of revenue on account. The ending balance in accounts receivable was $10,300. Based on this information alone, determine the amount of cash collections from accounts receivable.

d. X Co. had a $22,000 beginning balance in accounts receivable on January 1, Year 4. During Year 4, the company collected $109,000 of revenue on account. The ending balance in accounts receivable was $21,300. Based on this information alone, determine the amount of cash collections from accounts receivable.

Exercise 2-16A *Determine missing amounts in the accounts payable account*

Required

Determine the missing amounts in each of the following four independent scenarios:

a. X Co. had a $4,700 beginning balance in accounts payable on January 1, Year 8. During Year 8, the company incurred $67,600 of operating expenses on account and paid $68,900 cash to settle accounts payable. Based on this information alone, determine the amount of the ending balance in accounts payable.

b. X Co. had a $5,300 ending balance in accounts payable on December 31, Year 8. During Year 8, the company incurred $66,400 of operating expenses on account and paid $64,100 cash to settle accounts payable. Based on this information alone, determine the amount of the beginning balance in accounts payable.

c. X Co. had a $4,100 beginning balance in accounts payable on January 1, Year 8. During Year 8, the company incurred $67,600 of operating expenses on account. The ending balance in accounts payable was $4,800. Based on this information alone, determine the amount of cash paid to settle accounts payable.

d. X Co. had a $7,700 beginning balance in accounts payable on January 1, Year 8. During Year 8, the company paid $77,300 cash to settle accounts payable. The ending balance in accounts payable was $9,800. Based on this information alone, determine the amount of expenses incurred on account.

LO 2-6

Exercise 2-17A *Missing information related to accounts receivable*

Harbert, Inc. had a beginning balance of $12,000 in its Accounts Receivable account. The ending balance of Accounts Receivable was $10,500. During the period, Harbert collects $72,000 of its accounts receivable. Harbert incurred $63,000 of cash expenses during the accounting period.

Required

a. Based on the information provided, determine the amount of revenue recognized during the accounting period.

b. Based on the information provided, determine the amount of net income earned during the accounting period.

c. Based on the information provided, determine the amount of cash flow from operating activities.

d. Explain why the amounts determined in Requirements *b* and *c* are different.

LO 2-6

Exercise 2-18A *Missing information related to accounts payable*

During Year 6, Kincaid, Inc. earned $85,000 of cash revenue. The company incurs all operating expenses on account. The Year 6 beginning balance in Kincaid's accounts payable account was $2,000, while the ending balance was $25,000. The company made cash payments of $40,000 to reduce accounts payable during Year 6.

Required

a. Based on the information provided, determine the amount of operating expenses recognized during the accounting period.

b. Based on the information provided, determine the amount of net income earned during the accounting period.

c. Based on the information provided, determine the amount of cash flow from operating activities.

d. Explain why the amounts determined in Requirements *b* and *c* are different.

LO 2-7

Exercise 2-19A *Ethical conduct*

Required

Name and provide a brief explanation of the six Principles of Professional Conduct of the AICPA Code of Professional Conduct.

PROBLEMS—SERIES A

Mc Graw Hill connect   All applicable Problems in Series A are available in *Connect*.

LO 2-1

CHECK FIGURES
a. Net Income: $23,000
e. Net Cash Flow from Operating Activities: $23,000

Problem 2-20A *Showing how events affect the horizontal financial statements model*

Maben Company was started on January 1, Year 1, and experienced the following events during its first year of operation:

1. Acquired $30,000 cash from the issue of common stock.
2. Borrowed $40,000 cash from National Bank.
3. Earned cash revenues of $48,000 for performing services.
4. Paid cash expenses of $25,000.
5. Paid a $1,000 cash dividend to the stockholders.
6. Acquired an additional $20,000 cash from the issue of common stock.
7. Paid $10,000 cash to reduce the principal balance of the bank note.
8. Paid $53,000 cash to purchase land.
9. Determined that the market value of the land is $75,000.

Required

a. Use a horizontal financial statements model to show how each event affects the balance sheet, income statement, and statement of cash flows. Also, in the Statement of Cash Flows column, classify the cash flows as operating activities (OA), investing activities (IA), or financing activities (FA). The first event is shown as an example.

	Balance Sheet								Income Statement			Statement of Cash Flows
	Assets		=	Liab.	+	Stk. Equity						
Event	Cash	+ Land	=	Notes Pay.	+	Com. Stk.	+ Ret. Earn.		Rev.	− Exp.	= Net Inc.	
1.	30,000	+ NA	=	NA	+	30,000	+ NA		NA	− NA	= NA	30,000 FA

b. Determine the amount of total assets that Maben would report on the December 31, Year 1, balance sheet.

c. Identify the asset source transactions and related amounts for Year 1.

d. Determine the net income that Maben would report on the Year 1 income statement. Explain why dividends do not appear on the income statement.

e. Determine the net cash flows from operating activities, financing activities, and investing activities that Maben would report on the Year 1 statement of cash flows.

f. Determine the percentage of assets that were provided by investors, creditors, and earnings.

g. What is the balance in the Retained Earnings account immediately after Event 3 is recorded?

Problem 2-21A   *Matching accounting events with horizontal financial statements model effects*   LO 2-1, 2-2, 2-3

Electronic Enterprises (EE) experienced eight accounting events during Year 6. These events affected EE's financial statements, as shown in the following horizontal financial statements model:

	Balance Sheet								Income Statement			Statement of Cash Flows
	Assets		=	Liab.	+	Stk. Equity						
Event	Cash	+ Accts. Rec.	=	Accts. Pay.	+	Com. Stk.	+ Ret. Earn.		Rev.	− Exp.	= Net Inc.	
1.	+	NA		NA		+	NA		NA	NA	NA	+ FA
2.	NA	+		NA		NA	+		+	NA	+	NA
3.	NA	NA		+		NA	−		NA	+	−	NA
4.	+	NA		NA		NA	+		+	NA	+	+ OA
5.	+	−		NA		NA	NA		NA	NA	NA	+ OA
6.	−	NA		NA		NA	−		NA	+	−	− OA
7.	−	NA		−		NA	NA		NA	NA	NA	− OA
8.	−	NA		NA		NA	−		NA	NA	NA	− FA

Required

Match the event number shown in the horizontal financial statements model above with the corresponding description of an event shown in the following table. The first event has been matched as an example.

Event No.	Description
	Incurred cash expenses.
	Earned revenue on account.
	Earned cash revenue.
1.	Issued common stock for cash.
	Paid a cash dividend.
	Collected cash from customer accounts receivable.
	Used cash to pay off accounts payable.
	Incurred expenses on account.

Problem 2-22A *Effect of events on financial statements*

Waddell Company had the following balances in its accounting records as of December 31, Year 1:

Assets		Liabilities and Equity	
Cash	$35,000	Accounts Payable	$ 7,500
Accounts Receivable	9,000	Common Stock	40,000
Land	51,000	Retained Earnings	47,500
Total	$95,000	Total	$95,000

The following accounting events apply to Waddell Company's Year 2 fiscal year:

Jan. 1   Acquired $20,000 cash from the issue of common stock.
Mar. 1   Paid a $2,000 cash dividend to the stockholders.
April 1   Purchased additional land that cost $15,000 cash.
May   1   Made a cash payment on accounts payable of $5,500.
Sept. 1   Sold land for $30,000 cash that had originally cost $30,000.
Dec. 31   Earned $58,000 of service revenue on account during the year.
     31   Received cash collections from accounts receivable amounting to $46,000.
     31   Incurred other operating expenses on account during the year that amounted to $28,000.
     31   The land purchased on April 1 had a market value of $20,000.

Required

Based on the preceding information, answer the following questions for Waddell Company. All questions pertain to the Year 2 financial statements. (*Hint:* Enter items in accounts under the horizontal financial statements model before answering the questions.)

a. What amount would Waddell report for land on the balance sheet?
b. What amount of net cash flow from operating activities would be reported on the statement of cash flows?
c. What amount of total liabilities would be reported on the balance sheet?
d. What amount of net cash flow from investing activities would be reported on the statement of cash flows?
e. What amount of total expenses would be reported on the income statement?
f. What amount of service revenue would be reported on the income statement?
g. What amount of cash flows from financing activities would be reported on the statement of cash flows?
h. What amount of net income would be reported on the income statement?
i. What amount of retained earnings would be reported on the balance sheet?

Problem 2-23A *Notes payable and accrued interest over two accounting cycles*

Sentry, Inc. was started on January 1, Year 1.

Year 1 Transactions

1. Acquired $20,000 cash by issuing common stock.
2. Earned $62,000 of revenue on account.
3. On October 1, Year 1, borrowed $12,000 cash from the local bank.
4. Incurred $3,700 of operating expenses on account.
5. Collected $5,000 cash from accounts receivable.
6. Paid $2,900 cash to pay off a portion of the accounts payable.
7. On December 31, Year 1, Sentry recognized accrued interest expense. The note had a one-year term and an 8 percent annual interest rate.

Year 2 Transactions

1. Collected cash for the remaining balance in accounts receivable.
2. Paid cash to settle the remaining balance of accounts payable.

3. On September 30, Year 2, recognized accrued interest expense.
4. On September 30, Year 2, paid cash to settle the balance of the interest payable account.
5. On September 30, Year 2, paid cash to settle the notes payable.

Required

a. Record the events for Year 1 and Year 2 in an accounting equation. At the end of Year 1, total the columns to determine the Year 1 account balances. The Year 1 ending balances become the Year 2 beginning balances. At the end of Year 2, total the columns to determine the account balances for Year 2.

b. Prepare an income statement, a statement of changes in stockholders' equity, a balance sheet, and a statement of cash flows for Year 1 and Year 2.

c. If the company were liquidated at the end of Year 2, how much cash would be distributed to creditors? How much cash would be distributed to investors?

Problem 2-24A *Identifying and arranging accounts on financial statements*   LO 2-2, 2-3, 2-4, 2-5, 2-6

The following information was drawn from the records of Bennett Company:

CHECK FIGURES
Total Assets $100,000
Net Income $8,000

Common stock issued	$ 5,000	Retained earnings (beginning)	$15,000
Cash flow from investing activities	(32,000)	Cash flow from financing activities	2,000
Notes payable (ending)	10,000	Accounts payable (ending)	17,000
Service revenue	42,000	Dividends	3,000
Other operating expenses	20,000	Cash (ending)	23,000
Salary expense	10,000	Accounts receivable (ending)	18,000
Interest payable (ending)	3,000	Interest expense	4,000
Common stock (beginning)	40,000	Accrued salaries payable (ending)	5,000
Cash flow from operating activities	33,000	Land (ending)	59,000
Cash (beginning)	20,000	Cash collected from accounts receivable	65,000
Paid cash to reduce accounts payable	18,000		

Required

a. Use the appropriate accounts and balances from Bennett Company to construct an end of period income statement, a statement of changes in stockholders' equity, a balance sheet, and a statement of cash flows (show only totals for each activity on the statement of cash flows).

b. Assume all revenue was recognized on account. Determine the beginning accounts receivable balance.

c. Assume the accounts payable account is associated with other operating expenses and that all other operating expenses are incurred on account. Determine the beginning accounts payable balance.

Problem 2-25A *Missing information related to accounts receivable and accounts payable*   LO 2-6

Castile Inc. had a beginning balance of $4,000 in its Accounts Receivable account. The ending balance of Accounts Receivable was $4,500. During the period, Castile recognized $68,000 of revenue on account. Castile's Salaries Payable account has a beginning balance of $2,600 and an ending balance of $1,500. During the period, the company recognized $46,000 of accrued salary expense.

Required

a. Based on the information provided, determine the amount of net income.
b. Based on the information provided, determine the amount of net cash flow from operating activities.
c. Explain why the amounts computed in Requirements *a* and *b* are different.

LO 2-7

Problem 2-26A *Ethics*

Pete Chalance is an accountant with a shady past. Suffice it to say that he owes some very unsavory characters a lot of money. Despite his past, Pete works hard at keeping up a strong professional image. He is a manager at Smith and Associates, a fast-growing CPA firm. Pete is highly regarded around the office because he is a strong producer of client revenue. Indeed, on several occasions he exceeded his authority in establishing prices with clients. This is typically a partner's job, but who could criticize Pete, who is most certainly bringing in the business. Indeed, Pete is so good that he is able to pull off the following scheme. He bills clients at inflated rates and then reports the ordinary rate to his accounting firm. Say, for example, the normal charge for a job is $2,500. Pete will smooth talk the client, and then charge him $3,000. He reports the normal charge of $2,500 to his firm and keeps the extra $500 for himself. Pete knows this isn't exactly right, because his firm receives its regular charges and the client willingly pays for the services rendered. Still, as he pockets his ill-gotten gains, he thinks to himself, "Who's getting hurt?"

Required

The text discusses three common features (conditions) that motivate ethical misconduct. Identify and explain each of the three features as they appear in the preceding scenario.

EXERCISES—SERIES B

Where applicable in all exercises, round computations to the nearest dollar.

LO 2-1

Exercise 2-1B *Recording events in a horizontal financial statements model*

The Bruce Spruce Co. experienced the following events during its first year of operations, Year 1:

1. Acquired $75,000 cash by issuing common stock.
2. Earned $48,000 cash revenue.
3. Paid $34,000 cash for operating expenses.
4. Borrowed $20,000 cash from a bank.
5. Paid $38,000 cash to purchase land.
6. Paid a $2,000 cash dividend.

Required

a. Use a horizontal financial statements model to show how each event affects the balance sheet, income statement, and statement of cash flows. More specifically, record the amounts of the events into the model. Also, in the Statement of Cash Flows column, classify the cash flows as operating activities (OA), investing activities (IA), or financing activities (FA). The first transaction is shown as an example.

	Balance Sheet									Income Statement						Statement of Cash Flows
	Assets			=	Liab.	+	Stk. Equity									
Event	Cash	+	Land	=	Notes Pay.	+	Com. Stk.	+	Ret. Earn.	Rev.	−	Exp.	=	Net Inc.		
1.	75,000	+	NA	=	NA	+	75,000	+	NA	NA	−	NA	=	NA	75,000	FA

b. Prepare a formal income statement, statement of changes in stockholders' equity, balance sheet, and statement of cash flows.

LO 2-1

Exercise 2-2B *Types of transactions and the horizontal financial statements model*

Pet Partners experienced the following events during its first year of operations, Year 1:

1. Acquired cash by issuing common stock.
2. Borrowed cash from a bank.
3. Signed a contract to provide services in the future.

4. Purchased land with cash.
5. Paid cash for operating expenses.
6. Paid a cash dividend to the stockholders.
7. Determined that the market value of the land is higher than the historical cost.

Required

a. Indicate whether each event is an asset source, use, or exchange transaction.

b. Use a horizontal financial statements model to show how each event affects the balance sheet, income statement, and statement of cash flows. Indicate whether the event increases (I), decreases (D), or does not affect (NA) each part of the financial statements model. Also, in the Statement of Cash Flows column, classify the cash flows as operating activities (OA), investing activities (IA), or financing activities (FA). The first transaction is shown as an example.

	Balance Sheet				Income Statement			Statement of Cash Flows
	Assets =	**Liab.** +	**Stk. Equity**					
Event	Cash + Land =	Notes Pay. +	Com. Stk. + Ret. Earn.		Rev. −	Exp. =	Net Inc.	
1.	I + NA =	NA +	I + NA		NA −	NA =	NA	I FA

Exercise 2-3B   *Calculate missing amounts and interpret results*   LO 2-1

The following horizontal financial statements model shows the transactions experienced by Surf's Up Industries during Year 1. The table contains missing data that are labeled with alphabetic characters (a) through (n). Assume all transactions shown in the accounting equation are cash transactions.

	Balance Sheet						Income Statement			Statement of Cash Flows
	Assets		=	**Liab.** +	**Stk. Equity**					
				Notes	**Com.**	**Ret.**				
Event	Cash +	Land	=	Pay. +	Stk. +	Earn.	Rev. −	Exp. =	Net Inc.	
Beg.	0 +	0	=	0 +	0 +	0	0 −	0 =	0	NA
1.	500,000 +	NA	=	NA +	(a) +	NA	(b) −	NA =	(c)	500,000 FA
2.	400,000 +	NA	=	400,000 +	NA +	NA	NA −	NA =	(d)	400,000 (e)
3.	(475,000) +	(f)	=	NA +	NA +	NA	NA −	NA =	NA	(475,000) (g)
4.	(h) +	NA	=	NA +	NA +	(i)	105,000 −	NA =	105,000	105,000 OA
5.	(80,000) +	NA	=	NA +	NA +	(j)	NA −	(k) =	(80,000)	(80,000) OA
6.	(15,000) +	NA	=	NA +	NA + (15,000)		NA −	NA =	NA	(15,000) (l)
End	(m) +	475,000	=	400,000 +	500,000 +	10,000	(n) −	80,000 =	25,000	435,000 NC

Required

a. Use amounts or alphabetic letters to fill in the blanks highlighted by each character (a) through (n). Use the letters NA to indicate that no amount is related to the alphabetic character shown in the model. Use the letters FA to represent financing activity; IA to represent investing activities; OA to represent operating activities, and NC to represent net change.

b. Determine the total amount of assets that will appear on the December 31, Year 1, balance sheet.

c. Determine the total amount of net income that will appear on the income statement.

d. Determine the amount of cash flow from investing activities that will appear on the statement of cash flows.

LO 2-2, 2-4

Exercise 2-4B   *Effect of collecting accounts receivable on the accounting equation*

Smith Company earned $12,000 of service revenue on account during Year 1. The company collected $9,800 cash from accounts receivable during Year 1.

Required

Based on this information alone, determine the following for Smith Company. (*Hint:* Record the events in a horizontal financial statements model before satisfying the requirements.)

a. The balance of the accounts receivable that Smith would report on the December 31, Year 1, balance sheet.

b. The amount of net income that Smith would report on the Year 1 income statement.

c. The amount of net cash flow from operating activities that would be reported on the Year 1 statement of cash flows.

d. The amount of retained earnings that would be reported on the Year 1 balance sheet.

e. Why are the answers to Requirements *b* and *c* different?

LO 2-1, 2-2, 2-4

Exercise 2-5B   *Recording accounts receivable and other events in a horizontal financial statements model*

The Woodstock Shop experienced the following events during its first year of operations, Year 1:

1. Acquired $38,000 cash by issuing common stock.
2. Earned $30,000 revenue on account.
3. Paid $25,000 cash for operating expenses.
4. Borrowed $15,000 cash from a bank.
5. Collected $25,000 of the balance in accounts receivable.
6. Paid a $2,000 cash dividend.

Required

a. Use a horizontal financial statements model to show how each event affects the balance sheet, income statement, and statement of cash flows. More specifically, record the amounts of the events into the model. Also, in the Statement of Cash Flows column, classify the cash flows as operating activities (OA), investing activities (IA), or financing activities (FA). The first transaction is shown as an example.

	Balance Sheet									Income Statement						Statement of Cash Flows
	Assets			=	Liab.	+	Stk. Equity									
Event	Cash	+	Accts. Rec.	=	Notes Pay.	+	Com. Stk.	+	Ret. Earn.	Rev.	−	Exp.	=	Net Inc.		
1.	38,000	+	NA	=	NA	+	38,000	+	NA	NA	−	NA	=	NA	38,000	FA

b. Would the accounts receivable account appear in the assets, liabilities, or stockholders' equity section of the December 31, Year 1, balance sheet?

c. Determine the balance of the accounts receivable account that would appear on the December 31, Year 1, balance sheet.

d. Determine the amount of net income that would appear in the Year 1 income statement.

e. Determine the amount of the cash flow from operating activities that would appear in the Year 1 statement of cash flows.

f. Explain why the amount determined in Requirement *d* differs from the amount determined in Requirement *e*.

LO 2-1, 2-3, 2-4

Exercise 2-6B   *Effect of collecting accounts payable on financial statements*

Kendall Company earned $20,000 of cash revenue. Kendall Co. incurred $10,000 of utility expense on account during Year 1. The company made cash payments of $5,000 to reduce its accounts payable during Year 1.

Required

Based on this information alone, determine the following for Kendall Company. (*Hint:* Record the events in a horizontal financial statements model before satisfying the requirements.)

a. The balance of the accounts payable that would be reported on the December 31, Year 1, balance sheet.

b. The amount of expenses that would be reported on the Year 1 income statement.

c. The amount of net cash flow from operating activities that would be reported on the Year 1 statement of cash flows.

d. The amount of retained earnings that would be reported on the Year 1 balance sheet.

e. Why are the answers to Requirements *b* and *c* different?

Exercise 2-7B *Effect of accrued expenses on the accounting equation and financial statements*

During Year 1, Star Corporation earned $5,000 of cash revenue and accrued $3,000 of salaries expense.

Required

(*Hint:* Record the events in accounts under an accounting equation before satisfying the requirements.) Based on this information alone:

a. Prepare the December 31, Year 1, balance sheet.

b. Determine the amount of net income that Star would report on the Year 1 income statement.

c. Determine the amount of net cash flow from operating activities that Star would report on the Year 1 statement of cash flows.

d. Why are the answers to Requirements *b* and *c* different?

Exercise 2-8B *Effect of accruals on the financial statements*

Talley Inc. experienced the following events in Year 1 in its first year of operation:

1. Received $20,000 cash from the issue of common stock.
2. Performed services on account for $38,000.
3. Paid the utility expense of $2,500.
4. Collected $21,000 of the accounts receivable.
5. Recorded $15,000 of accrued salaries at the end of the year.
6. Paid a $2,000 cash dividend to the shareholders.

Required

a. Record the events in accounts under an accounting equation. In the last column of the table, provide appropriate account titles for the Retained Earnings amounts. The first transaction has been recorded as an example.

TALLEY INC.
Accounting Equation

Event No.	Assets		=	Liabilities	+	Stockholders' Equity		Acct. Titles for Ret. Earn.
	Cash	Accounts Receivable	=	Salaries Payable	+	Common Stock	Retained Earnings	
1.	20,000	NA	=	NA	+	20,000	NA	

b. Prepare the income statement, statement of changes in stockholders' equity, balance sheet, and statement of cash flows for the Year 1 accounting period.

c. Why is the amount of net income different from the amount of net cash flow from operating activities?

Exercise 2-9B   *Effect of accounts receivable and accounts payable transactions on financial statements*

The following events apply to Parker and Moates, a public accounting firm, for the Year 1 accounting period:

1. Performed $96,000 of services for clients on account.
2. Performed $65,000 of services for cash.
3. Incurred $45,000 of other operating expenses on account.
4. Paid $26,000 cash to an employee for salary.
5. Collected $70,000 cash from accounts receivable.
6. Paid $38,000 cash on accounts payable.
7. Paid a $10,000 cash dividend to the stockholders.
8. Accrued salaries were $3,000 at the end of Year 1.

Required

a. Show the effects of the events on the financial statements using a horizontal financial statements model like the following one. In the Statements of Cash Flows column, use OA to designate operating activity, IA for investment activity, FA for financing activity, and NC for net change in cash. Use NA to indicate that the model is not affected by the event. The first event is recorded as an example.

	Balance Sheet								Income Statement				Statement of Cash Flows
	Assets		=	Liabilities		+ Stk. Equity							
Event	Cash +	Accts. Rec.	=	Accts. Pay.	+ Sal. Pay. +	Ret. Earn.			Rev.	− Exp.	=	Net Inc.	
1.	NA +	96,000	=	NA	+ NA +	96,000			96,000	− NA	=	96,000	NA

b. What is the amount of total assets at the end of Year 1?
c. What is the balance of accounts receivable at the end of Year 1?
d. What is the balance of accounts payable at the end of Year 1?
e. What is the difference between accounts receivable and accounts payable?
f. What is net income for Year 1?
g. What is the amount of net cash flow from operating activities for Year 1?

Exercise 2-10B   *Effect of accruals on the financial statements*

Rosewood Inc. experienced the following events in Year 1, its first year of operation:

1. Received $50,000 cash from the issue of common stock.
2. Performed services on account for $67,000.
3. Paid a $5,000 cash dividend to the stockholders.
4. Collected $45,000 of the accounts receivable.
5. Paid $49,000 cash for other operating expenses.
6. Performed services for $10,000 cash.
7. Recognized $2,000 of accrued utilities expense at the end of the year.

Required

a. Identify the events that result in revenue or expense recognition.
b. Based on your response to Requirement *a*, determine the amount of net income reported on the Year 1 income statement.
c. Identify the events that affect the statement of cash flows.
d. Based on your response to Requirement *c*, determine the amount of cash flow from operating activities reported on the Year 1 statement of cash flows.
e. What is the balance of the Retained Earnings account that appears on the Year 1 balance sheet?

Exercise 2-11B *Net income versus changes in cash*

In Year 1, Hall Inc. billed its customers $62,000 for services performed. The company collected $51,000 of the amount billed. Hall incurred $39,000 of other operating expenses on account. Hall paid $31,000 of the accounts payable. Hall acquired $40,000 cash from the issue of common stock. The company invested $21,000 cash in the purchase of land.

Required

(*Hint:* Identify the six events described in the paragraph and record them in accounts under an accounting equation before attempting to answer the questions.) Use the preceding information to answer the following questions:

a. What amount of revenue will be reported on the Year 1 income statement?
b. What amount of cash flow from revenue will be reported on the statement of cash flows?
c. What is the net income for the period?
d. What is the net cash flow from operating activities for the period?
e. Why is the amount of net income different from the net cash flow from operating activities for the period?
f. What is the amount of net cash flow from investing activities?
g. What is the amount of net cash flow from financing activities?
h. What amounts of total assets, liabilities, and equity will be reported on the year-end balance sheet?

Exercise 2-12B *Matching concept*

Companies make sacrifices known as *expenses* to obtain benefits called *revenues.* The accurate measurement of net income requires that expenses be matched with revenues. In some circumstances, matching a particular expense directly with revenue is difficult or impossible. In these circumstances, the expense is matched with the period in which it is incurred.

Required

Distinguish the following items that could be matched directly with revenues from the items that would be classified as period expenses:

a. Sales commissions paid to employees.
b. Advertising expense.
c. Supplies.
d. The cost of land that has been sold.

Exercise 2-13B *Effects of recognizing accrued interest on financial statements*

Carry Connelly started Connelly Company on January 1, Year 1. The company experienced the following events during its first year of operation:

1. Earned $6,200 of cash revenue.
2. Borrowed $10,000 cash from the bank.
3. Adjusted the accounting records to recognize accrued interest expense on the bank note. The note, issued on September 1, Year 1, had a one-year term and a 9 percent annual interest rate.

Required

a. What is the amount of interest payable at December 31, Year 1?
b. What is the amount of interest expense in Year 1?
c. What is the amount of interest paid in Year 1?
d. Use a horizontal financial statements model to show how each event affects the balance sheet, income statement, and statement of cash flows. Indicate whether the event increases (I), decreases (D), or does not affect (NA) each part of the financial statements model. Also, in the Statement of Cash Flows column, designate the cash flows as operating activities (OA), investing activities (IA), or financing activities (FA). The first transaction has been recorded as an example.

	Balance Sheet									Income Statement			Statement of Cash Flows
	Assets		=	Liab.	+		Stk. Equity						
Event	Cash	=	Notes Pay.	+	Int. Pay.	+	Com. Stk.	+	Ret. Earn.	Rev.	− Exp.	= Net Inc.	
1.	I	=	NA	+	NA	+	NA	+	I	I	− NA	= I	I OA

LO 2-5

Exercise 2-14B   *Recognizing accrued interest expense*

California Company borrowed $120,000 from the issuance of a note payable on August 1, Year 1. The note had a 7 percent annual rate of interest and a one-year term to maturity.

Required

a. What amount of interest expense will California recognize for the year ending December 31, Year 1?

b. Show how the recognition of accrued interest expense on December 31, Year 1, affects the accounting equation.

c. What amount of cash will California pay for interest expense in Year 1?

d. What is the amount of interest payable as of December 31, Year 1?

e. What amount of cash will California pay for interest expense in Year 2?

f. What amount of interest expense will California recognize in Year 2?

g. What is the amount of interest payable as of December 31, Year 2?

LO 2-6

Exercise 2-15B   *Determine missing amounts in the accounts receivable account*

Required

Determine the missing amounts in each of the following four independent scenarios:

a. W Co. had a $5,000 beginning balance in accounts receivable on January 1, Year 4. During Year 4, the company earned $72,500 of revenue on account and collected $70,000 cash from accounts receivable. Based on this information alone, determine the amount of the ending balance in accounts receivable.

b. W Co. had a $3,200 ending balance in accounts receivable on December 31, Year 4. During Year 4, the company earned $60,600 of revenue on account and collected $61,200 cash from accounts receivable. Based on this information alone, determine the amount of the beginning balance in accounts receivable.

c. W Co. had an $11,300 beginning balance in accounts receivable on January 1, Year 4. During Year 4, the company earned $102,400 of revenue on account. The ending balance in accounts receivable was $15,800. Based on this information alone, determine the amount of cash collections from accounts receivable.

d. W Co. had an $18,000 beginning balance in accounts receivable on January 1, Year 4. During Year 4, the company collected $125,000 of revenue on account. The ending balance in accounts receivable was $28,500. Based on this information alone, determine the amount of cash collections from accounts receivable.

LO 2-6

Exercise 2-16B   *Determine missing amounts in the accounts payable account*

Required

Determine the missing amounts in each of the following four independent scenarios:

a. W Co. had a $5,500 beginning balance in accounts payable on January 1, Year 8. During Year 8, the company incurred $45,200 of operating expenses on account and paid $43,100 cash to settle accounts payable. Based on this information alone, determine the amount of the ending balance in accounts payable.

b. W Co. had a $5,300 ending balance in accounts payable on December 31, Year 8. During Year 8, the company incurred $55,200 of operating expenses on account and paid $54,600 cash to settle accounts payable. Based on this information alone, determine the amount of the beginning balance in accounts payable.

c. W Co. had a $3,000 beginning balance in accounts payable on January 1, Year 8. During Year 8, the company incurred $73,000 of operating expenses on account. The ending balance in accounts payable was $8,500. Based on this information alone, determine the amount of cash paid to settle accounts payable.

d. W Co. had a $6,750 beginning balance in accounts payable on January 1, Year 8. During Year 8, the company paid $82,000 cash to settle accounts payable. The ending balance in accounts payable was $10,800. Based on this information alone, determine the amount of expenses incurred on account.

Exercise 2-17B   *Missing information related to accounts receivable*

LO 2-6

London Falls Inc. had a beginning balance of $15,000 in its Accounts Receivable account. The ending balance of Accounts Receivable was $8,500. During the period, London Falls collects $65,000 of its accounts receivable. London Falls incurred $53,000 of cash expenses during the accounting period.

Required

a. Based on the information provided, determine the amount of revenue recognized during the accounting period.

b. Based on the information provided, determine the amount of net income earned during the accounting period.

c. Based on the information provided, determine the amount of cash flow from operating activities.

d. Explain why the amounts determined in Requirements *b* and *c* are different.

Exercise 2-18B   *Missing information related to accounts payable*

LO 2-6

During Year 6, Shelby Enterprises earned $115,000 of cash revenue. The company incurs all operating expenses on account. The Year 6 beginning balance in Shelby's accounts payable account was $25,000 and the ending balance was $18,000. The company made cash payments of $85,000 to reduce accounts payable during Year 6.

Required

a. Based on the information provided, determine the amount of operating expenses recognized during the accounting period.

b. Based on the information provided, determine the amount of net income earned during the accounting period.

c. Based on the information provided, determine the amount of cash flow from operating activities.

d. Explain why the amounts determined in Requirements *b* and *c* are different.

Exercise 2-19B   *Ethical conduct*

LO 2-7

An October 31, 2012, news release from Hewlett-Packard Company (HP) included the following:

> HP recorded a non-cash charge for the impairment of goodwill and intangible assets within its Software segment of approximately $8.8 billion in the fourth quarter of its 2012 fiscal year. The majority of this impairment charge is linked to serious accounting improprieties, disclosure failures, and outright misrepresentations at Autonomy Corporation that occurred prior to HP's acquisition of Autonomy and the associated impact of those improprieties, failures, and misrepresentations on the expected future financial performance of the Autonomy business over the long term.

Required

Comment on the provisions of SOX that pertain to intentional misrepresentation and describe the maximum penalty the CFO could face.

PROBLEMS—SERIES B

LO 2-1

Problem 2-20B *Showing how events affect the horizontal financial statements model*

Daley Company was started on January 1, Year 1, and experienced the following events during its first year of operation:

1. Acquired $52,000 cash from the issue of common stock.
2. Borrowed $20,000 cash from National Bank.
3. Earned cash revenues of $42,000 for performing services.
4. Paid cash expenses of $23,000.
5. Paid a $6,000 cash dividend to the stockholders.
6. Acquired an additional $10,000 cash from the issue of common stock.
7. Paid $10,000 cash to reduce the principal balance of the bank note.
8. Paid $45,000 cash to purchase land.
9. Determined that the market value of the land is $55,000.

Required

a. Use a horizontal financial statements model to show how each event affects the balance sheet, income statement, and statement of cash flows. Also, in the Statement of Cash Flows column, classify the cash flows as operating activities (OA), investing activities (IA), or financing activities (FA). The first event is shown as an example.

	Balance Sheet								Income Statement			Statement of Cash Flows
	Assets		=	Liab.	+	Stk. Equity						
Event	Cash	+ Land	= Notes Pay.	+	Com. Stk.	+ Ret. Earn.			Rev. −	Exp. =	Net Inc.		
1.	52,000	+ NA	= NA	+	52,000	+ NA			NA −	NA =	NA		52,000 FA

b. Determine the amount of total assets that Daley would report on the December 31, Year 1, balance sheet.

c. Identify the asset source transactions and related amounts for Year 1.

d. Determine the net income that Daley would report on the Year 1 income statement. Explain why dividends do not appear on the income statement.

e. Determine the net cash flows from operating activities, financing activities, and investing activities that Daley would report on the Year 1 statement of cash flows.

f. Determine the percentage of assets provided by investors, creditors, and earnings.

g. What is the balance in the Retained Earnings account immediately after Event 3 is recorded?

LO 2-1

Problem 2-21B *Matching accounting with events the horizontal financial statements model affects*

Electronic Enterprises (EE) experienced eight accounting events during Year 6. These events affected EE's financial statements as shown in the following horizontal financial statements model:

Event	Assets		=	Liab.	+	Stk. Equity		Income Statement			Statement of Cash Flows
	Cash +	Accts. Rec.	=	Accts. Pay. +	Com. Stk. +	Ret. Earn.		Rev. –	Exp. =	Net Inc.	
1.	+	NA		NA	+	NA		NA	NA	NA	+ FA
2.	NA	+		NA	NA	+		+	NA	+	NA
3.	NA	NA		+	NA	–		NA	+	–	NA
4.	+	NA		NA	NA	+		+	NA	+	+ OA
5.	+	–		NA	NA	NA		NA	NA	NA	+ OA
6.	–	NA		NA	NA	–		NA	+	–	– OA
7.	–	NA		–	NA	NA		NA	NA	NA	– OA
8.	–	NA		NA	NA	–		NA	NA	NA	– FA

Balance Sheet columns: Assets (Cash, Accts. Rec.), Liab. (Accts. Pay.), Stk. Equity (Com. Stk., Ret. Earn.). Income Statement: Rev. – Exp. = Net Inc.

Required

Match the event number shown in the horizontal financial statements model given with the corresponding description of an event shown in the following table. The first event has been matched as an example.

Event No.	Description
	Earned cash revenue.
	Incurred expenses on account.
	Incurred cash expenses.
	Used cash to pay off accounts payable.
	Collected cash from customer accounts receivable.
	Paid a cash dividend.
1.	Issued common stock for cash.
	Earned revenue on account.

Problem 2-22B *Effect of events on financial statements*

LO 2-1, 2-2, 2-3, 2-4

CHECK FIGURES
b. $48,000
h. $31,000

Waddell Company had the following balances in its accounting records as of December 31, Year 1:

Assets		Liabilities and Stk. Equity	
Cash	$ 52,000	Accounts Payable	$ 12,500
Accounts Receivable	23,000	Common Stock	35,000
Land	45,000	Retained Earnings	72,500
Total	$120,000	Total	$120,000

The following accounting events apply to Waddell Company's Year 2 fiscal year:

Jan. 1   Acquired $35,000 cash from the issue of common stock.

Mar. 1   Paid a $4,000 cash dividend to the stockholders.

April 1   Purchased additional land that cost $20,000 cash.

May 1   Made a cash payment on accounts payable of $7,000.

Sept. 1   Sold land for $25,000 cash that had originally cost $25,000.

Dec. 31   Earned $65,000 of service revenue on account during the year.

31   Received cash collections from accounts receivable amounting to $55,000.

31   Incurred other operating expenses on account during the year that amounted to $34,000.

31   The land purchased on April 1 had a market value of $30,000.

Required

Based on the preceding information, answer the following questions for Waddell Company. All questions pertain to the Year 2 financial statements. (*Hint:* Enter items in accounts under the horizontal financial statements model before answering the questions.)

a. What amount would Waddell report for land on the balance sheet?

b. What amount of net cash flow from operating activities would be reported on the statement of cash flows?

c. What amount of total liabilities would be reported on the balance sheet?

d. What amount of net cash flow from investing activities would be reported on the statement of cash flows?

e. What amount of total expenses would be reported on the income statement?

f. What amount of service revenue would be reported on the income statement?

g. What amount of cash flows from financing activities would be reported on the statement of cash flows?

h. What amount of net income would be reported on the income statement?

i. What amount of retained earnings would be reported on the balance sheet?

LO 2-5

Problem 2-23B *Notes payable and accrued interest over two accounting cycles*

Matchstix was started on January 1, Year 1.

Year 1 Transactions

1. Acquired $50,000 cash by issuing common stock.

2. Earned $24,000 of revenue on account.

3. On October 1, Year 1, borrowed $22,000 cash from the local bank.

4. Incurred $10,500 of operating expenses on account.

5. Collected $7,000 cash from accounts receivable.

6. Paid $3,500 cash to pay off a portion of the accounts payable.

7. On December 31, Year 1, Matchstix recognized accrued interest expense. The note had a one-year term and a 6 percent annual interest rate.

Year 2 Transactions

1. Collected cash for the remaining balance in accounts receivable.

2. Paid cash to settle the remaining balance of accounts payable.

3. On September 30, Year 2, recognized accrued interest expense.

4. On September 30, Year 2, paid cash to settle the balance of the interest payable account.

5. On September 30, Year 2, paid cash to settle the notes payable.

Required

a. Record the events for Year 1 and Year 2 in an accounting equation. At the end of Year 1, total the columns to determine the Year 1 account balances. The Year 1 ending balances become the Year 2 beginning balances. At the end of Year 2, total the columns to determine the ending account balances for Year 2.

b. Prepare an income statement, a statement of changes in stockholders' equity, a balance sheet, and a statement of cash flows for Year 1 and Year 2.

c. If the company were liquidated at the end of Year 2, how much cash would be distributed to creditors? How much cash would be distributed to investors?

Problem 2-24B   *Identifying and arranging accounts on financial statements*

The following information was drawn from the records of Tristan Company:

Accounts payable (ending)	$12,000	Cash collected from accounts	$46,000
Accounts receivable (ending)	32,000	receivable	
Notes payable (ending)	13,000	Cash flow from financing activities	8,000
Common stock (beginning)	55,000	Common stock issued	10,000
Dividends	2,000	Other operating expenses	18,000
Land (ending)	75,000	Cash (ending)	35,000
Interest payable (ending)	5,000	Cash flow from investing activities	(36,000)
Service revenue	65,000	Interest expense	5,000
Cash flow from operating activities	45,000	Accrued salaries payable (ending)	9,000
Cash (beginning)	18,000	Salary expense	12,000
Paid cash to reduce accounts	23,000	Retained earnings (beginning)	10,000
payable			

Required

a. Use the appropriate accounts and balances from Tristan Company to construct an end of period income statement, a statement of changes in stockholders' equity, a balance sheet, and a statement of cash flows (show only totals for each activity on the statement of cash flows).

b. Assume all revenue was recognized on account. Determine the beginning accounts receivable balance.

c. Assume the accounts payable account is associated with other operating expenses and that all other operating expenses are incurred on account. Determine the beginning accounts payable balance.

Problem 2-25B   *Missing information related to accounts receivable and accounts payable*

Graphic Design Inc. had a beginning balance of $2,000 in its Accounts Receivable account. The ending balance of Accounts Receivable was $2,400. During the period, Graphic Design recognized $40,000 of revenue on account. The Salaries Payable account has a beginning balance of $1,300 and an ending balance of $900. During the period, the company recognized $35,000 of accrued salary expense.

Required

a. Based on the information provided, determine the amount of net income.

b. Based on the information provided, determine the amount of net cash flow from operating activities.

c. Explain why the amounts computed in Requirements *a* and *b* are different.

Problem 2-26B   *Ethics*

Raula Kato discovered a material reporting error in the accounting records of Sampoon, Inc. (SI) during the annual audit. The error was so significant that it will certainly have an adverse effect on the price of the client's stock, which is actively traded on the western stock exchange. After talking to his close friend, and president of SI, Kato agreed to withhold the information until the president had time to sell his SI stock. Kato leaked the information to his parents so they could sell their shares of stock as well. The reporting matter was a relatively complex issue that involved recently issued reporting standards. Kato told himself that if he were caught he would plead ignorance. He would simply say he did not have time to keep up with the rapidly changing standards, and so would be off the hook.

Required

a. Write a memo that identifies specific principles of the AICPA Code of Professional Conduct that were violated by Kato.

b. Would pleading ignorance relieve Kato from his audit responsibilities?

ANALYZE, THINK, COMMUNICATE

ATC 2-1   Business Applications Case   *Understanding real-world annual reports*

Required

Obtain Target Corporation's annual report for its 2018 fiscal year (year ended February 2, 2019) at http://investors.target.com using the instructions in Appendix B, and use it to answer the following questions:

a. Which accounts on Target's balance sheet are accrual type accounts?

b. Compare Target's *net income* to its *cash provided by operating activities* for the fiscal year ended February 2, 2019 (2018). Which is larger?

c. First, compare Target's 2017 net income to its 2018 net income. Next, compare Target's 2017 cash provided by operating activities to its 2018 cash provided by operating activities. Which changed the most from 2017 to 2018, net income or cash provided by operating activities?

[Target Corporation]

ATC 2-2   Group Assignment   *Impact of receivables and payables on financial statements*

The following information is drawn from the accounting records of Kristy Company:

	Year 1	Year 2
Revenue recognized on account	$50,000	$40,000
Cash collections from customers	40,000	50,000
Expenses incurred on account	30,000	25,000
Cash payments to reduce accounts payable	25,000	30,000

Divide the class into groups of four or five students. Organize the groups into four sections. Assign each section of groups the following tasks:

Required

Group Tasks

Section 1 Groups–Prepare a Year 1 income statement and determine the balance in the accounts receivable account as of December 31, Year 1.

Section 2 Groups–Prepare a Year 2 income statement and determine the balance in the accounts receivable account as of December 31, Year 2.

Section 3 Groups–Prepare the Year 1 operating activities section of the statement of cash flows and determine the balance in the accounts payable account as of December 31, Year 1.

Section 4 Groups–Prepare the Year 2 operating activities section of the statement of cash flows and determine the balance in the accounts payable account as of December 31, Year 2.

Class Discussion

Discuss the purpose of accrual accounting.

ATC 2-3   Real-World Case   *Analyzing earnings information using real-world data*

The following data are based on information in the 2018 annual report of Cracker Barrel Old Country Store. As of August 3, 2018, Cracker Barrel operated 655 restaurants and gift shops in 45 states. Dollar amounts are in thousands.

	2018	2017
Assets	$1,527,355	$1,521,942
Liabilities	945,574	977,435
Stockholders' equity	581,781	544,507
Revenues	3,030,445	2,926,289
Expenses	2,782,825	2,724,390
Dividends	207,649	197,544
Retained earnings at end of 2016		488,481

Required

a. Calculate the company's net income and retained earnings for 2017 and 2018.

b. Which increased (or decreased) by the greatest percentage amount: revenues or net income? Show your computations.

c. For each year, calculate the company's net income as a percentage of its revenues. Show your computations.

d. Did the company perform better in 2017 or 2018? Explain your answer.

ATC 2-4   Business Applications   *Analyzing cash flow information using real-world data*

The following data are based on information in the 2017 annual report of YUM! Brands, Inc. YUM! Brands is the parent company of KFC, Pizza Hut, and Taco Bell. As of December 31, 2017, the parent company owned or franchised over 45,000 restaurants in 135 countries. Dollar amounts are in millions.

	2017	2016
Assets	$ 5,311	$ 5,453
Liabilities	11,645	11,068
Stockholders' equity	(6,334)	(5,615)
Revenues	5,878	6,356
Expenses	4,538	4,713
Cash flows from operating activities	1,030	1,248
Cash flows from investing activities	1,472	(4)
Cash flows from financing activities	(1,734)	(778)
Cash balance at the beginning of 2016 was $365		

Required

a. Calculate the company's net change in cash for 2016 and 2017.

b. Calculate the company's ending cash balance for 2016 and 2017.

c. Notice that cash flows from financing activities were negative for each year. What could cause this to happen? Do you think this represents something positive or negative about the company? Explain your answer.

ATC 2-5   Writing Assignment   *Impact of receivables and payables on financial statements*

Corola Corporation reported $34,000 of net income and $25,000 of net cash flow from operating activities. All revenue is earned on account.

Required

Write a brief memo that explains how earning revenue on account could have caused the difference between net income and cash flow.

ATC 2-6   Ethical Dilemma   *What is a little deceit among friends?*

Glenn's Cleaning Services Company is experiencing cash flow problems and needs a loan. Glenn has a friend who is willing to lend him the money he needs, provided she can be convinced that he will be able to repay the debt. Glenn has assured his friend that his business is viable, but his friend has asked to see the company's financial statements. Glenn's accountant produced the following financial statements.

Income Statement	
Service Revenue	$ 38,000
Operating Expenses	(70,000)
Net Loss	$(32,000)

Balance Sheet	
Assets	$85,000
Liabilities	$35,000
Stockholders' Equity	
Common Stock	82,000
Retained Earnings	(32,000)
Total Liabilities and	
Stockholders' Equity	$85,000

Glenn made the following adjustments to these statements before showing them to his friend. He recorded $82,000 of revenue on account from Barrymore Manufacturing Company for a contract to clean its headquarters office building that was still being negotiated for the next month. Barrymore had scheduled a meeting to sign a contract the following week so Glenn was sure that he would get the job. Barrymore was a reputable company, and Glenn was confident he could ultimately collect the $82,000. Also, he subtracted $30,000 of accrued salaries expense and the corresponding liability. He reasoned that because he had not paid the employees, he had not incurred any expense.

Required

a. Reconstruct the income statement and balance sheet as they would appear after Glenn's adjustments. Comment on the accuracy of the adjusted financial statements.

b. Suppose you are Glenn and the $30,000 you owe your employees is due next week. If you are unable to pay them, they will quit and the business will go bankrupt. You are sure you will be able to repay your friend when your employees perform the $82,000 of services for Barrymore and you collect the cash. However, your friend is risk averse and is not likely to make the loan based on the financial statements your accountant prepared. Would you make the changes that Glenn made to get the loan and thereby save your company? Defend your position with a rational explanation.

c. Discuss the elements of the fraud triangle as they apply to Glenn's decision to change the financial statements to reflect more favorable results.

ATC 2-7   Research Assignment   *Identifying accruals at Netflix, Inc.*

This chapter defined and discussed accrual transactions. Complete the following requirements using the most recent financial statements available on the Internet for Netflix, Inc. Obtain the statements by following the steps given. (Be aware that the formatting of the company's website may have changed since these instructions were written.)

1. Go to **www.netflix.com**.
2. Click on "Investor Relations," which is at the bottom of the page in very small print.
3. Click on the "Annual Reports and Proxies" link at the bottom of the page.

4. Click on the "20xx Annual Report." Use the .pdf version of the annual report.

5. Find the company's balance sheet and complete the following requirements. In recent years, this has been shown toward the end of the Form 10-K section of the company's annual report, around page 43. The "Index" near the beginning of the report can help you locate the financial statements.

Required

a. Make a list of all the accounts on the balance sheet that you believe are accrual type accounts.

b. What was Netflix's net income for the year?

c. Did the balance in Netflix's retained earnings increase or decrease from the end of last year to the end of the current year, and by what amount?

CHAPTER 3

Accounting for Deferrals

Video lectures and accompanying self-assessment quizzes are available in *Connect* for all learning objectives.

Tableau Dashboard Activity is available in *Connect* for this chapter.

LEARNING OBJECTIVES

After you have mastered the material in this chapter, you will be able to:

LO 3-1   Show how accounting for supplies affects financial statements.

LO 3-2   Show how accounting for prepaid items affects financial statements.

LO 3-3   Show how accounting for unearned revenues affects financial statements.

LO 3-4   Use a list of accounts to prepare financial statements containing deferrals.

LO 3-5   Compute depreciation expense and show how it affects financial statements.

LO 3-6   Use a return-on-assets ratio, a debt-to-assets ratio, and a return-on-equity ratio to analyze financial statements.

CHAPTER OPENING

Recall that accrual accounting is composed of accruals (discussed in Chapter 2) and deferrals. This chapter introduces deferrals. What is a deferral? Let's start with the meaning of the term *defer*. Defer means to postpone, delay, or put off. As used in accounting, a deferral occurs when a company postpones, delays, or otherwise puts off the recognition of a revenue or an expense. More specifically, the term **deferral** describes a revenue or an expense event that is recognized after cash has been exchanged.

The Curious Accountant

On September 15, 2020, Mary Garcia purchased a subscription to *Parents* magazine for her daughter who is expecting her first child. She paid $12 for a one-year subscription to the **Meredith Corporation**, a company that publishes 25 major magazines, including *Better Homes and Gardens, People, Shape,* and *Martha Stewart Living.* The company also owns 17 television stations. Mary's daughter will receive her first issue of the magazine in October.

Kristoffer Tripplaar/Alamy Stock Photo

How should Meredith Corporation account for the receipt of this cash? How would this event be reported on its December 31, 2020, financial statements? (Answers on page 137.)

ALVARADO ADVISORY SERVICES ILLUSTRATION FOR YEAR 1

To examine the effects of deferrals on financial statements, we will analyze the accounting events experienced by Alvarado Advisory Services. The company has two divisions. One of the divisions provides logistical consulting services; the other provides installation services for automated warehouse equipment.

EVENT 1   **Alvarado was started on January 1, Year 1, when it acquired $55,000 cash by issuing common stock.**

This event type has been discussed previously. Its effects on the financial statements are shown in the following horizontal financial statements model. If you are having trouble understanding these effects, you should return to Chapter 1.

	Balance Sheet					Income Statement					Statement of Cash Flows
	Assets	=	Liab.	+	Stk. Equity						
	Cash	=			Com. Stk.	Rev.	−	Exp.	=	Net Inc.	
Beg. Bal.	55,000	=	NA	+	55,000	NA	−	NA	=	NA	55,000 FA

ACCOUNTING FOR SUPPLIES

Accrual accounting draws a distinction between the terms cost and expense. A **cost** might be either an asset or an expense. If a company has already consumed a purchased resource, the cost of the resource is an expense. For example, companies normally pay for electricity the month after using it. The cost of electric utilities is therefore usually recorded as an expense. In contrast, if a company purchases a resource it will use in the future, the cost of the resource represents an asset.

LO 3-1

Show how accounting for supplies affects financial statements.

EXHIBIT 3.1

Relationship between Costs, Assets, and Expenses

Accountants record such a cost in an asset account and defer recognizing an expense until the resource has been used to produce revenue. For example, if a company purchases supplies that will be used in the future, it records the initial purchase as an asset. Later after the supplies have been used, it will recognize supplies expense. Deferring the expense recognition provides for more accurate matching of revenues and expenses. These relationships are shown in Exhibit 3.1.

EVENT 2   Alvarado paid $800 cash to purchase supplies.

Paying cash to purchase supplies is an asset exchange transaction. The asset account Cash decreases and the asset account Supplies increases. The total amount of assets is not affected. Note that this event does not affect the income statement. Instead, the cost of the supplies is recorded as an asset. The expense recognition is deferred until the supplies are used. Because the supplies are expected to be consumed in the process of generating revenue within the coming year, the cash outflow is classified as an operating activity on the statement of cash flows. The effects on the financial statements are shown next:

Balance Sheet							Income Statement						Statement of Cash Flows
Assets			=	Liabilities	+	Stk. Equity	Rev.	−	Exp.	=	Net Inc.		
Cash	+	Supplies											
(800)	+	800	=	NA	+	NA	NA	−	NA	=	NA	(800)	OA

End-of-Period Adjustment

ADJ. 1   After determining through a physical count that $150 of unused supplies are on hand as of December 31, Alvarado recognizes supplies expense.

If a company were to attempt to record supplies expense each time a pencil, piece of paper, envelope, or other supply item were used, the cost of such tedious recordkeeping would far outweigh its benefits. Instead, accountants record an expense for the total cost of all supplies used during the entire accounting period in a single end-of-period adjustment. The cost of supplies used is determined as follows:

Beginning balance of supplies	$ 0
Plus: Supplies purchases	800
Supplies available for use	800
Less: Ending balance of supplies	(150)
Supplies used	$ 650

Recognizing supplies expense is an asset use transaction. On the balance sheet the asset account Supplies and the stockholders' equity account Retained Earnings decrease. The recognition of supplies expense would cause the amount of net income shown on the income statement to decrease. Recall that cash was paid when the supplies were purchased. There is no cash payment associated with the use of the supplies. Because the expense recognition did not involve the payment of cash, the statement of cash flows is not affected. The effects on the financial statements are shown next:

Balance Sheet						Income Statement					Statement of Cash Flows
Assets	=	Liab.	+	Stk. Equity							
Supplies				Ret. Earn.		Rev.	−	Exp.	=	Net Inc.	
(650)	=	NA	+	(650)		NA	−	650	=	(650)	NA

CHECK YOURSELF 3.1

Treadmore Company started the Year 4 accounting period with $580 of supplies on hand. During Year 4, the company paid cash to purchase $2,200 of supplies. A physical count of supplies indicated that there were $420 of supplies on hand at the end of Year 4. Treadmore pays cash for supplies at the time they are purchased. Based on this information alone, determine the amount of supplies expense to be recognized on the income statement and the amount of cash flow to be shown in the operating activities section of the statement of cash flows.

Answer   The amount of supplies expense recognized on the income statement is the amount of supplies used during the accounting period. This amount is computed next:

$580 Beginning balance + $2,200 Supplies purchases = $2,780 Supplies available for use

$2,780 Supplies available for use − $420 Ending supplies balance = $2,360 Supplies used

The cash flow from operating activities is the amount of cash paid for supplies during the accounting period. In this case, Treadmore paid $2,200 cash to purchase supplies. This amount would be shown as a cash outflow.

ACCOUNTING FOR PREPAID ITEMS

EVENT 3   On March 1, Year 1, Alvarado pays $12,000 cash to lease office space for one year beginning immediately.

The cost of the office space described in Event 3 is an asset. It is recorded in the asset account Prepaid Rent. Alvarado expects to benefit from incurring this cost by using the office to generate revenue over the next 12 months. Expense recognition is deferred until Alvarado actually uses the office space to help generate revenue. Other commonly deferred expenses include prepaid insurance and prepaid taxes. As these titles imply, deferred expenses are frequently called **prepaid items**.

Purchasing prepaid rent is an asset exchange transaction. The asset account Cash decreases and the asset account Prepaid Rent increases. The amount of total assets is not affected. Note that this event does not affect the income statement. Expense recognition is deferred until the office space is used. Because the cash outflow was incurred to purchase prepaid rent (a short-term asset) that will be used to operate the business, it is classified as an operating activity on the statement of cash flows. The effects on the financial statements are shown next:

LO 3-2

Show how accounting for prepaid items affects financial statements.

Balance Sheet						Income Statement					Statement of Cash Flows
	Assets		=	Liab.	+	Stk. Equity					
Cash	+	Prepaid Rent					Rev.	−	Exp.	=	Net Inc.	
(12,000)	+	12,000	=	NA	+	NA		NA	−	NA	=	NA	(12,000) OA

End-of-Period Adjustment

ADJ. 2   Alvarado recognizes rent expense for the office space used during the Year 1 accounting period.

At the end of Year 1, Alvarado is required to expense the amount of office space that has been used. Recall that Alvarado paid $12,000 on March 1, Year 1, to rent office space for one year. The portion of the lease cost that represents using office space from March 1 through December 31 is computed as follows:

$$\$12{,}000 \text{ Cost of annual lease} \div 12 \text{ Months} = \$1{,}000 \text{ Cost per month}$$
$$\$1{,}000 \text{ Cost per month} \times 10 \text{ Months used} = \$10{,}000 \text{ Rent expense}$$

The expense recognition is an asset use transaction. On the balance sheet, assets (Prepaid Rent) and stockholders' equity (Retained Earnings) decrease. The expense reduces the amount of net income shown on the income statement. The statement of cash flows is not affected. Recall that the cash flow effect was recorded in Event 3. The effects on the financial statements are shown next:

Balance Sheet					Income Statement					Statement of Cash Flows
Assets	=	Liab.	+	Stk. Equity	Rev.	−	Exp.	=	Net Inc.	
Prepaid Rent				Ret. Earn.						
(10,000)	=	NA	+	(10,000)	NA	−	10,000	=	(10,000)	NA

Note that while $12,000 cash was paid for rent, only $10,000 of that amount is recognized as an expense in Year 1. The deferral of the additional $2,000 causes a difference between the amounts of cash flow from operating activities versus the amount of net income reported in Year 1.

 CHECK YOURSELF 3.2

Rujoub Inc. paid $18,000 cash for one year of insurance coverage that began on November 1, Year 1. Based on this information alone, determine the cash flow from operating activities that Rujoub would report on the Year 1 and Year 2 statements of cash flows. Also, determine the amount of insurance expense Rujoub would report on the Year 1 income statement and the amount of prepaid insurance (an asset) that Rujoub would report on the December 31, Year 1, balance sheet.

Answer   Because Rujoub paid all of the cash in Year 1, the Year 1 statement of cash flows would report an $18,000 cash outflow from operating activities. The Year 2 statement of cash flows would report zero cash flow from operating activities. The expense would be recognized in the periods in which the insurance is used. In this case, insurance expense is recognized at the rate of $1,500 per month ($18,000 ÷ 12 months). Rujoub used two months of insurance coverage in Year 1 and therefore would report $3,000 (2 months × $1,500) of insurance expense on the Year 1 income statement. Rujoub would report a $15,000 (10 months × $1,500) asset, prepaid insurance, on the December 31, Year 1, balance sheet. The $15,000 of prepaid insurance would be recognized as insurance expense in Year 2 when the insurance coverage is used.

ACCOUNTING FOR UNEARNED REVENUE

EVENT 4   Alvarado receives $18,000 cash in advance from Westberry Company for installation services that Alvarado agrees to perform over a one-year period beginning June 1, Year 1.

Recall from Chapter 2 that revenue is only recognized after the work has been completed. Accordingly, Alvarado must defer (delay) recognizing any revenue until it performs the consulting services (does the work) for Westberry. From Alvarado's point of view, the deferred revenue is a liability because Alvarado is obligated to perform services in the future. The liability is called **unearned revenue.**

The cash receipt is an asset source transaction. The asset account Cash and the liability account Unearned Revenue both increase. Collecting the cash has no effect on the income statement. The revenue will be reported on the income statement after Alvarado performs the services. The statement of cash flows reflects a cash inflow from operating activities. The effects on the financial statements are shown next:

LO 3-3

Show how accounting for unearned revenues affects financial statements.

Balance Sheet					Income Statement					Statement of Cash Flows
Assets	=	Liab.	+	Stk. Equity	Rev.	−	Exp.	=	Net Inc.	
Cash		Unearned Rev.								
18,000	=	18,000	+	NA	NA	−	NA	=	NA	18,000 OA

End-of-Period Adjustment

ADJ. 3   Alvarado recognizes the portion of the unearned revenue it earned during the accounting period.

The $18,000 cash advance requires Alvarado to provide installations services from June 1, Year 1, to May 31, Year 2. By December 31, Alvarado has earned 7 months (June 1 through December 31) of the revenue related to this contract. Rather than recording the revenue continuously as the installation services are being performed, Alvarado can simply recognize the amount earned in a single adjustment to the accounting records *at the end of the accounting period*. The amount of the adjustment is computed as follows:

$18,000 ÷ 12 months = $1,500 installation revenue earned per month

$1,500 × 7 months = $10,500 installation revenue to be recognized in Year 2

The end-of-period adjustment moves $10,500 from the liability Unearned Revenue account to the Installation Revenue account. This adjustment is a claims exchange event. Assets are not affected. On the balance sheet, liabilities (Unearned Revenue) decrease and stockholders' equity (Retained Earnings) increases. On the income statement, revenue and net income increase. Cash flow is not affected by the adjustment. Recall that the impact on cash occurred previously when Alvarado received the cash from Westberry in Event 4. The effects on the financial statements are shown next:

Balance Sheet					Income Statement					Statement of Cash Flows
Assets	=	Liab.	+	Stk. Equity	Rev.	−	Exp.	=	Net Inc.	
		Unearned Rev.	+	Ret. Earn.						
NA	=	(10,500)	+	10,500	10,500	−	NA	=	10,500	NA

Recall that revenue was previously defined as an economic benefit a company obtains by providing customers with goods and services. In this case, the economic benefit is a decrease in the liability account Unearned Revenue. **Revenue** can therefore be more precisely defined as *an increase in assets or a decrease in liabilities that a company obtains by providing customers with goods or services.*

CHECK YOURSELF 3.3

Sanderson & Associates received a $24,000 cash advance as a retainer to provide legal services to a client. The contract called for Sanderson to render services during a one-year period beginning October 1, Year 1. Based on this information alone, determine the cash flow from operating activities Sanderson would report on the Year 1 and Year 2 statements of cash flows. Also determine the amount of revenue Sanderson would report on the Year 1 and Year 2 income statements.

Answer   Because Sanderson collected all of the cash in Year 1, the Year 1 statement of cash flows would report a $24,000 cash inflow from operating activities. The Year 2 statement of cash flows would report zero cash flow from operating activities. Revenue is recognized in the period in which it is earned. In this case, revenue is earned at the rate of $2,000 per month ($24,000 ÷ 12 months = $2,000 per month). Sanderson rendered services for three months in Year 1 and 9 months in Year 2. Sanderson would report $6,000 (3 months × $2,000) of revenue on the Year 1 income statement and $18,000 (9 months × $2,000) of revenue on the Year 2 income statement.

PREPARE FINANCIAL STATEMENTS

LO 3-4

 Use a list of accounts to prepare financial statements containing deferrals.

Also, during Year 1, Alvarado experienced Event Numbers 5 through 11, which are shown in Exhibit 3.2. The effects of these types of events on the accounting equation and the financial statements have been covered in previous sections of the text and will not be repeated here. However, for your convenience the transaction data have been recorded in accounts under an accounting equation as shown in Exhibit 3.2. To confirm your understanding, you should trace each transaction to the information shown in the accounting equation. The information in the accounting equation has been labeled with the event or adjustment numbers to simplify the tracing process.

The 11 events and 4 adjustments Alvarado experienced during Year 1 are summarized in Exhibit 3.2. Recall that all adjustments are made at the end of the accounting period so that all account balances are updated prior to their use in preparing the financial statements. The account balances shown in Exhibit 3.2 are used to prepare the Year 1 financial statements that are presented in Exhibit 3.3.

EXHIBIT 3.2   Summary of Year 1 Events and Adjustments

Accounting Events For Year 1

1. Alvarado acquired $55,000 cash from the issue of common stock.
2. Alvarado paid $800 cash to purchase supplies.
3. On March 1, Alvarado paid $12,000 cash to lease office space for one year.
4. Alvarado received $18,000 cash in advance from Westberry Company for installation services to be performed for one year beginning June 1.
5. Alvarado provided $110,400 of consulting services on account.
6. Alvarado collected $105,000 cash from customers as partial settlement of accounts receivable.
7. Alvarado paid $32,000 cash for salary expense.
8. Alvarado incurred $20,000 of other operating expenses on account.
9. Alvarado paid $18,200 in a partial settlement of accounts payable.
10. Alvarado paid $79,500 to purchase land it planned to use in the future as a building site for its home office.
11. Alvarado paid $21,000 in cash dividends to its stockholders.

The year-end adjustments are:

Adj. 1   After determining through a physical count that it had $150 of unused supplies on hand as of December 31, Alvarado recognized supplies expense. The amount of the expense is $650 ($0 beginning balance + $800 supplies purchased = $800 available for use − $150 ending balance).

Adj. 2   Alvarado recognized rent expense for the office space used during the accounting period. The amount of expense recognized is $10,000 ($12,000 / 12 = $1,000 per month × 10 = $10,000).

Adj. 3   Alvarado recognized the portion of the unearned revenue it earned during the accounting period. The amount of revenue recognized is $10,500 ($18,000 / 12 months = $1,500 per month × 7 months = $10,500).

Adj. 4   Alvarado recognized $4,000 of accrued salary expense.

continued

EXHIBIT 3.2 Concluded

Effects of Year 1 Events Shown Under an Accounting Equation

Event No.			Assets					=	Liabilities				+	Stk. Equity		Other Account Titles
	Cash	+ Acc. Rec.	+ Supp.	+ Prep. Rent	+ Land	=	Acc. Pay.	+ Unear. Rev.	+ Sal. Pay.	+ Com. Stock	+ Ret. Earn.					
Beg.	0 +	0 +	0 +	0 +	0 =		0 +	0 +	0 +	0 +	0					
1.	55,000 +	NA +	NA +	NA +	NA =		NA +	NA +	NA +	55,000 +	NA					
2.	(800) +	NA +	800 +	NA +	NA =		NA +	NA +	NA +	NA +	NA					
3.	(12,000) +	NA +	NA +	12,000 +	NA =		NA +	NA +	NA +	NA +	NA					
4.	18,000 +	NA +	NA +	NA +	NA =		NA +	18,000 +	NA +	NA +	NA					
5.	NA +	110,400 +	NA +	NA +	NA =		NA +	NA +	NA +	NA +	110,400	Consulting Rev.				
6.	105,000 +	(105,000) +	NA +	NA +	NA =		NA +	NA +	NA +	NA +	NA					
7.	(32,000) +	NA +	NA +	NA +	NA =		NA +	NA +	NA +	NA +	(32,000)	Salary Exp.				
8.	NA +	NA +	NA +	NA +	NA =		20,000 +	NA +	NA +	NA +	(20,000)	Other Oper. Exp.				
9.	(18,200) +	NA +	NA +	NA +	NA =		(18,200) +	NA +	NA +	NA +	NA					
10.	(79,500) +	NA +	NA +	NA +	79,500 =		NA +	NA +	NA +	NA +	NA					
11.	(21,000) +	NA +	NA +	NA +	NA =		NA +	NA +	NA +	NA +	(21,000)	Dividends				
Adj. 1	NA +	NA +	(650) +	NA +	NA =		NA +	NA +	NA +	NA +	(650)	Supplies Exp.				
Adj. 2	NA +	NA +	NA +	(10,000) +	NA =		NA +	NA +	NA +	NA +	(10,000)	Rent Exp.				
Adj. 3	NA +	NA +	NA +	NA +	NA =		NA +	(10,500) +	NA +	NA +	10,500	Installation Rev.				
Adj. 4	NA +	NA +	NA +	NA +	NA =		NA +	NA +	4,000 +	NA +	(4,000)	Salary Exp.				
End	14,500 +	5,400 +	150 +	2,000 +	79,500 =		1,800 +	7,500 +	4,000 +	55,000 +	33,250					
		Total Assets 101,550				=	Total Liabilities $13,300		+	Total Stk. Equity $88,250						

EXHIBIT 3.3 Financial Statements

ALVARADO ADVISORY SERVICES
Financial Statements
Balance Sheet
As of December 31

	Year 1
Assets	
Cash	$ 14,500
Accounts receivable	5,400
Supplies	150
Prepaid rent	2,000
Land	79,500
Total assets	$101,550
Liabilities	
Salaries Payable	$ 4,000
Accounts Payable	1,800
Unearned Revenue	7,500
Total Liabilities	13,300
Stockholders' equity	
Common stock	55,000
Retained earnings	33,250
Total stockholders' equity	88,250
Total liabilities and stockholders' equity	$101,550

continued

EXHIBIT 3.3   *Concluded*

Income Statement
For the Year Ended December 31

	Year 1
Consulting revenue	$110,400
Installation revenue	10,500
Salary expense	(36,000)
Rent expense	(10,000)
Supplies expense	(650)
Other operating expenses	(20,000)
Net income	$ 54,250

Statement of Changes in Stockholders' Equity
For the Year Ended December 31

	Year 1
Beginning common stock	$ 0
Plus: Common stock issued	55,000
Ending common stock	55,000
Beginning retained earnings	0
Plus: Net income	54,250
Less: Dividends	(21,000)
Ending retained earnings	33,250
Total stockholders' equity	$ 88,250

Statement of Cash Flows
For the Year Ended December 31

	Year 1
Cash flows from operating activities	
Cash receipts from receivables	$105,000
Cash receipts from unearned revenue	18,000
Cash payments for salaries	(32,000)
Cash payment to reduce payables	(18,200)
Cash paid for supplies	(800)
Cash payment for rent	(12,000)
Net cash flows from operating activities	60,000
Cash flows from investing activities	
Cash paid to purchase land	(79,500)
Cash flows from financing activities	
Cash receipt from issuing common stock	55,000
Cash paid for dividends	(21,000)
Net cash flow from financing activities	34,000
Net change in cash	14,500
Plus: Beginning cash balance	0
Ending cash balance	$ 14,500

Deferral Accounts on the Balance Sheet

Examine the balance sheet to identify the accounts related to deferrals. Your analysis should identify three accounts, including supplies, prepaid rent, and unearned revenue. What caused the creation of these accounts?

- During Year 1, Alvarado paid $800 cash to purchase supplies but used only $650 of the supplies. In this case, Alvarado would defer the recognition of $150 ($800 − $650) of supplies expense until Year 2 when the remaining supplies will be used. The $150 deferral is shown as an asset on the Year 1 balance sheet in an account titled Supplies.

- Alvarado paid $12,000 cash for the right to use office space for one year. The company recognized $10,000 of rent expense for the portion of the year it used the office space in Year 1. The remaining $2,000 of expense is deferred until Year 2 when the office will be used for the remainder of the time designated in the rental agreement. The $2,000 deferral is shown as an asset on the Year 1 balance sheet in an account titled Prepaid Rent.

- During Year 1, Alvarado collected $18,000 cash from its customers but recognized only $10,500 of revenue for the services that it provided in Year 1. The recognition of the remaining $7,500 of revenue is deferred until additional services are performed in Year 2. The deferral is shown as a liability in an account titled Unearned Revenue on the Year 1 balance sheet. The unearned revenue account is classified as a liability because it represents an obligation for the company to perform services in the future.

Comparing the Income Statement with the Statement of Cash Flows

Accruals and deferrals cause significant differences in what is reported on the income statement versus the statement of cash flows. Exhibit 3.4 provides a comparison of the items appearing on Alvarado's Year 1 income statement versus the corresponding items appearing on the Year 1 statement of cash flows.

The following is an item-by-item analysis of the accruals and deferrals that caused the differences between Alvarado's Year 1 income statement and the Year 1 statement of cash flows. The explanations are tied to the superscripted reference numbers shown in the income statement.

EXHIBIT 3.4   Income Statement versus Statement of Cash Flows

Income Statement	
Consulting Revenue[1]	$110,400
Installation Revenue[2]	10,500
Salary expense[3]	(36,000)
Other operating expenses[4]	(20,000)
Supplies expense[5]	(650)
Rent Expense[6]	(10,000)
Net Income	$ 54,250

Statement of Cash Flows	
Cash inflow from receivables	$105,000
Cash inflow from installation contract	18,000
Cash payment for salaries	(32,000)
Cash payments on accts. pay.	(18,200)
Cash payment for supplies	(800)
Cash payments for rent	(12,000)
Net cash flow from operating act.	$ 60,000

1. Alvarado provided $110,400 of consulting services but collected only $105,000 of cash. In other words, Alvarado recognized $5,400 ($110,400 − $105,000) of *accrued* consulting revenue during Year 1. This is confirmed by the balance in accounts receivable that is shown on the Year 1 balance sheet.

2. Alvarado collected $18,000 of cash for installation services but provided only $10,500 of consulting services. In other words, Alvarado *deferred* the recognition of $7,500 of installation revenue in Year 1. This is confirmed by the balance in the unearned revenue account shown on the Year 1 balance sheet.

3. Alvarado recognized $36,000 of salary expense but paid its employees only $32,000 cash. In other words, Alvarado accrued $4,000 ($36,000 − $32,000) of *accrued* salary expense. This is confirmed by the balance in the salaries payable account shown on the Year 1 balance sheet.

4. Alvarado recognized $20,000 of other operating expenses but paid its suppliers only $18,200 cash. In other words, Alvarado accrued $1,800 ($20,000 − $18,200) of *accrued* other operating expenses. This is confirmed by the balance in the accounts payable account shown on the Year 1 balance sheet.

5. Alvarado paid $800 cash for supplies but recognized only $650 of supplies expense in Year 1. In other words, Alvarado *deferred* $150 ($800 − $650) of supplies expense. This is confirmed by the balance in the supplies account shown on the Year 1 balance sheet.

REALITY BYTES

WHY DID THAT BIG EXPENSE CAUSE THE STOCK PRICE TO RISE?

If you follow business news, which you should if you are a business major, you have probably heard about a company reporting a big write-off of assets, sometimes called a "special charge." Such an announcement sends a signal to readers that the company's earnings will decrease as a result of the write-off. However, in many cases, this seemingly bad news does not cause the company's stock price to fall; in fact, it sometimes causes it to increase. Why?

Consider the following January 27, 2018, announcement from General Motors Company (GM) related to its plans to close several plants and eliminate almost 15,000 jobs:

Katherine Welles/Shutterstock

> On November 20, 2018, the General Motors Company . . . Board of Directors approved a plan to accelerate the Company's transformation for the future (the "Plan"). The Plan is expected to strengthen the Company's core business, capitalize on the future of personal mobility, and drive significant cost efficiencies, and it consists, in relevant part, of (i) restructuring the Global Product Development Group, (ii) realigning current manufacturing capacity and utilization, and (iii) reducing salaried and contract staff and capital expenditures. These actions are expected to be substantially completed by the end of 2019.
>
> The Company expects to record pre-tax charges of $3.0 billion to $3.8 billion related to these actions, including up to $1.8 billion of non-cash accelerated asset write-downs and pension charges, and up to $2.0 billion of employee-related and other cash-based expenses.

Despite this seemingly bad financial news about a reduction in earnings of over $3 billion, GM's stock price increased by 4.8 percent on the day of the announcement, while the overall market was up only 1.5 percent.

There are at least a couple of reasons why this seeming bad news may have a positive impact on a company's stock price. First, while write-offs do decrease earnings, they often do not decrease the company's cash flows, and cash flow is at least as important to investors as earnings. Much of GM's special charge did not decrease its cash outflows.

The second reason that writing off assets can sometimes have a positive effect on a company's stock price is because extra expenses that are recognized today may mean there will be fewer expenses recognized in the future; thus, future earnings will be higher than they otherwise would have been. This subject will be explained further in later chapters, but keep in mind that investors are more interested in the future than they are in the past, so lower current earnings that lead to higher future earnings are often viewed as good news.

So, when you hear a company make a big announcement about its business, always ask yourself two questions: How does this event affect cash flows? And, how will this event affect future earnings?

6. Alvarado paid $12,000 cash for the rental of office space but recognized only $10,000 of rent expense in Year 1. In other words, Alvarado *deferred* $2,000 ($12,000 − $10,000) of rent expense. This is confirmed by the balance in the prepaid rent account shown on the Year 1 balance sheet.

The difference between net income and cash flow from operations is summarized in Exhibit 3.5.

EXHIBIT 3.5

Reconciliation of Net Income with Cash Flow from Operating Activities

Net income	$54,250
Minus accrued consulting revenue	(5,400)
Plus deferred installation revenue	7,500
Plus accrued salary expense	4,000
Plus accrued other operating expense	1,800
Minus deferred supplies expense	(150)
Minus deferred rent expense	(2,000)
Cash flow from operating activities	$60,000

Answers to The Curious Accountant

Because the Meredith Corporation receives cash from customers before sending any magazines to them, the company has not earned any revenue when it receives the cash. Meredith has a liability called *unearned revenue*. If Meredith closed its books on December 31, then $3 of the subscription would be recognized as revenue in 2020. The remaining $9 would appear on the balance sheet as a liability.

Meredith actually ends its accounting year on June 30 each year. The June 30, 2018, balance sheet for the company is presented in Exhibit 3.6. The liability for unearned revenue was $484.5 million ($360.4 + $124.1)—which represented about 9.5 percent ($484.5 ÷ $5,107.1) of total liabilities.

Will Meredith need cash to pay these subscription liabilities? Not exactly. The liabilities will not be paid directly with cash. Instead, they will be satisfied by providing magazines to the subscribers. However, Meredith will need cash to pay for producing and distributing the magazines supplied to the customers. Even so, the amount of cash required to provide magazines will probably differ significantly from the amount of unearned revenues. In most cases, subscription fees do not cover the cost of producing and distributing magazines. By collecting significant amounts of advertising revenue, publishers can provide magazines to customers at prices well below the cost of publication. The amount of unearned revenue is not likely to coincide with the amount of cash needed to cover the cost of satisfying the company's obligation to produce and distribute magazines. Even though the association between unearned revenues and the cost of providing magazines to customers is not direct, a knowledgeable financial analyst can use the information to make estimates of future cash flows and revenue recognition.

EXHIBIT 3.6   Balance Sheet for Meredith Corporation

MEREDITH CORPORATION AND SUBSIDIARIES
Consolidated Balance Sheets
As of June 30 (amounts in millions)

	2018	2017
Assets		
Current assets		
Cash and cash equivalents	$ 437.6	$ 22.3
Accounts receivable (net of allowances of $14.4 in 2018 and $8.0 in 2017)	542.0	289.1
Inventories	44.2	21.9
Current portion of subscription acquisition costs	118.1	145.0
Current portion of broadcast rights	9.8	7.8
Other current assets	713.1	—
Assets held for sale	114.3	19.3
Total current assets	1,979.1	505.4
Property, plant, and equipment		
Land	$ 24.6	$ 24.7
Buildings and improvements	153.5	153.7
Machinery and equipment	359.8	316.6
Leasehold improvements	177.4	14.3
Capitalized software	125.9	38.5
Construction in progress	20.2	1.7
Total property, plant, and equipment	861.4	549.5
Less accumulated depreciation	(377.6)	(359.7)
Net property, plant, and equipment	483.8	189.8
Subscription acquisition costs	61.1	79.7
Broadcast rights	18.9	21.8
Other assets	263.3	69.6
Intangible assets, net	2,005.2	955.9
Goodwill	1,915.8	907.5
Total assets	$6,727.2	$2,729.7
Liabilities and shareholders' equity		
Current liabilities		
Current portion of long-term debt	$ 17.7	$ 62.5
Current portion of long-term broadcast rights payable	8.9	9.2
Accounts payable	194.7	66.6
Accrued expenses		
Compensation and benefits	122.3	69.0
Distribution expenses	10.0	5.3
Other taxes and expenses	277.9	28.1
Total accrued expenses	410.2	102.4
Current portion of unearned revenues	360.4	219.0
Liabilities associated with assets held for sale	198.4	—
Total current liabilities	1,190.3	459.7
Long-term debt	3,117.9	635.7
Long-term broadcast rights payable	20.8	22.5
Unearned revenues	124.1	106.5
Deferred income taxes	437.0	384.7
Other noncurrent liabilities	217.0	124.6
Total liabilities	5,107.1	1,733.7
Redeemable convertible Series A preferred stock, par value	522.6	—
$1 per share, $1,000 per share liquidation preference		
Shareholders' equity		
Series preferred stock, par value $1 per share	—	—
Common stock, par value $1 per share	39.8	39.4
Class B stock, par value $1 per share, convertible to common stock	5.1	5.1
Additional paid-in capital	199.5	54.8
Retained earnings	889.8	915.7
Accumulated other comprehensive (loss)	(36.7)	(19.0)
Total shareholders' equity	1,097.5	996.0
Total liabilities and shareholders' equity	$6,727.2	$2,729.7

ALVARADO ADVISORY SERVICES ILLUSTRATION FOR YEAR 2

In Year 1 we focused on short-term deferrals. This section introduces deferrals that are associated on long-term assets. Recall that Alvarado's Year 1 ending account balances become Year 2's beginning account balances. During Year 2, Alvarado experienced the following accounting events:

EVENT 1 On January 1, Year 2, Alvarado acquired $50,000 cash by issuing common stock.

This event type has been discussed previously. Its effects on the financial statements are shown in the following horizontal financial statements model.

Balance Sheet						Income Statement						Statement of Cash Flows
Assets	=	Liab.	+	Stk. Equity								
Cash				Com. Stk.		Rev.	−	Exp.	=	Net Inc.		
50,000	=	NA	+	50,000		NA	−	NA	=	NA		50,000 FA

EVENT 2 Alvarado paid cash to its employees to settle the $4,000 of salaries payable that was accrued in Year 1.

This event reduces assets (Cash) and liabilities (Salaries Payable) on the balance sheet. It does not affect the income statement because the expense associated with the salaries payable was recognized in Year 1. The statement of cash flows shows a $4,000 cash outflow. This outflow is classified as an operating activity because it is associated with expense recognition. The effects on the financial statements are shown next:

Balance Sheet						Income Statement						Statement of Cash Flows
Assets	=	Liab.	+	Stk. Equity								
Cash		Sal. Pay.				Rev.	−	Exp.	=	Net Inc.		
(4,000)	=	(4,000)	+	NA		NA	−	NA	=	NA		(4,000) OA

ACCOUNTING FOR DEPRECIATION

LO 3-5

 Compute depreciation expense and show how it affects financial statements.

Companies frequently purchase assets that are used for several years. These assets are called long-term assets. When a company purchases a long-term asset, it normally defers some of the expense recognition. The deferred expense is called depreciation. The following illustration shows how depreciation is calculated and how it affects financial statements.

EVENT 3 On January 1, Year 2, Alvarado paid $43,000 cash to purchase a computer.

Alvarado expected to use the computer for four years and then sell it for $3,000. The expected period of use is commonly called the **useful life.** The amount Alvarado expects to receive from the sale of the asset at the end of its useful life is called the **salvage value.**

The purchase of the computer is an asset exchange transaction. The balance in the Cash account decreases and the balance in a new asset account called Computer increases. The purchase does not affect the income statement. Because the asset has a long-term useful life, the cash outflow necessary to buy the asset is an investing activity. The effects on the financial statements are shown next:

Balance Sheet						Income Statement				Statement of Cash Flows
Assets			= Liab.	+ Stk. Equity						
Cash	+	Book Value of Computer				Rev.	− Exp.	=	Net Inc.	
(43,000)	+	43,000	= NA	+ NA		NA	− NA	=	NA	(43,000) IA

ADJ. 1   On December 31, Year 2, Alvarado will adjust its accounts to recognize the expense of using the computer during Year 2.

To measure the net economic benefit of running the business, Alvarado must estimate how much of the cost of the computer it used in the process of earning revenue during Year 2. Recall that the computer has a four-year useful life and a $3,000 salvage value. Because the salvage value is expected to be recovered at the end of the computer's useful life, only $40,000 ($43,000 cost − $3,000 salvage) worth of the computer is ultimately expected to be used. Assuming the computer is used evenly over its four-year life, it is logical to allocate an equal amount of the $40,000 to expense each year the computer is used. The allocation is computed as follows:

$$(\text{Asset cost} - \text{Salvage value}) / \text{Useful life} = \text{Depreciation expense}$$
$$(\$43,000 - \$3,000) / 4 \text{ years} = \$10,000 \text{ per year}$$

As indicated above, the portion of the cost that represents the use of the asset is commonly called **depreciation expense.** The method of computing the depreciation expense that is described above is called **straight-line depreciation.** Other methods of calculating depreciation will be discussed later in the text.

Recognizing depreciation expense is an asset use transaction. Assets and stockholders' equity decrease. On the income statement, expenses increase and net income decreases. There are no cash flow consequences. Recall that the cash outflow occurred at the time the asset was purchased. There is no cash flow when the expense is recognized. The effects on the financial statements are shown next:

Balance Sheet						Income Statement				Statement of Cash Flows
Assets			= Liab.	+	Stk. Equity					
Cash	+	Book Value of Computer =			Retained Earnings	Rev.	− Exp.	=	Net Inc.	
NA	+	(10,000)	= NA	+	(10,000)	NA	− 10,000	=	(10,000)	NA

In Exhibit 3.7 the effect of recognizing depreciation expense is shown as a decrease in the column titled "BV Comp." In practice, the asset account Computer is not decreased directly. Instead, the asset reduction is recorded in a contra asset account called **Accumulated Depreciation.** This approach is used because it increases the usefulness of the information. Specifically, the balance sheet shows the original cost of the asset, the portion of the asset that has been used, and the remaining portion of the asset that is available for use in the future. The initials "BV" in the column titled "BV Comp." represent the term *book value.* The **book value** of the asset is the difference between the balances in the Computer account and the related Accumulated Depreciation account as follows:

Computer	$43,000
Accumulated Depreciation	(10,000)
Book Value	$33,000

The book value may also be called the **carrying value.** In real-world financial statements the original cost, accumulated depreciation, and the book value may be shown in a variety of different ways. For example, some companies may show the actual amounts of all three of these account balances, while others may only report the book value. Regardless of how it is

EXHIBIT 3.7   Summary of Year 2 Events and Adjustments

Accounting Events For Year 2

1. Alvarado acquired $50,000 cash from the issue of common stock.
2. Alvarado paid cash to its employees to settle the $4,000 of salaries payable that was accrued in Year 1.
3. On January 1, Year 2, Alvarado paid $43,000 cash to purchase a computer.
4. Alvarado paid $1,000 cash to purchase supplies.
5. On March 1, Year 2, Alvarado paid $13,200 cash to renew its lease for office space. This represents an increase in the previous year's cost of rent. The term of the new lease was one year.
6. Alvarado received $14,400 cash in advance from Lacy Corp. for installation services to be performed for one year beginning June 1, Year 2.
7. Alvarado provided $128,000 of consulting services on account.
8. Alvarado collected $110,000 cash from customers as partial settlement of accounts receivable.
9. Alvarado paid $33,000 cash for salary expense.
10. Alvarado incurred $24,000 of other operating expenses on account.
11. Alvarado paid $21,000 in partial settlement of accounts payable.
12. Alvarado paid $17,000 in cash dividends to its stockholders. The year-end adjustments are:

Adj. 1 Alvarado recognized depreciation expense on the computer. The computer had a four-year useful life and a $3,000 salvage value. The amount of depreciation expense is $10,000 ($43,000 cost − $3,000 salvage) / 4-year useful life.

Adj. 2 After determining through a physical count that it had $200 of unused supplies on hand as of December 31, Alvarado recognized supplies expense. The amount of the expense is $950 ($150 beginning balance + $1,000 supplies purchased = $1,150 available for use − $200 ending balance).

Adj. 3 Alvarado recognized rent expense for the office space used during the accounting period. The amount of the expense is calculated as the $2,000 beginning balance of prepaid rent representing 2 months of rent remaining on the first rental contract plus 10 months of usage of the second rental agreement ($13,200 / 12 = $1,100 per month × 10 = $11,000). The total rent expense for Year 2 is $13,000 ($2,000 + $11,000).

Adj. 4 Alvarado recognized the portion of the unearned revenue it earned during the Year 2 accounting period. The amount recognized includes $7,500 beginning balance representing the work completed on the Westberry contract plus 7 months of earned revenue on the Lacy Corp. contract ($14,400 / 12 months = $1,200 per month × 7 months = $8,400). The total amount of earned revenue is $15,900 ($7,500 + $8,400).

Adj. 5 Alvarado recognized $6,500 of accrued salary expense.

Effects of Year 2 Events Shown Under an Accounting Equation

	Assets						=	Liabilities			+	Stk. Equity		
Event No.	Cash	+ Acc. Rec.	+ Supp.	+ Prep. Rent	+ BV Comp.	+ Land	=	Acc. Pay.	+ Unear. Rev.	+ Sal. Pay.	+ Com. Stock.	+ Ret. Earn.	Other Account Titles
Beg.	14,500 +	5,400 +	150 +	2,000 +	0 +	79,500 =	1,800 +	7,500 +	4,000 +	55,000 +	33,250	
1.	50,000 +	NA +	NA +	NA +	NA +	NA =	NA +	NA +	NA +	50,000 +	NA	
2.	(4,000) +	NA +	NA +	NA +	NA +	NA =	NA +	NA +	(4,000) +	NA +	NA	
3.	(43,000) +	NA +	NA +	NA +	43,000 +	NA =	NA +	NA +	NA +	NA +	NA	
4.	(1,000) +	NA +	1,000 +	NA +	NA +	NA =	NA +	NA +	NA +	NA +	NA	
5.	(13,200) +	NA +	NA +	13,200 +	NA +	NA =	NA +	NA +	NA +	NA +	NA	
6.	14,400 +	NA +	NA +	NA +	NA +	NA =	NA +	14,400 +	NA +	NA +	NA	
7.	NA +	128,000 +	NA +	NA +	NA +	NA =	NA +	NA +	NA +	NA +	128,000	Consulting Rev.
8.	110,000 +	(110,000) +	NA +	NA +	NA +	NA =	NA +	NA +	NA +	NA +	NA	
9.	(33,000) +	NA +	NA +	NA +	NA +	NA =	NA +	NA +	NA +	NA +	(33,000)	Salary Exp.
10.	NA +	NA +	NA +	NA +	NA +	NA =	24,000 +	NA +	NA +	NA +	(24,000)	Other Oper. Exp.
11.	(21,000) +	NA +	NA +	NA +	NA +	NA =	(21,000) +	NA +	NA +	NA +	NA	
12.	(17,000)	NA	NA	NA	NA	NA	NA	NA +	NA	NA	(17,000)	Dividends
Adj. 1	NA +	NA +	NA +	NA +	(10,000) +	NA =	NA +	NA +	NA +	NA +	(10,000)	Depreciation Exp.
Adj. 2	NA +	NA +	(950) +	NA +	NA +	NA =	NA +	NA +	NA +	NA +	(950)	Supplies Exp.
Adj. 3	NA +	NA +	NA +	(13,000) +	NA +	NA =	NA +	NA +	NA +	NA +	(13,000)	Rent Exp.
Adj. 4	NA +	NA +	NA +	NA +	NA +	NA =	NA +	(15,900) +	NA +	NA +	15,900	Installation Rev.
Adj. 5	NA +	NA +	NA +	NA +	NA +	NA =	NA +	NA +	6,500 +	NA +	(6,500)	Salary Exp.
End	56,700 +	23,400 +	200 +	2,200 +	33,000 +	79,500 =	4,800 +	6,000 +	6,500 +	105,000 +	72,700	

Total Assets	=	Total Liabilities	+	Total Stk. Equity
195,000		$17,300		$177,700

shown on the balance sheet, the book value of the asset is added to the other asset account balances to determine the total amount of assets.

Depreciation expense is recognized each year the computer is used. Like other expense accounts, the Depreciation Expense account shows the sacrifice for a single accounting period. In this case, the Depreciation Expense account will be $10,000 each year. In contrast, the Accumulated Depreciation account increases (accumulates) each time depreciation expense is recognized. For example, at the end of Year 3, Alvarado will recognize $10,000 of depreciation expense and the balance in the Accumulated Depreciation account will increase to $20,000. At the end of Year 4, Alvarado will recognize $10,000 of depreciation expense and the balance in the Accumulated Depreciation account will increase to $30,000, and so on. As the amount of the accumulated depreciation increases, the book value of the asset decreases.

Other Year 2 Events

Also, during Year 2, Alvarado experienced Event Numbers 4 through 12, which are shown in Exhibit 3.7. The effects of these types of events on the accounting equation and the financial statements have been covered in previous sections of the text and will not be repeated here. However, the effects of the transactions on the accounting equation are shown in Exhibit 3.7. To confirm your understanding, you should trace each transaction to the impact shown on the accounting equation. The information in the equation has been labeled with the event or adjustment number to simplify the tracing process.

PREPARE FINANCIAL STATEMENTS

The 12 events and five adjustments Alvarado experienced during Year 2 are summarized in Exhibit 3.7. Recall that all adjustments are made at the end of the accounting period so that all account balances are updated prior to their use in preparing the financial statements. The information in Exhibit 3.7 is used to prepare the Year 2 financial statements shown in Exhibit 3.8.

EXHIBIT 3.8 Financial Statements

ALVARADO ADVISORY SERVICES
Financial Statements
Balance Sheets
As of December 31

	Year 1	Year 2
Assets		
Cash	$ 14,500	$ 56,700
Accounts receivable	5,400	23,400
Supplies	150	200
Prepaid rent	2,000	2,200
Book value of computer	0	33,000
Land	79,500	79,500
Total assets	$101,550	$195,000
Liabilities		
Salaries payable	$ 4,000	$ 6,500
Accounts payable	1,800	4,800
Unearned revenue	7,500	6,000
Total liabilities	13,300	17,300
Stockholders' equity		
Common stock	55,000	105,000
Retained earnings	33,250	72,700
Total stockholders' equity	88,250	177,700
Total liabilities and stockholders' equity	$101,550	$195,000

continued

EXHIBIT 3.8   *Concluded*

Income Statements For the Year Ended December 31	Year 1	Year 2
Consulting revenue	$110,400	$128,000
Installation revenue	10,500	15,900
Depreciation Expense	0	(10,000)
Salary expense	(36,000)	(39,500)
Rent expense	(10,000)	(13,000)
Supplies expense	(650)	(950)
Other operating expenses	(20,000)	(24,000)
Net income	$ 54,250	$ 56,450

Statement of Changes in Stockholders' Equity For the Year Ended December 31	Year 1	Year 2
Beginning common stock	$ 0	$ 55,000
Plus: Common stock issued	55,000	50,000
Ending common stock	55,000	105,000
Beginning retained earnings	0	33,250
Plus: Net income	54,250	56,450
Less: Dividends	(21,000)	(17,000)
Ending retained earnings	33,250	72,700
Total stockholders' equity	$ 88,250	$177,700

Statement of Cash Flows For the Year Ended December 31	Year 1	Year 2
Cash flows from operating activities		
Cash receipts from receivables	$105,000	$110,000
Cash receipts from unearned revenue	18,000	14,400
Cash payments for salaries	(32,000)	(37,000)
Cash payment to reduce payables	(18,200)	(21,000)
Cash paid for supplies	(800)	(1,000)
Cash payment for rent	(12,000)	(13,200)
Net cash flows from operating activities	60,000	52,200
Cash flows from investing activities		
Cash paid to purchase land	(79,500)	
Cash paid to purchase computer		(43,000)
Cash flows from financing activities		
Cash receipt from issuing common stock	55,000	50,000
Cash paid for dividends	(21,000)	(17,000)
Net cash flow from financing activities	34,000	33,000
Net change in cash	14,500	42,200
Plus: Beginning cash balance	0	14,500
Ending cash balance	$ 14,500	$ 56,700

Effect of Depreciation on Financial Statements

The items affected by the purchase and depreciation of the long-term asset (computer) are highlighted with a red font in the financial statements shown in Exhibit 3.8. Recall that Alvarado paid $43,000 cash to purchase the computer on January 1, Year 2. Even though the computer is used in the operation of the business, the full purchase price is shown in the *investing activities* section of the statement of cash flows. Because the purchase of long-term assets is classified as an investment, the corresponding cash flow will never appear in the operating activities section of the statement of cash flows.

The income statement shows $10,000 of depreciation expense. This represents usage of the asset for one year. The $33,000 ($43,000 − $10,000 accumulated depreciation) book value appears in the assets section of the balance sheet. The book value minus the salvage value will be recognized as an expense over the remaining useful life of the asset.

In each succeeding year, Alvarado will recognize $10,000 of depreciation, which will cause the book value of the assets to decline. Exhibit 3.9 shows how the income statement and balance sheet will be affected over the four-year useful life of the computer. At the end of its four-year life, the computer is shown at its salvage value.

EXHIBIT 3.9

Effect of Depreciation on Financial Statements

Income statement	Year 2	Year 3	Year 4	Year 5
Depreciation expense	$10,000	$10,000	$10,000	$10,000
Balance sheet				
Computer	$43,000	$43,000	$43,000	$43,000
Less: Accumulated depreciation	(10,000)	(20,000)	(30,000)	(40,000)
Book value	$33,000	$23,000	$13,000	$ 3,000

The purpose of spreading the expense of the computer over the life of the asset is to match revenues with expenses. We assume that the computer will be used to generate an even stream of revenue over a four-year span of time. Therefore, to accomplish matching, the cost must be deferred and expensed evenly over the same four-year period.

CHECK YOURSELF 3.4

On January 1, Year 1, Health Care Associates (HCA) paid $42,000 cash to purchase x-ray equipment. The equipment has a five-year useful life and a $2,000 salvage value. HCA uses straight-line depreciation. Based on this information alone: (1) explain how the statement of cash flows would be affected in Year 1, Year 2, and Year 3; and (2) determine the amount of depreciation expense reported on the income statement and the book value of the equipment reported on the balance sheet in the Year 1, Year 2, and Year 3 financial statements.

Answer

(1) The full $42,000 purchase price would be shown as a cash outflow in the investing activities section of the Year 1 statement of cash flows. Cash flow would not be affected in Year 2 and Year 3.

(2) HCA will recognize $8,000 (($42,000 cost − $2,000 salvage) / 5-year life) of depreciation expense for each year of the assets' useful life. Accordingly, the Year 1, Year 2, and Year 3 income statements would show $8,000 of depreciation expense. The amount of depreciation recognized will be added to the accumulated depreciation each year, thereby reducing the book value of the equipment. Accordingly, the book value of the equipment shown on the balance sheets would be $34,000 for Year 1, $26,000 for Year 2, and $18,000 for Year 3.

The Financial Analyst

Evaluating income performance requires considering the size of the investment base used to produce the income. In other words, you expect that someone who has $10 million to invest will earn more than someone who has only $10,000 to invest. Financial analysts use financial ratios to compare the performance of companies with different-size investments. The following section of the text discusses three frequently used ratios, including the return-on-assets ratio, the debt-to-assets ratio, and the return-on-equity ratio.

LO 3-6

Use a return-on-assets ratio, a debt-to-assets ratio, and a return-on-equity ratio to analyze financial statements.

Assessing the Effective Use of Assets

The relationship between the level of income and the size of the investment can be expressed as the **return-on-assets ratio**, as follows:

$$\frac{\text{Net income}^{1}}{\text{Total assets}}$$

This ratio permits meaningful comparisons between different-size companies. Compare Dollar General Corporation, a retailer that carries mostly low-priced merchandise, to Wal-Mart Stores, Inc. In 2018, Dollar General reported net income of $1.6 billion, while Walmart reported net income of $7.2 billion. Walmart's earnings were almost seven times greater than the earnings of Dollar General. However, the return-on-assets ratios for the two companies reveal that Dollar General produced higher earnings relative to the assets invested. Walmart's ratio was 3.3 percent, while Dollar General's was 12.0 percent. Even though Dollar General earned fewer dollars of net income, the company used its assets more efficiently than Walmart.

The preceding example demonstrates the usefulness of the relationship between income and assets. Two more ratios that enhance financial statement analysis are discussed in the following paragraphs.

Assessing Debt Risk

Borrowing money can be a risky business. To illustrate, assume two companies have the following financial structures:

	Assets	=	Liabilities	+	Stockholders' Equity
Eastern Company	100	=	20	+	80
Western Company	100	=	80	+	20

Which company has the greater financial risk? If each company incurred a $30 loss, the financial structures would change as follows:

	Assets	=	Liabilities	+	Stockholders' Equity
Eastern Company	70	=	20	+	50
Western Company	70	=	80	+	(10)

Clearly, Western Company is at greater risk. Eastern Company could survive a $30 loss that reduced assets and stockholders' equity, because it would still have a $50 balance in stockholders' equity and more than enough assets ($70) to satisfy the $20 obligation to creditors. In contrast, a $30 loss would throw Western Company into bankruptcy. The company would have a $10 deficit (negative) balance in stockholders' equity, and the remaining assets ($70) would be less than the $80 obligation to creditors.

---

[1]The use of net income in this ratio ignores the effects of debt financing and income taxation. The effect of these variables on the return-on-assets ratio is explained in a later chapter.

The level of debt risk can be measured in part by using a **debt-to-assets ratio,** as follows:

$$\frac{\text{Total debt}}{\text{Total assets}}$$

For example, Eastern Company's debt-to-assets ratio is 20 percent ($20 ÷ $100), while Western Company's is 80 percent ($80 ÷ $100). Why would the owners of Western Company be willing to accept greater debt risk? Assume that both companies produce $12 of revenue and each must pay 10 percent interest on money owed to creditors. Income statements for the two companies appear as follows:[2]

	Eastern Company	Western Company
Revenue	$12	$12
Interest Expense	2	8
Net Income	$10	$ 4

At first glance, the owners of Eastern Company appear better off because Eastern produced higher net income. In fact, however, the owners of *Western* Company are better off. The owners of Eastern Company get $10 of income for investing $80 of their own money into the business, a return on their invested funds of 12.5 percent ($10 ÷ $80). In contrast, the owners of Western Company obtain $4 of net income for their $20 investment, a return on invested funds of 20 percent ($4 ÷ $20).

The relationship between net income and stockholders' equity used above is the **return-on-equity ratio,** computed as

$$\frac{\text{Net income}}{\text{Stockholders' equity}}$$

Using borrowed money to increase the return on stockholders' investment is called **financial leverage.** Financial leverage explains why companies are willing to accept the risk of debt. Companies borrow money to make money. If a company can borrow money at 10 percent and invest it at 12 percent, the owners will be better off by 2 percent of the amount borrowed. A business that does not borrow may be missing an opportunity to increase its return on equity.

Real-World Data

Exhibit 3.10 shows the debt-to-assets, return-on-assets, and return-on-equity ratios for six real-world companies in two different industries. The data are drawn from the companies' 2017 annual reports. Notice that Aflac's return-on-assets ratio was 3.4 percent and Aetna's was 3.5 percent. Neither ratio seems good; banks sometimes pay more than 2.0 percent interest on deposits in savings accounts. The *return-on-equity* ratios, however, show a different picture; Aflac's was 18.7 percent and Aetna's was 12.0 percent—much better than what banks pay depositors.

EXHIBIT 3.10

Three Ratios (in Percentages) for Six Real-World Companies				
Industry	Company	Debt to Assets	Return on Assets	Return on Equity
Insurance	Aetna	71	3.5	12.0
	Aflac	82	3.4	18.7
	Progressive	75	4.1	17.1
Oil	Chevron	44	3.6	6.2
	ExxonMobil	44	5.7	10.1
	Marathon Oil	47	(26.0)	(48.9)

[2]This illustration ignores the effect of income taxes on debt financing. This subject is discussed in a later chapter.

FOCUS ON **INTERNATIONAL ISSUES**

HOW DOES IFRS DIFFER FROM U.S. GAAP?

Chapter 1 discussed the progression toward a single global GAAP in the form of International Financial Reporting Standards (IFRS). That discussion noted that the United States does not currently allow domestic companies to use IFRS; they must follow GAAP. Let's briefly consider just how U.S. GAAP differs from IFRS.

The differences can be summarized in a few broad categories. First, some differences are relatively minor. Consider the case of bank overdrafts. Under IFRS, some bank overdrafts are included as a cash inflow and are reported on the statement of cash flows. U.S. GAAP does not permit this. Conversely, some differences relate to very significant issues. Both IFRS and GAAP use historical cost as their primary method for reporting information on financial statements, but both allow exceptions in some circumstances. However, IFRS permits more exceptions to historical cost than GAAP does. Some of these differences will be discussed in later chapters.

Some of the differences affect how financial statements are presented in annual reports. IFRS requires companies to report all financial statements for the current year and the prior year—two years of comparative data. Rules of the Securities and Exchange Commission require U.S. companies to report two years of balance sheets (the current and prior year) and three years of all other statements. See the financial statements of Target Corporation in Appendix B as an example. Of course, companies can show additional years if they wish.

As you would expect in the first course of accounting, some of the differences between IFRS and GAAP are simply too complex to be covered. Examples of such items relate

Corbis/Getty Images

to business combinations (when one company buys another) and foreign currency translations (when a company has subsidiaries that operate outside the United States).

Do not be overwhelmed by the differences between IFRS and GAAP. They have many more rules alike than different. A person who has a reasonable understanding of U.S. GAAP should be able to read financial statements prepared under IFRS without too much difficulty. If you are interested in more detailed, up-to-date information about IFRS versus GAAP, the large international accounting firms have websites that can help. Two examples are: www.iasplus.com, which is presented by the firm of Deloitte Touche Tohmatsu, and www.kpmg.com/global/en/topics/global-ifrs-institute/, which is presented by the firm of KPMG.

Exhibit 3.10 shows that while ExxonMobil's return-on-equity ratio is about two times higher than its return-on-assets ratio (10.1 percent versus 5.7 percent). By comparison, Aflac's return-on-equity ratio is almost six times higher than its return-on-assets ratio (18.7 percent versus 3.4 percent). How did this happen? Compare their debt-to-assets ratios. Aflac financed 82 percent of its assets with debt compared to Exxon's 44 percent. Financial leverage is the biggest factor causing these results, but it is not the only factor that affects this ratio.

Because financial leverage offers the opportunity to increase return on equity, why doesn't every company leverage itself to the maximum? There is a downside. When the

Comstock Images/Alamy Stock Photo

economy turns down, companies may not be able to produce investment returns that exceed interest rates. A company that has borrowed money at a fixed rate of 8 percent that can earn only 6 percent on its investments will suffer from financial leverage. In other words, financial leverage is a double-edged sword. It can have a negative as well as a positive impact on a company's return-on-equity ratio.

Finally, compare the ratios in Exhibit 3.10 for companies in the oil industry to the same ratios for companies in the insurance industry. There are significant differences *between* industries, but there are considerable similarities *within* each industry. The debt-to-assets ratio is much higher for the insurance industry than for the oil industry. However, within each industry, the ratios are clustered fairly close together. Distinct differences between industries and similarities within industries are common business features. When you compare accounting information for different companies, you must consider the industries in which those companies operate.

A Look Back

This chapter introduced deferrals which are a part of the accrual accounting. Our discussion included accounting for supplies, prepaids, and long-term assets. In each case, the expense recognition for the cost of an item purchased is deferred by holding it in an asset account. When the item is used to produce revenue, a portion of the cost representing the amount used is removed from the asset account and recognized as an expense.

We also discussed an event where cash is collected from customers before services are performed. In this case, revenue recognition is deferred until the work is performed. At the time cash is collected, a liability account titled Unearned Revenue is created. As work is performed, a proportionate amount is removed from the liability account and recognized as earned revenue. Accounting for deferred revenue has expanded our definition of revenue. Specifically, revenue is now defined as an increase in assets or a decrease in liabilities resulting from providing products or services to customers.

Finally, this chapter introduced ratios that facilitate the assessment of management performance—specifically, the return-on-assets ratio. In general, managers who produce high income with a relatively small amount of assets are considered to be the better performers. The return-on-equity ratio provides a measure of management's use of financial leverage to provide higher investor returns. Finally, we explained how the debt-to-assets ratio is used to measure liquidation risk. A higher ratio denotes higher risk.

A Look Forward

Chapters 1 through 3 focused on businesses that generate revenue by providing services to their customers. Examples of these types of businesses include consulting, real estate sales, medical, and legal services. The next chapter introduces accounting practices for businesses that generate revenue by selling goods. Examples of these companies include Walmart, Best Buy, Office Depot, and Lowe's.

Video lectures and accompanying self-assessment quizzes are available in *Connect* for all learning objectives.

 Tableau Dashboard Activity is available in *Connect* for this chapter.

 SELF-STUDY REVIEW PROBLEM

Gifford Company experienced the following accounting events during Year 1:

1. Started operations on January 1 when it acquired $20,000 cash by issuing common stock.
2. Paid $15,000 cash to purchase office furniture.
3. Earned $68,000 of cash revenue.
4. Paid cash operating expenses of $52,000.
5. On March 1, collected $36,000 cash as an advance for services to be performed in the future.
6. Paid a $2,700 cash dividend to stockholders.

Adj. 1   On December 31, Year 1, recognized depreciation expense on the office furniture. The furniture has a $3,000 salvage value and a six-year useful life.

Adj. 2   On December 31, Year 1, adjusted the books to recognize the revenue earned by providing services related to the advance described in Event 5. The contract required Gifford to provide services for a one-year period starting March 1.

Gifford Company experienced the following accounting events during Year 2:

1. Recognized $73,000 of cash revenue.
2. On April 1, paid $12,000 cash for an insurance policy that provides coverage for one year beginning immediately.
3. Paid cash operating expenses of $59,000.
4. Paid a $5,000 cash dividend to stockholders.

Adj. 1   On December 31, Year 2, recognized depreciation expense on the office furniture. The furniture has a $3,000 salvage value and a six-year useful life.

Adj. 2   On December 31, Year 2, adjusted the books to recognize the remaining revenue earned by providing services related to the advance described in Event 5 of Year 1.

Adj. 3   On December 31, Year 2, Gifford adjusted the books to recognize the amount of the insurance policy used during Year 2.

Required

a. Record the events in a financial statements model like the following one. Show the book value of the furniture in the third column under the assets category. The first event is recorded as an example.

	Balance Sheet							Income Statement			Statement of Cash Flows
	Assets			= Liab.	+	Stk. Equity					
Year 1	Cash +	Prep. Ins. +	BV Furn. =	Unearn. Rev.	+	Com. Stk.	+ Ret. Earn.	Rev. −	Exp. =	Net Inc.	
1.	20,000 +	NA +	NA =	NA	+	20,000	+ NA	NA −	NA =	NA	20,000 FA

b. What amount of revenue would Gifford report on the Year 1 income statement?
c. What amount of cash flow from customers would Gifford report on the Year 1 statement of cash flows?
d. What amount of unearned revenue would Gifford report on the Year 1 and Year 2 year-end balance sheets?
e. What are the Year 2 opening balances for the revenue and expense accounts?
f. What amount of total assets would Gifford report on the December 31, Year 1, balance sheet?
g. What obligations and commitments would Gifford report on the December 31, Year 2, balance sheet?
h. Determine the book value of the furniture as of December 31, Year 3.

Solution to Requirement *a*

The financial statements model follows:

Year 1	Cash	+	Prep. Ins.	+	BV Furn.	=	Unearn. Rev.	+	Com. Stk.	+	Ret. Earn.		Rev.	−	Exp.	=	Net Inc.		Statement of Cash Flows
						Balance Sheet — Assets = Liab. + Stk. Equity							**Income Statement**						
1	20,000	+	NA	+	NA	=	NA	+	20,000	+	NA		NA	−	NA	=	NA		20,000 FA
2	(15,000)	+	NA	+	15,000	=	NA	+	NA	+	NA		NA	−	NA	=	NA		(15,000) IA
3	68,000	+	NA	+	NA	=	NA	+	NA	+	68,000		68,000	−	NA	=	68,000		68,000 OA
4	(52,000)	+	NA	+	NA	=	NA	+	NA	+	(52,000)		NA	−	52,000	=	(52,000)		(52,000) OA
5	36,000	+	NA	+	NA	=	36,000	+	NA	+	NA		NA	−	NA	=	NA		36,000 OA
6	(2,700)	+	NA	+	NA	=	NA	+	NA	+	(2,700)		NA	−	NA	=	NA		(2,700) FA
Adj. 1*	NA	+	NA	+	(2,000)	=	NA	+	NA	+	(2,000)		NA	−	2,000	=	(2,000)		NA
Adj. 2^	NA	+	NA	+	NA	=	(30,000)	+	NA	+	30,000		30,000	−	NA	=	30,000		NA
End	54,300	+	0	+	13,000	=	6,000	+	20,000	+	41,300		98,000	−	54,000	=	44,000		54,300

Year 2 — Asset, liability, and stockholders' equity account balances carry forward. Revenue, expense, and div. accounts start each period with zero balances.

Year 2	Cash	+	Prep. Ins.	+	BV Furn.	=	Unearn. Rev.	+	Com. Stk.	+	Ret. Earn.		Rev.	−	Exp.	=	Net Inc.		Statement of Cash Flows
Beg.	54,300	+	0	+	13,000	=	6,000	+	20,000	+	41,300		0	−	0	=	0		54,300
1	73,000	+	NA	+	NA	=	NA	+	NA	+	73,000		73,000	−	NA	=	73,000		73,000 OA
2	(12,000)	+	12,000	+	NA	=	NA	+	NA	+	NA		NA	−	NA	=	NA		(12,000) OA
3	(59,000)	+	NA	+	NA	=	NA	+	NA	+	(59,000)		NA	−	59,000	=	(59,000)		(59,000) OA
4	(5,000)	+	NA	+	NA	=	NA	+	NA	+	(5,000)		NA	−	NA	=	NA		(5,000) FA
Adj. 1*	NA	+	NA	+	(2,000)	=	NA	+	NA	+	(2,000)		NA	−	2,000	=	(2,000)		NA
Adj. 2^	NA	+	NA	+	NA	=	(6,000)	+	NA	+	6,000		6,000	−	NA	=	6,000		NA
Adj. 3†	NA	+	(9,000)	+	NA	=	NA	+	NA	+	(9,000)		NA	−	9,000	=	(9,000)		NA
End	51,300	+	3,000	+	11,000	=	0	+	20,000	+	45,300		79,000	−	70,000	=	9,000		51,300 NC

*The column abbreviated as "BV Furn." stands for Book Value of the Furniture. Depreciation expense is $2,000 ($15,000 cost − $3,000 salvage / 6-year life). This amount will be recognized each year of the asset's useful life. Increases to accumulated depreciation are shown as a negative in the "BV Furn." column.

^Revenue is earned at the rate of $3,000 ($36,000 ÷ 12 months) per month. Revenue recognized in Year 1 is $30,000 ($3,000 × 10 months). Revenue recognized in Year 2 is $6,000 ($3,000 × 2 months).

†Rent expense is incurred at the rate of $1,000 ($12,000 ÷ 12 months) per month. Rent expense recognized in Year 2 is $9,000 ($1,000 × 9 months).

Solutions to Requirements *b–h*

b. Gifford would report $98,000 of revenue in Year 1 ($68,000 revenue on account plus $30,000 of the $36,000 of unearned revenue).

c. The cash inflow from customers in Year 1 is $104,000 ($68,000 cash revenue plus $36,000 when the unearned revenue was received).

d. The December 31, Year 1, balance sheet will report $6,000 of unearned revenue, which is the amount of the cash advance less the amount of revenue recognized in Year 1 ($36,000 − $30,000). The December 31, Year 2, unearned revenue balance is zero because all of the unearned revenue would have been recognized by the end of Year 2.

e. Because revenue and expense accounts contain information for only one accounting period, the beginning balances in these accounts are always zero.

f. Assets on the December 31, Year 1, balance sheet are $67,300 ($54,300 cash balance + $13,000 book value of furniture).

g. Because all unearned revenue would be recognized before the financial statements were prepared at the end of Year 2, there would be no liabilities on the Year 2 balance sheet. In this case, all of the assets are committed to the investors.

h. The book value as of December 31, Year 3, is $9,000 ($15,000 cost − $6,000 accumulated depreciation).

KEY TERMS

Accumulated depreciation 140	Debt-to-assets ratio 146	Return-on-assets ratio 145	Straight-line depreciation 140
Book Value 140	Deferral 126	Return-on-equity ratio 146	Unearned revenue 131
Carrying Value 140	Depreciation expense 140	Revenue 131	Useful life 139
Cost 127	Financial leverage 146	Salvage value 139	
	Prepaid items 129		

QUESTIONS

1. What does accrual accounting attempt to accomplish?

2. What does the term *deferral* mean?

3. If cash is collected in advance of performing services, when is the associated revenue recognized?

4. What effect does the issue of common stock have on the accounting equation?

5. When is revenue recognized under accrual accounting?

6. What is the effect on the right side of the accounting equation when cash is collected in advance of performing services?

7. What does the term *unearned revenue* mean?

8. What effect does expense recognition have on the accounting equation?

9. When are expenses recognized under accrual accounting?

10. Why may net cash flow from operating activities on the cash flow statement be different from the amount of net income reported on the income statement?

11. What is the relationship between the income statement and changes in assets and liabilities?

12. How does net income affect the stockholders' claims on the business's assets?

13. What is the difference between a cost and an expense?

14. When does a cost become an expense? Do all costs become expenses?

15. How and when is the cost of the *supplies used* recognized in an accounting period?

16. What does the term *expense* mean?

17. What does the term *revenue* mean?

18. What does the term *end-of-period adjustment* mean? Give an example.

19. Give several examples of period costs.

20. Give an example of a cost that can be directly matched with the revenue produced by an accounting firm from preparing a tax return.

EXERCISES—SERIES A

Exercise 3-1A *Supplies and the financial statements model*

LO 3-1

Pizza Express Inc. began the Year 2 accounting period with $2,500 cash, $1,400 of common stock, and $1,100 of retained earnings. Pizza Express was affected by the following accounting events during Year 2:

1. Purchased $3,600 of supplies on account.

2. Earned and collected $12,300 of cash revenue.

3. Paid $2,700 cash on accounts payable.

4. Adjusted the records to reflect the use of supplies. A physical count indicated that $250 of supplies was still on hand on December 31, Year 2.

Required

a. Show the effects of the events on the financial statements using a horizontal statements model like the following one. In the Statement of Cash Flows column, use OA to designate operating activity, IA for investing activity, FA for financing activity, and NC for net change in cash. Use NA to indicate accounts not affected by the event. The beginning balances are entered in the following example:

	Balance Sheet							Income Statement			Statement of Cash Flows
	Assets		=	Liab.	+	Stk. Equity					
Event No.	Cash	+ Supplies	=	Accts. Pay	+ Com. Stk	+ Ret. Earn.		Rev.	− Exp.	= Net Inc.	
Beg. bal.	2,500	+ 0	=	0	+ 1,400	+ 1,100		0	− 0	= 0	0

b. Explain the difference between the amount of net income and amount of net cash flow from operating activities.

LO 3-1

Exercise 3-2A *Supplies on financial statements*

Yard Professionals Inc. experienced the following events in Year 1, its first year of operation:

1. Performed services for $35,000 cash.
2. Purchased $6,000 of supplies on account.
3. A physical count on December 31, Year 1, found that there was $1,800 of supplies on hand.

Required

Based on this information alone:

a. Record the events in accounts under an accounting equation.
b. Prepare an income statement, balance sheet, and statement of cash flows for the Year 1 accounting period.
c. What is the balance in the Supplies account as of January 1, Year 2?

LO 3-2

Exercise 3-3A *Show how prepaid items affect a financial statements model*

On June 1, Year 1, Hamlin, Inc. paid $12,000 for 12 months rent on its warehouse in Huntsville, Alabama. In addition, on October 1, Year 1, Hamlin paid $3,000 for a one-year insurance policy on the warehouse. Hamlin's reporting period ends on December 31st of each year.

Required

Show how both prepaid purchases and the associated end-of-period adjustments at the end of Year 1 will affect a financial statements model.

LO 3-2

Exercise 3-4A *Prepaid items on financial statements*

Life, Inc. experienced the following events in Year 1, its first year of operation:

1. Performed counseling services for $36,000 cash.
2. On February 1, Year 1, paid $18,000 cash to rent office space for the coming year.
3. Adjusted the accounts to reflect the amount of rent used during the year.

Required

Based on this information alone:

a. Record the events in accounts under an accounting equation.
b. Prepare an income statement, balance sheet, and statement of cash flows for the Year 1 accounting period.
c. Ignoring all other future events, what is the amount of rent expense that would be recognized in Year 2?

LO 3-2

Exercise 3-5A *Effect of an error on financial statements*

On April 1, Year 1, Maine Corporation paid $18,000 cash in advance for a one-year lease on an office building. Assume that Maine records the prepaid rent as an asset and that the books are closed on December 31.

Required

a. Show the payment for the one-year lease and the related end-of-period adjustment to recognize rent expense in the accounting equation.
b. Assume that Maine Corporation failed to record the required end-of-period adjustment to reflect using the office building. How would the error affect the company's Year 1 income statement and balance sheet?

LO 3-3

Exercise 3-6A *Unearned revenue defined as a liability*

Lan, an accounting major, and Pat, a marketing major, are watching a *Matlock* rerun on late-night TV. Of course, there is a murder, and the suspect wants to hire Matlock as the defense attorney. Matlock will take the case but requires an advance payment of $150,000. Pat remarks that Matlock has earned income of $150,000 without lifting a finger. Lan corrects Pat telling him that Matlock has not earned anything but instead Matlock has a $150,000 liability that would appear on his balance sheet. Pat asks, "How can that be?"

Required

Assuming you are Lan, explain to Pat why Matlock has a liability on his balance sheet. When would Matlock actually recognize the $150,000 of revenue on his income statement?

Exercise 3-7A   *Unearned items on financial statements*   LO 3-3

Yard Designs (YD) experienced the following events in Year 1, its first year of operation:

1. On October 1, Year 1, YD collected $54,000 for consulting services it agreed to provide during the coming year.
2. Adjusted the accounts to reflect the amount of consulting service revenue recognized in Year 1.

Required

Based on this information alone:

a. Record the events under an accounting equation.
b. Prepare an income statement, balance sheet, and statement of cash flows for the Year 1 accounting period.
c. Ignoring all other future events, what is the amount of service revenue that would be recognized in Year 2?

Exercise 3-8A   *Unearned revenue and the financial statements model*   LO 3-3

Clark Bell started a personal financial planning business when he accepted $36,000 cash as advance payment for managing the financial assets of a large estate. Bell agreed to manage the estate for a one-year period beginning June 1, Year 1.

Required

a. Show the effects of the advance payment and revenue recognition on the Year 1 financial statements using a horizontal statements model like the following one. In the Statement of Cash Flows column, use OA to designate operating activity, IA for investing activity, FA for financing activity, and NC for net change in cash. Use NA if the account is not affected.

	Balance Sheet						Income Statement				Statement of Cash Flows
	Assets	=	Liab.	+		Stk. Equity					
Event	Cash	=	Unearn. Rev.	+		Ret. Earn.	Rev.	−	Exp.	=	Net Inc.	

b. How much revenue would Bell recognize on the Year 2 income statement?
c. What is the amount of cash flow from operating activities in Year 2?

Exercise 3-9A   *Supplies, unearned revenue, and the financial statements model*   LO 3-1, 3-3

Hart, Attorney at Law, experienced the following transactions in Year 1, the first year of operations:

1. Accepted $36,000 on April 1, Year 1, as a retainer for services to be performed evenly over the next 12 months.
2. Performed legal services for cash of $54,000.
3. Purchased $2,800 of office supplies on account.
4. Paid $2,400 of the amount due on accounts payable.
5. Paid a cash dividend to the stockholders of $5,000.
6. Paid cash for operating expenses of $31,000.
7. Determined that at the end of the accounting period $200 of office supplies remained on hand.
8. On December 31, Year 1, recognized the revenue that had been earned for services performed in accordance with Transaction 1.

Required

Show the effects of the events on the financial statements using a horizontal statements model like the following one. In the Statement of Cash Flows column, use the initials OA to designate operating activity, IA for investing activity, FA for financing activity, and NC for net change in cash. Use NA to indicate accounts not affected by the event. The first event has been recorded as an example.

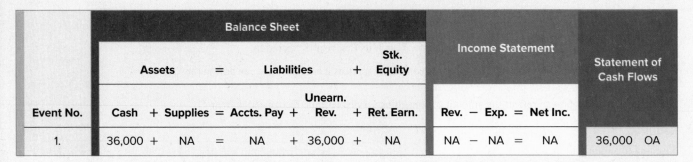

| | Balance Sheet | | | | | | Income Statement | | | Statement of Cash Flows |
| | Assets | | = | Liabilities | + | Stk. Equity | | | | |
Event No.	Cash +	Supplies =	Accts. Pay +	Unearn. Rev. +	Ret. Earn.		Rev. −	Exp. =	Net Inc.	
1.	36,000 +	NA =	NA +	36,000 +	NA		NA −	NA =	NA	36,000 OA

LO 3-2, 3-3

Exercise 3-10A   *Prepaid vs. unearned: the entity concept*

On October 1, Year 1, Josh Smith, attorney, accepted a $10,800 cash advance from his client, James Company, for services to be performed over the next six months.

Required

a. Record the deferral and the related December 31, Year 1, adjustment for Josh Smith in an accounting equation.

b. Record the deferral and the related December 31, Year 1, adjustment for James Company in an accounting equation.

LO 3-1, 3-2, 3-3

Exercise 3-11A   *Identifying deferral and accrual events*

Required

Identify each of the following events as an accrual, a deferral, or neither:

a. Paid cash in advance for a one-year insurance policy.

b. Paid cash to settle an account payable.

c. Collected accounts receivable.

d. Paid cash for current salaries expense.

e. Paid cash to purchase supplies.

f. Provided services on account.

g. Provided services and collected cash.

h. Paid cash to purchase land.

i. Recognized accrued salaries at the end of the accounting period.

j. Paid a cash dividend to the stockholders.

k. Recognized revenue on account at the end of the period.

l. Collected cash for services to be provided in the future.

LO 3-1, 3-2, 3-3

Exercise 3-12A   *Adjusting the accounts*

Norell Inc. experienced the following accounting events during its Year 1 accounting period:

1. Recognized revenue on account.

2. Issued common stock.

3. Paid cash to purchase supplies.

4. Collected a cash advance for services that will be provided during the coming year.

5. Paid a cash dividend to the stockholders.

6. Paid cash for an insurance policy that provides coverage during the next year.

7. Collected cash from accounts receivable.

8. Paid cash for operating expenses.

9. Paid cash to settle an account payable.

10. Paid cash to purchase land.

Required

Identify the events that would require an end-of-period adjustment.

Exercise 3-13A   *Classifying events on the statement of cash flows*

The following transactions pertain to the operations of Ewing Company for Year 2:

1. Acquired $30,000 cash from the issue of common stock.
2. Provided $65,000 of services on account.
3. Paid $22,000 cash on accounts payable.
4. Performed services for $8,000 cash.
5. Collected $51,000 cash from accounts receivable.
6. Incurred $37,000 of operating expenses on account.
7. Paid $6,500 cash for one year's rent in advance.
8. Paid a $4,000 cash dividend to the stockholders.
9. Paid $1,200 cash for supplies to be used in the future.
10. Recognized $3,100 of accrued salaries expense.

Required

a. Classify the cash flows from these transactions as operating activities (OA), investing activities (IA), or financing activities (FA). Use NA for transactions that do not affect the statement of cash flows.

b. Prepare a statement of cash flows. The beginning cash balance was $6,700.

Exercise 3-14A   *Effect of accounting events on the income statement and statement of cash flows*

Required

Explain how each of the following events or series of events and the related adjustments will affect the amount of *net income* and the amount of *cash flow from operating activities* reported on the year-end financial statements. Identify the direction of change (increase, decrease, or NA) and the amount of the change. Organize your answers according to the following table. The first event is recorded as an example. If an event does not have a related adjustment, record only the effects of the event.

	Net Income		Cash Flows from Operating Activities	
Event/Adjustment	Direction of Change	Amount of Change	Direction of Change	Amount of Change
a	NA	NA	Decrease	$9,000
Adj	Decrease	$2,250	NA	NA

a. Paid $9,000 cash on October 1 to purchase a one-year insurance policy.

b. Purchased $2,000 of supplies on account. Paid $500 cash on accounts payable. The ending balance in the Supplies account, after adjustment, was $300.

c. Provided services for $10,000 cash.

d. Collected $2,400 in advance for services to be performed in the future. The contract called for services to start on May 1 and to continue for one year.

e. Accrued salaries amounting to $5,600.

f. Sold land that cost $3,000 for $3,000 cash.

g. Acquired $15,000 cash from the issue of common stock.

h. Earned $12,000 of revenue on account. Collected $8,000 cash from accounts receivable.

i. Paid cash operating expenses of $4,500.

LO 3-1, 3-2, 3-5

Exercise 3-15A *Distinguishing between an expense and a cost*

Charlene Rose tells you that accountants where she works are real hair splitters. For example, they make a big issue over the difference between a cost and an expense. She says the two terms mean the same thing to her.

Required

a. Explain to Charlene the difference between a cost and expense from an accountant's perspective.

b. Explain whether each of the following events produces an asset or an expense:

   (1) Purchased a building for cash.

   (2) Paid cash to purchase supplies.

   (3) Used supplies on hand to produce revenue.

   (4) Paid cash in advance for insurance.

   (5) Recognized accrued salaries.

LO 3-1, 3-2, 3-3, 3-5

Exercise 3-16A *Revenue and expense recognition*

Required

a. Describe an end-of-period adjustment that results in an increase in liabilities.

b. Describe an end-of-period adjustment that results in a decrease in assets.

c. Describe an end-of-period adjustment that results in a decrease in liabilities.

d. Describe an end-of-period adjustment that reduces the book value of a long-term asset.

LO 3-4

CHECK FIGURES
a. BS
z. CF

Exercise 3-17A *Relationship of accounts to financial statements*

Required

Identify whether each of the following items would appear on the income statement (IS), statement of changes in stockholders' equity (SE), balance sheet (BS), or statement of cash flows (CF). Some items may appear on more than one statement; if so, identify all applicable statements. If an item would not appear on any financial statement, label it NA.

a. Supplies	t. Price/Earnings Ratio
b. Cash Flow from Financing Activities	u. Taxes Payable
c. "As of" Date Notation	v. Unearned Revenue
d. Ending Retained Earnings	w. Service Revenue
e. Net Income	x. Cash Flow from Investing Activities
f. Dividends Declared and Paid	y. Consulting Revenue
g. Net Change in Cash	z. Utilities Expense
h. "For the Period Ended"	aa. Ending Common Stock
i. Land	bb. Total Liabilities
j. Ending Common Stock	cc. Operating Cycle
k. Salaries Expense	dd. Cash Flow from Operating Activities
l. Prepaid Rent	ee. Operating Expenses
m. Accounts Payable	ff. Supplies Expense
n. Total Assets	gg. Beginning Retained Earnings
o. Salaries Payable	hh. Beginning Common Stock
p. Insurance Expense	ii. Prepaid Insurance
q. Notes Payable	jj. Salary Expense
r. Accounts Receivable	kk. Beginning Cash Balance
s. Rent Expense	ll. Ending Cash Balance

LO 3-1, 3-2, 3-3, 3-5

Exercise 3-18A *Recording events into a horizontal statements model*

The following is a partial list of transactions Bok Company experienced during its Year 3 accounting period:

1. Paid cash to purchase supplies.

2. Paid cash to purchase insurance coverage for the coming year.

3. Collected cash for services to be performed in the future.

4. Paid cash to purchase a long-term depreciable asset.

Required

Assume that each of the events requires an end-of-period adjustment. Use a horizontal financial statements model to show how the adjustments affect the financial statements. Use increase (I) and decrease (D) to indicate how the adjustment affects each part of the horizontal statements model. Use the letters NA to indicate that a part of the model is not affected by the adjustment. In the Statement of Cash Flows column, indicate whether cash increases (I) decreases (D), or is not affected (NA). Also, indicate whether the cash flow was caused by an operating activity (OA), an investing activity (IA), or a financing activity (FA).

Balance Sheet					Income Statement					Statement of Cash Flows
Assets	=	Liab.	+	Stk. Equity	Rev.	−	Exp.	=	Net Inc.	
+ −	=	NA	+	NA	NA	−	NA	=	NA	− OA

Exercise 3-19A   *Determining the impact of events on financial statements*   LO 3-1, 3-2, 3-3, 3-5

Required

Indicate whether each of the following statements is true or false:

a. The unearned revenue account appears on the income statement.
b. Supplies expense appears on the statement of cash flows.
c. Prepaid rent appears on the balance sheet.
d. The book value of a long-term asset appears on the statement of changes in stockholders' equity.
e. Depreciation expense appears on the income statement and in the operating activities section of the statement of cash flows.
f. Accrued salaries payable appears on the balance sheet.
g. Net income appears on the income statement and the statement of changes in stockholders' equity.
h. Dividends are deferrals because they delay the recognition of expenses.
i. Depreciation expense reduces net income but has no effect on the statement of cash flows.
j. The amount of accumulated depreciation is added to the corresponding asset account in order to determine the book value of the asset.
k. A decrease in unearned revenue is normally offset by an increase in retained earnings.

Exercise 3-20A   *Relationship between depreciation and the financial statements*   LO 3-5

On January 1, Year 2, LCJ Rental Cars purchased a car that is to be used to produce rental income. The car cost $35,000. It has an expected useful life of five years and a $5,000 salvage value. The car produced rental income of $9,000 per year throughout its useful life. Assume LCJ started the Year 2 accounting period with a beginning cash balance of $40,000.

Required

a. Prepare an income statement and a statement of cash flows for Year 2, Year 3, and Year 4.
b. Determine the book value of the car for Year 2, Year 3, and Year 4.

Exercise 3-21A   *Identifying transaction type and effect on the financial statements*   LO 3-1, 3-2, 3-3

Required

Identify whether each of the following transactions is an asset source (AS), asset use (AU), asset exchange (AE), or claims exchange (CE). Also, show the effects of the events on the financial statements using the horizontal statements model. Indicate whether the event increases (I), decreases (D), or does not affect (NA) each part of the financial statements model. In the Statement of Cash Flows column, designate the cash flows as operating activities (OA), investing activities (IA), or financing activities (FA). The first two transactions have been recorded as examples.

Event	Type of Event	Balance Sheet							Income Statement					Statement of Cash Flows
		Assets	=	Liabilities	+	C. Stk.	+	R. Earn.	Rev.	−	Exp.	=	Net Inc.	
a.	AS	I		NA		NA		I	I		NA		I	I OA
b.	AS	I		I		NA		NA	NA		NA		NA	NA

a. Provided services and collected cash.

b. Purchased supplies on account to be used in the future.

c. Paid cash in advance for one year's rent.

d. Paid cash to purchase land.

e. Paid a cash dividend to the stockholders.

f. Received cash from the issue of common stock.

g. Paid cash on accounts payable.

h. Collected cash from accounts receivable.

i. Received cash advance for services to be provided in the future.

j. Incurred other operating expenses on account.

k. Performed services on account.

l. Adjusted books to reflect the amount of pre-paid rent expired during the period.

m. Paid cash for operating expenses.

n. Adjusted the books to record the supplies used during the period.

o. Recorded accrued salaries.

p. Paid cash for salaries accrued at the end of a prior period.

q. Recognized revenue on account earned at the end of the accounting period.

LO 3-5

Exercise 3-22A   *Effect of depreciation on the accounting equation and financial statements*

The following events apply to Tracey's Restaurant for the Year 1 fiscal year:

1. Started the company when it acquired $21,000 cash from the issue of common stock.
2. Purchased a new cooktop that cost $22,000 cash.
3. Earned $32,000 in cash revenue.
4. Paid $16,000 cash for salaries expense.
5. Paid $7,000 cash for operating expenses.
6. Adjusted the records to reflect the use of the cooktop. The cooktop, purchased on January 1, Year 1, has an expected useful life of five years and an estimated salvage value of $2,000. Use straight-line depreciation. The adjustment was made as of December 31, Year 1.

Required

a. Record the events in accounts under an accounting equation.

b. What amount of depreciation expense would Tracey's report on the Year 2 income statement?

c. What amount of accumulated depreciation would Tracey's report on the December 31, Year 2, balance sheet?

d. Would the cash flow from operating activities be affected by depreciation in Year 2?

LO 3-5

Exercise 3-23A   *Depreciation affecting multiple cycles*

On January 1, Year 1, Your Ride Inc. paid $36,000 cash to purchase a taxi cab. The taxi had a four-year useful life and a $4,000 salvage value.

Required

a. Determine the amount of depreciation expense that would appear on the Year 1 and Year 2 income statements.

b. Determine the amount of accumulated depreciation that would appear on the Year 1 and Year 2 balance sheets.

c. Explain how the purchase of equipment would affect the Year 1 and Year 2 statements of cash flows.

LO 3-6

Exercise 3-24A   *Using ratio analysis to assess financial risk*

The following information was drawn from the balance sheets of two companies:

Company	Assets	=	Liabilities	+	Stockholders' Equity
East	200,000	=	84,000	+	116,000
West	600,000	=	168,000	+	432,000

Required

a. Compute the debt-to-assets ratio to measure the level of financial risk of both companies.

b. Compare the two ratios computed in Requirement *a* to identify which company has the higher level of financial risk.

Exercise 3-25A   *Using ratio analysis to assess return on equity*

LO 3-6

The following information was drawn from the Year 5 balance sheets of two companies:

Company	Assets	=	Liabilities	+	Common Stock	+	Retained Earnings
Butler	420,000	=	105,000	+	200,000	+	115,000
Lynch	600,000	=	240,000	+	100,000	+	260,000

During Year 5, Butler's net income was $25,200, while Lynch's net income was $43,200.

Required

a. Compute the return-on-equity ratio to measure the level of financial risk of both companies.

b. Compare the two ratios computed in Requirement *a* to identify which company is performing better.

PROBLEMS—SERIES A

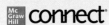 **All applicable Problems in Series A are available in *Connect*.**

Problem 3-26A   *Effect of end-of-period adjustments on the accounting equation*

LO 3-1, 3-2, 3-3

Required

Each of the following independent events requires an end-of-period adjustment. Show how each event and its related adjustment affect the accounting equation. Assume the fiscal year ends December 31. The first event is shown as an example.

CHECK FIGURES
d. Adjustment amount: $4,000

Event/ Adjustment	Total Assets				Stockholders' Equity		
	Cash	+	Other Assets	= Liabilities +	Common Stock	+	Retained Earnings
a	−4,800	+	+4,800	NA	NA		NA
Adj.	NA		−1,200	NA	NA		−1,200

a. Paid $4,800 cash in advance on October 1 for a one-year insurance policy.

b. Received a $3,600 cash advance for a contract to provide services in the future. The contract required a one-year commitment, starting April 1.

c. Purchased $1,200 of supplies on account. At year's end, $175 of supplies remained on hand.

d. Paid $9,600 cash in advance on August 1 for a one-year lease on office space.

Problem 3-27A   *Effect of events on financial statements*

LO 3-1, 3-2, 3-3

Simpson Company had the following balances in its accounting records as of December 31, Year 1:

CHECK FIGURES
b. $44,100
h. $42,450

Assets		Liabilities and Stk. Equity	
Cash	$ 40,000	Accounts Payable	$ 7,500
Accounts Receivable	9,000	Common Stock	45,000
Land	51,000	Retained Earnings	47,500
Total	$100,000	Total	$100,000

The following accounting events apply to Simpson Company's Year 2 fiscal year:

Jan.   1   Acquired $20,000 cash from the issue of common stock.
Feb.   1   Paid $6,000 cash in advance for a one-year lease for office space.
Mar.   1   Paid a $2,000 cash dividend to the stockholders.
April 1   Purchased additional land that cost $15,000 cash.
May   1   Made a cash payment on accounts payable of $5,500.
July   1   Received $9,600 cash in advance as a retainer for services to be performed monthly over the coming year.
Sept. 1   Sold land for $30,000 cash that had originally cost $30,000.
Oct.   1   Purchased $2,500 of supplies on account.
Dec. 31   Earned $58,000 of service revenue on account during the year.
      31   Received cash collections from accounts receivable amounting to $46,000.
      31   Incurred other operating expenses on account during the year that amounted to $28,000.
      31   Recognized accrued salaries expense of $6,500.
      31   Had $50 of supplies on hand at the end of the period.
      31   The land purchased on April 1 had a market value of $20,000.

Required

Based on the preceding information, answer the following questions for Simpson Company. All questions pertain to the Year 2 financial statements. (*Hint:* Enter items in accounts under the accounting equation before answering the questions.)

a. What amount would Simpson report for land on the balance sheet?
b. What amount of net cash flow from operating activities would be reported on the statement of cash flows?
c. What amount of rent expense would be reported on the income statement?
d. What amount of total liabilities would be reported on the balance sheet?
e. What amount of supplies expense would be reported on the income statement?
f. What amount of unearned revenue would be reported on the balance sheet?
g. What amount of net cash flow from investing activities would be reported on the statement of cash flows?
h. What amount of total expenses would be reported on the income statement?
i. What amount of service revenue would be reported on the income statement?
j. What amount of cash flows from financing activities would be reported on the statement of cash flows?
k. What amount of net income would be reported on the income statement?
l. What amount of retained earnings would be reported on the balance sheet?

LO 3-2, 3-3

Problem 3-28A   *Show how the events affect the financial statements using a horizontal statements model*

CHECK FIGURES
Net Income: $12,300
Ending Cash Balance: $19,000

The following events pertain to Super Cleaning Company:

1. Acquired $10,000 cash from the issue of common stock.
2. Provided $15,000 of services on account.
3. Provided services for $5,000 cash.
4. Received $2,800 cash in advance for services to be performed in the future.
5. Collected $12,200 cash from the account receivable created in Event 2.
6. Paid $1,900 for cash expenses.
7. Performed $1,400 of the services agreed to in Event 4.
8. Incurred $3,600 of expenses on account.
9. Paid $4,800 cash in advance for one-year contract to rent office space.
10. Paid $2,800 cash on the account payable created in Event 8.
11. Paid a $1,500 cash dividend to the stockholders.
12. Recognized rent expense for nine months' use of office space acquired in Event 9.

Required

Show the effects of the events on the financial statements using a horizontal statements model like the following one. In the Statement of Cash Flows column, use the letters OA to designate operating activity, IA for investing activity, FA for financing activity, and NC for net change in cash. Use NA to indicate accounts not affected by the event. The first event is shown as an example.

Event No.	Balance Sheet										Income Statement			Statement of Cash Flows
	Assets			=	Liabilities		+	Stk. Equity						
	Cash	+ Accts. Rec.	+ Prep. Ins.	=	Accts Pay.	+ Unearn. Rev.	+	Com. Stk.	+ Ret. Earn.		Rev.	− Exp.	= Net Inc.	
1.	10,000	+ NA	+ NA	=	NA	+ NA	+	10,000	+ NA		NA	− NA	= NA	10,000 FA

Problem 3-29A   *Relating titles and accounts to financial statements*   LO 3-4

Required

Identify the financial statements on which each of the following items (titles, date descriptions, and accounts) appears by placing a check mark in the appropriate column. If an item appears on more than one statement, place a check mark in every applicable column.

Item	Income Statement	Statement of Changes in Stockholders' Equity	Balance Sheet	Statement of Cash Flows
Unearned revenue				
Ending common stock				
Prepaid Insurance				
Accounts receivable				
Land				
Beginning cash balance				
Notes payable				
Beginning common stock				
Service revenue				
Utility expense				
Stock issue				
Operating activities				
For the period ended (date)				
Net income				
Investing activities				
Supplies				
Ending cash balance				
Salary expense				
Consulting revenue				
Dividends				
Net loss				
Accounts payable				
Interest expense				
As of (date)				
Financing activities				

Problem 3-30A   *Identifying and arranging the components of financial statements*

The following accounts and balances were drawn from the records of Barker Company at December 31, Year 2:

Supplies	$ 1,000	Beginning retained earnings	$ 9,300
Cash flow from investing act.	(5,200)	Cash flow from financing act.	(5,000)
Prepaid insurance	1,200	Rent expense	2,500
Service revenue	65,200	Dividends	3,000
Other operating expenses	41,000	Cash	48,000
Supplies expense	1,100	Accounts receivable	14,200
Insurance expense	2,100	Prepaid rent	4,800
Beginning common stock	40,000	Unearned revenue	6,400
Cash flow from operating act.	15,600	Land	24,000
Common stock issued	5,000	Accounts payable	17,000

Required

Use the accounts and balances from Barker Company to construct an income statement, statement of changes in stockholders' equity, balance sheet, and statement of cash flows (show only totals for each activity on the statement of cash flows).

Problem 3-31A   *Events for two complete accounting cycles*

Alcorn Service Company was formed on January 1, Year 1.

Events Affecting the Year 1 Accounting Period

1. Acquired $20,000 cash from the issue of common stock.
2. Purchased $800 of supplies on account.
3. Purchased land that cost $14,000 cash.
4. Paid $800 cash to settle accounts payable created in Event 2.
5. Recognized revenue on account of $10,500.
6. Paid $3,800 cash for other operating expenses.
7. Collected $7,000 cash from accounts receivable.

Information for Year 1 End-of-Period Adjustments

8. Recognized accrued salaries of $3,600 on December 31, Year 1.
9. Had $100 of supplies on hand at the end of the accounting period.

Events Affecting the Year 2 Accounting Period

1. Acquired $15,000 cash from the issue of common stock.
2. Paid $3,600 cash to settle the salaries payable obligation.
3. Paid $9,000 cash in advance to lease office space.
4. Sold the land that cost $14,000 for $14,000 cash.
5. Received $6,000 cash in advance for services to be performed in the future.
6. Purchased $2,400 of supplies on account during the year.
7. Provided services on account of $24,500.
8. Collected $12,600 cash from accounts receivable.
9. Paid a cash dividend of $2,000 to the stockholders.
10. Paid other operating expenses of $2,850.

Information for Year 2 End-of-Period Adjustments

11. The advance payment for rental of the office space (see Event 3) was made on March 1 for a one-year term.
12. The cash advance for services to be provided in the future was collected on October 1 (see Event 5). The one-year contract started on October 1.

13. Had $300 of supplies remaining on hand at the end of the period.
14. Recognized accrued salaries of $4,800 at the end of the accounting period.

Required

a. Identify each event affecting the Year 1 and Year 2 accounting periods as asset source (AS), asset use (AU), asset exchange (AE), or claims exchange (CE). Record the effects of each event under the appropriate account headings of the accounting equation.

b. Prepare an income statement, statement of changes in stockholders' equity, balance sheet, and statement of cash flows for Year 1 and Year 2.

Problem 3-32A   *Effect of depreciation on financial statements*

LO 3-5

On January 1, Year 2, Shapiro Company paid $70,000 cash to purchase a truck. The truck has a $10,000 salvage value and a five-year useful life. Assume that Shapiro earns $18,000 of cash revenue per year for Year 1 through Year 5 of the assets useful life. Shapiro began Year 2 with a beginning cash balance of $110,000.

Required

a. Determine the amount of net income for Year 2, Year 3, and Year 4.

b. Determine the amount of accumulated depreciation appearing on the Year 2, Year 3, and Year 4 balance sheet.

c. Determine the book value of the truck as of December 31, Year 2, Year 3, and Year 4.

d. Determine the cash flows shown on the statement of cash flows for Year 2, Year 3, and Year 4. For each cash flow item, indicate whether it is a cash inflow or cash outflow and whether the item would be shown in the financing, investing, or operating sections of the cash flow statement.

Problem 3-33A   *Effect of events on financial statements*

LO 3-1, 3-2, 3-3, 3-5

Porser Company had the following balances in its accounting records as of December 31, Year 1:

Assets		Claims	
Cash	$26,000	Accounts payable	$ 5,000
Accounts receivable	9,000	Common stock	28,000
Land	42,000	Retained earnings	44,000
Total	$77,000	Total	$77,000

The following accounting events apply to Porser Company's Year 2 fiscal year:

Jan. 1 Acquired $15,000 cash from the issue of common stock.
      1 Purchased a truck that cost $22,000 and had a $2,000 salvage value and a four-year useful life.
Feb. 1 Borrowed $12,000 by issuing a note that had a 9 percent annual interest rate and a one-year term.
      1 Paid $3,000 cash in advance for a one-year lease for office space.
Mar. 1 Paid a $2,000 cash dividend to the stockholders.
April 1 Purchased land that cost $28,000 cash.
May   1 Made a cash payment on accounts payable of $4,000.
July 1 Received $5,400 cash in advance as a retainer for services to be performed monthly over the next 12 months.
Sept. 1 Sold land for $42,000 that originally cost $42,000.
Oct. 1 Purchased $5,000 of supplies on account.
Dec. 31 Earned $42,000 of service revenue on account during the year.
     31 Received cash collections from accounts receivable amounting to $40,000.
     31 Incurred other operating expenses on account during the year that amounted to $6,000.
     31 Incurred accrued salaries expense of $5,200.
     31 Had $200 of supplies on hand at the end of the period.

Required

Based on the preceding information, answer the following questions. All questions pertain to the Year 2 financial statements. (*Hint:* Enter items in accounts under the accounting equation before answering the questions.)

a. Based on the preceding transaction, identify four additional adjustments and describe them.

b. What amount of interest expense would Porser report on the income statement?

c. What amount of net cash flow from operating activities would Porser report on the statement of cash flows?

d. What amount of rent expense would Porser report on the income statement?

e. What amount of total liabilities would Porser report on the balance sheet?

f. What amount of supplies expense would Porser report on the income statement?

g. What amount of unearned revenue would Porser report on the balance sheet?

h. What amount of net cash flow from investing activities would Porser report on the statement of cash flows?

i. What amount of interest payable would Porser report on the balance sheet?

j. What amount of total expenses would Porser report on the income statement?

k. What amount of retained earnings would Porser report on the balance sheet?

l. What amount of service revenues would Porser report on the income statement?

m. What amount of cash flows from financing activities would Porser report on the statement of cash flows?

n. What amount of net income would Porser report on the income statement?

LO 3-6

Problem 3-34A   *Using ratio analysis to assess return on equity*

The following information was drawn from the Year 8 balance sheets of two companies:

Company	Assets	=	Liabilities	+	Common Stock	+	Retained Earnings
Morris	500,000	=	125,000	+	300,000	+	75,000
Reeves	800,000	=	360,000	+	200,000	+	240,000

During Year 8, Morris's net income was $33,750, while Reeves's net income was $61,600.

Required

a. Compute the debt-to-assets ratio to measure the level of financial risk of both companies.

b. Compare the two ratios computed in Requirement *a* to identify which company has the higher level of financial risk.

c. Compute the return-on-equity ratio to measure the level of financial risk of both companies.

d. Compare the two ratios computed in Requirement *a* to identify which company is performing better.

e. Define the term *financial leverage*.

f. Identify the company that is using financial leverage to a greater extent.

EXERCISES—SERIES B

LO 3-1

Exercise 3-1B   *Supplies and the financial statements model*

Handy Andy Inc. began the Year 2 accounting period with $9,000 cash, $5,000 of common stock, and $4,000 of retained earnings. Handy Andy was affected by the following accounting events during Year 2:

1. Purchased $9,500 of supplies on account.

2. Earned and collected $32,500 of cash revenue.

3. Paid $7,200 cash on accounts payable.

4. Adjusted the records to reflect the use of supplies. A physical count indicated that $1,700 of supplies was still on hand on December 31, Year 2.

Required

a. Show the effects of the events on the financial statements using a horizontal statements model like the following one. In the Statement of Cash Flows column, use OA to designate operating activity, IA for investing activity, FA for financing activity, and NC for net change in cash. Use NA to indicate accounts not affected by the event. The beginning balances are entered in the following example:

	Balance Sheet								Income Statement			Statement of Cash Flows
	Assets		=	Liab.	+	Stk. Equity						
Event No.	Cash	+ Supplies	=	Accts. Pay.	+	Com. Stk.	+	Ret. Earn.	Rev.	− Exp.	= Net Inc.	
Beg. bal.	9,000 +	0	=	0	+	5,000	+	4,000	0	− 0	= 0	0

b. Explain the difference between the amount of net income and amount of net cash flow from operating activities.

Exercise 3-2B *Supplies on financial statements*

LO 3-1

Janitorial Professionals Inc. experienced the following events in Year 1, its first year of operation:

1. Performed services for $20,000 cash.
2. Purchased $4,000 of supplies on account.
3. A physical count on December 31, Year 1, found that there were $1,000 of supplies on hand.

Required

Based on this information alone:

a. Record the events in accounts under an accounting equation.
b. Prepare an income statement, balance sheet, and statement of cash flows for the Year 1 accounting period.
c. What is the balance in the Supplies account as of January 1, Year 2?

Exercise 3-3B *Show how prepaid items affect a financial statements model*

LO 3-2

On March 1, Year 1, Windy Mill Co. paid $48,000 for 12 months rent on its factory. In addition, on September 1, Year 1, the company paid $18,000 for a one-year insurance policy on the factory.

Required

Show how both purchases and the associated end-of-period adjustments at the end of Year 1 will affect a financial statements model.

Exercise 3-4B *Prepaid items on financial statements*

LO 3-2

Forestry Services Inc. experienced the following events in Year 1, its first year of operation:

1. Performed counseling services for $18,000 cash.
2. On February 1, Year 1, paid $12,000 cash to rent office space for the coming year.
3. Adjusted the accounts to reflect the amount of rent used during the year.

Required

Based on this information alone:

a. Record the events in accounts under an accounting equation.
b. Prepare an income statement, balance sheet, and statement of cash flows for the Year 1 accounting period.
c. Ignoring all other future events, what is the amount of rent expense that would be recognized in Year 2?

LO 3-2

Exercise 3-5B   *Effect of an error on financial statements*

On June 1, Year 1, Ark Corporation paid $8,400 to purchase a 24-month insurance policy. Assume that Ark records the purchase as an asset and that the books are closed on December 31.

Required

a. Show the purchase of the insurance policy and the related end-of-period adjustment to recognize insurance expense in the accounting equation.

b. Assume that Ark Corporation failed to record the end-of-period adjustment to reflect the expiration of insurance. How would the error affect the company's Year 1 income statement and balance sheet?

LO 3-3

Exercise 3-6B   *Unearned revenue defined as a liability*

Jake Lewis received $800 in advance for tutoring fees when he agreed to help Laura Dalton with her introductory accounting course. Upon receiving the cash, Jake mentioned that he would have to record the transaction as a liability within his year-end financial statements. Laura asked, "Why a liability? You don't owe me any money, do you?"

Required

Respond to Laura's question regarding Jake's liability.

LO 3-3

Exercise 3-7B   *Unearned items on financial statements*

Interior Design Consultants (IDC) experienced the following events in Year 1, its first year of operation:

1. On October 1, Year 1, IDC collected $24,000 for consulting services it agreed to provide during the coming year.

2. Adjusted the accounts to reflect the amount of consulting service revenue recognized in Year 1.

Required

Based on this information alone:

a. Record the events under an accounting equation.

b. Prepare an income statement, balance sheet, and statement of cash flows for the Year 1 accounting period.

c. Ignoring all other future events, what is the amount of service revenue that would be recognized in Year 2?

LO 3-3

Exercise 3-8B   *Unearned revenue and the financial statements model*

Brandon Baily started a personal financial planning business when he accepted $120,000 cash as advance payment for managing the financial assets of a large estate. Baily agreed to manage the estate for a one-year period beginning May 1, Year 1.

Required

a. Show the effects of the advance payment and revenue recognition on the Year 1 financial statements using a horizontal statements model like the following one. In the Statement of Cash Flows column, use OA to designate operating activity, IA for investing activity, FA for financing activity, and NC for net change in cash. Use NA if the account is not affected.

Event	Balance Sheet						Income Statement					Statement of Cash Flows
	Assets	=	Liab.	+	Stk. Equity							
	Cash	=	Unearn. Rev.	+	Ret. Earn.		Rev.	−	Exp.	=	Net Inc.	

b. How much revenue would Baily recognize on the Year 2 income statement?

c. What is the amount of cash flow from operating activities in Year 2?

Exercise 3-9B *Supplies, unearned revenue, and the financial statements model*

Warren, Attorney at Law, experienced the following transactions in Year 1, the first year of operations:

1. Purchased $1,500 of office supplies on account.
2. Accepted $36,000 on February 1, Year 1, as a retainer for services to be performed evenly over the next 12 months.
3. Performed legal services for cash of $84,000.
4. Paid cash for salaries expense of $32,000.
5. Paid a cash dividend to the stockholders of $8,000.
6. Paid $1,200 of the amount due on accounts payable.
7. Determined that at the end of the accounting period, $150 of office supplies remained on hand.
8. On December 31, Year 1, recognized the revenue that had been earned for services performed in accordance with Transaction 2.

Required

Show the effects of the events on the financial statements using a horizontal statements model like the following one. In the Statement of Cash Flows column, use the initials OA to designate operating activity, IA for investing activity, FA for financing activity, and NC for net change in cash. Use NA to indicate accounts not affected by the event. The first event has been recorded as an example.

	Balance Sheet									Income Statement				Statement of Cash Flows
	Assets			=	Liabilities			+	Stk. Equity					
Event No.	Cash	+	Supplies	=	Accts. Pay.	+	Unearn. Rev.	+	Ret. Earn.	Rev.	−	Exp.	=	Net Inc.	
1.	NA	+	1,500	=	1,500	+	NA	+	NA	NA	−	NA	=	NA	NA

Exercise 3-10B *Prepaid vs. unearned: the entity concept*

On October 1, Year 1, Stokes Company paid Eastport Rentals $4,800 for a 12-month lease on warehouse space.

Required

a. Record the deferral and the related December 31, Year 1, adjustment for Stokes Company in the accounting equation.
b. Record the deferral and the related December 31, Year 1, adjustment for Eastport Rentals in the accounting equation.

Exercise 3-11B *Identifying deferral and accrual events*

Required

Identify each of the following events as an accrual, deferral, or neither:

a. Incurred other operating expenses on account.
b. Recorded expense for salaries owed to employees at the end of the accounting period.
c. Paid a cash dividend to the stockholders.
d. Paid cash to purchase supplies to be used over the next several months.
e. Paid cash to purchase land.
f. Provided services on account.
g. Collected accounts receivable.
h. Paid one year's rent in advance.
i. Paid cash for utilities expense.
j. Collected $2,400 in advance for services to be performed over the next 12 months.
k. Recognized revenue on account at the end of the period.

LO 3-1, 3-2, 3-3

Exercise 3-12B *Adjusting the accounts*

Patal Inc. experienced the following accounting events during its Year 1 accounting period:

1. Paid cash to settle an account payable.
2. Collected a cash advance for services that will be provided during the coming year.
3. Paid a cash dividend to the stockholders.
4. Paid cash for a one-year lease to rent office space.
5. Collected cash from accounts receivable.
6. Recognized cash revenue.
7. Issued common stock.
8. Paid cash to purchase land.
9. Paid cash to purchase supplies.
10. Recognized operating expenses on account.

Required

Identify the events that would require an end-of-period adjustment.

LO 3-1, 3-2, 3-3

Exercise 3-13B *Classifying events on the statement of cash flows*

The following transactions pertain to the operations of Blair Company for Year 1:

1. Acquired $30,000 cash from the issue of common stock.
2. Performed services for $12,000 cash.
3. Paid a $7,200 cash advance for a one-year contract to rent equipment.
4. Recognized $15,000 of accrued salary expense.
5. Accepted a $21,000 cash advance for services to be performed in the future.
6. Provided $60,000 of services on account.
7. Incurred $28,000 of other operating expenses on account.
8. Collected $51,000 cash from accounts receivable.
9. Paid a $5,000 cash dividend to the stockholders.
10. Paid $22,000 cash on accounts payable.

Required

a. Classify the cash flows from these transactions as operating activities (OA), investing activities (IA), or financing activities (FA). Use NA for transactions that do not affect the statement of cash flows.

b. Prepare a statement of cash flows. (There is no beginning cash balance.)

LO 3-1, 3-2, 3-3

Exercise 3-14B *Effect of accounting events on the income statement and statement of cash flows*

Required

Explain how each of the following events or series of events and the related adjustments will affect the amount of *net income* and the amount of *cash flow from operating activities* reported on the year-end financial statements. Identify the direction of change (increase, decrease, or NA) and the amount of the change. Organize your answers according to the following table. The first event is recorded as an example. If an event does not have a related adjustment, record only the effects of the event.

	Net Income		Cash Flows from Operating Activities	
Event	Direction of Change	Amount of Change	Direction of Change	Amount of Change
a	NA	NA	NA	NA

a. Acquired $60,000 cash from the issue of common stock.

b. Earned $20,000 of revenue on account. Collected $15,000 cash from accounts receivable.

c. Paid $4,800 cash on October 1 to purchase a one-year insurance policy.

d. Collected $12,000 in advance for services to be performed in the future. The contract called for services to start on August 1 and to continue for one year.

e. Accrued salaries amounting to $5,000.

f. Sold land that cost $15,000 for $15,000 cash.

g. Provided services for $9,200 cash.

h. Purchased $2,000 of supplies on account. Paid $1,500 cash on accounts payable. The ending balance in the Supplies account, after adjustment, was $800.

i. Paid cash for other operating expenses of $2,200.

Exercise 3-15B *Distinguishing between an expense and a cost*   LO 3-1, 3-2, 3-5

A cost can be either an asset or an expense.

Required

a. Distinguish between a cost that is an asset and a cost that is an expense.

b. List three costs that are assets.

c. List three costs that are expenses.

Exercise 3-16B *Revenue and expense recognition*   LO 3-1, 3-2, 3-3, 3-5

Required

a. Describe an end-of-period adjustment that results in a decrease in liabilities.

b. Describe an end-of-period adjustment that reduces the book value of a long-term asset.

c. Describe an end-of-period adjustment that results in a decrease in assets.

d. Describe an end-of-period adjustment that results in an increase in liabilities.

Exercise 3-17B *Relationship of accounts to financial statements*   LO 3-4

Required

Identify whether each of the following items would appear on the income statement (IS), statement of changes in stockholders' equity (SE), balance sheet (BS), or statement of cash flows (CF). Some items may appear on more than one statement; if so, identify all applicable statements. If an item would not appear on any financial statement, label it NA.

a. Consulting Revenue

b. Market Value of Land

c. Supplies Expense

d. Salaries Payable

e. Notes Payable

f. Ending Common Stock

g. Beginning Cash Balance

h. Prepaid Rent

i. Net Change in Cash

j. Land

k. Operating Expenses

l. Total Liabilities

m. "As of" Date Notation

n. Salaries Expense

o. Net Income

p. Service Revenue

q. Cash Flow from Operating Activities

r. Rent Expense

s. Salary Expense

t. Total Stockholders' Equity

u. Unearned Revenue

v. Cash Flow from Investing Activities

w. Insurance Expense

x. Ending Retained Earnings

y. Interest Revenue

z. Supplies

aa. Beginning Retained Earnings

bb. Utilities Payable

cc. Cash Flow from Financing Activities

dd. Accounts Receivable

ee. Prepaid Insurance

ff. Ending Cash Balance

gg. Utilities Expense

hh. Accounts Payable

ii. Beginning Common Stock

jj. Dividends declared and paid

kk. Total Assets

LO 3-1, 3-2, 3-3, 3-5

Exercise 3-18B   *Recording events into a horizontal statements model*

The following is a partial list of transactions FRC Company experienced during its Year 4 accounting period:

1. Collected cash for services to be performed in the future.
2. Paid cash to purchase supplies.
3. Paid cash to purchase a long-term depreciable asset.
4. Paid cash to purchase insurance coverage for the coming year.

Required

Assume that each of the events requires an end-of-period adjustment. Use a horizontal financial statements model to show how the adjustments affect the financial statements. Use increase (I) and decrease (D) to indicate how the adjustment affects each part of the horizontal financial statements model. Use the letters NA to indicate that a part of the model is not affected by the adjustment. In the Statement of Cash Flows column, indicate whether cash increase (I) decreases (D), or is not affected (NA). Also, indicate whether the cash flow was caused by an operating activity (OA), an investing activity (IA), or financing activity (FA).

Balance Sheet					Income Statement					Statement of Cash Flows
Assets	=	Liab.	+	Stk. Equity	Rev.	−	Exp.	=	Net Inc.	
+ −	=	NA	+	NA	NA	−	NA	=	NA	− OA

LO 3-1, 3-2, 3-3, 3-5

Exercise 3-19B   *Determining the impact of events on financial statements*

Required

Indicate whether each of the following statements is true or false.

a. Prepaid rent appears on the balance sheet.
b. The book value of a long-term asset appears on the statement of changes in stockholders' equity.
c. Supplies expense appears on the statement of cash flows.
d. Net income appears on the income statement and the statement of changes in stockholders' equity.
e. Depreciation expense appears on the income statement and in the operating activities section of the statement of cash flows.
f. Accrued salaries payable appears on the balance sheet.
g. The amount of accumulated depreciation is added to the corresponding asset account in order to determine the book value of the asset.
h. The unearned revenue account appears on the income statement.
i. Depreciation expense reduces net income but has no effect on the statement of cash flows.
j. A decrease in unearned revenue is normally offset by an increase in retained earnings.
k. Dividends are deferrals because they delay the recognition of expenses.

LO 3-5

Exercise 3-20B   *Relationship between depreciation and the financial statements*

On January 1, Year 2, KimCom Boat Rentals purchased a boat that is to be used to produce rental income. The boat cost $120,000. It has an expected useful life of 10 years and a $20,000 salvage value. The boat produced rental income of $15,000 per year throughout its useful life. Assume that KimCom started Year 2 with a beginning cash balance of $130,000.

Required

a. Prepare an income statement and a statement of cash flows for Year 2, Year 3, and Year 4.
b. Determine the book value of the boat for Year 2, Year 3, and Year 4.

Exercise 3-21B *Identifying transaction type and effect on the financial statements*   LO 3-1, 3-2, 3-3

Required

Identify whether each of the following transactions is an asset source (AS), asset use (AU), asset exchange (AE), or claims exchange (CE). Also, show the effects of the events on the financial statements using the horizontal statements model. Indicate whether the event increases (I), decreases (D), or does not affect (NA) each part of the financial statements model. In the Statement of Cash Flows column, designate the cash flows as operating activities (OA), investing activities (IA), or financing activities (FA). The first two transactions have been recorded as examples.

Event	Type of Event	Balance Sheet					Income Statement			Statement of Cash Flows
		Assets	= Liabilities	+ C. Stk.	+	R. Earn.	Rev. −	Exp. =	Net Inc.	
a.	AE	I/D	NA	NA		NA	NA	NA	NA	D IA
b.	AS	I	NA	I		NA	NA	NA	NA	I FA

a. Purchased land for cash.

b. Acquired cash from the issue of common stock.

c. Collected cash from accounts receivable.

d. Paid cash for operating expenses.

e. Recorded accrued salaries.

f. Purchased supplies on account.

g. Performed services on account.

h. Paid cash in advance for rent on office space.

i. Adjusted the books to record supplies used during the period.

j. Performed services for cash.

k. Paid cash for salaries accrued at the end of a prior period.

l. Paid a cash dividend to the stockholders.

m. Adjusted books to reflect the amount of prepaid rent expired during the period.

n. Incurred operating expenses on account.

o. Paid cash on accounts payable.

p. Received cash advance for services to be provided in the future.

q. Recognized revenue on account at the end of the accounting period.

Exercise 3-22B *Effect of depreciation on the accounting equation and financial statements*   LO 3-5

The following events apply to Highland Grill for the Year 1 fiscal year:

1. Started the company when it acquired $40,000 cash by issuing common stock.

2. Purchased a new stove that cost $24,000 cash.

3. Earned $21,000 in cash revenue.

4. Paid $3,500 of cash for salaries expense.

5. Adjusted the records to reflect the use of the stove. Purchased on January 1, Year 1, the stove has an expected useful life of four years and an estimated salvage value of $4,000. Use straight-line depreciation. The adjustment was made as of December 31, Year 1.

Required

a. Record the events in accounts under an accounting equation.

b. Prepare a balance sheet and a statement of cash flows for the Year 1 accounting period.

c. What is the net income for Year 1?

d. What is the amount of depreciation expense Highland Grill would report on the Year 2 income statement?

e. What amount of accumulated depreciation would Highland Grill report on the December 31, Year 2, balance sheet?

f. Would the cash flow from operating activities be affected by depreciation in Year 2?

LO 3-5

Exercise 3-23B   *Depreciation affecting multiple cycles*

On January 1, Year 1, Yallow Cab Inc. paid $29,000 cash to purchase a taxi cab. The taxi had a three-year useful life and a $5,000 salvage value.

Required

a. Determine the amount of depreciation expense that would appear on the Year 1 and Year 2 income statements.

b. Determine the amount of accumulated depreciation that would appear on the Year 1 and Year 2 balance sheets.

c. Explain how the purchase of equipment would affect the Year 1 and Year 2 statements of cash flows.

LO 3-6

Exercise 3-24B   *Using ratio analysis to assess financial risk*

The following information was drawn from the balance sheets of two companies:

Company	Assets	=	Liabilities	+	Stockholders' Equity
North	100,000	=	24,500	+	75,500
South	500,000	=	220,000	+	280,000

Required

a. Compute the debt-to-assets ratio to measure the level of financial risk of both companies.

b. Compare the two ratios computed in Requirement *a* to identify which company has the higher level of financial risk.

LO 3-6

Exercise 3-25B   *Using ratio analysis to assess return on equity*

The following information was drawn from the Year 3 balance sheets of two companies:

Company	Assets	=	Liabilities	+	Common Stock	+	Retained Earnings
Williamson	550,000	=	300,000	+	180,000	+	70,000
Hendrix	680,000	=	120,000	+	120,000	+	440,000

During Year 3, Williamson's net income was $35,800, while Hendrix's net income was $22,900.

Required

a. Compute the return-on-equity ratio to measure the level of financial risk of both companies.

b. Compare the two ratios computed in Requirement *a* to identify which company is performing better.

PROBLEMS—SERIES B

Problem 3-26B   *Effect of end-of-period adjustments on the accounting equation*

LO 3-1, 3-2, 3-3

Required

Each of the following independent events requires an end-of-period adjustment. Show how each event and its related adjustment affect the accounting equation. Assume the fiscal year ends December 31. The first event is recorded as an example.

CHECK FIGURE
b. Adjustment amount:
   $2,200

	Total Assets			Stockholders' Equity	
Event/		Other		Common	Retained
Adjustment	Cash +	Assets =	Liabilities +	Stock +	Earnings
a	−6,000	+6,000	NA	NA	NA
Adj.	NA	−4,500	NA	NA	−4,500

a. Paid $6,000 cash in advance on April 1 for a one-year insurance policy.
b. Purchased $2,400 of supplies on account. At year's end, $200 of supplies remained on hand.
c. Paid $7,200 cash in advance on March 1 for a one-year lease on office space.
d. Received an $18,000 cash advance for a contract to provide services in the future. The contract required a one-year commitment starting September 1.

Problem 3-27B   *Effect of events on financial statements*

LO 3-1, 3-2, 3-3

Gossett Company had the following beginning balances in its accounting records as of January 1, Year 1:

Assets		Liabilities and Stk. Equity	
Cash	$ 60,000	Accounts Payable	$ 32,000
Accounts Receivable	45,000	Common Stock	60,000
Land	35,000	Retained Earnings	48,000
Totals	$140,000		$140,000

The following accounting events apply to Gossett for Year 1:

Jan. 1   Acquired an additional $30,000 cash from the issue of common stock.
April 1   Paid $7,200 cash in advance for a one-year lease for office space.
June 1   Paid a $5,000 cash dividend to the stockholders.
July 1   Purchased additional land that cost $40,000 cash.
Aug. 1   Made a cash payment on accounts payable of $21,000.
Sept. 1   Received $9,600 cash in advance as a retainer for services to be performed monthly during the next eight months.
Sept. 30 Sold land for $20,000 cash that had originally cost $20,000.
Oct. 1   Purchased $1,200 of supplies on account.
Dec. 31   Earned $75,000 of service revenue on account during the year.
   31   Received $62,000 cash collections from accounts receivable.
   31   Incurred $27,000 in other operating expenses on account during the year.
   31   Recognized accrued salaries expense of $18,000.
   31   Had $100 of supplies on hand at the end of the period.
   31   The land purchased on July 1 had a market value of $56,000.

Required

Based on the preceding information for Gossett Company, answer the following questions. All questions pertain to the Year 1 financial statements. (*Hint:* Record the events in accounts under an accounting equation before answering the questions.)

a. What amount would be reported for land on the balance sheet?
b. What amount of net cash flow from operating activities would be reported on the statement of cash flows?

c. What amount of rent expense would be reported on the income statement?

d. What amount of total liabilities would be reported on the balance sheet?

e. What amount of supplies expense would be reported on the income statement?

f. What amount of unearned revenue would be reported on the balance sheet?

g. What amount of net cash flow from investing activities would be reported on the statement of cash flows?

h. What amount of total expenses would be reported on the income statement?

i. What total amount of service revenue would be reported on the income statement?

j. What amount of cash flows from financing activities would be reported on the statement of cash flows?

k. What amount of net income would be reported on the income statement?

l. What amount of retained earnings would be reported on the balance sheet?

LO 3-2, 3-3

Problem 3-28B *Show how the events affect the financial statements using a horizontal statements model*

The following events pertain to Weaver Cleaning Company:

1. Acquired $15,000 cash from the issue of common stock.
2. Provided services for $6,000 cash.
3. Provided $18,000 of services on account.
4. Collected $11,000 cash from the account receivable created in Event 3.
5. Paid $1,400 cash to purchase supplies.
6. Had $100 of supplies on hand at the end of the accounting period.
7. Received $3,600 cash in advance for services to be performed in the future.
8. Performed one-half of the services agreed to in Event 7.
9. Paid $6,500 for salaries expense.
10. Incurred $2,800 of other operating expenses on account.
11. Paid $2,100 cash on the account payable created in Event 10.
12. Paid a $1,000 cash dividend to the stockholders.

Required

Show the effects of the events on the financial statements using a horizontal statements model like the following one. In the Statement of Cash Flows column, use the letters OA to designate operating activity, IA for investing activity, FA for financing activity, and NC for net change in cash. Use NA to indicate accounts not affected by the event. The first event is recorded as an example.

	Balance Sheet							Income Statement			Statement of Cash Flows
	Assets			=	Liabilities	+	Stk. Equity				
Event No.	Cash +	Accts. Rec. +	Supp. =	Accts. Pay. +	Unearn. Rev. +		Com. Stk. +	Ret. Earn.	Rev. − Exp. = Net Inc.			
1.	15,000 +	NA +	NA =	NA +	NA	+	15,000 +	NA	NA − NA = NA			15,000 FA

LO 3-4

Problem 3-29B *Relating titles and accounts to financial statements*

Required

Identify the financial statements on which each of the following items (titles, date descriptions, and accounts) appears by placing a check mark in the appropriate column. If an item appears on more than one statement, place a check mark in every applicable column.

Item	Income Statement	Statement of Changes in Stockholders' Equity	Balance Sheet	Statement of Cash Flows
Interest expense				
Net income				
Ending common stock				
Net loss				
Accounts receivable				
For the period ended (date)				
As of (date)				
Notes payable				
Stock issue				
Financing activities				
Utility expense				
Accounts payable				
Beginning common stock				
Unearned revenue				
Investing activities				
Supplies				
Ending cash balance				
Salary expense				
Consulting revenue				
Dividends				
Service revenue				
Land				
Prepaid Insurance				
Operating activities				
Beginning cash balance				

Problem 3-30B   *Identifying and arranging components of financial statements*   LO 3-4

The following accounts and balances were drawn from the records of Shearer Company at December 31, Year 2:

Cash	$22,100	Accounts receivable	$21,000
Land	43,000	Cash flow from operating act.	8,600
Insurance expense	2,500	Beginning retained earnings	47,200
Dividends	5,000	Beginning common stock	5,500
Prepaid insurance	3,500	Service revenue	86,000
Accounts payable	15,000	Cash flow from financing act.	9,000
Supplies	2,100	Ending common stock	14,500
Supplies expense	1,000	Cash flow from investing act.	(6,000)
Rent expense	3,500	Other operating expenses	59,000

Required

Use the accounts and balances from Shearer Company to construct an income statement, statement of changes in stockholders' equity, balance sheet, and statement of cash flows (show only totals for each activity on the statement of cash flows).

LO 3-1, 3-2, 3-3

Problem 3-31B *Events for two complete accounting cycles*

Iowa Service Company was formed on January 1, Year 1.

Events Affecting the Year 1 Accounting Period

1. Acquired cash of $60,000 from the issue of common stock.
2. Purchased $1,200 of supplies on account.
3. Purchased land that cost $18,000 cash.
4. Paid $800 cash to settle accounts payable created in Event 2.
5. Recognized revenue on account of $42,000.
6. Paid $21,000 cash for other operating expenses.
7. Collected $38,000 cash from accounts receivable.

Information for Year 1 End-of-Period Adjustments

8. Recognized accrued salaries of $3,200 on December 31, Year 1.
9. Had $200 of supplies on hand at the end of the accounting period.

Events Affecting the Year 2 Accounting Period

1. Acquired an additional $20,000 cash from the issue of common stock.
2. Paid $3,200 cash to settle the salaries payable obligation.
3. Paid $3,600 cash in advance for a lease on office facilities.
4. Sold land that had cost $15,000 for $15,000 cash.
5. Received $4,800 cash in advance for services to be performed in the future.
6. Purchased $1,000 of supplies on account during the year.
7. Provided services on account of $32,000.
8. Collected $33,000 cash from accounts receivable.
9. Paid a cash dividend of $5,000 to the stockholders.
10. Paid other operating expenses of $19,500.

Information for Year 2 End-of-Period Adjustments

11. The advance payment for rental of the office facilities (see Event 3) was made on March 1 for a one-year lease term.
12. The cash advance for services to be provided in the future was collected on October 1 (see Event 5). The one-year contract started October 1.
13. Had $300 of supplies on hand at the end of the period.
14. Recognized accrued salaries of $3,900 at the end of the accounting period.

Required

a. Identify each event affecting the Year 1 and Year 2 accounting periods as asset source (AS), asset use (AU), asset exchange (AE), or claims exchange (CE). Record the effects of each event under the appropriate account headings of the accounting equation.
b. Prepare an income statement, statement of changes in stockholders' equity, balance sheet, and statement of cash flows for Year 1 and Year 2.

LO 3-5

Problem 3-32B *Effect of depreciation on financial statements*

On January 1, Year 4, Franklin Company paid $200,000 cash to purchase a new theme ride. The ride has a $5,000 salvage value and a six-year useful life. Assume that Franklin earns $70,000 of cash revenue per year for Year 4 through Year 10 of the asset's useful life. Franklin Company began its Year 4 accounting period with a beginning cash balance of $150,000.

Required

a. Determine the amount of net income for Year 4, Year 5, and Year 6.

b. Determine the amount of accumulated depreciation appearing on the Year 4, Year 5, and Year 6 balance sheet.

c. Determine the book value of the theme ride as of December 31, Year 4, Year 5, and Year 6.

d. Determine the cash flows shown on the statement of cash flows for Year 4, Year 5, and Year 6. For each cash flow item, indicate whether it is a cash inflow or cash outflow, and whether the item would be shown in the financing, investing, or operating sections of the cash flow statement.

Problem 3-33B   *Effect of events on financial statements*   LO 3-1, 3-2, 3-3, 3-5

Oaks Company had the following balances in its accounting records as of December 31, Year 1:

Assets		Claims	
Cash	$ 61,000	Accounts payable	$ 25,000
Accounts receivable	45,000	Common stock	90,000
Land	27,000	Retained earnings	18,000
Totals	$133,000		$133,000

The following accounting events apply to Oaks's Year 2 fiscal year:

Jan. 1	Acquired an additional $70,000 cash from the issue of common stock.
1	Purchased a delivery van that cost $26,000 and that had a $7,000 salvage value and a five-year useful life.
Mar. 1	Borrowed $21,000 by issuing a note that had an 8 percent annual interest rate and a one-year term.
April 1	Paid $6,600 cash in advance for a one-year lease for office space.
June 1	Paid a $3,000 cash dividend to the stockholders.
July 1	Purchased land that cost $25,000 cash.
Aug. 1	Made a cash payment on accounts payable of $13,000.
Sept. 1	Received $8,400 cash in advance as a retainer for services to be performed monthly during the next eight months.
Oct. 1	Purchased $900 of supplies on account.
Dec. 31	Earned $80,000 of service revenue on account during the year.
31	Received $56,000 cash collections from accounts receivable.
31	Incurred $16,000 in other operating expenses on account during the year.
31	Incurred accrued salaries expense of $5,000.
31	Had $250 of supplies on hand at the end of the period.

Required

Based on the preceding information, answer the following questions. All questions pertain to the Year 2 financial statements. (*Hint:* Record the events in accounts under an accounting equation before answering the questions.)

a. What additional four end-of-period adjustments are required at the end of the year?

b. What amount of interest expense would Oaks report on the income statement?

c. What amount of net cash flow from operating activities would Oaks report on the statement of cash flows?

d. What amount of rent expense would Oaks report on the income statement?

e. What amount of total liabilities would Oaks report on the balance sheet?

f. What amount of supplies expense would Oaks report on the income statement?

g. What amount of unearned revenue would Oaks report on the balance sheet?

h. What amount of net cash flow from investing activities would Oaks report on the statement of cash flows?

i. What amount of interest payable would Oaks report on the balance sheet?

j. What amount of total expenses would Oaks report on the income statement?

k. What amount of retained earnings would Oaks report on the balance sheet?

l. What total amount of service revenues would Oaks report on the income statement?

m. What amount of cash flows from financing activities would Oaks report on the statement of cash flows?

n. What amount of net income would Oaks report on the income statement?

LO 3-6

Problem 3-34B   *Using ratio analysis to assess return on equity*

The following information was drawn from the Year 5 balance sheets of two companies:

Company	Assets	=	Liabilities	+	Common Stock	+	Retained Earnings
Steelman	720,000	=	400,000	+	200,000	+	120,000
Bingum	450,000	=	125,000	+	180,000	+	145,000

During Year 5, Steelman's net income was $45,800, while Bingum's net income was $22,300.

Required

a. Compute the debt-to-assets ratio to measure the level of financial risk of both companies.

b. Compare the two ratios computed in Requirement *a* to identify which company has the higher level of financial risk.

c. Compute the return-on-equity ratio to measure the level of financial risk of both companies.

d. Compare the two ratios computed in Requirement *a* to identify which company is performing better.

e. Define the term *financial leverage*.

f. Identify the company that is using financial leverage to a greater extent.

ANALYZE, THINK, COMMUNICATE

ATC 3-1   Business Applications Case   *Understanding real-world annual reports*

Required

Obtain Target Corporation's annual report for its 2018 fiscal year (year ended February 2, 2019) at http://investors.target.com using the instructions in Appendix B, and use it to answer the following questions:

a. What was Target's debt-to-assets ratio for its fiscal year ended February 2, 2019 (2018) and 2017?

b. What was Target's return-on-assets ratio for 2018 and 2017?

c. What was Target's return-on-equity ratio for 2018 and 2017?

d. Why was Target's return-on-equity ratio higher than its return-on-assets ratio for 2018 and 2017?

ATC 3-2   Group Assignment   *Missing information*

On January 1, Year 1, three companies purchased the same make and model copy machine. However, each company made different assumptions regarding the useful life and salvage value of its particular asset.

	Company A	Company B	Company C
Cost of copy machine	$45,000	$45,000	$45,000
Salvage value	5,000	5,000	10,000
Useful life	5 years	4 years	4 years

Required

a. Divide the class into groups of four or five students. Organize the groups into two sections. Assign one section of groups the copy machine data for Company A and Company B. Assign the other group the copy machine data for Company B and Company C.

Group Tasks

(1) Determine the amount of depreciation expense that each company will recognize on its Year 1 and Year 2 income statement.

(2) Determine the book value of the copy machine for each company as of December 31, Year 1 and Year 2.

(3) Have students in section one and two identify the company with the lowest depreciation expense and then explain why that company's depreciation is lower. Have students in section three and four identify the company with the copy machine that has the highest book value, and then explain why that company's book value is higher.

Class Discussion

b. Have the class discuss how managers can use salvage value and useful life to manipulate financial statement results.

ATC 3-3 Real-World Case *Performing ratio analysis using real-world data*

The following data were taken from Netflix, Inc.'s 2017 annual report. *All dollar amounts are in millions.*

	Fiscal Years Ending	
	December 31, 2017	December 31, 2016
Total assets	$19,013	$13,587
Total liabilities		
Stockholders' equity	3,582	2,680
Net income	559	187

Required

a. For each year, compute Netflix's debt-to-assets ratio, return-on-assets ratio, and return-on-equity ratio. You will need to compute total liabilities.

b. Did the company's level of financial risk increase or decrease from 2016 to 2017?

c. In which year did the company appear to manage its assets most efficiently?

d. Do the preceding ratios support the concept of financial leverage? Explain.

ATC 3-4 Business Applications *Performing ratio analysis using real-world data from two real-world companies*

The following data were taken from the 2017 annual reports of Biogen Idec, Inc. and Amgen, Inc. Both companies are leaders in biotechnology. *All dollar amounts are in millions.*

	Biogen Idec	Amgen
	December 31, 2017	December 31, 2017
Total assets	$23,652.6	$79,954
Total liabilities	11,054.5	54,713
Stockholders' equity	12,598.1	25,241
Net income	2,670.1	1,979

Required

a. For each company, compute the debt-to-assets ratio, return-on-assets ratio, and return-on-equity ratio.

b. Which company has the greatest level of financial risk? Explain.

c. Which company appears to have managed its assets most efficiently? Explain.

d. Which company performed better from the perspective of the owners? Explain.

ATC 3-5 Writing Assignment *How do deferrals affect net income versus cash flow?*

The following scenarios are independent of each other.

1. During Year 1, a company pays $3,000 cash to purchase supplies. There are $1,000 of supplies on hand at the end of Year 1.

2. On April 1, Year 1, a company pays $4,000 for a one-year insurance policy.

3. On October 1, Year 1, a company collects $12,000 in advance for services that will be performed over the next year.

4. On January 1, Year 1, a company pays $16,000 to purchase a long-term asset. The asset has a $4,000 salvage value and a three-year useful life.

Required

For each scenario, write a brief memo explaining why amounts recognized in the income statement will be different from amounts shown in the operating section of the cash flow statement for Year 1.

ATC 3-6 Ethical Dilemma *What is a little deceit among friends?*

Saul Sellers is the Chief Accountant for Bright Day Cafe (BDC) and is close to retirement. Traditionally, BDC provides a retirement plan that pays a bonus equal to 10 percent of the net income the restaurant reports in the year of retirement. BDC has just undertaken a remodeling project that involved the purchase of a significant amount of long-term assets. Saul is concerned that the depreciation associated with the new assets will reduce the company's income, thereby reducing his retirement bonus. Saul's friend, William, tells him to reduce the impact on income by adjusting the estimates of the useful lives and salvage values of the new assets. Saul knows he has the ability to manipulate the company's income, but is concerned that intentionally misrepresenting the useful life and salvage value is at best unethical and may even be illegal. Even so, he believes it is unfair for his retirement to be diminished simply because the restaurant has decided to remodel in the year he retires.

Required

a. How will net income be affected if Saul overstates the useful life of the asset?

b. How will net income be affected if Saul understates the useful life of the asset?

c. How will net income be affected if Saul overstates the salvage value of the asset?

d. How will net income be affected if Saul understates the salvage value of the asset?

e. Deliberately misrepresenting the useful life or salvage value would violate which provisions of the Code of Professional Conduct (summarized in Exhibit 2.7)?

f. Comment on how Saul's decision could be influenced by the components of the fraud triangle. (It will be helpful to review the Chapter 2 content on the fraud triangle.)

g. What is the maximum criminal penalty required if Saul falsely certifies the company's financial reports? (Reviewing the content in Chapter 2 pertaining to the Sarbanes–Oxley Act will help answer the question.)

ATC 3-7 Research Assignment *Investigating Nike's 10-K report*

A great number of companies must file financial reports with the SEC, and many of these reports are available electronically through the EDGAR database. EDGAR is an acronym for Electronic Data Gathering, Analysis, and Retrieval system, and its database is accessible via the Internet. Instructions for utilizing EDGAR are described in Appendix A.

Answer the following questions about Nike Company using its most current 10-K available on EDGAR or on the company's website at investors.nike.com:

a. In what year did Nike begin operations?

b. Other than the Nike brand, what business does Nike operate?

c. How many employees does Nike have?

d. Describe, in dollar amounts, Nike's accounting equation at the end of the most recent year.

e. Has Nike's performance been improving or deteriorating over the past three years? Explain your answer.

CHAPTER 4

Accounting for Merchandising Businesses

LEARNING OBJECTIVES

After you have mastered the material in this chapter, you will be able to:

Video lectures and accompanying self-assessment quizzes are available in *Connect* for all learning objectives.

Tableau Dashboard Activity is available in *Connect* for this chapter.

LO 4-1	Record and report on inventory transactions using the perpetual system.
LO 4-2	Show how purchase returns and allowances affect financial statements.
LO 4-3	Show how cash discounts affect financial statements.
LO 4-4	Show how transportation costs affect financial statements.
LO 4-5	Show how inventory shrinkage affects financial statements.
LO 4-6	Calculate gains and losses and show how they are presented on a multistep income statement.
LO 4-7	Determine the amount of net sales.
LO 4-8	Use common size financial statements and ratio analysis to evaluate managerial performance.

APPENDIX

LO 4-9	Identify the primary features of the periodic inventory system.

CHAPTER OPENING

Previous chapters have discussed accounting for service businesses. These businesses obtain revenue by providing some kind of service, such as medical or legal advice, to their customers. Other examples of service companies include dry cleaning companies, housekeeping companies, and car washes. This chapter introduces accounting for merchandising businesses. **Merchandising businesses** generate revenue by selling goods. They buy the merchandise they sell from companies called suppliers. The goods purchased for resale are called **merchandise inventory.** Merchandising businesses include **retail companies** (companies that sell goods to the final consumer) and **wholesale companies** (companies that sell to other businesses). Costco, JCPenney, Target, and Sam's Club are real-world merchandising businesses.

The Curious Accountant

Sergey Tikhomirov/123RF

Katie recently purchased a new Ford automobile from a dealer near her home. When she told her friend George that she was able to purchase the car for $1,000 less than the sticker price, George told Katie she had gotten a lousy deal. "Everybody knows there's a huge markup on cars," George said. "You could have gotten a much lower price if you'd shopped around."

Katie responded, "If there's such a big profit margin on cars, why did so many of the car manufacturers get into financial trouble?" George told her that she was confusing the maker of the car with the dealer. George argued that although the manufacturers may not have high profit margins, the dealers do, and told her again that she had paid too much.

Exhibit 4.1 presents the income statements for **AutoNation, Inc.** and **Ford Motor Company**. Based on these statements, do you think either of these friends is correct? For example, if you pay $20,000 for a vehicle from a dealership operated by AutoNation, the largest auto retailer in the United States, how much did the car cost the company? Also, how much did the car cost the Ford Motor Company to manufacture? (Answers on page 205.)

| EXHIBIT 4.1 | Comparative Income Statements |

AUTONATION, INC.
Consolidated Statements of Income (Partial)
For the Years Ended December 31
(In millions, except per share data)

	2017	2016	2015
Revenue:			
New vehicle	$12,180.8	$12,255.8	$ 11,995.0
Used vehicle	4,878.4	4,995.3	4,768.7
Parts and service	3,398.3	3,321.4	3,082.8
Finance and insurance, net	939.2	894.6	868.7
Other	137.9	141.9	146.8
Total revenue	21,534.6	21,609.0	20,862.0
Cost of Sales:			
New vehicle	11,592.4	11,620.0	11,321.9
Used vehicle	4,563.2	4,677.7	4,415.0
Parts and service	1,907.6	1,886.7	1,744.8
Other	112.4	111.4	118.8
Total cost of sales	18,175.6	18,295.8	17,600.5
Gross Profit:			
New vehicle	588.4	635.8	673.1
Used vehicle	315.2	317.6	353.7
Parts and service	1,490.7	1,434.7	1,338.0
Finance and insurance	939.2	894.6	868.7
Other	25.5	30.5	28.0
Total gross profit	3,359.0	3,313.2	3,261.5
Selling, general & administrative expenses	2,436.2	2,349.4	2,263.5
Depreciation and amortization	158.6	143.4	127.4
Franchise rights impairment	—	—	15.4
Other expenses (income), net	(79.2)	(69.1)	(17.9)
Operating income	843.4	889.5	873.1
Non-operating income (expense) items:			
Floorplan interest expense	(97.0)	(76.5)	(58.3)
Other interest expense	(120.2)	(115.5)	(90.9)
Interest income	1.0	1.1	0.1
Other income (losses), net	9.3	3.7	(1.3)
Income (loss) from continuing operations before income taxes	636.5	702.3	722.7
Income tax provision	201.5	270.6	279.0
Net income from continuing operations	435.0	431.7	443.7
Loss from discontinued operations, net of income taxes	(0.4)	(1.2)	(1.1)
Net income	$ 434.6	$ 430.5	$ 442.6

continued

EXHIBIT 4.1 *Concluded*

FORD MOTOR COMPANY AND SUBSIDIARIES
Consolidated Income Statements (Partial)
For the Years Ended December 31
(In millions except per share amounts)

	2017	2016	2015
Sales and revenues			
Automotive sales	$145,653	$141,546	$ 140,566
Financial Services revenues	11,113	10,253	8,992
Other	10	1	—
Total sales and revenues	156,776	151,800	149,558
Costs and expenses			
Cost of sales	131,332	126,183	124,446
Selling, administrative and other expenses	11,527	10,972	10,763
Financial Services interest, operating, and other services	9,104	8,904	7,368
Total costs and expenses	151,963	146,059	142,577
Interest expense on Automotive debt	1,133	894	773
Non–Financial Services interest income and other income (loss), net	3,060	(269)	1,854
Financial Services other income/(loss), net	207	438	372
Equity in income of affiliated companies	1,201	1,780	1,818
Income before income taxes	8,148	6,796	10,252
Provision for/(Benefit from) income taxes	520	2,189	2,881
Net income	7,628	4,607	7,371
Less: Income/(Loss) attributable to noncontrolling interests	26	11	(2)
Net income attributable to Ford Motor Company	$ 7,602	$ 4,596	$ 7,373

ACCOUNTING FOR INVENTORY TRANSACTIONS

Companies report inventory costs on the balance sheet in the asset account Merchandise Inventory. All costs incurred to acquire merchandise and ready it for sale are included in the inventory account. Examples of inventory costs include the price of goods purchased, shipping and handling costs, transit insurance, and storage costs. Because inventory items are referred to as products, inventory costs are frequently called **product costs.**

Costs that are not included in inventory are usually called **selling and administrative costs.** Examples of selling and administrative costs include advertising, administrative salaries, sales commissions, and insurance. Because selling and administrative costs are usually recognized as expenses *in the period* in which they are incurred, they are sometimes called **period costs.** In contrast, product costs are expensed when inventory is sold, regardless of when it was purchased. In other words, product costs are matched directly with sales revenue, while selling and administrative costs are matched with the period in which they are incurred.

LO 4-1

 Record and report on inventory transactions using the perpetual system.

Allocating Inventory Cost between Asset and Expense Accounts

The cost of inventory that is available for sale during a specific accounting period is determined as follows:

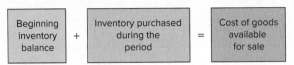

| Beginning inventory balance | + | Inventory purchased during the period | = | Cost of goods available for sale |

The **cost of goods available for sale** is allocated between the asset account Merchandise Inventory and an expense account called **Cost of Goods Sold.** The cost of inventory items that have not been sold (Merchandise Inventory) is reported as an asset on the balance sheet, and the cost of the items sold (Cost of Goods Sold) is expensed on the income statement. This allocation is depicted graphically as follows.

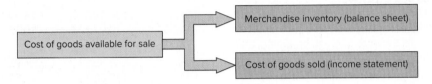

Cost of goods available for sale → Merchandise inventory (balance sheet)
Cost of goods available for sale → Cost of goods sold (income statement)

The difference between the sales revenue and the cost of goods sold is called **gross margin or gross profit.** The selling and administrative expenses (period costs) are subtracted from gross margin to obtain the net income.

Return to Exhibit 4.1 which displays income statements from the annual reports of AutoNation and Ford. For each company, review the most current income statement and determine the amount of gross margin on automobile sales. You should find a gross profit of $3,359.0 for AutoNation and a gross margin of $14,321 ($145,653 − $131,332) for Ford.

Perpetual Inventory System

Andreas Schindl/a4ndi/123RF

Most modern companies maintain their inventory records using the **perpetual inventory system,** so-called because the inventory account is adjusted perpetually (continually) throughout the accounting period. Each time merchandise is purchased, the inventory account is increased; each time it is sold, the inventory account is decreased. The following illustration demonstrates the basic features of the perpetual inventory system.

June Gardener loved plants and grew them with such remarkable success that she decided to open a small retail plant store. She started June's Plant Shop (JPS) on January 1, Year 1. The following discussion explains and illustrates the effects of the five events the company experienced during its first year of operation.

Effects of Year 1 Events on Financial Statements

EVENT 1   JPS acquired $15,000 cash by issuing common stock.

This event is an asset source transaction. It increases both assets (cash) and stockholders' equity (common stock). The income statement is not affected. The statement of cash flows reflects an inflow from financing activities. The effects on the financial statements are shown next:

Balance Sheet										Income Statement					Statement of Cash Flows
Assets			=	Liab.	+	Stk. Equity									
Cash	+	Inventory	+	Land	=	Accts. Pay.	+	Com. Stk.	+	Ret. Earn.	Rev.	−	Exp.	=	Net Inc.	
15,000	+	NA	+	NA	=	NA	+	15,000	+	NA	NA	−	NA	=	NA	15,000 FA

EVENT 2 JPS purchased merchandise inventory for $14,000 cash.

This event is an asset exchange transaction. One asset, cash, decreases, while another asset, merchandise inventory, increases; total assets remain unchanged. Because product costs are expensed when inventory is sold, not when it is purchased, the event does not affect the income statement. The cash outflow, however, is reported in the operating activities section of the statement of cash flows. The effects on the financial statements are shown next:

Balance Sheet						Income Statement			Statement of Cash Flows
Assets			= Liab.	+	Stk. Equity				
Cash	+ Inventory	+ Land	= Accts. Pay.	+ Com. Stk.	+ Ret. Earn.	Rev.	− Exp.	= Net Inc.	
(14,000) +	14,000	+ NA =	NA	+ NA	+ NA	NA	− NA	= NA	(14,000) OA

EVENT 3a JPS recognized sales revenue from selling inventory for $12,000 cash.

The revenue recognition is the first part of a two-part transaction. The *sales part* represents a source of assets (cash increases from earning sales revenue). Both assets (cash) and stockholders' equity (retained earnings) increase. Sales revenue on the income statement increases. The $12,000 cash inflow is reported in the operating activities section of the statement of cash flows. The effects on the financial statements are shown next:

Balance Sheet						Income Statement			Statement of Cash Flows
Assets			= Liab.	+	Stk. Equity				
Cash	+ Inventory	+ Land	= Accts. Pay.	+ Com. Stk.	+ Ret. Earn.	Rev.	− Exp.	= Net Inc.	
12,000 +	NA	+ NA =	NA	+ NA	+ 12,000	12,000	− NA	= 12,000	12,000 OA

EVENT 3b JPS recognized $8,000 of cost of goods sold.

The expense recognition is the second part of the two-part transaction. The *expense part* represents a use of assets. Both assets (merchandise inventory) and stockholders' equity (retained earnings) decrease. An expense account, Cost of Goods Sold, is reported on the income statement. This part of the transaction does not affect the statement of cash flows. A cash outflow occurred when the goods were bought, not when they were sold. The effects on the financial statements are shown next:

Balance Sheet						Income Statement			Statement of Cash Flows
Assets			= Liab.	+	Stk. Equity				
Cash	+ Inventory	+ Land	= Accts. Pay.	+ Com. Stk.	+ Ret. Earn.	Rev.	− Exp.	= Net Inc.	
NA +	(8,000)	+ NA =	NA	+ NA	+ (8,000)	NA	− 8,000	= (8,000)	NA

EVENT 4 JPS paid $1,000 cash for selling and administrative expenses.

This event is an asset use transaction. The payment decreases both assets (cash) and stockholders' equity (retained earnings). The increase in selling and administrative expenses decreases net income. The $1,000 cash payment is reported in the operating activities section of the statement of cash flows. The effects on the financial statements are shown next:

Balance Sheet										Income Statement			Statement of Cash Flows	
Assets			=	Liab.	+	Stk. Equity				Rev. −	Exp. =	Net Inc.		
Cash	+ Inventory	+ Land	= Accts. Pay.	+	Com. Stk.	+ Ret. Earn.								
(1,000) +	NA	+ NA	= NA	+	NA	+ (1,000)				NA −	1,000 =	(1,000)	(1,000)	OA

EVENT 5   JPS paid $5,500 cash to purchase land for a place to locate a future store.

Buying the land increases the Land account and decreases the Cash account on the balance sheet. The income statement is not affected. The statement of cash flow shows a cash outflow to purchase land in the investing activities section of the statement of cash flows. The effects on the financial statements are shown next:

Balance Sheet										Income Statement			Statement of Cash Flows	
Assets			=	Liab.	+	Stk. Equity				Rev. −	Exp. =	Net Inc.		
Cash	+ Inventory	+ Land	= Accts. Pay.	+	Com. Stk.	+ Ret. Earn.								
(5,500) +	NA	+ 5,500	= NA	+	NA	+ NA				NA −	NA =	NA	(5,500)	IA

Financial Statements for Year 1

JPS's financial statements for Year 1 are shown in Exhibit 4.2. JPS had no beginning inventory in its first year, so the cost of merchandise inventory available for sale was $14,000 (the amount of inventory purchased during the period). Recall that JPS must allocate the *Cost of Goods (Inventory) Available for Sale* between the *Cost of Goods Sold* ($8,000) and the ending balance ($6,000) in the *Merchandise Inventory* account. The cost of goods sold is reported as an expense on the income statement and the ending balance of merchandise inventory is reported as an asset on the balance sheet. The difference between the sales revenue ($12,000) and the cost of goods sold ($8,000) is labeled *gross margin* ($4,000) on the income statement.

EXHIBIT 4.2

Financial Statements

Year 1 Income Statement		12/31/Year 1 Balance Sheet			Year 1 Statement of Cash Flows	
Sales revenue	$12,000	Assets			Operating activities	
Cost of goods sold	(8,000)	Cash	$ 6,500		Inflow from	
Gross margin	4,000	Merchandise inventory	6,000		customers	$12,000
Less: Operating		Land	5,500		Outflow for	
expenses	(1,000)	Total assets		$18,000	inventory	(14,000)
Net income	$ 3,000	Liabilities		$ 0	Outflow for selling	
		Stockholders' equity			& admin. exp.	(1,000)
		Common stock	$15,000		Net cash outflow for	
		Retained earnings	3,000		operating activities	$(3,000)
		Total stockholders' equity		18,000	Investing activities	
		Total liab. and stk. equity		$18,000	Outflow to	
					purchase land	(5,500)
					Financing activities	
					Inflow from stock	
					issue	15,000
					Net change in cash	6,500
					Plus: Beginning cash	
					balance	0
					Ending cash balance	$ 6,500

CHECK YOURSELF 4.1

Phambroom Company began Year 1 with $35,600 in its Inventory account. During the year, it purchased inventory costing $356,800 and sold inventory that had cost $360,000 for $520,000. Based on this information alone, determine (1) the inventory balance as of December 31, Year 1, and (2) the amount of gross margin Phambroom would report on its Year 1 income statement.

Answer

1. $35,600 Beginning inventory + $356,800 Purchases = $392,400 Goods available for sale

$392,400 Goods available for sale − $360,000 Cost of goods sold = $32,400 Ending inventory

2. Sales revenue − Cost of goods sold = Gross margin
$520,000 − $360,000 = $160,000

TRANSPORTATION COST, PURCHASE RETURNS AND ALLOWANCES, AND CASH DISCOUNTS RELATED TO INVENTORY PURCHASES

Purchasing inventory often involves: (1) incurring transportation costs, (2) returning inventory or receiving purchase allowances (cost reductions), and (3) taking cash discounts (also cost reductions). During its second accounting cycle, JPS encountered these kinds of events. The final account balances on December 31, Year 1, become the January 1, Year 2, beginning balances: Cash, $6,500; Merchandise Inventory, $6,000; Land, $5,500; Common Stock, $15,000; and Retained Earnings, $3,000.

Steve Allen/Brand X Pictures/Alamy Stock Photo

Effects of the Year 2 Events on Financial Statements

JPS experienced the following events during its Year 2 accounting period. The effects of each of these events are explained and illustrated in the following discussion.

EVENT 1   JPS borrowed $4,000 cash by issuing a note payable.

JPS borrowed the money to enable it to purchase a plot of land for a site for a store it planned to build in the near future. Borrowing the money increases the Cash account and the Note Payable account on the balance sheet. The income statement is not affected. The statement of cash flow shows a cash flow from financing activities. The effects on the financial statements are shown next:

Balance Sheet							Income Statement			Statement of Cash Flows
Assets		=	Liabilities	+	Stk. Equity					
Cash + Inventory + Land	=	Accts. Pay. +	Notes Pay. +	Com. Stk. +	Ret. Earn.		Rev. − Exp. = Net Inc.			
4,000 + NA + NA	=	NA +	4,000 +	NA +	NA		NA − NA = NA			4,000 FA

EVENT 2 JPS purchased on account merchandise inventory with a list price of $11,000.

The inventory purchase increases both assets (merchandise inventory) and liabilities (accounts payable) on the balance sheet. The income statement is not affected until later, when inventory is sold. Because the inventory was purchased on account, there was no cash outflow. The effects on the financial statements are shown next:

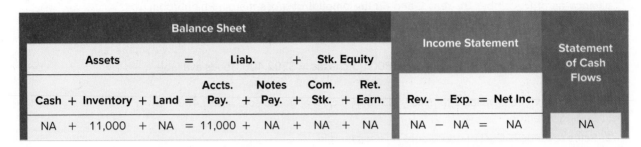

Balance Sheet								Income Statement			Statement of Cash Flows
Assets			=	Liab.		+	Stk. Equity				
Cash	+ Inventory	+ Land	=	Accts. Pay.	+ Notes Pay.	+ Com. Stk.	+ Ret. Earn.	Rev.	− Exp.	= Net Inc.	
NA	+ 11,000	+ NA	=	11,000	+ NA	+ NA	+ NA	NA	− NA	= NA	NA

ACCOUNTING FOR PURCHASE RETURNS AND ALLOWANCES

EVENT 3 JPS returned some of the inventory purchased in Event 2. The list price of the returned merchandise was $1,000.

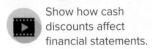

LO 4-2

Show how purchase returns and allowances affect financial statements.

To promote customer satisfaction, many businesses allow customers to return goods for reasons such as wrong size, wrong color, wrong design, or even simply because the purchaser changed his mind. The effect of a purchase return is the *opposite* of the original purchase. For JPS, the purchase return decreases both assets (merchandise inventory) and liabilities (accounts payable). There is no effect on either the income statement or the statement of cash flows. The effects on the financial statements are shown next:

Balance Sheet								Income Statement			Statement of Cash Flows
Assets			=	Liab.		+	Stk. Equity				
Cash	+ Inventory	+ Land	=	Accts. Pay.	+ Notes Pay.	+ Com. Stk.	+ Ret. Earn.	Rev.	− Exp.	= Net Inc.	
NA	+ (1,000)	+ NA	=	(1,000)	+ NA	+ NA	+ NA	NA	− NA	= NA	NA

Sometimes dissatisfied buyers will agree to keep goods instead of returning them if the seller offers to reduce the price. Such reductions are called allowances. *Purchase allowances* affect the financial statements the same way purchase returns do. On the financial statements, returns and allowances are combined in one account, called **Purchase Returns and Allowances**.

PURCHASE DISCOUNTS

EVENT 4 JPS received a cash discount on goods purchased in Event 2. The credit terms were 2/10, n/30.

LO 4-3

Show how cash discounts affect financial statements.

To encourage buyers to pay promptly, sellers sometimes offer **cash discounts.** To illustrate, assume JPS purchased the inventory in Event 2 under credit terms *2/10, n/30* (two-ten, net thirty). These terms mean the seller will allow a 2 percent cash discount if the purchaser pays cash within 10 days from the date of purchase. The amount not paid within the first 10 days is due at the end of 30 days from date of purchase. Recall that in Event 3, JPS returned $1,000 of the inventory purchased in Event 2, leaving a $10,000 balance ($11,000 list price − $1,000 purchase return). If JPS pays for the inventory within 10 days, the amount of the discount is $200 ($10,000 × .02).

When cash discounts are applied to purchases, they are called **purchase discounts.** When they are applied to sales, they are called sales discounts. Sales discounts will be discussed later in the chapter. A *purchase discount* reduces the cost of the inventory and the associated account payable on the balance sheet. A purchase discount does not directly affect the income statement or the statement of cash flows. The effects on the financial statements are shown next:

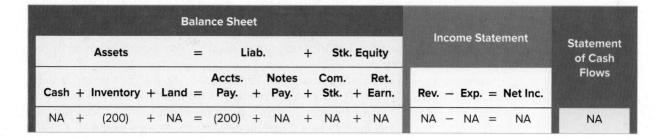

Balance Sheet										Income Statement			Statement of Cash Flows
Assets			=	Liab.		+	Stk. Equity						
Cash	+ Inventory	+ Land	=	Accts. Pay.	+ Notes Pay.	+	Com. Stk.	+ Ret. Earn.		Rev.	− Exp. =	Net Inc.	
NA	+ (200)	+ NA	=	(200)	+ NA	+	NA	+ NA		NA	− NA =	NA	NA

If JPS paid the account payable after 10 days, there would be no purchase discount. In this case, the balances in the Inventory and Accounts Payable accounts would remain at $10,000.

EVENT 5 JPS paid the $9,800 balance due on the account payable.

The remaining balance in the accounts payable is $9,800 ($10,000 list price − $200 purchase discount). Paying cash to settle the liability reduces cash and accounts payable on the balance sheet. The income statement is not affected. The cash outflow is shown in the operating section of the statement of cash flows. The effects on the financial statements are shown next:

Balance Sheet										Income Statement			Statement of Cash Flows
Assets			=	Liab.		+	Stk. Equity						
Cash	+ Inventory	+ Land	=	Accts. Pay.	+ Notes Pay.	+	Com. Stk.	+ Ret. Earn.		Rev.	− Exp. =	Net Inc.	
(9,800)	+ NA	+ NA	=	(9,800)	+ NA	+	NA	+ NA		NA	− NA =	NA	(9,800) OA

REALITY BYTES

Many real-world companies have found it more effective to impose a penalty for late payment than to use a cash discount to encourage early payment. The invoice from Arley Water Works is an example of the penalty strategy. Notice that the amount due, if paid by the due date, is $18.14. A $1.88 late charge is imposed if the bill is paid after the due date. The $1.88 late charge is, in fact, interest. If Arley Water Works collects the payment after the due date, the utility will receive cash of $20.02. The collection will increase cash ($20.02), reduce accounts receivable ($18.14), and increase interest revenue ($1.88).

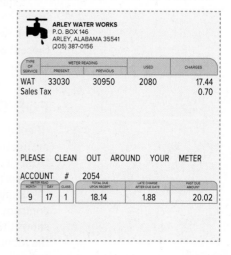

The Cost of Financing Inventory

Suppose you buy inventory this month and sell it next month. Where do you get the money to pay for the inventory at the time you buy it? One way to finance the purchase is to buy it on account and withhold payment until the last day of the term for the account payable. For example, suppose you buy inventory under terms 2/10, net/30. Under these circumstances, you could delay payment for 30 days after the day of purchase. This way, you may be able to collect enough money from the inventory you sell to pay for the inventory you purchased. Refusing the discount allows you the time needed to generate the cash necessary to pay off the liability (account payable). Unfortunately, this is usually a very expensive way to finance the purchase of inventory.

While the amount of a cash discount may appear small, the discount period is short. Consider the terms 2/10, net/30. Because you can pay on the tenth day and still receive the discount, you obtain financing for only 20 days (30-day full credit term − 10-day discount term). In other words, you must forgo a 2 percent discount to obtain a loan with a 20-day term. What is the size of the discount in annual terms? The answer is determined by the following formula:

$$\text{Annual rate} = \text{Discount rate} \times (365 \text{ days} \div \text{term of the loan})$$
$$\text{Annual rate} = 2\% \times (365 \div 20)$$
$$\text{Annual rate} = 36.5\%$$

This means that a 2 percent discount rate for 20 days is equivalent to a 36.5 percent annual rate of interest. So, if you do not have the money to pay the account payable, but can borrow money from a bank at less than 36.5 percent annual interest, you should borrow the money and pay off the account payable within the discount period.

ACCOUNTING FOR TRANSPORTATION COSTS

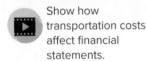

Show how transportation costs affect financial statements.

The terms *FOB shipping point* and *FOB destination* identify whether the buyer or the seller is responsible for transportation costs.

FOB Shipping Point

If goods are delivered **FOB shipping point**, the buyer accepts ownership of the merchandise at the shipping point. Since the buyer owns the goods, the buyer is responsible for the transportation cost paid to delivery companies such as UPS and Federal Express. Given that the buyer has to pay the transportation costs to bring the goods *into* its facilities, the transportation cost is called **transportation-in.**

Exhibit 4.3 provides a graphic depiction of goods that are delivered from a manufacturing company (Seller) to a merchandising company (Buyer) under FOB *shipping point.* The red "X" shows the point where the merchandising firm (Buyer) accepts ownership of the goods. Since the merchandising company (Buyer) owns the goods while they are in transit, the merchandising company (Buyer) is responsible for the transportation-in cost.

FOB Destination

If goods are delivered **FOB destination,** the seller maintains ownership all the way to the destination point. Since the seller has to pay the transportation costs to move goods *out* from its facilities to its customers' facilities, the transportation cost is called **transportation-out.**

Exhibit 4.4 provides a graphic depiction of goods that are delivered from a manufacturing company (Seller) to a merchandising company (Buyer) under *FOB destination.* The red "X" shows the point where the merchandising firm (Buyer) accepts ownership of the goods. Since the Manufacturing Company (Seller) owns the goods while they are in transit, the manufacturing company (Seller) is responsible for the transportation-out cost.

EXHIBIT 4.3

FOB Shipping Point

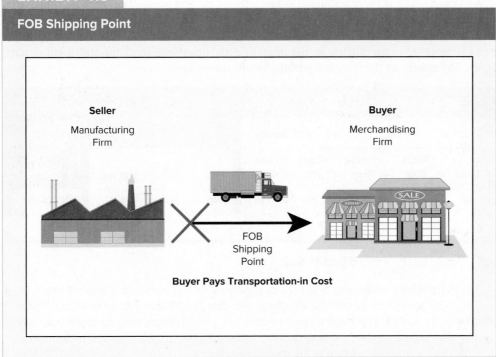

Seller
Manufacturing
Firm

Buyer
Merchandising
Firm

FOB
Shipping
Point

Buyer Pays Transportation-in Cost

EXHIBIT 4.4

FOB Destination

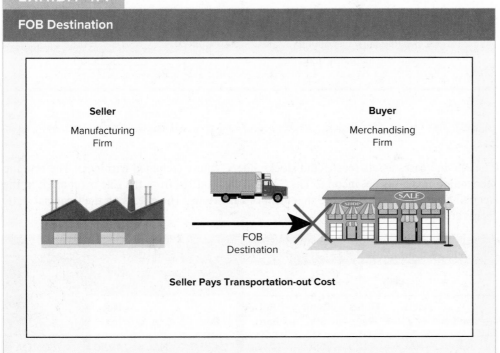

Seller
Manufacturing
Firm

Buyer
Merchandising
Firm

FOB
Destination

Seller Pays Transportation-out Cost

EVENT 6   The shipping terms for the inventory purchased in Event 2 were FOB shipping point. JPS paid the freight company $300 cash for delivering the merchandise.

Event 6 indicates the inventory was delivered FOB shipping point, so JPS (the buyer) is responsible for the $300 transportation cost. Because incurring transportation-in costs is necessary to obtain inventory, these costs are added to the inventory account. The transportation cost increases one asset account (Merchandise Inventory) and decreases another asset account (Cash). The income statement is not affected by this transaction because transportation-in costs are not expensed when they are incurred. Instead, they are expensed as part of *cost of goods sold* when the inventory is sold. However, the cash paid for transportation-in costs is reported as an outflow in the operating activities section of the statement of cash flows. The effects on the financial statements are shown next:

Balance Sheet									Income Statement				Statement of Cash Flows
Assets			=	Liab.		+	Stk. Equity						
				Accts.	Notes		Com.	Ret.					
Cash	+ Inventory	+ Land	=	Pay.	+ Pay.	+	Stk.	+ Earn.	Rev.	− Exp.	= Net Inc.		
(300) +	300	+ NA	=	NA	+ NA	+	NA	+ NA	NA	− NA	= NA		(300) OA

CHECK YOURSELF 4.2

Tsang Company purchased $32,000 of inventory on account with payment terms of 2/10, n/30 and freight terms FOB shipping point. Transportation costs were $1,100. Tsang obtained a $2,000 purchase allowance because the inventory was damaged upon arrival. Tsang paid for the inventory within the discount period. Based on this information alone, determine the balance in the Inventory account.

Answer

List price of inventory	$32,000
Plus: Transportation-in costs	1,100
Less: Purchase returns and allowances	(2,000)
Less: Purchase discount [($32,000 − $2,000) × .02]	(600)
Balance in inventory account	$30,500

EVENT 7a   JPS recognized $24,750 of revenue on the cash sale of merchandise that cost $11,500.

The sale increases assets (cash) and stockholders' equity (retained earnings). The revenue recognition increases net income. The $24,750 cash inflow from the sale is reported in the operating activities section of the statement of cash flows. The effects on the financial statements are shown next:

Balance Sheet									Income Statement			Statement of Cash Flows
Assets			=	Liab.		+	Stk. Equity				Net	
				Accts.	Notes		Com.	Ret.				Flows
Cash	+ Inventory	+ Land	=	Pay.	+ Pay.	+	Stk.	+ Earn.	Rev.	− Exp. =	Inc.	
24,750 +	NA	+ NA	=	NA	+ NA	+	NA	+ 24,750	24,750	− NA =	24,750	24,750 OA

EVENT 7b   JPS recognized $11,500 of cost of goods sold.

When goods are sold, the product cost—*including a proportionate share of transportation-in and adjustments for purchase returns and allowances*—is transferred from the Merchandise Inventory account to the expense account, Cost of Goods Sold. Recognizing cost of goods sold decreases both assets (merchandise inventory) and stockholders' equity (retained earnings). The expense recognition for cost of goods sold decreases net income. Cash flow is not affected. The effects on the financial statements are shown next:

Balance Sheet						Income Statement			Statement of Cash Flows
Assets	=	Liab.	+	Stk. Equity					
		Accts.	Notes	Com.	Ret.				
Cash + Inventory + Land =		Pay. +	Pay. +	Stk. +	Earn.	Rev. –	Exp.	= Net Inc.	
NA + (11,500) + NA =		NA +	NA +	NA +	(11,500)	NA –	11,500	= (11,500)	NA

EVENT 8 JPS paid $450 cash for transportation costs on inventory delivered to customers.

Assume the merchandise sold in Event 7a was shipped FOB destination. Also assume JPS paid the transportation cost in cash. FOB destination means the seller is responsible for the transportation cost, which is called transportation-out. Transportation-out is reported on the income statement as an operating expense in the section below gross margin. The cost of freight on goods shipped to customers is incurred *after* the goods are sold. It is not part of the costs to obtain goods or ready them for sale. Recognizing the expense of transportation-out reduces assets (cash) and stockholders' equity (retained earnings). Operating expenses increase and net income decreases. The cash outflow is reported in the operating activities section of the statement of cash flows. The effects on the financial statements are shown next:

Balance Sheet						Income Statement			Statement of Cash Flows
Assets	=	Liab.	+	Stk. Equity					
		Accts.	Notes	Com.	Ret.				
Cash + Inventory + Land =		Pay. +	Pay. +	Stk. +	Earn.	Rev. –	Exp.	= Net Inc.	
(450) + NA + NA =		NA +	NA +	NA +	(450)	NA –	450	= (450)	(450) OA

If the terms had been FOB shipping point, the customer would have been responsible for the transportation cost and JPS would not have recorded an expense.

EVENT 9 JPS paid $5,000 cash for selling and administrative expenses.

The effect on the balance sheet is to decrease both assets (cash) and stockholders' equity (retained earnings). Recognizing the selling and administrative expenses decreases net income. The $5,000 cash outflow is reported in the operating activities section of the statement of cash flows. The effects on the financial statements are shown next:

Balance Sheet						Income Statement			Statement of Cash Flows
Assets	=	Liab.	+	Stk. Equity					
		Accts.	Notes	Com.	Ret.				
Cash + Inventory + Land =		Pay. +	Pay. +	Stk. +	Earn.	Rev. –	Exp.	= Net Inc.	
(5,000) + NA + NA =		NA +	NA +	NA +	(5,000)	NA –	5,000	= (5,000)	(5,000) OA

EVENT 10 JPS paid $360 cash for interest expense on the note payable described in Event 1.

The effect on the balance sheet is to decrease both assets (cash) and stockholders' equity (retained earnings). Recognizing the interest expense decreases net income. The $360 cash outflow is reported in the operating activities section of the statement of cash flows. The effects on the financial statements are shown next:

Balance Sheet								Income Statement			Statement of Cash Flows
Assets			=	Liab.		+	Stk. Equity				
				Accts.	Notes		Com.	Ret.			
Cash +	Inventory +	Land =		Pay. +	Pay. +		Stk. +	Earn.	Rev. − Exp. =	Net Inc.	
(360) +	NA	+ NA =		NA +	NA +		NA +	(360)	NA − 360 =	(360)	(360) OA

ADJUSTMENT FOR LOST, DAMAGED, OR STOLEN INVENTORY

EVENT 11   JPS took a physical count of its inventory and found $4,100 of inventory on hand.

Show how inventory shrinkage affects financial statements.

Most merchandising companies experience some level of inventory **shrinkage,** a term that reflects decreases in inventory for reasons other than sales to customers. Inventory may be stolen by shoplifters, damaged by customers or employees, or even simply lost or misplaced. Because the *perpetual* inventory system is designed to record purchases and sales of inventory as they occur, the balance in the merchandise inventory account represents the amount of inventory that *should* be on hand at any given time. For example, based on the previous transactions, the book balance of JPS's Inventory account can be computed as follows:

Beginning balance	$ 6,000
Purchases	11,000
Purchase returns	(1,000)
Purchase discounts	(200)
Transportation-in	300
Goods available for sale	16,100
Cost of goods sold	(11,500)
Ending balance	$ 4,600

Assume that JPS takes a physical count of its inventory on hand and finds it has only $4,100 of inventory. By comparing the $4,600 book balance in the Merchandise Inventory account with the $4,100 of actual inventory counted, we determine that the company has experienced $500 of shrinkage. Under these circumstances, JPS must make an adjustment to write off the inventory shrinkage so that the balance of the Inventory account reported on the financial statements agrees with the amount of inventory actually on hand at the end of the period. The write-off decreases both assets (inventory) and stockholders' equity (retained earnings). The write-off increases expenses and decreases net income. Cash flow is not affected. The effects on the financial statements are shown next:

Balance Sheet								Income Statement			Statement of Cash Flows
Assets			=	Liab.		+	Stk. Equity		Rev./	Exp./	
				Accts.	Notes		Com.	Ret.	Gain −	Loss =	Net Inc.
Cash +	Inventory +	Land =		Pay. +	Pay. +		Stk. +	Earn.			
NA +	(500)	+ NA =		NA +	NA +		NA +	(500)	NA − 500 =	(500)	NA

Theoretically, inventory losses are operating expenses. However, because such losses are normally immaterial in amount, they are usually added to cost of goods sold for external reporting purposes.

GAINS, LOSSES, AND A MULTISTEP INCOME STATEMENT

EVENT 12 JPS sold the land that had cost $5,500 for $6,200 cash.

When JPS sells merchandise inventory for more than it cost, the difference between the sales revenue and the cost of the goods sold is called the *gross margin*. In contrast, when JPS sells land for more than it cost, the difference between the sales price and the cost of the land is called a **gain**. Why is one called *gross margin* and the other a *gain?* The terms are used to alert financial statement users to the fact that the nature of the underlying transactions is different.

JPS's primary business is selling inventory, not land. The term *gain* indicates profit resulting from transactions that are not likely to regularly recur. Similarly, had the land sold for less than cost, the difference would have been labeled **loss** rather than expense. This term also indicates the underlying transaction is not from normal, recurring operating activities. Gains and losses are shown separately on the income statement to communicate the expectation that they are nonrecurring.

The presentation of gains and losses in the income statement is discussed in more detail in a later section of the chapter. At this point, note that the sale increases cash, decreases land, and increases retained earnings on the balance sheet. The income statement shows a gain on the sale of land and net income increases. The $6,200 cash inflow is shown as an investing activity on the statement of cash flows. The effects on the financial statements are shown next:

LO 4-6

 Calculate gains and losses and show how they are presented on a multistep income statement.

Balance Sheet									Income Statement				Statement of Cash Flows	
Assets			=	Liab.		+	Stk. Equity		Rev./ Gain	−	Exp./ Loss	= Net Inc.		
Cash	+ Inventory	+ Land	=	Accts. Pay.	+ Notes Pay.	+	Com. Stk.	+ Ret. Earn.						
6,200 +	NA	+ (5,500) =		NA	+ NA	+	NA	+ 700	700	− NA	=	700	6,200	IA

For your convenience, the Year 2 transactions and their financial statement effects for JPS are summarized in Exhibit 4.5.

EXHIBIT 4.5

Summary of Year 2 Events and Their Financial Statement Effects

Accounting Events

Event 1	JPS borrowed $4,000 cash by issuing a note payable.
Event 2	JPS purchased on account merchandise inventory with a list price of $11,000.
Event 3	JPS returned some of the inventory purchased in Event 2. The list price of the returned merchandise was $1,000.
Event 4	JPS received a cash discount on goods purchased in Event 2. The credit terms were 2/10, n/30.
Event 5	JPS paid the $9,800 balance due on the account payable.
Event 6	The inventory purchased in Event 2 was delivered FOB shipping point. JPS paid the freight company $300 cash for delivering the merchandise.
Event 7a	JPS recognized $24,750 of revenue on the cash sale of merchandise that cost $11,500.
Event 7b	JPS recognized $11,500 of cost of goods sold.
Event 8	JPS paid $450 cash for transportation costs on inventory delivered to customers.
Event 9	JPS paid $5,000 cash for selling and administrative expenses.
Event 10	JPS paid $360 cash for interest expense on the note payable described in Event 1.
Event 11	JPS took a physical count of its inventory and found $4,100 of inventory on hand.
Event 12	JPS sold the land that had cost $5,500 for $6,200 cash.

continued

EXHIBIT 4.5 *Concluded*

Financial Statement Effects

	Balance Sheet									Income Statement			Statement of Cash Flows
	Assets			=	Liab.		+	Stk. Equity					
Event No.	Cash +	Inventory +	Land =		Accts. Pay. +	Notes Pay. +		Com. Stk. +	Ret. Earn.	Rev./ Gain −	Exp./ Loss =	Net Inc.	
Beg. Bal.	6,500 +	6,000 +	5,500		NA +	NA +		15,000 +	3,000	NA −	NA =	NA	6,500
1.	4,000 +	NA +	NA =		NA +	4,000 +		NA +	NA	NA −	NA =	NA	4,000 FA
2.	NA +	11,000 +	NA =		11,000 +	NA +		NA +	NA	NA −	NA =	NA	NA
3.	NA +	(1,000) +	NA =		(1,000) +	NA +		NA +	NA	NA −	NA =	NA	NA
4.	NA +	(200) +	NA =		(200) +	NA +		NA +	NA	NA −	NA =	NA	NA
5.	(9,800) +	NA +	NA =		(9,800) +	NA +		NA +	NA	NA −	NA =	NA	(9,800) OA
6.	(300) +	300 +	NA =		NA +	NA +		NA +	NA	NA −	NA =	NA	(300) OA
7a.	24,750 +	NA +	NA =		NA +	NA +		NA +	24,750	24,750 −	NA =	24,750	24,750 OA
7b.	NA +	(11,500) +	NA =		NA +	NA +		NA +	(11,500)	NA −	11,500 =	(11,500)	NA
8.	(450) +	NA +	NA =		NA +	NA +		NA +	(450)	NA −	450 =	(450)	(450) OA
9.	(5,000) +	NA +	NA =		NA +	NA +		NA +	(5,000)	NA −	5,000 =	(5,000)	(5,000) OA
10.	(360) +	NA +	NA =		NA +	NA +		NA +	(360)	NA −	360 =	(360)	(360) OA
11.	NA +	(500) +	NA =		NA +	NA +		NA +	(500)	NA −	500 =	(500)	NA
12.	6,200 +	NA +	(5,500) =		NA +	NA +		NA +	700	700 −	NA =	700	6,200 IA
End	25,540 +	4,100 +	0 =		0 +	4,000 +		15,000 +	10,640	25,450 − 17,810 =		7,640	25,540

The information shown in the horizontal financial statements model in Exhibit 4.5 is used to prepare the financial statements in Exhibits 4.6, 4.7, and 4.8. JPS's Year 2 income statement is shown in Exhibit 4.6. Observe the form of this statement carefully. It is more informative than one which simply subtracts expenses from revenues. First, it compares sales revenue with the cost of the goods that were sold to produce that revenue. The difference between the sales revenue and the cost of goods sold is called *gross margin*. Next, the operating expenses are subtracted from the gross margin to determine the *operating income*. **Operating income** is the amount of income generated from the normal recurring operations of a business. Items that are not expected to recur on a regular basis are subtracted from the operating income to determine the amount of *net income*.

EXHIBIT 4.6

JUNE'S PLANT SHOP
Income Statement
For the Period Ended December 31, Year 2

Sales revenue	$24,750
Cost of goods sold*	(12,000)
Gross margin	12,750
Less: Operating expenses	
Selling and administrative expense	(5,000)
Transportation-out	(450)
Operating income	7,300
Nonoperating items	
Interest expense	(360)
Gain on the sale of land	700
Net income	$ 7,640

*$11,500 inventory sold + $500 shrinkage.

EXHIBIT 4.7

JUNE'S PLANT SHOP
Balance Sheet
As of December 31, Year 2

Assets		
Cash	$25,540	
Merchandise inventory	4,100	
Total assets		$29,640
Liabilities		
Notes payable		$ 4,000
Stockholders' equity		
Common stock	$15,000	
Retained earnings	10,640	
Total stockholders' equity		25,640
Total liabilities and stockholders' equity		$29,640

EXHIBIT 4.8

JUNE'S PLANT SHOP
Statement of Cash Flows
For the Year Ended December 31, Year 2

Operating activities		
Inflow from customers	$24,750	
Outflow for inventory*	(10,100)	
Outflow for transportation-out	(450)	
Outflow for selling and administrative expense	(5,000)	
Outflow for interest expense	(360)	
Net cash outflow for operating activities		$ 8,840
Investing activities		
Inflow from sale of land		6,200
Financing activities		
Inflow from issue of note payable		4,000
Net change in cash		19,040
Plus beginning cash balance		6,500
Ending cash balance		$25,540

*Net cost of inventory $9,800 + Transportation-in $300 = $10,100

Income statements that show these additional relationships are called **multistep income statements.** Income statements that display a single comparison of all revenues minus all expenses are called **single-step income statements.** To this point in the text, we have shown only single-step income statements to promote simplicity. However, the multi-step form is used more frequently in practice. Exhibit 4.9 shows the percentage of companies that use the multistep versus the single-step format. Go to Exhibit 4.1 and identify the company that presents its income statement in the multistep format. You should have identified AutoNation as the company using the multistep format. Ford's statement is shown in the single-step format.

Note that interest is reported as a *nonoperating* item on the income statement in Exhibit 4.6. In contrast, it is shown in the *operating* activities section of the statement of cash flows in Exhibit 4.8. Generally accepted accounting principles (GAAP) require interest to be reported in the operating activities section of the statement of cash flows. There is no corresponding requirement for the treatment of interest on the income statement.

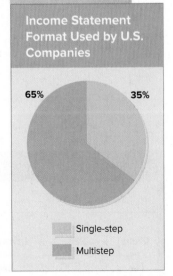

EXHIBIT 4.9

Income Statement Format Used by U.S. Companies

65%   35%

☐ Single-step
■ Multistep

REALITY BYTES

Good inventory management is essential for merchandising and manufacturing companies. Even if a company uses a perpetual inventory system, the amount of inventory believed to be on hand may be incorrect because of lost, damaged, or stolen goods, so a physical count is still required. Unfortunately, counting inventory is not a revenue-generating activity. If a company's employees are used to conduct the physical count, it takes time that may be better used for other activities. In fact, it may be so time-consuming that the business must close temporarily so employees will have the time to complete the inventory count.

©Roberts Publishing Services

To avoid this problem, many businesses hire outside companies to count their inventory. These outside vendors can bring in a large crew of specially trained workers and complete a count very quickly. There are many companies that provide inventory counting services, but **RGIS, LLC** claims to be the world's largest. RGIS (an acronym for Retail Grocery Inventory Service) reports that its 34,000 employees have counted over 400 billion items in the more than 4 million inventory counts it has conducted since beginning operations in 1958. On second thought, counting inventory *is* a revenue-producing activity if you are a company that counts inventory for others.

Prior to the requirement for reporting interest as an operating activity on the statement of cash flows, interest was considered to be a nonoperating item. Most companies continued to report interest as a nonoperating item on their income statements even though they were required to change how it was reported on the statement of cash flows. As a result, there is frequent inconsistency in the way interest is reported on the two financial statements.

Among the other accounts, you should observe that the ending inventory balance is shown in the assets section of the balance sheet in Exhibit 4.7. Adding the $25,540 cash balance to the $4,100 ending inventory balance yields total assets of $29,640. This amount balances with the total amount of liabilities plus stockholders' equity ($4,000 liabilities + $25,640 stockholders' equity = $29,640).

Also note that while the gain on the sale of land is shown on the income statement, it is not included in the operating activities section of the statement of cash flows. Because the gain is a nonoperating item, it is included in the cash inflow from the sale of land shown in the investing activities section. In this case, the full cash inflow from the sale of land ($6,200) is shown in the investing activities section of the statement of cash flows in Exhibit 4.8.

EVENTS AFFECTING SALES

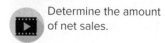

LO 4-7

Determine the amount of net sales.

To this point, we have assumed JPS did not offer cash discounts to its customers. However, sales, as well as purchases of inventory, can be affected by returns, allowances, and discounts. To illustrate, assume JPS engaged in the following selected events during Year 3.

EVENT 1a   JPS sold on account merchandise with a list price of $8,500. Payment terms were 1/10, n/30. The merchandise had cost JPS $4,000.

The sale increases both assets (accounts receivable) and shareholders' equity (retained earnings). Recognizing revenue increases net income. The statement of cash flows is not affected. The effects on the financial statements are shown next:

Balance Sheet									Income Statement			Statement of Cash Flows
Assets			=	Liab.	+	Stk. Equity						
Cash	+	Accts. Rec.	+	Inventory	=	Notes Pay.	+	Com. Stk.	+	Retained Earnings	Rev. − Exp. = Net Inc.	
NA	+	8,500	+	NA	=	NA	+	NA	+	8,500	8,500 − NA = 8,500	NA

EVENT 1b JPS recognized $4,000 of cost of goods sold.

Recognizing the expense decreases assets (merchandise inventory) and stockholders' equity (retained earnings). Cost of goods sold increases and net income decreases. Cash flow is not affected. The effects on the financial statements are shown next:

Balance Sheet								Income Statement				Statement of Cash Flows
Assets			=	Liab. +		Stk. Equity						
Cash +	Accts. Rec. +	Inventory	=	Notes Pay. +	Com. Stk. +	Retained Earnings		Rev. −	Exp.	= Net Inc.		
NA +	NA +	(4,000)	=	NA +	NA +	(4,000)		NA −	4,000	= (4,000)		NA

Accounting for Sales Returns and Allowances

Customers may return purchased merchandise for a variety of reasons. For example, after the purchase a customer may decide an item is the wrong color, size, or style. Under this scenario, the store reverses the original sales transaction. More specifically, the store accepts the returned item and reduces its accounts receivable balance.

Occasionally, a customer may receive damaged merchandise. For example, suppose a customer purchases a refrigerator, and when the refrigerator is delivered to the customer, it has a scratch visible enough that the customer decides to return the item. When the customer calls the store to complain, the store manager offers to reduce the sales price if the customer agrees to keep the refrigerator instead of returning it. In this case, the item is referred to as a sales allowance. The effects of **sales returns and allowances** on the financial statements are discussed further on.

EVENT 2a A customer from Event 1a returned inventory with a $1,000 list price. The merchandise had cost JPS $450.

The sales return decreases both assets (accounts receivable) and stockholders' equity (retained earnings) on the balance sheet. Sales and net income decrease. Cash flow is not affected. The effects on the financial statements are shown next:

Balance Sheet								Income Statement				Statement of Cash Flows
Assets			=	Liab. +		Stk. Equity						
Cash +	Accts. Rec. +	Inventory	=	Notes Pay. +	Com. Stk. +	Retained Earnings		Rev. −	Exp.	= Net Inc.		
NA +	(1,000) +	NA	=	NA +	NA +	(1,000)		(1,000) −	NA	= (1,000)		NA

EVENT 2b The cost of the goods ($450) is returned to the inventory account.

Because JPS got the inventory back, the sales return increases both assets (merchandise inventory) and stockholders' equity (retained earnings). The expense (cost of goods sold) decreases and net income increases. Cash flow is not affected. The effects on the financial statements are shown next:

Balance Sheet								Income Statement				Statement of Cash Flows
Assets			=	Liab. +		Stk. Equity						
Cash +	Accts. Rec. +	Inventory	=	Notes Pay. +	Com. Stk. +	Retained Earnings		Rev. −	Exp.	= Net Inc.		
NA +	NA +	450	=	NA +	NA +	450		NA −	(450)	= 450		NA

Accounting for Sales Discounts

Sales discounts are price reductions offered by sellers to encourage buyers to pay promptly. The same terminology used to describe purchase discounts is used to describe sales discounts. For example, the terms *1/10, net/30* mean that the seller will reduce the sales price by 1 percent if the buyer pays for the purchase within 10 days. If the payment is not made within 10 days, the full purchase price is due within 30 days from the day of purchase. The effects of **sales discounts** on the financial statements are discussed later in this section.

EVENT 3   JPS collected the balance of the accounts receivable generated in Event 1a. Recall the goods were sold under terms 1/10, net/30.

ALTERNATIVE 1   The collection occurs before the discount period has expired (within 10 days from the date of the sale).

JPS would give the buyer a 1 percent discount. Given the original sales amount of $8,500 and a sales return of $1,000, the amount of the discount is $75 [($8,500 − $1,000) × .01]. The sales discount reduces the amount of accounts receivable and retained earnings on the balance sheet. It also reduces the amount of revenue and the net income shown on the income statement. It does not affect the statement of cash flows. The effects on the financial statements are shown next:

Balance Sheet								Income Statement			Statement of Cash Flows
Assets			=	Liab.	+	Stk. Equity					
Cash	+	Accts. Rec.	+	Inventory	=	Notes Pay.	+	Com. Stk.	+	Retained Earnings	Rev. − Exp. = Net Inc.
NA	+	(75)	+	NA	=	NA	+	NA	+	(75)	(75) − NA = (75) / NA

The balance due on the account receivable is $7,425 ($8,500 original sales − $1,000 sales return − $75 discount). The collection increases the Cash account and decreases the Accounts Receivable account. The income statement is not affected. The cash inflow is shown in the operating activities section of the statement of cash flows. The effects on the financial statements are shown next:

Balance Sheet								Income Statement			Statement of Cash Flows
Assets			=	Liab.	+	Stk. Equity					
Cash	+	Accts. Rec.	+	Inventory	=	Notes Pay.	+	Com. Stk.	+	Retained Earnings	Rev. − Exp. = Net Inc.
7,425	+	(7,425)	+	NA	=	NA	+	NA	+	NA	NA − NA = NA / 7,425 OA

Net Sales

The gross amount of sales minus sales returns and allowances and sales discounts is commonly called **net sales**. Companies are not required by GAAP to show sales returns and allowances and sales discounts on their income statement. Indeed, most companies show only the amount of *net sales* on the income statement. In this case, the net sales amount to $7,425 ($8,500 original sales − $1,000 sales return − $75 discount).

ALTERNATIVE 2   The collection occurs after the discount period has expired (after 10 days from the date of the sale).

Under these circumstances, there is no sales discount. The amount collected is $7,500 ($8,500 original sale − $1,000 sales return). Net sales shown on the income statement would also be $7,500.

The Financial Analyst

How good is a $1 million increase in net income? The answer is not clear because there is no indication as to the size of the company. A million-dollar increase may be excellent for a small company but would be virtually meaningless for a company the size of ExxonMobil. Chapter 3 discussed the use of financial ratios to make comparisons of different-size companies. Here, we broaden the analytical tool set to include **common size financial statements.**

LO 4-8

Use common size financial statements and ratio analysis to evaluate managerial performance.

Common Size Financial Statements

Common size statements display information in percentages, as well as absolute dollar amounts. To illustrate, we expand the income statements for JPS to include percentages. The results are shown in Exhibit 4.10. The percentage data are computed by defining net sales as the base figure, or 100 percent. The other amounts on the statements are then shown as a percentage of net sales. For example, the *cost of goods sold percentage* is the dollar amount of *cost of goods sold* divided by the dollar amount of *net sales,* which produces a percentage of 66.7 percent ($8,000 ÷ $12,000) for Year 1 and 48.5 percent ($12,000 ÷ $24,750) for Year 2. Other income statement items are computed using the same approach.

Ratio Analysis

Two of the percentages shown in Exhibit 4.10 are used frequently in business to make comparisons within a specific company or between two or more different companies. These two commonly used percentages are the **gross margin percentage** and the **net income percentage.** The gross margin percentage provides insight about a company's pricing strategy. All other things being equal, a high gross margin percentage means that a company is charging high prices in relation to its cost of goods sold. These percentages are calculated as follows:

$$\text{Gross margin percentage} = \frac{\text{Gross margin}}{\text{Net sales}}$$

$$\text{Net income percentage} = \frac{\text{Net income}}{\text{Net sales}}$$

EXHIBIT 4.10   Common Size Financial Statements

JUNE'S PLANT SHOP
Income Statement
For the Years Ended December 31

	Year 1		Year 2	
Net sales*	$12,000	100.0%	$24,750	100.0%
Cost of goods sold	(8,000)	66.7	(12,000)	48.5
Gross margin	4,000	33.3	12,750	51.5
Less: Operating expenses				
Selling and administrative expense	(1,000)	8.3	(5,000)	20.2
Transportation-out			(450)	1.8
Operating income	3,000	25.0	7,300	29.5
Nonoperating items				
Interest expense			(360)	(1.5)
Gain on the sale of land			700	2.8
Net income	$ 3,000	25.0	$ 7,640	30.8

*Because JPS did not offer sales discounts or have sales returns and allowances during Year 1 or Year 2, the amount of sales revenue is equal to the amount of net sales. We use the term *net sales* here because it is more commonly used in business practice. Percentages do not add exactly because they have been rounded.

In practice, the *net income percentage* is frequently called the **return-on-sales** ratio. The return-on-sales ratio provides insight as to how much of each sales dollar remains as net income after all expenses are paid. All other things being equal, companies with high ratios are doing a better job of controlling expenses.

Comparisons within a Particular Company

To illustrate comparisons within a particular company, assume that JPS relocated its store in an upscale mall in early Year 2. Management realized that the company would have to pay more for operating expenses but believed those expenses could be offset by charging significantly higher prices. We use the gross margin percentage and the net income percentage to assess the success of JPS's strategy. Exhibit 4.10 shows an increase in the *gross margin percentage* from 33.3 to 51.5. This confirms that JPS was able to increase prices relative to its cost of goods sold. The increase in the *return-on-sales* ratio (25 percent to 30.8 percent) confirms that the increase in gross margin was larger than the increase in total expenses. We therefore conclude that JPS's strategy to relocate was successful. This may also explain why JPS sold its land in late Year 2. Considering the success the company experienced at the new location, there was no longer a motive to build a store on the land.

Because net income is affected by nonoperating items, some financial analysts would prefer to use *operating income* instead of *net income* when computing the *return-on-sales* ratio. In this case, the nonoperating items are immaterial. Indeed, to simplify the discussion in this chapter, we always assume immateriality when computing this ratio. However, when nonoperating items are significant, it is more insightful to use *operating income* as the numerator of the *return-on-sales* ratio.

Comparisons between Companies

Does Walmart sell merchandise at a higher or lower price than Target? The *gross margin percentage* is useful in answering questions such as this. Because Walmart's 2017 fiscal year annual report shows a gross margin percentage of 24.7, while Target's report shows a gross margin percentage of 28.9, we conclude that there is validity to Walmart's claim of having low prices. The next section of the chapter provides insight as to how the *gross margin percentage* and the *return-on-sales* ratio can be used to gain insight about the operations of several real-world companies.

 CHECK YOURSELF 4.3

The following sales data are from the records of two retail sales companies. All amounts are in thousands.

	Company A	Company B
Sales	$21,234	$43,465
Cost of goods sold	(14,864)	(34,772)
Gross margin	$ 6,370	$ 8,693

One company is an upscale department store, and the other is a discount store. Which company is the upscale department store?

Answer The gross margin percentage for Company A is approximately 30 percent ($6,370 ÷ $21,234). The gross margin percentage for Company B is 20 percent ($8,693 ÷ $43,465). These percentages suggest that Company A is selling goods with a higher markup than Company B, which implies that Company A is the upscale department store.

Answers to The Curious Accountant

As data from the income statement for AutoNation show, automobile dealers do not have big markups on the cars they sell. The new vehicles the company sold for $12,180.8 million in 2017 cost the company $11,592.4 to purchase, resulting in a gross margin of $588.4, or 4.8 percent. In other words, if you bought an "average" car from AutoNation for $20,000, the company's gross profit on it was only $960 ($20,000 × .048), meaning it paid Ford $19,040 ($20,000 − $960). Furthermore, the company still had other expenses to pay besides its cost of goods sold. In 2017, only 2.0 percent of each dollar of AutoNation's sales was net profit ($434.6 ÷ $21,534.6). Remember, the amount shown for sales on AutoNation's income statement is based on what customers actually paid for the cars the company sold, not the "sticker price."

Meanwhile, if Ford sold the car to AutoNation for $19,040, it earned a 10.5 percent gross margin on the sale, or $1,866 [$14,321 ÷ $145,653 = 9.8%; ($145,653 − $131,332 = $14,321)] [$19,040 × .098 = $1,866]. Like AutoNation, Ford still had other expenses to pay for besides the cost of goods sold. In 2017, Ford earned 4.8 percent of net profit on each dollar of sales ($7,602 ÷ $156,776).

Most consumers significantly overestimate the profit margins of the companies from which they buy goods. Retailers, especially, operate with small profit margins, so inventory management, discussed in Chapter 5, is very important to their success.

Real-World Data

Exhibit 4.11 shows the gross margin percentages and return-on-sales ratios for 10 companies. Three of the companies are manufacturers that produce pharmaceutical products, and the remaining 7 companies sell various products at the retail level. These data are for the companies' 2017 fiscal years.

EXHIBIT 4.11

Industry/Company	Gross Margin %	Return on Sales %
Pharmaceutical manufacturers		
GlaxoSmithKline	65.7	5.1
Johnson & Johnson	66.8	1.7
Merck & Co.	68.2	6.0
Retail pharmacies		
CVS	15.4	3.6
Rite Aid	22.2	4.4
Walgreens	23.4	3.8
Department stores		
Macy's	39.0	6.2
Walmart	24.7	2.0
Building supplies		
Home Depot	34.0	8.6
Lowe's	32.7	5.0

Marek Slusarczyk/123RF

A review of the data confirms our earlier finding that ratios for companies in the same industry are often more similar than are ratios for companies from different industries. For example, note that the manufacturers have much higher margins, both for gross profit and for net earnings, than do the retailers. Manufacturers are often able to charge higher prices than are retailers because they obtain patents that give them a legal monopoly on the products they create. When a company such as Merck develops a new drug, no one else can produce that drug until the patent expires, giving it lots of control over its price at the wholesale level. Conversely, when Rite Aid sells Merck's drug at the retail level, it faces price competition from CVS Caremark (CVS), a company that is trying to sell the same drug to the same consumers. One way CVS can try to get customers to shop at its store is to charge lower prices than its competitors, but this reduces its profit margins because it must pay the same price to get Merck's drug as did Rite Aid. However, a lower gross margin does not always mean a lower return on sales. As the data in Exhibit 4.11 show, in 2017 Rite Aid had a lower gross margin percentage than Walgreens, indicating it is charging lower prices for similar goods. However, Rite Aid still managed to generate a higher return on sales percentage.

It is difficult not to notice that Johnson & Johnson (J&J) had a much lower return on sales percentage than its direct competitors. This was the result of J&J having an unusually high income tax expense in 2017. In 2016, J&J's return on sales percent was 23.0 percent.

In the examples presented in Exhibit 4.11, some companies with higher gross margin percentages have higher return-on-sales ratios than their competitors, but this is not always the case. Finally, notice that Home Depot's gross margin percentage was only 4 percent higher than Lowe's [(34.0 − 32.7) ÷ 32.7], but its return-on-sales ratio was 72 percent higher. [(8.6 − 5.0) ÷ 5.0]. This is very unusual.

A Look Back

Merchandising companies earn profits by selling inventory at prices that are higher than the cost paid for the goods. Merchandising companies include *retail companies* (companies that sell goods to the final consumer) and *wholesale companies* (companies that sell to other merchandising companies). The products sold by merchandising companies are called *inventory*. The costs to purchase inventory, to receive it, and to ready it for sale are *product costs,* which are first accumulated in an inventory account (balance sheet asset account) and then recognized as cost of goods sold (income statement expense account) in the period in which goods are sold. Purchases and sales of inventory can be recorded continually as goods are bought and sold (perpetual system) or at the end of the accounting period (periodic system, discussed in the chapter Appendix).

Accounting for inventory includes the treatment of cash discounts, transportation costs, returns and allowances, and shrinkage. The cost of inventory is the list price less any purchase returns and allowances and purchase discounts, plus transportation-in costs. The cost of freight paid to acquire inventory (*transportation-in*) is considered a product cost. The cost of freight paid to deliver inventory to customers (*transportation-out*) is a selling expense. *Sales returns and allowances* and *sales discounts* are subtracted from sales revenue to determine the amount of *net sales* reported on the income statement. Purchase returns and allowances reduce product cost. Theoretically, the cost of lost, damaged, or stolen inventory (shrinkage) is an operating expense. However, because these costs are usually immaterial in amount, they are typically included as part of cost of goods sold on the income statement.

Some companies use a *multistep income statement*, which reports product costs separately from selling and administrative costs. Cost of goods sold is subtracted from sales revenue to determine *gross margin.* Selling and administrative expenses are subtracted from gross margin to determine income from operations. Other companies report income using a *single-step format,* in which the cost of goods sold is listed along with selling and administrative items in a single expense category that is subtracted in total from revenue to determine income from operations.

Managers of merchandising businesses operate in a highly competitive environment. They must manage company operations carefully to remain profitable. *Common size financial statements* (statements presented on a percentage basis) and ratio analysis are useful monitoring tools. Common size financial statements permit ready comparisons among different-size companies. Although a $1 million increase in sales may be good for a small company and bad for a large company, a 10 percent increase can apply to any size company. The two most common ratios used by merchandising companies are the *gross margin percentage* (gross margin ÷ net sales) and the *net income percentage* (net income ÷ net sales). Interpreting these ratios requires an understanding of industry characteristics. For example, a discount store such as Walmart would be expected to have a much lower gross margin percentage than an upscale store such as Neiman Marcus.

Managers should be aware of the financing cost of carrying inventory. By investing funds in inventory, a firm loses the opportunity to invest them in interest-bearing assets. The cost of financing inventory is an *opportunity cost.* To minimize financing costs, a company should minimize the amount of inventory it carries, the length of time it holds the inventory, and the time it requires to collect accounts receivable after the inventory is sold.

A Look Forward

To this point, the text has explained the basic accounting cycle for service and merchandising businesses. Future chapters more closely address specific accounting issues. For example, in Chapter 5 you will learn how to deal with inventory items that are purchased at differing prices. Other chapters will discuss a variety of specific practices widely used by real-world companies.

APPENDIX

Periodic Inventory System

Under certain conditions, it is impractical to record inventory sales transactions as they occur. Consider the operations of a fast-food restaurant. To maintain perpetual inventory records, the restaurant would have to transfer from the Inventory account to the Cost of Goods Sold account the *cost* of each hamburger, order of fries, soft drink, or other food items as they were sold. Obviously, recording the cost of each item at the point of sale would be impractical without using highly sophisticated computer equipment (recording the selling price the customer pays is captured by cash registers; the difficulty lies in capturing inventory cost).

LO 4-9

 Identify the primary features of the periodic inventory system.

The **periodic inventory system** offers a practical solution for recording inventory transactions in a low-technology, high-volume environment. Inventory costs are recorded in a Purchases account at the time of purchase. Purchase returns and allowances and transportation-in are recorded in separate accounts. No entries for the cost of merchandise purchases or sales are recorded in the Inventory account during the period. The cost of goods sold is determined at the end of the period, as shown in Exhibit 4.12.

The perpetual and periodic inventory systems represent alternative procedures for recording the same information. The amounts of cost of goods sold and ending inventory reported in the financial statements will be the same regardless of the method used.

The **schedule of cost of goods sold**, presented in Exhibit 4.12, is used for internal reporting purposes. It is normally not shown in published financial statements. The amount of cost of goods sold is reported as a single line item on the income statement. The income statement in Exhibit 4.6 will be the same whether JPS maintains perpetual or periodic inventory records.

EXHIBIT 4.12

Schedule of Cost of Goods Sold for 2019	
Beginning inventory	$ 6,000
Purchases	11,000
Purchase returns and allowances	(1,000)
Purchase discounts	(200)
Transportation-in	300
Cost of goods available for sale	16,100
Ending inventory	(4,100)
Cost of goods sold	$12,000

Advantages and Disadvantages of the Periodic System versus the Perpetual System

The chief advantage of the periodic method is recording efficiency. Recording inventory transactions occasionally (periodically) requires less effort than recording them continually (perpetually). Historically, practical limitations offered businesses like fast-food restaurants or grocery stores no alternative to using the periodic system. The sheer volume of transactions made recording individual decreases to the Inventory account balance as each item was sold impossible. Imagine the number of transactions a grocery store would have to record every business day to maintain perpetual records.

Although the periodic system provides a recordkeeping advantage over the perpetual system, perpetual inventory records provide significant control advantages over periodic records. With perpetual records, the book balance in the Inventory account should agree with the amount of inventory in stock at any given time. By comparing that book balance with the results of a physical inventory count, management can determine the amount of lost, damaged, destroyed, or stolen inventory. Perpetual records also permit more timely and accurate reorder decisions and profitability assessments.

When a company uses the *periodic* inventory system, lost, damaged, or stolen merchandise is automatically included in cost of goods sold. Because such goods are not included in the year-end physical count, they are treated as sold regardless of the reason for their absence. Because the periodic system does not separate the cost of lost, damaged, or stolen merchandise from the cost of goods sold, the amount of any inventory shrinkage is unknown. This feature is a major disadvantage of the periodic system. Without knowing the amount of inventory losses, management cannot weigh the costs of various security systems against the potential benefits.

Advances in such technology as electronic bar code scanning and increased computing power have eliminated most of the practical constraints that once prevented merchandisers with high-volume, low dollar-value inventories from recording inventory transactions on a continual basis. As a result, use of the perpetual inventory system has expanded rapidly in recent years, and continued growth can be expected. This text, therefore, concentrates on the perpetual inventory system.

Tableau Dashboard Activity is available in *Connect* for this chapter.

SELF-STUDY REVIEW PROBLEM

A step-by-step audio-narrated series of slides is available in *Connect*.

Academy Sales Company (ASC) started the Year 2 accounting period with the balances given in the following horizontal financial statements model. During Year 2, ASC experienced the following business events:

1. Purchased $16,000 of merchandise inventory on account, terms 2/10, n/30.
2. The goods that were purchased in Event 1 were delivered FOB shipping point. Transportation costs of $600 were paid in cash by the responsible party.
3. Returned $500 of goods purchased in Event 1.
4a. Recorded the cash discount on the goods purchased in Event 1.
4b. Paid the balance due on the account payable within the discount period.
5a. Recognized $21,000 of cash revenue from the sale of merchandise.
5b. Recognized $15,000 of cost of goods sold.
6. The merchandise in Event 5a was sold to customers FOB destination. Transportation costs of $950 were paid in cash by the responsible party.
7. Paid cash of $4,000 for selling and administrative expenses.
8. Sold the land for $5,600 cash.

Required

a. Record the preceding transactions in a horizontal financial statements model like the one that follows.

	Balance Sheet						Income Statement			Statement of Cash Flows
Event No.	Cash	+ Inventory	+ Land	= Accts. Pay.	+ Com. Stk.	+ Ret. Earn.	Rev./ Gain	− Exp./ Loss	= Net Inc.	
Bal.	25,000 +	3,000	+ 5,000 =	−0− +	18,000	+ 15,000	NA	− NA =	NA	NA

b. Prepare a schedule of cost of goods sold. (See the Appendix.)

c. Prepare a multistep income statement. Include common size percentages on the income statement.

d. ASC's gross margin percentage in Year 1 was 22 percent. Based on the common size data in the income statement, did ASC raise or lower its prices in Year 2?

e. Assuming a 10 percent rate of growth, what is the amount of net income expected for Year 3?

Answer

a.

	Balance Sheet						Income Statement			Statement of Cash Flows
Event No.	Cash	+ Inventory	+ Land	= Accts. Pay.	+ Com. Stk.	+ Ret. Earn.	Rev./ Gain	− Exp./ Loss	= Net Inc.	
Beg. Bal.	25,000 +	3,000	+5,000 =	−0−	+ 18,000	+ 15,000	NA	− NA =	NA	NA
1		+ 16,000	=	16,000 +	+		−	=		
2	(600) +	600	=	+	+		−	=		(600) OA
3	+	(500)	=	(500) +	+		−	=		
4a	+	(310)	=	(310) +	+		−	=		
4b	(15,190) +		=	(15,190) +	+		−	=		(15,190) OA
5a	21,000 +		=	+	+ 21,000	21,000 −	=	21,000	21,000 OA
5b	+	(15,000)	=	+	+ (15,000)	− 15,000	= (15,000)	
6	(950) +		=	+	+ (950)	− 950 =	(950)	(950) OA
7	(4,000) +		=	+	+ (4,000)	− 4,000 =	(4,000)	(4,000) OA
8	5,600 +		(5,000) =	+	+ 600	600 −	=	600	5,600 IA
End Bal.	30,860 +	3,790	−0− =	−0−	+ 18,000	+ 16,650	21,600 − 19,950 =	1,650	5,860 NC

b.

ACADEMY SALES COMPANY
Schedule of Cost of Goods Sold
For the Period Ended December 31, Year 2

Beginning inventory	$ 3,000
Plus purchases	16,000
Less: Purchase returns and allowances	(500)
Less: Purchases discounts	(310)
Plus: Transportation-in	600
Goods available for sale	18,790
Less: Ending inventory	(3,790)
Cost of goods sold	$15,000

c.

ACADEMY SALES COMPANY		
Income Statement*		
For the Period Ended December 31, Year 2		
Net sales	$21,000	100.0%
Cost of goods sold	(15,000)	71.4
Gross margin	6,000	28.6
Less: Operating expenses		
Selling and administrative expense	(4,000)	19.0
Transportation-out	(950)	4.5
Operating income	1,050	5.0
Nonoperating items		
Gain on the sale of land	600	2.9
Net income	$ 1,650	7.9

*Percentages do not add exactly because they have been rounded.

d. All other things being equal, the higher the gross margin percentage, the higher the sales prices. Because the gross margin percentage increased from 22 percent to 28.6 percent, the data suggest that Academy raised its sales prices.

e. $1,155 [$1,050 + (.10 × $1,050)]. Note that the gain is not expected to recur.

KEY TERMS

Cash discount 190
Common size financial
 statements 203
Cost of goods available for
 sale 186
Cost of Goods Sold 186
FOB destination 192
FOB shipping point 192
Gains 197
Gross margin 186
Gross margin percentage 203

Gross profit 186
Losses 197
Merchandise inventory 183
Merchandising businesses 182
Multistep income
 statement 199
Net income percentage 203
Net sales 202
Operating income (or loss) 198
Period costs 185
Periodic inventory system 207

Perpetual inventory system 186
Product costs 185
Purchase discount 191
Purchase Returns and
 Allowances 190
Retail companies 183
Return on sales 204
Sales discount 202
Sales returns and
 allowances 201

Schedule of cost of goods
 sold 207
Selling and administrative
 costs 185
Shrinkage 196
Single-step income
 statement 199
Transportation-in 192
Transportation-out 192
Wholesale companies 183

QUESTIONS

1. Define *merchandise inventory*. What types of costs are included in the Merchandise Inventory account?

2. What is the difference between a product cost and a selling and administrative cost?

3. How is the cost of goods available for sale determined?

4. What portion of cost of goods available for sale is shown on the balance

sheet? What portion is shown on the income statement?

5. When are period costs expensed? When are product costs expensed?

6. If Petco had net sales of $600,000, goods available for sale of $450,000, and cost of goods sold of $375,000, what is its gross margin? What amount of inventory will be shown on its balance sheet?

7. Describe how the perpetual inventory system works. What are some advantages of using the perpetual inventory system? Is it necessary to take a physical inventory when using the perpetual inventory system?

8. What are the effects of the following types of transactions on the accounting equation? Also identify the financial statements affected. (Assume that the

perpetual inventory system is used.)
 a. Acquisition of cash from the issue of common stock.
 b. Contribution of inventory by an owner of a company.
 c. Purchase of inventory with cash by a company.
 d. Sale of inventory for cash.

9. Northern Merchandising Company sold inventory that cost $12,000 for

$20,000 cash. How does this event affect the accounting equation? What financial statements and accounts are affected? (Assume that the perpetual inventory system is used.)

10. If goods are shipped FOB shipping point, which party (buyer or seller) is responsible for the transportation costs?

11. Define *transportation-in*. Is it a product or a period cost?

12. Why would a seller grant an allowance to a buyer of the seller's merchandise?

13. Dyer Department Store purchased goods with the terms 2/10, n/30. What do these terms mean?

14. Eastern Discount Stores incurred a $5,000 cash cost. How does the accounting

for this cost differ if the cash were paid for inventory versus commissions to sales personnel?

15. What is the purpose of giving credit terms to customers?

16. Define *transportation-out*. Is it a product cost or a period cost for the seller?

17. Ball Co. purchased inventory with a list price of $4,000 with the terms 2/10, n/30. What amount will be added to the Merchandise Inventory account?

18. Explain the difference between gains and revenues.

19. Explain the difference between losses and expenses.

20. Suda Company sold land that cost $40,000 for $37,000 cash. Explain how this transaction would be

shown on the statement of cash flows.

21. Explain the difference between purchase returns and sales returns. How do purchase returns affect the financial statements of both buyer and seller? How do sales returns affect the financial statements of both buyer and seller?

22. How is net sales determined?

23. What is the difference between a multistep income statement and a single-step income statement?

24. What is the advantage of using common size income statements to present financial information for several accounting periods?

25. What information is provided by the net income percentage (return-on-sales ratio)?

26. What is the purpose of preparing a schedule of cost of goods sold? (See the Appendix.)

27. Explain how the periodic inventory system works. What are some advantages of using the periodic inventory system? What are some disadvantages of using the periodic inventory system? Is it necessary to take a physical inventory when using the periodic inventory system? (See the Appendix.)

28. Why does the periodic inventory system impose a major disadvantage for management in accounting for lost, stolen, or damaged goods? (See the Appendix.)

EXERCISES—SERIES A

Mc Graw Hill **connect**   **All applicable Exercises in Series A are available in *Connect*.**

When the instructions for *any* exercise or problem call for the preparation of an income statement, use the *multistep format* unless otherwise indicated.

Exercise 4-1A   *Comparing a merchandising company with a service company*

LO 4-1

The following information is available for two different types of businesses for the Year 1 accounting year. Hopkins CPAs is a service business that provides accounting services to small businesses. Sports Clothing is a merchandising business that sells sports clothing to college students.

Data for Hopkins CPAs

1. Borrowed $90,000 from the bank to start the business.
2. Provided $50,000 of services to clients and collected $50,000 cash.
3. Paid salary expense of $32,000.

Data for Sports Clothing

1. Borrowed $90,000 from the bank to start the business.
2. Purchased $50,000 inventory for cash.
3. Inventory costing $26,000 was sold for $50,000 cash.
4. Paid $8,000 cash for operating expenses.

Required

a. Prepare an income statement, balance sheet, and statement of cash flows for each of the companies.

b. Which of the two businesses would have product costs? Why?

c. Why does Hopkins CPAs not compute gross margin on its income statement?

d. Compare the assets of both companies. What assets do they have in common? What assets are different? Why?

LO 4-1

Exercise 4-2A *Effect of inventory transactions on financial statements:* **perpetual system**

Dan Watson started a small merchandising business in Year 1. The business experienced the following events during its first year of operation. Assume that Watson uses the perpetual inventory system.

1. Acquired $30,000 cash from the issue of common stock.
2. Purchased inventory for $18,000 cash.
3. Sold inventory costing $15,000 for $32,000 cash.

Required

a. Record the events in a horizontal financial statements model like the one shown next.

Balance Sheet							Income Statement			Statement of Cash Flows
Assets			=	Stk. Equity						
Cash	+	Inv.	=	Com. Stk.	+	Ret. Earn.	Rev.	− Exp.	= Net Inc.	

b. Determine the amount of gross margin.
c. What is the amount of total assets at the end of the period?

LO 4-1

Exercise 4-3A *Effect of inventory transactions on the income statement and statement of cash flows:* **perpetual system**

During Year 1, Hardy Merchandising Company purchased $40,000 of inventory on account. Hardy sold inventory on account that cost $24,500 for $38,000. Cash payments on accounts payable were $22,000. There was $26,000 cash collected from accounts receivable. Hardy also paid $5,100 cash for operating expenses. Assume that Hardy started the accounting period with $20,000 in both cash and common stock.

Required

a. Identify the events described in the preceding paragraph and show them in a horizontal financial statements model like the following one:

Balance Sheet									Income Statement			Statement of Cash Flows
Assets				=	Liab.	+	Stk. Equity					
Cash	+ Accts. Rec.	+ Inv.		= Accts. Pay.	+	Com. Stk.	+ Ret. Earn.		Rev. − Exp. = Net Inc.			
20,000 +	NA	+ NA	=	NA	+	20,000	+ NA		NA − NA = NA			FA

b. What is the balance of accounts receivable at the end of Year 1?
c. What is the balance of accounts payable at the end of Year 1?
d. What are the amounts of gross margin and net income for Year 1?
e. Determine the amount of net cash flow from operating activities.
f. Explain why net income and retained earnings are the same for Hardy. Normally, would these amounts be the same? Why or why not?

LO 4-1

Exercise 4-4A *Recording inventory transactions in a horizontal financial statements model*

Milo Clothing experienced the following events during Year 1, its first year of operation:

1. Acquired $30,000 cash from the issue of common stock.
2. Purchased inventory for $15,000 cash.
3. Sold inventory costing $9,000 for $20,000 cash.
4. Paid $1,500 for advertising expense.

Required

Record the events in a horizontal financial statements model like the one shown next.

Balance Sheet						Income Statement			Statement of Cash Flows
Assets		=	Stk. Equity						
Cash	+ Inv.	=	Com. Stk.	+	Ret. Earn.	Rev.	− Exp.	= Net Inc.	

Exercise 4-5A   *Cash discounts and purchase returns*

LO 4-2, 4-3

On April 6, Year 1, Home Furnishings purchased $25,200 of merchandise from Una Imports, terms 2/10 n/45. On April 8, Home returned $2,400 of the merchandise to Una Imports. Home paid cash for the merchandise on April 15, Year 1.

Required

a. What is the amount that Home must pay Una Imports on April 15?

b. Show the events in a horizontal financial statements model like the following one:

Balance Sheet							Income Statement			Statement of Cash Flows
Assets		=	Liab.	+	Stk. Equity					
Cash	+ Inv.	=	Accts. Pay.	+	Com. Stk.	+ Ret. Earn.	Rev.	− Exp.	= Net Inc.	

c. How much must Home pay for the merchandise purchased if the payment is not made until April 20, Year 1?

d. Show the payment in Requirement *c* in a horizontal financial statements model like the previous one.

e. Why would Home want to pay for the merchandise by April 15?

Exercise 4-6A   *Understanding the freight terms FOB shipping point and FOB destination*

LO 4-4

Required

For each of the following events, indicate whether the freight terms are FOB destination or FOB shipping point.

a. Sold merchandise and the buyer paid the transportation costs.

b. Purchased merchandise and the seller paid the transportation costs.

c. Sold merchandise and paid the transportation costs.

d. Purchased merchandise and paid the transportation costs.

Exercise 4-7A   *Determining the cost of inventory*

LO 4-2, 4-3, 4-4

Required

For each of the following cases determine the ending balance in the inventory account. (*Hint:* First, determine the total cost of inventory available for sale. Next, subtract the cost of the inventory sold to arrive at the ending balance.)

a. Jill's Dress Shop had a beginning balance in its inventory account of $40,000. During the accounting period, Jill's purchased $75,000 of inventory, returned $5,000 of inventory, and obtained $750 of purchases discounts. Jill's incurred $1,000 of transportation-in cost and $600 of transportation-out cost. Salaries of sales personnel amounted to $31,000. Administrative expenses amounted to $35,600. Cost of goods sold amounted to $82,300.

b. Ken's Bait Shop had a beginning balance in its inventory account of $8,000. During the accounting period, Ken's purchased $36,900 of inventory, obtained $1,200 of purchases allowances, and received $360 of purchases discounts. Sales discounts amounted to $640. Ken's incurred $900 of transportation-in cost and $260 of transportation-out cost. Selling and administrative cost amounted to $12,300. Cost of goods sold amounted to $33,900.

LO 4-2, 4-3, 4-4

Exercise 4-8A *Accounting for product costs: perpetual inventory system*

Which of the following would be *added* to the Inventory account for a merchandising business using the perpetual inventory system?

Required

a. Transportation-out.

b. Purchase discount.

c. Transportation-in.

d. Purchase of a new computer to be used by the business.

e. Purchase of inventory.

f. Allowance received for damaged inventory.

LO 4-2, 4-3, 4-4

Exercise 4-9A *Determining the effect of inventory transactions on the horizontal financial statements model: perpetual system*

Bali Sales Company experienced the following events:

1. Purchased merchandise inventory for cash.

2. Purchased merchandise inventory on account.

3. Returned merchandise purchased on account.

4. Sold merchandise inventory for cash. Label the revenue recognition 4a and the expense recognition 4b.

5. Paid cash on accounts payable not within the discount period.

6. Sold merchandise inventory on account. Label the revenue recognition 6a and the expense recognition 6b.

7. Paid cash for selling and administrative expenses.

8. Paid cash for transportation-in.

9. Collected cash from accounts receivable.

10. Paid cash for transportation-out.

Required

Identify each event as asset source (AS), asset use (AU), asset exchange (AE), or claims exchange (CE). Also explain how each event affects the financial statements by placing a + for increase, − for decrease, or NA for not affected under each of the components in the following horizontal financial statements model. Assume the use of the perpetual inventory system. The first event is recorded as an example.

Event No.	Event Type	Balance Sheet					Income Statement					Statement of Cash Flows
		Assets	=	Liab.	+	Stk. Equity	Rev.	−	Exp.	=	Net Inc.	
1	AE	+ −	=	NA	+	NA	NA	−	NA	=	NA	− OA

LO 4-2, 4-4

Exercise 4-10A *Effect of product cost and period cost: horizontal financial statements model*

The Pet Store experienced the following events for the Year 1 accounting period:

1. Acquired $60,000 cash from the issue of common stock.

2. Purchased $65,000 of inventory on account.

3. Received goods purchased in Event 2 FOB shipping point; transportation cost of $900 paid in cash.

4. Sold inventory on account that cost $38,000 for $71,000.

5. Transportation cost on the goods sold in Event 4 was $620. The goods were shipped FOB destination. Cash was paid for the transportation cost.

6. Customer in Event 4 returned $4,200 worth of goods that had a cost of $2,150.

7. Collected $58,300 cash from accounts receivable.

8. Paid $59,200 cash on accounts payable.

9. Paid $2,600 for advertising expense.

10. Paid $3,100 cash for insurance expense.

Required

a. Which of these events affect period (selling and administrative) costs? Which result in product costs? If neither, label the transaction NA.

b. Show each event in a horizontal financial statements model like the following one. The first event is recorded as an example.

Balance Sheet									Income Statement			Statement of Cash Flows
Assets			=	Liab.	+		Stk. Equity					
Cash	+ Accts. Rec.	+ Inv.	=	Accts. Pay.	+	Com. Stk.	+	Ret. Earn.	Rev. –	Exp. =	Net Inc.	
60,000 +	NA	+ NA =		NA	+	60,000	+	NA	NA –	NA =	NA	60,000 FA

Exercise 4-11A   *Effect of inventory losses: perpetual system*   LO 4-5

Ho Designs experienced the following events during Year 1, its first year of operation:

1. Started the business when it acquired $70,000 cash from the issue of common stock.
2. Paid $41,000 cash to purchase inventory.
3. Sold inventory costing $37,500 for $56,200 cash.
4. Physically counted inventory showing $3,200 inventory was on hand at the end of the accounting period.

Required

a. Determine the amount of the difference between book balance and the actual amount of inventory as determined by the physical count.

b. Explain how differences between the book balance and the physical count of inventory could arise. Why is being able to determine whether differences exist useful to management?

Exercise 4-12A   *Effect of purchase returns and allowances and transportation costs on*   LO 4-2, 4-4, 4-6
the financial statements: perpetual system

The beginning account balances for Terry's Auto Shop as of January 1, Year 2, follow:

Account Titles	Beginning Balances
Cash	$16,000
Inventory	8,000
Common stock	20,000
Retained earnings	4,000

The following events affected the company during the Year 2 accounting period:

1. Purchased merchandise on account that cost $15,000.
2. The goods in Event 1 were purchased FOB shipping point with transportation cost of $800 cash.
3. Returned $2,600 of damaged merchandise.
4. Agreed to keep other damaged merchandise for which the company received a $1,100 allowance.
5. Sold merchandise that cost $15,000 for $31,000 cash.
6. Delivered merchandise to customers in Event 5 under terms FOB destination with transportation costs amounting to $500 cash.
7. Paid $8,000 on the merchandise purchased in Event 1.

Required

a. Organize appropriate accounts under an accounting equation. Record the beginning balances and the transaction data in the accounts.

b. Prepare an income statement and a statement of cash flows for Year 2.

c. Explain why a difference does or does not exist between net income and net cash flow from operating activities.

LO 4-6

Exercise 4-13A   *Multistep income statement*

In Year 1, Kim Company sold land for $80,000 cash. The land had originally cost $60,000. Also, Kim sold inventory that had cost $110,000 for $198,000 cash. Operating expenses amounted to $36,000.

Required

a. Prepare a Year 1 multistep income statement for Kim Company.

b. Assume that normal operating activities grow evenly by 10 percent during Year 2. Prepare a Year 2 multistep income statement for Kim Company.

c. Determine the percentage change in net income between Year 1 and Year 2.

d. Should the stockholders have expected the results determined in Requirement *c*? Explain your answer.

LO 4-6

Exercise 4-14A   *Single-step and multistep income statements*

The following information was taken from the accounts of Green Market, a small grocery store, at December 31, Year 1. The accounts are listed in alphabetical order, and all have normal balances. Dollar amounts are given in thousands.

Accounts payable	$ 800
Accounts receivable	2,250
Advertising expense	600
Cash	1,850
Common stock	2,000
Cost of goods sold	2,950
Gain on sale of land	200
Interest expense	120
Merchandise inventory	1,250
Prepaid rent	720
Rent expense	510
Retained earnings, 1/1/Year 1	2,610
Salaries expense	960
Sales revenue	5,600

Required

First, prepare an income statement for the year using the single-step approach. Then, prepare another income statement using the multistep approach.

LO 4-2, 4-3, 4-6

Exercise 4-15A   *Sales returns, discounts, gain, and a multistep income statement*

The following information was drawn from the Year 1 accounting records of Ozark Merchandisers:

1. Inventory that had cost $21,200 was sold for $39,900 under terms 2/20, net/30.

2. Customers returned merchandise to Ozark five days after the purchase. The merchandise had been sold for a price of $1,520. The merchandise had cost Ozark $920.

3. All customers paid their accounts within the discount period.

4. Selling and administrative expenses amounted to $4,200.

5. Interest expense paid amounted to $360.

6. Land that had cost $8,000 was sold for $9,250 cash.

Required

a. Determine the amount of net sales.

b. Prepare a multistep income statement.

c. Where would the interest expense be shown on the statement of cash flows?

d. How would the sale of the land be shown on the statement of cash flows?

e. Explain the difference between a gain and revenue.

Exercise 4-16A *Effect of sales returns and allowances and transportation costs on the financial statements: perpetual system*   LO 4-2, 4-4, 4-7

Powell Company began the Year 3 accounting period with $40,000 cash, $86,000 inventory, $60,000 common stock, and $66,000 retained earnings. During Year 3, Powell experienced the following events:

1. Sold merchandise costing $58,000 for $99,500 on account to Prentise Furniture Store.
2. Delivered the goods to Prentise under terms FOB destination. Transportation costs were $900 cash.
3. Received returned goods from Prentise. The goods cost Powell $4,000 and were sold to Prentise for $5,900.
4. Granted Prentise a $3,000 allowance for damaged goods that Prentise agreed to keep.
5. Collected partial payment of $81,000 cash from accounts receivable.

Required

a. Record the events in a horizontal financial statements model like the one shown as follows:

		Balance Sheet					Income Statement			Statement of Cash Flows
	Assets			=	Stk. Equity					
Cash	+	Accts. Rec.	+	Inv.	=	Com. Stk. + Ret. Earn.	Rev.	− Exp.	= Net Inc.	

b. Prepare an income statement, a balance sheet, and a statement of cash flows.
c. Why would Prentise agree to keep the damaged goods? Who benefits more?

Exercise 4-17A *Comprehensive exercise with sales discounts*   LO 4-2, 4- 3, 4-4, 4-6, 4-7, 4-8

Junker's Stash started the Year 2 accounting period with the balances given in the following horizontal financial statements model. During Year 2, Junker's Stash experienced the following business events:

1. Paid cash to purchase $70,000 of merchandise inventory.
2. The goods that were purchased in Event 1 were delivered FOB destination. Transportation costs of $1,400 were paid in cash by the responsible party.
3a. Sold merchandise for $72,000 under terms 1/10, n/30.
3b. Recognized $41,900 of cost of goods sold.
4a. Junker's Stash customers returned merchandise that was sold for $2,100.
4b. The merchandise returned in Event 4a had cost Junker's Stash $1,250.
5. The merchandise in Event 3a was sold to customers FOB destination. Transportation costs of $1,650 were paid in cash by the responsible party.
6a. The customers paid for the merchandise sold in Event 3a within the discount period. Recognized the sales discount.
6b. Collected the balance in the accounts receivable account.
7. Paid cash of $6,850 for selling and administrative expenses.
8. Sold the land for $9,100 cash.

Required

a. Show the given transactions in a horizontal financial statements model like the one shown next:

Event No.		Balance Sheet							Income Statement			Statement of Cash Flows
			Assets			=	Stk. Equity		Rev./ Exp./			
	Cash	+ Accts. Rec.	+ Inventory +	Land	=	Com. Stk	+ Ret. Earn.	Gain − Loss	= Net Inc.			
Bal.	80,000 +	0 +	15,000 + 11,000	=	70,000 +	36,000		NA − NA =	NA		NA	

b. Determine the amount of net sales.
c. Prepare a multistep income statement. Include common size percentages on the income statement.

d. The return-on-sales ratio for Junker's Stash during the prior year was 12 percent. Based on the common size data in the income statement, did the expenses for Junker's Stash increase or decrease in Year 2? Assume sales are same for both years.

e. Explain why the term *loss* is used to describe the results due to the sale of land.

LO 4-8

Exercise 4-18A *Using ratios to make comparisons*

The following income statements were drawn from the annual reports of the Atlanta Company and the Boston Company:

	Atlanta*	Boston*
Net sales	$210,000	$230,000
Cost of goods sold	(126,000)	(179,400)
Gross margin	84,000	50,600
Less: Operating exp.		
Selling and admin. exp.	(67,200)	(32,200)
Net income	$ 16,800	$ 18,400

*All figures are reported in thousands of dollars.

Required

a. One of the companies is a high-end retailer that operates in exclusive shopping malls. The other operates discount stores located in low-cost, standalone buildings. Identify the high-end retailer and the discounter. Support your answer with appropriate ratios.

b. If Atlanta and Boston have stockholders' equity of $168,000 and $122,700, respectively, which company is in the more profitable business?

LO 4-8

Exercise 4-19A *Using common size statements and ratios to make comparisons*

The following information is available for the Memphis and Billings companies:

	Memphis	Billings
Sales	$1,500,000	$1,500,000
Cost of goods sold	1,050,000	1,125,000
Operating expenses	350,000	250,000
Total assets	1,800,000	1,800,000
Stockholders' equity	720,000	720,000

Required

a. Prepare a common size income statement for each company.

b. Compute the return on assets and return on equity for each company.

c. Which company is more profitable from the stockholders' perspective?

d. One company is a high-end retailer, and the other operates a discount store. Which is the discounter? Support your selection by referring to the appropriate ratios.

LO 4-9

Exercise 4-20A *Effect of inventory transactions on the income statement and balance sheet: periodic system (Appendix)*

Bill Rose owns Rose Sporting Goods. At the beginning of the year, Rose Sporting Goods had $18,000 in inventory. During the year, Rose Sporting Goods purchased inventory that cost $66,000. At the end of the year, inventory on hand amounted to $28,500.

Required

Calculate the following:

a. Cost of goods available for sale during the year.

b. Cost of goods sold for the year.

c. Amount of inventory Rose Sporting Goods would report on the year-end balance sheet.

Exercise 4-21A *Determining cost of goods sold: periodic system (Appendix)* LO 4-9

Tippah Antiques uses the periodic inventory system to account for its inventory transactions. The following account titles and balances were drawn from Tippah's records for Year 2: beginning balance in inventory, $42,000; purchases, $128,000; purchase returns and allowances, $12,000; sales, $520,000; sales returns and allowances, $3,900; transportation-in, $1,000; and operating expenses, $130,000. A physical count indicated that $26,000 of merchandise was on hand at the end of the accounting period.

Required

a. Prepare a schedule of cost of goods sold.

b. Prepare a multistep income statement.

PROBLEMS—SERIES A

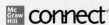 **All applicable Problems in Series A are available in *Connect*.**

Problem 4-22A *Identifying transportation costs* LO 4-4

Required

For each of the following events, determine the amount of transportation paid by The Box Company. Also indicate whether the transportation cost would be classified as a product or period (selling and administrative) cost.

a. Purchased merchandise with transportation costs of $650. The merchandise was shipped FOB shipping point.

b. Shipped merchandise to customers, freight terms FOB shipping point. The transportation costs were $310.

c. Purchased inventory with transportation costs of $1,500. The goods were shipped FOB destination.

d. Sold merchandise to a customer. Transportation costs were $520. The goods were shipped FOB destination.

Problem 4-23A *Identifying product and period costs* LO 4-4

Required

Indicate whether each of the following costs is a product cost or a period (selling and administrative) cost:

a. Goods purchased for resale.

b. Salaries of salespersons.

c. Advertising costs.

d. Transportation-out.

e. Interest on a note payable.

f. Salary of the company president.

g. Transportation-in.

h. Insurance on the office building.

i. Office supplies.

j. Costs incurred to improve the quality of goods available for sale.

Problem 4-24A *Basic transactions for three accounting cycles: perpetual system* LO 4-1, 4-6

Blooming Flower Company was started in Year 1 when it acquired $60,000 cash from the issue of common stock. The following data summarize the company's first three years' operating activities. Assume that all transactions were cash transactions.

CHECK FIGURES
Year 1 Net Income: $5,000
Year 2 Total Assets: $72,000

	Year 1	Year 2	Year 3
Purchases of inventory	$50,000	$60,000	$ 85,000
Sales	68,000	85,000	130,000
Cost of goods sold	34,000	43,000	71,000
Selling and administrative expenses	29,000	35,000	42,000

Required

Prepare an income statement (use multistep format) and balance sheet for each fiscal year. (*Hint:* Record the transaction data for each accounting period in the accounting equation before preparing the statements for that year.)

Problem 4-25A   *Comprehensive cycle problem: perpetual system*

At the beginning of Year 2, the Redd Company had the following balances in its accounts:

Cash	$16,900
Inventory	25,000
Common stock	30,000
Retained earnings	11,900

During Year 2, the company experienced the following events:

1. Purchased inventory that cost $15,200 on account from Ross Company under terms 1/10, n/30. The merchandise was delivered FOB shipping point. Transportation costs of $200 were paid in cash.
2. Returned $800 of the inventory it had purchased because the inventory was damaged in transit. The seller agreed to pay the return transportation cost.
3. Paid the amount due on its account payable to Ross Company within the cash discount period.
4. Sold inventory that had cost $18,000 for $32,000 on account, under terms 2/10, n/45.
5. Received merchandise returned from a customer. The merchandise originally cost $800 and was sold to the customer for $1,500 cash. The customer was paid $1,500 cash for the returned merchandise.
6. Delivered goods FOB destination in Event 4. Transportation costs of $140 were paid in cash.
7. Collected the amount due on the account receivable within the discount period.
8. Took a physical count indicating that $21,100 of inventory was on hand at the end of the accounting period.

Required

a. Identify these events as asset source (AS), asset use (AU), asset exchange (AE), or claims exchange (CE).
b. Record each event in a horizontal financial statements model like the following one:

	Balance Sheet						Income Statement			Statement of Cash Flows
	Assets			=	Liab.	+ Stk. Equity				
Event	Cash +	Acct. Rec. +	Mdse. Inv. =		Acct. Pay. +	Ret. Earn.	Rev. −	Exp. =	Net Inc.	

c. Prepare a multistep income statement, a statement of changes in stockholders' equity, a balance sheet, and a statement of cash flows.

Problem 4-26A   *Multistep and common size income statements*

The following information was drawn from the records of Toner Sales Company:

	Year 1	Year 2
Net sales	$200,000	$200,000
Cost of goods sold	(90,000)	(80,000)
Operating expenses	(60,000)	(50,000)
Loss on the sale of land	–0–	(24,000)

Required

a. Prepare a multistep income statement for each year.

b. Prepare a common size income statement for each year.

c. At a recent meeting of the stockholders, Toner's president stated Year 3 would be a very good year with net income rising significantly. Write a brief memo explaining whether you agree or disagree with the president. Assume that the operating trends between Year 1 and Year 2 continue through Year 3.

Problem 4-27A *Preparing schedule of cost of goods sold and multistep and single-step income statements: periodic system (Appendix)*

LO 4-9

The following account titles and balances were taken from the accounting records of King Co. for Year 2. The company uses the periodic inventory system.

Account Title	Balance
Sales returns and allowances	$ 3,500
Miscellaneous expense	900
Transportation-out	2,200
Sales	156,300
Advertising expense	6,200
Salaries expense	21,000
Transportation-in	3,800
Purchases	88,000
Interest expense	250
Merchandise inventory, January 1	11,200
Rent expense	12,000
Merchandise inventory, December 31	10,700
Purchase returns and allowances	2,100
Loss on sale of land	3,100
Utilities expense	1,850

Required

a. Prepare a schedule to determine the amount of cost of goods sold.

b. Prepare a multistep income statement.

c. Prepare a single-step income statement.

Problem 4-28A *Comprehensive cycle problem: periodic system (Appendix)*

LO 4-9

The following account balances pertain to Benji's Grocery as of January 1, Year 2:

Account Title	Beginning Balances
Cash	$64,000
Accounts receivable	12,000
Merchandise inventory	90,000
Accounts payable	7,500
Common stock	89,000
Retained earnings	69,500

CHECK FIGURES
a. Ending Cash: $161,994
b. Cost of Goods Sold: $262,986

The following events occurred in Year 2. Assume that Benji's uses the periodic inventory method.

1. Purchased land for $30,000 cash.

2. Purchased merchandise on account for $230,000, terms 1/10, n/45.

3. Paid transportation of $2,100 cash on merchandise purchased FOB shipping point.

4. Returned $8,600 of defective merchandise purchased in Event 2.

5. Sold merchandise for $186,000 cash.

6. Sold merchandise on account for $236,000, terms 2/10, n/30.
7. Paid cash within the discount period on accounts payable due on merchandise purchased in Event 2.
8. Paid $28,500 cash for selling expenses.
9. Collected $156,000 of the accounts receivable from Event 6 within the discount period.
10. Collected $56,000 of the accounts receivable but not within the discount period.
11. Paid $17,100 of other operating expenses.
12. A physical count indicated that $48,300 of inventory was on hand at the end of the accounting period.

Required

a. Record these transactions in a horizontal financial statements model like the following one:

			Balance Sheet						Income Statement			Statement of Cash Flows
		Assets			=	Liab. +	Stk. Equity					
Event	Cash +	Accts. Rec. +	Mdse. Inv. +	Land =		Accts. Pay. +	Com. Stk. +	Ret. Earn.	Rev. −	Exp. =	Net Inc.	

b. Prepare a schedule of cost of goods sold and an income statement.

EXERCISES—SERIES B

When the instructions for *any* exercise or problem call for the preparation of an income statement, use the *multistep format* unless otherwise indicated.

LO 4-1

Exercise 4-1B *Comparing a merchandising company with a service company*

The following information is available for two different types of businesses for the Year 1 accounting year. Diamond Consulting is a service business that provides consulting services to small businesses. University Bookstore is a merchandising business that sells books to college students.

Data for Diamond Consulting

1. Borrowed $80,000 by issuing a note to the bank to start the business.
2. Performed services for clients and collected $60,000 cash.
3. Paid salary expense of $38,400.

Data for University Bookstore

1. Borrowed $80,000 by issuing a note to the bank to start the business.
2. Purchased $38,000 of inventory for cash.
3. Inventory costing $33,600 was sold for $60,000 cash.
4. Paid $4,800 cash for operating expenses.

Required

a. Prepare an income statement, balance sheet, and statement of cash flows for each of the companies.
b. What is different about the income statements of the two businesses?
c. What is different about the balance sheets of the two businesses?
d. How are the statements of cash flow different for the two businesses?

LO 4-1

Exercise 4-2B *Effect of inventory transactions on financial statements: perpetual system*

Sara Bayer started a small merchandising business in Year 1. The business experienced the following events during its first year of operation. Assume that Bayer uses the perpetual inventory system.

1. Acquired $50,000 cash from the issue of common stock.
2. Purchased inventory for $22,000 cash.
3. Sold inventory costing $18,000 for $28,000 cash.

Required

a. Record the events in a horizontal financial statements model like the one shown next.

Balance Sheet						Income Statement			Statement of Cash Flows
Assets		=		Stk. Equity					
Cash	+	Inv.	=	Com. Stk.	+	Ret. Earn.	Rev.	−	Exp.	=	Net Inc.	

b. Determine the amount of gross margin.

c. What is the amount of total assets at the end of the period?

Exercise 4-3B *Effect of inventory transactions on the income statement and statement of cash flows: perpetual system*

LO 4-1

During Year 1, Rondor Merchandising Company purchased $40,000 of inventory on account. The company sold inventory on account that cost $30,000 for $50,000. Cash payments on accounts payable were $24,500. There was $38,000 cash collected from accounts receivable. Rondor also paid $9,000 cash for operating expenses. Assume that Rondor started the accounting period with $20,000 in both cash and common stock.

Required

a. Identify the events described in the preceding paragraph and record them in a horizontal financial statements model like the following one:

Balance Sheet										Income Statement			Statement of Cash Flows
Assets				=	Liab.	+	Stk. Equity						
Cash	+	Accts. Rec.	+	Inv.	=	Accts. Pay.	+	Com. Stk.	+	Ret. Earn.	Rev. − Exp. = Net Inc.		
20,000 +		NA	+	NA =	NA	+	20,000	+	NA		NA − NA = NA		NA

b. What is the balance of accounts receivable at the end of Year 1?

c. What is the balance of accounts payable at the end of Year 1?

d. What are the amounts of gross margin and net income for Year 1?

e. Determine the amount of net cash flow from operating activities.

f. Explain any differences between net income and net cash flow from operating activities.

Exercise 4-4B *Recording inventory transactions in a horizontal financial statements model*

LO 4-1

Farm Tractor Supply experienced the following events during Year 1, its first year of operation:

1. Acquired $85,000 cash from the issue of common stock.
2. Purchased inventory for $42,000 cash.
3. Sold inventory costing $25,000 for $56,000 cash.
4. Paid $3,000 for advertising expense.

Required

Record the events in a horizontal financial statements model like the one shown next.

Balance Sheet						Income Statement			Statement of Cash Flows
Assets		=		Stk. Equity					
Cash	+	Inv.	=	Com. Stk.	+	Ret. Earn.	Rev.	−	Exp.	=	Net Inc.	

Exercise 4-5B *Cash discounts and purchase returns*

LO 4-2, 4-3

On March 6, Year 1, Salon Express purchased merchandise from Hair Fashions with a list price of $19,000, terms 2/10, n/45. On March 10, Salon returned merchandise to Hair Fashions. The list price of the returned merchandise was $8,500. Salon paid cash to settle the accounts payable on March 15, Year 1.

Required

a. What is the amount of the check that Salon must write to Hair Fashions on March 15?

b. Show the events in a horizontal financial statements model like the following one:

Balance Sheet								Income Statement			Statement of Cash Flows
Assets		=	Liab.	+		Stk. Equity					
Cash	+ Inv.	=	Accts. Pay.	+ Com. Stk.	+	Ret. Earn.		Rev.	− Exp.	= Net Inc.	

c. How much would Salon pay for the merchandise purchased if the payment is not made until March 20, Year 1?

d. Show the payment of the merchandise in Requirement *c* in a horizontal financial statements model like the one shown previously.

e. Why would Hair Fashions sell merchandise with the terms 2/10, n/45?

LO 4-4

Exercise 4-6B *Determining which party is responsible for transportation cost*

Required

Determine which party (buyer or seller) is responsible for transportation charges in each of the following situations:

a. Purchased merchandise, transportation terms, FOB destination.

b. Purchased merchandise, transportation terms, FOB shipping point.

c. Sold merchandise, transportation terms, FOB destination.

d. Sold merchandise, transportatoin terms, FOB shipping point.

LO 4-3, 4-4

Exercise 4-7B *Purchase discounts and transportation costs*

Musgrove Basket Company had an $8,500 beginning balance in its Merchandise Inventory account. The following information regarding Musgrove's purchases and sales of inventory during its Year 1 accounting period was drawn from the company's accounting records:

1. Purchased $45,000 of inventory under terms 1/10, net/60. Transportation costs amounted to $700. The goods were delivered FOB shipping point. Musgrove paid for the inventory within the discount period.

2. Purchased $40,000 of inventory under terms 2/10, net/30. Transportation costs amounted to $900. The goods were delivered to Musgrove FOB destination. Musgrove paid for the inventory after the discount period had expired.

3. Sold inventory that cost $56,000 for $94,000. Transportation costs for goods delivered to customers amounted to $3,200. The goods were delivered FOB destination.

Required

a. Determine the balance in the Inventory account at the end of the accounting period.

b. Is Musgrove or its customers responsible for the transportation costs described in Event 3?

c. Determine the gross margin.

LO 4-2, 4-3, 4-4

Exercise 4-8B *Accounting for product costs: perpetual inventory system*

Which of the following would be *added* to the Inventory account for a merchandising business using the perpetual inventory system?

Required

a. Transportation-in.

b. Allowance received for damaged inventory.

c. Purchase of inventory.

d. Purchase of office supplies.

e. Transportation-out.

f. Cash discount given on goods sold.

Exercise 4-9B   *Determining the effect of inventory transactions on the horizontal*   **LO 4-2, 4-3, 4-4**
financial statements model: perpetual system

TRS Company experienced the following events:

1. Purchased merchandise inventory for cash.
2. Sold merchandise inventory on account. Label the revenue recognition 2a and the expense recognition 2b.
3. Returned merchandise purchased on account.
4. Purchased merchandise inventory on account.
5. Paid cash on accounts payable within the discount period.
6. Paid cash for selling and administrative expenses.
7. Sold merchandise inventory for cash. Label the revenue recognition 7a and the expense recognition 7b.
8. Paid cash for transportation-out.
9. Paid cash for transportation-in.
10. Collected cash from accounts receivable not within the discount period.

Required

Identify each event as asset source (AS), asset use (AU), asset exchange (AE), or claims exchange (CE). Also explain how each event affects the financial statements by placing a + for increase, − for decrease, or NA for not affected under each of the components in the following horizontal financial statements model. Assume the company uses the perpetual inventory system. The first event is recorded as an example.

		Balance Sheet					Income Statement					Statement of Cash Flows
Event No.	Event Type	Assets	=	Liab.	+	Stk. Equity	Rev.	−	Exp.	=	Net Inc.	
1	AE	+ −	=	NA	+	NA	NA	−	NA	=	NA	− OA

Exercise 4-10B   *Effect of product cost and period cost: horizontal financial statements model*   **LO 4-2, 4-4**

Wild Rose Co. experienced the following events for the Year 1 accounting period:

1. Acquired $20,000 cash from the issue of common stock.
2. Purchased $36,000 of inventory on account.
3. Received goods purchased in Event 2 FOB shipping point. Transportation cost of $900 paid in cash.
4. Returned $4,000 of goods purchased in Event 2 because of poor quality.
5. Sold inventory on account that cost $28,000 for $82,000.
6. Transportation cost on the goods sold in Event 5 was $200. The goods were shipped FOB destination. Cash was paid for the transportation cost.
7. Collected $33,000 cash from accounts receivable.
8. Paid $27,000 cash on accounts payable.
9. Paid $4,500 for advertising expense.
10. Paid $7,200 cash for insurance expense.

Required

a. Which of these transactions affect period (selling and administrative) costs? Which result in product costs? If neither, label the transaction NA.
b. Show each event in a horizontal financial statements model like the following one. The first event is recorded as an example.

Balance Sheet											Income Statement				Statement of Cash Flows
Assets			=	Liab.	+	Stk. Equity					Rev. − Exp. = Net Inc.				
Cash	+ Accts. Rec.	+ Inv.	=	Accts. Pay.	+	Com. Stk.	+	Ret. Earn.			Rev.	− Exp.	= Net Inc.		
20,000 +	NA	+ NA =		NA	+	20,000	+	NA			NA	− NA	= NA		20,000 FA

LO 4-5

Exercise 4-11B *Effect of inventory losses: perpetual system*

Alpine Ski Co. experienced the following events during Year 1, its first year of operation:

1. Started the business when it acquired $145,000 cash from the issue of common stock.
2. Paid $85,000 cash to purchase inventory.
3. Sold inventory costing $55,350 for $77,500 cash.
4. Physically counted inventory showing $28,000 inventory was on hand at the end of the accounting period.

Required

a. Determine the amount of the difference between book balance and the actual amount of inventory as determined by the physical count.

b. Explain how differences between the book balance and the physical count of inventory could arise. Why is being able to determine whether differences exist useful to management?

LO 4-2, 4-4, 4-6

Exercise 4-12B *Effect of purchase returns and allowances and transportation costs on the financial statements: perpetual system*

The beginning account balances for Franchoni's Body Shop as of January 1, Year 2, follow:

Account Titles	Beginning Balances
Cash	$15,000
Inventory	5,000
Common stock	18,000
Retained earnings	2,000

The following events affected the company during the Year 2 accounting period:

1. Purchased merchandise on account that cost $17,000.
2. The goods in Event 1 were purchased FOB shipping point with transportation cost of $1,200 cash.
3. Returned $2,200 of damaged merchandise.
4. Agreed to keep other damaged merchandise for which the company received a $900 allowance.
5. Sold merchandise that cost $12,000 for $27,000 cash.
6. Delivered merchandise to customers in Event 5 under terms FOB destination with transportation costs amounting to $800 cash.
7. Paid $7,800 on the merchandise purchased in Event 1.

Required

a. Organize appropriate accounts under an accounting equation. Record the beginning balances and the transaction data in the accounts.

b. Prepare an income statement and a statement of cash flows for Year 2.

c. Explain why a difference does or does not exist between net income and net cash flow from operating activities.

LO 4-6

Exercise 4-13B *Multistep income statement*

In Year 1, Image Incorporated sold land for $82,000 cash. The land had originally cost $50,000. Also, Image sold inventory that had cost $176,000 for $265,000 cash. Operating expenses amounted to $41,000.

Required

a. Prepare a Year 1 multistep income statement for Image Incorporated.

b. Assume that normal operating activities grow evenly by 10 percent during Year 2. Prepare a Year 2 multistep income statement for Image Incorporated.

c. Determine the percentage change in net income between Year 1 and Year 2.

d. Should the stockholders have expected the results determined in Requirement *c*? Explain your answer.

Exercise 4-14B   *Single-step and multistep income statements*   LO 4-6

The following information was taken from the accounts of Adams's Eatery, a delicatessen, at December 31, Year 1. The accounts are listed in alphabetical order, and each has a normal balance.

Accounts payable	$1,200
Accounts receivable	800
Advertising expense	400
Cash	820
Common stock	400
Cost of goods sold	1,200
Interest expense	140
Loss on sale of land	50
Merchandise inventory	900
Prepaid rent	80
Rent expense	220
Retained earnings	1,000
Salaries expense	260
Sales revenue	2,000

Required

First, prepare an income statement for the year using the single-step approach. Then, prepare another income statement using the multistep approach.

Exercise 4-15B   *Purchase returns, discounts, loss, and a multistep income statement*   LO 4-2, 4-3, 4-6

The following information was drawn from the Year 1 accounting records of Cozart Merchandisers.

1. Inventory with a list price of $40,000 was purchased under terms 2/10, net/30.
2. Cozart returned $4,200 of the inventory to the supplier five days after purchase.
3. The accounts payable was settled within the discount period.
4. The inventory was sold for $69,000.
5. Selling and administrative expenses amounted to $12,000.
6. Interest expense paid amounted to $800.
7. Land that cost $15,000 was sold for $20,000 cash.

Required

a. Determine the cost of the inventory sold.
b. Prepare a multistep income statement.
c. Where would the interest expense be shown on the statement of cash flows?
d. How would the sale of the land be shown on the statement of cash flows?
e. Explain the difference between a loss and an expense.

Exercise 4-16B   *Effect of sales returns and allowances and transportation costs on the*   LO 4-2, 4-4, 4-7
financial statements: perpetual system

McDowell Company began the Year 3 accounting period with $50,000 cash, $72,000 inventory, $55,000 common stock, and $67,000 retained earnings. During Year 3, McDowell experienced the following events:

1. Sold merchandise costing $52,000 for $85,700 on account to Anderson Sporting Goods.
2. Delivered the goods to Anderson under terms FOB destination. Transportation costs were $600 cash.
3. Received returned goods from Anderson. The goods cost McDowell $7,000 and were sold to Anderson for $9,200.
4. Granted Anderson a $2,000 allowance for damaged goods that Anderson agreed to keep.
5. Collected partial payment of $68,000 cash from accounts receivable.

Required

a. Record the events in a horizontal financial statements model like the one shown next.

Balance Sheet								Income Statement					Statement of Cash Flows
Assets				=	Stk. Equity								
Cash	+	Accts. Rec.	+	Inv.	=	Com. Stk.	+	Ret. Earn.	Rev.	−	Exp.	=	Net Inc.	

b. Prepare an income statement, a balance sheet, and a statement of cash flows.

c. Why would Anderson agree to keep the damaged goods? Who benefits more?

LO 4-2, 4-3, 4-4, 4-6, 4-7, 4-8

Exercise 4-17B   *Comprehensive exercise with purchases discounts*

Custom Auto Parts (CAP) started the Year 2 accounting period with the balances given in the following horizontal financial statements model. During Year 2, CAP experienced the following business events:

1. Purchased $60,000 of merchandise inventory on account, terms 2/10, n/30.
2. The goods that were purchased in Event 1 were delivered FOB shipping point. Transportation costs of $1,500 were paid in cash by the responsible party.
3. Returned $3,000 of goods purchased in Event 1.
4a. Recorded the cash discount on the goods purchased in Event 1.
4b. Paid the balance due on the account payable within the discount period.
5a. Recognized $59,000 of cash revenue from the sale of merchandise.
5b. Recognized $45,000 of cost of goods sold.
6. The merchandise in Event 5a was sold to customers FOB destination. Transportation costs of $1,400 were paid in cash by the responsible party.
7. Paid cash of $9,000 for selling and administrative expenses.
8. Sold the land for $14,500 cash.

Required

a. Show the given transactions in a horizontal financial statements model like the one shown next.

	Balance Sheet										Income Statement							Statement of Cash Flows
	Assets					= Liab. +		Stk. Equity										
Event No.	Cash	+ Inventory +	Land	=	Accts. Pay.	+	Com. Stk.	+	Ret. Earn.		Rev./ Gain	−	Exp./ Loss	=	Net Inc.			
Beg. Bal.	60,000 +	8,000	+ 12,000 =	−0−		+ 50,000 +		30,000			NA	−	NA	=	NA			NA

b. Prepare a multistep income statement. Include common size percentages on the income statement.

c. CAP's gross margin percentage in the prior year was 34 percent. Based on the common size data in the income statement, did CAP raise or lower its prices in Year 2?

d. Assuming a 5 percent rate of growth, what is the amount of net income expected for Year 3?

LO 4-8

Exercise 4-18B   *Using ratios to make comparisons*

The following income statements were drawn from the annual reports of Athens Company and Boulder Company:

	Athens*	Boulder*
Net sales	$32,600	$86,200
Cost of goods sold	(24,450)	(47,410)
Gross margin	8,150	38,790
Less: Operating exp.		
Selling and admin. exp.	(6,200)	(34,480)
Net income	$ 1,950	$ 4,310

*All figures are reported in thousands of dollars.

Required

a. One of the companies is a high-end retailer that operates in exclusive shopping malls. The other operates discount stores located in low-cost, standalone buildings. Identify the high-end retailer and the discounter. Support your answer with appropriate ratios.

b. If Athens and Boulder have equity of $22,000 and $39,000, respectively, which company is in the more profitable business?

Exercise 4-19B *Using common size statements and ratios to make comparisons*   LO 4-8

The following information is available for Billings and Phoenix companies:

	Billings	Phoenix
Sales	$3,000,000	$3,000
Cost of goods sold	1,800,000	2,100
Operating expenses	960,000	780
Total assets	3,750,000	3,750
Stockholders' equity	1,000,000	1,200

Required

a. Prepare a common size income statement for each company.

b. Compute the return on assets and return on equity for each company.

c. Which company is more profitable from the stockholders' perspective?

d. One company is a high-end retailer, and the other operates a discount store. Which is the discounter? Support your selection by referring to the appropriate ratios.

Exercise 4-20B *Effect of inventory transactions on the income statement and balance sheet: periodic system (Appendix)*   LO 4-9

Rick Dove is the owner of RD Cleaning. At the beginning of the year, RD Cleaning had $4,800 in inventory. During the year, RD Cleaning purchased inventory that cost $26,000. At the end of the year, inventory on hand amounted to $3,600.

Required

Calculate the following:

a. Cost of goods available for sale during the year.

b. Cost of goods sold for the year.

c. Inventory amount RD Cleaning would report on its year-end balance sheet.

Exercise 4-21B *Determining cost of goods sold: periodic system (Appendix)*   LO 4-9

Far East Retailers uses the periodic inventory system to account for its inventory transactions. The following account titles and balances were drawn from Far East's records for Year 2: beginning balance in inventory, $46,200; purchases, $352,400; purchase returns and allowances, $14,600; sales, $840,000; sales returns and allowances, $7,520; transportation-in, $2,150; and operating expenses, $65,100. A physical count indicated that $35,100 of merchandise was on hand at the end of the accounting period.

Required

a. Prepare a schedule of cost of goods sold.

b. Prepare a multistep income statement.

PROBLEMS—SERIES B

LO 4-4

Problem 4-22B *Identifying transportation cost*

Required

For each of the following events, determine the amount of transportation paid by Cycle Parts House. Also indicate whether the transportation is classified as a product or period cost.

a. Purchased merchandise with costs of $500, FOB shipping point.

b. Sold merchandise to a customer. Transportation costs were $800, FOB shipping point.

c. Purchased inventory with transportation costs of $1,400, FOB destination.

d. Shipped merchandise to customers with transportation costs of $300, FOB destination.

LO 4-4

Problem 4-23B *Identifying product and period costs*

Required

Indicate whether each of the following costs is a product cost or a period cost:

a. Cleaning supplies for the office.

b. Transportation on goods purchased for resale.

c. Salary of the marketing director.

d. Transportation on goods sold to customer with terms FOB destination.

e. Utilities expense incurred for office building.

f. Advertising expense.

g. Insurance on vans used to deliver goods to customers.

h. Salaries of sales supervisors.

i. Monthly maintenance expense for a copier.

j. Goods purchased for resale.

LO 4-1, 4-6

CHECK FIGURES
Year 1 Net Income: $2,000
Year 2 Total Assets: $105,000

Problem 4-24B *Basic transactions for three accounting cycles: perpetual system*

Singleton Company was started in Year 1 when it acquired $94,000 cash from the issue of common stock. The following data summarize the company's first three years' operating activities. Assume that all transactions were cash transactions.

	Year 1	Year 2	Year 3
Purchases of inventory	$45,000	$57,000	$71,000
Sales	63,000	76,000	118,000
Cost of goods sold	39,000	41,000	78,000
Selling and administrative expenses	22,000	26,000	36,000

Required

Prepare an income statement (use the multistep format) and balance sheet for each fiscal year. (*Hint:* Record the transaction data for each accounting period in the accounting equation before preparing the statements for that year.)

LO 4-2, 4-3, 4-4, 4-5, 4-6, 4-7

Problem 4-25B *Comprehensive cycle problem: perpetual system*

At the beginning of Year 2, the Dotson Company had the following balances in its accounts:

Cash	$14,500
Inventory	28,000
Common stock	18,000
Retained earnings	24,500

During Year 2, the company experienced the following events:

CHECK FIGURES
c. Net Income: $11,420
    Total Assets: $53,920

1. Purchased inventory that cost $18,600 on account from Richburg Company under terms 2/10, n/30. The merchandise was delivered FOB shipping point. Transportation costs of $300 were paid in cash.

2. Returned $600 of the inventory it had purchased because the inventory was damaged in transit. The seller agreed to pay the return transportation cost.

3. Paid the amount due on its account payable to Richburg Company within the cash discount period.

4. Sold inventory that had cost $14,000 for $27,000 on account, under terms 1/10, n/30.

5. Received merchandise returned from a customer. The merchandise originally cost $500 and was sold to the customer for $1,200 cash. The customer was paid $1,200 cash for the returned merchandise.

6. Delivered goods FOB destination in Event 4. Transportation costs of $170 were paid in cash.

7. Collected the amount due on the account receivable within the discount period.

8. Took a physical count indicating that $32,000 of inventory was on hand at the end of the accounting period.

Required

a. Identify these events as asset source (AS), asset use (AU), asset exchange (AE), or claims exchange (CE).

b. Record each event in a horizontal financial statements model like the following one:

	Balance Sheet						Income Statement			Statement of Cash Flows
	Assets			=	Liab.	+ Stk. Equity				
Event	Cash +	Acct. Rec. +	Mdse. Inv. =		Acct. Pay. +	Ret. Earn.	Rev. −	Exp. =	Net Inc.	

c. Prepare a multistep income statement, a statement of changes in stockholders' equity, a balance sheet, and a statement of cash flows.

Problem 4-26B   Multistep and common size income statements

LO 4-6, 4-8

The following information was drawn from the records of Moore Sales Company:

	Year 1	Year 2
Net sales	$60,000	$70,000
Cost of goods sold	(25,000)	(26,500)
Operating expenses	(13,200)	(16,100)
Gain on the sale of land	—0—	5,000

Required

a. Prepare a multistep income statement for each year.

b. Prepare a common size income statement for each year.

c. Assume that the operating trends between Year 1 and Year 2 continue through Year 3. Write a brief memo indicating whether you expect net income to increase or decrease in Year 3.

Problem 4-27B   Preparing a schedule of cost of goods sold and multistep and single-step income statements: periodic system (Appendix)

LO 4-9

eXcel

The following account titles and balances were taken from the accounting records of Hogan Sales Co. at December 31, Year 2. The company uses the periodic inventory method.

Account Title	Balance
Advertising expense	$ 20,800
Interest expense	10,000
Merchandise inventory, January 1	36,000
Merchandise inventory, December 31	40,200
Miscellaneous expense	1,600
Purchases	300,000
Purchase returns and allowances	5,400
Rent expense	36,000
Salaries expense	106,000
Sales	640,000
Sales returns and allowances	16,000
Transportation-in	12,400
Transportation-out	21,600
Gain on sale of land	8,000
Utilities expense	22,400

Required

a. Prepare a schedule to determine the amount of cost of goods sold.

b. Prepare a multistep income statement.

c. Prepare a single-step income statement.

LO 4-9

CHECK FIGURES
a. Ending Cash: $198,910
b. Cost of Goods Sold:
   $176,140

Problem 4-28B *Comprehensive cycle problem: periodic system (Appendix)*

The following account balances pertain to Frank's Hardware as of January 1, Year 2:

Account Title	Beginning Balances
Cash	$ 89,000
Accounts receivable	18,000
Merchandise inventory	110,000
Accounts payable	6,500
Common stock	95,000
Retained earnings	115,500

The following events occurred in Year 2. Assume that Frank's uses the periodic inventory method.

1. Purchased land for $45,000 cash.

2. Purchased merchandise on account for $190,000, terms 2/10, n/30.

3. Paid transportation cost of $1,700 cash on merchandise purchased FOB shipping point.

4. Returned $12,000 of defective merchandise purchased in Event 2.

5. Sold merchandise for $165,000 cash.

6. Sold merchandise on account for $210,000, terms 3/10, n/45.

7. Paid cash within the discount period on accounts payable due on merchandise purchased in Event 2.

8. Paid $22,000 cash for selling expenses.

9. Collected $145,000 of the accounts receivable from Event 6 within the discount period.

10. Collected $60,000 of the accounts receivable but not within the discount period.

11. Paid $12,600 of other operating expenses.

12. A physical count indicated that $110,000 of inventory was on hand at the end of the accounting period.

Required

a. Record these transactions in a horizontal financial statements model like the following one:

	Balance Sheet									Income Statement			Statement of Cash Flows
	Assets				**= Liab. +**		**Stk. Equity**						
Event	**Cash +**	**Accts. Rec. +**	**Mdse. Inv. +**	**Land =**	**Accts. Pay. +**		**Com. Stk. +**	**Ret. Earn.**		**Rev. −**	**Exp. =**	**Net Inc.**	

b. Prepare a schedule of cost of goods sold and an income statement.

ANALYZE, THINK, COMMUNICATE

ATC 4-1   Business Applications Case   *Understanding real-world annual reports*

Required

Obtain Target Corporation's annual report for its 2018 fiscal year (year ended February 2, 2019) at http://investors.target.com using the instructions in Appendix B, and use it to answer the following questions:

a. What was Target's gross margin percentage for the fiscal year ended February 2, 2019 (2018) and 2017? Use "Sales" for these computations.

b. What was Target's return on sales percentage for 2018 and 2017? Use "Total revenues" for these computations.

c. Target's return on sales percentage for 2017 was higher than it was in 2018. Ignoring taxes, how much higher would Target's 2018 net income have been if its return on sales percentage in 2018 had been the same as for 2017?

ATC 4-2   Group Assignment   *Multistep income statement*

The following quarterly information is given for Rossie for Year 1 (amounts shown are in millions):

	First Quarter	Second Quarter	Third Quarter	Fourth Quarter
Net Sales	$736.0	$717.4	$815.2	$620.1
Gross Margin	461.9	440.3	525.3	252.3
Net Income	37.1	24.6	38.6	31.4

Required

a. Divide the class into groups and organize the groups into four sections. Assign each section financial information for one of the quarters.

  (1) Each group should compute the cost of goods sold and operating expenses for the specific quarter assigned to its section and prepare a multistep income statement for the quarter.

  (2) Each group should compute the gross margin percentage and cost of goods sold percentage for its specific quarter.

  (3) Have a representative of each group put that quarter's sales, cost of goods sold percentage, and gross margin percentage on the board.

Class Discussion

b. Have the class discuss the change in each of these items from quarter to quarter and explain why the change might have occurred. Which was the best quarter and why?

ATC 4-3   Real-World Case   *Identifying companies based on financial statement information*

Presented here is selected information from the 2017 fiscal-year 10-K reports of four companies. The four companies, in alphabetical order, are Advance Micro Devices, a global semiconductor company; AT&T, Inc., a company that provides communications and digital entertainment; Caterpillar, Inc., a manufacturer of heavy machinery; and Pfizer, Inc., a pharmaceutical manufacturer. The data for the companies, presented in the order of the amount of their sales in millions of dollars, are:

	A	B	C	D
Sales	$5,329	$45,462	$52,546	$160,546
Cost of goods sold	3,506	31,049	11,240	77,379
Net earnings	43	754	21,307	29,450
Inventory	739	10,018	7,578	—
Accounts receivable	400	16,193	8,221	16,522
Total assets	3,540	76,962	171,797	444,097

Required

Based on these financial data and your knowledge and assumptions about the nature of the businesses that the companies operate, determine which data relate to which companies. Write a memorandum explaining your decisions. Include a discussion of which ratios you used in your analysis, and show the computations of these ratios in your memorandum.

ATC 4-4 Business Applications Case   *Performing ratio analysis using real-world data*

The Kroger Co. was founded in 1883 and is one of the largest retailers in the world, based on annual sales. Publix Super Markets, Inc. operates 1,167 grocery stores throughout the southeastern and mid-Atlantic United States. It is employee owned, and its stock is not available for purchase by the general public. Publix is usually rated in the top three for customer service among national grocery store chains.

The following data were taken from these companies' 2017 annual reports. All dollar amounts are in millions.

	Kroger Co. February 3, 2018	Publix December 31, 2017
Sales	$122,662	$34,837
Cost of goods sold	95,662	25,130
Net income	1,907	2,292

Required

a. Before performing any calculations, speculate as to which company will have the highest gross margin and return-on-sales percentage. Explain the rationale for your decision.

b. Calculate the gross margin percentages for Kroger and Publix.

c. Calculate the return-on-sales percentages for Kroger and Publix.

d. Do the calculations from Requirements *b* and *c* confirm your speculations in Requirement *a*?

ATC 4-5 Writing Assignment   *Effect of sales returns on financial statements*

Bell Farm and Garden Equipment Co. reported the following information for Year 1:

Net sales of equipment	$2,450,567
Other income	6,786
Cost of goods sold	(1,425,990)
Selling, general, and administrative expense	(325,965)
Depreciation and amortization	(3,987)
Net operating income	$ 701,411

Selected information from the balance sheet as of December 31, Year 1, follows:

Cash and marketable securities	$113,545
Inventory	248,600
Accounts receivable	82,462
Property, plant, and equipment—net	335,890
Other assets	5,410
Total assets	$785,907

Assume that a major customer returned a large order to Bell on December 31, Year 1. The amount of the sale had been $146,800, with a cost of sales of $94,623. The return was recorded in the books on January 1, Year 2. The company president does not want to correct the books. He argues that it makes no difference as to whether the return is recorded in Year 1 or Year 2. Either way, the return has been duly recognized.

Required

a. Assume you are the CFO for Bell Farm and Garden Equipment Co. Write a memo to the president explaining how the failure to recognize the return on December 31, Year 1, could cause the financial statements to be misleading to investors and creditors. Explain how omitting the return from the customer would affect net income and the balance sheet.

b. Why might the president want to record the return on January 1, Year 2, instead of December 31, Year 1?

c. Would the failure to record the customer return violate the AICPA Code of Professional Conduct? (See Exhibit 2.7 in Chapter 2.)

d. If the president of the company refuses to correct the financial statements, what action should you take?

ATC 4-6 Ethical Dilemma *Wait until I get mine*

Ada Fontanez is the president of a large company that owns a chain of athletic shoe stores. The company was in dire financial condition when she was hired three years ago. In an effort to motivate Fontanez, the board of directors included a bonus plan as part of her compensation package. According to her employment contract, on January 15 of each year, Fontanez is paid a cash bonus equal to 5 percent of the amount of net income reported on the preceding December 31 income statement. Fontanez was sufficiently motivated. Through her leadership, the company prospered. Her efforts were recognized throughout the industry, and she received numerous lucrative offers to leave the company. One offer was so enticing that she decided to change jobs. Her decision was made in late December, Year 5. However, she decided to resign effective February 1, Year 6, to ensure the receipt of her January bonus. On December 31, Year 1, the chief accountant, Walter Smith, advised Fontanez that the company had a sizable quantity of damaged inventory. A warehouse fire had resulted in smoke and water damage to approximately $600,000 of inventory. The warehouse was not insured, and the accountant recommended that the loss be recognized immediately. After examining the inventory, Fontanez argued that it could be sold as *damaged goods* to customers at reduced prices. Accordingly, she refused to allow the write-off the accountant recommended. She stated that so long as she is president, the inventory stays on the books at cost. She told the accountant that he could take up the matter with the new president in February.

Required

a. How would an immediate write-off of the damaged inventory affect the December 31, Year 5, income statement, balance sheet, and statement of cash flows?

b. How would the write-off affect Fontanez's bonus?

c. If the new president is given the same bonus plan, how will Fontanez's refusal to recognize the loss affect his or her bonus?

d. Assuming that the damaged inventory is truly worthless, comment on the ethical implications of Fontanez's refusal to recognize the loss in the Year 5 accounting period.

e. Assume that the damaged inventory is truly worthless and that you are Smith. How would you react to Fontanez's refusal to recognize the loss?

ATC 4-7 Research Assignment *Analyzing Coca-Cola's profit margins*

Using Coca-Cola Company's most current Form 10-K, answer the following questions. To obtain the Form 10-K, you can use the EDGAR system, following the instructions in Appendix A, or it can be found on the company's website.

Required

a. What was Coke's gross margin percentage for the most current year?

b. What was Coke's gross margin percentage for the previous year? Has it changed significantly?

c. What was Coke's return-on-sales percentage for the most current year?

d. What percentage of Coke's total net operating revenues for the most current year were from operations in the United States?

e. Comment on the appropriateness of comparing Coke's gross margin with that of Microsoft. If Microsoft has a higher or lower margin, does that mean Microsoft is a better-managed company?

CHAPTER 5

Accounting for Inventories

Video lectures and accompanying self-assessment quizzes are available in *Connect* for all learning objectives.

Tableau Dashboard Activity is available in *Connect* for this chapter.

LEARNING OBJECTIVES

After you have mastered the material in this chapter, you will be able to:

LO 5-1   Determine the amount of cost of goods sold and ending inventory using the specific identification, FIFO, LIFO, and weighted-average cost flow methods.

LO 5-2   Apply the lower-of-cost-or-market rule to inventory valuation.

LO 5-3   Show how fraud can be avoided through inventory control.

LO 5-4   Use the gross margin method to estimate ending inventory.

LO 5-5   Calculate and interpret the inventory turnover ratio.

CHAPTER OPENING

In the previous chapter, we used the simplifying assumption that identical inventory items cost the same amount. In practice, businesses often pay different amounts for identical items. Suppose The Mountain Bike Company (TMBC) sells high-end Model 201 helmets. Because all Model 201 helmets are identical, does the helmet supplier charge TMBC the same amount for each helmet? Probably not. You have likely observed that prices change frequently.

Assume TMBC purchases one Model 201 helmet at a cost of $100. Two weeks later, TMBC purchases a second Model 201 helmet. Because the supplier has raised prices, the second helmet costs $110. If TMBC sells one of its two helmets, should it record $100 or $110 as cost of goods sold? The following section of this chapter discusses several acceptable alternative methods for determining the amount of cost of goods sold from which companies may choose under generally accepted accounting principles.

The Curious Accountant

Albertsons Companies, Inc. is one of the nation's largest retail chains, operating about 2,318 stores under 13 different names, including Albertsons, Safeway, and Vons. As of February 24, 2018, the company reported approximately $4.6 billion of inventory on its balance sheet. In the notes to its financial statements, Albertsons reported that it uses an inventory method that assumes its newest goods are sold first and its oldest goods are kept in inventory.

Ken Wolter/123RF

Can you think of any reason why a company selling perishable goods, such as milk and vegetables, would use an inventory method that assumes older goods are kept, while newer goods are sold? (Answer on page 253.)

INVENTORY COST FLOW METHODS

Recall that when goods are sold, product costs flow (are transferred) from the Inventory account to the Cost of Goods Sold account. Four acceptable methods for determining the amount of cost to transfer are (1) specific identification; (2) first-in, first-out (FIFO); (3) last-in, first-out (LIFO); and (4) weighted average.

LO 5-1

Determine the amount of cost of goods sold and ending inventory using the specific identification, FIFO, LIFO, and weighted-average cost flow methods.

Specific Identification

Suppose The Mountain Bike Company (TMBC) tags inventory items so it can identify which one is sold at the time of sale. TMBC could then charge the actual cost of the specific item sold to cost of goods sold. Recall that the first inventory item TMBC purchased cost $100 and the second item cost $110. Using **specific identification,** cost of goods sold would be $100 if the first item purchased was sold, or $110 if the second item purchased was sold.

When a company's inventory consists of many low-priced, high-turnover goods, the recordkeeping necessary to use specific identification isn't practical. Imagine the difficulty of recording the cost of each specific food item in a grocery store. Another disadvantage of the specific identification method is the opportunity for managers to manipulate the income statement. For example, TMBC can report a lower cost of goods sold by selling the first instead of the second item. Specific identification is, however, frequently used for high-priced, low-turnover inventory items such as automobiles. For big ticket items like cars, customer demands for specific products limit management's ability to select which merchandise is sold, and volume is low enough to manage the recordkeeping.

Andersen Ross/Brand X Pictures/Getty Images

First-In, First-Out (FIFO)

The **first-in, first-out (FIFO) cost flow method** requires that the cost of the items purchased *first* be assigned to cost of goods sold. Using FIFO, TMBC's cost of goods sold is $100.

Last-In, First-Out (LIFO)

The **last-in, first-out (LIFO) cost flow method** requires that the cost of the items purchased *last* be charged to cost of goods sold. Using LIFO, TMBC's cost of goods sold is $110.

Weighted Average

To use the **weighted-average cost flow method,** first calculate the average cost per unit by dividing the *total cost* of the inventory available by the *total number* of units available. In the case of TMBC, the average cost per unit of the inventory is $105 [($100 + $110) ÷ 2]. Cost of goods sold is then calculated by multiplying the average cost per unit by the number of units sold. Using weighted average, TMBC's cost of goods sold is $105 ($105 × 1).

Physical Flow

The preceding discussion pertains to the flow of *costs* through the accounting records, *not* the actual **physical flow of goods.** Goods usually move physically on a FIFO basis, which means that the first items of merchandise acquired by a company (first-in) are the first items sold to its customers (first-out). The inventory items on hand at the end of the accounting period are typically the last items in (the most recently acquired goods). If companies did not sell their oldest inventory items first, inventories would include dated, less marketable merchandise. *Cost flow,* however, can differ from *physical flow.* For example, a company may use LIFO or weighted average for financial reporting even if its goods flow physically on a FIFO basis.

Effect of Cost Flow on Financial Statements

Effect on Income Statement

The cost flow method a company uses can significantly affect the gross margin reported in the income statement. To demonstrate, assume that TMBC sold the inventory item discussed previously for $120. The amounts of gross margin using the FIFO, LIFO, and weighted-average cost flow assumptions are shown in the following table:

	FIFO	LIFO	Weighted Average
Sales	$120	$120	$120
Cost of goods sold	100	110	105
Gross margin	$ 20	$ 10	$ 15

Even though the physical flow is assumed to be identical for each method, the gross margin reported under FIFO is double the amount reported under LIFO. Companies experiencing identical economic events (same units of inventory purchased and sold) can report significantly different results in their financial statements. Meaningful financial analysis requires an understanding of financial reporting practices.

Effect on Balance Sheet

Because total product costs are allocated between costs of goods sold and ending inventory, the cost flow method a company uses affects its balance sheet as well as its income statement. FIFO transfers the first cost to the income statement, so this leaves the last cost on the balance sheet. Similarly, by transferring the last cost to the income statement, LIFO leaves the first cost in ending inventory. The weighted-average method bases both cost of goods sold and ending inventory on the average cost per unit. To illustrate, the ending inventory TMBC would report on the balance sheet using each of the three cost flow methods is shown in the following table.

	FIFO	LIFO	Weighted Average
Ending inventory	$110	$100	$105

The FIFO, LIFO, and weighted-average methods are all used extensively in business practice. The same company may even use one cost flow method for some of its products and different cost flow methods for other products. Exhibit 5.1 illustrates the relative use of the different cost flow methods among U.S. companies.

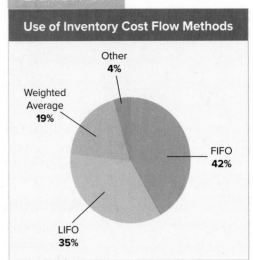

EXHIBIT 5.1

Use of Inventory Cost Flow Methods

The chart is based on data drawn from recent annual reports published by the 30 companies that comprise the Dow Jones Industrial Average. The category titled "Other" consisted of companies with relatively small quantities of inventory.

CHECK YOURSELF 5.1

Nash Office Supply (NOS) purchased two Model 303 copiers at different times. The first copier purchased cost $400 and the second copier purchased cost $450. NOS sold one of the copiers for $600. Determine the gross margin on the sale and the ending inventory balance assuming NOS accounts for inventory using (1) FIFO, (2) LIFO, and (3) weighted average.

Answer

	FIFO	LIFO	Weighted Average
Sales	$600	$600	$600
Cost of goods sold	(400)	(450)	(425)
Gross margin	$200	$150	$175
Ending inventory	$450	$400	$425

Multiple Layers with Multiple Quantities

The previous example illustrates different **inventory cost flow methods** using only two cost layers ($100 and $110) with only one unit of inventory in each layer. Actual business inventories are considerably more complex. Most real-world inventories are composed of multiple cost layers with different quantities of inventory in each layer. The underlying allocation concepts, however, remain unchanged.

For example, a different inventory item The Mountain Bike Company (TMBC) carries in its stores is a bike called the Eraser. TMBC's beginning inventory and two purchases of Eraser bikes are described next:

Jan. 1	Beginning inventory	10 units @ $200	=	$ 2,000
Mar. 18	First purchase	20 units @ $220	=	4,400
Aug. 21	Second purchase	25 units @ $250	=	6,250
Total cost of the 55 bikes available for sale				$12,650

The accounting records for the period show that TMBC paid cash for all Eraser bike purchases and sold 43 bikes at a cash price of $350 each.

Allocating Cost of Goods Available for Sale

The following discussion shows how to determine the cost of goods sold and ending inventory amounts using FIFO, LIFO, and weighted-average cost flow methods. We show all three methods to demonstrate how they affect the financial statements differently; TMBC would actually use only one of the methods.

Regardless of the cost flow method chosen, TMBC must allocate the cost of goods available for sale ($12,650) between cost of goods sold and ending inventory. The amounts assigned to each category will differ depending on TMBC's cost flow method. Computations for each method are shown in the next section.

FIFO Inventory Cost Flow

Recall that TMBC sold 43 Eraser bikes during the accounting period. The FIFO method transfers to the Cost of Goods Sold account the *cost of the first 43 bikes* TMBC had available to sell. The first 43 bikes acquired by TMBC were the 10 bikes in the beginning inventory (these were purchased in the prior period) plus the 20 bikes purchased in March and 13 of the bikes purchased in August. The expense recognized for the cost of these bikes ($9,650) is computed as follows:

Jan. 1	Beginning inventory	10 units @ $200	=	$2,000
Mar. 18	First purchase	20 units @ $220	=	4,400
Aug. 21	Second purchase	13 units @ $250	=	3,250
Total cost of the 43 bikes sold				$9,650

Because TMBC had 55 bikes available for sale, it would have 12 bikes (55 available − 43 sold) in ending inventory. The cost assigned to these 12 bikes (the ending balance in the Inventory account) equals the cost of goods available for sale minus the cost of goods sold as shown next:

Cost of goods available for sale	$12,650
Cost of goods sold	9,650
Ending inventory balance	$ 3,000

We show the allocation of the cost of goods available for sale between cost of goods sold and ending inventory graphically next:

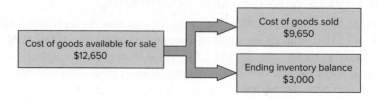

LIFO Inventory Cost Flow

Under LIFO, the cost of goods sold is the cost of the last 43 bikes acquired by TMBC, computed as follows:

Aug. 21	Second purchase	25 units @ $250	=	$ 6,250
Mar. 18	First purchase	18 units @ $220	=	3,960
Total cost of the 43 bikes sold				$10,210

The LIFO cost of the 12 bikes in ending inventory is computed as shown next:

Cost of goods available for sale	$12,650
Cost of goods sold	10,210
Ending inventory balance	$ 2,440

We show the allocation of the cost of goods available for sale between cost of goods sold and ending inventory graphically next:

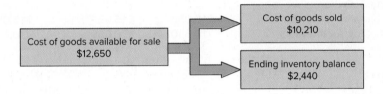

Weighted-Average Cost Flow

The weighted-average cost per unit is determined by dividing the *total cost of goods available for sale* by the *total number of units* available for sale. For TMBC, the weighted-average cost per unit is $230 ($12,650 ÷ 55). The weighted-average cost of goods sold is determined by multiplying the average cost per unit by the number of units sold ($230 × 43 = $9,890). The cost assigned to the 12 bikes in ending inventory is $2,760 (12 × $230).

We show the allocation of the cost of goods available for sale between cost of goods sold and ending inventory graphically next:

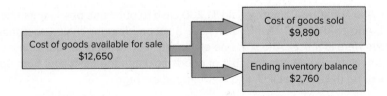

Financial Statements

Exhibit 5.2 displays partial financial statements for The Mountain Bike Company (TMBC). This exhibit includes only information pertaining to the Eraser bikes inventory item described previously. Other financial statement data are omitted.

Recall that assets are reported on the balance sheet in order of liquidity (how quickly they are expected to be converted to cash). Because companies frequently sell inventory on account, inventory is less liquid than accounts receivable. As a result, companies commonly report inventory below accounts receivable on the balance sheet.

Exhibit 5.2 demonstrates that the amounts reported for gross margin on the income statement and inventory on the balance sheet differ significantly. The cash flow from operating activities on the statement of cash flows, however, is identical under all three

EXHIBIT 5.2

TMBC COMPANY
Comparative Financial Statements

Partial Income Statements

	FIFO	LIFO	Weighted Average
Sales	$15,050	$15,050	$15,050
Cost of goods sold	(9,650)	(10,210)	(9,890)
Gross margin	5,400	4,840	5,160

Partial Balance Sheets

	FIFO	LIFO	Weighted Average
Assets			
Cash	$ XX	$ XX	$ XX
Accounts receivable	XX	XX	XX
Inventory	3,000	2,440	2,760

Partial Statements of Cash Flows

	FIFO	LIFO	Weighted Average
Operating Activities			
Cash inflow from customers	$15,050	$15,050	$15,050
Cash outflow for inventory	(10,650)	(10,650)	(10,650)

methods. TMBC paid $10,650 cash ($4,400 first purchase + $6,250 second purchase) to purchase inventory and received $15,050 cash for inventory sold. These cash flow consequences do not change regardless for whether TMBC uses FIFO, LIFO, or weighted average.

CHECK YOURSELF 5.2

In Year 1, Arlo Furniture Company paid $1,200 cash to purchase one leather chair. Later in Year 1, Arlo paid $1,400 cash to purchase a second leather chair. Other than price, both chairs were identical. Arlo sold one of the chairs on account in Year 1. Based on this information alone, determine the cost of goods sold and the cash flow from operating activities using (1) FIFO, (2) LIFO, and (3) weighted average.

Answer

	FIFO	LIFO	Weighted Average
Cost of Goods Sold	$1,200	$1,400	$1,300
Cash Flow for Operating Activities	$2,600	$2,600	$2,600

Note: *Cash flow* is not affected by *cost flow*. Regardless of what cost flow method is used to determine cost of goods sold, Arlo incurred a $2,600 cash outflow for the purchase of inventory in Year 1 .

Multiple Layers

The Impact of Income Tax

Based on the financial statement information in Exhibit 5.2, which cost flow method should TMBC use? Most people initially suggest FIFO because FIFO reports the highest gross margin and the largest balance in ending inventory. However, other factors are relevant. FIFO produces the highest gross margin; it also produces the highest net income and the highest income tax expense. In contrast, LIFO results in recognizing the lowest gross margin, lowest net income, and the lowest income tax expense.

Michael Kemp/Alamy Stock Photo

Will investors favor a company with more assets and higher net income or one with lower tax expense? Recognize that specific identification, FIFO, LIFO, and weighted average are *different methods of reporting the same information.* TMBC experienced only one set of events pertaining to Eraser bikes. Exhibit 5.2 reports those same events three different ways. However, if the FIFO reporting method causes TMBC to pay more taxes than the LIFO method, using FIFO will cause a real reduction in the value of the company. Paying more money in taxes leaves less money in the company. Knowledgeable investors would be more attracted to TMBC if it uses LIFO because the lower tax payments allow the company to keep more value in the business.

Research suggests that, as a group, investors are knowledgeable. They make investment decisions based on economic substance regardless of how information is reported in financial statements.

The Income Statement vs. the Tax Return

In some instances, companies may use one accounting method for financial reporting and a different method to compute income taxes (the tax return must explain any differences). With respect to LIFO, however, the Internal Revenue Service requires that companies using LIFO for income tax purposes must also use LIFO for financial reporting. A company could not, therefore, get both the lower tax benefit provided by LIFO and the financial reporting advantage offered under FIFO.

Inflation vs. Deflation

Our illustration assumes an inflationary environment (rising inventory prices). In a deflationary environment, the impact of using LIFO versus FIFO is reversed. LIFO produces tax advantages in an inflationary environment, while FIFO produces tax advantages in a deflationary environment. Companies operating in the computer industry—where prices are falling—would obtain a tax advantage by using FIFO. In contrast, companies that sell medical supplies in an inflationary environment would obtain a tax advantage by using LIFO.

Full Disclosure and Consistency

Generally accepted accounting principles allow each company to choose the inventory cost flow method best suited to its reporting needs. Because results can vary considerably among methods, however, the GAAP principle of **full disclosure** requires that financial statements disclose the method chosen. In addition, so that a company's financial statements are comparable from year to year, the GAAP principle of **consistency** generally requires that companies use the same cost flow method each period. The limited exceptions to the consistency principle are described in more advanced accounting courses.

CHECK YOURSELF 5.3

The following information was drawn from the inventory records of Fields, Inc.:

Beginning inventory	200 units @ $20
First purchase	400 units @ $22
Second purchase	600 units @ $24

Assume that Fields sold 900 units of inventory.

1. Determine the amount of cost of goods sold using FIFO.

2. Would using LIFO produce a higher or lower amount of cost of goods sold? Why?

Answer

1. Cost of goods sold using FIFO

Beginning inventory	200 units @ $20	=	$ 4,000
First purchase	400 units @ $22	=	8,800
Second purchase	300 units @ $24	=	7,200
Total cost of goods sold			$20,000

2. The inventory records reflect an inflationary environment of steadily rising prices. Because LIFO charges the latest costs (in this case, the highest costs) to the income statement, using LIFO (as opposed to FIFO) would produce a higher amount of cost of goods sold.

Inventory Cost Flow When Sales and Purchases Occur Intermittently

In the previous illustrations, all purchases were made before any goods were sold. This section addresses more realistic conditions, when sales transactions occur intermittently with purchases. Consider a third product that The Mountain Bike Company (TMBC) carries in its inventory: an energy bar called NeverStop. NeverStop is sold at concession booths sponsored by TMBC at bike races. TMBC purchases and sells NeverStop in bulk boxes. It refers to each box as a unit of product. TMBC's beginning inventory, purchases, and sales of NeverStop for the period are described next:

Date	Transaction	Description
Jan. 1	Beginning inventory	100 units @ $20.00
Feb. 14	Purchased	200 units @ $21.50
Apr. 5	Sold	220 units @ $30.00
June 21	Purchased	160 units @ $22.50
Aug. 18	Sold	100 units @ $30.00
Sep. 2	Purchased	280 units @ $23.50
Nov. 10	Sold	330 units @ $30.00

FIFO Cost Flow

Exhibit 5.3 displays the computations for cost of goods sold and inventory if TMBC uses the FIFO cost flow method. The inventory records are maintained in layers. Each time a sales transaction occurs, the unit cost in the first layer of inventory is assigned to the items sold. If the number of items sold exceeds the number of items in the first layer, the unit cost of the

EXHIBIT 5.3

Inventory Balance and Cost of Goods Sold Using FIFO Cost Flow Method

Date	Description	Units		Cost		Total	Cost of Goods Sold
Jan. 1	Beginning balance	100	@	$20.00	=	$2,000	
Feb. 14	Purchase	200	@	21.50	=	4,300	
Apr. 5	Sale of 220 units	(100)	@	20.00	=	(2,000)	
		(120)	@	21.50	=	(2,580)	$ 4,580
	Inventory balance after sale	80	@	21.50	=	1,720	
June 21	Purchase	160	@	22.50	=	3,600	
Aug. 18	Sale of 100 units	(80)	@	21.50	=	(1,720)	
		(20)	@	22.50	=	(450)	2,170
	Inventory balance after sale	140	@	22.50	=	3,150	
Sept. 2	Purchase	280	@	23.50	=	6,580	
Nov. 10	Sale of 330 units	(140)	@	22.50	=	(3,150)	
		(190)	@	23.50	=	(4,465)	7,615
	Ending inventory balance	90	@	23.50	=	$2,115	
	Total cost of goods sold						$14,365

next layer is assigned to the remaining number of units sold, and so on. For example, the cost assigned to the 220 units of inventory sold on April 5 is determined as follows:

100 units of inventory in the first layer × $20.00 per unit	=	$2,000
+ 120 units of inventory in the second layer × $21.50 per unit	=	2,580
220 units for total cost of goods sold for the April 5 sale	=	$4,580

The cost of goods sold for subsequent sales transactions is similarly computed.

Using FIFO, and assuming a selling price of $30 per unit, gross margin for the period is computed as follows:

Sales (650 units @ $30 each)	$19,500
Cost of goods sold	14,365
Gross margin	$ 5,135

Weighted-Average and LIFO Cost Flows

When maintaining perpetual inventory records, using the weighted-average or LIFO cost flow methods leads to timing difficulties. For example, under LIFO, the cost of the *last* items purchased *during an accounting period* is the first amount transferred to cost of goods sold. When sales and purchases occur intermittently, the cost of the last items purchased isn't known at the time earlier sales occur. For example, when TMBC sold merchandise in April, it did not know what the replacement inventory purchased in September would cost.

Accountants can solve cost flow timing problems by keeping perpetual records of the quantities (number of units) of items purchased and sold separately from the related costs. Keeping records of quantities moving in and out of inventory, even though cost information is unavailable, provides many of the benefits of a perpetual inventory system. For example, management can determine the quantity of lost, damaged, or stolen goods and the point at which to reorder merchandise. At the end of the accounting period, when the cost of all inventory purchases is available, costs are assigned to the quantity data that have been maintained perpetually. Although further discussion of the weighted-average and LIFO cost flow methods is beyond the scope of this text, recognize that timing problems associated with intermittent sales are manageable.

FOCUS ON INTERNATIONAL ISSUES

LIFO IN OTHER COUNTRIES

This chapter introduced a rather strange inventory cost flow assumption called LIFO. As explained, the primary advantage of LIFO is to reduce a company's income taxes. Given the choice, companies that use LIFO to reduce their taxes would probably prefer to use another method when preparing their GAAP-based financial statements, but the IRS does not permit this. Thus, they are left with no choice but to use the seemingly counterintuitive LIFO assumption for financial reporting purposes in order to reap the benefits of LIFO in their income tax reporting.

What happens in countries other than the United States? International Financial Reporting Standards (IFRS) do not allow the use of LIFO. Most industrialized nations are now using IFRS. You can

Weng lei-Imaginechina/AP Images

see the impact of this disparity if you review the annual report of a U.S. company that uses LIFO *and* has significant operations in other countries. Very often it will explain that LIFO is used to calculate inventory (and cost of goods sold) for domestic operations, but another method is used for activities outside the United States.

For example, here is an excerpt from General Electric's 2017 Form 10-K, Note 1.

*All inventories are stated at the lower of cost or realizable values. Cost for a portion of GE U.S. inventories is determined on a last-in, first-out (LIFO) basis. Cost of other GE inventories is determined on a first-in, first-out (FIFO) basis. LIFO was used for 34% and 32% of GE inventories in 2016 and 2017 respectively.**

If the company has its headquarters in the United States, why not simply use LIFO in its foreign operations? In addition to having to prepare financial statements for the United States, the company probably has to prepare statements for its local operations using the reporting standards of the local country.

Prior to the establishment of IFRS, each country was responsible for issuing its own, local GAAP. Even then, most countries did not allow for the use of LIFO.

*2017. General Electric Company Form 10-K. General Electric Company.

LOWER-OF-COST-OR-MARKET RULE

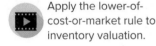

LO 5-2

Apply the lower-of-cost-or-market rule to inventory valuation.

Regardless of whether a company uses FIFO, LIFO, weighted average, or specific identification, once the cost of ending inventory has been determined, generally accepted accounting principles require that the cost be compared with the end of period market value and that the inventory be reported at *lower of cost or market. Market* is defined as the amount the company would have to pay to *replace* the merchandise. If the replacement cost is less than the actual cost, regardless of whether the decline in market value is due to physical damage, deterioration, obsolescence, or a general price-level decline, the loss must be recognized in the current period.

The **lower-of-cost-or-market rule** can be applied to (1) each individual inventory item, (2) major classes or categories of inventory, or (3) the entire stock of inventory in the aggregate. The most common practice is the individualized application. To illustrate applying the rule to individual inventory items, assume that The Mountain Bike Company (TMBC) has in ending inventory 100 T-shirts it purchased at a cost of $14 each. If the year-end replacement cost of the shirts is above $14, TMBC will report the ending inventory at cost (100 × $14 = $1,400). However, if outsourcing permits the manufacturer to reduce the unit price of the shirts to $11, then TMBC's replacement cost falls below the historical cost, and the inventory must be written down to $1,100 (100 × $11).

Exhibit 5.4 illustrates computing the ending inventory value on an item-by-item basis for a company that has four different inventory items. The company must write down the $30,020

REALITY BYTES

As previously noted in this chapter, the main incentive for a company to use the LIFO inventory assumption is to reduce, or at least defer, payment of income taxes. But, how much are U.S. companies really saving in taxes by using LIFO?

Some companies make it easy to estimate the amount of their taxes deferred by LIFO. Although **Kroger Company** uses the LIFO method for most of its merchandise inventory, it provides the difference between its ending inventory as measured by LIFO versus FIFO on its balance sheet. It refers to this difference as a "LIFO reserve." As of February 3, 2018, this reserve was $1,248 million. The federal income tax rate is currently 21 percent. So, multiplying $1,248 million by .21 suggests Kroger has been able to defer paying about $262 million in federal income taxes by using LIFO versus FIFO.

Jonathan Weiss/123RF

What about the tax savings for all of the companies in the United States who use LIFO? Various researchers have attempted to answer this question. One such recent study was authored by Daniel Tinkelman and Christine Tan. Their research used data from the IRS. These data revealed that while only about 1 percent of all U.S. companies use LIFO for most of their inventories, about 14 percent of the inventory on U.S. companies' balance sheets are measured with LIFO. Recall from Exhibit 5.1 that 35 percent of the large companies in the Dow Jones Industrial Average use LIFO. Tinkelman and Tan's analysis suggests that if LIFO method were no longer allowed by the IRS, companies would have to pay an additional $11 billion to $14 billion in taxes.

Sources: Kroger's Form 10-K and "Estimating the Potential Revenue Impact of Taxing LIFO Reserves in the Current Low Commodity Price Environment," *Journal of the American Taxation Association*, published online, January 2018.

EXHIBIT 5.4

Determination of Ending Inventory at Lower of Cost or Market

Item	Quantity (a)	Unit Cost (b)	Unit Market (c)	Total Cost (a × b)	Total Market (a × b)	Lower of Cost or Market
A	320	$21.50	$22.00	$ 6,880	$ 7,040	$ 6,880
B	460	18.00	16.00	8,280	7,360	7,360
C	690	15.00	14.00	10,350	9,660	9,660
D	220	20.50	23.00	4,510	5,060	4,510
				$30,020	$29,120	$28,410

historical cost of its ending inventory to $28,410. This $1,610 write-down reduces the company's gross margin for the period. If the company keeps perpetual inventory records, the effect of the write-down is as follows:

Balance Sheet				Income Statement				Statement of Cash Flows
Assets	=	Liab.	+ Stk. Equity	Rev.	− Exp.	=	Net Inc.	
Inventory			Ret. Earn.					
(1,610)	=	NA	+ (1,610)	NA	− 1,610	=	(1,610)	NA

FOCUS ON INTERNATIONAL ISSUES

THE LOWER-OF-COST-OR-MARKET RULE AND IFRS

Suppose a company has inventory with a historical cost of $1,000,000, the market value of which falls to $700,000. The company would have to write down the inventory and take a loss of $300,000. Now suppose that before the inventory was sold the market value recovered to $900,000. What would the company do? Nothing under U.S. GAAP; the inventory would remain on the books at $700,000 until it is sold or its market value declines further. However, under IFRS the inventory would be written up from $700,000 to $900,000, and a gain of $200,000 would be recognized.

Conceptually, the loss should be reported as an operating expense on the income statement. However, if the amount is immaterial, it can be included in cost of goods sold.

AVOIDING FRAUD IN MERCHANDISING BUSINESSES

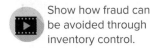

LO 5-3

Show how fraud can be avoided through inventory control.

For merchandising businesses, inventory is often the largest single asset reported on the balance sheet, and cost of goods sold is normally the largest single expense reported on the income statement. For example, a recent income statement for Publix (a large grocery store chain) reported $34.8 billion of sales and approximately $25.1 billion of cost of goods sold, which means cost of goods sold for Publix was about 72 percent of revenue. In contrast, the next largest expense (operating and administrative expense) was approximately $7.0 billion, or 20 percent of revenue. While cost of goods sold represents only one expense account, the operating and administrative expense category actually combines many, perhaps hundreds, of individual expense accounts, such as depreciation, salaries, utilities, and so on. Because the inventory and cost of goods sold accounts are so significant, they are attractive targets for concealing fraud. For example, suppose a manager attempts to perpetrate a fraud by deliberately understating expenses. The understatement is less likely to be detected if it is hidden in the $25.1 billion Cost of Goods Sold account than if it is recorded in one of the smaller operating expense accounts.

Because the inventory and cost of goods sold accounts are susceptible to abuse, auditors and financial analysts carefully examine them for signs of fraud. Using tools to detect possible inventory misstatements requires understanding how overstatement or understatement of inventory affects the financial statements. To illustrate, assume that a company overstates its year-end inventory balance by $1,000. This inventory overstatement results in a $1,000 understatement of cost of goods sold, as shown in the following schedule:

	Ending Inventory Is Accurate	Ending Inventory Is Overstated	Effect
Beginning inventory	$ 4,000	$ 4,000	
Purchases	6,000	6,000	
Cost of goods available for sale	10,000	10,000	
Ending inventory	(3,000)	(4,000)	$1,000 Overstated
Cost of goods sold	$ 7,000	$ 6,000	$1,000 Understated

The understatement of cost of goods sold results in the overstatement of gross margin, which leads to an overstatement of net earnings, as indicated in the following income statement:

	Ending Inventory Is Accurate	Ending Inventory Is Overstated	Effect
Sales	$11,000	$11,000	
Cost of goods sold	(7,000)	(6,000)	$1,000 Understated
Gross Margin	$ 4,000	$ 5,000	$1,000 Overstated

On the balance sheet, assets (inventory) and stockholders' equity (retained earnings) are overstated as follows:

	Ending Inventory Is Accurate	Ending Inventory Is Overstated	Effect
Assets			
Cash	$1,000	$ 1,000	
Inventory	3,000	4,000	$1,000 Overstated
Other assets	5,000	5,000	
Total assets	$9,000	$10,000	
Stockholders' equity			
Common stock	$5,000	$ 5,000	
Retained earnings	4,000	5,000	$1,000 Overstated
Total stockholders' equity	$9,000	$10,000	

Managers may be tempted to overstate the physical count of the ending inventory in order to report higher amounts of gross margin on the income statement and larger amounts of assets on the balance sheet. How can companies discourage managers from deliberately overstating the physical count of the ending inventory? The first line of defense is to assign the task of recording inventory transactions to different employees from those responsible for counting inventory.

Recall that under the perpetual system, increases and decreases in inventory are recorded at the time inventory is purchased and sold. If the records are maintained accurately, the balance in the inventory account should agree with the amount of physical inventory on hand. If a manager were to attempt to manipulate the financial statements by overstating the physical count of inventory, there would be a discrepancy between the accounting records and the physical count. In other words, a successful fraud requires controlling both the physical count and the recording process. If the counting and recording duties are performed by different individuals, fraud requires collusion, which reduces the likelihood of its occurrence. The separation of duties is an internal control procedure discussed further in the next chapter.

Because motives for fraud persist, even the most carefully managed companies cannot guarantee that no fraud will ever occur. As a result, auditors and financial analysts have developed tools to test for financial statement manipulation. The gross margin method of estimating the ending inventory balance is such a tool.

Digital Vision/Getty Images

ESTIMATING THE ENDING INVENTORY BALANCE

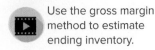

LO 5-4

Use the gross margin method to estimate ending inventory.

The **gross margin method** assumes that the percentage of gross margin to sales remains relatively stable over time. To the extent that this assumption is accurate, the gross margin ratio from prior periods can be used to accurately estimate the current period's ending inventory. To illustrate, first review the information in Exhibit 5.5, which pertains to The T-Shirt Company.

EXHIBIT 5.5

THE T-SHIRT COMPANY
Schedule for Estimating the Ending Inventory Balance
For the Six Months Ending June 30, Year 2

Beginning inventory	$ 5,100	
Purchases	18,500	
Cost of goods available for sale		$23,600
Sales through June 30, Year 2	22,000	
Less: Estimated gross margin*	?	
Estimated cost of goods sold		?
Estimated ending inventory		$?

*Historically, gross margin has amounted to approximately 25 percent of sales.

The estimated cost of ending inventory can be computed as follows:

1. Calculate the expected gross margin ratio using financial statement data from prior periods. Accuracy may be improved by averaging gross margin and sales data over several accounting periods. For The T-Shirt Company, assume the average gross margin for the prior five years ÷ the average sales for the same five-year period = 25% expected gross margin ratio.

2. Multiply the expected gross margin ratio by the current period's sales ($22,000 × 0.25 = $5,500) to estimate the amount of gross margin.

3. Subtract the estimated gross margin from sales ($22,000 − $5,500 = $16,500) to estimate the amount of cost of goods sold.

4. Subtract the estimated cost of goods sold from the amount of goods available for sale ($23,600 − $16,500 = $7,100) to estimate the amount of ending inventory.

The estimated amount of ending inventory ($7,100) can be compared to the book balance and the physical count of inventory. If the book balance or the physical count is significantly higher than the estimated inventory balance, the analysis suggests the possibility of financial statement manipulation.

Other analytical comparisons are also useful. For example, the current year's gross margin ratio can be compared to last year's ratio. If cost of goods sold has been understated (ending inventory overstated), the gross margin ratio will be inflated. If this year's ratio is significantly higher than last year's, further analysis is required.

Although it may seem common because of the intense publicity generated when it occurs, fraud is the exception rather than the norm. In fact, growth in the inventory account balance usually results from natural business conditions. For example, a company that is adding new stores is expected to report growth in its inventory balance. Nevertheless, significant growth in inventory that is not explained by accompanying sales growth signals the need to analyze further for evidence of manipulation.

Because one year's ending inventory balance becomes the next year's beginning inventory balance, inaccuracies carry forward from one accounting period to the next. Persistent inventory overstatements result in an inventory account balance that spirals higher and higher. A fraudulently increasing inventory balance is likely to be discovered eventually.

Answers to The Curious Accountant

Even though **Albertsons** uses the last-in, first-out *cost flow assumption* for financial reporting purposes, it, like most other companies, actually sells its oldest inventory first. As explained in the text material, GAAP allows a company to report its costs of goods sold in an order that is different from the actual physical flow of its goods. The primary reason some companies use the LIFO assumption is to reduce income taxes.

To avoid detection, a manager who has previously overstated inventory will need to write the inventory back down in a subsequent accounting period. Therefore, significant decreases, as well as increases, in the inventory balance or the gross margin ratio should be investigated. A manager may try to justify inventory write-downs by claiming that the inventory was lost, damaged, stolen, or had declined in value below historical cost. While there are valid reasons for writing down inventory, the possibility of fraud should be investigated.

CHECK YOURSELF 5.4

A physical count of Cantrell Inc.'s inventory revealed an ending balance of $6,020. The company's auditor decided to use the gross margin method to test the accuracy of the physical count. The accounting records indicate that the beginning inventory balance had been $20,000. During the period, Cantrell had purchased $70,000 of inventory and had recognized $140,000 of sales revenue. Cantrell's gross margin percentage is normally 40 percent of sales. Develop an estimate of the amount of ending inventory and comment on the accuracy of the physical count.

Answer Goods available for sale is $90,000 ($20,000 beginning inventory + $70,000 purchases). Estimated cost of goods sold is $84,000 [$140,000 sales − ($140,000 × 0.40) gross margin]. Estimated ending inventory is $6,000 ($90,000 goods available for sale − $84,000 cost of goods sold). The difference between the physical count and the estimated balance ($6,020 − $6,000 = $20) is immaterial. Therefore, the gross margin estimate is consistent with the physical count.

The Financial Analyst

Assume a grocery store sells two brands of kitchen cleansers: Zjax and Cosmos. Zjax costs $1.00 and sells for $1.25, resulting in a gross margin of $0.25 ($1.25 − $1.00). Cosmos costs $1.20 and sells for $1.60, resulting in a gross margin of $0.40 ($1.60 − $1.20). Is it more profitable to stock Cosmos than Zjax? Not if the store can sell significantly more cans of Zjax.

Suppose the lower price results in higher customer demand for Zjax. If the store can sell 7,000 units of Zjax but only 3,000 units of Cosmos, Zjax will provide a total gross margin of $1,750 (7,000 units × $0.25 per unit), while Cosmos will provide only $1,200 (3,000 units × $0.40 per unit). How fast inventory sells is as important as the spread between cost and selling price. To determine how fast inventory is selling, financial analysts calculate a ratio that measures the *average number of days it takes to sell inventory.*

LO 5-5

Calculate and interpret the inventory turnover ratio.

Average Number of Days to Sell Inventory

The first step in calculating the average number of days it takes to sell inventory is to compute the **inventory turnover,** as follows:

$$\frac{\text{Cost of goods sold}}{\text{Inventory}}$$

The result of this computation is the number of times the balance in the Inventory account is turned over (sold) each year. To more easily interpret the inventory turnover ratio, analysts often take a further step and determine the **average number of days to sell inventory** (also called the **average days in inventory**), computed as

$$\frac{365}{\text{Inventory turnover}}$$

Is It a Marketing or an Accounting Decision?

As suggested, overall profitability depends upon two elements: gross margin and inventory turnover. The most profitable combination would be to carry high-margin inventory that turns over rapidly. To be competitive, however, companies must often concentrate on one or the other of the elements. For example, *discount merchandisers* such as Costco offer lower prices to stimulate greater sales. In contrast, fashionable stores such as Neiman Marcus charge higher prices to compensate for their slower inventory turnover. These upscale stores justify their higher prices by offering superior style, quality, convenience, service, etc. While decisions about pricing, advertising, service, and so on are often viewed as marketing decisions, effective choices require understanding the interaction between the gross margin percentage and inventory turnover.

The Wallet Company Illustration

To examine the interaction between the gross margin percentage and inventory turnover from an accounting perspective, consider the case of The Wallet Company (TWC). TWC sells men's wallets. The following information was drawn from the company's accounting records:

	Year 7	Year 6
Sales revenue	$390,000	$320,000
Cost of goods sold	273,000	208,000
Gross margin	117,000	112,000
Average inventory balance	40,000	40,000

Comparing Year 7 with Year 6 data, how was TWC able to increase its total gross margin by $5,000 ($117,000 − $112,000)? First, note that TWC lowered the sales price of its products. This conclusion is supported by the fact that the company's gross margin percentage decreased from 35 percent ($112,000 gross margin / $320,000 sales revenue) to 30 percent ($117,000 gross margin / $390,000 sales revenue).

Next, note that inventory turnover increased from 5.2 ($208,000 cost of goods sold / $40,000 inventory balance) in Year 6 to 6.8 ($273,000 cost of goods sold / $40,000 inventory balance) in Year 7. Higher inventory turnover means that it requires less time to sell the inventory, restock it, and sell it again. In TWC's case, the number of days required to sell inventory in Year 6 was 70.19 (365 days in a year / 5.2 inventory turnover). In contrast, the number of days required to sell the inventory in Year 7 was only 53.7 (365 days in a year / 6.8 inventory turnover).

Decreasing the number of days required to sell inventory means that TWC sold inventory more rapidly in Year 7 than it did in Year 6. Increasing the speed at which inventory is sold means that more units are sold during an accounting period. In other words, higher inventory turnover lowers the number of days required to sell inventory and increases the number of units sold. The number of units sold is commonly called the sales volume. In summary, TWC was able to increase its profitability by lowering the sales price of its products, thereby increasing the sales volume.

Real-World Data

Exhibit 5.6 shows the *average number of days to sell inventory* for seven real-world companies in three different industries. The numbers pertain to the 2017 fiscal year. The data raise several questions.

EXHIBIT 5.6

Industry	Company	Average Number of Days to Sell Inventory
Fast Food	McDonald's	5
	Starbucks	50
	Restaurant Brands International	15
Department Stores	Macy's	124
	Walmart	43
Home Construction	D.R. Horton	344
	Toll Brothers	583

First, why do D.R. Horton and Toll Brothers take so long to sell their inventories compared with the other companies? Both of these companies build and sell houses. It takes a lot longer to build a house than it does to make a hamburger. Furthermore, once a house is built, it may take months to find a buyer. Finally, inventory of home builders includes the land on which the houses are constructed. A large subdivision may take several years to complete, but all of the land may have been purchased months, or even years, before the first house was started.

Why does Starbucks hold its inventory so much longer than the other two fast-food businesses? Starbucks's inventory is mostly coffee. It is more difficult for Starbucks to obtain coffee than it is for McDonald's or Restaurant Brands to obtain beef. Restaurant Brands International is the parent company of Burger King and Tim Horton. Very little coffee is grown in the United States. Because purchasing coffee requires substantial delivery time, Starbucks cannot order its inventory at the last minute. This problem is further complicated by the fact that coffee harvests are seasonal. Cattle, on the other hand, can be processed into hamburgers year-round. As a result, Starbucks must hold inventory longer than McDonald's or Restaurant Brands.

Why do department stores such as Macy's and Walmart take longer to sell inventory than McDonald's? Part of the answer is that food is perishable and clothing is not. But there is also the fact that department stores carry many more inventory items than do fast-food restaurants. It is much easier to anticipate customer demand if a company sells only 20 different items than if the company sells 20,000 different items. The problem of anticipating customer demand is solved by holding larger quantities of inventory.

Steve Pope/AP images

Finally, notice that Walmart sells its merchandise in 43 days, while Macy's takes 124. This would seem to be an advantage for Walmart, but recall from Chapter 4 that in its 2016 fiscal year, Walmart's gross margin percentage was 24.7, while Macy's was 39.0. Macy's higher gross margin percentage helps to make up for the additional time it takes to sell merchandise. Different companies use different business strategies to achieve their objectives. In the end, Macy's return on sales percentage, at 6.2 percent, was significantly higher than Walmart's, which was 2.0 percent, so Macy's higher gross margin did lead to higher bottom-line profit percentage in 2017.

Effects of Cost Flow on Ratio Analysis

Because the amounts of ending inventory and cost of goods sold are affected by the cost flow method (FIFO, LIFO, etc.) a company uses, the gross margin and inventory turnover ratios are also affected by the cost flow method used. Further, because cost of goods sold affects the amount of net income and retained earnings, many other ratios are also affected by the inventory cost flow method that a company uses. Financial analysts must consider that the ratios they use can be significantly influenced by which accounting methods a company chooses.

A Look Back

This chapter discussed the specific identification, first-in, first-out (FIFO), last-in, first-out (LIFO), and weighted-average inventory cost flow methods. Under *specific identification*, the actual cost of the goods is reported on the income statement and the balance sheet. Under *FIFO*, the cost of the items purchased first is reported on the income statement, and the cost of the items purchased last is reported on the balance sheet. Under *LIFO*, the cost of the items purchased last is reported on the income statement, and the cost of the items purchased first is reported on the balance sheet. Finally, under the *weighted-average method*, the average cost of inventory is reported on both the income statement and the balance sheet.

Generally accepted accounting principles often allow companies to account for the same types of events in different ways. The different cost flow methods presented in this chapter— FIFO, LIFO, weighted average, and specific identification—are examples of alternative accounting procedures allowed by GAAP. Financial analysts must be aware that financial statement amounts are affected by the accounting methods that a company uses, as well as the economic activity it experiences.

This chapter also explained how to calculate the time it takes a company to sell its inventory. The measure of how fast inventory sells is called *inventory turnover;* it is computed by dividing cost of goods sold by inventory. The result of this computation is the number of times the balance in the inventory account is turned over each year. The *average number of days to sell inventory* can be determined by dividing the number of days in a year (365) by the inventory turnover ratio.

A Look Forward

Chapter 6 examines accounting for cash and the system of internal controls. Internal controls are the accounting practices and procedures that companies use to protect assets and ensure that transactions are recorded accurately. You will learn that companies account for small disbursements of cash, called *petty cash disbursements,* differently than they do for large disbursements. You will also learn how to prepare a formal bank reconciliation.

Tableau Dashboard Activity is available in *Connect* for this chapter.

SELF-STUDY REVIEW PROBLEM

A step-by-step audio-narrated series of slides is available in *Connect*.

Erie Jewelers sells gold earrings. Its beginning inventory of Model 407 gold earrings consisted of 100 pairs of earrings at $50 per pair. Erie purchased two batches of Model 407 earrings during the year. The first batch purchased consisted of 150 pairs at $53 per pair; the second batch consisted of 200 pairs at $56 per pair. During the year, Erie sold 375 pairs of Model 407 earrings.

Required

Determine the amount of product cost Erie would allocate to cost of goods sold and ending inventory assuming that Erie uses (a) FIFO, (b) LIFO, and (c) weighted average.

Solution to Requirements a–c

Goods Available for Sale

Beginning inventory	100	@	$50	=	$ 5,000
First purchase	150	@	53	=	7,950
Second purchase	200	@	56	=	11,200
Goods available for sale	450				$24,150

a. FIFO

Cost of Goods Sold	Pairs		Cost per Pair		Cost of Goods Sold
From beginning inventory	100	@	$50	=	$5,000
From first purchase	150	@	53	=	7,950
From second purchase	125	@	56	=	7,000
Total pairs sold	375				$19,950

Ending inventory = Goods available for sale − Cost of goods sold
Ending inventory = $24,150 − $19,950 = $4,200

b. LIFO

Cost of Goods Sold	Pairs		Cost per Pair		Cost of Goods Sold
From second purchase	200	@	$56	=	$11,200
From first purchase	150	@	53	=	7,950
From beginning inventory	25	@	50	=	1,250
Total pairs sold	375				$20,400

Ending inventory = Goods available for sale − Cost of goods sold
Ending inventory = $24,150 − $20,400 = $3,750

c. Weighted average

Goods available for sale ÷ Total pairs = Cost per pair
$24,150 ÷ 450 = $53.6667
Cost of goods sold   375 units @ $53.6667 = $20,125
Ending inventory   75 units @ $53.6667 = $4,025

KEY TERMS

Average number of days
   to sell inventory
   (or average days in
   inventory) 254
Consistency 245

First-in, first-out (FIFO)
   cost flow method 240
Full disclosure 245
Gross margin
   method 252

Inventory cost flow
   methods 241
Inventory turnover 254
Last-in, first-out (LIFO) cost
   flow method 240

Lower-of-cost-or-market rule 248
Physical flow of goods 240
Specific identification 239
Weighted-average cost flow
   method 240

QUESTIONS

1. Name and describe the four cost flow methods discussed in this chapter.

2. What are some advantages and disadvantages of the specific identification method of accounting for inventory?

3. What are some advantages and disadvantages of using the FIFO method of inventory valuation?

4. What are some advantages and disadvantages of using the LIFO method of inventory valuation?

5. In an inflationary period, which inventory cost flow method will produce the highest net income? Explain.

6. In an inflationary period, which inventory cost flow method will produce the largest amount of total assets on the balance sheet? Explain.

7. What is the difference between the flow of costs and the physical flow of goods?

8. Does the choice of cost flow method (FIFO, LIFO, or weighted average) affect the statement of cash flows? Explain.

9. Assume that Key Co. purchased 1,000 units of merchandise in its first year of operations for $25 per unit. The company sold 850 units for $40. What is the amount of cost of goods sold using FIFO? LIFO? Weighted average?

10. Assume that Key Co. purchased 1,500 units of merchandise in its second year of operation for $27 per unit. Its beginning inventory was determined in Question 9. Assuming that 1,500 units are sold, what is the amount of cost of goods sold using FIFO? LIFO? Weighted average?

11. Refer to Questions 9 and 10. Which method might be preferable for financial statements? For income tax reporting? Explain.

12. In an inflationary period, which cost flow method—FIFO or LIFO—produces the larger cash flow? Explain.

13. Which inventory cost flow method produces the highest net income in a deflationary period?

14. How does the phrase *lower-of-cost-or-market* apply to inventory valuation?

15. If some merchandise declines in value because of damage or obsolescence, what effect will the lower-of-cost-or-market rule have on the income statement? Explain.

16. What is a situation in which estimates of the amount of inventory may

be useful or even necessary?

17. How can management manipulate net income using inventory fraud?

18. If the amount of goods available for sale is $123,000, the amount of sales is $130,000, and the gross margin is 25 percent of sales, what is the amount of ending inventory?

19. Assume that inventory is overstated by $1,500 at the end of Year 1 but is corrected in Year 2. What effect will this have on the Year 1 income statement? The Year 1 balance sheet? The Year 2 income statement? The Year 2 balance sheet?

20. What information does inventory turnover provide?

21. What is an example of a business that would have a high inventory turnover? A low inventory turnover?

EXERCISES—SERIES A

 connect All applicable Exercises in Series A are available in *Connect.*

LO 5-1

Exercise 5-1A   *Effect of inventory cost flow assumption on financial statements*

Required

For each of the following situations, indicate whether FIFO, LIFO, or weighted average applies:

a. In a period of falling prices, net income would be highest.

b. In a period of falling prices, the unit cost of goods would be the same for ending inventory and cost of goods sold.

c. In a period of rising prices, net income would be highest.

d. In a period of rising prices, cost of goods sold would be highest.

e. In a period of rising prices, ending inventory would be highest.

Exercise 5-2A *Allocating product cost between cost of goods sold and ending inventory*

Jones Co. started the year with no inventory. During the year, it purchased two identical inventory items at different times. The first purchase cost $1,060 and the other, $1,380. Jones sold one of the items during the year.

Required

Based on this information, how much product cost would be allocated to cost of goods sold and ending inventory on the year-end financial statements, assuming use of

a. FIFO?

b. LIFO?

c. Weighted average?

Exercise 5-3A *Allocating product cost between cost of goods sold and ending inventory: multiple purchases*

Cortez Company sells chairs that are used at computer stations. Its beginning inventory of chairs was 100 units at $60 per unit. During the year, Cortez made two batch purchases of this chair. The first was a 150-unit purchase at $68 per unit; the second was a 200-unit purchase at $72 per unit. During the period, it sold 270 chairs.

Required

Determine the amount of product costs that would be allocated to cost of goods sold and ending inventory, assuming that Cortez uses

a. FIFO.

b. LIFO.

c. Weighted average.

Exercise 5-4A *Effect of inventory cost flow (FIFO, LIFO, and weighted average) on gross margin*

The following information pertains to Mason Company for Year 2:

Beginning inventory	90 units @ $40
Units purchased	310 units @ $45

Ending inventory consisted of 30 units. Mason sold 370 units at $90 each. All purchases and sales were made with cash. Operating expenses amounted to $4,100.

Required

a. Compute the gross margin for Mason Company using the following cost flow assumptions: (1) FIFO, (2) LIFO, and (3) weighted average.

b. What is the amount of net income using FIFO, LIFO, and weighted average? (Ignore income tax considerations.)

c. Compute the amount of ending inventory using (1) FIFO, (2) LIFO, and (3) weighted average.

Exercise 5-5A *Effect of inventory cost flow on ending inventory balance and gross margin*

The Shirt Shop had the following transactions for T-shirts for Year 1, its first year of operations:

Jan. 20	Purchased 400 units @ $8	=	$3,200
Apr. 21	Purchased 200 units @ $10	=	2,000
July 25	Purchased 280 units @ $13	=	3,640
Sept. 19	Purchased 90 units @ $15	=	1,350

During the year, The Shirt Shop sold 810 T-shirts for $20 each.

Required

a. Compute the amount of ending inventory The Shirt Shop would report on the balance sheet, assuming the following cost flow assumptions: (1) FIFO, (2) LIFO, and (3) weighted average, rounded to two decimal places.

b. Compute the difference in gross margin between the FIFO and LIFO cost flow assumptions.

LO 5-1

Exercise 5-6A   *Income tax effect of shifting from FIFO to LIFO*

The following information pertains to the inventory of Parvin Company for Year 3:

Jan. 1	Beginning inventory	400 units @ $30
Apr. 1	Purchased	2,000 units @ $35
Oct. 1	Purchased	600 units @ $38

During Year 3, Parvin sold 2,700 units of inventory at $90 per unit and incurred $41,500 of operating expenses. Parvin currently uses the FIFO method but is considering a change to LIFO. All transactions are cash transactions. Assume a 30 percent income tax rate. Parvin started the period with cash of $75,000, inventory of $12,000, common stock of $50,000, and retained earnings of $37,000.

Required

a. Prepare income statements using FIFO and LIFO.

b. Determine the amount of income tax that Parvin would pay using each cost flow method.

c. Determine the cash flow from operating activities under FIFO and LIFO.

d. Why is the cash flow from operating activities different under FIFO and LIFO?

LO 5-1

Exercise 5-7A   *Effect of FIFO versus LIFO on income tax expense*

The Brick Company had cash sales of $280,000 for Year 1, its first year of operation. On April 2, the company purchased 210 units of inventory at $390 per unit. On September 1, an additional 160 units were purchased for $425 per unit. The company had 110 units on hand at the end of the year. The company's income tax rate is 40 percent. All transactions are cash transactions.

Required

a. The preceding paragraph describes five accounting events: (1) a sales transaction, (2) the first purchase of inventory, (3) a second purchase of inventory, (4) the recognition of cost of goods sold expense, and (5) the payment of income tax expense. Show the amounts of each event in horizontal statements models like the following ones, assuming first a FIFO and then a LIFO cost flow.

Effect of Events on Financial Statements
Panel 1: FIFO Cost Flow

Event No.	Balance Sheet					Income Statement					Statement of Cash Flows
	Cash	+	Inventory	=	Ret. Earn.	Rev.	−	Exp.	=	Net Inc.	

Panel 2: LIFO Cost Flow

Event No.	Balance Sheet					Income Statement					Statement of Cash Flows
	Cash	+	Inventory	=	Ret. Earn.	Rev.	−	Exp.	=	Net Inc.	

b. Compute net income using FIFO.

c. Compute net income using LIFO.

d. Explain the difference, if any, in the amount of income tax expense incurred using the two cost flow assumptions.

e. Which method, FIFO or LIFO, produced the larger amount of assets on the balance sheet?

Exercise 5-8A   *Recording inventory transactions using the perpetual method: intermittent sales and purchases*

LO 5-1

The following inventory transactions apply to Green Company for Year 2:

Jan. 1	Purchased	260 units @ $50
Apr. 1	Sold	130 units @ $85
Aug. 1	Purchased	390 units @ $56
Dec. 1	Sold	490 units @ $96

The beginning inventory consisted of 180 units at $48 per unit. All transactions are cash transactions.

Required

a. Record these transactions in a financial statements model, assuming Green uses the FIFO cost flow assumption and keeps perpetual records.

b. Compute cost of goods sold for Year 2.

Exercise 5-9A   *Effect of cost flow on ending inventory: intermittent sales and purchases*

LO 5-1

The Hat Store had the following series of transactions for Year 2:

Date	Transaction	Description
Jan. 1	Beginning inventory	50 units @ $40
Mar. 15	Purchased	200 units @ $42
May 30	Sold	170 units @ $95
Aug. 10	Purchased	275 units @ $46
Nov. 20	Sold	340 units @ $96

Required

a. Determine the quantity and dollar amount of inventory at the end of the year, assuming The Hat Store uses the FIFO cost flow assumption and keeps perpetual records.

b. Write a memo explaining why The Hat Store would have difficulty applying the weighted-average method on a perpetual basis.

Exercise 5-10A   *Lower-of-cost-or-market rule: perpetual system*

LO 5-2

The following information pertains to Hagen Metal Work's ending inventory for the current year:

Item	Quantity	Unit Cost	Unit Market Value
C	90	$24	$16
D	75	22	20
K	40	25	28
M	22	15	17

Required

a. Determine the value of the ending inventory using the lower-of-cost-or-market rule applied to (1) each individual inventory item and (2) the inventory in aggregate.

b. Calculate the adjustment required under both methods, assuming the decline in value is immaterial.

LO 5-2

Exercise 5-11A   *Lower-of-cost-or-market rule*

Brooks Company carries three inventory items. The following information pertains to the ending inventory:

Item	Quantity	Unit Cost	Unit Market Value
A	120	$60	$55
F	170	80	75
K	110	30	40

Required

a. Determine the ending inventory that Brooks will report on the balance sheet, assuming that it applies the lower-of-cost-or-market rule to individual inventory items.

b. Calculate the adjustment required under both methods, assuming the decline in value is immaterial.

LO 5-3

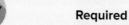

Exercise 5-12A   *Effect of inventory error on financial statements: perpetual system*

Stubbs Company failed to count $55,000 of inventory in its Year 1 year-end physical count.

Required

Write a memo explaining how Stubbs Company's balance sheet will be affected in Year 1. Assume Stubbs uses the perpetual inventory system.

LO 5-3

Exercise 5-13A   *Effect of inventory error on elements of financial statements*

The ending inventory for Carver Co. was incorrectly adjusted, which caused it to be understated by $15,300 for Year 2.

Required

Was each of the following amounts overstated, understated, or not affected by the error?

Item No.	Year	Amount
1	Year 2	Beginning inventory
2	Year 2	Purchases
3	Year 2	Goods available for sale
4	Year 2	Cost of goods sold
5	Year 2	Gross margin
6	Year 2	Net income
7	Year 3	Beginning inventory
8	Year 3	Purchases
9	Year 3	Goods available for sale
10	Year 3	Cost of goods sold
11	Year 3	Gross margin
12	Year 3	Net income

LO 5-4

Exercise 5-14A   *Estimating ending inventory*

A substantial portion of inventory owned by Prentiss Sporting Goods was recently destroyed when the roof collapsed during a rainstorm. Prentiss also lost some of its accounting records. Prentiss must estimate the loss from the storm for insurance reporting and financial statement purposes. Prentiss uses the periodic inventory system. The following accounting information was recovered from the damaged records:

Beginning inventory	$ 60,000
Purchases to date of storm	190,000
Sales to date of storm	250,000

The value of undamaged inventory counted was $3,600. Historically, Prentiss's gross margin percentage has been approximately 25 percent of sales.

Required

Estimate the following:

a. Gross margin in dollars.

b. Cost of goods sold.

c. Ending inventory.

d. Amount of lost inventory.

Exercise 5-15A *Estimating ending inventory: perpetual system*

LO 5-4

Brad Essary owned a small company that sold garden equipment. The equipment was expensive, and a perpetual system was maintained for control purposes. Even so, lost, damaged, and stolen merchandise normally amounted to 5 percent of the inventory balance. On June 14, Essary's warehouse was destroyed by fire. Just prior to the fire, the accounting records contained a $280,000 balance in the Inventory account. However, inventory costing $42,000 had been sold and delivered to customers but had not been recorded in the books at the time of the fire. The fire did not affect the showroom, which contained inventory that cost $58,000.

Required

Estimate the amount of inventory destroyed by fire.

Exercise 5-16A *Inventory turnover and average days to sell*

LO 5-5

The following accounting information pertains to two grocery store chains. One grocery store chain has a market strategy of selling only high-end organic food products while the other grocery store sells less expensive foods that are traditionally grown with the use of pesticides, synthetic fertilizers, and/or genetically modified organisms.

	Traditional	Organic
Sales	$600,000	?
Cost of Goods Sold	?	$300,000
Gross Margin	?	$200,000
Gross Margin Percentage	35%	?

The company selling traditional produced foods has an average inventory balance of $45,000, while the company selling organic foods has an average inventory balance of $40,000.

a. Complete the table by filling in the missing amounts.

b. Which grocery store chain is taking a lower cost/higher volume strategy as it relates to sales?

c. Calculate the inventory turnover and average days to sell inventory for each grocery store chain. Based on your calculations, which grocery chain will be required to reorder inventory more frequently?

Exercise 5-17A *Explaining multiple inventory methods at one real-world company*

IFRS

The following information related to accounting for inventory was taken from the 2016 annual report of Costco Wholesale Corporation:

Merchandise inventories consist of the following at the end of 2016 and 2015:

	2016	2015
United States	$6,422	$6,427
Foreign	2,547	2,481
Merchandise inventories	$8,969	$8,908

Merchandise inventories are valued at the lower of cost or market, as determined primarily by the retail inventory method, and are stated using the last-in, first-out (LIFO) method for substantially all U.S. merchandise inventories. Merchandise inventories for all foreign operations are primarily valued by the retail inventory method and are stated using the first-in, first-out (FIFO) method.

Required

Write a brief report explaining the reason or reasons that best explain why Costco uses the LIFO cost flow method for its inventories in the United States but the FIFO cost method for its other inventories.

IFRS

Exercise 5-18A *GAAP versus IFRS*

Generally accepted accounting principles (GAAP) and International Financial Reporting Standards (IFRS) treat the LIFO inventory cost flow method differently.

Required

a. Briefly describe the position GAAP takes with respect to LIFO.
b. Briefly describe the position IFRS takes with respect to LIFO.
c. Explain the primary force that motivates the different positions.

PROBLEMS—SERIES A

Mc Graw Hill **connect**   **All applicable Problems in Series A are available in *Connect*.**

LO 5-1

CHECK FIGURES
a. Cost of Goods Sold
  FIFO: $62,650
b. Net Income LIFO: $22,012

Problem 5-19A *Effect of different inventory cost flow methods on financial statements*

The accounting records of Wall's China Shop reflected the following balances as of January 1, Year 3:

Cash	$80,100
Beginning inventory	33,000 (220 units @ $150)
Common stock	50,000
Retained earnings	63,100

The following five transactions occurred in Year 3:

1. First purchase (cash): 150 units @ $155
2. Second purchase (cash): 160 units @ $160
3. Sales (all cash): 410 units @ $320
4. Paid $38,000 cash for salaries expense
5. Paid cash for income tax at the rate of 25 percent of income before taxes

Required

a. Compute the cost of goods sold and ending inventory, assuming (1) FIFO cost flow, (2) LIFO cost flow, and (3) weighted-average cost flow. Compute the income tax expense for each method.
b. Prepare the Year 3 income statement, balance sheet, and statement of cash flows under FIFO, LIFO, and weighted average. (*Hint:* Record the events under an accounting equation before preparing the statements.)

LO 5-1

CHECK FIGURES
a. Cost of Goods Sold: $49,250
c. Ending Inventory: $17,550

Problem 5-20A *Allocating product costs between cost of goods sold and ending inventory: intermittent purchases and sales of merchandise*

Pam's Creations had the following sales and purchase transactions during Year 2. Beginning inventory consisted of 60 items at $350 each. The company uses the FIFO cost flow assumption and keeps perpetual inventory records.

Date	Transaction	Description
Mar. 5	Purchased	50 items @ $370
Apr. 10	Sold	30 items @ $450
June 19	Sold	60 items @ $450
Sep. 16	Purchased	70 items @ $390
Nov. 28	Sold	45 items @ $480

Required

a. Record the inventory transactions in a financial statements model.

b. Calculate the gross margin Pam's Creations would report on the Year 2 income statement.

c. Determine the ending inventory balance Pam's Creations would report on the December 31, Year 2, balance sheet.

Problem 5-21A   *Inventory valuation based on the lower-of-cost-or-market rule*

At the end of the year, Randy's Parts Co. had the following items in inventory:

Item	Quantity	Unit Cost	Unit Market Value
P1	60	$ 85	$ 90
P2	40	70	72
P3	80	130	120
P4	70	125	130

LO 5-2

eXcel

CHECK FIGURES
a. $26,250
b. Decrease inventory
   by $800.

Required

a. Determine the amount of ending inventory using the lower-of-cost-or-market rule applied to each individual inventory item.

b. Provide the adjustment necessary to write down the inventory based on Requirement *a*. Assume that Randy's Parts Co. uses the perpetual inventory system.

c. Determine the amount of ending inventory, assuming that the lower-of-cost-or-market rule is applied to the total inventory in aggregate.

d. Provide the adjustment necessary to write down the inventory based on Requirement *c*. Assume that Randy's Parts Co. uses the perpetual inventory system.

e. Explain how the inventory loss would be reported when the periodic inventory system is used.

Problem 5-22A   *Effect of inventory errors on financial statements*

LO 5-3

The following income statement was prepared for Frame Supplies for Year 1:

FRAME SUPPLIES
Income Statement
For the Year Ended December 31, Year 1

Sales	$ 250,000
Cost of goods sold	(140,000)
Gross margin	110,000
Operating expenses	(69,500)
Net income	$ 40,500

During the year-end audit, the following errors were discovered:

1. A $2,500 payment for repairs was erroneously charged to the Cost of Goods Sold account. (Assume that the perpetual inventory system is used.)

2. Sales to customers for $1,800 at December 31, Year 1, were not recorded in the books for Year 1. Also, the $980 cost of goods sold was not recorded.

3. A mathematical error was made in determining ending inventory. Ending inventory was understated by $2,150. (The Inventory account was mistakenly written down to the Cost of Goods Sold account.)

Required

Determine the effect, if any, of each of the errors on the following items. Give the dollar amount of the effect and whether it would overstate (O), understate (U), or not affect (NA) the account. The first item for each error is recorded as an example.

Error No. 1	Amount of Error	Effect
Sales, Year 1	NA	NA
Ending inventory, December 31, Year 1		
Gross margin, Year 1		
Beginning inventory, January 1, Year 2		
Cost of goods sold, Year 1		
Net income, Year 1		
Retained earnings, December 31, Year 1		
Total assets, December 31, Year 1		

Error No. 2	Amount of Error	Effect
Sales, Year 1	$1,800	U
Ending inventory, December 31, Year 1		
Gross margin, Year 1		
Beginning inventory, January 1, Year 2		
Cost of goods sold, Year 1		
Net income, Year 1		
Retained earnings, December 31, Year 1		
Total assets, December 31, Year 1		

Error No. 3	Amount of Error	Effect
Sales, Year 1	NA	NA
Ending inventory, December 31, Year 1		
Gross margin, Year 1		
Beginning inventory, January 1, Year 2		
Cost of goods sold, Year 1		
Net income, Year 1		
Retained earnings, December 31, Year 1		
Total assets, December 31, Year 1		

LO 5-4

CHECK FIGURES
a. Gross Margin: $330,000
b. Total Inventory Loss:
$25,000

Problem 5-23A *Estimating ending inventory: gross margin method*

The inventory of Don's Grocery was destroyed by a tornado on October 6 of the current year. Fortunately, some of the accounting records were at the home of one of the owners and were not damaged. The following information was available for the period of January 1 through October 6:

Beginning inventory, January 1	$ 140,000
Purchases through October 6	670,000
Sales through October 6	1,100,000

Gross margin for Don's has traditionally been 30 percent of sales.

Required

a. For the period ending October 6, compute the following:

(1) Estimated gross margin.

(2) Estimated cost of goods sold.

(3) Estimated inventory at October 6.

b. Assume that $15,000 of the inventory was not damaged. What is the amount of the loss from the tornado?

c. If Don's had used the perpetual inventory system, how would it have determined the amount of the inventory loss?

Problem 5-24A *Estimating ending inventory: gross margin method*

Toyland wishes to produce quarterly financial statements, but it takes a physical count of inventory only at year-end. The following historical data were taken from the Year 1 and Year 2 accounting records:

	Year 1	Year 2
Net sales	$150,000	$190,000
Cost of goods sold	76,000	89,200

At the end of the first quarter of Year 3, Toyland had the following account balances:

Sales	$210,000
Purchases	90,000
Beginning inventory 1/1/Year 3	32,100
Ending inventory 3/31/Year 3	16,000

Based on purchases and sales, the Toyland accountant thinks inventory is low.

Required

Using the information provided, estimate the following for the first quarter of Year 3:

a. Cost of goods sold. (Use the average cost of goods sold percentage.)
b. Ending inventory at March 31.
c. What could explain the difference between actual and estimated inventory?

Problem 5-25A *Using ratios to make comparisons*

The following accounting information pertains to Boardwalk Taffy and Beach Sweets. The only difference between the two companies is that Boardwalk Taffy uses FIFO, while Beach Sweets uses LIFO.

	Boardwalk Taffy	Beach Sweets
Cash	$ 120,000	$ 120,000
Accounts receivable	480,000	480,000
Merchandise inventory	350,000	300,000
Accounts payable	360,000	360,000
Cost of goods sold	2,000,000	2,050,000
Building	500,000	500,000
Sales	3,000,000	3,000,000

Required

a. Compute the gross margin percentage for each company and identify the company that *appears* to be charging the higher prices in relation to its cost.
b. For each company, compute the inventory turnover ratio and the average days to sell inventory. Identify the company that *appears* to be incurring the higher financing cost.
c. Explain why a company with the lower gross margin percentage needs to have a higher inventory turnover ratio, assuming a period of inflation.

EXERCISES—SERIES B

LO 5-1

Exercise 5-1B *Effect of inventory cost flow assumption on financial statements*

Required

For each of the following situations, fill in the blank with *FIFO, LIFO,* or *weighted average:*

a. _____ would produce the highest amount of net income in an inflationary environment.

b. _____ would produce the highest amount of assets in an inflationary environment.

c. _____ would produce the lowest amount of net income in a deflationary environment.

d. _____ would produce the same unit cost for assets and cost of goods sold in an inflationary environment.

e. _____ would produce the lowest amount of net income in an inflationary environment.

f. _____ would produce an asset value that was the same regardless of whether the environment was inflationary or deflationary.

g. _____ would produce the lowest amount of assets in an inflationary environment.

h. _____ would produce the highest amount of assets in a deflationary environment.

LO 5-1

Exercise 5-2B *Allocating product cost between cost of goods sold and ending inventory*

Harris Co. started the year with no inventory. During the year, it purchased two identical inventory items. The inventory was purchased at different times. The first purchase cost $3,600 and the other, $4,200. One of the items was sold during the year.

Required

Based on this information, how much product cost would be allocated to cost of goods sold and ending inventory on the year-end financial statements, assuming use of

a. FIFO?

b. LIFO?

c. Weighted average?

LO 5-1

Exercise 5-3B *Allocating product cost between cost of goods sold and ending inventory: multiple purchases*

Marley Company sells coffee makers used in business offices. Its beginning inventory of coffee makers was 400 units at $50 per unit. During the year, Marley made two batch purchases of coffee makers. The first was a 500-unit purchase at $55 per unit; the second was a 600-unit purchase at $58 per unit. During the period, Marley sold 1,200 coffee makers.

Required

Determine the amount of product costs that would be allocated to cost of goods sold and ending inventory, assuming that Marley uses

a. FIFO.

b. LIFO.

c. Weighted average.

LO 5-1

Exercise 5-4B *Effect of inventory cost flow (FIFO, LIFO, and weighted average) on gross margin*

The following information pertains to Stanley Company for Year 2:

Beginning inventory	90 units @ $15
Units purchased	320 units @ $19

Ending inventory consisted of 40 units. Stanley sold 370 units at $30 each. All purchases and sales were made with cash.

Required

a. Compute the gross margin for Stanley Company using the following cost flow assumptions: (1) FIFO, (2) LIFO, and (3) weighted average.

b. What is the dollar amount of difference in net income between using FIFO versus LIFO? (Ignore income tax considerations.)

c. Determine the cash flow from operating activities, using each of the three cost flow assumptions listed in Requirement *a*. Ignore the effect of income taxes. Explain why these cash flows have no differences.

Exercise 5-5B *Effect of inventory cost flow on ending inventory balance and gross margin*   LO 5-1

The Shirt Shop had the following transactions for T-shirts for Year 1, its first year of operations:

Jan. 18	Purchased 300 units @ $7	=	$2,100
Apr. 15	Purchased 400 units @ $12	=	4,800
July 21	Purchased 220 units @ $14	=	3,080
Sept. 5	Purchased 60 units @ $18	=	1,080

During the year, The Shirt Shop sold 800 T-shirts for $25 each.

Required

a. Compute the amount of ending inventory The Shirt Shop would report on the balance sheet, assuming the following cost flow assumptions: (1) FIFO, (2) LIFO, and (3) weighted average, rounded to two decimal places.

b. Compute the difference in gross margin between the FIFO and LIFO cost-flow assumptions.

Exercise 5-6B *Income tax effect of shifting from FIFO to LIFO*   LO 5-1

The following information pertains to the inventory of Steelman Company for Year 2:

Jan. 1	Beginning inventory	500 units @ $28
Apr. 20	Purchased	1,800 units @ $32
Oct. 5	Purchased	400 units @ $35

During Year 3, Steelman sold 2,500 units of inventory at $85 per unit and incurred $38,600 of operating expenses. Steelman currently uses the FIFO method but is considering a change to LIFO. All transactions are cash transactions. Assume a 25 percent income tax rate. Steelman started the period with cash of $85,000, inventory of $22,000, common stock of $45,000, and retained earnings of $62,000.

Required

a. Prepare income statements using FIFO and LIFO.

b. Determine the amount of income tax that Steelman would pay using each cost flow method.

c. Determine the cash flow from operating activities under FIFO and LIFO.

d. Why is the cash flow from operating activities different under FIFO and LIFO?

Exercise 5-7B *Effect of FIFO versus LIFO on income tax expense*   LO 5-1

Home Gifts Inc. had cash sales of $112,500 for Year 1, its first year of operation. On April 2, the company purchased 150 units of inventory at $180 per unit. On September 1, an additional 200 units were purchased for $200 per unit. The company had 50 units on hand at the end of the year. The company's income tax rate is 40 percent. All transactions are cash transactions.

Required

a. The preceding paragraph describes five accounting events: (1) a sales transaction, (2) the first purchase of inventory, (3) a second purchase of inventory, (4) the recognition of cost of goods sold expense, and (5) the payment of income tax expense. Show the amounts of each event in horizontal statements models like the following ones, assuming first a FIFO and then a LIFO cost flow.

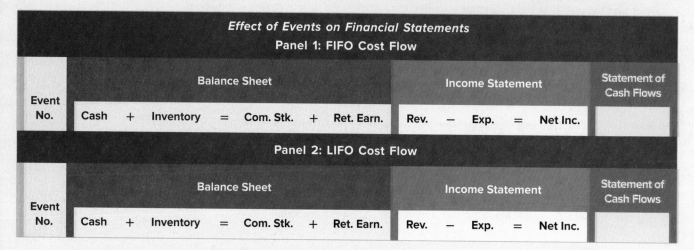

b. Compute net income using FIFO.
c. Compute net income using LIFO.
d. Explain the difference, if any, in the amount of income tax expense incurred using the two cost flow assumptions.
e. How does the use of the FIFO versus the LIFO cost flow assumptions affect the statement of cash flows?

LO 5-1

Exercise 5-8B *Recording inventory transactions using the perpetual system: intermittent sales and purchases*

The following inventory transactions apply to Duncan Steel Company for Year 2:

Jan. 1	Purchased	200 units @ $12
Apr. 1	Sold	150 units @ $20
Aug. 1	Purchased	300 units @ $15
Dec. 1	Sold	450 units @ $25

The beginning inventory consisted of 180 units at $10 per unit. All transactions are cash transactions.

Required

a. Record these transactions in a financial statements model, assuming Duncan uses the FIFO cost-flow assumption and keeps perpetual records.
b. Compute the ending balance in the Inventory account.

LO 5-1

Exercise 5-9B *Effect of cost flow on ending inventory: intermittent sales and purchases*

Nash Auto Parts, Inc. had the following transactions for Year 2:

Date	Transaction	Description
Jan. 1	Beginning inventory	40 units @ $22
Mar. 15	Purchased	150 units @ $24
May 30	Sold	175 units @ $48
Aug. 10	Purchased	320 units @ $26
Nov. 20	Sold	300 units @ $50

Required

a. Determine the quantity and dollar amount of inventory at the end of the year, assuming Nash Auto Parts, Inc. uses the FIFO cost flow assumption and keeps perpetual records.

b. Write a memo explaining why Nash Auto Parts, Inc. would have difficulty applying the LIFO method on a perpetual basis. Include a discussion of how to overcome these difficulties.

Exercise 5-10B   *Lower-of-cost-or-market rule: perpetual system*   LO 5-2

The following information pertains to James Hardware's ending inventory for the current year:

Item	Quantity	Unit Cost	Unit Market Value
M	200	$10	$ 8
N	100	12	10
O	40	8	9
P	30	5	10

Required

a. Determine the value of the ending inventory using the lower-of-cost-or-market rule applied to (1) each individual inventory item and (2) the inventory in aggregate.

b. Prepare any necessary adjustment, assuming the decline in value is immaterial, using the (1) individual method and (2) aggregate method. James Hardware uses the perpetual inventory system.

Exercise 5-11B   *Lower-of-cost-or-market rule*   LO 5-2

Harvey Company carries three inventory items. The following information pertains to the ending inventory:

Item	Quantity	Unit Cost	Unit Market Value
A	400	$20	$18
B	500	25	24
C	300	10	12

Required

a. Determine the ending inventory that will be reported on the balance sheet, assuming that Harvey applies the lower-of-cost-or-market rule to individual inventory items.

b. Prepare the necessary adjustment, assuming the decline in value is immaterial.

Exercise 5-12B   *Effect of inventory error on financial statements: perpetual system*   LO 5-3

Bosh Company failed to count $22,000 of inventory in its Year 1 year-end physical count.

Required

Explain how this error will affect Bosh's Year 1 financial statements, assuming that Bosh uses the perpetual inventory system.

Exercise 5-13B   *Effect of inventory misstatement on elements of financial statements*   LO 5-3

The ending inventory for Oak Co. was erroneously written down, causing an understatement of $6,500 at the end of Year 2.

Required

Was each of the following amounts overstated, understated, or not affected by the error?

Item No.	Year	Amount
1	Year 2	Beginning inventory
2	Year 2	Purchases
3	Year 2	Goods available for sale
4	Year 2	Cost of goods sold
5	Year 2	Gross margin
6	Year 2	Net income
7	Year 3	Beginning inventory
8	Year 3	Purchases
9	Year 3	Goods available for sale
10	Year 3	Cost of goods sold
11	Year 3	Gross margin
12	Year 3	Net income

LO 5-4

Exercise 5-14B *Estimating ending inventory using the gross margin method*

Frank Jones, the owner of Frank's Hunting Supplies, is surprised at the amount of actual inventory at the end of the year. He thought there should be more inventory on hand based on the amount of sales for the year. The following information is taken from the books of Frank's Hunting Supplies:

Beginning inventory	$250,000
Purchases for the year	500,000
Sales for the year	850,000
Inventory at the end of the year (based on actual count)	40,000

Historically, Frank has made a 20 percent gross margin on his sales. Frank thinks there may be some problem with the inventory. Evaluate the situation based on the historical gross profit percentage.

Required

Estimate the following:

a. Gross margin in dollars.

b. Cost of goods sold in dollars.

c. Estimated ending inventory.

d. Inventory shortage.

e. Provide an explanation for the shortage.

LO 5-4

Exercise 5-15B *Estimating ending inventory: perpetual system*

Beth Malone owned a small company that sold boating equipment. The equipment was expensive, and a perpetual system was maintained for control purposes. Even so, lost, damaged, and stolen merchandise normally amounted to 5 percent of the inventory balance. On June 14, Beth's warehouse was destroyed by fire. Just prior to the fire, the accounting records contained a $130,000 balance in the Inventory account. However, inventory that cost $20,000 had been sold and delivered to customers the day of the fire but had not been recorded in the books at the time of the fire. The fire did not affect the showroom, which contained inventory that cost $50,000.

Required

Estimate the amount of inventory destroyed by fire.

Exercise 5-16B   *Inventory turnover and average days to sell*

The following accounting information pertains to two retail stores that specialize in selling winter ski gear. Aspen Sports operates only a few locations and has a market strategy of selling only high-end ski gear. Discount Ski has many locations but sells lower-quality products than Aspen Sports.

	Discount Ski	Aspen Sports
Sales	$800,000	?
Cost of goods sold	?	$200,000
Gross margin	?	$300,000
Gross margin Percentage	20%	?

Discount Ski has an average inventory balance of $60,000, while Aspen Sports's average inventory balance is $55,000.

a. Complete the table by filling in the missing amounts.

b. Which retail store is using a higher cost/lower volume strategy regarding sales?

c. Calculate the inventory turnover and the average days to sale inventory for each retail store. Based on your calculations, which retail store will need to reorder inventory more frequently?

Exercise 5-17B   *Explaining multiple inventory methods at one real-world company*

IFRS

The following note related to accounting for inventory was taken from the 2016 annual report of Wal-Mart Stores, Inc.:

> *Inventories   The Company values inventories at the lower of cost or market as determined primarily by the retail inventory method of accounting, using the last-in, first-out ("LIFO") method for substantially all of the Walmart U.S. segment's inventories. The inventory at the Walmart International segment is valued primarily by the retail inventory method of accounting, using the first-in, first-out ("FIFO") method. The retail inventory method of accounting results in inventory being valued at the lower of cost or market since permanent markdowns are immediately recorded as a reduction of the retail value of inventory. The inventory at the Sam's Club segment is valued based on the weighted-average cost using the LIFO method. At January 31, 2016 and January 31, 2015, the Company's inventories valued at LIFO approximated those inventories as if they were valued at FIFO.*

*2016. Wal-Mart Stores, Inc. Annual Report. Walmart.

Required

Write a brief report explaining the reason or reasons that best explain why Walmart uses the LIFO cost flow method for its operations in the United States but the FIFO method for its non-U.S. operations.

Exercise 5-18B   *GAAP versus IFRS*

IFRS

Po River Winery Inc. has inventory that cost $500,000. The aging process for the inventory requires several years. At the end of Year 1, the inventory had a market value of $400,000. During Year 2, the market value recovered to an estimated $480,000.

Required

a. Assuming Po River uses GAAP, determine the book value and the amount of any gain or loss recognized on the Year 1 and Year 2 financial statements.

b. Assuming Po River uses IFRS, determine the book value and the amount of any gain or loss recognized on the Year 1 and Year 2 financial statements.

PROBLEMS—SERIES B

Problem 5-19B   *Effect of different inventory cost flow methods on financial statements*

LO 5-1

The accounting records of Octavia's Flower Shop reflected the following balances as of January 1, Year 3:

Cash	$92,500
Beginning inventory	36,000 (225 units @ $160)
Common stock	60,000
Retained earnings	68,500

CHECK FIGURES
a. Cost of Goods Sold FIFO: $58,325
b. Net Income LIFO: $18,340

The following five transactions occurred in Year 3:

1. First purchase (cash): 130 units @ $140
2. Second purchase (cash): 180 units @ $165
3. Sales (all cash): 380 units @ $335
4. Paid $42,000 cash for salaries expense
5. Paid cash for income tax at the rate of 30 percent of income before taxes

Required

a. Compute the cost of goods sold and ending inventory, assuming (1) FIFO cost flow, (2) LIFO cost flow, and (3) weighted-average cost flow. Compute the income tax expense for each method.

b. Prepare the Year 3 income statement, balance sheet, and statement of cash flows under FIFO, LIFO, and weighted average. (*Hint:* Record the events under an accounting equation before preparing the statements.)

LO 5-1

Problem 5-20B *Allocating product costs between cost of goods sold and ending inventory: intermittent purchases and sales of merchandise*

Donovan, Inc. had the following sales and purchase transactions during Year 2. Beginning inventory consisted of 120 items at $80 each. Donovan uses the FIFO cost flow assumption and keeps perpetual inventory records.

Date	Transaction	Description
Mar. 5	Purchased	100 items @ $90
Apr. 10	Sold	70 items @ $175
June 19	Sold	80 items @ $175
Sep. 16	Purchased	50 items @ $95
Nov. 28	Sold	60 items @ $180

Required

a. Record the inventory transactions in a financial statements model.

b. Calculate the gross margin Donovan would report on the Year 2 income statement.

c. Determine the ending inventory balance Donovan would report on the December 31, Year 2, balance sheet.

LO 5-2

Problem 5-21B *Inventory valuation based on the lower-of-cost-or-market rule*

At the end of the year, Ronaldo Jewelers had the following items in inventory:

Item	Quantity	Unit Cost	Unit Market Value
D1	30	$80	$90
D2	10	60	55
D3	41	30	32
D4	20	90	75

Required

a. Determine the amount of ending inventory using the lower-of-cost-or-market rule applied to each individual inventory item.

b. Provide the adjustment necessary to write down the inventory based on Requirement *a*. Assume that Ronaldo Jewelers uses the perpetual inventory system.

c. Determine the amount of ending inventory, assuming that the lower-of-cost-or-market rule is applied to the inventory in aggregate.

d. Provide the adjustment necessary to write down the inventory based on Requirement *c*. Assume that Ronaldo Jewelers uses the perpetual inventory system.

Problem 5-22B *Effect of inventory errors on financial statements*

The following income statement was prepared for Rice Company for Year 1:

RICE COMPANY	
Income Statement	
For the Year Ended December 31, Year 1	
Sales	$ 75,000
Cost of goods sold	(41,250)
Gross margin	33,750
Operating expenses	(10,120)
Net income	$ 23,630

During the year-end audit, the following errors were discovered:

1. An $1,800 payment for repairs was erroneously charged to the Cost of Goods Sold account. (Assume that the perpetual inventory system is used.)

2. Sales to customers for $3,400 at December 31, Year 1, were not recorded in the books for Year 1. Also, the $1,870 cost of goods sold was not recorded

3. A mathematical error was made in determining ending inventory. Ending inventory was understated by $1,700. (The Inventory account was written down in error to the Cost of Goods Sold account.)

Required

Determine the effect, if any, of each of the errors on the following items. Give the dollar amount of the effect and whether it would overstate (O), understate (U), or not affect (NA) the account. The effect on sales is recorded as an example.

Error No. 1	Amount of Error	Effect
Sales, Year 1	NA	NA
Ending inventory, December 31, Year 1		
Gross margin, Year 1		
Beginning inventory, January 1, Year 2		
Cost of goods sold, Year 1		
Net income, Year 1		
Retained earnings, December 31, Year 1		
Total assets, December 31, Year 1		

Error No. 2	Amount of Error	Effect
Sales, Year 1	$3,400	U
Ending inventory, December 31, Year 1		
Gross margin, Year 1		
Beginning inventory, January 1, Year 2		
Cost of goods sold, Year 1		
Net income, Year 1		
Retained earnings, December 31, Year 1		
Total assets, December 31, Year 1		

Error No. 3	Amount of Error	Effect
Sales, Year 1	NA	NA
Ending inventory, December 31, Year 1		
Gross margin, Year 1		
Beginning inventory, January 1, Year 2		
Cost of goods sold, Year 1		
Net income, Year 1		
Retained earnings, December 31, Year 1		
Total assets, December 31, Year 1		

LO 5-4

Problem 5-23B *Estimating ending inventory: gross margin method*

A hurricane destroyed the inventory of Coleman Feed Store on September 21 of the current year. Although some of the accounting information was destroyed, the following information was discovered for the period of January 1 through September 21:

Beginning inventory, January 1	$120,000
Purchases through September 21	450,000
Sales through September 21	800,000

The gross margin for Coleman Feed Store has traditionally been 35 percent of sales.

Required

a. For the period ending September 21, compute the following:

   (1) Estimated gross margin.

   (2) Estimated cost of goods sold.

   (3) Estimated inventory at September 21.

b. Assume that $8,000 of the inventory was not damaged. What is the amount of the loss from the hurricane?

c. Coleman Feed Store uses the perpetual inventory system. If some of the accounting records had not been destroyed, how would Coleman determine the amount of the inventory loss?

LO 5-4

Problem 5-24B *Estimating ending inventory: gross margin method*

Sam Todd, owner of Todd Company, is reviewing the quarterly financial statements and thinks the cost of goods sold is out of line with past years. The following historical data are available for Year 1 and Year 2:

	Year 1	Year 2
Net sales	$220,000	$250,000
Cost of goods sold	99,000	117,200

At the end of the first quarter of Year 3, Todd Company had the following account balances:

Sales	$280,000
Purchases	210,000
Beginning inventory, January 1, Year 3	70,000

Required

Using the information provided, estimate the following for the first quarter of Year 3:

a. Cost of goods sold. (Use average cost of goods sold percentage.)

b. Ending inventory at March 31 based on the historical cost of goods sold percentage.

c. Inventory shortage if the inventory balance as of March 31 is $125,000.

LO 5-5

Problem 5-25B *Using ratios to make comparisons*

The following accounting information pertains to Mobile and Casper companies. The only difference between the two companies is that Mobile uses FIFO, while Casper uses LIFO.

	Mobile Co.	Casper Co.
Cash	$ 70,000	$ 70,000
Accounts receivable	230,000	230,000
Merchandise inventory	220,000	190,000
Accounts payable	210,000	210,000
Cost of goods sold	1,350,000	1,380,000
Building	300,000	300,000
Sales	1,800,000	1,800,000

Required

a. Compute the gross margin percentage for each company and identify the company that *appears* to be charging the higher prices in relation to its cost.

b. For each company, compute the inventory turnover ratio and the average days to sell inventory. Identify the company that *appears* to be incurring the higher financing cost.

c. Explain why a company with the lower gross margin percentage needs to have a higher inventory turnover ratio assuming a period of inflation.

ANALYZE, THINK, COMMUNICATE

ATC 5-1   Business Applications Case   *Understanding real-world annual reports*

Required

Obtain Target Corporation's annual report for its 2018 fiscal year (year ended February 2, 2019) at http://investors.target.com using the instructions in Appendix B, and use it to answer the following questions:

a. What was Target's inventory turnover ratio and average days to sell inventory for the fiscal year ended February 2, 2019 (2018) and 2017?

b. Is the company's management of inventory getting better or worse?

c. What cost flow method(s) did Target use to account for inventory?

ATC 5-2   Group Assignment   *Inventory cost flow*

The accounting records of Blue Bird Co. showed the following balances at January 1, Year 2:

Cash	$30,000
Beginning inventory (100 units @ $50, 70 units @ $55)	8,850
Common stock	20,000
Retained earnings	18,850

Transactions for Year 2 were as follows:

> Purchased 100 units @ $54 per unit.
> Sold 220 units @ $80 per unit.
> Purchased 250 units @ $58 per unit.
> Sold 200 units @ $90 per unit.
> Paid operating expenses of $3,200.
> Paid income tax expense. The income tax rate is 30%.

Required

a. Organize the class into three sections, and divide each section into groups of three to five students. Assign each section one of the cost flow methods, FIFO, LIFO, or weighted average. The company uses the perpetual inventory system.

Group Tasks

Determine the amount of ending inventory, cost of goods sold, gross margin, and net income after income tax for the cost flow method assigned to your section. Also prepare an income statement using that cost flow assumption.

Class Discussion

b. Have a representative of each section put its income statement on the board. Discuss the effect that each cost flow method has on assets (ending inventory), net income, and cash flows. Which method is preferred for tax reporting? For financial reporting? What restrictions are placed on the use of LIFO for tax reporting?

ATC 5-3   Real-World Case   *Inventory management issues at the Penske Automotive Group*

The following data were extracted from the 2017 financial statements of Penske Automotive Group, Inc. This company operates automobile dealerships, mostly in the United States, Canada, and Western Europe, and commercial truck dealerships in Australia, New Zealand, and the United Kingdom. The company had 355 dealerships as of the end of 2017. Dollar amounts are in millions.

	December 31, 2017	December 31, 2016
Revenue	$21,387	$20,119
Cost of sale	18,164	17,152
Gross profit	3,223	2,967
Operating income before taxes	548	508
Net income	613	342
Ending inventory	3,944	3,408

Required

a. Compute Penske's gross margin percentage for 2017 and 2016.

b. Compute Penske's average days to sell inventory for 2017 and 2016.

c. How much higher or lower would *Penske's earnings before taxes* have been in 2017 if its gross margin percentage had been the same as it was in 2016? Show all supporting computations.

ATC 5-4   Business Applications Case   *Performing ratio analysis using real-world data*

Ruby Tuesday's, Inc. operated 605 casual dining restaurants across the United States as of June 6, 2017. Signet Jewelers Limited claims to be the world's largest retailer of diamond jewelry. Its stores include Zales, Jared, Kay Jewelers, and Piercing Pagoda. As of February 3, 2018, it had over 3,000 retail outlets.

The following data were taken from these companies' annual reports. All dollar amounts are in millions.

	Ruby Tuesday's June 6, 2017	Signet Jewelers February 3, 2018
Revenue	$952	$6,253
Cost of goods sold	269	4,063
Operating income before tax	(108)	202
Merchandise inventory	11	2,281

Required

a. Before performing any calculations, speculate as to which company will take the longest to sell its inventory. Explain the rationale for your decision.

b. Calculate the inventory turnover ratios for Ruby Tuesday's and Signet.

c. Calculate the average days to sell inventory for Ruby Tuesday's and Signet.

d. Do the calculations from Requirements *b* and *c* confirm your speculations in Requirement *a*?

ATC 5-5   Writing Assignment   *Use of LIFO*

The following information is available for Leno Company:

Sales	$695,000
Goods available for sale	535,000
Ending inventory (using FIFO)	246,000

Leno Company currently uses the FIFO cost flow method for financial statement reporting and tax reporting. It is considering changing to the LIFO cost flow method for tax reporting purposes. If Leno uses LIFO, its ending inventory would be $175,000.

Required

a. Why would Leno want to change to LIFO for tax reporting?

b. Discuss any changes that Leno would have to make for GAAP reporting if it does change to LIFO for tax reporting.

ATC 5-6 Ethical Dilemma *Show them only what you want them to see*

Clair Coolage is the chief accountant for a sales company called Far Eastern Imports. The company has been highly successful and is trying to increase its capital base by attracting new investors. The company operates in an inflationary environment and has been using the LIFO inventory cost flow method to minimize its net earnings and thereby reduce its income taxes. Katie Bailey, the vice president of finance, asked Coolage to estimate the change in net earnings that would occur if the company switched to FIFO. After reviewing the company's books, Coolage estimated that pretax income would increase by $1,200,000 if the company adopted the FIFO cost flow method. However, the switch would result in approximately $400,000 of additional taxes. The overall effect would result in an increase of $800,000 in net earnings. Bailey told Coolage to avoid the additional taxes by preparing the tax return on a LIFO basis but to prepare a set of statements on a FIFO basis to be distributed to potential investors.

Required

a. Comment on the legal and ethical implications of Bailey's decision.

b. How will the switch to FIFO affect Far Eastern's balance sheet?

c. If Bailey reconsiders and makes a decision to switch to FIFO for tax purposes as well as financial reporting purposes, net income will increase by $800,000. Comment on the wisdom of paying $400,000 in income taxes to obtain an additional $800,000 of net income.

ATC 5-7 Research Assignment *Analyzing inventory at Gap Company*

Using either Gap's most current Form 10-K or the company's annual report, answer the questions that follow. To obtain the Form 10-K, use either the EDGAR system, following the instructions in Appendix A, or the company's website. The company's annual report is available on its website.

Required

a. How many "company-operated" stores did Gap operate at year-end? (Do not include "Franchise store locations.")

b. What was the average amount of inventory per store? Use *all* stores operated by The Gap, Inc., not just those called *The Gap*. (*Hint:* The answer to this question must be computed. The number of stores in operation at the end of the most recent year can be found in the MD&A of the 10-K.)

c. Using the quarterly financial information in the 10-K, complete the following chart:

Quarter	Sales during Each Quarter
1	$
2	
3	
4	

d. Referring to the chart in Requirement *c*, explain why Gap's sales vary so widely throughout its fiscal year. Do you believe that Gap's inventory level varies throughout the year in relation to sales?

CHAPTER 6

Internal Control and Accounting for Cash

Video lectures and accompanying self-assessment quizzes are available in *Connect* for all learning objectives.

Tableau Dashboard Activity is available in *Connect* for this chapter.

LEARNING OBJECTIVES

After you have mastered the material in this chapter, you will be able to:

LO 6-1   Identify the key elements of a strong system of internal control.

LO 6-2   Identify special internal controls for cash.

LO 6-3   Prepare a bank reconciliation.

LO 6-4   Show how a petty cash fund affects financial statements.

LO 6-5   Describe the auditor's role in financial reporting.

CHAPTER OPENING

To operate successfully, businesses must establish systems of control. How can Walmart's upper-level managers ensure that every store will open on time? How can the president of General Motors be confident that the company's financial reports fairly reflect the company's operations? How can the owner of a restaurant prevent a waiter from serving food to his friends and relatives without charging them for it? The answer: by exercising effective control over company activities. The policies and procedures used to provide reasonable assurance that the objectives of an enterprise will be accomplished are called **internal controls.**

Internal controls can be divided into two categories: (1) **accounting controls** are designed to safeguard company assets and ensure reliable accounting records; and (2) **administrative controls** are concerned with evaluating performance and assessing the degree of compliance with company policies and public laws.

The Curious Accountant

jvdwolf/123RF

When many people think about the threats to a company's financial resources they imagine someone trying to steal its cash or other assets, or a hacker trying to drain its bank account. Although these are legitimate threats, the biggest threats facing business often come from within.

Consider the case of the **Volkswagen AG** (VW) emissions scandal that became widely known to the public in September 2015, when the Environmental Protection Agency (EPA) filed charges claiming VW had intentionally installed software to provide inaccurate results related to mileage and emissions performance in some of its vehicles with diesel engines. Within months of the charges by the EPA, VW admitted that its emissions-defeating software had been installed on about 11 million vehicles worldwide.

Companies' responsibilities under the Sarbanes–Oxley Act (SOX) were introduced in Chapter 2, and SOX is discussed further in this chapter. Do you think SOX was intended to require companies to protect their customers from the type of emissions-reporting frauds reported here? If not, are there other aspects of financial accounting systems that should protect a company's customers and investors? (Answers on page 286.)

KEY FEATURES OF INTERNAL CONTROL SYSTEMS

During the early 2000s, a number of accounting-related scandals cost investors billions. In 2001, Enron's share price went from $85 to $0.30 after it was revealed that the company had billions of dollars in losses that were not reported on the financial statements. Several months later, WorldCom reported an $11 billion accounting fraud, which included hundreds of millions in personal loans to then-CEO, Bernie Ebbers.

The Enron and WorldCom accounting scandals had such devastating effects that they led Congress to pass the Sarbanes–Oxley Act of 2002 (SOX). SOX requires public companies to evaluate their internal control and to publish those findings with their SEC filings. *Internal control* is the process designed to ensure reliable financial reporting, effective and efficient operations, and compliance with applicable laws and regulations. Safeguarding assets against theft and unauthorized use, acquisition, or disposal is also part of internal control.

Section 404 of Sarbanes-Oxley requires a statement of management's responsibility for establishing and maintaining adequate internal control over financial reporting by public companies. This section includes an assessment of the controls and the identification of the framework used for the assessment. The framework established by the Committee of Sponsoring

LO 6-1

Identify the key elements of a strong system of internal control.

Drew Angerer/Getty Images

Organizations (COSO) of the Treadway Commission in 1992 is the de facto standard by which SOX compliance is judged. COSO's framework, titled *Internal Control—An Integrated Framework,* recognizes five interrelated components, including:

1. *Control Environment.* The integrity and ethical values of the company, including its code of conduct, involvement of the board of directors, and other actions that set the tone of the organization.
2. *Risk Assessment.* Management's process of identifying potential risks that could result in misstated financial statements and developing actions to address those risks.
3. *Control Activities.* These are the activities usually thought of as "the internal controls." They include such things as segregation of duties, account reconciliations, and information processing controls designed to safeguard assets and enable an organization to prepare reliable financial statements in a timely manner.
4. *Information and Communication.* The internal and external reporting process, including an assessment of the technology environment.
5. *Monitoring.* Assessing the quality of a company's internal control over time and taking actions as necessary to ensure it continues to address the risks of the organization.

In 2004, COSO updated the framework to help entities design and implement effective enterprisewide approaches to risk management. The updated document is titled *Enterprise Risk Management (ERM)—An Integrated Framework.* The ERM framework introduces an enterprisewide approach to risk management, as well as concepts such as risk appetite, risk tolerance, and portfolio view. While SOX applies only to U.S. public companies, the ERM framework has been adopted by both public and private organizations around the world.

The ERM framework does not replace the internal control framework. Instead, it incorporates the internal control framework within it. Accordingly, companies may decide to look to the ERM framework both to satisfy their internal control needs and to move toward a fuller risk management process.

While a detailed discussion of the COSO documents is beyond the scope of this text, the following overview of the more common *control activities* of the internal control framework is insightful.

Segregation of Duties

The likelihood of fraud or theft is reduced if employees must work together to accomplish it. Clear **segregation of duties** is frequently used as a deterrent to corruption. When duties are segregated, the work of one employee can act as a check on the work of another employee. For example, a person selling seats to a movie may be tempted to steal money received from customers who enter the theater. This temptation is reduced if the person staffing the box office is required to issue tickets that a second employee collects as people enter the theater. If ticket stubs collected by the second employee are compared with the cash receipts from ticket sales, any cash shortages will become apparent. Furthermore, friends and relatives of the ticket agent cannot easily enter the theater without paying. Theft or unauthorized entry would require collusion between the ticket agent and the usher who collects the tickets. Both individuals would have to be dishonest enough to steal, yet trustworthy enough to convince each other they would keep the embezzlement secret. Whenever possible, the functions of *authorization, recording,* and *custody of assets* should be performed by separate individuals.

Quality of Employees

A business is only as good as the people it employs. Cheap labor is not a bargain if the employees are incompetent. Employees should be properly trained. In fact, they should be trained to perform a variety of tasks. The ability of employees to substitute for one another prevents disruptions when co-workers are absent because of illnesses, vacations, or other commitments. The capacity to rotate jobs also relieves boredom and increases respect for the contributions of other employees. Every business should strive to maximize the productivity of every employee. Ongoing training programs are essential to a strong system of internal control.

Bonded Employees

The best way to ensure employee honesty is to hire individuals with *high levels of personal integrity.* Employers should screen job applicants using interviews, background checks, and recommendations from prior employers or educators. Even so, screening programs may fail to identify character weaknesses. Further, unusual circumstances may cause honest employees to go astray. Therefore, employees in positions of trust should be bonded. A **fidelity bond** provides insurance that protects a company from losses caused by employee dishonesty.

Required Absences

Employees should be required to take regular vacations and their duties should be rotated periodically. Employees may be able to cover up fraudulent activities if they are always present at work. Consider the case of a parking meter collection agent who covered the same route for several years with no vacation. When the agent became sick, a substitute collected more money each day than the regular reader usually reported. Management checked past records and found that the ill meter reader had been understating the cash receipts and pocketing the difference. If management had required vacations or rotated the routes, the embezzlement would have been discovered much earlier.

Procedures Manual

Appropriate accounting procedures should be documented in a **procedures manual.** The manual should be routinely updated. Periodic reviews should be conducted to ensure that employees are following the procedures outlined in the manual.

Authority and Responsibility

Employees are motivated by clear lines of authority and responsibility. They work harder when they have the authority to use their own judgment, and they exercise reasonable caution when they are held responsible for their actions. Businesses should prepare an **authority manual** that establishes a definitive *chain of command.* The authority manual should guide both specific and general authorizations. **Specific authorizations** apply to specific positions within the organization. For example, investment decisions are authorized at the division level, while hiring decisions are authorized at the departmental level. In contrast, **general authority** applies across different levels of management. For example, employees at all levels may be required to fly economy class or to make purchases from specific vendors.

Prenumbered Documents

How would you know if a check were stolen from your checkbook? If you keep a record of your check numbers, the missing number would tip you off immediately. Businesses also use prenumbered checks to avoid the unauthorized use of their bank accounts. In fact, prenumbered forms are used for all important documents such as purchase orders, receiving reports, invoices, and checks. To reduce errors, prenumbered forms should be as simple and easy to use as possible. Also, the documents should allow for authorized signatures. For example, credit sales slips should be signed by the customer to clearly establish who made the purchase, reducing the likelihood of unauthorized transactions.

Physical Control

Employees walk away with billions of dollars of business assets each year. To limit losses, companies should establish adequate physical control over valuable assets. For example, inventory should be kept in a storeroom and not released without proper authorization. Serial numbers on equipment should be recorded along with the name of the individual who is responsible for the equipment. Unannounced physical counts should be conducted randomly to verify the presence of company-owned equipment. Certificates of deposit and marketable securities should be kept in fireproof vaults. Access to these vaults should be limited to authorized personnel. These procedures protect the documents from fire and limit access to only those individuals who have the appropriate security clearance to handle the documents.

In addition to safeguarding assets, there should be physical control over the accounting records. The accounting records should be kept in a fireproof safe. Only personnel responsible for recording transactions should have access to the points of data entry. With limited access, there is less chance that someone will change the records to conceal fraud or embezzlement.

Performance Evaluations

Because few people can evaluate their own performance objectively, internal controls should include independent verification of employee performance. For example, someone other than the person who has control over inventory should take a physical count of inventory. Internal and external audits serve as independent verification of performance. Auditors should evaluate the effectiveness of the internal control system, as well as verify the accuracy of the accounting records. In addition, the external auditors attest to the company's use of generally accepted accounting principles in the financial statements.

Limitations

A system of internal controls is designed to prevent or detect errors and fraud. However, no control system is foolproof. Internal controls can be circumvented by collusion among employees. Two or more employees working together can hide embezzlement by covering for each other. For example, if an embezzler goes on vacation, fraud will not be reported by a replacement who is in collusion with the embezzler. No system can prevent all fraud. However, a good system of internal controls minimizes illegal or unethical activities by reducing temptation and increasing the likelihood of early detection.

 CHECK YOURSELF 6.1

What are nine features of an internal control system?

Answer The nine features follow:

1. Separating duties so that fraud or theft requires collusion.
2. Hiring and training competent employees.
3. Bonding employees to recover losses through insurance.
4. Requiring employees to be absent from their jobs so that their replacements can discover errors or fraudulent activity that might have occurred.
5. Establishing proper procedures for processing transactions.
6. Establishing clear lines of authority and responsibility.
7. Using prenumbered documents.
8. Implementing physical controls such as locking cash in a safe.
9. Conducting performance evaluations through independent internal and external audits.

ACCOUNTING FOR CASH

For financial reporting purposes, **cash** generally includes currency and other items that are payable *on demand,* such as checks, money orders, bank drafts, and certain savings accounts. Savings accounts that impose substantial penalties for early withdrawal should be classified as *investments* rather than cash. Postdated checks or IOUs represent *receivables* and should not be included in cash. As illustrated in Exhibit 6.1, most companies combine currency and other receivable-on-demand items in a single balance sheet account with varying titles.

LO 6-2

Identify special internal controls for cash.

Companies must maintain a sufficient amount of cash to pay employees, suppliers, and other creditors. When a company fails to pay its legal obligations, its creditors can force the company into bankruptcy. Even so, management should avoid accumulating more cash than is needed. The failure to invest excess cash in earning assets reduces profitability. Cash inflows and outflows must be managed to prevent a shortage or surplus of cash.

Controlling Cash

Controlling cash, more than any other asset, requires strict adherence to internal control procedures. Cash has universal appeal. A relatively small suitcase filled with high-denomination currency can represent significant value. Furthermore, the rightful owner of currency is difficult to prove. In most cases, possession constitutes ownership. As a result, cash is highly susceptible to theft and must be carefully protected. Cash is most susceptible to embezzlement when it is received or disbursed. The following controls should be employed to reduce the likelihood of theft.

Cash Receipts

A record of all cash collections should be prepared immediately upon receipt. The amount of cash on hand should be counted regularly. Missing amounts of money can be detected by comparing the actual cash on hand with the book balance. Employees who receive cash should give customers a copy of a written receipt. Customers usually review their receipts to ensure they have gotten credit for the amount paid and call any errors to the receipts clerk's attention. This not only reduces errors but also provides a control on the clerk's honesty. Cash receipts should be deposited in a bank on a timely basis. Cash collected late in the day should be deposited in a night depository. Every effort should be made to minimize the amount of cash on hand. Keeping large amounts of cash on hand not only increases the risk of loss from theft but also places employees in danger of being harmed by criminals who may be tempted to rob the company.

Cash Payments

To effectively control cash, a company should make all disbursements using checks, thereby providing a record of cash payments. All checks should be prenumbered, and unused checks should be locked up. Using prenumbered checks allows companies to easily identify lost or stolen checks by comparing the numbers on unused and canceled checks with the numbers used for legitimate disbursements.

The duties of approving disbursements, signing checks, and recording transactions should be segregated. If one person is authorized to approve, sign, and record checks, he or she could falsify supporting documents, write an unauthorized check, and record a cover-up transaction in the accounting records. By separating these duties, the check signer reviews the documentation provided by the approving individual before signing the check. Likewise, the recording clerk reviews the work of both the approving person and the check signer when the disbursement is recorded in the accounting records. Thus, writing unauthorized checks requires trilevel collusion.

Supporting documents with authorized approval signatures should be required when checks are presented to the check signer. For example, a warehouse receiving order should be matched with a purchase order before a check is approved to pay a bill from a supplier.

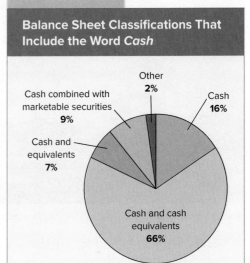

EXHIBIT 6.1

Balance Sheet Classifications That Include the Word *Cash*

- Cash combined with marketable securities 9%
- Cash and equivalents 7%
- Cash and cash equivalents 66%
- Other 2%
- Cash 16%

Note: The chart is based on data drawn from the recent annual reports published by the 30 companies that comprise the Dow Jones Industrial Average.

Answers to The Curious Accountant

Hirotaka Ihara/123RF

The Sarbanes–Oxley Act (SOX) placed a lot of emphasis on companies having a good system of internal controls, primarily to ensure proper financial reporting. But SOX was intended mostly to protect a company's investors, not its customers. Fraud that involves providing misleading information on emissions tests is not a financial reporting issue, but it can lead to financial problems. As this chapter has explained, good internal controls are about more than accurate financial reporting; they should also protect the company's resources, and customers are a major company resource.

The fraud that occurred at Volkswagen was bad for customers and the environment, but it was very costly to the company and its investors. By early 2017, *The Wall Street Journal* estimated that the emissions scandal would ultimately cost VW over $25 billion in direct compensation to car owners and fines to governments. As for stock investors, in the four years from February, 2015, until December, 2018, VW's stock price fell by about 18 percent. However, during this same period, the stock of Ford, General Motors, and Toyota also fell by an average of 18 percent. And, while these three automakers' sales increased by an average of 2.4 percent from 2014 through 2017, VW's sales increased by 14 percent. So, VW's program of buying back the affected cars at a fair price and firing the individuals involved in the scandal seemed to have satisfied its customers. In addition to the financial cost of fines and reparations, the scandal had human costs. By late 2018, eight current and former VW executives had been indicted in the United States, and one, Oliver Schmidt, had plead guilty and been sentenced to seven years in prison. VW's former CEO, Martin Winterkorn, had been indicted in Germany.

The problem at VW did not occur overnight, nor was it the work of one employee. VW initiated its "clean diesel" program in 2008, and as early as 2009, emissions-defeating devices had already been installed in cars. The problems even went beyond VW. Bosch, a parts supplier for VW, was also alleged to have known about the scheme, and Bosch agreed to pay $327.5 million to settle claims that it assisted in developing the software used to defeat emissions tests. One element of good internal control is to have a separation of duties so that if one person is behaving inappropriately, another is likely to see the misbehavior and take corrective action. This system does not work if many high-level employees are all willing to participate in the inappropriate behavior. Even the best systems of internal controls still rely on people.

Source: The emissions testing problems for VW vehicles were reported widely in the press. Many of the specifics for this Curious Accountant were from online postings of *The Wall Street Journal* dated January 9, 11, and 27, 2017, and the companies' public financial reporting.

REALITY BYTES

THE COST OF PROTECTING CASH

Could you afford to buy a safe like the one shown here? The vault is only one of many expensive security devices used by banks to safeguard cash. By using checking accounts, companies are able to avoid many of the costs associated with keeping cash safe. In addition to providing physical control, checking accounts enable companies to maintain a written audit trail of cash receipts and payments. Checking accounts represent the most widely used internal control device in modern society. It is difficult to imagine a business operating without the use of checking accounts.

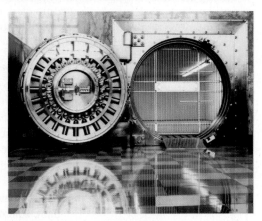

Digital Vision/Getty Images

Before payments are approved, invoice amounts should be checked and payees verified as valid vendors. Matching supporting documents with proper authorization discourages employees from creating phony documents for a disbursement to a friend or fictitious business. Also, the approval process serves as a check on the accuracy of the work of all employees involved.

Supporting documents should be marked *Paid* when the check is signed. If the documents are not indelibly marked, they could be retrieved from the files and resubmitted for a duplicate unauthorized payment. A payables clerk could collude with the payee to split extra cash paid out by submitting the same supporting documents for a second payment.

All spoiled and voided checks should be defaced and retained. If defaced checks are not retained, an employee could steal a check and then claim it was written incorrectly and thrown away. The clerk could then use the stolen check to make an unauthorized payment.

Checking Account Documents

The previous section explained the need for businesses to use checking accounts. Next, we will describe the four main types of forms associated with a bank checking account.

Signature Card

A bank **signature card** shows the bank account number and the signatures of the people authorized to sign checks. The card is retained in the bank's files. If a bank employee is unfamiliar with the signature on a check, he or she can refer to the signature card to verify the signature before cashing the check.

Deposit Ticket

Each deposit of cash or checks is accompanied by a **deposit ticket,** which normally identifies the account number and the name of the account. The depositor lists the individual amounts of currency, coins, and checks, as well as the total deposited, on the deposit ticket.

Bank Check

A written check affects three parties: (1) the person or business writing the check (the *payer*); (2) the bank on which the check is drawn; and (3) the person or business to whom the check is payable (the *payee*). Companies often write **checks** using multicopy, prenumbered forms, with the name of the issuing business preprinted on the face of each check. A remittance notice is usually attached to the check forms. This portion of the form provides the issuer space to record what the check is for (e.g., what invoices are being paid), the amount being disbursed, and the date of payment. When signed by the person whose signature is on the signature card, the check authorizes the bank to transfer the face amount of the check from the payer's account to the payee.

Bank Statement

Periodically, the bank sends its customers a **bank statement.** Bank statements frequently contain technical terms that are used to describe increases and decreases in the customer's account balance. Common terms include debit memos and credit memos. **Debit memos** describe transactions that reduce the customer's account balance. For example, bank services charges that are deducted from a customer's account balance are described in a debit memo. **Credit memos** describe activities that increase a customer's account balance. For example, when a bank pays interest that increases a customer's account balance the event is described in a credit memo.

Bank statements normally report (a) the balance of the account at the beginning of the period; (b) additions for customer deposits and credit memos occurring during the period; (c) subtractions for the payment of checks drawn on the account during the period and debit memos; (d) a running balance of the account; and (e) the balance of the account at the end of the period. The sample bank statement in Exhibit 6.2 illustrates these items with references to the preceding letters in parentheses.

EXHIBIT 6.2

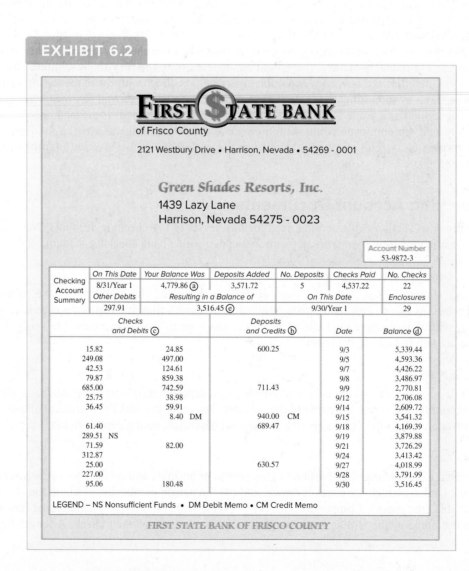

FIRST $ STATE BANK
of Frisco County

2121 Westbury Drive • Harrison, Nevada • 54269 - 0001

Green Shades Resorts, Inc.
1439 Lazy Lane
Harrison, Nevada 54275 - 0023

Account Number
53-9872-3

Checking Account Summary	On This Date	Your Balance Was	Deposits Added	No. Deposits	Checks Paid	No. Checks
	8/31/Year 1	4,779.86 (a)	3,571.72	5	4,537.22	22
	Other Debits	Resulting in a Balance of			On This Date	Enclosures
	297.91	3,516.45 (e)			9/30/Year 1	29

Checks and Debits (c)		Deposits and Credits (b)	Date	Balance (d)
15.82	24.85	600.25	9/3	5,339.44
249.08	497.00		9/5	4,593.36
42.53	124.61		9/7	4,426.22
79.87	859.38		9/8	3,486.97
685.00	742.59	711.43	9/9	2,770.81
25.75	38.98		9/12	2,706.08
36.45	59.91		9/14	2,609.72
	8.40 DM	940.00 CM	9/15	3,541.32
61.40		689.47	9/18	4,169.39
289.51 NS			9/19	3,879.88
71.59	82.00		9/21	3,726.29
312.87			9/24	3,413.42
25.00		630.57	9/27	4,018.99
227.00			9/28	3,791.99
95.06	180.48		9/30	3,516.45

LEGEND – NS Nonsufficient Funds • DM Debit Memo • CM Credit Memo

FIRST STATE BANK OF FRISCO COUNTY

RECONCILING THE BANK ACCOUNT

LO 6-3

Prepare a bank reconciliation.

Usually the ending balance reported on the bank statement differs from the balance in the depositor's Cash account as of the same date. The discrepancy is normally attributable to timing differences. For example, a depositor deducts the amount of a check from its Cash account when it writes the check. However, the bank does not deduct the amount of the check from the depositor's account until the payee presents it for payment, which may be days, weeks, or even months after the check is written. As a result, the balance on the depositor's books is lower than the balance on the bank's books. Companies prepare a **bank reconciliation** to explain the differences between the cash balance reported on the bank statement and the cash balance recorded in the depositor's accounting records.

Determining True Cash Balance

A bank reconciliation normally begins with the cash balance reported by the bank, which is called the **unadjusted bank balance.** The adjustments necessary to determine the amount of cash that the depositor actually owns as of the date of the bank statement are then added to and subtracted from the unadjusted bank balance. The final total is the **true cash balance.** The true cash balance is independently reached a second time by making adjustments to the **unadjusted book balance.** The bank account is reconciled when the true cash balance determined from the perspective of the unadjusted *bank* balance agrees with the true cash balance determined from the perspective of the unadjusted *book* balance. The procedures a company uses to determine the *true cash balance* from the two different perspectives are outlined here.

Adjustments to the Bank Balance

A typical format for determining the true cash balance beginning with the unadjusted bank balance is

> Unadjusted bank balance
> + Deposits in transit
> − Outstanding checks
> = True cash balance

Deposits in Transit

Companies frequently leave deposits in the bank's night depository or make them on the day following the receipt of cash. Such deposits are called **deposits in transit.** Because these deposits have been recorded in the depositor's accounting records but have not yet been added to the depositor's account by the bank, they must be added to the unadjusted bank balance.

Outstanding Checks

These are disbursements that have been properly recorded as cash deductions on the depositor's books. However, the bank has not deducted the amounts from the depositor's bank account because the checks have not yet been presented by the payee to the bank for payment; that is, the checks have not cleared the bank. **Outstanding checks** must be subtracted from the unadjusted bank balance to determine the true cash balance.

Adjustments to the Book Balance

A typical format for determining the true cash balance beginning with the unadjusted book balance is as follows:

> Unadjusted book balance
> + Accounts receivable collections
> + Interest earned
> − Bank service charges
> − Non-sufficient-funds (NSF) checks
> = True cash balance

Accounts Receivable Collections

To collect cash as quickly as possible, many companies have their customers send payments directly to the bank. The bank adds the collection directly to the depositor's account and notifies the depositor about the collection through a credit memo that is included on the bank statement. The depositor adds the amount of the cash collections to the unadjusted book balance in the process of determining the true cash balance.

Interest Earned

Banks pay interest on certain checking accounts. The amount of the interest is added directly to the depositor's bank account. The bank notifies the depositor about the interest through a credit memo that is included on the bank statement. The depositor adds the amount of the interest revenue to the unadjusted book balance in the process of determining the true cash balance.

Service Charges

Banks frequently charge depositors fees for services performed. They may also charge a penalty if the depositor fails to maintain a specified minimum cash balance throughout the period. Banks deduct such fees and penalties directly from the depositor's account and advise the depositor of the deduction through a debit memo that is included on the bank statement. The depositor deducts such **service charges** from the unadjusted book balance to determine the true cash balance.

Non-Sufficient-Funds (NSF) Checks

Non-sufficient-funds (NSF) checks are checks that a company obtains from its customers and deposits in its checking account. However, when the checks are submitted to the customers' banks for payment, the banks refuse payment because there is insufficient money in the customers' accounts. When such checks are returned, the amounts of the checks are deducted from the company's bank account balance. The company is advised of NSF checks through debit memos that appear on the bank statement. The depositor deducts the amounts of the NSF checks from the unadjusted book balance in the process of determining the true cash balance.

Correction of Errors

In the course of reconciling the bank statement with the Cash account, the depositor may discover errors in the bank's records, the depositor's records, or both. If an error is found on the bank statement, an adjustment for it is made to the unadjusted bank balance to determine the true cash balance, and the bank should be notified immediately to correct its records. Errors made by the depositor require adjustments to the book balance to arrive at the true cash balance.

Ryan McVay/Photodisc/Getty Images

Certified Checks

A **certified check** is guaranteed for payment by a bank. Whereas a regular check is deducted from the customer's account when it is presented for payment, a certified check is deducted from the customer's account when the bank certifies that the check is good. Certified checks, therefore, *have* been deducted by the bank in determining the unadjusted bank balance, whether they have cleared the bank or remain outstanding as of the date of the bank statement. Because certified checks are deducted both from bank and depositor records immediately, they do not cause differences between the depositor and bank balances. As a result, certified checks are not included in a bank reconciliation.

Illustrating a Bank Reconciliation

The following example illustrates a bank reconciliation for Green Shades Resorts, Inc. (GSRI). The bank statement for GSRI is displayed in Exhibit 6.2. Exhibit 6.3 illustrates the completed bank reconciliation. The items on the reconciliation are described in the discussion that follows.

EXHIBIT 6.3

GREEN SHADES RESORTS, INC.
Bank Reconciliation
September 30, Year 1

Unadjusted bank balance, September 30, Year 1		$3,516.45
Add: Deposits in transit		724.11
Bank error: Check drawn on Green Valley Resorts charged to GSRI		25.00
Less: Outstanding checks		

Check No.	Date	Amount
639	Sept. 18	$ 13.75
646	Sept. 20	29.00
672	Sept. 27	192.50

Total	(235.25)
True cash balance, September 30, Year 1	$4,030.31
Unadjusted book balance, September 30, Year 1	$3,361.22
Add: Receivable collected by bank	940.00
Error made by accountant (Check no. 633 recorded as $63.45 instead of $36.45)	27.00
Less: Bank service charges	(8.40)
NSF check	(289.51)
True cash balance, September 30, Year 1	$4,030.31

Adjustments to the Bank Balance

As of September 30, Year 1, the bank statement showed an unadjusted balance of $3,516.45. A review of the bank statement disclosed three adjustments that had to be made to the unadjusted bank balance to determine GSRI's true cash balance.

1. Comparing the deposits on the bank statement with deposits recorded in GSRI's accounting records indicated there was $724.11 of deposits in transit.

2. An examination of the returned checks disclosed that the bank had erroneously deducted a $25 check written by Green Valley Resorts from GSRI's bank account. This amount must be added back to the unadjusted bank balance to determine the true cash balance.

3. The checks returned with the bank statement were sorted and compared to the cash records. Three checks with amounts totaling $235.25 were outstanding.

   After these adjustments are made, GSRI's true cash balance is determined to be $4,030.31.

Adjustments to the Book Balance

As indicated in Exhibit 6.3, GSRI's unadjusted book balance as of September 30, Year 1, was $3,361.22. This balance differs from GSRI's true cash balance because of four unrecorded accounting events:

1. The bank collected a $940 account receivable for GSRI.

2. GSRI's accountant made a $27 recording error.

3. The bank charged GSRI an $8.40 service fee.

4. GSRI had deposited a $289.51 check from a customer who did not have sufficient funds to cover the check.

Two of these four adjustments increase the unadjusted cash balance. The other two decrease the unadjusted cash balance. After the adjustments have been recorded, the Cash account reflects the true cash balance of $4,030.31 ($3,361.22 unadjusted cash balance + $940.00 receivable collection + $27.00 recording error − $8.40 service charge − $289.51 NSF check). Because the true balance determined from the perspective of the bank statement agrees with the true balance determined from the perspective of GSRI's books, the bank statement has been successfully reconciled with the accounting records.

Updating GSRI's Accounting Records

Each of the adjustments to the book balance must be recorded in GSRI's financial records. The effects of each adjustment on the financial statements are as follows:

ADJUSTMENT 1   Recording the $940 receivable collection increases Cash and reduces Accounts Receivable.

It does not matter whether the bank or GSRI makes the collection; the effect of GSRI's records is the same. The balance in GSRI's Cash account increases and the balance in the Accounts Receivable account decreases. The event is an asset exchange transaction. The effects on the financial statements are shown next:

Balance Sheet							Income Statement					Statement of Cash Flows
Assets			=	Liab.	+	Stk. Equity						
Cash	+	Accts. Rec.					Rev.	−	Exp.	=	Net Inc.	
940	+	(940)	=	NA	+	NA	NA	−	NA	=	NA	940 OA

ADJUSTMENT 2   Assume the $27 recording error occurred because GSRI's accountant accidentally transposed two numbers when recording check no. 633 for utilities expense.

The check was written to pay utilities expense of $36.45 but was recorded as a $63.45 disbursement. Because cash payments are overstated by $27.00 ($63.45 − $36.45), this amount must be added back to cash and retained earnings on the balance sheet. On the income statement this reduces the amount of utility expense, thereby increasing net income. The effects on the financial statements are shown next:

Balance Sheet					Income Statement					Statement of Cash Flows
Assets	=	Liab.	+	Stk. Equity						
Cash	=			Ret. Earn.	Rev.	−	Exp.	=	Net Inc.	
27	=	NA	+	27	NA	−	(27)	=	27	27 OA

ADJUSTMENT 3   The $8.40 service charge is an expense.

The event reduces the Cash and Retained Earnings accounts, increases expenses, and reduces net income. The cash outflow is classified as an operating activity. The effects on the financial statements are shown next:

Balance Sheet					Income Statement					Statement of Cash Flows
Assets	=	Liab.	+	Stk. Equity						
Cash	=			Ret. Earn.	Rev.	−	Exp.	=	Net Inc.	
(8.40)	=	NA	+	(8.40)	NA	−	8.40	=	(8.40)	(8.40) OA

ADJUSTMENT 4 The $289.51 NSF check reduces GSRI's cash balance.

When it originally accepted the customer's check, GSRI increased its Cash account. Because there is not enough money in the customer's bank account to pay the check, GSRI didn't actually receive cash, so GSRI must reduce its Cash account. GSRI will still try to collect the money from the customer. In the meantime, it will show the amount of the NSF check as an account receivable. The adjustment to recognize the NSF check is an asset exchange transaction. Cash decreases and Accounts Receivable increases. The effects on the financial statements are shown next:

Balance Sheet							Income Statement					Statement of Cash Flows
Assets			=	Liab.	+	Stk. Equity	Rev.	−	Exp.	=	Net Inc.	
Cash	+	Accts. Rec.										
(289.51)	+	289.51	=	NA	+	NA	NA	−	NA	=	NA	(289.51) OA

Cash Short and Over

Sometimes employees make mistakes when collecting cash from or making change for customers. When such errors occur, the amount of money in the cash register will not agree with the amount of cash receipts recorded on the cash register tape. For example, suppose that when a customer paid for $17.95 of merchandise with a $20 bill, the sales clerk returned $3.05 in change instead of $2.05. If, at the end of the day, the cash register tape shows total receipts of $487.50, the cash drawer would contain only $486.50. The actual cash balance is less than the expected cash balance by $1. Any shortage of cash or excess of cash is recorded in a special account called **Cash Short and Over.** In this case, the company has a cash shortage which is treated as a miscellaneous expense. Its effects on the financial statements are shown next:

Balance Sheet					Income Statement					Statement of Cash Flows
Assets	=	Liab.	+	Stk. Equity	Rev.	−	Exp.	=	Net Inc.	
Cash				Ret. Earn.						
486.50	=	NA	+	486.50	487.50	−	1.00	=	486.50	486.50 OA

In contrast, a cash overage would be treated as miscellaneous revenue. Suppose a company provided $543 of service but collected $545 cash. In this scenario, the company would have $2 of cash short and over that would be recognized as miscellaneous revenue. In summary, cash shortages are treated as expenses, while cash overages are treated as revenues.

✓ CHECK YOURSELF 6.2

The following information was drawn from Reliance Company's October bank statement. The unadjusted bank balance on October 31 was $2,300. The statement showed that the bank had collected a $200 account receivable for Reliance. The statement also included $20 of bank service charges for October and a $100 check payable to Reliance that was returned NSF. A comparison of the bank statement with company accounting records indicates that there was a $500 deposit in transit and $1,800 of checks outstanding at the end of the month. Based on this information, determine the true cash balance on October 31.

Answer Because the unadjusted book balance is not given, start with the unadjusted bank balance to determine the true cash balance. The collection of the receivable, the bank service charges, and the NSF check are already recognized in the unadjusted bank balance, so these items are not used to determine the true cash balance. To determine the true cash balance, add the deposit in transit to the unadjusted bank balance and then subtract the outstanding checks. The true cash balance is $1,000 ($2,300 unadjusted bank balance + $500 deposit in transit − $1,800 outstanding checks).

USING PETTY CASH FUNDS

Although businesses use checks for most disbursements, they often pay for small items such as postage, delivery charges, taxi fares, employees' supper money, and so on with currency. They frequently establish a **petty cash fund** to maintain effective control over these small cash disbursements. The fund is established for a specified dollar amount, such as $300, and is controlled by one employee, called the *petty cash custodian.*

Petty cash funds are usually maintained on an **imprest basis,** which means that the money disbursed is periodically replenished. The fund is created by drawing a check on the regular checking account, cashing it, and giving the currency to the petty cash custodian. The custodian normally keeps the currency under lock and key. The amount of the petty cash fund depends on what it is used for, how often it is used, and how often it is replenished. It should be large enough to handle disbursements for a reasonable time period, such as several weeks or a month.

Establishing a Petty Cash Fund

EVENT 1   TUC Company established a $300 petty cash fund.

Establishing a petty cash fund merely transfers money from a bank to a safety box inside the company offices. The establishment is an asset exchange event. The Cash account decreases, and an account called Petty Cash increases. The effects on the financial statements are shown next:

Balance Sheet						Income Statement			Statement of Cash Flows
Assets			= Liab.	+	Stk. Equity				
Cash	+	Petty Cash				Rev.	− Exp.	= Net Inc.	
(300)	+	300	= NA	+	NA	NA	− NA	= NA	NA

Disbursing Petty Cash Funds

EVENT 2   TUC made cash payments from the petty cash fund.

When money is disbursed from the petty cash fund, the custodian should complete a **petty cash voucher,** such as the one in Exhibit 6.4. Any supporting documents, such as an invoice, restaurant bill, or parking fee receipt, should be attached to the petty cash voucher. The person who receives the money should sign the voucher as evidence of receiving the cash. The total of the amounts recorded on the petty cash vouchers, plus the remaining coins and currency, should equal the balance of the petty cash account. *There is no effect on the financial statements at the time petty cash funds are disbursed.* Instead, the effects on the financial statements occur at the time the petty cash fund is replenished.

EXHIBIT 6.4

Petty cash voucher no. _____

To: _____   Date _____, 20____

Explanation: Account No. _____   Amount _____

Approved by _____   Received by _____

Recognizing Petty Cash Expenses

EVENT 3   TUC recognized $216 of expenses that had been paid with cash from the petty fund.

When the amount of currency in the petty cash fund is relatively low, the fund is replenished in a two-step process. Step 1 is to recognize an expense. The amount of expense is determined by adding the amounts of the petty cash vouchers. For example, suppose the $300 petty cash fund is replenished when the total of the petty cash vouchers is $216. The vouchers can be classified according to different types of expenses or listed in total as miscellaneous expense. The effects on the financial statements are the same as those for any other cash expense. Assets and retained earnings decrease, expenses increase, net income decreases, and there is a cash outflow from operating activities.

Balance Sheet				Income Statement			Statement of Cash Flows
Assets	=	Liab.	+ Stk. Equity				
Petty Cash	=		Ret. Earn.	Rev. −	Exp. =	Net Inc.	
(216)	=	NA	+ (216)	NA −	216 =	(216)	(216) OA

Replenishing the Petty Cash Fund

EVENT 4   TUC replenished the petty cash fund.

Step 2 replenishes the petty cash fund. Specifically, a check is issued to the bank to obtain the currency needed to return the fund to its imprest balance. Then, the cash collected from the bank is placed into the petty cash fund safety box. The impact on the financial statements is the same as when the petty cash fund was established. Indeed, the same statement effects occur when the fund is established, replenished, or increased. All three events are asset exchanges. One asset account, Cash, decreases, while another asset account, Petty Cash, increases. There is no impact on the income statement or statement of cash flows. These effects are shown next:

Balance Sheet			Income Statement			Statement of Cash Flows
Assets	= Liab.	+ Stk. Equity				
Cash + Petty Cash			Rev. −	Exp. =	Net Inc.	
(216) + 216	= NA +	NA	NA −	NA =	NA	NA

If management desires more detailed information about petty cash expenditures, the vouchers can be sorted into specific expense items. In this case, we assume that the vouchers could be categorized as postage, $66; delivery charges, $78.40; taxi fares, $28; and supper money, $43.60. While each of these items could be recorded separately, the total impact on the financial statements is the same.

Once the replenishment is complete, the existing vouchers should be indelibly marked *Paid* so they cannot be reused.

Sometimes, cash shortages and overages are discovered when the money in the petty cash fund is physically counted. Cash shortages are recognized as expense, while cash overages are treated as revenues. If cash shortages or overages do not occur frequently and are of insignificant amounts, companies are likely to include them in miscellaneous expense or miscellaneous revenue.

CHECK YOURSELF 6.3

Cornerstone Corporation established a $400 petty cash fund that was replenished when it contained $30 of currency and coins and $378 of receipts for miscellaneous expenses. Based on this information, determine the amount of cash short or over to be recognized. Explain how the shortage or overage would be reported in the financial statements. Also determine the amount of petty cash expenses that were recognized when the fund was replenished.

Answer The fund contained $408 of currency and receipts ($30 currency + $378 of receipts), resulting in a cash overage of $8 ($408 total − $400 petty cash balance). The overage would be reported as miscellaneous revenue on the income statement. The amount of petty cash expenses recognized would equal the amount of the expense receipts, which is $378.

Alternative Approach to Petty Cash Expense Recognition and Replenishment

EVENTS 3 AND 4 COMBINED   JPS recognized expenses and replenished the petty cash fund simultaneously.

In practice, the recognition of petty cash expenses and the replenishment of the petty cash fund can be accomplished in a single event. Under this approach the petty cash account is not affected. Instead, the cash account is decreased at the time the miscellaneous expenses are recognized. The effects on the financial statements are the same as those previously shown. The only difference is a change in the account titles. The effects are shown next:

Balance Sheet			Income Statement			Statement of Cash Flows
Assets =	Liab. +	Stk. Equity				
Cash =		Ret. Earn.	Rev. −	Exp. =	Net Inc.	
(216) =	NA +	(216)	NA −	216 =	(216)	(216) OA

Under this approach, the petty cash account is affected only when management decides to add or decrease the size of the petty cash fund.

The Financial Analyst

LO 6-5

Describe the auditor's role in financial reporting.

Companies communicate information to analysts and other users through a document called the *annual report*. These reports are usually printed in color on high-quality paper and contain lots of photographs. However, in an effort to reduce cost, some companies issue their annual reports in black and white on low-grade paper or in electronic form. A company's annual report contains much more than the financial statements. Annual reports often have 40 or more pages. The financial statements require only four to six pages. What is printed on all those other pages? In general, the annual report of a large company has four major sections: (1) financial statements, (2) notes to the financial statements, (3) management's discussion and analysis, and (4) auditors' report. The notes and management's discussion and analysis make up the bulk of the report.

Notes to the Financial Statements

Accountants frequently have to make estimates when preparing financial statements. Also, GAAP may offer alternative ways of reporting certain transactions. **Notes to the financial statements** explain some of the estimates that were made, as well as which reporting options were used. Reading the notes is critical to understanding the financial statements. The financial statements include a caveat such as "the accompanying notes are an integral part of these financial statements."

Management's Discussion and Analysis

Management's discussion and analysis (MD&A) is located at the beginning of the annual report. MD&A is the section of the annual report in which management explains the company's past performance and future plans. For example, MD&A typically compares current-year earnings with those of past periods and explains the reasons for significant changes. If the company is planning significant acquisitions of assets or other businesses, this information is usually included in MD&A. Likewise, any plans to discontinue part of the existing business are outlined in MD&A.

Role of the Independent Auditor

As previously explained, financial statements are prepared in accordance with certain rules called *generally accepted accounting principles (GAAP)*. Thus, when General Electric publishes its financial statements, it is saying, "here are our financial statements prepared according to

GAAP." How can a financial analyst know that a company really did follow GAAP? Analysts and other statement users rely on **audits** conducted by **certified public accountants (CPAs).**

The primary roles of an independent auditor (CPA) are summarized as follows:

1. Conducts a financial audit (a detailed examination of a company's financial statements and underlying accounting records).

2. Assumes both legal and professional responsibilities to the public, as well as to the company paying the auditor.

3. Determines if financial statements are *materially* correct rather than *absolutely* correct.

4. Presents conclusions in an audit report that includes an opinion as to whether the statements are prepared in conformity with GAAP. In rare cases, the auditor issues a disclaimer.

5. Maintains professional confidentiality of client records. The auditor is not, however, exempt from legal obligations such as testifying in court.

The Financial Statements Audit

What is an audit? There are several different types of audits. The type most relevant to this course is a **financial statements audit.** The financial audit is a detailed examination of a company's financial statements and the documents that support those statements. It also tests the reliability of the accounting system used to produce the financial reports. A financial audit is conducted by an **independent auditor** who must be a CPA.

The term *independent auditor* typically refers to a *firm* of certified public accountants. CPAs are licensed by state governments to provide services to the public. They are to be independent of the companies they audit. To help ensure independence, CPAs may not be employees of the companies they audit. Further, they cannot have investments in the companies they audit. Although CPAs are paid by the companies they audit, the audit fee may not be based on the outcome of the audit.

Although the independent auditors are chosen by, paid by, and can be fired by their client companies, the auditors are primarily responsible to *the public.* In fact, auditors have a legal responsibility to those members of the public who have a financial interest in the company being audited. If investors in a company lose money, they sometimes sue the independent auditors in an attempt to recover their losses, especially if the losses were related to financial failure. A lawsuit against auditors will succeed only if the auditors failed in their professional responsibilities when conducting the audit. Auditors are not responsible for the success or failure of a company. Instead, they are responsible for the appropriate auditing of the reporting of that success or failure. While recent debacles such as Bernard L. Madoff Investment Securities produce spectacular headlines, auditors are actually not sued very often, considering the number of audits they perform.

Materiality and Financial Statements Audits

Auditors do not guarantee that financial statements are absolutely correct—only that they are *materially* correct. This is where things get a little fuzzy. What is a *material error?* The concept of materiality is very subjective. If Walmart inadvertently overstated its sales by $1 million, would this be material? In its 2018 fiscal year, Walmart had approximately $510 billion of sales! A $1 million error in computing sales at Walmart is like a $1 error in computing the pay of a person who makes $510,000 per year—not material at all! An error, or other reporting problem, is **material** if knowing about it would influence the decisions of an *average prudent investor.*

Financial audits are not directed toward the discovery of fraud. Auditors are, however, responsible for providing *reasonable assurance* that statements are free from material misstatements, whether caused by errors or fraud. Also, auditors are responsible for evaluating whether internal control procedures are in place to help prevent fraud. If fraud is widespread in a company, normal audit procedures should detect it.

Accounting majors take at least one and often two or more courses in auditing to understand how to conduct an audit. An explanation of auditing techniques is beyond the scope of this course, but at least be aware that auditors do not review how the company accounted for every transaction. Along with other methods, auditors use statistics to choose representative samples of transactions to examine.

Types of Audit Opinions

Once an audit is complete, the auditors present their conclusions in a report that includes an *audit opinion.* There are three basic types of audit opinions.

An **unqualified opinion,** despite its negative-sounding name, is the most favorable opinion auditors can express. It means the auditor believes the financial statements are in compliance with GAAP without material qualification, reservation, or exception. Most audits result in unqualified opinions because companies correct any material reporting deficiencies the auditors find before the financial statements are released.

The most negative report an auditor can issue is an **adverse opinion.** An adverse opinion means that one or more departures from GAAP are so material the financial statements do not present a fair picture of the company's status. The auditor's report explains the unacceptable accounting practice(s) that resulted in the adverse opinion being issued. Adverse opinions are very rare because public companies are required by law to follow GAAP.

A **qualified opinion** falls between an unqualified and an adverse opinion. A qualified opinion means that for the most part, the company's financial statements are in compliance with GAAP, but the auditors have reservations about something in the statements. The auditors' report explains why the opinion is qualified. A qualified opinion usually does not imply a serious accounting problem, but users should read the auditors' report and draw their own conclusions.

If an auditor is unable to perform the audit procedures necessary to determine whether the statements are prepared in accordance with GAAP, the auditor cannot issue an opinion on the financial statements. Instead, the auditor issues a **disclaimer of opinion.** A disclaimer is neither negative nor positive. It simply means that the auditor is unable to obtain enough information to confirm compliance with GAAP.

Regardless of the type of report they issue, auditors are only expressing their judgment about whether the financial statements present a fair picture of a company. They do not provide opinions regarding the investment quality of a company.

The ultimate responsibility for financial statements rests with the executives of the reporting company. Just like auditors, management can be sued by investors who believe they lost money due to improper financial reporting. This is one reason all businesspersons should understand accounting fundamentals.

Confidentiality

The **confidentiality** rules in the code of ethics for CPAs prohibit auditors from *voluntarily disclosing* information they have acquired as a result of their accountant–client relationships. However, accountants may be required to testify in a court of law. In general, federal law does not recognize an accountant–client privilege, as it does with attorneys and clergy. Some federal courts have taken exception to this position, especially as it applies to tax cases. State law varies with respect to accountant–client privilege. Furthermore, if auditors terminate a client relationship because of ethical or legal disagreements and they are subsequently contacted by a successor auditor, they may be required to inform the successor of the reasons for the termination. In addition, auditors must consider the particular circumstances of a case when assessing the appropriateness of disclosing confidential information. Given the diverse legal positions governing accountant–client confidentiality, auditors should seek legal counsel prior to disclosing any information obtained in an accountant–client relationship.

To illustrate, assume that Joe Smith, CPA, discovers that his client Jane Doe is misrepresenting information reported in her financial statements. Smith tries to convince Doe to correct the misrepresentations, but she refuses to do so. Smith is required by the code of ethics to terminate his relationship with Doe. However, Smith is not permitted to disclose Doe's dishonest reporting practices unless he is called on to testify in a legal hearing or to respond to an inquiry by Doe's successor accountant.

With respect to the discovery of significant fraud, the auditor is required to inform management at least one level above the position of the employee who is engaged in the fraud and to notify the board of directors of the company. Suppose that Joe Smith, CPA, discovers that Mary Adams, employee of Western Company, is embezzling money from Western. Smith is required to inform Adams' supervisor and to notify Western's board of directors. However, Smith is prohibited from publicly disclosing the fraud.

The Securities and Exchange Commission

The annual reports of public companies often differ from those of private companies because public companies are registered with the **Securities and Exchange Commission (SEC).** Public companies, sometimes called SEC companies, have to follow the reporting rules of the SEC as well as GAAP. SEC rules require some additional disclosures not required by GAAP. For example, an MD&A section is required by the SEC, but not by GAAP. As a result, annual reports of non-SEC companies usually do not include MD&A.

The SEC is a government agency authorized to establish and enforce the accounting rules for public companies. Although the SEC can overrule GAAP, it has very seldom done so. Recall that GAAP is established by the Financial Accounting Standards Board, a private professional accounting organization. While SEC rules seldom conflict with GAAP, they frequently require additional disclosures. All companies whose stock trades on public stock exchanges, and some whose stock does not, are required to register with the SEC. The SEC has no jurisdiction over non-SEC companies.

SEC companies must file specific information directly with the SEC annually, quarterly, and in-between if required. The most common reports are filed on Form 10-K (annually) and Form 10-Q (quarterly). The 10-Qs are less detailed than the 10-Ks. While there is significant overlap between the 10-Ks (SEC report) and the annual reports that companies issue directly to the public, the 10-Ks usually contain more information but fewer photographs. Most of the reports filed with the SEC are available electronically through the SEC's EDGAR database. EDGAR is an acronym for Electronic Data Gathering, Analysis, and Retrieval, and it is accessible on the Internet. Appendix A provides instructions for using EDGAR.

The SEC regulates audit standards as well as financial reporting. Prior to passage of the Sarbanes–Oxley Act in July 2002, the SEC left much of the regulation and oversight of independent auditors to the American Institute of Certified Public Accountants, a private professional organization. However, a key provision of Sarbanes–Oxley establishes the Public Company Accounting Oversight Board (PCAOB). This board assumes the primary responsibility for establishing and enforcing auditing standards for CPA firms that audit SEC companies. The board has five financially astute members, three of whom cannot be CPAs.

A Look Back

The policies and procedures used to provide reasonable assurance that the objectives of an enterprise will be accomplished are called *internal controls,* and they can be subdivided into two categories: accounting controls and administrative controls. *Accounting controls* are composed of procedures designed to safeguard the assets and ensure that the accounting records contain reliable information. *Administrative controls* are designed to evaluate performance and the degree of compliance with company policies and public laws. While the mechanics of internal control systems vary from company to company, the more prevalent features include the following: segregation of duties, quality of employees, bonded employees, required absence, a procedures manual, authority and responsibility, prenumbered documents, physical control, and performance evaluations.

Because cash is such an important business asset and because it is tempting to steal, much of the discussion of internal controls in this chapter focused on cash controls. Special procedures should be employed to control the receipts and payments of cash. One of the most common control policies is to use *checking accounts* for all except petty cash disbursements.

A *bank reconciliation* should be prepared each month to explain differences between the bank statement and a company's internal accounting records. A common reconciliation format determines the true cash balance based on both bank and book records. Items that typically appear on a bank reconciliation include the following:

Unadjusted bank balance	xxx	Unadjusted book balance	xxx
Add		Add	
Deposits in transit	xxx	Interest revenue	xxx
		Collection of receivables	xxx
Subtract		Subtract	
Outstanding checks	xxx	Bank service charges	xxx
		NSF checks	xxx
True cash balance	xxx	True cash balance	xxx

Agreement of the two true cash balances provides evidence that accounting for cash transactions has been accurate.

Another common internal control policy for protecting cash is using a *petty cash fund.* Normally, an employee who is designated as the petty cash custodian is entrusted with a small amount of cash. The custodian reimburses employees for small expenditures made on behalf of the company in exchange for authorized receipts from the employees at the time they are reimbursed. The total of these receipts, plus the remaining currency in the fund, should always equal the amount of funds entrusted to the custodian. Petty cash expenses are recognized at the time the fund is replenished.

Finally, the chapter discussed the auditor's role in financial reporting, including the materiality concept and the types of audit opinions that may be issued.

A Look Forward

Accounting for receivables and payables was introduced in Chapter 2 using relatively simple illustrations. For example, we assumed that customers who purchased services on account always paid their bills. In real business practice, some customers do not pay their bills. Among other topics, Chapter 7 examines how companies account for uncollectible accounts receivable.

Tableau Dashboard Activity is available in *Connect* for this chapter.

SELF-STUDY REVIEW PROBLEM

A step-by-step audio-narrated series of slides is available in *Connect*.

Part A: Bank Reconciliation

The following information pertains to Terry's Pest Control Company (TPCC) for July:

1. The unadjusted bank balance at July 31 was $870.
2. The bank statement included the following items:
   (a) A $60 credit memo for interest earned by TPCC.
   (b) A $200 NSF check made payable to TPCC.
   (c) A $110 debit memo for bank service charges.
3. The unadjusted book balance at July 31 was $1,400.
4. A comparison of the bank statement with company accounting records disclosed the following:
   (a) A $400 deposit in transit at July 31.
   (b) Outstanding checks totaling $120 at the end of the month.

Required

a. Prepare a bank reconciliation.

b. As a result of the bank reconciliation, TPCC made three adjustments to the book balance of its Cash account. These adjustments included (1) the recognition of interest revenue, (2) the recognition of an NSF check, and (3) the recognition of a service charge expense. Use a financial statements model like the one shown next to indicate how each of these adjustments affects the financial statements.

	Balance Sheet						Income Statement					Statement of Cash Flows
	Assets			=	Liab.	+	Stk. Equity					
Adj.	Cash	+	Accts. Rec.				Ret. Earn.	Rev.	−	Exp.	=	Net Inc.	

Solution to Requirement a

TERRY'S PEST CONTROL COMPANY
Bank Reconciliation
July 31

Unadjusted bank balance	$ 870
Add: Deposits in transit	400
Less: Outstanding checks	(120)
True cash balance	$1,150
Unadjusted book balance	$1,400
Add: Interest revenue	60
Less: NSF check	(200)
Less: Bank service charges	(110)
True cash balance	$1,150

Solution to Requirement b

	Balance Sheet							Income Statement					Statement of Cash Flows	
	Assets			=	Liab.	+	Stk. Equity							
Adj.	Cash	+	Accts. Rec.	=			Ret. Earn.	Rev.	−	Exp.	=	Net Inc.		
1.	60		NA	=	NA	+	60	60	−	NA	=	60	60	OA
2.	(200)	+	200	=	NA	+	NA	NA	−	NA	=	NA	(200)	OA
3.	(110)	+	NA	=	NA	+	(110)	NA	−	110	=	(110)	(110)	OA

Part B: Petty Cash

Terry's Pest Control Company established a $60 petty cash fund that was replenished when it contained $5 of currency and coins and $50 of receipts for miscellaneous expenses.

Required

Based on this information:

a. Use a financial statements model to show how establishing the petty cash fund will affect TPCC's financial statements.

b. Use a financial statements model to show how making a payment from the petty cash fund will affect TPCC's financial statements.

c. Use a financial statements model to show how recognizing expenses during the replenishment of TPCC's petty cash fund will affect TPCC's financial statements. Assume that all amounts of cash short and over are treated as miscellaneous expenses or revenues.

d. Use a financial statements model to show how transferring cash from a bank account to a petty cash safe box will affect TPCC's financial statements.

Solution to Requirement a

Balance Sheet						Income Statement			Statement of Cash Flows
Assets		= Liab.	+	Stk. Equity		Rev.	− Exp.	= Net Inc.	
Cash	+ Petty Cash								
(60)	+ 60	= NA	+	NA		NA	− NA	= NA	NA

Solution to Requirement b

There is no impact on the financial statements at the time petty cash payments (reimbursements) occur.

Solution to Requirement c

Balance Sheet						Income Statement			Statement of Cash Flows
Assets		= Liab.	+	Stk. Equity		Rev.	− Exp.	= Net Inc.	
Cash	+ Petty Cash								
(55)	+ NA	= NA	+	(55)		NA	− 55	= (55)	(55) OA

Solution to Requirement d

Balance Sheet						Income Statement			Statement of Cash Flows
Assets		= Liab.	+	Stk. Equity		Rev.	− Exp.	= Net Inc.	
Cash	+ Petty Cash								
(55)	+ 55	= NA	+	NA		NA	− NA	= NA	NA

Note: The effect on the financial statements is the same regardless of whether a petty cash fund is being established, replenished, or increased. In each case, the transaction is an asset exchange event. Cash is withdrawn from a checking account and placed into a petty cash safe box. One asset, Cash, decreases, while another asset, Petty Cash, increases. Total assets are not affected.

KEY TERMS

Accounting controls 280
Administrative controls 280
Adverse opinion 298
Audit 297
Authority manual 283
Bank reconciliation 289
Bank statement 288
Cash 285
Cash short and over 293
Certified check 290
Certified public accountant (CPA) 297

Checks 287
Confidentiality 298
Credit memo 288
Debit memo 288
Deposit ticket 287
Deposits in transit 289
Disclaimer of opinion 298
Fidelity bond 283
Financial statements audit 297
General authority 283
Imprest basis 294
Independent auditor 297

Internal controls 280
Management's discussion and analysis (MD&A) 296
Materiality 297
Non-sufficient-funds (NSF) checks 290
Notes to the financial statements 296
Outstanding checks 289
Petty cash fund 294
Petty cash voucher 294
Procedures manual 283

Qualified opinion 298
Securities and Exchange Commission (SEC) 299
Segregation of duties 282
Service charges 299
Signature card 287
Specific authorizations 283
True cash balance 289
Unadjusted bank balance 289
Unadjusted book balance 289
Unqualified opinion 298

QUESTIONS

1. What motivated Congress to pass the Sarbanes–Oxley Act (SOX) of 2002?
2. Define the term *internal control*.
3. Explain the relationship between SOX and COSO.
4. Name and briefly define the five components of COSO's internal control framework.
5. Explain how COSO's *Enterprise Risk Management—An Integrated Framework* project relates to COSO's *Internal Control—An Integrated Framework* project.
6. What is the difference between accounting controls and administrative controls?
7. What are several features of an effective internal control system?
8. What is meant by segregation of duties? Give an illustration.
9. What are the attributes of a high-quality employee?
10. What is a fidelity bond? Explain its purpose.

11. Why is it important that every employee periodically take a leave of absence or vacation?
12. What are the purpose and importance of a procedures manual?
13. What is the difference between specific and general authorizations?
14. Why should documents (checks, invoices, receipts) be prenumbered?
15. What procedures are important in the physical control of assets and accounting records?
16. What is the purpose of independent verification of performance?
17. What items are considered cash?
18. Why is cash more susceptible to theft or embezzlement than other assets?
19. Giving written copies of receipts to customers can help prevent what type of illegal acts?
20. What procedures can help protect cash receipts?

21. What procedures can help protect cash disbursements?
22. What effect does a debit memo in a bank statement have on the Cash account? What effect does a credit memo in a bank statement have on the Cash account?
23. What information is normally included in a bank statement?
24. Why might a bank statement reflect a balance that is larger than the balance recorded in the depositor's books? What could cause the bank balance to be smaller than the book balance?
25. What is the purpose of a bank reconciliation?
26. What is an outstanding check?
27. What is a deposit in transit?
28. What is a certified check?
29. How is an NSF check accounted for in the accounting records?
30. What is the purpose of the Cash Short and Over account?

31. What is the purpose of a petty cash fund?
32. What types of expenditures are usually made from a petty cash fund?
33. What is a financial statement audit? Who is qualified to perform it?
34. What is an independent auditor? Why must auditors be independent?
35. What makes an error in the financial statements material?
36. What three basic types of auditors' opinions can be issued on audited financial statements? Describe each.
37. What are the implications of an unqualified audit opinion?
38. When might an auditor issue a disclaimer on financial statements?
39. In what circumstances can an auditor disclose confidential information about a client without the client's permission?
40. What is the purpose of internal controls in an organization?

EXERCISES—SERIES A

 **All applicable Exercises in Series A are available in *Connect*.**

Exercise 6-1A *SOX and COSO's internal control frameworks*   LO 6-1

Required

a. Discuss the requirements of Section 404 of the Sarbanes–Oxley Act and how it relates to COSO.
b. What type of companies do these rules apply to?

Exercise 6-2A *Features of a strong internal control system*   LO 6-1

Required

List and describe nine features of a strong internal control system discussed in this chapter.

Exercise 6-3A *Internal control procedures to prevent embezzlement*   LO 6-1

Anna Chun was in charge of the returns department at The Luggage Company. She was responsible for evaluating returned merchandise. She sent merchandise that was reusable back to the warehouse, where it was restocked in inventory. Chun was also responsible for taking the merchandise that she determined to be defective to the city dump for disposal. She had agreed to buy a friend a tax planning program at a discount through her contacts at work. That is when the idea came to her. She could simply classify one of the reusable returns as defective and bring it home instead of taking it to the dump. She did so and made a quick $150. She was happy, and her friend was ecstatic; he was able to buy a $400 software package for only $150. He told his friends about the deal, and soon Chun had a regular set of customers. She was caught when a retail store owner complained to the marketing manager that his pricing strategy was being undercut by The Luggage Company's direct sales to the public. The marketing manager was suspicious because The Luggage Company had no direct marketing program. When the outside sales were ultimately traced back to Chun, the company discovered that it had lost over $10,000 in sales revenue because of her criminal activity.

Required

Identify an internal control procedure that could have prevented the company's losses. Explain how the procedure would have stopped the embezzlement.

LO 6-1

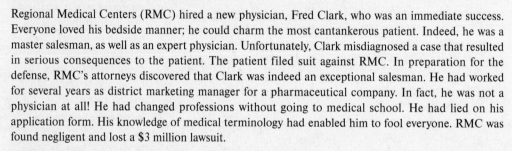

Exercise 6-4A   *Internal control procedures to prevent deception*

Regional Medical Centers (RMC) hired a new physician, Fred Clark, who was an immediate success. Everyone loved his bedside manner; he could charm the most cantankerous patient. Indeed, he was a master salesman, as well as an expert physician. Unfortunately, Clark misdiagnosed a case that resulted in serious consequences to the patient. The patient filed suit against RMC. In preparation for the defense, RMC's attorneys discovered that Clark was indeed an exceptional salesman. He had worked for several years as district marketing manager for a pharmaceutical company. In fact, he was not a physician at all! He had changed professions without going to medical school. He had lied on his application form. His knowledge of medical terminology had enabled him to fool everyone. RMC was found negligent and lost a $3 million lawsuit.

Required

Identify the relevant internal control procedures that could have prevented the company's losses. Explain how these procedures would have prevented Clark's deception.

LO 6-1

Exercise 6-5A   *Internal controls for small businesses*

Required

Assume you are the owner of a small business that has only two employees.

a. Which of the internal control procedures are most important to you?
b. How can you overcome the limited opportunity to use the segregation-of-duties control procedure?

LO 6-2

Exercise 6-6A   *Internal control for cash*

Required

a. Why are special controls needed for cash?
b. What is included in the definition of *cash*?

LO 6-3

Exercise 6-7A   *Treatment of NSF check*

Han's Supplies's bank statement contained a $270 NSF check that one of its customers had written to pay for supplies purchased.

Required

a. Show the effects of recognizing the NSF check on the financial statements by recording the appropriate amounts in a horizontal statements model like the following one:

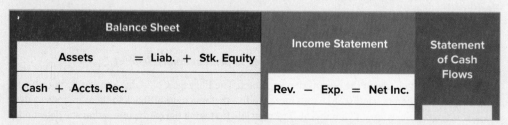

Balance Sheet			Income Statement	Statement of Cash Flows
Assets	= Liab. +	Stk. Equity		
Cash + Accts. Rec.			Rev. − Exp. = Net Inc.	

b. Is the recognition of the NSF check on Han's books an asset source, use, or exchange transaction?

c. Suppose the customer redeems the check by giving Han's $290 cash in exchange for the bad check. The additional $20 paid a service fee charged by Han's. Show the effects on the financial statements in the horizontal statements model in Requirement *a*.

d. Is the receipt of cash referenced in Requirement *c* an asset source, use, or exchange transaction?

Exercise 6-8A *Adjustments to the balance per books*

LO 6-3

Required

Identify which of the following items are added to or subtracted from the unadjusted *book balance* to arrive at the true cash balance. Distinguish the additions from the subtractions by placing a + beside the items that are added to the unadjusted book balance and a − beside those subtracted from it. The first item is recorded as an example.

Reconciling Items	Book Balance Adjusted?	Added or Subtracted?
Credit memo	Yes	+
Interest revenue		
Deposits in transit		
Debit memo		
Service charge		
Charge for printing checks		
NSF check from customer		
Note receivable collected by the bank		
Outstanding checks		

Exercise 6-9A *Adjustments to the balance per bank*

LO 6-3

Required

Identify which of the following items are added to or subtracted from the unadjusted *bank balance* to arrive at the true cash balance. Distinguish the additions from the subtractions by placing a + beside the items that are added to the unadjusted bank balance and a − beside those subtracted from it. The first item is recorded as an example.

Reconciling Items	Bank Balance Adjusted?	Added or Subtracted?
Bank service charge	No	NA
Outstanding checks		
Deposits in transit		
Debit memo		
Credit memo		
Certified checks		
Petty cash voucher		
NSF check from customer		
Interest revenue		

Exercise 6-10A *Adjusting the cash account*

LO 6-3

As of June 30, Year 1, the bank statement showed an ending balance of $19,500. The unadjusted Cash account balance was $15,200. The following information is available:

1. Deposit in transit: $2,400.
2. Credit memo in bank statement for interest earned in June: $30.
3. Outstanding check: $6,690.
4. Debit memo for service charge: $20.

Required

Determine the true cash balance by preparing a bank reconciliation as of June 30, Year 1, using the preceding information.

LO 6-3

Exercise 6-11A Determining the true cash balance, starting with the unadjusted bank balance

The following information is available for Trinkle Company for the month of June:

1. The unadjusted balance per the bank statement on June 30 was $81,500.
2. Deposits in transit on June 30 were $3,150.
3. A debit memo was included with the bank statement for a service charge of $40.
4. A $5,611 check written in June had not been paid by the bank.
5. The bank statement included a $950 credit memo for the collection of a note. The principal of the note was $900, and the interest collected amounted to $50.

Required

Determine the true cash balance as of June 30. (*Hint:* It is not necessary to use all of the preceding items to determine the true balance.)

LO 6-3

Exercise 6-12A Determining the true cash balance, starting with the unadjusted book balance

Nickleson Company had an unadjusted cash balance of $7,750 as of May 31. The company's bank statement, also dated May 31, included a $72 NSF check written by one of Nickleson's customers. There were $800 in outstanding checks and $950 in deposits in transit as of May 31. According to the bank statement, service charges were $50, and the bank collected an $800 note receivable for Nickleson. The bank statement also showed $13 of interest revenue earned by Nickleson.

Required

Determine the true cash balance as of May 31. (*Hint:* It is not necessary to use all of the preceding items to determine the true balance.)

LO 6-4

Exercise 6-13A Effect of establishing a petty cash fund

Chen Company established a $200 petty cash fund on January 1, Year 1.

Required

a. Is the establishment of the petty cash fund an asset source, use, or exchange transaction?
b. Show the establishment of the petty cash fund in a horizontal statements model like the following one:

Balance Sheet			Income Statement			Statement of Cash Flows
Assets	= Liab. + Stk. Equity					
Cash + Petty Cash			Rev. − Exp. = Net Inc.			

LO 6-4

Exercise 6-14A Effect of petty cash events on the financial statements

Fresh Foods established a petty cash fund of $100 on January 2. On January 31, the fund contained cash of $9.20 and vouchers for the following cash payments:

Maintenance expense	$61.50
Office supplies	12.50
Transportation expense	15.00

The four distinct accounting events affecting the petty cash fund for the period were (1) establishment of the fund, (2) reimbursements made to employees, (3) recognition of expenses (*Note:* all expenses are recorded in total as miscellaneous expense), and (4) replenishment of the fund.

Required

Show each of the four events in a horizontal statements model like the following one. In the Statement of Cash Flows column, indicate whether the item is an operating activity (OA), investing activity (IA), or a financing activity (FA). Use NA to indicate that an account was not affected by the event.

Balance Sheet			Income Statement			Statement of Cash Flows
Assets	=	Liab. + Stk. Equity				
Cash + Petty Cash			Rev. − Exp. = Net Inc.			

Exercise 6-15A   *Determining the amount of petty cash expense*

LO 6-4

Consider the following events:

1. A petty cash fund of $200 was established on April 1, Year 1.
2. Employees were reimbursed when they presented petty cash vouchers to the petty cash custodian.
3. On April 30, Year 1, the petty cash fund contained vouchers totaling $196.50 plus $2.20 of currency.

Required

Answer the following questions:

a. How did the establishment of the petty cash fund affect (increase, decrease, or have no effect on) total assets?

b. What is the amount of total petty cash expenses to be recognized during April?

c. When are petty cash expenses recognized (at the time of establishment, reimbursement, or replenishment)?

Exercise 6-16A   *Confidentiality and the auditor*

LO 6-5

Suzanne Hurley discovered significant fraud in the accounting records of a high-profile client. Due to her client's prestige, the story aired in the mainstream media. Unable to resolve her client's remaining concerns with the company's management team, Hurley ultimately resigned from the audit engagement. She knows she will be asked by several interested parties, including her friends and relatives, the successor auditor, and the prosecuting attorneys in a court of law, to tell what she knows. She has asked you for advice.

Required

Write a memo that explains Hurley's disclosure responsibilities to each of the interested parties.

PROBLEMS—SERIES A

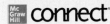 **CONNECT**   All applicable Problems in Series A are available in *Connect*.

Problem 6-17A   *Using internal control to restrict illegal or unethical behavior*

LO 6-1, 6-2

Required

For each of the following fraudulent acts, describe one or more internal control procedures that could have prevented (or helped prevent) the problems.

a. Everyone in the office has noticed what a dedicated employee Carley Trap is. She never misses work, not even for a vacation. Trap is in charge of the petty cash fund. She transfers funds from the company's bank account to the petty cash account on an as-needed basis. During a surprise audit, the petty cash fund was found to contain fictitious receipts. Over a three-year period, Trap had used more than $4,000 of petty cash to pay for personal expenses.

b. Doug Clampet was hired as the vice president of the manufacturing division of a corporation. His impressive resume listed a master's degree in business administration from a large state university and numerous collegiate awards and activities, but in truth Clampet only had a high school diploma. Soon, the company was in poor financial condition because of his inadequate knowledge and bad decisions.

c. Stone Manufacturing has good internal control over its manufacturing materials inventory. However, office supplies are kept on open shelves in the employee break room. The office supervisor has noticed that he is having to order paper, tape, staplers, and pens with increasing frequency.

LO 6-3

Problem 6-18A   *Preparing a bank reconciliation*

Rick Hall owns a card shop, Hall's Cards. The following cash information is available for the month of August Year 1:

As of August 31, the bank statement shows a balance of $16,140. The August 31 unadjusted balance in the Cash account of Hall's Cards is $14,100. A review of the bank statement revealed the following information:

1. A deposit of $4,150 on August 31, Year 1, does not appear on the August bank statement.
2. It was discovered that a check to pay for baseball cards was correctly written and paid by the bank for $4,500 but was recorded on the books as $5,400.
3. When checks written during the month were compared with those paid by the bank, three checks amounting to $5,370 were found to be outstanding.
4. A debit memo for $80 was included in the bank statement for the purchase of a new supply of checks.

Required

Prepare a bank reconciliation at the end of August showing the true cash balance.

LO 6-3

Problem 6-19A   *Missing information in a bank reconciliation*

The following data apply to Pro Beauty Supply Inc. for May Year 1:

1. Balance per the bank on May 31: $9,150.
2. Deposits in transit not recorded by the bank: $1,510.
3. Bank error; check written by Best Beauty Supply was charged to Pro Beauty Supply's account: $560.
4. The following checks written and recorded by Pro Beauty Supply were not included in the bank statement:

3013	$ 510
3054	640
3056	1,520

5. Note collected by the bank: $500.
6. Service charge for collection of note: $20.
7. The bookkeeper recorded a check for $230 when the May utilities expense was really $320.
8. Bank service charge in addition to the note collection fee: $40.
9. Customer checks returned by the bank as NSF: $310.

Required

Determine the amount of the unadjusted cash balance per Pro Beauty Supply's books.

LO 6-3

Problem 6-20A   *Adjustments to the cash account based on the bank reconciliation*

Required

Determine whether the following items included in Wong Company's January Year 1 bank reconciliation will require adjustments to the book balance of Wong's cash account and indicate the amount of any necessary adjustment.

a. Service charges of $50 for the month of January were listed on the bank statement.

b. The bank charged a $250 check drawn on Wing Restaurant to Wong's account. The check was included in Wong's bank statement.

c. A check of $62 was returned to the bank because of insufficient funds and was noted on the bank statement. Wong received the check from a customer and thought that it was good when it was deposited into the account.

d. A $990 deposit was recorded by the bank as $980.

e. Four checks totaling $810 written during the month of January were not included with the January bank statement.

f. A $75 check written to OfficeMax for office supplies was recorded as $57.

g. The bank statement indicated that the bank had collected a $450 note for Wong.

h. Wong recorded $900 of receipts on January 31, Year 1, which were deposited in the night depository of the bank. These deposits were not included in the bank statement.

Problem 6-21A   *Bank reconciliation and adjustments to the cash account*

LO 6-3

The following information is available for Park Valley Spa for July, Year 1:

CHECK FIGURE
a. True Cash Balance, July 31, Year 1: $16,234

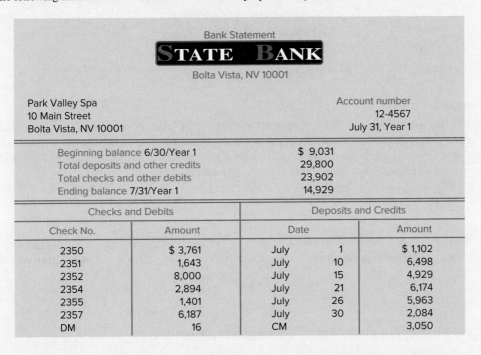

Bank Statement				
STATE BANK				
Bolta Vista, NV 10001				

Park Valley Spa		Account number
10 Main Street		12-4567
Bolta Vista, NV 10001		July 31, Year 1

Beginning balance 6/30/Year 1	$ 9,031
Total deposits and other credits	29,800
Total checks and other debits	23,902
Ending balance 7/31/Year 1	14,929

Checks and Debits		Deposits and Credits		
Check No.	Amount	Date		Amount
2350	$ 3,761	July	1	$ 1,102
2351	1,643	July	10	6,498
2352	8,000	July	15	4,929
2354	2,894	July	21	6,174
2355	1,401	July	26	5,963
2357	6,187	July	30	2,084
DM	16	CM		3,050

The following is a list of checks and deposits recorded on the books of the Park Valley Spa for July, Year 1:

Date		Check No.	Amount of Check	Date		Amount of Deposit
July	2	2351	$1,643	July	8	$6,498
July	4	2352	8,000	July	14	4,929
July	10	2353	1,500	July	21	6,174
July	10	2354	2,894	July	26	5,963
July	15	2355	1,401	July	29	2,084
July	20	2356	745	July	30	3,550
July	22	2357	6,187			

Other Information

1. Check no. 2350 was outstanding from June.

2. The credit memo was for collection of notes receivable.

3. All checks were paid at the correct amount.

4. The debit memo was for printed checks.
5. The June 30 bank reconciliation showed a deposit in transit of $1,102.
6. The unadjusted Cash account balance at July 31 was $13,200.

Required

Prepare the bank reconciliation for Park Valley Spa at the end of July.

LO 6-3

Problem 6-22A *Effect of adjustments to cash on the accounting equation*

After reconciling its bank account, Watson Company made the following adjustments to its cash account:

Event No.	Event Description
1.	Corrected overstatement of expense
2.	Recognized bank collection of an account receivable
3.	Recognized interest revenue
4.	Recognized bank service charge
5.	Recognized NSF check from Beat

Required

Identify the event depicted in each adjustment as asset source (AS), asset use (AU), asset exchange (AE), or claims exchange (CE). Also explain how each adjustment affects the accounting equation by placing a + for increase, − for decrease, or NA for not affected under the following components of the accounting equation. The first event is recorded as an example.

							Stockholders' Equity		
Event No.	Type of Event	Assets	=	Liabilities	+	Common Stock	+	Retained Earnings
1.	AS	+		NA		NA		+

LO 6-1, 6-2, 6-3

Problem 6-23A *Bank reconciliation and internal control*

Following is a bank reconciliation for Zocar Enterprises for June 30, Year 1:

	Cash Account	Bank Statement
Balance as of 6/30/Year 1	$1,918	$3,000
Deposit in transit		600
Outstanding checks		(1,507)
Note collected by bank	2,000	
Bank service charge	(25)	
NSF check	(1,800)	
Adjusted cash balance as of 6/30/Year 1	$2,093	$2,093

When reviewing the bank reconciliation, Zocar's auditor was unable to locate any reference to the NSF check on the bank statement. Furthermore, the clerk who reconciles the bank account and records the related adjustments could not find the actual NSF check that should have been included in the bank statement. Finally, there was no specific reference in the accounts receivable supporting records identifying a party who had written a bad check.

Required

a. Prepare the adjustment that the clerk would have made to record the NSF check.

b. Assume that the clerk who prepares the bank reconciliation and records adjustments also makes bank deposits. Explain how the clerk could use a fictitious NSF check to hide the theft of cash.

c. How could Zocar avoid the theft of cash that is concealed by the use of fictitious NSF checks?

Problem 6-24A   *Petty cash fund*

LO 6-4

Austin Co. established a petty cash fund by issuing a check for $300 and appointing Steve Mack as petty cash custodian. Mack had vouchers for the following petty cash payments during the month:

Stamps	$62
Miscellaneous items	20
Employee supper money	70
Taxi fare	50
Window-washing service	75

There was $21 of currency in the petty cash box at the time it was replenished.

Required

a. Show the effects of the following events on the financial statements using a horizontal statements model: (1) establish the fund, (2) reimburse employees, (3) recognize expenses (*Note:* all expenses are recorded in total as miscellaneous expense), and (4) replenish the fund. In the Statement of Cash Flows column, indicate whether the item is an operating activity (OA), investing activity (IA), or financing activity (FA). Use NA to indicate that an account was not affected by the event.

Balance Sheet				Income Statement			Statement of Cash Flows
Assets	= Liab. +	Stk. Equity					
Cash + Petty Cash				Rev. − Exp. =	Net Inc.		

b. Explain how the Cash Short and Over account required in this case will affect the income statement.

c. Identify the events depicted in Requirement *a* as asset source (AS), asset use (AU), asset exchange (AE), or claims exchange (CE).

Problem 6-25A   *Auditor responsibilities*

LO 6-5

You have probably heard it is unwise to bite the hand that feeds you. Independent auditors are chosen by, paid by, and can be fired by the companies they audit. What keeps the auditor independent? In other words, what stops an auditor from blindly following the orders of a client?

Required

Write a memo that explains the reporting responsibilities of an independent auditor.

EXERCISES—SERIES B

Exercise 6-1B   *SOX and COSO's internal control frameworks*

LO 6-1

Required

a. Explain what the acronym SOX refers to.

b. Define the acronym COSO and explain how it relates to SOX.

c. Name and briefly define the five components of COSO's internal control framework.

d. Define the acronym ERM and explain how it relates to COSO's internal control framework.

LO 6-1

Exercise 6-2B   *Internal control procedures*

Required

a. Name and describe the two categories of internal controls.

b. What is the purpose of internal controls?

LO 6-1

Exercise 6-3B   *Internal control procedures*

Stan Oden is opening a new business that will sell sporting goods. It will initially be a small operation, and he is concerned about the security of his assets. He will not be able to be at the business all of the time and will have to rely on his employees and internal control procedures to ensure that transactions are properly accounted for and assets are safeguarded. He will have a store manager and two other employees who will be sales personnel and stock personnel and who will also perform any other duties necessary. Stan will be in the business on a regular basis. He has come to you for advice.

Required

Write a memo to Stan outlining the procedures he should implement to ensure his store assets are protected and that the financial transactions are properly recorded.

LO 6-1

Exercise 6-4B   *Internal controls to prevent theft*

Sally Knox worked as the parts manager for East River Automobiles, a local automobile dealership. Sally was very dedicated and never missed a day of work. Because East River was a small operation, she was the only employee in the parts department. Her duties consisted of ordering parts for stock and those needed for repairs, receiving the parts and checking them in, distributing them as needed to the shop or to customers for purchase, and keeping track of and taking the year-end inventory of parts.

East River decided to expand and needed to secure additional financing. The local bank agreed to a loan contingent on an audit of the dealership. One requirement of the audit was to oversee the inventory count of both automobiles and parts on hand. Sally was clearly nervous, explaining she had just inventoried all parts in the parts department. She supplied the auditors with a detailed list. The inventory showed parts on hand worth $225,000. The auditors decided they needed to verify a substantial part of the inventory.

When the auditors began their counts, a pattern began to develop. Each type of part seemed to be one or two items short when the actual count was taken. This raised more concern. Although Sally assured the auditors the parts were just misplaced, the auditors continued the count. After completing the count of parts on hand, the auditors could document only $155,000 of actual parts. Suddenly, Sally quit her job and moved to another state.

Required

a. What do you suppose caused the discrepancy between the actual count and the count that Sally had supplied?

b. What procedures could be put into place to prevent this type of problem?

LO 6-1

Exercise 6-5B   *Internal controls for equipment*

Required

List the internal control procedures that pertain to the protection of business equipment.

LO 6-2

Exercise 6-6B   *Features of internal control procedures for cash*

Required

List and discuss effective internal control procedures that apply to cash.

LO 6-3

Exercise 6-7B   *Treatment of NSF check*

The bank statement of Hibbert Supplies included a $300 NSF check that one of Hibbert's customers had written to pay for services that were provided by Hibbert.

Required

a. Show the effects of recognizing the NSF check on the financial statements by recording the appropriate amounts in a horizontal statements model like the following one:

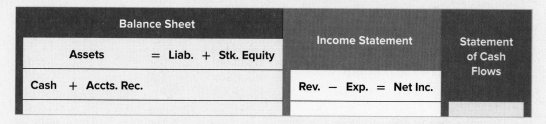

Balance Sheet			Income Statement	Statement of Cash Flows
Assets	= Liab. + Stk. Equity			
Cash + Accts. Rec.			Rev. − Exp. = Net Inc.	

b. Is the recognition of the NSF check on Hibbert's books an asset source, use, or exchange transaction?

c. Suppose the customer redeems the check by giving Hibbert $325 cash in exchange for the bad check. The additional $25 paid a service fee charged by Hibbert. Show the effects on the financial statements in the horizontal statements model in Requirement *a*.

d. Is the receipt of cash referred to in Requirement *c* an asset source, use, or exchange transaction?

Exercise 6-8B *Adjustments to the balance per books*

LO 6-3

Required

Identify which of the following items are added to or subtracted from the unadjusted *book balance* to arrive at the true cash balance. Distinguish the additions from the subtractions by placing a + beside the items that are added to the unadjusted book balance and a − beside those subtracted from it. The first item is recorded as an example.

Reconciling Items	Book Balance Adjusted?	Added or Subtracted?
Automatic debit for utility bill	Yes	−
Charge for printing new checks		
NSF check from customer		
ATM fee		
Outstanding checks		
Interest revenue earned on the account		
Deposits in transit		
Service charge		

Exercise 6-9B *Adjustments to the balance per bank*

LO 6-3

Required

Identify which of the following items are added to or subtracted from the unadjusted *bank balance* to arrive at the true cash balance. Distinguish the additions from the subtractions by placing a + beside the items that are added to the unadjusted bank balance and a − beside those subtracted from it. The first item is recorded as an example.

Reconciling Items	Bank Balance Adjusted?	Added or Subtracted?
Credit memo	No	N/A
ATM fee		
Petty cash voucher		
NSF check from customer		
Interest revenue		
Bank service charge		
Outstanding checks		
Deposits in transit		
Debit memo		

LO 6-3

Exercise 6-10B   *Adjusting the cash account*

As of May 31, Year 1, the bank statement showed an ending balance of $26,100. The unadjusted Cash account balance was $27,350. The following information is available:

1. Deposit in transit: $6,981.
2. Credit memo in bank statement for interest earned in May: $36.
3. Outstanding check: $5,720.
4. Debit memo for service charge: $25.

Required

Determine the true cash balance by preparing a bank reconciliation as of May 31, Year 1, using the preceding information.

LO 6-3

Exercise 6-11B   *Determining the true cash balance, starting with the unadjusted bank balance*

The following information is available for Jenkins Company for the month of August:

1. The unadjusted balance per the bank statement on August 31 was $35,200.
2. Deposits in transit on August 31 were $3,750.
3. A debit memo was included with the bank statement for a service charge of $35.
4. A $2,120 check written in August had not been paid by the bank.
5. The bank statement included a $1,550 credit memo for the collection of a note. The principal of the note was $1,500, and the interest collected was $50.

Required

Determine the true cash balance as of August 31. (*Hint:* It is not necessary to use all of the preceding items to determine the true balance.)

LO 6-3

Exercise 6-12B   *Determining the true cash balance, starting with the unadjusted book balance*

Burson Company had an unadjusted cash balance of $8,120 as of April 30. The company's bank statement, also dated April 30, included a $200 NSF check written by one of Burson's customers. There were $1,525 in outstanding checks and $900 in deposits in transit as of April 30. According to the bank statement, service charges were $50, and the bank collected a $500 note receivable for Burson. The bank statement also showed $31 of interest revenue earned by Burson.

Required

Determine the true cash balance as of April 30. (*Hint:* It is not necessary to use all of the preceding items to determine the true balance.)

LO 6-4

Exercise 6-13B   *Effect of establishing a petty cash fund*

Mountain Timber Company established a $180 petty cash fund on January 1, Year 1.

Required

a. Is the establishment of the petty cash fund an asset source, use, or exchange transaction?
b. Show the establishment of the petty cash fund in a horizontal statements model like the following one:

Balance Sheet			Income Statement	Statement of Cash Flows
Assets	= Liab. + Stk. Equity			
Cash + Petty Cash			Rev. − Exp. = Net Inc.	

Exercise 6-14B *Effect of petty cash events on the financial statements*

LO 6-4

Payton Inc. established a petty cash fund of $150 on January 2. On January 31, the fund contained cash of $8.20 and vouchers for the following cash payments:

Postage and office supplies	$76.30
Entertainment expense	36.50
Maintenance expense	25.00

The four distinct accounting events affecting the petty cash fund for the period were (1) establishment of the fund, (2) reimbursements made to employees, (3) recognition of expenses (*Note:* all expenses are recorded in total as miscellaneous expense), and (4) replenishment of the fund.

Required

Show each of the four events in a horizontal statements model like the following one. In the Statement of Cash Flows column, indicate whether the item is an operating activity (OA), investing activity (IA), or a financing activity (FA). Use NA to indicate that an account was not affected by the event.

Balance Sheet			Income Statement			Statement of Cash Flows
Assets	=	**Liab. + Stk. Equity**				
Cash + Petty Cash			**Rev. − Exp. = Net Inc.**			

Exercise 6-15B *Determining the amount of petty cash expense*

LO 6-4

Consider the following events:

1. A petty cash fund of $200 was established on April 1, Year 1.
2. Employees were reimbursed when they presented petty cash vouchers to the petty cash custodian.
3. On April 30, Year 1, the petty cash fund contained vouchers totaling $171.40 plus $26.10 of currency.

Required

Answer the following questions:

a. How did the establishment of the petty cash fund affect (increase, decrease, or have no effect on) total assets?

b. What is the amount of total petty cash expenses to be recognized during April?

c. When are petty cash expenses recognized (at the time of establishment, reimbursement, or replenishment)?

Exercise 6-16B *Materiality and the auditor*

LO 6-5

Sarah Bale is an auditor. Her work at two companies disclosed inappropriate recognition of revenue. Both cases involved dollar amounts in the $100,000 range. In one case, Bale considered the item material and required her client to restate earnings. In the other case, Bale dismissed the misstatement as being immaterial.

Required

Write a memo that explains how a $100,000 misstatement of revenue is acceptable for one company but unacceptable for a different company.

PROBLEMS—SERIES B

Problem 6-17B *Using internal control to restrict illegal or unethical behavior*

LO 6-1, 6-2

Required

For each of the following fraudulent acts, describe one or more internal control procedures that could have prevented (or helped prevent) the problems.

a. Linda Hinson, the administrative assistant in charge of payroll, created a fictitious employee, wrote weekly checks to the fictitious employee, and then personally cashed the checks for her own benefit.

b. Jim Stewart, the receiving manager of Western Lumber, created a fictitious supplier named B&A Building Supply. B&A regularly billed Western Lumber for supplies purchased. Stewart had printed shipping slips and billing invoices with the name of the fictitious company and opened a post office box as the mailing address. Stewart simply prepared a receiving report and submitted it for payment to the accounts payable department. The accounts payable clerk then paid the invoice when it was received because Stewart acknowledged receipt of the supplies.

c. Jalie Thomas works at a local hobby shop and usually operates the cash register. She has developed a way to give discounts to her friends. When they come by, she rings a lower price or does not charge the friend for some of the material purchased. At first, Thomas thought she would get caught, but no one seemed to notice. Indeed, she has become so sure that there is no way for the owner to find out that she has started taking home some supplies for her own personal use.

LO 6-3

Problem 6-18B *Preparing a bank reconciliation*

Bill Lewis owns a construction business, Lewis Supply Co. The following cash information is available for the month of October, Year 1.

As of October 31, the bank statement shows a balance of $21,400. The October 31 unadjusted balance in the Cash account of Lewis Supply Co. is $18,400. A review of the bank statement revealed the following information:

1. A deposit of $2,600 on October 31, Year 1, does not appear on the October 31 bank statement.
2. A debit memo for $75 was included in the bank statement for the purchase of a new supply of checks.
3. When checks written during the month were compared with those paid by the bank, three checks amounting to $2,075 were found to be outstanding.
4. It was discovered that a check to pay for repairs was correctly written and paid by the bank for $1,500 but was recorded on the books as $5,100.

Required

Prepare a bank reconciliation at the end of October showing the true cash balance.

LO 6-3

Problem 6-19B *Missing information in a bank reconciliation*

The following data apply to Woods Sports Inc. for April, Year 1:

1. Balance per the bank on April 30: $13,750.
2. Deposits in transit not recorded by the bank: $3,600.
3. Bank error; check written by Glen Woods on his personal checking account was drawn on Woods Sports Inc.'s account: $800.
4. The following checks written and recorded by Woods Sports Inc. were not included in the bank statement:

1901	$ 265
1920	650
1921	1,200

5. Credit memo for note collected by the bank: $1,100.
6. Service charge for collection of note: $50.
7. The bookkeeper recorded a check written for $760 to pay for April's office supplies as $670.
8. Bank service charge in addition to the note collection fee: $45.
9. NSF checks returned by the bank: $175.

Required

Determine the amount of the unadjusted cash balance per Woods Sports Inc.'s books.

Problem 6-20B   *Adjustments to the cash account based on the bank reconciliation*   **LO 6-3**

Determine whether the following items in China Imports's bank reconciliation will require adjustments to the book balance of China Imports's cash account and indicate the amount of any necessary adjustment.

a. The bank statement indicated that China Imports earned $60 of interest revenue.

b. China Imports' accountant mistakenly recorded a $430 check as $340.

c. Bank service charges for the month were $45.

d. The bank reconciliation disclosed that $800 had been stolen from China Imports's business.

e. Outstanding checks amounted to $2,600.

f. The bank collected $4,000 of China Imports's accounts receivable. China Imports had instructed its customers to send their payments directly to the bank.

g. The bank mistakenly gave Imports Inc. credit for a $800 deposit made by China Imports.

h. Deposits in transit were $6,200.

i. China Imports's bank statement contained a $525 NSF check. China Imports had received the check from a customer and had included it in one of its bank deposits.

Problem 6-21B   *Bank reconciliation and adjustments to the cash account*   **LO 6-3**

The following information is available for Pyle Garage for March Year 1:

BANK STATEMENT
HAZARD STATE BANK
215 MAIN STREET
HAZARD, GA 30321

Pyle Garage	Account number
629 Main Street	62-00062
Hazard, GA 30321	March 31, Year 1

Beginning balance 3/1/Year 1	$15,000.00
Total deposits and other credits	7,000.00
Total checks and other debits	6,000.00
Ending balance 3/31/Year 1	16,000.00

Checks and Debits		Deposits and Credits	
Check No.	Amount	Date	Amount
1462	$1,163.00	March 1	$1,000.00
1463	62.00	March 2	1,340.00
1464	1,235.00	March 6	210.00
1465	750.00	March 12	1,940.00
1466	1,111.00	March 17	855.00
1467	964.00	March 22	1,480.00
DM	15.00	CM	175.00
1468	700.00		

The following is a list of checks and deposits recorded on the books of Pyle Garage for March, Year 1:

Date	Check No.	Amount of Check	Date	Amount of Deposit
March 1	1463	$ 62.00	March 1	$1,340.00
March 5	1464	1,235.00	March 5	210.00
March 6	1465	750.00		
March 9	1466	1,111.00	March 10	1,940.00
March 10	1467	964.00		
March 14	1468	70.00	March 16	855.00
March 19	1469	1,500.00	March 19	1,480.00
March 28	1470	102.00	March 29	2,000.00

Other Information

1. Check no. 1462 was outstanding from February.
2. A credit memo for collection of accounts receivable was included in the bank statement.
3. All checks were paid at the correct amount.
4. The bank statement included a debit memo for service charges.
5. The February 28 bank reconciliation showed a deposit in transit of $1,000.
6. Check no. 1468 was for the purchase of equipment.
7. The unadjusted Cash account balance at March 31 was $16,868.

Required

Prepare the bank reconciliation for Pyle Garage at the end of March.

LO 6-3

Problem 6-22B   *Effect of adjustments to cash on the accounting equation*

After reconciling its bank account, Addy Equipment Company made the following adjustments to its cash account:

Event No.	Event Description
1.	Recognized NSF check from Wilson
2.	Corrected understatement of expense
3.	Recognized bank service charge
4.	Recognized bank collection of an account receivable
5.	Recognized interest revenue

Required

Identify the event depicted in each adjustment as asset source (AS), asset use (AU), asset exchange (AE), or claims exchange (CE). Also explain how each adjustment affects the accounting equation by placing a + for increase, − for decrease, or NA for not affected under the following components of the accounting equation. The first event is recorded as an example.

						Stockholders' Equity		
Event No.	Type of Event	Assets	=	Liabilities	+	Common Stock	+	Retained Earnings
1.	AE	+/−		NA		NA		

LO 6-1, 6-2, 6-3

Problem 6-23B   *Bank reconciliation and internal control*

The following is a bank reconciliation for BBQ Express for May 31, Year 1:

	Cash Account	Bank Statement
Balance as of 5/31/Year 1	$25,000	$22,000
Deposit in transit		4,250
Outstanding checks		(465)
Note collected by bank	1,815	
Bank service charge	(30)	
Automatic payment on loan	(1,000)	
Adjusted cash balance as of 5/31/Year 1	$25,785	$25,785

Because of limited funds, BBQ Express employed only one accountant who was responsible for receiving cash, recording receipts and disbursements, preparing deposits, and preparing the bank reconciliation. The accountant left the company on June 8, Year 1, after preparing the May 31 bank reconciliation. His replacement compared the checks returned with the bank statement to the cash disbursement records and found the total of the outstanding checks to be $4,600.

Required

a. Prepare a corrected bank reconciliation.

b. What is the total amount of cash missing, and how was the difference between the "true cash" per the bank and the "true cash" per the books hidden on the reconciliation prepared by the former employee?

c. What could BBQ Express do to avoid cash theft in the future?

Problem 6-24B *Petty cash fund*

LO 6-4

The following data pertain to the petty cash fund of Marsh Company:

CHECK FIGURE
a. Cash Short: $3

1. The petty cash fund was established on an imprest basis at $250 on March 1.

2. On March 31, a physical count of the fund disclosed $13 in currency and coins, vouchers authorizing meal allowances totaling $120, vouchers authorizing purchase of postage stamps of $21, and vouchers for payment of delivery charges of $93.

Required

a. Show the effects of the following events on the financial statements using a horizontal statements model: (1) establish the fund, (2) reimburse employees, (3) recognize expenses (*Note:* all expenses are recorded in total as miscellaneous expense), and (4) replenish the fund. In the Statement of Cash Flows column, indicate whether the item is an operating activity (OA), investing activity (IA), or financing activity (FA). Use NA to indicate that an account was not affected by the event.

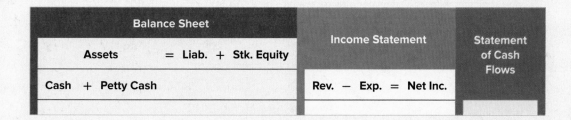

b. Explain how the Cash Short and Over account required in this case will affect the income statement.

c. Identify the events depicted in Requirement *a* as asset source (AS), asset use (AU), asset exchange (AE), or claims exchange (CE).

Problem 6-25B *Types of audit reports*

LO 6-5

Connie Stevens is a partner in a regional accounting firm. Stevens was hired by a client to audit the company's books. After extensive work, Stevens determined that she was unable to perform the appropriate audit procedures.

Required

a. Name the type of audit report that Stevens should issue with respect to the work that she did accomplish.

b. If Stevens had been able to perform the necessary audit procedures, there are three types of audit reports she could have issued depending on the outcome of the audit. Name and describe these three types of audit reports.

ANALYZE, THINK, COMMUNICATE

ATC 6-1   Business Applications Case   *Understanding real-world annual reports*

Required

Obtain Target Corporation's annual report for its 2018 fiscal year (year ended February 2, 2019) at http://investors.target.com using the instructions in Appendix B, and use it to answer the following questions:

a. Who are the independent auditors for Target?

b. What type of opinion did the independent auditors issue on Target's financial statements?

c. On what date does it appear the independent auditors completed their work related to Target's financial statements for the fiscal year ended February 2, 2019 (2018)?

d. Does the auditors' report give any information about how the audit was conducted? If so, what does it suggest was done?

e. Does the auditors' report tell the reader that the audit was concerned with materiality rather than absolute accuracy in the financial statements?

ATC 6-2   Group Assignment   *Bank reconciliations*

The following cash and bank information is available for three companies at June 30, Year 1:

Cash and Adjustment Information	Peach Co.	Apple Co.	Pear Co.
Unadjusted cash balance per books, 6/30	$45,620	$32,450	$23,467
Outstanding checks	1,345	2,478	2,540
Service charge	50	75	35
Balance per bank statement, 6/30	48,632	37,176	24,894
Credit memo for collection of notes receivable	4,500	5,600	3,800
NSF check	325	145	90
Deposits in transit	2,500	3,200	4,800
Credit memo for interest earned	42	68	12

Required

a. Organize the class into three sections and divide each section into groups of three to five students. Assign Peach Co. to section 1, Apple Co. to section 2, and Pear Co. to section 3.

Group Tasks

(1) Prepare a bank reconciliation for the company assigned to your group.

(2) Select a representative from a group in each section to put the bank reconciliation on the board.

Class Discussion

b. Discuss the cause of the difference between the unadjusted cash balance and the ending balance for the bank statement. Also, discuss types of adjustments that are commonly made to the bank balance and types of adjustments commonly made to the unadjusted book balance.

ATC 6-3   Real-World Case   *Evaluating management's responsibilities*

The following excerpt was taken from Alphabet, Inc.'s 10-K report for its 2017 fiscal year. Alphabet, Inc. is the parent company of Google, Inc.

CONTROLS AND PROCEDURES

Evaluation of Disclosure Controls and Procedures

Our management, with the participation of our chief executive officer and chief financial officer, evaluated the effectiveness of our disclosure controls and procedures. . . .

Based on this evaluation, our chief executive officer and chief financial officer concluded that, as of December 31, 2017, our disclosure controls and procedures are designed at a reasonable assurance level and are effective to provide reasonable assurance that information we are required to disclose in reports that we file or submit under the Exchange Act is recorded, processed, summarized, and reported within the time periods specified in the SEC's rules and forms, and that such information is accumulated and communicated to our management, including our chief executive officer and chief financial officer, as appropriate, to allow timely decisions regarding required disclosure. . . .

Management's Report on Internal Control over Financial Reporting

Our management is responsible for establishing and maintaining adequate internal control over financial reporting, as defined in Rule 13a-15(f) of the Exchange Act. Our management conducted an evaluation of the effectiveness of our internal control over financial reporting based on the framework in Internal Control–Integrated Framework issued by the Committee of Sponsoring Organizations of the Treadway Commission (2013 framework). Based on this evaluation, management concluded that our internal control over financial reporting was effective as of December 31, 2017. Management reviewed the results of its assessment with our Audit Committee. The effectiveness of our internal control over financial reporting as of December 31, 2017, has been audited by Ernst & Young LLP, an independent registered public accounting firm, as stated in its report which is included in Item 8 of this Annual Report on Form 10-K.

Limitations on Effectiveness of Controls and Procedures

In designing and evaluating the disclosure controls and procedures, management recognizes that any controls and procedures, no matter how well designed and operated, can provide only reasonable assurance of achieving the desired control objectives. In addition, the design of disclosure controls and procedures must reflect the fact that there are resource constraints and that management is required to apply its judgment in evaluating the benefits of possible controls and procedures relative to their costs.[1]

Required

Based on information in the text, list some of the elements of internal control you would expect the company's management to have established. You do not need to read the report of the Treadway Commission.

ATC 6-4 Business Applications Case *Decisions about materiality*

The accounting firm of Brooke & Doggett, CPAs, recently completed the audits of three separate companies. During these audits, the following events were discovered, and Brooke & Doggett is trying to decide if each event is material. If an item is material, the CPA firm will insist that the company modify the financial statements.

1. In 2020, Major Company reported service revenues of $7,000,000 and earnings before tax of $560,000. Because of an accounting error, the company recorded $42,000 as revenue in 2020 for services that will not be performed until early 2021.
2. Willis Company plans to report a cash balance of $150,000. Because of an accounting error, this amount is $10,700 too high. Willis also plans to report total assets of $8,600,000 and net earnings of $890,000.
3. Adams Company's 2020 balance sheet shows a cash balance of $500,000 and total assets of $19,000,000. For 2020, the company had a net income of 1,700,000. These balances are all correct, but they would have been $14,000 higher if the president of the company had not claimed business travel expenses that were, in fact, the cost of personal vacations for him and his family. He charged the costs of these trips on the company's credit card. The president of Adams Company owns 25 percent of the business.

Required

Write a memorandum to the partners of Brooke & Doggett, explaining whether each of these events is material.

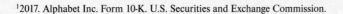

[1]2017. Alphabet Inc. Form 10-K. U.S. Securities and Exchange Commission.

ATC 6-5   Writing Assignment   *Internal control procedures*

Sarah Johnson was a trusted employee of Evergreen Trust Bank. She was involved in everything. She worked as a teller, accounted for the cash at the other teller windows, and recorded many of the transactions in the accounting records. She was so loyal that she never took a day off, even when very sick. She routinely worked late to see that all the day's work was properly recorded in the accounting records, and never took a day's vacation because they might need her at the bank.

Adam and Jammie, CPAs, were hired to perform an audit, the first complete audit that had been done in several years. Johnson seemed somewhat upset by the upcoming audit, saying that everything had been properly accounted for and that the audit was a needless expense. When Adam and Jammie examined some of the bank's internal control procedures, the firm discovered problems. In fact, as the audit progressed, it became apparent that a large amount of cash was missing. Numerous adjustments had been made to customer accounts with credit memorandums, and many of the transactions had been entered several days late. In addition, there were numerous cash payments for "office expenses."

When the audit was complete, it was determined that more than $100,000 of funds was missing or improperly accounted for. All fingers pointed to Johnson. The bank's president, who was a close friend of Johnson, was bewildered. How could this type of thing happen at this bank?

Required

Prepare a written memo to the bank president, outlining the procedures that should be followed to prevent this type of problem in the future.

ATC 6-6   Ethical Dilemma   *I need just a little extra money*

John Riley, a certified public accountant, has worked for the past eight years as a payroll clerk for Southeast Industries, a small furniture manufacturing firm in the northeast. John recently experienced unfortunate circumstances. His teenage son required minor surgery and the medical bills not covered by John's insurance have financially strained John's family.

John works hard and is a model employee. Although he received regular performance raises during his first few years with Southeast, John's wages have not increased in three years. John asked his supervisor, Bill Jameson, for a raise. Bill agreed that John deserved a raise, but told him he could not currently approve one because of sluggish sales.

A disappointed John returned to his duties while the financial pressures in his life continued. Two weeks later, Larry Tyler, an assembly worker at Southeast, quit over a dispute with management. John conceived an idea. John's duties included not only processing employee terminations but also approving time cards before paychecks were issued and then distributing the paychecks to firm personnel. John decided to delay processing Larry's termination, to forge timecards for Larry for the next few weeks, and to cash the checks himself. Because he distributed paychecks, no one would find out, and John reasoned that he was really entitled to the extra money anyway. In fact, no one did discover his maneuver and John stopped the practice after three weeks.

Required

a. Does John's scheme affect Southeast's balance sheet? Explain your answer.

b. Review the AICPA's Articles of Professional Conduct (see Chapter 2) and comment on any of the standards that have been violated.

c. Identify the three elements of unethical and criminal conduct recognized in the fraud triangle.

ATC 6-7   Research Assignment   *Investigating cash and management issues at Smucker's*

Using the most current annual report available on the company's website, answer the following questions about the J. M. Smucker Company. Note that Smucker's "annual report" is more user friendly than its Form 10-K, but the needed information can be found in either.

Required

a. Instead of "Cash," the company's balance sheet uses the account name "Cash and cash equivalents." How does the company define cash equivalents?

b. The annual report has two reports in which management clearly acknowledges its responsibility for the company's financial reporting and internal controls. What are the names of these reports and on what pages are they located?

CHAPTER 7

Accounting for Receivables

LEARNING OBJECTIVES

After you have mastered the material in this chapter, you will be able to:

Video lectures and accompanying self-assessment quizzes are available in *Connect* for all learning objectives.

Tableau Dashboard Activity is available in *Connect* for this chapter.

LO 7-1 Under the allowance method use the percent of revenue method to account for uncollectible accounts expense.

LO 7-2 Use the percent of receivables method to estimate uncollectible accounts expense.

LO 7-3 Use aging of accounts receivable to estimate uncollectible accounts expense.

LO 7-4 Show how the direct write-off method of accounting for uncollectible accounts affects financial statements.

LO 7-5 Show how accounting for notes receivable and accrued interest affects financial statements.

LO 7-6 Show how accounting for credit card sales affects financial statements.

LO 7-7 Calculate and interpret the accounts receivable turnover ratio.

CHAPTER OPENING

Many people buy on impulse. If they must wait, the desire to buy wanes. To take advantage of impulse buyers, most merchandising companies offer customers credit because it increases their sales. A disadvantage of this strategy occurs when some customers are unable or unwilling to pay their bills. Nevertheless, the widespread availability of credit suggests that the advantages of increased sales outweigh the disadvantages of some uncollectible accounts.

When a company allows a customer to "buy now and pay later," the company's right to collect cash in the future is called an **account receivable.** Typically, amounts due from individual accounts receivable are relatively small and the collection period is short. Most accounts receivable are collected within 30 days. When a longer credit term is needed or when a receivable is large, the seller usually requires the buyer to issue a note reflecting a credit agreement between the parties. The note specifies the maturity date, interest rate, and other credit terms. Receivables evidenced by such notes are called **notes receivable.** Accounts and notes receivable are reported as assets on the balance sheet.

The Curious Accountant

Super Nova Images/Alamy Stock Photo

General Dynamics Corporation is an aerospace and defense company that provides both products and services in business aviation; combat vehicles; weapons systems and munitions; shipbuilding; and communications and information technology. Its products include **Gulfstream** business jet airplanes. Its largest customer is the U.S. government. In 2017, 61 percent of its revenue came from sales to the U.S. government, and another 11 percent came from sales to governments of other countries. The remaining 28 percent of its revenues were from commercial customers.

Suppose the U.S. government contracted with General Dynamics to purchase four Gulfstream airplanes at a total cost of $200 million. Assume the government offers to pay for the airplanes on the day they are delivered (a cash purchase) or 60 days later (a purchase on account). Assume that General Dynamics is absolutely sure the government will pay its account when due.

Do you think the company should care whether the government pays for the services upon delivery or 60 days later? Why? (Answer on page 327.)

ESTIMATING UNCOLLECTIBLE ACCOUNTS EXPENSE* USING THE PERCENT OF REVENUE METHOD

Most companies do not expect to collect the full amount (face value) of their accounts receivable. Even carefully screened credit customers sometimes don't pay their bills. The **net realizable value** of accounts receivable represents the amount of receivables a company estimates it will actually collect. The net realizable value is the *face value* less an *allowance for doubtful accounts.*

The **allowance for doubtful accounts** represents a company's estimate of the amount of uncollectible receivables. To illustrate, assume a company with total accounts receivable of $50,000 estimates that $2,000 of its receivables will not be collected. The net realizable value of receivables is computed as follows:

Accounts receivable	$50,000
Less: Allowance for doubtful accounts	(2,000)
Net realizable value of receivables	$48,000

A company cannot know today, of course, the exact amount of the receivables it will not be able to collect in the future. The *allowance for doubtful accounts* and the *net realizable value* are necessarily *estimated amounts.* The net realizable value, however, more closely measures the cash that will ultimately be collected than does the face value. To avoid overstating assets, companies report receivables on their balance sheets at the net realizable value.

Reporting accounts receivable in the financial statements at net realizable value is commonly called the **allowance method of accounting for uncollectible accounts.** As indicated earlier, the allowance method requires accountants to estimate the amount of uncollectible accounts. How do accountants make these estimates? One approach is to base the estimates on a percentage of revenue. The following section of this chapter illustrates accounting for uncollectible accounts when the percentage of revenue approach is employed.

Accounting Events Affecting the Year 1 Period

Allen's Tutoring Services (ATS) is a small company that provides tutoring services to college students. ATS started operations on January 1, Year 1. During Year 1, ATS experienced three types of accounting events. These events are discussed in the following.

EVENT 1   Revenue Recognition
Allen's Tutoring Services (ATS) recognized $3,750 of service revenue earned on account during Year 1.

This is an asset source transaction. ATS obtained assets (accounts receivable) by providing services to customers. Both assets and stockholders' equity (retained earnings) increase. The event increases revenue and net income. Cash flow is not affected. The effects on the financial statements are shown next:

Balance Sheet					Income Statement					Statement of Cash Flows
Assets	=	Liab.	+	Stk. Equity						
Accts. Rec.	=			Ret. Earn.	Rev.	−	Exp.	=	Net Inc.	
3,750	=	NA	+	3,750	3,750	−	NA	=	3,750	NA

*In practice the estimated amount of uncollectible accounts expense is frequently called **bad debts expense**. While frequently used, the bad debts expense term is a misnomer because it is a receivable rather than a debt that has turned bad. To avoid confusion in the early stages of the learning process the author team has chosen to use a term that provides an accurate description of true expense.

Answers to The Curious Accountant

General Dynamics would definitely prefer to make the sale to the government in cash rather than on account. Even though it may be certain to collect its accounts receivable, the sooner the company gets its cash, the sooner the cash can be reinvested.

The interest cost related to a small accounts receivable of $50 that takes 40 days to collect may seem immaterial. At 3 percent, the lost interest amounts to $.16. However, when one considers that General Dynamics had approximately $3.6 billion of accounts receivable on December 31, 2017, and took an average of 43 days to collect them, the cost of financing receivables for a real-world company becomes apparent. At 3 percent, the cost of waiting 43 days to collect $3.6 billion of cash is $12.7 million ($3.6 billion × .03 × 43/365). For a full year, the cost to General Dynamics would be $108 million ($3.6 billion × .03). In 2017, the weighted-average interest rate on General Dynamic's debt was approximately 2.6 percent.

EVENT 2   Collection of Receivables

ATS collected $2,750 cash from accounts receivable in Year 1.

This event is an asset exchange transaction. The asset cash increases; the asset accounts receivable decreases. Total assets remain unchanged. Net income is not affected because the revenue was recognized in the previous transaction. The cash inflow is reported in the operating activities section of the statement of cash flows. The effects on the financial statements are shown next:

Balance Sheet						Income Statement			Statement of Cash Flows
Assets			= Liab.	+	Stk. Equity				
Cash	+	Accts. Rec.				Rev.	− Exp.	= Net Inc.	
2,750	+	(2,750)	= NA	+	NA	NA	− NA	= NA	2,750 OA

EVENT 3   Recognizing Uncollectible Accounts Expense

ATS recognized uncollectible accounts expense for accounts expected to be uncollectible in the future.

While ATS has collected cash for some of the revenue earned in Year 1, some of the remaining receivables may never be collected. ATS will not know the *actual amount* of uncollectible accounts until Year 1 when the customers fail to pay. However, the company can estimate the amount of revenue that it expects will be uncollectible. The *estimated amount* of uncollectible accounts can then be recognized as an expense on the Year 1 income statement. Recognizing the amount of **uncollectible accounts expense** (frequently called *bad debts expense*) improves the matching of revenues and expenses and therefore increases the accuracy of the financial statements.

Many accountants determine the estimated uncollectible accounts expense by taking a percentage of revenue. This approach is commonly called the **percent of revenue method.** The percentage used to make the estimate is usually based on the company's past collection experiences. However, the percentage may be adjusted for anticipated future circumstances. For example, the percentage may be reduced if the company plans to adopt more rigorous credit approval standards. Alternatively, the percentage may be increased if economic forecasts signal an economic downturn that would make customer defaults more likely.

Because this is ATS's first year of operation, there is no prior experience for determining the estimated percentage of uncollectible accounts. Instead, ATS will have to base its estimate on industry averages. To illustrate the accounting procedures for recognizing uncollectible accounts expense, assume that ATS estimates that 2 percent of revenue will be uncollectible. Under these circumstances, ATS would recognize $75 ($3,750 of revenue × 2 percent) of uncollectible accounts expense on the Year 1 income statement.

The estimated amount of uncollectible accounts expense is recognized in a year-end adjustment. The adjustment reduces the net realizable value of receivables, stockholders' equity, and the amount of reported net income. The statement of cash flows is not affected. The effects on the financial statements are shown next:

Balance Sheet					Income Statement					Statement of Cash Flows
Assets	=	Liab.	+	Stk. Equity						
Net Realizable Value of Receivables	=			Ret. Earn.	Rev.	–	Exp.	=	Net Inc.	
(75)	=	NA	+	(75)	NA	–	75	=	(75)	NA

The Accounts Receivable account is not reduced directly because none of the receivables have *actually* been determined to be uncollectible. The decrease in the net realizable value of receivables represents an *estimate* of what will be uncollectible some time in the future. To distinguish the actual balance in accounts receivable from the net realizable value, accountants use a **contra asset account** called Allowance for Doubtful Accounts. The balance in the Allowance for Doubtful Accounts is subtracted from the balance in the Accounts Receivable account to determine the net realizable value of receivables that is shown on the balance sheet. The net realizable value of receivables for ATS is determined as follows:

Accounts receivable	$1,000*
Less: Allowance for doubtful accounts	(75)
Net realizable value of receivables	$ 925

*($3,750 revenue on account – $2,750 of collections)

Generally accepted accounting principles require disclosure of both the net realizable value and the amount of the allowance account. Many companies disclose these amounts directly in the balance sheet in a manner similar to that shown in the text box. Other companies disclose allowance information in the notes to the financial statements.

Analysis of the Year 1 Financial Statements

Exhibit 7.1, Panel A shows a summary of the Year 1 transactions for ATS. Panel B contains the financial statements. As previously indicated, estimating uncollectible accounts improves the usefulness of the Year 1 financial statements in two ways. First, the balance sheet reports the amount of cash ($1,000 – $75 = $925) the company actually expects to collect (net realizable value of accounts receivable). Second, the income statement provides a clearer picture of managerial performance because it better *matches* the uncollectible accounts expense with the revenue it helped produce. The statements in Exhibit 7.1 show that the cash flow from operating activities ($2,750) differs from net income ($3,675). The statement of cash flows reports only cash collections, whereas the income statement reports revenues earned on account less the estimated amount of uncollectible accounts expense.

EXHIBIT 7.1

The Big Picture

Panel A Transactions Summary

Event 1   ATS earned $3,750 of revenue on account.
Event 2   ATS collected $2,750 cash from accounts receivable.
Event 3   ATS adjusted its accounts to reflect management's estimate that uncollectible accounts expense would be $75.

Panel B Financial Statements for Year 1

Income Statement		Balance Sheet			Statement of Cash Flows	
Service revenue	$3,750	Assets			**Operating Activities**	
Uncollectible accts. exp.	(75)	Cash		$2,750	Inflow from customers	$2,750
Net income	$3,675	Accounts receivable	$1,000		**Investing Activities**	0
		Less: Allowance	(75)		**Financing Activities**	0
		Net realizable value		925	Net change in cash	2,750
		Total assets		$3,675	Plus: Beginning cash balance	0
		Stockholders' equity			Ending cash balance	$2,750
		Retained earnings		$3,675		

CHECK YOURSELF 7.1

Pamlico Inc. began operations on January 1, Year 1. During Year 1, it earned $400,000 of revenue on account. The company collected $370,000 of accounts receivable. At the end of the year, Pamlico estimates uncollectible accounts expense will be 1 percent of revenue. Based on this information alone, what is the net realizable value of accounts receivable as of December 31, Year 1?

Answer   Accounts receivable at year-end are $30,000 ($400,000 sales on account − $370,000 collection of receivables). The recognition of uncollectible accounts expense would result in a $4,000 ($400,000 × 0.01) balance in the allowance account. The net realizable value of accounts receivable is therefore $26,000 ($30,000 − $4,000).

Accounting Events Affecting the Year 2 Period

To further illustrate accounting for uncollectible accounts, we discuss six accounting events affecting Allen's Tutoring Services (ATS) during Year 2.

EVENT 1   Write-Off of Uncollectible Accounts Receivable
ATS wrote off $70 of uncollectible accounts receivable.

This is an asset exchange transaction. The amount of the uncollectible accounts is removed from the Accounts Receivable account and from the Allowance for Doubtful Accounts account. Because the balances in both the Accounts Receivable and the Allowance accounts decrease, the net realizable value of receivables—and therefore total assets—remains unchanged. The write-off does not affect the income statement. Because the uncollectible accounts expense was recognized in the previous year, the expense would be double counted if it were recognized again at the time an uncollectible account is written off. Finally, the statement of cash flows is not affected by the write-off. The effects on the financial statements are shown next:

Balance Sheet						Income Statement						Statement of Cash Flows
Assets		=	Liab.	+	Stk. Equity							
Net Realizable Value of Receivables						Rev.	−	Exp.	=	Net Inc.		
NA		=	NA	+	NA	NA	−	NA	=	NA		NA

The computation of the *net realizable value,* before and after the write-off, is shown next:

	Before Write-Off	After Write-Off
Accounts receivable	$1,000	$930
Less: Allowance for doubtful accounts	(75)	(5)
Net realizable value	$ 925	$925

EVENT 2   Revenue Recognition
ATS provided $10,000 of tutoring services on account during Year 2.

Assets (accounts receivable) and stockholders' equity (retained earnings) increase. Recognizing revenue increases net income. Cash flow is not affected. The effects on the financial statements are shown next:

Balance Sheet						Income Statement						Statement of Cash Flows
Assets	=	Liab.	+	Stk. Equity								
Accts. Rec.	=			Ret. Earn.		Rev.	−	Exp.	=	Net Inc.		
10,000	=	NA	+	10,000		10,000	−	NA	=	10,000		NA

EVENT 3   Collection of Accounts Receivable
ATS collected $8,430 cash from accounts receivable.

The balance in the Cash account increases, and the balance in the Accounts Receivable account decreases. Total assets are unaffected. Net income is not affected because revenue was recognized previously. The cash inflow is reported in the operating activities section of the statement of cash flows. The effects on the financial statements are shown next:

Balance Sheet							Income Statement					Statement of Cash Flows
Assets			=	Liab.	+	Stk. Equity						
Cash	+	Accts. Rec.					Rev.	−	Exp.	=	Net Inc.	
8,430	+	(8,430)	=	NA	+	NA	NA	−	NA	=	NA	8,430 OA

EVENT 4   Recovery of an Uncollectible Account: Reinstate Receivable
ATS recovered a receivable that it had previously written off.

Occasionally, a company receives payment from a customer whose account was previously written off. In such cases, the customer's account should be reinstated and the cash received should be recorded the same way as any other collection on account. The account receivable is reinstated because a complete record of the customer's payment history may be useful if the customer requests credit again at some future date. To illustrate, assume that ATS received a $10 cash payment from a customer whose account had previously been written off. The first step is to **reinstate** the account receivable by reversing the previous write-off. The balances in the Accounts Receivable and the Allowance accounts increase. Because the Allowance is a contra asset account, the increase in it offsets the increase in the Accounts Receivable account, and total assets are unchanged. Net income and cash flow are unaffected. The effects on the financial statements are shown next:

Balance Sheet					Income Statement				Statement of Cash Flows
Assets	=	Liab.	+	Stk. Equity					
Net Realizable Value of Receivables					Rev.	−	Exp.	=	Net Inc.	
NA	=	NA	+	NA	NA	−	NA	=	NA	NA

EVENT 5   Recovery of an Uncollectible Account: Collection of Receivable
ATS recorded collection of the reinstated receivable.

The collection of $10 is recorded like any other collection of a receivable account: Cash increases and Accounts Receivable decreases. The income statement is not affected. There is a $10 cash inflow from operating activities. The effects on the financial statements are shown next:

Balance Sheet							Income Statement				Statement of Cash Flows
Assets			=	Liab.	+	Stk. Equity					
Cash	+	Accts. Rec.					Rev.	−	Exp.	=	Net Inc.	
10	+	(10)	=	NA	+	NA	NA	−	NA	=	NA	10 OA

EVENT 6   Adjustment for Recognition of Uncollectible Accounts Expense
Using the percent of revenue method, ATS recognized uncollectible accounts expense for Year 2.

Assuming management continues to estimate uncollectible accounts expense at 2 percent of revenue, ATS will recognize $200 ($10,000 revenue × .02) of uncollectible accounts expense in a year-end adjustment. The allowance for doubtful accounts increases, which causes the net realizable value of receivables to decrease. Uncollectible accounts expense increases, which causes net income and retained earnings to decrease. There is no effect on cash flow. The effects on the financial statements are shown next:

photastic/Shutterstock

Balance Sheet					Income Statement				Statement of Cash Flows
Assets	=	Liab.	+	Stk. Equity					
Net Realizable Value of Receivables	=			Ret. Earn.	Rev.	−	Exp.	=	Net Inc.	
(200)	=	NA	+	(200)	NA	−	200	=	(200)	NA

Analysis of the Year 2 Financial Statements

Panel A of Exhibit 7.2 shows a summary of the Year 2 accounting events for ATS. Panel B displays the Year 2 financial statements. The amount of uncollectible accounts expense ($200) differs from the ending balance of the Allowance account ($215). The balance in the Allowance account was $15 before the Year 2 adjustment for uncollectible accounts expense

EXHIBIT 7.2

The Big Picture

Panel A Transactions Summary

Event 1 ATS wrote off $70 of uncollectible accounts receivable.
Event 2 ATS earned $10,000 of revenue on account.
Event 3 ATS collected $8,430 cash from accounts receivable.
Event 4 ATS reinstated a $10 account receivable it had previously written off.
Event 5 ATS recorded the collection of $10 from the reinstated receivable referenced in Event 4.
Event 6 ATS adjusted its accounts to recognize $200 of uncollectible accounts expense.

Panel B Financial Statements for Year 2

Income Statement		Balance Sheet		Statement of Cash Flows	
Service revenue	$10,000	Assets		**Operating Activities**	
Uncollectible accts. exp.	(200)	Cash	$11,190	Inflow from customers	$ 8,440
Net income	$ 9,800	Accounts receivable $2,500		**Investing Activities**	0
		Less: Allowance (215)		**Financing Activities**	0
		Net realizable value	2,285	Net change in cash	8,440
		Total assets	$13,475	Plus: Beginning cash balance	2,750
		Stockholders' equity		Ending cash balance	$11,190
		Retained earnings	$13,475		

was recorded. At the end of Year 1, Allen's Tutoring Services estimated there would be $75 of uncollectible accounts as a result of Year 1 credit sales. Actual write-offs, however, amounted to $70, and $10 of that amount was recovered, indicating the actual uncollectible accounts expense for Year 1 was only $60. Hindsight shows the expense for Year 1 was overstated by $15. However, if no estimate had been made, the amount of uncollectible accounts expense would have been understated by $60. In some accounting periods, estimated uncollectible accounts expense will likely be overstated; in others, it may be understated. The allowance method cannot produce perfect results, but it does improve the accuracy of the financial statements.

Because no dividends were paid, retained earnings at the end of Year 2 equals the December 31, Year 1, retained earnings plus Year 2 net income (that is, $3,675 + $9,800 = $13,475). Again, the cash flow from operating activities ($8,440) differs from net income ($9,800) because the statement of cash flows does not include the effects of revenues earned on account or the recognition of uncollectible accounts expense.

 CHECK YOURSELF 7.2

Maher Company had beginning balances in Accounts Receivable and Allowance for Doubtful Accounts of $24,200 and $2,000, respectively. During the accounting period, Maher earned $230,000 of revenue on account and collected $232,500 of cash from receivables. The company also wrote off $1,950 of uncollectible accounts during the period. Maher estimates uncollectible accounts expense will be 1 percent of credit sales. Based on this information, what is the net realizable value of receivables at the end of the period?

Answer The balance in the Accounts Receivable account is $19,750 ($24,200 + $230,000 − $232,500 − $1,950). The amount of uncollectible accounts expense for the period is $2,300 ($230,000 × 0.01). The balance in the Allowance for Doubtful Accounts is $2,350 ($2,000 − $1,950 + $2,300). The net realizable value of receivables is therefore $17,400 ($19,750 − $2,350).

ESTIMATING UNCOLLECTIBLE ACCOUNTS EXPENSE USING THE PERCENT OF RECEIVABLES METHOD

Some accountants believe they can better estimate the amount of uncollectible accounts expense by basing their estimates on a percentage of accounts receivable rather than a percentage of revenue. This approach is commonly called the **percent of receivables method** of estimating uncollectible accounts expense. The approach focuses on estimating the most accurate balance for the Allowance for Doubtful Accounts account that appears on the year-end balance sheet.

LO 7-2

Use the percent of receivables method to estimate uncollectible accounts expense.

To illustrate, assume that before adjusting its accounts on December 31, Year 1, Pyramid Corporation had a $56,000 balance in its Accounts Receivable account and a $500 balance in its Allowance for Doubtful Accounts account. Further assume that Pyramid estimates it will be unable to collect 6 percent of its accounts receivable. In other words, Pyramid estimates that $3,360 ($56,000 × .06) of the accounts receivable will be uncollectible. Accordingly, the *ending balance* in the Allowance for Doubtful Accounts account that appears on the December 31, Year 1, balance sheet must be $3,360.

Because the Allowance account currently has a $500 balance, Pyramid must recognize an adjustment that adds $2,860 ($3,360 − $500) to the Allowance account before preparing the financial statements. Likewise, Pyramid will recognize $2,860 of uncollectible accounts expense. In other words, *the amount of the uncollectible accounts expense is determined by calculating the amount necessary to achieve the required $3,360 ending balance in the Allowance account.* The adjustment causes the Allowance for Doubtful Accounts to increase, which causes the net realizable value of receivables and retained earnings to decrease. On the income statement, uncollectible accounts expense increases, which causes net income to decrease. There is no effect on cash flow. The effects on the financial statements are shown next:

Balance Sheet					Income Statement						Statement of Cash Flows
Assets		=	Liab.	+	Stk. Equity						
Net Realizable Value of Receivables	=				Ret. Earn.	Rev.	−	Exp.	=	Net Inc.	
(2,860)		=	NA	+	(2,860)	NA	−	2,860	=	(2,860)	NA

✔ CHECK YOURSELF 7.3

During Year 1, Oron Company earned $100,000 of revenue. Before adjusting its accounts on December 31, Year 1, Oron had a $20,000 balance in its Accounts Receivable Account and a $50 balance in its Allowance for Doubtful Accounts account. Determine the amount of uncollectible accounts expense Oron will recognize on its Year 1 income statement assuming the company estimates uncollectible accounts expense to be 4 percent of receivables.

Answer The ending balance in the Allowance for Doubtful Accounts account after the year-end adjustment must be $800 ($20,000 accounts receivable × .04). Because there is an existing balance of $50 in the Allowance account, the adjustment must add $750 to the Allowance account balance. The adjustment to the Allowance account is offset by the recognition of Uncollectible Accounts Expense. Accordingly, the amount of uncollectible accounts expense recognized on the Year 1 income statement is $750.

Aging Accounts Receivable

History suggests that an account receivable that is past its due date is less likely to be collected than one that is not yet currently due. The longer an account receivable remains past due, the less likely it is to be collected. Accordingly, the accuracy of the amount of estimated uncollectible accounts expense can be improved by **aging of accounts receivable,** which involves applying higher uncollectible percentage estimates to older receivables. To illustrate, assume that Pyramid Corporation prepared the aging of accounts receivable schedule shown in Exhibit 7.3.

The amount of accounts receivable that is estimated to be uncollectible (the ending balance in the Allowance for Doubtful Accounts account) is determined by applying different percentages to each category in the aging schedule. The percentage for each category is based on a company's previous collection experience for each of the categories. The percentages become progressively higher as the accounts become older. Exhibit 7.4 illustrates computing the ending balance required for Pyramid Corporation's December 31, Year 1, balance sheet.

The computations in Exhibit 7.4 show that the *ending balance* in the Allowance for Doubtful Accounts account shown must be $3,760. Because Pyramid has an unadjusted $500 balance in its Allowance account, the amount of uncollectible accounts expense to be recognized in the adjustment is $3,260 ($3,760 required ending balance − $500 current unadjusted balance). Except for the amount of the estimated expense, the effects on the financial statement would be

EXHIBIT 7.3

PYRAMID CORPORATION
Accounts Receivable Aging Schedule
December 31, Year 1

Customer Name	Total Balance	Current	Number of Days Past Due			
			0–30	31–60	61–90	Over 90
J. Davis	$ 6,700	$ 6,700				
B. Diamond	4,800	2,100	$ 2,700			
K. Eppy	9,400	9,400				
B. Gilman	2,200				$1,000	$1,200
A. Kelly	7,300	7,300				
L. Niel	8,600	1,000	6,000	$ 1,600		
L. Platt	4,600			4,600		
J. Turner	5,500			3,000	2,000	500
H. Zachry	6,900		3,000	3,900		
Total	$56,000	$26,500	$11,700	$13,100	$3,000	$1,700

EXHIBIT 7.4

Balance Required in the Allowance for Doubtful Accounts at December 31, Year 1

Number of Days Past Due	Receivables Amount	Percentage Likely to Be Uncollectible	Required Allowance Account Balance
Current	$26,500	.01	$ 265
0–30	11,700	.05	585
31–60	13,100	.10	1,310
61–90	3,000	.25	750
Over 90	1,700	.50	850
Total	$56,000		$3,760

the same as previously shown. Remember that aging is designed to improve the estimated amount of uncollectible accounts expense. It does not affect how the recognition of the expense affects the financial statements.

Matching Revenues and Expenses versus Asset Measurement

The *percent of revenue* method, with its focus on determining the uncollectible accounts expense, is often called the income statement approach. The *percent of receivables* method, focused on determining the best estimate of the allowance balance, is frequently called the balance sheet approach. Which estimating method is better? In any given year, the results will vary slightly between approaches. In the long run, however, the percentages used in either approach are based on a company's actual history of uncollectible accounts. Accountants routinely revise their estimates as more data become available, using hindsight to determine if the percentages should be increased or decreased. Either approach provides acceptable results.

RECOGNIZING UNCOLLECTIBLE ACCOUNTS EXPENSE USING THE DIRECT WRITE-OFF METHOD

If uncollectible accounts are not material, generally accepted accounting principles allow companies to account for them using the **direct write-off method.** Under the direct write-off method, a company simply recognizes uncollectible accounts expense *in the period in which it identifies and writes off uncollectible accounts.* No estimates, allowance account, or adjustments are needed.

The direct write-off method fails to match revenues with expenses. Revenues are recognized in one period and any related uncollectible accounts expense is recognized in a later period. Also, the direct write-off method overstates assets because receivables are reported at *face value* rather than *net realizable value.* If the amount of uncollectible accounts is immaterial, however, companies accept the minor reporting inaccuracies as a reasonable trade-off for recording convenience.

To illustrate the direct write-off method, return to Allen's Tutoring Services (ATS) Year 1 accounting period. However, to highlight the differences between the direct write-off method and the allowance method, we will focus on the events that relate to the differences in the two methods. More specifically, note that this discussion does not include all events contained in the original Allen's Tutoring Services illustration. The specific events covered are discussed as follows.

Assume Allen's Tutoring Services (ATS) employs the direct write-off method. Recall that, during Year 1, ATS recognized $3,750 of revenue on account. The effects on the financial statements are shown next:

LO 7-4

Show how the direct write-off method of accounting for uncollectible accounts affects financial statements.

Balance Sheet				Income Statement				Statement of Cash Flows
Assets	=	Liab.	+ Stk. Equity					
Accts. Rec. =			Ret. Earn.	Rev.	− Exp.	= Net Inc.		
3,750	=	NA	+ 3,750	3,750	− NA	= 3,750		NA

ATS believed only an immaterial amount of the $3,750 of accounts receivable would prove uncollectible. It therefore made no year-end adjustment for estimated uncollectible accounts. Instead, ATS recognizes uncollectible accounts expense when it determines an account is uncollectible.

In the Year 2 accounting period, ATS determined that $70 of accounts receivable were uncollectible. ATS recognized the uncollectible accounts expense in the write-off the uncollectible receivables. With the direct write-off method, the write-off reduces the asset account Accounts Receivable and decreases the stockholders' equity account Retained Earnings. On the income statement, expenses increase and net income decreases. The statement of cash flows is not affected by the write-off. The effects on the financial statements are shown next:

Balance Sheet						Income Statement						Statement of Cash Flows
Assets	=	Liab.	+	Stk. Equity								
Accts. Rec.	=			Ret. Earn.		Rev.	−	Exp.	=	Net Inc.		
(70)	=	NA	+	(70)		NA	−	70	=	(70)		NA

Also, in Year 2, ATS recovered a $10 account receivable it had previously written off. Recording the recovery of a previously written-off account requires the recognition of two events. First, ATS must *reinstate* the receivable (merely reverse the write-off above) because it has proven to be collectible after all. Second, ATS must record collecting the reinstated account. With the direct write-off method, reinstating the receivable increases the asset account Accounts Receivable and increases the stockholders' equity account Retained Earnings. On the income statement, expenses decrease and net income increases. The statement of cash flows is not affected. The effects on the financial statements are shown next:

Balance Sheet						Income Statement						Statement of Cash Flows
Assets	=	Liab.	+	Stk. Equity								
Accts. Rec.	=			Ret. Earn.		Rev.	−	Exp.	=	Net Inc.		
10	=	NA	+	10		NA	−	(10)	=	10		NA

Like the collection of any other receivable, collection of the reinstated account receivable increases the asset account Cash and decreases the asset account Accounts Receivable. The income statement is not affected. The cash inflow is reported in the operating activities section of the statement of cash flows. The effects on the financial statements are shown next:

Balance Sheet							Income Statement					Statement of Cash Flows
Assets			=	Liab.	+	Stk. Equity						
Cash	−	Accts. Rec.					Rev.	−	Exp.	=	Net Inc.	
10		(10)	=	NA	+	NA	NA	−	NA	=	NA	10 OA

ACCOUNTING FOR NOTES RECEIVABLE

Companies typically do not charge their customers interest on accounts receivable that are not past due. When a company extends credit for a long time or when the amount of credit it extends is large, however, the cost of granting free credit and the potential for disputes about payment terms both increase. To address these concerns, the parties frequently enter into a credit agreement, the terms of which are legally documented in a **promissory note.**

To illustrate, assume in Year 3 Allen's Tutoring Services (ATS) generates excess cash that it loans to an individual, Stanford Cummings, so Cummings can buy a car. ATS and Cummings agree that Cummings will repay the money borrowed plus interest at the end of one year. They also agree that ATS will hold the title to the car to secure the debt. Exhibit 7.5 illustrates a promissory note that outlines this credit agreement. For ATS, the credit arrangement represents a *note receivable.*

EXHIBIT 7.5

Promissory Note

Promissory Note

$15,000 (3)   *November 1, Year 3*

Amount   **Date**

For consideration received, Stanford Cummings (1) **hereby promises to pay to the order of:**

Allen's Tutoring Services (2)

Fifteen thousand and no/100 (3)   **Dollars**

payable on   October 31, Year 4 (5)

plus interest thereon at the rate of 6 **percent per year.** (4)

Collateral Description   Automobile title (6)

Signature   *Stanford Cummings* (1)

Features of this note are discussed next. Each feature is cross-referenced with a number that corresponds to an item on the promissory note in Exhibit 7.5. Locate each feature in Exhibit 7.5 and read the corresponding description of the feature that follows:

1. Maker—The person responsible for making payment on the due date is the **maker** of the note. The maker may also be called the *borrower* or *debtor.*

2. Payee—The person to whom the note is made payable is the **payee.** The payee may also be called the *creditor* or *lender.* The payee loans money to the maker and expects the return of the principal and the interest due.

3. Principal—The amount of money loaned by the payee to the maker of the note is the **principal.**

4. Interest—The economic benefit earned by the payee for loaning the principal to the maker is **interest,** which is normally expressed as an annual percentage of the principal amount. For example, a note with a 6 percent interest rate requires interest payments equal to 6 percent of the principal amount every year the loan is outstanding.

5. Maturity Date—The date on which the maker must repay the principal and make the final interest payment to the payee is the **maturity date.**

6. Collateral—Assets belonging to the maker that are assigned as security to ensure that the principal and interest will be paid when due are called **collateral.** In this example, if Cummings fails to pay ATS the amount due, ownership of the car Cummings purchased will be transferred to ATS.

Reporting Transactions Related to Notes Receivable

We illustrate accounting for notes receivable using the credit agreement evidenced by the promissory note in Exhibit 7.5. Allen's Tutoring Services engaged in many transactions during Year 3 and Year 4; we discuss here only transactions directly related to the note receivable.

EVENT 1   Loan of Money

The note shows that ATS loaned $15,000 to Stanford Cummings on November 1, Year 3. This event is an asset exchange. The asset account Cash decreases, and the asset account Notes Receivable increases. The income statement is not affected. The statement of cash flows shows a cash outflow for investing activities. The effects on the financial statements are shown next:

	Balance Sheet							Income Statement			Statement of Cash Flows
	Assets				= Liab. +	Stk. Equity					
Date	Cash	+	Notes Rec.	+ Int. Rec. =		Ret. Earn.		Rev. −	Exp. =	Net Inc.	
11/01/Year 3	(15,000)	+	15,000	+ NA	= NA +	NA		NA −	NA =	NA	(15,000) IA

EVENT 2   Accrual of Interest

For ATS, loaning money represents an investment in the note receivable. ATS will collect the principal ($15,000) plus interest of 6 percent of the principal amount ($0.06 \times \$15,000 = \$900$), or a total of $15,900, on October 31, Year 4, one year from the date the loan was made.

Conceptually, lenders *earn* interest continually even though they do not *collect* cash continually. Each day, the amount of interest due, called **accrued interest**, is greater than the day before. Companies would find it highly impractical to attempt to record (recognize) accrued interest continually as the amount due increased.

Businesses typically solve the recordkeeping problem by only recognizing accrued interest when it is time to prepare financial statements or when the interest is due. At such times, the accounts are *adjusted* to reflect the amount of interest currently due. For example, ATS recorded the asset exchange immediately upon investing in the Note Receivable on November 1, Year 3. ATS did not, however, recognize any interest earned on the note until the balance sheet date, December 31, Year 3. At year-end, ATS made an adjustment to recognize the interest it had earned during the previous two months (November 1 through December 31).

ATS computed the amount of accrued interest by multiplying the principal amount of the note by the annual interest rate and by the length of time for which the note has been outstanding.

$$\text{Principal} \times \text{Annual interest rate} \times \text{Time outstanding} = \text{Interest revenue}$$
$$\$15,000 \times \quad 0.06 \quad \times \quad (2/12) \quad = \quad \$150$$

ATS recognized the $150 of interest revenue in Year 3 although ATS will not collect the cash until Year 4. This practice illustrates the **matching concept.** Interest revenue is recognized in (matched with) the period in which it is earned regardless of when the related cash is collected. The adjustment is an asset source transaction. The asset account Interest Receivable increases, and the stockholders' equity account Retained Earnings increases. The income statement reflects an increase in revenue and net income. The statement of cash flows is not affected because ATS will not collect cash until the maturity date (October 31, Year 4). The effects on the financial statements are shown next:

	Balance Sheet							Income Statement			Statement of Cash Flows
	Assets				= Liab. +	Stk. Equity					
Date	Cash	+	Notes Rec.	+ Int. Rec. =		Ret. Earn.		Rev. −	Exp. =	Net Inc.	
12/31/Year 3	NA	+	NA	+ 150	= NA +	150		150 −	NA =	150	NA

EVENT 3   Collection of Principal and Interest on the Maturity Date

ATS collected $15,900 cash on the maturity date. The collection included $15,000 for the principal plus $900 for the interest. Recall that ATS previously accrued interest in the December 31, Year 3, adjustment for the two months in Year 3 that the note was outstanding. Since year-end, ATS has earned an additional 10 months of interest revenue. ATS must recognize this interest revenue before recording the cash collection. The amount of interest earned in Year 4 is computed as follows:

$$\text{Principal} \times \text{Annual interest rate} \times \text{Time outstanding} = \text{Interest revenue}$$
$$\$15,000 \times \quad 0.06 \quad \times \quad (10/12) \quad = \quad \$750$$

The effects on the financial statements are shown next:

	Balance Sheet								Income Statement					Statement of Cash Flows
	Assets					= Liab. +	Stk. Equity							
Date	Cash	+	Notes Rec.	+	Int. Rec.	=		Ret. Earn.	Rev.	−	Exp.	=	Net Inc.	
10/31/Year 4	NA	+	NA	+	750	= NA +		750	750	−	NA	=	750	NA

The total amount of accrued interest is now $900 ($150 accrued in Year 3 plus $750 accrued in Year 4). The $15,900 cash collection is an asset exchange transaction. The asset account Cash increases, and two asset accounts, Notes Receivable and Interest Receivable, decrease. The income statement is not affected. The statement of cash flows shows a $15,000 inflow from investing activities (recovery of principal) and a $900 inflow from operating activities (interest collection). The effects on the financial statements are shown next:

	Balance Sheet								Income Statement					Statement of Cash Flows
	Assets					= Liab. +	Stk. Equity							
Date	Cash	+	Notes Rec.	+	Int. Rec.	=		Ret. Earn.	Rev.	−	Exp.	=	Net Inc.	
10/31/Year 4	15,900	+	(15,000)	+	(900)	= NA +		NA	NA	−	NA	=	NA	15,000 IA 900 OA

Financial Statements

The financial statements reveal key differences between the timing of revenue recognition and the exchange of cash. These differences are highlighted next:

	Year 3	Year 4	Total
Interest revenue recognized	$150	$750	$900
Cash inflow from operating activities	0	900	900

Accrual accounting calls for recognizing revenue in the period in which it is earned regardless of when cash is collected.

Income Statement

Although generally accepted accounting principles require reporting receipts of, or payments for, interest on the statement of cash flows as operating activities, they do not specify how to classify interest on the income statement. In fact, companies traditionally report interest on the income statement as a nonoperating item. Interest is therefore frequently reported in two different categories within the same set of financial statements.

Balance Sheet

As with other assets, companies report interest receivable and notes receivable on the balance sheet in order of their liquidity. **Liquidity** refers to how quickly assets are expected to be converted to cash during normal operations. In the preceding example, Allen's Tutoring Services expects to convert its accounts receivable to cash before it collects the interest receivable and note receivable. Companies commonly report interest and notes receivable after accounts receivable. Exhibit 7.6 shows a partial balance sheet for ATS to illustrate the presentation of receivables.

EXHIBIT 7.6

Typical Balance Sheet Presentation of Receivables

ALLEN'S TUTORING SERVICES
Partial Balance Sheet
As of December 31, Year 3

Cash		xxxx
Accounts receivable	xxxx	
Less: Allowance for doubtful accounts	(xxxx)	
Net realizable value of accounts receivable		xxxx
Interest receivable		xxxx
Notes receivable		xxxx

 CHECK YOURSELF 7.4

On October 1, Year 1, Mei Company accepted a promissory note for a loan it made to the Asia Pacific Company. The note had a $24,000 principal amount, a four-month term, and an annual interest rate of 4 percent. Determine the amount of interest revenue and the cash inflow from operating activities Mei will report in its Year 1 and Year 2 financial statements.

Answer The computation of accrued interest revenue is shown next. The interest rate is stated in annual terms even though the term of the note is only four months. Interest rates are commonly expressed as an annual percentage regardless of the term of the note. The *time outstanding* in the following formulas is therefore expressed as a fraction of a year. Mei charged annual interest of 4 percent, but the note was outstanding for only 3/12 of a year in Year 1 and 1/12 of a year in Year 2.

Year 1

Principal	×	Annual interest rate	×	Time outstanding	=	Interest revenue
$24,000	×	0.04	×	(3/12)	=	$240

Year 2

Principal	×	Annual interest rate	×	Time outstanding	=	Interest revenue
$24,000	×	0.04	×	(1/12)	=	$80

In Year 1, Mei's cash inflow from interest revenue will be zero.
   In Year 2, Mei will report a $320 ($240 + $80) cash inflow from operating activities for interest revenue.

ACCOUNTING FOR CREDIT CARD SALES

LO 7-6

Show how accounting for credit card sales affects financial statements.

Many businesses accept third-party credit cards instead of offering credit directly to their customers. Credit card companies normally charge merchants a fee that typically ranges between 1 and 5 percent of their credit sales. Why would merchants pay credit card fees instead of offering credit directly to their customers? Credit card sales offer three distinct advantages over direct credit sales. (1) Accepting credit cards tends to increase sales because customers with an existing credit card can buy goods without having to apply for store credit. (2) Merchants do not have to incur the expense of credit approval and record maintenance. (3) Credit companies accept the risk of slow collections or defaults, thereby eliminating the uncollectible accounts expense that merchants would otherwise incur.
   The credit card company usually provides customers with plastic cards that permit cardholders to charge purchases at various retail outlets. When a sale takes place, the seller

records the transaction on a receipt the customer usually signs. The receipt is forwarded to the credit card company, which immediately pays the merchant.

Piotr Adamowicz/123RF

The credit card company deducts its service fee from the gross amount of the sale and pays the merchant the net balance (gross amount of sale less credit card fee) in cash. The credit card company collects the gross sale amount directly from the customer. The merchant avoids the risk of uncollectible accounts, as well as the cost of maintaining customer credit records. To illustrate, assume that Allen's Tutoring Services experiences the following events.

EVENT 1 Recognition of Revenue and Expense on Credit Card Sales

ATS accepts a credit card payment for $1,000 of services rendered.

Assume the credit card company charges a 5 percent fee for handling the transaction ($1,000 × 0.05 = $50). ATS's income increases by the amount of revenue ($1,000) and decreases by the amount of the credit card expense ($50). Net income increases by $950. The event increases an asset, accounts receivable, due from the credit card company, and stockholders' equity (retained earnings) by $950 ($1,000 revenue − $50 credit card expense). Cash flow is not affected. The effects on the financial statements are shown next:

Balance Sheet					Income Statement					Statement of Cash Flows
Assets	=	Liab.	+	Stk. Equity						
Accts. Rec.	=			Ret. Earn.	Rev.	−	Exp.	=	Net Inc.	
950	=	NA	+	950	1,000	−	50	=	950	NA

EVENT 2 Collection of Credit Card Receivable

The collection of the receivable due from the credit card company is recorded like any other receivable collection.

When ATS collects the net amount of $950 ($1,000 − $50) from the credit card company, one asset account (Cash) increases and another asset account (Accounts Receivable) decreases. Total assets are not affected. The income statement is not affected. A $950 cash inflow is reported in the operating activities section of the statement of cash flows. The effects on the financial statements are shown next:

Balance Sheet							Income Statement					Statement of Cash Flows
Assets			=	Liab.	+	Stk. Equity						
Cash	+	Accts. Rec.					Rev.	−	Exp.	=	Net Inc.	
950	+	(950)	=	NA	+	NA	NA	−	NA	=	NA	950 OA

The Financial Analyst

LO 7-7

Calculate and interpret the accounts receivable turnover ratio.

As mentioned earlier, two costs of extending credit to customers are uncollectible accounts expense and recordkeeping costs. These costs can be significant. Large companies spend literally millions of dollars to buy the equipment and pay the staff necessary to operate entire departments devoted to managing accounts receivable. Further, there is an implicit interest cost associated with extending credit. When a customer is permitted to delay payment, the creditor forgoes the opportunity to invest the amount the customer owes.

Exhibit 7.7 presents part of a note from the 2017 annual report of Rent-A-Center. This excerpt provides insight into the credit costs real companies incur. First, observe that Rent-A-Center has $74 million of receivables. These receivables represent money that could be in the bank earning interest if all sales had been made in cash. If Rent-A-Center could have earned interest at 5 percent on that money, the opportunity cost of this lost interest is approximately $3.7 million ($74 million × .05) a year. Next, observe that Rent-A-Center expects to have uncollectible accounts amounting to approximately $4.2 million (balance in the allowance account). These are significant costs to a company that reported a net income of $6.7 million on their 2017 income statement.

EXHIBIT 7.7

Rent-A-Center, Inc. December 31, 2017
Partial Note C Regarding Accountants Receivable and Allowance for Doubtful Accounts
(amounts shown in thousands)

Receivables consist of the following:

	2017	2016
Installment sales receivable	$55,516	$55,834
Trade and notes receivables	18,474	14,067
Other receivables	—	3,477
Total	73,990	73,378
Less allowance for doubtful accounts	(4,167)	(3,593)
Net receivables	$69,823	$69,785

Changes in the company's allowance for doubtful accounts are as follows:

	2017	2016
Beginning balance	$ 3,593	$ 3,614
Uncollectible accounts expense	15,702	15,449
Accounts written off	(15,791)	(16,095)
Recoveries	663	625
Ending balance	$ 4,167	$ 3,593

Average Number of Days to Collect Accounts Receivable

The longer it takes to collect accounts receivable, the greater the opportunity cost of lost income. Also, business experience indicates that the older an account receivable becomes, the less likely it is to be collected. Finally, taking longer to collect an account typically costs more for salaries, equipment, and supplies used in the process of trying to collect it. Businesses are therefore concerned about how long it takes to collect their receivables.

Two ratios help management, or other users, measure a company's collection period. One is the **accounts receivable turnover ratio,** computed as:[1]

$$\frac{\text{Sales}}{\text{Net accounts receivable}}$$

Net accounts receivable is also known as net realizable value of receivable, which is the amount of accounts receivable minus the allowance for doubtful accounts. Dividing a company's sales by its net accounts receivable tells how many times the net accounts receivable balance is "turned over" (converted into cash) each year. The higher the turnover, the shorter the collection period. To simplify its interpretation, the accounts receivable turnover ratio is

---

[1]To be more precise, the ratio could be computed using only credit sales and average accounts receivable. Usually, however, companies do not report credit sales separately from cash sales in published financial statements. Average accounts receivable, if desired, is computed as [(Beginning receivables + Ending receivables) ÷ 2]. For this course, use the simpler computation shown here (Sales ÷ Accounts receivable).

often taken one step further to determine the **average number of days to collect accounts receivable,** sometimes called the *average collection period.* This is computed as:

$$\frac{365}{\text{Accounts receivable turnover ratio}}$$

This ratio measures how many days, on average, it takes a company to collect its accounts receivable. Because longer collection periods increase costs, shorter periods are obviously more desirable. To illustrate computing the *average number of days to collect accounts receivable* for Allen's Tutoring Services, refer to the Year 2 financial statements in Exhibit 7.2. On average, the company takes 83 days to collect its receivables, computed in two steps:

1. The accounts receivable turnover is 4.376 ($10,000 ÷ $2,285) times.
2. The average number of days to collect receivables is 83 (365 ÷ 4.376) days.

In the preceding computations, the net realizable value of accounts receivable was used because that is the amount typically reported in published financial statements. The results would not have been materially different had total accounts receivable been used.

Real-World Data

What is the collection period for real companies? The time required to collect receivables varies among industries and among companies within industries. The fourth column in Exhibit 7.8 displays the average number of days to collect receivables for seven companies in three different industries. These numbers are for 2017.

Because customers in fast-food restaurants typically pay cash when they purchase hamburgers or coffee, why do these companies have accounts receivable? The accounts receivable for McDonald's and Restaurant Brands arise because these companies sell goods to restaurants that are independent franchisees. (Restaurant Brands is the parent company of Burger King and Tim Horton.) So, for example, McDonald's accounts receivable represents future collections from restaurant owners, not only from customers who purchase hamburgers.

Although there are many franchised Starbucks coffee shops, most of the company's revenues come from shops that are owned and operated by the company itself. Starbucks does not have accounts receivable from its own shops; its receivables come from sales to outside customers and from credit card sales in its own shops. In addition to accounts receivable related to franchised coffee shops, Starbucks sells coffee products such as coffee beans to retailers such as grocery stores. Most of these companies do not pay Starbucks "cash on delivery," but purchase their goods on account. One way companies manage their cash flow is to take time to pay their bills, and large companies such as Kroger can essentially force their suppliers to sell them goods on credit.

EXHIBIT 7.8

Industry	Company	Average Days to Sell Inventory	Average Days to Collect Receivables	Length of Operating Cycle
Fast Food	McDonald's	5	32	37
	Starbucks	50	10	60
	Restaurant Brands International	15	36	51
Department Stores	Macy's	124	5	129
	Walmart	43	4	47
Home Construction	D.R. Horton	344	0	344
	Toll Brothers	583	0	583

Some companies allow their customers extended time to pay their bills because the customers would otherwise have difficulty coming up with the money. Many small companies do not have cash available to pay up front. Buying on credit is the only way they can obtain the inventory they need. If a manufacturer or wholesaler wants to sell to such companies, credit sales represent the only option available.

The length of the **operating cycle** is the average time it takes a business to convert inventory to accounts receivable plus the time it takes to convert accounts receivable into cash. The average number of days to collect receivables is one component of the operating cycle for a particular company. The other component is the average number of days to sell inventory, which was explained in Chapter 5. The length of the operating cycles for the real-world companies in Exhibit 7.8 is shown in the last column.

What is the significance of the different operating cycle lengths in Exhibit 7.8? As previously explained, the longer the operating cycle takes, the more it costs the company. Exhibit 7.8 shows it takes Macy's an average of 82 days longer than Walmart to complete an operating cycle. All other things being equal, approximately how much did this longer time reduce Macy's earnings? Assume Macy's could invest excess cash at 8 percent (or alternatively, assume it pays 8 percent to finance its inventory and accounts receivable). Using the accounting information reported in Macy's 2017 financial statements, we can answer the question as follows:

$$\text{Macy's investment in inventory} \times \text{Interest rate} \times \text{Time} = \text{Cost}$$
$$\$5,178,000,000 \times 8\% \times 82/365 = \$93,062,137$$

With 2.8 operating cycles per year ($365 \div 129$), the extended operating cycle costs Macy's $261 million annually. Based on the assumptions used here, Macy's would have increased its after-tax earnings by approximately 17 percent, if it could have reduced its operating cycle by 82 days. Although this illustration is a rough estimate, it demonstrates that it is important for businesses to minimize the length of their operating cycles.

REALITY BYTES

This chapter explains that, in general, companies want to collect their receivables as quickly as possible. There is a notable exception to this generalization. If a company charges its customers interest on unpaid receivables, the company makes money on the unpaid balance. Many sellers of "big-ticket" goods like furniture, large appliances, and automobiles offer to finance their customers' purchases, allowing customers extended time to pay off their receivables in exchange for the customers' paying additional charges for interest.

For example, most people probably think of Harley-Davidson as a company that makes its profits selling motorcycles, and that is largely true. However, Harley-Davidson also made a substantial amount of profit from financing the motorcycles that it sells. During 2015, 2016, and 2017, the company earned 73 percent of its operating income

Tofudevil/Shutterstock

from motorcycle sales and 27 percent from financing those sales. This amounted to $831 million of income before taxes. Therefore, the fact that it took Harley-Davidson 181 days to collect its receivables in 2017 was probably not a reason for concern.

CHECK YOURSELF 7.5

Randolph Corporation had sales for the year of $535,333 and a net realizable value of receivables at year-end of $22,000. Determine Randolph's average number of days to collect accounts receivable.

Answer The accounts receivable turnover is 24.33 ($535,333 ÷ $22,000) times per year. The average number of days to collect accounts receivable is 15 (365 ÷ 24.33).

FOCUS ON INTERNATIONAL ISSUES

A ROSE BY ANY OTHER NAME . . .

If a person who studied U.S. GAAP wanted to look at the financial statements of a non-U.S. company, choosing statements of a company from another English-speaking country might seem logical. Presumably, this would eliminate language differences, and only the differences in GAAP would remain. However, this is not true.

Andriy Blokhin/Shutterstock   Torontonian/Shutterstock   DSGNSR1/Shutterstock

When an accountant in the United States uses the term *turnover,* she or he is usually thinking of a financial ratio, such as the accounts receivable turnover ratio. However, in the United Kingdom, the term *turnover* refers to what U.S. accountants call *sales.* UK balance sheets do not usually show an account named *Inventory;* rather, they use the term *Stocks.* In the United States, accountants typically use the term *stocks* to refer to certificates representing ownership in a corporation. Finally, if an accountant or banker from the United Kingdom should ever ask you about your *gearing ratio,* he or she probably is not interested in your bicycle but in your debt-to-assets ratio.

Although IFRS has significantly increased the uniformity of financial reporting throughout the world, it does not seek to impose absolute uniformity. IFRS often allows alternate ways of accounting for the same business event, as will be discussed in Chapter 8. Even when different companies choose the same IFRS option for accounting for a given event, they are allowed some flexibility in the application of the IFRS rule, as are companies in the United States who follow GAAP. And, obviously, companies in different countries are allowed to prepare financial reports in their own language. As we will see in Chapter 9, companies in different countries may even use significantly different formats for their balance sheets.

A Look Back

We first introduced accounting for receivables in Chapter 2. This chapter presented additional complexities related to accounts receivable, such as the *allowance method of accounting for uncollectible accounts.* The allowance method improves matching of expenses with revenues. It also provides a more accurate measure of the value of accounts receivable on the balance sheet.

Under the allowance method, estimated uncollectible accounts expense is recorded in a year-end adjustment. There are two methods commonly used to estimate the amount of uncollectible accounts expense: the percent of revenue method and the percent of receivables method. With the percent of revenue method, uncollectible accounts expense is measured as a percent of the period's sales. With the percent of receivables method, a company analyzes its accounts receivable at the end of the period, usually classifying them by age, to estimate the amount of the accounts receivable balance that is likely to be uncollectible. The balance in the Allowance for Doubtful Accounts account is then adjusted to equal the estimated amount of uncollectible accounts. Uncollectible accounts expense decreases the net realizable value of receivables (accounts receivable − allowance for doubtful accounts), stockholders' equity, and net income.

The allowance method of accounting for uncollectible accounts is conceptually superior to the *direct write-off method,* in which uncollectible accounts expense is recognized when an account is determined to be uncollectible. The direct write-off method fails to match revenues with expenses and overstates accounts receivable on the balance sheet. It is easier to use, however, and is permitted by generally accepted accounting principles if the amount of uncollectible accounts expense is immaterial.

The chapter also introduced notes receivable and accounting for *accrued interest.* When the term of a promissory note extends over more than one accounting period, companies must make adjustments to recognize interest in the appropriate accounting period, even if the cash exchange of interest occurs in a different accounting period.

We also discussed accounting for credit card sales, a vehicle that shifts uncollectible accounts expense to the credit card issuer. Many companies find the benefits of accepting major credit cards to be worth the credit card expense consequently incurred.

Finally, we addressed the costs of making credit sales. In addition to uncollectible accounts expense, interest is a major cost of financing receivables. The length of the collection period provides a measure of the quality of receivables. Short collection periods usually indicate lower amounts of uncollectible accounts and interest cost. Long collection periods imply higher costs. The collection period can be measured in two steps. First, divide sales by the accounts receivable balance to determine the accounts receivable turnover ratio. Then, divide the number of days in the year (365) by the accounts receivable turnover ratio.

 # A Look Forward

Chapter 8 discusses accounting for long-term assets such as buildings and equipment. As with inventory cost flow, discussed in Chapter 5, GAAP allows companies to use different accounting methods to report on similar types of business events. Life would be easier for accounting students if all companies used the same accounting methods. However, the business world is complex. For the foreseeable future, people are likely to continue to have diverse views as to the best way to account for a variety of business transactions. To function effectively in today's business environment, it is important for you to be able to recognize differences in reporting practices.

 Tableau Dashboard Activity is available in *Connect* for this chapter.

 ## SELF-STUDY REVIEW PROBLEM

 A step-by-step audio-narrated series of slides is available in *Connect*.

During Year 4, Calico Company experienced the following accounting events:

1. Provided $120,000 of services on account.
2. Collected $85,000 cash from accounts receivable.
3. Wrote off $1,800 of accounts receivable that were uncollectible.
4. Loaned $3,000 to an individual, Emma Gardner, in exchange for a note receivable.
5. Paid $90,500 cash for operating expenses.
6. Estimated that uncollectible accounts expense would be 2 percent of credit sales. Recorded the year-end adjustment.
7. Recorded the year-end adjustment for accrued interest on the note receivable (see Event 4). Calico made the loan on August 1. It had a six-month term and a 6 percent rate of interest.

Calico's account balances on January 1, Year 4, were as follows:

Event No.	Assets								=	Liab.	+	Stk. Equity		
	Cash	+	Net Realizable Value of Receivables	+	Notes Rec.	+	Int. Rec.	=			+	Com. Stk.	+	Ret. Earn.
Beg. Bal.	12,000	+	15,800	+	NA	+	NA	=	NA		+	20,000	+	7,800

Required

a. Record the Year 4 events in accounts using the horizontal format shown in the preceding example.

b. Determine net income for Year 4.

c. Determine net cash flow from operating activities for Year 4.

d. Assuming the balance in the Allowance for Doubtful Accounts account was $2,000 on January 1, Year 4, determine the balance in the Accounts Receivable account as of December 31, Year 4.

e. What amount of interest revenue will Calico recognize on its note receivable in Year 5?

Solution to Requirement *a*

Event No.	Assets								=	Liab.	+	Stk. Equity		
	Cash	+	Net Realizable Value of Receivables	+	Notes Rec.	+	Int. Rec.	=			+	Com. Stk.	+	Ret. Earn.
Beg. Bal.	12,000	+	15,800	+	NA	+	NA	=	NA		+	20,000	+	7,800
1.	NA	+	120,000	+	NA	+	NA	=	NA		+	NA	+	120,000
2.	85,000	+	(85,000)	+	NA	+	NA	=	NA		+	NA	+	NA
3.	NA	+	NA	+	NA	+	NA	=	NA		+	NA	+	NA
4.	(3,000)	+	NA	+	3,000	+	NA	=	NA		+	NA	+	NA
5.	(90,500)	+	NA	+	NA	+	NA	=	NA		+	NA	+	(90,500)
6.	NA	+	(2,400)	+	NA	+	NA	=	NA		+	NA	+	(2,400)
7.	NA	+	NA	+	NA	+	75*	=	NA		+	NA	+	75
Totals	3,500	+	48,400	+	3,000	+	75	=	NA		+	20,000	+	34,975

*$3,000 × .06 × 5/12 = $75

Solution to Requirements *b–e*

b. Net income is $27,175 ($120,000 − $90,500 − $2,400 + $75).

c. Net cash flow from operating activities is an outflow of $5,500 ($85,000 − $90,500).

d. First, determine the December 31, Year 4, balance in the Allowance for Doubtful Accounts account, which is $2,600 ($2,000 beginning balance − $1,800 write-off + $2,400 expense recognition). Next, determine the December 31 balance in the Accounts Receivable account, which is $51,000 ($48,400 Net Realizable Value + $2,600 Allowance for Doubtful Accounts).

e. In Year 5, Calico will recognize interest revenue for one month: $3,000 × .06 × 1/12 = $15.

KEY TERMS

Account receivable 324	Allowance method of accounting	Direct write-off method 335	Payee 337
Accounts receivable turnover	for uncollectible	Interest 337	Percent of receivables
ratio 342	accounts 326	Liquidity 339	method 333
Accrued interest 338	Average number of days to	Maker 337	Percent of revenue method 327
Aging of accounts	collect accounts	Matching concept 338	Principal 337
receivable 334	receivable 343	Maturity date 337	Promissory note 336
Allowance for doubtful	Bad debts expense 326	Net realizable value 326	Reinstate 330
accounts 326	Collateral 337	Notes receivable 325	Uncollectible accounts
	Contra asset account 328	Operating cycle 344	expense 327

QUESTIONS

1. What is the difference between accounts receivable and notes receivable?

2. What is the *net realizable value* of receivables?

3. What type of account is the Allowance for Doubtful Accounts?

4. What are two ways in which estimating uncollectible accounts improves the accuracy of the financial statements?

5. When using the allowance method, why is uncollectible accounts expense an estimated amount?

6. What is the most common format for reporting accounts receivable on the balance sheet? What information does this method provide beyond showing only the net amount?

7. Why is it necessary to make an adjustment to reinstate a previously written-off account receivable before the collection is recorded?

8. What are some factors considered in estimating the amount of uncollectible accounts receivable?

9. What is the effect on the accounting equation of recognizing uncollectible accounts expense?

10. What is the effect on the accounting equation of writing off an uncollectible account receivable when the allowance method is used? When the direct write-off method is used?

11. How does the recovery of a previously written-off account affect the income statement when the allowance method is used? How does the recovery of a previously written-off account affect the statement of cash flows when the allowance method is used?

12. What is the advantage of using the allowance method of accounting for uncollectible accounts? What is the advantage of using the direct write-off method?

13. How do companies determine the percentage estimate of uncollectible accounts when using the percent of revenue method?

14. What is an advantage of using the percent of receivables method of estimating uncollectible accounts expense?

15. What is "aging of accounts receivable"?

16. What is the difference between the allowance method and the direct write-off method of accounting for uncollectible accounts?

17. When is it acceptable to use the direct write-off method of accounting for uncollectible accounts?

18. What is a promissory note?

19. Define the following terms:
    a. Maker
    b. Payee
    c. Principal
    d. Interest
    e. Maturity date
    f. Collateral

20. What is the formula for computing interest revenue?

21. What is accrued interest?

22. When is an adjustment for accrued interest generally recorded?

23. Assume that on July 1, Year 1, Big Corp. loaned Little Corp. $12,000 for a period of one year at 6 percent interest. What amount of interest revenue will Big report for Year 1? What amount of cash will Big receive upon maturity of the note?

24. In which section of the statement of cash flows will Big report the cash collected in Question 23?

25. Why is it generally beneficial for a business to accept major credit cards as payment for goods and services even when the fee charged by the credit card company is substantial?

26. What types of costs do businesses avoid when they accept major credit cards as compared with handling credit sales themselves?

27. How is the accounts receivable turnover ratio computed? What information does the ratio provide?

28. How is the average number of days to collect accounts receivable computed? What information does the ratio provide?

29. Is accounting terminology standard in all countries? What term is used in the United Kingdom to refer to *sales*? What term is used to refer to *inventory*? What is a *gearing ratio*? Is it important to know about these differences?

30. What is the operating cycle of a business?

EXERCISES—SERIES A

McGraw Hill connect   All applicable Exercises in Series A are available in *Connect*.

Exercise 7-1A   *Analysis of financial statement effects of accounting for uncollectible accounts under the allowance method*   **LO 7-1**

Businesses using the allowance method for the recognition of uncollectible accounts expense commonly experience four accounting events:

1. Recognition of uncollectible accounts expense through a year-end adjustment.
2. Write-off of uncollectible accounts.
3. Recognition of revenue on account.
4. Collection of cash from accounts receivable.

Required

Show the effect of each event on the elements of the financial statements, using a horizontal statements model like the one shown next. Use the following coding scheme to record your answers: increase is +, decrease is −, not affected is NA. In the Statement of Cash Flows column, indicate whether the item is an operating activity (OA), investing activity (IA), or financing activity (FA). The first transaction is entered as an example.

Event No.	Balance Sheet			Income Statement			Statement of Cash Flows
	Assets	= Liab. +	Stk. Equity	Rev. −	Exp. =	Net Inc.	
1.	−	NA	−	NA	+	−	NA

Exercise 7-2A   *Accounting for uncollectible accounts: allowance method*   **LO 7-1**

Holmes Cleaning Service began operation on January 1, Year 1. The company experienced the following events for its first year of operations:

Events Affecting Year 1:

1. Provided $84,000 of cleaning services on account.
2. Collected $76,000 cash from accounts receivable.
3. Paid salaries of $28,500 for the year.
4. Adjusted the accounts to reflect management's expectations that uncollectible accounts expense would be $1,650. The expense was determined using the percent of revenue method.

Required

a. Organize the transaction data in accounts under an accounting equation.
b. Prepare an income statement, a balance sheet, and a statement of cash flows for Year 1.

Exercise 7-3A   *Analyzing account balances for a company using the allowance method of accounting for uncollectible accounts*   **LO 7-1**

The following account balances come from the records of Ourso Company:

	Beginning Balance	Ending Balance
Accounts Receivable	$2,800	$3,600
Allowance for Doubtful Accounts	280	350

During the accounting period, Ourso recorded $14,000 of sales revenue on account. The company also wrote off a $150 account receivable.

Required

a. Determine the amount of cash collected from receivables.

b. Determine the amount of uncollectible accounts expense recognized during the period.

LO 7-1

Exercise 7-4A   *Effect of recognizing uncollectible accounts expense on financial statements: percent of revenue allowance method*

Rosie Dry Cleaning was started on January 1, Year 1. It experienced the following events during its first two years of operation:

Events Affecting Year 1

1. Provided $45,000 of cleaning services on account.
2. Collected $39,000 cash from accounts receivable.
3. Adjusted the accounting records to reflect the estimate that uncollectible accounts expense would be 1 percent of the cleaning revenue on account.

Events Affecting Year 2

1. Wrote off a $300 account receivable that was determined to be uncollectible.
2. Provided $62,000 of cleaning services on account.
3. Collected $61,000 cash from accounts receivable.
4. Adjusted the accounting records to reflect the estimate that uncollectible accounts expense would be 1 percent of the cleaning revenue on account.

Required

a. Organize the transaction data in accounts under an accounting equation.

b. Determine the following amounts:

   (1) Net income for Year 1.

   (2) Net cash flow from operating activities for Year 1.

   (3) Balance of accounts receivable at the end of Year 1.

   (4) Net realizable value of accounts receivable at the end of Year 1.

c. Repeat Requirement *b* for the Year 2 accounting period.

LO 7-1

Exercise 7-5A   *Analyzing financial statement effects of accounting for uncollectible accounts using the percent of revenue allowance method*

Grover Inc. uses the allowance method to account for uncollectible accounts expense. Grover Inc. experienced the following four accounting events in Year 1:

1. Recognized $92,000 of revenue on account.
2. Collected $78,000 cash from accounts receivable.
3. Wrote off uncollectible accounts of $720.
4. Recognized uncollectible accounts expense. Grover estimated that uncollectible accounts expense will be 1 percent of sales on account.

Required

Show the effect of each event on the elements of the financial statements, using a horizontal statements model like the one shown next. Use + for increase, − for decrease, and NA for not affected. In the Statement of Cash Flows column, indicate whether the item is an operating activity (OA), investing activity (IA), or financing activity (FA). The first transaction is entered as an example.

Event No.	Balance Sheet					Income Statement					Statement of Cash Flows
	Assets	=	Liab.	+	Stk. Equity	Rev.	−	Exp.	=	Net Inc.	
1.	+		NA		+	+		NA		+	NA

Exercise 7-6A   *Effect of recovering a receivable previously written off*

Renue Spa had the following balances at December 31, Year 2: Cash of $15,000, Accounts Receivable of $61,000, Allowance for Doubtful Accounts of $3,750, and Retained Earnings of $72,250. During Year 3, $2,100 of accounts receivable were written off as uncollectible. In addition, Renue unexpectedly collected $500 of receivables that had been written off in a previous accounting period. Services provided on account during Year 3 were $215,000, and cash collections from receivables were $218,000. Uncollectible accounts expense was estimated to be 2 percent of the sales on account for the period.

Required

a.   Organize the information in accounts under an accounting equation.

b.   Based on the preceding information, compute (after year-end adjustment):

   (1) Balance of Allowance for Doubtful Accounts at December 31, Year 3.

   (2) Balance of Accounts Receivable at December 31, Year 3.

   (3) Net realizable value of Accounts Receivable at December 31, Year 3.

c.   What amount of uncollectible accounts expense will Renue Spa have for Year 3?

d.   Explain how the $500 recovery of receivables affected the accounting equation.

Exercise 7-7A   *Effect of recognizing uncollectible accounts on the financial statements:*
                  percent of receivables allowance method

Leach Inc. experienced the following events for the first two years of its operations:

Year 1:

1.   Issued $10,000 of common stock for cash.

2.   Provided $78,000 of services on account.

3.   Provided $36,000 of services and received cash.

4.   Collected $69,000 cash from accounts receivable.

5.   Paid $38,000 of salaries expense for the year.

6.   Adjusted the accounting records to reflect uncollectible accounts expense for the year. Leach estimates that 5 percent of the ending accounts receivable balance will be uncollectible.

Year 2:

1.   Wrote off an uncollectible account for $650.

2.   Provided $88,000 of services on account.

3.   Provided $32,000 of services and collected cash.

4.   Collected $81,000 cash from accounts receivable.

5.   Paid $65,000 of salaries expense for the year.

6.   Adjusted the accounts to reflect uncollectible accounts expense for the year. Leach estimates that 5 percent of the ending accounts receivable balance will be uncollectible.

Required

a.   Organize the transaction data in accounts under an accounting equation.

b.   Prepare the income statement, statement of changes in stockholders' equity, balance sheet, and statement of cash flows for Year 1.

c.   What is the net realizable value of the accounts receivable at December 31, Year 1?

d.   Repeat Requirements *a, b,* and *c* for Year 2.

Exercise 7-8A   *Accounting for uncollectible accounts: percent of receivables allowance*
                  method

Vulcan Service Co. experienced the following transactions for Year 1, its first year of operations:

1.   Provided $91,000 of services on account.

2.   Collected $72,000 cash from accounts receivable.

3. Paid $36,000 of salaries expense for the year.

4. Adjusted the accounts using the following information from an accounts receivable aging schedule:

Number of Days Past Due	Amount	Percent Likely to Be Uncollectible	Allowance Balance
Current	$7,800	.01	
0–30	4,500	.05	
31–60	2,000	.10	
61–90	2,200	.20	
Over 90 days	2,500	.50	

Required

a. Organize the transaction data in accounts under an accounting equation.

b. Prepare the income statement for Vulcan Service Co. for Year 1.

c. What is the net realizable value of the accounts receivable at December 31, Year 1?

LO 7-4

Exercise 7-9A *Accounting for uncollectible accounts: direct write-off method*

Patel Service Co. does make a few sales on account but is mostly a cash business. Consequently, it uses the direct write-off method to account for uncollectible accounts. During Year 1, Patel Service Co. earned $35,000 of cash revenue and $4,500 of revenue on account. Cash operating expenses were $19,000. After numerous attempts to collect a $120 account receivable from Sam Stephens, the account was determined to be uncollectible in Year 1.

Required

a. Show the effects of (1) cash revenue, (2) revenue on account, (3) cash expenses, and (4) write off of the uncollectible account on the financial statements using a horizontal statements model like the one shown here. In the Statement of Cash Flows column, indicate whether the item is an operating activity (OA), investing activity (IA), or financing activity (FA). Use NA to indicate that an element is not affected by the event.

Balance Sheet			Income Statement			Statement of Cash Flows
Assets	= Liab. +	Stk. Equity				
Cash + Accts. Rec.			Rev. − Exp. =	Net Inc.		

b. What amount of net income did Patel Service Co. report on the Year 1 income statement?

LO 7-1, 7-4

Exercise 7-10A *Accounting for uncollectible accounts: percent of revenue allowance versus direct write-off method*

Joey's Bike Shop sells new and used bicycle parts. Although a majority of its sales are cash sales, it makes a significant amount of credit sales. During Year 1, its first year of operations, Joey's Bike Shop experienced the following:

Sales on account	$260,000
Cash sales	580,000
Collections of accounts receivable	235,000
Uncollectible accounts charged off during the year	1,250

Required

a. Assume that Joey's Bike Shop uses the allowance method of accounting for uncollectible accounts and estimates that 1 percent of its sales on account will not be collected. Answer the following questions:

   (1) What is the Accounts Receivable balance at December 31, Year 1?

   (2) What is the ending balance of the Allowance for Doubtful Accounts at December 31, Year 1, after all transactions and adjustments are recorded?

   (3) What is the amount of uncollectible accounts expense for Year 1?

   (4) What is the net realizable value of accounts receivable at December 31, Year 1?

b. Assume that Joey's Bike Shop uses the direct write-off method of accounting for uncollectible accounts. Answer the following questions:

   (1) What is the Accounts Receivable balance at December 31, Year 1?

   (2) What is the amount of uncollectible accounts expense for Year 1?

   (3) What is the net realizable value of accounts receivable at December 31, Year 1?

Exercise 7-11A *Accounting for notes receivable*

LO 7-5

Rainey Enterprises loaned $20,000 to Small Co. on June 1, Year 1, for one year at 6 percent interest.

Required

Show the effects of the following transactions in a horizontal statements model like the one shown next:

1. The loan to Small Co.
2. The adjustment at December 31, Year 1.
3. The adjustment and collection of the note on June 1, Year 2.

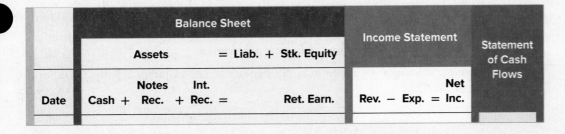

Exercise 7-12A *Notes receivable–accrued interest*

LO 7-5

On May 1, Year 1, Benz's Sandwich Shop loaned $10,000 to Mark Henry for one year at 6 percent interest.

Required

Answer the following questions:

a. What is Benz's interest income for Year 1?

b. What is Benz's total amount of receivables at December 31, Year 1?

c. How will the loan and interest be reported on Benz's Year 1 statement of cash flows?

d. What is Benz's interest income for Year 2?

e. What is the total amount of cash that Benz's will collect in Year 2 from Mark Henry?

f. How will the loan and interest be reported on Benz's Year 2 statement of cash flows?

g. What is the total amount of interest that Benz's earned on the loan to Mark Henry?

Exercise 7-13A *Effect of credit card sales on financial statements*

LO 7-6

Ultra Day Spa provided $120,000 of services during Year 1. All customers paid for the services with credit cards. Ultra submitted the credit card receipts to the credit card company immediately. The credit card company paid Ultra cash in the amount of face value less a 5 percent service charge.

Required

a. Show the credit card sales and the subsequent collection of accounts receivable in a horizontal statements model like the one shown next. In the Statement of Cash Flows column, indicate whether the item is an operating activity (OA), investing activity (IA), or financing activity (FA). Use NA to indicate that an element is not affected by the event.

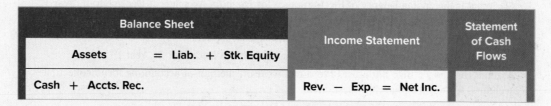

Balance Sheet			Income Statement	Statement of Cash Flows
Assets	= Liab.	+ Stk. Equity		
Cash + Accts. Rec.			Rev. − Exp. = Net Inc.	

b. Based on this information alone, answer the following questions:

(1) What is the amount of total assets at the end of the accounting period?

(2) What is the amount of revenue reported on the income statement?

(3) What is the amount of cash flow from operating activities reported on the statement of cash flows?

(4) What costs would a business incur if it maintained its own accounts receivable? What cost does a business incur by accepting credit cards?

LO 7-6

Exercise 7-14A   *Recording credit card sales*

Luna Company accepted credit cards in payment for $6,000 of services performed during July. The credit card company charged Luna a 4 percent service fee; it paid Luna as soon as it received the invoices.

Required

Based on this information alone, what is the amount of net income earned during the month of July?

LO 7-1, 7-5, 7-6

Exercise 7-15A   *Comprehensive single-cycle problem*

The following trial balance was drawn from the accounts of Little Grocery Supplier (LGS) as of December 31, Year 2:

Cash	$ 9,000
Accounts Receivable	41,000
Allowance for Doubtful Accounts	2,500
Inventory	78,000
Accounts Payable	21,000
Common Stock	50,000
Retained Earnings	54,500

Transactions for Year 3

1. Acquired an additional $20,000 cash from the issue of common stock.

2. Purchased $85,000 of inventory on account.

3. Sold inventory that cost $91,000 for $160,000. Sales were made on account.

4. The company wrote off $900 of uncollectible accounts.

5. On September 1, LGS loaned $18,000 to Eden Co. The note had an 8 percent interest rate and a one-year term.

6. Paid $19,000 cash for operating expenses.

7. The company collected $161,000 cash from accounts receivable.

8. A cash payment of $92,000 was paid on accounts payable.

9. The company paid a $5,000 cash dividend to the stockholders.

10. Uncollectible accounts are estimated to be 1 percent of sales on account.

11. Recorded the accrued interest at December 31, Year 3 (see item 5).

Required

a. Organize the transaction data in accounts under an accounting equation.

b. Prepare an income statement, a statement of changes in stockholders' equity, a balance sheet, and a statement of cash flows for Year 3.

Exercise 7-16A *Accounts receivable turnover and average days to collect accounts receivable*

LO 7-7

The following information is available for Market, Inc. and Supply, Inc. at December 31:

Accounts	Market, Inc.	Supply, Inc.
Accounts Receivable	$ 56,200	$ 75,400
Allowance for Doubtful Accounts	2,248	2,256
Sales Revenue	606,960	867,100

Required

a. What is the accounts receivable turnover for each of the companies?

b. What is the average days to collect the receivables?

c. Assuming both companies use the percent of receivables allowance method, what is the estimated percentage of uncollectible accounts for each company?

PROBLEMS—SERIES A

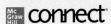 **All applicable Problems in Series A are available in Connect.**

Problem 7-17A *Accounting for uncollectible accounts: two cycles using the percent of revenue allowance method*

LO 7-1

The following transactions apply to Jova Company for Year 1, the first year of operation:

1. Issued $10,000 of common stock for cash.
2. Recognized $210,000 of service revenue earned on account.
3. Collected $162,000 from accounts receivable.
4. Paid operating expenses of $125,000.
5. Adjusted accounts to recognize uncollectible accounts expense. Jova uses the allowance method of accounting for uncollectible accounts and estimates that uncollectible accounts expense will be 1 percent of sales on account.

The following transactions apply to Jova for Year 2:

1. Recognized $320,000 of service revenue on account.
2. Collected $335,000 from accounts receivable.
3. Determined that $2,150 of the accounts receivable were uncollectible and wrote them off.
4. Collected $800 of an account that had previously been written off.
5. Paid $205,000 cash for operating expenses.
6. Adjusted the accounts to recognize uncollectible accounts expense for Year 2. Jova estimates uncollectible accounts expense will be 0.5 percent of sales on account.

CHECK FIGURES
c. Ending Accounts
   Receivable, Year 1: $48,000
d. Net Income, Year 2: $113,400

Required

Complete the following requirements for Year 1 and Year 2. Complete all requirements for Year 1 prior to beginning the requirements for Year 2.

a. Identify the type of each transaction (asset source, asset use, asset exchange, or claims exchange).

b. Show the effect of each transaction on the elements of the financial statements, using a horizontal statements model like the one shown here. Use + for increase, − for decrease, and NA for not affected. Also, in the Statement of Cash Flows column, indicate whether the item is an operating activity (OA), investing activity (IA), or financing activity (FA). The first transaction is entered as an example.

	Balance Sheet				Income Statement				Statement of Cash Flows
Event No.	Assets	=	Liab.	+ Stk. Equity	Rev.	−	Exp.	= Net Inc.	
1.	+		NA	+	+		NA	+	NA

c. Organize the transaction data in accounts under an accounting equation.

d. Prepare the income statement, statement of changes in stockholders' equity, balance sheet, and statement of cash flows.

LO 7-1

Problem 7-18A *Determining account balances and their effect on the horizontal statements model: percent of revenue allowance method of accounting for uncollectible accounts*

CHECK FIGURE
d. Net Realizable Value: $43,100

During the first year of operation, Year 1, Direct Service Co. recognized $290,000 of service revenue on account. At the end of Year 1, the accounts receivable balance was $46,000. For this first year in business, the owner believes uncollectible accounts expense will be about 1 percent of sales on account.

Required

a. What amount of cash did Direct Service collect from accounts receivable during Year 1?

b. Assuming Direct Service uses the allowance method to account for uncollectible accounts, what amount should Direct Service record as uncollectible accounts expense for Year 1?

c. Show the effects of the following three transactions on the financial statements by recording the appropriate amounts in a horizontal statements model like the one shown next. In the Statement of Cash Flows column, indicate whether the item is an operating activity (OA), investing activity (IA), or financing activity (FA). Use NA for not affected.

   (1) Record service revenue on account.
   (2) Record collections from accounts receivable.
   (3) Record the event to recognize uncollectible accounts expense.

Balance Sheet				Income Statement				Statement of Cash Flows
Assets		= Liab.	+ Stk. Equity					
Cash + Net Realizable Value of Receivables				Rev.	−	Exp.	= Net Inc.	

d. What is the net realizable value of receivables at the end of Year 1?

LO 7-2

Problem 7-19A *Determination of account balances: percent of receivables allowance method of accounting for uncollectible accounts*

CHECK FIGURE
a. Net Realizable Value: $65,040

The following information is available for Quality Book Sales' sales on account and accounts receivable:

Accounts receivable balance, January 1, Year 2	$ 78,500
Allowance for doubtful accounts, January 1, Year 2	4,710
Sales on account, Year 2	550,000
Collection on accounts receivable, Year 2	556,000

After several collection attempts, Quality Book Sales wrote off $2,850 of accounts that could not be collected. Quality Book Sales estimates that 0.5 percent of sales on account will be uncollectible.

Required

a. Compute the following amounts:

   (1) Using the allowance method, the amount of uncollectible accounts expense for Year 2.

   (2) The net realizable value of receivables at the end of Year 2.

b. Explain why the uncollectible accounts expense amount is different from the amount that was written off as uncollectible.

Problem 7-20A   *Accounting for uncollectible accounts: percent of receivables allowance method*

Sage Inc. experienced the following transactions for Year 1, its first year of operations:

1. Issued common stock for $50,000 cash.
2. Purchased $140,000 of merchandise on account.
3. Sold merchandise that cost $110,000 for $250,000 on account.
4. Collected $236,000 cash from accounts receivable.
5. Paid $118,000 on accounts payable.
6. Paid $50,000 of salaries expense for the year.
7. Paid other operating expenses of $28,000.
8. Sage adjusted the accounts using the following information from an accounts receivable aging schedule:

Number of Days Past Due	Amount	Percent Likely to Be Uncollectible	Allowance Balance
Current	$10,000	0.01	
0–30	2,000	0.05	
31–60	1,200	0.10	
61–90	500	0.20	
Over 90 days	300	0.50	

Required

a. Organize the transaction data in accounts under an accounting equation.
b. Prepare the income statement, statement of changes in stockholders' equity, balance sheet, and statement of cash flows for Sage Inc. for Year 1.
c. What is the net realizable value of the accounts receivable at December 31, Year 1?

Problem 7-21A   *Multistep income statement and balance sheet*

Required

Use the following information to prepare a multistep income statement and a balance sheet for Sherman Equipment Co. for Year 2. (*Hint:* Some of the items will *not* appear on either statement, and ending retained earnings must be calculated.)

Salaries Expense	$ 69,000	Operating Expenses	62,000
Common Stock	100,000	Cash Flow from Investing Activities	78,400
Notes Receivable (short term)	24,000	Prepaid Rent	12,500
Allowance for Doubtful Accounts	7,800	Land	40,000
Uncollectible Accounts Expense	8,100	Cash	48,100
Supplies	1,200	Inventory	98,300
Interest Revenue	5,400	Accounts Payable	46,000
Sales Revenue	320,000	Salaries Payable	12,000
Dividends	3,500	Cost of Goods Sold	148,000
Interest Receivable (short term)	1,500	Accounts Receivable	56,000
Beginning Retained Earnings	81,000		

Problem 7-22A   *Accounting for notes receivable and uncollectible accounts using the direct write-off method*

The following transactions apply to Hooper Co. for Year 1, its first year of operations:

1. Issued $60,000 of common stock for cash.
2. Provided $90,000 of services on account.
3. Collected $78,000 cash from accounts receivable.

4. Loaned $20,000 to Mosby Co. on November 30, Year 1. The note had a one-year term to maturity and a 6 percent interest rate.

5. Paid $26,000 of salaries expense for the year.

6. Paid a $2,000 dividend to the stockholders.

7. Recorded the accrued interest on December 31, Year 1 (see item 4).

8. Estimated that 1 percent of service revenue will be uncollectible.

Required

a. Show the effects of these transactions in a horizontal statements model like the one shown next:

	Balance Sheet							Income Statement			Statement of Cash Flows
	Assets				=	Stk. Equity					
Event No.	Cash +	Net Realizable Value of Receivable +	Notes Rec. +	Int. Rec. =		Com. Stk. +	Ret. Earn.	Rev. −	Exp. =	Net Inc.	

b. Prepare the income statement, balance sheet, and statement of cash flows for Year 1.

LO 7-1, 7-5

Problem 7-23A *Missing information*

The following information comes from the accounts of James Company:

Account Title	Beginning Balance	Ending Balance
Accounts Receivable	$36,000	$34,000
Allowance for Doubtful Accounts	1,800	1,600
Note Receivable	40,000	40,000
Interest Receivable	1,400	2,800

Required

a. There were $190,000 of sales on account during the accounting period. Write-offs of uncollectible accounts were $1,450. What was the amount of cash collected from accounts receivable? What amount of uncollectible accounts expense was reported on the income statement? What was the net realizable value of receivables at the end of the accounting period?

b. The note receivable has a two-year term with a 7 percent interest rate. What amount of interest revenue was recognized during the period? How much cash was collected from interest?

LO 7-2, 7-6

Problem 7-24A *Accounting for credit card sales and uncollectible accounts: percent of receivables allowance method*

Northwest Sales had the following transactions in Year 1:

1. The business was started when it acquired $200,000 cash from the issue of common stock.

2. Northwest purchased $900,000 of merchandise for cash in Year 1.

3. During the year, the company sold merchandise for $1,200,000. The merchandise cost $710,000. Sales were made under the following terms:

a. $520,000	Cash sales
b. 380,000	Credit card sales (The credit card company charges a 4 percent service fee.)
c. 300,000	Sales on account

4. The company collected all the amount receivable from the credit card company.
5. The company collected $210,000 of accounts receivable.
6. The company paid $190,000 cash for selling and administrative expenses.
7. Determined that 5 percent of the ending accounts receivable balance would be uncollectible.

Required

a. Show the effects of each of the transactions on the elements of the financial statements, using a horizontal statements model like the following one. Use + for increase, − for decrease, and NA for not affected. The first transaction is entered as an example.

Event No.	Balance Sheet			Income Statement			Statement of Cash Flows
	Assets	= Liab.	+ Stk. Equity	Rev.	− Exp.	= Net Inc.	
1.	+	NA	+	NA	NA	NA	+ FA

b. Prepare an income statement, statement of changes in stockholders' equity, balance sheet, and statement of cash flows for Year 1.

Problem 7-25A *Effect of transactions on the elements of financial statements*   LO 7-4, 7-5, 7-6

Required

Identify each of the following independent transactions as asset source (AS), asset use (AU), asset exchange (AE), or claims exchange (CE). Also explain how each event affects assets, liabilities, stockholders' equity, net income, and cash flow by placing a + for increase, − for decrease, or NA for not affected under each of the categories. The first event is recorded as an example.

Event	Type of Event	Assets	Liabilities	Common Stock	Retained Earnings	Net Income	Cash Flow
a	AS	+	NA	NA	+	+	NA

a. Provided services on account.
b. Wrote off an uncollectible account (use the direct write-off method).
c. Loaned cash to H. Phillips for one year at 6 percent interest.
d. Collected cash from customers paying their accounts.
e. Paid cash for land.
f. Sold merchandise at a price above cost. Accepted payment by credit card. The credit card company charges a service fee. The receipts have not yet been forwarded to the credit card company.
g. Provided services for cash.
h. Paid cash for operating expenses.
i. Paid cash for salaries expense.
j. Recovered an uncollectible account that had been previously written off (assume the direct write-off method is used to account for uncollectible accounts).
k. Paid cash to creditors on accounts payable.
l. Recorded three months of accrued interest on the note receivable (see item c).
m. Submitted receipts to the credit card company (see item f) and collected cash.
n. Sold land at its cost.

LO 7-1, 7-5, 7-6

Problem 7-26A   *Comprehensive accounting cycle problem (uses percent of revenue allowance method)*

The following trial balance was prepared for Tile, Etc., Inc. on December 31, Year 2, after all account adjustments had been made:

Account Title	
Cash	$110,000
Accounts Receivable	125,000
Allowance for Doubtful Accounts	18,000
Inventory	425,000
Accounts Payable	95,000
Common Stock	450,000
Retained Earnings	97,000

Tile, Etc. had the following transactions in Year 3:

1. Purchased merchandise on account for $580,000.
2. Sold merchandise that cost $420,000 for $890,000 on account.
3. Sold for $245,000 cash merchandise that had cost $160,000.
4. Sold merchandise for $190,000 to credit card customers. The merchandise had cost $96,000. The credit card company charges a 4 percent fee.
5. Collected $620,000 cash from accounts receivable.
6. Paid $610,000 cash on accounts payable.
7. Paid $145,000 cash for selling and administrative expenses.
8. Collected cash for the full amount due from the credit card company (see item 4).
9. Loaned $60,000 to J. Parks. The note had an 8 percent interest rate and a one-year term to maturity.
10. Wrote off $7,500 of accounts as uncollectible.
11. Made the following adjustments:
    (a) Recorded uncollectible accounts expense estimated at 1 percent of sales on account.
    (b) Recorded seven months of accrued interest on the note at December 31, Year 3 (see item 9).

Required

a. Organize the transaction data in accounts under an accounting equation.
b. Prepare an income statement, a statement of changes in stockholders' equity, a balance sheet, and a statement of cash flows for Year 3.

EXERCISES—SERIES B

LO 7-1

Exercise 7-1B   *Analysis of financial statement effects of accounting for uncollectible accounts under the allowance method*

Hardin Services Co. experienced the following events in Year 1:

1. Provided services on account.
2. Collected cash for accounts receivable.
3. Attempted to collect an account and, when unsuccessful, wrote off the amount to uncollectible accounts expense.

Required

Show the effect of each event on the elements of the financial statements, using a horizontal statements model like the one shown next. Use + for increase, − for decrease, and NA for not affected. In the Statement of Cash Flows column, indicate whether the item is an operating activity (OA), investing activity (IA), or financing activity (FA).

	Balance Sheet			Income Statement			Statement of Cash Flows
Event No.	Assets	= Liab.	+ Stk. Equity	Rev.	− Exp.	= Net Inc.	

Exercise 7-2B   *Accounting for uncollectible accounts: allowance method*

LO 7-1

Sandy's Accounting Service began operation on January 1, Year 1. The company experienced the following events for its first year of operations:

Events Affecting Year 1:

1. Provided $96,000 of accounting services on account.
2. Collected $80,000 cash from accounts receivable.
3. Paid salaries of $32,000 for the year.
4. Adjusted the accounts to reflect management's expectations that uncollectible accounts expense would be $1,600.

Required

a. Organize the transaction data in accounts under an accounting equation.

b. Prepare an income statement, balance sheet, and statement of cash flows for Year 1.

Exercise 7-3B   *Analyzing account balances for a company using the allowance method of accounting for uncollectible accounts*

LO 7-1

The following account balances come from the records of Stone Company:

	Beginning Balance	Ending Balance
Accounts Receivable	$4,000	$4,500
Allowance for Doubtful Accounts	150	250

During the accounting period, Stone recorded $21,000 of service revenue on account. The company also wrote off a $180 account receivable.

Required

a. Determine the amount of cash collected from receivables.

b. Determine the amount of uncollectible accounts expense recognized during the period.

Exercise 7-4B   *Effect of recognizing uncollectible accounts expense on financial statements: percent of revenue allowance method*

LO 7-1

Reliable Auto Service was started on January 1, Year 1. The company experienced the following events during its first two years of operation:

Events Affecting Year 1

1. Provided $52,000 of repair services on account.
2. Collected $32,000 cash from accounts receivable.
3. Adjusted the accounting records to reflect the estimate that uncollectible accounts expense would be 2 percent of the service revenue on account.

Events Affecting Year 2

1. Wrote off a $320 account receivable that was determined to be uncollectible.
2. Provided $65,000 of repair services on account.
3. Collected $66,000 cash from accounts receivable.
4. Adjusted the accounting records to reflect the estimate that uncollectible accounts expense would be 1 percent of the service revenue on account.

Required

a. Organize the transaction data in accounts under an accounting equation.

b. Determine the following amounts:

    (1) Net income for Year 1.

    (2) Net cash flow from operating activities for Year 1.

    (3) Balance of accounts receivable at the end of Year 1.

    (4) Net realizable value of accounts receivable at the end of Year 1.

c. Repeat Requirements *a* and *b* for the Year 2 accounting period.

LO 7-1

Exercise 7-5B *Analyzing financial statement effects of accounting for uncollectible accounts using the percent of revenue allowance method*

Tull Bros. uses the allowance method to account for uncollectible accounts expense. Tull experienced the following four events in Year 1:

1. Recognized $68,000 of revenue on account.

2. Collected $62,000 cash from accounts receivable.

3. Determined that $500 of accounts receivable were not collectible and wrote them off.

4. Recognized uncollectible accounts expense for the year. Tull estimates that uncollectible accounts expense will be 2 percent of its sales.

Required

Show the effect of each of these events on the elements of the financial statements, using a horizontal statements model like the following one. Use + for increase, − for decrease, and NA for not affected. In the Statement of Cash Flows column, indicate whether the item is an operating activity (OA), investing activity (IA), or financing activity (FA).

	Balance Sheet					Income Statement				Statement of Cash Flows
	Assets		= Liab.	+	Stk. Equity					
Event No.	Cash +	Net Realizable Value of Rec. =			Ret. Earn.	Rev. −	Exp. =	Net Inc.		

LO 7-1

Exercise 7-6B *Effect of recovering a receivable previously written off*

Edd's Shoe Repair had the following balances at December 31, Year 1: Cash of $22,000, Accounts Receivable of $76,000, Allowance for Doubtful Accounts of $3,200, and Retained Earnings of $94,800. During Year 2, $2,900 of accounts receivable were written off as uncollectible. In addition, Edd's Shoe Repair unexpectedly collected $200 of receivables that had been written off in a previous accounting period. Sales on account during Year 2 were $210,000, and cash collections from receivables were $215,000. Uncollectible accounts expense was estimated to be 1 percent of the sales on account for the period.

Required

a. Organize the information in accounts under an accounting equation.

b. Based on the preceding information, compute (after year-end adjustment):

    (1) Balance of Allowance for Doubtful Accounts at December 31, Year 2.

    (2) Balance of Accounts Receivable at December 31, Year 2.

    (3) Net realizable value of Accounts Receivable at December 31, Year 2.

c. What amount of uncollectible accounts expense will Edd's Shoe Repair report for Year 2?

d. Explain how the $200 recovery of receivables affected the accounting equation.

LO 7-2

Exercise 7-7B *Effect of recognizing uncollectible accounts on the financial statements: percent of receivables allowance method*

Juno Inc. experienced the following events for the first two years of its operations:

Year 1:

1. Issued $5,000 of common stock for cash.

2. Provided $80,000 of services on account.

3. Provided $22,000 of services and received cash.

4. Collected $65,000 cash from accounts receivable.

5. Paid $24,000 of salaries expense for the year.

6. Adjusted the accounting records to reflect uncollectible accounts expense for the year. Juno estimates that 5 percent of the ending accounts receivable balance will be uncollectible.

Year 2:

1. Wrote off an uncollectible account of $620.

2. Provided $95,000 of services on account.

3. Provided $15,000 of services and collected cash.

4. Collected $90,000 cash from accounts receivable.

5. Paid $35,000 of salaries expense for the year.

6. Adjusted the accounts to reflect uncollectible accounts expense for the year. Juno estimates that 5 percent of the ending accounts receivable balance will be uncollectible.

Required

a. Organize the transaction data in accounts under an accounting equation.

b. Prepare the income statement, statement of changes in stockholders' equity, balance sheet, and statement of cash flows for Year 1.

c. What is the net realizable value of the accounts receivable at December 31, Year 1?

d. Repeat Requirements a, b, and c for Year 2.

Exercise 7-8B *Accounting for uncollectible accounts: percent of receivables allowance method*

LO 7-2, 7-3

Pollard Service Co. experienced the following transactions for Year 1, its first year of operations:

1. Provided $86,000 of services on account.

2. Collected $72,000 cash from accounts receivable.

3. Paid $39,000 of salaries expense for the year.

4. Pollard adjusted the accounts using the following information from an accounts receivable aging schedule:

Number of Days Past Due	Amount	Percent Likely to Be Uncollectible	Allowance Balance
Current	$7,500	.01	
0–30	2,000	.05	
31–60	1,500	.10	
61–90	1,000	.30	
Over 90 days	2,000	.50	

Required

a. Organize the transaction data in accounts under an accounting equation.

b. Prepare the income statement for Pollard Service Co. for Year 1.

c. What is the net realizable value of the accounts receivable at December 31, Year 1?

Exercise 7-9B *Accounting for uncollectible accounts: direct write-off method*

LO 7-4

Applied Business Systems has a small number of sales on account but is mostly a cash business. Consequently, it uses the direct write-off method to account for uncollectible accounts. During Year 1, Applied Business Systems earned $46,000 of cash revenue and $9,000 of revenue on account. Cash operating expenses were $32,100. After numerous attempts to collect a $325 account receivable from J.C. Mims, the account was determined to be uncollectible in Year 2.

Required

a. Show the effects of (1) cash revenue, (2) revenue on account, (3) cash expenses, and (4) write-off of the uncollectible account on the financial statements using a horizontal statements model like the following one. In the Statement of Cash Flows column, indicate whether the item is an operating activity (OA), investing activity (IA), or financing activity (FA). Use NA to indicate that an element is not affected by the event.

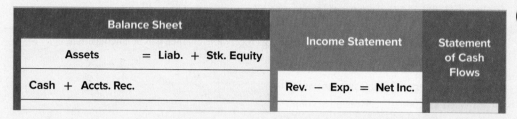

b. What amount of net income did Applied Business Systems report on the Year 1 income statement?

LO 7-1, 7-4

Exercise 7-10B *Accounting for uncollectible accounts: percent of revenue allowance versus direct write-off method*

Classic Auto Parts sells new and used auto parts. Although a majority of its sales are cash sales, it makes a significant amount of credit sales. During Year 1, its first year of operations, Classic Auto Parts experienced the following:

Sales on account	$320,000
Cash sales	680,000
Collections of accounts receivable	295,000
Uncollectible accounts charged off during the year	1,400

Required

a. Assume that Classic Auto Parts uses the allowance method of accounting for uncollectible accounts and estimates that 1 percent of its sales on account will not be collected. Answer the following questions:

   (1) What is the Accounts Receivable balance at December 31, Year 1?
   (2) What is the ending balance of the Allowance for Doubtful Accounts at December 31, Year 1, after all transactions and adjustments are recorded?
   (3) What is the amount of uncollectible accounts expense for Year 1?
   (4) What is the net realizable value of accounts receivable at December 31, Year 1?

b. Assume that Classic Auto Parts uses the direct write-off method of accounting for uncollectible accounts. Answer the following questions:

   (1) What is the Accounts Receivable balance at December 31, Year 1?
   (2) What is the amount of uncollectible accounts expense for Year 1?
   (3) What is the net realizable value of accounts receivable at December 31, Year 1?

LO 7-5

Exercise 7-11B *Accounting for notes receivable*

Cachet Enterprises loaned $30,000 to Craft Co. on September 1, Year 1, for one year at 6 percent interest.

Required

Show the effects of the following transactions in a horizontal statements model like the one shown next.

1. The loan to Craft Co.
2. The adjustment at December 31, Year 1.
3. The adjustment and collection of the note on September 1, Year 2.

	Balance Sheet					Income Statement			Statement of Cash Flows
	Assets			= Liab. +	Stk. Equity				
Date	Cash +	Notes Rec. +	Int. Rec. =		Ret. Earn.	Rev. −	Exp. =	Net Inc.	

LO 7-5

Exercise 7-12B *Notes receivable—accrued interest*

On March 1, Year 1, Taylor's Deli loaned $18,000 to Style Studio for one year at 5 percent interest.

Required

Answer the following questions:

a. What is Taylor's interest income for Year 1?

b. What is Taylor's total amount of receivables at December 31, Year 1?

c. How will the loan and interest be reported on Taylor's Year 1 statement of cash flows?

d. What is Taylor's interest income for Year 2?

e. What is the total amount of cash that Taylor's will collect in Year 2 from Style Studio?

f. How will the loan and interest be reported on Taylor's Year 2 statement of cash flows?

g. What is the total amount of interest Taylor's Deli earned from the loan to Style Studio?

Exercise 7-13B   *Effect of credit card sales on financial statements*   LO 7-6

Advanced Carpet Cleaning provided $76,000 of services during Year 1, its first year of operations. All customers paid for the services with major credit cards. Advanced Carpet submitted the credit card receipts to the credit card company immediately. The credit card company paid Advanced Carpet cash in the amount of face value less a 3 percent service charge.

Required

a. Show the credit card sales and the subsequent collection of accounts receivable in a horizontal statements model like the one shown next. In the Statement of Cash Flows column, indicate whether the item is an operating activity (OA), investing activity (IA), or financing activity (FA). Use NA to indicate that an element is not affected by the event.

Balance Sheet			Income Statement			Statement of Cash Flows
Assets	= Liab.	+ Stk. Equity				
Cash + Accts. Rec.			Rev. − Exp. = Net Inc.			

b. Answer the following questions:

(1) What is the amount of total assets at the end of the accounting period?

(2) What is the amount of revenue reported on the income statement?

(3) What is the amount of cash flow from operating activities reported on the statement of cash flows?

(4) Why would Advanced Carpet Cleaning accept credit cards instead of providing credit directly to its customers? In other words, why would Advanced Carpet be willing to pay 3 percent of sales to have the credit card company handle its sales on account?

Exercise 7-14B   *Recording credit card sales*   LO 7-6

Jung Company accepted credit cards in payment for $8,650 of services performed during March, Year 1. The credit card company charged Jung a 4 percent service fee. The credit card company paid Jung as soon as it received the invoices.

Required

Based on this information alone, what is the amount of net income earned during the month of March?

Exercise 7-15B   *Comprehensive single-cycle problem*   LO 7-1, 7-5, 7-6

The following trial balance was drawn from the accounts of Southern Timber Co. as of December 31, Year 1:

Cash	$16,000
Accounts receivable	18,000
Allowance for doubtful accounts	2,000
Inventory	25,000
Accounts payable	9,200
Common stock	30,000
Retained earnings	17,800

Transactions for Year 2

1. Acquired an additional $20,000 cash from the issue of common stock.

2. Purchased $80,000 of inventory on account.

3. Sold inventory that cost $61,000 for $98,000. Sales were made on account.

4. Wrote off $1,500 of uncollectible accounts.

5. On September 1, Southern loaned $10,000 to Pine Co. The note had a 6 percent interest rate and a one-year term.

6. Paid $24,500 cash for salaries expense.

7. Collected $99,000 cash from accounts receivable.

8. Paid $78,000 cash on accounts payable.

9. Paid a $5,000 cash dividend to the stockholders.

10. Accepted credit cards for sales amounting to $5,000. The cost of goods sold was $3,500. The credit card company charges a 4 percent service charge. The cash has not been received.

11. Estimated uncollectible accounts expense to be 1 percent of sales on account.

12. Recorded the accrued interest at December 31, Year 1.

Required

a. Organize the transaction data in accounts under an accounting equation.

b. Prepare an income statement, statement of changes in stockholders' equity, balance sheet, and statement of cash flows for Year 2.

LO 7-7

Exercise 7-16B *Accounts receivable turnover and average days to collect accounts receivable*

The following information is available for Bradford Inc. and Windsor Inc. at December 31:

Accounts	Bradford	Windsor
Accounts Receivable	$ 92,500	$ 220,200
Allowance for Doubtful Accounts	3,250	8,100
Sales Revenue	716,500	1,978,200

Required

a. What is the accounts receivable turnover for each of the companies?

b. What is the average days to collect the receivables?

c. Assuming both companies use the percent of receivables allowance method, what is the estimated percentage of uncollectible accounts for each company?

PROBLEMS—SERIES B

LO 7-1

Problem 7-17B *Accounting for uncollectible accounts—two cycles using the percent of revenue allowance method*

CHECK FIGURES
c. Ending Accounts
   Receivable, Year 1: $8,000
d. Net Income, Year 2: $31,960

The following transactions apply to Sports Consulting for Year 1, the first year of operation:

1. Issued $5,000 of common stock for cash.

2. Recognized $70,000 of service revenue earned on account.

3. Collected $62,000 from accounts receivable.

4. Adjusted accounts to recognize uncollectible accounts expense. Sports uses the allowance method of accounting for uncollectible accounts and estimates that uncollectible accounts expense will be 2 percent of sales on account.

The following transactions apply to Sports Consulting for Year 2:

1. Recognized $84,000 of service revenue on account.
2. Collected $70,000 from accounts receivable.
3. Determined that $1,100 of the accounts receivable were uncollectible and wrote them off.
4. Collected $200 of an account that had been previously written off.
5. Paid $51,200 cash for operating expenses.
6. Adjusted accounts to recognize uncollectible accounts expense for Year 2. Sports estimates that uncollectible accounts expense will be 1 percent of sales on account.

Required

Complete all the following requirements for Year 1 and Year 2. Complete all requirements for Year 1 prior to beginning the requirements for Year 2.

a. Identify the type of each transaction (asset source, asset use, asset exchange, or claims exchange).
b. Show the effect of each transaction on the elements of the financial statements, using a horizontal statements model like the one shown next. Use + for increase, – for decrease, and NA for not affected. Also, in the Statement of Cash Flows column, indicate whether the item is an operating activity (OA), investing activity (IA), or financing activity (FA). The first transaction is entered as an example.

Event No.	Balance Sheet					Income Statement					Statement of Cash Flows
	Assets	=	Liab.	+	Stk. Equity	Rev.	–	Exp.	=	Net Inc.	
1.	+		NA		+	+		NA		+	NA

c. Organize the transaction data in accounts under an accounting equation.
d. Prepare the income statement, statement of changes in stockholders' equity, balance sheet, and statement of cash flows.

Problem 7-18B *Determination of account balances and their effect on the horizontal statements model: percent of receivables allowance method of accounting for uncollectible accounts*

LO 7-2

During the first year of operation, Year 1, Home Renovation recognized $261,000 of service revenue on account. At the end of Year 1, the accounts receivable balance was $46,300. Even though this is his first year in business, the owner believes he will collect all but about 4 percent of the ending balance.

Required

a. What amount of cash was collected by Home Renovation during Year 1?
b. Assuming the use of an allowance system to account for uncollectible accounts, what amount should Home Renovation record as uncollectible accounts expense in Year 1?
c. Show the effects of the following three transactions on the financial statements by recording the appropriate amounts in a horizontal statements model like the one shown next. In the Statement of Cash Flows column, indicate whether the item is an operating activity (OA), investing activity (IA), or financing activity (FA). Use NA for not affected.
   (1) Record service revenue on account.
   (2) Record collection of accounts receivable.
   (3) Record the event to recognize uncollectible accounts expense.

Balance Sheet					Income Statement					Statement of Cash Flows
Assets		=	Liab.	+	Stk. Equity	Rev.	–	Exp.	=	Net Inc.	
Cash	+	Net Realizable Value of Receivables									

d. What is the net realizable value of receivables at the end of Year 1?

LO 7-1

Problem 7-19B *Determining account balances: percent of revenue allowance method of accounting for uncollectible accounts*

The following information pertains to Kee Cabinet Company's sales on account and accounts receivable:

Accounts Receivable Balance, January 1, Year 2	$ 96,200
Allowance for Doubtful Accounts, January 1, Year 2	6,250
Sales on Account, Year 2	726,000
Cost of Goods Sold, Year 2	473,000
Collections of Accounts Receivable, Year 2	715,000

After several collection attempts, Kee Cabinet Company wrote off $3,100 of accounts that could not be collected. Kee estimates that uncollectible accounts expense will be 0.5 percent of sales on account.

Required

a. Compute the following amounts:

   (1) Using the allowance method, the amount of uncollectible accounts expense for Year 2.

   (2) The net realizable value of receivables at the end of Year 2.

b. Explain why the uncollectible accounts expense amount is different from the amount that was written off as uncollectible.

LO 7-2, 7-3

Problem 7-20B *Accounting for uncollectible accounts: percent of receivables allowance method*

Thorne Inc. experienced the following transactions for Year 1, its first year of operations:

1. Issued common stock for $60,000 cash.
2. Purchased $210,000 of merchandise on account.
3. Sold merchandise that cost $165,000 for $310,000 on account.
4. Collected $288,000 cash from accounts receivable.
5. Paid $190,000 on accounts payable.
6. Paid $46,000 of salaries expense for the year.
7. Paid other operating expenses of $62,000.
8. Thorne adjusted the accounts using the following information from an accounts receivable aging schedule:

Number of Days Past Due	Amount	Percent Likely to Be Uncollectible	Allowance Balance
Current	$15,700	.01	
0–30	8,500	.05	
31–60	4,000	.10	
61–90	2,600	.20	
Over 90 days	1,200	.50	

Required

a. Organize the transaction data in accounts under an accounting equation.

b. Prepare the income statement, statement of changes in stockholders' equity, balance sheet, and statement of cash flows for Thorne Inc. for Year 1.

c. What is the net realizable value of the accounts receivable at December 31, Year 1?

Problem 7-21B *Multistep income statement and balance sheet*   LO 7-1, 7-5

Required

Use the following information to prepare a multistep income statement and a balance sheet for Trias Company for Year 2. (*Hint:* Some of the items will *not* appear on either statement, and ending retained earnings must be calculated.)

Operating Expenses	$ 45,000	Allowance for Doubtful Accounts	$ 6,500
Accounts Payable	48,000	Sales Revenue	350,000
Land	45,000	Uncollectible Accounts Expense	9,600
Dividends	10,000	Accounts Receivable	92,000
Beginning Retained Earnings	120,100	Salaries Payable	10,500
Interest Revenue	12,000	Supplies	4,500
Inventory	105,000	Prepaid Rent	16,000
Notes Receivable (short term)	15,000	Common Stock	60,000
Cash	16,700	Cost of Goods Sold	225,000
Interest Receivable (short term)	2,100	Salaries Expense	61,200
Cash Flow from Investing Activities	(91,600)	Unearned Revenue	40,000

Problem 7-22B *Accounting for notes receivable and uncollectible accounts using the direct write-off method*   LO 7-4, 7-5

The following transactions apply to Cheng Co. for Year 1, its first year of operations:

1. Issued $60,000 of common stock for cash.
2. Provided $94,000 of services on account.
3. Collected $84,500 cash from accounts receivable.
4. Loaned $10,000 to Swan Co. on October 1, Year 1. The note had a one-year term to maturity and a 6 percent interest rate.
5. Paid $41,000 of salaries expense for the year.
6. Paid a $3,000 dividend to the stockholders.
7. Recorded the accrued interest on December 31, Year 1 (see item 4).
8. Determined that $990 of accounts receivable were uncollectible. The company uses the direct write-off method.

Required

a. Show the effects of the preceding transactions in a horizontal statements model like the one shown next.

	Balance Sheet							Income Statement			Statement of Cash Flows
	Assets				=	Stk. Equity					
Event No.	Cash +	Accts. Rec. +	Notes Rec. +	Int. Rec.	=	Com. Stk. +	Ret. Earn.	Rev. −	Exp. =	Net Inc.	

b. Prepare the income statement, balance sheet, and statement of cash flows for Year 1.

Problem 7-23B *Missing information*   LO 7-1, 7-5

The following information comes from the accounts of Legoria Company:

Account Title	Beginning Balance	Ending Balance
Accounts Receivable	$36,000	$32,000
Allowance for Doubtful Accounts	2,000	2,200
Notes Receivable	50,000	50,000
Interest Receivable	2,000	5,000

Required

a. There were $160,000 in sales on account during the accounting period. Write-offs of uncollectible accounts were $1,200. What was the amount of cash collected from accounts receivable? What amount of uncollectible accounts expense was reported on the income statement? What was the net realizable value of receivables at the end of the accounting period?

b. The note has a 6 percent interest rate and 24 months to maturity. What amount of interest revenue was recognized for the year? How much cash was collected for interest?

LO 7-2, 7-6

Problem 7-24B *Accounting for credit card sales and uncollectible accounts: percent of receivables allowance method*

Diamond Supply Company had the following transactions in Year 1:

1. Acquired $50,000 cash from the issue of common stock.
2. Purchased $120,000 of merchandise for cash in Year 1.
3. Sold merchandise that cost $95,000 for $180,000 during the year under the following terms:

$ 50,000	Cash sales
115,000	Credit card sales (Credit card company charges a 3 percent service fee.)
15,000	Sales on account

4. Collected all the amount receivable from the credit card company.
5. Collected $11,300 of accounts receivable.
6. Paid selling and administrative expenses of $51,500.
7. Determined that 5 percent of the ending accounts receivable balance would be uncollectible.

Required

a. Show the effects of each of the transactions on the elements of the financial statements, using a horizontal statements model like the one shown next. Use + for increase, − for decrease, and NA for not affected. The first transaction is entered as an example.

Event No.	Balance Sheet				Income Statement					Statement of Cash Flows
	Assets	=	Liab.	+ Stk. Equity	Rev.	−	Exp.	=	Net Inc.	
1.	+		NA	+	NA		NA		NA	+ FA

b. Prepare an income statement, statement of changes in stockholders' equity, balance sheet, and statement of cash flows for Year 1.

LO 7-4, 7-5, 7-6

Problem 7-25B *Effect of transactions on the elements of financial statements*

Required

Identify each of the following independent transactions as an asset source (AS), asset use (AU), asset exchange (AE), or claims exchange (CE). Also explain how each event affects assets, liabilities, stockholders' equity, net income, and cash flow by placing a + for increase, − for decrease, or NA for not affected under each of the categories. The first event is recorded as an example.

Event	Type of Event	Assets	Liabilities	Common Stock	Retained Earnings	Net Income	Cash Flow
a	AS/AU	+/−	NA	NA	+	+	NA

a. Sold merchandise at a price above cost. Accepted payment by credit card. The credit card company charges a service fee. The receipts have not yet been forwarded to the credit card company.

b. Sold land for cash at its cost.

c. Paid cash to satisfy salaries payable.

d. Submitted receipts to the credit card company (see item *a*) and collected cash.

e. Loaned Carl Maddox cash. The loan had a 5 percent interest rate and a one-year term to maturity.

f. Paid cash to creditors on accounts payable.

g. Accrued three months' interest on the note receivable (see item *e*).

h. Provided services for cash.

i. Paid cash for salaries expense.

j. Provided services on account.

k. Wrote off an uncollectible account (use direct write-off method).

l. Collected cash from customers paying their accounts.

m. Recovered an uncollectible account that was previously written off (assume direct write-off method was used).

n. Paid cash for land.

o. Paid cash for other operating expenses.

Problem 7-26B *Comprehensive accounting cycle problem (uses percent of revenue allowance method)*   LO 7-1, 7-5, 7-6

The following trial balance was prepared for Village Cycle Sales and Service on December 31, Year 1:

Account Title	
Cash	$46,200
Accounts Receivable	21,300
Allowance for Doubtful Accounts	1,350
Inventory	85,600
Accounts Payable	28,000
Common Stock	80,000
Retained Earnings	43,750

Village Cycle had the following transactions in Year 2:

1. Purchased merchandise on account for $260,000.
2. Sold merchandise that cost $243,000 on account for $340,000.
3. Performed $80,000 of services for cash.
4. Sold merchandise for $60,000 to credit card customers. The merchandise cost $41,250. The credit card company charges a 5 percent fee.
5. Collected $348,000 cash from accounts receivable.
6. Paid $265,000 cash on accounts payable.
7. Paid $115,000 cash for selling and administrative expenses.
8. Collected cash for the full amount due from the credit card company (see item 4).
9. Loaned $50,000 to Lee Supply. The note had a 9 percent interest rate and a one-year term to maturity.
10. Wrote off $830 of accounts as uncollectible.
11. Made the following adjustments:
    (a) Recorded three months' interest on the note at December 31, Year 2 (see item 9).
    (b) Estimated uncollectible accounts expense to be .5 percent of sales on account.

Required

a. Organize the transaction data in accounts under an accounting equation.

b. Prepare an income statement, a statement of changes in stockholders' equity, a balance sheet, and a statement of cash flows for Year 2.

ANALYZE, THINK, COMMUNICATE

ATC 7-1 Business Applications Case *Understanding real-world annual reports*

Required

Obtain Target Corporation's annual report for its 2018 fiscal year (year ended February 2, 2019) at http://investors.target.com using the instructions in Appendix B. Anyone who has shopped at Target knows that many of its customers use a credit card to pay for their purchases. There is even a Target brand credit card. However, Target did not report any accounts receivables or credit card receivables on its February 2, 2019 (2018), balance sheet.

a. Review Target's Form 10-K and explain why Target does not report any accounts receivables, even though there is a Target branded credit card.

b. In addition to a Target branded credit card, there is also a Target branded debit card. What percentage of Target's sales are made to customers using a target branded credit card and debit card?

c. In 2018, how much revenue did Target generate from its credit card profit sharing program?

Hint: It will be much easier to answer these questions if you do a word search on Target's Form 10-K rather than trying to find the answers by reading through the report.

ATC 7-2 Group Assignment *Missing information*

The following selected financial information is available for three companies:

	Expo	White	Zina
Total sales	$125,000	$210,000	?
Cash sales	?	26,000	$120,000
Sales on account	40,000	?	75,000
Accounts receivable, January 1, Year 2	6,200	42,000	?
Accounts receivable, December 31, Year 2	5,600	48,000	7,500
Allowance for doubtful accounts, January 1, Year 2	?	?	405
Allowance for doubtful accounts, December 31, Year 2	224	1,680	?
Uncollectible accounts expense, Year 2	242	1,200	395
Uncollectible accounts written off	204	1,360	365
Collections of accounts receivable, Year 2	?	?	75,235

Required

a. Divide the class into three sections and divide each section into groups of three to five students. Assign one of the companies to each of the sections.

Group Tasks

(1) Determine the missing amounts for your company.

(2) Determine the percentage of accounts receivable estimated to be uncollectible at the end of Year 1 and Year 2 for your company.

(3) Determine the percentage of total sales that are sales on account for your company.

(4) Determine the accounts receivable turnover for your company.

Class Discussion

a. Have a representative of each section put the missing information on the board and explain how it was determined.

b. Which company has the highest percentage of sales that are on account?

c. Which company is doing the best job of collecting its accounts receivable? What procedures and policies can a company use to better collect its accounts receivable?

ATC 7-3 Real-World Case *Time needed to collect accounts receivable*

Presented here are the average days to collect accounts receivable for four companies in different industries. The data are for 2017.

Company	Average Days to Collect Accounts Receivable
Boeing (aircraft manufacturer)	41
Ford (auto sales only)	27
Haverty Furniture (furniture retailer)	1
Procter & Gamble (consumer products manufacturer)	26

Required

Write a brief memorandum that provides possible answers to each of the following questions:

a. Why would a company that manufactures and sells airplanes (Boeing) and a company that manufactures and sells automobiles (Ford) collect their accounts receivables in such relatively short times?

b. Why would a company that sells furniture (Haverty) collect its receivables so much quicker than a company that sells toothpaste and soap (Procter & Gamble)?

ATC 7-4 Business Applications Case *Performing ratio analysis using real-world data*

AutoZone, Inc. claims to be the nation's leading auto parts retailer. It sells replacement auto parts directly to the consumer. BorgWarner, Inc. has over 30,000 employees and produces automobile parts, such as transmissions and cooling systems, for the world's vehicle manufacturers. The following data were taken from these companies' 2018 and 2017 annual reports. All dollar amounts are in thousands.

	Fiscal Years Ending	
	AutoZone August 25, 2018	BorgWarner December 31, 2017
Sales	$11,221,077	$9,799,300
Accounts receivable	256,136	1,735,700

Required

a. Before performing any calculations, speculate as to which company will take the longest to collect its accounts receivable. Explain the rationale for your decision.

b. Calculate the accounts receivable turnover ratios for AutoZone and BorgWarner.

c. Calculate the average days to collect accounts receivable for AutoZone and BorgWarner.

d. Do the calculations from Requirements *b* and *c* confirm your speculations in Requirement *a*?

ATC 7-5   Writing Assignment   *Cost of charge sales*

Paul Smith is opening a plumbing supply store in University City. He plans to sell plumbing parts and materials to both wholesale and retail customers. Because contractors (wholesale customers) prefer to charge parts and materials and pay at the end of the month, Paul expects he will have to offer charge accounts. He plans to offer charge sales to the wholesale customers only and to require retail customers to pay with either cash or credit cards. Paul wondered what expenses his business would incur relative to the charge sales and the credit cards.

Required

a. What issues will Paul need to consider if he allows wholesale customers to buy plumbing supplies on account?

b. Write a memo to Paul Smith outlining the potential cost of accepting charge customers. Discuss the difference between the allowance method for uncollectible accounts and the direct write-off method. Also discuss the cost of accepting credit cards.

ATC 7-6   Ethical Dilemma   *How bad can it be?*

Alonzo Saunders owns a small training services company that is experiencing growing pains. The company has grown rapidly by offering liberal credit terms to its customers. Although his competitors require payment for services within 30 days, Saunders permits his customers to delay payment for up to 90 days. Saunders' customers thereby have time to fully evaluate the training that employees receive before they must pay for that training. Saunders guarantees satisfaction. If a customer is unhappy, the customer does not have to pay. Saunders works with reputable companies, provides top-quality training, and rarely encounters dissatisfied customers.

The long collection period, however, has created a cash flow problem. Saunders has a $100,000 accounts receivable balance but needs cash to pay current bills. He has recently negotiated a loan agreement with National Bank of Brighton County that should solve his cash flow problems. The loan agreement requires that Saunders pledge the accounts receivable as collateral for the loan. The bank agreed to loan Saunders 70 percent of the receivables balance, thereby giving him access to $70,000 cash. Saunders is satisfied with this arrangement because he estimates he needs approximately $60,000.

On the day Saunders was to execute the loan agreement, he heard a rumor that his biggest customer was experiencing financial problems and might declare bankruptcy. The customer owed Saunders $45,000. Saunders promptly called the customer's chief accountant and learned "off the record" that the rumor was true. The accountant told Saunders that the company's net worth was negative and most of its assets were pledged as collateral for bank loans. In his opinion, Saunders was unlikely to collect the balance due. Saunders' immediate concern was the impact the circumstances would have on his loan agreement with the bank.

Saunders uses the direct write-off method to recognize uncollectible accounts expense. Removing the $45,000 receivable from the collateral pool would leave only $55,000 of receivables, reducing the available credit to $38,500 ($55,000 × 0.70). Even worse, recognizing the uncollectible accounts expense would so adversely affect his income statement that the bank might further reduce the available credit by reducing the percentage of receivables allowed under the loan agreement. Saunders will have to attest to the quality of the receivables at the date of the loan but reasons that, because the information he obtained about the possible bankruptcy was "off the record," he is under no obligation to recognize the uncollectible accounts expense until the receivable is officially uncollectible.

Required

a. How are income and assets affected by the decision not to act on the bankruptcy information?

b. Review the AICPA's Articles of Professional Conduct (see Chapter 2) and comment on any of the standards that would be violated by the actions Saunders is contemplating.

c. Identify the elements of unethical and criminal conduct recognized in the fraud triangle (see Chapter 2), and explain how they apply to this case.

ATC 7-7 Research Assignment *Comparing Whirlpool Corporation's and Chipotle's time to collect accounts receivable*

Using the most current annual reports or Forms 10-K for Whirlpool Corporation and Chipotle Mexican Grill, Inc., complete the requirements that follow. To obtain the Forms 10-K, use either the EDGAR system, following the instructions in Appendix A, or the companies' websites. The annual reports can be found on the companies' websites.

Required

a. What was Whirlpool's average days to collect accounts receivable? Show your computations.
b. What percentage of accounts receivable did Whirlpool estimate would not be collected?
c. What was Chipotle's average days to collect accounts receivable? Show your computations.
d. What percentage of accounts receivable did Chipotle estimate would not be collected?
e. Briefly explain why Whirlpool would take longer than Chipotle to collect its accounts receivable.

CHAPTER 8

Accounting for Long-Term Operational Assets

LEARNING OBJECTIVES

After you have mastered the material in this chapter, you will be able to:

Video lectures and accompanying self-assessment quizzes are available in *Connect* for all learning objectives.

Tableau Dashboard Activity is available in *Connect* for this chapter.

LO 8-1	Identify and determine the cost of long-term operational assets.
LO 8-2	Calculate straight-line depreciation and show how it affects financial statements.
LO 8-3	Calculate double-declining-balance depreciation and show how it affects financial statements.
LO 8-4	Calculate units-of-production depreciation and show how it affects financial statements.
LO 8-5	Show how gains and losses on disposals of long-term operational assets affect financial statements.
LO 8-6	Identify some of the tax issues that affect long-term operational assets.
LO 8-7	Show how revising estimates affects financial statements.
LO 8-8	Show how continuing expenditures for operational assets affect financial statements.
LO 8-9	Calculate depletion and show how it affects financial statements.
LO 8-10	Identify and determine the cost of intangible assets.
LO 8-11	Show how the amortization of intangible assets affects financial statements.
LO 8-12	Show how expense recognition choices and industry characteristics affect financial performance measures.

CHAPTER OPENING

Companies use assets to produce revenue. Some assets, like inventory or office supplies, are called **current assets** because they are used relatively quickly (within a single accounting period). Other assets, like equipment or buildings, are used for extended periods of time (two or more accounting periods). These assets are called **long-term operational assets.**[1] Accounting for long-term assets raises several questions. For example, what is the cost of the asset? Is it the list price only or should the cost of transportation, transit insurance, setup, and so on be added to the list price? Should the cost of a long-term asset be recognized as expense in the period the asset is purchased or should the cost be expensed over the useful life of the asset? What happens in the accounting records when a long-term asset is retired from use? This chapter answers these questions. It explains accounting for long-term operational assets from the date of purchase through the date of disposal.

The Curious Accountant

Most companies have various types of long-term assets that they use to operate their business. Common types of long-term assets include buildings, machinery, and equipment. But there are other types as well. A major category of long-term assets for a mining company is the mineral reserves from which they extract ore.

Brad Sauter/Shutterstock

Freeport-McMoRan Copper & Gold, Inc. (referred to as FCX) is one of the largest mining operations in the world. It produces copper, gold, and molybdenum from 12 major mines located on four continents. As of December 31, 2017, it owned proven mineral reserves that cost $4.0 billion, as well as buildings, machinery, and equipment that cost $23.4 billion.

As you learned in Chapters 3 and 4, except for land, over time most assets are consumed in a company's efforts to produce revenues, and as they are consumed, the asset account is decreased and an expense account is increased. How do you think the way a mining company uses its buildings and equipment differs from the way it uses its mineral reserves, and how do you think these differences affect the way these assets are accounted for? (Answers on page 394.)

---

[1]Classifying assets as current versus long term is explained in more detail in Chapter 9.

TANGIBLE VERSUS INTANGIBLE ASSETS

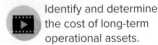

LO 8-1

Identify and determine the cost of long-term operational assets.

Long-term assets may be tangible or intangible. **Tangible assets** have a physical presence; they can be seen and touched. Tangible assets include equipment, machinery, natural resources, and land. In contrast, intangible assets have no physical form. Although they may be represented by physical documents, **intangible assets** are, in fact, rights or privileges. They cannot be seen or touched. For example, a patent represents an exclusive legal *privilege* to produce and sell a particular product. It protects inventors by making it illegal for others to profit by copying their inventions. Although a patent may be represented by legal documents, the privilege is the actual asset. Because the privilege cannot be seen or touched, the patent is an intangible asset.

Tangible Long-Term Assets

Tangible long-term assets are classified as (1) property, plant, and equipment or (2) natural resources.

Property, Plant, and Equipment

Property, plant, and equipment is sometimes called *plant assets* or *fixed assets.* Examples of property, plant, and equipment include furniture, cash registers, machinery, delivery trucks, computers, mechanical robots, buildings, and land. The level of detail used to account for these assets varies. One company may include all office equipment in one account, whereas another company might divide office equipment into computers, desks, chairs, and so on. The term used to recognize expense for consuming plant and equipment is **depreciation.**

While land is normally classified as a component of property, plant, and equipment, it is not subject to depreciation. Land has an infinite life. It is not worn out or consumed as it is used. When buildings or other assets are purchased simultaneously with land, the amount paid must be divided between the land and the other assets because of the nondepreciable nature of the land.

Natural Resources

Mineral deposits, oil and gas reserves, timber stands, coal mines, and stone quarries are examples of **natural resources.** Conceptually, natural resources are inventories. When sold, the cost of these assets is frequently expensed as *cost of goods sold.* Although inventories are usually classified as short-term assets, natural resources are normally classified as long term because the resource deposits generally have long lives. For example, it may take decades to extract all of the diamonds from a diamond mine. The term used to recognize expense for natural resources is **depletion.**

Intangible Assets

Intangible assets fall into two categories, those with *identifiable useful lives* and those with *indefinite useful lives.*

Intangible Assets with Identifiable Useful Lives

Intangible assets with identifiable useful lives include patents and copyrights. These assets may become obsolete (a patent may become worthless if new technology provides a superior product) or may reach the end of their legal lives. The term used when recognizing expense for intangible assets with identifiable useful lives is called **amortization**.

Intangible Assets with Indefinite Useful Lives

The benefits of some intangible assets may extend so far into the future that their useful lives cannot be estimated. For how many years will the Coca-Cola trademark attract customers? When will the value of a McDonald's franchise end? There are no answers to these questions.

Intangible assets such as renewable franchises, trademarks, and goodwill have indefinite useful lives. The costs of such assets are not expensed unless the value of the assets becomes impaired.

DETERMINING THE COST OF LONG-TERM ASSETS

The **historical cost concept** requires that an asset be recorded at the amount paid for it. This amount includes the purchase price plus any costs necessary to get the asset in the location and condition for its intended use. Common cost components are:

- **Buildings:** (1) purchase price, (2) sales taxes, (3) title search and transfer document costs, (4) realtor's and attorney's fees, and (5) remodeling costs.
- **Land:** (1) purchase price, (2) sales taxes, (3) title search and transfer document costs, (4) realtor's and attorney's fees, (5) costs for removal of old buildings, and (6) grading costs.
- **Equipment:** (1) purchase price (less discounts), (2) sales taxes, (3) delivery costs, (4) installation costs, and (5) costs to adapt for intended use.

The cost of an asset does not include payments for fines, damages, and so on that could have been avoided.

 CHECK YOURSELF 8.1

Sheridan Construction Company purchased a new bulldozer that had a $260,000 list price. The seller agreed to allow a 4 percent cash discount in exchange for immediate payment. The bulldozer was delivered FOB shipping point at a cost of $1,200. Sheridan hired a new employee to operate the dozer for an annual salary of $36,000. The employee was trained to operate the dozer for a one-time training fee of $800. The cost of the company's theft insurance policy increased by $300 per year as a result of adding the dozer to the policy. The dozer had a five-year useful life and an expected salvage value of $26,000. Determine the asset's cost.

Answer

List price	$260,000
Less: Cash discount ($260,000 × 0.04)	(10,400)
Shipping cost	1,200
Training cost	800
Total asset cost (amount capitalized)	$251,600

Basket Purchase Allocation

Acquiring a group of assets in a single transaction is known as a **basket purchase.** The total price of a basket purchase must be allocated among the assets acquired. Accountants commonly allocate the purchase price using the **relative market value method.** To illustrate, assume that Beatty Company purchased land and a building for $240,000 cash. A real estate appraiser determined the market value of each asset to be

Building	$270,000
Land	90,000
Total	$360,000

The appraisal indicates that the land is worth 25 percent ($90,000 ÷ $360,000) of the total value and the building is worth 75 percent ($270,000 ÷ $360,000). Using these percentages, the actual purchase price is allocated as follows:

Building	0.75 × $240,000 =	$180,000
Land	0.25 × $240,000 =	60,000
Total		$240,000

METHODS OF RECOGNIZING DEPRECIATION EXPENSE

The life cycle of an operational asset involves (1) acquiring the funds to buy the asset, (2) purchasing the asset, (3) using the asset, and (4) retiring (disposing of) the asset. These stages are illustrated in Exhibit 8.1. The stages involving (1) acquiring funds and (2) purchasing assets have been discussed previously. This section of the chapter describes how accountants recognize the *use* of assets (Stage 3). As they are used, assets suffer from wear and tear called *depreciation*. Ultimately, assets depreciate to the point that they are no longer useful in the process of earning revenue. This process usually takes several years. The amount of an asset's cost that is allocated to expense during an accounting period is called **depreciation expense.**

An asset that is fully depreciated by one company may still be useful to another company. For example, a rental car that is no longer useful to Hertz may still be useful to a local delivery company. As a result, companies are frequently able to sell their fully depreciated assets to other companies or individuals. The expected market value of a fully depreciated asset is called its **salvage value.** The total amount of depreciation a company recognizes for an asset, its **depreciable cost,** is the difference between its original cost and its salvage value.

For example, assume a company purchases an asset for $5,000. The company expects to use the asset for 5 years (the **estimated useful life**) and then to sell it for $1,000 (salvage value). The depreciable cost of the asset is $4,000 ($5,000 − $1,000). The portion of the depreciable cost ($4,000) that represents its annual usage is recognized as depreciation expense.

Accountants must exercise judgment to estimate the amount of depreciation expense to recognize each period. For example, suppose you own a personal computer. You know how much the computer cost, and you know you will eventually need to replace it. How would you determine the amount the computer depreciates each year you use it? Businesses may use any of several acceptable methods to estimate the amount of depreciation expense to recognize each year.

The method used to recognize depreciation expense should match the asset's usage pattern. More expense should be recognized in periods when the asset is used more, and less in periods when the asset is used less. Because assets are used to produce revenue, matching expense recognition with asset usage also matches expense recognition with revenue recognition. Three alternative methods for recognizing depreciation expense are (1) straight-line, (2) double-declining-balance, and (3) units-of-production.

The *straight-line* method produces the same amount of depreciation expense each accounting period. *Double-declining-balance,* an accelerated method, produces more depreciation expense in the early years of an asset's life, with a declining amount of expense in later years. *Units-of-production* produces varying amounts of depreciation expense in different accounting periods (more in some accounting periods and less in others). Exhibit 8.2 contrasts the different depreciation methods that U.S. companies use.

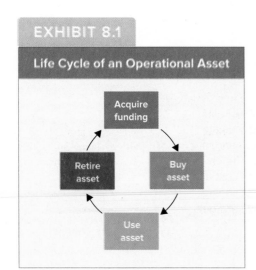

EXHIBIT 8.1

Life Cycle of an Operational Asset

Acquire funding

Buy asset

Use asset

Retire asset

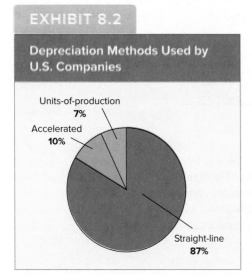

EXHIBIT 8.2

Depreciation Methods Used by U.S. Companies

Units-of-production 7%

Accelerated 10%

Straight-line 87%

The chart is based on data drawn from recent annual reports published by the 30 companies that comprise the Dow Jones Industrial Average. The percentages add to more than 100% because one company used two depreciation methods and therefore was included in two categories.

Dryden Enterprises Illustration

To illustrate the different depreciation methods, consider a van purchased by Dryden Enterprises. Dryden plans to use the van as rental property. The van had a list price of $23,500. Dryden obtained a 10 percent cash discount from the dealer. The van was delivered FOB shipping point, and Dryden paid an additional $250 for transportation costs. Dryden also paid $2,600 for a custom accessory package to increase the van's appeal as a rental vehicle. The cost of the van is computed as follows:

List price	$23,500	
Less: Cash discount	(2,350)	$23,500 × 0.10
Plus: Transportation costs	250	
Plus: Cost of customization	2,600	
Total	$24,000	

The van has an estimated *salvage value* of $4,000 and an *estimated useful life* of four years. The following section examines three different patterns of expense recognition for this van.

STRAIGHT-LINE DEPRECIATION

The first scenario assumes the van is used evenly over its four-year life. The revenue from renting the van is assumed to be $8,000 per year. The matching concept calls for the expense recognition pattern to match the revenue stream. Because the same amount of revenue is recognized in each accounting period, Dryden should use **straight-line depreciation** because it produces equal amounts of depreciation expense each year.

LO 8-2

Calculate straight-line depreciation and show how it affects financial statements.

EVENT 1 Issued common stock to acquire cash.

The first phase of the asset life cycle is to acquire funds to purchase the asset. Assume Dryden acquired $25,000 cash on January 1, Year 1, by issuing common stock. The effects on the financial statements are shown next:

Balance Sheet						Income Statement				Statement of Cash Flows
Assets			=	Stk. Equity						
Cash	+	Book Value of Van	=	Com. Stk.	+	Ret. Earn.	Rev.	−	Exp.	=	Net Inc.	
25,000	+	NA	=	25,000	+	NA	NA	−	NA	=	NA	25,000 FA

EVENT 2 Paid cash to purchase a van.

The second phase of the life cycle is to purchase the van. Assume Dryden bought the van on January 1, Year 1, using funds from the stock issue. The cost of the van, previously computed, was $24,000 cash. The effects on the financial statements are shown next:

Balance Sheet						Income Statement				Statement of Cash Flows
Assets			=	Stk. Equity						
Cash	+	Book Value of Van	=	Com. Stk.	+	Ret. Earn.	Rev.	−	Exp.	=	Net Inc.	
(24,000)	+	24,000	=	NA	+	NA	NA	−	NA	=	NA	(24,000) IA

In the third phase of the life cycle of an asset, revenue is generated through the use of the asset. We will label the generation of revenue Event 3a and the use of the asset Event 3b. Although illustrated only once, these effects occur four times—once for each year Dryden earns revenue by renting the van.

EVENT 3a   Earned cash revenue by renting the van.

Dryden used the van by renting it to customers. The rent revenue each year is $8,000 cash. The effects on the financial statements are shown next:

Balance Sheet						Income Statement				Statement of Cash Flows
Assets			=	Stk. Equity						
Cash	+	Book Value of Van	=	Com. Stk.	+	Ret. Earn.	Rev.	−	Exp.	=	Net Inc.	
8,000	+	NA	=	NA	+	8,000	8,000	−	NA	=	8,000	8,000 OA

EVENT 3b   Adjusted records to show that the van is being consumed in the process of earning revenue.

Dryden's van will not last forever. Indeed, the van will experience wear and tear as it is being used by customers. Eventually, the van will become so dilapidated that customers will no longer be willing to rent it. The gradual deterioration in the usefulness of the van is called depreciation. Dryden adjusts its accounts at the end of each accounting period to recognize depreciation expense (consumption of the asset). When an asset is assumed to be used (consumed) equally during each year of its useful life, an equal amount of depreciation expense is recognized each year. The technique used to determine an equal amount of expense recognition is called the *straight-line method*. The amount of straight-line depreciation expense recognized for the van is calculated as follows:

$$\text{(Asset cost} - \text{Salvage value)} \div \text{Useful life} = \text{Depreciation expense}$$
$$(\$24,000 - \$4,000) \quad \div \quad 4 \text{ years} \quad = \quad \$5,000 \text{ per year}$$

Recognizing depreciation expense is an asset use transaction that reduces assets and stockholders' equity. The asset reduction is reported using a **contra asset account** called **Accumulated Depreciation**. The **book value** of a long-term tangible asset is determined by subtracting the balance in the Accumulated Depreciation account from the balance in the associated asset account. The book value may also be called the **carrying value**.

While recognizing depreciation expense decreases net income, it *does not affect cash flow*. The $24,000 cash outflow occurred in January, Year 1, when Dryden purchased the van. In contrast, the $5,000 depreciation expense is recognized each year as the van is used. The December 31, Year 1, effects on the financial statements are shown next:

Balance Sheet						Income Statement				Statement of Cash Flows
Assets			=	Stk. Equity						
Cash	+	Book Value of Van	=	Com. Stk.	+	Ret. Earn.	Rev.	−	Exp.	=	Net Inc.	
NA	+	(5,000)	=	NA	+	(5,000)	NA	−	5,000	=	(5,000)	NA

The book value of the van as of December 31, Year 1, is $19,000, computed as shown:

Van	$24,000
Accumulated depreciation	(5,000)
Book value	$19,000

Recall that expense accounts reflect information occurring during a single accounting period. In this case, Dryden will recognize $5,000 of depreciation expense each year of the asset's useful life. As a result, the Depreciation Expense account will never have a balance that is larger than $5,000. In contrast, the Accumulated Depreciation account is a balance sheet account. As its name implies, the total amount in the Accumulated Depreciation account increases (accumulates) each time depreciation expense is recognized. For example, at the end of Year 2, Dryden will recognize $5,000 of depreciation expense and the balance in the Accumulated Depreciation account will increase to $10,000. At the end of Year 3, Dryden will recognize $5,000 of depreciation expense and increase the balance in the Accumulated Depreciation account to $15,000, and so on.

Financial Statements

Exhibit 8.3 contains the financial statements for the Dryden illustration from Year 1 through Year 4. Study the exhibit until you understand how all the figures were derived. The amount of depreciation expense ($5,000) reported on the income statement is constant each year from Year 1 through Year 4. The amount of accumulated depreciation reported on the balance sheet grows from $5,000 to $10,000, to $15,000, and finally to $20,000. The Accumulated Depreciation account is a *contra asset account* that is subtracted from the Van account in determining total assets.

EXHIBIT 8.3	Financial Statements under Straight-Line Depreciation			
DRYDEN ENTERPRISES Financial Statements				
	Year 1	**Year 2**	**Year 3**	**Year 4**
Income Statements				
Rent revenue	$ 8,000	$ 8,000	$ 8,000	$ 8,000
Depreciation expense	(5,000)	(5,000)	(5,000)	(5,000)
Net income	$ 3,000	$ 3,000	$ 3,000	$ 3,000
Balance Sheets				
Assets				
Cash	$ 9,000	$17,000	$25,000	$33,000
Van	24,000	24,000	24,000	24,000
Accumulated depreciation	(5,000)	(10,000)	(15,000)	(20,000)
Total assets	$28,000	$31,000	$34,000	$37,000
Stockholders' equity				
Common stock	$25,000	$25,000	$25,000	$25,000
Retained earnings	3,000	6,000	9,000	12,000
Total stockholders' equity	$28,000	$31,000	$34,000	$37,000
Statements of Cash Flows				
Operating Activities				
Inflow from customers	$ 8,000	$ 8,000	$ 8,000	$ 8,000
Investing Activities				
Outflow to purchase van	(24,000)			
Financing Activities				
Inflow from stock issue	25,000			
Net Change in Cash	9,000	8,000	8,000	8,000
Beginning cash balance	0	9,000	17,000	25,000
Ending cash balance	$ 9,000	$17,000	$25,000	$33,000

Notice the differences between cash flow from operating activities and the income statement. For example, in Year 1 Dryden paid $24,000 cash to purchase the van. However, only $5,000 of this cost is shown as an operating expense on the income statement. Further, there is no effect on cash flow from operating activities. Instead, the entire $24,000 cash outflow is shown as an investing activity. These differences highlight the fact that cash flow from operating activities and the income statement are purposefully designed to inform users about different aspects of the business's operations.

DOUBLE-DECLINING-BALANCE DEPRECIATION

LO 8-3

Calculate double-declining-balance depreciation and show how it affects financial statements.

Guy Sagi/123RF

For the second scenario, assume demand for the van is strong when it is new, but fewer people rent the van as it ages. As a result, the van produces smaller amounts of revenue as time goes by. To match expenses with revenues, it is reasonable to recognize more depreciation expense in the van's early years and less as it ages.

Double-declining-balance depreciation produces a large amount of depreciation in the first year of an asset's life and progressively smaller levels of expense in each succeeding year. Because the double-declining-balance method recognizes depreciation expense more rapidly than the straight-line method does, it is called an **accelerated depreciation method**. Depreciation expense recognized using double-declining-balance is computed in three steps.

1. *Determine the straight-line rate.* Divide one by the asset's useful life. Because the estimated useful life of Dryden's van is four years, the straight-line rate is 25 percent ($1 \div 4$) per year.

2. *Determine the double-declining-balance rate.* Multiply the straight-line rate by 2 (*double* the rate). The double-declining-balance rate for the van is 50 percent (25 percent $\times$ 2).

3. *Determine the depreciation expense.* Multiply the double-declining-balance rate by the book value of the asset *at the beginning of the period* (recall that book value is historical cost minus *accumulated depreciation*). The following table shows the amount of depreciation expense that Dryden will recognize over the van's useful life (Year 1 — Year 4).

Year	Book Value at Beginning of Period	×	Double the Straight-Line Rate	=	Annual Depreciation Expense	
Year 1	($24,000 − $ 0)	×	0.50	=	$12,000	
Year 2	(24,000 − 12,000)	×	0.50	=	6,000	
Year 3	(24,000 − 18,000)	×	0.50	=	~~3,000~~	2,000
Year 4	(24,000 − 20,000)	×	0.50	=	~~2,000~~	0

Regardless of the depreciation method used, *an asset cannot be depreciated below its salvage value.* This restriction affects depreciation computations for the third and fourth years. Because the van had a cost of $24,000 and a salvage value of $4,000, the total amount of depreciable cost (historical cost − salvage value) is $20,000 ($24,000 − $4,000). Because $18,000 ($12,000 + $6,000) of the depreciable cost is recognized in the first two years, only $2,000 ($20,000 − $18,000) remains to be recognized after the second year. Depreciation expense recognized in the third year is therefore $2,000 even though double-declining-balance computations suggest that $3,000 should be recognized. Similarly, zero depreciation expense is recognized in the fourth year even though the computations indicate a $2,000 charge.

Effects on the Financial Statements

Exhibit 8.4 displays financial statements for the life of the asset assuming Dryden uses double-declining-balance depreciation. The illustration assumes a cash revenue stream of $15,000, $9,000, $5,000, and $3,000 for Year 1, Year 2, Year 3, and Year 4, respectively. Trace the depreciation expense from the preceding table to the income statements. Reported depreciation expense is greater in the earlier years, and smaller in the later years of the asset's life.

The double-declining-balance method smooths the amount of net income reported over the asset's useful life. In the early years, when heavy asset use produces higher revenue, depreciation expense is also higher. Similarly, in the later years, lower levels of revenue are matched with lower levels of depreciation expense. Net income is constant at $3,000 per year.

The depreciation method a company uses *does not* affect how it acquires the financing, invests the funds, and retires the asset. For Dryden's van, the accounting effects of these life cycle phases are the same as under the straight-line approach. Except for the amount of depreciation expense recognized, financial statement effects are the same regardless of the depreciation method used.

EXHIBIT 8.4	Financial Statements under Double-Declining-Balance Depreciation

DRYDEN ENTERPRISES
Financial Statements

	Year 1	Year 2	Year 3	Year 4
Income Statements				
Rent revenue	$15,000	$ 9,000	$ 5,000	$ 3,000
Depreciation expense	(12,000)	(6,000)	(2,000)	0
Net income	$ 3,000	$ 3,000	$ 3,000	$ 3,000
Balance Sheets				
Assets				
Cash	$16,000	$25,000	$30,000	$33,000
Van	24,000	24,000	24,000	24,000
Accumulated depreciation	(12,000)	(18,000)	(20,000)	(20,000)
Total assets	$28,000	$31,000	$34,000	$37,000
Stockholders' equity				
Common stock	$25,000	$25,000	$25,000	$25,000
Retained earnings	3,000	6,000	9,000	12,000
Total stockholders' equity	$28,000	$31,000	$34,000	$37,000
Statements of Cash Flows				
Operating Activities				
Inflow from customers	$15,000	$ 9,000	$ 5,000	$ 3,000
Investing Activities				
Outflow to purchase van	(24,000)			
Financing Activities				
Inflow from stock issue	25,000			
Net Change in Cash	16,000	9,000	5,000	3,000
Beginning cash balance	0	16,000	25,000	30,000
Ending cash balance	$16,000	$25,000	$30,000	$33,000

CHECK YOURSELF 8.2

Olds Company purchased an asset that cost $36,000 on January 1, Year 1. The asset had an expected useful life of five years and an estimated salvage value of $5,000. Assuming Olds uses the double-declining-balance method, determine the amount of depreciation expense and the amount of accumulated depreciation Olds would report on the Year 3 financial statements.

Answer

Year	Book Value at Beginning of Period	×	Double the Straight-Line Rate*	=	Annual Depreciation Expense
Year 1	($36,000 – $ 0)	×	0.40	=	$14,400
Year 2	(36,000 – 14,400)	×	0.40	=	8,640
Year 3	(36,000 – 23,040)	×	0.40	=	5,184
Total accumulated depreciation at December 31, Year 3					$28,224

*Double-declining-balance rate = 2 × Straight-line rate = 2 × (1 ÷ 5 years) = 0.40

UNITS-OF-PRODUCTION DEPRECIATION

LO 8-4

Calculate units-of-production depreciation and show how it affects financial statements.

Suppose rental demand for Dryden's van depends on general economic conditions. In a robust economy, travel increases, and demand for renting vans is high. In a stagnant economy, demand for van rentals declines. In such circumstances, revenues fluctuate from year to year. To accomplish the matching objective, depreciation should also fluctuate from year to year. A method of depreciation known as **units-of-production depreciation** accomplishes this goal by basing depreciation expense on actual asset usage.

Computing depreciation expense using units-of-production begins with identifying a measure of the asset's productive capacity. For example, the number of miles Dryden expects its van to be driven may be a reasonable measure of its productive capacity. If the depreciable asset were a saw, an appropriate measure of productive capacity could be the number of board feet the saw was expected to cut during its useful life. In other words, the basis for measuring production depends on the nature of the depreciable asset.

To illustrate computing depreciation using the units-of-production depreciation method, assume that Dryden measures productive capacity based on the total number of miles the van will be driven over its useful life. Assume Dryden estimates this productive capacity to be 100,000 miles. The first step in determining depreciation expense is to compute the cost per unit of production. For Dryden's van, this amount is total depreciable cost (historical cost − salvage value) divided by total units of expected productive capacity (100,000 miles). The depreciation cost per mile is therefore $0.20 [($24,000 cost − $4,000 salvage) ÷ 100,000 miles]. Annual depreciation expense is computed by multiplying the cost per mile by the number of miles driven. Odometer readings indicate the van was driven 40,000 miles, 20,000 miles, 30,000 miles, and 15,000 miles in Year 1, Year 2, Year 3, and Year 4, respectively. Based on these data, Dryden developed the following schedule of depreciation charges:

Year	Cost per Mile (a)	Miles Driven (b)	Depreciation Expense (a × b)
Year 1	$.20	40,000	$8,000
Year 2	.20	20,000	4,000
Year 3	.20	30,000	6,000
Year 4	.20	15,000	~~3,000~~ 2,000

As pointed out in the discussion of the double-declining-balance method, an asset cannot be depreciated below its salvage value. Because $18,000 of the $20,000 ($24,000 cost − $4,000 salvage) depreciable cost is recognized in the first three years of using the van, only $2,000 ($20,000 − $18,000) remains to be charged to depreciation in the fourth year, even though the depreciation computations suggest the charge should be $3,000. As the preceding table indicates, the general formula for computing units-of-production depreciation is

$$\frac{\text{Cost − Salvage value}}{\text{Total estimated units of production}} \times \begin{array}{c}\text{Units of production}\\ \text{in current}\\ \text{year}\end{array} = \begin{array}{c}\text{Annual}\\ \text{depreciation}\\ \text{expense}\end{array}$$

Exhibit 8.5 displays financial statements that assume Dryden uses units-of-production depreciation. The exhibit assumes a cash revenue stream of $11,000, $7,000, $9,000, and $5,000 for Year 1, Year 2, Year 3, and Year 4, respectively. Trace the depreciation expense from the preceding schedule to the income statements. Depreciation expense is greater in years the van is driven more, and smaller in years the van is driven less, providing a reasonable matching of depreciation expense with revenue produced. Net income is again constant at $3,000 per year.

EXHIBIT 8.5   Financial Statements under Units-of-Production Depreciation

DRYDEN ENTERPRISES
Financial Statements

	Year 1	Year 2	Year 3	Year 4
Income Statements				
Rent revenue	$11,000	$ 7,000	$ 9,000	$ 5,000
Depreciation expense	(8,000)	(4,000)	(6,000)	(2,000)
Net income	$ 3,000	$ 3,000	$ 3,000	$ 3,000
Balance Sheets				
Assets				
Cash	$12,000	$19,000	$28,000	$33,000
Van	24,000	24,000	24,000	24,000
Accumulated depreciation	(8,000)	(12,000)	(18,000)	(20,000)
Total assets	$28,000	$31,000	$34,000	$37,000
Stockholders' equity				
Common stock	$25,000	$25,000	$25,000	$25,000
Retained earnings	3,000	6,000	9,000	12,000
Total stockholders' equity	$28,000	$31,000	$34,000	$37,000
Statements of Cash Flows				
Operating Activities				
Inflow from customers	$11,000	$ 7,000	$ 9,000	$ 5,000
Investing Activities				
Outflow to purchase van	(24,000)			
Financing Activities				
Inflow from stock issue	25,000			
Net Change in Cash	12,000	7,000	9,000	5,000
Beginning cash balance	0	12,000	19,000	28,000
Ending cash balance	$12,000	$19,000	$28,000	$33,000

ACCOUNTING FOR THE DISPOSAL OF LONG-TERM OPERATIONAL ASSETS

LO 8-5

Show how gains and losses on disposals of long-term operational assets affect financial statements.

Regardless of which method of depreciation a company chooses to use, the van will ultimately cease to be useful for the purpose of generating revenue. At this point, the company will have to dispose of the asset. To illustrate accounting for the disposal of the asset, assume Dryden retires the van from service and sells it on January 1, Year 5, for $4,500 cash. On this date, the van's book value is $4,000 ($24,000 cost − $20,000 accumulated depreciation). Under these circumstances, Dryden would recognize a $500 gain ($4,500 sales price − $4,000 book value) on the sale.

Like revenue, gains benefit the stockholders. In this case, assets and stockholders' equity increase. More specifically, the Cash account increases by $4,500, the book value of the van decreases by $4,000 ($24,000 Van account − $20,000 Accumulated Depreciation account) and Retained Earnings increases by $500. The gain increases the amount of net income. Because selling vans is not part of Dryden's normal operations, the gain will be reported separately, after operating income, on the income statement. The amount of the gain is not reported on the statement of cash flows. Instead, the entire $4,500 is shown in the statement of cash flows as an inflow from investing activities. The effects on financial statements are shown next.

Balance Sheet						Income Statement				Statement of Cash Flows
Assets			=	Stk. Equity						
Cash	+	Book Value of Van	=	Com. Stk.	+	Ret. Earn.	Rev./ Gain	−	Exp./ Loss	=	Net Inc.	
4,500	+	(4,000)	=	NA	+	500	500	−	NA	=	500	4,500 IA

Comparing the Depreciation Methods

The total amount of depreciation expense Dryden recognized using each of the three methods was $20,000 ($24,000 cost − $4,000 salvage value). The different methods affect the *timing*, but not the *total amount*, of expense recognized. The different methods simply assign the $20,000 to different accounting periods. Exhibit 8.6 presents graphically the differences among the three depreciation methods discussed earlier. A company should use the method that most closely matches expenses with revenues.

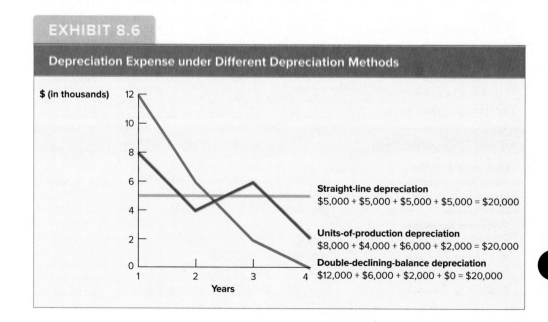

EXHIBIT 8.6

Depreciation Expense under Different Depreciation Methods

Straight-line depreciation
$5,000 + $5,000 + $5,000 + $5,000 = $20,000

Units-of-production depreciation
$8,000 + $4,000 + $6,000 + $2,000 = $20,000

Double-declining-balance depreciation
$12,000 + $6,000 + $2,000 + $0 = $20,000

INCOME TAX CONSIDERATIONS

The matching principle is not relevant to income tax reporting. The objective of tax reporting is to minimize tax expense. For tax purposes, the most desirable depreciation method is the one that produces the highest amount of depreciation expense. Higher expenses mean lower taxes.

The maximum depreciation currently allowed by tax law is computed using an accelerated depreciation method known as the **modified accelerated cost recovery system (MACRS).** MACRS specifies the useful life for designated categories of assets. For example, under the law, companies must base depreciation computations for automobiles, light trucks, technological equipment, and other similar asset types on a 5-year useful life. In contrast, a 7-year life must be used for office furniture, fixtures, and many types of conventional machinery. The law classifies depreciable property, excluding real estate, into one of six categories: 3-year property, 5-year property, 7-year property, 10-year property, 15-year property, and 20-year property. Tables have been established for each category that specify the percentage of cost that can be expensed (deducted) in determining the amount of taxable income. A tax table for 5- and 7-year property is shown next as an example.

Year	5-Year Property, %	7-Year Property, %
1	20.00	14.29
2	32.00	24.49
3	19.20	17.49
4	11.52	12.49
5	11.52	8.93
6	5.76	8.92
7		8.93
8		4.46

The amount of depreciation a company can deduct each year for tax purposes is determined by multiplying the cost of a depreciable asset by the percentage shown in the table. For example, the depreciation expense for Year 1 of a 7-year property asset is the cost of the asset multiplied by 14.29 percent. Depreciation for Year 2 is the cost multiplied by 24.49 percent.

The tables present some apparent inconsistencies. For example, if MACRS is an accelerated depreciation method, why is less depreciation permitted in Year 1 than in Years 2 and 3? Also, why is depreciation computed in Year 6 for property with a 5-year life, and in Year 8 for property with a 7-year life? These conditions are the consequence of using the **half-year convention.**

The half-year convention is designed to simplify computing taxable income. Instead of requiring taxpayers to calculate depreciation from the exact date of purchase to the exact date of disposal, the tax code requires one-half year's depreciation to be charged in the year in which an asset is acquired and one-half year's depreciation in the final year of depreciation. As a result, the percentages shown in the table for the first and last years represent depreciation for one-half year instead of the actual time of usage.

To illustrate computing depreciation using MACRS, assume that Wilson Company purchased furniture (7-year property) for $10,000 cash on July 21. Tax depreciation charges over the useful life of the asset are computed as shown:

Year	Table Factor, %	×	Cost	=	Depreciation Amount
1	14.29		$10,000		$ 1,429
2	24.49		10,000		2,449
3	17.49		10,000		1,749
4	12.49		10,000		1,249
5	8.93		10,000		893
6	8.92		10,000		892
7	8.93		10,000		893
8	4.46		10,000		446
Total over useful life					$10,000

FOCUS ON INTERNATIONAL ISSUES

As you have learned, U.S. GAAP requires companies to use historical cost when accounting for property, plant, and equipment (PPE). Once a company begins depreciating its buildings and equipment, expenses increase (due to depreciation expense), which causes net income and retained earnings to decrease. This, of course, ignores the revenue the company hopes to generate by using the asset.

Under IFRS, a company has two options regarding accounting of PPE. First, it can use a historical cost accounting method that is virtually identical to that required by U.S. GAAP. Second, it can use the "revaluation model," which reports PPE at its fair value. There can be different ways of determining fair value, but the preferred approach is to base fair value on a market-based appraisal, performed by professional appraisers. These revaluations must be conducted frequently enough that the fair value of an asset is not materially different from its recorded book value.

Skip Nall/Digital Vision/Getty Images

Basically, the revaluation model works as follows. The company periodically compares the current book value of its PPE to the fair value at that same date. This fair value relates to the value of the used asset, not the amount required to replace it with a new asset. If the fair value of an asset is higher than its currently recorded book value, the recorded amount for the asset is increased, which increases total assets. However, the increase in the asset's fair value is *not* reported on the company's income statement, as would a gain from selling the asset. Rather, the increase is reported in a special section of stockholders' equity, which balances the increase that was recorded for assets. But, if the new fair value is *lower* than the asset's current book value, the decrease is charged to net income, as well as to assets. This is another example of the conservatism principle at work. Not surprisingly, there are exceptions to these rules. Once a new fair value is established, future depreciation expense is based on these values.

One concern might be that companies, hoping to manipulate earnings, would pick and choose some assets to account for under historical costs and others to account for under the revaluation model. This is not permitted. Although a company does not have to use a single method for all its assets, it must use a single method for all the assets in a given class of assets. For example, historical costs could be used for all factory equipment, and the revaluation model used for all its buildings.

As significant as the difference between the historical cost method and the fair value approach might be, the majority of companies continue to use historical costs. Professors H. B. Christensen and V. Nikolaev conducted a study of the use of revaluation accounting for nonfinancial assets by companies in Germany and the United Kingdom. Their research found that only 3.2 percent of the 1,539 companies surveyed used the revaluation model for property, plant, and equipment.*

*Source: Christensen, H. B. and Nikolaev, V., "Who Uses Fair Value Accounting for Nonfinancial Assets after IFRS Adoption?" The University of Chicago Booth School of Business Working Paper No. 09-12, February 2009.

As an alternative to MACRS, the tax code permits using straight-line depreciation. For certain types of assets such as real property (Buildings), the tax code requires using straight-line depreciation.

There is no requirement that depreciation methods used for financial reporting be consistent with those used in preparing the income tax return. For example, a company may use straight-line depreciation in its financial statements and MACRS for the tax return. A company making this choice would reduce taxes in the early years of an asset's life because it would report higher depreciation charges on the tax return than in the financial statements. In later years, however, taxes will be higher because, under MACRS, the amount of depreciation declines as the asset becomes older. Taxes are delayed but not avoided. The amount of taxes delayed for future payment represent a **deferred tax liability.** Delaying tax payments is advantageous. During the delay period, the money that would have been used to pay taxes can be used instead to make revenue-generating investments.

REVISION OF ESTIMATES

LO 8-7

Show how revising estimates affects financial statements.

In order to report useful financial information on a timely basis, accountants must make many estimates of future results, such as the salvage value and useful life of depreciable assets. Estimates are frequently revised when new information surfaces. Because revisions of estimates are common, generally accepted accounting principles call for incorporating the revised information into present and future calculations. Prior reports are not corrected.

To illustrate, assume that McGraw Company purchased a machine on January 1, Year 1, for $50,000. McGraw estimated the machine would have a useful life of 8 years and a salvage value of $3,000. Using the straight-line method, McGraw determined the annual depreciation charge as follows:

$$(\$50{,}000 - \$3{,}000) \div 8 \text{ years} = \$5{,}875 \text{ per year}$$

At the beginning of the fifth year, accumulated depreciation on the machine is $23,500 ($5,875 × 4). The machine's book value is $26,500 ($50,000 − $23,500). At this point, what happens if McGraw changes its estimates of useful life or the salvage value? Consider the following revision examples independently of each other.

Revision of Life

Assume McGraw revises the expected life to 14 years, rather than 8. The machine's *remaining* life would then be 10 more years instead of 4 more years. Assume salvage value remains $3,000. Depreciation for each remaining year is

$$(\$26{,}500 \text{ book value} - \$3{,}000 \text{ salvage}) \div 10\text{-year remaining life} = \$2{,}350$$

Revision of Salvage

Alternatively, assume the original expected life remained 8 years, but McGraw revised its estimate of salvage value to $6,000. Depreciation for each of the remaining 4 years would be

$$(\$26{,}500 \text{ book value} - \$6{,}000 \text{ salvage}) \div 4\text{-year remaining life} = \$5{,}125$$

The revised amounts are determined for the full year, regardless of when McGraw revised its estimates. For example, if McGraw decides to change the estimated useful life on October 1, Year 3, the change would be effective as of January 1, Year 3. The year-end adjustment for depreciation would include a full year's depreciation calculated on the basis of the revised estimated useful life.

CONTINUING EXPENDITURES FOR PLANT ASSETS

LO 8-8

Show how continuing expenditures for operational assets affect financial statements.

Most plant assets require additional expenditures for maintenance or improvement during their useful lives. Accountants must determine if these expenditures should be expensed or capitalized (recorded as assets).

Costs That Are Expensed

The costs of routine maintenance and minor repairs that are incurred to *keep* an asset in good working order are expensed in the period in which they are incurred. Because they reduce net income when incurred, accountants often call repair and maintenance costs **revenue expenditures** (companies subtract them from revenue).

With respect to the previous example, assume McGraw spent $500 for routine lubrication and to replace minor parts. The effects on the financial statements are shown next:

Balance Sheet					Income Statement					Statement of Cash Flows
Assets	=		Stk. Equity							
Cash	=	Com. Stk.	+	Ret. Earn.	Rev.	−	Exp.	=	Net Inc.	
(500)	=	NA	+	(500)	NA	−	500	=	(500)	(500) OA

Costs That Are Capitalized

Substantial amounts spent to improve the quality or extend the life of an asset are described as **capital expenditures.** Capital expenditures are accounted for in one of two ways, depending on whether the cost incurred *improves the quality* or *extends the life* of the asset.

Improving Quality

Expenditures such as adding air conditioning to an existing building or installing a trailer hitch on a vehicle improve the quality of service these assets provide. If a capital expenditure improves an asset's quality, the amount is added to the historical cost of the asset. The additional cost is expensed through higher depreciation charges over the asset's remaining useful life.

To demonstrate, return to the McGraw Company example. Recall that the machine originally cost $50,000, had an estimated salvage value of $3,000, and had a predicted life of 8 years. Recall further that accumulated depreciation at the beginning of the fifth year is $23,500 ($5,875 × 4), so the book value is $26,500 ($50,000 − $23,500). Assume McGraw makes a major expenditure of $4,000 in the machine's fifth year to improve its productive capacity. The effects on the financial statements are shown next:

Balance Sheet							Income Statement					Statement of Cash Flows
Assets			=	Stk. Equity								
Cash	+	Book Value of Mach.	=	Com. Stk.	+	Ret. Earn.	Rev.	−	Exp.	=	Net Inc.	
(4,000)	+	4,000	=	NA	+	NA	NA	−	NA	=	NA	(4,000) IA

After recording the expenditure, the machine account balance is $54,000 and the asset's book value is $30,500 ($54,000 − $23,500). The depreciation charges for each of the remaining 4 years are

$$(\$30{,}500 \text{ book value} - \$3{,}000 \text{ salvage}) \div 4\text{-year remaining life} = \$6{,}875$$

Extending Life

Expenditures such as replacing the roof of an existing building or putting a new engine in an older vehicle extend the useful life of these assets. If a capital expenditure extends the life of an asset rather than improving the asset's quality of service, accountants view the expenditure as canceling some of the depreciation previously charged to expense. The event is still an asset exchange; cash decreases, and the book value of the machine increases. However, the increase in the book value of the machine results from reducing the balance in the contra asset account, Accumulated Depreciation.

To illustrate, assume that instead of increasing productive capacity, McGraw's $4,000 expenditure had extended the useful life of the machine by 2 years. The effects on the financial statements are shown next:

Balance Sheet							Income Statement					Statement of Cash Flows
Assets			=	Stk. Equity								
Cash	+	Book Value of Mach.	=	Com. Stk.	+	Ret. Earn.	Rev.	−	Exp.	=	Net Inc.	
(4,000)	+	4,000	=	NA	+	NA	NA	−	NA	=	NA	(4,000) IA

After the expenditure is recorded, the book value is the same as if the $4,000 had been added to the Machine account ($50,000 cost − $19,500 adjusted balance in Accumulated Depreciation = $30,500). Depreciation expense for each of the remaining 6 years follows:

($30,500 book value − $3,000 salvage) ÷ 6-year remaining life = $4,583

CHECK YOURSELF 8.3

On January 1, Year 1, Dager Inc. purchased an asset that cost $18,000. It had a 5-year useful life and a $3,000 salvage value. Dager uses straight-line depreciation. On January 1, Year 3, it incurred a $1,200 cost related to the asset. With respect to this asset, determine the amount of expense and accumulated depreciation Dager would report in the Year 3 financial statements under each of the following assumptions:

1. The $1,200 cost was incurred to repair damage resulting from an accident.

2. The $1,200 cost improved the operating capacity of the asset. The total useful life and salvage value remained unchanged.

3. The $1,200 cost extended the useful life of the asset by one year. The salvage value remained unchanged.

Answer

1. Dager would report the $1,200 repair cost as an expense. Dager would also report depreciation expense of $3,000 [($18,000 − $3,000) ÷ 5]. Total expenses related to this asset in Year 3 would be $4,200 ($1,200 repair expense + $3,000 depreciation expense). Accumulated depreciation at the end of Year 3 would be $9,000 ($3,000 depreciation expense × 3 years).

2. The $1,200 cost would be capitalized in the asset account, increasing both the book value of the asset and the annual depreciation expense.

	After-Effects of Capital Improvement
Amount in asset account ($18,000 + $1,200)	$19,200
Less: Salvage value	(3,000)
Accumulated depreciation on January 1, Year 3	(6,000)
Remaining depreciable cost before recording Year 3 depreciation	$10,200
Depreciation for Year 3 ($10,200 ÷ 3 years)	$ 3,400
Accumulated depreciation at December 31, Year 3 ($6,000 + $3,400)	$ 9,400

3. The $1,200 cost would be subtracted from the Accumulated Depreciation account, increasing the book value of the asset. The remaining useful life would increase to 4 years, which would decrease the depreciation expense.

	After-Effects of Capital Improvement
Amount in asset account	$18,000
Less: Salvage value	(3,000)
Accumulated depreciation on January 1, Year 3 ($6,000 − $1,200)	(4,800)
Remaining depreciable cost before recording Year 3 depreciation	$10,200
Depreciation for Year 3 ($10,200 ÷ 4 years)	$ 2,550
Accumulated depreciation at December 31, Year 3 ($4,800 + $2,550)	$ 7,350

Answers to The Curious Accountant

As assets lose their productive capacity, either from being used or due to obsolescence, the asset account is reduced and an expense account is increased. Assets such as buildings and equipment may decline faster if they are used, but, due to obsolescence, they usually continue to decline even if they are not used. For this reason, a time-based depreciation method, such as straight-line or double-declining-balance, is almost always used for buildings and more often than not for equipment. In contrast, a mineral reserve does not lose its capacity unless ore is extracted. After all, the gold the FCX is mining today has been in the earth for millions of years. For this reason, companies typically use the units-of-production method to calculate depletion on mineral reserves. In both cases, the objective should be to achieve the best matching of expenses incurred with the revenues they generate.

NATURAL RESOURCES

LO 8-9

Calculate depletion and show how it affects financial statements.

The cost of natural resources includes not only the purchase price but also related items such as the cost of exploration, geographic surveys, and estimates. The process of expensing natural resources is commonly called depletion.[2] The most common method used to calculate depletion is units-of-production.

To illustrate, assume Apex Coal Mining paid $4,000,000 cash to purchase a mine with an estimated 16,000,000 tons of coal. The unit depletion charge is

$$\$4,000,000 \div 16,000,000 \text{ tons} = \$0.25 \text{ per ton}$$

If Apex mines 360,000 tons of coal in the first year, the depletion charge is

$$360,000 \text{ tons} \times \$0.25 \text{ per ton} = \$90,000$$

The depletion of a natural resource has the same effect on the accounting equation as other expense recognition events. Assets (in this case, a *coal mine*) and stockholders' equity decrease. The depletion expense reduces net income. The effects of the acquisition and depletion of the coal mine on the financial statements are shown next:

Balance Sheet						Income Statement					Statement of Cash Flows
Assets			=	Stk. Equity							
Cash	+	Coal Mine	=	Com. Stk.	+	Ret. Earn.	Rev.	−	Exp.	=	Net Inc.	
(4,000,000)	+	4,000,000	=	NA	+	NA	NA	−	NA	=	NA	(4,000,000) IA
NA	+	(90,000)	=	NA	+	(90,000)	NA	−	90,000	=	(90,000)	NA

INTANGIBLE ASSETS

LO 8-10

Identify and determine the cost of intangible assets.

Intangible assets provide rights, privileges, and special opportunities to businesses. Common intangible assets include trademarks, patents, copyrights, franchises, and goodwill. Some of the unique characteristics of these intangible assets are described in the following sections.

[2]In practice, the depletion charge is considered a product cost and is allocated between inventory and cost of goods sold. This text uses the simplifying assumption that all resources are sold in the same accounting period in which they are extracted. The full depletion charge is therefore expensed in the period in which the resources are extracted.

FOCUS ON INTERNATIONAL ISSUES

RESEARCH *AND* DEVELOPMENT VS. RESEARCH *OR* DEVELOPMENT

For many years, some thought the companies that followed U.S. GAAP were at a disadvantage when it came to research and development (R&D) costs, because these companies had to immediately expense such cost, while the accounting rules of some other countries allowed R&D cost to be capitalized. Remember, recording costs as an asset—capitalizing it—means that net income is not immediately reduced. The global movement toward using IFRS is reducing, but not eliminating, the different accounting treatments for R&D.

Adam Gault/OJO Images/Getty Images

Like U.S. GAAP, IFRS requires *research* costs to be expensed, but it allows *development* costs to be capitalized. This IFRS rule itself can present challenges, because sometimes it is not clear where research ends and development begins. Basically, once research has produced a product, patent, and so forth that the company believes will result in a revenue-generating outcome, any additional costs to get it ready for market are development costs.

Trademarks

A **trademark** is a name or symbol that identifies a company or a product. Familiar trademarks include the Polo emblem, the name *Coca-Cola*, and the Nike slogan, "Just do it." Trademarks are registered with the federal government and have an indefinite legal lifetime.

The costs incurred to design, purchase, or defend a trademark are capitalized in an asset account called Trademarks. Companies want their trademarks to become familiar, but they also face the risk of a trademark being used as the generic name for a product. To protect a trademark, companies in this predicament spend large sums on legal fees and extensive advertising programs to educate consumers. Well-known trademarks that have been subject to this problem include Coke, Xerox, Kleenex, and Vaseline.

Patents

A **patent** grants its owner an exclusive legal right to produce and sell a product that has one or more unique features. Patents issued by the U.S. Patent Office have a legal life of 20 years. Companies may obtain patents through purchase, lease, or internal development. The costs capitalized in the Patent account are usually limited to the purchase price and legal fees to obtain and successfully defend the patent. The research and development costs incurred to develop patentable products are usually expensed in the period in which they are incurred.

Copyrights

A **copyright** protects writers' works, musical compositions, works of art, and other intellectual property for the exclusive benefit of the creator or persons assigned the right by the creator. The cost of a copyright includes the purchase price and any legal costs associated with obtaining and defending the copyright. Copyrights granted by the federal government extend for the life of the creator plus 70 years. A radio commercial could legally use a Bach composition as background music; it could not, however, use the theme song from the most recent Academy Award–winning movie without obtaining permission from the copyright owner. The cost of a copyright is often expensed early because future royalties may be uncertain.

REALITY BYTES

In 2017, **Reckitt Benckiser Group, PLC** reported that it had paid $17.9 billion to acquire **Mead Johnson Nutrition Co.** (M-J), even though the company's assets were reported on its December 31, 2016, balance sheet to be only $4.1 billion. Reckitt is a British-based company that owns numerous consumer brands, including Air Wick, French's, Lysol, and Dr. Scholl's. M-J's brands include Enfamil infant formulas. Why would Reckitt pay the owners of M-J over four times the value of the assets shown on the company's balance sheet?

Jill Braaten/McGraw-Hill Education

Reckitt was willing to pay well above the book value of the assets for several reasons. First, the value of the assets on M-J's balance sheet represented the historical cost of the assets. The current market value of these assets was probably higher than their historical cost, especially for intangible assets such as its trademarks and research in progress. Second, Reckitt believed that the two companies combined could operate at a lower cost than the two could as separate companies, thus increasing the total earnings they could generate. It estimated these savings would be over $200 million per year by the third year after the acquisition. Third, M-J had a bigger presence than Reckitt in developing markets, especially China, so this would make it easier to get Reckitt's existing products into those markets. Finally, Reckitt probably believed that M-J had *goodwill* that enables a company to use its assets in a manner that will generate above-average earnings. In other words, Reckitt was paying for a hidden asset not shown on M-J's balance sheet.

Source: Companies' reports.

Franchises

Franchises grant exclusive rights to sell products or perform services in certain geographic areas. Franchises may be granted by governments or private businesses. Franchises granted by governments include federal broadcasting licenses. Private business franchises include fast-food restaurant chains and brand labels such as Healthy Choice. The legal and useful lives of a franchise are frequently difficult to determine. Judgment is often crucial to establishing the estimated useful life for franchises.

Goodwill

Goodwill is the value attributable to favorable factors such as reputation, location, and superior products. Consider the most popular restaurant in your town. If the owner sold the restaurant, do you think the acquisition price would be simply the total value of the chairs, tables, kitchen equipment, and building? Certainly not, because much of the restaurant's value lies in its popularity; in other words, its ability to generate a high return is based on the goodwill (reputation) of the business.

Calculating goodwill can be complex; here we present a simple example to illustrate how it is determined. Suppose the accounting records of a restaurant named Bendigo's show

$$\text{Assets} = \text{Liabilities} + \text{Stockholders' equity}$$
$$\$200,000 = \$50,000 + \$150,000$$

Assume a buyer agrees to acquire the restaurant by paying the owner $300,000 cash and assuming the existing liabilities. In other words, the restaurant is acquired at a price of $350,000 ($300,000 cash + $50,000 assumed liabilities). Now assume that the assets of the business (tables, chairs, kitchen equipment, etc.) have a fair value of only $280,000. Why would the buyer pay $350,000 to purchase assets with a fair value of $280,000? Obviously, the buyer is purchasing more than just the assets. The buyer is acquiring the business's goodwill.

The amount of the goodwill is the difference between the purchase price and the fair value of the assets. In this case, the goodwill is $70,000 ($350,000 − $280,000). The effects of the acquisition on the financial statements are shown next:

Balance Sheet						Income Statement			Statement of Cash Flows
Assets			=	Liab.	+ Stk. Equity				
Cash	+ Rest. Assets	+ Goodwill	= N. Pay.	+	C. Stk.	Rev. −	Exp. =	Net Inc.	
(300,000) +	280,000	+ 70,000	= 50,000	+	NA	NA −	NA =	NA	(300,000) IA

The fair value of the restaurant assets represents the historical cost to the new owner. It becomes the basis for future depreciation charges.

Expense Recognition for Intangible Assets

As mentioned earlier, intangible assets fall into two categories, those with *identifiable useful lives* and those with *indefinite useful lives.* Expense recognition for intangible assets depends on which classification applies.

LO 8-11

Show how the amortization of intangible assets affects financial statements.

Expensing Intangible Assets with Identifiable Useful Lives

The costs of intangible assets with identifiable useful lives are normally expensed on a straight-line basis using a process called *amortization.* An intangible asset should be amortized over the shorter of two possible time periods: (1) its legal life or (2) its useful life.

To illustrate, assume that Flowers Industries purchased a newly granted patent for $44,000 cash. Although the patent has a legal life of 20 years, Flowers estimates that it will be useful for only 11 years. The annual amortization charge is therefore $4,000 ($44,000 ÷ 11 years). The effects of the patent purchase and first-year amortization on the financial statements are shown next:

Balance Sheet						Income Statement			Statement of Cash Flows
Assets		=	Stk. Equity						
Cash	+ Patent	= Com. Stk.	+	Ret. Earn.		Rev. −	Exp. =	Net Inc.	
(44,000)	+ 44,000	= NA	+	NA		NA −	NA =	NA	(44,000) IA
NA	+ (4,000)	= NA	+	(4,000)		NA −	4,000 =	(4,000)	NA

Impairment Losses for Intangible Assets with Indefinite Useful Lives

Intangible assets with indefinite useful lives must be tested for impairment annually. The impairment test consists of comparing the fair value of the intangible asset to its carrying value (book value). If the fair value is less than the book value, an impairment loss must be recognized.

To illustrate, return to the example of the Bendigo's restaurant acquisition. Recall that the buyer of Bendigo's paid $70,000 for goodwill. Assume the restaurant experiences a significant decline in revenue because many of its former regular customers are dissatisfied with the food prepared by the new chef. Suppose the decline in revenue is so substantial that the new owner believes the Bendigo's name is permanently impaired. The owner decides to hire a different chef and change the name of the restaurant. In this case, the business has suffered a permanent decline in value of goodwill. The company must recognize an impairment loss.

The restaurant's name has lost its value, but the owner believes the location continues to provide the opportunity to produce above-average earnings. Some, but not all, of the goodwill has been lost. Assume the fair value of the remaining goodwill is determined to be $40,000. The impairment loss to recognize is $30,000 ($70,000 − $40,000). The loss

EXHIBIT 8.7

Balance Sheet Presentation of Operational Assets

Partial Balance Sheet			
Long-Term Assets			
Plant and equipment			
Buildings	$4,000,000		
Less: Accumulated depreciation	(2,500,000)	$1,500,000	
Equipment	1,750,000		
Less: Accumulated depreciation	(1,200,000)	550,000	
Total plant and equipment			$2,050,000
Land			850,000
Natural resources			
Mineral deposits (Less: Depletion)		2,100,000	
Oil reserves (Less: Depletion)		890,000	
Total natural resources			2,990,000
Intangibles			
Patents (Net of amortization)		38,000	
Goodwill		175,000	
Total intangible assets			213,000
Total long-term assets			$6,103,000

reduces the intangible asset (Goodwill), stockholder's equity (Retained Earnings), and net income. The statement of cash flows is not affected. The effects on the financial statements are shown next:

Balance Sheet				Income Statement				Statement of Cash Flows
Assets	=	Liab.	+ Stk. Equity					
Goodwill =			Ret. Earn.	Rev.	−	Exp.	= Net Inc.	
(30,000)	=	NA	+ (30,000)	NA	−	(30,000)	= (30,000)	NA

Balance Sheet Presentation

This chapter explained accounting for the acquisition, expense recognition, and disposal of a wide range of long-term assets. Exhibit 8.7 illustrates the typical balance sheet presentation of many of the assets discussed.

The Financial Analyst

LO 8-12

Show how expense recognition choices and industry characteristics affect financial performance measures.

Managers may have differing opinions about which allocation method (straight-line, accelerated, or units-of-production) best matches expenses with revenues. As a result, one company may use straight-line depreciation, while another company in similar circumstances uses double-declining-balance. Because the allocation method a company uses affects the amount of expense it recognizes, analysts reviewing financial statements must consider the accounting procedures companies use in preparing the statements.

Assume that two companies, Alpha and Zeta, experience identical economic events in Year 1 and Year 2. Both generate revenue of $50,000 and incur cost of goods sold of $30,000 during each year. In Year 1, each company pays $20,000 for an asset with an expected useful life of five years and no salvage value. How will the companies' financial statements differ if one uses straight-line depreciation and the other uses the double-declining-balance method? To answer this question, first compute the depreciation expense for both companies for Year 1 and Year 2.

Effect of Judgment and Estimation

If Alpha Company uses the straight-line method, depreciation for Year 1 and Year 2 is

$$(\text{Cost} - \text{Salvage}) \div \text{Useful life} = \text{Depreciation expense per year}$$

$$(\$20,000 - \$0) \div 5 \text{ years} = \$4,000$$

In contrast, if Zeta Company uses the double-declining-balance method, Zeta recognizes the following amounts of depreciation expense for Year 1 and Year 2.

	(Cost − Accumulated Depreciation)	×	2 × (Straight-Line Rate)	=	Depreciation Expense
Year 1	($20,000 − $ 0)	×	[2 × (1 ÷ 5)]	=	$8,000
Year 2	($20,000 − $8,000)	×	[2 × (1 ÷ 5)]	=	$4,800

Based on these computations, the income statements for the two companies are

Income Statements				
	Year 1		**Year 2**	
	Alpha Co.	**Zeta Co.**	**Alpha Co.**	**Zeta Co.**
Sales	$50,000	$50,000	$50,000	$50,000
Cost of goods sold	(30,000)	(30,000)	(30,000)	(30,000)
Gross margin	20,000	20,000	20,000	20,000
Depreciation expense	(4,000)	(8,000)	(4,000)	(4,800)
Net income	$16,000	$12,000	$16,000	$15,200

The relevant sections of the balance sheets are

Plant Assets				
	Year 1		**Year 2**	
	Alpha Co.	**Zeta Co.**	**Alpha Co.**	**Zeta Co.**
Asset	$20,000	$20,000	$20,000	$20,000
Accumulated depreciation	(4,000)	(8,000)	(8,000)	(12,800)
Book value	$16,000	$12,000	$12,000	$ 7,200

The depreciation method is not the only aspect of expense recognition that can vary between companies. Companies may also make different assumptions about the useful lives and salvage values of long-term operational assets. Thus, even if the same depreciation method is used, depreciation expense may still differ.

Because the depreciation method and the underlying assumptions regarding useful life and salvage value affect the determination of depreciation expense, they also affect the amounts of net income, retained earnings, and total assets. Financial statement analysis is affected if it is based on ratios that include these items. Previously defined ratios that are affected include the (1) debt-to-assets ratio, (2) return-on-assets ratio, (3) return-on-equity ratio, and (4) return-on-sales ratio.

Chris Parypa/Essentials/rypson/iStockphoto

To promote meaningful analysis, GAAP requires companies to disclose all significant accounting policies used to prepare their financial statements. This disclosure is provided in the notes that accompany the financial statements.

Effect of Industry Characteristics

As indicated in previous chapters, industry characteristics affect financial performance measures. For example, companies in manufacturing industries invest heavily in machinery, while insurance companies rely more on human capital. Manufacturing companies therefore have relatively higher depreciation charges than insurance companies. To illustrate how the type of industry affects financial reporting, examine Exhibit 8.8. This exhibit compares the ratio of sales to property, plant, and equipment for two companies in each of three different industries. These data are for 2017.

EXHIBIT 8.8

Industry Data Reflecting the Use of Long-Term Tangible Assets

Industry	Company	Sales ÷ Property, Plant, and Equipment
Broadband Communications	Comcast Corp.	2.20
	Verizon Communications	1.21
Airlines	Alaska Air Group	1.26
	Southwest Airlines	1.14
Employment Agencies	Kelly Services	62.42
	Manpower, Inc.	133.38

The table indicates that for every $1.00 invested in property, plant, and equipment, **Manpower** produced $133.38 of sales. In contrast, **Verizon** and **Southwest Airlines** produced only $1.21 and $1.14, respectively, for each $1.00 they invested in operational assets. Does this mean the management of Manpower is doing a better job than the management of Verizon or Southwest Airlines? Not necessarily. It means that these companies operate in different economic environments. In other words, it takes significantly more equipment to operate a cable company or an airline than it takes to operate an employment agency.

Effective financial analysis requires careful consideration of industry characteristics, accounting policies, and the reasonableness of assumptions such as useful life and salvage value.

 ## A Look Back

This chapter explains that the primary objective of recognizing depreciation is to match the cost of a long-term tangible asset with the revenues the asset is expected to generate. The matching concept also applies to natural resources (depletion) and intangible assets (amortization). The chapter explains how alternative methods can be used to account for the same event (e.g., straight-line versus double-declining-balance depreciation). Companies experiencing exactly the same business events could produce different financial statements. The alternative accounting methods for depreciating, depleting, or amortizing assets include the (1) straight-line, (2) double-declining-balance, and (3) units-of-production methods.

The *straight-line method* produces equal amounts of expense in each accounting period. The amount of the expense recognized is determined using the formula [(cost − salvage) ÷ number of years of useful life]. The *double-declining-balance method* produces proportionately larger amounts of expense in the early years of an asset's useful life and increasingly smaller amounts of expense in the later years of the asset's useful life. The formula for calculating double-declining-balance depreciation is [book value at beginning of period × (2 × the straight-line rate)]. The *units-of-production method* produces expense in direct proportion to the number of units produced during an accounting period. The formula for the amount of expense recognized each period is [(cost − salvage) ÷ total estimated units of production = allocation rate × units of production in current accounting period].

The chapter also discussed *MACRS depreciation,* an accelerated tax reporting method. MACRS is not acceptable under GAAP for public reporting. A company may use MACRS depreciation for tax purposes and straight-line or one of the other methods for public reporting. As a result, differences may exist between the amount of tax expense and the amount of tax liability. Such differences are reported as *deferred income taxes.*

This chapter showed how to account for *changes in estimates* such as the useful life or the salvage value of a depreciable asset. Changes in estimates do not affect the amount of depreciation recognized previously. Instead, the remaining book value of the asset is expensed over its remaining useful life.

After an asset has been placed into service, companies typically incur further costs for maintenance, quality improvement, and extensions of useful life. *Maintenance costs* are expensed in the period in which they are incurred. *Costs that improve the quality* of an asset are added to the cost of the asset, increasing the book value and the amount of future depreciation charges. *Costs that extend the useful life* of an asset are subtracted from the asset's Accumulated Depreciation account, increasing the book value and the amount of future depreciation charges.

A Look Forward

In Chapter 9, we move from the assets section of the balance sheet to issues in accounting for short-term liabilities. You will also study the basic components of a payroll accounting system.

 Tableau Dashboard Activity is available in *Connect* for this chapter.

SELF-STUDY REVIEW PROBLEM

A step-by-step audio-narrated series of slides is available in *Connect*.

The following information pertains to a machine purchased by Bakersfield Company on January 1, Year 1:

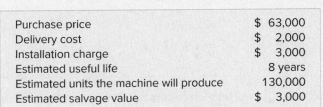

Purchase price	$ 63,000
Delivery cost	$ 2,000
Installation charge	$ 3,000
Estimated useful life	8 years
Estimated units the machine will produce	130,000
Estimated salvage value	$ 3,000

The machine produced 14,400 units during Year 1 and 17,000 units during Year 2.

Required

Determine the depreciation expense Bakersfield would report for Year 1 and Year 2 using each of the following methods:

a. Straight-line

b. Double-declining-balance

c. Units-of-production

d. MACRS, assuming that the machine is classified as a seven-year property

Solution to Requirements *a–d*

a. Straight-line

Purchase price	$63,000	
Delivery cost	2,000	
Installation charge	3,000	
Total cost of machine	68,000	
Less: Salvage value	(3,000)	
	$65,000 ÷ 8 = $8,125 Depreciation per year	
Year 1	$ 8,125	
Year 2	$ 8,125	

b. Double-declining-balance

Year	Cost	−	Accumulated Depreciation at Beginning of Year	×	2 × S-L Rate	=	Annual Depreciation
Year 1	$68,000	−	$ 0	×	(2 × 0.125)	=	$17,000
Year 2	68,000	−	17,000	×	(2 × 0.125)	=	12,750

c. Units-of-production

(1) (Cost − Salvage value) ÷ Estimated units of production = Depreciation cost per unit produced

$$\frac{\$68,000 - \$3,000}{130,000} = \$0.50 \text{ per unit}$$

(2) Cost per unit × Annual units produced = Annual depreciation expense

$$\text{Year 1} \quad \$0.50 \times 14,400 = \$7,200$$
$$\text{Year 2} \quad 0.50 \times 17,000 = \ \ 8,500$$

d. MACRS

$$\text{Cost} \times \text{MACRS percentage} = \text{Annual depreciation}$$
$$\text{Year 1} \quad \$68,000 \times 0.1429 = \quad \$ \ 9,717$$
$$\text{Year 2} \quad 68,000 \times 0.2449 = \quad 16,653$$

KEY TERMS

QUESTIONS

1. What is the difference between the functions of long-term operational assets and investments?

2. What is the difference between tangible and intangible assets? Give an example of each.

3. What is the difference between goodwill and specifically identifiable intangible assets?

4. Define *depreciation*. What kind of asset depreciates?

5. Why do you think natural resources are called *wasting assets?*

6. Is land a depreciable asset? Why or why not?

7. Define *amortization*. Which kinds of assets are amortized?

8. Explain the historical cost concept as it applies to long-term operational assets. Why is the book value of an asset likely to be different from the current fair market value of the asset?

9. What different kinds of expenditures might be included in the recorded cost of a building?

10. What is a basket purchase of assets? When a basket purchase is made, how is cost assigned to individual assets?

11. What are the stages in the life cycle of a long-term operational asset?

12. Explain straight-line, units-of-production, and double-declining-balance depreciation. When is it appropriate to use each of these depreciation methods?

13. What effect does the recognition of depreciation expense have on total assets? On total equity?

14. Does the recognition of depreciation expense affect cash flows? Why or why not?

15. MalMax purchased a depreciable asset. What would be the difference in total assets at the end of the first year if MalMax chooses straight-line depreciation versus double-declining-balance depreciation?

16. John Smith mistakenly expensed the cost of a long-term tangible fixed asset. Specifically, he charged the cost of a truck to a delivery expense account. How will this error affect the income statement and the balance sheet in the year in which the mistake is made?

17. What is *salvage value?*

18. What type of account (classification) is Accumulated Depreciation?

19. How is the book value of an asset determined?

20. Why is depreciation that has been recognized over the life of an asset shown in a contra account? Why not just reduce the asset account?

21. Assume that a piece of equipment cost $5,000 and had accumulated depreciation recorded of $3,000. What is the book value of the equipment? Is the book value equal to the fair market value of the equipment? Explain.

22. Why would a company choose to depreciate one piece of equipment using the double-declining-balance method and another piece of equipment using straight-line depreciation?

23. Explain MACRS depreciation. When is its use appropriate?

24. Does the method of depreciation required to be used for tax purposes reflect the use of a piece of equipment? Can you use double-declining-balance depreciation for tax purposes?

25. Define *deferred taxes*. Where does the account *Deferred Taxes* appear in the financial statements?

26. Why may it be necessary to revise the estimated life of a plant asset? When the estimated life is revised, does it affect the amount of depreciation per year? Why or why not?

27. How are capital expenditures made to improve the quality of a capital asset accounted for? Would the answer change if the expenditure extended the life of the asset but did not improve quality? Explain.

28. When a long-term operational asset is sold at a gain, how is the balance sheet affected? Is the statement of cash flows affected? If so, how?

29. Define *depletion*. What is the most commonly used method of computing depletion?

30. List several common intangible assets. How is the life determined that is to be used to compute amortization?

31. List some differences between U.S. GAAP and IFRS for long-term operational assets.

32. How do differences in expense recognition and industry characteristics affect financial performance measures?

EXERCISES—SERIES A

 **All applicable Exercises in Series A are available in *Connect*.**

Unless specifically included, ignore income tax considerations in all exercises and problems.

Exercise 8-1A   *Long-term operational assets used in a business*   LO 8-1

Required

Give some examples of long-term operational assets that each of the following companies is likely to own: *(a)* Caterpillar, *(b)* Amtrak, *(c)* Facebook, and *(d)* Bank of America Corp.

LO 8-1

Exercise 8-2A *Identifying long-term operational assets*

Required

Which of the following items should be classified as long-term operational assets?

a. Prepaid insurance

b. Coal mine

c. Office equipment

d. Accounts receivable

e. Supplies

f. Copyright

g. Delivery van

h. Land used in the business

i. Goodwill

j. Cash

k. Filing cabinet

l. Tax library of accounting firm

LO 8-1

Exercise 8-3A *Classifying tangible and intangible assets*

Required

Identify each of the following long-term operational assets as either tangible (T) or intangible (I):

a. Pizza oven

b. Land

c. Franchise

d. Filing cabinet

e. Copyright

f. Silver mine

g. Office building

h. Drill press

i. Patent

j. Oil well

k. Desk

l. Goodwill

LO 8-1

Exercise 8-4A *Determining the cost of an asset*

Southwest Milling Co. purchased a front-end loader to move stacks of lumber. The loader had a list price of $140,000. The seller agreed to allow a 4 percent discount because Southwest Milling paid cash. Delivery terms were FOB shipping point. Transportation cost amounted to $1,200. Southwest Milling had to hire a specialist to calibrate the loader. The specialist's fee was $1,800. The loader operator is paid an annual salary of $60,000. The cost of the company's theft insurance policy increased by $800 per year as a result of acquiring the loader. The loader had a four-year useful life and an expected salvage value of $6,000.

Required

Determine the amount to be capitalized in an asset account for the purchase of the front-end loader.

LO 8-1

Exercise 8-5A *Allocating costs on the basis of relative market values*

Carver Inc. purchased a building and the land on which the building is situated for a total cost of $700,000 cash. The land was appraised at $320,000 and the building at $480,000.

Required

a. What is the accounting term for this type of acquisition?

b. Determine the amount of the purchase cost to allocate to the land and the amount to allocate to the building.

c. Would the company recognize a gain on the purchase? Why or why not?

d. Record the purchase in a statements model like the following one:

Balance Sheet							Income Statement			Statement of Cash Flows
Assets			=	Liab.	+	Stk. Equity				
Cash	+ Land	+ Building					Rev.	− Exp.	= Net Inc.	

Exercise 8-6A   *Allocating costs for a basket purchase*   LO 8-1

Pitney Co. purchased an office building, land, and furniture for $500,000 cash. The appraised value of
the assets was as follows:

Land	$180,000
Building	300,000
Furniture	120,000
Total	$600,000

Required

a. Compute the amount to be recorded on the books for each asset.

b. Show the purchase in a horizontal statements model like the following one:

Balance Sheet						Income Statement			Statement of Cash Flows
Assets				= Liab. +	Stk. Equity				
Cash +	Land +	Building +	Furn.			Rev. −	Exp. =	Net Inc.	

Exercise 8-7A   *Effect of depreciation on the accounting equation and financial
statements*   LO 8-2

The following events apply to Gulf Seafood for the Year 1 fiscal year:

1. The company started when it acquired $60,000 cash by issuing common stock.

2. Purchased a new cooktop that cost $40,000 cash.

3. Earned $72,000 in cash revenue.

4. Paid $25,000 cash for salaries expense.

5. Adjusted the records to reflect the use of the cooktop. Purchased on January 1, Year 1, the cooktop
    has an expected useful life of four years and an estimated salvage value of $4,000. Use straight-line
    depreciation. The adjustment was made as of December 31, Year 1.

Required

a. Record the previous transactions in a horizontal statements model like the following one.

	Balance Sheet					Income Statement			Statement of Cash Flows
	Assets		=	Stk. Equity					
Event	Cash +	Book Value of Equip. =	Com. Stk. +	Ret. Earn.		Rev. −	Exp. =	Net Inc.	

b. What amount of depreciation expense would Gulf Seafood report on the Year 1 income statement?

c. What amount of accumulated depreciation would Gulf Seafood report on the December 31, Year 2,
    balance sheet?

d. Would the cash flow from operating activities be affected by depreciation in Year 1?

Exercise 8-8A   *Effect of double-declining-balance depreciation on financial statements*   LO 8-3

Golden Manufacturing Company started operations by acquiring $150,000 cash from the issue of com-
mon stock. On January 1, Year 1, the company purchased equipment that cost $120,000 cash, had an
expected useful life of six years, and had an estimated salvage value of $4,000. Golden Manufacturing
earned $72,000 and $83,000 of cash revenue during Year 1 and Year 2, respectively. Golden Manufacturing uses double-declining-balance depreciation.

Required

a. Record the preceding transactions in a horizontal statements model like the following one:

	Balance Sheet						Income Statement					Statement of Cash Flows
	Assets		=	Stk. Equity								
Event	Cash +	Book Value of Equip.	=	Com. Stk. +	Ret. Earn.		Rev. −	Exp.	=	Net Inc.		

b. Prepare income statements, balance sheets, and statements of cash flows for Year 1 and Year 2.

LO 8-2, 8-3

Exercise 8-9A *Computing and recording straight-line versus double-declining-balance depreciation*

At the beginning of Year 1, Copeland Drugstore purchased a new computer system for $52,000. It is expected to have a five-year life and a $7,000 salvage value.

Required

a. Compute the depreciation for each of the five years, assuming that the company uses
   (1) Straight-line depreciation.
   (2) Double-declining-balance depreciation.
b. Record the purchase of the computer system and the depreciation expense for the first year under straight-line and double-declining-balance methods in a financial statements model like the following one:

	Balance Sheet					Income Statement					Statement of Cash Flows
	Assets		=	Stk. Equity							
Cash +	Book Value of Comp. Sys.		=	Ret. Earn.		Rev. −	Exp.	=	Net Inc.		

LO 8-3, 8-4, 8-5

Exercise 8-10A *Double-declining-balance and units-of-production depreciation: gain or loss on disposal*

Exact Photo Service purchased a new color printer at the beginning of Year 1 for $38,000. The printer is expected to have a four-year useful life and a $3,500 salvage value. The expected print production is estimated at 1,500,000 pages. Actual print production for the four years was as follows:

Year 1	390,000
Year 2	410,000
Year 3	420,000
Year 4	300,000
Total	1,520,000

The printer was sold at the end of Year 4 for $1,650.

Required

a. Compute the depreciation expense for each of the four years, using double-declining-balance depreciation.
b. Compute the depreciation expense for each of the four years, using units-of-production depreciation.
c. Calculate the amount of gain or loss from the sale of the asset under each of the depreciation methods.

Exercise 8-11A *Events related to the acquisition, use, and disposal of a tangible plant asset: straight-line depreciation*

City Taxi Service purchased a new auto to use as a taxi on January 1, Year 1, for $36,000. In addition, City paid sales tax and title fees of $1,200 for the vehicle. The taxi is expected to have a five-year life and a salvage value of $4,000.

Required

a. Using the straight-line method, compute the depreciation expense for Year 1 and Year 2.

b. Assume the auto was sold on January 1, Year 3, for $21,000. Determine the amount of gain or loss that would be recognized on the asset disposal.

Exercise 8-12A *Effect of the disposal of plant assets on the financial statements*

Un Company sold office equipment with a cost of $23,000 and accumulated depreciation of $12,000 for $14,000.

Required

a. What is the book value of the asset at the time of sale?

b. What is the amount of gain or loss on the disposal?

c. How would the sale affect net income (increase, decrease, no effect) and by how much?

d. How would the sale affect the amount of total assets shown on the balance sheet (increase, decrease, no effect) and by how much?

e. How would the event affect the statement of cash flows (inflow, outflow, no effect) and in what section?

Exercise 8-13A *Effect of gains and losses on the accounting equation and financial statements*

On January 1, Year 1, Prairie Enterprises purchased a parcel of land for $28,000 cash. At the time of purchase, the company planned to use the land for a warehouse site. In Year 3, Prairie Enterprises changed its plans and sold the land.

Required

a. Assume that the land was sold for $29,500 in Year 3.

   (1) Show the effect of the sale on the accounting equation.

   (2) What amount would Prairie report on the Year 3 income statement related to the sale of the land?

   (3) What amount would Prairie report on the Year 3 statement of cash flows related to the sale of the land?

b. Assume that the land was sold for $24,000 in Year 3.

   (1) Show the effect of the sale on the accounting equation.

   (2) What amount would Prairie report on the Year 3 income statement related to the sale of the land?

   (3) What amount would Prairie report on the Year 3 statement of cash flows related to the sale of the land?

Exercise 8-14A *Computing depreciation for tax purposes*

Crossroads Eye Care Company purchased $60,000 of equipment on March 1, Year 1.

Required

a. Compute the amount of depreciation expense that is deductible under MACRS for Year 1 and Year 2, assuming that the equipment is classified as a seven-year property.

b. Compute the amount of depreciation expense that is deductible under MACRS for Year 1 and Year 2, assuming that the equipment is classified as a five-year property.

Exercise 8-15A *Revision of estimated useful life*

On January 1, Year 1, Poultry Processing Company purchased a freezer and related installation equipment for $42,000. The equipment had a three-year estimated life with a $3,000 salvage value. Straight-line depreciation was used. At the beginning of Year 3, Poultry Processing revised the expected life of the asset to four years rather than three years. The salvage value was revised to $2,000.

Required

Compute the depreciation expense for each of the four years, Year 1 through Year 4.

LO 8-8

Exercise 8-16A *Distinguishing between revenue expenditures and capital expenditures*

Bill's Wrecker Service has just completed a minor repair on a tow truck. The repair cost was $1,550, and the book value prior to the repair was $6,500. In addition, the company spent $12,000 to replace the roof on a building. The new roof extended the life of the building by five years. Prior to the roof replacement, the company's accounts reflected the Building account at $85,000 and related Accumulated Depreciation account at $32,000.

Required

After the work was completed, what book value should appear on the balance sheet for the tow truck and the building?

LO 8-8

Exercise 8-17A *Effect of revenue expenditures versus capital expenditures on financial statements*

Sellers Construction Company purchased a compressor for $28,000 cash. It had an estimated useful life of four years and a $4,000 salvage value. At the beginning of the third year of use, the company spent an additional $6,000 related to the equipment. The company's financial condition just prior to this expenditure is shown in the following statements model:

Balance Sheet							Income Statement					Statement of Cash Flows
Assets			=	Stk. Equity								
Cash	+	Book Value of Compressor	=	Com. Stk.	+	Ret. Earn.	Rev.	−	Exp.	=	Net Inc.	
45,000	+	16,000	=	40,000	+	21,000	NA	−	NA	=	NA	NA

Required

Record the $6,000 expenditure in the statements model under each of the following *independent* assumptions:

a. The expenditure was for routine maintenance.
b. The expenditure extended the compressor's life.
c. The expenditure improved the compressor's operating capacity.

LO 8-8

Exercise 8-18A *Effect of revenue expenditures versus capital expenditures on financial statements*

On January 1, Year 1, Webb Construction Company overhauled four cranes, resulting in a slight increase in the life of the cranes. Such overhauls occur regularly at two-year intervals and have been treated as a maintenance expense in the past. Management is considering whether to capitalize this year's $22,000 cash cost in the Cranes asset account or to expense it as a maintenance expense. Assume that the cranes have a remaining useful life of two years and no expected salvage value. Assume straight-line depreciation.

Required

a. Determine the amount of additional depreciation expense Webb would recognize in Year 1 and Year 2 if the cost were capitalized in the Cranes account.
b. Determine the amount of expense Webb would recognize in Year 1 and Year 2 if the cost were recognized as maintenance expense.
c. Determine the effect of the overhaul on cash flow from operating activities for Year 1 and Year 2 if the cost were capitalized and expensed through depreciation charges.
d. Determine the effect of the overhaul on cash flow from operating activities for Year 1 and Year 2 if the cost were recognized as maintenance expense.

Exercise 8-19A *Computing and recording depletion expense*   LO 8-9

Colorado Mining paid $600,000 to acquire a mine with 40,000 tons of coal reserves. The following statements model reflects Colorado Mining's financial condition just prior to purchasing the coal reserves. The company extracted 15,000 tons of coal in Year 1 and 18,000 tons in Year 2.

Balance Sheet						Income Statement					Statement of Cash Flows
Assets			=	Stk. Equity							
Cash	+	Coal Reserve	=	Com. Stk.	+	Ret. Earn.	Rev.	−	Exp.	=	Net Inc.	
800,000	+	NA	=	800,000	+	NA	NA	−	NA	=	NA	NA

Required
a. Compute the depletion charge per unit.
b. Record the acquisition of the coal reserves and the depletion expense for Years 1 and 2 in a financial statements model like the preceding one.

Exercise 8-20A *Computing and recording goodwill*   LO 8-10

Arizona Corp. acquired the business Data Systems for $320,000 cash and assumed all liabilities at the date of purchase. Data's books showed tangible assets of $260,000, liabilities of $40,000, and stockholders' equity of $220,000. An appraiser assessed the fair market value of the tangible assets at $250,000 at the date of acquisition. Arizona Corp.'s financial condition just prior to the acquisition is shown in the following statements model:

Balance Sheet								Income Statement				Statement of Cash Flows
Assets					=	Liab.	+ Stk. Equity					
Cash	+	Tangible Assets	+	Goodwill				Rev.	−	Exp.	=	Net Inc.	
450,000	+	NA	+	NA	=	NA	+ 450,000	NA	−	NA	=	NA	NA

Required
a. Compute the amount of goodwill acquired.
b. Record the acquisition in a financial statements model like the preceding one.

Exercise 8-21A *Computing and recording the amortization of intangibles*   LO 8-10, 8-11

Dynamo Manufacturing paid cash to acquire the assets of an existing company. Among the assets acquired were the following items:

Patent with 4 remaining years of legal life	$40,000
Goodwill	35,000

Dynamo's financial condition just prior to the acquisition of these assets is shown in the following statements model:

Balance Sheet								Income Statement				Statement of Cash Flows
Assets					=	Liab.	+ Stk. Equity					
Cash	+	Patent	+	Goodwill				Rev.	−	Exp.	=	Net Inc.	
90,000	+	NA	+	NA	=	NA	+ 90,000	NA	−	NA	=	NA	NA

Required
a. Compute the annual amortization expense for these items.
b. Show the acquisition of the intangible assets and the related amortization expense for Year 1 in a horizontal statements model like the one shown earlier.

LO 8-12

Exercise 8-22A *Identifying companies using property, plant, and equipment*

Executive Jets, LLC operates a charter flight-service company in the northwestern United States. Classic Steps, LLC is a company that provides dance lessons to students of all ages. Classic Steps has dance studios in several cities throughout the western United States. The following data are from the companies' most recent financial statements but are not identified as to which company they relate.

	Company 1	Company 2
Sales	$10,000,000	$10,000,000
Depreciation expense	70,000	500,000
Net earnings	850,000	800,000
Current assets	950,000	900,000
Property, plant, and equipment	700,000	6,000,000
Total assets	2,500,000	7,900,000

Required

a. Calculate the ratio of sales to property, plant, and equipment for each company.

b. Based on the ratios calculated in Requirement *a*, decide which is the charter flight-service company and which is the dance studio business. Explain your answer.

c. Based on the ratios calculated in Requirement *a*, which company appears to be using its property, plant, and equipment more efficiently? Explain your answer.

d. Explain why two companies with such different amounts of property, plant, and equipment might have the same amount of current assets.

IFRS

Exercise 8-23A *R&D costs: GAAP vs. IFRS*

The Paris Corp. incurred $3,600,000 of research cost and $800,000 of development cost during the current year.

Required

a. Determine the amount of expense recognized on its income statement assuming Paris uses U.S. GAAP.

b. Determine the amount of expense recognized on its income statement assuming Paris uses IFRS.

IFRS

Exercise 8-24A *Accounting for land and buildings under IFRS*

Assume the following. Queensland Company purchased a parcel of land on January 1, Year 1, for $400,000. It constructed a building on the land at a cost of $2,000,000. The building was occupied on January 1, Year 4, and is expected to have a useful life of 40 years and an estimated salvage value of $600,000.

As of December 31, Year 5 and Year 6, the fair value of the land had not been formally revalued because the real estate market had not changed significantly. Due to a jump in real estate prices, during Year 7 the value of the land had increased to $450,000, and the fair value of the building was $2,000,000. The salvage value of the building is still estimated at $600,000. The land and the building were reevaluated by the company in Year 7.

Required

a. Under U.S. accounting rules, what amount would be reported on the company's Year 6 and Year 7 balance sheets for the land and for the building? Show any necessary computations.

b. Under U.S. accounting rules, what amount of depreciation expense would be reported in Year 7 for the building? Show any necessary computations.

c. Under the IFRS revaluation model, what amount would be reported on the company's Year 6 and Year 7 balance sheets for the land and for the building? Show any necessary computations.

d. Under the IFRS revaluation model, what amount of depreciation expense would be reported in Year 7 for the building? Show any necessary computations.

PROBLEMS—SERIES A

Problem 8-25A   *Accounting for acquisition of assets including a basket purchase*   **LO 8-1**

Trinkle Co., Inc. made several purchases of long-term assets in Year 1. The details of each purchase are presented here.

New Office Equipment

1. List price: $60,000; terms: 2/10 n/30; paid within discount period.
2. Transportation-in: $1,500.
3. Installation: $2,500.
4. Cost to repair damage during unloading: $650.
5. Routine maintenance cost after six months: $350.

Basket Purchase of Copier, Computer, and Scanner for $30,000 with Fair Market Values

1. Copier, $22,000.
2. Computer, $10,000.
3. Scanner, $8,000.

Land for New Warehouse with an Old Building Torn Down

1. Purchase price, $250,000.
2. Demolition of building, $18,000.
3. Lumber sold from old building, $6,000.
4. Grading in preparation for new building, $22,000.
5. Construction of new building, $510,000.

Required

In each of these cases, determine the amount of cost to be capitalized in the asset accounts.

Problem 8-26A   *Determining the effect of depreciation expense on financial statements*   **LO 8-2, 8-3, 8-4**

Three different companies each purchased trucks on January 1, Year 1, for $50,000. Each truck was expected to last four years or 200,000 miles. Salvage value was estimated to be $5,000. All three trucks were driven 66,000 miles in Year 1, 42,000 miles in Year 2, 40,000 miles in Year 3, and 60,000 miles in Year 4. Each of the three companies earned $40,000 of cash revenue during each of the four years. Company A uses straight-line depreciation, company B uses double-declining-balance depreciation, and company C uses units-of-production depreciation.

Required

Answer each of the following questions. Ignore the effects of income taxes.

a. Which company will report the highest amount of net income for Year 1?
b. Which company will report the lowest amount of net income for Year 4?
c. Which company will report the highest book value on the December 31, Year 3, balance sheet?
d. Which company will report the highest amount of retained earnings on the December 31, Year 4, balance sheet?
e. Which company will report the lowest amount of cash flow from operating activities on the Year 3 statement of cash flows?

Problem 8-27A   *Effect of straight-line versus double-declining-balance depreciation on the recognition of expense and gains or losses*   **LO 8-2, 8-3, 8-5**

Becker Office Service purchased a new computer system in Year 1 for $40,000. It is expected to have a five-year useful life and a $5,000 salvage value. The company expects to use the system more extensively in the early years of its life.

Required

a. Calculate the depreciation expense for each of the five years, assuming the use of straight-line depreciation.

b. Calculate the depreciation expense for each of the five years, assuming the use of double-declining-balance depreciation.

c. Would the choice of one depreciation method over another produce a different amount of cash flow for any year? Why or why not?

d. Assume that Becker Office Service sold the computer system at the end of the fourth year for $15,000. Compute the amount of gain or loss using each depreciation method.

e. Explain any differences in gain or loss due to using the different methods.

LO 8-2, 8-5

Problem 8-28A *Accounting for depreciation over multiple accounting cycles: straight-line depreciation*

Bensen Company started business by acquiring $60,000 cash from the issue of common stock on January 1, Year 1. The cash acquired was immediately used to purchase equipment for $50,000 that had a $10,000 salvage value and an expected useful life of four years. The equipment was used to produce the following revenue stream (assume that all revenue transactions are for cash). At the beginning of the fifth year, the equipment was sold for $8,800 cash. Bensen uses straight-line depreciation.

	Year 1	Year 2	Year 3	Year 4	Year 5
Revenue	$26,100	$28,500	$32,000	$31,300	$0

Required

Prepare income statements, statements of changes in stockholders' equity, balance sheets, and statements of cash flows for each of the five years.

LO 8-4, 8-5

Problem 8-29A *Computing and recording units-of-production depreciation*

Sabel Co. purchased assembly equipment for $500,000 on January 1, Year 1. Sabel's financial condition immediately prior to the purchase is shown in the following horizontal statements model:

Balance Sheet						Income Statement				Statement of Cash Flows
Assets			=	Stk. Equity						
Cash	+	Book Value of Equip.	=	Com. Stk.	+	Ret. Earn.	Rev.	− Exp.	= Net Inc.	
800,000	+	NA	=	800,000	+	NA	NA	− NA	= NA	NA

The equipment is expected to have a useful life of 200,000 machine hours and a salvage value of $20,000. Actual machine-hour use was as follows:

Year 1	56,000
Year 2	61,000
Year 3	42,000
Year 4	36,000
Year 5	10,000

Required

a. Compute the depreciation for each of the five years, assuming the use of units-of-production depreciation.

b. Assume that Sabel earns $230,000 of cash revenue during Year 1. Record the purchase of the equipment and the recognition of the revenue and the depreciation expense for the first year in a financial statements model like the preceding one.

c. Assume that Sabel sold the equipment at the end of the fifth year for $20,600. Calculate the amount of gain or loss on the sale of equipment.

Problem 8-30A   *Calculating depreciation expense using four different methods*

Banko Inc. manufactures sporting goods. The following information applies to a machine purchased on January 1, Year 1:

Purchase price	$ 70,000
Delivery cost	$ 3,000
Installation charge	$ 1,000
Estimated life	5 years
Estimated units	140,000
Salvage estimate	$ 4,000

During Year 1, the machine produced 36,000 units, and during Year 2 it produced 38,000 units.

Required

Determine the amount of depreciation expense for Year 1 and Year 2 using each of the following methods:

a. Straight-line
b. Double-declining-balance
c. Units of production
d. MACRS, assuming that the machine is classified as 7-year property

Problem 8-31A   *Purchase and use of tangible asset: three accounting cycles, straight-line depreciation*

The following transactions relate to Academy Towing Service. Assume the transactions for the purchase of the wrecker and any capital improvements occur on January 1 of each year.

Year 1

1. Acquired $70,000 cash from the issue of common stock.
2. Purchased a used wrecker for $32,000. It has an estimated useful life of three years and a $5,000 salvage value.
3. Paid sales tax on the wrecker of $3,000.
4. Collected $56,100 in towing fees.
5. Paid $12,000 for gasoline and oil.
6. Recorded straight-line depreciation on the wrecker for Year 1.
7. Closed the revenue and expense accounts to Retained Earnings at the end of Year 1.

Year 2

1. Paid for a tune-up for the wrecker's engine, $900.
2. Bought four new tires, $1,250.
3. Collected $62,000 in towing fees.
4. Paid $18,000 for gasoline and oil.
5. Recorded straight-line depreciation for Year 2.
6. Closed the revenue and expense accounts to Retained Earnings at the end of Year 2.

Year 3

1. Paid to overhaul the wrecker's engine, $4,800, which extended the life of the wrecker to a total of four years. The salvage value did not change.
2. Paid for gasoline and oil, $19,100.
3. Collected $65,000 in towing fees.
4. Recorded straight-line depreciation for Year 3.
5. Closed the revenue and expense accounts at the end of Year 3.

Required

a. Use a horizontal statements model like the following one to show the effect of these transactions on the elements of financial statements. Use + for increase, − for decrease, and NA for not affected. The first event is recorded as an example.

Year 1 Event No.	Assets	=	Liabilities	+	Stk. Equity	Net Inc.	Cash Flow
1	+		NA		+	NA	+ FA

b. Prepare an income statement, a statement of changes in stockholders' equity, a balance sheet, and a statement of cash flows for Year 1, Year 2, and Year 3.

Problem 8-32A *Recording continuing expenditures for plant assets*

Morris Inc. recorded the following transactions over the life of a piece of equipment purchased in Year 1:

Jan. 1, Year 1	Purchased equipment for $90,000 cash. The equipment was estimated to have a five-year life and $5,000 salvage value and was to be depreciated using the straight-line method.
Dec. 31, Year 1	Recorded depreciation expense for Year 1.
Sept. 30, Year 2	Undertook routine repairs costing $900.
Dec. 31, Year 2	Recorded depreciation expense for Year 2.
Jan. 1, Year 3	Made an adjustment costing $2,500 to the equipment. It improved the quality of the output but did not affect the life and salvage value estimates.
Dec. 31, Year 3	Recorded depreciation expense for Year 3.
June 1, Year 4	Incurred $850 cost to oil and clean the equipment.
Dec. 31, Year 4	Recorded depreciation expense for Year 4.
Jan. 1, Year 5	Had the equipment completely overhauled at a cost of $9,000. The overhaul was estimated to extend the total life to seven years. The salvage value did not change.
Dec. 31, Year 5	Recorded depreciation expense for Year 5.
Oct. 1, Year 6	Received and accepted an offer of $19,000 for the equipment.

Required

a. Use a horizontal statements model like the following one to show the effects of these transactions on the elements of the financial statements. Use + for increase, − for decrease, and NA for not affected. The first event is recorded as an example.

Date	Assets	=	Liabilities	+	Stk. Equity	Net Inc.	Cash Flow
Jan. 1, Year 1	+ −		NA		NA	NA	− IA

b. Determine the amount of depreciation expense to be reported on the income statements for Year 1 through Year 5.

c. Determine the book value (cost − accumulated depreciation) Morris will report on the balance sheets at the end of the years Year 1 through Year 6.

d. Determine the amount of the gain or loss Morris will report on the disposal of the equipment on October 1, Year 6.

Problem 8-33A *Continuing expenditures with statements model*

Tower Company owned a service truck that was purchased at the beginning of Year 1 for $31,000. It had an estimated life of three years and an estimated salvage value of $4,000. Tower Company uses straight-line depreciation. Its financial condition as of January 1, Year 3, is shown in the following financial statements model:

Balance Sheet								Income Statement					Statement of Cash Flows
Assets				=	Stk. Equity								
Cash	+	Book Value of Truck		=	Com. Stk.	+	Ret. Earn.	Rev.	−	Exp.	=	Net Inc.	
20,000	+	13,000		=	9,000	+	24,000	NA	−	NA	=	NA	NA

In Year 3, Tower Company spent the following amounts on the truck:

Jan. 4 Overhauled the engine for $6,000. The estimated life was extended one additional year, and the salvage value was revised to $3,000.

July 6 Obtained oil change and transmission service, $250.

Aug. 7 Replaced the fan belt and battery, $350.

Dec. 31 Purchased gasoline for the year, $7,500.

Dec. 31 Recognized Year 3 depreciation expense.

Required

Record the Year 3 transactions in a statements model like the preceding one.

Problem 8-34A *Accounting for depletion*

LO 8-7, 8-9

Flannery Company engages in the exploration and development of many types of natural resources. In the last two years, the company has engaged in the following activities:

Jan. 1, Year 1 Purchased for $1,500,000 a silver mine estimated to contain 100,000 tons of silver ore.

July 1, Year 1 Purchased for $1,700,000 cash a tract of land containing timber estimated to yield 1,000,000 board feet of lumber. At the time of purchase, the land had an appraised of $100,000.

Feb. 1, Year 2 Purchased for $2,700,000 a gold mine estimated to yield 50,000 tons of gold-veined ore.

Sept. 1, Year 2 Purchased oil reserves for $1,300,000. The reserves were estimated to contain 270,000 barrels of oil, of which 10,000 would be unprofitable to pump.

CHECK FIGURES
a. Silver Mine Depletion, Year 1: $210,000
c. Total Natural Resources: $4,844,000

Required

a. Determine the amount of depletion expense that would be recognized on the Year 1 income statement for each of the two reserves, assuming 14,000 tons of silver were mined and 500,000 board feet of lumber were cut.

b. Determine the amount of depletion expense that would be recognized on the Year 2 income statement for each of the four reserves, assuming 20,000 tons of silver are mined, 300,000 board feet of lumber are cut, 4,000 tons of gold ore are mined, and 50,000 barrels of oil are extracted.

c. Prepare the portion of the December 31, Year 2, balance sheet that reports natural resources.

Problem 8-35A *Accounting for intangible assets*

LO 8-10

Mitre Company acquired Midwest Transportation Co. for $1,400,000. The fair market values of the assets acquired were as follows. No liabilities were assumed.

CHECK FIGURE
Goodwill acquired: $180,000

Equipment	$510,000
Land	150,000
Building	520,000
Franchise (10-year life)	40,000

Required

Calculate the amount of goodwill acquired.

Problem 8-36A *Accounting for goodwill*

LO 8-11

Rossie Equipment Manufacturing Co. acquired the assets of Alba Inc., a competitor, in Year 1. It recorded goodwill of $70,000 at acquisition. Because of defective machinery Alba had produced prior to the acquisition, it has been determined that all of the acquired goodwill has been permanently impaired.

Required

Explain how the recognition of the impairment of the goodwill will affect the Year 1 balance sheet, income statement, and statement of cash flows.

EXERCISES—SERIES B

Unless specifically included, ignore income tax considerations in all exercises and problems.

LO 8-1

Exercise 8-1B *Long-term operational assets used in a business*

Required

Give some examples of long-term operational assets that each of the following companies is likely to own: (*a*) Sears, (*b*) Princess Cruise Lines, (*c*) Southwest Airlines, and (*d*) Harley-Davidson Co.

LO 8-1

Exercise 8-2B *Identifying long-term operational assets*

Required

Which of the following items should be classified as long-term operational assets?

a. Cash	**g.** Inventory
b. Buildings	**h.** Patent
c. Production machinery	**i.** Tract of timber
d. Accounts receivable	**j.** Land
e. Prepaid rent	**k.** Computer
f. Franchise	**l.** Goodwill

LO 8-1

Exercise 8-3B *Classifying tangible and intangible assets*

Required

Identify each of the following long-term operational assets as either tangible (T) or intangible (I).

a. Retail store building	**g.** 18-wheel truck
b. Shelving for inventory	**h.** Timber
c. Trademark	**i.** Log loader
d. Gas well	**j.** Dental chair
e. Drilling rig	**k.** Goodwill
f. FCC license for TV station	**l.** Computer software

LO 8-1

Exercise 8-4B *Determining the cost of an asset*

Oregon Logging Co. purchased an electronic saw to cut various types and sizes of logs. The saw had a list price of $160,000. The seller agreed to allow a 5 percent discount because Oregon paid cash. Delivery terms were FOB shipping point. Transportation cost amounted to $3,200. Oregon hired an individual to operate the saw at an annual salary of $50,000. Oregon had to build a special platform to mount the saw at a cost of $2,500. The cost of the company's theft insurance policy increased by $1,800 per year as a result of acquiring the saw. The saw had a five-year useful life and an expected salvage value of $25,000.

Required

Determine the amount to be capitalized in an asset account for the purchase of the saw.

LO 8-1

Exercise 8-5B *Allocating costs on the basis of relative market values*

Florida Company purchased a building and the land on which the building is situated for a total cost of $800,000 cash. The land was appraised at $300,000 and the building at $700,000.

Required

a. What is the accounting term for this type of acquisition?

b. Determine the amount of the purchase cost to allocate to the land and the amount to allocate to the building.

c. Would the company recognize a gain on the purchase? Why or why not?

d. Record the purchase in a statements model like the following one:

Balance Sheet						Income Statement			Statement of Cash Flows
Assets			= Liab.	+	Stk. Equity				
Cash +	Land +	Building				Rev. −	Exp. =	Net Inc.	

Exercise 8-6B *Allocating costs for a basket purchase*   LO 8-1

Usrey Company purchased a restaurant building, land, and equipment for $600,000 cash. The appraised value of the assets was as follows:

Land	$200,000
Building	480,000
Equipment	120,000
Total	$800,000

Required

a. Compute the amount to be recorded on the books for each of the assets.

b. Show the purchase in a horizontal statements model like the following one:

Balance Sheet						Income Statement			Statement of Cash Flows
Assets				= Liab.	+ Stk. Equity				
Cash + Land + Building + Equip.						Rev. − Exp. = Net Inc.			

Exercise 8-7B *Effect of depreciation on the accounting equation and financial statements*   LO 8-2

The following events apply to The Soda Shop for the Year 1 fiscal year:

1. The company started when it acquired $20,000 cash from the issue of common stock.
2. Purchased a new ice cream machine that cost $20,000 cash.
3. Earned $36,000 in cash revenue.
4. Paid $21,000 cash for salaries expense.
5. Paid $6,000 cash for operating expenses.
6. Adjusted the records to reflect the use of the machine to make ice cream sodas. The machine, purchased on January 1, Year 1, has an expected useful life of five years and an estimated salvage value of $5,000. Use straight-line depreciation. The adjustment was made as of December 31, Year 1.

Required

a. Record the previous transactions in a horizontal statements model like the following one:

	Balance Sheet				Income Statement			Statement of Cash Flows
	Assets	=	Stk. Equity					
Event	Cash + Book Value of Equip.	=	Com. Stk. + Ret. Earn.		Rev. − Exp. = Net Inc.			

b. What amount of depreciation expense would The Soda Shop report on the Year 2 income statement?

c. What amount of accumulated depreciation would The Soda Shop report on the December 31, Year 2, balance sheet?

d. Would the cash flow from operating activities be affected by depreciation in Year 2?

Exercise 8-8B *Effect of double-declining-balance depreciation on financial statements*   LO 8-3

Hinds Company started operations by acquiring $120,000 cash from the issue of common stock. On January 1, Year 1, the company purchased equipment that cost $110,000 cash. The equipment had an expected useful life of five years and an estimated salvage value of $10,000. Hinds Company earned $85,000 and $72,000 of cash revenue during Year 1 and Year 2, respectively. Hinds Company uses double-declining-balance depreciation.

Required

a. Record the previous transactions in a horizontal statements model like the following one:

	Balance Sheet						Income Statement					Statement of Cash Flows
	Assets			=	Stk. Equity							
Event	Cash	+	Book Value of Equip.	=	Com. Stk.	+	Ret. Earn.	Rev.	−	Exp.	=	Net Inc.	

b. Prepare income statements, balance sheets, and statements of cash flows for Year 1 and Year 2.

LO 8-2, 8-3

Exercise 8-9B *Computing and recording straight-line versus double-declining-balance depreciation*

At the beginning of Year 1, Hill Manufacturing purchased a new computerized drill press for $75,000. It is expected to have a five-year life and a $15,000 salvage value.

Required

a. Compute the depreciation for each of the five years, assuming that the company uses

   (1) Straight-line depreciation.

   (2) Double-declining-balance depreciation.

b. Record the purchase of the drill press and the depreciation expense for the first year under the straight-line and double-declining-balance methods in a financial statements model like the following one:

	Balance Sheet					Income Statement					Statement of Cash Flows
	Assets			=	Stk. Equity						
Cash	+	Book Value of Drill Press	=	Ret. Earn.		Rev.	−	Exp.	=	Net Inc.	

LO 8-3, 8-4, 8-5

Exercise 8-10B *Double-declining-balance and units-of-production depreciation: gain or loss on disposal*

Design Service Co. purchased a new color copier at the beginning of Year 1 for $47,000. The copier is expected to have a five-year useful life and a $7,000 salvage value. The expected copy production was estimated at 2,000,000 copies. Actual copy production for the five years was as follows:

Year 1	560,000
Year 2	490,000
Year 3	430,000
Year 4	350,000
Year 5	210,000
Total	2,040,000

The copier was sold at the end of Year 5 for $7,600.

Required

a. Compute the depreciation expense for each of the five years, using double-declining-balance depreciation.

b. Compute the depreciation expense for each of the five years, using units-of-production depreciation. (Round cost per unit to three decimal places.)

c. Calculate the amount of gain or loss from the sale of the asset under each of the depreciation methods.

Exercise 8-11B   *Events related to the acquisition, use, and disposal of a tangible plant asset: straight-line depreciation*   LO 8-2, 8-5

Pete's Pizza purchased a delivery van on January 1, Year 1, for $35,000. In addition, Pete's paid sales tax and title fees of $1,500 for the van. The van is expected to have a four-year life and a salvage value of $6,500.

Required

a.   Using the straight-line method, compute the depreciation expense for Year 1 and Year 2.

b.   Assume the van was sold on January 1, Year 4, for $21,000. Determine the amount of gain or loss that would be recognized on the asset disposal.

Exercise 8-12B   *Effect of the disposal of plant assets on the financial statements*   LO 8-5

A plant asset with a cost of $50,000 and accumulated depreciation of $41,000 is sold for $10,000.

Required

a.   What is the book value of the asset at the time of sale?

b.   What is the amount of gain or loss on the disposal?

c.   How would the sale affect net income (increase, decrease, no effect) and by how much?

d.   How would the sale affect the amount of total assets shown on the balance sheet (increase, decrease, no effect) and by how much?

e.   How would the event affect the statement of cash flows (inflow, outflow, no effect) and in what section?

Exercise 8-13B   *Effect of gains and losses on the accounting equation and financial statements*   LO 8-5

On January 1, Year 1, Heflin Enterprises purchased a parcel of land for $20,000 cash. At the time of purchase, the company planned to use the land for future expansion. In Year 2, Heflin Enterprises changed its plans and sold the land.

Required

a.   Assume that the land was sold for $22,500 in Year 2.

  (1) Show the effect of the sale on the accounting equation.

  (2) What amount would Heflin report on the income statement related to the sale of the land?

  (3) What amount would Heflin report on the statement of cash flows related to the sale of the land?

b.   Assume that the land was sold for $18,500 in Year 2.

  (1) Show the effect of the sale on the accounting equation.

  (2) What amount would Heflin report on the income statement related to the sale of the land?

  (2) What amount would Heflin report on the statement of cash flows related to the sale of the land?

Exercise 8-14B   *Computing depreciation for tax purposes*   LO 8-6

Ripley Lumber Company purchased $240,000 of equipment on September 1, Year 1.

Required

a.   Compute the amount of depreciation expense that is deductible under MACRS for Year 1 and Year 2, assuming that the equipment is classified as a seven-year property.

b.   Compute the amount of depreciation expense that is deductible under MACRS for Year 1 and Year 2, assuming that the equipment is classified as a five-year property.

Exercise 8-15B   *Revision of estimated useful life*   LO 8-7

On January 1, Year 1, Mead Machining Co. purchased a compressor and related installation equipment for $72,500. The equipment had a three-year estimated life with a $12,500 salvage value. Straight-line depreciation was used. At the beginning of Year 3, Mead revised the expected life of the asset to four years rather than three years. The salvage value was revised to $2,500.

Required

Compute the depreciation expense for each of the four years.

LO 8-8

Exercise 8-16B *Distinguishing between revenue expenditures and capital expenditures*

Efficient Shredding Service has just completed a minor repair on a shredding machine. The repair cost was $1,900, and the book value prior to the repair was $6,000. In addition, the company spent $12,000 to replace the roof on a building. The new roof extended the life of the building by five years. Prior to the roof replacement, the company's accounts reflected the Building account at $110,000 and related Accumulated Depreciation account at $30,000.

Required

After the work was completed, what book value should Efficient have reported on the balance sheet for the shredding machine and the building?

LO 8-8

Exercise 8-17B *Effect of revenue expenditures versus capital expenditures on financial statements*

Ford Construction Company purchased a forklift for $150,000 cash. It had an estimated useful life of four years and a $10,000 salvage value. At the beginning of the third year of use, the company spent an additional $9,000 that was related to the forklift. The company's financial condition just prior to this expenditure is shown in the following statements model:

Balance Sheet							Income Statement					Statement of Cash Flows
Assets			=	Stk. Equity								
Cash	+	Book Value of Forklift	=	Com. Stk.	+	Ret. Earn.	Rev.	−	Exp.	=	Net Inc.	
15,000	+	80,000	=	45,000	+	50,000	NA	−	NA	=	NA	NA

Required

Record the $9,000 expenditure in the statements model under each of the following *independent* assumptions:

a. The expenditure was for routine maintenance.
b. The expenditure extended the forklift's life.
c. The expenditure improved the forklift's operating capacity.

LO 8-8

Exercise 8-18B *Effect of revenue expenditures versus capital expenditures on financial statements*

On January 1, Year 1, Midstate Power Company overhauled four turbine engines that generate power for customers. The overhaul resulted in a slight increase in the capacity of the engines to produce power. Such overhauls occur regularly at two-year intervals and have been treated as a maintenance expense in the past. Management is considering whether to capitalize this year's $22,000 cash cost in the engine asset account or to expense it as a maintenance expense. Assume that the engines have a remaining useful life of two years and no expected salvage value. Assume straight-line depreciation.

Required

a. Determine the amount of additional depreciation expense Midstate would recognize in Year 1 and Year 2 if the cost were capitalized in the Engine account.
b. Determine the amount of expense Midstate would recognize in Year 1 and Year 2 if the cost were recognized as maintenance expense.
c. Determine the effect of the overhaul on cash flow from operating activities for Year 1 and Year 2 if the cost were capitalized and expensed through depreciation charges.
d. Determine the effect of the overhaul on cash flow from operating activities for Year 1 and Year 2 if the cost were recognized as maintenance expense.

LO 8-9

Exercise 8-19B *Computing and recording depletion expense*

Fulton Sand and Gravel paid $800,000 to acquire 1,200,000 cubic yards of sand reserves. The following statements model reflects Fulton's financial condition just prior to purchasing the sand reserves. The company extracted 650,000 cubic yards of sand in Year 1 and 450,000 cubic yards in Year 2.

Balance Sheet							Income Statement			Statement of Cash Flows
Assets		=	Stk. Equity							
Cash	+	Sand Reserve	=	Com. Stk.	+	Ret. Earn.	Rev.	−	Exp.	=	Net Inc.	
900,000	+	NA	=	900,000	+	NA	NA	−	NA	=	NA	NA

Required

a. Compute the depletion charge per cubic yard.

b. Record the acquisition of the sand reserves and the depletion expense for Years 1 and 2 in a financial statements model like the preceding one.

Exercise 8-20B   *Computing and recording goodwill*   LO 8-10

Horn Co. acquired the business Medical Supply Co. for $275,000 cash and assumed all liabilities at the date of acquisition. Medical's books showed tangible assets of $250,000, liabilities of $10,000, and stockholders' equity of $240,000. An appraiser assessed the fair market value of the tangible assets at $265,000 at the date of acquisition. Horn's financial condition just prior to the acquisition is shown in the following statements model:

Balance Sheet								Income Statement			Statement of Cash Flows
Assets				=	Liab.	+	Stk. Equity				
Cash	+	Tangible Assets	+	Goodwill				Rev.	−	Exp.	=	Net Inc.	
450,000	+	NA	+	NA	=	NA	+	450,000	NA	−	NA	=	NA	NA

Required

a. Compute the amount of goodwill acquired.

b. Record the acquisition in a financial statements model like the preceding one.

Exercise 8-21B   *Computing and recording the amortization of intangibles*   LO 8-10, 8-11

Garth Manufacturing paid cash to acquire the assets of an existing company. Among the assets acquired were the following items:

Patent with 5 remaining years of legal life	$48,000
Goodwill	35,000

Garth's financial condition just prior to the purchase of these assets is shown in the following statements model:

Balance Sheet								Income Statement			Statement of Cash Flows
Assets				=	Liab.	+	Stk. Equity				
Cash	+	Patent	+	Goodwill				Rev.	−	Exp.	=	Net Inc.	
94,000	+	NA	+	NA	=	NA	+	94,000	NA	−	NA	=	NA	NA

Required

a. Compute the annual amortization expense for these items if applicable.

b. Show the acquisition of the intangible assets and the related amortization expense for year 1 in a horizontal statements model like the preceding one.

Exercise 8-22B   *Identifying companies using property, plant, and equipment*

Tri-Cities Equipment Rentals, LLC rents equipment such as cranes and bulldozers to construction companies, while Sam's Tax Services, LLC provides income tax and accounting services to individuals and small businesses. Sam's has offices in several cities throughout the mid-Atlantic states. The data that follow are from the companies' most recent financial statements, but are not identified as to which company they relate.

	Company 1	Company 2
Sales	$13,500,000	$13,500,000
Depreciation expense	700,000	90,000
Net earnings	1,050,000	1,100,000
Current assets	1,000,000	850,000
Property, plant, and equipment	8,100,000	900,000
Total assets	10,700,000	2,700,000

Required

a. Calculate the ratio of sales to property, plant, and equipment for each company.

b. Based on the ratios calculated in Requirement *a*, decide which is the equipment rental company and which is the tax and accounting business. Explain your answer.

c. Based on the ratios calculated in Requirement *a*, which company appears to be using its property, plant, and equipment more efficiently? Explain your answer.

d. Explain why two companies with such different amounts of property, plant, and equipment might have the same amount of current assets.

Exercise 8-23B   *Depreciable assets under IFRS*

The Transnational Business Inc. (TBI) purchased an asset that cost $60,000 on January 1, Year 1. The asset had a four-year useful life and a $10,000 salvage value.

Required

a. Determine the amount of expense recognized on the Year 1 income statement, assuming TBI uses U.S. GAAP.

b. Determine the amount of expense or gain recognized on the income statement, assuming TBI uses the IFRS revaluation model and the asset is determined to have a fair value of $55,000 as of December 31, Year 1.

c. Determine the amount of expense or gain recognized on the income statement, assuming TBI uses the IFRS revaluation model and the asset is determined to have a fair value of $65,000 as of December 31, Year 1.

Exercise 8-24B   *Accounting for land and buildings under IFRS*

Assume the following. Madrid Company purchased a parcel of land on January 1, Year 1, for $600,000. It constructed a building on the land at a cost of $3,000,000. The building was occupied on January 1, Year 4, and is expected to have a useful life of 40 years and an estimated salvage value of $1,000,000.

As of December 31, Year 5 and Year 6, the fair value of the land had not been formally revalued because the real estate market had not changed significantly. Due to a jump in real estate prices, during Year 7 the value of the land had increased to $650,000, and the fair value of the building was $3,000,000. The salvage value of the building is still estimated at $1,000,000. The land and the building were reevaluated by the company in Year 7.

Required

a. Under U.S. accounting rules, what amount would be reported on the company's Year 6 and Year 7 balance sheets for the land and for the building? Show any necessary computations.

b. Under U.S. accounting rules, what amount of depreciation expense would be reported in Year 7 for the building? Show any necessary computations.

c. Under the IFRS revaluation model, what amount would be reported on the company's Year 6 and Year 7 balance sheets for the land and for the building? Show any necessary computations.

d. Under the IFRS revaluation model, what amount of depreciation expense would be reported in Year 7 for the building? Show any necessary computations.

PROBLEMS—SERIES B

Problem 8-25B   *Accounting for acquisition of assets including a basket purchase*

LO 8-1

Floyd Company made several purchases of long-term assets in Year 1. The details of each purchase are presented here.

New Office Equipment

1. List price: $50,000; terms: 1/10 n/30; paid within the discount period.
2. Transportation-in: $1,200.
3. Installation: $1,000.
4. Cost to repair damage during unloading: $700.
5. Routine maintenance cost after eight months: $240.

Basket Purchase of Office Furniture, Copier, Computers, and Laser Printers for $70,000 with Fair Market Values

1. Office furniture, $48,000.
2. Copier, $12,000.
3. Computers and printers, $20,000.

Land for New Headquarters with Old Barn Torn Down

1. Purchase price, $100,000.
2. Demolition of barn, $7,000.
3. Lumber sold from old barn, $2,000.
4. Grading in preparation for new building, $11,000.
5. Construction of new building, $310,000.

Required

In each of these cases, determine the amount of cost to be capitalized in the asset accounts.

Problem 8-26B   *Determining the effect of depreciation expense on financial statements*

LO 8-2, 8-3, 8-4

Three different companies each purchased a machine on January 1, Year 1, for $64,000. Each machine was expected to last five years or 200,000 hours. Salvage value was estimated to be $6,000. All three machines were operated for 50,000 hours in Year 1, 55,000 hours in Year 2, 40,000 hours in Year 3, 44,000 hours in Year 4, and 31,000 hours in Year 5. Each of the three companies earned $30,000 of cash revenue during each of the five years. Company A uses straight-line depreciation, company B uses double-declining-balance depreciation, and company C uses units-of-production depreciation.

Required

Answer each of the following questions. Ignore the effects of income taxes.

a. Which company will report the highest amount of net income for Year 1?

b. Which company will report the lowest amount of net income for Year 3?

c. Which company will report the highest book value on the December 31, Year 3, balance sheet?

d. Which company will report the highest amount of retained earnings on the December 31, Year 4, balance sheet?

e. Which company will report the lowest amount of cash flow from operating activities on the Year 3 statement of cash flows?

Problem 8-27B   *Effect of straight-line versus double-declining-balance depreciation on the recognition of expense and gains or losses*

LO 8-2, 8-3, 8-5

National Laundry Services purchased a new steam press on January 1 for $42,000. It is expected to have a five-year useful life and a $4,000 salvage value. National expects to use the steam press more extensively in the early years of its life.

Required

a. Calculate the depreciation expense for each of the five years, assuming the use of straight-line depreciation.

b. Calculate the depreciation expense for each of the five years, assuming the use of double-declining-balance depreciation.

c. Would the choice of one depreciation method over another produce a different amount of cash flow for any year? Why or why not?

d. Assume that National Laundry Services sold the steam press at the end of the third year for $22,000. Compute the amount of gain or loss using each depreciation method.

LO 8-2, 8-5

Problem 8-28B *Accounting for depreciation over multiple accounting cycles: straight-line depreciation*

Scott Company began operations when it acquired $40,000 cash from the issue of common stock on January 1, Year 1. The cash acquired was immediately used to purchase equipment for $40,000 that had a $4,000 salvage value and an expected useful life of four years. The equipment was used to produce the following revenue stream (assume all revenue transactions are for cash). At the beginning of the fifth year, the equipment was sold for $4,500 cash. Scott uses straight-line depreciation.

	Year 1	Year 2	Year 3	Year 4	Year 5
Revenue	$9,500	$10,000	$10,500	$8,500	$0

Required

Prepare income statements, statements of changes in stockholders' equity, balance sheets, and statements of cash flows for each of the five years.

LO 8-4, 8-5

Problem 8-29B *Computing and recording units-of-production depreciation*

Friendly Corporation purchased a delivery van for $28,500 in Year 1. The firm's financial condition immediately prior to the purchase is shown in the following horizontal statements model:

Balance Sheet							Income Statement						Statement of Cash Flows
Assets			=	Stk. Equity									
Cash	+	Book Value of Van	=	Com. Stk.	+	Ret. Earn.	Rev.	−	Exp.	=	Net Inc.		
50,000	+	NA	=	50,000	+	NA	NA	−	NA	=	NA		NA

The van was expected to have a useful life of 200,000 miles and a salvage value of $2,500. Actual mileage was as follows:

Year 1	60,000
Year 2	50,000
Year 3	55,000

Required

a. Compute the depreciation for each of the three years, assuming the use of units-of-production depreciation.

b. Assume that Friendly earns $26,000 of cash revenue during Year 1. Record the purchase of the van and the recognition of the revenue and the depreciation expense for the first year in a financial statements model like the one shown earlier.

c. Assume that Friendly sold the van at the end of the third year for $8,000. Calculate the amount of gain or loss on the sale of equipment.

Problem 8-30B   *Calculating depreciation expense using four different methods*   LO 8-2, 8-3, 8-4, 8-6

Todd Service Company purchased a copier on January 1, Year 1, for $25,000 and paid an additional $500 for delivery charges. The copier was estimated to have a life of four years or 1,000,000 copies. Salvage value was estimated at $1,500. The copier produced 250,000 copies in Year 1 and 270,000 copies in Year 2.

Required

Compute the amount of depreciation expense for the copier for calendar years Year 1 and Year 2, using the following methods:

a. Straight-line
b. Units-of-production
c. Double-declining-balance
d. MACRS, assuming that the copier is classified as five-year property

Problem 8-31B   *Purchase and use of tangible asset: three accounting cycles,*   LO 8-3, 8-7, 8-8
double-declining-balance depreciation

The following transactions pertain to Accounting Solutions Inc. Assume the transactions for the purchase of the computer and any capital improvements occur on January 1 each year.

Year 1

1. Acquired $80,000 cash from the issue of common stock.
2. Purchased a computer system for $35,000. It has an estimated useful life of five years and a $5,000 salvage value.
3. Paid $2,450 sales tax on the computer system.
4. Collected $65,000 in fees from clients.
5. Paid $1,500 in fees to service the computers.
6. Recorded double-declining-balance depreciation on the computer system for Year 1.
7. Closed the revenue and expense accounts to Retained Earnings at the end of Year 1.

Year 2

1. Paid $1,000 for repairs to the computer system.
2. Bought off-site backup services to maintain the computer system, $1,500.
3. Collected $68,000 in fees from clients.
4. Paid $1,500 in fees to service the computers.
5. Recorded double-declining-balance depreciation for Year 2.
6. Closed the revenue and expense accounts to Retained Earnings at the end of Year 2.

Year 3

1. Paid $6,000 to upgrade the computer system, which extended the total life of the system to six years. The salvage value did not change.
2. Paid $1,200 in fees to service the computers.
3. Collected $70,000 in fees from clients.
4. Recorded double-declining-balance depreciation for Year 3.
5. Closed the revenue and expense accounts at the end of Year 3.

Required

a. Use a horizontal statements model like the following one to show the effect of these transactions on the elements of the financial statements. Use + for increase, − for decrease, and NA for not affected. The first event is recorded as an example.

Year 1 Event No.	Assets	=	Liabilities	+	Stk. Equity	Net Inc.	Cash Flow
1	+		NA		+	NA	+ FA

b. Prepare an income statement, a statement of changes in stockholders' equity, a balance sheet, and a statement of cash flows for Year 1, Year 2, and Year 3.

LO 8-2, 8-8

Problem 8-32B *Recording continuing expenditures for plant assets*

Tringle Inc. recorded the following transactions over the life of a piece of equipment purchased in Year 1:

Jan. 1, Year 1   Purchased the equipment for $38,000 cash. The equipment is estimated to have a five-year life and $3,000 salvage value and was to be depreciated using the straight-line method.

Dec. 31, Year 1   Recorded depreciation expense for Year 1.

May 5, Year 2   Undertook routine repairs costing $900.

Dec. 31, Year 2   Recorded depreciation expense for Year 2.

Jan. 1, Year 3   Made an adjustment costing $4,000 to the equipment. It improved the quality of the output but did not affect the life and salvage value estimates.

Dec. 31, Year 3   Recorded depreciation expense for Year 3.

Mar. 1, Year 4   Incurred $410 cost to oil and clean the equipment.

Dec. 31, Year 4   Recorded depreciation expense for Year 4.

Jan. 1, Year 5   Had the equipment completely overhauled at a cost of $9,000. The overhaul was estimated to extend the total life to seven years and revised the salvage value to $2,500.

Dec. 31, Year 5   Recorded depreciation expense for Year 5.

July 1, Year 6   Sold the equipment for $8,500 cash.

Required

a. Use a horizontal statements model like the following one to show the effects of these transactions on the elements of the financial statements. Use + for increase, − for decrease, and NA for not affected. The first event is recorded as an example.

Date	Assets	=	Liabilities	+	Stk. Equity	Net Inc.	Cash Flow
Jan. 1, Year 1	+ −		NA		NA	NA	− IA

b. Determine the amount of depreciation expense Tringle will report on the income statements for Year 1 through Year 5.

c. Determine the book value (cost − accumulated depreciation) Tringle will report on the balance sheets at the end of Year 1 through Year 5.

d. Determine the amount of the gain or loss Tringle will report on the disposal of the equipment on July 1, Year 6.

LO 8-2, 8-8

Problem 8-33B *Accounting for continuing expenditures*

Delta Manufacturing paid $62,000 to purchase a computerized assembly machine on January 1, Year 1. The machine had an estimated life of eight years and a $2,000 salvage value. Delta's financial condition as of January 1, Year 4, is shown in the following financial statements model. Delta uses the straight-line method for depreciation.

Balance Sheet								Income Statement				Statement of Cash Flows
Assets				=	Stk. Equity							
Cash	+	Book Value of Mach.	=	Com. Stk.	+	Ret. Earn.		Rev.	− Exp.	=	Net Inc.	
15,000	+	39,500	=	10,500	+	44,000		NA	− NA	=	NA	NA

Delta Manufacturing made the following expenditures on the computerized assembly machine in Year 4:

Jan. 2   Added an overdrive mechanism for $8,000 that would improve the overall quality of the performance of the machine but would not extend its life. The salvage value was revised to $2,500.
Aug. 1   Performed routine maintenance, $1,250.
Oct. 2   Replaced some computer chips (considered routine), $800.
Dec. 31 Recognized Year 4 depreciation expense.

Required

Record the Year 4 transactions in a statements model like the preceding one.

Problem 8-34B   *Accounting for depletion*

LO 8-7, 8-9

Metals Exploration Corporation engages in the exploration and development of many types of natural resources. In the last two years, the company has engaged in the following activities:

Jan. 1, Year 1   Purchased a coal mine estimated to contain 300,000 tons of coal for $900,000.
July 1, Year 1   Purchased for $2,000,000 cash a tract of land containing timber estimated to yield 3,000,000 board feet of lumber. At the time of purchase, the land had an appraised value of $200,000.
Feb. 1, Year 2   Purchased a silver mine estimated to contain 50,000 tons of silver for $850,000.
Aug. 1, Year 2   Purchased for $875,000 oil reserves estimated to contain 270,000 barrels of oil, of which 20,000 would be unprofitable to pump.

Required

a.   Determine the amount of depletion expense that would be recognized on the Year 1 income statement for each of the two reserves, assuming 80,000 tons of coal were mined, and 1,000,000 board feet of lumber were cut.

b.   Determine the amount of depletion expense that would be recognized on the Year 2 income statement for each of the four reserves, assuming 68,000 tons of coal are mined, 1,200,000 board feet of lumber are cut, 9,000 tons of silver are mined, and 80,000 barrels of oil are extracted.

c.   Prepare the portion of the December 31, Year 2, balance sheet that reports natural resources.

Problem 8-35B   *Accounting for intangible assets*

LO 8-10

Doug's Diner acquired a fast-food restaurant for $1,500,000. The fair market values of the assets acquired were as follows. No liabilities were assumed.

Equipment	$380,000
Land	200,000
Building	680,000
Franchise (5-year life)	120,000

Required

Calculate the amount of goodwill acquired.

Problem 8-36B   *Accounting for goodwill*

LO 8-11

Bostick Co. acquired the assets of Belk Co. for $1,200,000 in Year 1. The estimated fair market value of the assets at the acquisition date was $1,000,000. Goodwill of $200,000 was recorded at acquisition. In Year 2, because of negative publicity, one-half of the goodwill acquired from Belk Co. was judged to be permanently impaired.

Required

How will Bostick account for the impairment of the goodwill?

ANALYZE, THINK, COMMUNICATE

ATC 8-1   Business Applications Case   *Understanding real-world annual reports*

Required

Obtain Target Corporation's annual report for its 2018 fiscal year (year ended February 2, 2019) at http://investors.target.com using the instructions in Appendix B, and use it to answer the following questions:

a. What method of depreciation does Target use?

b. What types of intangible assets does Target have?

c. What are the estimated lives that Target uses for the various types of long-term assets?

d. As of February 2, 2019 (2018 fiscal year), what is the original cost of Target's land, buildings and improvements, and fixtures and equipment?

e. What was Target's depreciation and amortization expense for 2018?

ATC 8-2   Group Assignment   *Different depreciation methods*

Sweet's Bakery makes cakes, pies, and other pastries that it sells to local grocery stores. The company experienced the following transactions during Year 1.

1. Started business by acquiring $60,000 cash from the issue of common stock.
2. Purchased bakery equipment for $46,000.
3. Had sales in Year 1 amounting to $42,000.
4. Paid $8,200 of cash for supplies, which were all used during the year to make baked goods.
5. Incurred other operating expenses of $12,000 for Year 1.
6. Recorded depreciation assuming the equipment had a four-year life and a $6,000 salvage value. The MACRS recovery period is five years.
7. Paid income tax. The rate is 30 percent.

Required

a. Organize the class into three sections and divide each section into groups of three to five students. Assign each section a depreciation method: straight-line, double-declining-balance, or MACRS.

Group Task

Prepare an income statement and balance sheet using the preceding information and the depreciation method assigned to your group.

Class Discussion

b. Have a representative of each section put its income statement on the board. Are there differences in net income? In the amount of income tax paid? How will these differences in the amount of depreciation expense change over the life of the equipment?

ATC 8-3   Real-World Case   *Identifying companies based on financial statement information*

The following ratios are for four companies in different industries. Some of these ratios have been discussed in the textbook, others have not, but their names explain how the ratio was computed. These data are for the companies' 2017 fiscal years. The four sets of ratios, presented randomly are:

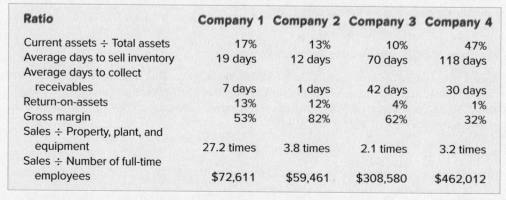

Ratio	Company 1	Company 2	Company 3	Company 4
Current assets ÷ Total assets	17%	13%	10%	47%
Average days to sell inventory	19 days	12 days	70 days	118 days
Average days to collect receivables	7 days	1 days	42 days	30 days
Return-on-assets	13%	12%	4%	1%
Gross margin	53%	82%	62%	32%
Sales ÷ Property, plant, and equipment	27.2 times	3.8 times	2.1 times	3.2 times
Sales ÷ Number of full-time employees	$72,611	$59,461	$308,580	$462,012

The four companies to which these ratios relate, listed in alphabetical order, are:

Anheuser-Busch InBev SA/NV is a company that produces beer and related products.

Caterpillar, inc. is a company that manufactures heavy construction equipment.

Denny's Corp. operates approximately 1,735 restaurants as of December 27, 2017.

Weight Watchers International, Inc. is a company that provides weight loss services and products. Its fiscal year-end was December 31, 2017, during which 83 percent of its revenues came from services and 17 percent from product sales.

Required

Determine which company should be matched with each set of ratios. Write a memorandum explaining the rationale for your decisions.

ATC 8-4 Business Applications Case *Performing ratio analysis using real-world data*

Electronic Arts, Inc. (commonly know as EA Sports) develops, markets, and publishes electronic games. Union Pacific Corporation is one of the largest railway networks in the nation, with 32,122 miles of railroads. The following data were taken from one of the companies' December 31, 2017, annual reports. Revealing which data relate to which company was intentionally omitted. The dollar amounts are in millions.

	Company 1	Company 2
Sales	$21,240	$5,150
Depreciation costs	2,105	136
Net earnings	10,712	1,043
Current assets	4,006	6,004
Property, plant, and equipment	51,605	453
Total assets	57,806	8,584

Required

a. Calculate depreciation costs as a percentage of sales for each company.

b. Calculate property, plant, and equipment as a percentage of total assets for each company.

c. Based on the information now available to you, decide which data relate to which company. Explain the rationale for your decision.

d. Which company appears to be using its assets most efficiently? Explain your answer.

ATC 8-5 Writing Assignment *Impact of historical cost on asset presentation on the balance sheet*

Assume you are examining the balance sheets of two companies and note the following information:

	Company A	Company B
Equipment	$1,130,000	$900,000
Accumulated Depreciation	(730,000)	(500,000)
Book Value	$ 400,000	$400,000

Maxie Smith, a student who has had no accounting courses, remarks that Company A and Company B have the same amount of equipment.

Required

In a short paragraph, explain to Maxie that the two companies do not have equal amounts of equipment. In your discussion comments regarding the possible age of each company's equipment, you may want to include the impact of the historical cost concept on balance sheet information, as well as the impact of different depreciation methods on book value.

ATC 8-6   Ethical Dilemma   *What's an expense?*

Several years ago, Wilson Blowhard founded a communications company. The company became successful and grew by expanding its customer base and acquiring some of its competitors. In fact, most of its growth resulted from acquiring other companies. Mr. Blowhard is adamant about continuing the company's growth and increasing its net worth. To achieve these goals, the business's net income must continue to increase at a rapid pace.

If the company's net worth continues to rise, Mr. Blowhard plans to sell the company and retire. He is, therefore, focused on improving the company's profit any way he can.

In the communications business, companies often use the lines of other communications companies. This line usage is a significant operating expense for Mr. Blowhard's company. Generally accepted accounting principles require operating costs like line use be expensed as they are incurred each year. Each dollar of line cost reduces net income by a dollar.

After reviewing the company's operations, Mr. Blowhard concluded that the company did not currently need all of the line use it was paying for. It was really paying the owner of the lines now so that the line use would be available in the future for all of Mr. Blowhard's expected new customers. Mr. Blowhard instructed his accountant to capitalize all of the line cost charges and depreciate them over 10 years. The accountant reluctantly followed Mr. Blowhard's instructions, and the company's net income for the current year showed a significant increase over the prior year's net income. Mr. Blowhard had found a way to report continued growth in the company's net income and increase the value of the company.

Required

a. How does Mr. Blowhard's scheme affect the amount of income that the company would otherwise report in its financial statements, and how does the scheme affect the company's balance sheet? Explain your answer.

b. Review the AICPA's Articles of Professional Conduct (see Chapter 2) and comment on any of the principles that were violated.

c. Review the elements of the fraud triangle (see Chapter 2) and comment on which of these features are evident in this case.

ATC 8-7   Research Assignment   *Comparing Microsoft's and Intel's operational assets*

This chapter discussed how companies in different industries often use different proportions of current versus long-term assets to accomplish their business objective. The technology revolution resulting from the silicon microchip has often been led by two well-known companies: Microsoft and Intel. Although often thought of together, these companies are really very different. Using either the most current Forms 10-K or annual reports for Microsoft Corporation and Intel Corporation, complete the requirements requested as follows. Obtain the Forms 10-K using either the EDGAR system, following the instructions in Appendix A, or the company's website. Microsoft's annual report is available on its website; Intel's annual report is its Form 10-K.

Required

a. Fill in the missing data in the following table. The percentages must be computed; they are not included in the companies' 10-Ks. (*Note:* The percentages for current assets and property, plant, and equipment will not sum to 100.)

	Current Assets	Property, Plant, and Equipment	Total Assets
Microsoft			
Dollar Amount	$ _____	$ _____	$ _____
% of Total Assets	_____ %	_____ %	100%
Intel			
Dollar Amount	$ _____	$ _____	$ _____
% of Total Assets	_____ %	_____ %	100%

b. Briefly explain why these two companies have different percentages of their assets in current assets versus property, plant, and equipment.

CHAPTER 9

Accounting for Current Liabilities and Payroll

LEARNING OBJECTIVES

After you have mastered the material in this chapter, you will be able to:

Video lectures and accompanying self-assessment quizzes are available in *Connect* for all learning objectives.

Tableau Dashboard Activity is available in *Connect* for this chapter.

LO 9-1   Show how notes payable and related interest expense affect financial statements.

LO 9-2   Show how sales tax liabilities affect financial statements.

LO 9-3   Define contingent liabilities and explain how they are reported in financial statements.

LO 9-4   Explain how warranty obligations affect financial statements.

LO 9-5   Determine payroll taxes and explain how they affect financial statements.

LO 9-6   Prepare a classified balance sheet.

LO 9-7   Use the current ratio to assess the level of liquidity.

APPENDIX

LO 9-8   Show how discount notes and related interest charges affect financial statements.

CHAPTER OPENING

Chapter 7 explained the need to estimate the net realizable value of receivables (the amount of receivables a company expects to actually collect). Do companies also estimate the net realizable value of payables (the amount they expect to actually pay)? The answer is no. Unless there is evidence to the contrary, companies are assumed to be going concerns that will continue to operate. Under this **going concern assumption,** companies expect to pay their obligations in full.

Accounts and notes payable are therefore reported at face value. In addition to reporting liabilities for which the amounts due are known, companies report liabilities for which the amounts due are uncertain. Liabilities that are uncertain as to amount are contingent liabilities.

Chapter 2 discussed several types of liabilities with known amounts due, including accounts payable, salaries payable, and unearned revenue. This chapter introduces other liabilities with known amounts due: notes payable, sales tax payable, and payroll liabilities; and contingent liabilities including warranties payable and vacation pay. We limit the discussion in this chapter to *current liabilities,* those that are payable within one year or the operating cycle, whichever is longer.

The Curious Accountant

Komenton/Shutterstock

On March 10, 2019, a **Boeing** 737 MAX, owned and operated by **Ethiopian Airlines**, crashed soon after take-off. All passengers and flight crew, 157 in total, died in this crash. Another Boeing 737 Max, operated by **Lion Air** of Indonesia, had crashed on October 29, 2018, killing 189 persons.

Given that neither of these airplanes were being operated by Boeing, does Boeing have any financial responsibility for the crashes? How should Boeing, or other companies in similar circumstances, report such events to their investors? (Answers on page 439.)

ACCOUNTING FOR NOTES PAYABLE

LO 9-1

Show how notes payable and related interest expense affect financial statements.

Our discussion of promissory notes in Chapter 7 focused on the lender. Recall that the lender is the entity that loans the money and recognizes a note receivable on its books. In this chapter, we focus on the borrower. The borrower receives cash and issues (gives) a note to the lender as evidence of an obligation to return the borrowed money at sometime in the future. Since the borrower issues the note, the borrower is sometimes called the **issuer.** The issuer's obligation to repay the borrowed money is shown as a note payable on the borrower's books. The following illustration examines three events occurring over two accounting cycles that are experienced by an issuer of a note payable.

EVENT 1   During Year 1, Herrera Supply Company (HSC) borrowed cash and issued a note payable acknowledging its obligation to repay the money in the future.

Assume that on September 1, Year 1, Herrera Supply Company (HSC) borrowed $90,000 (the principal amount) from National Bank. As evidence of the debt, Herrera issued a **note payable** that had a one-year term and an annual interest rate of 9 percent.

Issuing the note is an asset source transaction. The asset account Cash increases and the liability account Notes Payable increases. The income statement is not affected. The statement of cash flows shows a $90,000 cash inflow from financing activities. The effects on the financial statements are shown next:

	Balance Sheet						Income Statement			Statement of Cash Flows
	Assets =	Liabilities			+	Stk. Equity				
Date	Cash =	Notes Pay. +	Int. Pay. +	Com. Stk. +		Ret. Earn.	Rev. −	Exp. =	Net Inc.	
09/01/ Year 1	90,000 =	90,000 +	NA +	NA +		NA	NA −	NA =	NA	90,000 FA

EVENT 2   On December 31, Year 1, HSC adjusted its records to recognize accrued interest expense.

On December 31, Year 1, HSC would record an adjustment to recognize four months (September 1 through December 31) of accrued interest expense. The accrued interest is $2,700 [$90,000 × 0.09 × (4 ÷ 12)]. The adjustment is a claims exchange. The liability account Interest Payable increases, and the stockholders' equity account Retained Earnings decreases. The income statement would report interest expense, even though HSC had not paid any cash for interest in Year 1. The effects on the financial statements are shown next:

	Balance Sheet						Income Statement			Statement of Cash Flows
	Assets =	Liabilities			+	Stk. Equity				
Date	Cash =	Notes Pay. +	Int. Pay. +	Com. Stk. +		Ret. Earn.	Rev. −	Exp. =	Net Inc.	
12/31/ Year 1	NA =	NA +	2,700 +	NA +		(2,700)	NA −	2,700 =	(2,700)	NA

The third event occurs on August 31, Year 2 when the note matures. For clarity we divide the maturity event into three components as follows:

EVENT 3a   HSC recognized interest expense that accrued during Year 2.

This event requires the recognition of $5,400 [$90,000 × 0.09 × (8 ÷ 12)] for eight months of interest expense that accrued from January 1 through August 31 of Year 2. The effects on the financial statements are shown next:

	Balance Sheet					Income Statement			Statement of Cash Flows
	Assets =	Liabilities	+	Stk. Equity					
Date	Cash =	Notes Pay. + Int. Pay. +		Com. Stk. + Ret. Earn.		Rev. − Exp. = Net Inc.			
08/31/ Year 2	NA =	NA + 5,400 +		NA + (5,400)		NA − 5,400 = (5,400)			NA

EVENT 3b   HSC paid cash for the total amount of interest expense that was accrued in Year 1 and Year 2.

This event recognizes HSC's August 31, Year 2 cash payment for interest. The event is an asset use transaction that reduces both the Cash and Interest Payable accounts for the total amount of interest due: $8,100 [$90,000 × 0.09 × (12 ÷ 12)]. The interest payment includes the four months' interest accrued in Year 1 and the eight months accrued in Year 2 ($2,700 + $5,400 = $8,100). There is no effect on the income statement because HSC recognized the accrued interest expense in two previous events. The statement of cash flows would show an $8,100 cash outflow from operating activities. The effects on the financial statements are shown next:

	Balance Sheet					Income Statement			Statement of Cash Flows
	Assets =	Liabilities	+	Stk. Equity					
Date	Cash =	Notes Pay. + Int. Pay. +		Com. Stk. + Ret. Earn.		Rev. − Exp. = Net Inc.			
08/31/ Year 2	(8,100) =	NA + (8,100) +		NA + NA		NA − NA = NA			(8,100) OA

EVENT 3c   HSC paid off the $90,000 principal balance.

This August 31, Year 2 event reflects repaying the principal (original amount borrowed). The event is an asset use transaction. The Cash account and the Notes Payable account each decrease by $90,000. There is no effect on the income statement. The statement of cash flows would show a $90,000 cash outflow from financing activities. Recall that paying interest is classified as an operating activity even though repaying the principal is a financing activity. The effects on the financial statements are shown next:

	Balance Sheet					Income Statement			Statement of Cash Flows
	Assets =	Liabilities	+	Stk. Equity					
Date	Cash =	Notes Pay. + Int. Pay. +		Com. Stk. + Ret. Earn.		Rev. − Exp. = Net Inc.			
08/31/ Year 2	(90,000) =	(90,000) + NA +		NA + NA		NA − NA = NA			(90,000) FA

CHECK YOURSELF 9.1

On October 1, Year 1, Mellon Company issued an interest-bearing note payable to Better Banks Inc. The note had a $24,000 principal amount, a four-month term, and an annual interest rate of 4 percent. Determine the amount of interest expense and the cash outflow from operating activities Mellon will report in its Year 1 and Year 2 financial statements.

Answer The total cash payment for interest expense is due in Year 2. Accordingly, there is zero cash flow shown in the operating activities section of the Year 1 statement of cash flows. The total $320 [$24,000 × 0.04 × (4/12)] cash outflow for interest will appear in the operating activities section of Mellon's Year 2 statement of cash flows.

The computation of accrued interest expense is shown as follows. Unless otherwise specified, the interest rate is stated in annual terms, even though the term of the note is only four months. Interest rates are commonly expressed as an annual percentage regardless of the term of the note. The *time outstanding* in the following formulas is therefore expressed as a fraction of a year. Mellon paid interest at an annual rate of 4 percent, but the note was outstanding for only 3/12 of a year in Year 1 and 1/12 of a year in Year 2.

Year 1

Principal × Annual interest rate × Time outstanding = Interest expense
$24,000 ×   0.04   ×   (3/12)   = $240

Year 2

Principal × Annual interest rate × Time outstanding = Interest expense
$24,000 ×   0.04   ×   (1/12)   = $80

The statement effects are summarized next:

Financial Statement Items	Year 1	Year 2
Cash Flow from Operating Activities	0	$320
Interest Expense	$240	80

ACCOUNTING FOR SALES TAX

Show how sales tax liabilities affect financial statements.

Most cities, counties, and/or states require retail companies to collect a sales tax on items sold to their customers. The retailer collects the tax from its customers and remits the tax to the taxing authority at regular intervals. The retailer has a current liability for the amount of sales tax collected but not yet paid to the state.

EVENT 1   Herrera Supply Company (HSC) sells merchandise for $2,000 cash. The merchandise is subject to a 6% sales tax.

Herrera Supply Company (HSC) must collect cash for not only the $2,000 sales price of merchandise but also must collect an additional $120 ($2,000 × .06) cash for the sales tax. The $120 represents a liability due to the city, county, and/or state taxing authority. The effects on the financial statements are shown next:

Balance Sheet							Income Statement						Statement of Cash Flows
Assets	=	Liab.	+		Stk. Equity								
Cash	=	Sales Tax Pay.	+	Com. Stk.	+	Ret. Earn.	Rev.	−	Exp.	=	Net Inc.		
2,120	=	120	+	NA	+	2,000	2,000	−	NA	=	2,000		2,120 OA

EVENT 2   Herrera Supply Company (HSC) remits (pays) the amount it owes the taxing authorities.

Remitting the tax (paying cash to the tax authority) is an asset use transaction. Both the Cash account and the Sales Tax Payable account decrease. The effects on the financial statements are shown next:

Balance Sheet							Income Statement				Statement of Cash Flows
Assets	=	Liab.	+	Stk. Equity							
Cash	=	Sales Tax Pay.	+	Com. Stk.	+	Ret. Earn.	Rev.	−	Exp.	= Net Inc.	
(120)	=	(120)	+	NA	+	NA	NA	−	NA	= NA	(120) OA

CONTINGENT LIABILITIES

A **contingent liability** is a potential obligation arising from a past event. The amount or existence of the obligation depends on some future event. A pending lawsuit, for example, is a contingent liability. Depending on the outcome, a defendant company could be required to pay a monetary settlement or could be relieved of any obligation. Generally accepted accounting principles require that companies classify contingent liabilities into three different categories depending on the likelihood of their becoming actual liabilities. The categories and the accounting for each are described in the following:

LO 9-3

Define contingent liabilities and explain how they are reported in financial statements.

1. If the likelihood of a future obligation arising is *probable* (likely) and its amount can be *reasonably estimated,* a liability is recognized in the financial statements. Contingent liabilities in this category include warranties, vacation pay, and sick leave.

2. If the likelihood of a future obligation arising is *reasonably possible* but not likely, or if it is probable but *cannot be reasonably estimated,* no liability is reported on the balance sheet. The potential liability is, however, disclosed in the notes to the financial statements. Contingent liabilities in this category include legal challenges, environmental damages, and government investigations.

3. If the likelihood of a future obligation arising is *remote,* no liability need be recognized in the financial statements or disclosed in the notes to the statements.[1]

Source: USGS photo by Don Becker

Determining whether a contingent liability is probable, reasonably possible, or remote requires professional judgment. Even seasoned accountants seek the advice of attorneys, engineers, insurance agents, and government regulators before classifying significant contingent liabilities. Professional judgment is also required to distinguish between contingent liabilities and **general uncertainties.** All businesses face uncertainties such as competition and damage from floods or storms. Such uncertainties are not contingent liabilities, however, because they do not arise from past events.

Exhibit 9.1 summarizes the three categories of contingent liabilities and the accounting for each category.

---

[1]Companies may, if desired, voluntarily disclose contingent liabilities classified as remote.

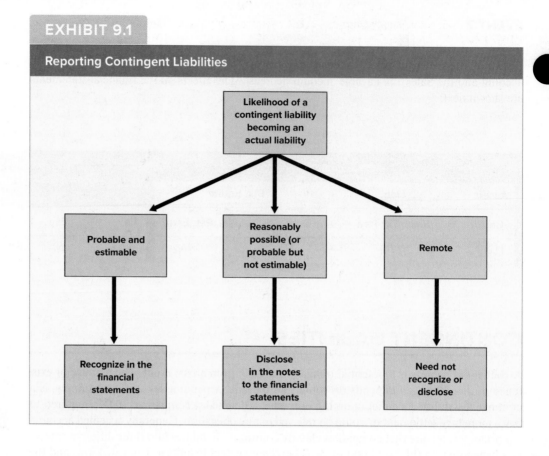

EXHIBIT 9.1

Reporting Contingent Liabilities

Likelihood of a contingent liability becoming an actual liability

- **Probable and estimable** → **Recognize in the financial statements**
- **Reasonably possible (or probable but not estimable)** → **Disclose in the notes to the financial statements**
- **Remote** → **Need not recognize or disclose**

WARRANTY OBLIGATIONS

LO 9-4

Explain how warranty obligations affect financial statements.

To attract customers, many companies guarantee their products or services. Such guarantees are called **warranties,** and they take many forms. Usually, they extend for a specified period of time. Within this period, the seller promises to replace or repair defective products without charge. Although the amount and timing of warranty obligations are uncertain, warranties usually represent liabilities that must be reported in the financial statements.

To illustrate accounting for warranty obligations, assume Herrera Supply Company (HSC) had cash of $2,000, inventory of $6,000, common stock of $5,000, and retained earnings of $3,000 on December 31, Year 1. The Year 2 accounting period is affected by three accounting events: (1) sale of merchandise under warranty; (2) recognition of warranty obligations to customers who purchased the merchandise; and (3) settlement of a customer's warranty claim.

EVENT 1   During Year 2, HSC sold for $7,000 cash merchandise that had cost $4,000.

In the following statements model, revenue from the sale is labeled 1a, while the cost of the sale is labeled 1b. The effects of the sale on the financial statements are shown next:

Event No.	Balance Sheet							Income Statement					Statement of Cash Flows
	Assets			=	Liab.	+	Stk. Equity						
	Cash	+	Inventory	=		+	Ret. Earn.	Rev.	−	Exp.	=	Net Inc.	
1a.	7,000	+	NA	=	NA	+	7,000	7,000	−	NA	=	7,000	7,000 OA
1b.	NA	+	(4,000)	=	NA	+	(4,000)	NA	−	4,000	=	(4,000)	NA

Answers to The Curious Accountant

As explained in this chapter, what **Boeing** was facing as a result of these crashes was a contingent liability. If a defect with the Boeing 737 MAX's design or manufacture is proven to have contributed to the crashes, Boeing will likely have to pay significant damages. But, at the time of the events, it was not clear if Boeing would be held responsible. As previously explained, in this situation companies must assess the probability of being held responsible, and try to estimate the amount of any possible damages. If the company believes these amounts are material, they will usually disclose their conclusions in one or more of three ways. First, they may file a Form 8-K, called a "Current Report" with the SEC. Second, they may issue a news release. Third, they will recognize a loss and a liability on their next financial statements that are released, assuming they can estimate the amount of the possible losses.

After the October 2018 Lion Air crash, Boeing released a statement expressing sympathy for the victims, but it did not file an 8-K. Also, Boeing did not disclose an estimated loss or contingent liability related to the event on its December 31, 2018 quarterly statements. After the March 10, 2019 crash, Boeing released a statement expressing sympathy for the victims and support for the Federal Aviation Administration's decision to temporarily ground the 737 MAX airplanes, but it did not discuss the financial impact the crashes might have on Boeing. However, when it released its results for the first quarter of 2019, in its Form 10-Q dated April 24, 2019, it acknowledged that its earnings had already been reduced by approximately $1 billion as a result of the issues related to the 737 MAX. On that same day Boeing released a Form 8-K, in which it stated, "The previously issued 2019 financial guidance does not reflect 737 MAX impacts. Due to the uncertainty of the timing and conditions surrounding return to service of the 737 MAX fleet, new guidance will be issued at a future date."

Suppose a company does not believe it will be held financially responsible for a contingent loss and therefore does not disclose the potential liability to investors. What happens if later the company is found to be responsible for that liability? Typically, the company will face lawsuits from investors claiming that they suffered personal, financial losses due to the non-disclosure. Companies facing contingent losses and liabilities are in very difficult positions.

Sources: Company SEC filings.

EVENT 2 **HSC guaranteed the merchandise sold in Event 1 to be free from defects for one year following the date of sale.**

Although the exact amount of future warranty claims is unknown, HSC must inform financial statement users of the company's obligation. HSC must estimate the amount of the warranty liability and report the estimate in the Year 2 financial statements. Assume the warranty obligation is estimated to be $100. Recognizing this obligation increases liabilities (warranties payable) and reduces stockholders' equity (retained earnings). Recognizing the warranty expense reduces net income. The statement of cash flows is not affected when the obligation and the corresponding expense are recognized. The effects on the financial statements are shown next:

	Balance Sheet			Income Statement			Statement of Cash Flows
	Assets =	Liab.	+ Stk. Equity				
Event No.		Warr. Pay.	+ Ret. Earn.	Rev. −	Exp. =	Net Inc.	
2.	NA =	100	+ (100)	NA −	100 =	(100)	NA

EVENT 3   HSC paid $40 cash to repair defective merchandise returned by a customer.

The cash payment for the repair is not an expense. Recall that the warranty expense was recognized in the period in which the sale was recognized, not when the payment was made. The payment reduces an asset (Cash) and a liability (Warranties Payable). The income statement is not affected by the repairs payment. However, there is a $40 cash outflow reported in the operating activities section of the statement of cash flows. The effects on the financial statements are shown next:

	Balance Sheet			Income Statement			Statement of Cash Flows
	Assets =	Liab.	+ Stk. Equity				
Event No.	Cash =	Warr. Pay.	+ Ret. Earn.	Rev. −	Exp. =	Net Inc.	
3.	(40) =	(40)	+ NA	NA −	NA =	NA	(40) OA

Financial Statements

The financial statements for HSC's Year 2 accounting period are shown in Exhibit 9.2.

EXHIBIT 9.2

Financial Statements for Year 2

Income Statement		Balance Sheet		Statement of Cash Flows	
Sales revenue	$ 7,000	Assets		**Operating Activities**	
Cost of goods sold	(4,000)	Cash	$ 8,960	Inflow from customers	$7,000
Gross margin	3,000	Inventory	2,000	Outflow for warranty	(40)
Warranty expense	(100)	Total assets	$10,960	Net inflow from	
Net income	$ 2,900	Liabilities		operating activities	6,960
		Warranties payable	$ 60	**Investing Activities**	0
		Stockholders' equity		**Financing Activities**	0
		Common stock	5,000	Net change in cash	6,960
		Retained earnings	5,900	Plus: Beginning cash balance	2,000
		Total liab. and	$10,960	Ending cash balance	$8,960
		stockholders' equity			

REALITY BYTES

Many of the items we purchase come with a manufacturer's warranty, but companies that sell electronics and electrical appliances often offer to sell you an extended warranty that provides protection after the manufacturer's warranty has expired. Why do they offer this option to customers, and how do these warranties differ from the standard manufacturers' warranties?

Companies, such as **Best Buy**, offer to sell customers extended warranties because they make a significant profit on them. If you buy an extended warranty from Best Buy, the retailer is not actually the one who is promising to repair your product; that will be done by a third party. Best Buy simply receives a commission for selling the warranty. In 2018, such commissions accounted for 2.0 percent of the company's total revenues, and because it had to incur very little expense to earn these revenues, they are mostly profit.

A katz/Shutterstock

The typical manufacturer's warranty, as you have learned in this chapter, is an expense recognized at the time of the sale. However, companies that provide extended warranties must recognize the warranty revenue over the life of the warranty, not immediately upon sale. Remember, this is referring to the third-party warranty provider, not Best Buy. Because Best Buy is simply earning a commission from selling the warranty, it gets to recognize all of the revenue at the time of the sale.

CHECK YOURSELF 9.2

Flotation Systems, Inc. (FSI) began operations in Year 1. Its sales were $360,000 in Year 1 and $410,000 in Year 2. FSI estimates the cost of its one-year product warranty will be 2 percent of sales. Actual cash payments for warranty claims amounted to $5,400 during Year 1 and $8,500 during Year 2. Determine the amount of warranty expense that FSI would report on its Year 1 and Year 2 year-end income statements. Also, determine the amount of warranties payable that FSI would report on its Year 1 and Year 2 year-end balance sheet.

Answer   FSI would report Warranty Expense on the December 31, Year 1, income statement of $7,200 ($360,000 × 0.02). Warranty Expense on the December 31, Year 2, income statement is $8,200 ($410,000 × 0.02).

FSI would report Warranties Payable on the December 31, Year 1, balance sheet of $1,800 ($7,200 − $5,400). Warranties Payable on the December 31, Year 2, balance sheet is $1,500 ($1,800 + $8,200 − $8,500).

ACCOUNTING FOR PAYROLL

If you've had a job, you know the amount of your paycheck is less than the amount of your salary. Employers are required to withhold part of each employee's earnings. The money withheld is used to pay such items as income taxes, union dues, and medical insurance premiums for which the *employee* is responsible. The *employer* is also required to make matching payments for certain items such as Social Security and to pay additional amounts for unemployment taxes. This section of the chapter explains how employers account for *employee withholdings,* as well as *employer payroll expenses.*

LO 9-5

 Determine payroll taxes and explain how they affect financial statements.

Identifying Employees

Businesses use the services of independent contractors as well as employees. They must distinguish between the two because payroll taxes apply only to employees. When a business supervises, directs, and controls an individual's work, the individual is an **employee** of the business. When a business pays an individual for specific services, but the individual supervises and controls the work, then that individual is an **independent contractor.**

The distinction between independent contractor and employee depends upon control and supervision rather than the type of work performed. A company's chief financial officer (CFO) is a company *employee;* the company's outside auditor is an *independent contractor.* Although both individuals provide accounting services, the company controls the CFO's work while the auditor is independent.

Employees' Gross Earnings

The compensation earned by employees who are paid based on the number of hours they work is normally called **wages.** The compensation earned by employees who are paid a set amount per week, month, or other earnings period regardless of the number of hours worked is normally called **salaries.** The total amount of wages or salaries earned, before any deductions for withholding, represents employees' **gross earnings.** Gross earnings is the sum of regular pay plus any bonuses, overtime, or other additions.

Deductions from Employees' Gross Earnings

Employers withhold money from employees' gross earnings and are obligated (have liabilities) to pay the funds withheld on behalf of the employees. Employers determine each employee's net pay (cash paid to the employee) by *deducting* the withholdings from the gross earnings. This section of the chapter introduces common withholdings.

Federal Income Taxes

To help the federal government collect income taxes due on a timely basis, the tax laws adopted by Congress require employers to withhold income taxes from employee earnings. The employers then pay the withheld taxes directly to the government.

For example, assume an employee earns $2,000. Assume further that the employee owes $300 of income tax on these earnings. On payday, the employer withholds $300 of the earnings and pays the employee $1,700 cash. The employer then has a $300 liability (obligation) to the federal government for the income tax withheld. In the future, the employer will use the money withheld to pay the employee's federal income tax liability. The statement effects of recognizing the salary expense, accruing the liability, and paying the employee are shown next:

Balance Sheet			Income Statement		Statement of Cash Flows
Assets =	Liab. +	Stk. Equity			
Cash =	EIT Pay. +	Com. Stk. + Ret. Earn.	Rev. − Exp. = Net Inc.		
(1,700) =	300 +	NA + (2,000)	NA − 2,000 = (2,000)		(1,700) OA

When the employer pays the liability, both cash and liabilities will decrease. The income statement will not be affected. The statement of cash flows will show a cash outflow from operating activities. The effects on the financial statements are shown next:

Balance Sheet			Income Statement		Statement of Cash Flows
Assets =	Liab. +	Stk. Equity			
Cash =	EIT Pay. +	Com. Stk. + Ret. Earn.	Rev. − Exp. = Net Inc.		
(300) =	(300) +	NA + NA	NA − NA = NA		(300) OA

The federal tax laws require employers to withhold funds for employee Social Security and Medicare (FICA) taxes, as well as income taxes. Employers may also be required to withhold amounts to pay state, county, and municipal government taxes from employees' paychecks. These withholdings have the same effects on the financial statements as those described earlier for federal income taxes.

Federal Income Tax Documents

The amount withheld from an employee's salary depends on the employee's *gross pay* and the number of *withholding allowances* the employee claims. Each allowance reduces the amount the employer must withhold. Employees are generally allowed to claim one allowance for themselves and one for each legal dependent. For example, a married person with two dependent children could claim four allowances (the employee, the dependent spouse, and the two dependent children). Exhibit 9.3 shows an **Employee's Withholding Allowance Certificate, Form W-4,** the form used to document the number of allowances claimed by an employee.

The federal government provides tax withholding tables that indicate the amount to withhold for any amount of earnings and any number of allowances. At the end of the calendar year, the employer must notify each employee of the amount of his or her gross earnings for the year, as well as the amounts the employer withheld. Employers provide this information to employees on a **Wage and Tax Statement, Form W-2,** illustrated in Exhibit 9.4. The employer sends one copy of Form W-2 to the Social Security Administration and other copies to the employee.

EXHIBIT 9.3

Employee's Withholding Allowance Certificate Form W-4

------------------ Separate here and give Form W-4 to your employer. Keep the worksheet(s) for your records. ------------------

Form W-4
Department of the Treasury
Internal Revenue Service

Employee's Withholding Allowance Certificate

▶ Whether you're entitled to claim a certain number of allowances or exemption from withholding is subject to review by the IRS. Your employer may be required to send a copy of this form to the IRS.

OMB No. 1545-0074

2019

1 Your first name and middle initial	Last name	2 Your social security number

Home address (number and street or rural route)	3 ☐ Single ☐ Married ☐ Married, but withhold at higher Single rate. **Note:** If married filing separately, check "Married, but withhold at higher Single rate."
City or town, state, and ZIP code	4 If your last name differs from that shown on your social security card, check here. You must call 800-772-1213 for a replacement card. ▶ ☐

5	Total number of allowances you're claiming (from the applicable worksheet on the following pages)	**5**	
6	Additional amount, if any, you want withheld from each paycheck	**6** $	
7	I claim exemption from withholding for 2019, and I certify that I meet **both** of the following conditions for exemption.		

• Last year I had a right to a refund of **all** federal income tax withheld because I had **no** tax liability, **and**
• This year I expect a refund of **all** federal income tax withheld because I expect to have **no** tax liability.
If you meet both conditions, write "Exempt" here . . . . ▶ **7**

Under penalties of perjury, I declare that I have examined this certificate and, to the best of my knowledge and belief, it is true, correct, and complete.

Employee's signature
(This form is not valid unless you sign it.) ▶   **Date** ▶

8 Employer's name and address (**Employer:** Complete boxes 8 and 10 if sending to IRS and complete boxes 8, 9, and 10 if sending to State Directory of New Hires.)	9 First date of employment	10 Employer identification number (EIN)

For Privacy Act and Paperwork Reduction Act Notice, see page 4.   Cat. No. 10220Q   Form **W-4** (2019)

Source: Internal Revenue Service, www.irs.gov

EXHIBIT 9.4

EXHIBIT 9.4

Wage and Tax Statement Form W-2

22222	Void ☐	**a** Employee's social security number	For Official Use Only ▶ OMB No. 1545-0008	
b Employer identification number (EIN)			**1** Wages, tips, other compensation	**2** Federal income tax withheld
c Employer's name, address, and ZIP code			**3** Social security wages	**4** Social security tax withheld
			5 Medicare wages and tips	**6** Medicare tax withheld
			7 Social security tips	**8** Allocated tips
d Control number			**9**	**10** Dependent care benefits
e Employee's first name and initial Last name Suff.			**11** Nonqualified plans	**12a** See instructions for box 12
			13 Statutory employee ☐ Retirement plan ☐ Third-party sick pay ☐	**12b**
			14 Other	**12c**
				12d
f Employee's address and ZIP code				

15 State Employer's state ID number	16 State wages, tips, etc.	17 State income tax	18 Local wages, tips, etc.	19 Local income tax	20 Locality name

Form W-2 Wage and Tax Statement   **2019**   Department of the Treasury—Internal Revenue Service

Copy A For Social Security Administration — Send this entire page with Form W-3 to the Social Security Administration; photocopies are **not** acceptable.

For Privacy Act and Paperwork Reduction Act Notice, see the separate instructions.

Cat. No. 10134D

Do Not Cut, Fold, or Staple Forms on This Page

Source: Internal Revenue Service, www.irs.gov

Employers are required to file the **Employer's Quarterly Federal Tax Return, Form 941** no later than one month after each quarter ends. This form reports the amounts due and paid to the government for federal withholdings. Failure to pay withheld taxes in a timely manner is serious. The government has the right to impose significant penalties and can even close a business, seize its assets, and take legal action against those who fail to pay taxes due.

Social Security and Medicare Taxes (FICA)

Congress adopted the Federal Insurance Contributions Act (FICA) to provide funding for the Social Security and Medicare programs. **Social Security** provides qualified individuals with old age, survivor's, and disability insurance (OASDI); **Medicare** provides health insurance. During their working years, employees pay a percentage of their earnings (up to a specified limit) to the federal government for Social Security. At retirement, a qualified person is entitled to receive monthly Social Security payments. Workers who become disabled before retirement are eligible to receive disability benefits. If a worker or retired person dies, any legal dependents are eligible to receive survivor benefits.

In order to meet the required benefit payments, Congress has frequently increased the amount of earnings to which the rates apply. Future changes in FICA tax rates and earnings maximums are likely. These changes will affect only the amount of FICA taxes, however, not how to account for them. *To simplify computations, this text assumes a Social Security rate of 6 percent on the first $130,000 of income and a Medicare rate of 1.5 percent on all earnings.*[2] For example, an employee earning $100,000 per year will have the following FICA taxes withheld from his or her salary:

Social Security	$100,000	×	6.0%	=	$6,000
Medicare	100,000	×	1.5%	=	1,500
Total withheld					$7,500

Not only employees are required to pay FICA taxes; the FICA legislation requires employers to pay a matching amount. The total FICA tax paid to the federal government for an employee earning $100,000 per year is $15,000 ($7,500 × 2), half paid by the employee and half paid by the employer. We discuss accounting for employer taxes later in the chapter.

CHECK YOURSELF 9.3

Jose Hernandez works for First Financial Services, Inc. (FFSI). During the first year of his employment Mr. Hernandez earned $12,000 per month. Determine the total amount of Social Security and Medicare tax that Mr. Hernandez will be required to pay for the year. Determine the total amount of tax that FFSI will have to pay for the year. Base your answer on the tax rates and limitations used in this text.

Answer

Even though Mr. Hernandez will earn $144,000 ($12,000 × 12 months) for the year, he will be required to pay Social Security tax only on $130,000. Accordingly, his Social Security tax for the year is $7,800 ($130,000 × 6.0%). Since there is no cap on Medicare tax, Mr. Hernandez will have to pay the Medicare tax rate on the entire $144,000 of his income. Specifically, he will have to pay $2,160 ($144,000 × 1.5%). FFSI is required to match Mr. Hernandez payment. As a result, FFSI will also have to pay $7,800 in Social Security tax and $2,160 Medicare tax for the year. FFSI's portion of these taxes are commonly called payroll taxes. Payroll taxes will be discussed in more detail in a subsequent section of this text.

Voluntary Withholdings (Deductions)

One reason governments require employers to withhold taxes from employee earnings is that many people have difficulty managing their spending. If employees received their gross earnings amount, they might not be able to pay their taxes because they would spend the money on other things first. Many people have this tendency with regard to other spending responsibilities as well. To ensure they make important payments, they voluntarily allow their employer to withhold money from their salaries. The employer then uses the money withheld to make payment in the employees' names for such items as medical insurance premiums, union dues, charitable contributions, and contributions to private retirement funds or savings accounts. Even employees who manage their personal finances without difficulty find it convenient to allow their employers to withhold funds and make payments on their behalf.

Withholding voluntary deductions from an employee's gross earnings represents a service on the employer's part. The employer must deduct the amounts authorized by each employee and remit the withheld money to the proper recipients. The employer must maintain additional records and undertake additional transactions to ensure the proper amounts are withheld and paid as specified on a timely basis. Employers normally itemize all deductions from gross pay on the pay stub to explain how an employee's net pay was determined.

[2]The actual rates for 2019 are 6.2 percent for the first $132,900 for Social Security and 1.45 percent on all earnings for Medicare.

Computing Employee Net Pay

Net pay is the employee's gross earnings less all deductions (withholdings). Net pay, often called take-home pay, is the amount of cash the employee receives from the employer.

To illustrate, assume that Herrera Supply Company (HSC) has an employee named Sarah Jennings. Ms. Jennings earns a monthly salary of $6,000. Based on Ms. Jennings's Form W-4, the tax tables require withholding $450 per month for income taxes. Because Ms. Jennings earns less than $130,000 per year, her full monthly salary is subject to FICA withholdings. Ms. Jennings has authorized HSC to deduct $320 per month for medical insurance and $25 per month for a charitable contribution to the American Cancer Society. Ms. Jennings's net pay is computed as follows:

Gross monthly salary		$6,000
Deductions		
Federal income taxes	$450	
FICA Tax—Social Security ($6,000 × 6%)	360	
FICA Tax—Medicare ($6,000 × 1.5%)	90	
Medical insurance premiums	320	
American Cancer Society	25	
Total deductions		1,245
Net pay		$4,755

The statement effects of recognizing salary expense for Ms. Jennings are shown next:

Balance Sheet					Income Statement				Statement of Cash Flows
Assets =	Liab.	+	Stk. Equity						
	Various		Com.	Ret.					
Cash =	Payables	+	Stk. +	Earn.	Rev. −	Exp.	= Net Inc.		
(4,755) =	1,245	+	NA +	(6,000)	NA −	6,000	= (6,000)		(4,755) OA

Employer Payroll Taxes

As mentioned earlier, employers are required to match employees' FICA taxes, and FICA tax rates are subject to change. This text uses the same assumed tax rates for employers as it uses for employees. *Assume a Social Security rate of 6 percent on the first $130,000 of each employee's earnings and a Medicare rate of 1.5 percent on all earnings.* The employer's portion of FICA taxes is a payroll tax expense to the employer.

Employers also incur a payroll tax expense for *unemployment* taxes. Congress adopted the **Federal Unemployment Tax Act (FUTA)** to finance temporary relief to qualified *unemployed* persons. The tax is determined by multiplying the wages of employees (up to a specified maximum limit) by a specified rate. The FUTA tax provides money to both state and federal government workforce agencies. States may enact supplemental unemployment tax laws based on higher maximum earnings or tax rates and could assess employees, rather than employers, for all or part of the supplemental coverage.

As of January 2017, the unemployment tax rate was 6.0 percent of the first $7,000 of wages earned by each employee during a calendar year. FUTA allows employers a credit of up to 5.4 percent for amounts paid to a state unemployment program, leaving a rate of 0.6 percent to be paid to the federal government. For example, on a tax of $420 (6.0% × $7,000), an employer would pay $42 (0.6% × $7,000) to the federal government and $378 (5.4% × $7,000) to the state government. State governments receive a larger percentage because they are responsible for administering the unemployment programs. The rates may be reduced to reward employers with few or no unemployment claims.

Recording and Reporting Payroll Taxes

To illustrate computing employer payroll tax expense, return to HSC's employee, Ms. Jennings, who earns $6,000 per month. HSC's February payroll tax expense for Ms. Jennings is computed as follows:

FICA tax expense—Social Security ($6,000 × 6%)	$360
FICA tax expense—Medicare ($6,000 × 1.5%)	90
Federal unemployment tax expense ($1,000 × 0.6%)	6
State unemployment tax expense ($1,000 × 5.4%)	54
Total payroll tax expense	$510

The unemployment taxes apply only to the first $7,000 of income earned each year by each employee. Because Ms. Jennings earned $6,000 in January, unemployment tax only applies to $1,000 of her February salary. The statement effects of recognizing payroll tax expense are shown next:

Balance Sheet						Income Statement					Statement of Cash Flows
Assets	=	Liab.	+		Stk. Equity						
Cash	=	Various Payables	+	Com. Stk.	+	Ret. Earn.	Rev.	−	Exp.	=	Net Inc.	
NA	=	510	+	NA	+	(510)	NA	−	510	=	(510)	NA

✓ CHECK YOURSELF 9.4

Bill Chavez, an employee of Bay Town Boat Company (BTBC), earns a salary of $150,000 per year. Based on the tax rates assumed in this chapter, determine the annual payroll tax expense BTBC would incur with respect to Mr. Chavez. How much payroll tax would Mr. Chavez be required to pay?

Answer

Payroll Tax Expense for BTBC	
FICA tax expense—Social Security ($130,000 × 6%)	$ 7,800
FICA tax expense—Medicare ($150,000 × 1.5%)	2,250
Federal unemployment tax expense ($7,000 × 0.6%)	42
State unemployment tax expense ($7,000 × 5.4%)	378
Total payroll tax expense	$10,470

Recall that FICA (Social Security) tax is limited to the first $130,000 of earnings. Mr. Chavez would not pay any payroll taxes. Payroll taxes apply to employers, not employees.

Employee Fringe Benefits

In addition to salaries and wages, many employers provide their employees with a variety of fringe benefits such as paid vacations, sick leave, maternity leave, and medical, dental, life, and disability insurance. These benefits plus payroll taxes frequently amount to as much as 25 percent of the employees' gross salaries and wages. Fringe benefits are reported as expenses on the income statement.

To illustrate, assume HSC provides the following fringe benefits to an employee, Alice Worthington. Ms. Worthington accrues $200 per month in vacation pay. HSC pays $250 per month for Ms. Worthington's medical insurance and contributes $150 per month to a pension (retirement) program for Ms. Worthington. Based on this information, HSC would recognize the following expenses and corresponding liabilities each month:

Fringe Benefits Expenses		
Vacation Pay Expense	$200	
Employee Medical Insurance Expense	250	
Employee Pension Expense	150	
Total Expenses		$600
Fringe Benefits Liabilities		
Vacation Pay Payable	$200	
Employee Medical Insurance Payable	250	
Employee Pension Liability	150	
Total Liabilities		$600

The statement effects of recognizing the monthly accrual of fringe benefits expenses are shown next:

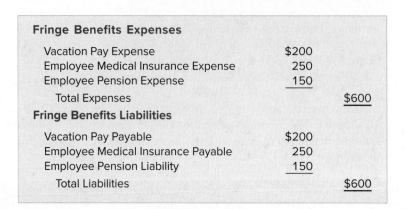

Balance Sheet					Income Statement			Statement of Cash Flows
Assets	=	Liab.	+	Stk. Equity				
		Various	Com.	Ret.				
Cash	=	Payables	+ Stk. +	Earn.	Rev. −	Exp. =	Net Inc.	
NA	=	600	+ NA +	(600)	NA −	600 =	(600)	NA

The Financial Analyst

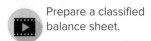
Because meeting obligations on time is critical to business survival, financial analysts and creditors are interested in whether companies will have enough money available to pay bills when they are due. Most businesses provide information about their bill-paying ability by classifying their assets and liabilities according to liquidity. The more quickly an asset is converted to cash or consumed, the more *liquid* it is. Assets are usually divided into two major classifications: *current* and *noncurrent*. Current items are also referred to as *short term* and noncurrent items as *long term*.

Preparing a Classified Balance Sheet

A **current (short-term) asset** is expected to be converted to cash or consumed within one year or an operating cycle, whichever is longer. An **operating cycle** is defined as the average time it takes a business to convert cash to inventory, inventory to accounts receivable, and accounts receivable back to cash. The financial tools used to measure the length of an operating cycle for particular businesses are discussed in Chapter 7. For most businesses, the operating cycle is less than one year. As a result, the one-year rule normally prevails with respect to classifying assets as current. The current assets section of a balance sheet typically includes the following items:

> Current Assets
>   Cash
>   Marketable securities
>   Accounts receivable
>   Short-term notes receivable
>   Interest receivable
>   Inventory
>   Supplies
>   Prepaid items

Given the definition of current assets, it seems reasonable to assume that **current (short-term) liabilities** would be those due within one year or an operating cycle, whichever is longer. This assumption is usually correct. However, an exception is made for long-term renewable debt. For example, consider a liability that was issued with a 20-year term to maturity. After 19 years, the liability becomes due within one year and is, therefore, a current liability. Even so, the liability will be classified as long term if the company plans to issue new long-term debt and to use the proceeds from that debt to repay the maturing liability. This situation is described as *refinancing short-term debt on a long-term basis*. In general, if a business does not plan to use any of its current assets to repay a debt, that debt is listed as long term even if it is due within one year. The current liabilities section of a balance sheet typically includes the following items:

> Current Liabilities
>   Accounts payable
>   Short-term notes payable
>   Wages payable
>   Taxes payable
>   Interest payable

Balance sheets that distinguish between current and noncurrent items are called **classified balance sheets.** To enhance the usefulness of accounting information, most real-world balance sheets are classified. Exhibit 9.5 displays an example of a classified balance sheet.

Liquidity versus Solvency

Liquidity describes the ability to generate sufficient short-term cash flows to pay obligations as they come due. **Solvency** is the ability to repay liabilities in the long run. Liquidity and solvency are both important to the survival of a business. Financial analysts rely on several ratios to help them evaluate a company's liquidity and solvency. The *debt-to-assets* ratio introduced in Chapter 3 is one tool used to measure solvency. The primary ratio used to evaluate liquidity is the current ratio.

The **current ratio** is defined as:

$$\frac{\text{Current assets}}{\text{Current liabilities}}$$

Because current assets normally exceed current liabilities, this ratio is usually greater than 100 percent. For example, if a company has $250 in current assets and $100 in current liabilities, current assets are 250 percent of current liabilities. The current ratio is traditionally expressed as a decimal rather than as a percentage, however; most analysts would describe this example as a current ratio of 2.5 to 1 ($250 ÷ $100 = $2.50 in current assets for every $1 in current liabilities). This book uses the traditional format when referring to the current ratio.

LO 9-7

Use the current ratio to assess the level of liquidity.

EXHIBIT 9.5

LIMBAUGH COMPANY
Classified Balance Sheet
As of December 31, Year 1

Assets

Current Assets			
Cash		$ 20,000	
Accounts receivable		35,000	
Inventory		230,000	
Prepaid rent		3,600	
Total current assets			$288,600
Property, Plant, and Equipment			
Office equipment	$ 80,000		
Less: Accumulated depreciation	(25,000)	55,000	
Building	340,000		
Less: Accumulated depreciation	(40,000)	300,000	
Land		120,000	
Total property, plant, and equipment			475,000
Total assets			$763,600

Liabilities and Stockholders' Equity

Current Liabilities			
Accounts payable		$ 32,000	
Notes payable		120,000	
Salaries payable		32,000	
Unearned revenue		9,800	
Total current liabilities			$193,800
Long-Term Liabilities			
Note payable			100,000
Total liabilities			293,800
Stockholders' Equity			
Common stock		200,000	
Retained earnings		269,800	469,800
Total liabilities and stockholders' equity			$763,600

The current ratio is among the most widely used ratios in analyzing financial statements. Current ratios can be too high, as well as too low. A low ratio suggests that the company may have difficulty paying its short-term obligations. A high ratio suggests that a company is not maximizing its earnings potential because investments in liquid assets usually do not earn as much money as investments in other assets. Companies must try to maintain an effective balance between liquid assets (so they can pay bills on time) and nonliquid assets (so they can earn a good return).

Real-World Data

Exhibit 9.6 presents the current ratios and debt-to-assets ratios for six companies in three different industries. These data are for the 2017 fiscal year.

Upon reviewing the data in Exhibit 9.6, one might conclude that the two electric utilities have more credit risks than the two clothing stores. After all, Dominion Energy and American Electric Power have much lower current ratios and higher debt-to-assets ratios, but they do not necessarily have higher credit risk. The ratios of clothing stores and electric utilities may not be comparable because their industries are very different. If the economy turns downward,

FOCUS ON INTERNATIONAL ISSUES

WHY ARE THESE BALANCE SHEETS BACKWARD?

As discussed in earlier chapters, most industrialized countries require companies to use international financial accounting standards (IFRS), which are similar to the GAAP used in the United States. The globalization of accounting standards should, therefore, make it easier to read a company's annual report regardless of its country of origin. However, there are still language differences between companies; German companies prepare their financial reports using IFRS (but in German), while UK companies use English.

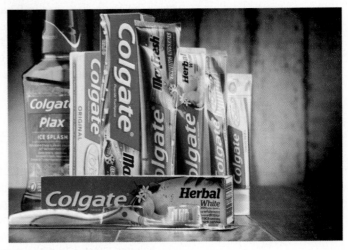

Monticello/Shutterstock

Suppose language is not an issue. For example, companies in the United States, the United Kingdom (UK), and even India prepare their annual reports in English. Thus, one would expect to find few differences between financial reports prepared by companies in these countries. However, if a person who learned accounting in the United States looks at the balance sheet of a UK company, he or she might think thte statement is a bit "backward," and likewise, the balance sheet of an Indian company might seem upside down.

Like U.S. companies, UK companies report assets at the top, or left, of the balance sheet and liabilities and stockholders' equity on the bottom or right. However, unlike the United States, UK companies typically show long-term assets before current assets. Even more different are balance sheets of Indian companies, which begin with stockholders' equity and then liabilities at the top or left, and then show assets on the bottom or right. Like the UK statements, those in India show long-term assets before current assets. Realize that most of the accounting rules established by IFRS or U.S. GAAP deal with measurement issues. Assets can be measured using the same rules but they may be disclosed in different ways. IFRS requires companies to classify assets and liabilities as current versus noncurrent, but the order in which these categories are listed on the balance sheet is not specified.

For an example of a financial statement for a UK company, go to www.itvplc.com. Click on "Investors" and then "Annual Report." For an example of an Indian company's annual report, go to www.colgatepalmolive.co.in. Click on "For Investors," then "Annual Report."

---

people are more likely to continue to use electricity than they are to spend money on new clothes. Because utility companies have a stable source of revenue, creditors are likely to feel comfortable with higher levels of debt for these companies than they would for clothing companies. Utilities have traditionally had relatively high debt-to-assets ratios.

What about the high debt-to-assets ratios of the companies in the building supplies business? When the economy is bad, housing construction is often one of the first industries to feel the effects, so why are Home Depot's and Lowe's debt-to-assets ratios so high? In this situ-

EXHIBIT 9.6

Industry	Company	Current Ratio	Debt-to-Assets Ratio
Electric utilities	American Electric Power	0.51	0.72
	Dominion Energy	0.45	0.75
Clothing stores	American Eagle Outfitters	2.00	0.31
	The Gap	1.86	0.60
Building supplies	Home Depot	1.17	0.97
	Lowe's	1.06	0.83

ation, the cause is due to macroeconomic policy. In 2017, and the few preceding years, interest rates were very low due to the policies of the Federal Reserve. The low interest rates caused many companies to increase their financing through debt and decrease their financing through equity. This was accomplished by buying back some of their outstanding common stock, an issue discussed in Chapter 11. Just four years earlier, in 2013, Home Depot's and Lowe's debt-to-assets ratios were only 0.57 and 0.58, respectively. Finally, notice that while the building supplies companies have debt-to-assets ratios in line with the electric utilities, their current ratios are much higher, and similar to each other's. As the data in Exhibit 9.6 demonstrate, financial ratios are often grouped by industry.

A Look Back

Chapter 9 discussed accounting for current liabilities and payroll. Current liabilities are obligations due within one year or the company's operating cycle, whichever is longer. The chapter expanded the discussion of promissory notes begun in Chapter 7. Chapter 7 introduced accounting for the note payee, the lender; Chapter 9 discussed accounting for the note maker (issuer), the borrower. Notes payable and related interest payable are reported as liabilities on the balance sheet. Chapter 9 also discussed accounting for sales tax liabilities, warranty obligations, and contingent liabilities.

Payroll costs and payroll taxes constitute a major expense for most businesses. An employer is responsible for withholding money from an employee's salary. The most common withholdings are for federal income taxes, FICA taxes, insurance premiums, savings or retirement contributions, union dues, and charitable donations. The employer uses the withholdings to pay the employees' obligations. The difference between the *gross pay* and the money withheld is called net pay. The *net pay* is the amount of cash the employer pays to the employee.

In addition to making payments for its employees, the employer is responsible for certain taxes on its employees' salaries and wages. These taxes are called payroll taxes. They include matching FICA Social Security and Medicare taxes, and federal and state unemployment taxes. Governments periodically change the rates of these taxes. The accounting for them, however, is not affected by rate changes. The rates used in this text are as follows: FICA Social Security—6 percent of the first $130,000 of each employee's wages with a matching payment for the employer; FICA Medicare—1.5 percent of the total wages of each employee with a matching payment for the employer; federal unemployment taxes—0.6 percent (6.0 percent less a 5.4 percent credit for state unemployment taxes) of the first $7,000 of each employee's wages; and state unemployment—5.4 percent of the first $7,000 of each employee's wages.

Finally, Chapter 9 discussed assessing companies' liquidity. The current ratio is current assets divided by current liabilities. The higher the current ratio, the more liquid the business.

A Look Forward

Chapter 10 investigates issues related to accounting for long-term liabilities. As you will learn, income tax consequences enter into decisions to borrow money.

APPENDIX

Accounting for Discount Notes

LO 9-8

Show how discount notes and related interest charges affect financial statements.

All notes payable discussed previously have been "add-on" **interest-bearing notes.** The amount due at maturity for add-on notes is the *face value* of the note *plus accrued interest.* In contrast, the interest on a **discount note** is included in the face value of the note. A $5,000 face value discount note is repaid with $5,000 cash at maturity. This payment includes both principal and accrued interest.

Accounting Events Affecting Year 1

To illustrate, assume Beacon Management Services experienced the following four events in Year 1: (1) borrowed money by issuing a discount note; (2) recognized operating expenses; (3) recognized revenue; and (4) recognized accrued interest.

EVENT 1   Beacon Management Services was started when it issued a $10,000 face value discount note to State Bank on March 1, Year 1.

The note had a 9 percent *discount rate* and a one-year term to maturity. As with interest-bearing notes, the *issuer* of a discount note exchanges the promissory note for cash. Accounting for the discount note requires dividing the face amount between the **discount** and the **principal,** or **proceeds** (amount of cash borrowed). The discount is computed by multiplying the face value of the note by the interest rate by the time period. Subtracting the discount from the face value of the note determines the principal (proceeds). The computations follow:

Face value of note	$10,000
Less discount ($10,000 × 0.09 × 1) =	900
Proceeds (amount borrowed)	$ 9,100

On the issue date, both assets and liabilities increase by the amount borrowed (the $9,100 principal). The borrowing transaction on the issue date has no effect on the income statement. The $9,100 cash inflow is reported in the financing activities section of the statement of cash flows. The effects on the financial statements are shown next:

Event No.	Balance Sheet						Income Statement					Statement of Cash Flows
	Assets =	Liabilities	+	Stk. Equity								
	Cash =	Carrying Value of Note Pay.	+	Com. Stk.	+	Ret. Earn.	Rev.	−	Exp.	=	Net Inc.	
1	9,100 =	9,100	+	NA	+	NA	NA	−	NA	=	NA	9,100 FA

The discount is recorded in a **contra liability account** called **Discount on Notes Payable.** The *carrying value* of the liability is the difference between the Notes Payable and Discount accounts. Carrying value, also called *book value,* is the amount at which the liability is carried on the books. The carrying value on the issue date is as follows:

Note Payable	$10,000
Discount on Note Payable	(900)
Carrying value of Note Payable	$ 9,100

EVENT 2   Beacon incurred $8,000 of cash operating expenses.

Paying these expenses reduces both assets and stockholders' equity. The effect on the income statement is to increase expenses and decrease net income. The cash outflow is reported in the operating activities section of the statement of cash flows. The effects on the financial statements are shown next:

Event No.	Balance Sheet						Income Statement					Statement of Cash Flows
	Assets =	Liabilities	+	Stk. Equity								
	Cash =	Carrying Value of Note Pay.	+	Com. Stk.	+	Ret. Earn.	Rev.	−	Exp.	=	Net Inc.	
2	(8,000) =	NA	+	NA	+	(8,000)	NA	−	(8,000)	=	(8,000)	(8,000) OA

EVENT 3   Beacon recognized $12,000 of cash service revenue.

Recognizing revenue increases both assets and stockholders' equity. Net income increases. The cash inflow is reported in the operating activities section of the statement of cash flows. The effects on the financial statements are shown next:

Event No.	Balance Sheet						Income Statement			Statement of Cash Flows
	Assets =	Liabilities	+	Stk. Equity						
	Cash =	Carrying Value of Note Pay.	+	Com. Stk.	+	Ret. Earn.	Rev.	− Exp. =	Net Inc.	
3	12,000 =	NA	+	NA	+	12,000	12,000 −	NA =	12,000	12,000 OA

EVENT 4   Beacon made an adjustment to recognize interest accrued since March 1.

The bookkeeping technique of converting the discount to interest expense over the term of the loan is described as **amortizing** the discount. On December 31, Year 1, Beacon must adjust its accounting records to amortize the 10 months of interest expense it incurred in Year 1. For this note, interest expense accrues at $75 per month ($900 discount ÷ 12). As of December 31, $750 ($75 × 10) of interest expense has accrued. Because no cash payment is due until the note matures in Year 2, the reduction in stockholders' equity from recognizing the interest expense is accompanied by an increase in liabilities. The effect of the interest recognition on the income statement is to increase expenses and decrease net income by $750. The statement of cash flows is not affected by the accrual. Beacon recognizes the cash effects of the interest on the maturity date when it pays the maturity (face) value of the note to State Bank. The effects of amortizing $750 of the discount on the financial statements are shown next:

Event No.	Balance Sheet						Income Statement			Statement of Cash Flows
	Assets =	Liabilities	+	Stk. Equity						
	Cash =	Carrying Value of Note Pay.	+	Com. Stk.	+	Ret. Earn.	Rev. −	Exp. =	Net Inc.	
4	NA =	750	+	NA	+	(750)	NA −	750 =	(750)	NA

The increase in liabilities is recognized by *reducing the contra liability account,* Discount on Notes Payable. Recall that the carrying value of the liability was $9,100 on the day the note was issued. The adjustment to recognize the accrued interest expense removes $750 from the Discount account, leaving a discount balance of $150 ($900 − $750) after the adjustment.

General Financial Statements

Panel A of Exhibit 9.7 summarizes the Year 1 accounting events. The financial statements are shown in Panel B of the exhibit. You should study Exhibit 9.7 to strengthen your understanding of how the accounting for discount notes affects the financial statements. First, notice that after amortizing 10 months' interest expense, the carrying value of the liability reported on the December 31, Year 1, balance sheet is $9,850 ($10,000 face value − $150 discount). Also, note that while the income statement shows $750 of interest expense, there is no corresponding cash flow for interest shown in the statement of cash flows. Recall that the cash paid for interest occurs on the maturity date in Year 2.

Accounting Events Affecting Year 2

In Year 2, Beacon Management Services experienced the following four accounting events: (1) recognized accrued interest for Year 2; (2) paid the face value of the note; (3) recognized revenue; and (4) recognized operating expenses.

EVENT 1   Beacon made an adjustment to recognize interest accrued since December 31.

Because the note had a one-year term, interest for two months remains to be accrued at the maturity date on February 28, Year 2. Interest on this note accrues at $75 per month ($900 discount ÷ 12), so there is $150 ($75 × 2) of interest expense to recognize in Year 2.

EXHIBIT 9.7

The Big Picture

Panel A: Transaction Summary

1. Beacon issued a $10,000 face value, one-year, discount note with a 9 percent discount rate.
2. Beacon paid $8,000 cash for operating expenses.
3. Beacon earned cash service revenue of $12,000.
4. Beacon recognized $750 of accrued interest expense.

Panel B: Financial Statements for Year 1

Income Statement			Balance Sheet			Statement of Cash Flows	
Service revenue	$12,000		Assets			**Operating Activities**	
Operating expenses	(8,000)		Cash		$13,100	Inflow from customers	$12,000
Operating income	4,000		Liabilities			Outflow for expenses	(8,000)
Interest expense	(750)		Notes payable	$10,000		Net inflow from	
Net income	$ 3,250		Less: Disc. on notes pay.	(150)		operating activities	4,000
			Total liabilities		$ 9,850	**Investing Activities**	0
			Stockholders' equity			**Financing Activities**	
			Retained earnings		3,250	Inflow from creditors	9,100
			Total liab. and stockholders' equity		$13,100	Net change in cash	13,100
						Plus: Beginning cash balance	0
						Ending cash balance	$13,100

Recognizing the interest increases liabilities (the Discount account is reduced to zero) and decreases stockholders' equity. The effect on the income statement of recognizing interest is to increase expenses and decrease net income by $150. The statement of cash flows is not affected by the interest recognition. The effects on the financial statements are shown next:

Event No.	Balance Sheet						Income Statement			Statement of Cash Flows
	Assets =	Liabilities		+	Stk. Equity					
	Cash =	Carrying Value of Note Pay.	+	Com. Stk.	+	Ret. Earn.	Rev. −	Exp. =	Net Inc.	
1.	NA =	150	+	NA	+	(150)	NA −	150 =	(150)	NA

EVENT 2   Beacon paid the face value of the note.

The face value ($10,000) of the note is due on the maturity date. Paying the maturity value is an asset use transaction that decreases both assets and liabilities. The income statement is not affected by the payment. The $10,000 cash payment includes $900 for interest and $9,100 for principal. On the statement of cash flows, a $900 outflow for interest is reported in the operating activities section and a $9,100 outflow for repaying the loan is reported in the financing activities section. The effects on the financial statements are shown next:

Event No.	Balance Sheet						Income Statement			Statement of Cash Flows
	Assets =	Liabilities		+	Stk. Equity					
	Cash =	Carrying Value of Note Pay.	+	Com. Stk.	+	Ret. Earn.	Rev. −	Exp. =	Net Inc.	
2.	(10,000) =	(10,000)	+	NA	+	NA	NA −	NA =	NA	(900) OA (9,100) FA

EVENT 3   Beacon recognized $13,000 of cash service revenue.

Recognizing the revenue increases both assets and stockholders' equity. Net income also increases. The cash inflow is reported in the operating activities section of the statement of cash flows. The effects on the financial statements are shown next:

	Balance Sheet						Income Statement			Statement of Cash Flows
Event No.	Assets =	Liabilities	+	Stk. Equity						
	Cash =	Carrying Value of Note Pay.	+	Com. Stk.	+	Ret. Earn.	Rev. −	Exp. =	Net Inc.	
3.	13,000 =	NA	+	NA	+	13,000	13,000 −	NA =	13,000	13,000 OA

EVENT 4   Beacon incurred $8,500 of cash operating expenses.

This event decreases both assets and stockholders' equity. Net income also decreases. The cash outflow is reported in the operating activities section of the statement of cash flows. The effects on the financial statements are shown next:

	Balance Sheet						Income Statement			Statement of Cash Flows
Event No.	Assets =	Liabilities	+	Stk. Equity						
	Cash =	Carrying Value of Note Pay.	+	Com. Stk.	+	Ret. Earn.	Rev. −	Exp. =	Net Inc.	
4.	(8,500) =	NA	+	NA	+	(8,500)	NA −	8,500 =	(8,500)	(8,500) OA

Financial Statements

Panel A of Exhibit 9.8 summarizes the Year 2 accounting events. The financial statements are shown in Panel B of the exhibit. You should study Exhibit 9.8 to strengthen your understanding of how accounting for discount notes affects the financial statements. Observe that no liabilities are reported in the balance sheet because Beacon has paid off the note and interest. Because Beacon has not paid dividends since its inception, retained earnings represents the sum of net income recognized for Year 1 and Year 2.

EXHIBIT 9.8

The Big Picture

Panel A: Transaction Summary

Event 1	Recognized accrued interest for Year 2.
Event 2	Paid face value of note.
Event 3	Recognized revenue.
Event 4	Recognized operating expenses.

Panel B: Financial Statements for Year 2

Income Statement		Balance Sheet		Statement of Cash Flows	
Service revenue	$13,000	Assets		**Operating Activities**	
Operating expenses	(8,500)	Cash	$7,600	Inflow from customers	$13,000
Operating income	4,500	Liabilities	$ 0	Outflow for expenses	(8,500)
Interest expense	(150)	Stockholders' equity		Outflow for interest	(900)
Net income	$ 4,350	Retained earnings	7,600	Net inflow from	
		Total liab. and stockholders' equity	$7,600	operating activities	3,600
				Investing Activities	0
				Financing Activities	
				Outflow to creditors	(9,100)
				Net change in cash	(5,500)
				Plus: Beginning cash balance	13,100
				Ending cash balance	$ 7,600

Tableau Dashboard Activity is available in *Connect* for this chapter.

SELF-STUDY REVIEW PROBLEM

A step-by-step audio-narrated series of slides is available in *Connect*.

Perfect Picture Inc. (PPI) experienced the following selected events during Year 1. The events are summarized (transaction data pertain to the full year) and limited to those that affect the company's current liabilities.

1. PPI had cash sales of $820,000. The state requires that PPI charge customers an 8 percent sales tax (ignore cost of goods sold). PPI paid the state sales tax authority $63,000.

2. On March 1, PPI issued a note payable to County Bank. PPI received $50,000 cash (principal balance). The note had a one-year term and a 6 percent annual interest rate. On December 31, PPI recognized accrued interest on the note.

3. On December 31, PPI recognized warranty expense at the rate of 3 percent of sales. PPI paid $22,000 cash to settle warranty claims.

4. PPI has five employees. Four of the employees each earn $40,000 per year. The fifth employee, the store manager, earns $140,000 per year. The annual amount withheld for income tax for all employees is $54,000. Each of the five employees has volunteered to have $50 per month withheld as a charitable contribution to the United Way. Record the net pay as a liability.

5. PPI pays $320 per month for medical insurance premiums for each employee. The company also contributes an amount equal to 4 percent of salaries to a pension fund for each employee. Each employee accrues vacation pay at a rate of $300 per month.

Required

a. Determine the amount of sales tax expense recognized by PPI and the ending balance in the sales tax liability account.

b. As of December 31, Year 1, determine the total amount of liabilities associated with the note described in Event 2.

c. Determine the amount of warranties payable as of December 31, Year 1.

d. Determine the annual amount of net pay associated with Event 4.

e. Based on the salary data described in Event 4, determine the annual payroll tax expense for FICA and unemployment taxes.

f. Determine the amount of fringe benefits expense associated with Event 5.

Solution

Requirement *a*

The amount of sales tax expense recognized by PPI is zero. PPI is not responsible for the sales tax expense. Instead, PPI's customers are responsible for the sales tax expense. At the time of the sale, PPI withholds the sales tax and incurs a liability to pay the taxing authority. In this case, the amount of the liability is $65,600 ($820,000 × .08). Because PPI paid the taxing authority $63,000, the ending balance in the Sales Tax Payable account is $2,600.

Requirement *b*

The amount of accrued interest payable as of December 31, Year 1, is $2,500 [$50,000 × .06 × (10/12)]. Total liabilities as of December 31, Year 1, is $52,500, which includes the $50,000 principal balance of the note plus the $2,500 of accrued interest payable.

Requirement *c*

The total warranty liability for Year 1 is $24,600 ($820,000 sales × .03). Because PPI paid $22,000 in warranty claims during Year 1, the ending balance in the Warranties Payable account is $2,600 ($24,600 − $22,000).

Requirement d

Computation of Net Pay	
Salary Expense [(4 × $40,000) + $140,000]	$300,000
Employee Income Tax Payable	(54,000)
FICA Tax—Social Security Payable*	(17,400)
FICA Tax—Medicare Payable ($300,000 × 0.015)	(4,500)
United Way Payable ($50 × 5 × 12)	(3,000)
Net Pay	$224,100

*Recall that the chapter assumes Social Security tax is applied to a maximum limit of $130,000. [($40,000 × 0.06 = $2,400 × 4 = $9,600) + ($130,000 × 0.06 = $7,800)] = $17,400

Requirement e

Computation of Payroll Tax Expense	
FICA Tax—Social Security Payable*	$17,400
FICA Tax—Medicare Payable ($300,000 × 0.015)	4,500
Federal Unemployment Tax Payable ($7,000 × 5 × 0.006)	210
State Unemployment Tax Payable ($7,000 × 5 × 0.054)	1,890
Payroll Tax Expense	$24,000

*Recall that the chapter assumes Social Security tax is applied to a maximum limit of $130,000. [($40,000 × 0.06 = $2,400 × 4 = $9,600) + ($130,000 × 0.06 = $7,800)] = $17,400

Requirement f

Computation of Fringe Benefits Expense	
Medical Insurance Payable ($320 × 12 × 5)	$19,200
Employee Pension Fund Payable ($300,000 × 0.04)	12,000
Vacation Pay Payable ($300 × 12 × 5)	18,000
Fringe Benefits Expense	$49,200

KEY TERMS

QUESTIONS

1. What type of transaction is a cash payment to creditors? How does this type of transaction affect the accounting equation?

2. What is a current liability? Distinguish between a current liability and a long-term debt.

3. What is included in the adjustment to record accrued interest expense? How does it affect the accounting equation?

4. Who is the maker of a note payable?

5. What is the going concern assumption? Does it affect the way liabilities are reported in the financial statements?

6. Why is it necessary to make an adjustment at the end of the accounting period for unpaid interest on a note payable?

7. Assume that on October 1, Year 1, Big Company borrowed $10,000 from the local bank at 6 percent interest. The note is due on October 1, Year 2. How much interest does Big pay in Year 1? How much interest does Big pay in Year 2? What amount of cash does Big pay back in Year 2?

8. When a business collects sales tax from customers, is it revenue? Why or why not?

9. What is a contingent liability?

10. List the three categories of contingent liabilities.

11. Are contingent liabilities recorded on a company's books? Explain.

12. What is the difference in accounting procedures for a liability that is probable and estimable and one that is reasonably possible but not estimable?

13. What type of liabilities are not recorded on a company's books?

14. What does the term *warranty* mean?

15. What effect does recognizing future warranty obligations have on the balance sheet? On the income statement?

16. When is warranty cost reported on the statement of cash flows?

17. What is the difference between an employee and an independent contractor?

18. What is the difference between wages and salaries?

19. What is the purpose of the W-2 form? What is the purpose of the W-4 form?

20. What two taxes are components of the FICA tax? What programs do they fund?

21. Who pays the FICA tax? Is there a ceiling on the amount of tax that is paid?

22. What is the difference between gross pay and net pay for an employee?

23. Why are amounts withheld from employees' pay considered liabilities of the employer?

24. What is the purpose of the Federal Unemployment Tax? What is the maximum amount of wages subject to the tax?

25. What items are included in compensation cost for a company in addition to the gross salaries of the employees?

26. Give two examples of fringe benefits.

27. What is a classified balance sheet?

28. What is the difference between the liquidity and the solvency of a business?

29. The higher the company's current ratio, the better the company's financial condition. Do you agree with this statement? Explain.

30. What is the difference between an interest-bearing note and a discount note?

31. How is the carrying value of a discount note computed?

32. Will the effective rate of interest be the same on a $10,000 face value, 6 percent interest-bearing note and a $10,000 face value, 6 percent discount note? Is the amount of cash received upon making these two loans the same? Why or why not?

33. How does the *amortization* of a discount affect the income statement, balance sheet, and statement of cash flows?

34. How does issuing an $8,000 discount note with an 8 percent discount rate and a one-year term to maturity affect the accounting equation?

35. What type of account is Discount on Notes Payable?

EXERCISES—SERIES A

 All applicable Exercises in Series A are available in *Connect*.

Exercise 9-1A   *Recognizing accrued interest expense*   LO 9-1

Abardeen Corporation borrowed $90,000 from the bank on October 1, Year 1. The note had an 8 percent annual rate of interest and matured on March 31, Year 2. Interest and principal were paid in cash on the maturity date.

Required

a. What amount of cash did Abardeen pay for interest in Year 1?

b. What amount of interest expense was recognized on the Year 1 income statement?

c. What amount of total liabilities was reported on the December 31, Year 1, balance sheet?

d. What total amount of cash was paid to the bank on March 31, Year 2, for principal and interest?

e. What amount of interest expense was reported on the Year 2 income statement?

Exercise 9-2A *Effects of recognizing accrued interest on financial statements*

Bill Darby started Darby Company on January 1, Year 1. The company experienced the following events during its first year of operation:

1. Earned $16,200 of cash revenue.
2. Borrowed $12,000 cash from the bank.
3. Adjusted the accounting records to recognize accrued interest expense on the bank note. The note, issued on September 1, Year 1, had a one-year term and an 8 percent annual interest rate.

Required

a. What is the amount of interest payable at December 31, Year 1?
b. What is the amount of interest expense in Year 1?
c. What is the amount of interest paid in Year 1?
d. Use a horizontal statements model to show how each event affects the balance sheet, income statement, and statement of cash flows. Indicate whether the event increases (I), decreases (D), or does not affect (NA) each element of the financial statements. In the Statement of Cash Flows column, designate the cash flows as operating activities (OA), investing activities (IA), or financing activities (FA). The first transaction has been recorded as an example.

Event No.	Balance Sheet											Income Statement					Statement of Cash Flows
	Cash	=	Notes Pay.	+	Int. Pay.	+	Com. Stk.	+	Ret. Earn.			Rev.	−	Exp.	=	Net Inc.	
1.	I	=	NA	+	NA	+	NA	+	I			I	−	NA	=	I	I OA

Exercise 9-3A *Recording sales tax*

Vail Book Mart sells books and other supplies to students in a state where the sales tax rate is 8 percent. Vail Book Mart engaged in the following transactions for Year 1. Sales tax of 8 percent is collected on all sales.

1. Book sales, not including sales tax, for Year 1 amounted to $250,000 cash.
2. Cash sales of miscellaneous items in Year 1 were $85,000, not including tax.
3. Cost of goods sold was $190,000 for the year.
4. Paid $117,000 in operating expenses for the year.
5. Paid the sales tax collected to the state agency.

Required

a. What is the total amount of sales tax Vail Book Mart collected and paid for the year?
b. What is Vail Book Mart's net income for the year?

Exercise 9-4A *Recognizing sales tax payable*

The following selected transactions apply to Topeca Supply for November and December Year 1. November was the first month of operations. Sales tax is collected at the time of sale but is not paid to the state sales tax agency until the following month.

1. Cash sales for November Year 1 were $165,000, plus sales tax of 7 percent.
2. Topeca Supply paid the November sales tax to the state agency on December 10, Year 1.
3. Cash sales for December Year 1 were $180,000, plus sales tax of 7 percent.

Required

a. Show the effect of the preceding transactions on a horizontal statements model like the one shown next:

Balance Sheet								Income Statement					Statement of Cash Flows
Assets	=	Liabilities	+		Stk. Equity								
Cash	=	Sales Tax Pay.	+	Com. Stk.	+	Ret. Earn.		Rev.	−	Exp.	=	Net Inc.	

b. What was the total amount of sales tax paid in Year 1?

c. What was the total amount of sales tax collected in Year 1?

d. What is the amount of the sales tax liability as of December 31, Year 1?

e. On which financial statement will the sales tax liability appear?

Exercise 9-5A *Contingent liabilities*

LO 9-3

The following three independent sets of facts relate to contingent liabilities:

1. In November of the current year, an automobile manufacturing company recalled all pickup trucks manufactured during the past two years. A flaw in the battery cable was discovered and the recall provides for replacement of the defective cables. The estimated cost of this recall is $2 million.

2. The EPA has notified a company of violations of environmental laws relating to hazardous waste. These actions seek cleanup costs, penalties, and damages to property. The company is reasonably certain there will be cost associated with the cleanup, but cannot estimate the amount. The cleanup cost could be as high as $4,000,000 or as little as $500,000, and insurance could reimburse all or part of the cost. There is no way to more accurately estimate the cost to the company at this time.

3. Holland Company does not carry property damage insurance because of the cost. The company has suffered substantial losses each of the past three years. However, it has had no losses for the current year. Management thinks this is too good to be true and is sure there will be significant losses in the coming year, but the exact amount cannot be determined.

Required

a. Discuss the various categories of contingent liabilities.

b. For each item in the preceding list, determine the correct accounting treatment.

Exercise 9-6A *Effect of warranties on income and cash flow*

LO 9-4

To support herself while attending school, Daun Deloch sold stereo systems to other students. During the first year of operations, Daun purchased the stereo systems for $140,000 and sold them for $250,000 cash. She provided her customers with a one-year warranty against defects in parts and labor. Based on industry standards, she estimated that warranty claims would amount to 2 percent of sales. During the year, she paid $2,820 cash to replace a defective tuner.

Required

Prepare an income statement and statement of cash flows for Daun's first year of operation. Based on the information given, what is Daun's total warranties liability at the end of the accounting period?

Exercise 9-7A *Effect of warranty obligations and payments on financial statements*

LO 9-4

The Chair Company provides a 120-day parts-and-labor warranty on all merchandise it sells. The Chair Company estimates the warranty expense for the current period to be $2,650. During this period, a customer returned a product that cost $1,830 to repair.

Required

a. Show the effects of these transactions on the financial statements using a horizontal statements model like the example shown next. Use + for increase, − for decrease, and NA for not affected. In the Statement of Cash Flows column, indicate whether the item is an operating activity (OA), investing activity (IA), or financing activity (FA).

Balance Sheet					Income Statement				Statement of Cash Flows
Assets	=	Liab.	+	Stk. Equity	Rev.	−	Exp.	= Net Inc.	

b. Discuss the advantage of estimating the amount of warranty expense.

Exercise 9-8A *Current liabilities*

The following transactions apply to Ozark Sales for Year 1:

1. The business was started when the company received $50,000 from the issue of common stock.
2. Purchased equipment inventory of $380,000 on account.
3. Sold equipment for $510,000 cash (not including sales tax). Sales tax of 8 percent is collected when the merchandise is sold. The merchandise had a cost of $330,000.
4. Provided a six-month warranty on the equipment sold. Based on industry estimates, the warranty claims would amount to 2 percent of sales.
5. Paid the sales tax to the state agency on $400,000 of the sales.
6. On September 1, Year 1, borrowed $50,000 from the local bank. The note had a 4 percent interest rate and matured on March 1, Year 2.
7. Paid $6,200 for warranty repairs during the year.
8. Paid operating expenses of $78,000 for the year.
9. Paid $250,000 of accounts payable.
10. Recorded accrued interest on the note issued in transaction no. 6. Round answer to nearest whole dollar.

Required

a. Show the effect of these transactions on the financial statements using a horizontal statements model like the one shown next. Use + for increase, − for decrease, and NA for not affected. In the Statement of Cash Flows column, indicate whether the item is an operating activity (OA), investing activity (IA), or financing activity (FA). The first transaction is recorded as an example.

Balance Sheet				Income Statement				Statement of Cash Flows
Assets	=	Liabilities	+ Stk. Equity	Rev.	− Exp.	=	Net Inc.	
+		NA	+	NA	NA		NA	+ FA

b. Prepare the income statement, balance sheet, and statement of cash flows for the period ended December 31, Year 1.

c. What is the total amount of current liabilities at December 31, Year 1?

Exercise 9-9A *Calculating payroll*

Zolnick Enterprises has two hourly employees: Kelly and Jon. Both employees earn overtime at the rate of 1½ times the hourly rate for hours worked in excess of 40 per week. Assume the Social Security tax rate is 6 percent on the first $130,000 of wages, and the Medicare tax rate is 1.5 percent on all earnings. Federal income tax withheld for Kelly and Jon was $260 and $220, respectively, for the first week of January. The following information is for the first week in January, Year 1:

Employee	Hours Worked	Wage Rate per Hour
Kelly	54	$32
Jon	44	$26

Required

a. Calculate the gross pay for each employee for the week.
b. Calculate the net pay for each employee for the week.

Exercise 9-10A *Calculating payroll*

Old Town Entertainment has two employees in Year 1. Clay earns $3,600 per month, and Philip, the manager, earns $10,800 per month. Neither is paid extra for working overtime. Assume the Social Security tax rate is 6 percent on the first $130,000 of earnings and the Medicare tax rate is 1.5 percent on all earnings. The federal income tax withholding is 15 percent of gross earnings for Clay and 20 percent for Philip. Both Clay and Philip have been employed all year.

Required

a. Calculate the net pay for both Clay and Philip for March.

b. Calculate the net pay for both Clay and Philip for December.

c. Is the net pay the same in March and December for both employees? Why or why not?

d. What amounts will Old Town report on the Year 1 W-2s for each employee?

Exercise 9-11A   *Calculating employee and employer payroll taxes*   LO 9-5

Sky Co. employed Tom Mills in Year 1. Tom earned $5,100 per month and worked the entire year. Assume the Social Security tax rate is 6 percent for the first $130,000 of earnings, and the Medicare tax rate is 1.5 percent. Tom's federal income tax withholding amount is $900 per month. Use 5.4 percent for the state unemployment tax rate and .06 percent for the federal unemployment tax rate on the first $7,000 of earnings per employee.

Required

a. Answer the following questions:

(1) What is Tom's net pay per month?

(2) What amount does Tom pay monthly in FICA taxes?

(3) What is the total payroll tax expense for Sky Co. for January, Year 1? February, Year 1? March, Year 1? December, Year 1?

b. Assume that instead of $5,100 per month Tom earned $11,000 per month. Based on this new level of income Tom's new federal income tax withholding is $2,000. Answer the questions in Requirement *a*.

Exercise 9-12A   *Fringe benefits and payroll expense*   LO 9-5

The two employees of Silver Co. receive various fringe benefits. Silver Co. provides vacation at the rate of $315 per day. Each employee earns one day of vacation per month worked. In addition, Silver Co. pays a total amount of $650 per month in medical insurance premiums. Silver also contributes a total amount of $400 per month into an employee retirement plan. The federal unemployment tax rate is 6 percent, while the state unemployment tax rate is 4 percent. Unemployment taxes apply to the first $7,000 of earnings per employee. Assume a Social Security tax rate of 6 percent and a Medicare tax rate of 1.5 percent.

Required

a. Prepare the computation of accrued fringe benefits per month.

b. Show the effect of accrued fringe benefits per month on a horizontal statements model like the one shown next:

Balance Sheet						Income Statement			Statement of Cash Flows
Assets	=	Liabilities	+		Stk. Equity				
Cash	=	Various Payables	+	Com. Stk.	+	Ret. Earn.	Rev. − Exp. =	Net Inc.	

c. If the two employees each worked 250 days, what is Silver Co.'s total payroll cost (salary, payroll taxes, and fringe benefits) for the year? (Assume that each employee earns $315 per day.)

Exercise 9-13A   *Computation of net pay and payroll expense*   LO 9-5

The following information is available for the employees of Webber Packing Company for the first week of January, Year 1:

1. Kayla earns $28 per hour and 1½ times her regular rate for hours over 40 per week. Kayla worked 52 hours the first week in January. Kayla's federal income tax withholding is equal to 15 percent of her gross pay. Webber pays medical insurance of $50 per week for Kayla and contributes $50 per week to a retirement plan for her.

2. Paula earns a weekly salary of $1,600. Paula's federal income tax withholding is 18 percent of her gross pay. Webber pays medical insurance of $80 per week for Paula and contributes $100 per week to a retirement plan for her.

3. Vacation pay is accrued at the rate of 2 hours per week (based on the regular pay rate) for Kayla and $60 per week for Paula.

Assume the Social Security tax rate is 6 percent on the first $130,000 of salaries, and the Medicare tax rate is 1.5 percent of total salaries. The state unemployment tax rate is 5.4 percent and the federal unemployment tax rate is 0.6 percent of the first $7,000 of salary for each employee.

Required

a. Compute the gross pay for Kayla for the first week in January.

b. Compute the net pay for both Kayla and Paula for the first week in January.

c. What is the total cost of compensation expense for the first week of January Year 1 for Webber Company?

LO 9-6

Exercise 9-14A *Preparing a classified balance sheet*

Required

Use the following information to prepare a classified balance sheet for Alpha Co. at the end of Year 1.

Accounts receivable	$26,500
Accounts payable	12,200
Cash	20,500
Common stock	30,000
Land	10,000
Long-term notes payable	17,500
Merchandise inventory	26,300
Retained earnings	23,600

LO 9-7

Exercise 9-15A *Using the current ratio to make comparisons*

The following information was drawn from the balance sheets of the Kansas and Montana companies:

	Kansas	Montana
Current assets	$59,000	$78,000
Current liabilities	40,000	43,000

Required

a. Compute the current ratio for each company.

b. Which company has the greater likelihood of being able to pay its bills?

c. Assume that both companies have the same amount of total assets. Speculate as to which company would produce the higher return-on-assets ratio.

LO 9-8

Exercise 9-16A *Effect of a discount note on financial statements (Appendix)*

Helen Parish started a design company on January 1, Year 1. On April 1, Year 1, Parish borrowed cash from a local bank by issuing a one-year $120,000 face value note with annual interest based on an 8 percent discount. During Year 1, Parish provided services for $72,000 cash.

Required

Answer the following questions. (*Hint:* Record the events in an accounting equation prior to answering the questions.)

a. What is the amount of total liabilities on the December 31, Year 1, balance sheet?

b. What is the amount of net income on the Year 1 income statement?

c. What is the amount of cash flow from operating activities on the Year 1 statement of cash flows?

Exercise 9-17A *Comparing effective interest rates on discount versus interest-bearing notes (Appendix)*

Sheldon Jones borrowed money by issuing two notes on March 1, Year 1. The financing transactions are described next.

1. Borrowed funds by issuing a $52,000 face value discount note to Farmers Bank. The note had an 8 percent discount rate, a one-year term to maturity, and was paid off on March 1, Year 2.
2. Borrowed funds by issuing a $52,000 face value, interest-bearing note to Valley Bank. The note had an 8 percent stated rate of interest, a one-year term to maturity, and was paid off on March 1, Year 2.

Required

a. Show the effects of issuing the two notes on the financial statements using separate horizontal financial statement models like those shown next. Record the transaction amounts under the appropriate categories. In the Statement of Cash Flows column, indicate whether the item is an operating activity (OA), investing activity (IA), or financing activity (FA). Record only the events occurring on the date of issue. Do not record accrued interest or the repayment at maturity.

Discount Note

Balance Sheet					Income Statement			Statement of Cash Flows
Assets	=	Liabilities	+	Stk. Equity				
Cash	=	Carrying Value of Note Pay.	+	Ret. Earn.	Rev. −	Exp. =	Net Inc.	

Interest-Bearing Note

Balance Sheet					Income Statement			Statement of Cash Flows
Assets	=	Liabilities	+	Stk. Equity				
Cash	=	Notes Pay.	+	Ret. Earn.	Rev. −	Exp. =	Net Inc.	

a. What is the total amount of interest to be paid on each note?
b. What amount of cash was received from each note when it was issued?
c. Which note has the higher effective interest rate? Support your answer with appropriate computations.

Exercise 9-18A *Recording accounting events for a discount note (Appendix)*

Harden Co. issued a $60,000 face value discount note to National Bank on July 1, Year 1. The note had a 6 percent discount rate and a one-year term to maturity.

Required

Show the effects of the following transactions (a–c) on the financial statements using a horizontal financial statement model such as the following one. Record the transaction amounts under the appropriate categories. In the Statement of Cash Flows column, indicate whether the item is an operating activity (OA), investing activity (IA), or financing activity (FA).

Balance Sheet					Income Statement			Statement of Cash Flows
Assets	=	Liabilities	+	Stk. Equity				
Cash	=	Carrying Value of Note Pay.	+	Ret. Earn.	Rev. −	Exp. =	Net Inc.	

a. The issuance of the note on July 1, Year 1.
b. The adjustment for accrued interest at the end of the year, December 31, Year 1.
c. Recording interest expense for Year 2 and repaying the principal on June 30, Year 2.

PROBLEMS—SERIES A

Mc Graw Hill **connect** All applicable Problems in Series A are available in *Connect*.

Problem 9-19A   *Effect of accrued interest on financial statements*

Malco Enterprises issued $10,000 of common stock when the company was started. In addition, Malco borrowed $36,000 from a local bank on July 1, Year 1. The note had a 6 percent annual interest rate and a one-year term to maturity. Malco Enterprises recognized $72,500 of revenue on account in Year 1 and $85,200 of revenue on account in Year 2. Cash collections of accounts receivable were $61,300 in Year 1 and $71,500 in Year 2. Malco paid $39,000 of other operating expenses in Year 1 and $45,000 of other operating expenses in Year 2. Malco repaid the loan and interest at the maturity date.

Required

Based on this information, answer the following questions. (*Hint:* Record the events in the accounting equation before answering the questions.)

a.   What amount of interest expense would Malco report on the Year 1 income statement?

b.   What amount of net cash flow from operating activities would Malco report on the Year 1 statement of cash flows?

c.   What amount of total liabilities would Malco report on the December 31, Year 1, balance sheet?

d.   What amount of retained earnings would Malco report on the December 31, Year 1, balance sheet?

e.   What amount of net cash flow from financing activities would Malco report on the Year 1 statement of cash flows?

f.   What amount of interest expense would Malco report on the Year 2 income statement?

g.   What amount of net cash flow from operating activities would Malco report on the Year 2 statement of cash flows?

h.   What amount of total assets would Malco report on the December 31, Year 2, balance sheet?

i.   What amount of net cash flow from investing activities would Malco report on the Year 2 statement of cash flows?

j.   If Malco Enterprises paid a $2,000 dividend during Year 2, what retained earnings balance would it report on the December 31, Year 2, balance sheet?

Problem 9-20A   *Account for short-term debt and sales tax—two accounting cycles*

The following transactions apply to Walnut Enterprises for Year 1, its first year of operations:

1.   Received $50,000 cash from the issue of a short-term note with a 6 percent interest rate and a one-year maturity. The note was made on April 1, Year 1.

2.   Received $130,000 cash plus applicable sales tax from performing services. The services are subject to a sales tax rate of 6 percent.

3.   Paid $62,000 cash for other operating expenses during the year.

4.   Paid the sales tax due on $110,000 of the service revenue for the year. Sales tax on the balance of the revenue is not due until Year 2.

5.   Recognized the accrued interest at December 31, Year 1.

The following transactions apply to Walnut Enterprises for Year 2:

1.   Paid the balance of the sales tax due for Year 1.

2.   Received $201,000 cash plus applicable sales tax from performing services. The services are subject to a sales tax rate of 6 percent.

3.   Repaid the principal of the note and applicable interest on April 1, Year 2.

4.   Paid $102,500 of other operating expenses during the year.

5.   Paid the sales tax due on $185,000 of the service revenue. The sales tax on the balance of the revenue is not due until Year 3.

Required

a. Organize the transaction data in accounts under an accounting equation.

b. Prepare a balance sheet, statement of changes in stockholders' equity, income statement, and statement of cash flows for Year 1 and Year 2.

Problem 9-21A   *Contingent liabilities*

LO 9-3

Required

a. Give an example of a contingent liability that is probable and reasonably estimable. How would this type of liability be shown in the accounting records?

b. Give an example of a contingent liability that is reasonably possible or probable but not reasonably estimable. How would this type of liability be shown in the accounting records?

c. Give an example of a contingent liability that is remote. How is this type of liability shown in the accounting records?

Problem 9-22A   *Current liabilities*

LO 9-1, 9-2, 9-3, 9-4

The following selected transactions were taken from the books of Ripley Company for Year 1:

CHECK FIGURE
b. Total Current Liabilities:
$22,600

1. On February 1, Year 1, borrowed $70,000 cash from the local bank. The note had a 6 percent interest rate and was due on June 1, Year 1.

2. Cash sales for the year amounted to $240,000 plus sales tax at the rate of 7 percent.

3. Ripley provides a 90-day warranty on the merchandise sold. The warranty expense is estimated to be 1 percent of sales.

4. Paid the sales tax to the state sales tax agency on $210,000 of the sales.

5. Paid the note due on June 1 and the related interest.

6. On November 1, Year 1, borrowed $20,000 cash from the local bank. The note had a 6 percent interest rate and a one-year term to maturity.

7. Paid $2,100 in warranty repairs.

8. A customer has filed a lawsuit against Ripley for $1 million for breach of contract. The company attorney does not believe the suit has merit.

Required

a. Answer the following questions:

(1) What amount of cash did Ripley pay for interest during Year 1?

(2) What amount of interest expense is reported on Ripley's income statement for Year 1?

(3) What is the amount of warranty expense for Year 1?

b. Prepare the current liabilities section of the balance sheet at December 31, Year 1.

c. Show the effect of these transactions on the financial statements using a horizontal statements model like the one shown next. Use + for increase, − for decrease, and NA for not affected. In the Statement of Cash Flows column, indicate whether the item is an operating activity (OA), investing activity (IA), or financing activity (FA). The first transaction has been recorded as an example.

Balance Sheet			Income Statement			Statement of Cash Flows
Assets	= Liabilities	+ Stk. Equity	Rev.	− Exp.	= Net Inc.	
+	+	NA	NA	NA	NA	+ FA

Problem 9-23A   *Accounting for payroll and payroll taxes*

LO 9-5

Electronics Service Co. pays salaries monthly on the last day of the month. The following information is available from Electronics for the month ended December 31, Year 1:

Administrative salaries	$96,000
Sales salaries	57,000
Office salaries	38,000

Assume the Social Security tax rate is 6 percent on the first $130,000 of salaries. Duke reached the $130,000 amount in December. His salary is $11,500 per month and is included in the $96,000. No one else will reach the $130,000 amount for the year. None of the employee salaries are subject to unemployment tax in December.

Other amounts withheld from salaries in December were as follows:

Federal income tax	$21,500
State income tax	11,200
Employee savings plan	4,000

Required

a. Determine the net pay for employee salary expenses on December 31, Year 1.

b. Determine the amount of payroll tax expense for Electronics Service Co. for December, Year 1.

LO 9-1, 9-2, 9-4, 9-5

Problem 9-24A *Comprehensive single-cycle problem*

The following transactions apply to Park Co. for Year 1:

1. Received $50,000 cash from the issue of common stock.
2. Purchased inventory on account for $180,000.
3. Sold inventory for $250,000 cash that had cost $140,000. Sales tax was collected at the rate of 5 percent on the inventory sold.
4. Borrowed $50,000 from First State Bank on March 1, Year 1. The note had a 7 percent interest rate and a one-year term to maturity.
5. Paid the accounts payable (see transaction 2).
6. Paid the sales tax due on $190,000 of sales. Sales tax on the other $60,000 is not due until after the end of the year.
7. Salaries for the year for one employee amounted to $46,000. Assume the Social Security tax rate is 6 percent and the Medicare tax rate is 1.5 percent. Federal income tax withheld was $5,300.
8. Paid $5,800 for warranty repairs on account during the year.
9. Paid $36,000 of other operating expenses during the year.
10. Paid a dividend of $2,000 to the shareholders.

Adjustments

11. The products sold in transaction 3 were warranted. Park estimated that the warranty cost would be 3 percent of sales.
12. Record the accrued interest at December 31, Year 1.
13. Record the accrued payroll tax at December 31, Year 1. Assume no payroll taxes have been paid for the year and that the unemployment tax rate is 6 percent (federal unemployment tax rate is 0.6 percent and the state unemployment tax rate is 5.4 percent on the first $7,000 of earnings per employee).

Required

a. Create an accounting equation. Record the events under the equation. Number the entries with the related event numbers. The following is a partial list of accounts with the first two events shown as examples. Create new accounts as needed to record the events. The final solution should have 21 accounts. Use parentheses to indicate decreases to an account.

Event No.	Assets			=	Liabilities			+	Stk. Equity		
	Cash	+	Inventory	=	Acc. Pay.	+	Sales Tax Pay.	+	Com. Stk.	+	Ret. Earn.
1.	50,000	+	NA	=	NA	+	NA	+	50,000	+	NA
2.	NA	+	180,000	=	180,000	+	NA	+	NA	+	NA

b. Prepare an income statement, statement of changes in stockholders' equity, balance sheet, and statement of cash flows for Year 1.

Problem 9-25A   *Multistep income statement and classified balance sheet*

LO 9-6

Required

Use the following information to prepare a multistep income statement and a classified balance sheet for Eller Equipment Co. for Year 1. (*Hint:* Some of the items will *not* appear on either statement, and ending retained earnings must be calculated.)

CHECK FIGURES
Total Current Assets: $212,700
Total Current Liabilities:
$67,500

Salaries expense	$ 72,000	Beginning retained earnings	$134,150
Common stock	50,000	Warranties payable (short term)	2,500
Notes receivable (short term)	10,000	Gain on sale of equipment	8,500
Allowance for doubtful accounts	6,500	Operating expenses	96,000
Accumulated depreciation	42,300	Cash flow from investing activities	125,000
Notes payable (long term)	80,000	Prepaid rent	14,000
Salvage value of building	6,000	Land	70,000
Interest payable (short term)	1,500	Cash	26,300
Uncollectible accounts expense	7,150	Inventory	110,500
Supplies	1,800	Accounts payable	32,000
Equipment	97,500	Interest expense	8,600
Interest revenue	3,600	Salaries payable	5,200
Sales revenue	510,000	Unearned revenue	26,300
Dividends	11,500	Cost of goods sold	310,000
Warranty expense	9,600	Accounts receivable	56,000
Interest receivable (short term)	600	Depreciation expense	1,000

Problem 9-26A   *Using ratios to make comparisons*

LO 9-7

CHECK FIGURE
a. Aspen Current Ratio:
1.53 to 1.0

The following accounting information exists for the Aspen and Willow companies:

	Aspen	Willow
Cash	$ 30,000	$ 20,000
Wages payable	30,000	25,000
Merchandise inventory	65,000	35,000
Building	95,000	95,000
Accounts receivable	35,000	40,000
Long-term notes payable	145,000	110,000
Land	60,000	55,000
Accounts payable	55,000	50,000
Sales revenue	325,000	265,000
Expenses	295,000	230,000

Required

a. Identify the current assets and current liabilities and compute the current ratio for each company.

b. Assuming that all assets and liabilities are listed here, compute the debt-to-assets ratios for each company.

c. Determine which company has the greater financial risk in both the short term and the long term.

Problem 9-27A   *Accounting for a discount note across two accounting cycles (Appendix)*

LO 9-8

Don Terry opened Terry Company, an accounting practice, in Year 1. The following summarizes transactions that occurred during Year 1:

1. Issued a $120,000 face value discount note to First National Bank on July 1, Year 1. The note had an 8 percent discount rate and a one-year term to maturity.

2. Recognized cash revenue of $310,000.

CHECK FIGURES
b. Net Income, Year 1:
$160,200
Total Assets, Year 2:
$323,400

3. Incurred and paid $145,000 of operating expenses.

4. Adjusted the books to recognize interest expense at December 31, Year 1.

The following summarizes transactions that occurred in Year 2:

1. Recognized $346,000 of cash revenue.

2. Incurred and paid $178,000 of operating expenses.

3. Recognized the interest expense for Year 2 and paid the face value of the note.

Required

a. Show the effects of each of the transactions on the elements of the financial statements, using a horizontal statements model like the following one. Use + for increase, − for decrease, and NA for not affected. The first transaction is entered as an example.

Event No.	Balance Sheet			Income Statement			Statement of Cash Flows
	Assets	= Liab.	+ Stk. Equity	Rev.	− Exp.	= Net Inc.	
1	+	+	NA	NA	NA	NA	+ FA

b. Prepare an income statement, statement of changes in stockholders' equity, balance sheet, and statement of cash flows for Year 1 and Year 2.

EXERCISES—SERIES B

LO 9-1

Exercise 9-1B   *Recognizing accrued interest expense*

Union Corporation borrowed $60,000 from the bank on November 1, Year 1. The note had a 6 percent annual rate of interest and matured on April 30, Year 2. Interest and principal were paid in cash on the maturity date.

Required

a. What amount of cash did Union pay for interest in Year 1?

b. What amount of interest expense was reported on the Year 1 income statement?

c. What amount of total liabilities was reported on the December 31, Year 1, balance sheet?

d. What total amount of cash was paid to the bank on April 30, Year 2, for principal and interest?

e. What amount of interest expense was reported on the Year 2 income statement?

LO 9-1

Exercise 9-2B   *Effects of recognizing accrued interest on financial statements*

Danny Bell started Bell Company on January 1, Year 1. The company experienced the following events during its first year of operation:

1. Earned $3,000 of cash revenue for performing services.

2. Borrowed $4,800 cash from the bank.

3. Adjusted the accounting records to recognize accrued interest expense on the bank note. The note, issued on August 1, Year 1, had a one-year term and a 6 percent annual interest rate.

Required

a. What is the amount of interest expense in Year 1?

b. What amount of cash was paid for interest in Year 1?

c. Use a horizontal statements model to show how each event affects the balance sheet, income statement, and statement of cash flows. Indicate whether the event increases (I), decreases (D), or does not affect (NA) each element of the financial statements. In the Statement of Cash Flows column, designate the cash flows as operating activities (OA), investing activities (IA), or financing activities (FA). The first transaction has been recorded as an example.

Event No.	Balance Sheet												Income Statement					Statement of Cash Flows
	Cash	=	Notes Pay.	+	Int. Pay.	+	Com. Stk.	+	Ret. Earn.				Rev.	−	Exp.	=	Net Inc.	
1.	I	=	NA	+	NA	+	NA	+	I				I	−	NA	=	I	I OA

Exercise 9-3B *Recording sales tax*   LO 9-2

The Tiger Book Store sells books and other supplies to students in a state where the sales tax rate is 7 percent. The Tiger Book Store engaged in the following transactions for Year 1. Sales tax of 7 percent is collected on all sales.

1. Book sales, not including sales tax, for Year 1 amounted to $215,000 cash.
2. Cash sales of miscellaneous items in Year 1 were $160,000, not including tax.
3. Cost of goods sold amounted to $195,000 for the year.
4. Paid $95,000 in operating expenses for the year.
5. Paid the sales tax collected to the state agency.

Required

a. What is the total amount of sales tax the Tiger Book Store collected and paid for the year?
b. What is the Tiger Book Store's net income for the year?

Exercise 9-4B *Recognizing sales tax payable*   LO 9-2

The following selected transactions apply to Fast Stop for November and December, Year 1. November was the first month of operations. Sales tax is collected at the time of sale but is not paid to the state sales tax agency until the following month.

1. Cash sales for November, Year 1 were $85,000 plus sales tax of 8 percent.
2. Fast Stop paid the November sales tax to the state agency on December 10, Year 1.
3. Cash sales for December, Year 1 were $98,000 plus sales tax of 8 percent.

Required

a. Show the effect of the preceding transactions on a horizontal statements model like the one shown next:

Balance Sheet								Income Statement					Statement of Cash Flows
Assets	=	Liabilities	+		Stk. Equity								
Cash	=	Sales Tax Pay.	+	Com. Stk.	+	Ret. Earn.		Rev.	−	Exp.	=	Net Inc.	

b. What was the total amount of sales tax paid in Year 1?
c. What was the total amount of sales tax collected in Year 1?
d. What is the amount of the sales tax liability as of December 31, Year 1?
e. On what financial statement will the sales tax liability appear?

Exercise 9-5B *Contingent liabilities*   LO 9-3

The following legal situations apply to Zier Corp. for Year 1:

1. A customer slipped and fell on a slick floor while shopping in the retail store. The customer has filed a $5 million lawsuit against the company. Zier's attorney knows that the company will have to pay some damages but is reasonably certain that the suit can be settled for $750,000.
2. The EPA has assessed a fine against Zier of $320,000 for hazardous emissions from one of its manufacturing plants. The EPA had previously issued a warning to Zier and required Zier to make repairs within six months. Zier began to make the repairs but was not able to complete them within the six-month period. Because Zier has started the repairs, Zier's attorney thinks the fine will be reduced to $120,000. He is approximately 80 percent certain that he can negotiate the fine reduction because of the repair work that has been completed.

3. One of Zier's largest manufacturing facilities is located in "tornado alley." Property is routinely damaged by storms. Zier estimates it may have property damage of as much as $450,000 this coming year.

Required

For each of the preceding items, determine the correct accounting treatment.

LO 9-4

Exercise 9-6B *Effect of warranties on income and cash flow*

To support himself while attending school, Steve Owens sold computers to other students. During the year, Steve purchased computers for $150,000 and sold them for $280,000 cash. He provided his customers with a one-year warranty against defects in parts and labor. Based on industry standards, he estimated that warranty claims would amount to 5 percent of sales. During the year, he paid $1,545 cash to replace a defective hard drive.

Required

a. Prepare an income statement and statement of cash flows for Steve's first year of operation.

b. Explain the difference between net income and the amount of cash flow from operating activities.

LO 9-4

Exercise 9-7B *Effect of warranty obligations and payments on financial statements*

The Malon Appliance Co. provides a 120-day parts-and-labor warranty on all merchandise it sells. Malon estimates the warranty expense for the current period to be $2,450. During this period, a customer returned a product that cost $1,950 to repair.

Required

a. Show the effects of these transactions on the financial statements using a horizontal statements model like the example shown next. Use + for increase, − for decrease, and NA for not affected. In the Statement of Cash Flows column, indicate whether the item is an operating activity (OA), investing activity (IA), or financing activity (FA).

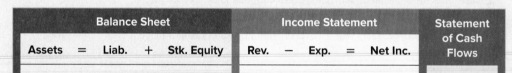

b. Discuss the advantage of estimating the amount of warranty expense.

LO 9-1, 9-2, 9-4

Exercise 9-8B *Current liabilities*

The following transactions apply to Farmer's Equipment Sales Corp. for Year 1:

1. The business was started when Farmer's received $60,000 from the issue of common stock.
2. Purchased $160,000 of merchandise on account.
3. Sold merchandise for $220,000 cash (not including sales tax). Sales tax of 8 percent is collected when the merchandise is sold. The merchandise had a cost of $140,000.
4. Provided a six-month warranty on the merchandise sold. Based on industry estimates, the warranty claims would amount to 4 percent of merchandise sales.
5. Paid the sales tax to the state agency on $180,000 of the sales.
6. On September 1, Year 1, borrowed $40,000 from the local bank. The note had a 6 percent interest rate and matures on March 1, Year 2.
7. Paid $6,600 for warranty repairs during the year.
8. Paid operating expenses of $61,000 for the year.
9. Paid $145,000 of accounts payable.
10. Recorded accrued interest at the end of the year.

Required

a. Show the effect of these transactions on the financial statements using a horizontal statements model like the one shown next. Use + for increase, − for decrease, and NA for not affected. In the Statement of Cash Flows column, indicate whether the item is an operating activity (OA), investing activity (IA), or financing activity (FA). The first transaction is recorded as an example.

Balance Sheet			Income Statement			Statement of Cash Flows
Assets =	Liabilities +	Stk. Equity	Rev. −	Exp. =	Net Inc.	
+	NA	+	NA	NA	NA	+ FA

b. Prepare the income statement, balance sheet, and statement of cash flows for the period ended December 31, Year 1.

c. What is the total amount of current liabilities at December 31, Year 1?

Exercise 9-9B *Calculating payroll*

LO 9-5

Wilkins Enterprises has two hourly employees: Marcia and Clark. Both employees earn overtime at the rate of 1½ times the hourly rate for hours worked in excess of 40 per week. Assume the Social Security tax rate is 6 percent on the first $130,000 of wages, and the Medicare tax rate is 1.5 percent on all earnings. Federal income tax withheld for Marcia and Clark was $280 and $250, respectively. The following information is for the first week in January, Year 1:

Employee	Hours Worked	Wage Rate per Hour
Marcia	54	$25
Clark	48	$35

Required

a. Calculate the gross pay for each employee for the week.

b. Calculate the net pay for each employee for the week.

Exercise 9-10B *Calculating payroll*

LO 9-5

Easy Stop has two employees in Year 1. Catherine earns $4,500 per month and Jordan, the manager, earns $11,000 per month. Neither is paid extra if they work overtime. Assume the Social Security tax rate is 6 percent on the first $130,000 of earnings, and the Medicare tax rate is 1.5 percent on all earnings. The federal income tax withholding is 15 percent of gross earnings for Catherine and 20 percent for Jordan. Both Catherine and Jordan have been employed all year.

Required

a. Calculate the net pay for both Catherine and Jordan for March.

b. Calculate the net pay for both Catherine and Jordan for December.

c. Is the net pay the same in March and December for both employees? Why or why not?

d. What amounts will Easy Stop report on the Year 1 W-2s for each employee?

Exercise 9-11B *Calculating employee and employer payroll taxes*

LO 9-5

Culver Co. employed Jen Sing in Year 1. Jen earned $5,200 per month and worked the entire year. Assume the Social Security tax rate is 6 percent on the first $130,000 of earnings, and the Medicare tax rate is 1.5 percent. Jen's federal income tax withholding amount is $800 per month. Use 6.0 percent for the unemployment tax rate for the first $7,000 of earnings per employee.

Required

a. Answer the following questions:

(1) What is Jen's net pay per month?

(2) What amount does Jen pay monthly in FICA taxes?

(3) What is the total payroll tax expense for Culver Co. for January, Year 1? February, Year 1? March, Year 1? December, Year 1?

b. Assume that instead of $5,200 per month, Jen earned $11,200 per month. Jen's new federal income tax withholding amount is $1,800. Answer the questions in Requirement *a.*

LO 9-5

Exercise 9-12B *Fringe benefits and payroll expense*

The two employees at Oswald Co. receive various fringe benefits. Oswald Co. provides vacation at the rate of $500 per day, and each employee earns one day of vacation per month worked. In addition, Oswald Co. pays a total amount of $780 per month in medical insurance premiums. Oswald also contributes a total amount of $400 per month into an employee retirement plan. The federal unemployment tax rate is 6 percent, while the state unemployment tax rate is 4.5 percent. Unemployment taxes apply to the first $7,000 of earnings per employee. Assume a Social Security tax rate of 6.0 percent and a Medicare tax rate of 1.5 percent.

Required

a. Prepare the computation for the accrued fringe benefits per month.

b. Show the effect of accrued fringe benefits per month on a statements model like the one shown next:

Balance Sheet									Income Statement					Statement of Cash Flows
Assets	=	Liabilities	+			Stk. Equity								
Cash	=	Various Payables	+	Com. Stk.	+	Ret. Earn.			Rev.	−	Exp.	=	Net Inc.	

c. If the two employees each worked 250 days for the year, what is Oswald Co.'s total payroll cost (salary, payroll taxes, and fringe benefits) for the year? (Assume that each employee earns $500 per day.)

LO 9-5

Exercise 9-13B *Computation of net pay and payroll expense*

The following information is available for the employees of Yui Company for the first week of January, Year 1:

1. Sam earns $32 per hour and 1½ times his regular rate for hours over 40 per week. He worked 46 hours the first week in January. Sam's federal income tax withholding is equal to 10 percent of his gross pay. Yui pays medical insurance of $75 per week for Sam and contributes $50 per week to a retirement plan for him.

2. Adam earns a weekly salary of $1,200. Adam's federal income tax withholding is 15 percent of his gross pay. Yui pays medical insurance of $110 per week for Adam and contributes $100 per week to a retirement plan for him.

3. Vacation pay is accrued at the rate of 1/4 of the regular pay rate per hour for Sam and $60 per week for Adam.

Assume the Social Security tax rate is 6 percent on the first $130,000 of salaries, and the Medicare tax rate is 1.5 percent of total salaries. The state unemployment tax rate is 5.4 percent and the federal unemployment tax rate is 0.6 percent of the first $7,000 of salary for each employee.

Required

a. Compute the gross pay for Sam for the first week in January.

b. Compute the net pay for both Sam and Adam for the first week in January.

c. What is the total cost of compensation expense for the first week of January, Year 1, for Yui Company?

LO 9-6

Exercise 9-14B *Preparing a classified balance sheet*

Required

Use the following information to prepare a classified balance sheet for Latimer Co. at the end of Year 1:

Accounts receivable	$36,200
Accounts payable	12,400
Cash	29,650
Common stock	50,000
Long-term notes payable	45,500
Merchandise inventory	38,300
Office equipment	36,400
Retained earnings	36,250
Prepaid insurance	3,600

Exercise 9-15B   *Using the current ratio to make comparisons*   LO 9-7

The following information was drawn from the balance sheets of the Augusta and Reno Companies:

	Augusta Company	Reno Company
Current assets	$45,000	$72,000
Current liabilities	28,000	54,000

Required

a. Compute the current ratio for each company.

b. Which company has the greater likelihood of being able to pay its bills?

c. Assume that both companies have the same amount of total assets. Speculate as to which company would produce the higher return-on-assets ratio.

Exercise 9-16B   *Effect of a discount note on financial statements (Appendix)*   LO 9-8

Mark Miller started a moving company on January 1, Year 1. On March 1, Year 1, Miller borrowed cash from a local bank by issuing a one-year $80,000 face value note with annual interest based on a 12 percent discount. During Year 1, Miller provided services for $65,400 cash.

Required

Answer the following questions. (*Hint:* Record the events in an accounting equation prior to answering the questions.)

a. What is the amount of total liabilities on the December 31, Year 1, balance sheet?

b. What is the amount of net income on the Year 1 income statement?

c. What is the amount of cash flow from operating activities on the Year 1 statement of cash flows?

Exercise 9-17B   *Comparing effective interest rates on discount versus interest-bearing notes (Appendix)*   LO 9-1, 9-8

Jim Hanks borrowed money by issuing two notes on January 1, Year 1. The financing transactions are described as follows.

1. Borrowed funds by issuing a $60,000 face value discount note to State Bank. The note had an 8 percent discount rate, a one-year term to maturity, and was paid off on December 31, Year 1.

2. Borrowed funds by issuing a $60,000 face value, interest-bearing note to Community Bank. The note had an 8 percent stated rate of interest, a one-year term to maturity, and was paid off on December 31, Year 1.

Required

a. Show the effects of issuing the two notes on the financial statements using separate horizontal financial statement models like those shown next. Record the transaction amounts under the appropriate categories. In the Statement of Cash Flows column, indicate whether the item is an operating activity (OA), investing activity (IA), or financing activity (FA). Record only the events occurring on the date of issue. Do not record accrued interest or the repayment at maturity.

Discount Note

Balance Sheet					Income Statement				Statement of Cash Flows
Assets	=	Liabilities	+	Stk. Equity					
Cash	=	Carrying Value of Note Pay.	+	Ret. Earn.	Rev.	−	Exp.	=	Net Inc.	

Interest-Bearing Note

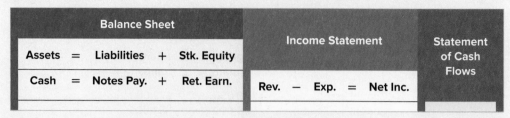

b. What is the total amount of interest to be paid on each note?

c. What amount of cash was received from each note when it was issued?

d. Which note has the higher effective interest rate? Support your answer with appropriate computations.

LO 9-8

Exercise 9-18B   *Recording accounting events for a discount note (Appendix)*

Bricca Co. issued a $60,000 face value discount note to First Bank on June 1, Year 1. The note had a 6 percent discount rate and a one-year term to maturity.

Required

Show the effects of the following transactions (a–c) on the financial statements using a horizontal financial statement model such as the following one. Record the transaction amounts under the appropriate categories. In the Statement of Cash Flows column, indicate whether the item is an operating activity (OA), investing activity (IA), or financing activity (FA).

Balance Sheet					Income Statement				Statement of Cash Flows
Assets	=	Liabilities	+	Stk. Equity					
Cash	=	Carrying Value of Note Pay.	+	Ret. Earn.	Rev.	−	Exp.	= Net Inc.	

a. The issuance of the note on June 1, Year 1.

b. The adjustment for accrued interest at the end of the year, December 31, Year 1.

c. Recording interest expense for Year 2 and repaying the principal on May 31, Year 2.

PROBLEMS—SERIES B

LO 9-1

Problem 9-19B   *Effect of accrued interest on financial statements*

Ingals Co. issued $10,000 of common stock when the company was started. In addition, Ingals borrowed $20,000 from the local bank on April 1, Year 1. The note had an 8 percent annual interest rate and a one-year term to maturity. Ingals Co. recognized $54,000 of revenue on account in Year 1 and $65,000 of revenue on account in Year 2. Cash collections from accounts receivable were $46,000 in Year 1 and $63,000 in Year 2. Ingals Co. paid $27,000 of salaries expense in Year 1 and $36,000 of salaries expense in Year 2. Ingals Co. paid the loan and interest at the maturity date.

Required

Based on the preceding information, answer the following questions. (*Hint:* Record the events in the accounting equation before answering the questions.)

a. What amount of net cash flow from operating activities would Ingals report on the Year 1 cash flow statement?

b. What amount of interest expense would Ingals report on the Year 1 income statement?

c. What amount of total liabilities would Ingals report on the December 31, Year 1, balance sheet?

d. What amount of retained earnings would Ingals report on the December 31, Year 1, balance sheet?

e. What amount of cash flow from financing activities would Ingals report on the Year 1 statement of cash flows?

f. What amount of interest expense would Ingals report on the Year 2 income statement?

g. What amount of cash flows from operating activities would Ingals report on the Year 2 cash flows statement?

h. What amount of total assets would Ingals report on the December 31, Year 2, balance sheet?

Problem 9-20B *Accounting for short-term debt and sales tax—two accounting cycles*   LO 9-1, 9-2

The following transactions apply to Barclay Co. for Year 1, its first year of operations:

1. Received $50,000 cash from the issue of a short-term note with a 5 percent interest rate and a one-year maturity. The note was made on April 1, Year 1.
2. Received $140,000 cash plus applicable sales tax from performing services. The services are subject to a sales tax rate of 6 percent.
3. Paid $84,000 cash for other operating expenses during the year.
4. Paid the sales tax due on $110,000 of the service revenue for the year. Sales tax on the balance of the revenue is not due until Year 2.
5. Recognized the accrued interest at December 31, Year 1.

The following transactions apply to Barclay Co. for Year 2:

1. Paid the balance of the sales tax due for Year 1.
2. Received $155,000 cash plus applicable sales tax from performing services. The services are subject to a sales tax rate of 6 percent.
3. Repaid the principal of the note and applicable interest on April 1, Year 2.
4. Paid $96,000 of other operating expenses during the year.
5. Paid the sales tax due on $135,000 of the service revenue. The sales tax on the balance of the revenue is not due until Year 3.

Required

a. Organize the transaction data in accounts under an accounting equation.
b. Prepare a balance sheet, statement of changes in stockholders' equity, income statement, and statement of cash flows for Year 1 and Year 2.

Problem 9-21B *Contingent liabilities*   LO 9-3

Required

How should each of the following situations be reported in the financial statements?

a. It has been determined that one of the company's products has caused a safety hazard. It is considered probable that liabilities have been incurred and a reasonable estimate of the amount can be made.
b. A company warehouse is located in a section of the city that has routinely flooded in the past. Consequently, the company can no longer find a source of insurance for the warehouse. No flood has yet occurred this year.
c. Because of newly passed legislation, a company will have to upgrade its facilities over the next two years. Significant expenditures will occur, but at this time the amount has not been determined.

Problem 9-22B *Current liabilities*   LO 9-1, 9-2, 9-3, 9-4

The following selected transactions were taken from the books of Dodson Company for Year 1:

1. On March 1, Year 1, borrowed $60,000 cash from the local bank. The note had a 6 percent interest rate and was due on September 1, Year 1.
2. Cash sales for the year amounted to $240,000 plus sales tax at the rate of 7 percent.
3. Dodson provides a 90-day warranty on the merchandise sold. The warranty expense is estimated to be 2 percent of sales.
4. Paid the sales tax to the state sales tax agency on $200,000 of the sales.
5. Paid the note due on September 1 and the related interest.
6. On October 1, Year 1, borrowed $50,000 cash from the local bank. The note had a 7 percent interest rate and a one-year term to maturity.
7. Paid $3,800 in warranty repairs.
8. A customer has filed a lawsuit against Dodson for $150,000 for breach of contract. The company attorney does not believe the suit has merit.

Required

a. Answer the following questions:

   (1) What amount of cash did Dodson pay for interest during the year?

   (2) What amount of interest expense is reported on Dodson's income statement for the year?

   (3) What is the amount of warranty expense for the year?

b. Prepare the current liabilities section of the balance sheet at December 31, Year 1.

c. Show the effect of these transactions on the financial statements using a horizontal statements model like the one shown next. Use + for increase, − for decrease, and NA for not affected. In the Statement of Cash Flows column, indicate whether the item is an operating activity (OA), investing activity (IA), or financing activity (FA). The first transaction is recorded as an example.

Balance Sheet			Income Statement			Statement of Cash Flows
Assets	= Liabilities	+ Stk. Equity	Rev.	− Exp.	= Net Inc.	
+	+	NA	NA	NA	NA	+ FA

LO 9-5

Problem 9-23B *Accounting for payroll and payroll taxes*

Maddox Co. pays salaries monthly on the last day of the month. The following information is available from Maddox Co. for the month ended December 31, Year 1.

Administrative salaries	$85,000
Sales salaries	66,000
Office salaries	48,000

Assume the Social Security tax rate is 6 percent on the first $130,000 of salaries, while the Medicare tax rate is 1.5 percent on all salaries. James reached the $130,000 amount in December. His salary is $11,000 per month and is included in the $85,000. No one else will reach the $130,000 amount for the year. None of the employee salaries are subject to unemployment tax in December.

Other amounts withheld from salaries in December were as follows:

Federal income tax	$24,500
State income tax	7,200
Employee savings plan	3,000

Required

a. Determine the net pay for employee salary expenses on December 31, Year 1.

b. Determine the amount of payroll tax expense for Maddox Co. for December, Year 1.

LO 9-1, 9-2, 9-4, 9-5

Problem 9-24B *Comprehensive single-cycle problem*

The following transactions apply to Ritter Co. for Year 1:

1. Received $40,000 cash from the issue of common stock.
2. Purchased inventory on account for $128,000.
3. Sold inventory for $200,000 cash that had cost $110,000. Sales tax was collected at the rate of 5 percent on the inventory sold.
4. Borrowed $40,000 from First State Bank on October 1, Year 1. The note had a 6 percent interest rate and a one-year term to maturity.
5. Paid the accounts payable (see transaction 2).
6. Paid the sales tax due on $160,000 of sales. Sales tax on the other $40,000 is not due until after the end of the year.

7. Salaries for the year for one employee amounted to $45,000. Assume the Social Security tax rate is 6 percent and the Medicare tax rate is 1.5 percent. Federal income tax withheld was $5,600.

8. Paid $3,200 for warranty repairs on account during the year.

9. Paid $24,000 of other operating expenses during the year.

10. Paid a dividend of $5,000 to the shareholders.

Adjustments

11. The products sold in transaction 3 were warranted. Ritter estimated that the warranty cost would be 3 percent of sales.

12. Record the accrued interest at December 31, Year 1.

13. Record the accrued payroll tax at December 31, Year 1. Assume no payroll taxes have been paid for the year and that the unemployment tax rate is 6.0 percent (the federal unemployment tax rate is 0.6 percent and the state unemployment tax rate is 5.4 percent on the first $7,000 of earnings per employee).

Required

a. Create an accounting equation. Record the events under the equation. Number the entries with the related event numbers. The following is a partial list of accounts with the first two events shown as examples. Create new accounts as needed to record the events. The final solution should have 21 accounts. Use parentheses to indicate decreases to an account.

Event No.	Assets			=	Liabilities			+	Stk. Equity		
	Cash	+	Inventory	=	Acc. Pay.	+	Sales Tax Pay.	+	Com. Stk.	+	Ret. Earn.
1.	40,000	+	NA	=	NA	+	NA	+	40,000	+	NA
2.	NA	+	128,000	=	128,000	+	NA	+	NA	+	NA

b. Prepare an income statement, statement of changes in stockholders' equity, balance sheet, and statement of cash flows for Year 1.

Problem 9-25B   *Multistep income statement and classified balance sheet*   LO 9-6

Required

Use the following information to prepare a multistep income statement and a classified balance sheet for Brown Company for Year 1. (*Hint:* Some of the items will *not* appear on either statement, and ending retained earnings must be calculated.)

Operating expenses	$ 45,000	Cash	$ 46,000
Land	75,000	Interest receivable (short term)	1,600
Accumulated depreciation	46,000	Cash flow from investing activities	(96,000)
Accounts payable	35,000	Allowance for doubtful accounts	14,000
Unearned revenue	27,000	Interest payable (short term)	6,000
Warranties payable (short term)	4,500	Sales revenue	900,000
Equipment	96,000	Uncollectible accounts expense	25,000
Notes payable (long term)	140,000	Interest expense	16,000
Salvage value of equipment	10,000	Accounts receivable	88,000
Dividends	15,000	Salaries payable	48,000
Warranty expense	7,200	Supplies	4,500
Beginning retained earnings	41,100	Prepaid rent	18,000
Interest revenue	4,200	Common stock	90,000
Gain on sale of equipment	7,000	Cost of goods sold	575,000
Inventory	126,000	Salaries expense	102,000
Notes receivable (short term)	12,500	Building	110,000

LO 9-7

Problem 9-26B   *Using ratios to make comparisons*

The following accounting information exists for Collie and Spaniel companies:

	Collie	Spaniel
Cash	$ 12,000	$ 15,000
Wages payable	10,000	12,000
Merchandise inventory	20,000	55,000
Building	90,000	80,000
Accounts receivable	22,000	25,000
Long-term notes payable	80,000	100,000
Land	35,000	40,000
Accounts payable	25,000	35,000
Sales revenue	220,000	250,000
Expenses	190,000	230,000

Required

a. Identify the current assets and current liabilities and compute the current ratio for each company.

b. Assuming that all assets and liabilities are listed here, compute the debt-to-assets ratios for each company.

c. Determine which company has the greater financial risk in both the short term and the long term.

LO 9-8

Problem 9-27B   *Accounting for a discount note—two accounting cycles (Appendix)*

Ball Company was started in Year 1. The following summarizes transactions that occurred during Year 1:

1. Issued a $40,000 face value discount note to Golden Savings Bank on April 1, Year 1. The note had a 6 percent discount rate and a one-year term to maturity.
2. Recognized revenue from services performed for cash, $130,000.
3. Incurred and paid $98,000 cash for selling and administrative expenses.
4. Amortized the discount on the note at the end of the year, December 31, Year 1.

The following summarizes transactions that occurred in Year 2:

1. Recognized $215,000 of service revenue in cash.
2. Incurred and paid $151,000 for selling and administrative expenses.
3. Amortized the remainder of the discount for Year 2 and paid the face value of the note.

Required

a. Show the effects of each of the transactions on the elements of the financial statements, using a horizontal statements model like the one shown next. Use + for increase, − for decrease, and NA for not affected. The first transaction is entered as an example.

Event No.	Balance Sheet			Income Statement			Statement of Cash Flows
	Assets	= Liab.	+ Stk. Equity	Rev.	− Exp.	= Net Inc.	
1	+	+	NA	NA	NA	NA	+ FA

b. Prepare an income statement, statement of changes in stockholders' equity, balance sheet, and statement of cash flows for Year 1 and Year 2.

ANALYZE, THINK, COMMUNICATE

ATC 9-1   Business Applications Case   *Understanding real-world annual reports*

Required

Obtain Target Corporation's annual report for its 2018 fiscal year (year ended February 2, 2019) at http://
investors.target.com using the instructions in Appendix B, and use it to answer the following questions:

a. What was Target's current ratio for its fiscal year ended February 2, 2019 (2018) and 2017?

b. Did the current ratio get stronger or weaker from 2017 to 2018? Explain briefly why this happened.

c. Target's balance sheet reports "Accrued and other current liabilities." What is included in this category? (See the notes to the financial statements.)

ATC 9-2   Group Assignment   *Accounting for payroll*

The following payroll information is available for three companies for Year 1. Each company has two
employees. Assume that the Social Security tax rate is 6 percent on the first $130,000 of earnings and
that the Medicare tax rate is 1.5 percent on all earnings.

Brooks Company				
Brooks Company	Hourly Rate	Regular Hours	Overtime Rate	Overtime Hours
Employee No. 1	$40	2,000	$60	300
Employee No. 2	20	2,000	30	100

Other benefits provided for the employees:

Medical insurance	$250 per month for each employee
Pension benefits	$100 per month for one employee

Federal income tax withheld is 15 percent of gross earnings for each employee. The state unemployment tax rate is 5.4 percent and the federal unemployment tax rate is 0.6 percent on the first $7,000 of
earnings per employee.

Hill Company				
Hill Company	Weekly Rate/ Hourly Rate	Weeks/Hours Worked	Overtime Rate	Overtime Hours
Employee No. 1	$2,000	52	NA	NA
Employee No. 2	18/hr.	2,000	$27/hr.	60

Other benefits provided for the employees:

Medical and dental insurance	$325 per month for each employee
Pension benefits	$150 per month for one employee and $100 per month for the other employee

Federal income tax withheld is 15 percent of gross earnings for each employee. The state unemployment tax rate is 5.4 percent and the federal unemployment tax rate is 0.6 percent on the first $7,000 of
earnings per employee.

Valley Company				
Valley Company	Monthly Rate/ Hourly Rate	Monthly/Hours Worked	Overtime Rate	Overtime Hours
Employee No. 1	$10,500	12	NA	NA
Employee No. 2 (part time)	20/hr.	860	NA	NA

Other benefits provided for the employees:	
Medical and dental insurance	$375 per month for only one employee
Pension benefits	10% of gross salary for the full-time employee

Federal income tax withheld is 15 percent of gross earnings for each employee. The state unemployment tax rate is 5.4 percent and the federal unemployment tax rate is 0.6 percent on the first $7,000 of earnings per employee.

Required

a. Divide the class into groups of four or five students. Organize the groups into three sections. Assign each section of the groups the payroll data for one of the given companies.

Group Tasks

(1) Determine the gross and net payroll for your company for the year.

(2) Determine the total compensation cost for your company for the year.

(3) Have a representative from each section put the compensation on the board broken down by salaries cost, payroll tax, and fringe benefit cost.

Class Discussion

b. Have the class discuss how the categories of compensation cost are similar and why some are more or less than those of the other companies.

ATC 9-3   Real-World Case   *Unusual types of liabilities*

In the liabilities section of its 2017 balance sheet, Bank of America reported "Deposits in U.S. offices: Noninterest-bearing" in U.S. offices of over $430 billion. Bank of America is a very large banking company. In the liabilities section of its 2017 balance sheet, Newmont Mining Corporation reported "reclamation and remediation liabilities" of $2.3 billion. Newmont Mining is involved in gold mining and refining activities. In its 2017 balance sheet, Delta Air Lines's largest current liability reported was $4.9 billion for "air traffic liability."

Required

a. For each of the preceding liabilities, write a brief explanation of what you believe the nature of the liability to be and how the company will pay it off. To develop your answers, think about the nature of the industry in which each of the companies operates.

b. Of the three liabilities described, which do you think poses the most risk for the company? In other words, for which liability are actual costs most likely to exceed the liability reported on the balance sheet? Uncertainty creates risk.

ATC 9-4   Business Applications Case   *Performing ratio analysis using real-world data*

Advanced Micro Devices, Inc. (AMD) is "a global semiconductor company with facilities around the world." AMD began operations in 1969. Texas Instruments, Inc. is the company that invented the integrated circuit over 45 years ago. It has more than 100,000 customers in over 30 countries. The following data were taken from the companies' 2017 annual reports. Dollar amounts are in millions.

	Advanced Micro Devices	Texas Instruments
Current assets	$2,622	$ 8,734
Current liabilities	1,486	2,258
Total assets	3,540	17,642
Total liabilities	2,929	7,305

Required

a. Compute the current ratio for each company.

b. Compute the debt-to-assets ratio for each company.

c. Based on the ratios computed in Requirements *a* and *b*, which company had the better liquidity in 2017?

d. Based on the ratios computed in Requirements *a* and *b*, which company had the better solvency in 2017?

ATC 9-5   Writing Assignment   *Payroll tax costs*

Nancy, who graduated from State University in June, Year 1, has just landed her first real job. She is excited because her salary is $4,000 per month. Nancy is single and has been planning all month about how she will spend her $4,000. When she received her first paycheck on June 30, Year 1, she was very disappointed. The amount of her check was only $3,100. Explain to Nancy why (generally) her check will not be for $4,000.

ATC 9-6   Ethical Dilemma   *Who pays FICA taxes?*

Scott Putman owns and operates a lawn care company. Like most companies in the lawn care business, his company experiences a high level of employee turnover. However, he finds it relatively easy to replace employees because he pays above-market wages. He attributes his ability to pay high wages to a little accounting trick he discovered several years ago. Instead of paying his half of each employee's FICA taxes to the government, he decided to pay that money to the employees in the form of higher wages. He then doubles their FICA tax payroll deduction and uses half of the deduction to pay his share of the Social Security tax. For example, suppose he plans to pay an employee $2,000 per month. Technically, the employee would have to pay 7.5 percent FICA and Medicare tax ($2,000 × .075 = $150) and Mr. Putman's company would have to make a $150 matching payment. Instead of doing it this way, he devised the following plan. He pays the employee $2,150 and then deducts $300 for FICA and Medicare tax from the employee's salary. The end result is the same. Either way, the employee ends up with net pay of $1,850 ($2,000 − $150 = $1,850 or $2,150 − $300 = $1,850). Also, the government gets $300 FICA tax, regardless of how it gets divided between the employee and the employer. Mr. Putman is convinced that he is right in what he is doing. Certainly, it benefits his company by allowing him to offer higher starting salaries. Further, he believes it is a more honest way of showing the real cost of Social Security and Medicare.

Required

a. Is Mr. Putnam right in his assumption that the total tax paid is the same under his approach as it would be if proper accounting procedures were applied? Explain.

b. Assuming that Mr. Putman is a CPA, do his actions violate any of the articles of the AICPA Code of Professional Conduct shown in Chapter 2 (Exhibit 2.7)? If so, discuss some of the articles that are violated.

c. Discuss Mr. Putman's actions within the context of the fraud triangle's elements of ethical misconduct that were outlined in Chapter 2.

ATC 9-7   Research Assignment   *Analyzing AutoZone's liquidity*

Using either the most current Form 10-K for AutoZone, Inc. or the company's annual report, answer the following questions. To obtain the Form 10-K, either use the EDGAR system (following the instructions in Appendix A), or the company's website. The company's annual report is available on its website.

Required

a. What is AutoZone's current ratio?

b. Which of AutoZone's current assets had the largest balance?

c. What percentage of AutoZone's total assets consisted of current assets?

d. If AutoZone were a company that manufactured auto parts rather than a retailer of auto parts, how do you think its balance sheet would be different?

Accounting for Long-Term Debt

Video lectures and accompanying self-assessment quizzes are available in *Connect* for all learning objectives.

Tableau Dashboard Activity is available in *Connect* for this chapter.

LEARNING OBJECTIVES

After you have mastered the material in this chapter, you will be able to:

LO 10-1   Show how an installment note affects financial statements.

LO 10-2   Show how a line of credit affects financial statements.

LO 10-3   Describe bond features and show how bonds issued at face value affect financial statements.

LO 10-4   Use the straight-line method to amortize bond discounts.

LO 10-5   Use the straight-line method to amortize bond premiums.

LO 10-6   Use the effective interest rate method to amortize bond discounts.

LO 10-7   Use the effective interest rate method to amortize bond premiums.

LO 10-8   Explain the advantages and disadvantages of debt financing.

CHAPTER OPENING

Most businesses finance their investing activities with long-term debt. Recall that current liabilities mature within one year or a company's operating cycle, whichever is longer. Other liabilities are long-term liabilities. Long-term debt agreements vary with respect to requirements for paying interest charges and repaying principal (the amount borrowed). Interest payments may be due monthly, annually, at some other interval, or at the maturity date. Interest charges may be based on a **fixed interest rate** that remains constant during the term of the loan or on a **variable interest rate** that fluctuates up or down during the loan period.

Principal repayment is generally required either in one lump sum at the maturity date or in installments that are spread over the life of the loan. For example, each monthly payment on your car loan probably includes both paying interest and repaying some of the principal. Repaying a portion of the principal with regular payments that also include interest is often called loan **amortization.**[1] This chapter explains accounting for interest and principal with respect to the major forms of long-term debt financing.

[1]In Chapter 8, the term *amortization* described the expense recognized when the cost of an intangible asset is systematically allocated to expense over the useful life of the asset. This chapter shows that the term *amortization* refers more broadly to a variety of allocation processes. Here, it means the systematic process of allocating interest to the periods in which the loan is outstanding.

The Curious Accountant

In 2017, **Dell Technologies, Inc.** reported a net loss of $3.9 billion. The previous year it had reported a loss of $1.7 billion. The company had $2.4 billion of interest expense in 2017.

With such a huge loss on its income statement, do you think Dell was able to make the interest payments on its debt? If so, how? (Answers on page 487.)

Lukmanazis/Shutterstock

INSTALLMENT NOTES PAYABLE

LO 10-1

Show how an installment note affects financial statements.

Loans that require payments of principal and interest at regular intervals (amortizing loans) are typically represented by **installment notes.** The terms of installment notes usually range from two to five years. To illustrate accounting for installment notes, assume Blair Company was started on January 1, Year 1, when it borrowed $100,000 cash from National Bank. In exchange for the money, Blair issued the bank a five-year installment note with a 9 percent fixed interest rate. The effects of issuing the note on the financial statements are shown next:

	Balance Sheet						Income Statement					Statement of Cash Flows
	Assets	=	Liab.	+		Stk. Equity						
Date	Cash	=	Notes Pay.	+	Com. Stk.	+	Ret. Earn.	Rev.	−	Exp.	=	Net Inc.	
Year 1													
Jan. 1	100,000	=	100,000	+	NA	+	NA	NA	−	NA	=	NA	100,000 FA

The loan agreement required Blair to pay five equal installments of $25,709[2] on December 31 of Year 1 through Year 5. Exhibit 10.1 shows the allocation of each payment between principal and interest. When Blair pays the final installment, both the principal and interest will be paid in full. The amounts shown in Exhibit 10.1 are computed as follows:

1. The Interest Expense (Column D) is computed by multiplying the Principal Balance on Jan. 1 (Column B) by the interest rate. For example, interest expense for Year 1 is $100,000 \times 0.09 = $9,000; for Year 2 it is $83,291 \times 0.09 = $7,496; and so on.

2. The Principal Repayment (Column E) is computed by subtracting the Interest Expense (Column D) from the Cash Payment on Dec. 31 (Column C). For example, the Principal Repayment for Year 1 is $25,709 − $9,000 = $16,709; for Year 2 it is $25,709 − $7,496 = $18,213; and so on.

3. The Principal Balance on Dec. 31 (Column F) is computed by subtracting the Principal Repayment (Column E) from the Principal Balance on Jan. 1 (Column B). For example, the Principal Balance on Dec. 31 for Year 1 is $100,000 − $16,709 = $83,291; on December 31, Year 2, the principal balance is $83,291 − $18,213 = $65,078; and so on.

EXHIBIT 10.1

Amortization Schedule for Installment Note Payable

Accounting Period Column A	Principal Balance on Jan. 1 Column B	Cash Payment on Dec. 31 Column C	Interest Expense Column D	Principal Repayment Column E	Principal Balance on Dec. 31 Column F
Year 1	$100,000	$25,709	$9,000	$16,709	$83,291
Year 2	83,291	25,709	7,496	18,213	65,078
Year 3	65,078	25,709	5,857	19,852	45,226
Year 4	45,226	25,709	4,070	21,639	23,587
Year 5	23,587	25,710*	2,123	23,587	0

*All computations are rounded to the nearest dollar. To fully liquidate the liability, the final payment is one dollar more than the others because of rounding differences.

[2]The amount of the annual payment is determined using the present value concepts presented in Appendix G at the end of this textbook. Usually, the lender (bank or other financial institution) calculates the amount of the payment for the customer.

Answers to The Curious Accountant

Even though **Dell Technologies** reported a $3.9 billion loss in 2017, it was able to make the interest payments on its debt with no difficulty for two reasons. First, interest is paid with cash, not accrual earnings. Some of the expenses on the company's income statement did not require the use of cash in 2017. For example, Dell reported a depreciation and amortization expense of $8.6 billion, which did not require cash payments.

Second, the net loss the company incurred was *after* the interest expense of $2.4 billion had been deducted. The company's statement of cash flows shows that net cash flow from operating activities in 2017, *after making interest payments,* was a positive $6.8 billion. The capacity of operations to support interest payments is measured by the amount of earnings before interest deductions. For example, look at the Year 1 income statement for Blair Company in Exhibit 10.2. This statement shows only $3,000 of net income, but $12,000 of cash revenue was available for the payment of interest. Similarly, Dell's 2017 net loss is not an indication of the company's ability to pay interest in the short run.

The Principal Balance on Dec. 31 (ending balance) for Year 1 ($83,291) is also the Principal Balance on Jan. 1 (beginning balance) for Year 2; the principal balance on December 31, Year 2, is the principal balance on January 1, Year 3, and so on.

Although the amounts for interest expense and principal repayment differ each year, the effects of the annual payment on the financial statements are the same. On the balance sheet, assets (Cash) decrease by the total amount of the payment; liabilities (Notes Payable) decrease by the amount of the principal repayment; and stockholders' equity (Retained Earnings) decreases by the amount of interest expense. Net income decreases from recognizing interest expense. On the statement of cash flows, the portion of the cash payment applied to interest is reported in the operating activities section, and the portion applied to principal is reported in the financing activities section. The effects on the Year 1 financial statements are shown next. While the amounts will differ in subsequent years, the impacts on the financial statements will be the same.

Date	Balance Sheet								Income Statement						Statement of Cash Flows
	Assets	=	Liab.	+		Stk. Equity									
	Cash	=	Notes Pay.	+	Com. Stk.	+	Ret. Earn.		Rev.	−	Exp.	=	Net Inc.		
Year 1 Dec. 31	(25,709)	=	(16,709)	+	NA	+	(9,000)		NA	−	9,000	=	(9,000)		(9,000) OA (16,709) FA

Exhibit 10.2 displays income statements, balance sheets, and statements of cash flows for Blair Company for the accounting periods Year 1 through Year 5. The illustration assumes that Blair earned $12,000 of rent revenue each year. Because some of the principal is repaid each year, the note payable amount reported on the balance sheet and the amount of the interest expense on the income statement both decline each year.

EXHIBIT 10.2

BLAIR COMPANY
Financial Statements

	Year 1	Year 2	Year 3	Year 4	Year 5
Income Statements					
Rent revenue	$ 12,000	$12,000	$12,000	$12,000	$12,000
Interest expense	(9,000)	(7,496)	(5,857)	(4,070)	(2,123)
Net income	$ 3,000	$ 4,504	$ 6,143	$ 7,930	$ 9,877
Balance Sheets					
Assets					
Cash	$ 86,291	$72,582	$58,873	$45,164	$31,454
Liabilities					
Note payable	$ 83,291	$65,078	$45,226	$23,587	$ 0
Stockholders' equity					
Retained earnings	3,000	7,504	13,647	21,577	31,454
Total liabilities and stk. equity	$ 86,291	$72,582	$58,873	$45,164	$31,454
Statements of Cash Flows					
Operating Activities					
Inflow from customers	$ 12,000	$12,000	$12,000	$12,000	$12,000
Outflow for interest	(9,000)	(7,496)	(5,857)	(4,070)	(2,123)
Investing Activities	0	0	0	0	0
Financing Activities					
Inflow from note issue	100,000	0	0	0	0
Outflow to repay note	(16,709)	(18,213)	(19,852)	(21,639)	(23,587)
Net change in cash	86,291	(13,709)	(13,709)	(13,709)	(13,710)
Plus: Beginning cash balance	0	86,291	72,582	58,873	45,164
Ending cash balance	$ 86,291	$72,582	$58,873	$45,164	$31,454

 CHECK YOURSELF 10.1

On January 1, Year 1, Krueger Company issued a $50,000 installment note to State Bank. The note had a 10-year term and an 8 percent interest rate. Krueger agreed to repay the principal and interest in 10 annual payments of $7,451.47 at the end of each year. Determine the amount of principal and interest Krueger paid during the first and second year that the note was outstanding.

Answer

Accounting Period	Principal Balance January 1 A	Cash Payment December 31 B	Applied to Interest C = A × 0.08	Applied to Principal B − C
Year 1	$50,000.00	$7,451.47	$4,000.00	$3,451.47
Year 2	46,548.53	7,451.47	3,723.88	3,727.59

LINE OF CREDIT

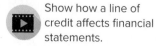

A **line of credit** enables a company to borrow or repay funds as needed. For example, a business may borrow $50,000 one month and make a partial repayment of $10,000 the next month. Credit agreements usually specify a limit on the amount that can be borrowed. Exhibit 10.3 shows that credit agreements are widely used.

Interest rates on lines of credit normally vary with fluctuations in some designated interest rate benchmark such as the rate paid on U.S. Treasury bills. For example, a company may pay 4 percent interest one month and 4.5 percent the next month, even if the principal balance remains constant.

Lines of credit typically have one-year terms. Although they are classified on the balance sheet as short-term liabilities, lines of credit are frequently extended indefinitely by simply renewing the credit agreement.

To illustrate accounting for a line of credit, assume Lagoon Company owns a wholesale jet-ski distributorship. In the spring, Lagoon borrows money using a line of credit to finance building up its inventory. Lagoon repays the loan over the summer months using cash generated from jet-ski sales. Borrowing or repaying events occur on the first of the month. Interest payments occur at the end of each month. Exhibit 10.4 presents all Year 1 line of credit events.

Each borrowing event (March 1, April 1, and May 1) is an asset source transaction. Both cash and the line of credit liability increase. Each repayment (June 1, July 1, and August 1) is an asset use transaction. Both cash and the line of credit liability decrease. Each month's interest expense recognition and payment is an asset use transaction. Assets (Cash) and stockholders' equity (Retained Earnings) decrease, as does net income. The effects of these events on the financial statements are shown in Exhibit 10.5.

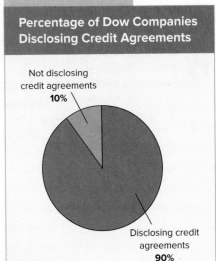

EXHIBIT 10.3

Percentage of Dow Companies Disclosing Credit Agreements

Not disclosing credit agreements
10%

Disclosing credit agreements
90%

Source: Dow Jones Industrial Average

EXHIBIT 10.4

Summary of Line of Credit Events

Date	Amount Borrowed (Repaid)	Loan Balance at End of Month	Effective Interest Rate per Month (%)	Interest Expense (rounded to nearest $1)
Mar. 1	$ 20,000	$ 20,000	0.09 ÷ 12	$150
Apr. 1	30,000	50,000	0.09 ÷ 12	375
May 1	50,000	100,000	0.105 ÷ 12	875
June 1	(10,000)	90,000	0.10 ÷ 12	750
July 1	(40,000)	50,000	0.09 ÷ 12	375
Aug. 1	(50,000)	0	0.09 ÷ 12	0

EXHIBIT 10.5

Effects on Financial Statements

Date	Balance Sheet					Income Statement					Statement of Cash Flows	
	Assets	=	Liabilities	+	Equity	Rev.	–	Exp.	=	Net Inc.		
Mar. 1	20,000	=	20,000	+	NA	NA	–	NA	=	NA	20,000	FA
31	(150)	=	NA	+	(150)	NA	–	150	=	(150)	(150)	OA
Apr. 1	30,000	=	30,000	+	NA	NA	–	NA	=	NA	30,000	FA
30	(375)	=	NA	+	(375)	NA	–	375	=	(375)	(375)	OA
May 1	50,000	=	50,000	+	NA	NA	–	NA	=	NA	50,000	FA
31	(875)	=	NA	+	(875)	NA	–	875	=	(875)	(875)	OA
June 1	(10,000)	=	(10,000)	+	NA	NA	–	NA	=	NA	(10,000)	FA
30	(750)	=	NA	+	(750)	NA	–	750	=	(750)	(750)	OA
July 1	(40,000)	=	(40,000)	+	NA	NA	–	NA	=	NA	(40,000)	FA
31	(375)	=	NA	+	(375)	NA	–	375	=	(375)	(375)	OA
Aug. 1	(50,000)	=	(50,000)	+	NA	NA	–	NA	=	NA	(50,000)	FA
31	NA	=	NA	+	NA	NA	–	NA	=	NA	NA	

BOND LIABILITIES

Describe bond features and show how bonds issued at face value affect financial statements.

Many companies borrow money directly from the public by selling **bond certificates,** otherwise called *issuing* bonds. Bond certificates describe a company's obligation to pay interest and to repay the principal. The seller, or **issuer,** of a bond is the borrower; the buyer of a bond, or **bondholder,** is the lender.

From the issuer's point of view, a bond represents an obligation to pay a sum of money to the bondholder on the bond's maturity date. The amount due at maturity is the **face value** of the bond. Most bonds also require the issuer to make cash interest payments based on a **stated interest rate** at regular intervals over the life of the bond. Exhibit 10.6 shows a typical bond certificate.

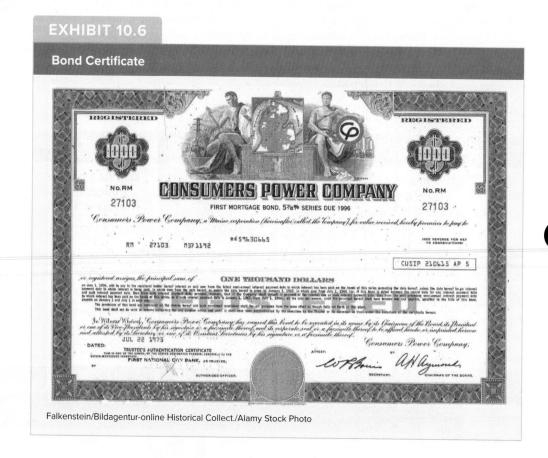

EXHIBIT 10.6

Bond Certificate

Falkenstein/Bildagentur-online Historical Collect./Alamy Stock Photo

Advantages of Issuing Bonds

Bond financing offers companies the following advantages:

1. Bonds usually have longer terms than notes issued to banks. While typical bank loan terms range from 2 to 5 years, bonds normally have 20-year terms to maturity. Longer terms to maturity allow companies to implement long-term strategic plans without having to worry about frequent refinancing arrangements.

2. Bond interest rates may be lower than bank interest rates. Banks earn profits by borrowing money from the public (depositors) at low interest rates, then loaning that money to companies at higher rates. By issuing bonds directly to the public, companies can pay lower interest costs by eliminating the middleman (banks).

Security of Bonds

Bonds may be either secured or unsecured.

1. **Secured bonds** grant their holders a priority legal claim on specified identifiable assets should the issuer default. A common type of secured bond is a **mortgage bond,** which conditionally transfers the title of designated property to the bondholder until the bond is paid.

2. **Unsecured bonds,** also called **debentures,** are issued based on the general strength of the borrower's credit. Bond certificates often specify the priority of debenture holders' claims relative to other creditors. Holders of **subordinated debentures** have lower priority claims than other creditors, whereas holders of **unsubordinated debentures** have equal claims.

Timing of Maturity

The maturity dates of bonds can be specified in various ways. Even bonds sold as separate components of a single issue may have different maturity dates.

1. **Term bonds** mature on a specified date in the future.

2. **Serial bonds** mature at specified intervals throughout the life of the total issue. For example, bonds with a total face value of $1,000,000 may mature in increments of $100,000 every year for 10 years.

To ensure there is enough cash available at maturity to pay off the debt, a bond agreement may require the issuer to make regular payments into a **sinking fund.** Money deposited in the sinking fund is usually managed by an independent trustee who invests the funds until the bonds mature. At maturity, the funds and the proceeds from the investments are used to repay the bond debt.

REALITY BYTES

Throughout this textbook, various financial ratios have been discussed, along with explanations of how they are used by financial analysts. Ratios are also often included as covenants in loan agreements when a company borrows money. If the company violates a ratio covenant in the loan agreement, the lender can force the company to renegotiate the loan or pay back the borrowed funds much earlier than originally agreed. This can have dire consequences for the company. Consider the following excerpts taken from the "Management's Discussion and Analysis . . . - *Capital Financing Overview*" of the **Las Vegas Sands Corporation**'s 2017 Form 10-K.

Jacob Andrzejczak/Getty Images

> We fund our development projects primarily through borrowings from our credit facilities . . . and operating cash flows. Our U.S., Macao and Singapore credit facilities, as amended, contain various financial covenants. The U.S. credit facility requires our Las Vegas operations to comply with a financial covenant at the end of each quarter to the extent that any revolving loans or certain letters of credit are outstanding. This financial covenant requires our Las Vegas operations to maintain a maximum leverage ratio of net debt, as defined, to trailing twelve-month adjusted earnings before interest, income taxes, depreciation and amortization, as defined ("Adjusted EBITDA"). The maximum leverage ratio is 5.5x for all quarterly periods through maturity. . . . Our Macao credit facility requires our Macao operations to comply with similar financial covenants, including maintaining a maximum leverage ratio of debt to Adjusted EBITDA. The maximum leverage ratio is 3.5x for the quarterly periods ending December 31, 2017 through September 30, 2019 and then decreases to, and remains at, 3.0x for all quarterly periods thereafter through maturity. Our Singapore credit facility requires our Marina Bay Sands operations to comply with similar financial covenants. . . .[3]

Simply put, the company is warning investors that if it violates the ratio covenants, which it seems likely to do, the company could go into bankruptcy. Ratios matter!

[3]U.S. Securities and Exchange Commission.

Special Features

Some bonds feature one or both of the following characteristics:

1. **Convertible bonds** are liabilities that can be exchanged at the option of the bondholder for common stock or some other specified ownership interest. The issuing company benefits because bondholders (investors) are willing to accept a lower interest rate in exchange for the conversion feature. Bondholders benefit because they obtain the option to share in potential rewards of ownership. If the market value of the company's stock increases, bondholders can convert their bonds to stock. If the stock price does not increase, bondholders are still guaranteed interest payments and priority claims in bankruptcy settlements.

2. **Callable bonds** allow the issuing company to redeem (pay off) the bond debt before the maturity date. If interest rates decline, this feature benefits the issuing company because it could borrow additional money at a lower rate and use the proceeds to pay off its higher rate bonds. Because an early redemption would eliminate their higher-interest bond investments, bondholders consider call features undesirable. To encourage investors to buy callable bonds, the **call price** normally exceeds the *face value* of the bonds. For example, the issuing company may agree to pay the holder of a $1,000 face-value bond a call price of $1,050 if the bond is redeemed before its maturity date. The difference between the call price and the face value ($50 [$1,050 − $1,000] in this case) is commonly called a **call premium.**

Bond Ratings

Three financial services analyze the risk of default for corporate bond issues and publish ratings of the risk as guides to bond investors. These agencies are Fitch, Moody's, and Standard & Poor's. The highest rating (lowest risk) a company can achieve is AAA, the next highest is AA, and so forth. Bond issuers try to maintain high credit ratings because lower ratings require them to pay higher interest rates.

Restrictive Covenants

In general, large loans with long terms to maturity pose more risk to lenders (creditors) than small loans with short terms. To reduce the risk that they won't get paid, lenders frequently require borrowers (debtors) to pledge designated assets as **collateral** for loans. For example, when a bank makes a car loan, it usually retains legal title to the car until the loan is fully repaid. If the borrower fails to make the monthly payments, the bank repossesses the car, sells it to someone else, and uses the proceeds to pay the original owner's debt. Similarly, assets like accounts receivable, inventory, equipment, buildings, and land may be pledged as collateral for business loans.

Besides requiring collateral, creditors often obtain additional protection by including **restrictive covenants** in loan agreements. Such covenants may restrict additional borrowing, limit dividend payments, or restrict salary increases. If the loan restrictions are violated, the borrower is in default and the loan balance is due immediately.

Finally, creditors often ask owners and executives of nonpublic companies to provide copies of their personal tax returns and financial statements. The financial condition of the owners and executives is important because they may be asked to pledge personal property as collateral for business loans.

Bonds Issued at Face Value

Assume Sandra Mason needs cash in order to seize a business opportunity. Mason knows of a company seeking a plot of land on which to store its inventory of crushed stone. Mason also knows of a suitable tract of land she could purchase for $100,000. The company has agreed to lease the land it needs from Mason for $12,000 per year. Mason lacks the funds to buy the land.

Some of Mason's friends recently complained about the low interest rates banks were paying on certificates of deposit. Mason suggested that her friends invest in bonds instead of CDs. She offered to sell them bonds with a 9 percent stated interest rate. The terms specified in the bond agreement Mason drafted included making interest payments in cash on December 31 of each year, a five-year term to maturity, and pledging the land as collateral for the bonds.[4] Her friends were favorably impressed, and Mason issued the bonds to them in exchange for cash on January 1, Year 1.

Mason used the bond proceeds to purchase the land, and then immediately contracted to lease it for five years. On December 31, Year 5, the maturity date of the bonds, Mason sold the land for its $100,000 book value and used the proceeds from the sale to repay the bond liability.

Financial Statement Effects

Mason's business venture involved six distinct accounting events, described as follows.

EVENT 1   Issued bonds for $100,000 cash.

Assets (Cash) and liabilities (Bonds Payable) increase. Net income is not affected. The $100,000 cash inflow is reported in the financing activities section of the statement of cash flows. The effects on the financial statements are shown next:

Balance Sheet					Income Statement				Statement of Cash Flows
Assets	=	Liab.	+	Stk. Equity					
Cash	=	Bonds Pay.			Rev.	− Exp.	=	Net Inc.	
100,000	=	100,000	+	NA	NA	− NA	=	NA	100,000 FA

EVENT 2   Paid $100,000 cash to purchase land.

The asset cash decreases and the asset land increases. The income statement is not affected. The cash outflow is reported in the investing activities section of the statement of cash flows. The effects on the financial statements are shown next:

Balance Sheet				Income Statement				Statement of Cash Flows
Assets		= Liab. + Stk. Equity						
Cash	+	Land		Rev.	− Exp.	=	Net Inc.	
(100,000)	+	100,000 = NA + NA		NA	− NA	=	NA	(100,000) IA

EVENT 3   Recognized $12,000 cash revenue from renting the land.

This event is repeated each year from Year 1 through Year 5. The event increases assets and stockholders' equity. Recognizing revenue increases net income. The cash inflow is reported in the operating activities section of the statement of cash flows. The effects on the financial statements are shown next:

Balance Sheet					Income Statement				Statement of Cash Flows
Assets	=	Liab.	+	Stk. Equity					
Cash	=			Ret. Earn.	Rev.	− Exp.	=	Net Inc.	
12,000	=	NA	+	12,000	12,000	− NA	=	12,000	12,000 OA

[4]In practice, bonds are usually issued for much larger sums of money, often hundreds of millions of dollars. Also, terms to maturity are normally long, with 20 years being common. Using such large amounts for such long terms is unnecessarily cumbersome for instructional purposes. The effects of bond issues can be illustrated efficiently by using smaller amounts of debt with shorter maturities, as assumed in the case of Sandra Mason.

EVENT 4   Paid $9,000 cash for interest.

This event is also repeated each year from Year 1 through Year 5. The interest payment is an asset use transaction. Cash and stockholders' equity (Retained Earnings) decrease. The expense recognition decreases net income. The cash outflow is reported in the operating activities section of the statement of cash flows. The effects on the financial statements are shown next:

Balance Sheet				Income Statement			Statement of Cash Flows
Assets	=	Liab.	+ Stk. Equity				
Cash	=		Ret. Earn.	Rev.	− Exp.	= Net Inc.	
(9,000)	=	NA	+ (9,000)	NA	− 9,000	= (9,000)	(9,000) OA

EVENT 5   Sold the land for cash equal to its $100,000 book value.

Cash increases and land decreases. Because there was no gain or loss on the sale, the income statement is not affected. The cash inflow is reported in the investing activities section of the statement of cash flows. The effects on the financial statements are shown next:

Balance Sheet			Income Statement		Statement of Cash Flows
Assets	= Liab. + Stk. Equity				
Cash + Land			Rev. − Exp. = Net Inc.		
100,000 + (100,000) = NA + NA			NA − NA = NA		100,000 IA

EVENT 6   Repaid the face value of the bond liability.

Cash and bonds payable decrease. The income statement is not affected. The cash outflow is reported in the financing activities section of the statement of cash flows. The effects on the financial statements are shown next:

Balance Sheet				Income Statement			Statement of Cash Flows
Assets	=	Liab.	+ Stk. Equity				
Cash	=	Bonds Pay.		Rev.	− Exp.	= Net Inc.	
(100,000)	=	(100,000)	+ NA	NA	− NA	= NA	(100,000) FA

Financial Statements

Exhibit 10.7 displays Mason Company's financial statements. For simplicity, the income statement does not distinguish between operating and other items. Rent revenue and interest expense are constant across all accounting periods, so Mason recognizes $3,000 of net income in each accounting period. On the balance sheet, cash increases by $3,000 each year because cash revenue exceeds cash paid for interest. Land remains constant each year at its $100,000 historical cost until it is sold in Year 5. Similarly, the bonds payable liability is reported at $100,000 from the date the bonds were issued in Year 1 until they are paid off on December 31, Year 5.

Compare Blair Company's income statements in Exhibit 10.2 with Mason Company's income statements in Exhibit 10.7. Both Blair and Mason borrowed $100,000 cash at a 9 percent stated interest rate for five-year terms. Blair, however, repaid its liability under the terms of an installment note, while Mason did not repay any principal until the end of the five-year bond term. Because Blair repaid part of the principal balance on the installment loan each year, Blair's interest expense declined each year. The interest expense on Mason's bond liability, however, remained constant because the full principal amount was outstanding for the entire five-year bond term.

EXHIBIT 10.7

Mason Company Financial Statements

Bonds Issued at Face Value

	Year 1	Year 2	Year 3	Year 4	Year 5
Income Statements					
Rent revenue	$ 12,000	$ 12,000	$ 12,000	$ 12,000	$ 12,000
Interest expense	(9,000)	(9,000)	(9,000)	(9,000)	(9,000)
Net income	$ 3,000	$ 3,000	$ 3,000	$ 3,000	$ 3,000
Balance Sheets					
Assets					
Cash	$ 3,000	$ 6,000	$ 9,000	$ 12,000	$ 15,000
Land	100,000	100,000	100,000	100,000	0
Total assets	$103,000	$106,000	$109,000	$112,000	$ 15,000
Liabilities					
Bonds payable	$100,000	$100,000	$100,000	$100,000	$ 0
Stockholders' equity					
Retained earnings	3,000	6,000	9,000	12,000	15,000
Total liabilities and stockholders' equity	$103,000	$106,000	$109,000	$112,000	$ 15,000
Statements of Cash Flows					
Operating Activities					
Inflow from customers	$ 12,000	$ 12,000	$ 12,000	$ 12,000	$ 12,000
Outflow for interest	(9,000)	(9,000)	(9,000)	(9,000)	(9,000)
Investing Activities					
Outflow to purchase land	(100,000)				
Inflow from sale of land					100,000
Financing Activities					
Inflow from bond issue	100,000				
Outflow to repay bond liab.					(100,000)
Net Change in Cash	3,000	3,000	3,000	3,000	3,000
Plus: Beginning cash balance	0	3,000	6,000	9,000	12,000
Ending cash balance	$ 3,000	$ 6,000	$ 9,000	$ 12,000	$ 15,000

AMORTIZATION USING THE STRAIGHT-LINE METHOD

Bonds Issued at a Discount

Return to the Mason Company illustration with one change. Assume Mason's bond certificates have a 9 percent stated rate of interest printed on them. Suppose Mason's friends find they can buy bonds from another entrepreneur willing to pay a higher rate of interest. They explain to Mason that business decisions cannot be made on the basis of friendship. Mason provides a counteroffer. There is no time to change the bond certificates, so Mason offers to accept $95,000 for the bonds today and still repay the full face value of $100,000 at the maturity date. The $5,000 difference is called a **bond discount.** Mason's friends agree to buy the bonds for $95,000.

LO 10-4

Use the straight-line method to amortize bond discounts.

Effective Interest Rate

The bond discount increases the interest Mason must pay. First, Mason must still make the annual cash payments described in the bond agreement. In other words, Mason must pay cash of $9,000

(0.09 × $100,000) annually even though she actually borrowed only $95,000. Second, Mason will have to pay back $5,000 more than she received ($100,000 − $95,000). The extra $5,000 (bond discount) is additional interest. Although the $5,000 of additional interest is not paid until maturity, when spread over the life of the bond, it amounts to $1,000 of additional interest expense per year.

The actual rate of interest that Mason must pay is called the **effective interest rate.** A rough estimate of the effective interest rate for the discounted Mason bonds is 10.5 percent ([$9,000 annual stated interest + $1,000 annual amortization of the discount] ÷ $95,000 amount borrowed). Selling the bonds at a $5,000 discount permits Mason to raise the 9 percent stated rate of interest to an effective rate of roughly 10.5 percent. Deeper discounts would raise the effective rate even higher. More shallow discounts would reduce the effective rate of interest. Mason can set the effective rate of interest to any level desired by adjusting the amount of the discount.

Bond Prices

It is common business practice to use discounts to raise the effective rate of interest above the stated rate. Bonds frequently sell for less than face value. Bond prices are normally expressed *as a percentage of the face value.* For example, Mason's discounted bonds sold for 95, meaning the bonds sold at 95 percent of face value ($100,000 × 0.95 = $95,000). Amounts of less than 1 percentage point are usually expressed as a fraction. Therefore, a bond priced at 98 3/4 sells for 98.75 percent of face value.

Financial Statement Effects

To illustrate accounting for bonds issued at a discount, return to the Mason Company example using the assumption the bonds are issued for 95 instead of face value. We examine the same six events using this revised assumption. This revision changes some amounts reported on the financial statements. For example, Event 1 in Year 1 reflects receiving only $95,000 cash from the bond issue. Because Mason had only $95,000 available to invest in land, the illustration assumes that Mason acquired a less desirable piece of property that generated only $11,400 of rent revenue per year.

EVENT 1 Bonds with a face value of $100,000 are issued at 95.

Because Mason must pay the face value at maturity, the $100,000 face value of the bonds is recorded in the Bonds Payable account. The $5,000 discount is recorded in a separate contra liability account called **Discount on Bonds Payable.** As shown next, the contra account is subtracted from the face value to determine the **carrying value** (book value) of the bond liability on January 1, Year 1.

Bonds payable	$100,000
Less: Discount on bonds payable	(5,000)
Carrying value	$ 95,000

The bond issue is an asset source transaction. Both assets and total liabilities increase by $95,000. Net income is not affected. The cash inflow is reported in the financing activities section of the statement of cash flows. The effects on the financial statements are shown next:

Balance Sheet				Income Statement			Statement of Cash Flows
Assets =	Liabilities	+ Stk. Equity					
Cash =	Carrying Value of Bond Liability +	Equity		Rev. −	Exp. =	Net Inc.	
(95,000) =	95,000	+ NA		NA −	NA =	NA	95,000 FA

EVENT 2 Paid $95,000 cash to purchase land.

The asset cash decreases and the asset land increases. The income statement is not affected. The cash outflow is reported in the investing activities section of the statement of cash flows. The effects on the financial statements are shown next:

Balance Sheet			Income Statement			Statement of Cash Flows
Assets	= Liab. + Stk. Equity		Rev. – Exp. = Net Inc.			
Cash + Land						
(95,000) + 95,000 = NA +	NA		NA – NA =	NA		(95,000) IA

EVENT 3 Recognized $11,400 cash revenue from renting the land.

This event is repeated each year from Year 1 through Year 5. The event is an asset source transaction that increases assets and stockholders' equity. Recognizing revenue increases net income. The cash inflow is reported in the operating activities section of the statement of cash flows. The effects on the financial statements are shown next:

Balance Sheet				Income Statement				Statement of Cash Flows
Assets	=	Liab.	+	Stk. Equity				
Cash	=			Ret. Earn.	Rev.	– Exp.	= Net Inc.	
11,400	=	NA	+	11,400	11,400	– NA	= 11,400	11,400 OA

EVENT 4 Recognized interest expense. The interest cost of borrowing has two components: the $9,000 paid in cash each year and the $5,000 discount paid at maturity.

Using **straight-line amortization,** the amount of the discount recognized as expense in each accounting period is $1,000 ($5,000 discount ÷ 5 years). Mason will therefore recognize $10,000 of interest expense each year ($9,000 at the stated interest rate plus $1,000 amortization of the bond discount). On the balance sheet, the asset cash decreases by $9,000, the carrying value of the bond liability increases by $1,000 (through a decrease in the bond discount), and retained earnings (Interest Expense) decreases by $10,000. The effects on the financial statements are shown next:

Balance Sheet			Income Statement			Statement of Cash Flows
Assets =	Liab.	+ Stk. Equity				
Cash =	Carrying Value of Bond Liability	+ Ret. Earn.	Rev. –	Exp.	= Net Inc.	
(9,000) =	1,000	+ (10,000)	NA –	10,000	= (10,000)	(9,000) OA

EVENT 5 Sold the land for cash equal to its $95,000 book value.

Cash increases and land decreases. Because there was no gain or loss on the sale, the income statement is not affected. The cash inflow is reported in the investing activities section of the statement of cash flows. The effects on the financial statements are shown next:

Balance Sheet			Income Statement			Statement of Cash Flows
Assets	= Liab. + Stk. Equity		Rev. – Exp. = Net Inc.			
Cash + Land						
95,000 + (95,000) = NA +	NA		NA – NA =	NA		95,000 IA

EVENT 6 Paid the bond liability.

Cash and bonds payable decrease. The income statement is not affected. For reporting purposes, the cash outflow is separated into two parts on the statement of cash flows: $95,000 of the cash outflow is reported in the financing activities section because it represents repaying the principal amount borrowed; the remaining $5,000 cash outflow is reported in the operating activities section because it represents the interest arising from issuing the bonds at a discount. In practice, the amount of the discount is frequently immaterial and is combined in the financing activities section with the principal repayment. The effects on the financial statements are shown next:

Balance Sheet			Income Statement			Statement of Cash Flows
Assets = Liab. + Stk. Equity			Rev. − Exp. = Net Inc.			
Cash = Bonds Pay.						
(100,000) = (100,000) + NA			NA − NA = NA			(95,000) FA (5,000) OA

Financial Statements

Exhibit 10.8 displays Mason Company's financial statements, assuming the bonds were issued at a discount. Contrast the net income reported in Exhibit 10.8 (bonds issued at a

EXHIBIT 10.8

Mason Company Financial Statements

	Bonds Issued at a Discount				
	Year 1	Year 2	Year 3	Year 4	Year 5
Income Statements					
Rent revenue	$ 11,400	$ 11,400	$ 11,400	$ 11,400	$ 11,400
Interest expense	(10,000)	(10,000)	(10,000)	(10,000)	(10,000)
Net income	$ 1,400	$ 1,400	$ 1,400	$ 1,400	$ 1,400
Balance Sheets					
Assets					
Cash	$ 2,400	$ 4,800	$ 7,200	$ 9,600	$ 7,000
Land	95,000	95,000	95,000	95,000	0
Total assets	$ 97,400	$ 99,800	$102,200	$104,600	$ 7,000
Liabilities					
Bonds payable	$100,000	$100,000	$100,000	$100,000	$ 0
Discount on bonds payable	(4,000)	(3,000)	(2,000)	(1,000)	0
Carrying value of bond liab.	96,000	97,000	98,000	99,000	0
Stockholders' equity					
Retained earnings	1,400	2,800	4,200	5,600	7,000
Total liabilities and stockholders' equity	$ 97,400	$ 99,800	$102,200	$104,600	$ 7,000
Statements of Cash Flows					
Operating Activities					
Inflow from customers	$ 11,400	$ 11,400	$ 11,400	$ 11,400	$ 11,400
Outflow for interest	(9,000)	(9,000)	(9,000)	(9,000)	(14,000)
Investing Activities					
Outflow to purchase land	(95,000)				
Inflow from sale of land					95,000
Financing Activities					
Inflow from bond issue	95,000				
Outflow to repay bond liab.					(95,000)
Net Change in Cash	2,400	2,400	2,400	2,400	(2,600)
Plus: Beginning cash balance	0	2,400	4,800	7,200	9,600
Ending cash balance	$ 2,400	$ 4,800	$ 7,200	$ 9,600	$ 7,000

discount) with the net income reported in Exhibit 10.7 (bonds sold at face value). Two factors cause the net income in Exhibit 10.8 to be lower. First, because the bonds were sold at a discount, Mason Company had less money to spend on its land investment. It bought less desirable land, which generated less revenue. Second, the effective interest rate was higher than the stated rate, resulting in higher interest expense. Lower revenues coupled with higher expenses result in less profitability.

On the balance sheet, the carrying value of the bond liability increases each year until the maturity date, December 31, Year 5, when it is equal to the $100,000 face value of the bonds (the amount Mason is obligated to pay). Because Mason did not pay any dividends, retained earnings ($7,000) on December 31, Year 5, is equal to the total amount of net income reported over the five-year period ($1,400 × 5). All earnings were retained in the business.

Several factors account for the differences between net income and cash flow. First, although $10,000 of interest expense is reported on each income statement, only $9,000 of cash was paid for interest each year until Year 5, when $14,000 was paid for interest ($9,000 based on the stated rate + $5,000 for discount). The $1,000 difference between interest expense and cash paid for interest in Year 1, Year 2, Year 3, and Year 4 results from amortizing the bond discount. The cash outflow for the interest related to the discount is included in the $100,000 payment made at maturity on December 31, Year 5. Even though $14,000 of cash is paid for interest in Year 5, only $10,000 is recognized as interest expense on the income statement that year. Although the total increase in cash over the five-year life of the business ($7,000) is equal to the total net income reported for the same period, there are significant timing differences between when the interest expense is recognized and when the cash outflows occur to pay for it.

✓ CHECK YOURSELF 10.2

On January 1, Year 1, Moffett Company issued bonds with a $600,000 face value at 98. The bonds had a 9 percent annual interest rate and a 10-year term. Interest is payable in cash on December 31 of each year. What amount of interest expense will Moffett report on the Year 3 income statement? What carrying value for bonds payable will Moffett report on the December 31, Year 3, balance sheet?

Answer The bonds were issued at a $12,000 ($600,000 × 0.02) discount. The discount will be amortized over the 10-year life at the rate of $1,200 ($12,000 ÷ 10 years) per year. The amount of interest expense for Year 3 is $55,200 ($600,000 × 0.09 = $54,000 annual cash interest + $1,200 discount amortization).

The carrying value of the bond liability is equal to the face value less the unamortized discount. By the end of Year 3, $3,600 of the discount will have been amortized ($1,200 × 3 years = $3,600). The unamortized discount as of December 31, Year 3, will be $8,400 ($12,000 − $3,600). The carrying value of the bond liability as of December 31, Year 3, will be $591,600 ($600,000 − $8,400).

Effect of Semiannual Interest Payments

The previous examples assumed that interest payments were made annually. In practice, most bond agreements call for interest to be paid semiannually, which means that interest is paid in cash twice each year. If Mason's bond certificate had stipulated semiannual interest payments, her company would have paid $4,500 ($100,000 × 0.09 = $9,000; $9,000 ÷ 2 = $4,500) cash to bondholders for interest on June 30 and December 31 of each year. The amortization of the discount would be $500 semiannually ($5,000 discount ÷ 5 years = $1,000; $1,000 ÷ 2 = $500). Accordingly, on June 30 and December 31 of each year, the company will recognize

$5,000 of interest expense ($4,500 cash payment + $500 discounts amortization). The effects of each semiannual payment on the financial statements are shown next:

Balance Sheet				Income Statement				Statement of Cash Flows	
Assets =	Liab.	+ Stk. Equity							
Cash =	Carrying Value of Bond Liability +	Ret. Earn.		Rev. −	Exp.	= Net Inc.			
(4,500) =	500	+ (5,000)		NA −	5,000	= (5,000)		(4,500)	OA

Bonds Issued at a Premium

LO 10-5

Use the straight-line method to amortize bond premiums.

When bonds are sold for more than their face value, the difference between the amount received and the face value is called a **bond premium.** Bond premiums reduce the effective interest rate. For example, assume Mason Company issued its 9 percent bonds at 105, receiving $105,000 cash on the issue date. The company is still only required to repay the $100,000 face value of the bonds at the maturity date. The $5,000 difference between the amount received and the amount repaid at maturity reduces the total amount of interest expense. The premium is recorded in a separate liability account called **Premium on Bonds Payable.** This account is reported on the balance sheet as an addition to Bonds Payable, increasing the carrying value of the bond liability. On the issue date, the bond liability would be reported on the balance sheet as follows:

Bonds payable	$100,000
Plus: Premium on bonds payable	5,000
Carrying value	$105,000

The entire $105,000 cash inflow is reported in the financing activities section of the statement of cash flows even though the $5,000 premium is conceptually an operating activities cash flow because it pertains to interest. In practice, premiums are usually so small they are immaterial and the entire cash inflow is normally classified as a financing activity. Assuming annual interest payments, the financial statement effects for issuing the bonds at a premium and the first interest payment are shown next:

	Balance Sheet				Income Statement				Statement of Cash Flows	
	Assets =	Liabilities	+ Stk. Equity							
Date	Cash =	Carrying Value of Bond Liability			Rev. −	Exp.	= Net Inc.			
Jan. 1	105,000 =	105,000	+ NA		NA −	NA	= NA		105,000	FA
Dec. 31	(9,000) =	(1,000)	(8,000)			8,000	(8,000)		(9,000)	OA

The Market Rate of Interest

When a bond is issued, the effective interest rate is determined by current market conditions. Market conditions are influenced by many factors, such as the state of the economy, government policy, and the law of supply and demand. These conditions are collectively reflected in the **market interest rate.** The *effective rate of interest* investors are willing to accept *for a* *particular bond* equals the *market rate of interest* for other investments with similar levels of risk at the time the bond is issued. When the market rate of interest is higher than the stated rate of interest, bonds will sell at a discount so as to increase the effective rate of interest to the market rate. When the market rate is lower than the stated rate, bonds will sell at a premium so as to reduce the effective rate to the market rate.

Bond Redemptions

In the previous illustration, Mason Company's five-year, 9 percent bonds were redeemed (paid off) on the maturity date. After Mason Company paid the bondholders the face value of the bonds, the balance in the bonds payable account was zero. The balance in the fully amortized discount account was also zero.

Companies may redeem bonds with a *call provision* prior to the maturity date. If a company calls bonds prior to maturity, it must pay the bondholders the call price. As explained previously, the call price is normally above face value. For example, suppose Mason Company's bond certificate allows it to call the bonds at 103. Assume Mason's client breaks the land rental contract two years early, at the end of Year 3. Mason is forced to sell the land and pay off the bonds. Assuming the bonds were originally issued at a $5,000 discount, Exhibit 10.8 shows there is a $2,000 balance in the Discount on Bonds Payable account at the end of Year 3.

To redeem the bonds on January 1, Year 4, Mason must pay the bondholders $103,000 ($100,000 face value × 1.03 call price). Because the book value of the bond liability is $98,000 ($100,000 face value − $2,000 remaining discount), Mason recognizes a $5,000 loss ($103,000 redemption price − $98,000 book value) when the bonds are called. The early redemption decreases cash, the carrying value of the bond liability, and stockholders' equity.

The entire $103,000 cash outflow is reported in the financing activities section of the statement of cash flows. Conceptually, some of this outflow is attributable to activities other than financing. In practice, the amounts paid in an early redemption which are not attributable to financing activities are usually immaterial and the entire cash outflow is therefore classified as a financing activity. The effects on the financial statements are shown as follows:

Balance Sheet					Income Statement				Statement of Cash Flows
Assets	=	Liabilities	+	Stk. Equity					
Cash	=	Carrying Value of Bond Liability	+	Ret. Earn.	Rev. −	Loss	=	Net Inc.	
(103,000)	=	(98,000)	+	(5,000)	NA −	5,000	=	(5,000)	(103,000) FA

AMORTIZATION USING THE EFFECTIVE INTEREST RATE METHOD

Up to this point, we have demonstrated the straight-line method for amortizing bond discounts and premiums. While this method is easy to understand, it is inaccurate because it does not show the correct amount of interest expense incurred during each accounting period. To illustrate, return to the case of Mason Company, demonstrated in Exhibit 10.8. Recall that the exhibit shows the effects of accounting for a $100,000 face-value bond with a 9 percent stated rate of interest that was issued at a price of 95. The carrying value of the bond liability on the January 1, Year 1, issue date was $95,000. The bond discount was amortized using the straight-line method.

Recall that the straight-line method amortizes the discount equally over the life of the bond. Specifically, there is a $5,000 discount that is amortized over a five-year life, resulting in a $1,000 amortization per year. As the discount is amortized, the bond liability (carrying value of the bond) increases. Specifically, the carrying value of the bond liability shown in Exhibit 10.8 increases as follows:

Accounting Period	Year 1	Year 2	Year 3	Year 4
Carrying value as of December 31	$96,000	$97,000	$98,000	$99,000

While the carrying value of the bond liability increases steadily, the straight-line method recognizes the same amount of interest expense ($9,000 stated rate of interest + $1,000 discount amortization = $10,000 interest expense) per year. This straight-line recognition pattern is irrational because the amount of interest expense recognized should increase as the carrying value of the bond liability increases. A more accurate recognition pattern can be accomplished by using an approach called the **effective interest rate method.**

Amortizing Bond Discounts

LO 10-6

Use the effective interest rate method to amortize bond discounts.

The effective interest rate is determined by the price that the buyer of a bond is willing to pay on the issue date. In the case of Mason Company, the issue price of $95,000 for bonds with a $100,000 face value, a 9 percent stated rate of interest, and a five-year term produces an effective interest rate of approximately 10.33 percent.[5] Because the effective interest rate is based on the market price of the bonds on the day of issue, it is sometimes called *the market rate of interest.*
   Interest recognition under the effective interest rate method is accomplished as follows:

1. Determine the cash payment for interest by multiplying the stated rate of interest times the face value of the bonds.

2. Determine the amount of interest expense by multiplying the effective rate of interest times the carrying value of the bond liability.

3. Determine the amount of the amortization of the bond discount by subtracting the cash payment from the interest expense.

4. Update the carrying value of the liability by adding the amount of the discount amortization to the amount of the carrying value at the beginning of the accounting period.

Applying these procedures to the Mason Company illustration produces the amortization schedule shown in Exhibit 10.9.

EXHIBIT 10.9

Amortization Schedule for Bond Discount

	(A) Cash Payment	(B) Interest Expense	(C) Discount Amortization	(D) Carrying Value
January 1, Year 1				$ 95,000
December 31, Year 1	$ 9,000	$ 9,814	$ 814	95,814
December 31, Year 2	9,000	9,898	898	96,712
December 31, Year 3	9,000	9,990	990	97,702
December 31, Year 4	9,000	10,093	1,093	98,795
December 31, Year 5	9,000	10,205	1,205	100,000
Totals	$45,000	$50,000	$5,000	

(A) Stated rate of interest times the face value of the bonds ($100,000 × 0.09).
(B) Effective interest rate times the carrying value at the beginning of the period. For the Year 1 accounting period, the amount is $9,814 ($95,000 × 0.1033).
(C) Interest Expense − Cash Payment. For Year 1, the discount amortization is $814 ($9,814 − $9,000 = $814).
(D) Carrying value at the beginning of the period plus the portion of the discount amortized. For the accounting period ending December 31, Year 1, the amount is $95,814 ($95,000 + $814).

[5]In practice, the effective rate of interest is calculated using software programs, interest formulas, or interest tables. For further discussion, see Appendix G, which is located at the end of this textbook.

The recognition of interest expense at the end of each accounting period has the following effects on the financial statements. On the balance sheet, assets decrease, liabilities increase, and retained earnings decrease. On the income statement, expenses increase and net income decreases. There is a cash outflow in the operating activities section of the statement of cash flows. These effects on the financial statements are shown next:

Balance Sheet						Income Statement					Statement of Cash Flows
Assets	=	Liabilities		+	Stk. Equity						
Cash	=	Carrying Value of Bond Liability		+	Ret. Earn.	Rev.	−	Exp.	=	Net Inc.	
(9,000)	=	814		+	(9,814)	NA	−	9,814	=	(9,814)	(9,000) OA

Exhibit 10.10 shows the financial statements for Mason Company for Year 1 through Year 5. The statements assume the same events as those used to construct Exhibit 10.8. These events are summarized next.

EXHIBIT 10.10

Financial Statements

Under the Assumption That Bonds Are Issued at a Discount

	Year 1	Year 2	Year 3	Year 4	Year 5
Income Statements					
Rent revenue	$ 11,400	$ 11,400	$ 11,400	$ 11,400	$11,400
Interest expense	(9,814)	(9,898)	(9,990)	(10,093)	(10,205)
Net income	$ 1,586	$ 1,502	$ 1,410	$ 1,307	$ 1,195
Balance Sheets					
Assets					
Cash	$ 2,400	$ 4,800	$ 7,200	$ 9,600	$ 7,000
Land	95,000	95,000	95,000	95,000	0
Total assets	$ 97,400	$ 99,800	$102,200	$104,600	$ 7,000
Liabilities					
Bonds payable	$100,000	$100,000	$100,000	$100,000	$ 0
Discount on bonds payable	(4,186)	(3,288)	(2,298)	(1,205)	0
Carrying value of bond liab.	95,814	96,712	97,702	98,795	0
Equity					
Retained earnings	1,586	3,088	4,498	5,805	7,000
Total liabilities and equity	$ 97,400	$ 99,800	$102,200	$104,600	$ 7,000
Statements of Cash Flows					
Operating Activities					
Inflow from customers	$ 11,400	$ 11,400	$ 11,400	$ 11,400	$11,400
Outflow for interest	(9,000)	(9,000)	(9,000)	(9,000)	(14,000)
Investing Activities					
Outflow to purchase land	(95,000)				
Inflow from sale of land					95,000
Financing Activities					
Inflow from bond issue	95,000				
Outflow to repay bond liab.					(95,000)
Net Change in Cash	2,400	2,400	2,400	2,400	(2,600)
Plus: Beginning cash balance	0	2,400	4,800	7,200	9,600
Ending cash balance	$ 2,400	$ 4,800	$ 7,200	$ 9,600	$ 7,000

1. Mason issues a $100,000 face-value bond with a 9 percent stated rate of interest. The bond has a five-year term and is issued at a price of 95. Annual interest is paid with cash on December 31 of each year.

2. Mason uses the proceeds from the bond issue to purchase land.

3. Leasing the land produces rent revenue of $11,400 cash per year.

4. On the maturity date of the bond, the land is sold and the proceeds from the sale are used to repay the bond liability.

The only difference between the two exhibits is that Exhibit 10.8 was constructed assuming that the bond discount was amortized using the straight-line method, while Exhibit 10.10 assumes that the discount was amortized using the effective interest rate method.

Notice that interest expense under the effective interest rate method (Exhibit 10.10) increases each year, while interest expense under the straight-line method (Exhibit 10.8) remains constant for all years. This result occurs because the effective interest rate method amortizes increasingly larger amounts of the discount (see Column C of Exhibit 10.9) as the carrying value of the bond liability increases. In contrast, the straight-line method amortized the bond discount at a constant rate of $1,000 per year over the life of the bond. Even so, the total amount of interest expense recognized over the life of the bond is the same ($50,000) under both methods. Because the effective interest rate method matches the interest expense with the carrying value of the bond liability, it is the theoretically preferred approach. Indeed, accounting standards require the use of the effective interest rate method when the differences between it and the straight-line method are material.

The amortization of the discount affects the carrying value of the bond, as well as the amount of interest expense. Under the effective interest rate method, the rate of growth of the carrying value of the bond increases as the maturity date approaches. In contrast, under the straight-line method the rate of growth of the carrying value of the bond remains constant at $1,000 per year throughout the life of the bond.

Finally, notice that cash flow is not affected by the method of amortization. The exact same cash flow consequences occur under both the straight-line (Exhibit 10.8) and the effective interest rate method (Exhibit 10.10).

Amortizing Bond Premiums

LO 10-7

Use the effective interest rate method to amortize bond premiums.

Bond premiums can also be amortized using the effective interest rate method. To illustrate, assume United Company issued a $100,000 face-value bond with a 10 percent stated rate of interest. The bond had a five-year term, was issued at a price of $107,985, and the effective rate of interest is 8 percent. United's accountant prepared the amortization schedule shown in Exhibit 10.11.

EXHIBIT 10.11

Amortization Schedule for Bond Premium

	(A) Cash Payment	(B) Interest Expense	(C) Premium Amortization	(D) Carrying Value
January 1, Year 1				$107,985
December 31, Year 1	$10,000	$ 8,639	$1,361	106,624
December 31, Year 2	10,000	8,530	1,470	105,154
December 31, Year 3	10,000	8,413	1,587	103,567
December 31, Year 4	10,000	8,285	1,715	101,852
December 31, Year 5	10,000	8,148	1,852	100,000
Totals	$50,000	$42,015	$7,985	

(A) Stated rate of interest times the face value of the bonds ($100,000 × 0.10).

(B) Effective interest times the carrying value at the beginning of the period. For the Year 1 accounting period, the amount is $8,639 ($107,985 × 0.08).

(C) Cash Payment − Interest Expense. For Year 1, the premium amortization is $1,361 ($10,000 − $8,639 = $1,361).

(D) Carrying value at the beginning of the period minus the portion of the premium amortized. For the accounting period ending December 31, Year 1, the amount is $106,624 ($107,985 − $1,361).

The recognition of interest expense at the end of each accounting period has the following effects on the financial statements. On the balance sheet, assets decrease, liabilities decrease, and retained earnings decrease. On the income statement, expenses increase and net income decreases. There is a cash outflow in the operating activities section of the statement of cash flows. These effects on the financial statements are shown next:

Balance Sheet						Income Statement				Statement of Cash Flows
Assets	=	Liabilities		+	Stk. Equity					
Cash	=	Carrying Value of Bond Liability		+	Ret. Earn.	Rev.	−	Exp.	= Net Inc.	
(10,000)	=	(1,361)		+	(8,639)	NA	−	8,639	= (8,639)	(10,000) OA

The Financial Analyst

Bond financing has advantages and disadvantages for the stockholders of a business. Assessing a company's investment potential requires understanding both the potential rewards and the potential risks of debt financing.

LO 10-8

 Explain the advantages and disadvantages of debt financing.

Financial Leverage and Tax Advantage of Debt Financing

As with other forms of credit, bonds may provide companies increased earnings through **financial leverage.** If a company can borrow money at 7 percent through a bond issue and invest the proceeds at 12 percent, the company's earnings benefit from the 5 percent (12 percent − 7 percent) **spread.**

Also, bond interest expense, like other forms of interest expense, is tax deductible, making the effective cost of borrowing less than the interest expense because the interest expense reduces the tax expense. Because dividend payments are not tax deductible, equity financing (e.g., issuing common stock) does not offer this advantage.

To illustrate, assume its organizers obtain $100,000 to start Maduro Company. During its first year of operation, Maduro earns $60,000 of revenue and incurs $40,000 of expenses other than interest expense. Consider two different forms of financing. First, assume the initial $100,000 is obtained by issuing common stock (equity financing) and Maduro pays an 8 percent dividend ($100,000 × 0.08 = $8,000 dividend). Second, assume Maduro issues $100,000 of bonds that pay 8 percent annual interest ($100,000 × 0.08 = $8,000). Assuming a 30 percent tax rate, which form of financing produces the larger increase in retained earnings? Refer to the following computations:

Computation of Addition to Retained Earnings		
	Equity Financing	Debt Financing
Revenue	$60,000	$60,000
Expense (excluding interest)	(40,000)	(40,000)
Earnings before interest and taxes	20,000	20,000
Interest ($100,000 × 8%)	0	(8,000)
Pretax income	20,000	12,000
Income tax (30%)	(6,000)	(3,600)
Net income	14,000	8,400
Dividend	(8,000)	0
Addition to retained earnings	$ 6,000	$ 8,400

Debt financing produces $2,400 more retained earnings than equity financing. If equity financing is obtained, the company pays $6,000 in income taxes; debt financing requires only $3,600 of income taxes. Maduro's cost of financing, whether paid in dividends to investors or interest to creditors, is $8,000. With debt financing, however, the Internal Revenue Service receives $2,400 less.

The after-tax interest cost of debt can be computed as

$$\text{Total interest expense} \times (1.0 - \text{Tax rate})$$
$$\$8,000 \times (1.0 - 0.30) = \$5,600$$

The after-tax interest rate that Maduro is paying can be computed using the same logic:

$$\text{Debt interest rate} \times (1.0 - \text{Tax rate})$$
$$8\% \times (1.0 - 0.30) = 5.6\%$$

Unlike interest expense, there is no difference in the before-tax and after-tax effects of a dividend. For Maduro, $1 of dividends costs the company a full $1 of retained earnings, while $1 of interest has an after-tax cost of only $0.70 (assuming a 30 percent tax rate). This tax benefit only applies to profitable businesses. There are no tax savings if a company has no income because businesses that produce losses pay no taxes.

EBIT and Ratio Analysis

The tax consequences of debt financing can influence ratio analysis. For example, consider the *return-on-assets* (*ROA*) ratio discussed in Chapter 3. In that chapter, ROA was defined as:

$$\text{Net income} \div \text{Total assets}$$

Recall that the ROA ratio is used to measure the effectiveness of asset management. In general, higher ROAs suggest better performance. However, the Maduro example demonstrates that a higher ROA can be obtained by using equity financing rather than debt financing without regard to how assets are managed. Recall that Maduro obtained $100,000 of assets whether through equity or debt financing. The assets were used exactly the same way regardless of the financing method used. With equity financing, Maduro's ROA is 14 percent ($14,000 ÷ $100,000), and with debt financing it is 8.4 percent ($8,400 ÷ $100,000). The difference in the ROA results from the financing approach rather than asset management.

The effects of the financing strategy can be avoided in ROA calculations by using *earnings before interest and taxes* (*EBIT*) rather than net income when computing the ratio. For example, if Maduro uses EBIT to compute ROA, the result is 20 percent ($20,000 ÷ $100,000) regardless of whether debt or equity financing is used. Using EBIT to compute ROA provides a less biased measure of asset utilization. For simplicity, however, this text uses net income to determine ROA unless otherwise indicated.

Times-Interest-Earned Ratio

Financing with bonds also has disadvantages. The issuer is legally obligated to make interest payments on time and to repay the principal at maturity. If a company fails to make scheduled payments, the creditors (bondholders) can force the company into bankruptcy. The claims on a company's assets held by bondholders and other creditors have priority over the claims of the owners. If a company in bankruptcy is forced to liquidate its assets, creditor claims must be fully paid before any owner claims can be paid. Bond issues therefore increase the owners' risk.

Financial analysts use several ratios to help assess the risk of bankruptcy. One is the *debt-to-assets ratio,* explained in Chapter 3. Another is the **times-interest-earned** ratio, defined as

$$\text{EBIT} \div \text{Interest expense}$$

This ratio measures *how many times* a company would be able to pay its interest using its earnings. The *times-interest-earned ratio* is based on EBIT rather than net income because it is the amount of earnings before interest and taxes that is available to pay interest. The higher the ratio, the less likely a company will be unable to make its interest payments. Higher times-interest-earned ratios suggest lower levels of risk. Examples of times-interest-earned ratios and debt-to-assets ratios for six real-world companies follow. These numbers are based on financial data for 2017.

Industry	Company	Times Interest Earned	Debt to Assets
Breakfast cereal	Kellogg's	7.5	0.86
	General Mills	6.4	0.76
Cosmetics	Avon	1.9	1.07
	Esteé Lauder	16.5	0.63
Hotels	Marriott International	10.8	0.84
	Hilton Worldwide	3.5	0.85

Because bills are paid with cash, not income, a company may be able to make interest payments even if it has a negative times-interest-earned ratio. A company with no EBIT may yet have cash. Meaningful financial statement analysis cannot rely on any single ratio or any set of ratios. Making sound business decisions requires considering other information in addition to the insights provided from analyzing ratios. A company with inferior ratios and a patent on a newly discovered drug that cures cancer may be a far better investment than a company with great ratios and a patent on a chemotherapy product that will soon be out of date. Ratio computations are based on historical data. They are useful only to the extent that history is likely to repeat itself.

CHECK YOURSELF 10.3

Selected financial data pertaining to Shaver Company and Goode Company follow (amounts are in thousands):

	Shaver Company	Goode Company
Earnings before interest and taxes	$750,720	$2,970,680
Interest expense	234,600	645,800

Based on this information, which company is more likely to be able to make its interest payments?

Answer   The times-interest-earned ratio for Shaver Company is 3.2 ($750,720 ÷ $234,600) times. The times-interest-earned ratio for Goode Company is 4.6 ($2,970,680 ÷ $645,800) times. Based on these data, Goode Company is more likely to be able to make its interest payments.

A Look Back

This chapter explained basic accounting for long-term debt. *Long-term notes payable* usually mature in two to five years and require payments that include a return of principal plus interest. *Lines of credit* enable companies to borrow limited amounts on an as-needed basis. Although lines of credit normally have one-year terms, companies frequently renew them, extending the effective maturity date to the intermediate range of five or more years. Interest on a line of credit is normally paid monthly.

Long-term debt financing for more than 10 years usually requires issuing *bonds.* Bond agreements normally commit a company to pay *semiannual interest* at a fixed percentage of the bond face value. The amount of interest required by the bond agreement is based on the *stated interest rate.* If bonds are issued when the *market interest rate* is different from the stated interest rate, companies will receive more or less than the face value in order for the effective rate of interest to be consistent with market conditions. Selling bonds at a *discount* (below face value) increases the effective interest rate above the stated rate. Selling bonds at a *premium* decreases the effective rate of interest.

This chapter explained the tax advantages of using debt versus equity financing. Interest is a *tax-deductible expense* subtracted prior to determining taxable income. In contrast, dividends paid to owners are not deductible in determining taxable income.

 # A Look Forward

A company seeking long-term financing might choose to use debt, such as the types of bonds or term loans that were discussed in this chapter. Owners' equity is another source of long-term financing. Several equity alternatives are available, depending on the type of business organization the owners choose to establish. For example, a company could be organized as a sole proprietorship, partnership, or corporation. Chapter 11 presents accounting issues related to equity transactions for each of these types of business structures.

 Tableau Dashboard Activity is available in *Connect* for this chapter.

 ## SELF-STUDY REVIEW PROBLEM

 A step-by-step audio-narrated series of slides is available in *Connect*.

During Year 1 and Year 2, Herring Corp. completed the following selected transactions relating to its bond issue. The corporation's fiscal year ends on December 31.

Year 1

Jan.   1   Sold $400,000 of 10-year, 9 percent bonds at 97. Interest is payable in cash on December 31 each year.

Dec. 31   Paid the bond interest and recorded the amortization of the discount using the straight-line method.

Year 2

Dec. 31   Paid the bond interest and recorded the amortization of the discount using the straight-line method.

Required

a. Show how these events would affect Herring's financial statements by recording them in a financial statements model like the following one:

	Balance Sheet			Income Statement			Statement of Cash Flows
	Assets =	Liab.	+ Stk. Equity				
Date	Cash =	Carrying Value of Bond Liability +	Ret. Earn.	Rev. −	Exp. =	Net Inc.	
1/1/Year 1							
12/31/Year 1							
12/31/Year 2							

b. Determine the carrying value of the bond liability as of December 31, Year 2.

c. Assuming Herring had earnings before interest and taxes of $198,360 in Year 2, calculate the times-interest-earned ratio.

Solution

a.

	Balance Sheet			Income Statement		Statement of Cash Flows	
	Assets =	Liab.	+ Stk. Equity				
Date	Cash =	Carrying Value of Bond Liability	+ Ret. Earn.	Rev. — Exp. = Net Inc.			
1/1/Year 1	388,000 =	388,000	+ NA	NA — NA = NA		388,000	FA
12/31/Year 1	(36,000) =	1,200	+ (37,200)	NA — 37,200 = (37,200)		(36,000)	OA
12/31/Year 2	(36,000) =	1,200	+ (37,200)	NA — 37,200 = (37,200)		(36,000)	OA

b. The unamortized discount as of December 31, Year 2, is $9,600 ($12,000 − $1,200 − $1,200). The carrying value of the bond liability is $390,400 ($400,000 − $9,600).

c. The times-interest-earned ratio is 5.3 times ($198,360 ÷ $37,200).

KEY TERMS

Amortization 485
Bond certificate 490
Bond discount 495
Bond premium 500
Bondholder 490
Call premium 492
Call price 492
Callable bonds 492
Carrying value 496
Collateral 492
Convertible bonds 492

Debenture 491
Discount on Bonds
  Payable 496
Effective interest rate 496
Effective interest rate
  method 502
Face value 490
Financial leverage 505
Fixed interest rate 484
Installment notes 486
Issuer 490

Line of credit 488
Market interest rate 500
Mortgage bond 491
Premium on Bonds
  Payable 500
Restrictive covenants 492
Secured bonds 491
Serial bonds 491
Sinking fund 491
Spread 505
Stated interest rate 490

Straight-line amortization 497
Subordinated debentures 491
Term bonds 491
Times interest earned 506
Unsecured bonds 491
Unsubordinated
  debentures 491
Variable interest rate 484

QUESTIONS

1. What is the difference between classification of a note as short term or long term?

2. At the beginning of Year 1, B Co. has a note payable of $72,000 that calls for an annual payment of $16,246, which includes both principal and interest. If the interest rate is 8 percent, what is the amount of interest expense in Year 1 and in Year 2? What is the balance of the note at the end of Year 2?

3. What is the purpose of a line of credit for a business? Why would a company choose to obtain a line of credit instead of issuing bonds?

4. What are the primary sources of debt financing for most large companies?

5. What are some advantages of issuing bonds versus borrowing from a bank?

6. What are some disadvantages of issuing bonds?

7. Why can a company usually issue bonds at a lower interest rate than the company would pay if the funds were borrowed from a bank?

8. What effect does income tax have on the cost of borrowing funds for a business?

9. What is the concept of financial leverage?

10. Which type of bond, secured or unsecured, is likely to have a lower interest rate? Explain.

11. What is the function of restrictive covenants attached to bond issues?

12. What is the difference between term bonds and serial bonds?

13. What is the purpose of establishing a sinking fund?

14. What is the call price of a bond? Is it usually higher or lower than the face amount of the bond? Explain.

15. If Roc Co. issued $100,000 of 5 percent, 10-year bonds at the face amount, what is the effect of the issuance of the bonds on the financial

statements? What amount of interest expense will Roc Co. recognize each year?

16. What mechanism is used to adjust the stated interest rate to the market rate of interest?

17. When the effective interest rate is higher than the stated interest rate on a bond issue, will the bond sell at a discount or premium? Why?

18. What type of transaction is the issuance of bonds by a company?

19. What factors may cause the effective interest rate and the stated interest rate to be different?

20. If a bond is selling at 97½, how much cash will the company receive from the sale of a $1,000 bond?

21. How is the carrying value of a bond computed?

22. Gay Co. has a balance in the Bonds Payable account of $25,000 and a balance in the Discount on Bonds Payable account of $5,200. What is the carrying value of the bonds? What is the total amount of the liability?

23. When the effective interest rate is higher than the stated interest rate, will interest expense be higher or lower than the amount of interest paid?

24. Assuming that the selling price of the bond and the face value are the same, would the issuer of a bond prefer to make annual or semiannual interest payments? Why?

25. Rato Co. called some bonds and had a loss on the redemption of the bonds of $2,850. How is this amount reported on the income statement?

26. Which method of financing, debt or equity, is generally more advantageous from a tax standpoint? Why?

27. If a company has a tax rate of 30 percent, and interest expense was $10,000, what is the after-tax cost of the debt?

28. Which type of financing, debt or equity, increases the risk factor of a business? Why?

29. What information does the times-interest-earned ratio provide?

EXERCISES—SERIES A

All applicable Exercises in Series A are available in *Connect*.

LO 10-1

Exercise 10-1A   *Interest only versus an installment note*

Sanders Co. is planning to finance an expansion of its operations by borrowing $150,000. City Bank has agreed to loan Sanders the funds. Sanders has two repayment options: (1) to issue a note with the principal due in 10 years and with interest payable annually or (2) to issue a note to repay $15,000 of the principal each year along with the annual interest based on the unpaid principal balance. Assume the interest rate is 8 percent for each option.

Required

a. What amount of interest will Sanders pay in Year 1
 (1) Under option 1?
 (2) Under option 2?
b. What amount of interest will Sanders pay in Year 2
 (1) Under option 1?
 (2) Under option 2?
c. Explain the advantage of each option.

LO 10-1

Exercise 10-2A   *Amortization schedule for an installment note*

On January 1, Year 1, Beatie Co. borrowed $200,000 cash from Central Bank by issuing a five-year, 6 percent note. The principal and interest are to be paid by making annual payments in the amount of $47,479. Payments are to be made December 31 of each year, beginning December 31, Year 1.

Required

Prepare an amortization schedule for the interest and principal payments for the five-year period.

LO 10-1

Exercise 10-3A   *Financial statement effects of an installment note*

Dan Dayle started a business by issuing an $80,000 face-value note to First State Bank on January 1, Year 1. The note had an 8 percent annual rate of interest and a five-year term. Payments of $20,037 are to be made each December 31 for five years.

Required

a. What portion of the December 31, Year 1, payment is applied to
 (1) Interest expense?
 (2) Principal?

b. What is the principal balance on January 1, Year 2?

c. What portion of the December 31, Year 2, payment is applied to

    (1) Interest expense?

    (2) Principal?

Exercise 10-4A   *Financial statement effects of an installment note*   LO 10-1

A partial amortization schedule for a 10-year note payable issued on January 1, Year 1, is shown next:

Accounting Period	Principal Balance January 1	Cash Payment	Applied to Interest	Applied to Principal
Year 1	$200,000	$27,174	$12,000	$15,174
Year 2	184,826	27,174	11,090	16,084
Year 3	168,742	27,174	10,125	17,049

Required

a. Using a financial statements model like the following one, record the appropriate amounts for the following two events:

    (1) January 1, Year 1, issue of the note payable.

    (2) December 31, Year 1, payment on the note payable.

Event No.	Balance Sheet			Income Statement			Statement of Cash Flows
	Assets	= Liab.	+ Stk. Equity	Rev.	− Exp.	= Net Inc.	
1.							

b. If the company earned $62,000 cash revenue and paid $45,000 in cash expenses in addition to the interest in Year 1, what is the amount of each of the following?

    (1) Net income for Year 1

    (2) Cash flow from operating activities for Year 1

    (3) Cash flow from financing activities for Year 1

c. What is the amount of interest expense on this loan for Year 4?

Exercise 10-5A   *Calculations for a line of credit*   LO 10-2

Colson Company has a line of credit with Federal Bank. Colson can borrow up to $800,000 at any time over the course of the Year 1 calendar year. The following table shows the prime rate expressed as an annual percentage, along with the amounts borrowed and repaid during the first four months of Year 1. Colson agreed to pay interest at an annual rate equal to 2 percent above the bank's prime rate. Funds are borrowed or repaid on the first day of each month. Interest is payable in cash on the last day of the month. The interest rate is applied to the outstanding monthly balance. For example, Colson pays 6 percent (4 percent + 2 percent) annual interest on $80,000 for the month of January.

Month	Amount Borrowed or (Repaid)	Prime Rate for the Month
January	$80,000	4.0%
February	50,000	4.25
March	(30,000)	4.5
April	20,000	4.25

Required

a. Compute the amount of interest that Colson will pay on the line of credit for the first four months of Year 1. Round answers to nearest whole dollar.

b. Compute the amount of Colson's liability at the end of each of the first four months.

LO 10-3

Exercise 10-6A   *Two accounting cycles for bonds issued at face value*

Doyle Company issued $500,000 of 10-year, 7 percent bonds on January 1, Year 2. The bonds were issued at face value. Interest is payable in cash on December 31 of each year. Doyle immediately invested the proceeds from the bond issue in land. The land was leased for an annual $125,000 of cash revenue, which was collected on December 31 of each year, beginning December 31, Year 2.

Required

a. Organize the transaction data in accounts under the accounting equation for Year 2 and Year 3.

b. Prepare the income statement, balance sheet, and statement of cash flows for Year 2 and Year 3.

LO 10-3

Exercise 10-7A   *Two accounting cycles for bonds issued at face value*

On January 1, Year 1, Bell Corp. issued $180,000 of 10-year, 6 percent bonds at their face amount. Interest is payable on December 31 of each year with the first payment due December 31, Year 1.

Required

Show the effects of these bonds on the accounting equation for Year 1 and Year 2.

LO 10-3

Exercise 10-8A   *Calculations for callable bonds*

Nivan Co. issued $500,000 of 5 percent, 10-year, callable bonds on January 1, Year 1, at their face value. The call premium was 3 percent (bonds are callable at 103). Interest was payable annually on December 31. The bonds were called on December 31, Year 5.

Required

a. Calculate the amount of interest expense for Year 5.

b. Determine the amount of loss on bond redemption recognized on December 31, Year 5.

LO 10-3

Exercise 10-9A   *Annual versus semiannual interest for bonds issued at face value*

Milan Company issued bonds with a face value of $200,000 on January 1, Year 1. The bonds had a 7 percent stated rate of interest and a six-year term. The bonds were issued at face value. Interest is payable on an annual basis.

Required

Write a memo explaining whether the total cash outflow for interest would be more, less, or the same if the bonds pay semiannual versus annual interest.

LO 10-4, 10-5

Exercise 10-10A   *Determining cash receipts from bond issues*

Required

Compute the cash proceeds from bond issues under the following terms. For each case, indicate whether the bonds sold at a premium or discount.

a. Pear, Inc. issued $400,000 of 10-year, 8 percent bonds at 103.

b. Apple, Inc. issued $200,000 of five-year, 12 percent bonds at 97½.

c. Cherry Co. issued $100,000 of five-year, 6 percent bonds at 102¼.

d. Grape, Inc. issued $120,000 of four-year, 8 percent bonds at 96.

LO 10-3, 10-4, 10-5

Exercise 10-11A   *Stated rate of interest versus the market rate of interest*

Required

Indicate whether a bond will sell at a premium (P), discount (D), or face value (F) for each of the following conditions:

a. _____ The stated rate of interest is higher than the market rate.

b. _____ The market rate of interest is equal to the stated rate.

c. _____ The market rate of interest is less than the stated rate.

d. _____ The stated rate of interest is less than the market rate.

e. _____ The market rate of interest is higher than the stated rate.

Exercise 10-12A   *Identifying bond premiums and discounts*

LO 10-4, 10-5

Required

In each of the following situations, state whether the bonds will sell at a premium or discount.

a. Valley issued $300,000 of bonds with a stated interest rate of 7 percent. At the time of issue, the market rate of interest for similar investments was 6 percent.

b. Spring issued $220,000 of bonds with a stated interest rate of 5 percent. At the time of issue, the market rate of interest for similar investments was 6 percent.

c. River Inc. issued $150,000 of callable bonds with a stated interest rate of 5 percent. The bonds were callable at 102. At the date of issue, the market rate of interest was 6 percent for similar investments.

Exercise 10-13A   *Determining the amount of bond premiums and discounts*

LO 10-4, 10-5

Required

For each of the following situations, calculate the amount of bond discount or premium, if any:

a. Gray Co. issued $80,000 of 6 percent bonds at 101¼.

b. Bush, Inc. issued $200,000 of 10-year, 6 percent bonds at 97½.

c. Oak, Inc. issued $100,000 of 20-year, 6 percent bonds at 103.

d. Willow Co. issued $180,000 of 15-year, 7 percent bonds at 99.

Exercise 10-14A   *Straight-line amortization of a bond discount*

LO 10-4

Diaz Company issued bonds with a $180,000 face value on January 1, Year 1. The bonds had a 7 percent stated rate of interest and a five-year term. Interest is paid in cash annually, beginning December 31, Year 1. The bonds were issued at 98. The straight-line method is used for amortization.

Required

a. Use a financial statements model like the one shown next to demonstrate how (1) the January 1, Year 1, bond issue and (2) the December 31, Year 1, recognition of interest expense, including the amortization of the discount and the cash payment, affect the company's financial statements. Use + for increase, – for decrease, and NA for not affected.

Event No.	Balance Sheet			Income Statement			Statement of Cash Flows
	Assets	= Liab.	+ Stk. Equity	Rev.	– Exp.	= Net Inc.	
1.							

b. Determine the carrying value (face value less discount or plus premium) of the bond liability as of December 31, Year 1.

c. Determine the amount of interest expense reported on the Year 1 income statement.

d. Determine the carrying value (face value less discount or plus premium) of the bond liability as of December 31, Year 2.

e. Determine the amount of interest expense reported on the Year 2 income statement.

Exercise 10-15A   *Straight-line amortization of a bond premium*

LO 10-5

The Square Foot Grill, Inc. issued $200,000 of 10-year, 6 percent bonds on January 1, Year 2, at 102. Interest is payable in cash annually on December 31. The straight-line method is used for amortization.

Required

a. Use a financial statements model like the one shown next to demonstrate how (1) the January 1, Year 2, bond issue and (2) the December 31, Year 2, recognition of interest expense, including the amortization of the premium and the cash payment, affects the company's financial statements. Use + for increase, − for decrease, and NA for not affected.

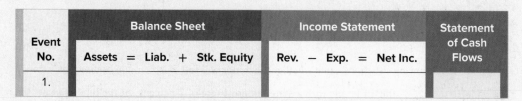

Event No.	Balance Sheet			Income Statement			Statement of Cash Flows
	Assets	= Liab. +	Stk. Equity	Rev. −	Exp. =	Net Inc.	
1.							

b. Determine the carrying value (face value less discount or plus premium) of the bond liability as of December 31, Year 2.

c. Determine the amount of interest expense reported on the Year 2 income statement.

d. Determine the carrying value of the bond liability as of December 31, Year 3.

e. Determine the amount of interest expense reported on the Year 3 income statement.

LO 10-4

Exercise 10-16A *Straight-line amortization for bonds issued at a discount*

On January 1, Year 1, Price Co. issued $190,000 of five-year, 6 percent bonds at 96½. Interest is payable annually on December 31. The discount is amortized using the straight-line method.

Required

a. Determine the amount of cash proceeds received by Price Co. on January 1, Year 1.

b. Calculate the amount of interest expense reported on the December 31, Year 2, income statement.

c. What is the carrying value of the bond liability as of December 31, Year 2?

LO 10-5

Exercise 10-17A *Straight-line amortization of a bond premium*

Stuart Company issued bonds with a $150,000 face value on January 1, Year 1. The bonds had a 6 percent stated rate of interest and a five-year term. Interest is paid in cash annually, beginning December 31, Year 1. The bonds were issued at 103. The straight-line method is used for amortization.

Required

a. Use a financial statements model like the following one to demonstrate how (1) the January 1, Year 1, bond issue and (2) the December 31, Year 1, recognition of interest expense, including the amortization of the premium and the cash payment, affect the company's financial statements. Use + for increase, − for decrease, and NA for not affected.

Event No.	Balance Sheet			Income Statement			Statement of Cash Flows
	Assets	= Liab. +	Stk. Equity	Rev. −	Exp. =	Net Inc.	
1.							

b. Determine the carrying value (face value less discount or plus premium) of the bond liability as of December 31, Year 1.

c. Determine the amount of interest expense reported on the Year 1 income statement.

d. Determine the carrying value of the bond liability as of December 31, Year 2.

e. Determine the amount of interest expense reported on the Year 2 income statement.

LO 10-5

Exercise 10-18A *Straight-line amortization for bonds issued at a premium*

On January 1, Year 1, Sayers Company issued $280,000 of five-year, 6 percent bonds at 102. Interest is payable semiannually on June 30 and December 31. The premium is amortized using the straight-line method.

Required

a. Determine the amount of cash proceeds received by Sayers Company on January 1, Year 1.

b. Calculate the amount of interest expense as of June 30, Year 2.

c. What is the carrying value of the bond liability as of December 31, Year 2?

Exercise 10-19A   *Effective interest amortization of a bond discount*

LO 10-6

On January 1, Year 1, the Diamond Association issued bonds with a face value of $300,000, a stated rate of interest of 6 percent, and a 10-year term to maturity. Interest is payable in cash on December 31 of each year. The effective rate of interest was 7 percent at the time the bonds were issued. The bonds sold for $278,932. Diamond used the effective interest rate method to amortize the bond discount.

Required

a. Determine the amount of the discount on the day of issue.

b. Determine the amount of interest expense recognized on December 31, Year 1.

c. Determine the carrying value of the bond liability on December 31, Year 1.

Exercise 10-20A   *Effective interest amortization of a bond discount*

LO 10-6

On January 1, Year 1, Parker Company issued bonds with a face value of $80,000, a stated rate of interest of 8 percent, and a five-year term to maturity. Interest is payable in cash on December 31 of each year. The effective rate of interest was 9 percent at the time the bonds were issued. The bonds sold for $76,888. Parker used the effective interest rate method to amortize the bond discount.

Required

a. Prepare an amortization table as shown next:

	Cash Payment	Interest Expense	Discount Amortization	Carrying Value
January 1, Year 1				$76,888
December 31, Year 1	$ 6,400	$ 6,920	$ 520	77,408
December 31, Year 2	?	?	?	?
December 31, Year 3	?	?	?	?
December 31, Year 4	?	?	?	?
December 31, Year 5	?	?	?	?
Totals	$32,000	$35,112	$3,112	

b. What item(s) in the table would appear on the Year 4 balance sheet?

c. What item(s) in the table would appear on the Year 4 income statement?

d. What item(s) in the table would appear on the Year 4 statement of cash flows?

Exercise 10-21A   *Effective interest amortization of a bond premium*

LO 10-7

On January 1, Year 1, Young Company issued bonds with a face value of $300,000, a stated rate of interest of 7 percent, and a 10-year term to maturity. Interest is payable in cash on December 31 of each year. The effective rate of interest was 6 percent at the time the bonds were issued. The bonds sold for $322,081. Young used the effective interest rate method to amortize the bond premium.

Required

a. Determine the amount of the premium on the day of issue.

b. Determine the amount of interest expense recognized on December 31, Year 1.

c. Determine the carrying value of the bond liability on December 31, Year 1.

Exercise 10-22A   *Effective interest amortization for a bond premium*

LO 10-7

On January 1, Year 1, Hart Company issued bonds with a face value of $150,000, a stated rate of interest of 8 percent, and a five-year term to maturity. Interest is payable in cash on December 31 of each year. The effective rate of interest was 7 percent at the time the bonds were issued. The bonds sold for $156,150. Hart used the effective interest rate method to amortize the bond premium.

Required

a. Prepare an amortization table as shown next:

	Cash Payment	Interest Expense	Premium Amortization	Carrying Value
January 1, Year 1				$156,150
December 31, Year 1	$12,000	$10,931	$1,069	155,081
December 31, Year 2	?	?	?	?
December 31, Year 3	?	?	?	?
December 31, Year 4	?	?	?	?
December 31, Year 5	?	?	?	?
Totals	$60,000	$53,850	$6,150	

b. What item(s) in the table would appear on the Year 4 balance sheet?

c. What item(s) in the table would appear on the Year 4 income statement?

d. What item(s) in the table would appear on the Year 4 statement of cash flows?

LO 10-5, 10-7

Exercise 10-23A   *Effective interest versus straight-line amortization*

On January 1, Year 1, the Christie Companies issued bonds with a face value of $500,000, a stated rate of interest of 10 percent, and a 20-year term to maturity. Interest is payable in cash on December 31 of each year. The effective rate of interest was 8 percent at the time the bonds were issued.

Required

Write a brief memo explaining whether the effective interest rate method or the straight-line method will produce the highest amount of interest expense recognized on the Year 1 income statement.

LO 10-8

Exercise 10-24A   *Determining the after-tax cost of debt*

The following information is available for three companies:

	Rope Co.	Chain Co.	Line Co.
Face value of bonds payable	$400,000	$700,000	$600,000
Interest rate	8%	7%	6%
Income tax rate	35%	20%	25%

Required

a. Determine the annual before-tax interest cost for each company *in dollars.*

b. Determine the annual after-tax interest cost for each company *in dollars.*

c. Determine the annual after-tax interest cost for each company as *a percentage* of the face value of the bonds.

LO 10-8

Exercise 10-25A   *Determining the effects of financing alternatives on ratios*

Clayton Industries has the following account balances:

Current assets	$20,000	Current liabilities	$10,000
Noncurrent assets	80,000	Noncurrent liabilities	50,000
		Stockholders' equity	40,000

The company wishes to raise $40,000 in cash and is considering two financing options: Clayton can sell $40,000 of bonds payable, or it can issue additional common stock for $40,000. To help in the decision process, Clayton's management wants to determine the effects of each alternative on its current ratio and debt-to-assets ratio.

Required

a. Help Clayton's management by completing the following chart:

Ratio	Currently	If Bonds Are Issued	If Stock Is Issued
Current ratio			
Debt-to-assets ratio			

b. Assume that after the funds are invested, EBIT amounts to $12,000. Also assume the company pays $4,000 in dividends or $4,000 in interest depending on which source of financing is used. Based on a 30 percent tax rate, determine the amount of the increase in retained earnings that would result under each financing option.

PROBLEMS—SERIES A

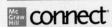 **connect** All applicable Problems in Series A are available in *Connect*.

Problem 10-26A   *Effect of an installment note on financial statements*

On January 1, Year 1, Brown Co. borrowed cash from First Bank by issuing a $100,000 face value, four-year term note that had an 8 percent annual interest rate. The note is to be repaid by making annual cash payments of $30,192 that include both interest and principal on December 31 of each year. Brown used the proceeds from the loan to purchase land that generated rental revenues of $52,000 cash per year.

Required

a. Prepare an amortization schedule for the four-year period. Round answers to nearest whole dollar.

b. Organize the information in accounts under an accounting equation.

c. Prepare an income statement, a balance sheet, and a statement of cash flows for each of the four years.

d. Does cash outflow from operating activities remain constant or change each year? Explain.

Problem 10-27A   *Effect of a line of credit on financial statements*

Boyd Company has a line of credit with State Bank. Boyd can borrow up to $400,000 at any time over the course of the Year 1 calendar year. The following table shows the prime rate expressed as an annual percentage along with the amounts borrowed and repaid during Year 1. Boyd agreed to pay interest at an annual rate equal to 2 percent above the bank's prime rate. Funds are borrowed or repaid on the first day of each month. Interest is payable in cash on the last day of the month. The interest rate is applied to the outstanding monthly balance. For example, Boyd pays 7 percent (5 percent + 2 percent) annual interest on $100,000 for the month of January.

Month	Amount Borrowed or (Repaid)	Prime Rate for the Month
January	$100,000	5%
February	70,000	6
March	(30,000)	7
April through October	No change	No change
November	(50,000)	6
December	(40,000)	5

Boyd earned $45,000 of cash revenue during Year 1.

Required

a. Prepare an income statement, balance sheet, and statement of cash flows for Year 1. (*Note:* Round computations to the nearest dollar.)

b. Write a memo to explain how the business was able to generate retained earnings when the owner contributed no assets to the business.

Problem 10-28A   *Recording transactions for callable bonds*

Arnold Corp. issued $600,000 of 20-year, 8 percent, callable bonds on January 1, Year 1, with interest payable annually on December 31. The bonds were issued at their face amount. The bonds are callable at 104. The fiscal year of the corporation ends December 31.

Required

Show the effect of the following events on the financial statements by recording the appropriate amounts in a horizontal statements model like the following one. In the Statement of Cash Flows column, indicate whether the item is an operating activity (OA), investing activity (IA), or financing activity (FA). Use NA if an element was not affected by the event.

(1) Issued the bonds on January 1, Year 1.

(2) Paid interest due to bondholders on December 31, Year 1.

(3) On January 1, Year 6, Arnold Corp. called the bonds. Assume that all interim entries were correctly recorded.

Event No.	Balance Sheet			Income Statement			Statement of Cash Flows
	Assets	= Liab.	+ Stk. Equity	Rev.	− Exp.	= Net Inc.	
1.							

LO 10-5

Problem 10-29A   *Straight-line amortization of a bond premium*

Pine Land Co. was formed when it acquired cash from the issue of common stock. The company then issued bonds at a premium on January 1, Year 1. Interest is payable annually on December 31 of each year, beginning December 31, Year 1. On January 2, Year 1, Pine Land Co. purchased a piece of land and leased it for an annual rental fee. The rent is received annually on December 31, beginning December 31, Year 1. At the end of the eight-year period (December 31, Year 8), the land was sold at a gain, and the bonds were paid off. A summary of the transactions for each year follows:

Year 1

1. Acquired cash from the issue of common stock.
2. Issued eight-year bonds.
3. Purchased land.
4. Received land rental income.
5. Recognized interest expense including the straight-line amortization of the premium and made the cash payment for interest on December 31.

Year 2 through Year 7

6. Received land rental income.
7. Recognized interest expense, including the straight-line amortization of the premium, and made the cash payment for interest on December 31.

Year 8

8. Sold land at a gain.
9. Retired bonds at face value.

Required

Identify each of these events and transactions as an asset source (AS), asset use (AU), asset exchange (AE), or claims exchange (CE). Explain how each event affects assets, liabilities, equity, net income, and cash flow by placing a + for increase, − for decrease, or NA for not affected under each category. In the Statement of Cash Flows column, indicate whether the item is an operating activity (OA), investing activity (IA), or financing activity (FA). The first event is recorded as an example.

Event No.	Types of Event	Assets	=	Liabilities	+	Common Stock	+	Retained Earnings	Net Income	Cash Flows
1.	AS	+		NA		+		NA	NA	+ FA

Problem 10-30A *Straight-line amortization of a bond discount*

During Year 1 and Year 2, Agatha Corp. completed the following transactions relating to its bond issue. The corporation's fiscal year is the calendar year.

LO 10-4

CHECK FIGURES
c. Year 1 Interest
  Expense: $18,600
d. Year 1 Interest Paid: $18,000

Year 1

Jan. 1   Issued $300,000 of 10-year, 6 percent bonds for $294,000. The annual cash payment for interest is due on December 31.

Dec. 31   Recognized interest expense, including the straight-line amortization of the discount, and made the cash payment for interest.

Dec. 31   Closed the interest expense account.

Year 2

Dec. 31   Recognized interest expense, including the straight-line amortization of the discount, and made the cash payment for interest.

Dec. 31   Closed the interest expense account.

Required

a. When the bonds were issued, was the market rate of interest more or less than the stated rate of interest? If Agatha had sold the bonds at their face amount, what amount of cash would Agatha have received?

b. Prepare the liabilities section of the balance sheet at December 31, Year 1 and Year 2.

c. Determine the amount of interest expense that will be reported on the income statements for Year 1 and Year 2.

d. Determine the amount of interest that will be paid in cash to the bondholders in Year 1 and Year 2.

Problem 10-31A *Straight-line amortization of a bond discount*

LO 10-4

OZ Company was started when it issued bonds with a $500,000 face value on January 1, Year 1. The bonds were issued for cash at 96. OZ uses the straight-line method of amortization. They had a 20-year term to maturity and an 8 percent annual interest rate. Interest was payable on December 31 of each year. OZ Company immediately purchased land with the proceeds (cash received) from the bond issue. OZ leased the land for $60,000 cash per year. On January 1, Year 4, the company sold the land for $500,000 cash. Immediately after the sale of the land, OZ redeemed the bonds at 98. Assume that no other accounting events occurred during Year 4.

Required

a. Record the events associated with this bond in an accounting equation for Year 1, Year 2, Year 3, and Year 4. Total the amounts in each account at the end of each year.

b. Prepare an income statement, statement of changes in equity, balance sheet, and statement of cash flows for the Year 1, Year 2, Year 3, and Year 4 accounting periods. Assume that the company's fiscal year ends on December 31 of each year.

Problem 10-32A *Effect of bond transactions on financial statements*

LO 10-4, 10-5

The three typical accounting events associated with borrowing money through a bond issue are:

1. Exchanging the bonds for cash on the day of issue.
2. Making cash payments for interest expense and recording amortization when applicable.
3. Repaying the principal at maturity.

Required

a. Assuming the bonds are issued at face value, show the effect of each of the three events on the financial statements using a horizontal statements model like the following one. Use + for increase, − for decrease, and NA for not affected.

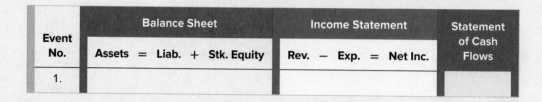

Event No.	Balance Sheet			Income Statement			Statement of Cash Flows
	Assets	= Liab.	+ Stk. Equity	Rev.	− Exp.	= Net Inc.	
1.							

b. Repeat the requirements in Requirement *a,* but assume instead that the bonds are issued at a discount.

c. Repeat the requirements in Requirement *a,* but assume instead that the bonds are issued at a premium.

LO 10-4, 10-6

Problem 10-33A   *Effective interest versus straight-line amortization*

On January 1, Year 1, Twain Corp. sold $500,000 of its own 7 percent, 10-year bonds. Interest is payable annually on December 31. The bonds were sold to yield an effective interest rate of 8 percent. Twain uses the effective interest rate method. The bonds sold for $466,450.

Required

a. Determine the cash proceeds received and the discount on bonds payable.

b. Calculate interest expense and bond discount amortization for Year 1 and Year 2. (Assume effective interest amortization.)

c. Calculate interest expense and bond discount amortization for December 31, Year 1. (Assume straight-line amortization.)

d. Calculate the amount of interest expense for Year 2. (Assume effective interest amortization.)

e. Calculate the amount of interest expense for Year 2. (Assume straight-line amortization.)

LO 10-8

Problem 10-34A   *Using ratios to make comparisons*

The following information pertains to Austin, Inc. and Huston Company:

Account Title	Austin	Huston
Current assets	$ 40,000	$ 40,000
Total assets	300,000	300,000
Current liabilities	15,000	20,000
Total liabilities	200,000	240,000
Stockholders' equity	100,000	60,000
Interest expense	14,000	17,000
Income tax expense	28,000	27,000
Net income	52,000	50,000

Required

a. Compute each company's debt-to-assets ratio, current ratio, and times interest earned (EBIT must be computed). Identify the company with the greater financial risk.

b. Compute each company's return-on-equity ratio and return-on-assets ratio. Use EBIT instead of net income when computing the return-on-assets ratio. Identify the company that is managing its assets more effectively. Identify the company that is producing the higher return from the stockholders' perspective. Explain how one company was able to produce a higher return on equity than the other.

EXERCISES—SERIES B

Exercise 10-1B   *Interest only versus an installment note*

LO 10-1

Pare Co. borrowed $80,000 from National Bank by issuing a note with a five-year term. Pare has two options with respect to the payment of interest and principal. Option 1 requires the payment of interest only on an annual basis with the full amount of the principal due at maturity. Option 2 calls for an annual payment that includes interest due plus a partial repayment of the principal balance. The effective annual interest rate on both notes is identical.

Required

Write a memo explaining how the two alternatives will affect *(a)* the carrying value of liabilities, *(b)* the amount of annual interest expense, *(c)* the total amount of interest that will be paid over the life of the note, and *(d)* the cash flow consequences.

Exercise 10-2B   *Amortization schedule for an installment note*

LO 10-1

On January 1, Year 1, Monroe Co. borrowed $80,000 cash from First Bank by issuing a four-year, 6 percent note. The principal and interest are to be paid by making annual payments in the amount of $23,087. Payments are to be made December 31 of each year, beginning December 31, Year 1.

Required

Prepare an amortization schedule for the interest and principal payments for the four-year period.

Exercise 10-3B   *Financial statement effects of an installment note*

LO 10-1

Lek Hood started a business by issuing a $70,000 face-value note to State National Bank on January 1, Year 1. The note had a 6 percent annual rate of interest and a 10-year term. Payments of $9,511 are to be made each December 31 for 10 years.

Required

a. What portion of the December 31, Year 1, payment is applied to
   (1) Interest expense?
   (2) Principal?
b. What is the principal balance on January 1, Year 2?
c. What portion of the December 31, Year 2, payment is applied to
   (1) Interest expense?
   (2) Principal?

Exercise 10-4B   *Financial statement effects of an installment note*

LO 10-1

A partial amortization schedule for a five-year note payable that Mercury Co. issued on January 1, Year 1, is shown next:

Accounting Period	Principal Balance January 1	Cash Payment	Applied to Interest	Applied to Principal
Year 1	$60,000	$13,858	$3,000	$10,858
Year 2	49,142	13,858	2,457	11,401

Required

a. What rate of interest is Mercury Co. paying on the note?
b. Using a financial statements model like the one shown next, record the appropriate amounts for the following two events:
   (1) January 1, Year 1, issue of the note payable
   (2) December 31, Year 2, payment on the note payable

Event No.	Balance Sheet			Income Statement			Statement of Cash Flows
	Assets	= Liab. +	Stk. Equity	Rev. −	Exp. =	Net Inc.	
1.							

c. If the company earned $75,000 cash revenue and paid $32,000 in cash expenses in addition to the interest in Year 1, what is the amount of each of the following?

(1) Net income for Year 1

(2) Cash flow from operating activities for Year 1

(3) Cash flow from financing activities for Year 1

d. What is the amount of interest expense on this loan for Year 3?

LO 10-2

Exercise 10-5B   *Calculations for a line of credit*

Singer Company has a line of credit with United Bank. Singer can borrow up to $400,000 at any time over the course of the Year 1 calendar year. The following table shows the prime rate expressed as an annual percentage along with the amounts borrowed and repaid during the first three months of Year 1. Singer agreed to pay interest at an annual rate equal to 2 percent above the bank's prime rate. Funds are borrowed or repaid on the first day of each month. Interest is payable in cash on the last day of the month. The interest rate is applied to the outstanding monthly balance. For example, Singer pays 6.5 percent (4.5 percent + 2 percent) annual interest on $140,000 for the month of February.

Month	Amount Borrowed or (Repaid)	Prime Rate for the Month
January	$80,000	4.0%
February	60,000	4.5
March	(20,000)	4.0

Required

a. Compute the amount of interest that Singer will pay on the line of credit for the three months of Year 1. Round answers to nearest whole dollar.

b. Compute the amount of Singer's liability at the end of each of the first three months.

LO 10-3

Exercise 10-6B   *Two accounting cycles for bonds issued at face value*

Pluto Company issued $300,000 of 20-year, 6 percent bonds on January 1, Year 1. The bonds were issued at face value. Interest is payable in cash on December 31 of each year. Pluto immediately invested the proceeds from the bond issue in land. The land was leased for an annual $50,000 of cash revenue, which was collected on December 31 of each year, beginning December 31, Year 1.

Required

a. Organize the transaction data in accounts under the accounting equation for Year 1 and Year 2.

b. Prepare the income statement, balance sheet, and statement of cash flows for Year 1 and Year 2.

LO 10-3

Exercise 10-7B   *Two accounting cycles for bonds issued at face value*

On January 1, Year 1, Hazman Corp. issued $200,000 of 10-year, 6 percent bonds at their face value. Interest is payable on December 31 of each year with the first payment due December 31, Year 1.

Required

Show the effects of these bonds on the accounting equation for Year 1 and Year 2.

LO 10-3

Exercise 10-8B   *Calculations for callable bonds*

Tyler Co. issued $250,000 of 6 percent, 10-year, callable bonds on January 1, Year 1, at their face value. The call premium was 2 percent (bonds are callable at 102). Interest was payable annually on December 31. The bonds were called on December 31, Year 4.

Required

a. Calculate the amount of interest expense for Year 4.

b. Determine the amount of loss on bond redemption recognized on December 31, Year 4.

Exercise 10-9B   *Annual versus semiannual interest for bonds issued at face value*

LO 10-3

Jupiter Co. issued bonds with a face value of $150,000 on January 1, Year 1. The bonds had a 6 percent stated rate of interest and a five-year term. The bonds were issued at face value.

Required

a. What total amount of interest will Jupiter pay in Year 1 if bond interest is paid annually each December 31?

b. What total amount of interest will Jupiter pay in Year 1 if bond interest is paid semiannually each June 30 and December 31?

c. Write a memo explaining which option Jupiter would prefer.

Exercise 10-10B   *Determining cash receipts from bond issues*

LO 10-4, 10-5

Required

Compute the cash proceeds from bond issues under the following terms. For each case, indicate whether the bonds sold at a premium or discount.

a. Hett, Inc. issued $400,000 of eight-year, 8 percent bonds at 101.

b. Holt Co. issued $250,000 of four-year, 6 percent bonds at 98.

c. Holmes Co. issued $300,000 of 10-year, 7 percent bonds at 102¼.

d. Hart, Inc. issued $200,000 of five-year, 6 percent bonds at 97½.

Exercise 10-11B   *Stated rate of interest versus the market rate of interest*

LO 10-3, 10-4, 10-5

Required

Indicate whether a bond will sell at a premium (P), discount (D), or face value (F) for each of the following conditions:

a. _____ The stated rate of interest is less than the market rate.

b. _____ The market rate of interest is equal to the stated rate.

c. _____ The market rate of interest is less than the stated rate.

d. _____ The market rate of interest is higher than the stated rate.

e. _____ The stated rate of interest is higher than the market rate.

Exercise 10-12B   *Identifying bond premiums and discounts*

LO 10-4, 10-5

Required

In each of the following situations, state whether the bonds will sell at a premium or discount:

a. Carver issued $400,000 of bonds with a stated interest rate of 7 percent. At the time of issue, the market rate of interest for similar investments was 6 percent.

b. Herring issued $200,000 of bonds with a stated interest rate of 6 percent. At the time of issue, the market rate of interest for similar investments was 8 percent.

c. Watson, Inc. issued callable bonds with a stated interest rate of 6 percent. The bonds were callable at 102. At the date of issue, the market rate of interest was 7 percent for similar investments.

Exercise 10-13B   *Determining the amount of bond premiums and discounts*

LO 10-4, 10-5

Required

For each of the following situations, calculate the amount of bond discount or premium, if any:

a. Jones Co. issued $120,000 of 6 percent bonds at 101.

b. Jude, Inc. issued $80,000 of 10-year, 8 percent bonds at 98.

c. James, Inc. issued $200,000 of 15-year, 9 percent bonds at 102¼.

d. Jolly Co. issued $400,000 of 20-year, 8 percent bonds at 99¾.

LO 10-4

Exercise 10-14B   *Straight-line amortization of a bond discount*

Frey Company issued bonds of $300,000 face value on January 1, Year 1. The bonds had a 6 percent stated rate of interest and a 10-year term. Interest is paid in cash annually, beginning December 31, Year 1. The bonds were issued at 98. Frey uses the straight-line method of amortization.

Required

a. Use a financial statements model like the one shown next to demonstrate how (1) the January 1, Year 1, bond issue and (2) the December 31, Year 1, recognition of interest expense, including the amortization of the discount and the cash payment, affect the company's financial statements. Use + for increase, − for decrease, and NA for not affected.

Event No.	Balance Sheet			Income Statement			Statement of Cash Flows
	Assets	= Liab.	+ Stk. Equity	Rev.	− Exp.	= Net Inc.	
1.							

b. Determine the amount of interest expense reported on the Year 1 income statement.

c. Determine the carrying value (face value less discount or plus premium) of the bond liability as of December 31, Year 1.

d. Determine the amount of interest expense reported on the Year 2 income statement.

e. Determine the carrying value (face value less discount or plus premium) of the bond liability as of December 31, Year 2.

LO 10-4

Exercise 10-15B   *Straight-line amortization of a bond discount*

Dixon Construction, Inc. issued $300,000 of 10-year, 6 percent bonds on July 1, Year 1, at 96. Interest is payable in cash semiannually on June 30 and December 31. Dixon uses the straight-line method of amortization.

Required

a. Use a financial statements model like the one shown next to demonstrate how (1) the January 1, Year 2, bond issue and (2) the December 31, Year 2, recognition of interest expense, including the amortization of the premium and the cash payment, affect the company's financial statements. Use + for increase, − for decrease, and NA for not affected.

Event No.	Balance Sheet			Income Statement			Statement of Cash Flows
	Assets	= Liab.	+ Stk. Equity	Rev.	− Exp.	= Net Inc.	
1.							

b. Determine the carrying value (face value less discount or plus premium) of the bond liability as of December 31, Year 1.

c. Determine the amount of interest expense reported on the Year 1 income statement.

d. Determine the carrying value of the bond liability as of December 31, Year 2.

e. Determine the amount of interest expense reported on the Year 2 income statement.

LO 10-4

Exercise 10-16B   *Straight-line amortization for bonds issued at a discount*

On January 1, Year 1, Files Co. issued $400,000 of five-year, 6 percent bonds at 97. Interest is payable annually on December 31. The discount is amortized using the straight-line method.

Required

a. Determine the amount of cash proceeds received by Files Co. on January 1, Year 1.

b. Calculate the amount of interest expense reported on the December 31, Year 2, income statement.

c. What is the carrying value of the bond liability as of December 31, Year 2?

Exercise 10-17B   *Straight-line amortization of a bond premium*

LO 10-5

Ramsey Company issued bonds of $300,000 face value on January 1, Year 1. The bonds had a 6 percent stated rate of interest and a 10-year term. Interest is paid in cash annually, beginning December 31, Year 1. The bonds were issued at 101½. The straight-line method is used for amortization.

Required

a. Use a financial statements model like the one shown next to demonstrate how (1) the January 1, Year 1, bond issue and (2) the December 31, Year 1, recognition of interest expense, including the amortization of the premium and the cash payment, affect the company's financial statements. Use + for increase, − for decrease, and NA for not affected.

Event No.	Balance Sheet			Income Statement			Statement of Cash Flows
	Assets	= Liab.	+ Stk. Equity	Rev.	− Exp.	= Net Inc.	
1.							

b. Determine the carrying value (face value plus premium) of the bond liability as of December 31, Year 1.

c. Determine the amount of interest expense reported on the Year 1 income statement.

d. Determine the carrying value of the bond liability as of December 31, Year 2.

e. Determine the amount of interest expense reported on the Year 2 income statement.

Exercise 10-18B   *Straight-line amortization for bonds issued at a premium*

LO 10-5

On January 1, Year 1, Chen Company issued $300,000 of five-year, 6 percent bonds at 101. Interest is payable annually on December 31. The premium is amortized using the straight-line method.

Required

a. Determine the amount of cash proceeds received by Chen Company on January 1, Year 1.

b. Calculate the amount of interest expense as of December 31, Year 2.

c. What is the carrying value of the bond liability as of December 31, Year 2?

Exercise 10-19B   *Effective interest amortization of a bond discount*

LO 10-6

On January 1, Year 1, Seaside Condo Association issued bonds with a face value of $250,000, a stated rate of interest of 8 percent, and a 10-year term to maturity. Interest is payable in cash on December 31 of each year. The effective rate of interest was 10 percent at the time the bonds were issued. The bonds sold for $219,277. Seaside used the effective interest rate method to amortize the bond discount:

Required

a. Determine the amount of the discount on the day of issue.

b. Determine the amount of interest expense recognized on December 31, Year 1.

c. Determine the carrying value of the bond liability on December 31, Year 1.

Exercise 10-20B   *Effective interest amortization of a bond discount*

LO 10-6

On January 1, Year 1, Valley Enterprises issued bonds with a face value of $60,000, a stated rate of interest of 8 percent, and a five-year term to maturity. Interest is payable in cash on December 31 of each year. The effective rate of interest was 9 percent at the time the bonds were issued. The bonds sold for $57,666. Valley used the effective interest rate method to amortize the bond discount.

Required

a. Prepare an amortization table as shown next:

	Cash Payment	Interest Expense	Discount Amortization	Carrying Value
January 1, Year 1				$57,666
December 31, Year 1	$ 4,800	$ 5,190	$ 390	58,056
December 31, Year 2	?	?	?	?
December 31, Year 3	?	?	?	?
December 31, Year 4	?	?	?	?
December 31, Year 5	?	?	?	?
Totals	$24,000	$26,334	$2,334	

b. What item(s) in the table would appear on the Year 2 balance sheet?

c. What item(s) in the table would appear on the Year 2 income statement?

d. What item(s) in the table would appear on the Year 2 statement of cash flows?

LO 10-7

Exercise 10-21B   *Effective interest amortization of a bond premium*

On January 1, Year 1, Omega Company issued bonds with a face value of $200,000, a stated rate of interest of 6 percent, and a 10-year term to maturity. Interest is payable in cash on December 31 of each year. The effective rate of interest was 5 percent at the time the bonds were issued. The bonds sold for $215,443. Omega used the effective interest rate method to amortize the bond discount.

Required

a. Determine the amount of the premium on the day of issue.

b. Determine the amount of interest expense recognized on December 31, Year 1.

c. Determine the carrying value of the bond liability on December 31, Year 1.

LO 10-7

Exercise 10-22B   *Effective interest amortization for a bond premium*

On January 1, Year 1, Reese Incorporated issued bonds with a face value of $120,000, a stated rate of interest of 8 percent, and a five-year term to maturity. Interest is payable in cash on December 31 of each year. The effective rate of interest was 7 percent at the time the bonds were issued. The bonds sold for $124,920. Reese used the effective interest rate method to amortize the bond discount.

Required

a. Prepare an amortization table as shown next:

	Cash Payment	Interest Expense	Discount Amortization	Carrying Value
January 1, Year 1				$124,920
December 31, Year 1	$ 9,600	$ 8,744	$ 856	124,064
December 31, Year 2	?	?	?	?
December 31, Year 3	?	?	?	?
December 31, Year 4	?	?	?	?
December 31, Year 5	?	?	?	?
Totals	$48,000	$43,080	$4,920	

b. What item(s) in the table would appear on the Year 3 balance sheet?

c. What item(s) in the table would appear on the Year 3 income statement?

d. What item(s) in the table would appear on the Year 3 statement of cash flows?

Exercise 10-23B   *Effective interest versus straight-line amortization*

On January 1, Year 1, Wright and Associates issued bonds with a face value of $800,000, a stated rate of interest of 8 percent, and a 20-year term to maturity. Interest is payable in cash on December 31 of each year. The effective rate of interest was 9 percent at the time the bonds were issued.

Required

Write a brief memo explaining whether the effective interest rate method or the straight-line method will produce the highest amount of interest expense recognized on the Year 1 income statement.

Exercise 10-24B   *Determining the after-tax cost of debt*

The following information is available for three companies:

	Bass Co.	Carp Co.	Perch Co.
Face value of bonds payable	$300,000	$600,000	$500,000
Interest rate	10%	9%	8%
Income tax rate	40%	30%	35%

Required

a. Determine the annual before-tax interest cost for each company *in dollars*.

b. Determine the annual after-tax interest cost for each company *in dollars*.

c. Determine the annual after-tax interest cost for each company as *a percentage* of the face value of the bonds.

Exercise 10-25B   *Determining the effects of financing alternatives on ratios*

Cascade Industries has the following account balances:

Current assets	$ 30,000	Current liabilities	$15,000
Noncurrent assets	120,000	Noncurrent liabilities	75,000
		Stockholders' equity	60,000

The company wishes to raise $50,000 in cash and is considering two financing options: Cascade can sell $50,000 of bonds payable, or it can issue additional common stock for $50,000. To help in the decision process, Cascade's management wants to determine the effects of each alternative on its current ratio and debt-to-assets ratio.

Required

a. Help Cascade's management by completing the following chart:

Ratio	Currently	If Bonds Are Issued	If Stock Is Issued
Current ratio			
Debt-to-assets ratio			

b. Assume that after the funds are invested, EBIT amounts to $18,000. Also assume the company pays $5,000 in dividends or $5,000 in interest, depending on which source of financing is used. Based on a 30 percent tax rate, determine the amount of the increase in retained earnings that would result under each financing option.

PROBLEMS—SERIES B

LO 10-1

Problem 10-26B   *Effect of an installment note on financial statements*

On January 1, Year 1, Kramer Co. borrowed cash from First City Bank by issuing a $90,000 face-value, three-year term note that had a 7 percent annual interest rate. The note is to be repaid by making annual payments of $34,295 that include both interest and principal on December 31. Kramer invested the proceeds from the loan in land that generated lease revenues of $45,000 cash per year.

Required

a. Prepare an amortization schedule for the three-year period.

b. Organize the information in accounts under an accounting equation.

c. Prepare an income statement, balance sheet, and statement of cash flows for each of the three years.

d. Does cash outflow from operating activities remain constant or change each year? Explain.

LO 10-2

Problem 10-27B   *Effect of a line of credit on financial statements*

Mott Company has a line of credit with Bay Bank. Mott can borrow up to $400,000 at any time over the course of the Year 1 calendar year. The following table shows the prime rate expressed as an annual percentage, along with the amounts borrowed and repaid during Year 1. Mott agreed to pay interest at an annual rate equal to 1 percent above the bank's prime rate. Funds are borrowed or repaid on the first day of each month. Interest is payable in cash on the last day of the month. The interest rate is applied to the outstanding monthly balance. For example, Mott pays 6 percent (5 percent + 1 percent) annual interest on $60,000 for the month of January.

Month	Amount Borrowed or (Repaid)	Prime Rate for the Month
January	$60,000	5%
February	40,000	5
March	(30,000)	6
April through October	No change	No change
November	(20,000)	6
December	(10,000)	5

Mott earned $25,000 of cash revenue during Year 1.

Required

a. Prepare an income statement, balance sheet, and statement of cash flows for Year 1.

b. Write a memo discussing the advantages to a business of arranging a line of credit.

LO 10-3

Problem 10-28B   *Recording transactions for callable bonds*

Dame Co. issued $250,000 of 10-year, 6 percent, callable bonds on January 1, Year 1, with interest payable annually on December 31. The bonds were issued at their face amount. The bonds are callable at 101½. The fiscal year of the corporation is the calendar year.

Required

Show the effect of the following events on the financial statements by recording the appropriate amounts in a horizontal statements model like the following one. In the Statement of Cash Flows column, indicate whether the item is an operating activity (OA), investing activity (IA), or financing activity (FA). Use NA if an element was not affected by the event.

(1) Issued the bonds on January 1, Year 1.

(2) Paid interest due to bondholders on December 31, Year 1.

(3) On January 1, Year 5, Dame Co. called the bonds. Assume that all interim entries were correctly recorded.

	Balance Sheet			Income Statement			Statement of Cash Flows
Event No.	Assets	= Liab. +	Stk. Equity	Rev.	− Exp. =	Net Inc.	
1.							

Problem 10-29B *Straight-line amortization of a bond discount*

LO 10-4

White Co. was formed when it acquired cash from the issue of common stock. The company then issued bonds at a discount on January 1, Year 1. Interest is payable on December 31 with the first payment made December 31, Year 1. On January 2, Year 1, White Co. purchased a piece of land that produced rent revenue annually. The rent is collected on December 31 of each year, beginning December 31, Year 1. At the end of the six-year period (January 1, Year 7), the land was sold at a gain and the bonds were paid off at face value. A summary of the transactions for each year follows:

Year 1

1. Acquired cash from the issue of common stock.
2. Issued six-year bonds.
3. Purchased land.
4. Received land rental income.
5. Recognized interest expense, including the straight-line amortization of the discount, and made the cash payment for interest on December 31.

Year 2 through Year 6

6. Received land rental income.
7. Recognized interest expense, including the straight-line amortization of the discount, and made the cash payment for interest December 31.

Year 7

8. Sold the land at a gain.
9. Retired the bonds at face value.

Required

Identify each of these events and transactions as an asset source (AS), asset use (AU), asset exchange (AE), or claims exchange (CE). Explain how each event affects assets, liabilities, equity, net income, and cash flow by placing a + for increase, − for decrease, or NA for not affected under each of the categories. In the Statement of Cash Flows column, indicate whether the item is an operating activity (OA), investing activity (IA), or financing activity (FA). The first event is recorded as an example.

Event No.	Types of Event	Assets	=	Liabilities	+	Common Stock	+	Retained Earnings	Net Income	Cash Flow
1.	AS	+		NA		+		NA	NA	+ FA

Problem 10-30B *Straight-line amortization of a bond discount*

LO 10-4

During Year 1 and Year 2, Kale Co. completed the following transactions relating to its bond issue. The company's fiscal year ends on December 31.

Year 1

Mar. 1 Issued $200,000 of eight-year, 6 percent bonds for $194,000. The semiannual cash payment for interest is due on March 1 and September 1, beginning September Year 1.

Sept. 1 Recognized interest expense, including the straight-line amortization of the discount, and made the semiannual cash payment for interest.

Dec. 31 Recognized accrued interest expense, including the straight-line amortization of the discount.

Dec. 31 Closed the interest expense account.

Year 2

Mar.1   Recognized interest expense, including the straight-line amortization of the discount, and made the semiannual cash payment for interest.

Sept. 1   Recognized interest expense, including the straight-line amortization of the discount, and made the semiannual cash payment for interest.

Dec. 31   Recognized accrued interest expense, including the amortization of the discount.

Dec. 31   Closed the interest expense account.

Required

a. When the bonds were issued, was the market rate of interest more or less than the stated rate of interest? If the bonds had sold at face value, what amount of cash would Kale Co. have received?

b. Prepare the liabilities section of the balance sheet at December 31, Year 1 and Year 2.

c. Determine the amount of interest expense Kale would report on the income statements for Year 1 and Year 2.

d. Determine the amount of interest Kale would pay to the bondholders in Year 1 and Year 2.

LO 10-5

Problem 10-31B   *Straight-line amortization of a bond premium*

Whitten Company was started when it issued bonds with $300,000 face value on January 1, Year 1. The bonds were issued for cash at 103. Whitten uses the straight-line method of amortization. They had a 15-year term to maturity and a 6 percent annual interest rate. Interest was payable annually. Whitten immediately purchased land with the proceeds (cash received) from the bond issue. Whitten leased the land for $36,000 cash per year. On January 1, Year 4, the company sold the land for $310,000 cash. Immediately after the sale, Whitten repurchased its bonds (repaid the bond liability) at 104. Assume that no other accounting events occurred in Year 4.

Required

a. Record the events associated with this bond in an accounting equation for Year 1, Year 2, Year 3, and Year 4. Total the amounts in each account at the end of each year.

b. Prepare an income statement, statement of changes in equity, balance sheet, and statement of cash flows for each of the Year 1, Year 2, Year 3, and Year 4 accounting periods. Assume that the company's fiscal year ends on December 31 of each year.

LO 10-1, 10-2, 10-4, 10-5

Problem 10-32B   *Effect of financing transactions on financial statements*

Required

Show the effect of each of the following independent accounting events on the financial statements using a horizontal statements model like the following one. Use + for increase, − for decrease, and NA for not affected. The first event is recorded as an example.

Event No.	Balance Sheet			Income Statement			Statement of Cash Flows
	Assets	= Liab.	+ Stk. Equity	Rev.	− Exp.	= Net Inc.	
1.	+	+	NA	NA	NA	NA	FA +

a. Issued a bond at a premium.

b. Made an interest payment on a bond that had been issued at a premium and amortized the premium.

c. Borrowed funds using a line of credit.

d. Made an interest payment for funds that had been borrowed against a line of credit.

e. Made a cash payment on a note payable for both interest and principal.

f. Issued a bond at face value.

g. Made an interest payment on a bond that had been issued at face value.

h. Issued a bond at a discount.

i. Made an interest payment on a bond that had been issued at a discount and amortized the discount.

Problem 10-33B   *Effective interest versus straight-line amortization*   LO 10-5, 10-7

On January 1, Year 1, Mason Corp. sold $100,000 of its own 6 percent, 5-year bonds. Interest is payable annually on December 31. The bonds were sold to yield an effective interest rate of 5 percent. Mason Corp. uses the effective interest rate method. The bonds sold for $104,330.

Required

a. Determine the cash proceeds received and the premium on bonds payable.

b. Calculate interest expense and bond premium amortization for Year 1 and Year 2. (Assume effective interest amortization.)

c. Calculate interest expense and bond premium amortization for December 31, Year 1. (Assume straight-line amortization.)

d. Calculate the amount of interest expense for Year 4. (Assume effective interest amortization.)

e. Calculate the amount of interest expense for Year 4. (Assume straight-line amortization.)

Problem 10-34B   *Using ratios to make comparisons*   LO 10-8

The following information pertains to the Tacoma and Olympia companies:

Account Title	Tacoma Co.	Olympia Co.
Current assets	$ 60,000	$ 60,000
Total assets	1,000,000	1,000,000
Current liabilities	55,000	50,000
Total liabilities	800,000	600,000
Stockholders' equity	200,000	400,000
Interest expense	60,000	45,000
Income tax expense	95,000	100,000
Net income	145,000	155,000

Required

a. Compute each company's debt-to-assets ratio, current ratio, and times interest earned (EBIT must be computed). Identify the company with the greater financial risk.

b. Compute each company's return-on-equity ratio and return-on-assets ratio. Use EBIT instead of net income when computing the return-on-assets ratio. Identify the company that is managing its assets more effectively. Identify the company that is producing the higher return from the stockholders' perspective. Explain how one company was able to produce a higher return on equity than the other.

ANALYZE, THINK, COMMUNICATE

ATC 10-1   **Business Applications Case**   *Understanding real-world annual reports*

Obtain Target Corporation's annual report for its 2018 fiscal year (year ended February 2, 2019) at http://investors.target.com using the instructions in Appendix B, and use it to answer the following questions:

Required

a. What was the average interest rate on Target's long-term debt in the fiscal-year ended February 2, 2019 (2018)?

b. Target has an "unsecured revolving credit facility" (i.e., a line of credit). What is the total amount of credit available under this facility? How much of this total amount available had Target used as of February 2, 2019?

c. Target's balance sheet shows a line titled "Other noncurrent liabilities." What are the types of debt included in this category?

ATC 10-2   **Group Assignment**   *Missing information*

The following three companies issued the following bonds:

1. Carr, Inc. issued $100,000 of 8 percent, five-year bonds at 102¼ on January 1, Year 1. Interest is payable annually on December 31.

2. Kim, Inc. issued $100,000 of 8 percent, five-year bonds at 98 on January 1, Year 1. Interest is payable annually on December 31.

3. Jay, Inc. issued $100,000 of 8 percent, five-year bonds at 104 on January 1, Year 1. Interest is payable annually on December 31.

Required

a. Organize the class into three sections and divide each section into groups of three to five students. Assign each of the sections one of the companies.

Group Tasks

(1) Compute the following amounts for your company (use straight-line amortization):

(a) Cash proceeds from the bond issue

(b) Interest paid in Year 1

(c) Interest expense for Year 1

(2) Prepare the liabilities section of the balance sheet as of December 31, Year 1.

Class Discussion

b. Have a representative of each section put the liabilities section for its company on the board.

c. Is the amount of interest expense different for the three companies? Why or why not?

d. Is the amount of interest paid different for each of the companies? Why or why not?

e. Is the amount of total liabilities different for each of the companies? Why or why not?

ATC 10-3   Real-World Case   *Using accounting numbers to assess creditworthiness*

Advance Auto Parts, Inc. is ". . . a leading automotive aftermarket parts provider in North America. . . . We were founded in 1929 as Advance Stores Company. . . . As of January 2, 2016 . . . we operated 5,171 total stores and 122 branches primarily under the trade names 'Advance Auto Parts,' 'Autopart International,' 'Carquest,' and 'Worldpac.'"

Foot Locker, Inc. ". . . incorporated under the laws of the State of New York[6] in 1989, is a leading global retailer of athletically inspired shoes and apparel, operating 3,383 primarily mall-based stores in the United States, Canada, Europe, Australia, and New Zealand as of January 30, 2016."

Johnson & Johnson, Inc. ". . . and its subsidiaries have approximately 127,100[7] employees worldwide engaged in the research and development, manufacture and sale of a broad range of products in the health care field. . . . The Company's primary focus is products related to human health and well-being. Johnson & Johnson was incorporated in the State of New Jersey in 1887."

Tesla, Inc.: "We design, develop, manufacture and sell high-performance[8] fully electric vehicles, and energy storage systems, as well as install, operate and maintain solar and energy storage products. We are the world's only vertically integrated energy company, offering end-to-end clean energy products, including generation, storage and consumption."

Each company received a different rating from Standard & Poor's (S&P). In descending order, the ratings for these companies were AAA, BBB−, BB+, and B−. These rating are as of March 16, 2017. All dollar amounts are in millions.

	Net Income	Cash Flow from Operations	Current Ratio	Debt-to-Assets Ratio	Times Interest Earned	Return-on-Assets Ratio
Advance Auto Parts						
2015	$ 473	$ 690	1.30	0.70	12.57	0.058
2016	460	501	1.41	0.65	13.32	0.055
Foot Locker						
2015	520	712	3.53	0.30	162.80	0.145
2016	541	745	3.72	0.32	210.25	0.143
Jonnson & Johnson						
2015	15,409	19,279	2.17	0.47	35.78	0.116
2016	16,540	18,767	2.47	0.50	28.28	0117
Tesla						
2015	(889)	(524)	0.99	0.87	−6.37	−0.110
2016	(773)	(124)	1.07	0.79	−2.75	−0.034

[6]U.S. Securities and Exchange Commission.

[7]U.S. Securities and Exchange Commission.

[8]U.S. Securities and Exchange Commission.

Required

Determine which credit rating was assigned to which company. Write a memorandum explaining the rationale for your decisions. The logic you present to support your conclusions is more important than correctly matching the companies with their ratings.

ATC 10-4 Business Applications Case *Performing ratio analysis using real-world data*

Apple, Inc. manufactures and markets mobile phones, personal computers, and related software. The following data were taken from the company's 2018 and 2015 annual reports. All dollar amounts are in millions.

	Fiscal Years Ending	
Account Title	September 29, 2018	September 26, 2015
Current assets	$ 131,339	$ 89,378
Total assets	365,725	290,479
Current liabilities	116,866	80,610
Total liabilities	258,578	171,124
Interest expense	3,240	733
Income tax expense	13,372	19,121
Net income	59,531	53,394

Required

a. Calculate the EBIT for each year.

b. Calculate the times-interest-earned ratio for each year.

c. Calculate the current ratio and debt-to-assets ratio for each year.

d. Did the company's level of financial risk increase or decrease from 2015 to 2018? Explain.

ATC 10-5 Writing Assignment *Debt versus equity financing*

Mack Company plans to invest $50,000 in land that will produce annual rent revenue equal to 15 percent of the investment, starting on January 1, Year 1. The revenue will be collected in cash at the end of each year, starting December 31, Year 1. Mack can obtain the cash necessary to purchase the land from two sources. Funds can be obtained by issuing $50,000 of 10 percent, five-year bonds at their face amount. Interest due on the bonds is payable on December 31 of each year with the first payment due on December 31, Year 1. Alternatively, the $50,000 needed to invest in land can be obtained from equity financing. In this case, the stockholders (holders of the equity) will be paid a $5,000 annual cash dividend. Mack Company is in a 30 percent income tax bracket.

Required

a. Prepare an income statement and statement of cash flows for Year 1 under the two alternative financing proposals.

b. Write a short memorandum explaining why one financing alternative provides more net income but less cash flow than the other.

ATC 10-6 Ethical Dilemma *I don't want to pay taxes*

Dana Harbert recently started a very successful small business. Indeed, the business had grown so rapidly that she was no longer able to finance its operations by investing her own resources in the business. She needed additional capital but had no more of her own money to put into the business. A friend, Gene Watson, was willing to invest $100,000 in the business. Harbert estimated that, with Watson's investment, the company would be able to increase revenue by $40,000. Furthermore, she believed that operating expenses would increase by only 10 percent. Harbert and Watson agreed that Watson's investment should entitle him to receive a cash dividend equal to 20 percent of net income. A set of forecasted statements with and without Watson's investment is presented next. (Assume that all transactions involving revenue, expense, and dividends are cash transactions.)

Financial Statements

	Forecast 1 without Watson's Investment	Forecast 2 with Watson's Investment
Income Statements		
Revenue	$120,000	$160,000
Operating expenses	(70,000)	(77,000)
Income before interest and taxes	50,000	83,000
Income tax expense (effective tax rate is 30%)	(15,000)	(24,900)
Net income	$ 35,000	$ 58,100
Statements of Changes in Stockholders' Equity		
Beginning retained earnings	$ 15,000	$ 15,000
Plus: Net income	35,000	58,100
Less: Dividend to Watson (20% of $58,100)	0	(11,620)
Ending retained earnings	$ 50,000	$ 61,480
Balance Sheets		
Assets (computations explained in following paragraph)	$400,000	$511,480
Liabilities	$ 0	$ 0
Equity		
Common stock	350,000	450,000
Retained earnings	50,000	61,480
Total liabilities and equity	$400,000	$511,480

The balance for assets in Forecast 1 is computed as the beginning balance of $365,000 plus net income of $35,000. The balance for assets in Forecast 2 is computed as the beginning balance of $365,000, plus the $100,000 cash investment, plus net income of $58,100, less the $11,620 dividend. Alternatively, total assets can be computed by determining the amount of total claims (total assets = total claims).

Harbert tells Watson that there would be a $3,486 tax advantage associated with debt financing. She says that if Watson is willing to become a creditor instead of an owner, she could pay him an additional $697.20 (that is, 20 percent of the tax advantage). Watson tells Harbert that he has no interest in participating in the management of the business, but Watson wants an ownership interest to guarantee that he will always receive 20 percent of the profits of the business. Harbert suggests that they execute a formal agreement in which Watson is paid 11.62 percent interest on his $100,000 loan to the business. This agreement will be used for income tax reporting. In addition, Harbert says that she is willing to establish a private agreement to write Watson a personal check for any additional amount necessary to make Watson's total return equal to 20 percent of all profits plus a $697.20 bonus for his part of the tax advantage. She tells Watson, "It's just like ownership. The only difference is that we call it debt for the Internal Revenue Service. If they want to have some silly rule that says if you call it debt, you get a tax break, then we'd be foolish *not* to call it debt. I will call it anything they want, just as long as I don't have to pay taxes on it."

Required

a. Construct a third set of forecasted financial statements (Forecast 3) at 11.62 percent annual interest, assuming that Watson is treated as creditor (he loans the business $100,000).

b. Verify the tax advantage of debt financing by comparing the balances of the Retained Earnings account in Forecast 2 and Forecast 3.

c. If you were Watson, would you permit Harbert to classify the equity transaction as debt to provide a higher return to the business and to you?

d. Comment on the ethical implications of misnaming a financing activity for the sole purpose of reducing income taxes.

ATC 10-7   Research Assignment   *Analyzing debt financing at Home Depot*

Interest rates in the United States were at historic lows for much of the period from 2013 through 2019. The economy was slowly recovering from the recession of 2008 and 2009, and the Federal Reserve kept interest rates low to encourage this recovery. Because of these low interest rates, many companies increased their long-term financing from debt, while lowering their financing with owners' equity. Home Depot, Inc., the building supplies company, was one of these firms.

Use Home Depot's 2017 Form 10-K to obtain the data for 2016 and 2017, and its 2015 Form 10-K to obtain the data for 2014 and 2015. (*Note:* Home Depot ends its fiscal year in late January or early February, so for the purposes of this assignment, the fiscal year ending on January 28, 2018, is considered the company's 2017 fiscal year. All other fiscal years are treated the same, so 2015 will be the year ended January 31, 2016.) To obtain the 10-Ks, you can either use the EDGAR system, following the instructions in Appendix A, or they can be found on the company's website.

Required

a. For each year, 2014 through 2017, calculate the following ratios:

   (1) Debt to assets

   (2) Return on assets

   (3) Return on equity

b. List the company's interest expense for each year from 2014 through 2017.

c. Write a brief memorandum discussing all of the effects that Home Depot's strategy of increasing its financing with debt had on the company from 2014 through 2017.

CHAPTER 11

Proprietorships, Partnerships, and Corporations

LEARNING OBJECTIVES

After you have mastered the material in this chapter, you will be able to:

LO 11-1	Identify the primary characteristics of sole proprietorships, partnerships, and corporations.
LO 11-2	Identify the characteristics of capital stock.
LO 11-3	Differentiate between common and preferred stock.
LO 11-4	Show how issuing different classes of stock affects financial statements.
LO 11-5	Show how treasury stock affects financial statements.
LO 11-6	Show how declaring and paying cash dividends affect financial statements.
LO 11-7	Show how stock dividends and stock splits affect financial statements.
LO 11-8	Show how the appropriation of retained earnings affects financial statements.
LO 11-9	Show how accounting information is used to make stock investment decisions.
LO 11-10	Use financial statements to analyze the impact of business liquidations on creditors and owners.

Video lectures and accompanying self-assessment quizzes are available in *Connect* for all learning objectives.

Tableau Dashboard Activity is available in *Connect* for this chapter.

CHAPTER OPENING

You want to start a business. How should you structure it? Should it be a sole proprietorship, partnership, or corporation? Each form of business structure presents advantages and disadvantages. For example, a sole proprietorship allows maximum independence and control, while partnerships and corporations allow individuals to pool resources and talents with other people. This chapter discusses these and other features of the three primary forms of business structure.

The Curious Accountant

Stockbyte/Getty Images

Imagine your rich uncle rewarded you for doing well in your first accounting course by giving you $10,000 to invest in the common stock of one company. After reviewing many recent annual reports, you narrowed your choice to two companies with the following characteristics:

Mystery Company A: This company began operations in 2007 and began selling its stock to the public on March 23, 2018. It has lost money every year it has been in existence. In 2017 alone, its losses were $112 million, and by December 31, 2017, it had total lifetime losses of approximately $1.1 billion. Even so, the company provides services that are used by millions of individuals every day. At its current price of $22.31, you could buy about 450 shares. A friend tells you that a person whose head was "in the clouds" anyway would be crazy not to buy this company's stock.

Mystery Company B: This company has been in existence since 1837 and has been incorporated since 1905. It has made a profit and paid dividends for as long as anyone can remember. In its 2018 fiscal-year alone, its net earnings were $9.8 billion, and it paid dividends of $7.1 billion. Almost every home in America uses one or more of its products or services. Its stock is selling for about $102.57 per share, so you can buy 97 shares. Your friend says that owning this company's stock would be about as exciting as brushing your teeth.

The names of the real-world companies described here are disclosed later. Based on the information provided, which company's stock would you buy? (Answers on page 538.)

FORMS OF BUSINESS ORGANIZATIONS

Sole proprietorships are owned by a single individual who is responsible for making business and profit distribution decisions. If you want to be the absolute master of your destiny, you should organize your business as a proprietorship. Establishing a sole proprietorship is usually as simple as obtaining a business license from local government authorities. Usually no legal ownership agreement is required.

Partnerships allow persons to share their talents, capital, and the risks and rewards of business ownership. Because two or more individuals share ownership, partnerships require clear agreements about how authority, risks, and profits will be shared. Prudent partners minimize misunderstandings by hiring attorneys to prepare a **partnership agreement** that defines the responsibilities of each partner and describes how income or losses will be divided. Because the measurement of income affects the distribution of profits, partnerships frequently hire accountants to ensure that records are maintained in accordance with

LO 11-1

Identify the primary characteristics of sole proprietorships, partnerships, and corporations.

generally accepted accounting principles (GAAP). Partnerships (and sole proprietorships) also may need professional advice to deal with tax issues.

A **corporation** is a separate legal entity created by the authority of a state government. The paperwork to start a corporation is complex. For most laypersons, engaging professional attorneys and accountants to assist with the paperwork is well worth the fees charged.

Each state has separate laws governing establishing corporations. Many states follow the standard provisions of the Model Business Corporation Act. All states require the initial application to provide **articles of incorporation**, which normally include the following information: (1) the corporation's name and proposed date of incorporation; (2) the purpose of the corporation; (3) the location of the business and its expected life (which can be *perpetuity,* meaning *endless*); (4) provisions for capital stock; and (5) the names and addresses of the members of the first board of directors, the individuals with the ultimate authority for operating the business. If the articles are in order, the state establishes the legal existence of the corporation by issuing a charter of incorporation. The charter and the articles are public documents.

Each form of business organization presents a different combination of advantages and disadvantages. Persons wanting to start a business or invest in one should consider the characteristics of each type of business structure.

Regulation

Few laws specifically affect the operations of proprietorships and partnerships. Corporations, however, are usually heavily regulated. The extent of government regulation depends on the size and distribution of a company's ownership interests. Ownership interests in corporations are normally evidenced by **stock certificates.**

Ownership of corporations can be transferred from one individual to another through exchanging stock certificates. As long as the exchanges (buying and selling of shares of stock, often called *trading*) are limited to transactions between individuals, a company is defined as a **closely held corporation.** However, once a corporation reaches a certain size, it may list its stock on a stock exchange such as the New York Stock Exchange. Trading on a stock exchange is limited to the stockbrokers who are members of the exchange. These brokers represent buyers and sellers who are willing to pay the brokers commissions for exchanging stock certificates on their behalf. Although closely held corporations are relatively free from government regulation, companies whose stock is publicly traded on the exchanges by brokers are subject to extensive regulation.

The extensive regulation of trading on stock exchanges began in the 1930s. The stock market crash of 1929 and the subsequent Great Depression led Congress to pass the **Securities Act of 1933** and the **Securities Exchange Act of 1934** to regulate issuing stock and to govern the exchanges. The 1934 act also created the Securities and Exchange Commission (SEC) to enforce the securities laws. Congress gave the SEC legal authority to establish accounting principles for corporations that are registered on the exchanges. However, the

---

Answers to The Curious Accountant

Mystery Company A is Dropbox, Inc., as of March 15, 2019. For its initial public offering on March 23, 2018, its stock was priced at $21 per share; by the end of the day it was selling for $22.31. One-year later, the stock was trading at $22.81, an increase of 6 percent.

Mystery Company B is Procter & Gamble Company, as of March 15, 2019. It manufactures and sells numerous personal care and household care products, including toothpaste, shampoo, and laundry detergent. During the one-year of trading when Dropbox's stock price increased by 6 percent, Procter & Gamble's stock price increased by 35 percent, from $75.91 to $102.57. Of course, only the future will reveal which company is the better investment in the long run.

SEC has generally deferred its rule-making authority to the independent, private sector Financial Accounting Standards Board (FASB).

A number of high-profile business failures around the turn of this century raised questions about the effectiveness of financial statement audits to protect the public. The **Sarbanes-Oxley Act of 2002** was adopted to address these concerns. The act created a five-member Public Company Accounting Oversight Board (PCAOB) with the authority to set and enforce auditing, attestation, quality control, and ethics standards for auditors of public companies. The PCAOB is empowered to impose disciplinary and remedial sanctions for violations of its rules, securities laws, and professional auditing and accounting standards. Public corporations operate in a complex regulatory environment that requires the services of attorneys and professional accountants.

Double Taxation

Corporations pay income taxes on their earnings and then owners pay income taxes on distributions (dividends) received from corporations. As a result, distributed corporate profits are taxed twice—first when income is reported on the corporation's income tax return and a second time when distributions are reported on individual owners' tax returns. This phenomenon is commonly called **double taxation** and is a significant disadvantage of the corporate form of business organization.

To illustrate, assume Glide Corporation earns pretax income of $100,000. Glide is in a 21 percent tax bracket. The corporation itself will pay income tax of $21,000 ($100,000 × 0.21). Next, assume that the corporation distributes the after-tax income of $79,000 ($100,000 − $21,000) to individual stockholders who are in a personal federal income tax bracket of 22 percent. The $79,000 dividend will be reported on the stockholders' individual income tax returns, requiring tax payments of $17,380 ($79,000 × 0.22). Ultimately, total income tax of $38,380 ($21,000 + $17,380) is paid on the $100,000 of income earned by the corporation. In contrast, consider a proprietorship that is owned by an individual in a 22 percent federal income tax bracket. If the proprietorship earns and distributes $100,000 profit, the total tax would be only $22,000 ($100,000 × 0.22).

Double taxation can be a burden for small companies. To reduce that burden, tax laws permit small closely held corporations to elect "S Corporation" status. S Corporation income is not taxed at the corporate level but instead flows through to the owners who pay individual income taxes. Also, many states have enacted laws permitting the formation of **limited liability companies (LLCs),** which offer many of the benefits of corporate ownership yet are, in general, taxed as sole proprietorships or partnerships. Because proprietorships and partnerships are not separate taxable entities, company earnings are taxable to the owners rather than the company itself.

Limited Liability

Given the disadvantages of increased regulation and double taxation, why would anyone choose the corporate form of business structure over a partnership or proprietorship? A major reason is that the corporate form limits an investor's potential liability as an owner of a business venture. Because a corporation is legally separate from its owners, creditors cannot claim owners' personal assets as payment for the company's debts. Also, plaintiffs must sue the corporation, not its owners. The most that owners of a corporation can lose is the amount they have invested in the company (the value of the company's stock).

Unlike corporate stockholders, the owners of proprietorships and partnerships are *personally liable* for actions they take in the name of their companies. In fact, partners are responsible not only for their own actions but also for those taken by any other partner on behalf of the partnership. The benefit of **limited liability** is one of the most significant reasons limited liability companies and corporations are so popular.

Continuity

Unlike partnerships or proprietorships, which terminate with the departure of their owners, a corporation's life continues when a shareholder dies or sells his or her stock. Because of **continuity** of existence, many corporations formed in the 1800s still thrive today.

Transferability of Ownership

The **transferability** of corporate ownership is easy. An investor simply buys or sells stock to acquire or give up an ownership interest in a corporation. Hundreds of millions of shares of stock are bought and sold on the major stock exchanges each day.

Transferring the ownership of proprietorships is much more difficult. To sell an ownership interest in a proprietorship, the proprietor must find someone willing to purchase the entire business. Because most proprietors also run their businesses, transferring ownership also requires transferring management responsibilities. Consider the difference in selling $1 million of ExxonMobil stock versus selling a locally owned gas station. The stock could be sold on the New York Stock Exchange within minutes. In contrast, it could take years to find a buyer who is financially capable of and interested in owning and operating a gas station.

Transferring ownership in partnerships can also be difficult. As with proprietorships, ownership transfers may require a new partner to make a significant investment and accept management responsibilities in the business. Further, a new partner must accept and be accepted by the other partners. Personality conflicts and differences in management style can cause problems in transferring ownership interests in partnerships.

Management Structure

Partnerships and proprietorships are usually managed by their owners. Corporations, in contrast, have three tiers of management authority. The *owners* (**stockholders**) represent the highest level of organizational authority. The stockholders *elect* a **board of directors** to oversee company operations. The directors then *hire* professional executives to manage the company on a daily basis. Because large corporations can offer high salaries and challenging career opportunities, they can often attract superior managerial talent.

Ability to Raise Capital

Because corporations can have millions of owners (shareholders), they have the opportunity to raise huge amounts of capital. Few individuals have the financial means to build and operate a telecommunications network such as AT&T or a marketing distribution system

Jonathan Weiss/Alamy Stock Photo

such as Walmart. However, by pooling the resources of millions of owners through public stock and bond offerings, corporations generate the billions of dollars of capital needed for such massive investments. In contrast, the capital resources of proprietorships and partnerships are limited to a relatively small number of private owners. Although proprietorships and partnerships can also obtain resources by borrowing, the amount creditors are willing to lend them is usually limited by the size of the owners' net worth.

Appearance of Capital Structure in Financial Statements

The ownership interest (equity) in a business is composed of two elements: (1) owner/investor contributions and (2) retained earnings. The way these two elements are reported in the financial statements differs for each type of business structure (proprietorship, partnership, or corporation).

Presentation of Equity in Proprietorships

Owner contributions and retained earnings are combined in a single Capital account on the balance sheets of proprietorships. To illustrate, assume that Worthington Sole Proprietorship was started on January 1, Year 1, when it acquired a $5,000 capital contribution from its owner, Phil Worthington. During the first year of operation, the company generated $4,000 of cash revenues, incurred $2,500 of cash expenses, and distributed $1,000 cash to the owner.

EXHIBIT 11.1

WORTHINGTON SOLE PROPRIETORSHIP
Financial Statements
As of December 31, Year 1

Income Statement		Capital Statement		Balance Sheet	
Revenue	$4,000	Beginning capital balance	$ 0	Assets	
Expenses	2,500	Plus: Investment by owner	5,000	Cash	$5,500
Net income	$1,500	Plus: Net income	1,500	Owners' equity	
		Less: Withdrawal by owner	(1,000)	Worthington, capital	$5,500
		Ending capital balance	$5,500		

Exhibit 11.1 displays Year 1 financial statements for Worthington's company. Note on the *capital statement* that distributions are called **withdrawals.** Verify that the $5,500 balance in the Capital account on the balance sheet includes the $5,000 owner contribution and the retained earnings of $500 ($1,500 net income − $1,000 withdrawal).

CHECK YOURSELF 11.1

Weiss Company was started on January 1, Year 1, when it acquired $50,000 cash from its owner(s). During Year 1, the company earned $72,000 of net income. Explain how the equity section of Weiss's December 31, Year 1, balance sheet would differ if the company were a proprietorship versus a corporation.

Answer *Proprietorship* records combine capital acquisitions from the owner and earnings from operating the business in a single capital account. In contrast, *corporation* records separate capital acquisitions from the owners and earnings from operating the business. If Weiss were a proprietorship, the equity section of the year-end balance sheet would report a single capital component of $122,000. If Weiss were a corporation, the equity section would report two separate equity components, most likely common stock of $50,000 and retained earnings of $72,000.

Presentation of Equity in Partnerships

The financial statement format for reporting partnership equity is similar to that used for proprietorships. Contributed capital and retained earnings are combined. However, a separate capital account is maintained for each partner in the business to reflect each partner's ownership interest.

To illustrate, assume that Sara Slater and Jill Johnson formed a partnership on January 1, Year 2. The partnership acquired $2,000 of capital from Slater and $4,000 from Johnson. The partnership agreement called for each partner to receive an annual distribution equal to 10 percent of her capital contribution. Any further earnings were to be retained in the business and divided equally between the partners. During Year 2, the company earned $5,000 of cash revenue and incurred $3,000 of cash expenses, for net income of $2,000 ($5,000 − $3,000). As specified by the partnership agreement, Slater received a $200 ($2,000 × 0.10) cash withdrawal and Johnson received $400 ($4,000 × 0.10). The remaining $1,400 ($2,000 − $200 − $400) of income was retained in the business and divided equally, adding $700 to each partner's capital account.

Exhibit 11.2 displays financial statements for the Slater and Johnson partnership. Again, note that distributions are called *withdrawals.* Also find on the balance sheet a *separate capital*

EXHIBIT 11.2

SLATER AND JOHNSON PARTNERSHIP
Financial Statements
As of December 31, Year 2

Income Statement		Capital Statement		Balance Sheet	
Revenue	$5,000	Beginning capital balance	$ 0	Assets	
Expenses	3,000	Plus: Investment by owner	6,000	Cash	$7,400
Net income	$2,000	Plus: Net income	2,000	Owners' equity	
		Less: Withdrawal by owner	(600)	Slater, capital	$2,700
		Ending capital balance	$7,400	Johnson, capital	4,700
				Total capital	$7,400

account for each partner. Each capital account includes the amount of the partner's contributed capital plus her proportionate share of the earnings.

Presentation of Stockholders' Equity in Corporations

Corporations have more complex capital structures than proprietorships and partnerships. Explanations of some of the more common features of corporate capital structures and transactions follow.

ACCOUNTING FOR CAPITAL STOCK

LO 11-2

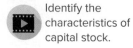

Identify the characteristics of capital stock.

Stock issued by corporations may have a variety of different characteristics. For example, a company may issue different classes of stock that grant owners different rights and privileges. Also, the number of shares a corporation can legally issue may differ from the number it actually has issued. Further, a corporation can even buy back its own stock. Finally, a corporation may assign different values to the stock it issues. Accounting for corporate equity transactions is discussed in the next section of the text.

Par Value

Many states require assigning a **par value** to stock. Historically, par value represented the maximum liability of the investors. Par value multiplied by the number of shares of stock issued represents the minimum amount of assets that must be retained in the company as protection for creditors. This amount is known as **legal capital**. To ensure that the amount of legal capital is maintained in a corporation, many states require that purchasers pay at least the par value for a share of stock initially purchased from a corporation. To minimize the amount of assets that owners must maintain in the business, many corporations issue stock with very low par values, often $1 or less. Therefore, *legal capital* as defined by par value has come to have very little relevance to investors or creditors. As a result, many states allow corporations to issue no-par stock.

Stated Value

No-par stock may have a stated value. Like par value, **stated value** is an arbitrary amount assigned by the board of directors to the stock. It also has little relevance to investors and creditors. Stock with a par value and stock with a stated value are accounted for exactly the same way. When stock has no par or stated value, accounting for it is slightly different. These accounting differences are illustrated later in this chapter.

Stock: Authorized, Issued, and Outstanding

As part of the regulatory function, states approve the maximum number of shares of stock that corporations are legally permitted to issue. This maximum number is called **authorized stock.** Authorized stock that has been sold to the public is called **issued stock.** When a corporation buys back some of its issued stock from the public, the repurchased stock is called **treasury stock.** Treasury stock is still considered to be issued stock, but it is no longer outstanding. **Outstanding stock** (total issued stock minus treasury stock) is stock owned by investors outside the corporation. For example, assume that Alpha, Incorporated is authorized to issue 150,000 shares of stock, issues 100,000 shares to investors, and then buys back 20,000 shares of treasury stock. In this scenario, there are 150,000 shares authorized, 100,000 shares issued, and 80,000 shares outstanding.

Other Valuation Terminology

The price an investor must pay to purchase a share of stock is the **market value.** The sales price of a share of stock may be more or less than the par value. Another term analysts frequently associate with stock is *book value.* **Book value per share** is calculated by dividing total stockholders' equity (assets − liabilities) by the number of shares of stock owned by investors. Book value per share differs from market value per share because equity is measured in historical dollars and market value reflects investors' estimates of a company's current value.

To illustrate, return to the scenario where Alpha, Incorporated has 150,000 shares authorized, 100,000 shares issued, and 80,000 shares outstanding. At this point, assume that Alpha has $520,000 of assets, $120,000 in liabilities, $240,000 of common stock, and $160,000 of retained earnings. Further, assume that the market value of Alpha's common stock is $6 per share. Based on this scenario, Alpha's book value per share is $5 [($520,000 assets − $120,000 liabilities) / 80,000 shares outstanding]. The most likely explanation for the market value ($6 per share) being higher than the book value ($5 per share) is that book value is a measure of historical cost, while market value is a measure of current values.

COMMON VERSUS PREFERRED STOCK

The corporate charter defines the number of shares of stock authorized, the par value or stated value (if any), and the classes of stock that a corporation can issue. Most stock issued is classified as either *common or preferred.*

LO 11-3

Differentiate between common and preferred stock.

Common Stock

All corporations issue **common stock.** Common stockholders bear the highest risk of losing their investment if a company is forced to liquidate. On the other hand, they reap the greatest rewards when a corporation prospers. Common stockholders generally enjoy several rights, including: (1) the right to buy and sell stock, (2) the right to share in the distribution of profits, (3) the right to share in the distribution of corporate assets in the case of liquidation, (4) the right to vote on significant matters that affect the corporate charter, and (5) the right to participate in the election of directors.

Preferred Stock

Many corporations issue **preferred stock** in addition to common stock. Holders of preferred stock receive certain privileges relative to holders of common stock. In exchange for special privileges in some areas, preferred stockholders give up rights in other areas. Preferred stockholders usually have no voting rights and the amount of their dividends is usually limited. Preferences granted to preferred stockholders include the following:

1. *Preference as to assets.* Preferred stock often has a liquidation value. In case of bankruptcy, preferred stockholders must be paid the liquidation value before any assets are distributed to common stockholders. However, preferred stockholder claims still fall behind creditor claims.

2. *Preference as to dividends.* Preferred shareholders are frequently guaranteed the right to receive dividends before common stockholders. The amount of the preferred dividend is normally stated on the stock certificate. It may be stated as a dollar value (say, $5) per share or as a percentage of the par value. Most preferred stock has **cumulative dividends,** meaning that if a corporation is unable to pay the preferred dividend in any year, the dividend is not lost but begins to accumulate. Cumulative dividends that have not been paid are called **dividends in arrears.** When a company pays dividends, any preferred stock arrearages must be paid before any other dividends are paid. Noncumulative preferred stock is not often issued because preferred stock is much less attractive if missed dividends do not accumulate.

To illustrate the effects of preferred dividends, consider Dillion, Incorporated, which has the following shares of stock outstanding:

> Preferred stock, 4%, $10 par, 10,000 shares
> Common stock, $10 par, 20,000 shares

Assume the preferred stock dividend has not been paid for two years. If Dillion pays $22,000 in dividends, how much will each class of stock receive? It depends on whether the preferred stock is cumulative.

Allocation of Distribution for Cumulative Preferred Stock		
	To Preferred	**To Common**
Dividends in arrears	$ 8,000	$ 0
Current year's dividends	4,000	10,000
Total distribution	$12,000	$10,000
Allocation of Distribution for Noncumulative Preferred Stock		
	To Preferred	**To Common**
Dividends in arrears	$ 0	$ 0
Current year's dividends	4,000	18,000
Total distribution	$ 4,000	$18,000

The total annual dividend on the preferred stock is $4,000 (0.04 × $10 par × 10,000 shares). If the preferred stock is cumulative, the $8,000 in arrears must be paid first. Then, $4,000 for the current year's dividend is paid next. The remaining $10,000 goes to common stockholders. If the preferred stock is noncumulative, the $8,000 of dividends from past periods is ignored. This year's $4,000 preferred dividend is paid first, with the remaining $18,000 going to common.

Other features of preferred stock may include the right to participate in distributions beyond the established amount of the preferred dividend, the right to convert preferred stock to common stock or to bonds, and the potential for having the preferred stock called (repurchased) by the corporation. Detailed discussion of these topics is left to more advanced courses. Exhibit 11.3 indicates that roughly 20 percent of U.S. companies have preferred shares outstanding.

EXHIBIT 11.3

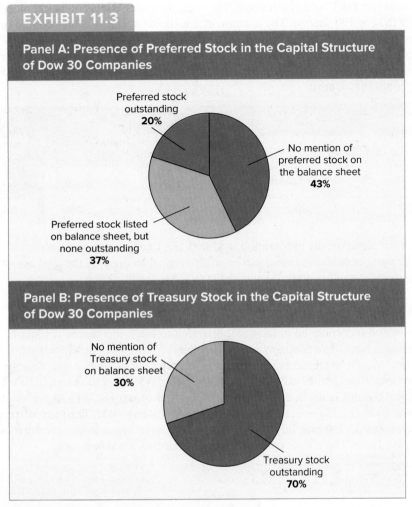

Panel A: Presence of Preferred Stock in the Capital Structure of Dow 30 Companies

Preferred stock outstanding **20%**

No mention of preferred stock on the balance sheet **43%**

Preferred stock listed on balance sheet, but none outstanding **37%**

Panel B: Presence of Treasury Stock in the Capital Structure of Dow 30 Companies

No mention of Treasury stock on balance sheet **30%**

Treasury stock outstanding **70%**

Source: Dow Jones Industrial Average

Other Classes of Stock

There can be different classes of common or preferred stock. For example, a company could issue class A common stock that provides its stockholders with rights to vote in the elections of the members of the board of directors. The same company could also issue class B common stock that does not provide voting rights. In conclusion, a company can have many classes of stock, with each type offering the shareholders a different set of rights and privileges.

ACCOUNTING FOR STOCK TRANSACTIONS ON THE DAY OF ISSUE

Issuing stock with a par or stated value is accounted for differently from issuing no-par stock. For stock with either a par or stated value, the total amount acquired from the owners is divided between two separate equity accounts. The amount of the par or stated value is recorded in the stock account. Any amount received above the par or stated value is recorded in an account called **Paid-in Capital in Excess of Par** (or **Stated**) **Value.**

LO 11-4

Show how issuing different classes of stock affects financial statements.

Issuing Par Value Stock

To illustrate the issue of common stock with a par value, assume that Nelson Incorporated is authorized to issue 250 shares of common stock. During Year 1, Nelson issued 100 shares of

$10 par common stock for $22 per share. The event increases assets and stockholders' equity by $2,200 ($22 × 100 shares). The increase in stockholders' equity is divided into two parts, $1,000 of par value ($10 per share × 100 shares) and $1,200 ($2,200 − $1,000) received in excess of par value. The income statement is not affected. The $2,200 cash inflow is reported in the financing activities section of the statement of cash flows. The effects on the financial statements are shown next:

Balance Sheet								Income Statement					Statement of Cash Flows
Assets	=	Liab.	+			Stk. Equity							
Cash	=			Com. Stk.	+	PIC in Excess		Rev.	−	Exp.	=	Net Inc.	
2,200	=	NA	+	1,000	+	1,200		NA	−	NA	=	NA	2,200 FA

The *legal capital* of the corporation is $1,000, the total par value of the issued common stock. The number of shares issued can be easily verified by dividing the total amount in the common stock account by the par value ($1,000 ÷ $10 = 100 shares).

Stock Classification

Assume Nelson Incorporated obtains authorization to issue 400 shares of Class B, $20 par value common stock. The company issues 150 shares of this stock at $25 per share. The impact on the financial statements is the same as in the previous transaction. Specifically, the event increases assets and stockholders' equity by $3,750 ($25 × 150 shares). The increase in stockholders' equity is divided into two parts, $3,000 of par value ($20 per share × 150 shares) and $750 ($3,750 − $3,000) received in excess of par value. The income statement is not affected. The $3,750 cash inflow is reported in the financing activities section of the statement of cash flows. The effects on the financial statements are shown next:

Balance Sheet								Income Statement					Statement of Cash Flows
Assets	=	Liab.	+			Stk. Equity							
Cash	=			Com. Stk.	+	PIC in Excess		Rev.	−	Exp.	=	Net Inc.	
3,750	=	NA	+	3,000	+	750		NA	−	NA	=	NA	3,750 FA

As the preceding event suggests, companies can issue numerous classes of common stock. The specific rights and privileges for each class are described in the individual stock certificates.

Stock Issued at Stated Value

Assume Nelson Incorporated is authorized to issue 300 shares of a third class of stock, 7 percent cumulative preferred stock with a stated value of $10 per share. Nelson issued 100 shares of the preferred stock at a price of $22 per share. The effect on the financial statements is identical to that described for the issue of the $10 par value common stock. The differences pertain to the rights and privileges of the investors rather than the financial statement impacts. While it is only the account names that change, the effects on the financial statements are shown next for your review:

Balance Sheet								Income Statement					Statement of Cash Flows
Assets	=	Liab.	+			Stk. Equity							
Cash	=			Pfd. Stk.	+	PIC in Excess		Rev.	−	Exp.	=	Net Inc.	
2,200	=	NA	+	1,000	+	1,200		NA	−	NA	=	NA	2,200 FA

Stock Issued with No Par Value

Assume that Nelson Incorporated is authorized to issue 150 shares of a fourth class of stock. This stock is no-par common stock. Nelson issues 100 shares of this no-par stock at $22 per share. The entire amount received ($22 × 100 = $2,200) is recorded in the stock account. The effects on the financial statements are shown next:

Balance Sheet						Income Statement						Statement of Cash Flows	
Assets	=	Liab.	+	Stk. Equity									
Cash	=			Com. Stk.	+	PIC in Excess	Rev.	−	Exp.	=	Net Inc.		
2,200	=	NA	+	2,200	+	NA	NA	−	NA	=	NA	2,200	FA

Financial Statement Presentation

Exhibit 11.4 displays Nelson Incorporated's balance sheet after the four stock issuances described earlier. The exhibit assumes that Nelson earned and retained $5,000 of income during Year 1. The stock accounts are presented first, followed by the paid-in capital in excess of par (or stated) value accounts. A wide variety of reporting formats are used in practice. For example, another popular format is to group accounts by stock class, with the paid-in capital in excess accounts listed with their associated stock accounts. Alternatively, many companies combine the different classes of stock into a single amount and provide the detailed information in notes to the financial statements.

EXHIBIT 11.4

NELSON INCORPORATED
Balance Sheet
As of December 31, Year 1

Assets	
Cash	$15,350
Stockholders' equity	
Preferred stock, $10 stated value, 7% cumulative, 300 shares authorized, 100 issued and outstanding	$ 1,000
Common stock, $10 par value, 250 shares authorized, 100 issued and outstanding	1,000
Common stock, class B, $20 par value, 400 shares authorized, 150 issued and outstanding	3,000
Common stock, no par, 150 shares authorized, 100 issued and outstanding	2,200
Paid-in capital in excess of stated value—Preferred	1,200
Paid-in capital in excess of par value—Common	1,200
Paid-in capital in excess of par value—Class B common	750
Total paid-in capital	10,350
Retained earnings	5,000
Total stockholders' equity	$15,350

TREASURY STOCK

LO 11-5

Show how treasury stock affects financial statements.

When a company buys its own stock, the stock purchased is called *treasury stock*. Why would a company buy its own stock? Common reasons include (1) to have stock available to give employees pursuant to stock option plans, (2) to accumulate stock in preparation for a merger or business combination, (3) to reduce the number of shares outstanding in order to increase earnings per share, (4) to keep the price of the stock high when it appears to be falling, and (5) to avoid a hostile takeover (removing shares from the open market reduces the opportunity for outsiders to obtain enough voting shares to gain control of the company).

Conceptually, purchasing treasury stock is the reverse of issuing stock. When a business issues stock, the assets and stockholders' equity of the business increase. When a business buys treasury stock, the assets and stockholders' equity of the business decrease. To illustrate, return to the Nelson Incorporated example. Assume that in Year 2 Nelson paid $20 per share to buy back 50 shares of the $10 par value common stock that it originally issued at $22 per share. The purchase of treasury stock is an asset use transaction. Assets and stockholders' equity decrease by the cost of the purchase ($20 × 50 shares = $1,000). The income statement is not affected. The cash outflow is reported in the financing activities section of the statement of cash flows. The effects on the financial statements are shown next:

Balance Sheet							Income Statement					Statement of Cash Flows
Assets	=	Liab.	+	Stk. Equity								
Cash	=			Other Equity Accts.	−	Treasury Stk.	Rev.	−	Exp.	=	Net Inc.	
(1,000)	=	NA	+	NA	−	1,000	NA	−	NA	=	NA	(1,000) FA

The Treasury Stock account is a contra equity account. It is deducted from the other equity accounts in determining total stockholders' equity. In this example, the Treasury Stock account is recorded at the full amount paid ($1,000). The original issue price and the par value of the stock are not considered. Recording the full amount paid in the Treasury Stock account is called the **cost method of accounting for treasury stock** transactions. Although other methods could be used, the cost method is the most common.

Assume Nelson reissues 30 shares of treasury stock at a price of $25 per share. As with any other stock issue, the sale of treasury stock is an asset source transaction. In this case, assets and stockholders' equity increase by $750 ($25 × 30 shares). The income statement is not affected. The cash inflow is reported in the financing activities section of the statement of cash flows. The effects on the financial statements are shown next:

Balance Sheet									Income Statement					Statement of Cash Flows
Assets	=	Liab.	+	Stk. Equity										
Cash	=			Other Equity Accts.	−	Treasury Stk.	+	PIC from Treasury Stk.	Rev.	−	Exp.	=	Net Inc.	
750	=	NA	+	NA	−	(600)	+	150	NA	−	NA	=	NA	750 FA

The decrease in the Treasury Stock account increases stockholders' equity. The $150 difference between the cost of the treasury stock ($20 per share × 30 shares = $600) and the sales price ($750) is *not* reported as a gain. The sale of treasury stock is a capital acquisition, not a revenue transaction. The $150 is additional paid-in capital. *Corporations do not recognize gains or losses on the sale of treasury stock.*

After selling 30 shares of treasury stock, 20 shares remain in Nelson's possession. These shares cost $20 each, so the balance in the Treasury Stock account is now $400 ($20 × 20 shares). Treasury stock is reported on the balance sheet directly below retained earnings. Although this placement suggests that treasury stock reduces retained earnings, the reduction actually applies to the entire stockholders' equity section. In the following section, we continue our discussion of Nelson Incorporated and show the presentation of treasury stock in the balance sheet. (See Exhibit 11.5.)

REALITY BYTES

HOW MUCH TREASURY STOCK CAN A COMPANY PURCHASE?

A common practice in recent years has been for companies to purchase treasury stock frequently. Whereas in past years companies wishing to distribute more of their equity back to shareholders might have increased dividends, today they are more likely to use stock buybacks. Some companies seem to take the practice to extremes. Consider the excerpt that follows, taken from the shareholders' equity section of **McDonald's Corporation**'s recent balance sheets.

First, notice that the company has a balance in its Treasury Stock account that is much larger than the balance in its Common Stock account. How can this be? Remember, when stock is issued to shareholders it is recorded in Common Stock at its issuance price, but it is recorded in Treasury Stock at the price the company paid to buy it back. The stock prices of successful companies rise over time.

Second, notice that McDonald's has purchased so much treasury stock that its total shareholders' equity is negative. This is unusual. When a company has negative shareholders' equity, it is usually because of a negative balance in Retained Earnings, but McDonald's had $48.3 billion of retained earnings as of December 31, 2017. The fact that the company had negative shareholders' equity means that, at least on paper, its liabilities were more than its assets. While this can present a problem for a company that is struggling, McDonald's reported approximately $9.6 billion of earnings before interest and taxes (EBIT) and $5.6 billion of cash flow from operating activities in 2017, so it was able to meet its debt obligations with no difficulty.

Aaron Roeth/Aaron Roeth Photography

McDonald's Corporation Partial Balance Sheets For the years ended (in millions)		
	December 31, 2017	December 31, 2016
Shareholders' deficit		
Class A common stock	$ 16.6	$ 16.6
Additional paid-in capital	7,072.4	6,757.9
Retained earnings	48,325.8	46,222.7
Accumulated other comprehensive loss	(2,178.4)	(3,092.9)
Common stock held in treasury	(56,504.4)	(52,108.6)
Total shareholders' equity	(3,268.0)	(2,204.3)
Total liabilities and stockholders' equity	$33,803.7	$31,023.9

CHECK YOURSELF 11.2

On January 1, Year 1, Janell Company's Common Stock account balance was $20,000. On April 1, Year 1, Janell paid $12,000 cash to purchase some of its own stock. Janell resold this stock on October 1, Year 1, for $14,500. What is the effect on the company's cash and stockholders' equity from both the April 1 purchase and the October 1 resale of the stock?

Answer The April 1 purchase would reduce both cash and stockholders' equity by $12,000. The treasury stock transaction represents a return of invested capital to those owners who sold stock back to the company.

The sale of the treasury stock on October 1 would increase both cash and stockholders' equity by $14,500. The difference between the sales price of the treasury stock and its cost ($14,500 − $12,000) represents additional paid-in capital from treasury stock transactions. The stockholders' equity section of the balance sheet would include Common Stock, $20,000, and Additional Paid-in Capital from Treasury Stock Transactions, $2,500.

CASH DIVIDENDS

LO 11-6

Show how declaring and paying cash dividends affect financial statements.

Cash dividends are affected by three significant dates: *the declaration date, the date of record, and the payment date.* Assume that on October 15, Year 2, the board of Nelson Incorporated declared the cash dividend on the 100 outstanding shares of its $10 stated value preferred stock. The dividend will be paid to stockholders of record as of November 15, Year 2. The cash payment will be made on December 15, Year 2.

Declaration Date

Although corporations are not required to declare dividends, they are legally obligated to pay dividends once they have been declared. They must recognize a liability on the **declaration date** (in this case, October 15, Year 2). The increase in liabilities is accompanied by a decrease in retained earnings. The income statement and statement of cash flows are not affected. The effects of *declaring* the $70 (0.07 × $10 × 100 shares) dividend on the financial statements are shown next:

Balance Sheet								Income Statement					Statement of Cash Flows
Assets	=	Liab.	+		Stk. Equity								
Cash	=	Div. Pay.	+	Com. Stk.	+	Ret. Earn.		Rev.	−	Exp.	=	Net Inc.	
NA	=	70	+	NA	+	(70)		NA	−	NA	=	NA	NA

Date of Record

Cash dividends are paid to investors who owned the preferred stock on the **date of record** (in this case, November 15, Year 2). Any stock sold after the date of record but before the payment date (in this case, December 15, Year 2) is traded **ex-dividend,** meaning the buyer will not receive the upcoming dividend. The date of record is merely a cutoff date. It does not affect the financial statements.

Payment Date

Nelson Incorporated actually paid the cash dividend on the **payment date.** This event has the same effect as paying any other liability. Assets (cash) and liabilities (dividends payable) both decrease. The income statement is not affected. The cash outflow is reported in the financing activities section of the statement of cash flows. The effects on the financial statements are shown next:

REALITY BYTES

As you have learned, dividends, unlike interest on bonds, do not have to be paid. In fact, a company's board of directors must vote to pay dividends before they can be paid. Even so, once a company establishes a practice of paying a dividend of a given amount each period, usually quarterly, the company is reluctant to not pay the dividend. The amount of dividends that companies pay, relative to their earnings, varies widely.

Large, well-established companies usually do pay dividends, while young, growing companies often do not. Consider the 30 companies that make up the Dow Jones Industrial Average. In 2017, all of these companies paid dividends. VISA paid out the lowest percentage of its earnings in dividends (18.6 percent). At the other extreme was Chevron, which paid dividends of $0.84

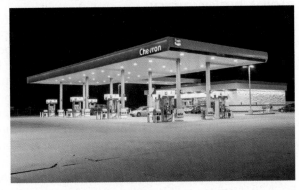

Trong Nguyen/Shutterstock

per share even though it reported a net loss of $0.72 per share. The average percentage of earnings paid out as dividends for all 30 companies in the Dow was about 58 percent in 2017, but seven of the companies paid out more in dividends than they earned in profit.

For comparison, consider two large, relatively young, technology companies: Alphabet, Inc., the parent company of Google, and Facebook. Although both of these companies have had large, positive earnings in recent years (Google alone had $12.7 billion in earnings in 2017), neither has ever paid a dividend to its common shareholders. They are using their cash to grow their businesses, often by purchasing other companies.

Balance Sheet							Income Statement					Statement of Cash Flows
Assets	=	Liab.	+		Stk. Equity							
Cash	=	Div. Pay.	+	Com. Stk.	+	Ret. Earn.	Rev.	−	Exp.	=	Net Inc.	
(70)	=	(70)	+	NA	+	NA	NA	−	NA	=	NA	(70) FA

STOCK DIVIDENDS AND SPLITS

Stock Dividends

Dividends are not always paid in cash. Companies sometimes choose to issue **stock dividends**, wherein they distribute additional shares of stock to the stockholders. To illustrate, assume that Nelson Incorporated decided to issue a 10 percent stock dividend on its class B, $20 par value common stock. Because dividends apply to outstanding shares only, Nelson will issue 15 (150 outstanding shares × 0.10) additional shares of class B stock.

Assume the new shares are distributed when the market value of the stock is $30 per share. As a result of the stock dividend, Nelson will transfer $450 ($30 × 15 new shares) from retained earnings to paid-in capital.[1] The stock dividend is an equity exchange transaction. The income statement and statement of cash flows are not affected. The effects on the financial statements are shown next:

LO 11-7

Show how stock dividends and stock splits affect financial statements.

Balance Sheet									Income Statement					Statement of Cash Flows
Assets	=	Liab.	+			Stk. Equity								
				Com. Stk.	+	PIC in Excess	+	Ret. Earn.	Rev.	−	Exp.	=	Net Inc.	
NA	=	NA	+	300	+	150	+	(450)	NA	−	NA	=	NA	NA

[1]The accounting here applies to small stock dividends. Accounting for large stock dividends is explained in a more advanced course.

FOCUS ON INTERNATIONAL ISSUES

PICKY, PICKY, PICKY . . .

Considering the almost countless number of differences that could exist between U.S. GAAP and IFRS, it is not surprising that some of those that do exist relate to very specific issues. Consider the case of the timing of stock splits.

Assume a company that ends its fiscal year on December 31, 2020, declares a 2-for-1 stock split on January 15, 2021, before it has issued its 2020 annual report. Should the company apply the effects of the stock split retroactively to its 2020 financial statements or begin showing the effects of the split on its 2021 statements? Under U.S. GAAP, the split must be applied retroactively to the 2020 statements because they had not been issued at the time of the split. Under IFRS, the 2020 statements would not show the effects of the split, but the 2021 statements would. By the way, an event that occurs between a company's fiscal year-end and the date its annual report is released is called a *subsequent event* by accountants.

Obviously, no one can know every rule under GAAP, much less all of the differences between GAAP and IFRS. This is why it is important to learn how to find answers to specific accounting questions, as well as to develop an understanding of the basic accounting rules. Most important, if you are not sure you know the answer, do not assume you do.

Stock dividends have no effect on assets. They merely increase the number of shares of stock outstanding. Because a greater number of shares represents the same ownership interest in the same amount of assets, the market value per share of a company's stock normally declines when a stock dividend is distributed. A lower market price makes the stock more affordable and may increase demand for the stock, which benefits both the company and its stockholders.

Stock Splits

A corporation may also reduce the market price of its stock through a **stock split.** A stock split replaces existing shares with a greater number of new shares. Any par or stated value of the stock is proportionately reduced to reflect the new number of shares outstanding. For example, assume Nelson Incorporated declared a 2-for-1 stock split on the 165 outstanding shares (150 originally issued + 15 shares distributed in a stock dividend) of its $20 par value, class B common stock. Nelson notes in the accounting records that the 165 old $20 par shares are replaced with 330 new $10 par shares. Investors who owned the 165 shares of old common stock would now own 330 shares of the new common stock.

Stock splits have no effect on the dollar amounts of assets, liabilities, and stockholders' equity. They affect only the number of shares of stock outstanding and the par value per share. In Nelson's case, the ownership interest that was previously represented by 165 shares of stock is now represented by 330 shares. Because twice as many shares now represent the same ownership interest, the market value per share should be one-half as much as it was prior to the split. However, as with a stock dividend, the lower market price will probably stimulate demand for the stock. As a result, doubling the number of shares will likely reduce the market price to slightly more than one-half of the pre-split value. For example, if the stock were selling for $30 per share before the 2-for-1 split, it might sell for $15.50 after the split.

APPROPRIATION OF RETAINED EARNINGS

LO 11-8

Show how the appropriation of retained earnings affects financial statements.

The board of directors may restrict the amount of retained earnings available to distribute as dividends. The restriction may be required by credit agreements, or it may be discretionary. A retained earnings restriction, often called an *appropriation*, is an equity exchange event. It transfers a portion of existing retained earnings to **appropriated retained earnings.** Total retained earnings remains unchanged. To illustrate, assume that Nelson Incorporated appropriates $1,000 of retained earnings for future expansion. The income statement and the statement of cash flows are not affected. The effects on the financial statements are shown next:

Balance Sheet								Income Statement			Statement of Cash Flows
Assets	=	Liab.	+	Stk. Equity				Rev.	−	Exp.	=	Net Inc.	
				Com. Stk.	+	Ret. Earn.	+	App. Ret. Earn.					
NA	=	NA	+	NA	+	(1,000)	+	1,000	NA	−	NA	=	NA	FA

Financial Statement Presentation

The Year 1 and Year 2 events for Nelson Incorporated are summarized as follows. Events 1 through 8 are cash transactions. The results of the Year 1 transactions (nos. 1–5) were shown in Exhibit 11.4. The results of the Year 2 transactions (nos. 6–11) are shown in Exhibit 11.5.

1. Issued 100 shares of $10 par value common stock at a market price of $22 per share.
2. Issued 150 shares of class B, $20 par value common stock at a market price of $25 per share.
3. Issued 100 shares of $10 stated value, 7 percent cumulative preferred stock at a market price of $22 per share.
4. Issued 100 shares of no-par common stock at a market price of $22 per share.
5. Earned and retained $5,000 cash from operations.
6. Purchased 50 shares of $10 par value common stock as treasury stock at a market price of $20 per share.
7. Sold 30 shares of treasury stock at a market price of $25 per share.

EXHIBIT 11.5

NELSON INCORPORATED
Balance Sheet
As of December 31, Year 2

Assets		
Cash		$21,030
Stockholders' equity		
Preferred stock, $10 stated value, 7% cumulative, 300 shares authorized, 100 issued and outstanding	$1,000	
Common stock, $10 par value, 250 shares authorized, 100 issued, and 80 outstanding	1,000	
Common stock, class B, $10 par, 800 shares authorized, 330 issued and outstanding	3,300	
Common stock, no par, 150 shares authorized, 100 issued and outstanding	2,200	
Paid-in capital in excess of stated value—Preferred	1,200	
Paid-in capital in excess of par value—Common	1,200	
Paid-in capital in excess of par value—Class B common	900	
Paid-in capital in excess of cost of treasury stock	150	
Total paid-in capital		$10,950
Retained Earnings		
Appropriated	1,000	
Unappropriated	9,480	
Total retained earnings		10,480
Less: Treasury stock, 20 shares @ $20 per share		(400)
Total stockholders' equity		$21,030

8. Declared and paid a $70 cash dividend on the preferred stock.

9. Issued a 10 percent stock dividend on the 150 shares of outstanding class B, $20 par value common stock (15 additional shares). The additional shares were issued when the market price of the stock was $30 per share. There are 165 (150 + 15) class B common shares outstanding after the stock dividend.

10. Issued a 2-for-1 stock split on the 165 shares of class B, $20 par value common stock. After this transaction, there are 330 shares outstanding of the class B common stock with a $10 par value.

11. Appropriated $1,000 of retained earnings.

The illustration assumes that Nelson earned net income of $6,000 in Year 2. The ending retained earnings balance is determined as follows: Beginning balance $5,000 + $6,000 Net income − $70 Cash dividend − $450 Stock dividend = $10,480.

The Financial Analyst

STOCK INVESTMENT DECISIONS

LO 11-9

Show how accounting information is used to make stock investment decisions.

Stockholders may benefit in two ways when a company generates earnings. The company may distribute the earnings directly to the stockholders in the form of dividends. Alternatively, the company may retain some or all of the earnings to finance growth and increase its potential for future earnings. If the company retains earnings, the market value of its stock should increase to reflect its greater earnings prospects. How can analysts use financial reporting to help assess the potential for dividend payments or growth in market value?

Receiving Dividends

Is a company likely to pay dividends in the future? The financial statements can help answer this question. They show if dividends were paid in the past. Companies with a history of paying dividends usually continue to pay dividends. Also, to pay dividends in the future, a company must have sufficient cash and retained earnings. These amounts are reported on the balance sheet and the statement of cash flows.

Increasing the Price of Stock

Is the market value (price) of a company's stock likely to increase? Increases in a company's stock price occur when investors believe the company's earnings will grow. Financial statements provide information that is useful in predicting the prospects for earnings growth. Here also, a company's earnings history is an indicator of its growth potential. However, because published financial statements report historical information, investors must recognize their limitations. Investors want to know about the future. Stock prices are therefore influenced more by forecasts than by history.

For example:

Helen89/Shutterstock

■ On December 14, 2018, Costco Wholesale Corporation announced that revenues for the quarter ended November 25, 2018, were 10.2 percent higher than for the same quarter of the previous year, and its earnings were up 19.9 percent. In reaction to this seemingly good news, the price of its stock *fell* by 4.9 percent. Why did the market respond in this way? Even though the quarterly earnings per share (EPS) of $1.61 were higher than last year, analysts had expected Costco's EPS to be $1.62, and they were concerned that increased competition would reduce the rate of Costco's future growth.

■ On November 27, 2018, salesforce.com, Inc. announced that EPS for the quarter ended October 31, 2018 were 65 percent lower than for the previous quarter, and 4.3 percent lower than for the same quarter of 2017. The market's reaction to this seemingly negative news was to *increase* the price of the company's stock by 7.4 percent. The market reacted this way because even though earnings were down significantly, total revenues increased by around 26 from the prior year, and 3.4 percent from the previous quarter.

In each case, investors reacted to the potential for earnings growth rather than the historical earnings reports. Because investors find forecasted statements more relevant to decision making than historical financial statements, most companies provide forecasts in addition to historical financial statements.

The value of a company's stock is also influenced by nonfinancial information that financial statements cannot provide. For example, suppose ExxonMobil announced in the middle of its fiscal year that it had just discovered substantial oil reserves on property to which it held drilling rights. Consider the following questions:

■ What would happen to the price of ExxonMobil's stock on the day of the announcement?

■ What would happen to ExxonMobil's financial statements on that day?

The price of ExxonMobil's stock would almost certainly increase as soon as the discovery was made public. However, nothing would happen to its financial statements on that day. There would probably be very little effect on its financial statements for that year. Only after the company began to develop the oil field and sell the oil would its financial statements reflect the discovery. Changes in financial statements tend to lag behind the announcements companies make regarding their earnings potential.

To illustrate the hypothetical Exxon story with a real-world example, consider the events at Apache Corporation in September 2016. Apache, like Exxon, is in the gas and oil business, but it is less well known. On September 7, 2016, Apache announced that it had confirmed the discovery of an oil and gas field on property it controlled in Texas. The estimated reserves of this field were three billion barrels of oil and 75 billion cubic feet of natural gas, which are worth billions of dollars. However, a comparison of Apache's quarterly balance sheet of June 30, 2016, issued just before the announcement, with its quarterly balance sheet dated September 30, 2016, issued just after the announcement, shows that reported gas and oil properties *fell* by $102 million. The stock market's reaction? From September 6, 2016 until September 8, 2016, the price of Apache's stock increased by 14.3 percent, while the stock market as a whole fell by 0.2 percent.

Price-Earnings Ratio

The **price-earnings ratio,** frequently called the *P/E ratio*, is the most commonly reported measure of a company's value. The P/E ratio is a company's market price per share of stock divided by the company's annual earnings per share (EPS).[2]

Assume Western Company recently reported annual earnings per share of $3. Western's stock is currently selling for $54 per share. Western's stock is therefore selling at a P/E ratio of 18 ($54 market price ÷ $3 EPS). What does a P/E ratio of 18 mean? If Western continued earning $3 per share of stock each year and paid out all its earnings to stockholders in the form of cash dividends, it would take 18 years for an investor to recover the price paid for the stock.

In contrast, assume the stock of Eastern Company, which reported EPS of $4, is currently selling for $48 per share. Eastern's P/E ratio is 12 ($48 market price ÷ $4 EPS). Investors who buy Eastern Company stock would get their money back six years faster (18 − 12) than investors who buy Western Company stock.

Why would investors buy a stock with a P/E ratio of 18 when they could buy one with a P/E ratio of 12? If investors expect Western Company's earnings to grow faster than Eastern Company's earnings, the higher P/E ratio makes sense. For example, suppose Western Company's earnings

---

[2]The amount of earnings per share is provided on the face of the income statement. In its simplest form, it is computed by dividing the company's net income (net earnings) by the number of shares of common stock outstanding.

were to double to $6 per share, while Eastern's remained at $4 per share. Western's P/E ratio would drop to 9 ($54 market price ÷ $6 EPS), while Eastern's remains at 12. This explains why high-growth companies sell for higher P/E multiples than do low-growth companies.

Caution must be used when interpreting P/E ratios. A company can have a high P/E ratio due to very low earnings, rather than high optimism by investors. For example, if a company's EPS is $0.02, and its stock is selling for $0.50, it will have a P/E ratio of 25, which is high. In this case, the high P/E ratio is the result of very low earnings, not optimism. If a company has a net loss, the P/E ratio is not computed.

Also, be aware that P/E ratios reported in the financial press are often based on *projected* EPS, rather than historical earnings. Sometimes P/E ratios based on historical earnings are referred to as being based on trailing earnings. In this course, compute the P/E ratio using the company's most recent, actual earnings amount rather than its forecasted earnings.

Exercising Control through Stock Ownership

The more influence an investor has over the operations of a company, the more the investor can benefit from owning stock in the company. For example, consider a power company that needs coal to produce electricity. The power company may purchase some common stock in a coal mining company to ensure a stable supply of coal. What percentage of the mining company's stock must the power company acquire to exercise significant influence over the mining company? The answer depends on how many investors own stock in the mining company and how the number of shares is distributed among the stockholders.

The greater its number of stockholders, the more *widely held* a company is. If stock ownership is concentrated in the hands of a few persons, a company is *closely held*. Widely held companies can generally be controlled with smaller percentages of ownership than closely held companies. Consider a company in which no existing investor owns more than 1 percent of the voting stock. A new investor who acquires a 5 percent interest would immediately become, by far, the largest shareholder and would likely be able to significantly influence board decisions. In contrast, consider a closely held company in which one current shareholder owns 51 percent of the company's stock. Even if another investor acquired the remaining 49 percent of the company, that investor could not control the company.

Financial statements contain some, but not all, of the information needed to help an investor determine ownership levels necessary to permit control. For example, the financial statements disclose the total number of shares of stock outstanding, but they normally contain little information about the number of shareholders and even less information about any relationships between shareholders. Relationships between shareholders are critically important because related shareholders, whether bound by family or business interests, might exercise control by voting as a bloc. For publicly traded companies, information about the number of shareholders and the identity of some large shareholders is disclosed in reports filed with the Securities and Exchange Commission.

BUSINESS LIQUIDATIONS

LO 11-10

Use financial statements to analyze the impact of business liquidations on creditors and owners.

Why is the income statement important? Because the income statement measures profitability, and profitability is vital to the survival of a business. Recall that revenues increase assets, and expenses decrease assets. If the decreases (expenses) exceed the increases (revenue), the asset base declines. If this condition persists, the company will ultimately run out of assets and will be forced to cease operations.

Business Liquidations Resulting from Net Losses

If a business ceases to operate, its remaining assets are sold and the sale proceeds are returned to the creditors and investors through a process called business **liquidation.** Creditors have priority in business liquidations. This means the business uses its assets first to settle the obligations to the creditors. Any assets remaining after the creditors have been paid are then distributed to the investors.

Investor Loss

To illustrate, consider the case of Cruz Company. At the end of Year 1, Cruz had $300 cash, $200 note payable, and $100 common stock. During Year 2, the company generated $280 of cash revenue and incurred $355 of cash expenses. Based on this information, Cruz's Year 2 income statement and its Year 1 and Year 2 balance sheets are shown in Exhibit 11.6. The $75 loss reduces the balances in the cash and retained earnings accounts. See the footnotes in the financial statements for details.

EXHIBIT 11.6

Income Statement for Cruz Company for the Period Ended December 31, Year 2

Revenue (asset increases)	$ 280
Less: Expenses (asset decreases)	(355)
Net Loss (change in assets)	$ (75)

Balance Sheets for Cruz Company as of December 31

	Year 1	Year 2
Assets		
Cash	$300	$ 225*
Total Assets	$300	$ 225
Liabilities		
Notes Payable	$200	$ 200
Stockholders' Equity		
Common Stock	100	100
Retained Earnings	0	(75)**
Total Liabilities and Stockholders' Equity	$300	$ 225

*$300 Beginning Balance + $280 Cash Revenue − $355 Cash Expenses = $225 Ending Balance
**$0 Beginning Balance − $75 Net Loss = ($75) Ending Balance

If Cruz is forced to liquidate at the end of Year 2, its total assets of $225 would be distributed first to creditors in the amount of $200, with the remaining amount going to the owners (investors), who would receive only $25 ($100 − $75). In this case, the investors alone suffer the entire loss.

Investor/Creditor Shared Loss

Now return to the original scenario, where on December 31, Year 1, Cruz had $300 cash, $200 note payable, and $100 common stock. However, in this scenario we will assume that during Year 2 the company generated $320 of cash revenue and incurred $440 of cash expenses. Based on the new earnings data, Cruz's income statement and its Year 1 and Year 2 balance sheets will appear as shown in Exhibit 11.7. The $120 loss reduces the balances in the cash and retained earnings accounts. See the footnotes in the financial statements for details.

Now if Cruz is forced to liquidate at the end of Year 2, the investors would receive zero and the creditors would receive only $180 even though the business owes them $200. Simply stated, Cruz cannot distribute assets it does not have. This case shows that creditors, as well as investors, are at risk of losing some or all of the resources they provide to businesses. However, creditors are at lesser risk because they are first in line to receive assets in case of liquidation.

EXHIBIT 11.7

Income Statement for Cruz Company for the Period Ended December 31, Year 2

Revenue (asset increases)	$ 320
Less: Expenses (asset decreases)	(440)
Net Loss (change in assets)	$ (120)

Balance Sheets for Cruz Company as of December 31

	Year 1	Year 2
Assets		
Cash	$ 300	$ 180*
Total Assets	$ 300	$ 180
Liabilities		
Notes Payable	$ 200	$ 200
Stockholders' Equity		
Common Stock	100	100
Retained Earnings	0	(120)**
Total Liabilities and Stockholders' Equity	$ 300	$ 180

*$300 Beginning Balance + $320 Cash Revenue − $440 Cash Expenses = $180 Ending Balance

**$0 Beginning Balance − $120 Net Loss = ($120) Ending Balance

Business Liquidations Resulting from the Mismanagement of Assets

It is interesting to note that even profitable companies can be forced to liquidate. To illustrate, assume Bandera Company's December 31, Year 1, balance sheet shows $800 cash, $300 notes payable, and $500 common stock. During Year 2, Bandera earns $300 of cash revenue and incurs $100 of cash expenses. Also, assume Bandera pays $950 to purchase land in Year 2. Based on this information alone, Bandera's Year 2 income statement and its Year 1 and Year 2 balance sheets will appear as shown in Exhibit 11.8.

EXHIBIT 11.8

Income Statement for Bandera Company for the Period Ended December 31, Year 2

Revenue (asset increases)	$ 300
Less: Expenses (asset decreases)	(100)
Net Income (change in assets)	$ 200

Balance Sheets for Bandera Company as of December 31

	Year 1	Year 2
Assets		
Cash	$800	$ 50*
Land	0	950
Total Assets	$800	$1,000
Liabilities		
Notes Payable	$300	$ 300
Stockholders' Equity		
Common Stock	500	500
Retained Earnings	0	200**
Total Liabilities and Stockholders' Equity	$800	$1,000

*$800 Beginning Bal. + $300 Cash Revenue − $100 Cash Expenses − $950 Purchase = $50 Ending Bal.

**$0 Beginning Balance + $200 Net Income = $200 Ending Balance

Assuming the land could not be sold immediately, Bandera has only $50 cash available to settle a $300 debt. If the liabilities are due at the end of Year 2 and the creditors demand payment, Bandera could be forced into bankruptcy. A company must properly manage its assets, as well as its income, in order to remain a going concern.

The **going concern** doctrine assumes that a business is able to continue its operations into the foreseeable future. Many procedures and practices used by accountants are based on a going concern assumption. If a company's going concern status becomes uncertain, accountants are required to notify creditors and investors.

Clearly, profitability is of critical importance to investors and creditors alike. They stand to lose all or a significant amount of their investment if a company is forced to liquidate. However, they are not the only entities at risk. Employees will lose jobs; suppliers will lose customers; governments will lose tax revenue; and customers will lose services. These and other stakeholders suffer when businesses fail. Because business survival depends on profitability, many business professionals consider the income statement to be the most important financial statement that companies issue.

A Look Back

Starting a business requires obtaining financing; it takes money to make money. Although some money may be borrowed, lenders are unlikely to make loans to businesses that lack some degree of owner financing. Equity financing is therefore critical to virtually all profit-oriented businesses. This chapter has examined some of the issues related to accounting for equity transactions.

The idea that a business must obtain financing from its owners was one of the first events presented in this textbook. This chapter discussed the advantages and disadvantages of organizing a business as a sole proprietorship versus a partnership versus a corporation. These advantages and disadvantages include the following:

- *Double taxation*—Income of corporations is subject to double taxation, but that of proprietorships and partnerships is not.
- *Regulation*—Corporations are subject to more regulation than are proprietorships and partnerships.
- *Limited liability*—An investor's personal assets are not at risk as a result of owning corporate securities. The investor's liability is limited to the amount of the investment. In general, proprietorships and partnerships do not offer limited liability. However, laws in some states permit the formation of limited liability companies, which operate like proprietorships and partnerships yet place some limits on the personal liability of their owners.
- *Continuity*—Proprietorships and partnerships dissolve when one of the owners leaves the business. Corporations are separate legal entities that continue to exist regardless of changes in ownership.
- *Transferability*—Ownership interests in corporations are easier to transfer than those of proprietorships or partnerships.
- *Management structure*—Corporations are more likely to have independent professional managers than are proprietorships or partnerships.
- *Ability to raise capital*—Because they can be owned by millions of investors, corporations have the opportunity to raise more capital than proprietorships or partnerships.

Corporations issue different classes of common stock and preferred stock as evidence of ownership interests. In general, *common stock* provides the widest range of privileges, including the right to vote and participate in earnings. *Preferred stockholders* usually give up the right to vote in exchange for preferences such as the right to receive dividends or assets upon liquidation before common stockholders. Stock may have a *par value* or *stated value*, which relates to legal requirements governing the amount of capital that must be maintained in the corporation. Corporations may also issue *no-par stock*, avoiding some of the legal requirements that pertain to par or stated value stock.

Stock that a company issues and then repurchases is called *treasury stock*. Purchasing treasury stock reduces total assets and stockholders' equity. Reselling treasury stock represents a capital acquisition. The difference between the reissue price and the cost of the treasury stock is recorded directly in the equity accounts. Treasury stock transactions do not result in gains or losses on the income statement.

Companies may issue *stock splits* or *stock dividends*. These transactions increase the number of shares of stock without changing the net assets of a company. The per share market value usually drops when a company issues stock splits or dividends.

Purchasing the stock of a company is frequently called an investment. Investing in a company's stock offers two primary benefits. First, an investor may share in a company's earnings via the receipt of dividends. Second, the market value of the investment may increase. Both of these benefits are dependent of the company's ability to produce earnings. If a company cannot produce earnings it will eventually be forced to cease operations and to liquidate its assets. Both investors and creditors may lose some or all of their invested capital when a business is forced to liquidate. Because business survival depends on profitability, many business professionals consider the income statement to be the most important financial statement that companies issue.

 # A Look Forward

Chapter 12 examines the statement of cash flows in more detail than past chapters have. It introduces a more practical way to prepare the statement than analyzing every single event affecting the Cash account, and it presents the more formal format for the statement of cash flows used by most real-world companies.

 Tableau Dashboard Activity is available in *Connect* for this chapter.

 ## SELF-STUDY REVIEW PROBLEM

 A step-by-step audio-narrated series of slides is available in *Connect*.

Edwards Inc. experienced the following events:

1. Issued common stock for cash.
2. Declared a cash dividend.
3. Issued noncumulative preferred stock for cash.
4. Appropriated retained earnings.
5. Distributed a stock dividend.
6. Paid cash to purchase treasury stock.
7. Distributed a 2-for-1 stock split.
8. Issued cumulative preferred stock for cash.
9. Paid a cash dividend that had previously been declared.
10. Sold treasury stock for cash at a higher amount than the cost of the treasury stock.

Required

Show the effect of each event on the elements of the financial statements using a horizontal statements model like the one shown next. Use + for increase, − for decrease, and NA for not affected. In the Statement of Cash Flows column, indicate whether the item is an operating activity (OA), investing activity (IA), or financing activity (FA). The first transaction is entered as an example.

Event	Assets	=	Liab.	+	Stk. Equity	Rev.	−	Exp.	=	Net Inc.	Cash Flow
1.	+		NA		+	NA		NA		NA	+ FA

Solution to Self-Study Review Problem

Event	Assets	= Liab.	+ Stk. Equity	Rev.	− Exp.	= Net Inc.	Cash Flow
1.	+	NA	+	NA	NA	NA	+ FA
2.	NA	+	−	NA	NA	NA	NA
3.	+	NA	+	NA	NA	NA	+ FA
4.	NA	NA	− +	NA	NA	NA	NA
5.	NA	NA	− +	NA	NA	NA	NA
6.	−	NA	−	NA	NA	NA	− FA
7.	NA	NA	NA	NA	NA	NA	NA
8.	+	NA	+	NA	NA	NA	+ FA
9.	−	−	NA	NA	NA	NA	− FA
10.	+	NA	+	NA	NA	NA	+ FA

KEY TERMS

Appropriated retained earnings 552
Articles of incorporation 538
Authorized stock 543
Board of directors 540
Book value per share 543
Closely held corporation 538
Common stock 543
Continuity 539
Corporation 538
Cost method of accounting for treasury stock 548
Cumulative dividends 544

Date of record 550
Declaration date 550
Dividends in arrears 544
Double taxation 539
Ex-dividend 550
Going concern assumption 559
Issued stock 543
Legal capital 542
Limited liability 539
Limited liability company (LLC) 539
Liquidation 556
Market value 543

Outstanding stock 543
Paid-in Capital in Excess of Par Value 545
Par value 542
Partnership 537
Partnership agreement 537
Payment date 550
Preferred stock 543
Price-earnings (P/E) ratio 550
Sarbanes–Oxley Act of 2002 539
Securities Act of 1933 538

Securities Exchange Act of 1934 538
Sole proprietorship 537
Stated value 542
Stock certificate 538
Stock dividend 551
Stock split 552
Stockholders 540
Transferability 540
Treasury stock 543
Withdrawals 541

QUESTIONS

1. What are the three major forms of business organizations? Describe each.

2. How are sole proprietorships formed?

3. Discuss the purpose of a partnership agreement. Is such an agreement necessary for partnership formation?

4. What is meant by the phrase *separate legal entity?* To which type of business organization does it apply?

5. What is the purpose of the articles of incorporation? What information do they provide?

6. What is the function of the stock certificate?

7. What prompted Congress to pass the Securities Act of 1933 and the Securities Exchange Act of 1934? What is the purpose of these laws?

8. What are the advantages and disadvantages of the corporate form of business organization?

9. What is a limited liability company? Discuss its advantages and disadvantages.

10. How does the term *double taxation* apply to corporations? Give an example of double taxation.

11. What is the difference between contributed capital and retained earnings for a corporation?

12. What are the similarities and differences in the equity structure of a sole proprietorship, a partnership, and a corporation?

13. Why is it easier for a corporation to raise large amounts of capital than it is for a partnership?

14. What is the meaning of each of the following terms with respect to the corporate form of organization?
    (a) Legal capital
    (b) Par value of stock
    (c) Stated value of stock
    (d) Market value of stock
    (e) Book value of stock
    (f) Authorized shares of stock
    (g) Issued stock
    (h) Outstanding stock
    (i) Treasury stock
    (j) Common stock
    (k) Preferred stock
    (l) Dividends

15. What is the difference between cumulative preferred stock and noncumulative preferred stock?

16. What is no-par stock? How is it recorded in the accounting records?

17. Assume that Best Co. has issued and outstanding 1,000 shares of $100 par value, 10 percent, cumulative preferred stock. What is the dividend per share? If the preferred dividend is two years in arrears, what total amount of dividends must be paid before the common shareholders can receive any dividends?

18. If Best Co. issued 10,000 shares of $20 par value common stock for $30 per share, what amount is recorded in the Common Stock account? What amount of cash is received?

19. What is the difference between par value stock and stated value stock?

20. Why might a company repurchase its own stock?

21. What effect does the purchase of treasury stock have on the stockholders' equity of a company?

22. Assume that Day Company repurchased 1,000 of its own shares for $30 per share and sold the shares two weeks later for $35 per share. What is the amount of gain on the sale? How is it reported on the balance sheet? What type of account is treasury stock?

23. What is the importance of the declaration date, record date, and payment date in conjunction with corporate dividends?

24. What is the difference between a stock dividend and a stock split?

25. Why would a company choose to distribute a stock dividend instead of a cash dividend?

26. What is the primary reason that a company would declare a stock split?

27. If Best Co. had 10,000 shares of $20 par value common stock outstanding and declared a 5-for-1 stock split, how many shares would then be outstanding

and what would be their par value after the split?

28. When a company appropriates retained earnings, does the company set aside cash for a specific use? Explain.

29. What is the largest source of financing for most U.S. businesses?

30. What is meant by *equity financing?* What is meant by *debt financing?*

31. What is a widely held corporation? What is a closely held corporation?

32. What are some reasons that a corporation might not pay dividends?

EXERCISES—SERIES A

 connect All applicable Exercises in Series A are available in *Connect.*

LO 11-1

Exercise 11-1A *Characteristics of sole proprietorships, partnerships, and corporations*

Required

The three primary types of business organization are proprietorship, partnership, and corporation. Each type has characteristics that distinguish it from the other types. In the left column of the following table, write the name of the type of business organization that is most likely to possess the characteristic described in the right column of the table. The first item is shown as an example.

Business Type	Characteristic
Proprietorship	Owned and operated by a single individual
	Subject to double taxation
	Has a retained earnings account on its balance sheet
	One owner may be held personally liable for actions taken on behalf of the business by different owner
	Profits benefit a single individual
	Frequently uses legal agreements to define profit distribution for two or more owners
	Most highly regulated form of business
	The business dissolves with the death of its only owner
	Offers the least capacity to raise capital
	Provides the best opportunity to benefit a few people
	Has only one capital account on its balance sheet
	Provides for easy transfer of ownership
	Offers the highest level of control over operating decisions
	Has multiple capital accounts but no retained earnings account on its balance sheet
	Provides the greatest capacity to raise capital
	Least regulated form of business
	Usually operated by a professional management team that is separated from the owners
	Has two or more owners who are not stockholders

Exercise 11-2A *Effect of accounting events on the financial statements of a sole* *proprietorship*

A sole proprietorship was started on January 1, Year 1, when it received $60,000 cash from Marlin Jones, the owner. During Year 1, the company earned $35,300 in cash revenues and paid $16,200 in cash expenses. Jones withdrew $1,000 cash from the business during Year 1.

Required

Prepare an income statement, capital statement (statement of changes in equity), balance sheet, and statement of cash flows for Jones's Year 1 fiscal year.

Exercise 11-3A *Effect of accounting events on the financial statements of a partnership*

Faith Busby and Jeremy Beatty started the B&B partnership on January 1, Year 1. The business acquired $44,000 cash from Busby and $66,000 from Beatty. During Year 1, the partnership earned $42,000 in cash revenues and paid $18,400 for cash expenses. Busby withdrew $2,000 cash from the business, and Beatty withdrew $2,500 cash. The net income was allocated to the capital accounts of the two partners in proportion to the amounts of their original investments in the business.

Required

Prepare an income statement, capital statement, balance sheet, and statement of cash flows for B&B's Year 1 fiscal year.

Exercise 11-4A *Capital stock authorized, issued, and outstanding*

Enscoe Enterprises, Inc. (EEI) has 225,000 shares authorized, 150,000 shares issued, and 30,000 shares of treasury stock. At this point, EEI has $780,000 of assets. $180,000 liabilities, $360,000 of common stock, and $240,000 of retained earnings. Further, assume that the market value of EEI's common stock is $7 per share.

Required

a. Determine the number of shares of stock that is outstanding.

b. Determine the book value per share.

c. Provide a rational explanation for the difference between the book value per share and the market value per share of EEI's common stock.

Exercise 11-5A *Characteristics of capital stock*

The stockholders' equity section of Creighton Company's balance sheet is shown as follows:

CREIGHTON COMPANY
As of December 31, Year 3

Stockholders' equity	
Preferred stock, $10 stated value, 7% cumulative,	
300 shares authorized, 50 issued and outstanding	$ 500
Common stock, $10 par value, 250 shares authorized,	
100 issued and outstanding	1,000
Common stock, class B, $20 par value, 400 shares authorized,	
150 issued and outstanding	3,000
Common stock, no par, 150 shares authorized,	
100 issued and outstanding	2,200
Paid-in capital in excess of stated value—preferred	600
Paid-in capital in excess of par value—common	1,200
Paid-in capital in excess of par value—class B common	750
Retained earnings	7,000
Total stockholders' equity	$16,250

Required

a. Assuming the preferred stock was originally issued for cash, determine the amount of cash collected when the stock was issued.

b. Based on the class B common stock alone, determine the amount of the company's legal capital.

c. Based on the class B common stock alone, determine the minimum amount of assets that must be retained in the company as protection for creditors.

d. Determine the number of shares of class B common stock that are available to sell as of December 31, Year 3.

e. Assuming Creighton purchases treasury stock consisting of 25 shares of its no par common stock on January 1, Year 4, determine the amount of the no-par common stock that would be outstanding immediately after the purchase.

f. Based on the stockholders' equity section shown earlier, can you determine the market value of the preferred stock? If yes, what is the market value of one share of this stock?

LO 11-3

Exercise 11-6A *Accounting for cumulative preferred dividends*

When Crossett Corporation was organized in January, Year 1, it immediately issued 4,000 shares of $50 par, 6 percent, cumulative preferred stock and 50,000 shares of $20 par common stock. Its earnings history is as follows: Year 1, net loss of $35,000; Year 2, net income of $125,000; Year 3, net income of $215,000. The corporation did not pay a dividend in Year 1.

Required

a. How much is the dividend arrearage as of January 1, Year 2?

b. Assume that the board of directors declares a $25,000 cash dividend at the end of Year 2 (remember that the Year 1 and Year 2 preferred dividends are due). How will the dividend be divided between the preferred and common stockholders?

LO 11-3

Exercise 11-7A *Cash dividends for preferred and common shareholders*

Weaver Corporation had the following stock issued and outstanding at January 1, Year 1.

1. 150,000 shares of $1 par common stock.
2. 15,000 shares of $100 par, 6 percent, noncumulative preferred stock.

On June 10, Weaver Corporation declared the annual cash dividend on its 15,000 shares of preferred stock and a $0.50 per share dividend for the common shareholders. The dividends will be paid on July 1 to the shareholders of record on June 20.

Required

Determine the total amount of dividends to be paid to the preferred shareholders and common shareholders.

LO 11-4

Exercise 11-8A *Effect of issuing common stock on the balance sheet*

Newly formed S&J Iron Corporation has 50,000 shares of $10 par common stock authorized. On March 1, Year 1, S&J Iron issued 6,000 shares of the stock for $16 per share. On May 2, the company issued an additional 10,000 shares for $18 per share. S&J Iron was not affected by other events during Year 1.

Required

a. Record the transactions in a horizontal statements model like the following one. In the Statement of Cash Flows column, indicate whether the item is an operating activity (OA), investing activity (IA), or financing activity (FA). Use NA to indicate that an element was not affected by the event.

Balance Sheet						Income Statement				Statement of Cash Flows
Assets	=	Liab.	+		Stk. Equity					
Cash	=			Com. Stk.	+	PIC in Excess	Rev.	−	Exp.	=	Net Inc.	

b. Determine the amount S&J Iron would report for common stock on the December 31, Year 1, balance sheet.

c. Determine the amount S&J Iron would report for paid-in capital in excess of par.

d. What is the total amount of capital contributed by the owners?

e. What amount of total assets would S&J Iron report on the December 31, Year 1, balance sheet?

Exercise 11-9A   *Recording and reporting common and preferred stock transactions*   LO 11-4

Eastport Inc. was organized on June 5, Year 1. It was authorized to issue 300,000 shares of $10 par common stock and 50,000 shares of 5 percent cumulative class A preferred stock. The class A stock had a stated value of $50 per share. The following stock transactions pertain to Eastport Inc.:

1. Issued 15,000 shares of common stock for $12 per share.
2. Issued 5,000 shares of the class A preferred stock for $51 per share.
3. Issued 60,000 shares of common stock for $15 per share.

Required

Prepare the stockholders' equity section of the balance sheet immediately after these transactions.

Exercise 11-10A   *Effect of no-par common and par preferred stock on the horizontal*   LO 11-4
statements model

Mercury Corporation issued 6,000 shares of no-par common stock for $45 per share. Mercury also issued 3,000 shares of $50 par, 5 percent noncumulative preferred stock at $52 per share.

Required

Record these events in a horizontal statements model like the following one. In the Statement of Cash Flows column, indicate whether the item is an operating activity (OA), investing activity (IA), or financing activity (FA). Use NA to indicate that an element was not affected by the event.

Balance Sheet					Income Statement			Statement of Cash Flows
Assets =			Stk. Equity					
Cash =	Pfd. Stk. +		Com. Stk. +	PIC in Excess	Rev. −	Exp. =	Net Inc.	

Exercise 11-11A   *Issuing stock for assets other than cash*   LO 11-4

Tom Yuppy, a wealthy investor, exchanged a plot of land that originally cost him $25,000 for 1,000 shares of $10 par common stock issued to him by Leuig Corp. On the same date, Leuig Corp. issued an additional 2,000 shares of stock to Yuppy for $25 per share.

Required

a. What was the value of the land at the date of the stock issue?

b. Show the effect of the two stock issues on Leuig's books in a horizontal statements model like the following one. In the Statement of Cash Flows column, indicate whether the item is an operating activity (OA), investing activity (IA), or financing activity (FA). Use NA to indicate that an element was not affected by the event.

Balance Sheet						Income Statement			Statement of Cash Flows
Assets			=	Stk. Equity					
Cash +	Land	=	Com. Stk. +		PIC in Excess	Rev. −	Exp. =	Net Inc.	

LO 11-5

Exercise 11-12A   *Treasury stock transactions*

Elroy Corporation repurchased 4,000 shares of its own stock for $30 per share. The stock has a par of $10 per share. A month later, Elroy resold 900 shares of the treasury stock for $32 per share.

Required

What is the balance of the treasury stock account after these transactions?

LO 11-5

Exercise 11-13A   *Recording and reporting treasury stock transactions*

The following information pertains to JAE Corp. at January 1, Year 1:

Common stock, $10 par, 20,000 shares authorized, 2,000 shares issued and outstanding	$20,000
Paid-in capital in excess of par, common stock	15,000
Retained earnings	82,000

JAE Corp. completed the following transactions during Year 1:

1. Issued 3,000 shares of $10 par common stock for $25 per share.
2. Repurchased 500 shares of its own common stock for $26 per share.
3. Resold 200 shares of treasury stock for $30 per share.

Required

a. How many shares of common stock were outstanding at the end of the period?
b. How many shares of common stock had been issued at the end of the period?
c. Organize the transactions data in accounts under the accounting equation.
d. Prepare the stockholders' equity section of the balance sheet reflecting these transactions. Include the number of shares authorized, issued, and outstanding in the description of the common stock.

LO 11-6

Exercise 11-14A   *Effect of cash dividends on financial statements*

On May 1, Year 1, Love Corporation declared a $50,000 cash dividend to be paid on May 31 to shareholders of record on May 15.

Required

Record the events occurring on May 1, May 15, and May 31 in a horizontal statements model like the following one. In the Statement of Cash Flows column, indicate whether the item is an operating activity (OA), investing activity (IA), or financing activity (FA).

	Balance Sheet								Income Statement				Statement of Cash Flows
Date	Assets	=	Liab.	+	Com. Stk.	+	Ret. Earn.		Rev.	−	Exp.	= Net Inc.	

LO 11-7

Exercise 11-15A   *Accounting for stock dividends*

Beacon Corporation issued a 5 percent stock dividend on 30,000 shares of its $10 par common stock. At the time of the dividend, the market value of the stock was $15 per share.

Required

a. Compute the amount of the stock dividend.
b. Show the effects of the stock dividend on the financial statements using a horizontal statements model like the following one:

	Balance Sheet										Income Statement				Statement of Cash Flows
Assets	=	Liab.	+	Com. Stk.	+	PIC in Excess	+	Ret. Earn.			Rev.	−	Exp.	= Net Inc.	

Exercise 11-16A *Determining the effects of stock splits on the accounting records*   LO 11-7

The market value of Yeates Corporation's common stock had become excessively high. The stock was currently selling for $240 per share. To reduce the market price of the common stock, Yeates declared a 3-for-1 stock split for the 100,000 outstanding shares of its $10 par value common stock.

Required

a. How will Yeates Corporation's books be affected by the stock split?

b. Determine the number of common shares outstanding and the par value after the split.

c. Explain how the market value of the stock will be affected by the stock split.

Exercise 11-17A *Determining how the appropriation of retained earnings affects financial statements*   LO 11-8

On December 30, Billy's Boat Yard (BBY) had $90,000 of cash, $20,000 of liabilities, $30,000 of common stock, and $40,000 of unrestricted retained earnings. On December 31, BBY appropriated retained earnings in the amount of $18,000 for a future remodeling project.

Required

a. Record the December 31 appropriation in the following statements model:

Balance Sheet										Income Statement					Statement of Cash Flows
Assets	=	Liab.	+	Com. Stk.	+	Ret. Earn.	+	App. Ret. Earn.		Rev.	−	Exp.	=	Net Inc.	

b. Determine the amount of dividends that BBY can pay immediately after the December 31 appropriation.

c. Determine the total amount of retained earnings immediately after the December 31 appropriation.

d. Determine the total amount of cash immediately after the December 31 appropriation.

Exercise 11-18A *Corporate announcements*   LO 11-9

Discount Drugs (one of the three largest drug makers) just reported that its Year 2 third-quarter profits are essentially the same as the Year 1 third-quarter profits. In addition to this announcement, Discount Drugs also announced the same day that the Food and Drug Administration has just approved a new drug used to treat high blood pressure that Discount Drugs developed. This new drug has been shown to be extremely effective and has few or no side effects. It will also be less expensive than the other drugs currently on the market.

Required

Using the preceding information, answer the following questions:

a. What do you think will happen to the stock price of Discount Drugs on the day these two announcements are made? Explain your answer.

b. How will the balance sheet be affected on that day by the preceding announcements?

c. How will the income statement be affected on that day by the preceding announcements?

d. How will the statement of cash flows be affected on that day by the preceding announcements?

Exercise 11-19A *Using the P/E ratio*   LO 11-9

Lake Inc. and River Inc. reported net incomes of $800,000 and $1,000,000, respectively, for the most recent fiscal year. Both companies had 200,000 shares of common stock issued and outstanding. The market price per share of Lake's stock was $50, while River's sold for $85 per share.

Required

a. Determine the P/E ratio for each company.

b. Based on the P/E ratios computed in Requirement *a*, which company do investors believe has the greater potential for growth in income?

LO 11-9

Exercise 11-20A   *The P/E ratio*

Required

Write a memo explaining why one company's P/E ratio may be higher than another company's P/E ratio.

LO 11-10

Exercise 11-21A   *Interpreting the effects of business liquidation on creditors and owners*

Assume that Harris Company acquires $3,600 cash from creditors and $4,200 cash from investors.

Required

a. Explain the primary differences between investors and creditors.

b. If Harris Company has net income of $2,000 and then liquidates, what amount of cash will the creditors receive? What amount of cash will the investors receive?

c. If Harris Company has a net loss of $2,000 cash and then liquidates, what amount of cash will the creditors receive? What amount of cash will the investors receive?

d. If Harris Company has a net loss of $4,900 cash and then liquidates, what amount of cash will the creditors receive? What amount of cash will the investors receive?

PROBLEMS—SERIES A

Mc Graw Hill connect   All applicable Problems in Series A are available in *Connect*.

LO 11-1

Problem 11-22A   *Different forms of business organization*

Cal Cagle was working to establish a business enterprise with four of his wealthy friends. Each of the five individuals would receive a 20 percent ownership interest in the company. A primary goal of establishing the enterprise was to minimize the amount of income taxes paid. Assume that the five investors are in a 35 percent personal tax bracket and that the corporate tax rate is 25 percent. Also assume that the new company is expected to earn $220,000 of cash income before taxes during its first year of operation. All earnings are expected to be immediately distributed to the owners.

Required

Calculate the amount of after-tax cash flow available to each investor if the business is established as a partnership versus a corporation. Write a memo explaining the advantages and disadvantages of these two forms of business organization. Explain why a limited liability company may be a better choice than either a partnership or a corporation.

LO 11-1

eXcel

CHECK FIGURES
a. Net Income: $16,900
b. Cascade: $29,160

Problem 11-23A   *Effect of business structure on financial statements*

Cascade Company was started on January 1, Year 1, when it acquired $60,000 cash from the owners. During Year 2, the company earned cash revenues of $35,000 and incurred cash expenses of $18,100. The company also paid cash distributions of $4,000.

Required

Prepare a Year 1 income statement, capital statement (statement of changes in equity), balance sheet, and statement of cash flows under each of the following assumptions. (Consider each assumption separately.)

a. Cascade is a sole proprietorship owned by Carl Cascade.

b. Cascade is a partnership with two partners, Carl Cascade and Beth Cascade. Carl Cascade invested $24,000 and Beth Cascade invested $36,000 of the $60,000 cash that was used to start the business. Beth was expected to assume the vast majority of the responsibility for operating the business. The partnership agreement called for Beth to receive 60 percent of the profits and Carl to get the remaining 40 percent. With regard to the $4,000 distribution, Beth withdrew $2,400 from the business and Carl withdrew $1,600.

c. Cascade is a corporation. It issued 5,000 shares of $5 par common stock for $60,000 cash to start the business.

Problem 11-24A   *Cash dividends: common and preferred stock*

LO 11-3

Nowell Inc. had the following stock issued and outstanding at January 1, Year 1:

1. 150,000 shares of no-par common stock.
2. 30,000 shares of $50 par, 4 percent, cumulative preferred stock. (Dividends are in arrears for one year.)

On March 8, Year 1, Nowell declared a $175,000 cash dividend to be paid March 31 to shareholders of record on March 20.

Required

What amount of dividends will be paid to the preferred shareholders versus the common shareholders?

Problem 11-25A   *Analyzing financial statement effects for treasury stock transactions*

LO 11-4, 11-5

The Corners Corporation experienced three events that affected its financial statements as shown below. Assume that the original issue (Event 1) was for 400,000 shares, and the treasury stock was acquired for $5 per share (Event 2).

CHECK FIGURE
b. 4,800

Balance Sheet							Income Statement			Statement of Cash Flows	
Assets	=			Stk. Equity							
Cash	=	Com. Stk. +	PIC in Excess of Par	−	Treasury Stock	+	PIC from Treasury Stk.	Rev. − Exp. = Net Inc.			
1,000,000	=	600,000 +	400,000	−	NA	+	NA	NA − NA = NA		1,000,000	FA
(24,000)	=	NA +	NA	−	24,000	+	NA	NA − NA = NA		(24,000)	FA
21,000	=	NA +	NA	−	(18,000)	+	3,000	NA − NA = NA		21,000	FA

Required

a. What was the sales price per share of the original stock issue?
b. How many shares of stock did the corporation acquire in Event 2?
c. How many shares were reissued in Event 3?
d. How many shares are outstanding immediately following Events 2 and 3, respectively?

Problem 11-26A   *Recording and reporting stock transactions and cash dividends across two accounting cycles*

LO 11-3, 11-6

eXcel

Sun Corporation received a charter that authorized the issuance of 100,000 shares of $10 par common stock and 50,000 shares of $50 par, 5 percent cumulative preferred stock. Sun Corporation completed the following transactions during its first two years of operation.

CHECK FIGURES
b. Preferred Stock, Year 1: $50,000
c. Common Shares Outstanding, Year 2: 35,100

Year 1

Jan. 5	Sold 6,000 shares of the $10 par common stock for $15 per share.
12	Sold 1,000 shares of the 5 percent preferred stock for $55 per share.
Apr. 5	Sold 30,000 shares of the $10 par common stock for $21 per share.
Dec. 31	During the year, earned $150,000 in cash revenue and paid $88,000 for cash operating expenses.
31	Declared the cash dividend on the outstanding shares of preferred stock for Year 1. The dividend will be paid on February 15 to stockholders of record on January 10, Year 2.

Year 2

Feb. 15	Paid the cash dividend declared on December 31, Year 1.
Mar. 3	Sold 15,000 shares of the $50 par preferred stock for $53 per share.
May 5	Purchased 900 shares of the common stock as treasury stock at $24 per share.
Dec. 31	During the year, earned $210,000 in cash revenues and paid $98,000 for cash operating expenses.
31	Declared the annual dividend on the preferred stock and a $0.50 per share dividend on the common stock.

Required

a. Organize the transaction data in accounts under an accounting equation.

b. Prepare the balance sheets at December 31, Year 1 and Year 2.

c. What is the number of common shares *outstanding* at the end of Year 1? At the end of Year 2? How many common shares had been *issued* at the end of Year 1? At the end of Year 2? Explain any differences between issued and outstanding common shares for Year 1 and for Year 2.

LO 11-2, 11-3, 11-7

CHECK FIGURES
a. Par Value per Share: $20
b. Dividend per Share: $1.20

Problem 11-27A *Analyzing the stockholders' equity section of the balance sheet*

The stockholders' equity section of the balance sheet for Mann Equipment Co. at December 31, Year 1, is as follows:

Stockholders' Equity		
Paid-in capital		
Preferred stock, ? par value, 6% cumulative, 100,000 shares authorized, 10,000 shares issued and outstanding	$ 200,000	
Common stock, $10 stated value, 200,000 shares authorized, 100,000 shares issued and outstanding	1,000,000	
Paid-in capital in excess of par—Preferred	25,000	
Paid-in capital in excess of stated value—Common	500,000	
Total paid-in capital		$1,725,000
Retained earnings		420,000
Total stockholders' equity		$2,145,000

Note: The market value per share of the common stock is $42, and the market value per share of the preferred stock is $26.

Required

a. What is the par value per share of the preferred stock?

b. What is the dividend per share on the preferred stock?

c. What was the average issue price per share (price for which the stock was issued) of the common stock?

d. Explain the difference between the par value and the market price of the preferred stock.

e. If Mann declares a 2-for-1 stock split on the common stock, how many shares will be outstanding after the split? What amount will be transferred from the retained earnings account because of the stock split? Theoretically, what will be the market price of the common stock immediately after the stock split?

LO 11-4, 11-6, 11-7

CHECK FIGURE
b. Total Paid-In Capital: $608,000

Problem 11-28A *Recording and reporting stock dividends*

Brice Co. completed the following transactions in Year 1, the first year of operation.

1. Issued 40,000 shares of no-par common stock for $10 per share.

2. Issued 8,000 shares of $20 par, 6 percent, preferred stock for $20 per share.

3. Paid a cash dividend of $9,600 to preferred shareholders.

4. Issued a 10 percent stock dividend on no-par common stock. The market value at the dividend declaration date was $12 per share.

5. Later that year, issued a 2-for-1 split on the shares of outstanding common stock. The market price of the stock at that time was $50 per share.

6. Produced $140,000 of cash revenues and incurred $72,000 of cash operating expenses.

7. Closed the revenue, expense, and dividend accounts to retained earnings.

Required

a. Record each of these events in a horizontal statements model like the following one. In the Statement of Cash Flows column, indicate whether the item is an operating activity (OA), investing activity (IA), or financing activity (FA). Use NA to indicate that an element is not affected by the event.

Balance Sheet						Income Statement				Statement of Cash Flows
Assets	=			Stk. Equity						
		Pfd. Stk.	+	Com. Stk.	+	Ret. Earn.	Rev.	−	Exp.	=	Net Inc.	

b. Prepare the stockholders' equity section of the balance sheet at the end of Year 1. (Include all necessary information.)

c. Theoretically, what is the market value of the common stock after the stock split?

Problem 11-29A *Recording and reporting treasury stock transactions*

Choctaw Co. completed the following transactions in Year 1, the first year of operation.

1. Issued 20,000 shares of $10 par common stock for $10 per share.
2. Issued 3,000 shares of $20 stated value preferred stock for $20 per share.
3. Purchased 1,000 shares of common stock as treasury stock for $12 per share.
4. Declared a $2,000 cash dividend on preferred stock.
5. Sold 500 shares of treasury stock for $14 per share.
6. Paid $2,000 cash for the preferred dividend declared in Event 4.
7. Earned cash revenues of $78,000 and incurred cash expenses of $41,000.
8. Appropriated $8,000 of retained earnings.

Required

a. Organize the transaction in accounts under an accounting equation.

b. Prepare a balance sheet as of December 31, Year 1.

LO 11-3, 11-4, 11-5, 11-6, 11-8

CHECK FIGURE
b. Total Paid-In Capital: $261,000

Problem 11-30A *Effects of equity transactions on financial statements*

The following events were experienced by Sequoia, Inc.:

1. Issued cumulative preferred stock for cash.
2. Issued common stock for cash.
3. Issued noncumulative preferred stock for cash.
4. Paid cash to purchase treasury stock.
5. Sold treasury stock for an amount of cash that was more than the cost of the treasury stock.
6. Declared a cash dividend.
7. Declared a 2-for-1 stock split on the common stock.
8. Distributed a stock dividend.
9. Appropriated retained earnings.
10. Paid a cash dividend that was previously declared.

LO 11-3, 11-4, 11-5, 11-6, 11-7, 11-8

Required

Show the effect of each event on the elements of the financial statements using a horizontal statements model like the following one. Use + for increase, − for decrease, and NA for not affected. In the Statement of Cash Flows column, indicate whether the item is an operating activity (OA), investing activity (IA), or financing activity (FA). The first transaction is entered as an example.

Event No.	Balance Sheet					Income Statement					Statement of Cash Flows
	Assets	=	Liab.	+	Stk. Equity	Rev.	−	Exp.	=	Net Inc.	
1	+		NA		+	NA		NA		NA	+ FA

Problem 11-31A *Using accounting information to make investment decisions*

Sea Coast Plumbing Company (SCPC) is a national company that provides residential plumbing services. SCPC is considering making a substantial investment in Rakeland Distributors, Inc. (RDI). RDI sells plumbing supplies throughout the United States.

LO 11-9

Required

a. Identify two financial benefits that SCPC could receive from an investment in RDI.
b. What types of information would be helpful in evaluating SCPC's investment opportunity?
c. Speculate as to how owning RDI stock could benefit SCPC's capacity to conduct its operations.

LO 11-10

Problem 11-32A *Interpreting the effects of business liquidations*

On January 1, Year 1, Eastwood Company is started when it issues 100 shares of $10 par value stock for a cash price of $15 per share. Also, on January 1 Year 1, Eastwood borrows $35,000 cash by issuing a note payable to the Metropolitan Bank. Eastwood immediately purchases land that costs $36,000 cash. During Year 1 Eastwood earns $7,000 of cash revenue and incurs $4,000 of cash expenses. No other transaction occurred during Year 1.

Required

a. If the bank demands repayment of the note on January 1, Year 2, does Eastwood have the funds available to repay the loan?
b. Determine the amount of cash on hand as of January 1, Year 2.
c. Determine the total amount of liabilities as of January 1, Year 2.
d. Assume that Eastwood is forced to liquidate its business on January 1, Year 2. Further, assume that in the process of liquidation Eastwood has to sell the land for $27,000. Under these circumstances:
   1. Determine the amount of cash that the bank would receive in the liquidation.
   2. Determine the amount of cash that the investors would receive in the liquidation.

EXERCISES—SERIES B

LO 11-1

Exercise 11-1B *Characteristics of sole proprietorships, partnerships, and corporations*

Required

The three primary types of business organization are proprietorship, partnership, and corporation. Each type has characteristics that distinguish it from the other types. In the left column of the following table, write the name of the type of business organization that is most likely to possess the characteristic described in the right column of the table. The first item is shown as an example.

Business Type	Characteristic
Proprietorship	Offers the highest level of control over operating decisions
	The business dissolves with the death of its only owner
	Has a retained earnings account on its balance sheet
	Has two or more owners who are not stockholders
	Profits benefit a single individual
	Frequently uses legal agreements to define profit distribution for two or more owners
	Most highly regulated form of business
	Subject to double taxation
	Has multiple capital accounts but no retained earnings account on its balance sheet
	Provides the best opportunity to benefit a few people
	Has only one capital account on its balance sheet
	Provides for easy transfer of ownership
	Owned and operated by a single individual
	Offers the least capacity to raise capital
	Provides the greatest capacity to raise capital
	Least regulated form of business
	One owner may be held personally liable for actions taken on behalf of the business by a different owner
	Usually operated by a professional management team that is separated from the owners

Exercise 11-2B   Effect of accounting events on the financial statements of a sole proprietorship

A sole proprietorship was started on January 1, Year 1, when it received $30,000 cash from Maria Lopez, the owner. During Year 1, the company earned $50,000 in cash revenues and paid $22,300 in cash expenses. Lopez withdrew $10,000 cash from the business during Year 1.

Required

Prepare an income statement, capital statement (statement of changes in equity), balance sheet, and statement of cash flows for Lopez's Year 1 fiscal year.

Exercise 11-3B   Effect of accounting events on the financial statements of a partnership

D. Reed and J. Files started the RF partnership on January 1, Year 1. The business acquired $70,000 cash from Reed and $140,000 from Files. During Year 1, the partnership earned $75,000 in cash revenues and paid $39,000 for cash expenses. Reed withdrew $2,000 cash from the business, and Files withdrew $4,000 cash. The net income was allocated to the capital accounts of the two partners in proportion to the amounts of their original investments in the business.

Required

Prepare an income statement, capital statement, balance sheet, and statement of cash flows for the RF partnership for the Year 1 fiscal year.

Exercise 11-4B   Capital stock authorized, issued, and outstanding

Bronson Inc. has 300,000 shares authorized, 175,000 shares issued, and 25,000 shares of treasury stock. At this point, Bronson has $820,000 of assets. $250,000 liabilities, $400,000 of common stock, and $170,000 of retained earnings. Further, assume that the market value of Bronson's common stock is $6 per share.

Required

a. Determine the number of shares of stock that is outstanding.

b. Determine the book value per share.

c. Provide a rational explanation for the difference between the book value per share and the market value per share of Bronson Inc. common stock.

Exercise 11-5B   Characteristics of capital stock

The stockholders' equity section of Creighton Company's balance sheet is shown as follows:

CREIGHTON COMPANY	
As of December 31, Year 3	
Stockholders' equity	
Preferred stock, $6 stated value, 6% cumulative,	
250 shares authorized, 100 issued and outstanding	$ 600
Common stock, $6 par value, 200 shares authorized,	
150 issued and outstanding	900
Common stock, class B, $8 par value, 450 shares	
authorized, 100 issued and outstanding	800
Common stock, no par, 200 shares authorized,	
150 issued and outstanding	1,800
Paid-in capital in excess of stated value—preferred	400
Paid-in capital in excess of par value—common	900
Paid-in capital in excess of par value—class B common	800
Retained earnings	9,000
Total stockholders' equity	$15,200

Required

a. Assuming the preferred stock was originally issued for cash, determine the amount of cash that was collected when the stock was issued.

b. Based on the class B common stock alone, determine the amount of the company's legal capital.

c. Based on the class B common stock alone, determine the minimum amount of assets that must be retained in the company as protection for creditors.

d. Determine the number of shares of class B common stock that are available to sell as of December 31, Year 3.

e. Assuming Creighton purchases treasury stock consisting of 50 shares of its no par common stock on January 1, Year 4, determine the amount of the no-par common stock that would be outstanding immediately after the purchase.

f. Based on the stockholders' equity section shown earlier, can you determine the market value of the preferred stock? If yes, what is the market value of one share of this stock?

LO 11-3

Exercise 11-6B *Accounting for cumulative preferred dividends*

When Ching Corporation was organized in January, Year 1, it immediately issued 10,000 shares of $50 par, 5 percent, cumulative preferred stock and 15,000 shares of $10 par common stock. The company's earnings history is as follows: Year 1, net loss of $18,000; Year 2, net income of $95,000; Year 3, net income of $90,000. The corporation did not pay a dividend in Year 1.

Required

a. How much is the dividend arrearage as of January 1, Year 2?

b. Assume that the board of directors declares a $65,000 cash dividend at the end of Year 2 (remember that the Year 1 and Year 2 preferred dividends are due). How will the dividend be divided between the preferred and common stockholders?

LO 11-3

Exercise 11-7B *Cash dividends for preferred and common shareholders*

ALR Corporation had the following stock issued and outstanding at January 1, Year 1.

1. 200,000 shares of $10 par common stock.
2. 8,000 shares of $100 par, 4 percent, noncumulative preferred stock.

On May 10, ALR Corporation declared the annual cash dividend on its 8,000 shares of preferred stock and a $0.50 per share dividend for the common shareholders. The dividends will be paid on June 15 to the shareholders of record on May 30.

Required

Determine the total amount of dividends to be paid to the preferred shareholders and common shareholders.

LO 11-4

Exercise 11-8B *Effect of issuing common stock on the balance sheet*

Newly formed Irwin Services Corporation has 100,000 shares of $10 par common stock authorized. On March 1, Year 1, Irwin Services issued 20,000 shares of the stock for $12 per share. On May 2, the company issued an additional 30,000 shares for $15 per share. Irwin Services was not affected by other events during Year 1.

Required

a. Record the transactions in a horizontal statements model like the following one. In the Statement of Cash Flows column, indicate whether the item is an operating activity (OA), investing activity (IA), or financing activity (FA). Use NA to indicate that an element was not affected by the event.

Balance Sheet						Income Statement					Statement of Cash Flows
Assets	=	Liab.	+		Stk. Equity						
Cash	=			Com. Stk.	+	PIC in Excess	Rev.	−	Exp.	=	Net Inc.

b. Determine the amount Irwin Services would re*port for common* stock on the December 31, Year 1, balance sheet.

c. Determine the amount Irwin Services would report for paid-in capital in excess of par.

d. What is the total amount of capital contributed by the owners?

e. What amount of total assets would Irwin Services report on the December 31, Year 1, balance sheet?

Exercise 11-9B *Recording and reporting common and preferred stock transactions*   LO 11-4

Reiss Inc. was organized on June 1, Year 1. It was authorized to issue 500,000 shares of $10 par common stock and 100,000 shares of 4 percent cumulative class A preferred stock. The class A stock had a stated value of $50 per share. The following stock transactions pertain to Reiss Inc.

1. Issued 40,000 shares of common stock for $16 per share.
2. Issued 20,000 shares of the class A preferred stock for $52 per share.
3. Issued 60,000 shares of common stock for $20 per share.

Required

Prepare the stockholders' equity section of the balance sheet immediately after these transactions.

Exercise 11-10B *Effect of no-par common and par preferred stock on the horizontal statements model*   LO 11-4

Rice Corporation issued 10,000 shares of no-par common stock for $25 per share. Rice also issued 3,000 shares of $40 par, 6 percent noncumulative preferred stock at $42 per share.

Required

Record these events in a horizontal statements model like the following one. In the Statement of Cash Flows column, indicate whether the item is an operating activity (OA), investing activity (IA), or financing activity (FA). Use NA to indicate that an element was not affected by the event.

Balance Sheet						Income Statement					Statement of Cash Flows
Assets	=			Stk. Equity							
Cash	=	Pfd. Stk.	+	Com. Stk.	+	PIC in Excess	Rev.	−	Exp.	=	Net Inc.	

Exercise 11-11B *Issuing stock for assets other than cash*   LO 11-4

Carroll Corporation was formed when it issued shares of common stock to two of its shareholders. Carroll issued 10,000 shares of $5 par common stock to R. Flowler in exchange for $80,000 cash (the issue price was $8 per share). Carroll also issued 3,500 shares of stock to P. Jones in exchange for a one-year-old delivery van on the same day. Jones had originally paid $39,000 for the van.

Required

a. What was the market value of the delivery van on the date of the stock issue?
b. Show the effect of the two stock issues on Carroll's books in a horizontal statements model like the following one. In the Statement of Cash Flows column, indicate whether the item is an operating activity (OA), investing activity (IA), or financing activity (FA). Use NA to indicate that an element was not affected by the event.

Balance Sheet							Income Statement					Statement of Cash Flows
Assets			=		Stk. Equity							
Cash	+	Van	=	Com. Stk.	+	PIC in Excess	Rev.	−	Exp.	=	Net Inc.	

Exercise 11-12B *Treasury stock transactions*   LO 11-5

Earles Corporation repurchased 4,000 shares of its own stock for $30 per share. The stock has a par value of $10 per share. A month later, Earles resold 2,500 shares of the treasury stock for $35 per share.

Required

What is the balance of the treasury stock account after these transactions?

LO 11-5

Exercise 11-13B *Recording and reporting treasury stock transactions*

The following information pertains to Ming Corp. at January 1, Year 1:

Common stock, $10 par, 50,000 shares authorized,	
3,000 shares issued and outstanding	$30,000
Paid-in capital in excess of par, common stock	12,000
Retained earnings	46,000

Ming Corp. completed the following transactions during Year 1:

1. Issued 2,000 shares of $10 par common stock for $16 per share.
2. Repurchased 500 shares of its own common stock for $18 per share.
3. Resold 120 shares of treasury stock for $20 per share.

Required

a. How many shares of common stock were outstanding at the end of the period?
b. How many shares of common stock had been issued at the end of the period?
c. Organize the transactions data in accounts under the accounting equation.
d. Prepare the stockholders' equity section of the balance sheet reflecting these transactions. Include the number of shares authorized, issued, and outstanding in the description of the common stock.

LO 11-6

Exercise 11-14B *Effect of cash dividends on financial statements*

On October 1, Year 1, Nicholes Corporation declared a $50,000 cash dividend to be paid on December 15 to shareholders of record on November 1.

Required

Record the events occurring on October 1, November 1, and December 15 in a horizontal statements model like the following one. In the Statement of Cash Flows column, indicate whether the item is an operating activity (OA), investing activity (IA), or financing activity (FA).

	Balance Sheet							Income Statement				Statement of Cash Flows
Date	Assets	=	Liab.	+	Com. Stk.	+	Ret. Earn.	Rev.	−	Exp.	= Net Inc.	

LO 11-7

Exercise 11-15B *Accounting for stock dividends*

Egrett Corporation issued a 4 percent stock dividend on 20,000 shares of its $10 par common stock. At the time of the dividend, the market value of the stock was $30 per share.

Required

a. Compute the amount of the stock dividend.
b. Show the effects of the stock dividend on the financial statements using a horizontal statements model like the following one:

	Balance Sheet								Income Statement			Statement of Cash Flows
Assets	=	Liab.	+	Com. Stk.	+	PIC in Excess	+	Ret. Earn.	Rev.	−	Exp.	= Net Inc.

LO 11-7

Exercise 11-16B *Determining the effects of stock splits on the accounting records*

The market value of Granger Corporation's common stock had become excessively high. The stock was currently selling for $240 per share. To reduce the market price of the common stock, Granger declared a 3-for-1 stock split for the 200,000 outstanding shares of its $15 par common stock.

Required

a. How will Granger Corporation's books be affected by the stock split?
b. Determine the number of common shares outstanding and the par value after the split.
c. Explain how the market value of the stock will be affected by the stock split.

Exercise 11-17B *Determining how the appropriation of retained earnings affects financial statements*

On December 30, Odom Enterprises (OE) had $120,000 in cash, $35,000 in liabilities, $50,000 of common stock, and $35,000 in unrestricted retained earnings. On December 31, OE appropriated retained earnings in the amount of $15,000 for a future remodeling project.

Required

a. Record the December 31 appropriation in the following statements model:

Balance Sheet											Income Statement					Statement of Cash Flows
Assets	=	Liab.	+	Com. Stk.	+	Ret. Earn.	+	App. Ret. Earn.			Rev.	–	Exp.	=	Net Inc.	

b. Determine the amount of dividends that OE can pay immediately after the December 31 appropriation.

c. Determine the total amount of retained earnings immediately after the December 31 appropriation.

d. Determine the total amount of cash immediately after the December 31 appropriation.

Exercise 11-18B *Accounting information*

The Cutting Edge (TCE) is one of the world's largest lawn mower distributors. TCE is concerned about maintaining an adequate supply of the economy-line mowers it sells in its stores. TCE currently obtains its economy-line mowers from two suppliers. To ensure a steady supply of mowers, the management of TCE is considering the purchase of an ownership interest in one of the companies that supplies its mowers. More specifically, TCE wants to own enough stock of one of the suppliers to enable it to exercise significant influence over the management of the company. The following is a description of the two suppliers.

The first supplier, Dobbs Incorporated, is a closely held company. Large blocks of the Dobbs stock are held by individual members of the Dobbs family. TCE's investment advisor has discovered that one of the members of the Dobbs family is interested in selling her 5 percent share of the company's stock.

The second supplier, National Mowers Inc., has widely disbursed ownership with no one single stockholder owning more than 1 percent of the stock. TCE's investment advisor believes that 5 percent of this company's stock could be acquired gradually over an extended period of time without having a significant effect on the company's stock price.

Required

Provide a recommendation to TCE's management as to whether it should pursue the purchase of 5 percent of Dobbs Incorporated, or 5 percent of National Mowers Inc. Your answer should be supported by an explanation of your recommendation.

Exercise 11-19B *Using the P/E ratio*

Davis, Inc. and Royal, Inc. reported net incomes of $81,000 and $93,000, respectively, for their most recent fiscal years. Both companies had 10,000 shares of common stock issued and outstanding. The market price per share of Davis's stock was $130, while Royal's sold for $120 per share.

Required

a. Determine the P/E ratio for each company. (Round to the nearest whole number.)

b. Based on the P/E ratios computed in Requirement *a*, which company do investors believe has the greater potential for growth in income?

Exercise 11-20B *The P/E ratio*

Pepper Company's earnings were approximately the same in Year 1 and Year 2. Even so, the company's P/E ratio dropped significantly.

Required

Speculate about why Pepper's P/E ratio dropped significantly while its earnings remained constant.

Exercise 11-21B *Interpreting the effects of business liquidation on creditors and owners*

Assume that Alvin Company acquires $5,000 cash from creditors and $2,500 cash from investors.

Required

a. Explain the primary differences between investors and creditors.

b. If Alvin Company has net income of $1,500 and then liquidates, what amount of cash will the creditors receive? What amount of cash will the investors receive?

c. If Alvin Company has a net loss of $1,500 cash and then liquidates, what amount of cash will the creditors receive? What amount of cash will the investors receive?

d. If Alvin Company has a net loss of $5,500 cash and then liquidates, what amount of cash will the creditors receive? What amount of cash will the investors receive?

PROBLEMS—SERIES B

LO 11-1

Problem 11-22B   *Different forms of business organization*

Bill Wheeler established a partnership with June Cramer. The new company, W&C Fuels, purchased coal directly from mining companies and contracted to ship the coal via waterways to a seaport where it was delivered to ships that were owned and operated by international utilities companies. Wheeler was primarily responsible for running the day-to-day operations of the business. Cramer negotiated the buy-and-sell agreements. She recently signed a deal to purchase and deliver $2,000,000 of coal to Solar Utilities. W&C Fuels purchased the coal on account from Miller Mining Company. After accepting title to the coal, W&C Fuels agreed to deliver the coal under terms FOB destination, Port of Long Beach. Unfortunately, Cramer failed to inform Wheeler of the deal in time for Wheeler to insure the shipment. While in transit, the vessel carrying the coal suffered storm damage that rendered the coal virtually worthless by the time it reached its destination. W&C Fuels immediately declared bankruptcy. The company not only was responsible for the $2,000,000 due to Miller Mining Company but also was sued by Solar for breach of contract. Cramer had a personal net worth of virtually zero, but Wheeler was a wealthy individual with a net worth approaching $2,500,000. Accordingly, Miller Mining and Solar filed suit against Wheeler's personal assets. Wheeler claimed that he was not responsible for the problem because Cramer had failed to inform him of the contracts in time to obtain insurance coverage. Cramer admitted that she was personally responsible for the disaster.

Required

Write a memo describing Wheeler's risk associated with his participation in the partnership. Comment on how other forms of ownership would have affected his level of risk.

LO 11-1, 11-2

Problem 11-23B   *Effect of business structure on financial statements*

Best Auto Parts Company was started on January 1, Year 1, when the owners invested $120,000 cash in the business. During Year 1, the company earned cash revenues of $80,000 and incurred cash expenses of $56,000. The company also paid cash distributions of $5,000.

Required

Prepare a Year 1 income statement, capital statement (statement of changes in equity), balance sheet, and statement of cash flows using each of the following assumptions. (Consider each assumption separately.)

a. Best Auto Parts is a sole proprietorship owned by J. Smart.

b. Best Auto Parts is a partnership with two partners: Beth Song and J. Smart. Song invested $72,000 and Smart invested $48,000 of the $120,000 cash used to start the business. Smart was expected to assume the vast majority of the responsibility for operating the business. The partnership agreement called for Smart to receive 60 percent of the profits and Song the remaining 40 percent. With regard to the $5,000 distribution, Smart withdrew $1,500 from the business and Song withdrew $3,500.

c. Best Auto Parts is a corporation. The owners were issued 10,000 shares of $10 par common stock when they invested the $120,000 cash in the business.

LO 11-3

Problem 11-24B   *Cash dividends: Common and preferred stock*

Tyler Corp. had the following stock issued and outstanding at January 1, Year 1.

1. 60,000 shares of no-par common stock.

2. 15,000 shares of $100 par, 4 percent, cumulative preferred stock. (Dividends are in arrears for one year.)

On February 1, Year 1, Tyler declared a $150,000 cash dividend to be paid March 31 to shareholders of record on March 10.

Required

What amount of dividends will be paid to the preferred shareholders versus the common shareholders?

Problem 11-25B *Analyzing financial statement effects for treasury stock transactions*   LO 11-4, 11-5

The Corners Corporation experienced three events that affected its financial statements, as shown in
the following table. Assume that the original issue (Event 1) was for 400,000 shares, and the treasury
stock was acquired for $4 per share (Event 2).

CHECK FIGURE
b. 7,500

Balance Sheet							Income Statement			Statement of Cash Flows	
Assets	=			Stk. Equity							
Cash	=	Com. Stk. +	PIC in Excess of Par	−	Treasury Stock	+	PIC from Treasury Stk.	Rev. −	Exp. =	Net Inc.	
800,000	=	600,000 +	200,000	−	NA	+	NA	NA − NA =		NA	800,000 FA
(30,000)	=	NA +	NA	−	30,000	+	NA	NA − NA =		NA	(30,000) FA
12,000	=	NA +	NA	−	(10,000)	+	2,000	NA − NA =		NA	12,000 FA

Required

a. What was the sales price per share of the original stock issue?

b. How many shares of stock did the corporation acquire in Event 2?

c. How many shares were reissued in Event 3?

d. How many shares are outstanding immediately following Entries 2 and 3, respectively?

Problem 11-26B *Recording and reporting stock transactions and cash dividends across two accounting cycles*   LO 11-3, 11-6

Edgar Corporation was authorized to issue 100,000 shares of $8 par common stock and 50,000 shares
of $80 par, 4 percent, cumulative preferred stock. Edgar Corporation completed the following transac-
tions during its first two years of operation.

Year 1

Jan. 2	Issued 25,000 shares of $8 par common stock for $10 per share.
15	Issued 2,000 shares of $80 par preferred stock for $90 per share.
Feb. 14	Issued 20,000 shares of $8 par common stock for $12 per share.
Dec. 31	During the year, earned $280,000 of cash revenues and paid $165,000 of cash operating expenses.
31	Declared the cash dividend on outstanding shares of preferred stock for Year 1. The dividend will be paid on January 31 to stockholders of record on January 15, Year 2.
31	Closed revenue, expense, and dividend accounts to the retained earnings account.

Year 2

Jan. 31	Paid the cash dividend declared on December 31, Year 1.
Mar. 1	Issued 4,000 shares of $80 par preferred stock for $92 per share.
June 1	Purchased 1,000 shares of common stock as treasury stock at $14 per share.
Dec. 31	During the year, earned $185,000 of cash revenues and paid $110,000 of cash operating expenses.
31	Declared the dividend on the preferred stock and a $1.00 per share dividend on the common stock.
31	Closed revenue, expense, and dividend accounts to the retained earnings account.

Required

a. Organize the transaction data in accounts under an accounting equation.

b. Prepare the stockholders' equity section of the balance sheet at December 31, Year 1.

c. Prepare the balance sheet at December 31, Year 2.

LO 11-2, 11-3, 11-7

Problem 11-27B   *Analyzing the stockholders' equity section of the balance sheet*

The stockholders' equity section of the balance sheet for Stinson Company at December 31, Year 1, is as follows:

Stockholders' Equity

Paid-in capital
  Preferred stock, ? par value, 5% cumulative,
    100,000 shares authorized, 40,000 shares
    issued and outstanding $400,000
  Common stock, $20 stated value, 150,000 shares
    authorized, 40,000 shares issued and ? outstanding   800,000
  Paid-in capital in excess of par—Preferred   30,000
  Paid-in capital in excess of stated value—Common   100,000

  Total paid-in capital $1,330,000
  Retained earnings   250,000
  Treasury stock, 2,000 shares   (25,000)
  Total stockholders' equity $1,555,000

Note: The market value per share of the common stock is $40, and the market value per share of the preferred stock is $12.

Required

a. What is the par value per share of the preferred stock?
b. What is the dividend per share on the preferred stock?
c. What is the number of common stock shares outstanding?
d. What was the average issue price per share (price for which the stock was issued) of the common stock?
e. Explain the difference between the average issue price and the market price of the common stock.
f. If Stinson declared a 2-for-1 stock split on the common stock, how many shares would be outstanding after the split? What amount would be transferred from the retained earnings account because of the stock split? Theoretically, what would be the market price of the common stock immediately after the stock split?

LO 11-4, 11-6, 11-7

Problem 11-28B   *Recording and reporting stock dividends*

Burk Corp. completed the following transactions in Year 1, the first year of operation:

1. Issued 30,000 shares of $10 par common stock for $15 per share.
2. Issued 6,000 shares of $100 par, 5 percent, preferred stock at $101 per share.
3. Paid the annual cash dividend to preferred shareholders.
4. Issued a 5 percent stock dividend on the common stock. The market value at the dividend declaration date was $19 per share.
5. Later that year, issued a 2-for-1 split on the 31,500 shares of outstanding common stock.
6. Earned $165,000 of cash revenues and paid $98,000 of cash operating expenses.
7. Closed the revenue, expense, and dividend accounts to retained earnings.

Required

a. Record each of these events in a horizontal statements model like the following one. In the Statement of Cash Flows column, indicate whether the item is an operating activity (OA), investing activity (IA), or financing activity (FA). Use NA to indicate that an element is not affected by the event.

Balance Sheet							Income Statement			Statement of Cash Flows
Assets =			Stk. Equity							
	Pfd. Stk. +	Com. Stk. +	PIC in Excess PS +	PIC in Excess CS +	Ret. Earn.		Rev. −	Exp. =	Net Inc.	

b. Prepare the stockholders' equity section of the balance sheet at the end of Year 1.

Problem 11-29B *Recording and reporting treasury stock transactions*

LO 11-3, 11-4, 11-5, 11-6, 11-8

Rabern Corp. completed the following transactions in Year 1, the first year of operation.

1. Issued 15,000 shares of $10 par common stock at par.
2. Issued 5,000 shares of $50 stated value preferred stock at $52 per share.
3. Purchased 800 shares of common stock as treasury stock for $12 per share.
4. Declared a 5 percent cash dividend on preferred stock.
5. Sold 300 shares of treasury stock for $16 per share.
6. Paid the cash dividend on preferred stock that was declared in Event 4.
7. Earned revenue of $80,000 and incurred operating expenses of $48,000.
8. Appropriated $6,000 of retained earnings.

Required

a. Organize the transaction in accounts under an accounting equation.
b. Prepare the stockholders' equity section of the balance sheet as of December 31, Year 1.

Problem 11-30B *Effects of equity transactions on financial statements*

LO 11-3, 11-4, 11-5, 11-6, 11-7, 11-8

The following events were experienced by Halbart Inc.

1. Issued common stock for cash.
2. Distributed a 2-for-1 stock split on the common stock.
3. Appropriated retained earnings.
4. Issued cumulative preferred stock for cash.
5. Sold treasury stock for an amount of cash that was more than the cost of the treasury stock.
6. Issued noncumulative preferred stock for cash.
7. Paid cash to purchase treasury stock.
8. Declared a cash dividend.
9. Distributed a stock dividend.
10. Paid the cash dividend declared in Event 8.

Required

Show the effect of each event on the elements of the financial statements using a horizontal statements model like the following one. Use + for increase, − for decrease, and NA for not affected. In the Statement of Cash Flows column, indicate whether the item is an operating activity (OA), investing activity (IA), or financing activity (FA). The first transaction is entered as an example.

Event No.	Balance Sheet			Income Statement			Statement of Cash Flows
	Assets	= Liab.	+ Stk. Equity	Rev.	− Exp.	= Net Inc.	
1	+	NA	+	NA	NA	NA	+ FA

Problem 11-31B *Using accounting information to make investment decisions*

LO 11-9

An investor is trying to decide whether to purchase stock in Henderson Inc. or Glover Corporation. Glover Corporation reported annual earnings per share of $8, and the current market price of Glover stock is $64 per share. Henderson Inc. has annual earnings per share of $4, and the current market price for Henderson stock is $84 per share. Based on this information, complete the requirements to assist the investor in making his decision.

Required

a. Determine the P/E ratio for Glover Corporation.
b. Determine the P/E ratio for Henderson Inc.
c. Assume the growth prospects for the two companies are identical. Further, assume both companies plan to distribute all future earnings as cash dividends. Under these circumstances, which company represents the best investment opportunity?

LO 11-10

Problem 11-32B *Interpreting the effects of business liquidations*

On January 1, Year 1, Lakeview Company is started when it issues 100 shares of $20 par value stock for a cash price of $25 per share. Also, on January 1 Year 1, Lakeview borrows $45,000 cash by issuing a note payable to the Metropolitan Bank. Lakeview immediately purchases land that costs $40,000 cash. During Year 1 Lakeview earns $10,000 of cash revenue and incurs $5,000 of cash expenses. No other transaction occurred during Year 1.

Required

a. If the bank demands repayment of the note on January 1, Year 2, does Lakeview have the funds available to repay the loan?

b. Determine the amount of cash on hand as of January 1, Year 2.

c. Determine the total amount of liabilities as of January 1, Year 2.

d. Assume that Lakeview is forced to liquidate its business on January 1, Year 2. Further, assume that in the process of liquidation Lakeview has to sell the land for $30,000. Under these circumstances:

1. Determine the amount of cash that the bank would receive in the liquidation.
2. Determine the amount of cash that the investors would receive in the liquidation.

ANALYZE, THINK, COMMUNICATE

ATC 11-1 **Business Applications Case** *Understanding real-world annual reports*

Obtain Target Corporation's annual report for its 2018 fiscal year (year ended February 2, 2019) at http://investors.target.com using the instructions in Appendix B, and use it to answer the following questions:

Required

a. What is the par value per share of Target's stock?

b. How many shares of Target's common stock were *outstanding* as of February 2, 2019?

c. Target's annual report provides some details about the company's executive officers. How many are identified? What is their minimum, maximum, and average age? How many are females?

d. Target's balance sheet does not show a balance for treasury stock. Does this mean the company has not repurchased any of its own stock? Explain.

ATC 11-2 **Group Assignment** *Missing information*

Listed here are the stockholders' equity sections of three public companies for fiscal years ending in 2017 and 2016. Note that for General Mills these data are for the fiscal years ended on May 27, 2018 (2017) and May 28, 2017 (2016).

	2017	2016
The Wendy's Company (in thousands)		
Stockholders' equity		
Common stock, ? par value per share, authorized:		
1,500,000; 470,424 shares issued	$ 47,042	$ 47,042
Additional paid-in capital	2,885,955	2,878,589
Retained earnings	(163,289)	(290,857)
Accumulated other comp. income (loss)	(46,198)	(63,241)
Treasury stock, at cost: 229,912 in 2017		
and 223,850 in 2016	(2,150,307)	(2,043,797)
Coca-Cola (in millions)		
Stockholders' equity		
Common stock, ? par value per share, authorized:		
11,200; issued: 7,040 shares in 2017 and 2016	1,760	1,760
Capital surplus	15,864	14,993
Reinvested earnings	60,430	65,502
Accumulated other comp. inc. (loss)	(10,305)	(11,205)
Treasury stock, at cost: (2,781 shares in 2017 and		
2,752 shares in 2016)	(50,677)	(47,988)

General Mills (in millions)		
Stockholders' equity		
Common stock, ? par value per share,		
754.6 issued in 2018 and 2017	75.5	75.5
Additional paid-in capital	1,202.5	1,120.9
Retained earnings	14,459.6	13,138.9
Accumulated other comp. inc. (loss)	(2,429.0)	(2,244.5)
Treasury stock, at cost: 161.5 and 177.7		
shares in 2018 and 2017, respectively, at cost	(7,167.5)	(7,762.9)

Required

a. Divide the class into three sections and divide each section into groups of three to five students. Assign each section one of the companies.

Group Tasks

Based on the company assigned to your group, answer the following questions.

b. What is the per share par or stated value of the common stock in 2017?

c. What was the average issue price of the common stock for each year?

d. How many shares of stock are outstanding at the end of each year?

e. What is the average cost per share of the treasury stock for 2017?

f. Do the data suggest that your company was profitable in 2017?

g. Can you determine the amount of net income from the information given? What is missing?

h. What is the total stockholders' equity of your company for each year?

Class Discussion

i. Have each group select a representative to present the information about its company. Compare the share issue price and the par or stated value of the companies.

j. Compare the average issue price to the current market price for each of the companies. Speculate about what might cause the difference.

ATC 11-3 Real-World Case *Which stock is most valuable?*

Listed here are data for five companies. These data are for the companies' 2017 fiscal years. The market price per share is the closing price of the companies' stock as of February 28, 2018, two months after the end of their fiscal years. Except for market price per share, all amounts are in millions. The shares outstanding number is the weighted-average number of shares the company used to compute basic earnings per share. Note that Berkshire has only 1.645 million shares outstanding, not 1,645 million.

Company	Net Earnings	Stockholders' Equity	Shares Outstanding	Market Price per Share
Amazon.com	$ 3,033	$ 27,209	484	$ 1,512.45
Berkshire Hathaway	45,353	351,954	1.645	310,250.00
ExxonMobil	19,848	194,5000	4,329	75.74
PepsiCo	4,908	10,981	1,420	109.73
Verizon Communications	30,550	44,6870	4,079	47.74

Required

a. Compute the earnings per share (EPS) for each company.

b. Compute the P/E ratio for each company.

c. Using the P/E ratios, rank the companies' stock in the order that the stock market appears to value the companies, from most valuable to least valuable. Identify reasons the ranking based on P/E ratios may not represent the market's optimism for some companies.

d. Compute the book value per share for each company.

e. Compare each company's book value per share to its market price per share. Based on the data, rank the companies from most valuable to least valuable. (The higher the ratio of market value to book value, the greater the value the stock market appears to be assigning to a company's stock.)

ATC 11-4   Business Applications Case   *Performing ratio analysis using real-world data*

There were 37,855 McDonald's Company restaurants in over 100 countries as of December 31, 2018. Chipotle Mexican Grill, Inc., a much newer fast-food restaurant company, began operations with one restaurant in 1993. At one time, McDonald's was one of its largest investors, but McDonald's divested its Chipotle stock in 2006. As of December 31, 2018, it had 2,452 restaurants operating in the United States. The following data were taken from the companies' December 31, 2018, annual reports.

	McDonald's	Chipotle
Net earnings (in thousands)	$5,924,300	$176,5536
Earnings per share	$ 7.61	$ 6.35
The following data were taken from public stock-price quotes:		
Stock price per share on February 28, 2019	$ 182.81	$ 607.65
(Two months after the end of their 2018 fiscal years)		

Required

a. Compute the price-earnings ratios for each company as of February 28, 2019.

b. Which company's future performance did the financial markets appear to be more optimistic about as of February 28, 2019?

c. Provide some reasons why the market may view one company's future more optimistically than the other.

ATC 11-5   Writing Assignment   *Comparison of organizational forms*

Jim Baku and Scott Hanson are thinking about opening a new restaurant. Baku has extensive marketing experience but does not know that much about food preparation. However, Hanson is an excellent chef. Both will work in the business, but Baku will provide most of the funds necessary to start the business. At this time, they cannot decide whether to operate the business as a partnership or a corporation.

Required

Prepare a written memo to Baku and Hanson describing the advantages and disadvantages of each organizational form. Also, from the limited information provided, recommend the organizational form you think they should use.

ATC 11-6   Ethical Dilemma   *Bad news versus very bad news*

Louise Stinson, the chief financial officer of Bostonian Corporation, was on her way to the president's office. She was carrying the latest round of bad news. There would be no executive bonuses this year. Corporate profits were down. Indeed, if the latest projections held true, the company would report a small loss on the year-end income statement. Executive bonuses were tied to corporate profits. The executive compensation plan provided for 10 percent of net earnings to be set aside for bonuses. No profits meant no bonuses. While things looked bleak, Stinson had a plan that might help soften the blow.

After informing the company president of the earnings forecast, Stinson made the following suggestion: Because the company was going to report a loss anyway, why not report a big loss? She reasoned that the directors and stockholders would not be much angrier if the company reported a large loss than if it reported a small one. There were several questionable assets that could be written down in the current year. This would increase the current year's loss but would reduce expenses in subsequent accounting periods. For example, the company was carrying damaged inventory that was estimated to have a value of $2,500,000. If this estimate were revised to $500,000, the company would have to recognize a $2,000,000 loss in the current year. However, next year when the goods were sold, the expense for cost of goods sold would be $2,000,000 less and profits would be higher by that amount. Although the directors would be angry this year, they would certainly be happy next year. The strategy would also have the benefit of adding $200,000 to next year's executive bonus pool ($2,000,000 × 0.10). Furthermore, it could not hurt this year's bonus pool because there would be no pool this year due to the company reporting a loss.

Some of the other items that Stinson is considering include (1) converting from straight-line to accelerated depreciation, (2) increasing the percentage of receivables estimated to be uncollectible in the current year and lowering the percentage in the following year, and (3) raising the percentage of estimated warranty claims in the current period and lowering it in the following period. Finally, Stinson notes that two of the company's department stores have been experiencing losses. The company could sell these stores this year and thereby improve earnings next year. Stinson admits that the sale would result in significant losses this year, but she smiles as she thinks of next year's bonus check.

Required

a. Explain how each of the three numbered strategies for increasing the amount of the current year's loss would affect the stockholders' equity section of the balance sheet in the current year. How would the other elements of the balance sheet be affected?

b. If Stinson's strategy were effectively implemented, how would it affect the stockholders' equity in subsequent accounting periods?

c. Comment on the ethical implications of running the company for the sake of management (maximization of bonuses) versus the maximization of return to stockholders.

d. Formulate a bonus plan that will motivate managers to maximize the value of the firm instead of motivating them to manipulate the reporting process.

e. How would Stinson's strategy of overstating the amount of the reported loss in the current year affect the company's current P/E ratio?

ATC 11-7 Research Assignment *Analyzing Bed Bath & Beyond's equity structure*

Using either Bed Bath & Beyond, Inc.'s most current Form 10-K or the company's annual report, answer the following questions. To obtain the Form 10-K, use either the EDGAR system, following the instructions in Appendix A, or the company's website. The company's annual report is available on its website.

Required

a. What is the *book value* of Bed Bath & Beyond's stockholders' equity that is shown on the company's balance sheet? What is its book value per share?

b. What is the par value of Bed Bath & Beyond's common stock?

c. Does Bed Bath & Beyond have any treasury stock? If so, how many shares of treasury stock does the company hold?

d. In recent years, the market price of Bed Bath & Beyond's stock has often been lower than its book value. What does this say about investors' opinion of the company's future prospects?

CHAPTER 12

Statement of Cash Flows

Video lectures and accompanying self-assessment quizzes are available in *Connect* for all learning objectives.

Tableau Dashboard Activity is available in *Connect* for this chapter.

LEARNING OBJECTIVES

After you have mastered the material in this chapter, you will be able to:

LO 12-1 Prepare the operating activities section of a statement of cash flows using the indirect method.

LO 12-2 Prepare the operating activities section of a statement of cash flows using the direct method.

LO 12-3 Prepare the investing activities section of a statement of cash flows.

LO 12-4 Prepare the financing activities section of a statement of cash flows.

CHAPTER OPENING

To make informed investment and credit decisions, financial statement users need information to help them assess the amounts, timing, and uncertainty of a company's prospective cash flows. This chapter explains more about the items reported on the statement of cash flows and describes a more practical way to prepare the statement than analyzing every event affecting the cash account. As previously shown, the statement of cash flows reports how a company obtained and spent cash during an accounting period. Sources of cash are **cash inflows**, and uses are **cash outflows**. Cash receipts (inflows) and payments (outflows) are reported as operating activities, investing activities, or financing activities.

The Curious Accountant

As described in The Curious Accountant for Chapter 11, **Dropbox, Inc.** began operations in 2007 and began selling its stock to the public on March 23, 2018. It has lost money every year it has been in existence. In 2017 alone, its losses were $112 million, and by December 31, 2017, it had total lifetime losses of approximately $1.1 billion.

How could Dropbox lose so much money and still be able to pay its bills? (Answers on page 592.)

Wirul Kengthankan/123RF

AN OVERVIEW OF THE STATEMENT OF CASH FLOWS

The statement of cash flows provides information about cash coming into and going out of a business during an accounting period. Cash flows are classified into one of three categories: operating activities, investing activities, or financing activities. A separate section also displays any significant noncash investing and financing activities. Descriptions of these categories and how they are presented in the statement of cash flows follow.

Operating Activities

Routine cash inflows and outflows resulting from running (operating) a business are reported in the **operating activities** section of the statement of cash flows. Cash flows reported as operating activities include:

1. Cash receipts from revenues, including interest and dividend revenue.

2. Cash payments for expenses, including interest expense. Recall that dividend payments are not expenses. Dividend payments are reported in the financing activities section.

EXHIBIT 12.1

Operating Activities—Direct Method

Cash Flows from Operating Activities

Cash receipts from customers	$400
Cash payments for expenses	(350)
Net cash flow from operating activities	$ 50

Under generally accepted accounting principles, the operating activities section of the statement of cash flows can be presented using either the *direct* or the *indirect* method. The **direct method** explicitly (*directly*) identifies the major *sources* and *uses* of cash. To illustrate, assume that, during Year 1, New South Company earns revenue on account of $500 and collects $400 cash from customers. Further assume the company incurs $390 of expenses on account and pays $350 cash to settle accounts payable. Exhibit 12.1 shows the operating activities section of the statement of cash flows using the *direct method.*

In contrast, the **indirect method** starts with net income as reported on the income statement, followed by the adjustments necessary to convert the accrual-based net income figure to a cash-basis equivalent. To illustrate, begin with New South Company's income statement based on the earlier assumptions:

Revenues	$500
Expenses	(390)
Net income	$110

Converting the net income of $110 to the net cash flow from operating activities of $50 requires the following adjustments:

1. New South earned $500 of revenue but collected only $400 in cash. The remaining $100 will be collected in the next accounting period. This $100 *increase in accounts receivable* must be *subtracted* from net income to determine cash flow because it increased net income but did not increase cash.

2. New South incurred $390 of expense but paid only $350 in cash. The remaining $40 will be paid in the next accounting period. This $40 *increase in accounts payable* must be *added* back to net income to determine cash flow because it decreased net income but did not use cash.

EXHIBIT 12.2

Operating Activities—Indirect Method

Cash Flows from Operating Activities

Net income	$110
Subtract: Increase in accounts receivable	(100)
Add: Increase in accounts payable	40
Net cash flow from operating activities	$ 50

Exhibit 12.2 shows the operating activities section of the statement of cash flows using the *indirect method*.

Compare the direct method presented in Exhibit 12.1 with the indirect method presented in Exhibit 12.2. Both methods report $50 of net cash flow from operating activities. They represent two different approaches to computing the same amount.

Because people typically find the direct method easier to understand, the Financial Accounting Standards Board (FASB) recommends it. Most companies, however, use the indirect method. Why? Back when the FASB adopted a requirement for companies to include a statement of cash flows in their published financial statements, most companies used accounting systems that were compatible with the indirect method. It was therefore easier to prepare the new statement under the indirect method using existing systems than to create new recordkeeping systems compatible with the direct method.

The FASB continues to advocate the direct method, and a growing number of companies use it. Because the majority of companies continue to use the indirect method, however, financial statement users should understand both methods.

 CHECK YOURSELF 12.1

Hammer, Inc. had a beginning balance of $22,400 in its Accounts Receivable account. During the accounting period, Hammer earned $234,700 of net income. The ending balance in the Accounts Receivable account was $18,200. Based on this information alone, determine the amount of cash flow from operating activities.

Answer

Account Title	Ending	Beginning	Change
Accounts receivable	$18,200	$22,400	$(4,200)

Applicable Rule	Cash Flow from Operating Activities	Amount
	Net Income	$234,700
Rule 1	Add: Decrease in accounts receivable	4,200
	Cash flow from operating activities	$238,900

Investing Activities

For a business, long-term assets are investments. Cash flows related to acquiring or disposing of long-term assets are therefore reported in the **investing activities** section of the statement of cash flows. Cash flows reported as investing activities include:

1. Cash receipts (inflows) from selling property, plant, equipment, or marketable securities, as well as collections from credit instruments such as notes or mortgages receivable.

2. Cash payments (outflows) for purchasing property, plant, equipment, or marketable securities, as well as for making loans to borrowers.

Financing Activities

Cash flows related to borrowing (short- or long-term) and stockholders' equity are reported in the **financing activities** section of the statement of cash flows. Cash flows reported as financing activities include:

Ryan McVay/Photodisc/Getty Images

1. Cash receipts (inflows) from borrowing money and issuing stock.
2. Cash payments (outflows) to repay debt, purchase treasury stock, and pay dividends.

The classification of cash flows is based on the type of activity, not the type of account. For example, buying another company's common stock is an investing activity, but issuing a company's own common stock is a financing activity. Receiving dividends from a common stock investment is an operating activity, and paying dividends to a company's own stockholders is a financing activity. Similarly, loaning money is an investing activity, although borrowing it is a financing activity. Focus on the type of activity rather than the type of account when classifying cash flows as operating, investing, or financing activities.

Noncash Investing and Financing Activities

Companies sometimes undertake significant **noncash investing and financing activities** such as acquiring a long-term asset in exchange for common stock. Because these types of transactions do not involve exchanging cash, they are not reported in the main body of the statement of cash flows. However, because the FASB requires that all material investing and financing activities be disclosed, whether or not they involve exchanging cash, companies must include with the statement of cash flows a separate schedule of any noncash investing and financing activities.

Reporting Format for the Statement of Cash Flows

Cash flow categories are reported in the following order: (1) operating activities; (2) investing activities; and (3) financing activities. In each category, the difference between the inflows and outflows is presented as a net cash inflow or outflow for the category. These net amounts are combined to determine the net change (increase or decrease) in the company's cash for the period. The net change in cash is combined with the beginning cash balance to determine the ending cash balance. The ending cash balance on the statement of cash flows is the same as the cash balance reported on the balance sheet. The schedule of noncash investing and financing activities is typically presented at the bottom of the statement of cash flows. Exhibit 12.3 outlines this format.

As indicated in Exhibit 12.4, 50 percent of the companies that make up the Dow Jones Industrial Average show the statement of cash flows as the third statement presented, with the remaining 50 percent presenting it as the fourth statement. However, a sizable number of companies present it after the income statement and balance sheet but before the statement of changes in stockholders' equity. Some companies place the statement of cash flows first, before the other three statements.

EXHIBIT 12.3	Format for Statement of Cash Flows

WESTERN COMPANY	
Statement of Cash Flows	
For the Year Ended December 31, Year 5	
Cash flows from operating activities	
Net Inflow (outflow) from operating activities	XXX
Cash flows from investing activities	
Net Inflow (outflow) from investing activities	XXX
Cash flows from financing activities	
Net Inflow (outflow) from financing activities	<u>XXX</u>
Net Inflow (outflow) in cash	XXX
Plus: Beginning cash balance	<u>XXX</u>
Ending cash balance	<u>XXX</u>
Schedule of Noncash Investing and Financing Activities	
List of significant noncash transactions	<u>XXX</u>

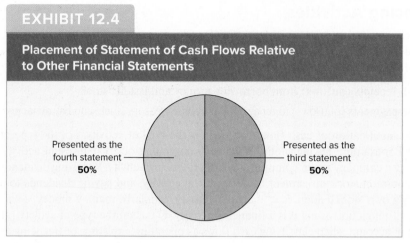

EXHIBIT 12.4

Placement of Statement of Cash Flows Relative to Other Financial Statements

Presented as the fourth statement — 50%

Presented as the third statement — 50%

Source: Dow Jones Industrial Average

PREPARING A STATEMENT OF CASH FLOWS

Most of the data needed to construct a statement of cash flows can be obtained from two successive balance sheets and the intervening income statement. Certain information from the long-term asset records is also usually required. To illustrate, refer to the financial statements for New South Company presented in Exhibit 12.5. Notice that cash decreased from $400 at the end of Year 1 to $300 at the end of Year 2. The statement of cash flows explains what caused this $100 decrease.

EXHIBIT 12.5   Financial Statements for New South Company

NEW SOUTH COMPANY
Balance Sheets
As of December 31

	Year 2	Year 1
Current assets:		
Cash	$ 300	$ 400
Accounts receivable	1,000	1,200
Interest receivable	400	300
Inventory	8,900	8,200
Prepaid insurance	1,100	1,400
Total current assets	11,700	11,500
Long-term assets		
Investment securities	5,100	3,500
Store fixtures	5,400	4,800
Accumulated depreciation	(900)	(1,200)
Land	8,200	6,000
Total long-term assets	17,800	13,100
Total assets	$29,500	$24,600
Current liabilities:		
Accounts payable—inventory purchases	$ 800	$ 1,100
Salaries payable	1,000	900
Other operating expenses payable	1,500	1,300
Interest payable	300	500
Unearned rent revenue	600	1,600
Total current liabilities	4,200	5,400

continued

EXHIBIT 12.5	*Concluded*

NEW SOUTH COMPANY
Balance Sheets
As of December 31

	Year 2	Year 1
Long-term liabilities		
Mortgage payable	2,200	0
Bonds payable	1,000	4,000
Total long-term liabilities	3,200	4,000
Stockholders' equity		
Common stock	10,000	8,000
Retained earnings	12,700	7,200
Treasury stock	(600)	0
Total stockholders' equity	22,100	15,200
Total liabilities and stockholders' equity	$29,500	$24,600

NEW SOUTH COMPANY
Income Statement
For the Year Ended December 31, Year 2

Sales revenue		$20,600
Cost of goods sold		(10,500)
Gross margin		10,100
Operating expenses		
Depreciation expense	$ (1,000)	
Salaries expense	(2,700)	
Insurance expense	(1,300)	
Other operating expenses	(1,400)	
Total operating expenses		(6,400)
Income from sales business		3,700
Other income—rent revenue		2,400
Operating income		6,100
Nonoperating revenue and expense		
Interest revenue	700	
Interest expense	(400)	
Gain on sale of store fixtures	600	
Total nonoperating items		900
Net income		$ 7,000

Note 1: No investment securities were sold during Year 2.

Note 2: During Year 2, New South sold store fixtures that had originally cost $1,700. At the time of sale, accumulated depreciation on the fixtures was $1,300.

Note 3: Land was acquired during Year 2 by issuing a mortgage note payable. No land sales occurred during Year 2.

PREPARING THE OPERATING ACTIVITIES SECTION OF A STATEMENT OF CASH FLOWS USING THE INDIRECT METHOD

LO 12-1

 Prepare the operating activities section of a statement of cash flows using the indirect method.

Recall that the indirect approach begins with the amount of net income. Many aspects of accrual accounting, such as recognizing revenues and expenses on account, can cause differences between the amount of net income reported on a company's income statement and the amount of net cash flow it reports from operating activities. Most of the differences between

Answers to The Curious Accountant

First, it should be remembered that GAAP requires earnings and losses be computed on an accrual basis. A company can have negative earnings and still have positive cash flows from operating activities. This was the case at Dropbox. For 2016 and 2017, the company's cash flows from operating activities totaled a positive $582.918 million.

In its early years of operations, Dropbox, like many new companies, was also able to stay in business because of the cash it raised through financing activities. Obviously, a company cannot operate indefinitely without generating cash from operating activities. Individuals and institutions who are willing to buy a company's stock or loan it cash in its early years will disappear if they do not believe the company will eventually begin earning profits and generating positive cash flows from operations. Exhibit 12.6 presents Dropbox's statements of cash flows for 2016 and 2017.

EXHIBIT 12.6

DROPBOX, INC.
Consolidated Statements of Cash Flows (partial)
(in thousands)

	Year Ended December 31	
	2016	2017
Cash flows from operating activities		
Net loss	$ (210.2)	$ (111.7)
Adjustments to reconcile net loss to net cash provided by operating activities:		
Depreciation and amortization	191.6	181.8
Stock-based compensation	147.6	164.6
Amortization of deferred commissions	3.7	6.6
Donation of common stock to charitable foundation	—	9.4
Other	1.1	(1.7)
Changes in operating assets and liabilities:		
Trade and other receivables, net	1.0	(14.4)
Prepaid expenses and other current assets	—	(18.2)
Other assets	(7.8)	(10.6)
Accounts payable	5.5	16.2
Accrued and other current liabilities	(12.4)	34.0
Accrued compensation and benefits	35.6	14.4
Deferred revenue	87.6	64.3
Non-current liabilities	9.3	(4.4)
Net cash provided by operating activities	252.6	330.3
Cash flows from investing activities		
Capital expenditures	(115.2)	(25.3)
Purchase of intangible assets	(8.5)	(0.8)
Cash received from equipment rebates	3.6	2.2
Cash received from sales of equipment	2.1	—
Net cash used in investing activities	(118.0)	(23.9)

continued

EXHIBIT 12.6   *Concluded*

DROPBOX, INC.
Consolidated Statements of Cash Flows (partial)
(in thousands)

	Year Ended December 31	
	2016	2017
Cash flows from financing activities		
Principle payments on capital lease obligations	(137.9)	(133.0)
Principle payments against note payable	(3.8)	(3.9)
Principle payments against financing lease obligation	(1.6)	(2.3)
Proceeds from sale-leaseback agreement	8.8	—
Fees paid for revolving credit facility	—	(2.6)
Shares repurchased for tax withholding on release of restricted stock	—	(87.9)
Proceeds from issuance of common stock, net of repurchases	—	0.5
Payments of deferred offering costs	—	(2.5)
Net cash provided by financing activities	(134.5)	(231.7)
Effect of exchange rates on cash and cash equivalents	(4.3)	2.6
Changes in cash and cash equivalents	(4.2)	77.3
Cash, cash equivalents, and restricted cash – beginning of period	356.9	352.7
Cash, cash equivalents, and restricted cash – end of period	$ 352.7	$430.0

revenue and expense recognition and cash flows are related to changes in the balances of the noncash current assets and current liabilities.

Indirect Method—Reconciliation Approach

The following section of this chapter examines the relationships between items reported on the income statement and the related assets and liabilities. Begin by reconciling the *noncash current asset and current liability* amounts shown on the balance sheets in Exhibit 12.5. *Do not include Cash in this analysis.* The amount of the change in the cash balance is the result of not only operating activities but also investing and financing activities.

Reconciliation of Accounts Receivable

Use the information in Exhibit 12.5 to prepare the following reconciliation of Accounts Receivable. The beginning and ending balances appear on the balance sheets. The *increase due to revenue recognized on account* is the sales revenue reported on the income statement.

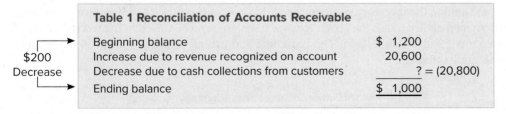

Table 1 Reconciliation of Accounts Receivable

Beginning balance	$ 1,200
Increase due to revenue recognized on account	20,600
Decrease due to cash collections from customers	? = (20,800)
Ending balance	$ 1,000

$200 Decrease

To balance Accounts Receivable, the *decrease due to cash collections from customers* must be $20,800.[1]

The reconciliation shows that the $200 decrease in the accounts receivable balance occurred because *cash collections from customers* were $200 more than the amount of *revenue recognized on account* ($20,800 versus $20,600). Because the amount of cash collected is more than the amount of revenue recognized, we add $200 to the amount of net income to determine net cash flow from operating activities (Reference No. 1 in Exhibit 12.7).

[1]This text uses the simplifying assumption that all sales occur on account.

Reconciliation of Interest Receivable

The beginning and ending balances appear on the balance sheets in Exhibit 12.5. The *increase due to interest revenue recognized on account* is the interest revenue reported on the income statement.

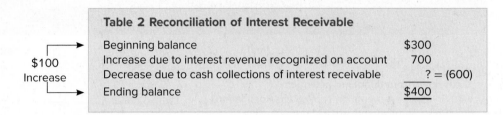

Table 2 Reconciliation of Interest Receivable	
Beginning balance	$300
Increase due to interest revenue recognized on account	700
Decrease due to cash collections of interest receivable	? = (600)
Ending balance	$400

To balance Interest Receivable, the *decrease due to cash collections of interest receivable* must be $600.

The reconciliation shows that the $100 increase in the interest receivable balance occurred because *cash collections of interest* were $100 less than the *interest revenue recognized on account* ($600 versus $700). Because the amount of cash collected is less than the amount of revenue recognized, we subtract the $100 from the amount of net income to determine net cash flow from operating activities (Reference No. 2 in Exhibit 12.7).

Reconciliation of Inventory and Accounts Payable

To simplify computing the amount of cash paid for inventory purchases, assume that all inventory purchases are made on account. The computation requires two steps. First, Inventory must be analyzed to determine the amount of inventory purchased. Second, Accounts Payable must be analyzed to determine the amount of cash paid to purchase inventory.

Use the financial statement information in Exhibit 12.5 to prepare the following Inventory reconciliation. The beginning and ending balances appear on the balance sheets. The *decrease due to recognizing cost of goods sold* is the cost of goods sold reported on the income statement.

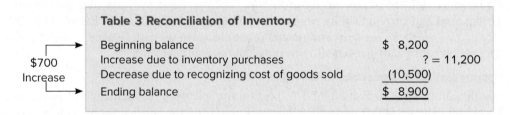

Table 3 Reconciliation of Inventory	
Beginning balance	$ 8,200
Increase due to inventory purchases	? = 11,200
Decrease due to recognizing cost of goods sold	(10,500)
Ending balance	$ 8,900

To balance Inventory, the *increase due to inventory purchases* must be $11,200.

Assuming the inventory was purchased on account, the $11,200 of inventory purchases determined earlier equals the *increase due to inventory purchases* used in the reconciliation of Accounts Payable that follows. The beginning and ending balances appear on the balance sheets in Exhibit 12.5.

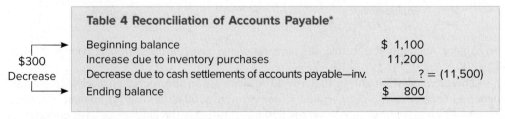

Table 4 Reconciliation of Accounts Payable*	
Beginning balance	$ 1,100
Increase due to inventory purchases	11,200
Decrease due to cash settlements of accounts payable—inv.	? = (11,500)
Ending balance	$ 800

*Assume that Accounts Payable is used for purchases of inventory only.

To balance Accounts Payable, the *decrease due to cash settlements of accounts payable–inventory* (cash paid to purchase inventory) must be $11,500.

Because the amount of *cash paid to purchase inventory* is $1,000 more than the amount of *cost of goods sold* recognized on the income statement ($11,500 versus $10,500), we subtract the $1,000 difference from the amount of net income to determine net cash flow from operating activities. In Exhibit 12.7, the $1,000 subtraction is divided between a $700 increase in inventory (Reference No. 3 in Exhibit 12.7) and a $300 decrease in accounts payable (Reference No. 4 in Exhibit 12.7).

Reconciliation of Prepaid Insurance

Use the financial statement information in Exhibit 12.5 to reconcile Prepaid Insurance. The beginning and ending balances appear on the balance sheets. The *decrease due to recognizing insurance expense* is the insurance expense reported on the income statement.

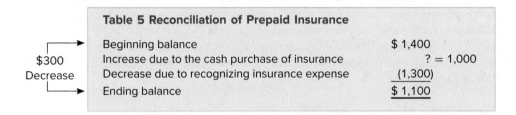

Table 5 Reconciliation of Prepaid Insurance	
Beginning balance	$ 1,400
Increase due to the cash purchase of insurance	? = 1,000
Decrease due to recognizing insurance expense	(1,300)
Ending balance	$ 1,100

$300 Decrease

To balance Prepaid Insurance, the amount of the *increase due to the cash purchase of insurance* must be $1,000.

The reconciliation shows that the $300 decrease in the prepaid insurance balance occurred because *cash paid to purchase insurance* was $300 less than the amount of *insurance expense recognized* ($1,000 versus $1,300). Because the amount of cash paid is less than the amount of expense recognized, we add $300 to the amount of net income to determine the net cash flow from operating activities (Reference No. 5 in Exhibit 12.7).

Reconciliation of Salaries Payable

Use the financial statement information in Exhibit 12.5 to reconcile Salaries Payable. The beginning and ending balances appear on the balance sheets. The *increase due to recognizing salary expense on account* is the salaries expense reported on the income statement.

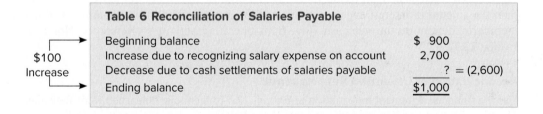

Table 6 Reconciliation of Salaries Payable	
Beginning balance	$ 900
Increase due to recognizing salary expense on account	2,700
Decrease due to cash settlements of salaries payable	? = (2,600)
Ending balance	$1,000

$100 Increase

To balance Salaries Payable, the amount of the *decrease due to cash settlements of salaries payable* (cash paid for salaries expense) must be $2,600. The reconciliation shows that the $100 increase in the salaries payable balance occurred because the *cash paid for salary expense* is $100 less than the amount of *salary expense recognized on account* ($2,600 versus $2,700). Because the amount of cash paid is less than the amount of expense recognized, we add $100 to the amount of net income to determine the cash flow from operating activities (Reference No. 6 in Exhibit 12.7).

Reconciliation of Other Operating Expenses Payable

Use the financial statement information in Exhibit 12.5 to reconcile Other Operating Expenses Payable. The beginning and ending balances appear on the balance sheets. The *increase due to recognizing other operating expenses on account* is the other operating expenses amount reported on the income statement.

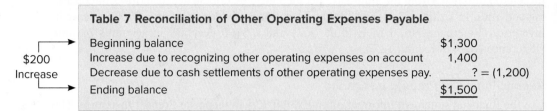

Table 7 Reconciliation of Other Operating Expenses Payable

Beginning balance	$1,300
Increase due to recognizing other operating expenses on account	1,400
Decrease due to cash settlements of other operating expenses pay.	? = (1,200)
Ending balance	$1,500

$200 Increase

To balance Other Operating Expenses Payable, the amount of the *decrease due to cash settlements of other operating expenses payable* must be $1,200.

The reconciliation shows that the $200 increase in the other operating expenses payable balance occurred because the *cash paid for other operating expenses* was $200 less than the amount of *other operating expenses recognized on account* ($1,200 versus $1,400). Because the amount of cash paid is less than the amount of expense recognized, we add $200 to the amount of net income to determine the net cash flow from operating activities (Reference No. 7 in Exhibit 12.7).

Reconciliation of Interest Payable

Use the financial statement information in Exhibit 12.5 to reconcile Interest Payable. The beginning and ending balances appear on the balance sheets. The *increase due to recognizing interest expense on account* is the interest expense reported on the income statement.

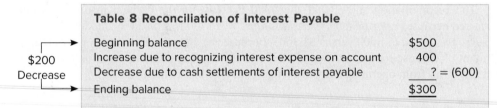

Table 8 Reconciliation of Interest Payable

Beginning balance	$500
Increase due to recognizing interest expense on account	400
Decrease due to cash settlements of interest payable	? = (600)
Ending balance	$300

$200 Decrease

To balance Interest Payable, the amount of the *decrease due to cash settlements of interest payable* (cash paid for interest expense) must be $600.

The reconciliation shows that the $200 decrease in the interest payable balance occurred because the amount of *cash paid for interest expense* is $200 more than the amount of *interest expense recognized on account* ($600 versus $400). Because the amount of cash paid is more than the amount of interest expense recognized, we subtract $200 from the amount of net income to determine the net cash flow from operating activities (Reference No. 8 in Exhibit 12.7).

Reconciliation of Unearned Rent Revenue

Use the financial statement information in Exhibit 12.5 to reconcile Unearned Rent Revenue. The beginning and ending balances appear on the balance sheets. The *decrease due to recognizing other income–rent revenue* is the other income–rent revenue reported on the income statement.

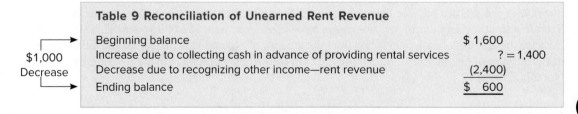

Table 9 Reconciliation of Unearned Rent Revenue

Beginning balance	$ 1,600
Increase due to collecting cash in advance of providing rental services	? = 1,400
Decrease due to recognizing other income–rent revenue	(2,400)
Ending balance	$ 600

$1,000 Decrease

To balance Unearned Rent Revenue, the amount of the *increase due to collecting cash in advance of providing rental services* must be $1,400.

EXHIBIT 12.7

	Cash Flows from Operating Activities—Indirect Method	
Reference No.	**Cash Flows from Operating Activities**	
	Net income	$ 7,000
	Adjustments to reconcile net income to net cash flow from operating activities:	
1	Decrease in accounts receivable	200
2	Increase in interest receivable	(100)
3	Increase in inventory	(700)
4	Decrease in accounts payable for inventory purchases	(300)
5	Decrease in prepaid insurance	300
6	Increase in salaries payable	100
7	Increase in other operating expenses payable	200
8	Decrease in interest payable	(200)
9	Decrease in unearned rent revenue	(1,000)
10	Depreciation expense	1,000
11	Gain on sale of store fixtures	(600)
	Net cash flow from operating activities	$ 5,900

The reconciliation shows that the $1,000 decrease in the unearned rent revenue balance occurred because the amount of *cash collected in advance of providing rental services* is $1,000 less than the amount of *rent revenue recognized* ($1,400 versus $2,400). Because the amount of cash collected is less than the amount of revenue recognized, we subtract $1,000 from the amount of net income to determine the net cash flow from operating activities (Reference No. 9 in Exhibit 12.7).

Noncash Expenses

The calculation of accrual-based net income frequently includes noncash expenses such as depreciation expense. Because noncash expenses are deducted in determining net income, they must be added back to the amount of net income when computing net cash flow from operating activities (Reference No. 10 in Exhibit 12.7).

Gains and Losses

When a company retires a long-term asset, the company may receive cash from the sale of the asset being retired. If the asset is sold for more than book value (cost — accumulated depreciation), the gain increases net income; if the asset is sold for less than book value, the loss decreases net income. In either case, the cash inflow is the total amount of cash collected from selling the asset, not the amount of the gain or loss, and this cash inflow is reported in the investing activities section of the statement of cash flows. Because gains increase net income and losses decrease net income, but neither represents the amount of cash received from an asset sale, gains must be subtracted from and losses added back to net income to determine net cash flow from operating activities (Reference No. 11 in Exhibit 12.7).

Indirect Method—Rule-Based Approach

The reconciliation process described in the previous section of this chapter leads to a set of rules that can be used to convert accrual-based revenues and expenses to their cash flow equivalents. These rules are summarized in Exhibit 12.8.

Although the rule-based approach offers less insight, it is easy to apply. To illustrate, return to the financial statement data in Exhibit 12.5. The *noncash* current assets and current liabilities reported on the balance sheets are summarized in Exhibit 12.9 for your convenience. The amount of the change in each balance is shown in the *Change* column.

EXHIBIT 12.8

Cash Flows from Operating Activities—Indirect Method

	Net income	XXX
Rule 1	Add decreases and subtract increases in noncash current assets.	XXX
Rule 2	Add increases and subtract decreases in noncash current liabilities.	XXX
Rule 3	Add noncash expenses (e.g., depreciation).	XXX
Rule 4	Add losses and subtract gains.	XXX
	Net cash flow from operating activities	XXX

EXHIBIT 12.9

Noncash Current Assets and Current Liabilities

Account Title	Year 2	Year 1	Change
Accounts receivable	$1,000	$1,200	$ (200)
Interest receivable	400	300	100
Inventory	8,900	8,200	700
Prepaid insurance	1,100	1,400	(300)
Accounts payable—inventory purchases	800	1,100	(300)
Salaries payable	1,000	900	100
Other operating expenses payable	1,500	1,300	200
Interest payable	300	500	(200)
Unearned rent revenue	600	1,600	(1,000)

Refer to the income statement to identify the amounts of net income, noncash expenses, gains, and losses. The income statement for New South Company in Exhibit 12.5 includes three relevant figures: net income of $7,000; depreciation expense of $1,000; and a $600 gain on the sale of store fixtures. Applying the rules in Exhibit 12.8 produces the operating activities section of the statement of cash flows shown in Exhibit 12.10. The applicable rule for each item is referenced in the first column of the exhibit.

EXHIBIT 12.10 — Cash Flows from Operating Activities—Indirect Method, Operating Activities

NEW SOUTH COMPANY
Statement of Cash Flows
For the Year Ended December 31, Year 2

Applicable Rule	Cash Flows from Operating Activities	
	Net income	$7,000
	Adjustments to reconcile net income to net cash flow from operating activities:	
Rule 1	Decrease in accounts receivable	200
Rule 1	Increase in interest receivable	(100)
Rule 1	Increase in inventory	(700)
Rule 2	Decrease in accounts payable for inventory purchases	(300)
Rule 1	Decrease in prepaid insurance	300
Rule 2	Increase in salaries payable	100
Rule 2	Increase in other operating expenses payable	200
Rule 2	Decrease in interest payable	(200)
Rule 2	Decrease in unearned rent revenue	(1,000)
Rule 3	Depreciation expense	1,000
Rule 4	Gain on sale of store fixtures	(600)
	Net cash flow from operating activities	$5,900

The operating activities section of the statements of cash flows shown in Exhibits 12.10 and 12.7 are identical. The rule-based approach is an alternative way to prepare this section when using the indirect method.

CHECK YOURSELF 12.2

Q Magazine, Inc. reported $369,000 of net income for the month. At the beginning of the month, its Unearned Revenue account had a balance of $78,000. At the end of the month, the account had a balance of $67,000. Based on this information alone, determine the amount of net cash flow from operating activities.

Answer

Account Title	Ending	Beginning	Change
Unearned revenue	$67,000	$78,000	$(11,000)

Applicable Rule	Cash Flows from Operating Activities	Amount
	Net income	$369,000
Rule 2	Deduct: Decrease in unearned revenue	(11,000)
	Net cash flow from operating activities	$358,000

CHECK YOURSELF 12.3

The following account balances were drawn from the accounting records of Loeb, Inc.:

Account Title	Ending Balance	Beginning Balance
Prepaid rent	$3,000	$4,200
Interest payable	2,650	2,900

Loeb reported $7,400 of net income during the accounting period. Based on this information alone, determine the amount of net cash flow from operating activities.

Answer Based on Rule 1, the $1,200 decrease ($4,200 − $3,000) in Prepaid Rent (current asset) must be added to net income to determine the amount of net cash flow from operating activities. Rule 2 requires that the $250 decrease ($2,900 − $2,650) in interest Payable (current liability) must be deducted from net income. Accordingly, the cash flow from operating activities is $8,350 ($7,400 + $1,200 − $250). Note that paying interest is defined as an operating activity and should not be confused with dividend payments, which are classified as financing activities.

CHECK YOURSELF 12.4

Arley Company's income statement reported net income (all amounts are in millions) of $326 for the year. The income statement included depreciation expense of $45 and a net loss on the sale of long-term assets of $22. Based on this information alone, determine the net cash flow from operating activities.

Answer Based on Rule 3 and Rule 4, both the depreciation expense and the loss would have to be added to net income to determine net cash flow from operating activities. Net cash flow from operating activities would be $393 million ($326 + $45 + $22).

PREPARING THE OPERATING ACTIVITIES SECTION OF A STATEMENT OF CASH FLOWS USING THE DIRECT METHOD

The reconciliation tables developed earlier to determine net cash flow from operating activities under the *indirect method* also disclose the information needed to present the amount of net cash flow from operating activities under the *direct method*. Remember that the amount of net cash flow from operating activities is the same whether it is presented using the indirect or the direct method.

The direct method shows the specific sources and uses of cash that are associated with operating activities. It does not show adjustments to net income. To illustrate, examine Exhibit 12.11. The information in the reference column identifies the reconciliation table from which the cash flow amounts were drawn.

EXHIBIT 12.11		
Cash Flows from Operating Activities—Direct Method		
Reference	**Cash Flows from Operating Activities**	
Table 1	Inflow from customers	$20,800
Table 2	Inflow from interest revenue	600
Table 4	Outflow for inventory purchases	(11,500)
Table 5	Outflow to purchase insurance	(1,000)
Table 6	Outflow to pay salary expense	(2,600)
Table 7	Outflow for other operating expenses	(1,200)
Table 8	Outflow to pay interest expense	(600)
Table 9	Inflow from rent revenue	1,400
	Net cash flow from operating activities	$ 5,900

Table 3 is not included in Exhibit 12.11 because it does not directly involve a cash flow. Also, noncash expenses, gains, and losses are not used in the determination of net cash flow from operating activities when using the direct method.

PREPARING THE INVESTING ACTIVITIES SECTION OF A STATEMENT OF CASH FLOWS

The direct and indirect methods discussed earlier pertain only to the presentation of operating activities. The *investing activities* section of the statement of cash flows is the same regardless of whether the direct or indirect method is used for operating activities. The information necessary to identify cash inflows and outflows from investing activities is obtained by reconciling changes in a company's long-term assets. In general:

- Increases in long-term asset balances suggest cash outflows to purchase assets.
- Decreases in long-term asset balances suggest cash inflows from selling assets.

It is usually necessary to analyze data from the long-term asset records to determine details about long-term asset purchases and sales. In the New South Company example, these details are presented as notes at the bottom of the balance sheets.

To illustrate, return to the financial statements in Exhibit 12.5. New South Company reports the following three long-term assets on its balance sheets. *It is not necessary to reconcile accumulated depreciation because it does not affect cash flow.*

Long-Term Asset	Year 2	Year 1
Investment securities	$5,100	$3,500
Store fixtures	5,400	4,800
Land	8,200	6,000

For each long-term asset, reconcile the beginning and ending balances by identifying purchases and sales affecting it. Review the notes for additional relevant information. Begin with investment securities.

Reconciliation of Investment Securities

Reconciliation of Investment Securities	
Beginning balance in investment securities	$3,500
Increase due to purchase of investment securities	? = 1,600
Decrease due to sale of investment securities	0
Ending balance in investment securities	$5,100

Because Note 1 below the balance sheets indicates no investment securities were sold during Year 2, the *decrease due to sale of investment securities* is zero. To balance Investment Securities, the *increase due to purchase of investment securities* must be $1,600. In the absence of contrary information, assume New South used cash to purchase the investment securities. This cash outflow is reported in the investing activities section of the statement of cash flows in Exhibit 12.12.

EXHIBIT 12.12

Cash Flows from Investing Activities

Cash Flows from Investing Activities	
Cash outflow to purchase investment securities	$(1,600)
Cash inflow from the sale of store fixtures	1,000
Cash outflow to purchase store fixtures	(2,300)
Net cash outflow from investing activities	$(2,900)

Reconciliation of Store Fixtures

Reconciliation of Store Fixtures	
Beginning balance in store fixtures	$ 4,800
Increase due to purchase of store fixtures	? = 2,300
Decrease due to sale of store fixtures	(1,700)
Ending balance in store fixtures	$ 5,400

Note 2 below the balance sheets indicates that the *decrease due to sale of store fixtures* is $1,700. What is the cash flow from this sale? The book value of these fixtures was $400 ($1,700 cost − $1,300 accumulated depreciation). Because the income statement reports a $600 gain on the sale of store fixtures, the cash collected from the sale was more than the book value of the store fixtures. Compute the amount of cash collected from the sale of store fixtures as follows:

$$\text{Cash inflow} = \text{Book value} + \text{Gain} = \$400 + \$600 = \$1,000$$

The $1,000 cash inflow from the sale of store fixtures is reported in the investing activities section of the statement of cash flows in Exhibit 12.12.

To balance Store Fixtures, the *increase due to purchase of store fixtures* must be $2,300. In the absence of contrary information, assume New South used cash to purchase store fixtures. The cash outflow is reported in the investing activities section of the statement of cash flows in Exhibit 12.12.

Reconciliation of Land

Reconciliation of Land	
Beginning balance in land	$6,000
Increase due to purchase of land	? = 2,200
Decrease due to sale of land	0
Ending balance in land	$8,200

Because Note 3 below the balance sheets indicates no land was sold during Year 2, the *decrease due to sale of land* is zero. To balance Land, the *increase due to purchase of land* must be $2,200. Because the land was acquired by issuing a mortgage note payable, New South did not use cash for the purchase. This type of transaction is reported in the *noncash investing and financing activities* section of the statement of cash flows, discussed in more detail later in the chapter. The cash inflows and outflows from investing activities are summarized in Exhibit 12.12.

CHECK YOURSELF 12.5

On January 1, Year 7, Wyatt Company had an Equipment balance of $124,000. During Year 7, Wyatt purchased equipment that cost $50,000. The balance in Equipment on December 31, Year 7, was $90,000. The Year 7 income statement included a $7,000 loss from the sale of equipment. On the date of sale, accumulated depreciation on the equipment sold was $49,000.

Required

a. Determine the cost of the equipment sold during Year 7.

b. Determine the amount of cash flow from the sale of equipment that should be reported in the investing activities section of the Year 7 statement of cash flows.

Solution

a.

Reconciliation of Equipment	
Beginning balance	$124,000
Increase due to the purchase of equipment	50,000
Decrease due to sale of equipment	? = (84,000)
Ending balance	$ 90,000

To balance Equipment, the *decrease due to sale of equipment* must be $84,000.

b. The book value of the equipment sold was $35,000 ($84,000 − $49,000 accumulated depreciation). Because Wyatt recognized a loss on the equipment sale, the amount of cash collected from the sale was less than the book value of the equipment. The cash collected from the sale of the equipment was $28,000 ($35,000 book value − $7,000 loss on sale).

PREPARING THE FINANCING ACTIVITIES SECTION OF A STATEMENT OF CASH FLOWS

Because the differences between the direct and the indirect methods of presenting the statement of cash flows pertain only to operating activities, the *financing activities* section is the same under either approach. The information necessary to identify cash inflows and outflows from financing activities is obtained by reconciling changes in short-term notes payable, long-term liabilities, and stockholders' equity. In general:

LO 12-4

Prepare the financing activities section of a statement of cash flows.

- Increases in short-term notes payable or long-term debt balances suggest cash inflows occurred from issuing debt instruments (notes or bonds).

- Decreases in short-term notes payable or long-term debt balances suggest cash outflows occurred for payment of debt (notes or bonds).

- Increases in contributed capital (common stock, preferred stock, or paid-in capital) suggest cash inflows occurred from issuing equity instruments.

- Increases or decreases in treasury stock suggest cash outflows or inflows occurred to purchase or sell a company's own stock.

- Decreases in retained earnings from cash dividends suggest cash outflows occurred to pay dividends.

larryhw/123RF

To illustrate, return to the financial statements of the New South Company in Exhibit 12.5. The following long-term liability and stockholders' equity balances are reported on the New South balance sheets:

Account Title	Year 2	Year 1
Mortgage payable	$ 2,200	$ 0
Bonds payable	1,000	4,000
Common stock	10,000	8,000
Retained earnings	12,700	7,200
Treasury stock	600	0

For each account, reconcile the beginning and ending balances by identifying the increases and decreases affecting it. Review the notes for additional relevant information. Begin with the mortgage payable liability.

Reconciliation of Mortgage Payable

Reconciliation of Mortgage Payable	
Beginning balance in mortgage payable	$ 0
Increase due to issuing mortgage payable	? = 2,200
Decrease due to payment of mortgage payable	0
Ending balance in mortgage payable	$2,200

As previously discussed, Note 3 indicates a mortgage note payable was issued to acquire land. The *increase due to issuing mortgage payable* is $2,200. Because New South received land, not cash, by issuing the mortgage, the transaction is reported in the noncash investing and financing activities section of the statement of cash flows.

Reconciliation of Bonds Payable

Bonds Payable	
Beginning balance in bonds payable	$4,000
Increase due to issuing bonds payable	0
Decrease due to payment of bonds payable	? = (3,000)
Ending balance in bonds payable	$1,000

Because there is no indication that New South issued bonds during Year 2, assume the *increase due to issuing bonds payable* is zero. To balance Bonds Payable, the *decrease due to payment of bonds payable* must be $3,000. The cash outflow is reported in the financing activities section in Exhibit 12.13.

EXHIBIT 12.13

Cash Flows from Financing Activities

Cash Flows from Financing Activities	
Cash outflow to reduce bonds payable	$(3,000)
Cash inflow from issuing common stock	2,000
Cash outflow to pay dividends	(1,500)
Cash outflow to purchase treasury stock	(600)
Net cash outflow from financing activities	$(3,100)

Reconciliation of Common Stock

Reconciliation of Common Stock	
Beginning balance in common stock	$ 8,000
Increase due to issuing common stock	? = 2,000
Ending balance in common stock	$10,000

To balance Common Stock, the *increase due to issuing common stock* has to be $2,000. The cash inflow is reported in the financing activities section in Exhibit 12.13.

Reconciliation of Retained Earnings

Reconciliation of Retained Earnings	
Beginning balance in retained earnings	$ 7,200
Increase due to net income	7,000
Decrease due to payment of dividends	? = (1,500)
Ending balance in retained earnings	$12,700

The *increase due to net income* comes from the income statement. To balance Retained Earnings, the decrease due to payment of dividends must be $1,500. In the absence of information to the contrary, assume the decrease is due to the cash payment of dividends. The cash outflow for payment of dividends is reported in the financing activities section of the statement of cash flows in Exhibit 12.13.

Reconciliation of Treasury Stock

Reconciliation of Treasury Stock	
Beginning balance in treasury stock	$ 0
Increase due to purchasing treasury stock	? = 600
Decrease due to reissuing treasury stock	0
Ending balance in treasury stock	$600

Because there is no indication that New South reissued treasury stock during Year 2, the *decrease due to reissuing treasury stock* is zero. To balance Treasury Stock, the increase due to purchasing treasury stock must be $600. The cash outflow is reported in the financing activities section in Exhibit 12.13.

Exhibits 12.14 and 12.15 illustrate the complete statement of cash flows for New South Company under the two alternative methods. Exhibit 12.14 presents operating activities using

EXHIBIT 12.14   Statement of Cash Flows—Indirect Method

NEW SOUTH COMPANY
Statement of Cash Flows
For the Year Ended December 31, Year 2

Cash Flows from Operating Activities		
Net income	$ 7,000	
Adjustments to reconcile net income to net cash flow from operating activities:		
Decrease in accounts receivable	200	
Increase in interest receivable	(100)	
Increase in inventory	(700)	
Decrease in accounts payable for inventory purchases	(300)	
Decrease in prepaid insurance	300	
Increase in salaries payable	100	
Increase in other operating expenses payable	200	
Decrease in interest payable	(200)	
Decrease in unearned rent revenue	(1,000)	
Depreciation expense	1,000	
Gain on sale of store fixtures	(600)	
Net cash inflow from operating activities		$5,900
Cash Flows from Investing Activities		
Cash outflow to purchase investment securities	(1,600)	
Cash inflow from the sale of store fixtures	1,000	
Cash outflow to purchase store fixtures	(2,300)	
Net cash outflow from investing activities		(2,900)
Cash Flows from Financing Activities		
Cash outflow to reduce bonds payable	(3,000)	
Cash inflow from issuing common stock	2,000	
Cash outflow to pay dividends	(1,500)	
Cash outflow to purchase treasury stock	(600)	
Net cash outflow from financing activities		(3,100)
Net outflow in cash		(100)
Plus: Beginning cash balance		400
Ending cash balance		$ 300
Schedule of Noncash Investing and Financing Activities		
Issue mortgage for land		$2,200

EXHIBIT 12.15	Statement of Cash Flows—Direct Method

NEW SOUTH COMPANY
Statement of Cash Flows
For the Year Ended December 31, Year 2

Cash Flows from Operating Activities		
Inflow from customers	$ 20,800	
Inflow from interest revenue	600	
Outflow for inventory purchases	(11,500)	
Outflow to purchase insurance	(1,000)	
Outflow to pay salary expense	(2,600)	
Outflow for other operating expenses	(1,200)	
Outflow to pay interest expense	(600)	
Inflow from rent revenue	1,400	
Net cash inflow from operating activities		$5,900
Cash Flows from Investing Activities		
Cash outflow to purchase investment securities	(1,600)	
Cash inflow from the sale of store fixtures	1,000	
Cash outflow to purchase store fixtures	(2,300)	
Net cash outflow from investing activities		(2,900)
Cash Flows from Financing Activities		
Cash outflow to reduce bonds payable	(3,000)	
Cash inflow from issuing common stock	2,000	
Cash outflow to pay dividends	(1,500)	
Cash outflow to purchase treasury stock	(600)	
Net cash outflow from financing activities		(3,100)
Net outflow in cash		(100)
Plus: Beginning cash balance		400
Ending cash balance		$ 300
Schedule of Noncash Investing and Financing Activities		
Issue mortgage for land		$2,200

the indirect method. Exhibit 12.15 presents operating activities using the direct method. The investing and financing activities do not differ between methods. Under either method, the combined effects of operating, investing, and financing activities result in a net decrease in cash of $100 for Year 2. This $100 decrease is necessarily consistent with the difference between the December 31, Year 2, and the December 31, Year 1, cash balances shown in the balance sheets in Exhibit 12.5.

CHECK YOURSELF 12.6

On January 1, Year 4, Sterling Company had a balance of $250,000 in Bonds Payable. During Year 4, Sterling issued bonds with a $75,000 face value. The bonds were issued at face value. The balance in Bonds Payable on December 31, Year 4, was $150,000.

Required

a. Determine the cash outflow for repayment of bond liabilities assuming the bonds were retired at face value.

b. Prepare the financing activities section of the Year 4 statement of cash flows.

Solution

a.

Reconciliation of Bonds Payable	
Beginning balance	$250,000
Increase due to issuing bonds payable	75,000
Decrease due to payment of bonds payable	? = (175,000)
Ending balance	$150,000

In order to balance Bonds Payable, the *decrease due to payment of bonds payable* must be $175,000. In the absence of information to the contrary, assume cash was used to pay the bond liabilities.

b.

Cash Flows from Financing Activities	
Inflow from issuing bond liabilities	$ 75,000
Outflow for reduction of bond liabilities	(175,000)
Net cash outflow from financing activities	$(100,000)

Preparing the Schedule of Noncash Investing and Financing Activities

As mentioned earlier, companies may engage in significant noncash investing and financing activities. For example, New South Company acquired land by issuing a $2,200 mortgage note. Because these types of transactions do not involve exchanging cash, they are not reported in the main body of the statement of cash flows. However, the Financial Accounting Standards Board (FASB) requires disclosure of all material investing and financing activities, whether or not they involve exchanging cash. Companies must therefore include with the statement of cash flows a separate schedule that reports noncash investing and financing activities. See the *Schedule of Noncash Investing and Financing Activities* at the bottom of Exhibits 12.14 and 12.15 for an example.

REALITY BYTES

How did **Amazon.com** acquire $13.2 billion of assets in 2017 *without* spending cash? Oddly enough, the answer can be found on its statement of cash flows.

The supplemental "noncash transactions" information included at the bottom of Amazon's statement of cash flows reveals that it acquired the assets by using long-term leases, a form of debt.

Had Amazon issued $13.2 billion of long-term debt for cash, and then used this cash to purchase $13.2 billion of assets, it would have reported two separate cash events in the body of its statement of cash flows. A cash inflow would have been reported in the financing activities section for the issuance of the debt, and a cash outflow would have been reported in the investing activities section for the purchase of the assets. Acquiring large amounts of assets is considered

Evan Lorne/Shutterstock

important, even if there is no immediate exchange of cash, so generally accepted accounting principles require such events to be reported with the statement of cash flows or disclosed in the notes.

Juan Carlos Baena/Alamy Stock Photo

Anthony Correia/Shutterstock

The Financial Analyst

Why are financial analysts interested in the statement of cash flows? Understanding the cash flows of a business is essential because cash is used to pay the bills. A company, especially one experiencing rapid growth, can be short of cash in spite of earning substantial net income. To illustrate, assume you start a computer sales business. You borrow $2,000 and spend the money to purchase two computers for $1,000 each. You sell one of the computers on account for $1,500. If your loan required a payment at this time, you could not make it. Even though you have net income of $500 ($1,500 sales − $1,000 cost of goods sold), you have no cash until you collect the $1,500 account receivable. A business cannot survive without managing cash flow carefully. It is little wonder that financial analysts are keenly interested in cash flow.

Real-World Data

The statement of cash flows frequently provides a picture of business activity that otherwise would be lost in the complexities of accrual accounting. For example, as *The Curious Accountant* in Chapter 10 explained, even though Dell Technologies reported a loss of approximately $3.9 billion in 2017 on its income statement, its net cash flow from operating activities was a positive $6.8 billion.

Investors consider cash flow information so important they are willing to pay for it. Even though the FASB *prohibits* companies from disclosing *cash flow per share* in audited financial statements, one prominent stock analysis service, *Value Line Investment Survey*, sells this information to a significant customer base. Clearly, Value Line's customers value information about cash flows.

Exhibit 12.16 compares income from operations to cash flows from operating activities for six real-world companies for 2015 through 2018. Several things are apparent from this exhibit. Notice that the cash flow from operating activities exceeds income from operations for all but 5 of the 24 comparisons, and all but one of these relate to one company: Netflix. Cash flows often exceed earnings because depreciation, a noncash expense, is usually significant. There are two dramatic examples of the differences between cash flow and earnings. First, for the four years shown in Exhibit 12.16, Twitter had cumulative net earnings of $0.1 billion, but its cash flows from operations were a positive $3.3 billion. Second, Chevron had cumulative net earnings of $28.4 billion for the four years reported, but its net cash flows from operations were $83.4 billion, more than twice as large. The difference between cash flows from operating activities and net earnings helps explain how some companies can have significant losses over a few years and continue to stay in business and pay their bills.

The exhibit also shows that cash flow from operating activities can be more stable than operating income. The results for Caterpillar demonstrate this clearly. Caterpillar's earnings ranged from a negative $59 million to a positive $6.1 billion, a range of $6.2 billion, which is 280 percent of its average earnings of $2.2 billion for these four years. However, operating cash flows were not only positive in every year, but their total variation over the four years of $1.1 billion was only 18 percent of the average cash flows from operations ($6.1 billion).

So, what could explain why Netflix had *negative* cash flow from operating activities in all four years, even though it had *positive* and growing net earnings in each year? The company was experiencing the kind of growth described earlier for your computer business. Its cash outflows were supporting growth in Netflix's "content assets"—essentially, its inventory. Netflix's revenues more than doubled from 2015 to 2018, going

EXHIBIT 12.16

Net Income versus Cash Flow from Operations _(in millions)_				
	2018	**2017**	**2016**	**2015**
Caterpillar				
Net income	$ 6,148	$ 759	$ (59)	$ 2,113
Cash flow—operations	6,558	5,706	5,608	6,675
Chevron				
Net income	$14,860	9,269	(431)	4,710
Cash flow—operations	30,618	20,515	12,846	19,456
Facebook				
Operating income	6,882	4,268	10,217	3,688
Cash flow—operations	7,684	7,670	16,108	8,599
Netflix				
Net income	1,211	559	187	123
Cash flow—operations	(2,680)	(1,786)	(1,474)	(749)
Twitter				
Net income	1,206	(109)	(457)	(521)
Cash flow—operations	1,340	832	763	383
Wendy's				
Net income	460	194	130	161
Cash flow—operations	224	251	181	212

from $6.8 billion to $15.8 billion. To support this growth, the company had to increase its inventory. From 2015 to 2018, Netflix's content assets increased from $7.2 billion to $20.1 billion.

The Netflix situation highlights a potential weakness in the format of the statement of cash flows. Some accountants consider it misleading to classify all increases in long-term assets as _investing activities_ and all changes in inventory as affecting cash flow from operating activities. In the case of Netflix, they would argue that the increase in inventory that relates to expanding its business should be classified as an investing activity, just as the cost of a new warehouse is. Although inventory is classified as a current asset and buildings are classified as long-term assets, in reality there is a certain level of inventory a company must permanently maintain to stay in business. The GAAP format of the statement of cash flows penalizes cash flow from operating activities for increases in inventory that are really a permanent investment in assets.

Conversely, the same critics might argue that some purchases of long-term assets are not actually _investments_ but merely replacements of old, existing property, plant, and equipment. In other words, the _investing activities_ section of the statement of cash flows makes no distinction between expenditures that expand the business and those that simply replace old equipment (sometimes called _capital maintenance_ expenditures).

Users of the statement of cash flows must exercise the same care interpreting it as when they use the balance sheet or the income statement. Numbers alone are insufficient. Users must evaluate numbers based on knowledge of the particular business and industry they are analyzing.

Accounting information alone cannot guide a businessperson to a sound decision. Making good business decisions requires an understanding of the business in question, the environmental and economic factors affecting the operation of that business, and the accounting concepts on which the financial statements of that business are based.

A Look Back

This chapter examined in detail only one financial statement, the statement of cash flows. The chapter provided a more comprehensive discussion of how accrual accounting relates to cash-based accounting. Effective use of financial statements requires understanding not only accrual and cash-based accounting systems but also how they relate to each other. That relationship is why a statement of cash flows can begin with a reconciliation of net income, an accrual measurement, to net cash flow from operating activities, a cash measurement. Finally, this chapter explained how the conventions for classifying cash flows as operating, investing, or financing activities require analysis and understanding to make informed decisions with the financial information.

A Look Forward

In previous chapters we have focused on how business events affect financial statements. The primary goal was to provide you with a conceptual framework of accounting that would enable you to think like business professionals. Accordingly, we have used lay terminology such as increase and decrease or plus and minus to illustrate the effects of business events on financial statements. This chapter focuses on the technical terms and procedures that accountants use in the recordkeeping process. In practice, accountants usually maintain records using a system known as *double-entry bookkeeping*. Chapter 13 introduces the basic components of this bookkeeping system. You will learn how to record business events using a debit/credit format. You will be introduced to ledgers, journals, and trial balances. You will learn how the closing process works and how information is transferred from one accounting period to the next.

 Tableau Dashboard Activity is available in *Connect* for this chapter.

 SELF-STUDY REVIEW PROBLEM

 A step-by-step audio-narrated series of slides is available in *Connect*.

The following financial statements pertain to Schlemmer Company:

Balance Sheets As of December 31		
	Year 2	Year 1
Cash	$48,400	$ 2,800
Accounts receivable	2,200	1,200
Inventory	5,600	6,000
Equipment	18,000	22,000
Accumulated depreciation—equip.	(13,650)	(17,400)
Land	17,200	10,400
Total assets	$77,750	$25,000
Accounts payable (inventory)	$ 5,200	$ 4,200
Long-term debt	5,600	6,400
Common stock	19,400	10,000
Retained earnings	47,550	4,400
Total liabilities and equity	$77,750	$25,000

Income Statement For the Year Ended December 31, Year 2	
Sales revenue	$67,300
Cost of goods sold	(24,100)
Gross margin	43,200
Depreciation expense	(1,250)
Operating income	41,950
Gain on sale of equipment	2,900
Loss on disposal of land	(100)
Net income	$44,750

Additional Data

1. During Year 2, equipment that had originally cost $11,000 was sold. Accumulated depreciation on this equipment was $5,000 at the time of sale.
2. Common stock was issued in exchange for land valued at $9,400 at the time of the exchange.

Required

Using the indirect method, prepare in good form a statement of cash flows for the year ended December 31, Year 2.

Solution

SCHLEMMER COMPANY Statement of Cash Flows For the Year Ended December 31, Year 2		
Cash Flows from Operating Activities		
Net income	$44,750	
Add:		
Decrease in inventory (1)	400	
Increase in accounts payable (2)	1,000	
Depreciation expense (3)	1,250	
Loss on disposal of land (4)	100	
Subtract:		
Increase in accounts receivable (1)	(1,000)	
Gain on sale of equipment (4)	(2,900)	
Net cash inflow from operating activities		$43,600
Cash Flows from Investing Activities		
Cash inflow from the sale of equipment (5)	8,900	
Cash outflow for the purchase of equipment (5)	(7,000)	
Cash inflow from sale of land (6)	2,500	
Net cash inflow from investing activities		4,400
Cash Flows from Financing Activities		
Cash outflow to repay long-term debt (7)	(800)	
Cash outflow to pay dividends (8)	(1,600)	
Net cash outflow from financing activities		(2,400)
Net Increase in Cash		45,600
Plus: Beginning cash balance		2,800
Ending cash balance		$48,400
Schedule of Noncash Investing and Financing Activities		
Issue of common stock for land (9)		$ 9,400

(1) Add decreases and subtract increases in current asset account balances to net income.
(2) Add increases and subtract decreases in current liability account balances to net income.
(3) Add noncash expenses (depreciation) to net income.
(4) Add losses on the sale of noncurrent assets to net income and subtract gains on the sale of long-term assets from net income.
(5) Information regarding the Equipment account is summarized in the following table:

Equipment Account Information	
Beginning balance in equipment	$22,000
Purchases of equipment (cash outflows)	? = 7,000
Sales of equipment (cash inflows)	(11,000)
Ending balance in equipment	$18,000

To balance the account, equipment costing $7,000 must have been purchased. In the absence of information to the contrary, we assume cash was used to make the purchase.

Note 1 to the financial statement shows that equipment sold had a book value of $6,000 ($11,000 cost − $5,000 accumulated depreciation). The amount of the cash inflow from this sale is computed as follows:

$$\text{Cash inflow} = \text{Book value} + \text{Gain} = \$6,000 + \$2,900 = \$8,900$$

(6) The information regarding the Land account is as follows:

Land Account Information

Beginning balance in land	$10,400
Purchases of land (issue of common stock)	9,400
Sales of land (cash inflows)	? = (2,600)
Ending balance in land	$17,200

Note 2 indicates that land valued at $9,400 was acquired by issuing common stock. Because there was no cash flow associated with this purchase, the event is shown in the *noncash investing and financing activities* section of the statement of cash flows.

To balance the account, the cost (book value) of land sold had to be $2,600. Because the income statement shows a $100 loss on the sale of land, the cash collected from the sale is computed as follows:

$$\text{Cash inflow} = \text{Book value} - \text{Loss} = \$2,600 - \$100 = \$2,500$$

(7) The information regarding the Long-Term Debt account is as follows:

Long-Term Debt Information

Beginning balance in long-term debt	$6,400
Issue of long-term debt instruments (cash inflow)	0
Payment of long-term debt (cash outflow)	? = (800)
Ending balance in long-term debt	$5,600

There is no information in the financial statements that suggests long-term debt was issued. Therefore, to balance the account, $800 of long-term debt had to be paid off, thereby resulting in a cash outflow.

(8) The information regarding the Retained Earnings account is as follows:

Retained Earnings Information

Beginning balance in retained earnings	$ 4,400
Net income	44,750
Dividends (cash outflow)	? = (1,600)
Ending balance in retained earnings	$47,550

To balance the account, $1,600 of dividends had to be paid, thereby resulting in a cash outflow.

(9) Note 2 states that common stock was issued to acquire land valued at $9,400. This is a noncash investing and financing activity.

KEY TERMS

Cash inflows 586	Financing	Investing activities 588	Operating activities 587
Cash outflows 586	activities 589	Noncash investing and	
Direct method 587	Indirect method 587	financing activities 589	

QUESTIONS

1. What is the purpose of the statement of cash flows?

2. What are the three categories of cash flows reported on the cash flow statement? Discuss each and give an example of an inflow and an outflow for each category.

3. What are noncash investing and financing activities? Provide an example. How are such transactions shown on the statement of cash flows?

4. Albring Company had a beginning balance in accounts receivable of $12,000 and an ending balance of $14,000. Net income amounted to $110,000. Based on this information alone, determine the amount of net cash flow from operating activities.

5. Forsyth Company had a beginning balance in utilities payable of $3,300 and an ending balance of $5,200. Net income amounted to $87,000. Based on this information alone, determine the amount of net cash flow from operating activities.

6. Clover Company had a beginning balance in unearned revenue of $4,300 and an ending balance of $3,200. Net income amounted to $54,000. Based on this information alone, determine the amount of net cash flow from operating activities.

7. Which of the following activities are financing activities?
   (a) Payment of accounts payable.
   (b) Payment of interest on bonds payable.
   (c) Sale of common stock.
   (d) Sale of preferred stock at a premium.
   (e) Payment of a cash dividend.

8. Does depreciation expense affect net cash flow? Explain.

9. If Best Company sold land that cost $4,200 at a $500 gain, how much cash did it collect from the sale of land?

10. If Best Company sold office equipment that originally cost $7,500 and had $7,200 of accumulated

depreciation at a $100 loss, what was the selling price for the office equipment?

11. In which section of the statement of cash flows would the following transactions be reported using the indirect method?
   (a) The amount of the change in the balance of accounts receivable.
   (b) Cash purchase of investment securities.
   (c) Cash purchase of equipment.
   (d) Cash sale of merchandise.
   (e) Cash sale of common stock.
   (f) The amount of net income.
   (g) Cash proceeds from loan.
   (h) Cash payment on bonds payable.
   (i) Cash receipt from sale of old equipment.
   (j) The amount of the change in the balance of accounts payable.

12. What is the difference between preparing the

statement of cash flows using the direct method and using the indirect method?

13. Which method (direct or indirect) of presenting the statement of cash flows is more intuitively logical? Why?

14. What is the major advantage of using the indirect method to present the statement of cash flows?

15. What is the advantage of using the direct method to present the statement of cash flows?

16. How would Best Company report the following transactions on the statement of cash flows?
   (a) Purchased new equipment for $46,000 cash.
   (b) Sold old equipment for $8,700 cash. The equipment had a book value of $4,900.

17. Can a company report negative net cash flows from operating activities for the year on the statement of cash flows but still have positive net income on the income statement? Explain.

EXERCISES—SERIES A

Exercise 12-1A   *Use the indirect method to determine cash flows from operating activities*   LO 12-1

An accountant for Southern Manufacturing Companies (SMC) computed the following information by making comparisons between SMC's Year 1 and Year 2 balance sheets. Further information was determined by examining the company's Year 2 income statement.

1. The amount of cash dividends paid to the stockholders.
2. The amount of a decrease in the balance of an Unearned Revenue account.
3. The amount of an increase in the balance of an Inventory account.
4. The amount of an increase in the balance of a Land account.
5. The amount of a decrease in the balance of a Prepaid Rent account.
6. The amount of an increase in the balance of a Treasury Stock account.
7. The amount of an increase in the balance of the Accounts Receivable account.
8. The amount of a loss arising from the sale of land.
9. The amount of an increase in the balance of the Other Operating Expenses Payable account.
10. The amount of a decrease in the balance of the Bonds Payable account.
11. The amount of depreciation expense shown on the income statement.

Required

For each item described in the preceding list, indicate whether the amount should be added to or subtracted from the amount of net income when determining the amount of net cash flow from operating activities using the indirect method. Also identify any items that do not affect net cash flow from operating activities because they are reported as investing or financing activities.

LO 12-1

Exercise 12-2A   *Use the indirect method to determine cash flows from operating activities*

Alfonza Incorporated presents its statement of cash flows using the indirect method. The following accounts and corresponding balances were drawn from the company's Year 2 and Year 1 year-end balance sheets:

Account Title	Year 2	Year 1
Accounts receivable	$16,200	$17,800
Accounts payable	7,600	9,100

The Year 2 income statement showed net income of $31,600.

Required

a. Prepare the operating activities section of the statement of cash flows.
b. Explain why the change in the balance in accounts receivable was added to or subtracted from the amount of net income when you completed Requirement *a*.
c. Explain why the change in the balance in accounts payable was added to or subtracted from the amount of net income when you completed Requirement *a*.

LO 12-1

Exercise 12-3A   *Use the indirect method to determine cash flows from operating activities*

Shim Company presents its statement of cash flows using the indirect method. The following accounts and corresponding balances were drawn from Shim's Year 2 and Year 1 year-end balance sheets.

Account Title	Year 2	Year 1
Accounts receivable	$36,000	$37,200
Prepaid rent	2,400	1,800
Interest receivable	600	400
Accounts payable	9,300	10,400
Salaries payable	4,500	5,200
Unearned revenue	3,600	5,400

The income statement reported a $1,500 gain on the sale of equipment, an $800 loss on the sale of land, and $3,600 of depreciation expense. Net income for the period was $47,300.

Required

Prepare the operating activities section of the statement of cash flows.

LO 12-2

Exercise 12-4A   *Use the direct method to determine cash flows from operating activities*

The following accounts and corresponding balances were drawn from Avia Company's Year 2 and Year 1 year-end balance sheets:

Account Title	Year 2	Year 1
Unearned revenue	$7,600	$6,200
Prepaid rent	2,400	3,600

During the year, $46,000 of unearned revenue was recognized as having been earned. Rent expense for Year 2 was $18,000.

Required

Based on this information alone, prepare the operating activities section of the statement of cash flows assuming the direct approach is used.

Exercise 12-5A   *Use the direct method to determine cash flows from operating activities*

LO 12-2

The following accounts and corresponding balances were drawn from Marinelli Company's Year 2 and Year 1 year-end balance sheets:

Account Title	Year 2	Year 1
Accounts receivable	$35,200	$31,600
Interest receivable	4,200	4,800
Other operating expenses payable	21,000	18,500
Salaries payable	6,500	7,200

The Year 2 income statement is shown next:

Income Statement	
Sales	$530,000
Salaries expense	(214,000)
Other operating expenses	(175,000)
Operating income	141,000
Nonoperating items: Interest revenue	16,500
Net income	$157,500

Required

a. Use the direct method to compute the amount of cash inflows from operating activities.
b. Use the direct method to compute the amount of cash outflows from operating activities.

Exercise 12-6A   *Direct versus indirect method of determining cash flows from operating activities*

LO 12-1, 12-2

Expert Electronics, Inc. (EEI) recognized $3,800 of sales revenue on account and collected $2,100 of cash from accounts receivable. Further, EEI recognized $900 of operating expenses on account and paid $700 cash as partial settlement of accounts payable.

Required

Based on this information alone:

a. Prepare the operating activities section of the statement of cash flows under the direct method.
b. Prepare the operating activities section of the statement of cash flows under the indirect method.

Exercise 12-7A   *The direct versus the indirect method of determining cash flows from operating activities*

LO 12-1, 12-2

The following accounts and corresponding balances were drawn from Jogger Company's Year 2 and Year 1 year-end balance sheets:

Account Title	Year 2	Year 1
Accounts receivable	$57,000	$62,000
Prepaid rent	1,100	1,300
Utilities payable	900	750
Other operating expenses payable	21,300	22,400

The Year 2 income statement is shown next:

Income Statement	
Sales	$268,000
Rent expense	(36,000)
Utilities expense	(18,300)
Other operating expenses	(79,100)
Net Income	$134,600

Required

a. Prepare the operating activities section of the statement of cash flows using the direct method.

b. Prepare the operating activities section of the statement of cash flows using the indirect method.

LO 12-3

Exercise 12-8A *Determining cash flow from investing activities*

On January 1, Year 1, Shelton Company had a balance of $325,000 in its Land account. During Year 1, Shelton sold land that had cost $106,500 for $132,000 cash. The balance in the Land account on December 31, Year 1, was $285,000.

Required

a. Determine the cash outflow for the purchase of land during Year 1.

b. Prepare the investing activities section of the Year 1 statement of cash flows.

LO 12-3

Exercise 12-9A *Determining cash flows from investing activities*

On January 1, Year 1, Bacco Company had a balance of $72,350 in its Delivery Equipment account. During Year 1, Bacco purchased delivery equipment that cost $22,100. The balance in the Delivery Equipment account on December 31, Year 1, was $69,400. The Year 1 income statement reported a gain from the sale of equipment of $5,000. On the date of sale, accumulated depreciation on the equipment sold amounted to $22,000.

Required

a. Determine the original cost of the equipment that was sold during Year 1.

b. Determine the amount of cash flow from the sale of delivery equipment that should be shown in the investing activities section of the Year 1 statement of cash flows.

LO 12-3

Exercise 12-10A *Determining cash flows from investing activities*

The following accounts and corresponding balances were drawn from Delsey Company's Year 2 and Year 1 year-end balance sheets:

Account Title	Year 2	Year 1
Investment securities	$110,000	$116,500
Machinery	486,000	437,000
Land	160,000	100,000

Other information drawn from the accounting records:

1. Delsey incurred a $6,000 loss on the sale of investment securities during Year 2.

2. Old machinery with a book value of $8,000 (cost of $36,000 minus accumulated depreciation of $28,000) was sold. The income statement showed a gain on the sale of machinery of $4,500.

3. Delsey did not sell land during the year.

Required

a. Compute the amount of cash flow associated with the sale of investment securities.

b. Compute the amount of cash flow associated with the purchase of machinery.

c. Compute the amount of cash flow associated with the sale of machinery.

d. Compute the amount of cash flow associated with the purchase of land.

e. Prepare the investing activities section of the statement of cash flows.

Exercise 12-11A   *Determining cash flows from financing activities*   LO 12-4

On January 1, Year 1, DIBA Company had a balance of $450,000 in its Bonds Payable account. During Year 1, DIBA issued bonds with a $200,000 face value. There was no premium or discount associated with the bond issue. The balance in the Bonds Payable account on December 31, Year 1, was $400,000.

Required

a. Determine the cash outflow for the repayment of bond liabilities assuming that the bonds were retired at face value.

b. Prepare the financing activities section of the Year 1 statement of cash flows.

Exercise 12-12A   *Determining cash flows from financing activities*   LO 12-4

On January 1, Year 1, Hardy Company had a balance of $150,000 in its Common Stock account. During Year 1, Hardy paid $20,000 to purchase treasury stock. Treasury stock is accounted for using the cost method. The balance in the Common Stock account on December 31, Year 1, was $175,000. Assume that the common stock is no par stock.

Required

a. Determine the cash inflow from the issue of common stock.

b. Prepare the financing activities section of the Year 1 statement of cash flows.

Exercise 12-13A   *Determining cash flows from financing activities*   LO 12-4

The following accounts and corresponding balances were drawn from Dexter Company's Year 2 and Year 1 year-end balance sheets:

Account Title	Year 2	Year 1
Bonds payable	$350,000	$400,000
Common stock	450,000	420,000

Other information drawn from the accounting records:

1. Dividends paid during the period amounted to $50,000.

2. There were no bond liabilities issued during the period.

Required

a. Compute the amount of cash flow associated with the repayment of bond liabilities.

b. Compute the amount of cash flow associated with the issue of common stock.

c. Prepare the financing activities section of the statement of cash flows.

PROBLEMS—SERIES A

 All applicable Problems in Series A are available in *Connect*.

Problem 12-14A   *The direct versus the indirect method of determining cash flow from*   LO 12-1, 12-2
                      operating activities

Green Brands, Inc. (GBI) presents its statement of cash flows using the indirect method. The following accounts and corresponding balances were drawn from GBI's Year 2 and Year 1 year-end balance sheets:

Account Title	Year 2	Year 1
Accounts receivable	$48,000	$52,000
Merchandise inventory	78,000	72,000
Prepaid insurance	24,000	32,000
Accounts payable	31,000	28,000
Salaries payable	8,200	7,800
Unearned service revenue	2,400	3,600

The Year 2 income statement is shown next:

Income Statement	
Sales	$720,000
Cost of goods sold	(398,000)
Gross margin	322,000
Service revenue	6,000
Insurance expense	(36,000)
Salaries expense	(195,000)
Depreciation expense	(12,000)
Operating income	85,000
Gain on sale of equipment	4,500
Net income	$ 89,500

Required

a. Prepare the operating activities section of the statement of cash flows using the direct method.

b. Prepare the operating activities section of the statement of cash flows using the indirect method.

Problem 12-15A   *Determining cash flows from investing activities*

The following information was drawn from the year-end balance sheets of Mass Trading Company:

Account Title	Year 2	Year 1
Investment securities	$ 47,200	$ 42,400
Equipment	246,000	218,000
Buildings	646,000	720,000
Land	95,000	72,000

The following is additional information regarding transactions that occurred during Year 2:

1. Investment securities that had cost $6,100 were sold. The Year 2 income statement contained a loss on the sale of investment securities of $1,400.

2. Equipment with a cost of $38,000 was purchased.

3. The income statement showed a gain on the sale of equipment of $8,000. On the date of sale, accumulated depreciation on the equipment sold amounted to $8,000.

4. A building that had originally cost $210,000 was demolished.

5. Land that had cost $30,000 was sold for $27,000.

Required

a. Determine the amount of cash flow for the purchase of investment securities during Year 2.

b. Determine the amount of cash flow from the sale of investment securities during Year 2.

c. Determine the cost of the equipment that was sold during Year 2.

d. Determine the amount of cash flow from the sale of equipment during Year 2.

e. Determine the amount of cash flow for the purchase of buildings during Year 2.

f. Determine the amount of cash flow for the purchase of land during Year 2.

g. Prepare the investing activities section of the Year 2 statement of cash flows.

Problem 12-16A *Determining cash flows from financing activities*

The following information was drawn from the year-end balance sheets of Fox River, Inc.

Account Title	Year 2	Year 1
Bonds payable	$600,000	$800,000
Common stock	210,000	180,000
Treasury stock	20,000	5,000
Retained earnings	86,000	75,000

The following is additional information regarding transactions that occurred during Year 2:

1. Fox River, Inc. issued $100,000 of bonds during Year 2. The bonds were issued at face value. All bonds retired were retired at face value.
2. Common stock did not have a par value.
3. Fox River, Inc. uses the cost method to account for treasury stock.
4. The amount of net income shown on the Year 2 income statement was $32,000.

Required

a. Determine the amount of cash flow for the retirement of bonds that should appear on the Year 2 statement of cash flows.
b. Determine the amount of cash flow from the issue of common stock that should appear on the Year 2 statement of cash flows.
c. Determine the amount of cash flow for the purchase of treasury stock that should appear on the Year 2 statement of cash flows.
d. Determine the amount of cash flow for the payment of dividends that should appear on the Year 2 statement of cash flows.
e. Prepare the financing activities section of the Year 2 statement of cash flows.

Problem 12-17A *Preparing a statement of cash flows*

The following information can be obtained by examining a company's balance sheet and income statement information:

a. Increases in current asset account balances, other than cash.
b. Decreases in current asset account balances, other than cash.
c. Cash outflows to purchase long-term assets.
d. Decreases in current liability account balances.
e. Cash outflows to repay long-term debt.
f. Gains recognized on the sale of long-term assets.
g. Noncash expenses (e.g., depreciation).
h. Cash outflows to purchase treasury stock.
i. Increases in current liability account balances.
j. Cash inflows from the sale of long-term assets.
k. Cash inflows from the issue of common stock.
l. Cash outflows to pay dividends.
m. Losses incurred from the sale of long-term assets.
n. Cash inflows from the issue of long-term debt.

Required

Construct a table like the following one. For each item, indicate whether it would be used in the computation of net cash flows from operating, investing, or financing activities. Also, indicate whether the item would be added or subtracted when determining the net cash flow from operating, investing, or financing activities. Assume the indirect method is used to prepare the operating activities section of the statement of cash flows. The first item has been completed as an example.

Item	Type of Activity	Add or Subtract
a.	Operating	Subtract
b.		

Problem 12-18A *Using financial statements to prepare a statement of cash flows—indirect method*

The comparative balance sheets and income statements for Gypsy Company follow.

	Year 2	Year 1
Balance Sheets		
As of December 31		
Assets		
Cash	$ 32,500	$16,300
Accounts receivable	4,750	2,800
Inventory	11,200	9,800
Equipment	45,000	52,000
Accumulated depreciation—equipment	(17,800)	(21,800)
Land	28,000	12,000
Total assets	$103,650	$71,100
Liabilities and stockholders' equity		
Accounts payable (inventory)	$ 3,750	$ 4,900
Long-term debt	5,800	7,800
Common stock	47,000	25,000
Retained earnings	47,100	33,400
Total liabilities and stockholders' equity	$103,650	$71,100

Income Statement	
For the Year Ended December 31, Year 2	
Sales revenue	$61,200
Cost of goods sold	(24,500)
Gross margin	36,700
Depreciation expense	(12,000)
Operating income	24,700
Gain on sale of equipment	1,500
Loss on disposal of land	(100)
Net income	$26,100

Additional Data

1. During Year 2, the company sold equipment for $21,500; it had originally cost $36,000. Accumulated depreciation on this equipment was $16,000 at the time of the sale. Also, the company purchased equipment for $29,000 cash.

2. The company sold land that had cost $6,000. This land was sold for $5,900, resulting in the recognition of a $100 loss. Also, common stock was issued in exchange for title to land that was valued at $22,000 at the time of exchange.

3. Paid dividends of $12,400.

Required

Prepare a statement of cash flows using the indirect method.

eXcel

Problem 12-19A *Using financial statements to prepare a statement of cash flows—indirect method*

The comparative balance sheets and an income statement for Raceway Corporation follow:

Balance Sheets
As of December 31

	Year 2	Year 1
Assets		
Cash	$ 6,300	$ 48,400
Accounts receivable	10,200	7,260
Merchandise inventory	45,200	56,000
Prepaid rent	700	2,140
Equipment	140,000	144,000
Accumulated depreciation	(73,400)	(118,000)
Land	116,000	50,000
Total assets	$245,000	$189,800
Liabilities		
Accounts payable (inventory)	$ 37,200	$ 40,000
Salaries payable	12,200	10,600
Stockholders' equity		
Common stock, $50 par value	150,000	120,000
Retained earnings	45,600	19,200
Total liabilities and stockholders' equity	$245,000	$189,800

Income Statement
For the Year Ended December 31, Year 2

Sales	$480,000
Cost of goods sold	(264,000)
Gross profit	216,000
Operating expenses	
Depreciation expense	(11,400)
Rent expense	(7,000)
Salaries expense	(95,200)
Other operating expenses	(76,000)
Net income	$ 26,400

Other Information

1. Purchased land for $66,000.
2. Purchased new equipment for $62,000.
3. Sold old equipment that cost $66,000 with accumulated depreciation of $56,000 for $10,000 cash.
4. Issued common stock for $30,000.

Required

Prepare the statement of cash flows for Year 2 using the indirect method.

Problem 12-20A *Using transaction data to prepare a statement of cash flows—direct method*

York Company engaged in the following transactions for Year 1. The beginning cash balance was $86,000 and the ending cash balance was $59,100.

1. Sales on account were $548,000. The beginning receivables balance was $128,000 and the ending balance was $90,000.
2. Salaries expense for the period was $232,000. The beginning salaries payable balance was $16,000 and the ending balance was $8,000.
3. Other operating expenses for the period were $236,000. The beginning other operating expenses payable balance was $16,000 and the ending balance was $10,000.
4. Recorded $30,000 of depreciation expense. The beginning and ending balances in the Accumulated Depreciation account were $12,000 and $42,000, respectively.

5. The Equipment account had beginning and ending balances of $44,000 and $56,000, respectively. There were no sales of equipment during the period.

6. The beginning and ending balances in the Notes Payable account were $36,000 and $44,000, respectively. There were no payoffs of notes during the period.

7. There was $4,600 of interest expense reported on the income statement. The beginning and ending balances in the Interest Payable account were $8,400 and $7,500, respectively.

8. The beginning and ending Merchandise Inventory account balances were $22,000 and $29,400, respectively. The company sold merchandise with a cost of $83,600 (cost of goods sold for the period was $83,600). The beginning and ending balances in the Accounts Payable account were $8,000 and $6,400, respectively.

9. The beginning and ending balances in the Notes Receivable account were $60,000 and $100,000, respectively. Notes receivable result from long-term loans made to employees. There were no collections from employees during the period.

10. The beginning and ending balances in the Common Stock account were $120,000 and $160,000, respectively. The increase was caused by the issue of common stock for cash.

11. Land had beginning and ending balances of $24,000 and $14,000, respectively. Land that cost $10,000 was sold for $6,000, resulting in a loss of $4,000.

12. The tax expense for the period was $6,600. The Taxes Payable account had a $2,400 beginning balance and a $2,200 ending balance.

13. The Investments account had beginning and ending balances of $20,000 and $60,000, respectively. The company purchased investments for $50,000 cash during the period, and investments that cost $10,000 were sold for $22,000, resulting in a $12,000 gain.

Required

a. Determine the amount of cash flow for each item and indicate whether the item should appear in the operating, investing, or financing activities section of a statement of cash flows. Also identify any items that do not affect the cash flow statement. Assume York Company uses the direct method for showing net cash flow from operating activities.

b. Prepare a statement of cash flows based on the information you developed in Requirement *a*.

LO 12-2, 12-3, 12-4

Problem 12-21A *Using financial statements to prepare a statement of cash flows— direct method*

CHECK FIGURES
Net Cash Flow from Operating Activities: $56,200
Net Increase in Cash: $80,200

The following financial statements were drawn from the records of Matrix Shoes.

Balance Sheets As of December 31		
	Year 2	**Year 1**
Assets		
Cash	$ 94,300	$ 14,100
Accounts receivable	36,000	40,000
Merchandise inventory	72,000	64,000
Notes receivable	0	16,000
Equipment	98,000	170,000
Accumulated depreciation—equipment	(47,800)	(94,000)
Land	46,000	30,000
Total assets	$298,500	$240,100
Liabilities		
Accounts payable	$ 24,000	$ 26,400
Salaries payable	15,000	10,000
Utilities payable	800	1,400
Interest payable	0	1,000
Notes payable (long-term)	0	24,000
Common stock	150,000	110,000
Retained earnings	108,700	67,300
Total liabilities and stockholders' equity	$298,500	$240,100

Income Statement For the Year Ended December 31, Year 2	
Sales revenue	$300,000
Cost of goods sold	(144,000)
Gross margin	156,000
Operating expenses	
Salaries expense	(88,000)
Depreciation expense	(9,800)
Utilities expense	(6,400)
Operating income	51,800
Nonoperating items	
Interest expense	(2,400)
Loss on the sale of equipment	(800)
Net income	$ 48,600

Additional Information

1. Sold equipment costing $72,000 with accumulated depreciation of $56,000 for $15,200 cash.
2. Paid a $7,200 cash dividend to owners.

Required

Analyze the data and prepare a statement of cash flows using the direct method.

EXERCISES—SERIES B

Exercise 12-1B   *Use the indirect method to determine cash flows from operating activities*   **LO 12-1**

An accountant for Farve Enterprise Companies (FEC) computed the following information by making comparisons between FEC's Year 2 and Year 1 balance sheets. Further information was determined by examining the company's Year 2 income statement.

1. The amount of an increase in the balance of a Prepaid Rent account.
2. The amount of an increase in the balance of a Treasury Stock account.
3. The amount of a decrease in the balance of the Accounts Receivable account.
4. The amount of a gain arising from the sale of land.
5. The amount of an increase in the balance of the Salaries Payable account.
6. The amount of an increase in the balance of the Bonds Payable account.
7. The amount of depreciation expense shown on the income statement.
8. The amount of cash dividends paid to the stockholders.
9. The amount of an increase in the balance of an Unearned Revenue account.
10. The amount of a decrease in the balance of an Inventory account.
11. The amount of a decrease in the balance of a Land account.

Required

For each item in the preceding list, indicate whether the amount should be added to or subtracted from the amount of net income when determining the amount of net cash flow from operating activities using the indirect method. Also identify any items that do not affect net cash flow from operating activities because they are reported as investing or financing activities.

Exercise 12-2B   *Use the indirect method to determine cash flows from operating activities*   **LO 12-1**

Napoleon Incorporated presents its statement of cash flows using the indirect method. The following accounts and corresponding balances were drawn from the company's Year 2 and Year 1 year-end balance sheets:

Account Title	Year 2	Year 1
Accounts receivable	$31,400	$28,600
Accounts payable	10,300	9,800

The Year 2 income statement showed net income of $41,500.

Required

a. Prepare the operating activities section of the statement of cash flows.

b. Explain why the change in the balance in accounts receivable was added to or subtracted from the amount of net income when you completed Requirement *a*.

c. Explain why the change in the balance in accounts payable was added to or subtracted from the amount of net income when you completed Requirement *a*.

LO 12-1

Exercise 12-3B   *Use the indirect method to determine cash flows from operating activities*

Pella Company presents its statement of cash flows using the indirect method. The following accounts and corresponding balances were drawn from Pella's Year 2 and Year 1 year-end balance sheets:

Account Title	Year 2	Year 1
Accounts receivable	$24,000	$21,000
Prepaid rent	1,650	1,900
Interest receivable	900	1,200
Accounts payable	10,200	8,500
Salaries payable	2,700	2,900
Unearned revenue	2,000	1,800

The income statement reported a $700 loss on the sale of equipment, a $900 gain on the sale of land, and $2,500 of depreciation expense. Net income for the period was $36,500.

Required

Prepare the operating activities section of the statement of cash flows.

LO 12-2

Exercise 12-4B   *Use the direct method to determine cash flows from operating activities*

The following accounts and corresponding balances were drawn from Osprey Company's Year 2 and Year 1 year-end balance sheets:

Account Title	Year 2	Year 1
Unearned revenue	$4,500	$6,000
Prepaid rent	5,200	3,600

During the year, $84,000 of unearned revenue was recognized as having been earned. Rent expense for Year 2 was $24,000.

Required

Based on this information alone, prepare the operating activities section of the statement of cash flows assuming the direct approach is used.

LO 12-2

Exercise 12-5B   *Use the direct method to determine cash flows from operating activities*

The following accounts and corresponding balances were drawn from Pixi Company's Year 2 and Year 1 year-end balance sheets:

Account Title	Year 2	Year 1
Accounts receivable	$62,000	$56,000
Interest receivable	8,000	6,000
Other operating expenses payable	26,000	29,000
Salaries payable	12,000	9,000

The Year 2 income statement is shown next:

Income Statement	
Sales	$650,000
Salaries expense	(420,000)
Other operating expenses	(110,000)
Operating income	120,000
Nonoperating items: Interest revenue	15,000
Net income	$135,000

Required

a. Use the direct method to compute the amount of cash inflows from operating activities.

b. Use the direct method to compute the amount of cash outflows from operating activities.

Exercise 12-6B   *Direct versus indirect method of determining cash flows from operating activities*   LO 12-1, 12-2

Ragg Shop, Inc. (RSI) recognized $3,800 of sales revenue on account and collected $2,950 of cash from accounts receivable. Further, RSI recognized $1,200 of operating expenses on account and paid $900 cash as partial settlement of accounts payable.

Required

Based on this information alone:

a. Prepare the operating activities section of the statement of cash flows under the direct method.

b. Prepare the operating activities section of the statement of cash flows under the indirect method.

Exercise 12-7B   *The direct versus the indirect method of determining cash flows from operating activities*   LO 12-1, 12-2

The following accounts and corresponding balances were drawn from Geneses Company's Year 2 and Year 1 year-end balance sheets:

Account Title	Year 2	Year 1
Accounts receivable	$65,000	$72,000
Prepaid rent	1,400	1,950
Utilities payable	3,200	3,800
Other operating expenses payable	27,000	31,500

The Year 2 income statement is shown next:

Income Statement	
Sales	$420,000
Rent expense	(52,000)
Utilities expense	(45,300)
Other operating expenses	(195,000)
Net income	$127,700

Required

a. Prepare the operating activities section of the statement of cash flows using the direct method.

b. Prepare the operating activities section of the statement of cash flows using the indirect method.

LO 12-3

Exercise 12-8B   *Determining cash flow from investing activities*

On January 1, Year 1, Poole Company had a balance of $178,000 in its Land account. During Year 1, Poole sold land that had cost $71,000 for $95,000 cash. The balance in the Land account on December 31, Year 1, was $210,000.

Required

a. Determine the cash outflow for the purchase of land during Year 1.

b. Prepare the investing activities section of the Year 1 statement of cash flows.

LO 12-3

Exercise 12-9B   *Determining cash flow from investing activities*

On January 1, Year 1, Sanita Company had a balance of $76,300 in its Office Equipment account. During Year 1, Sanita purchased office equipment that cost $30,300. The balance in the Office Equipment account on December 31, Year 1, was $75,400. The Year 1 income statement contained a gain from the sale of equipment of $6,000. On the date of sale, accumulated depreciation on the equipment sold amounted to $14,400.

Required

a. Determine the cost of the equipment that was sold during Year 1.

b. Determine the amount of cash flow from the sale of office equipment that should be shown in the investing activities section of the Year 1 statement of cash flows.

LO 12-3

Exercise 12-10B   *Determining cash flows from investing activities*

The following accounts and corresponding balances were drawn from Teva Company's Year 2 and Year 1 year-end balance sheets:

Account Title	Year 2	Year 1
Investment securities	$102,000	$110,000
Machinery	480,000	465,000
Land	75,000	95,000

Other information drawn from the accounting records:

1. Teva incurred a $3,000 loss on the sale of investment securities during Year 2.

2. Old machinery with a book value of $8,000 (cost of $34,000 minus accumulated depreciation of $26,000) was sold. The income statement showed a gain on the sale of machinery of $7,500.

3. Teva incurred a loss of $4,000 on the sale of land in Year 2.

Required

a. Compute the amount of cash flow associated with the sale of investment securities.

b. Compute the amount of cash flow associated with the purchase of machinery.

c. Compute the amount of cash flow associated with the sale of machinery.

d. Compute the amount of cash flow associated with the sale of land.

e. Prepare the investing activities section of the statement of cash flows.

LO 12-4

Exercise 12-11B   *Determining cash flows from financing activities*

On January 1, Year 1, Van Company had a balance of $800,000 in its Bonds Payable account. During Year 1, Van issued bonds with a $300,000 face value. There was no premium or discount associated with the bond issue. The balance in the Bonds Payable account on December 31, Year 1, was $600,000.

Required

a. Determine the cash outflow for the repayment of bond liabilities assuming that the bonds were retired at face value.

b. Prepare the financing activities section of the Year 1 statement of cash flows.

Exercise 12-12B *Determining cash flows from financing activities*

LO 12-4

On January 1, Year 1, Milam Company had a balance of $300,000 in its Common Stock account. During Year 1, Milam paid $18,000 to purchase treasury stock. Treasury stock is accounted for using the cost method. The balance in the Common Stock account on December 31, Year 1, was $350,000. Assume that the common stock is no par stock.

Required

a. Determine the cash inflow from the issue of common stock.

b. Prepare the financing activities section of the Year 1 statement of cash flows.

Exercise 12-13B *Determining cash flows from financing activities*

LO 12-4

The following accounts and corresponding balances were drawn from Cushing Company's Year 2 and Year 1 year-end balance sheets:

Account Title	Year 2	Year 1
Bonds payable	$200,000	$150,000
Common stock	650,000	400,000

Other information drawn from the accounting records:

1. Dividends paid during the period amounted to $50,000.
2. There were no bond liabilities repaid during the period.

Required

a. Compute the amount of cash flow associated with the issue of bond liabilities.

b. Compute the amount of cash flow associated with the issue of common stock.

c. Prepare the financing activities section of the statement of cash flows.

PROBLEMS—SERIES B

Problem 12-14B *The direct versus the indirect method of determining cash flows from operating activities*

LO 12-1, 12-2

The following accounts and corresponding balances were drawn from Crimson Sports, Inc.'s Year 2 and Year 1 year-end balance sheets:

Account Title	Year 2	Year 1
Accounts receivable	$31,000	$36,000
Merchandise inventory	70,000	65,000
Prepaid insurance	25,000	24,000
Accounts payable	18,000	20,000
Salaries payable	5,100	4,500
Unearned service revenue	10,200	9,500

The Year 2 income statement is shown next:

Income Statement	
Sales	$495,000
Cost of goods sold	(215,000)
Gross margin	280,000
Service revenue	20,000
Insurance expense	(42,000)
Salaries expense	(122,000)
Depreciation expense	(12,000)
Operating income	124,000
Gain on sale of equipment	1,500
Net income	$125,500

Required

a. Prepare the operating activities section of the statement of cash flows using the direct method.

b. Prepare the operating activities section of the statement of cash flows using the indirect method.

LO 12-3

Problem 12-15B *Determining cash flows from investing activities*

The following information was drawn from the year-end balance sheets of Vigotti Company:

Account Title	Year 2	Year 1
Investment securities	$ 51,000	$ 60,000
Equipment	310,000	275,000
Buildings	980,000	950,000
Land	135,000	110,000

The following is additional information regarding transactions that occurred during Year 2:

1. Investment securities that had cost $11,300 were sold. The Year 2 income statement contained a loss on the sale of investment securities of $800.

2. Equipment with a cost of $80,000 was purchased.

3. The income statement showed a gain on the sale of equipment of $9,500. On the date of sale, accumulated depreciation on the equipment sold amounted to $38,000.

4. A building that had originally cost $90,000 was demolished.

5. Land that had cost $20,000 was sold for $15,000.

Required

a. Determine the amount of cash flow for the purchase of investment securities during Year 2.

b. Determine the amount of cash flow from the sale of investment securities during Year 2.

c. Determine the cost of the equipment that was sold during Year 2.

d. Determine the amount of cash flow from the sale of equipment during Year 2.

e. Determine the amount of cash flow for the purchase of buildings during Year 2.

f. Determine the amount of cash flow for the purchase of land during Year 2.

g. Prepare the investing activities section of the Year 2 statement of cash flows.

LO 12-4

Problem 12-16B *Determining cash flows from financing activities*

The following information was drawn from the year-end balance sheets of Long's Wholesale, Inc.:

Account Title	Year 2	Year 1
Bonds payable	$400,000	$600,000
Common stock	190,000	150,000
Treasury stock	20,000	15,000
Retained earnings	96,000	80,000

The following is additional information regarding transactions that occurred during Year 2:

1. Long's Wholesale, Inc. issued $90,000 of bonds during Year 2. The bonds were issued at face value. All bonds retired were retired at face value.
2. Common stock did not have a par value.
3. Long's Wholesale, Inc. uses the cost method to account for treasury stock. Long's Wholesale, Inc. did not resell any treasury stock in Year 2.
4. The amount of net income shown on the Year 2 income statement was $49,000.

Required

a. Determine the amount of cash flow for the retirement of bonds that should appear on the Year 2 statement of cash flows.
b. Determine the amount of cash flow from the issue of common stock that should appear on the Year 2 statement of cash flows.
c. Determine the amount of cash flow for the purchase of treasury stock that should appear on the Year 2 statement of cash flows.
d. Determine the amount of cash flow for the payment of dividends that should appear on the Year 2 statement of cash flows.
e. Prepare the financing activities section of the Year 2 statement of cash flows.

Problem 12-17B *Preparing a statement of cash flows*

LO 12-1, 12-3, 12-4

The following information can be obtained by examining a company's balance sheet and income statement information:

a. Increases in current asset account balances, other than cash.
b. Cash outflows to purchase noncurrent assets.
c. Decreases in current liability account balances.
d. Noncash expenses (e.g., depreciation).
e. Cash outflows to purchase treasury stock.
f. Gains recognized on the sale of noncurrent assets.
g. Cash outflows to pay dividends.
h. Cash inflows from the issue of common stock.
i. Cash inflows from the sale of noncurrent assets.
j. Increases in current liability account balances.
k. Cash inflows from the issue of noncurrent debt.
l. Losses incurred from the sale of noncurrent assets.
m. Decreases in current asset account balances, other than cash.
n. Cash outflows to repay noncurrent debt.

Required

Construct a table like the following one. For each item, indicate whether it would be used in the computation of net cash flows from operating, investing, or financing activities. Also, indicate whether the item would be added or subtracted when determining the net cash flow from operating, investing, or financing activities. Assume the indirect method is used to prepare the operating activities section of the statement of cash flows. The first item has been completed as an example.

Item	Type of Activity	Add or Subtract
a.	Operating	Subtract
b.		

LO 12-1, 12-3, 12-4

Problem 12-18B *Using financial statements to prepare a statement of cash flows—indirect method*

The following financial statements were drawn from the records of Culinary Products Co.:

Balance Sheets As of December 31		
	Year 2	**Year 1**
Assets		
Cash	$24,200	$ 2,800
Accounts receivable	2,000	1,200
Inventory	6,400	6,000
Equipment	19,000	42,000
Accumulated depreciation—equipment	(9,000)	(17,400)
Land	18,400	10,400
Total assets	$61,000	$45,000
Liabilities and stockholders' equity		
Accounts payable (inventory)	$ 2,600	$ 4,200
Long-term debt	2,800	6,400
Common stock	22,000	10,000
Retained earnings	33,600	24,400
Total liabilities and stockholders' equity	$61,000	$45,000

Income Statement For the Year Ended December 31, Year 2	
Sales revenue	$35,700
Cost of goods sold	(14,150)
Gross margin	21,550
Depreciation expense	(3,600)
Operating income	17,950
Gain on sale of equipment	500
Loss on disposal of land	(50)
Net income	$18,400

Additional Data

1. During Year 2, the company sold equipment for $18,500; it had originally cost $30,000. Accumulated depreciation on this equipment was $12,000 at the time of the sale. Also, the company purchased equipment for $7,000 cash.

2. The company sold land that had cost $4,000. This land was sold for $3,950, resulting in the recognition of a $50 loss. Also, common stock was issued in exchange for title to land that was valued at $12,000 at the time of exchange.

3. Paid dividends of $9,200.

Required

Prepare a statement of cash flows using the indirect method.

LO 12-1, 12-3, 12-4

Problem 12-19B *Using financial statements to prepare a statement of cash flows—indirect method*

The comparative balance sheets and an income statement for Wang Beauty Products, Inc. are shown next:

Balance Sheets As of December 31		
	Year 2	**Year 1**
Assets		
Cash	$ 68,800	$ 40,600
Accounts receivable	30,000	22,000
Merchandise inventory	160,000	176,000
Prepaid rent	2,400	4,800
Equipment	256,000	288,000
Accumulated depreciation	(146,800)	(236,000)
Land	192,000	80,000
Total assets	$562,400	$375,400
Liabilities and stockholders' equity		
Accounts payable (inventory)	$ 67,000	$ 76,000
Salaries payable	28,000	24,000
Stockholders' equity		
Common stock, $50 par value	250,000	200,000
Retained earnings	217,400	75,400
Total liabilities and stockholders' equity	$562,400	$375,400

Income Statement For the Year Ended December 31, Year 2	
Sales	$1,500,000
Cost of goods sold	(797,200)
Gross profit	702,800
Operating expenses	
Depreciation expense	(22,800)
Rent expense	(24,000)
Salaries expense	(256,000)
Other operating expenses	(258,000)
Net income	$ 142,000

Other Information

1. Purchased land for $112,000.
2. Purchased new equipment for $100,000.
3. Sold old equipment that cost $132,000 with accumulated depreciation of $112,000 for $20,000 cash.
4. Issued common stock for $50,000.

Required

Prepare the statement of cash flows for Year 2 using the indirect method.

Problem 12-20B   *Using transaction data to prepare a statement of cash flows—direct method*   LO 12-2, 12-3, 12-4

The Electric Company engaged in the following transactions during Year 2. The beginning cash balance was $43,000 and the ending cash balance was $48,600.

1. Sales on account were $274,000. The beginning receivables balance was $86,000 and the ending balance was $74,000.
2. Salaries expense was $115,000. The beginning salaries payable balance was $9,600 and the ending balance was $7,500.
3. Other operating expenses were $118,000. The beginning Other Operating Expenses Payable balance was $8,500 and the ending balance was $6,000.
4. Recorded $25,000 of depreciation expense. The beginning and ending balances in the Accumulated Depreciation account were $18,000 and $43,000, respectively.

5. The Equipment account had beginning and ending balances of $28,000 and $42,000, respectively. There were no sales of equipment during the period.

6. The beginning and ending balances in the Notes Payable account were $38,000 and $32,000, respectively. There were no notes payable issued during the period.

7. There was $4,600 of interest expense reported on the income statement. The beginning and ending balances in the Interest Payable account were $6,400 and $6,200, respectively.

8. The beginning and ending Merchandise Inventory account balances were $26,000 and $32,500, respectively. The company sold merchandise with a cost of $119,000. The beginning and ending balances in the Accounts Payable account were $10,000 and $12,500, respectively.

9. The beginning and ending balances in the Notes Receivable account were $80,000 and $20,000, respectively. Notes receivable result from long-term loans made to creditors. There were no loans made to creditors during the period.

10. The beginning and ending balances in the Common Stock account were $140,000 and $190,000, respectively. The increase was caused by the issue of common stock for cash.

11. Land had beginning and ending balances of $48,000 and $28,000, respectively. Land that cost $20,000 was sold for $16,000, resulting in a loss of $4,000.

12. The tax expense for the period was $6,600. The Tax Payable account had a $3,200 beginning balance and a $2,800 ending balance.

13. The Investments account had beginning and ending balances of $10,000 and $30,000, respectively. The company purchased investments for $40,000 cash during the period, and investments that cost $20,000 were sold for $26,000, resulting in a $6,000 gain.

Required

a. Determine the amount of cash flow for each item and indicate whether the item should appear in the operating, investing, or financing activities section of a statement of cash flows. Also identify any items that do not affect the cash flow statement. Assume The Electric Company uses the direct method for showing net cash flow from operating activities.

b. Prepare a statement of cash flows based on the information you developed in Requirement *a*.

LO 12-2, 12-3, 12-4   **Problem 12-21B**   *Using financial statements to prepare a statement of cash flows—direct method*

The following financial statements were drawn from the records of Boston Materials, Inc.:

Balance Sheets As of December 31		
	Year 2	Year 1
Assets		
Cash	$ 99,700	$ 25,400
Accounts receivable	72,000	60,000
Inventory	86,000	75,000
Notes receivable (long-term)	0	24,000
Equipment	104,000	152,000
Accumulated depreciation—equipment	(67,500)	(75,000)
Land	60,000	45,000
Total assets	$354,200	$306,400
Liabilities and stockholders' equity		
Accounts payable	$ 35,300	$ 36,200
Salaries payable	18,200	15,500
Utilities payable	1,400	2,800
Interest payable	600	1,200
Notes payable (long-term)	0	36,000
Common stock	120,000	100,000
Retained earnings	178,700	114,700
Total liabilities and stockholders' equity	$354,200	$306,400

Income Statement For the Year Ended December 31, Year 2	
Sales revenue	$450,000
Cost of goods sold	(212,000)
Gross margin	238,000
Operating expenses	
Salaries expense	(96,000)
Depreciation expense	(18,500)
Utilities expense	(7,500)
Operating income	116,000
Nonoperating items	
Interest expense	(3,500)
Gain on sale of equipment	1,500
Net income	$114,000

Additional Information

1. Sold equipment costing $48,000 with accumulated depreciation of $26,000 for $23,500 cash.
2. Paid a $50,000 cash dividend to owners.

Required

Analyze the data and prepare a statement of cash flows using the direct method.

ANALYZE, THINK, COMMUNICATE

ATC 12-1   Business Applications Case   *Understanding real-world annual reports*

Required

Obtain Target Corporation's annual report for its 2018 fiscal year (year ended February 2, 2019) at http://investors.target.com using the instructions in Appendix B, and use it to answer the following questions:

a. For the year ended February 2, 2019 (2018), which was larger, Target's *net income* or its *cash flow from operating activities?* By what amount did they differ?

b. What two items are most responsible for the difference between Target's *net income* and its *cash flow from operating activities* in 2018?

c. In 2018, Target generated approximately $6.0 billion of cash from operating activities, and its cash balance decreased by $1.1 billion. How did the company use this $7.1 billion of cash?

ATC 12-2   Real-World Case   *Following the cash*

Tesla, Inc. began operations in 2003 but did not begin selling its stock to the public until June 28, 2010. It has lost money every year it has been in existence, and by December 31, 2016, it had total lifetime losses of approximately $5 billion. In addition to making automobiles, Tesla makes energy storage systems. Tesla's statements of cash flows for 2015, 2016, and 2017 follow.

a. As this chapter explained, many companies that report net losses on their earnings statements report positive cash flows from operating activities. How do Tesla's net incomes compare to its cash flows from operating activities?

b. Based only on the information in the statements of cash flows, does Tesla appear to be growing the capacity of its business? Explain.

c. In 2017, Tesla paid off $3.995 billion of "convertible and other debt." Where did it get the funds to repay this debt?

d. All things considered, based on the information in its statements of cash flows, does Tesla's cash position appear to be improving or deteriorating?

TESLA, INC.
Consolidated Statements of Cash Flows
(in thousands)

	For the Years Ending December 31		
	2017	2016	2015
Cash flows from operating activities:			
Net loss	$(2,240,578)	$ (773,046)	$ (888,663)
Adjustments to reconcile net loss to net cash used in operating activities:			
Depreciation and amortization	1,636,003	947,099	422,590
Stock-based compensation	466,760	334,225	197,999
Amortization of debt discount and issuance costs	91,037	94,690	78,054
Inventory write-downs	131,665	65,520	44,940
Loss on disposal of fixed assets	105,770	34,633	37,723
Foreign currency transaction loss (gains)	52,309	(29,183)	55,765
Loss (gain) related to SolarCity acquisition	57,746	(88,727)	—
Non-cash interest and other operating activities	135,237	(15,179)	20,382
Changes in operating assets and liabilities, net of effect of business combinations:			
Accounts receivable	(24,635)	(216,565)	46,267
Inventories	(178,850)	(632,867)	(369,364)
Operating lease vehicles	(1,522,573)	(1,832,836)	(1,204,496)
Prepaid expenses and other current assets	(72,084)	56,806	(29,595)
MyPower customer notes receivable and other assets	(15,453)	(49,353)	(24,362)
Accounts payable and accrued liabilities	388,206	750,640	263,345
Deferred revenue	468,902	382,962	322,203
Customer deposits	170,027	388,361	36,721
Resale value guarantee	208,718	326,934	442,295
Other long-term liabilities	81,139	132,057	23,697
Net cash flows from operating activities	(60,654)	(123,829)	(524,499)
Cash flows from investing activities:			
Purchases of property and equipment excluding capital leases, net of sales	(3,414,814)	(1,280,802)	(1,634,850)
Maturities of short-term marketable securities	—	16,667	—
Purchase of solar energy systems, leased and to be leased	(666,540)	(159,669)	—
Increase in restricted cash	(223,090)	(206,149)	(26,441)
Business combinations, net of cash acquired	(114,523)	213,523	(12,260)
Net cash flows from investing activities	(4,418,967)	(1,416,430)	(1,673,551)
Cash flows from financing activities:			
Proceeds from issuance of common stock in public offering	400,175	1,701,734	730,000
Proceeds from issuance of convertible and other debt	7,138,055	2,852,964	318,972
Repayments of convertible and other debt	(3,995,484)	(1,857,594)	—
Repayments of borrowings under Solar Bonds issued to related parties	(165,000)	—	—
Collateralized lease borrowing	511,321	769,709	568,745
Proceeds from exercise of stock options and other stock issuances	259,116	163,817	106,611
Principal payments on capital leases	(103,304)	(46,889)	(203,780)
Common stock and debt issuance costs	(63,111)	(20,042)	(17,025)
Purchase of convertible note hedges	(204,102)	—	—
Proceeds from settlement of convertible note hedges	287,213	—	—
Proceeds from issuance of warrants	52,883	—	—
Proceeds from issuance of common stock in private placements	—	—	20,000
Payments for settlements of warrants	(230,385)	—	—
Proceeds from investment by noncontrolling interests in subsidiaries	789,704	201,527	—
Distributions paid to noncontrolling interests in subsidiaries	(261,844)	(21,250)	—
Payments for buyouts of noncontrolling interests in subsidiaries	(373)	—	—
Net cash flows from financing activities	4,414,864	3,743,976	1,523,523
Effect of exchange rate changes on cash and cash equivalents	39,455	(7,409)	(34,278)
Net (decrease) increase in cash and cash equivalents	(25,302)	2,196,308	(708,805)
Cash and cash equivalents at beginning of period	3,393,216	1,196,908	1,905,713
Cash and cash equivalents at end of period	$ 3,367,914	$3,393,216	$1,196,908

ATC 12-3 Group Assignment *Preparing a statement of cash flows*

The following financial statements and information are available for Blythe Industries Inc.:

Balance Sheets As of December 31		
	Year 3	**Year 2**
Assets		
Cash	$ 160,200	$120,600
Accounts receivable	103,200	85,000
Inventory	186,400	171,800
Marketable securities (available for sale)	284,000	220,000
Equipment	650,000	490,000
Accumulated depreciation	(310,000)	(240,000)
Land	80,000	120,000
Total assets	$1,153,800	$967,400
Liabilities and stockholders' equity		
Liabilities		
Accounts payable (inventory)	$ 36,400	$ 66,200
Notes payable—Long-term	230,000	250,000
Bonds payable	200,000	100,000
Total liabilities	466,400	416,200
Stockholders' equity		
Common stock, no par	240,000	200,000
Preferred stock, $50 par	110,000	100,000
Paid-in capital in excess of par—Preferred stock	34,400	26,800
Total paid-In capital	384,400	326,800
Retained earnings	333,000	264,400
Less: Treasury stock	(30,000)	(40,000)
Total stockholders' equity	687,400	551,200
Total liabilities and stockholders' equity	$1,153,800	$967,400

Income Statement For the Year Ended December 31, Year 3		
Sales revenue		$1,050,000
Cost of goods sold		(766,500)
Gross profit		283,500
Operating expenses		
Supplies expense	$20,400	
Salaries expense	92,000	
Depreciation expense	90,000	
Total operating expenses		(202,400)
Operating income		81,100
Nonoperating items		
Interest expense		(16,000)
Gain from the sale of marketable securities		30,000
Gain from the sale of land and equipment		12,000
Net income		$ 107,100

Additional Information

1. Sold land that cost $40,000 for $44,000.
2. Sold equipment that cost $30,000 and had accumulated depreciation of $20,000 for $18,000.
3. Purchased new equipment for $190,000.
4. Sold marketable securities that were classified as available-for-sale and that cost $40,000 for $70,000.

5. Purchased new marketable securities, classified as available-for-sale, for $104,000.

6. Paid $20,000 on the principal of the long-term note.

7. Paid off a $100,000 bond issue and issued new bonds for $200,000.

8. Sold 100 shares of treasury stock at its cost.

9. Issued some new common stock.

10. Issued some new $50 par preferred stock.

11. Paid dividends. (*Note:* The only transactions to affect retained earnings were net income and dividends.)

Required

Organize the class into three sections and divide each section into groups of three to five students. Assign each section of groups an activity section of the statement of cash flows (operating activities, investing activities, or financing activities).

Group Task

Prepare your assigned portion of the statement of cash flows. Have a representative of your section put your activity section of the statement of cash flows on the board. As each section adds its information on the board, the full statement of cash flows will be presented.

Class Discussion

Have the class finish the statement of cash flows by computing the net change in cash. Also have the class answer the following questions.

a. What is the cost per share of the treasury stock?

b. What was the issue price per share of the preferred stock?

c. What was the book value of the equipment sold?

ATC 12-4   Business Applications Case   *Calculating cash flows using real-world data*

The following information was taken from the annual reports of Pfizer, Inc. and Ford Motor Company. These data are for 2018, and all amounts are in millions.

Information from Pfizer, Inc.	
Inventory on December 31, 2017	$ 7,508
Inventory on December 31, 2018	7,578
Cost of goods sold for 2018	11,248
Accounts payables on December 31, 2017	4,656
Accounts payables on December 31, 2018	4,674

Information from Ford Motor Company	
Accounts receivables on December 31, 2017	$ 11,195
Accounts receivables on December 31, 2018	10,599
Sales (automobiles)	148,294

Required

a. Calculate the amount of inventory that Pfizer purchased during 2018.

b. Calculate how much cash Pfizer spent on inventory purchases. Assume that all inventory purchases were on account, and that accounts payables related only to the purchase of inventory.

c. Calculate how much cash Ford collected as a result of sales of automobiles. Assume that all sales were made on account, and that accounts receivables related only to sales of automobiles.

ATC 12-5 Writing Assignment *Explaining discrepancies between cash flow and operating income*

The following selected information was drawn from the records of Fleming Company:

Assets	2016	2017
Accounts receivable	$ 400,000	$ 840,200
Merchandise inventory	720,000	1,480,000
Equipment	1,484,000	1,861,200
Accumulated depreciation	(312,000)	(402,400)

Fleming is experiencing cash flow problems. Despite the fact that it reported significant increases in operating income, operating activities produced a net cash outflow. Recent financial forecasts predict that Fleming will have insufficient cash to pay its current liabilities within three months.

Required

Write an explanation of Fleming's cash shortage. Include a recommendation to remedy the problem.

ATC 12-6 Ethical Dilemma *Would I lie to you, baby?*

Andy and Jean Crocket are involved in divorce proceedings. When discussing a property settlement, Andy told Jean that he should take over their investment in an apartment complex because she would be unable to absorb the loss that the apartments are generating. Jean was somewhat distrustful and asked Andy to support his contention. He produced the following income statement, which was supported by a CPA's unqualified opinion that the statement was prepared in accordance with generally accepted accounting principles.

CROCKET APARTMENTS		
Income Statement		
For the Year Ended December 31, Year 3		
Rent revenue		$580,000
Less: Expenses		
Depreciation expense	$280,000	
Interest expense	184,000	
Operating expense	88,000	
Management fees	56,000	
Total expenses		(608,000)
Net loss		$ (28,000)

All revenue is earned on account. Interest and operating expenses are incurred on account. Management fees are paid in cash. The following accounts and balances were drawn from the Year 2 and Year 3 year-end balance sheets:

Account Title	Year 2	Year 3
Rent receivable	$40,000	$44,000
Interest payable	12,000	18,000
Accounts payable (oper. exp.)	6,000	4,000

Jean is reluctant to give up the apartments but feels that she must do so because her present salary is only $40,000 per year. She says that if she takes the apartments, the $28,000 loss would absorb a significant portion of her salary, leaving her only $12,000 with which to support herself. She tells you that, while the figures seem to support her husband's arguments, she believes that she is failing to see something. She knows that she and her husband collected a $20,000 distribution from the business on December 1, Year 3. Also, $150,000 cash was paid in Year 3 to reduce the principal balance on a mortgage that was taken out to finance the purchase of the apartments two years ago. Finally, $24,000 cash was paid during Year 3 to purchase a computer system used in the business. She wonders, "If the apartments are losing money, where is my husband getting all the cash to make these payments?"

Required

a. Prepare a statement of cash flows for the Year 3 accounting period.

b. Compare the cash flow statement prepared in Requirement *a* with the income statement and provide Jean Crocket with recommendations.

c. Comment on the value of an unqualified audit opinion when using financial statements for decision-making purposes.

ATC 12-7 Research Assignment *Analyzing cash flow information*

In 2017 and 2016, Sears Holding Corporation reported net losses and negative cash flows from operating activities. Using the company's Form 10-K for the fiscal year ended February 3, 2018 (2017), complete the requirements shown as follows. The Form 10-K can be found on the company's website. It can also be obtained using the EDGAR system following the instructions in Appendix A.

Required

a. Determine Sears's net incomes and cash flow from operating activities for 2017 and 2016.

b. How was Sears able to pay its bills given that it has such large, negative net cash flows from operating activities in 2017 and 2016? Provide a separate answer for each year.

CHAPTER 13

The Double-Entry Accounting System

LEARNING OBJECTIVES

After you have mastered the material in this chapter, you will be able to:

Video lectures and accompanying self-assessment quizzes are available in *Connect* for all learning objectives.

LO 13-1   Record business events in T-accounts using debit/credit terminology.

LO 13-2   Record transactions using the general journal format.

LO 13-3   Prepare a trial balance and explain how it is used to prepare financial statements.

LO 13-4   Prepare closing entries in general journal format.

LO 13-5   Maintain accounting records for a complete accounting cycle containing an advanced set of business events.

CHAPTER OPENING

To prepare financial statements, a company must have a system for accurately capturing the vast numbers of business transactions in which it engages each year. The most widely used system, double-entry accounting, is so effective it has been in use for hundreds of years! This chapter explains the rules for recording transactions using double-entry accounting.

Double-entry accounting rules are analogous to other rules people adopt to achieve various goals, such as rules governing traffic signals. A red signal means "stop," but it could just as easily mean "go." What matters is that all drivers agree on what red means. Similarly, double-entry accounting rules could have developed differently. In fact, the rules sometimes seem backward at first. You likely use accounting terms like *debit* or *credit* from a consumer's point of view. To learn the accounting rules, however, you must view them from a business perspective. With practice, they will become second nature and you will know them as well as you know traffic signals.

The Curious Accountant

Most companies prepare financial statements at least once each year. The year that financial statements report upon is called a **fiscal year.** Illustrations in this textbook usually assume the fiscal year coincides with the calendar year; that is, it ends on December 31. In practice, the fiscal years of many companies do not end on December 31. For example, **Ralph Lauren Corp.**, a company that produces clothing, ends its fiscal year on the last

Tea/123RF

Saturday in March or the first Saturday in April. **Abercrombie & Fitch Co.**, a company that sells clothing, ends its fiscal year on the last Saturday in January or the first Saturday in February.

Why would these companies choose these dates to end their fiscal years? (Answers on page 655.)

DEBIT/CREDIT TERMINOLOGY

By now you know that the accounting equation is composed of three primary *elements* including assets, liabilities, and stockholders' equity. Further, each element may be divided into subcomponents called *accounts*. For example, the element assets may be subdivided in specific accounts such as cash, accounts receivable, inventory, equipment, etc. Likewise, the liabilities element may contain accounts such as payables, warranty obligations, bond liabilities, etc. Finally, the stockholders' equity element may include common stock and retained earnings accounts.

 LO 13-1

Record business events in T-accounts using debit/credit terminology.

As you have learned, accounting events cause increases and/or decreases in the elements of the accounting equation. For example, the event of *acquiring cash from the issue of common stock* will cause the assets and stockholders' equity to increase. In practice, accountants describe the increases and/or decreases with technical terminology. For example, instead of saying that an account is increased or decreased, an accountant would say the account is debited or credited to reflect the impact a transaction has on the elements of the accounting equation.

Rules for Debits and Credits

An account form known as a **T-account** is a good starting point for learning how to describe increases and decreases with debit and credit terminology. A T-account gets its name from the fact that it is shaped like the letter T. The account title is written across the top of the horizontal bar of the T. The left side of the vertical bar is the **debit** side, and the right side is the **credit** side. The following diagram uses T-accounts to show when the terms *debit* and *credit* are used to designate increases or decreases in each element of the accounting equation.

Assets		=	Liabilities		+	Stockholders' Equity	
Debit	Credit		Debit	Credit		Debit	Credit
+	–		–	+		–	+

Notice that a debit can represent an increase or a decrease. Likewise, a credit can represent an increase or a decrease. Whether a debit or credit represents an increase or a decrease depends on the element (asset, liability, or stockholders' equity) in question.

RECORDING TRANSACTIONS IN T-ACCOUNTS

To facilitate the learning process, we suggest that you develop a systematic three-step approach for recording accounting events in T-accounts.

Step 1: Determine how an event affects each *element* of the accounting equation. Specifically, does the event cause the element assets, liabilities, and/or stockholders' equity to increase, decrease, or remain unaffected.

Step 2: Use the rules for debits and credits to convert the increase/decrease terminology to debit/credit terminology.

Step 3: Identify the specific asset, liability, and/or stockholders' equity *accounts* affected by the event and record the debits or credits in the appropriate T-accounts.

To illustrate this step-wise approach, we record the Year 2 accounting events for a small business: Collins Brokerage Services, Inc. Collins begins the accounting period with the following balances in its balance sheet accounts: Cash, $5,000; Common Stock, $4,000; and Retained Earnings, $1,000. These account balances are shown later in Exhibit 13.2.

We will now record the Year 2 events in T-accounts. The Year 2 events are organized into four categories, including asset source, asset exchange, asset use, and claims exchange.

Asset Source Transactions

Recall that a business may obtain assets from three primary sources: stockholders, creditors, or operations (retained earnings). An asset source transaction increases assets and increases liabilities or stockholders' equity. The increase in assets is recorded with a debit entry. The increase in liabilities or stockholders' equity is recorded with a credit entry. The following section demonstrates recording procedures for common asset source transactions.

EVENT 1   Acquired $25,000 cash from the issue of common stock.

We use the three-step systematic approach described previously to record this event in T-accounts.

(1) This accounting event increases both assets and stockholders' equity. (*These effects are highlighted by the plus signs shown above the designated elements in the green bar above the accounting equation.*)

(2) In accordance with the rules of debits and credits, the increase in assets is recorded with a debit, and the increase in stockholders' equity is recorded with a credit.

(3) Accordingly, the asset account Cash is debited and the stockholders' equity account Common Stock is credited.

The recording process is summarized as follows:

+			+	
Assets	**=**	**Liabilities**	**+**	**Stockholders' Equity**
Cash				**Common Stock**
Debit	Credit			Debit	Credit
25,000					25,000

Notice the entry included both debiting an account and crediting an account. This system is called **double-entry accounting.** Recording any transaction requires at least one debit and at least one credit. The total of the debit amounts must equal the total of the credit amounts. These requirements provide accountants with a built-in error detection tool.

The effects of recording the issue of common stock on the financial statements are shown next:

Balance Sheet					Income Statement					Statement of Cash Flows
Assets	=	Liab.	+	Stk. Equity						
Cash	=			Com. Stk.	Rev.	−	Exp.	=	Net Inc.	
25,000	=	NA	+	25,000	NA	−	NA	=	NA	25,000 FA

EVENT 2   Purchased $850 of supplies on account.

Purchasing supplies on account increases the elements, assets and liabilities. Debits increase assets and credits increase liability accounts. Accordingly, the asset account Supplies is debited and the liability account Accounts Payable is credited. The recording process is summarized here:

+			+	
Assets	**=**	**Liabilities**	**+**	**Stockholders' Equity**
Supplies		**Account Payable**		
Debit	Credit	Debit	Credit	
850			850	

The effects of this entry on the financial statements are shown next:

Balance Sheet					Income Statement					Statement of Cash Flows
Assets	=	Liab.	+	Stk. Equity						
Supplies	=	Accts. Pay.			Rev.	−	Exp.	=	Net Inc.	
850	=	850	+	NA	NA	−	NA	=	NA	NA

EVENT 3   Collected $1,800 cash as an advance to provide future services over a one-year period starting March 1.

Accepting the $1,800 in advance creates an obligation for Collins. The obligation is to provide future services to a customer. Collins will recognize a liability called *unearned revenue.* Recording the event increases the elements, assets and liabilities. Debits increase assets and credits increase liabilities. Accordingly, the asset account Cash is debited, and the liability account Unearned Revenue is credited. The recording process is summarized here:

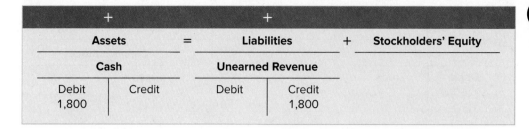

The effects of this entry on the financial statements are shown next:

Balance Sheet				Income Statement			Statement of Cash Flows
Assets	=	Liab.	+ Stk. Equity				
Cash	=	Unearned Revenue		Rev.	− Exp.	= Net Inc.	
1,800	=	1,800	+ NA	NA	− NA	= NA	1,800 OA

EVENT 4   Provided $15,760 of services on account.

To promote a conceptual understanding of accounting in previous chapters, we have recorded revenue, expense, and dividend events directly into retained earnings. In practice, the volume of activity makes it impractical to record all transactions affecting these accounts into a single account. Instead, separate Revenue, Expense, and Dividend accounts are used to capture the transactions occurring during each accounting period. Indeed, depending on the volume of activity, it is usually necessary to establish numerous revenue and expense accounts, with each account representing a specific type of revenue, expense, or dividend. At the end of the accounting period, after the statements are prepared, the information is transferred from the separate accounts to the Retained Earnings account. The procedures for transferring the balance in the revenue account to retained earnings is called closing. Closing is discussed further in Learning Objective 13-4 of this chapter.

Recognizing revenue earned on account increases the assets and stockholders' equity. Debits increase assets and credits increase stockholders' equity. Accordingly, the asset account Accounts Receivable is debited, and the Service Revenue account is credited. The recording process is summarized here:

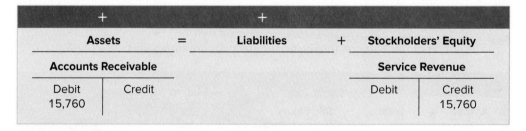

The effects of this entry on the financial statements are shown next:

Balance Sheet				Income Statement			Statement of Cash Flows
Assets	=	Liab.	+ Stk. Equity				
Accts. Rec.	=		Ret. Earn.	Rev.	− Exp.	= Net Inc.	
15,760	=	NA	+ 15,760	15,760	− NA	= 15,760	NA

CHECK YOURSELF 13.1

What are the three sources of assets? Which accounts are debited and credited when a business acquires an asset?

Answer The three sources of assets are creditors, investors, and earnings. When a company acquires an asset, the asset account is debited and the source account is credited. For example, if a company earns revenue on account, the Receivables account is debited and the Revenue account is credited.

Asset Exchange Transactions

Asset exchange transactions involve trading one asset for another asset. One asset increases; the other decreases. The total amount of assets remains unchanged. Recall that debits increase assets, whereas credits decrease assets. Accordingly, asset exchange transactions are recorded by debiting the asset that is increasing, while crediting the asset that is decreasing.

EVENT 5   Purchased land for $26,000 cash.

Purchasing land with cash increases one asset account and decreases another asset account. Because credits decrease assets, the asset account Cash is credited, and because debits increase assets, the asset account Land is debited. The recording process is summarized here:

−		+		=	Claims
Assets					
Cash		**Land**			
Debit	Credit	Debit	Credit		
	26,000	26,000			

The effects of this entry on the financial statements are shown next:

Balance Sheet			Income Statement			Statement of Cash Flows
Assets	**= Liab. + Stk. Equity**					
Cash + Land			**Rev. − Exp. = Net Inc.**			
(26,000) + 26,000 = NA +	NA		NA − NA =	NA		(26,000) IA

EVENT 6   Paid $1,200 cash for a one-year insurance policy with coverage starting August 1.

Purchasing prepaid insurance with cash increases one asset account and decreases another asset account. Because credits decrease assets, the asset account Cash is credited, and because debits increase assets, the asset account Prepaid Insurance is debited. The recording process is summarized here:

−		+		=	Claims
Assets					
Cash		**Prepaid Insurance**			
Debit	Credit	Debit	Credit		
	1,200	1,200			

The effects of this entry on the financial statements are shown next:

Balance Sheet			Income Statement			Statement of Cash Flows
Assets	= Liab. + Stk. Equity					
Cash + Prepaid Insurance			Rev. − Exp. = Net Inc.			
(1,200) + 1,200	= NA + NA		NA − NA = NA			(1,200) OA

EVENT 7   Collected $13,400 cash from accounts receivable.

Collecting an account receivable increases one asset account and decreases another asset account. Because debits increase assets, the asset account Cash is debited, and because credits decrease assets, the asset account Accounts Receivable is credited. The recording process is summarized here:

+			−		=	Claims
Assets						
Cash			Accounts Receivable			
Debit	Credit		Debit	Credit		
13,400				13,400		

The effects of this entry on the financial statements are shown next:

Balance Sheet			Income Statement			Statement of Cash Flows
Assets	= Liab. + Stk. Equity					
Cash + Accts. Rec.			Rev. − Exp. = Net Inc.			
13,400 + (13,400)	= NA + NA		NA − NA = NA			13,400 OA

Asset Use Transactions

There are three primary asset use transactions: paying expenses may use assets, paying dividends may use assets, or settling liabilities may use assets. An asset use transaction decreases assets and also decreases liabilities or stockholders' equity. The decrease in assets is recorded with a credit, while the decrease in liabilities or stockholders' equity is recorded with a debit.

EVENT 8   Paid $9,500 cash for salaries expense.

Recognizing cash expenses decreases both elements, assets and stockholders' equity. Because credits decrease assets, the asset account Cash is credited, and because debits decrease stockholders' equity, the stockholders' equity account Salaries Expense is debited. Notice that the decrease in stockholders' equity is not recorded directly into the retained earnings account but is instead held in a separate expense account. The balance in the expense account will be transferred to retained earnings at the end of the accounting period. The procedures for transferring the balance in the expense account to retained earnings is called closing. Closing is discussed further in Learning Objective 13-4 of this chapter. The recording process is summarized here:

−		=	Liabilities	+	−	
Assets					Stockholders' Equity	
Cash					Salaries Expense	
Debit	Credit				Debit	Credit
	9,500				9,500	

The effects of this entry on the financial statements are shown next:

Balance Sheet				Income Statement				Statement of Cash Flows
Assets	=	Liab.	+ Stk. Equity					
Cash	=		Ret. Earn.	Rev.	− Exp.	=	Net Inc.	
(9,500)	=	NA	+ (9,500)	NA	− 9,500	=	(9,500)	(9,500) OA

EVENT 9   Paid an $800 cash dividend.

Recognizing cash dividends decreases both elements, assets and stockholders' equity. Because credits decrease assets, the decrease in the asset account Cash is credited, and because debits decrease stockholders' equity, the stockholders' equity account Dividends is debited. Notice that the decrease in stockholders' equity is not recorded directly into the retained earnings account but is instead held in a separate dividends account. The balance in the dividends account will be transferred to retained earnings at the end of the accounting period. The procedures for transferring the balance in the dividend account to retained earnings is called closing. Closing is discussed further in Learning Objective 13-4 of this chapter. The recording process is summarized here:

Assets	=	Liabilities	+	Stockholders' Equity	
Cash				**Dividends**	
Debit	Credit			Debit	Credit
	800			800	

Recall that dividends are wealth transfers, not expenses. Therefore, the income statement is not affected. The effects of this entry on the financial statements are shown next:

Balance Sheet				Income Statement				Statement of Cash Flows
Assets	=	Liab.	+ Stk. Equity					
Cash	=		Ret. Earn.	Rev.	− Exp.	=	Net Inc.	
(800)	=	NA	+ (800)	NA	− NA	=	NA	(800) FA

EVENT 10   Paid $850 cash to settle accounts payable.

Paying cash to reduce liabilities decreases both elements, assets and liabilities. Because credits decrease assets, the asset account Cash is credited, and because debits decrease liabilities, the liability account Accounts Payable is debited. The recording process is summarized here:

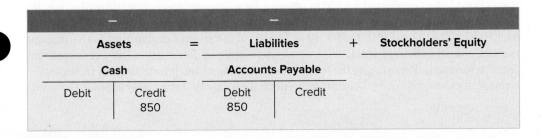

Assets	=	Liabilities	+	Stockholders' Equity
Cash		**Accounts Payable**		
Debit	Credit	Debit	Credit	
	850	850		

The effects of this entry on the financial statements are shown next:

Balance Sheet					Income Statement					Statement of Cash Flows
Assets	=	Liab.	+	Stk. Equity						
Cash	=	Accts. Pay.			Rev.	−	Exp.	=	Net Inc.	
(850)	=	(850)	+	NA	NA	−	NA	=	NA	(850) OA

Claims Exchange Transactions

Claims exchange transactions involve trading one claim for another claim. The total amount of claims remains unchanged. Recall that debits decrease claims and that credits increase claims. Accordingly, claims exchange transactions are recorded by debiting the decrease in liabilities or stockholders' equity and crediting the increase in liabilities or stockholders' equity.

EVENT 11   Recognized $1,900 other operating expenses on account.

This event increases the element liabilities and decreases the element stockholders' equity. Because credits increase liabilities, the liability account Accounts Payable is credited, and because debits decrease stockholders' equity, the stockholders' equity account Other Operating Expense is debited. The recording process is summarized here:

		+		−	
Assets	=	Liabilities	+	Stockholders' Equity	
		Accounts Payable		Other Operating Expense	
		Debit	Credit	Debit	Credit
			1,900	1,900	

The effects of this entry on the financial statements are shown next:

Balance Sheet						Income Statement					Statement of Cash Flows
Assets	=	Liab.		+	Stk. Equity						
		Accts. Pay.	+		Ret. Earn.	Rev.	−	Exp.	=	Net Inc.	
NA	=	1,900	+		(1,900)	NA	−	1,900	=	(1,900)	NA

Adjusting the Accounts

Assume Collins's fiscal year ends on December 31, Year 2. Collins has several unrecorded accruals and deferrals that must be recognized before the financial statements can be prepared. The appropriate adjustments are discussed in the following.

ADJUSTMENT 1   As of December 31, Year 2, Collins had earned $1,500 of the $1,800 in revenue it deferred in Event 3.

Recall that Collins's collected $1,800 in advance for a one-year contract starting March 1. By December 31, Year 2, Collins would have provided professional services for 10 months, earning $1,500 ($1,800 ÷ 12 = $150; $150 × 10 = $1,500) of the revenue during Year 2. This amount must be transferred from the liability account (Unearned Revenue) to an equity account (Service Revenue). Recognizing the revenue decreases the element liabilities and increases the element stockholders' equity. Because debits decrease liabilities, the liability account Unearned

Revenue is debited, and because credits increase stockholders' equity, the stockholders' equity account Service Revenue is credited. The recording process is summarized here:

Assets	=	Liabilities	+	Stockholders' Equity
		−		**+**
		Unearned Revenue		**Service Revenue**
		Debit | Credit		Debit | Credit
		1,500 |		| 1,500

The effects of this entry on the financial statements are shown next:

Balance Sheet					Income Statement				Statement of Cash Flows
Assets	=	Liab.	+	Stk. Equity					
		Unearned Revenue	+	Ret. Earn.	Rev.	−	Exp.	= Net Inc.	
NA	=	(1,500)	+	1,500	1,500	−	NA	= 1,500	NA

ADJUSTMENT 2   As of December 31, Year 2, Collins had $800 of accrued salary expenses that will be paid in Year 2.

Assume that Collins owes $800 to employees for work done in Year 2. Collins will pay these salaries in Year 3. The required adjusting entry increases the element liabilities and decreases the element stockholders' equity. Because credits increase liabilities, the liability account Salaries Payable is credited, and because debits decrease stockholders' equity, the stockholders' equity account Salaries Expense is debited. The recording process is summarized here:

Assets	=	Liabilities	+	Stockholders' Equity
		+		**−**
		Salaries Payable		**Salaries Expense**
		Debit | Credit		Debit | Credit
		| 800		800 |

The effects of this entry on the financial statements are shown next:

Balance Sheet					Income Statement				Statement of Cash Flows
Assets	=	Liab.	+	Stk. Equity					
		Sal. Pay.	+	Ret. Earn.	Rev.	−	Exp.	= Net Inc.	
NA	=	800	+	(800)	NA	−	800	= (800)	NA

ADJUSTMENT 3   As of December 31, Year 2, Collins had used $500 of the $1,200 of insurance coverage that was prepaid in Event 6.

Recall that Collins paid $1,200 in advance for insurance coverage for one year. The monthly insurance cost is therefore $100 ($1,200 ÷ 12 months). By December 31, Collins had *used* the insurance coverage for five months in Year 2. Insurance expense for those five months is therefore $500 ($100 × 5). Recognizing the insurance expense decreases the elements assets and stockholders' equity. Because credits decrease assets, the asset account Prepaid Insurance is credited, and because debits decrease stockholders' equity, the stockholders' equity Insurance Expense is debited. The recording process is summarized here:

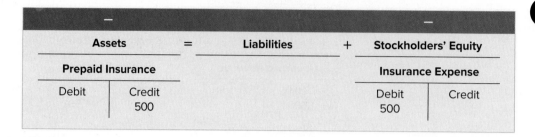

Assets	=	Liabilities	+	Stockholders' Equity	
Prepaid Insurance				**Insurance Expense**	
Debit	Credit 500			Debit 500	Credit

The effects of this entry on the financial statements are shown next:

Balance Sheet					Income Statement				Statement of Cash Flows
Assets	=	Liab.	+	Stk. Equity					
Prep. Ins.	=			Ret. Earn.	Rev.	−	Exp.	= Net Inc.	
(500)	=	NA	+	(500)	NA	−	500	= (500)	NA

ADJUSTMENT 4   As of December 31, Year 2, a physical count of the supplies on hand revealed that $125 of unused supplies were available for future use.

Collins used $725 ($850 − $125) of supplies during the period. Recognizing the supplies expense decreases both elements, assets and stockholders' equity. Because credits decrease assets, the asset account Supplies is credited, and because debits decrease stockholders' equity, the stockholders' equity account Supplies Expense is debited. The recording process is summarized here:

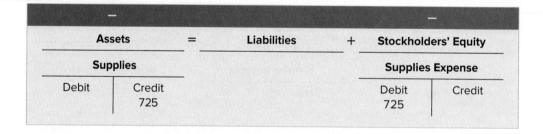

Assets	=	Liabilities	+	Stockholders' Equity	
Supplies				**Supplies Expense**	
Debit	Credit 725			Debit 725	Credit

The effects of this entry on the financial statements are shown next:

Balance Sheet					Income Statement				Statement of Cash Flows
Assets	=	Liab.	+	Stk. Equity					
Supplies	=			Ret. Earn.	Rev.	−	Exp.	= Net Inc.	
(725)	=	NA	+	(725)	NA	−	725	= (725)	NA

 CHECK YOURSELF 13.2

Can an asset exchange transaction be an adjusting entry?

Answer   No. Adjusting entries always involve revenue or expense accounts. Because an asset exchange transaction involves only asset accounts, it cannot be an adjusting entry.

THE GENERAL JOURNAL

LO 13-2

Record transactions using the general journal format.

Businesses find it impractical to record every individual transaction directly into general ledger accounts. Imagine the number of cash transactions a grocery store has each day. To simplify recordkeeping, businesses rely on **source documents**, such as cash register tapes, as the basis for entering transaction data into the accounting system. Other source documents include invoices, time cards, check registers, and deposit tickets.

Accountants further simplify recordkeeping by initially recording data from source documents into **journals.** Journals provide a chronological record of business transactions. *Transactions are recorded in journals before they are entered into ledger accounts.* Journals are therefore **books of original entry.** Companies may use different **special journals** to record specific types of recurring transactions. For example, a company may use one special journal to record sales on account, another to record purchases on account, a third to record cash receipts, and a fourth to record cash payments. Transactions that do not fall into any of these categories are recorded in the **general journal.** Although special journals are useful, companies can keep records without them by recording all transactions in the general journal. For simplicity, this text illustrates a general journal only.

At a minimum, the general journal shows the dates, the account titles, and the amounts of each transaction. The date is recorded in the first column, followed by the title of the account to be debited. The title of the account to be credited is indented and written on the line directly below the account to be debited. The dollar amount of the transaction is recorded in the Debit and Credit columns. Dollar signs are not used when recording journal entries. For example, providing services for $1,000 cash on August 1 would be recorded in general journal format as follows:

Date	Account Title	Debit	Credit
Aug. 1	Cash	1,000	
	Service Revenue		1,000

Exhibit 13.1 shows a summary of Collins's Year 2 transactions and demonstrates how the transactions are recorded in general journal format. For easy reference, the journal column

REALITY BYTES

Do all accounting systems require using debits and credits? The answer is a definite no. Many small businesses use a single-entry system. A checkbook constitutes a sufficient accounting system for many business owners. Deposits represent revenues, and payments constitute expenses. Many excellent automated accounting systems do not require data entry through a debit/credit recording scheme. QuickBooks is a good example of this type of system. Data are entered into the QuickBooks software program through a user-friendly computer interface that does not require knowledge of debit/credit terminology. Even so, the QuickBooks program produces traditional financial reports such as an income statement, balance sheet, and statement of cash flows. How is this possible? Before you become too ingrained

Paul Sakuma/AP Images

in the debit/credit system, recall that throughout the first two chapters of this text, we illustrated accounting records without using debits and credits. Financial reports can be produced in many ways without using a double-entry system. Having recognized this point, we also note that the vast majority of medium- to large-sized companies use the double-entry system. Indeed, debit/credit terminology is a part of common culture. Most people have an understanding of what is happening when a business tells them that their account is being debited or credited. It is important for you to embrace the double-entry system as well as other financial reporting systems.

EXHIBIT 13.1

Transaction Summary

Event 1   Acquired $25,000 cash from the issue of common stock.
Event 2   Purchased $850 of supplies on account.
Event 3   Collected $1,800 cash as an advance to provide future services over a one-year period starting March 1.
Event 4   Provided $15,760 of services on account.
Event 5   Purchased land for $26,000 cash.
Event 6   Paid $1,200 cash for a one-year insurance policy with coverage starting August 1.
Event 7   Collected $13,400 cash from accounts receivable.
Event 8   Paid $9,500 cash for salaries expense.
Event 9   Paid an $800 cash dividend.
Event 10 Paid $850 cash to settle accounts payable.
Event 11 Recognized $1,900 other operating expenses on account.

Adjustments

Adj. 1   Recognized $1,500 of deferred service revenue.
Adj. 2   Recognized $800 of accrued salaries expense.
Adj. 3   Recognized $500 of deferred insurance expense.
Adj. 4   Recognized $725 of deferred supplies expense.

General Journal Entries

Event No.	Account Titles	Debit	Credit
1	Cash	25,000	
	Common Stock		25,000
2	Supplies	850	
	Accounts Payable		850
3	Cash	1,800	
	Unearned Service Revenue		1,800
4	Accounts Receivable	15,760	
	Service Revenue		15,760
5	Land	26,000	
	Cash		26,000
6	Prepaid Insurance	1,200	
	Cash		1,200
7	Cash	13,400	
	Accounts Receivable		13,400
8	Salaries Expense	9,500	
	Cash		9,500
9	Dividends	800	
	Cash		800
10	Accounts Payable	850	
	Cash		850
11	Other Operating Expenses	1,900	
	Accounts Payable		1,900
Adj. 1	Unearned Service Revenue	1,500	
	Service Revenue		1,500
Adj. 2	Salaries Expense	800	
	Salaries Payable		800
Adj. 3	Insurance Expense	500	
	Prepaid Insurance		500
Adj. 4	Supplies Expense	725	
	Supplies		725

EXHIBIT 13.2

General Ledger

| | Assets | | = | | Liabilities | | + | | Stockholders' Equity | | |

Assets

Cash

Bal.	5,000	26,000	(5)
(1)	25,000	1,200	(6)
(3)	1,800	9,500	(8)
(7)	13,400	800	(9)
		850	(10)
Bal.	6,850		

Accounts Receivable

(4)	15,760	13,400	(7)
Bal.	2,360		

Prepaid Insurance

(6)	1,200	500	(Adj. 3)
Bal.	700		

Supplies

(2)	850	725	(Adj. 3)
Bal.	125		

Land

(5)	26,000	

Liabilities

Accounts Payable

(10)	850	850	(2)
		1,900	(11)
		1,900	Bal.

Salaries Payable

	800	(Adj. 2)

Unearned Service Revenue

(Adj. 1)	1,500	1,800	(3)
		300	Bal.

Stockholders' Equity

Common Stock

	4,000	Bal.
	25,000	(1)
	29,000	Bal.

Retained Earnings

	1,000	Bal.

Dividends

(9)	800	

Service Revenue

	15,760	(4)
	1,500	(Adj. 1)
	17,260	Bal.

Other Operating Expenses

(11)	1,900	

Salaries Expense

(8)	9,500	
(Adj. 2)	800	
Bal.	10,300	

Insurance Expense

(Adj. 3)	500	

Supplies Expense

(Adj. 4)	725	

normally used for the transaction date contains the event numbers and the references for the adjusting entries. After transactions are initially recorded in a journal, the dollar amounts of each debit and credit are copied into the ledger accounts through a process called **posting.**

Most companies today use computer technology to record transactions and prepare financial statements. Computers can record and post data pertaining to vast numbers of transactions with incredible speed and unparalleled accuracy. Both manual and computerized accounting systems, however, use the same underlying design. Analyzing a manual account-ing system is a useful way to gain insight into how computer-based systems work.

The collection of all the accounts used by a particular business is called the **general ledger.** The general ledger for Collins is displayed in Exhibit 13.2. In a manual system, the ledger could be a book with pages for each account, where entries are recorded by hand. In more sophisticated systems, the general ledger is maintained in electronic form. Data are entered into electronic ledgers using computer keyboards or scanners. Companies typically assign each ledger account a name and a number. A list of all ledger accounts and their account numbers is called the **chart of accounts.**

TRIAL BALANCE AND FINANCIAL STATEMENTS

LO 13-3

Prepare a trial balance and explain how it is used to prepare financial statements.

To test whether debits equal credits in the general ledger, accountants regularly prepare an internal accounting schedule called a **trial balance.** A trial balance lists every ledger account and its balance. Debit balances are listed in one column, and credit balances are listed in an adjacent column. The columns are totaled and the totals are compared. Exhibit 13.3 displays the trial balance for Collins Brokerage Services, Inc. after the adjusting entries have been posted to the ledger.

If the debit total does not equal the credit total, the accountant knows to search for an error. Even if the totals are equal, however, there may be errors in the accounting records. For example, equal trial balance totals would not disclose errors like the following: failure to record transactions; misclassifications, such as debiting the wrong account; or incorrectly recording the amount of a transaction, such as recording a $200 transaction as $2,000. Equal debits and credits in a trial balance provide evidence rather than proof of accuracy.

Supplemented with details from the Cash and Common Stock ledger accounts, the adjusted trial balance (Exhibit 13.3) provides the information to prepare the financial statements for Collins Brokerage Services, Inc. The income statement, statement of changes in stockholders' equity, balance sheet, and statement of cash flows are shown in Exhibits 13.4, 13.5, 13.6, and 13.7, respectively.

EXHIBIT 13.3

COLLINS BROKERAGE SERVICES, INC.
Adjusted Trial Balance
December 31, Year 2

Account Title	Debit	Credit
Cash	$ 6,850	
Accounts receivable	2,360	
Prepaid insurance	700	
Supplies	125	
Land	26,000	
Accounts payable		$ 1,900
Salaries payable		800
Unearned service revenue		300
Common stock		29,000
Retained earnings		1,000
Dividends	800	
Service revenue		17,260
Salaries expense	10,300	
Insurance expense	500	
Supplies expense	725	
Other operating expense	1,900	
Totals	$50,260	$50,260

EXHIBIT 13.4

COLLINS BROKERAGE SERVICES, INC.
Income Statement
For the Year Ended December 31, Year 2

Revenue		$17,260
Expenses		
Salaries expense	$(10,300)	
Other operating expenses	(1,900)	
Insurance expense	(500)	
Supplies expense	(725)	
Total expenses		(13,425)
Net income		$ 3,835

EXHIBIT 13.5

COLLINS BROKERAGE SERVICES, INC.
Statement of Changes in Stockholders' Equity
For the Year Ended December 31, Year 2

Beginning common stock	$ 4,000	
Plus: Common stock issued	25,000	
Ending common stock		$29,000
Beginning retained earnings	1,000	
Plus: Net income	3,835	
Less: Dividends	(800)	
Ending retained earnings		4,035
Total stockholders' equity		$33,035

EXHIBIT 13.6

COLLINS BROKERAGE SERVICES, INC.
Balance Sheet
As of December 31, Year 2

Assets		
Cash	$ 6,850	
Accounts receivable	2,360	
Prepaid insurance	700	
Supplies	125	
Land	26,000	
Total assets		$36,035
Liabilities		
Accounts payable	$ 1,900	
Salaries payable	800	
Unearned service revenue	300	
Total liabilities		$ 3,000
Stockholders' equity		
Common stock	29,000	
Retained earnings	4,035	
Total stockholders' equity		33,035
Total liabilities and stockholders' equity		$36,035

EXHIBIT 13.7

COLLINS BROKERAGE SERVICES, INC.
Statement of Cash Flows
For the Year Ended December 31, Year 2

Cash flows from operating activities		
Cash receipts from customers	$15,200*	
Cash payments for salaries expense	(9,500)	
Cash payments for insurance expense	(1,200)	
Cash payments for supplies	(850)	
Net cash flow from operating activities		$ 3,650
Cash flows from investing activities		
Cash payment to purchase land		(26,000)
Cash flows from financing activities		
Cash receipts from issue of common stock	25,000	
Cash payment for dividends	(800)	
Net cash flow from financing activities		24,200
Net increase in cash		1,850
Plus: Beginning cash balance		5,000
Ending cash balance		$ 6,850

*$13,400 accounts receivable collections + $1,800 unearned service revenue collection.

Answers to The Curious Accountant

Part 1

The process of closing the books and going through a year-end audit is time-consuming for a business. Also, it is time spent that does not produce revenue. Thus, companies whose business is highly seasonal often choose "slow" periods to end their fiscal year. **Abercrombie & Fitch** does heavy business during the Christmas season, so it might find December 31 an inconvenient time to close its books. Toward the end of January, business activity is slow, and inventory levels are at their low points. This is a good time to count the inventory and to assess the financial condition of the company. For these reasons, Abercrombie & Fitch has chosen to close its books to end its fiscal year around the end of January.

Now that you know why a business like Abercrombie & Fitch might choose to end its fiscal year at the end of January, can you think of a reason why **Ralph Lauren** closes its books at the end of March?

PERMANENT VERSUS TEMPORARY ACCOUNTS

The process of transferring information from the revenue, expense, and dividend accounts to the Retained Earnings account is called *closing*. Because the Revenue, Expense, and Dividend information is held in the accounts temporarily, these accounts are called **temporary accounts.** Because the balances in the temporary accounts are closed at the end of each accounting period, these accounts have a zero balance at the beginning of each new accounting period. In contrast, the Retained Earnings account balance carries forward from one accounting period to the next. Because this account is not closed, it is called a **permanent account.**

LO 13-4

 Prepare closing entries in general journal format.

Closing Entries

Exhibit 13.8 shows **closing entries** for Collins Brokerage Services, Inc. These entries move all Year 2 data from the temporary accounts (revenues, expenses, and dividends) into the Retained Earnings account. For example, the first closing entry in Exhibit 13.8 moves the balance in the Service Revenue account to the Retained Earnings account. As shown in the adjusted trial balance (Exhibit 13.3), the Service Revenue account has a $17,260 credit balance before it is closed. Debiting the account for $17,260 brings its after-closing balance to zero. The corresponding $17,260 credit to Retained Earnings increases the balance in that account.

The second closing entry moves the balance in the Salaries Expense account to the Retained Earnings account. Before closing, the Salaries Expense account has a $10,300 debit balance; crediting the account for $10,300 leaves it with an after-closing balance of zero. The corresponding $10,300 debit to the Retained Earnings account reduces the balance in that account. The remaining entries close the other revenue, expense, and dividend accounts to the Retained Earnings account.

EXHIBIT 13.8

Closing Entries

Date	Account Titles	Debit	Credit
Dec. 31	Service Revenue	17,260	
	Retained Earnings		17,260
31	Retained Earnings	10,300	
	Salaries Expense		10,300
31	Retained Earnings	1,900	
	Other Operating Expenses		1,900
31	Retained Earnings	500	
	Insurance Expense		500
31	Retained Earnings	725	
	Supplies Expense		725
31	Retained Earnings	800	
	Dividends		800

Closing entries can be recorded more efficiently than in Exhibit 13.8. For example, all revenue, expense, and dividend accounts can be closed to the retained earning accounts in a single compound journal entry, as shown next:

Date	Account Title	Debit	Credit
Dec. 31	Service Revenue	17,260	
	Salary Expense		10,300
	Other Operating Expenses		1,900
	Insurance Expense		500
	Supplies Expense		725
	Dividends		800
	Retained Earnings		3,035

Answers to The Curious Accountant

Part 2

Late March or early April probably is a relatively slow time of year for Ralph Lauren, which sells most of its goods through retailers. It must deliver clothing to stores such as Abercrombie & Fitch weeks before it will be sold to holiday shoppers. By April, the Christmas season has passed and much of the spring clothing will have already been shipped to retailers, so this is a good time for Ralph Lauren to close its books. Tommy Hilfiger another clothing manufacturer, closes its books around the end of March of each year, and Levi Strauss closes its books around the end of November.

The form of the closing entries is not important. What matters is that all revenue, expense, and dividend amounts be moved to the Retained Earnings account. After the closing entries are posted to the ledger accounts, all revenue, expense, and dividend accounts have zero balances. The temporary accounts are then ready to capture revenue, expense, and dividend data for the next fiscal year.

If all companies closed their books on December 31 each year, accountants, printers, lawyers, government agencies, and others would be overburdened by the effort to produce the accounting reports of all companies at the same time. In an effort to balance the workload, many companies close their books at the end of the natural business year. A natural business year ends when operating activities are at their lowest point. For many companies, the lowest point in the operating cycle occurs on a date other than December 31. A recent survey found that almost one-half of the companies sampled closed their books in months other than December (see Exhibit 13.9).

Post-Closing Trial Balance

How often should companies prepare a trial balance? Some companies prepare a trial balance daily; others may prepare one monthly, quarterly, or annually, depending on the needs of management. The heading of a trial balance describes the status of the account balances in it. For example, the trial balance in Exhibit 13.10 is described as a *Post-Closing Trial Balance* because it reflects the account balances immediately after the closing entries were posted. Further, since this trial balance shows the account balances after closing, it contains no revenue, expense, or dividend accounts. In contrast, the trial balance in Exhibit 13.3 is described as an *Adjusted Trial Balance* because it shows the account balances immediately after the adjusting entries were posted. A trial balance prepared at the end of each day may be described as a *Daily Trial Balance*.

EXHIBIT 13.9

Distribution of Fiscal Closing Dates

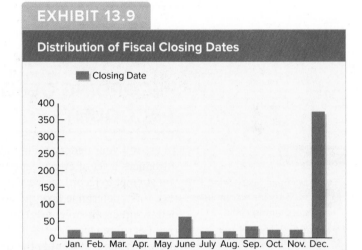

Source: Dow Jones Industrial Average

EXHIBIT 13.10

COLLINS BROKERAGE SERVICES, INC.
Post-Closing Trial Balance
December 31, Year 2

Account Title	Debit	Credit
Cash	$ 6,850	
Accounts receivable	2,360	
Prepaid insurance	700	
Supplies	125	
Land	26,000	
Accounts payable		$ 1,900
Salaries payable		800
Unearned service revenue		300
Common stock		29,000
Retained earnings		4,035
Totals	$36,035	$36,035

CHECK YOURSELF 13.3

Describe an error that would not cause a trial balance to be out of balance.

Answer Many potential errors would not cause a trial balance to be out of balance, such as debiting or crediting the wrong account. For example, if revenue earned on account were recorded with a debit to Cash instead of Accounts Receivable, total assets would be correct and the totals in the trial balance would equal each other even though the balances in the Cash and Accounts Receivable accounts would be incorrect. Recording the same incorrect amount in both the debit and credit part of an entry also would not cause a trial balance to be out of balance. For example, if $20 of revenue earned on account were recorded as a $200 debit to Accounts Receivable and a $200 credit to Consulting Revenue, the totals in the trial balance would equal each other, although the Accounts Receivable and Consulting Revenue amounts would be incorrect.

RECORDING DEBITS AND CREDITS IN T-ACCOUNTS FOR OTHER EVENTS

LO 13-5

Maintain accounting records for a complete accounting cycle containing an advanced set of business events.

To expand your understanding of the rules of debits and credits, this section of the chapter introduces a set of events experienced by The Shoe Store (TSS) during Year 4. We suggest you attempt to record each event in T-accounts before reading the explanation provided in the text. First, determine how the event affects the accounting equation. Next, use the rules for debits and credits to convert the increase/decrease terminology to debit/credit terminology (see Learning Objective 13-1). Finally, identify the accounts affected. Using this approach, you will be able to identify the debits and credits associated with any accounting event, even those not covered in this text.

On January 1, Year 4, the balance sheet for The Shoe Store showed $65,000 of cash, $25,000 of common stock, and $40,000 of retained earnings.

T-Account Entries for the Purchase and Sale of Merchandise Inventory

EVENT 1 TSS purchased merchandise inventory (shoes) for $26,000 cash.

Purchasing inventory is an asset exchange transaction. One asset, cash, decreases, while another asset, merchandise inventory, increases; total assets remain unchanged. Because credits decrease assets, the decrease in assets (Cash) is recorded with a credit, and because debits increase assets, the increase in assets (Merchandise Inventory) is recorded with a debit. The recording process is summarized here:

–	+		=	Claims
Assets			=	**Claims**
Cash		**Merchandise Inventory**		
Debit	Credit	Debit	Credit	
	26,000	26,000		

The effects of this entry on the financial statements are shown next:

Balance Sheet						Income Statement			Statement of Cash Flows
Assets	=	Liab.	+		Stk. Equity				
Cash	+ Inventory	= Accts. Pay.	+ Com. Stk.	+ Ret. Earn.		Rev.	− Exp.	= Net Inc.	
(26,000) +	26,000	= NA	+ NA	+ NA		NA	− NA	= NA	(26,000) OA

EVENT 2a   TSS recognized revenue from selling inventory for $33,000 on account.

Selling inventory is a two-part transaction that includes the recognition of sales revenue and the recognition of cost of goods sold expense. The *sales part* is an asset source event. Both assets and stockholders' equity increase. Because debits increase assets, the increase in assets (Accounts Receivable) is recorded with a debit, and because credits increase stockholders' equity, the increase in stockholders' equity (Sales Revenue) is recorded with a credit. The recording process is summarized here:

+				+	
Assets	=	Liabilities	+	Stockholders' Equity	
Accounts Receivable				Sales Revenue	
Debit	Credit			Debit	Credit
33,000					33,000

The effects of this entry on the financial statements are shown next:

Balance Sheet						Income Statement			Statement of Cash Flows
Assets	=	Liab.	+		Stk. Equity				
Ac. Rec.	+ Inventory	= Accts. Pay.	+ Com. Stk.	+ Ret. Earn.		Rev.	− Exp.	= Net Inc.	
33,000 +	NA	= NA	+ NA	+ 33,000		33,000	− NA	= 33,000	NA

EVENT 2b   TSS recognized $18,000 of cost of goods sold.

The expense recognition is the second part of the two-part transaction. The *expense part* represents an asset use event. Both assets and stockholders' equity decrease. Because credits decrease assets, the decrease in assets (Merchandise Inventory) is recorded with a credit, and because debits decrease stockholders' equity, the decrease in stockholders' equity (Cost of Goods Sold) is recorded with a debit. The recording process is summarized here:

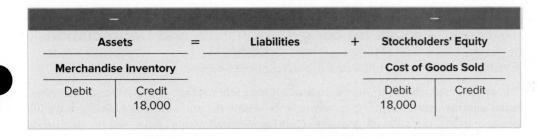

−				−	
Assets	=	Liabilities	+	Stockholders' Equity	
Merchandise Inventory				Cost of Goods Sold	
Debit	Credit			Debit	Credit
	18,000			18,000	

The effects of this entry on the financial statements are shown next:

Balance Sheet										Income Statement					Statement of Cash Flows
Assets			=	Liab.	+	Stk. Equity									
Ac. Rec.	+	Inventory	=	Accts. Pay.	+	Com. Stk.	+	Ret. Earn.		Rev.	−	Exp.	=	Net Inc.	
NA	+	(18,000)	=	NA	+	NA	+	(18,000)		NA	−	18,000	=	(18,000)	NA

For additional information related to accounting for merchandising transactions, see Learning Objective 4-1.

EVENT 3   In a year-end adjusting entry, TSS recognized $1,650 of Uncollectible Accounts Expense.

The expense recognition is an asset use event. Both assets and stockholders' equity decrease. Because credits decrease assets, the decrease in assets (Allowance for Doubtful Accounts) is recorded with a credit, and because debits decrease stockholders' equity, the decrease in stockholders' equity (Uncollectible Accounts Expense) is recorded with a debit. The recording process is summarized here:

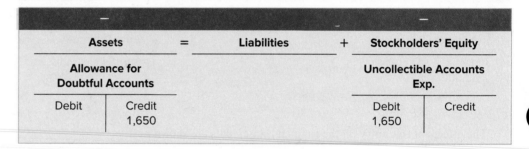

Recall that the balance of the Allowance for Doubtful Accounts account is subtracted from the balance of the Accounts Receivable account, thereby decreasing the total amount of assets shown on the balance sheet. The difference between the balance in the Accounts Receivable account and the Allowance for Doubtful Accounts is titled the "net realizable value of receivables." Accordingly, the financial statement effects of the entry to recognize uncollectible accounts expense are shown next:

Balance Sheet						Income Statement					Statement of Cash Flows
Assets	=	Liab.	+	Stk. Equity							
Net Realizable Value of Receivables	=	Ac. Pay.	+	Ret. Earn.		Rev.	−	Exp.	=	Net Inc.	
(1,650)	=	NA	+	(1,650)		NA	−	1,650	=	(1,650)	NA

For additional information related to accounting for uncollectible accounts, see Learning Objective 7-1.

T-Account Entries for Long-Term Assets and Depreciation

EVENT 4   TSS paid $34,000 cash to purchase store furniture.

Paying cash to purchase furniture is an asset exchange transaction. One asset, cash, decreases, while another asset, furniture, increases; total assets remain unchanged. Because credits decrease assets, the decrease in assets (Cash) is recorded with a credit, and because debits increase assets, the increase in assets (furniture) is recorded with a debit. The recording process is summarized here:

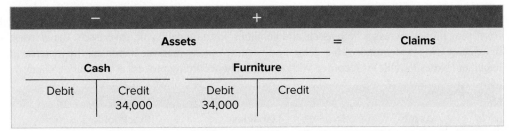

	Assets			=	Claims
	−		+		
Cash			**Furniture**		
Debit	Credit 34,000	Debit 34,000	Credit		

The effects of this entry on the financial statements are shown next:

Balance Sheet						Income Statement					Statement of Cash Flows
Assets			=	Stk. Equity							
Cash	+	Furniture	=	Com. Stk.	+	Ret. Earn.	Rev.	−	Exp.	=	Net Inc.	
(34,000)	+	34,000	=	NA	+	NA	NA	−	NA	=	NA	(34,000) IA

EVENT 5   TSS recognized depreciation expense associated with the furniture purchased in Event 4.

Assuming the furniture has a $4,000 salvage value and a three-year useful life depreciation expense is determined as follows:

($34,000 cost − $4,000 salvage) / 3-year useful life = $10,000 per year

The expense recognition is an asset use event. Both assets and stockholders' equity decrease. Because credits decrease assets, the decrease in assets (Accumulated Depreciation) is recorded with a credit, and because debits decrease stockholders' equity, the decrease in stockholders' equity (Depreciation Expense) is recorded with a debit. The recording process is summarized here:

Assets		=	Liabilities	+	Stockholders' Equity	
−					−	
Accumulated Depreciation					**Depreciation Expense**	
Debit	Credit 10,000				Debit 10,000	Credit

Recall that the balance in the Accumulated Depreciation account is subtracted from the balance in the asset account, Furniture, thereby decreasing the total amount of assets shown on the balance sheet. The difference between the balance in the Furniture account and the Accumulated Depreciation account is titled the Book Value of the Furniture. Accordingly, the financial statement effects of the entry to recognize depreciation expense are shown next:

Balance Sheet						Income Statement					Statement of Cash Flows
Assets			=	Stk. Equity							
Cash	+	Book Value of Furniture	=	Com. Stk.	+	Ret. Earn.	Rev.	−	Exp.	=	Net Inc.	
NA	+	(10,000)	=	NA	+	(10,000)	NA	−	10,000	=	(10,000)	NA

For additional information related to accounting for depreciation, see Learning Objective 8-2.

Journal Entries for Notes Payable and Interest Expense

EVENT 6 TSS acquired $20,000 cash by issuing a note to the State Bank.

Borrowing money increases both assets and liabilities. Because debits increase assets, the increase in assets (Cash) is recorded with a debit, and because credits increase liabilities, the increase in liabilities (Notes Payable) is recorded with a credit, The recording process is summarized here:

	+			+	
Assets		**=**	**Liabilities**	**+**	**Stockholders' Equity**
Cash			Notes Payable		
Debit	Credit		Debit	Credit	
20,000				20,000	

The effects of this entry on the financial statements are shown next:

Balance Sheet							Income Statement					Statement of Cash Flows
Assets	=	Liabilities			+	Stk. Equity						
Cash	=	Notes Pay.	+	Int. Pay.		Ret. Earn.	Rev.	−	Exp.	=	Net Inc.	
20,000	=	20,000		NA	+	NA	NA	−	NA	=	NA	20,000 FA

EVENT 7 Recognized accrued interest expense for the note issued in Event 6.

Assume the note was issued on October 1 and carried a 9 percent annual interest rate. Under these circumstances, the accrued interest as of December 31, Year 4, is computed as follows:

$$\$20,000 \text{ principal} \times .09 \text{ annual interest} \times 3/12 = \$450$$

Recognizing accrued interest expense increases liabilities and decreases stockholders' equity. Because credits increase liabilities, the increase in liabilities (Interest Payable) is recorded with a credit, and because debits decrease stockholders' equity, the decrease in stockholders' equity (Interest Expense) is recorded with a debit. The recording process is summarized here:

		+		−	
Assets	**=**	**Liabilities**	**+**	**Stockholders' Equity**	
		Interest Payable		Interest Expense	
		Debit	Credit	Debit	Credit
			450	450	

The effects of this entry on the financial statements are shown next:

Balance Sheet							Income Statement					Statement of Cash Flows
Assets	=	Liabilities			+	Stk. Equity						
Cash	=	Notes Pay.	+	Int. Pay.		Ret. Earn.	Rev.	−	Exp.	=	Net Inc.	
NA	=	NA		450	+	(450)	NA	−	450	=	(450)	NA

For additional information related to accounting for notes payable, see Learning Objective 9-1.

General Ledger and Adjusted Trial Balance

A summary of the Year 4 events experienced by TSS is shown in the general ledger in Exhibit 13.11.

EXHIBIT 13.11

General Ledger

Assets	=	Liabilities	+	Stockholders' Equity

Cash

Bal.	65,000	26,000	(1)
(6)	20,000	34,000	(4)
Bal.	25,000		

Notes Payable

		20,000	(6)
		20,000	Bal.

Common Stock

		25,000	Bal.
		25,000	Bal.

Service Revenue

		33,000	(2a)
		33,000	Bal.

Accounts Receivable

(2a)	33,000	
Bal.	33,000	

Interest Payable

		450	(7)
		450	Bal.

Retained Earnings

		40,000	Bal.
		40,000	Bal.

Cost of Goods Sold

(2b)	18,000	
Bal.	18,000	

Allowance for Doubtful Accts.

	1,650	(3)
	1,650	Bal.

Uncollectible Accounts Expense

(3)	1,650	
Bal.	1,650	

Merchandise Inventory

(1)	26,000	18,000	(2b)
Bal.	8,000		

Depreciation Expense

(5)	10,000	
Bal.	10,000	

Furniture

(4)	34,000	
Bal.	34,000	

Interest Expense

(7)	450	
Bal.	450	

Accumulated Depreciation

	10,000	(5)
	10,000	Bal.

Adjusted Trial Balance

Exhibit 13.12 displays the trial balance for The Shoe Store after the adjusting entries have been posted to the ledger. To ensure your understanding of the source of the account balance shown in the adjusted trial balance, you should trace the balances shown in Exhibit 13.11 to those shown in Exhibit 13.12.

Financial Statements

Supplemented with details from the Cash and Common Stock ledger accounts, the adjusted trial balance (Exhibit 13.3) provides the information to prepare the financial statements for The Shoe Store. The income statement, statement of changes in stockholders' equity, balance sheet, and statement of cash flows are shown in Exhibits 13.13, 13.14, 13.15, and 13.16, respectively.

EXHIBIT 13.12

THE SHOE STORE
Adjusted Trial Balance
December 31, Year 4

Account Title	Debit	Credit
Cash	$ 25,000	
Accounts receivable	33,000	
Allowance for doubtful accounts		$ 1,650
Merchandise inventory	8,000	
Furniture	34,000	
Accumulated depreciation		10,000
Note payable		20,000
Interest payable		450
Common stock		25,000
Retained earnings		40,000
Service revenue		33,000
Cost of goods sold	18,000	
Uncollectible accounts expense	1,650	
Depreciation expense	10,000	
Interest expense	450	
Totals	$130,100	$130,100

EXHIBIT 13.13

THE SHOE STORE
Income Statement
For the Year Ended December 31, Year 4

Revenue		$ 33,000
Expenses:		
Cost of goods sold	$(18,000)	
Uncollectible accounts exp.	(1,650)	
Depreciation expense	(10,000)	
Interest expense	(450)	
Total expenses		(30,100)
Net income		$ 2,900

EXHIBIT 13.15

THE SHOE STORE
Balance Sheet
As of December 31, Year 4

Assets			
Cash		$25,000	
Accounts receivable	$33,000		
Allow. for doubtful accts.	(1,650)		
Net real. value of rec.		31,350	
Merchandise Inventory		8,000	
Furniture	34,000		
Accumulated depreciation	(10,000)		
Book value of furniture		24,000	
Total assets			$88,350
Liabilities			
Interest payable		$ 450	
Notes payable		20,000	
Total liabilities			$20,450
Stockholders' equity			
Common stock		25,000	
Retained earnings		$42,900	
Total stockholders' equity			67,900
Total liabilities and stockholders' equity			$88,350

EXHIBIT 13.14

THE SHOE STORE
Statement of Changes in Stockholders' Equity
For the Year Ended December 31, Year 4

Beginning common stock	$25,000	
Plus: Common stock issued	0	
Ending common stock		$25,000
Beginning retained earnings	40,000	
Plus: Net income	2,900	
Less: Dividends	0	
Ending retained earnings		42,900
Total stockholders' equity		$67,900

EXHIBIT 13.16

THE SHOE STORE
Statement of Cash Flows
For the Year Ended December 31, Year 4

Cash flows from operating activities	
Cash payment to purchase inventory	$(26,000)
Cash flows from investing activities	
Cash payment to purchase furniture	(34,000)
Cash flows from financing activities	
Cash receipt from issue of note payable	20,000
Net decrease in cash	(40,000)
Plus: Beginning cash balance	65,000
Ending cash balance	$ 25,000

Closing Entries

At the end of the accounting period, the balances in the revenue and expense accounts are transferred to the retained earnings account. The required closing entry for this transfer is shown in general journal format in Exhibit 13.17. While it is not shown here, the closing entry would be posted to the ledger accounts, thereby leaving zero balances in the revenue and expense accounts as of January 1, Year 5.

EXHIBIT 13.17

Closing Entries

Event No.	Account Titles	Debit	Credit
Closing Entry	Revenue	33,000	
	Cost of Goods Sold		18,000
	Uncollectible Accounts Expense		1,650
	Depreciation Expense		10,000
	Interest Expense		450
	Retained Earnings		2,900

A Look Back

This chapter introduced the *double-entry accounting system*. This system was first documented in the 1400s, and is used by most companies today. Key components of the double-entry system are summarized as follows.

Accounting professionals use debit/credit terminology to describe the effects that business events have on the elements of an accounting equation. *Debits* are used to record increases in asset accounts, as well as decreases in liability and stockholders' equity accounts. *Credits* are used to record decreases in asset accounts and increases in liability and stockholders' equity accounts.

T-accounts are frequently used to analyze and communicate account activity. The account title is placed at the top of the horizontal bar of the T, and increases and decreases are placed on either side of the vertical bar. In a T-account, debits are recorded on the left side and credits are recorded on the right side. The rules of debits and credits are shown in T-account for are summarized here:

Assets		=	Liabilities		+	Stockholders' Equity	
Debit	Credit		Debit	Credit		Debit	Credit
+	−		−	+		−	+

The chapter employs a three-step approach for learning how to use debit and credit terminology to describe increases and decreases in various accounts. These steps include the following:

Step 1: Determine how an event affects each *element* of the accounting equation. Specifically, does the event cause the element assets, liabilities, and/or stockholders' equity to increase, decrease, or remain unaffected?

Step 2: Use the rules for debits and credits to convert the increase/decrease terminology to debit/credit terminology.

Step 3: Identify the specific asset, liability, and/or stockholders' equity *accounts* affected by the event and record the debits or credits in the appropriate T-accounts.

Accountants initially record transaction data in journals. The *general journal* is used not only for data entry but also as a shorthand communication tool. Each journal entry includes at least one debit and one credit. An entry is recorded using at least two lines, with the debit recorded on the top line and the credit on the bottom line. The credit is indented to distinguish it from the debit. The general journal format is illustrated next:

Debit	xxx	
Credit		xxx

Information is posted (copied) from the journals to *ledger* accounts. The ledger accounts provide the information used to prepare the financial statements.

Trial balances are used to check the mathematical accuracy of the recording process. Ledger accounts with their associated debit and credit balances are listed in the trial balance. The debit and credit amounts are totaled and compared. An equal amount of debits and credits provides evidence but not proof that transactions have been recorded correctly. If the debits and credits are *not* equal, it is proof that errors exist.

A Look Forward

Chapter 14, which is available online only, provides expanded coverage of financial statement analysis. Your instructor will provide guidance as to how to access this chapter if he or she decides to cover it. If your journey ends here, we sincerely hope this text provided a meaningful learning experience that will serve you well as you progress through your academic training and, ultimately, your career. Good luck and best wishes.

SELF-STUDY REVIEW PROBLEM

A step-by-step audio-narrated series of slides is available in *Connect*.

The following events apply to the first year of operations for Mestro Financial Services Company:

1. Acquired $28,000 cash by issuing common stock on January 1, Year 1.
2. Purchased $1,100 of supplies on account.
3. Paid $12,000 cash in advance for a one-year lease on office space.
4. Earned $23,000 of consulting revenue on account.
5. Incurred $16,000 of general operating expenses on account.
6. Collected $20,000 cash from receivables.
7. Paid $13,000 cash on accounts payable.
8. Paid a $1,000 cash dividend to stockholders.

Information for Adjusting Entries

9. There was $200 of supplies on hand at the end of the accounting period.
10. The one-year lease on the office space was effective beginning on October 1, Year 1.
11. There was $1,200 of accrued salaries at the end of Year 1.

Required

a. Record the preceding events in general journal format.
b. Post the transaction data from the general journal into general ledger T-accounts.
c. Prepare an adjusted trial balance.
d. Prepare an income statement, statement of changes in stockholders' equity, balance sheet, and statement of cash flows.
e. Prepare the appropriate closing entries in general journal format.

Solution to Requirement *a*

Event No.	Account Title	Debit	Credit
1.	Cash	28,000	
	Common Stock		28,000
2.	Supplies	1,100	
	Accounts Payable		1,100
3.	Prepaid Rent	12,000	
	Cash		12,000
4.	Accounts Receivable	23,000	
	Consulting Revenue		23,000
5.	General Operating Expenses	16,000	
	Accounts Payable		16,000
6.	Cash	20,000	
	Accounts Receivable		20,000
7.	Accounts Payable	13,000	
	Cash		13,000
8.	Dividends	1,000	
	Cash		1,000
9.	Supplies Expense	900	
	Supplies		900
10.	Rent Expense	3,000	
	Prepaid Rent		3,000
11.	Salaries Expense	1,200	
	Salaries Payable		1,200

Solution to Requirement *b*

MESTRO FINANCIAL SERVICES COMPANY
T-Accounts, Year 1

Assets = Liabilities + Stockholders' Equity

Cash

(1)	28,000	(3)	12,000
(6)	20,000	(7)	13,000
		(8)	1,000
Bal.	22,000		

Accounts Receivable

(4)	23,000	(6)	20,000
Bal.	3,000		

Supplies

(2)	1,100	(9)	900
Bal.	200		

Prepaid Rent

(3)	12,000	(10)	3,000
Bal.	9,000		

Accounts Payable

(7)	13,000	(2)	1,100
		(5)	16,000
		Bal.	4,100

Salaries Payable

		(11)	1,200
		Bal.	1,200

Common Stock

		(1)	28,000
		Bal.	28,000

Dividends

(8)	1,000	

Consulting Revenue

		(4)	23,000

General Operating Expenses

(5)	16,000	

Salaries Expense

(11)	1,200	

Supplies Expense

(9)	900	

Rent Expense

(10)	3,000	

Solution to Requirement *c*

MESTRO FINANCIAL SERVICES COMPANY
Trial Balance
December 31, Year 1

Account Titles	Debit	Credit
Cash	$22,000	
Accounts receivable	3,000	
Supplies	200	
Prepaid rent	9,000	
Accounts payable		$ 4,100
Salaries payable		1,200
Common stock		28,000
Dividends	1,000	
Consulting revenue		23,000
General operating expenses	16,000	
Salaries expense	1,200	
Supplies expense	900	
Rent expense	3,000	
Totals	$56,300	$56,300

Solution to Requirement *d*

MESTRO FINANCIAL SERVICES COMPANY
Financial Statements

Income Statement
For the Year Ended December 31, Year 1

Consulting revenue		$23,000
Expenses		
General operating expenses	$16,000	
Salaries expense	1,200	
Supplies expense	900	
Rent expense	3,000	
Total expenses		(21,100)
Net income		$ 1,900

Statement of Changes in Stockholders' Equity
For the Year Ended December 31, Year 1

Beginning common stock	$ 0	
Plus: Common stock issued	28,000	
Ending common stock		$28,000
Beginning retained earnings	0	
Plus: Net income	1,900	
Less: Dividends	(1,000)	
Ending retained earnings		900
Total stockholders' equity		$28,900

continued

Balance Sheet
As of December 31, Year 1

Assets		
Cash	$22,000	
Accounts receivable	3,000	
Supplies	200	
Prepaid rent	9,000	
Total assets		$34,200
Liabilities		
Accounts payable	$ 4,100	
Salaries payable	1,200	
Total liabilities		$ 5,300
Stockholders' equity		
Common stock	28,000	
Retained earnings	900	
Total stockholders' equity		28,900
Total liabilities and stockholders' equity		$34,200

Statement of Cash Flows
For the Year Ended December 31, Year 1

Cash flows from operating activities		
Inflow from customers	$20,000	
Outflow for expenses	(25,000)	
Net cash flow from operating activities		$ (5,000)
Cash flows from investing activities		0
Cash flows from financing activities		
Inflow from issue of common stock	28,000	
Outflow for dividends	(1,000)	
Net cash flow from financing activities		27,000
Net change in cash		22,000
Plus: Beginning cash balance		0
Ending cash balance		$22,000

Solution to Requirement e

Date	Account Title	Debit	Credit
Dec. 31	Consulting Revenue	23,000	
	Retained Earnings		23,000
Dec. 31	Retained Earnings	21,100	
	General Operating Expenses		16,000
	Salaries Expense		1,200
	Supplies Expense		900
	Rent Expense		3,000
Dec. 31	Retained Earnings	1,000	
	Dividends		1,000

KEY TERMS

Books of original entry 651	Double-entry accounting 643	Permanent account 656	Temporary accounts 655
Chart of accounts 653	Fiscal year 641	Posting 653	Trial balance 653
Closing entries 656	General journal 651	Source document 651	
Credit 641	General ledger 653	Special journals 651	
Debit 641	Journal 651	T-account 641	

QUESTIONS

1. What are the two fundamental equality require-
ments of the double-entry
accounting system?

2. Define *debit* and *credit*.
How are assets, liabilities,
and stockholders' equity
affected (increased or
decreased) by debits and
by credits?

3. How is the balance of an
account determined?

4. What are the three primary
sources of business assets?

5. What are the three primary
ways a business may use
assets?

6. Give an example of an asset
exchange transaction.

7. How does a debit to an
expense account ulti-
mately affect retained
earnings? Stockholders'
equity?

8. What accounts normally
have debit balances? What
accounts normally have
credit balances?

9. What is the primary
source of information for
preparing the financial
statements?

10. What is the purpose of a
journal?

11. What is the difference
between the *general
journal* and special
journals?

12. What is a ledger?
What is its function in
the accounting
system?

13. What is the purpose of
closing entries?

14. Do all companies close
their books on December
31? Why or why not?

15. At a minimum, what
information is recorded
in the general journal?

16. What is the purpose of a
trial balance?

17. When should a trial
balance be prepared?

18. What does the term *posting*
mean?

EXERCISES—SERIES A

Mc Graw Hill **connect** All applicable Exercises in Series A are available in *Connect*.

LO 13-1

Exercise 13-1A *Matching debit and credit terminology with accounting equation elements*

Required

Complete the following table by indicating whether a debit or credit is used to increase or decrease the balance of accounts belonging to each category of financial statement elements. The appropriate debit/credit terminology has been identified for the first category (assets) as an example.

Category of Elements	Used to Increase This Element	Used to Decrease This Element
Assets	Debit	Credit
Liabilities		
Stockholders' Equity		

LO 13-1

Exercise 13-2A *Debit/credit terminology*

Two introductory accounting students were arguing about how to record a transaction involving an exchange of cash for land. Laura stated that the transaction should have a debit to Land and a credit to Cash; Clark argued that the reverse (debit to Cash and credit to Land) represented the appropriate treatment.

Required

Which student was correct? Defend your position.

LO 13-1

Exercise 13-3A *Matching debit and credit terminology with account titles*

Required

Indicate whether each of the following accounts normally has a debit balance or a credit balance:
a. Salaries Expense
b. Consulting Revenue
c. Unearned Revenue
d. Accounts Payable
e. Dividends
f. Land
g. Salaries Payable
h. Cash

i. Prepaid Insurance
j. Common Stock
k. Interest Revenue
l. Rent Expense

Exercise 13-4A   *Applying debit/credit terminology to accounting events*

Required

a. In parallel columns, list the accounts that would be debited and credited for each of the following unrelated transactions:

(1) Acquired cash from the issue of common stock.

(2) Provided services for cash.

(3) Paid cash for salaries expense.

(4) Purchased supplies for cash.

(5) Paid in advance for two-year lease on office space.

(6) Provided services on account.

(7) Recognized expense for prepaid rent that had been used up by the end of the accounting period.

(8) Recorded accrued salaries at the end of the accounting period.

b. Use a horizontal statements model to show how each event affects the balance sheet, income statement, and statement of cash flows. Indicate whether the event increases (+), decreases (−), or does not affect (NA) each element of the financial statements. Also, in the Statement of Cash Flows column, use the letters OA to designate operating activity, IA for investing activity, and FA for financing activity. The first event is shown as an example.

Balance Sheet				Income Statement			Statement of Cash Flows
Assets	=	Liab.	+ Stk. Equity	Rev.	− Exp.	= Net Inc.	
+		NA	+	NA	NA	NA	+ FA

Exercise 13-5A   *Debit/credit terminology*

Required

For each of the following independent events, identify the account that would be debited and the account that would be credited. The accounts for the first event are identified as an example.

Event	Account Debited	Account Credited
a	Cash	Common Stock

a. Received cash by issuing common stock.

b. Received cash for services to be performed in the future.

c. Paid salaries payable.

d. Provided services on account.

e. Paid cash for operating expenses.

f. Purchased supplies on account.

g. Recognized revenue for services completed. Cash had been collected in Event *b*.

h. Recognized accrued salaries expense.

i. Recognized expense for supplies used during the period.

j. Performed services for cash.

k. Paid accounts payable.

l. Received cash in payment of accounts receivable.

m. Paid a cash dividend to the stockholders.

Exercise 13-6A *Identifying transaction type, its effect on the accounting equation, and whether the effect is recorded with a debit or credit*

Required

Identify whether each of the following transactions is an asset source (AS), asset use (AU), asset exchange (AE), or claims exchange (CE). Also explain how each event affects the accounting equation by placing a + for increase, − for decrease, and NA for not affected under each of the elements of the accounting equation. Finally, indicate whether the effect requires a debit or credit entry. The first event is recorded as an example.

						Stockholders' Equity		
Event	Type of Event	Assets	=	Liabilities	+	Common Stock	+	Retained Earnings
a	AS	+ Debit		+ Credit		NA		NA

  a. Purchased supplies on account.

  b. Acquired cash from the issue of common stock.

  c. Paid cash in advance for one year of rent.

  d. Paid salaries payable.

  e. Received cash for services to be performed in the future.

  f. Paid a cash dividend to the stockholders.

  g. Received cash in payment of accounts receivable.

  h. Paid accounts payable.

  i. Provided services for cash.

  j. Recognized expense for supplies used during the period.

  k. Recognized revenue for services completed for which cash had been collected previously.

  l. Incurred other operating expenses on account.

  m. Purchased land with cash.

Exercise 13-7A *Identifying increases and decreases in T-accounts*

Required

For each of the following T-accounts, indicate the side of the account that should be used to record an increase or decrease in the account balance:

Cash		Accounts Payable		Common Stock	
Debit	Credit	Debit	Credit	Debit	Credit

Accounts Receivable		Salaries Payable		Retained Earnings	
Debit	Credit	Debit	Credit	Debit	Credit

Supplies	
Debit	Credit

Exercise 13-8A *T-accounts and the accounting equation*

Required

Record each of the following Fred Co. events in T-accounts, and then explain how the event affects the elements of the accounting equation.

  a. Received $20,000 cash by issuing common stock.

  b. Purchased supplies for $1,000 cash.

c. Purchased land for $10,000 cash.

d. Performed services for $3,200 cash.

Exercise 13-9A   *Recording receivables and identifying their effect on financial statements*

LO 13-1

Davos Company performed services on account for $160,000 in Year 1. Davos collected $120,000 cash from accounts receivable during Year 1, and the remaining $40,000 was collected in cash during Year 2.

Required

a. Record the Year 1 transactions in T-accounts.

b. Show the Year 1 transactions in a horizontal statements model like the following one:

Balance Sheet				Income Statement			Statement of Cash Flows
Assets		= Liab. +	Stk. Equity				
Cash + Accts. Rec. =			Ret. Earn.	Rev. − Exp. = Net Inc.			

c. Determine the amount of revenue Davos would report on the Year 1 income statement.

d. Determine the amount of cash flow from operating activities Davos would report on the Year 1 statement of cash flows.

e. Open a T-account for Retained Earnings, and close the Year 1 Service Revenue account to the Retained Earnings account.

f. Record the Year 2 cash collection in the appropriate T-accounts.

g. Show the Year 2 transaction in a horizontal statements model like the one shown in Requirement *b*.

h. Assuming no other transactions occur in Year 2, determine the amount of net income and the net cash flow from operating activities for Year 2.

Exercise 13-10A   *Recording supplies and identifying their effect on financial statements*

LO 13-1, 13-3, 13-4

Sye Chase started and operated a small family architectural firm in Year 1. The firm was affected by two events: (1) Chase provided $25,000 of services on account, and (2) he purchased $2,800 of supplies on account. There were $250 of supplies on hand as of December 31, Year 1.

Required

a. Open T-accounts and record the two transactions in the accounts.

b. Record the required year-end adjusting entry to reflect the use of supplies.

c. Show the preceding transactions in a horizontal statements model like the following one:

Balance Sheet				Income Statement			Statement of Cash Flows
Assets		= Liab. +	Stk. Equity				
Accts. Rec. + Supplies =		Accts. Pay. +	Ret. Earn.	Rev. − Exp. = Net Inc.			

d. Explain why the amounts of net income and net cash flow from operating activities differ.

e. Record and post the required closing entries, and prepare a post-closing trial balance.

Exercise 13-11A   *Recording unearned revenue and identifying its effect on financial statements*

LO 13-1

Raylan received a $60,000 cash advance payment on June 1, Year 1, for consulting services to be performed in the future. Services were to be provided for a one-year term beginning June 1, Year 1.

Required

a. Record the June 1 cash receipt in T-accounts.

b. Record in T-accounts the adjustment required as of December 31, Year 1.

c. Show the preceding transaction and related adjustment in a horizontal statements model like the following one:

Balance Sheet			Income Statement			Statement of Cash Flows
Assets	= Liab.	+ Stk. Equity	Rev.	− Exp.	= Net Inc.	

d. Determine the amount of net income on the Year 1 income statement. What is the amount of net cash flow from operating activities for Year 1?

e. What amount of liabilities would Raylan report on the Year 1 balance sheet?

LO 13-1

Exercise 13-12A *Using a T-account to determine cash flow from operating activities*

River Co. began the accounting period with a $132,000 debit balance in its Accounts Receivable account. During the accounting period, River Co. earned revenue on account of $180,000. The ending Accounts Receivable balance was $116,000.

Required

Based on this information alone, determine the amount of cash inflow from operating activities during the accounting period. (*Hint:* Use a T-account for Accounts Receivable. Enter the debits and credits for the given events, and solve for the missing amount.)

LO 13-1

Exercise 13-13A *Using a T-account to determine cash flow from operating activities*

The Garden Company began the accounting period with a $60,000 credit balance in its Accounts Payable account. During the accounting period, Garden Company incurred expenses on account of $152,000. The ending Accounts Payable balance was $64,000.

Required

Based on this information, determine the amount of cash outflow for expenses during the accounting period. (*Hint:* Use a T-account for Accounts Payable. Enter the debits and credits for the given events, and solve for the missing amount.)

LO 13-2

Exercise 13-14A *Recording events in the general journal and identifying their effect on financial statements*

Required

Record each of the following transactions in general journal form and then show the effect of the transaction in a horizontal statements model. The first transaction is shown as an example.

Account Title	Debit	Credit
Accounts Receivable	8,200	
Service Revenue		8,200

Balance Sheet			Income Statement			Statement of Cash Flows
Assets	= Liab.	+ Stk. Equity	Rev.	− Exp.	= Net Inc.	
8,200		8,200	8,200	NA	8,200	NA

a. Performed $8,200 of services on account.

b. Collected $5,600 cash on accounts receivable.

c. Paid $1,450 cash in advance for an insurance policy.

d. Paid $400 on accounts payable.

e. Recorded the adjusting entry to recognize $300 of insurance expense.

f. Received $1,600 cash for services to be performed at a later date.

g. Purchased land for $9,000 cash.

h. Purchased supplies for $350 cash.

Exercise 13-15A   *Recording prepaid items and identifying their effect on financial*   LO 13-2
statements

Cherokee Company began operations when it issued common stock for $80,000 cash. It paid $60,000 cash in advance for a one-year contract to lease delivery equipment for the business. It signed the lease agreement on March 1, Year 1, which was effective immediately. Cherokee received $98,000 of cash revenue in Year 1.

Required

a. Record the March 1 cash payment in general journal format.
b. Record in general journal format the adjustment required as of December 31, Year 1.
c. Show all events in a horizontal statements model like the following one:

Balance Sheet							Income Statement			Statement of Cash Flows
Assets		=	Liab.	+		Stk. Equity				
Cash	+ Prep. Rent	=			Common Stock	+ Ret. Earn.	Rev.	− Exp.	= Net Inc.	

d. What amount of net income will Cherokee Company report on the Year 1 income statement? What is the amount of net cash flow from operating activities for Year 1?
e. Determine the amount of prepaid rent Cherokee Company would report on the December 31, Year 1, balance sheet.

Exercise 13-16A   *Recording accrued salaries and identifying their effect on financial*   LO 13-2
statements

On December 31, Year 1, BIG Company had accrued salaries of $6,400.

Required

a. Record in general journal format the adjustment required as of December 31, Year 1.
b. Show the above adjustment in a horizontal statements model like the following one:

Balance Sheet				Income Statement			Statement of Cash Flows
Assets	=	Liab.	+ Stk. Equity				
		Sal. Pay.	+ Ret. Earn.	Rev.	− Exp.	= Net Inc.	

c. Determine the amount of net income BIG would report on the Year 1 income statement, assuming that BIG received $36,000 of cash revenue. What is the amount of net cash flow from operating activities for Year 1?
d. What amount of salaries payable would BIG report on the December 31, Year 1, balance sheet?

Exercise 13-17A   *Recording transactions in the general journal and T-accounts*   LO 13-1, 13-2

The following events apply to Montgomery Company for Year 1, its first year of operation:

1. Received cash of $36,000 from the issue of common stock.
2. Performed $48,000 of services on account.
3. Incurred $6,500 of other operating expenses on account.
4. Paid $21,000 cash for salaries expense.
5. Collected $34,500 of accounts receivable.
6. Paid a $3,000 dividend to the stockholders.
7. Performed $9,500 of services for cash.
8. Paid $5,500 of the accounts payable.

Required

a. Record the preceding transactions in general journal form.

b. Post the entries to T-accounts and determine the ending balance in each account.

c. Determine the amount of total assets at the end of Year 1.

d. Determine the amount of net income for Year 1.

LO 13-1, 13-2, 13-3

Exercise 13-18A *Recording events in the general journal, posting to T-accounts, and preparing a trial balance*

The following events apply to Equipment Services Inc. in its first year of operation:

1. Acquired $60,000 cash from the issue of common stock.
2. Received an $8,200 cash advance for services to be provided in the future.
3. Purchased $2,000 of supplies on account.
4. Earned $36,000 of service revenue on account.
5. Incurred $16,100 of operating expenses on account.
6. Collected $28,500 cash from accounts receivable.
7. Made a $15,100 payment on accounts payable.
8. Paid a $2,000 cash dividend to stockholders.
9. Recognized $1,600 of supplies expense.
10. Recorded $3,100 of accrued salaries expense.
11. Recognized $3,100 of revenue for services provided to the customer in Event 2.

Required

a. Record the events in T-accounts and determine the ending account balances.

b. Test the equality of the debit and credit balances of the T-accounts by preparing a trial balance.

LO 13-3

Exercise 13-19A *Prepare a trial balance*

Required

On December 31, Year 2, Morgan Company had the following normal account balances in its general ledger. Use this information to prepare a trial balance.

Land	$30,000
Unearned Revenue	32,000
Dividends	8,000
Prepaid Rent	5,600
Cash	90,000
Salaries Expense	18,000
Accounts Payable	7,000
Common Stock	80,000
Operating Expense	41,000
Office Supplies	2,500
Advertising Expense	3,500
Retained Earnings, 1/1/Year 2	9,000
Service Revenue	86,000
Accounts Receivable	15,400

LO 13-3

Exercise 13-20A *Determining the effect of errors on the trial balance*

Required

Explain how each of the following posting errors affects a trial balance. State whether the trial balance will be out of balance because of the posting error, and indicate which side of the trial balance will have a higher amount after each independent entry is posted. If the posting error does not affect the equality of debits and credits in the trial balance, state that the error will not cause an inequality and explain why.

a. A $900 credit to Unearned Revenue was credited to Service Revenue.

b. A $3,400 credit to Accounts Payable was not posted.

c. A $900 debit to Rent Expense was posted twice.

d. A $1,250 debit to Office Supplies was debited to Office Supplies Expense.

e. A $560 debit to Cash was posted as a $650 debit.

Exercise 13-21A   *Preparing closing entries*   LO 13-4

The following financial information was taken from the books of Zone Health Club, a small spa and fitness club:

Account Balances as of December 31, Year 2	
Accounts Receivable	$12,450
Accounts Payable	6,200
Salaries Payable	3,150
Cash	36,750
Dividends	2,000
Operating Expense	35,300
Prepaid Rent	1,200
Rent Expense	8,400
Retained Earnings 1/1/Year 2	41,250
Salaries Expense	14,500
Service Revenue	65,400
Supplies	650
Supplies Expense	3,150
Common Stock	7,000
Unearned Revenue	6,400
Land	15,000

Required

a. Prepare the journal entries necessary to close the temporary accounts at December 31, Year 2, for Zone Health Club.

b. What is the balance in the Retained Earnings account after the closing entries are posted?

Exercise 13-22A   *Recording events in the general journal, posting to T-accounts, and preparing closing entries*   LO 13-1, 13-2, 13-3, 13-4

At the beginning of Year 2, Oak Consulting had the following normal balances in its accounts:

Account	Balance
Cash	$42,000
Accounts Receivable	25,000
Accounts Payable	8,400
Common Stock	24,000
Retained Earnings	34,600

The following events apply to Oak Consulting for Year 2:

1. Provided $185,000 of services on account.

2. Incurred $45,800 of operating expenses on account.

3. Collected $140,000 of accounts receivable.

4. Paid $120,000 cash for salaries expense.

5. Paid $31,400 cash as a partial payment on accounts payable.

6. Paid a $10,000 cash dividend to the stockholders.

Required

a. Record these transactions in a general journal.

b. Open T-accounts, and post the beginning balances and the preceding transactions to the appropriate accounts.

c. Show the beginning balances and the transactions in a horizontal statements model such as the following one:

Balance Sheet										Income Statement					Statement of Cash Flows
Assets			=	Liab.	+		Stk. Equity								
Cash	+	Accts. Rec.	=	Accts. Pay.	+	Com. Stk.	+	Ret. Earn.		Rev.	−	Exp.	=	Net Inc.	

d. Record the closing entries in the general journal and post them to the T-accounts. What is the amount of net income for the year?

e. What is the amount of *change* in retained earnings for the year? Is the change in retained earnings different from the amount of net income? If so, why?

f. Prepare a post-closing trial balance.

LO 13-5

Exercise 13-23A   *Adjusting Entries*

The following information was drawn from the accounting records of Chapin Company.

1. On January 1, Year 1, Chapin paid $56,000 cash to purchase a truck. The truck had a five-year useful life and a $6,000 salvage value.

2. As of December 31, Year 1, Chapin Company had a $68,000 balance in its Accounts Receivable account and a zero balance in its Allowance for Doubtful Accounts account. Sales on account for Year 1 amounted to $320,000. Chapin estimates that 5 percent of credit sales will be uncollectible.

Required

a. Record the year-end adjusting entry for depreciation expense on the truck in T-accounts.

b. Determine the book value of the truck that will appear on the December 31, Year 1, balance sheet.

c. Record the year-end adjusting entry of uncollectible accounts expense.

d. Determine the net realizable value of receivables that will appear on the December 31, Year 1, balance sheet.

LO 13-5

Exercise 13-24A   *Adjusted trial balance*

The following balances were drawn from the accounts of Carter Company. The accounts and balances shown here are presented in random order: Equipment–$14,000; Cash–$25,000; Depreciation Expense–$7,000; Notes Payable–$22,000; Common Stock–$41,000; Accumulated Depreciation–$7,000; Interest Expense–$1,000; Cost of Goods Sold–$32,000; Retained Earnings–$12,000; Allowance for Doubtful Accounts–$2,000; Merchandise Inventory–$19,000; Interest Payable–$1,000; Sales Revenue–$52,000; Uncollectible Accounts Expense–$2,000; and Accounts Receivable–$37,000.

Required

Prepare an adjusted trial balance.

IFRS

Exercise 13-25A   *IFRS and U.S. GAAP*

1. Describe some ways that U.S. GAAP and IFRS are different.

2. How are U.S. GAAP and IFRS alike for reporting purposes?

PROBLEMS—SERIES A

Mc Graw Hill **connect** All applicable Problems in Series A are available in *Connect*.

Problem 13-26A *Identifying debit and credit balances*

Required

Indicate whether each of the following accounts normally has a debit or credit balance:

a. Interest Receivable
b. Interest Revenue
c. Prepaid Insurance
d. Land
e. Salaries Payable
f. Salaries Expense
g. Supplies Expense
h. Consulting Revenue
i. Utilities Payable
j. Supplies
k. Service Revenue

l. Accounts Payable
m. Operating Expense
n. Unearned Revenue
o. Dividends
p. Cash
q. Insurance Expense
r. Accounts Receivable
s. Utilities Expense
t. Retained Earnings
u. Common Stock

CHECK FIGURES
a. Interest Receivable: Debit
j. Supplies: Debit

Problem 13-27A *Transaction type and debit/credit terminology*   LO 13-1

The following events apply to Kate Enterprises:

1. Collected $16,200 cash for services to be performed in the future.
2. Acquired $50,000 cash from the issue of common stock.
3. Paid salaries to employees: $3,500 cash.
4. Paid cash to rent office space for the next 12 months: $12,000.
5. Paid cash of $17,500 for other operating expenses.
6. Paid on accounts payable: $1,752.
7. Paid cash for utilities expense: $804.
8. Recognized $45,000 of service revenue on account.
9. Paid a $2,500 cash dividend to the stockholders.
10. Purchased $3,200 of supplies on account.
11. Received $12,500 cash for services rendered.
12. Recognized $5,200 of accrued salaries expense.
13. Recognized $3,000 of rent expense. Cash had been paid in a prior transaction (see Event 4).
14. Recognized $5,000 of revenue for services performed. Cash had been previously collected (see Event 1).

Required

Identify each event as an asset source (AS), asset use (AU), asset exchange (AE), or claims exchange (CE). Also identify the account to be debited and the account to be credited when the transaction is recorded. The first event is recorded as an example.

Event No.	Type of Event	Account Debited	Account Credited
1	AS	Cash	Unearned Revenue

CHECK FIGURE
b. Total debits: $207,000

Problem 13-28A *Showing events in a statements model, recording them in T-accounts, and preparing a trial balance*

The following accounting events apply to Mary's Designs for Year 1:

Asset Source Transactions

1. Began operations by acquiring $90,000 of cash from the issue of common stock.
2. Performed services and collected cash of $9,000.
3. Collected $36,000 of cash in advance for services to be provided over the next 12 months.
4. Provided $58,000 of services on account.
5. Purchased supplies of $5,200 on account.

Asset Exchange Transactions

6. Purchased $21,000 of land for cash.
7. Collected $49,000 of cash from accounts receivable.
8. Purchased $3,150 of supplies with cash.
9. Paid $12,000 for one year's rent in advance.

Asset Use Transactions

10. Paid $24,000 cash for salaries of employees.
11. Paid a cash dividend of $5,000 to the stockholders.
12. Paid off $3,600 of the accounts payable with cash.

Claims Exchange Transactions

13. Placed an advertisement in the local newspaper for $2,600 on account.
14. Incurred utility expense of $1,800 on account.

Adjusting Entries

15. Recognized $12,000 of revenue for performing services. The collection of cash for these services occurred in a prior transaction. (See Event 3.)
16. Recorded $8,000 of accrued salary expense at the end of Year 1.
17. Recorded supplies expense. Had $1,900 of supplies on hand at the end of the accounting period.
18. Recognized four months of expense for prepaid rent that had been used up during the accounting period.

Required

a. Record each of the preceding events in T-accounts.
b. Prepare a before-closing trial balance.
c. Use a horizontal statements model to show how each event affects the balance sheet, income statement, and statement of cash flows. Indicate whether the event increases (+), decreases (−), or does not affect (NA) each element of the financial statements. Also, in the Statement of Cash Flows column, use the letters OA to designate operating activity, IA for investing activity, and FA for financing activity. The first event is recorded as an example.

Balance Sheet				Income Statement					Statement of Cash Flows
Assets	=	Liab.	+	Stk. Equity	Rev.	−	Exp.	=	Net Inc.	
+		NA		+	NA		NA		NA	+ FA

Problem 13-29A   *Effect of journal entries on financial statements*   LO 13-2

Event No.	Account Title	Debit	Credit
1.	Cash	xxx	
	Common Stock		xxx
2.	Prepaid Rent	xxx	
	Cash		xxx
3.	Accounts Receivable	xxx	
	Service Revenue		xxx
4.	Cash	xxx	
	Unearned Revenue		xxx
5.	Cash	xxx	
	Accounts Receivable		xxx
6.	Supplies	xxx	
	Accounts Payable		xxx
7.	Salaries Expense	xxx	
	Cash		xxx
8.	Utilities Expense	xxx	
	Cash		xxx
9.	Supplies Expense	xxx	
	Supplies		xxx
10.	Unearned Revenue	xxx	
	Service Revenue		xxx
11.	Cash	xxx	
	Service Revenue		xxx
12.	Dividends	xxx	
	Cash		xxx
13.	Rent Expense	xxx	
	Prepaid Rent		xxx

Required

The preceding 13 different accounting events are presented in general journal format. Use a horizontal statements model to show how each event affects the balance sheet, income statement, and statement of cash flows. Indicate whether the event increases (+), decreases (−), or does not affect (NA) each element of the financial statements. Also, in the Statement of Cash Flows column, use the letters OA to designate operating activity, IA for investing activity, and FA for financing activity. The first event is recorded as an example.

Balance Sheet				Income Statement			Statement of Cash Flows
Assets	=	Liab.	+ Stk. Equity	Rev.	− Exp.	= Net Inc.	
+		NA	+	NA	NA	NA	+ FA

Problem 13-30A   *Identifying accounting events from journal entries*   LO 13-2

Required

The following information is from the records of attorney Glenn Price. Write a brief explanation of the accounting event represented in each of the general journal entries.

Date	Account Titles	Debit	Credit
Jan. 1	Cash	40,000	
	Common Stock		40,000
Feb. 1	Cash	24,000	
	Service Revenue		24,000
Mar. 1	Prepaid Rent	1,600	
	Cash		1,600
Apr. 1	Accounts Receivable	48,000	
	Service Revenue		48,000
May 1	Supplies	2,000	
	Cash		2,000
June 10	Cash	8,000	
	Unearned Revenue		8,000
July 10	Cash	8,800	
	Accounts Receivable		8,800
Aug. 1	Salaries Expense	4,000	
	Cash		4,000
Oct. 1	Dividends	2,000	
	Cash		2,000
Nov. 1	Property Tax Expense	3,000	
	Cash		3,000
Dec. 31	Rent Expense	4,400	
	Prepaid Rent		4,400
31	Unearned Revenue	2,240	
	Service Revenue		2,240
31	Supplies Expense	800	
	Supplies		800

LO 13-2

Problem 13-31A   *Recording adjusting entries in general journal format*

Required

Each of the following independent events requires a year-end adjusting entry. Record each event and the related adjusting entry in general journal format. The first event is recorded as an example. Assume a December 31 closing date.

Event No.	Date	Account Titles	Debit	Credit
a	July 1	Prepaid Rent	48,000	
		Cash		48,000
a	Dec. 31	Rent Expense (48,000 × 6/12)	24,000	
		Prepaid Rent		24,000

a. Paid $48,000 cash in advance on July 1 for a one-year lease on office space.

b. Purchased $5,000 of supplies on account on April 15. At year-end, $500 of supplies remained on hand.

c. Received a $9,600 cash advance on July 1 for a contract to provide services for one year beginning immediately.

d. Paid $5,400 cash in advance on February 1 for a one-year insurance policy.

Problem 13-32A   *Effect of errors on the trial balance*

The following trial balance was prepared from the ledger accounts of Ricardo Company:

LO 13-3

CHECK FIGURE
Corrected Cash Balance: $69,710

RICARDO COMPANY
Trial Balance
April 30, Year 1

Account Title	Debit	Credit
Cash	$ 68,900	
Accounts Receivable	30,000	
Supplies	1,800	
Prepaid Insurance	3,600	
Land		$ 12,000
Accounts Payable		9,600
Common Stock		100,000
Retained Earnings		27,510
Dividends	8,000	
Service Revenue		60,000
Rent Expense	9,600	
Salaries Expense	31,500	
Operating Expense	32,400	
Totals	$185,800	$209,110

When the trial balance failed to balance, the accountant reviewed the records and discovered the following errors:

1. The company received $560 as payment for services rendered. The credit to Service Revenue was recorded correctly, but the debit to Cash was recorded as $650.

2. A $900 receipt of cash that was received from a customer on accounts receivable was not recorded.

3. A $600 purchase of supplies on account was properly recorded as a debit to the Supplies account. However, the credit to Accounts Payable was not recorded.

4. Land valued at $12,000 was contributed to the business in exchange for common stock. The entry to record the transaction was recorded as a $12,000 credit to both the Land account and the Common Stock account.

5. A $500 rent payment was properly recorded as a credit to Cash. However, the Salaries Expense account was incorrectly debited for $500.

Required

Based on this information, prepare a corrected trial balance for Ricardo Company.

Problem 13-33A   *Comprehensive problem: single cycle*

The following transactions pertain to Smith Training Company for Year 1:

LO 13-1, 13-2, 13-3, 13-4

CHECK FIGURES
d. Net Income: $50,880
Total Assets: $98,180

Jan. 30	Established the business when it acquired $45,000 cash from the issue of common stock.
Feb. 1	Paid rent for office space for two years, $24,000 cash.
Apr. 10	Purchased $3,200 of supplies on account.
July 1	Received $24,000 cash in advance for services to be provided over the next year.
20	Paid $1,500 of the accounts payable from April 10.
Aug. 15	Billed a customer $18,000 for services provided during August.
Sept. 15	Completed a job and received $8,400 cash for services rendered.
Oct. 1	Paid employee salaries of $12,000 cash.
15	Received $15,000 cash from accounts receivable.
Nov. 16	Billed customers $42,000 for services rendered on account.
Dec. 1	Paid a dividend of $15,000 cash to the stockholders.
31	Adjusted records to recognize the services provided on the contract of July 1.
31	Recorded $3,600 of accrued salaries as of December 31.
31	Recorded the rent expense for the year. (See February 1.)
31	Physically counted supplies; $280 was on hand at the end of the period.

Required

a. Record the preceding transactions in the general journal.

b. Post the transactions to T-accounts and calculate the account balances.

c. Prepare a trial balance.

d. Prepare the income statement, statement of changes in stockholders' equity, balance sheet, and statement of cash flows.

e. Prepare the closing entries at December 31.

f. Prepare a trial balance after the closing entries are posted.

<table>
<tr><td>LO 13-1, 13-2, 13-3, 13-4</td></tr>
</table>

Problem 13-34A *Two complete accounting cycles*

CHECK FIGURES
b. Ending Cash Balance, Year 1: $29,500
g. Net Income, Year 2: $20,750

Colton Enterprises experienced the following events for Year 1, the first year of operation:

1. Acquired $35,000 cash from the issue of common stock.
2. Paid $12,000 cash in advance for rent. The payment was for the period April 1, Year 1, to March 31, Year 2.
3. Performed services for customers on account for $72,000.
4. Incurred operating expenses on account of $35,000.
5. Collected $55,500 cash from accounts receivable.
6. Paid $21,000 cash for salary expense.
7. Paid $28,000 cash as a partial payment on accounts payable.

Adjusting Entries

8. Made the adjusting entry for the expired rent. (See Event 2.)
9. Recorded $2,400 of accrued salaries at the end of Year 1.

Events for Year 2

1. Paid $2,400 cash for the salaries accrued at the end of the prior accounting period.
2. Performed services for cash of $21,000.
3. Purchased $2,800 of supplies on account.
4. Paid $13,200 cash in advance for rent. The payment was for one year beginning April 1, Year 2.
5. Performed services for customers on account for $88,000.
6. Incurred operating expenses on account of $41,500.
7. Collected $89,000 cash from accounts receivable.
8. Paid $39,000 cash as a partial payment on accounts payable.
9. Paid $31,500 cash for salary expense.
10. Paid a $10,000 cash dividend to stockholders.

Adjusting Entries

11. Made the adjusting entry for the expired rent. (*Hint:* Part of the rent was paid in Year 1.)
12. Recorded supplies expense. A physical count showed that $450 of supplies were still on hand.

Required

a. Record the events and adjusting entries for Year 1 in general journal form.

b. Post the Year 1 events to T-accounts.

c. Prepare a trial balance for Year 1.

d. Prepare an income statement, statement of changes in stockholders' equity, balance sheet, and statement of cash flows for Year 1.

e. Record the entries to close the Year 1 temporary accounts to Retained Earnings in the general journal and post to the T-accounts.

f. Prepare a post-closing trial balance for December 31, Year 1.

g. Repeat Requirements *a* through *f* for Year 2.

Problem 13-35A   *Recording events in the general ledger*

LO 13-5

As of January 1, Year 5, the accounting records for Antique Art, Inc. (AAI) showed Cash of $130,000, Common Stock of $100,000, and Retained Earnings of $30,000. During Year 5, AAI experienced the following accounting events:

1. AAI purchased merchandise inventory for $94,000 cash.
2a. AAI recognized revenue from selling inventory for $104,000 on account.
2b. AAI recognized $76,000 of cost of goods sold.
3. AAI paid $28,000 cash to purchase a warehouse. The warehouse had a five-year useful life and a $4,000 salvage value.
4. On May 1, Year 5, AAI acquired $30,000 cash by issuing a note to the State Bank. The note had a 6 percent annual interest rate and a one-year term to maturity.
5. AAI recognized accrued interest expense for the note issued in Event 4.
6. AAI estimated its uncollectible accounts expense to be 5 percent of credit sales.
7. AAI recognized depreciation expense associated with the warehouse purchased in Event 3.

Required

a. Record the events in a general journal.
b. Determine the net realizable value of receivables that will appear on the December 31, Year 5, balance sheet.
c. Determine the book value of the warehouse that will appear on the December 31, Year 5, balance sheet.

Problem 13-36A   *Recording events and preparing financial statements*

LO 13-5

The December 31, Year 2, balance sheet for Shannon's Lamps, Inc. (SLI) showed Cash of $64,000, Common Stock of $24,000, and Retained Earnings of $40,000. During Year 3, SLI experienced the following accounting events:

1. SLI purchased merchandise inventory (lamps) for $47,000 cash.
2a. SLI recognized revenue from selling inventory for $52,000 on account.
2b. SLI recognized $38,000 of cost of goods sold.
3. In a year-end adjusting entry, SLI recognized $1,520 of uncollectible accounts expense.
4. SLI paid $14,000 cash to purchase display equipment. The equipment had a four-year useful life and a $2,000 salvage value.
5. SLI recognized depreciation expense associated with the equipment purchased in Event 4.
6. On September 1, Year 3, SLI acquired $16,000 cash by issuing a note to the State Bank. The note had a 6 percent annual interest rate and a one-year term to maturity.
7. SLI recognized accrued interest expense for the note issued in Event 6.

Required

a. Record the events in T-accounts and determine the ending account balances.
b. Prepare an income statement, a balance sheet, and a statement of cash flows.

EXERCISES—SERIES B

Exercise 13-1B   *Matching debit and credit terminology with accounts*

LO 13-1

Required

Complete the following table by indicating whether a debit or credit is used to increase or decrease the balance of the following accounts. The appropriate debit/credit terminology has been identified for the first account as an example.

Account Titles	Used to Increase This Account	Used to Decrease This Account
Insurance Expense	Debit	Credit
Rent Expense		
Prepaid Rent		
Interest Revenue		
Accounts Receivable		
Accounts Payable		
Common Stock		
Land		
Unearned Revenue		
Service Revenue		
Retained Earnings		

LO 13-1

Exercise 13-2B *Debit/credit rules*

Jake, Mollie, and Neil, three accounting students, are discussing the rules of debits and credits. Jake says that debits increase account balances and credits decrease account balances. Mollie says that Jake is wrong, that credits increase account balances and debits decrease account balances. Neil interrupts and declares that they are both correct.

Required

Explain what Neil means and give examples of transactions where debits increase account balances, credits decrease account balances, credits increase account balances, and debits decrease account balances.

LO 13-1

Exercise 13-3B *Matching debit and credit terminology with account titles*

Required

Indicate whether each of the following accounts normally has a debit balance or a credit balance:

a. Unearned Revenue
b. Service Revenue
c. Dividends
d. Land
e. Accounts Receivable
f. Cash

g. Common Stock
h. Prepaid Rent
i. Supplies
j. Accounts Payable
k. Interest Revenue
l. Rent Expense

LO 13-1

Exercise 13-4B *Applying debit/credit terminology to accounting events*

Required

a. In parallel columns, list the accounts that would be debited and credited for each of the following unrelated transactions:

(1) Provided services for cash.
(2) Recognized accrued salaries at the end of the period.
(3) Provided services on account.
(4) Paid cash for operating expenses.
(5) Acquired cash from the issue of common stock.
(6) Purchased supplies on account.
(7) Purchased land for cash.
(8) Paid a cash dividend to the stockholders.

b. Use a horizontal statements model to show how each event affects the balance sheet, income sheet, and statement of cash flows. Indicate whether the event increases (+), decreases (−), or does not affect (NA) each element of the financial statements. Also, in the Statement of Cash Flows column, use the letters OA to designate operating activity, IA for investing activity, and FA for financing activity. The first event is recorded as an example.

Balance Sheet					Income Statement					Statement of Cash Flows
Assets	=	Liab.	+	Stk. Equity	Rev.	−	Exp.	=	Net Inc.	
+		NA		+	+		NA		+	+ OA

Exercise 13-5B *Debit/credit terminology*

LO 13-1

Required

For each of the following independent events, identify the account that would be debited and the account that would be credited. The accounts for the first event are identified as an example.

Event	Account Debited	Account Credited
a	Cash	Unearned Revenue

a. Received cash for services to be performed in the future.
b. Purchased supplies on account.
c. Paid cash in advance for one year's rent.
d. Received cash by issuing common stock.
e. Provided services on account.
f. Paid accounts payable.
g. Paid salaries payable.
h. Recognized revenue for services completed; previously collected the cash in Event *a*.
i. Paid cash for operating expenses.
j. Paid salaries expense.
k. Received cash in payment of accounts receivable.
l. Recognized expense for prepaid rent that had been used up by the end of the accounting period.
m. Paid cash dividends to the stockholders.

Exercise 13-6B *Identifying transaction type, its effect on the accounting equation, and whether the effect is recorded with a debit or credit*

LO 13-1

Required

Identify whether each of the following transactions is an asset source (AS), asset use (AU), asset exchange (AE), or claims exchange (CE). Also explain how each event affects the accounting equation by placing a (+) for increase, (−) for decrease, and NA for not affected under each of the components of the accounting equation. Finally, indicate whether the effect requires a debit or credit entry. The first event is recorded as an example.

						Stockholders' Equity		
Event	Type of Event	Assets	=	Liabilities	+	Common Stock	+	Retained Earnings
a	AS	+ Debit		NA		NA		+ Credit

a. Provided services for cash.
b. Received cash in payment of accounts receivable.
c. Recognized revenue for services completed; cash collected previously.
d. Purchased land by paying cash.
e. Purchased supplies on account.
f. Paid salaries payable.

g. Recognized expense for prepaid rent that had been used up by the end of the accounting period.

h. Incurred other operating expenses on account.

i. Recognized expense for supplies used during the period.

j. Received cash for services to be performed in the future.

k. Paid a cash dividend to the stockholders.

l. Paid cash in advance for one year's rent.

m. Provided services on account.

LO 13-1

Exercise 13-7B   *Identifying increases and decreases in T-accounts*

Required

For each of the following T-accounts, indicate the side of the account that should be used to record an increase or decrease in the financial statement element:

Assets		=	Liabilities		+	Stockholders' Equity	
Debit	Credit		Debit	Credit		Debit	Credit

LO 13-1

Exercise 13-8B   *T-accounts and the accounting equation*

Required

Record each of the following Wilson Co. events in T-accounts and then explain how the event affects the accounting equation:

a. Received $40,000 cash by issuing common stock.

b. Purchased supplies for $1,800 cash.

c. Performed services on account for $14,000.

d. Paid cash for $8,000 of salaries expense.

LO 13-1

Exercise 13-9B   *Recording receivables and identifying their effect on financial statements*

Ross Company performed services on account for $30,000 in Year 1, its first year of operations. Ross collected $24,000 cash from accounts receivable during Year 1 and the remaining $6,000 in cash during Year 2.

Required

a. Record the Year 1 transactions in T-accounts.

b. Show the Year 1 transactions in a horizontal statements model like the following one:

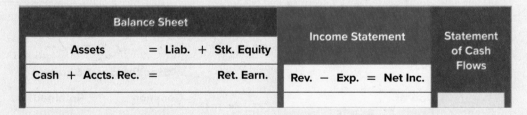

c. Determine the amount of revenue that would be reported on the Year 1 income statement.

d. Determine the amount of cash flow from operating activities that would be reported on the Year 1 statement of cash flows.

e. Open a T-account for Retained Earnings, and close the Year 1 Service Revenue account to the Retained Earnings account.

f. Record the Year 2 cash collection in the appropriate T-accounts.

g. Show the Year 2 transaction in a horizontal statements model like the one shown in Requirement *b*.

h. Assuming no other transactions occur in Year 2, determine the amount of net income and the net cash flow from operating activities for Year 2.

Exercise 13-10B   *Recording supplies and identifying their effect on financial statements*   LO 13-1, 13-3, 13-4

Laura Moss started and operated a small family consulting firm in Year 1. The firm was affected by two events: (1) Moss provided $36,000 of services on account, and (2) she purchased $10,000 of supplies on account. There were $1,800 of supplies on hand as of December 31, Year 1.

Required

a. Open T-accounts and record the two transactions in the accounts.
b. Record the required year-end adjusting entry to reflect the use of supplies.
c. Show the above transactions in a horizontal statements model like the following one:

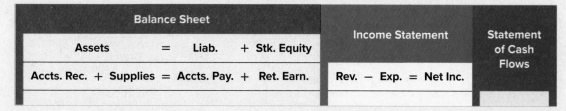

Balance Sheet					Income Statement			Statement of Cash Flows
Assets		=	Liab.	+ Stk. Equity				
Accts. Rec. + Supplies	=	Accts. Pay. +	Ret. Earn.		Rev. −	Exp. =	Net Inc.	

d. Explain why the amounts of net income and net cash flow from operating activities differ.
e. Record and post the required closing entries, and prepare a post-closing trial balance.

Exercise 13-11B   *Recording unearned revenue and identifying its effect on financial statements*   LO 13-1

James Jones received a $90,000 cash advance on March 1, Year 1, for legal services to be performed in the future. Services were to be provided for a one-year term beginning March 1, Year 1.

Required

a. Record the March 1 cash receipt in T-accounts.
b. Record in T-accounts the adjustment required as of December 31, Year 1.
c. Show the preceding transaction and related adjustment in a horizontal statements model like the following one:

Balance Sheet				Income Statement			Statement of Cash Flows
Assets =	Liab.	+	Stk. Equity	Rev. −	Exp. =	Net Inc.	

d. Determine the amount of net income on the Year 1 income statement. What is the amount of net cash flow from operating activities for Year 1?
e. What amount of unearned revenue would Jones report on the December 31, Year 1, balance sheet?

Exercise 13-12B   *Using a T-account to determine cash flow from operating activities*   LO 13-1

Barnes Inc. began the accounting period with a $105,000 debit balance in its Accounts Receivable account. During the accounting period, Barnes earned revenue on account of $448,000. The ending Accounts Receivable balance was $86,000.

Required

Based on this information alone, determine the amount of cash inflow from operating activities during the accounting period. (*Hint:* Use a T-account for Accounts Receivable. Enter the debits and credits for the given events, and solve for the missing amount.)

Exercise 13-13B   *Using a T-account to determine cash flow from operating activities*   LO 13-1

Hun Company began the accounting period with a $36,000 credit balance in its Accounts Payable account. During the accounting period, Hun incurred expenses on account of $108,000. The ending Accounts Payable balance was $48,000.

Required

Based on this information, determine the amount of cash outflow for expenses during the accounting period. (*Hint:* Use a T-account for Accounts Payable. Enter the debits and credits for the given events, and solve for the missing amount.)

LO 13-2

Exercise 13-14B   *Recording events in the general journal and identifying their effect on financial statements*

Required

Record each of the following transactions in general journal form and then show the effect of the transaction in the horizontal statements model. The first transaction is shown as an example.

Account Title	Debit	Credit
Accounts Receivable	50,000	
Service Revenue		50,000

Balance Sheet				Income Statement						Statement of Cash Flows
Assets	=	Liab.	+	Stk. Equity	Rev.	−	Exp.	=	Net Inc.	
50,000		NA		50,000	50,000		NA		50,000	NA

a.   Performed $50,000 worth of services on account.
b.   Charged $2,000 on account for operating expense.
c.   Collected $27,000 cash on accounts receivable.
d.   Paid $700 on accounts payable.
e.   Paid $6,800 cash in advance for an insurance policy.
f.   Recorded the adjusting entry to recognize $4,500 of insurance expense.
g.   Received $4,000 cash for services to be performed at a later date.
h.   Purchased supplies for $2,400 cash.

LO 13-2

Exercise 13-15B   *Recording accrued salaries and identifying their effect on financial statements*

On December 31, Year 1, Zeal Company had accrued salaries of $12,000.

Required

a.   Record in general journal format the adjustment required as of December 31, Year 1.
b.   Show the above adjustment in a horizontal statements model like the following one:

Balance Sheet					Income Statement				Statement of Cash Flows
Assets	=	Liab.	+	Stk. Equity					
		Sal. Pay.	+	Ret. Earn.	Rev.	−	Exp.	=	Net Inc.	

c.   Determine the amount of net income Zeal would report on the Year 1 income statement, assuming that Zeal received $29,000 of cash revenue. What is the amount of net cash flow from operating activities for Year 1?
d.   What amount of salaries payable would Zeal report on the December 31, Year 1, balance sheet?

Exercise 13-16B   *Recording prepaid items and identifying their effect on financial*   LO 13-2
statements

Virginia Mining began operations by issuing common stock for $150,000. The company paid $135,000 cash in advance for a one-year contract to lease machinery for the business. The lease agreement was signed on March 1, Year 1, and was effective immediately. Virginia Mining received $172,500 of cash revenue in Year 1.

Required

a. Record the March 1 cash payment in general journal format.

b. Record in general journal format the adjustment required as of December 31, Year 1.

c. Show all Year 1 events in a horizontal statements model like the following one:

Balance Sheet						Income Statement			Statement of Cash Flows
Assets		=	Liab. +	Stk. Equity					
Cash +	Prep. Rent =			Common Stock +	Ret. Earn.	Rev. –	Exp. =	Net Inc.	

d. What amount of net income would be reported on the Year 1 income statement? What is the amount of net cash flow from operating activities for Year 1?

e. Determine the amount of prepaid rent that would be reported on the December 31, Year 1, balance sheet.

Exercise 13-17B   *Recording transactions in general journal and T-accounts*   LO 13-1, 13-2

The following events apply to Colton Training Co. for Year 1, its first year of operation:

1. Received cash of $60,000 from the issue of common stock.
2. Performed $100,000 worth of services on account.
3. Paid $74,000 cash for salaries expense.
4. Purchased supplies for $13,000 on account.
5. Collected $79,000 of accounts receivable.
6. Paid $9,500 of the accounts payable.
7. Paid a $6,000 dividend to the stockholders.
8. Had $2,500 of supplies on hand at the end of the period.

Required

a. Record these events in general journal form.

b. Post the entries to T-accounts and determine the ending balance in each account.

c. Determine the amount of total assets at the end of Year 1.

d. Determine the amount of net income for Year 1.

Exercise 13-18B   *Recording events in the general journal, posting to T-accounts, and*   LO 13-1, 13-2, 13-3
preparing a trial balance

The following events apply to Perry Carpet Cleaners in its first year of operations:

1. Received $45,000 cash from the issue of common stock.
2. Earned $37,500 of service revenue on account.
3. Incurred $15,000 of operating expenses on account.
4. Received $30,000 cash for performing services.

5. Paid $12,000 cash to purchase land.

6. Collected $33,000 of cash from accounts receivable.

7. Received a $9,000 cash advance for services to be provided in the future.

8. Purchased $1,350 of supplies on account.

9. Made an $11,250 payment on accounts payable.

10. Paid a $7,500 cash dividend to the stockholders.

11. Recognized $750 of supplies expense.

12. Recognized $7,500 of revenue for services provided to the customer in Event 7.

Required

a. Record the events in the general journal.

b. Post the events to T-accounts and determine the ending account balances.

c. Test the equality of the debit and credit balances of the T-accounts by preparing a trial balance.

LO 13-3

Exercise 13-19B   *Preparing a trial balance*

Required

On December 31, Year 2, Wages Company had the following normal account balances in its general ledger. Use this information to prepare a trial balance.

Common Stock	$ 50,000
Salaries Expense	32,000
Office Supplies	3,600
Advertising Expense	5,000
Retained Earnings, 1/1/Year 2	28,400
Unearned Revenue	36,000
Accounts Receivable	13,000
Cash	120,000
Service Revenue	152,000
Dividends	10,000
Prepaid Insurance	12,800
Land	44,000
Rent Expense	30,000
Accounts Payable	4,000

LO 13-3

Exercise 13-20B   *Determining the effect of errors on the trial balance*

Required

Explain how each of the following posting errors affects a trial balance. State whether the trial balance will be out of balance because of the posting error, and indicate which side of the trial balance will have a higher amount after each independent entry is posted. If the posting error does not affect the equality of debits and credits in the trial balance, state that the error will not cause an inequality and explain why.

a. A $2,000 credit to Salaries Payable was not posted.

b. A $5,400 debit to Cash was posted as a $4,500 debit.

c. A $3,000 debit to Prepaid Rent was debited to Rent Expense.

d. A $2,500 credit to Accounts Payable was posted as a credit to Cash.

e. The collection of $400 of accounts receivable was posted to Accounts Receivable twice.

LO 13-4

Exercise 13-21B   *Preparing closing entries*

The following financial information was taken from the books of Serenity Spa:

Account Balances as of December 31, Year 2	
Accounts Receivable	$ 54,000
Accounts Payable	15,000
Advertising Expense	7,000
Cash	80,600
Common Stock	40,000
Dividends	10,000
Land	27,000
Prepaid Rent	6,400
Rent Expense	15,600
Retained Earnings 1/1/Year 2	38,800
Salaries Expense	64,000
Salaries Payable	23,600
Service Revenue	153,000
Supplies	800
Supplies Expense	5,000

Required

a. Prepare the journal entries necessary to close the temporary accounts December 31, Year 2, for Serenity Spa.

b. What is the balance in the Retained Earnings account after the closing entries are posted?

Exercise 13-22B *Recording events in the general journal, posting to T-accounts, and preparing closing entries*   LO 13-1, 13-2, 13-3, 13-4

At the beginning of Year 2, Event Services Co. had the following normal balances in its accounts:

Account	Balance
Cash	$60,000
Accounts Receivable	38,000
Accounts Payable	24,800
Common Stock	48,000
Retained Earnings	25,200

The following events apply to Event Services Co. for Year 2:

1. Provided $130,000 of services on account.
2. Incurred $6,200 of operating expenses on account.
3. Collected $112,000 of accounts receivable.
4. Paid $72,000 cash for salaries expense.
5. Paid $30,000 cash as a partial payment on accounts payable.
6. Paid a $16,000 cash dividend to the stockholders.

Required

a. Record these events in a general journal.

b. Open T-accounts and post the beginning balances and the preceding transactions to the appropriate accounts. Determine the balance of each account.

c. Show the beginning balances and the events in a horizontal statements model such as the following one:

Balance Sheet									Income Statement			Statement of Cash Flows
Assets		=	Liab.	+		Stk. Equity						
Cash	+ Accts. Rec.	=	Accts. Pay.	+	Common Stock	+	Ret. Earn.		Rev.	− Exp.	= Net Inc.	

d. Record the closing entries in the general journal and post them to the T-accounts. What is the amount of net income for the year?

e. What is the amount of *change* in retained earnings for the year? Is the change in retained earnings different from the amount of net income? If so, why?

f. Prepare a post-closing trial balance.

LO 13-5

Exercise 13-23B *Determining the book value of assets*

The following information was drawn from the accounting records of Schafer Company:

1. On January 1, Year 1, Schafer paid $72,000 cash to purchase a truck. The truck had a seven-year useful life and a $9,000 salvage value.

2. As of December 31, Year 1, Schafer Company had an $84,000 balance in its Accounts Receivable account and a zero balance in its Allowance for Doubtful Accounts account. Sales on account for Year 1 amounted to $450,000. Schafer estimates that 3 percent of credit sales will be uncollectible.

Required

a. Record the year-end adjusting entry for depreciation expense on the truck in T-accounts.

b. Determine the book value of the truck that will appear on the December 31, Year 1, balance sheet.

c. Record the year-end adjusting entry of uncollectible accounts expense.

d. Determine the net realizable value of receivables that will appear on the December 31, Year 1, balance sheet.

LO 13-5

Exercise 13-24B *Adjusted trial balance*

The following balances were drawn from the accounts of Carter Company. The accounts and balances shown here are presented in random order: Equipment—$26,000; Cash—$18,000; Depreciation Expense—$3,000; Notes Payable—$26,000; Common Stock—$35,000; Accumulated Depreciation—$3,000; Interest Expense—$500; Cost of Goods Sold—$36,000; Retained Earnings—$14,000; Allowance for Doubtful Accounts—$3,000; Merchandise Inventory—$16,000; Interest Payable—$2,000; Sales Revenue—$47,000; Uncollectible Accounts Expense—$3,000; and Accounts Receivable—$27,500.

Required

Prepare an adjusted trial balance.

IFRS

Exercise 13-25B *IFRS and U.S. GAAP*

Define the IASB and describe its function.

PROBLEMS—SERIES B

LO 13-1

Problem 13-26B *Identifying debit and credit balances*

Required

Indicate whether each of the following accounts normally has a debit or credit balance:

a. Retained Earnings	**k.** Interest Receivable
b. Prepaid Insurance	**l.** Interest Revenue
c. Insurance Expense	**m.** Dividends
d. Accounts Receivable	**n.** Operating Expense
e. Salaries Payable	**o.** Unearned Revenue
f. Cash	**p.** Accounts Payable
g. Common Stock	**q.** Supplies
h. Rent Expense	**r.** Service Revenue
i. Salaries Expense	**s.** Prepaid Rent
j. Land	**t.** Supplies Expense

Problem 13-27B   *Transaction type and debit/credit terminology*   LO 13-1

The following events apply to Un Enterprises:

1. Acquired $30,000 cash from the issue of common stock.
2. Recognized $28,000 of service revenue on account.
3. Paid cash to rent office space for the next 12 months: $7,800.
4. Paid cash of $9,200 for operating expenses.
5. Collected $9,000 cash for services to be performed in the future.
6. Paid salaries to employees: $8,000 cash.
7. Paid cash for utilities expense: $1,200.
8. Paid on accounts payable: $1,200.
9. Paid a $5,000 cash dividend to the stockholders.
10. Purchased $2,000 of supplies on account.
11. Received $18,000 cash for services rendered.
12. Recognized $3,250 of rent expense related to cash paid in a prior transaction (see Event 3).
13. Recognized $6,000 of revenue for services performed for which cash had been previously collected (see Event 5).
14. Recognized $4,800 of accrued salaries expense.

Required

Identify each event as asset source (AS), asset use (AU), asset exchange (AE), or claims exchange (CE). Also identify the account to be debited and the account to be credited when the transaction is recorded. The first event is recorded as an example.

Event No.	Type of Event	Account Debited	Account Credited
1	AS	Cash	Common Stock

Problem 13-28B   *Showing events in a statements model, recording them in T-accounts, and preparing a trial balance*   LO 13-1, 13-3

The following accounting events apply to Little Co. for Year 1:

Asset Source Transactions

1. Began operations when the business acquired $40,000 cash from the issue of common stock.
2. Performed services and collected cash of $2,000.
3. Collected $9,000 of cash in advance for services to be provided over the next 12 months.
4. Provided $24,000 of services on account.
5. Purchased supplies of $840 on account.

Asset Exchange Transactions

6. Purchased $8,000 of land for cash.
7. Collected $17,000 of cash from accounts receivable.
8. Purchased $1,000 of supplies with cash.
9. Paid $7,200 in advance for one year's rent.

Asset Use Transactions

10. Paid $6,000 cash for salaries of employees.
11. Paid a cash dividend of $4,000 to the stockholders.
12. Paid $840 for supplies that had been purchased on account.

Claims Exchange Transactions

13. Placed an advertisement in the local newspaper for $300 and agreed to pay for the ad later.
14. Incurred utilities expense of $250 on account.

Adjusting Entries

15. Recognized $6,000 of revenue for performing services. The collection of cash for these services occurred in a prior transaction. (See Event 3.)
16. Recorded $1,800 of accrued salary expense at the end of Year 1.
17. Recorded supplies expense. Had $240 of supplies on hand at the end of the accounting period.
18. Recognized that three months of prepaid rent had been used up during the accounting period.

Required

a. Record each of the preceding transactions in T-accounts and determine the balance of each account.
b. Prepare a before-closing trial balance.
c. Use a horizontal statements model to show how each event affects the balance sheet, income statement, and statement of cash flows. Indicate whether the event increases (+), decreases (−), or does not affect (NA) each element of the financial statements. Also, in the Statement of Cash Flows column, use the letters OA to designate operating activity, IA for investing activity, and FA for financing activity. The first event is recorded as an example.

Balance Sheet				Income Statement			Statement of Cash Flows
Assets	=	Liab.	+ Stk. Equity	Rev.	− Exp.	= Net Inc.	
+		NA	+	NA	NA	NA	+ FA

LO 13-2

Problem 13-29B   *Effect of journal entries on financial statements*

Event No.	Account Title	Debit	Credit
1.	Cash	xxx	
	Common Stock		xxx
2.	Accounts Receivable	xxx	
	Service Revenue		xxx
3.	Cash	xxx	
	Accounts Receivable		xxx
4.	Supplies	xxx	
	Accounts Payable		xxx
5.	Cash	xxx	
	Unearned Revenue		xxx
6.	Cash	xxx	
	Service Revenue		xxx
7.	Property Tax Expense	xxx	
	Cash		xxx
8.	Prepaid Rent	xxx	
	Cash		xxx
9.	Salaries Expense	xxx	
	Cash		xxx
10.	Unearned Revenue	xxx	
	Service Revenue		xxx
11.	Rent Expense	xxx	
	Prepaid Rent		xxx
12.	Supplies Expense	xxx	
	Supplies		xxx
13.	Dividends	xxx	
	Cash		xxx

Required

The preceding 13 different accounting events are presented in general journal format. Use a horizontal statements model to show how each event affects the balance sheet, income statement, and statement of cash flows. Indicate whether the event increases (+), decreases (−), or does not affect (NA) each element of the financial statements. Also, in the Statement of Cash Flows column, use the letters OA to designate operating activity, IA for investing activity, and FA for financing activity. The first event is recorded as an example.

Balance Sheet				Income Statement				Statement of Cash Flows
Assets	=	Liab.	+ Stk. Equity	Rev.	− Exp.	=	Net Inc.	
+		NA	+	NA	NA		NA	+ FA

Problem 13-30B *Identifying accounting events from journal entries*

LO 13-2

Required

The following information is from the records of Floral Design. Write a brief explanation of the accounting event represented in each of the general journal entries.

Date	Account Titles	Debit	Credit
Jan. 1	Cash	18,750	
	Common Stock		18,750
Feb. 1	Prepaid Rent	15,300	
	Cash		15,300
Mar. 1	Cash	19,500	
	Unearned Revenue		19,500
Apr. 1	Accounts Receivable	27,600	
	Service Revenue		27,600
May 1	Supplies	2,325	
	Accounts Payable		2,325
31	Salaries Expense	9,150	
	Cash		9,150
June 30	Property Tax Expense	4,500	
	Cash		4,500
Sept. 1	Cash	13,000	
	Service Revenue		13,000
Oct. 2	Cash	16,000	
	Accounts Receivable		16,000
Dec. 1	Dividends	4,000	
	Cash		4,000
Dec. 31	Supplies Expense	2,100	
	Supplies		2,100
31	Rent Expense	9,600	
	Prepaid Rent		9,600
31	Unearned Revenue	12,500	
	Service Revenue		12,500

Problem 13-31B *Recording adjusting entries in general journal format*

LO 13-2

Required

Each of the following independent events requires a year-end adjusting entry. Record each event and the related adjusting entry in general journal format. The first event is recorded as an example. Assume a December 31 closing date.

Date	Account Titles	Debit	Credit
Oct. 1	Prepaid Rent	8,400	
	Cash		8,400
Dec. 31	Rent Expense (8,400 × 3/12)	2,100	
	Prepaid Rent		2,100

a. Paid $8,400 cash in advance on October 1 for a one-year lease on office space.

b. Paid $4,800 cash in advance on May 1 for a one-year insurance policy.

c. Purchased $1,600 of supplies on account on June 15. At year end, $200 of supplies remained on hand.

d. Received a $4,800 cash advance on September 1 for a contract to provide services for one year beginning immediately.

LO 13-3

Problem 13-32B *Effect of errors on the trial balance*

The following trial balance was prepared from the ledger accounts of Klein Inc.

KLEIN INC.
Trial Balance
May 31, Year 1

Account Titles	Debit	Credit
Cash	$ 7,200	
Accounts Receivable	3,000	
Supplies	420	
Prepaid Insurance	2,400	
Land	5,000	
Accounts Payable		$ 1,500
Common Stock		1,800
Retained Earnings		7,390
Dividends	400	
Service Revenue		$20,830
Rent Expense	3,600	
Salaries Expense	9,000	
Operating Expenses	2,500	
Totals	$33,520	$31,520

The accountant for Klein Inc. made the following errors during May, Year 1:

1. The cash purchase of land for $3,000 was recorded as a $5,000 debit to Land and a $3,000 credit to Cash.

2. A $1,600 purchase of supplies on account was properly recorded as a debit to the Supplies account but was incorrectly recorded as a credit to the Cash account.

3. The company provided services valued at $7,800 to a customer on account. The accountant recorded the transaction in the proper accounts but in the incorrect amount of $8,700.

4. A $1,200 cash receipt from a customer on an account receivable was not recorded.

5. An $800 cash payment of an account payable was not recorded.

6. The May utility bill, which amounted to $1,050 on account, was not recorded.

Required

a. Identify the errors that would cause a difference in the total amounts of debits and credits that would appear in a trial balance. Indicate whether the Debit or Credit column would be larger as a result of the error.

b. Indicate whether each of the preceding errors would overstate, understate, or have no effect on the amount of total assets, liabilities, and stockholders' equity. Your answer should take the following form:

Event No.	Assets	=	Liabilities	+	Stockholders' Equity
1	Overstate		No effect		No effect

c. Prepare a corrected trial balance.

Problem 13-33B   *Comprehensive problem: single cycle*

LO 13-1, 13-2, 13-3, 13-4

The following transactions pertain to Price Corporation for Year 1:

Jan. 1   Began operations when the business acquired $25,000 cash from the issue of common stock.
Mar. 1   Paid rent for office space for two years: $8,400 cash.
Apr. 14   Purchased $400 of supplies on account.
June 30   Received $12,000 cash in advance for services to be provided over the next year.
July 5   Paid $300 of the accounts payable from April 14.
Aug. 1   Billed a customer $4,800 for services provided during July.
       8   Completed a job and received $1,600 cash for services rendered.
Sept. 1   Paid employee salaries of $18,000 cash.
       9   Received $4,250 cash from accounts receivable.
Oct. 5   Billed customers $17,000 for services rendered on account.
Nov. 2   Paid a $500 cash dividend to the stockholders.
Dec. 31   Adjusted records to recognize the services provided on the contract of June 30.
       31   Recorded $1,100 of accrued salaries as of December 31.
       31   Recorded the rent expense for the year. (See March 1.)
       31   Physically counted supplies; $50 was on hand at the end of the period.

Required

a. Record the preceding transactions in the general journal.
b. Post the transactions to T-accounts and calculate the account balances.
c. Prepare a trial balance.
d. Prepare the income statement, statement of changes in stockholders' equity, balance sheet, and statement of cash flows.
e. Prepare the closing entries at December 31.
f. Prepare a trial balance after the closing entries are posted.

Problem 13-34B   *Two complete accounting cycles*

LO 13-1, 13-2, 13-3, 13-4

Anchor Machining experienced the following events during Year 1:

1. Started operations by acquiring $100,000 of cash from the issue of common stock.
2. Paid $12,000 cash in advance for rent during the period from February 1, Year 1, to February 1, Year 2.
3. Received $9,600 cash in advance for services to be performed evenly over the period from September 1, Year 1, to September 1, Year 2.
4. Performed services for customers on account for $130,400.
5. Incurred operating expenses on account of $63,000.
6. Collected $113,800 cash from accounts receivable.
7. Paid $44,000 cash for salaries expense.
8. Paid $56,000 cash as a partial payment on accounts payable.

Adjusting Entries

9. Made the adjusting entry for the expired rent. (See Event 2.)
10. Recognized revenue for services performed in accordance with Event 3.
11. Recorded $4,200 of accrued salaries at the end of Year 1.

Events for Year 2

1. Paid $4,200 cash for the salaries accrued at the end of the previous year.
2. Performed services for cash of $81,000.
3. Paid $50,000 cash to purchase land.
4. Paid $10,800 cash in advance for rent during the period from February 1, Year 2, to February 1, Year 3.
5. Performed services for customers on account for $164,000.
6. Incurred operating expenses on account of $98,200.
7. Collected $152,600 cash from accounts receivable.
8. Paid $96,000 cash as a partial payment on accounts payable.
9. Paid $82,000 cash for salaries expense.
10. Paid a $10,000 cash dividend to the stockholders.

Adjusting Entries

11. Recognized revenue for services performed in accordance with Event 3 in Year 1.
12. Made the adjusting entry for the expired rent. (*Hint:* Part of the rent was paid in Year 1.)
13. Recorded $7,000 of accrued salaries at the end of Year 2.

Required

a. Record the events and adjusting entries for Year 1 in general journal form.
b. Post the events for Year 1 to T-accounts.
c. Prepare a trial balance for Year 1.
d. Prepare an income statement, statement of changes in stockholders' equity, balance sheet, and statement of cash flows for Year 1.
e. Record the entries to close the Year 1 temporary accounts to Retained Earnings in the general journal and post to the T-accounts.
f. Prepare a post-closing trial balance for December 31, Year 1.
g. Repeat Requirements a through f for Year 2.

LO 13-5

Problem 13-35B *Recording events in the general ledger*

As of January 1, Year 5, the accounting records for High Tech Supply (HTS) showed Cash of $180,000, Common Stock of $120,000, and Retained Earnings of $60,000. During Year 5, HTS experienced the following accounting events:

1. HTS purchased merchandise inventory for $78,000 cash.
2a. HTS recognized revenue from selling inventory for $97,000 on account.
2b. HTS recognized $82,000 of cost of goods sold.
3. HTS paid $38,000 cash to purchase a warehouse. The warehouse had a 10-year useful life and an $8,000 salvage value.
4. On April 1, Year 5, HTS acquired $35,000 cash by issuing a note to the State Bank. The note had a 5 percent annual interest rate and a one-year term to maturity.
5. HTS recognized accrued interest expense for the note issued in Event 4.
6. HTS estimated its uncollectible accounts expense to be 3 percent of credit sales.
7. HTS recognized depreciation expense associated with the warehouse purchased in Event 3.

Required

a. Record the events in a general journal.
b. Determine the net realizable value of receivables that will appear on the December 31, Year 5, balance sheet.
c. Determine the book value of the warehouse that will appear on the December 31, Year 5, balance sheet.

Problem 13-36B   *Recording events and preparing financial statements*

The December 31, Year 2, balance sheet for Mason Dixon Corp. (MDC) showed Cash of $80,000, Common Stock of $30,000, and Retained Earnings of $50,000. During Year 3, MDC experienced the following accounting events:

1. MDC purchased merchandise inventory for $52,000 cash.

2a. MDC recognized revenue from selling inventory for $75,000 on account.

2b. MDC recognized $45,000 of cost of goods sold.

3. In a year-end adjusting entry MDC recognized $1,600 of uncollectible accounts expense.

4. MDC paid $25,000 cash to purchase display equipment. The equipment had a five-year useful life and a $5,000 salvage value.

5. MDC recognized depreciation expense associated with the equipment purchased in Event 4.

6. On October 1, Year 3, MDC acquired $30,000 cash by issuing a note to the State Bank. The note had a 5 percent annual interest rate and a one-year term to maturity.

7. MDC recognized accrued interest expense for the note issued in Event 6.

Required

a. Record the events in T-accounts and determine the ending account balances.

b. Prepare an income statement, a balance sheet, and a statement of cash flows.

ACCESSING THE EDGAR DATABASE THROUGH THE INTERNET

Successful business managers need many different skills, including communication, interpersonal, computer, and analytical skills. Most business students become very aware of the data analysis skills used in accounting, but they may not be as aware of the importance of "data-finding" skills. There are many sources of accounting and financial data. The more sources you are able to use, the better.

One very important source of accounting information is the EDGAR database. Others are probably available at your school through the library or business school network. Your accounting instructor will be able to identify these for you and make suggestions regarding their use. By making the effort to learn to use electronic databases, you will enhance your abilities as a future manager and your marketability as a business graduate.

These instructions assume that you know how to access and use an Internet browser. Follow the instructions to retrieve data from the Securities and Exchange Commission's EDGAR database. Be aware that the SEC may have changed its interface since this appendix was written. Accordingly, be prepared for slight differences between the following instructions and what appears on your computer screen. Take comfort in the fact that changes are normally designed to simplify user access. If you encounter a conflict between the following instructions and the instructions provided in the SEC interface, remember that the SEC interface is more current and should take precedence over the following instructions.

Most companies provide links to their SEC filings from their corporate website. These links are often simpler to use and provide more choices regarding file formats than the SEC's EDGAR site. On company websites, links to SEC filings are usually found under one of the following links: "Investor Relations," "Company Info," or "About Us."

1. Connect to the EDGAR database through the following address: http://www.sec.gov/.

2. After the SEC homepage appears, click on **Company Filings.**

3. On the screen that appears, enter the name of the company whose file you wish to retrieve.

4. The next screen will present a list of companies that have the same name as the one you entered, along with companies that have similar names. Identify the company you want and click on the CIK number beside it.

5. Enter the SEC form number that you want to retrieve in the window titled **Filing Type** that appears in the upper left portion of the screen. For example, if you want Form 10-K, which will usually be the case, enter **10-K** and click on the **Search** button.

6. A list of the forms you requested will be presented, along with the date they were filed. Click on the **Document** button next to the file you wish to retrieve.

7. Once the 10-K has been retrieved, you can search it online or save it on your computer.

8. Often, the 10-K will have a table of contents that can help locate the part of the report you need. The financial statements are seldom located at the beginning of the Form 10-K. They are usually in either Section 8 or Section 15.

PORTION OF THE FORM 10-K FOR TARGET CORPORATION

UNITED STATES
SECURITIES AND EXCHANGE COMMISSION
Washington, D.C. 20549
FORM 10-K

(Mark One)

☒   **ANNUAL REPORT PURSUANT TO SECTION 13 OR 15(d) OF THE SECURITIES EXCHANGE ACT OF 1934**

For the fiscal year ended February 2, 2019

OR

☐   **TRANSITION REPORT PURSUANT TO SECTION 13 OR 15(d) OF THE SECURITIES EXCHANGE ACT OF 1934**

For the transition period from   to

Commission file number **1-6049**

**TARGET CORPORATION**

(Exact name of registrant as specified in its charter)

Minnesota	**41-0215170**
(State or other jurisdiction of incorporation or organization)	(I.R.S. Employer Identification No.)
1000 Nicollet Mall, Minneapolis, Minnesota	**55403**
(Address of principal executive offices)	(Zip Code)

Registrant's telephone number, including area code: 612/304-6073

Securities Registered Pursuant To Section 12(B) Of The Act:

Title of Each Class	**Name of Each Exchange on Which Registered**
Common Stock, par value $0.0833 per share	**New York Stock Exchange**

Securities registered pursuant to Section 12(g) of the Act: **None**

Source: U.S. Securities and Exchange Commission.

Indicate by check mark if the registrant is a well-known seasoned issuer, as defined in Rule 405 of the Securities Act. Yes ☒ No ☐

Indicate by check mark if the registrant is not required to file reports pursuant to Section 13 or Section 15(d) of the Act. Yes ☐ No ☒

Note – Checking the box above will not relieve any registrant required to file reports pursuant to Section 13 or 15(d) of the Exchange Act from their obligations under those Sections.

Indicate by check mark whether the registrant (1) has filed all reports required to be filed by Section 13 or 15(d) of the Securities Exchange Act of 1934 during the preceding 12 months (or for such shorter period that the registrant was required to file such reports), and (2) has been subject to such filing requirements for the past 90 days. Yes ☒ No ☐

Indicate by check mark whether the registrant has submitted electronically every Interactive Data File required to be submitted pursuant to Rule 405 of Regulation S-T (§232.405 of this chapter) during the preceding 12 months (or for such shorter period that the registrant was required to submit such files). Yes ☒ No ☐

Indicate by check mark if disclosure of delinquent filers pursuant to Item 405 of Regulation S-K (§229.405 of this chapter) is not contained herein, and will not be contained, to the best of registrant's knowledge, in definitive proxy or information statements incorporated by reference in Part III of this Form 10-K or any amendment to this Form 10-K. ☒

Indicate by check mark whether the registrant is a large accelerated filer, an accelerated filer, a non-accelerated filer, smaller reporting company, or an emerging growth company (as defined in Rule 12b-2 of the Exchange Act).

Large accelerated filer   ☒   Accelerated filer   ☐   Non-accelerated filer   ☐

Smaller reporting company   ☐   Emerging growth company   ☐

If an emerging growth company, indicate by check mark if the registrant has elected not to use the extended transition period for complying with any new or revised financial accounting standards provided pursuant to Section 13(a) of the Exchange Act. ☐

Indicate by check mark whether the registrant is a shell company (as defined in Rule 12b-2 of the Act). Yes ☐ No ☒

The aggregate market value of the voting stock held by non-affiliates of the registrant as of August 4, 2018, was $42,763,636,334 based on the closing price of $81.45 per share of Common Stock as reported on the New York Stock Exchange Composite Index.

Indicate the number of shares outstanding of each of registrant's classes of Common Stock, as of the latest practicable date. Total shares of Common Stock, par value $0.0833, outstanding at March 7, 2019, were 516,333,213.

DOCUMENTS INCORPORATED BY REFERENCE

Portions of Target's Proxy Statement for the Annual Meeting of Shareholders to be held on June 12, 2019, are incorporated into Part III.

Item 8. Financial Statements and Supplementary Data

Report of Management on the Consolidated Financial Statements

Management is responsible for the consistency, integrity, and presentation of the information in the Annual Report. The consolidated financial statements and other information presented in this Annual Report have been prepared in accordance with accounting principles generally accepted in the United States and include necessary judgments and estimates by management.

To fulfill our responsibility, we maintain comprehensive systems of internal control designed to provide reasonable assurance that assets are safeguarded and transactions are executed in accordance with established procedures. The concept of reasonable assurance is based upon recognition that the cost of the controls should not exceed the benefit derived. We believe our systems of internal control provide this reasonable assurance.

The Board of Directors exercised its oversight role with respect to the Corporation's systems of internal control primarily through its Audit Committee, which is comprised of independent directors. The Committee oversees the Corporation's systems of internal control, accounting practices, financial reporting and audits to assess whether their quality, integrity, and objectivity are sufficient to protect shareholders' investments.

In addition, our consolidated financial statements have been audited by Ernst & Young LLP, independent registered public accounting firm, whose report also appears on this page.

/s/ Brian C. Cornell	/s/ Cathy R. Smith
Brian C. Cornell	Cathy R. Smith
Chairman and Chief Executive Officer	Executive Vice President and
March 13, 2019 March 13, 2019	Chief Financial Officer

Report of Independent Registered Public Accounting Firm

To the Shareholders and the Board of Directors of Target Corporation

Opinion on the Financial Statements

We have audited the accompanying consolidated statements of financial position of Target Corporation (the Corporation) as of February 2, 2019 and February 3, 2018, the related consolidated statements of operations, comprehensive income, cash flows and shareholders' investment for each of the three years in the period ended February 2, 2019, and the related notes (collectively referred to as the "consolidated financial statements"). In our opinion, the consolidated financial statements present fairly, in all material respects, the financial position of the Corporation at February 2, 2019 and February 3, 2018, and the results of its operations and its cash flows for each of the three years in the period ended February 2, 2019, in conformity with U.S. generally accepted accounting principles.

We also have audited, in accordance with the standards of the Public Company Accounting Oversight Board (United States) (PCAOB), the Corporation's internal control over financial reporting as of February 2, 2019, based on criteria established in *Internal Control-Integrated Framework* issued by the Committee of Sponsoring Organizations of the Treadway Commission (2013 framework) and our report dated March 13, 2019, expressed an unqualified opinion thereon.

Adoption of New Accounting Standards

ASU No. 2014-09
As discussed in Note 2 to the consolidated financial statements, the Corporation changed its method for recognizing revenue in 2018 due to the adoption of ASU No. 2014-09, Revenue from Contracts with Customers (Topic 606), as amended, effective February 4, 2018, using the full retrospective approach.

ASU No. 2016-02
As discussed in Note 2 to the consolidated financial statements, the Corporation changed its method of accounting for leases in 2018 due to the adoption of ASU No. 2016-02, Leases (Topic 842), as amended, effective February 4, 2018, using the modified retrospective approach.

Basis for Opinion

These financial statements are the responsibility of the Corporation's management. Our responsibility is to express an opinion on the Corporation's financial statements based on our audits. We are a public accounting firm registered with the PCAOB and are required to be independent with respect to the Corporation in accordance with the U.S. federal securities laws and the applicable rules and regulations of the Securities and Exchange Commission and the PCAOB.

We conducted our audits in accordance with the standards of the PCAOB. Those standards require that we plan and perform the audit to obtain reasonable assurance about whether the financial statements are free of material misstatement, whether due to error or fraud. Our audits included performing procedures to assess the risks of material misstatement of the financial statements, whether due to error or fraud, and performing procedures that respond to those risks. Such procedures included examining, on a test basis, evidence regarding the amounts and disclosures in the financial statements. Our audits also included evaluating the accounting principles used and significant estimates made by management, as well as evaluating the overall presentation of the financial statements. We believe that our audits provide a reasonable basis for our opinion.

/s/ Ernst & Young LLP

We have served as the Corporation's auditor since 1931.

Minneapolis, Minnesota
March 13, 2019

Report of Management on Internal Control over Financial Reporting

Our management is responsible for establishing and maintaining adequate internal control over financial reporting, as such term is defined in Exchange Act Rules 13a-15(f). Under the supervision and with the participation of our management, including our chief executive officer and chief financial officer, we assessed the effectiveness of our internal control over financial reporting as of February 2, 2019, based on the framework in *Internal Control–Integrated Framework (2013)*, issued by the Committee of Sponsoring Organizations of the Treadway Commission (2013 framework). Based on our assessment, we conclude that the Corporation's internal control over financial reporting is effective based on those criteria.

Our internal control over financial reporting as of February 2, 2019, has been audited by Ernst & Young LLP, the independent registered public accounting firm who has also audited our consolidated financial statements, as stated in their report which appears on this page.

/s/ Brian C. Cornell	/s/ Cathy R. Smith
Brian C. Cornell Chairman and Chief Executive Officer March 13, 2019	Cathy R. Smith Executive Vice President and Chief Financial Officer

Report of Independent Registered Public Accounting Firm

To the Shareholders and the Board of Directors of Target Corporation

Opinion on Internal Control over Financial Reporting

We have audited Target Corporation's internal control over financial reporting as of February 2, 2019, based on criteria established in Internal Control–Integrated Framework issued by the Committee of Sponsoring Organizations of the Treadway Commission (2013 framework) (the COSO criteria). In our opinion, Target Corporation (the Corporation) maintained, in all material respects, effective internal control over financial reporting as of February 2, 2019, based on the COSO criteria.

We also have audited, in accordance with the standards of the Public Company Accounting Oversight Board (United States) (PCAOB), the consolidated statements of financial position of the Corporation as of February 2, 2019 and February 3, 2018, the related consolidated statements of operations, comprehensive income, cash flows and shareholders' investment for each of the three years in the period ended February 2, 2019, and the related notes and our report dated March 13, 2019 expressed an unqualified opinion thereon.

Basis for Opinion

The Corporation's management is responsible for maintaining effective internal control over financial reporting and for its assessment of the effectiveness of internal control over financial reporting included in the accompanying Report of Management on Internal Control over Financial Reporting. Our responsibility is to express an opinion on the Corporation's internal control over financial reporting based on our audit. We are a public accounting firm registered with the PCAOB and are required to be independent with respect to the Corporation in accordance with the U.S. federal securities laws and the applicable rules and regulations of the Securities and Exchange Commission and the PCAOB.

We conducted our audit in accordance with the standards of the PCAOB. Those standards require that we plan and perform the audit to obtain reasonable assurance about whether effective internal control over financial reporting was maintained in all material respects.

Our audit included obtaining an understanding of internal control over financial reporting, assessing the risk that a material weakness exists, testing and evaluating the design and operating effectiveness of internal control based on the assessed risk, and performing such other procedures as we considered necessary in the circumstances. We believe that our audit provides a reasonable basis for our opinion.

Definition and Limitations of Internal Control Over Financial Reporting

A company's internal control over financial reporting is a process designed to provide reasonable assurance regarding the reliability of financial reporting and the preparation of financial statements for external purposes in accordance with generally accepted accounting principles. A company's internal control over financial reporting includes those policies and procedures that (1) pertain to the maintenance of records that, in reasonable detail, accurately and fairly reflect the transactions and dispositions of the assets of the company; (2) provide reasonable assurance that transactions are recorded as necessary to permit preparation of financial statements in accordance with generally accepted accounting principles, and that receipts and expenditures of the company are being made only in accordance with authorizations of management and directors of the company; and (3) provide reasonable assurance regarding prevention or timely detection of unauthorized acquisition, use, or disposition of the company's assets that could have a material effect on the financial statements.

Because of its inherent limitations, internal control over financial reporting may not prevent or detect misstatements. Also, projections of any evaluation of effectiveness to future periods are subject to the risk that controls may become inadequate because of changes in conditions, or that the degree of compliance with the policies or procedures may deteriorate.

/s/ Ernst & Young LLP

Minneapolis, Minnesota
March 13, 2019

Consolidated Statements of Operations

(millions, except per share data)	2018	2017 As Adjusted[a]	2016 As Adjusted[a]
Sales	$74,433	$71,786	$69,414
Other revenue	923	928	857
Total revenue	75,356	72,714	70,271
Cost of sales	53,299	51,125	49,145
Selling, general and administrative expenses	15,723	15,140	14,217
Depreciation and amortization (exclusive of depreciation included in cost of sales)	2,224	2,225	2,045
Operating income	4,110	4,224	4,864
Net interest expense	461	653	991
Net other (income)/expense	(27)	(59)	(88)
Earnings from continuing operations before income taxes	3,676	3,630	3,961
Provision for income taxes	746	722	1,295
Net earnings from continuing operations	2,930	2,908	2,666
Discontinued operations, net of tax	7	6	68
Net earnings	$ 2,937	$ 2,914	$ 2,734
Basic earnings per share			
Continuing operations	$ 5.54	$ 5.32	$ 4.61
Discontinued operations	0.01	0.01	0.12
Net earnings per share	$ 5.55	$ 5.32	$ 4.73
Diluted earnings per share			
Continuing operations	$ 5.50	$ 5.29	$ 4.58
Discontinued operations	0.01	0.01	0.12
Net earnings per share	$ 5.51	$ 5.29	$ 4.69
Weighted average common shares outstanding			
Basic	528.6	546.8	577.6
Diluted	533.2	550.3	582.5
Antidilutive shares	—	4.1	0.1

Note: Per share amounts may not foot due to rounding.
See accompanying Notes to Consolidated Financial Statements.
[a]Refer to Note 2 regarding the adoption of new accounting standards for revenue recognition, leases, and pensions.

Consolidated Statements of Comprehensive Income

(millions)	2018	2017 As Adjusted[a]	2016 As Adjusted[a]
Net earnings	$2,937	$ 2,914	$2,734
Other comprehensive (loss)/income, net of tax			
Pension and other benefit liabilities, net of tax	(52)	2	(13)
Currency translation adjustment and cash flow hedges, net of tax	(6)	6	4
Other comprehensive (loss)/income	(58)	8	(9)
Comprehensive income	$2,879	$2,922	$2,725

See accompanying Notes to Consolidated Financial Statements.
[a]Refer to Note 2 regarding the adoption of new accounting standards for revenue recognition, leases, and pensions.

Consolidated Statements of Financial Position

(millions, except footnotes)	February 2, 2019	February 3, 2018 As Adjusted [a]
Assets		
Cash and cash equivalents	$ 1,556	$ 2,643
Inventory	9,497	8,597
Other current assets	1,466	1,300
Total current assets	12,519	12,540
Property and equipment		
Land	6,064	6,095
Buildings and improvements	29,240	28,131
Fixtures and equipment	5,912	5,623
Computer hardware and software	2,544	2,645
Construction-in-progress	460	440
Accumulated depreciation	(18,687)	(18,398)
Property and equipment, net	25,533	24,536
Operating lease assets	1,965	1,884
Other noncurrent assets	1,273	1,343
Total assets	$41,290	$40,303
Liabilities and shareholders' investment		
Accounts payable	$ 9,761	$ 8,677
Accrued and other current liabilities	4,201	4,094
Current portion of long-term debt and other borrowings	1,052	281
Total current liabilities	15,014	13,052
Long-term debt and other borrowings	10,223	11,117
Noncurrent operating lease liabilities	2,004	1,924
Deferred income taxes	972	693
Other noncurrent liabilities	1,780	1,866
Total noncurrent liabilities	14,979	15,600
Shareholders' investment		
Common stock	43	45
Additional paid-in capital	6,042	5,858
Retained earnings	6,017	6,495
Accumulated other comprehensive loss	(805)	(747)
Total shareholders' investment	11,297	11,651
Total liabilities and shareholders' investment	$41,290	$40,303

Common Stock Authorized 6,000,000,000 shares, $0.0833 par value; 517,761,600 shares issued and outstanding at February 2, 2019; 541,681,670 shares issued and outstanding at February 3, 2018.

Preferred Stock Authorized 5,000,000 shares, $0.01 par value; no shares were issued or outstanding at February 2, 2019 or February 3, 2018.

See accompanying Notes to Consolidated Financial Statements.

[a]Refer to Note 2 regarding the adoption of new accounting standards for revenue recognition, leases, and pensions.

Consolidated Statements of Cash Flows

(millions)	2018	2017 As Adjusted[a]	2016 As Adjusted[a]
Operating activities			
Net earnings	$2,937	$2,914	$2,734
Earnings from discontinued operations, net of tax	7	6	68
Net earnings from continuing operations	2,930	2,908	2,666
Adjustments to reconcile net earnings to cash provided by operations:			
Depreciation and amortization	2,474	2,476	2,318
Share-based compensation expense	132	112	113
Deferred income taxes	322	(188)	40
Loss on debt extinguishment	—	123	422
Noncash losses/(gains) and other, net	95	208	(11)
Changes in operating accounts:			
Inventory	(900)	(348)	293
Other assets	(299)	(156)	56
Accounts payable	1,127	1,307	(166)
Accrued and other liabilities	89	419	(394)
Cash provided by operating activities—continuing operations	5,970	6,861	5,337
Cash provided by operating activities—discontinued operations	3	74	107
Cash provided by operations	5,973	6,935	5,444
Investing activities			
Expenditures for property and equipment	(3,516)	(2,533)	(1,547)
Proceeds from disposal of property and equipment	85	31	46
Cash paid for acquisitions, net of cash assumed	—	(518)	—
Other investments	15	(55)	28
Cash required for investing activities	(3,416)	(3,075)	(1,473)
Financing activities			
Additions to long-term debt	—	739	1,977
Reductions of long-term debt	(281)	(2,192)	(2,649)
Dividends paid	(1,335)	(1,338)	(1,348)
Repurchase of stock	(2,124)	(1,046)	(3,706)
Stock option exercises	96	108	221
Cash required for financing activities	(3,644)	(3,729)	(5,505)
Net (decrease)/increase in cash and cash equivalents	(1,087)	131	(1,534)
Cash and cash equivalents at beginning of period	2,643	2,512	4,046
Cash and cash equivalents at end of period	$1,556	$2,643	$2,512
Supplemental information			
Interest paid, net of capitalized interest	$ 476	$ 678	$ 999
Income taxes paid	373	934	1,514
Leased assets obtained in exchange for new finance lease liabilities	130	139	252
Leased assets obtained in exchange for new operating lease liabilities	246	212	148

See accompanying Notes to Consolidated Financial Statements.

[a]Refer to Note 2 regarding the adoption of new accounting standards for revenue recognition, leases, and pensions.

Consolidated Statements of Shareholders' Investment

(millions)	Common Stock Shares	Stock Par Value	Additional Paid-in Capital	Retained Earnings As Adjusted[a]	Accumulated Other Comprehensive (Loss)/Income	Total
January 30, 2016	602.2	$50	$5,348	$8,196	$(629)	$12,965
Adoption of ASC Topic 842 (Leases)	—	—	—	(43)	—	(43)
Net earnings	—	—	—	2,734	—	2,734
Other comprehensive loss	—	—	—	—	(9)	(9)
Dividends declared	—	—	—	(1,359)	—	(1,359)
Repurchase of stock	(50.9)	(4)	—	(3,682)	—	(3,686)
Stock options and awards	4.9	—	313	—	—	313
January 28, 2017	556.2	$46	$ 5,661	$5,846	$(638)	$ 10,915
Net earnings	—	—	—	2,914	—	2,914
Other comprehensive income	—	—	—	—	8	8
Dividends declared	—	—	—	(1,356)	—	(1,356)
Repurchase of stock	(17.6)	(1)	—	(1,026)	—	(1,027)
Stock options and awards	3.1	—	197	—	—	197
Reclassification of tax effects to retained earnings	—	—	—	117	(117)	—
February 3, 2018	541.7	$45	$5,858	$6,495	$ (747)	$ 11,651
Net earnings	—	—	—	2,937	—	2,937
Other comprehensive loss	—	—	—	—	(58)	(58)
Dividends declared	—	—	—	(1,347)	—	(1,347)
Repurchase of stock	(27.2)	(2)	—	(2,068)	—	(2,070)
Stock options and awards	3.3	—	184	—	—	184
February 2, 2019	517.8	$43	$6,042	$6,017	$(805)	$ 11,297

We declared $2.54, $2.46, and $2.36 dividends per share for the twelve months ended February 2, 2019, February 3, 2018, and January 28, 2017, respectively.

See accompanying Notes to Consolidated Financial Statements.

[a]Refer to Note 2 regarding the adoption of new accounting standards for revenue recognition, leases, and pensions.

SUMMARY OF FINANCIAL RATIOS

CHAPTER 3

Debt-to-Assets Ratio

The debt-to-assets ratio reveals the percentage of a company's assets that is financed with borrowed money. The higher the debt-to-assets ratio is, the greater its financial risk, other things being equal. The debt-to-assets ratio is defined as

$$\frac{\text{Total debt}}{\text{Total assets}}$$

Return-on-Assets Ratio

The return-on-assets ratio (ROA) helps measure how well a company is using the assets available to it. The greater the amount of earnings that can be obtained for a given amount of assets, the better a company is doing at utilizing its assets. So, in general, the higher a company's ROA, the better. The ROA ratio is defined as

$$\frac{\text{Net income}}{\text{Total assets}}$$

Return-on-Equity Ratio

The return-on-equity ratio (ROE) helps to measure how much the owners of a company are earning on the money they have invested in the business. The higher a company's ROE, the better. The ROE is defined as

$$\frac{\text{Net income}}{\text{Stockholders' equity}}$$

CHAPTER 4

Gross Margin Percentage

The gross margin percentage helps explain a company's pricing strategy. It compares the amount a company pays for the goods it sells to the price the company is able to charge for those goods. The more a company marks up its goods, the higher the gross margin percentage will be. Specialty shops tend to have higher gross margin percentages, while discount stores tend to have lower percentages. This ratio is sometimes called the gross profit percentage. The gross margin percentage is defined as

$$\frac{\text{Gross margin}}{\text{Net sales}}$$

Return-on-Sales Ratio

The return-on-sales ratio, expressed as a percentage, indicates how much of each dollar of sales remains as profit after all expenses have been deducted. Discount stores do not necessarily have lower return-on-sales percentages than specialty shops. The higher the return-on-sales ratio percentage, the better. The return-on-sales ratio is defined as

$$\frac{\text{Net income}}{\text{Net sales}}$$

CHAPTER 5

Inventory Turnover Ratio and Average Days to Sell Inventory

The inventory turnover ratio and the average days to sell inventory ratio indicate how long a company takes to sell the goods it has in merchandise inventory. The first ratio, inventory turnover, explains how many times per year a company's inventory is sold, or "turned over"; generally, the *higher* this ratio is, the better. Because the inventory turnover ratio is not easily understood by everyone, the second ratio, average days to sell inventory, is often used. However, the average days to sell inventory ratio cannot be computed without first computing the inventory turnover ratio. Generally, the *lower* the average days to sell inventory ratio is, the better. The inventory turnover ratio is defined as

$$\frac{\text{Cost of goods sold}}{\text{Inventory}}$$

The average days to sell inventory ratio is defined as

$$\frac{365 \text{ days}}{\text{Inventory turnover}}$$

A company's operating cycle is the time it takes it to convert cash into inventory, sell the inventory, and collect the cash from accounts receivable that resulted from the sale of the inventory. The time it takes a business to do this can be computed by adding the *average days to sell inventory* and the *average number of days to collect accounts receivable.*

CHAPTER 7

Accounts Receivable Turnover Ratio and Average Number of Days to Collect Receivables

The accounts receivable turnover ratio and the average number of days to collect receivables ratio indicate how long a company takes to collect its accounts receivable. The first ratio, accounts receivable turnover, explains how many times per year a company's receivables are collected, or "turned over"; generally, the *higher* this ratio is, the better. Because the accounts receivable turnover ratios are not easily understood by everyone, the second ratio, average days to collect receivables, is often used. However, the average number of days to collect receivables ratio cannot be computed without first computing the accounts receivable turnover ratio. Generally, the *lower* the average days to collect receivables ratio is, the better. The accounts receivable turnover ratio is defined as

$$\frac{\text{Sales}}{\text{Accounts receivable}}$$

The average number of days to collect receivables ratio is defined as

$$\frac{365 \text{ days}}{\text{Accounts receivable turnover ratio}}$$

CHAPTER 9

Current Ratio

Liquidity refers to how quickly noncash assets can be converted into cash. The more quickly assets can be converted into cash, the more liquid they are and the more useful they are for paying liabilities that must be paid in the near future. The current ratio provides a measure of how much liquidity a company has. Specifically, it compares a company's more liquid assets (current assets) to its current liabilities. Other things being equal, the higher a company's current ratio, the easier it can pay its currently maturing debts. The current ratio is defined as

$$\frac{\text{Current assets}}{\text{Current liabilities}}$$

CHAPTER 10

Times-Interest-Earned Ratio

The times-interest-earned ratio helps assess a company's ability to make interest payments on its debt. Failure to make interest (or principal) payments can cause a company to be forced into bankruptcy. Other things being equal, a company with a higher times interest earned ratio is considered to have lower financial risk than a company with a lower ratio.

EBIT is an acronym for "earnings before interest and taxes." In other words, it is what net earnings would have been if the company had no interest expense or income tax expense. Because net earnings are calculated after interest has been subtracted, a company might have $0 of earnings and still have been able to make its interest payments. Thus, the times-interest-earned ratio is based on EBIT and is defined as

$$\frac{\text{EBIT}}{\text{Interest expense}}$$

Return-on-Assets Ratio (refined)

As discussed in detail in Chapter 3, the return-on-assets ratio (ROA) helps measure how well a company is using the assets available to it. The greater the amount of earnings that can be obtained for a given amount of assets, the better a company is doing at utilizing its assets, so the higher this ratio is, the better. Throughout most of this textbook, ROA has been based on net earnings. However, the use of net earnings creates an ROA that is biased against companies with relatively more debt versus equity financing. Because the ROA ratio is intended to help assess how efficiently a company is using its assets, not how it is financed, the ROA that is used in the business world is often defined as

$$\frac{\text{EBIT}}{\text{Total assets}}$$

CHAPTER 11

Price-Earnings Ratio

The price-earnings ratio (P/E ratio) gives an indication of how optimistic the financial markets are about a company's future earnings. The higher a company's P/E ratio is, the more investors are willing to pay for each dollar of earnings that the company generates. Typically, investors are willing to pay this higher price because they think the company will grow in the future. Lower P/E ratios indicate investors are less optimistic about the company's future growth. The price-earnings ratio is defined as

$$\frac{\text{Market price of one share of stock}}{\text{Earnings per share}}$$

Earnings per Share Ratio

The earnings per share ratio (EPS) provides an indication of the amount of a company's earnings that are attributable to each share of common stock outstanding. Obviously, the higher this ratio is, the better. In companies that have complex equity structures, such as convertible preferred stock and stock option plans, the computation of EPS can be very complex, but in its simplest form, EPS is defined as

$$\frac{\text{Net earnings}}{\text{Outstanding shares of common stock}}$$

APPENDIX D

GENERAL LEDGER CAPSTONE PROJECT (AN ELECTRONIC VERSION OF THIS PROJECT IS AVAILABLE IN *CONNECT*.)

INTRODUCTION AND INSTRUCTIONS

Pacilio Security Services, Inc. provides security services for concerts and other events. The company has been in business for two years. For Years 3 through 11 complete the following:

a. Record the transactions in general journal form. When necessary, round all amounts to the nearest whole dollar.

b. Post the transactions to T-accounts and determine the account balances.

c. Prepare a trial balance.

d. Prepare an income statement, statement of changes in stockholders' equity, balance sheet, and statement of cash flows for Year 3.

e. Prepare the closing entries and post to the T-accounts.

f. Prepare a post-closing trial balance.

To assist you, a beginning of the year trial balance is provided for each year.

YEAR 3 ACCOUNTING PERIOD

Reference: Chapters 1–3

The account balances of Pacilio Security Services, Inc. as of January 1, Year 3, are shown here:

Cash	$8,900
Accounts Receivable	1,500
Supplies	65
Prepaid Rent	800
Land	4,000
Accounts Payable	1,050
Unearned Revenue	200
Salaries Payable	1,200
Notes Payable	2,000
Common Stock	8,000
Retained Earnings	2,815

During Year 3, Pacilio Security Services experienced the following transactions:

1. Paid the salaries payable from Year 2.

2. Paid the balance of $2,000 on the debt owed to the Small Business Government Agency. The loan is interest-free.

3. Performed $32,000 of security services for numerous local events during the year; $21,000 was on account and $11,000 was for cash.

4. On May 1, paid $3,000 for 12 months' rent in advance.

5. Purchased supplies on account for $700.

6. Paid salaries expense for the year of $9,000.

7. Incurred other operating expenses on account, $4,200.

8. On October 1, Year 3, a customer paid $1,200 for services to be provided over the next 12 months.

9. Collected $19,000 of accounts receivable during the year.

10. Paid $5,950 on accounts payable.

11. Paid $1,800 of advertising expenses for the year.

12. Paid a cash dividend to the shareholders of $4,650.

13. The market value of the land was determined to be $5,500 at December 31, Year 3.

Adjustments

14. There was $120 of supplies on hand at the end of the year.

15. Recognized the expired rent.

16. Recognized the earned revenue from Year 2 and transaction no. 8.

17. Accrued salaries were $1,000 at December 31, Year 3.

YEAR 4 ACCOUNTING PERIOD

Reference: Chapter 4

The account balances of Pacilio Security Services, Inc. as of January 1, Year 4, are shown here:

Cash	$12,500
Accounts Receivable	3,500
Supplies	120
Prepaid Rent	1,000
Land	4,000
Unearned Revenue	900
Salaries Payable	1,000
Common Stock	8,000
Retained Earnings	11,220

In Year 4, Pacilio Security Services decided to expand its business to sell security systems and offer 24-hour alarm monitoring services. It plans to phase out its current service of providing security personnel at various events. The following summary transactions occurred during Year 4:

1. Paid the salaries payable from Year 3.

2. Acquired an additional $42,000 cash from the issue of common stock.

3. Rented a larger building on May 1; paid $6,000 for 12 months' rent in advance.

4. Paid $800 cash for supplies to be used over the next several months by the business.

5. Purchased alarm systems for resale at a cost of $12,000. The alarm systems were purchased on account with the terms 2/10, n/30.

6. Returned alarm systems that had a cost of $240.

7. Installed alarm systems during the year for a total sales amount of $20,000. The cost of these systems amounted to $9,440. Sales of $15,000 were on account, while $5,000 were cash sales.

8. Paid the installers and other employees a total of $9,500 in salaries.

9. Sold $36,000 of monitoring services for the year. The services are billed to the customers each month.

10. Paid cash on accounts payable. The payment was made before the discount period expired. At the time of purchase, the inventory had a cost of $8,000.

11. Paid cash to settle additional accounts payable. The payment was made after the discount period expired. At the time of purchase, the inventory had a cost of $2,780.

12. Collected $43,000 of accounts receivable during the year.
13. Performed $12,000 of security services for area events; $9,000 was on account and $3,000 was for cash.
14. Paid advertising cost of $1,620 for the year.
15. Paid $1,100 for utilities expense for the year.
16. Paid a dividend of $12,000 to the shareholders.

Adjustment Information

17. Supplies of $150 were on hand at the end of the year.
18. Recognized the expired rent for the year.
19. Recognized the balance of the unearned revenue; cash was received in Year 3.
20. Accrued salaries at December 31, Year 4, were $1,500.

YEAR 5 ACCOUNTING PERIOD

Reference: Chapter 5

The account balances of Pacilio Security Services, Inc. as of January 1, Year 5, are shown here:

Cash	$62,860
Accounts receivable	20,500
Supplies	150
Prepaid rent	2,000
Merchandise inventory (9 @ $240)	2,160
Land	4,000
Accounts payable	980
Salaries payable	1,500
Common stock	50,000
Retained earnings	39,190

During Year 5, Pacilio Security Services experienced the following transactions:

1. Paid the salaries payable from Year 4.
2. On January 15, purchased 20 standard alarm systems for cash at a cost of $250 each.
3. On February 1, paid the accounts payable of $980, but not within the discount period. (The company uses the gross method.)
4. On March 1, leased a business van. Paid $4,800 for one year's lease in advance.
5. Paid $7,200 on May 1 for one year's rent on the office in advance.
6. Purchased with cash $500 of supplies to be used over the next several months by the business.
7. Purchased with cash another 25 alarm systems on August 1 for resale at a cost of $260 each.
8. On September 5, purchased on account 30 standard alarm systems at a cost of $265 each.
9. Installed 60 standard alarm systems for $33,000. Sales of $22,000 were on account, while $11,000 were cash sales. (*Note:* Be sure to record cost of goods sold using the perpetual FIFO method.)
10. Made a full refund to a dissatisfied customer who returned her alarm system. The sale had been a cash sale for $550 with a cost of $260.
11. Paid installers and other employees a total of $21,000 cash for salaries.
12. Sold $45,000 of monitoring services during the year. The services are billed to the customers each month.
13. Sold an additional monitoring service for $1,200 for one year's service. The customer paid the full amount of $1,200 on October 1.
14. Collected $74,000 of accounts receivable during the year.

15. Paid an additional $6,000 to settle some of the accounts payable.
16. Paid $3,500 of advertising expense during the year.
17. Paid $2,320 of utilities expense for the year.
18. Paid a dividend of $15,000 to the shareholders.

Adjustments

19. There was $200 of supplies on hand at the end of the year.
20. Recognized the expired rent for both the van and the office building for the year.
21. Recognized the revenue earned from transaction 13.
22. Accrued salaries at December 31, Year 5, were $1,000.

YEAR 6 ACCOUNTING PERIOD

Reference: Chapter 6

The account balances of Pacilio Security Services, Inc. as of January 1, Year 6, are shown here:

Cash	$74,210
Accounts Receivable	13,500
Supplies	200
Prepaid Rent	3,200
Merchandise Inventory (24 @ $265; 1 @ $260)	6,620
Land	4,000
Accounts Payable	1,950
Unearned Revenue	900
Salaries Payable	1,000
Common Stock	50,000
Retained Earnings	47,880

During Year 6, Pacilio Security Services experienced the following transactions:

1. Paid the salaries payable from Year 5.
2. On March 1, Year 6, Pacilio established a $100 petty cash fund to handle small expenditures.
3. Paid $4,800 on March 1, Year 6, for a one-year lease on the company van in advance.
4. Paid $7,200 on May 2, Year 6, for one year's office rent in advance.
5. Purchased $400 of supplies on account.
6. Purchased 100 alarm systems for $28,000 cash during the year.
7. Sold 102 alarm systems for $57,120. All sales were on account. (Compute cost of goods sold using the FIFO cost flow method.)
8. Paid $2,100 on accounts payable during the year.
9. Replenished the petty cash fund on August 1. At this time, the petty cash fund had only $7 of currency left. It contained the following receipts: office supplies expense, $23; cutting grass, $55; and miscellaneous expense, $14.
10. Billed $52,000 of monitoring services for the year.
11. Paid installers and other employees a total of $25,000 cash for salaries.
12. Collected $89,300 of accounts receivable during the year.
13. Paid $3,600 of advertising expense during the year.
14. Paid $2,500 of utilities expense for the year.
15. Paid a dividend of $10,000 to the shareholders.

Adjustments

16. There was $160 of supplies on hand at the end of the year.
17. Recognized the expired rent for both the van and the office building for the year. (The rent for both the van and the office remained the same for Year 5 and Year 6.)

18. Recognized the balance of the revenue earned in Year 6 where cash had been collected in Year 5.

19. Accrued salaries at December 31, Year 6, were $1,400.

Special Instructions for Year 6

1. Record the given transactions in general journal form.

2. Post the transactions to the T-accounts.

3. Prepare a bank reconciliation at the end of the year. The following information is available for the bank reconciliation:

   (1) Checks written but not paid by the bank, $8,350.

   (2) A deposit of $6,500 made on December 31, Year 6, had been recorded but was not shown on the bank statement.

   (3) A debit memo for $55 for a new supply of checks. (*Hint:* Use Office Supplies Expense account.)

   (4) A credit memo for $30 for interest earned on the checking account.

   (5) An NSF check for $120.

   (6) The balance shown on the bank statement was $80,822.

4. Record and post any adjustments necessary from the bank reconciliation.

5. Prepare a trial balance.

6. Prepare an income statement, statement of changes in stockholders' equity, balance sheet, and statement of cash flows.

7. Close the temporary accounts to retained earnings.

8. Post the closing entries to the T-accounts and prepare a post-closing trial balance.

YEAR 7 ACCOUNTING PERIOD

Reference: Chapter 7

The account balances of Pacilio Security Services, Inc. as of January 1, Year 7, are shown here:

Cash	$78,972
Petty Cash	100
Accounts Receivable	33,440
Supplies	160
Prepaid Rent	3,200
Merchandise Inventory (23 @ $280)	6,440
Land	4,000
Accounts Payable	250
Salaries Payable	1,400
Common Stock	50,000
Retained Earnings	74,662

During Year 7, Pacilio Security Services experienced the following transactions:

1. Paid the salaries payable from Year 6.

2. Paid $4,800 on March 1, Year 7, for one year's lease in advance on the company van.

3. Paid $8,400 on May 2, Year 7, for one year's office rent in advance.

4. Purchased $550 of supplies on account.

5. Paid cash to purchase 105 alarm systems at a cost of $285 each.

6. Pacilio has noticed its accounts receivable balance is growing more than desired and some collection problems exist. It appears that uncollectible accounts expense is approximately 3 percent of total credit sales. Pacilio has decided it will, starting this year, adopt the allowance method of accounting for uncollectible accounts. It will record an adjusting entry to recognize the estimate at the end of the year.

7. In trying to collect several of its delinquent accounts, Pacilio has learned that these customers have either declared bankruptcy or moved and left no forwarding address. These uncollectible accounts amount to $1,900.

8. Sold 110 alarm systems for $63,800. All sales were on account. (Compute cost of goods sold using the FIFO cost flow method.)

9. Paid the balance of the accounts payable.

10. Pacilio began accepting credit cards for some of its monitoring service sales. The credit card company charges a fee of 4 percent. Total monitoring services for the year were $68,000. Pacilio accepted credit cards for $24,000 of this amount. The other $44,000 was sales on account.

11. On July 1, Year 7, Pacilio replenished the petty cash fund. The fund contained $21 of currency and receipts of $50 for yard mowing, $22 for office supplies expense, and $9 for miscellaneous expenses.

12. Collected the amount due from the credit card company.

13. Paid installers and other employees a total of $45,000 cash for salaries.

14. Collected $116,800 of accounts receivable during the year.

15. Paid $9,500 of advertising expense during the year.

16. Paid $5,200 of utilities expense for the year.

17. Paid a dividend of $20,000 to the shareholders.

Adjustments

18. There was $250 of supplies on hand at the end of the year.

19. Recognized the expired rent for both the van and the office for the year.

20. Recognized the uncollectible accounts expense for the year using the allowance method.

21. Accrued salaries at December 31, Year 7, were $2,100.

YEAR 8 ACCOUNTING PERIOD

Reference: Chapter 8

The account balances of Pacilio Security Services, Inc. as of January 1, Year 8, are shown here:

Cash	$93,708
Petty cash	100
Accounts receivable	22,540
Allowance for doubtful accounts	1,334
Supplies	250
Prepaid rent	3,600
Merchandise inventory (18 @ $285)	5,130
Land	4,000
Salaries payable	2,100
Common stock	50,000
Retained earnings	75,894

During Year 8, Pacillo Security Services experienced the following transactions:

1. Paid the salaries payable from Year 7.

2. Purchased equipment and a van for a lump sum of $36,000 cash on January 2, Year 8. The equipment was appraised for $10,000 and the van was appraised for $30,000.

3. Paid $9,000 on May 1, Year 8, for one year's office rent in advance.

4. Purchased $300 of supplies on account.

5. Purchased 120 alarm systems at a cost of $280 each. Paid cash for the purchase.

6. After numerous attempts to collect from customers, wrote off $2,350 of uncollectible accounts receivable.

7. Sold 115 alarm systems for $580 each. All sales were on account. (Be sure to compute cost of goods sold using the FIFO cost flow method)

8. Billed $86,000 of monitoring services for the year. Credit card sales amounted to $36,000, and the credit card company charged a 4 percent fee. The remaining $50,000 were sales on account.

9. Replenished the petty cash fund on June 30. The fund had $12 cash and receipts of $45 for yard mowing, $28 for office supplies expense, and $11 for miscellaneous expenses.

10. Collected the amount due from the credit card company.

11. Paid installers and other employees a total of $52,000 cash for salaries.

12. Collected $115,500 of accounts receivable during the year.

13. Paid $12,500 of advertising expense during the year.

14. Paid $6,800 of utilities expense for the year.

15. Sold the land, which was originally purchased for $12,000.

16. Paid the accounts payable.

17. Paid a dividend of $10,000 to the shareholders.

Adjustments

18. Determined that $180 of supplies were on hand at the end of the year.

19. Recognized the expired rent for both the old van and the office building for the year. The lease on the van was not renewed. Rent paid on March 1, Year 7, for the van was $4,800.

20. Recognized uncollectible accounts expense for the year using the allowance method. Pacilio estimates that 3 percent of sales on account will not be collected.

21. Recognized depreciation expense on the equipment and the van. The equipment has a five-year life and a $2,000 salvage value. The van has a four-year life and a $6,000 salvage value. The company uses double-declining-balance for the van and straight-line for the equipment.

22. Accrued salaries at December 31, Year 8, were $1,500.

YEAR 9 ACCOUNTING PERIOD

Reference: Chapter 9

The account balances of Pacilio Security Services, Inc. as of January 1, Year 9, are shown here:

Cash	$93,380
Petty Cash	100
Accounts receivable	21,390
Allowance for doubtful accounts	2,485
Supplies	180
Prepaid rent	3,000
Merchandise inventory (23 @ $280)	6,440
Equipment	9,000
Van	27,000
Accumulated depreciation	14,900
Salaries payable	1,500
Common stock	50,000
Retained earnings	91,605

During Year 9, Pacilio Security Services experienced the following transactions:

1. Paid the salaries payable from Year 8.

2. Paid $9,000 on May 2, Year 9, for one year's office rent in advance.

3. Purchased $425 of supplies on account.

4. Purchased 145 alarm systems at a cost of $290 each. Paid cash for the purchase.

5. After numerous attempts to collect from customers, wrote off $2,060 of uncollectible accounts receivable.

6. Sold 130 alarm systems for $580 each plus sales tax of 5 percent. All sales were on account. (Be sure to compute cost of goods sold using the FIFO cost flow method.)

7. Billed $107,000 of monitoring services for the year. Credit card sales amounted to $42,000, and the credit card company charged a 4 percent fee. The remaining $65,000 were sales on account. Sales tax is not charged on this service.

8. Replenished the petty cash fund on June 30. The fund had $5 cash and has receipts of $60 for yard mowing, $15 for office supplies expense, and $17 for miscellaneous expenses.

9. Collected the amount due from the credit card company.

10. Paid the sales tax collected on $69,600 of the alarm sales.

11. Paid installers and other employees a total of $65,000 for salaries for the year. Assume the Social Security tax rate is 6 percent and the Medicare tax rate is 1.5 percent. Federal income taxes withheld amounted to $7,500. Cash was paid for the net amount of salaries due.

12. Pacilio now offers a one-year warranty on its alarm systems. Paid $1,950 in warranty repairs during the year.

13. On September 1, borrowed $12,000 from State Bank. The note had an 8 percent interest rate and a one-year term to maturity.

14. Collected $136,100 of accounts receivable during the year.

15. Paid $15,000 of advertising expense during the year.

16. Paid $7,200 of utilities expense for the year.

17. Paid the payroll taxes, both the amounts withheld from the salaries plus the employer share of Social Security tax and Medicare tax, on $60,000 of the salaries plus $7,000 of the federal income tax that was withheld. (Unemployment taxes were not paid at this time.)

18. Paid the accounts payable.

19. Paid a dividend of $10,000 to the shareholders.

Adjustments

20. There was $165 of supplies on hand at the end of the year.

21. Recognized the expired rent for the office building for the year.

22. Recognized uncollectible accounts expense for the year using the allowance method. The company revised its estimate of uncollectible accounts based on prior years' experience. This year, Pacilio estimates that 2.75 percent of sales on account will not be collected.

23. Recognized depreciation expense on the equipment and the van. The equipment has a five-year life and a $2,000 salvage value. The van has a four-year life and a $6,000 salvage value. The company uses double-declining-balance for the van and straight-line for the equipment. (A full year's depreciation was taken in Year 8, the year of acquisition.)

24. The alarm systems sold in transaction 6 were covered with a one-year warranty. Pacilio estimated that the warranty cost would be 3 percent of alarm sales.

25. Recognized the accrued interest on the note payable at December 31, Year 9.

26. The unemployment tax on salaries has not been paid. Recorded the accrued unemployment tax on the salaries for the year. The unemployment tax rate is 4.5 percent. ($14,000 of salaries is subject to this tax.)

27. Recognized the employer Social Security and Medicare payroll tax that has not been paid on $5,000 of salaries expense.

YEAR 10 ACCOUNTING PERIOD

Reference: Chapter 10

The account balances of Pacilio Security Services, Inc. as of January 1, Year 10, are shown here:

Cash	$122,475
Petty cash	100
Accounts receivable	27,400
Allowance for doubtful accounts	4,390
Supplies	165
Prepaid rent	3,000
Merchandise inventory (38 @ $290)	11,020
Equipment	9,000
Van	27,000
Accumulated depreciation	23,050
Sales tax payable	290
Employee income tax payable	500
FICA—Social Security tax payable	600
FICA—Medicare tax payable	150
Warranty payable	312
Unemployment tax payable	630
Interest payable	320
Notes payable	12,000
Common stock	50,000
Retained earnings	107,918

During Year 10, Pacilio Security Services experienced the following transactions:

1. Paid the sales tax payable from Year 9.
2. Paid the balance of the payroll liabilities due for Year 9 (federal income tax, FICA taxes, and unemployment taxes).
3. On January 1, Year 10, purchased land and a building for $150,000. The building was appraised at $125,000 and the land at $25,000. Pacilio paid $50,000 cash and financed the balance. The balance was financed with a 10-year installment note. The note had an interest rate of 7 percent and annual payments of $14,238 due on the last day of the year.
4. On January 1, Year 10, issued $50,000 of 6 percent, five year bonds. The bonds were issued at 98.
5. Purchase $660 of supplies on account.
6. Purchased 170 alarm systems at a cost of $300. Cash was paid for the purchase.
7. After numerous attempts to collect from customers, wrote off $2,450 of uncollectible accounts receivable.
8. Sold 160 alarm systems for $580 each plus sales tax of 5 percent. All sales were on account. (Be sure to compute cost of goods sold using the FIFO cost flow method.)
9. Billed $120,000 of monitoring services for the year. Credit card sales amounted to $36,000, and the credit card company charged a 4 percent fee. The remaining $84,000 were sales on account. Sales tax is not charged on this service.
10. Replenished the petty cash fund on June 30. The fund had $11 cash and receipts of $65 for yard mowing and $24 for office supplies expense.
11. Collected the amount due from the credit card company.
12. Paid the sales tax collected on $85,000 of the alarm sales.
13. Collected $167,000 of accounts receivable during the year.
14. Paid installers and other employees a total of $82,000 for salaries for the year. Assume the Social Security tax rate is 6 percent and the Medicare tax rate is 1.5 percent. Federal income taxes withheld amounted to $9,600. The net amount of salaries was paid in cash.
15. Paid $1,250 in warranty repairs during the year.
16. On September 1, paid the note and interest owed to State Bank.
17. Paid $18,000 of advertising expense during the year.
18. Paid $5,600 of utilities expense for the year.
19. Paid the payroll liabilities, both the amounts withheld from the salaries plus the employer share of Social Security tax and Medicare tax, on $75,000 of the salaries plus $8,600 of the federal income tax that was withheld. (Disregard unemployment taxes in this entry.)

20. Paid the accounts payable.
21. Paid bond interest and amortized the discount.
22. Paid the annual installment on the amortized note.
23. Paid a dividend of $10,000 to the shareholders.

Adjustments

24. There was $210 of supplies on hand at the end of the year.
25. Recognized the expired rent for the office building for the year.
26. Recognized the uncollectible accounts expense for the year using the allowance method. Pacilio now estimates that 1.5 percent of sales on account will not be collected.
27. Recognized depreciation expense on the equipment, van, and building. The equipment has a 5-year life and a $2,000 salvage value. The van has a 4-year life and a $6,000 salvage value. The building has a 40-year life and a $10,000 salvage value. The company uses double-declining-balance for the van and straight-line for the equipment and the building. The equipment and van were purchased in Year 8 and a full year of depreciation was taken for both in Year 8.
28. The alarms systems sold in transaction 8 were covered with a one-year warranty. Pacilio estimated that the warranty cost would be 2 percent of alarm sales.
29. The unemployment tax on the three employees has not been paid. Record the accrued unemployment tax on the salaries for the year. The unemployment tax rate is 4.5 percent and gross wages for all employees exceeded $7,000.
30. Recognized the employer Social Security and Medicare payroll tax that has not been paid on $7,000 of salaries expense.

YEAR 11 ACCOUNTING PERIOD

Reference: Chapter 11

The account balances of Pacilio Security Services, Inc. as of January 1, Year 11, are shown here:

Cash	$113,718
Petty cash	100
Accounts receivable	39,390
Allowance for doubtful accounts	4,662
Supplies	210
Merchandise inventory (48 @ $300)	14,400
Equipment	9,000
Van	27,000
Building	125,000
Accumulated depreciation	28,075
Land	25,000
Sales tax payable	390
Employee income tax payable	1,000
FICA—Social Security tax payable	840
FICA—Medicare tax payable	210
Warranty payable	918
Unemployment tax payable	945
Notes payable—Building	92,762
Bonds payable	50,000
Discount on bonds payable	800
Common stock	50,000
Retained earnings	124,816

During Year 11, Pacilio Security Services experienced the following transactions:

1. Paid the sales tax payable from Year 10.
2. Paid the balance of the payroll liabilities due for Year 10 (federal income tax, FICA taxes, and unemployment taxes).
3. Issued 5,000 additional shares of the $5 par value common stock for $8 per share and 1,000 shares of $50 stated value, 5 percent cumulative preferred stock for $52 per share.

4. Purchased $500 of supplies on account.

5. Purchased 190 alarm systems at a cost of $310. Cash was paid for the purchase.

6. After numerous attempts to collect from customers, wrote off $3,670 of uncollectible accounts receivable.

7. Sold 210 alarm systems for $600 each plus sales tax of 5 percent. All sales were on account. (Be sure to compute cost of goods sold using the FIFO cost flow method.)

8. Billed $125,000 of monitoring services for the year. Credit card sales amounted to $58,000, and the credit card company charged a 4 percent fee. The remaining $67,000 were sales on account. Sales tax is not charged on this service.

9. Replenished the petty cash fund on June 30. The fund had $10 cash and receipts of $75 for yard mowing and $15 for office supplies expense.

10. Collected the amount due from the credit card company.

11. Paid the sales tax collected on $105,000 of the alarm sales.

12. Collected $198,000 of accounts receivable during the year.

13. Paid installers and other employees a total of $96,000 for salaries for the year. Assume the Social Security tax rate is 6 percent and the Medicare tax rate is 1.5 percent. Federal income taxes withheld amounted to $10,600. No employee exceeded $110,000 in total wages. The net salaries were paid in cash.

14. On October 1, declared a dividend on the preferred stock and a $1 per share dividend on the common stock to be paid to shareholders of record on October 15, payable on November 1, Year 11.

15. Paid $1,625 in warranty repairs during the year.

16. On November 1, Year 11, paid the dividends that had been previously declared.

17. Paid $18,500 of advertising expense during the year.

18. Paid $6,100 of utilities expense for the year.

19. Paid the payroll liabilities, both the amounts withheld from the salaries plus the employer share of Social Security tax and Medicare tax, on $88,000 of the salaries plus $9,200 of the federal income tax that was withheld.

20. Paid the accounts payable.

21. Paid bond interest and amortized the discount. The bond was issued in Year 10 and pays interest at 6 percent.

22. Paid the annual installment of $14,238 on the amortized note. The interest rate for the note is 7 percent.

Adjustments

23. There was $190 of supplies on hand at the end of the year.

24. Recognized the uncollectible accounts expense for the year using the allowance method. Pacilio now estimates that 1 percent of sales on account will not be collected.

25. Recognized depreciation expense on the equipment, van, and building. The equipment, purchased in Year 8, has a 5-year life and a $2,000 salvage value. The van has a 4-year life and a $6,000 salvage value. The building has a 40-year life and a $10,000 salvage value. The company uses straight-line for the equipment and the building. The van is fully depreciated.

26. The alarm systems sold in transaction 7 were covered with a one-year warranty. Pacilio estimated that the warranty cost would be 2 percent of alarm sales.

27. The unemployment tax on the three employees has not been paid. Record the accrued unemployment tax on the salaries for the year. The unemployment tax rate is 4.5 percent and gross wages for all three employees exceeded $7,000.

28. Recognized the employer Social Security and Medicare payroll tax that has not been paid on $8,000 of salaries expense.

CAPSTONE FINANCIAL STATEMENT ANALYSIS AND ANNUAL REPORT PROJECTS

ANNUAL REPORT PROJECT FOR THE TARGET CORPORATION (OBTAIN **TARGET CORPORATION'S** ANNUAL REPORT FOR ITS 2018 FISCAL YEAR (YEAR ENDED FEBRUARY 2, 2019) AT HTTP:// INVESTORS.TARGET.COM).

Target's 2016, 2017, and 2018 Statements of Operations and Statements of Financial Position have been loaded in Excel spreadsheets and are available in the *Connect* library. The statements in the spreadsheets have been revised to better reflect the format and wording used in the course textbook. The Excel spreadsheets provide a starting point for the vertical and horizontal analysis required in the project.

Please note: All references to the company's year-end data pertain to the fiscal year-end. For example, the company's 2018 financial statements are dated February 2, 2019, which is the company's fiscal closing date. Likewise, the 2017 financial statements apply to the fiscal year ending February 3, 2018. Also, Target reports "Sales" and "Total revenue" on it earnings statements. For the sake of simplicity, for this project use the "Total revenue" amounts anytime an answer requires the use of "Sales." For example, when computing the gross margin percentage.

Company Overview and Management's Discussion and Analysis

The annual report for Target Corporation opens with a general description of business operations, risk factors, stock market registration, and selected financial data. This is followed by Management's Discussion and Analysis of Financial Condition, in which management talks about financial results, including segment results, liquidity, and other matters deemed necessary to provide adequate disclosure to users of the report. Refer to these items to answer Questions 1–6.

1. How many employees did Target have in 2018?
2. Identify at least five risk factors for Target.
3. On what stock market exchange is the company's stock traded? What is Target's symbol?
4. Who operates the pharmacies located in Target's stores?
5. When, and in what state, was Target incorporated?
6. Target provides information about its capital expenditures related to three major categories: existing stores, new stores, and technology and supply chain. What percentage of capital expenditures were spent on each category in 2018 and in 2016? What has been the trend in Target's capital expenditures over the past three years?

Report of Independent Registered Public Accounting Firm on Consolidated Financial Statements (Auditors)

7. What is the name of the company's independent auditors?
8. Who is responsible for the financial statements?
9. What is the outside auditors' responsibility?

10. What type of opinion did the independent auditors issue on the financial statements (unqualified, qualified, adverse, or disclaimer)? What does this opinion mean?

11. The auditors' report indicates the audit was concerned with material misstatements rather than absolute accuracy in the financial statements. What does "material" mean?

Income Statement—Vertical Analysis

12. Using Excel, compute common-size income statements for all three fiscal years. In common-size income statements, total revenue is 100 percent and every other number is a percentage of total revenue. Attach the spreadsheet to the end of this project. (To help you get started, you can find Target's financial statements in Excel format in *Connect*. The financial statements have been slightly reformatted to conform to the multistep income statement format utilized throughout the textbook.)

13. Using the common-size income statements, identify the significant trends.

14. What was the gross margin (gross profit) and the gross margin percentage for fiscal years 2018, 2017, and 2016?

15. If the gross margin percentage changed over the three-year period, what caused the change? (*Hint*: Changes in either the numerator or denominator reveal what caused the change in the gross margin percentage.)

16. What was the return on sales percentage for fiscal years 2018, 2017, and 2016? What do these ratios indicate about Target?

Income Statement—Horizontal Analysis

17. Using Excel, compute annual changes for each line item on the income statement. For each of the two most recent years, insert a column for changes in absolute dollars and insert another column for the percentage changes. Attach the spreadsheet to the end of this project. (You can find Target's financial statements in Excel format in *Connect*.)

18. What were the absolute dollar and the percentage changes in revenues between fiscal years 2018 and 2017 and between 2017 and 2016?

19. Describe the trend in revenues. Be specific (e.g., slight/steady/drastic increase or decrease each year, or fluctuating with an initial modest/significant increase or decrease followed by a modest/significant increase or decrease, etc.) to precisely describe the company's situation.

20. What were the absolute dollar and the percentage changes in cost of sales (cost of goods sold) between fiscal years 2018 and 2017 and between 2017 and 2016?

21. Describe the trend in cost of sales (cost of goods sold). Be specific (e.g., slight/steady/ drastic increase or decrease each year, or fluctuating with an initial modest/significant increase or decrease followed by a modest/significant increase or decrease, etc.) to precisely describe the company's situation.

22. What were the absolute dollar and the percentage changes in selling, general, and administrative expenses (operating expenses) between fiscal years 2018 and 2017 and between 2017 and 2016?

23. Describe the trend in selling, general, and administrative expenses. Be specific (e.g., slight/steady/drastic increase or decrease each year, or fluctuating with an initial modest/ significant increase or decrease followed by a modest/significant increase or decrease, etc.) to precisely describe the company's situation.

24. What were the absolute dollar and the percentage changes in net income from fiscal years 2017 to 2018 and 2016 to 2017?

25. How would you describe the trend for net income? Be specific (e.g., slight/steady/drastic increase or decrease each year, or fluctuating with an initial modest/significant increase or decrease followed by a modest/significant increase or decrease, etc.) to precisely describe the company's situation. Do you expect the trend to continue?

26. Which items had the largest percentage change from 2016 through 2018, revenues or expenses (such as selling, general, and administrative expenses or cost of sales)?

27. Summarize what is causing the changes in net income from fiscal years 2016 to 2017 and 2017 to 2018 based on the percentages computed in Questions 18 through 26. Do you expect the trend to continue?

Balance Sheet—Vertical Analysis

28. Using Excel, compute common-size balance sheets for the years ended February 2, 2019, and February 3, 2018. In common-size balance sheets, total assets is 100 percent and every other number is a percentage of total assets. Attach the spreadsheet to the end of this project. (You can find Target's financial statements in Excel format in *Connect*.)

29. Current assets constituted what percentage of total assets at February 2, 2019, and February 3, 2018? Which current asset had the largest balance at each fiscal year-end?

30. Long-term assets constituted what percentage of total assets at February 2, 2019, and February 3, 2018? (*Note:* solutions for percentages calculated for items 29 and 30 should total 100 percent.) Which long-term asset had the largest balance at each fiscal year-end?

31. Which category of assets (single line item) on the balance sheet is the largest as of February 3, 2018? Explain why a simple comparison of the percentage amounts for each asset line may lead to misleading results for answering the question, "Which category is largest?"

32. Current liabilities constituted what percentage of total assets at February 2, 2019, and February 3, 2018? Which long-term liability had the largest balance at each fiscal year-end?

33. Long-term liabilities constituted what percentage of total assets at February 2, 2019, and February 3, 2018? Which long-term liability had the largest balance at each fiscal year-end?

34. Calculate the ratio of stockholders' equity to total assets on February 2, 2019, and February 3, 2018. Identify whether Target finances its assets mostly with debt or equity.

Balance Sheet—Horizontal Analysis

35. Using Excel, compute annual changes for each line item on the balance sheet. Insert a column for changes in absolute dollars and insert another column for the percentage changes. Attach the spreadsheet to the end of this project. (You can find Target's financial statements in Excel format in *Connect*.)

36. Which liability account had the greatest change from 2017 to 2018 in terms of (a) absolute dollars, and (b) percentage? Were the changes increases or decreases?

37. What was the absolute dollar and the percentage change between the February 2, 2019, and February 3, 2018, balances for inventory? Was the change an increase or decrease? What line item (account) on the income statement is directly related to inventory? Did this account change in a similar direction as inventory?

38. Compared to the February 3, 2018, balances, did the amounts reported for the following long-term assets increase or decrease? By how much? Include dollar amounts for each item.

	Year Ended February 2, 2019	
	Dollar Amount	Increase or Decrease
Property, plant, and equipment, net		
Other noncurrent assets		
Total long-term assets		

What line item on the income statement is directly related to property, plant, and equipment? Did this account change in a similar direction as property, plant, and equipment?

39. What were the absolute dollar and the percentage changes of long-term liabilities from February 2, 2019, to February 3, 2018? Were the changes increases or decreases? What line item (account) on the income statement is closely related to the long-term liabilities? Did this account change in the same direction as long-term liabilities?

40. What was the amount of the change in the balance in retained earnings between February 2, 2019, and February 3, 2018? What caused this change?

Balance Sheet—Ratio Analysis

41. Compute the current ratio at February 2, 2019, and February 3, 2018. What does this ratio indicate about Target?

42. Calculate the debt-to-assets ratios for the years ended February 2, 2019, and February 3, 2018. In which year did Target appear to have the highest financial risk?

43. Calculate the inventory turnover ratios and the average number of days to sell inventory for the years ended February 2, 2019, and February 3, 2018. In which year was the turnover and days to sell inventory more favorable?

Balance Sheet—Stockholders' Equity Section

44. Does the company's common stock have a par value? If so, how much was the par value per share?

45. How many shares of common stock were issued as of February 2, 2019, and February 3, 2018?

46. How many shares of treasury stock did the company have as of February 2, 2019, and February 3, 2018? How were the treasury stock purchases reflected on the statement of cash flows? Include the type of cash flow activity.

47. What percentage of stockholders' equity do the following items represent at each year-end (February 2, 2019, and February 3, 2018)?

	February 2, 2019	February 3, 2018
Total paid-in capital	%	%
Retained earnings		
Other items	100%	100%

Statement of Cash Flows

48. Does Target report cash flows from operating activities using the direct or the indirect method? Describe how you can tell.

49. What was the dollar amount of the increase or decrease in cash and cash equivalents for the fiscal years 2018, 2017, and 2016?

50. Does the ending balance of cash and cash equivalents agree with the amount reported on the balance sheet for years ended February 2, 2019, and February 3, 2018?

	February 2, 2019	February 3, 2018
Balance sheet	$	$
Statement of cash flows		

51. Identify the four largest individual cash flow items (inflows or outflows) for the year ended February 2, 2019.

52. On which statement(s) would you expect to find information regarding the declaration and payment of dividends? What amount of dividends did Target pay in 2018? What amount of dividends did Target declare in 2018? Briefly explain why these amounts are not the same.

Notes to the Financial Statements

53. In your own words, briefly summarize two significant accounting policies.

54. When does Target recognize the revenue earned from the sale and use of "gift cards"?

55. While there are Target-brand credit cards, Target does not actually own or administer them. Who does, and how much did Target earn in 2018 and 2017 from Target-branded credit cards?

56. Using the following schedule, identify which accounts on the balance sheet and income statement are affected by a company's inventory cost flow assumption. Also, identify the effects that the three inventory cost flow assumptions, FIFO, weighted-average, and LIFO have on the amounts reported on the balance sheet and income statement. Specifically, identify which cost flow assumption results in the highest, lowest, and middle dollar amount that is reported in the relevant account on each statement. Assume that prices are rising.

	Effect of Cost Flow Assumptions		
Account Affected	**FIFO**	**AVG**	**LIFO**
1. Balance Sheet:			
2. Income Statement:			

57. What inventory cost flow method does Target use?

58. What are the estimated useful lives of the company's depreciable assets?

59. Using the following schedule, identify which accounts on the balance sheet and income statement are affected, given the two types of depreciation methods a company may use (accelerated versus straight-line). Also, assuming it is the first year a depreciable asset is used, identify the effects that the two depreciation methods have on the amounts reported on the balance sheet and income statement. Specifically, identify which method results in the highest dollar amount reported and which results in the lowest.

	Effect of Depreciation Methods	
Account Affected	**Accelerated**	**Straight-Line**
1. Balance Sheet:		
2. Income Statement:		

60. What method of depreciation does Target use?

61. Did the balance in the goodwill account increase or decrease? Speculate as to what caused this change.

62. In addition to goodwill, what kinds of intangible assets does the company have? What are their estimated lives?

63. Identify three different accrued expenses.

64. Identify two kinds of commitments and contingencies.

65. What is the amount of available unsecured revolving credit? What was the balance outstanding at the end of each fiscal year?

66. What is the amount of total long-term borrowings at February 2, 2019? What was the weighted-average interest rate on Target's notes payable and debentures for 2018? Other than "long-term debt and other borrowings," what are the other long-term liability items reported on the balance sheet?

Performance Measures

67. Compute the return-on-assets ratio (use net income rather than EBIT in the numerator) for the years ended February 2, 2019, and February 3, 2018.

68. Compute the return-on-equity ratio for the years ended February 2, 2019, and February 3, 2018.

69. Were the return-on-equity ratios greater or lesser than the return-on-assets ratios? Explain why.

70. What were Target's basic earnings per share (EPS) for the years ended February 2, 2019, and February 3, 2018? Identify what caused the ratio to change.

FINANCIAL STATEMENTS PROJECT (SELECTION OF COMPANY TO BE DECIDED BY INSTRUCTOR)

Date Due: _____

Required

Based on the annual report of the company you are reviewing, answer the following questions. If you cannot answer a particular question, briefly explain why. If the question is not applicable to your company's financial statements, answer "N/A."

Show all necessary computations in good form. Label all numbers in your computations. If relevant, reference your answers to page(s) in the annual report.

"Current year" means the most recent fiscal year in the company's annual report. "Prior year" means the fiscal year immediately preceding the current year.

1. What products or services does the company sell? Be specific.

2. What do you think the outlook is for these products or services? Why do you think so?

3. By what percentage have sales increased or decreased in each of the last two fiscal years?

4. If the company reported sales by segments, which segment had the largest percentage of total sales? Which segment had the smallest percentage of total sales? **Show computations of the relevant percentages.**

   Largest segment _____ Percentage of total sales _____

   Smallest segment _____ Percentage of total sales _____

5. What is net income for the current year? _____

6. Did the current year's net income increase or decrease since the prior year? By how much? What caused the change?

7. If the company reported earnings by segments, which segment had the largest percentage of total earnings? Which segment had the smallest percentage of total earnings? **Show computations of the relevant percentages.**

   Largest segment _____ Percentage of total earnings _____

   Smallest segment _____ Percentage of total earnings _____

8. Did the company report any special, unusual, or otherwise nonroutine items in either current or prior year net income? If so, explain the item(s).

9. For the current year, how does net income compare to net cash provided (used) by operating activities?

10. For the current year, what one or two items were most responsible for the difference between net income and net cash provided (used) by operating activities?

11. Did the company pay cash dividends during the current year? If so, how much were they?

12. If the company paid cash dividends, what percentage of net income were the cash dividends? If the company did not pay cash dividends, why do you think it did not?

13. Which of the following is the company's largest asset category: accounts receivable, inventory, or land? What is the amount of that asset category?

14. If the company reported assets by segments, which segment had the largest percentage of total assets? Which segment had the smallest percentage of total assets? **Show computations of the relevant percentages.**

   Largest segment _____ Percentage of total assets _____

   Smallest segment _____ Percentage of total assets _____

15. How much **cash** did the company invest in property, plant, and equipment during the current year?

16. Which inventory method(s) did the company use?

17. Which depreciation method(s) did the company use?
18. If the company has any intangible assets, what kind are they?
19. Did the company report any contingent liabilities ("contingencies")? If so, briefly explain.
20. Does the company have any preferred stock authorized? If so, how many shares were authorized?
21. Does the company's common stock have a par value? If so, what was it?
22. In what price range was the company's common stock trading during the last quarter of the current year?
23. What was the market price of the company's common stock on DD/MM/Year?
24. Where (on what stock exchange) is the company's stock traded?
25. Who was the company's independent auditor?
26. Develop one question about the company's financial report that you do not know how to answer.
27. Compute the following ratios for the current year and the prior year. Show the appropriate formulas in the first column. Show all supporting computations in the second and third columns.

Ratio	Current Year	Prior Year
Gross Profit Formula:		
Inventory Turnover Formula:		
Current Ratio Formula:		
Debt to Equity Formula:		
Return on Assets Formula:		
Return on Equity Formula:		

ACCOUNTING FOR INVESTMENT SECURITIES

TYPES OF INVESTMENT SECURITIES

A financial investment occurs when one entity provides assets or services to another entity in exchange for a certificate known as a *security.* The entity that provides the assets and receives the security certificate is called the **investor.** The entity that receives the assets or services and gives the security certificate is called the **investee.** This appendix discusses accounting practices that apply to securities held by investors.

There are two primary types of investment securities: debt securities and equity securities. An investor receives a **debt security** when assets *are loaned* to the investee. In general, a debt security describes the investee's obligation to return the assets and to pay interest for the use of the assets. Common types of debt securities include bonds, notes, certificates of deposit, and commercial paper.

An **equity security** is obtained when an investor acquires an *ownership interest* in the investee. An equity security usually describes the rights of ownership, including the right to influence the operations of the investee and to share in profits or losses that accrue from those operations. The most common types of equity securities are common stock and preferred stock. In summary, **investment securities** are certificates that describe the rights and privileges that investors receive when they loan or give assets or services to investees.

Transactions between the investor and the investee constitute the **primary securities market.** There is a **secondary securities market** in which investors exchange (buy and sell) investment securities with other investors. Securities that regularly trade in established secondary markets are called **marketable securities.** Investee companies are affected by secondary-market transactions only to the extent that their obligations are transferred to a different party. For example, assume that Tom Williams (investor) loans assets to American Can Company (investee). Williams receives a bond (investment security) from American Can that describes American Can's obligation to return assets and pay interest to Williams. This exchange represents a primary securities market transaction. Now assume that, in a secondary-market transaction, Williams sells his investment security (bond) to Tina Tucker. American Can Company is affected by this transaction only to the extent that the company's obligation transfers from Williams to Tucker. In other words, American Can's obligation to repay principal and interest does not change. The only thing that changes is the party to whom American Can makes payments. *An investee's financial statements are not affected when the securities it has issued to an investor are traded in the secondary market.*

The **fair value,** also called **market value,** is the amount that the investor would receive if the securities were sold in an orderly transaction. More specifically, the fair value is based on the amount that would be collected (an exit value) from the sale of an asset as opposed to the cost necessary to acquire a comparable asset. For a more detailed definition of fair value, see *FASB Accounting Standards Codification Topic 820,* "Fair Value Measurements and Disclosures." Whether securities are reported at fair value or historical cost depends on whether the investor intends to sell or hold the securities. Generally accepted accounting principles require companies to classify their investment securities into one of three categories: (1) held-to-maturity securities, (2) trading securities, and (3) available-for-sale securities.

Held-to-Maturity Securities

Because equity securities representing ownership interests have no maturity date, the held-to-maturity classification applies only to debt securities. Debt securities should be classified as held-to-maturity securities if the investor has a *positive intent* and the *ability* to hold the securities until the maturity date. **Held-to-maturity securities** are reported on the balance sheet at *amortized historical cost.*[1]

Trading Securities

Both debt and equity securities can be classified as *trading securities.* **Trading securities** are bought and sold for the purpose of generating profits on the short-term appreciation of stock or bond prices. They are usually traded frequently and within short time spans from the time when they are acquired. Trading securities are reported on the investor's balance sheet at their fair value on the investor's fiscal closing date.

Available-for-Sale Securities

All marketable securities that are not classified as held-to-maturity or trading securities must be classified as **available-for-sale securities.** These securities are also reported on the investor's balance sheet at fair value as of the investor's fiscal closing date.

Two of the three classifications, therefore, must be reported at fair value, which is a clear exception to the historical cost concept. Other exceptions to the use of historical cost measures for asset valuation are discussed in later sections of this appendix.

REPORTING EVENTS THAT AFFECT INVESTMENT SECURITIES

The effects on the investor's financial statements of four distinct accounting events involving marketable investment securities are illustrated in the following section. The illustration assumes that the investor, Arapaho Company, started the accounting period with cash of $10,000 and common stock of $10,000.

EVENT 1   Arapaho paid $9,000 cash to purchase marketable investment securities.

This event is an asset exchange. One asset (cash) decreases, and another asset (investment securities) increases. The income statement is not affected. The $9,000 cash outflow is reported as either an operating activity or an investing activity, depending on how the securities are classified. Because *trading securities* are short-term assets that are regularly traded for the purpose of producing income, cash flows from the purchase or sale of trading securities are reported in the operating activities section of the statement of cash flows. In contrast, cash flows involving the purchase or sale of securities classified as *held to maturity* or *available for sale* are reported in the investing activities section of the statement of cash flows. The only difference among the three alternatives lies in the classification of the cash outflow reported on the statement of cash flows, as shown in the following statements model:

Event No.	Type	Assets			=	Liab. + Stk. Equity		Rev.	−	Exp.	=	Net Inc.	Statement of Cash Flows	
		Cash	+	Inv. Sec.										
1.	Held	(9,000)	+	9,000	=	NA +	NA	NA	−	NA	=	NA	(9,000)	IA
1.	Trading	(9,000)	+	9,000	=	NA +	NA	NA	−	NA	=	NA	(9,000)	OA
1.	Available	(9,000)	+	9,000	=	NA +	NA	NA	−	NA	=	NA	(9,000)	IA

[1]Debt securities are frequently purchased for amounts that are more or less than their face value (the amount of principal due at the maturity date). If the purchase price is above the face value, the difference between the face value and the purchase price is called a *premium.* If the purchase price is below the face value, the difference is called a *discount.* Premiums and discounts increase or decrease the amount of interest revenue earned and affect the carrying value of the bond investment reported on the balance sheet. The presentation in this appendix makes the simplifying assumption that the bonds are purchased at a price equal to their face value. Accounting for discounts and premiums is discussed in Chapter 10.

EVENT 2 Arapaho earned $1,600 of cash investment revenue.

Investment revenue is reported the same way regardless of whether the investment securities are classified as held to maturity, trading, or available for sale. Investment revenue comes in two forms. Earnings from equity investments are called **dividends.** Revenue from debt securities is called **interest.** Both forms have the same impact on the financial statements. Recognizing the investment revenue increases both assets and stockholders' equity. Revenue and net income increase. The cash inflow from investment revenue is reported in the operating activities section of the statement of cash flows regardless of how the investment securities are classified.

Event No.	Balance Sheet			Income Statement			Statement of Cash Flows
	Assets =	Liab. +	Stk. Equity	Rev. –	Exp. =	Net Inc.	
	Cash =		Ret. Earn.				
2.	1,600 =	NA +	1,600	1,600 –	NA =	1,600	1,600 OA

EVENT 3 Arapaho sold securities that cost $2,000 for $2,600 cash.

This event results in recognizing a $600 realized (actual) gain that increases both total assets and stockholders' equity. The asset cash increases by $2,600 and the asset investment securities decreases by $2,000, resulting in a $600 increase in total assets. The $600 realized gain is reported on the income statement, increasing net income and retained earnings. The $600 gain does not appear on the statement of cash flows. Instead, the entire $2,600 cash inflow is reported in one section of the statement of cash flows. Cash inflows from the sale of held-to-maturity and available-for-sale securities are reported as investing activities. Cash flows involving trading securities are reported as operating activities. These effects are shown next:

Event No.	Type	Assets			= Liab. +	Stk. Equity	Rev. or Gain –	Exp. or Loss =	Net Inc.	Statement of Cash Flows
		Cash	+	Inv. Sec.						
3.	Held	2,600	+	(2,000)	= NA +	600	600 –	NA =	600	2,600 IA
3.	Trading	2,600	+	(2,000)	= NA +	600	600 –	NA =	600	2,600 OA
3.	Available	2,600	+	(2,000)	= NA +	600	600 –	NA =	600	2,600 IA

EVENT 4 Arapaho recognized a $700 unrealized gain.

After Event 3, the historical cost of Arapaho's portfolio of remaining investment securities is $7,000 ($9,000 purchased less $2,000 sold). Assume that at Arapaho's fiscal closing date, these securities have a fair value of $7,700, giving Arapaho a $700 unrealized gain on its investment. This type of gain (sometimes called a *paper profit*) is classified as *unrealized* because the securities have not been sold. The treatment of **unrealized gains or losses** in the financial statements depends on whether the securities are classified as held to maturity, trading, or available for sale. Unrealized gains or losses on securities classified as *held to maturity* are not recognized in the financial statements; they have no effect on the balance sheet, income statement, and statement of cash flows. Even so, many companies choose to disclose the market value of the securities as part of the narrative description or in the notes that accompany the financial statements. Whether or not the market value is disclosed, held-to-maturity securities are reported on the balance sheet at amortized cost.

Investments classified as trading securities are reported in the financial statements at fair value. Unrealized gains or losses on *trading securities* are recognized in net income even though the securities have not been sold. In Arapaho's case, the $700 gain increases the carrying value of the investment securities. The gain increases net income, which in turn increases retained earnings. Unrealized gains and losses have no effect on cash flows.

Investments classified as available-for-sale securities are also reported in the financial statements at fair value. However, an important distinction exists with respect to how the unrealized gains and losses affect the financial statements. Even though unrealized gains or losses on available-for-sale securities are included in the assets on the balance sheet, they *are not* recognized in determining net income.[2] On Arapaho's balance sheet, the $700 gain increases the carrying value of the investment securities. A corresponding increase is reported in a separate equity account called Unrealized Gain or Loss on Available-for-Sale Securities. The statement of cash flows is not affected by recognizing unrealized gains and losses on available-for-sale securities.

The effects of these alternative treatments of unrealized gains and losses on Arapaho's financial statements are shown next:

Event No.	Type	Assets	=	Liab.	+	Stk. Equity			Rev. or Gain	−	Exp. or Loss	=	Net Inc.	Statement of Cash Flows
		Inv. Sec.	=			Ret. Earn.	+	Unreal. Gain						
4.	Held	NA	=	NA	+	NA	+	NA	NA	−	NA	=	NA	NA
4.	Trading	700	=	NA	+	700	+	NA	700	−	NA	=	700	NA
4.	Available	700	=	NA	+	NA	+	700	NA	−	NA	=	NA	NA

FINANCIAL STATEMENTS

As the preceding discussion implies, the financial statements of Arapaho Company are affected by not only the business events relating to its security transactions but also the accounting treatment used to report those events. In other words, the same economic events are reflected differently in the financial statements depending on whether the securities are classified as held to maturity, trading, or available for sale. Exhibit F.1 displays the financial statements for Arapaho under each investment classification alternative.

The net income reported under the trading securities alternative is $700 higher than that reported under the held-to-maturity and available-for-sale alternatives because unrealized gains and losses on trading securities are recognized on the income statement. Similarly, total assets and total stockholders' equity are $700 higher under the trading and available-for-sale alternatives than they are under the held-to-maturity category because the $700 unrealized gain is recognized on the balance sheet for those two classifications. The gain is not reported on the income statement for available-for-sale securities; it is reported on the balance sheet in a special equity account called Unrealized Gain on Investment Securities. The statements of cash flows report purchases and sales of trading securities as operating activities, while purchases and sales of available-for-sale and held-to-maturity securities are investing activities. Exhibit F.2 summarizes the reporting differences among the three classifications of investment securities.

[2]GAAP permits companies to report unrealized gains and losses on available-for-sale securities as additions to or subtractions from net income, with the result being titled *comprehensive income*. Alternatively, the unrealized gains and losses can be reported on a separate statement of net income and other comprehensive income.

EXHIBIT F.1

ARAPAHO COMPANY
Comparative Financial Statements

Income Statements

Investment Securities Classified as	Held	Trading	Available
Investment revenue	$1,600	$1,600	$1,600
Realized gain	600	600	600
Unrealized gain		700	
Net income	$2,200	$2,900	$2,200

Balance Sheets

	Held	Trading	Available
Assets			
Cash	$ 5,200	$ 5,200	$ 5,200
Investment securities, at cost (market value $7,700)	7,000		
Investment securities, at market (cost $7,000)		7,700	7,700
Total assets	$12,200	$12,900	$12,900
Stockholders' equity			
Common stock	$10,000	$10,000	$10,000
Retained earnings	2,200	2,900	2,200
Unrealized gain on investment securities			700
Total stockholders' equity	$12,200	$12,900	$12,900

Statements of Cash Flows

	Held	Trading	Available
Operating Activities			
Cash inflow from investment revenue	$ 1,600	$ 1,600	$ 1,600
Outflow to purchase securities		(9,000)	
Inflow from sale of securities		2,600	
Investing Activities			
Outflow to purchase securities	(9,000)		(9,000)
Inflow from sale of securities	2,600		2,600
Financing Activities*	0	0	0
Net decrease in cash	(4,800)	(4,800)	(4,800)
Beginning cash balance	10,000	10,000	10,000
Ending cash balance	$ 5,200	$ 5,200	$ 5,200

*The $10,000 of common stock is assumed to have been issued prior to the start of the accounting period.

EXHIBIT F.2

Investment Category	Types of Securities	Types of Revenue Recognized	Reported on Balance Sheet at	Recognition of Unrealized Gains and Losses on the Income Statement	Cash Flow from Purchase or Sale of Securities Classified as
Held to maturity	Debt	Interest	Amortized cost	No	Investing activity
Trading	Debt and equity	Interest and dividends	Market value	Yes	Operating activity
Available for sale	Debt and equity	Interest and dividends	Market value	No	Investing activity

Alternative Reporting Practices for Equity Securities

If an investor owns 20 percent or more of an investee's equity securities, the investor is presumed able, unless there is evidence to the contrary, to exercise *significant influence* over the investee company. Investors owning more than 50 percent of the stock of an investee company are assumed to have control over the investee. The previous discussion of accounting rules for equity securities assumed the investor did not significantly influence or control the investee. Alternative accounting rules apply to securities owned by investors who exercise significant influence or control over an investee company. Accounting for equity investment securities differs depending on the level of the investor's ability to influence or control the operating, investing, and financing activities of the investee.

As previously demonstrated, investors who do not have significant influence (they own less than 20 percent of the stock of the investee) account for their investments in equity securities at fair value. Investors exercising significant influence (they own 20 to 50 percent of the investee's stock) must account for their investments using the **equity method.** A detailed discussion of the equity method is beyond the scope of this text. However, *be aware that investments reported using the equity method represent a measure of the book value of the investee rather than the cost or fair value of the equity securities owned.*

Investors that have a controlling interest (they own more than 50 percent of the investee's stock) in an investee company are required to issue **consolidated financial statements.** The company that holds the controlling interest is referred to as the **parent company,** and the company that is controlled is called the **subsidiary company.** Usually, the parent and subsidiary companies maintain separate accounting records. However, a parent company is also required to report to the public its accounting data along with that of its subsidiaries in a single set of combined financial statements. These consolidated statements represent a separate accounting entity consisting of the parent and its subsidiaries. A parent company that owns one subsidiary will produce three sets of financial statements: statements for the parent company, statements for the subsidiary company, and statements for the consolidated entity.

KEY TERMS

Available-for-sale securities 733	Equity security 732	Investor 732	Secondary securities market 732
Consolidated financial statements 737	Fair value 732	Market value 732	Subsidiary company 737
Debt security 732	Held-to-maturity securities 733	Marketable securities 732	Trading securities 733
Dividend 734	Interest 734	Parent company 737	Unrealized gains or losses 734
Equity method 737	Investee 732	Primary securities market 732	
	Investment securities 732		

EXERCISES

 **All applicable Exercises are available in Connect.**

Exercise F1 *Identifying asset values for financial statements*

Required

Indicate whether each of the following assets should be valued at fair market value (FMV), lower of cost or market (LCM), or historical cost (HC) on the balance sheet. For certain assets, historical cost may be called amortized cost (AC).

Asset	FMV	LCM	HC/AC
Buildings			
Available-for-sale securities			
Office equipment			
Inventory			
Supplies			
Land			
Trading securities			
Cash			
Held-to-maturity securities			

Exercise F2 *Accounting for investment securities*

Norris Co. purchased $36,000 of marketable securities on March 1, Year 1. On the company's fiscal year closing date, December 31, Year 1, the securities had a market value of $27,000. During Year 1, Norris Co. recognized $10,000 of revenue and $2,000 of expenses.

Required

a. Record a +, −, or NA in a horizontal statements model to show how the purchase of the securities affects the financial statements, assuming that the securities are classified as (1) held to maturity, (2) trading, or (3) available for sale. In the Statement of Cash Flows column, indicate whether the event is an operating activity (OA), investing activity (IA), or financing activity (FA). Record only the effects of the purchase event.

Event No.	Type	Cash	+	Inv. Sec.	=	Liab.	+	Stk. Equity	Rev.	−	Exp.	=	Net Inc.	Statement of Cash Flows
1.	Held													
2.	Trading													
3.	Available													

b. Determine the amount of net income that would be reported on the Year 1 income statement, assuming that the marketable securities are classified as (1) held to maturity, (2) trading, or (3) available for sale.

Exercise F3 *Effect of investment securities transactions on financial statements*

The following information pertains to Botter Supply Co. for Year 1:

1. Purchased $100,000 of marketable investment securities.
2. Earned $10,000 of cash investment revenue.
3. Sold for $30,000 securities that cost $25,000.
4. The fair value of the remaining securities at December 31, Year 1, was $89,000.

Required

a. Record the four events in a statements model like the following one. Use a separate model for each classification: (1) held to maturity, (2) trading, and (3) available for sale. The first event for the first classification is shown as an example.

Held to Maturity

	Balance Sheet									Income Statement						Statement of Cash Flows
Event No.	Cash	+	Inv. Sec.	=	Liab.	+	Ret. Earn.	+	Unreal. Gain.	Rev. or Gains.	−	Exp. or Loss	=	Net Inc.		Statement of Cash Flows
1	(100,000)	+	100,000	=	NA	+	NA	+	NA	NA	−	NA	=	NA		(100,000) IA

b. What is the amount of net income under each of the three classifications?

c. What is the change in cash from operating activities under each of the three classifications?

d. Are the answers to Requirements *b* and *c* different for each of the classifications? Why or why not?

Exercise F4   *Preparing financial statements for investment securities*

Molten, Inc. began Year 2 with $100,000 in both cash and common stock. The company engaged in the following investment transactions during Year 2:

1. Purchased $20,000 of marketable investment securities.
2. Earned $600 cash from investment revenue.
3. Sold investment securities for $14,000 that cost $10,000.
4. Purchased $7,000 of additional marketable investment securities.
5. Determined that the investment securities had a fair value of $22,000 at the end of Year 2.

Required

Use a vertical statements model to prepare income statements, balance sheets, and statements of cash flow for Molten, Inc., assuming the securities were (*a*) held to maturity, (*b*) trading, and (*c*) available for sale.

Exercise F5   *Differences among marketable investment securities classifications*

Complete the following table for the three categories of marketable investment securities:

Investment Category	Types of Securities	Types of Revenue Recognized	Value Reported on Balance Sheet	Recognition of Unrealized Gains and Losses on the Income Statement	Cash Flow from Purchase or Sale of Securities Is Classified as
Held to maturity	Debt	Interest	Amortized cost	No	Investing activity
Trading					
Available for sale					

Exercise F6   *Effect of marketable investment securities transactions on financial statements*

The following transactions pertain to Harrison Imports for Year 1:

1. Started business by acquiring $30,000 cash from the issue of common stock.
2. Provided $90,000 of services for cash.
3. Invested $35,000 in marketable investment securities.
4. Paid $18,000 of operating expense.
5. Received $500 of investment income from the securities.
6. Invested an additional $16,000 in marketable investment securities.
7. Paid a $2,000 cash dividend to the stockholders.
8. Sold investment securities that cost $8,000 for $14,000.
9. Received another $1,000 in investment income.
10. Determined the market value of the investment securities at the end of the year was $42,000.

Required

Use a vertical statements model to prepare a Year 1 income statement, balance sheet, and statement of cash flows, assuming that the marketable investment securities were classified as (a) held to maturity, (b) trading, and (c) available for sale.

Exercise F7   *Comprehensive horizontal statements model*

Woody's Catering experienced the following independent events:

1. Acquired cash from issuing common stock.
2. Purchased inventory on account.
3. Paid cash to purchase marketable securities classified as trading securities.
4. Recorded unrealized loss on marketable securities that were classified as available-for-sale securities.
5. Recorded unrealized loss on marketable securities that were classified as trading securities.
6. Recorded unrealized loss on marketable securities that were classified as held-to-maturity securities.
7. Wrote down inventory to comply with lower-of-cost-or-market rule. (Assume that the company uses the perpetual inventory system.)
8. Recognized cost of goods sold under the weighted-average method.
9. Recognized cost of goods sold under FIFO.

Required

a. Show the effect of each event on the elements of the financial statements using a horizontal statements model like the following one. Use + for increase, − for decrease, and NA for not affected. In the Statement of Cash Flows column, indicate whether the item is an operating activity (OA), investing activity (IA), or financing activity (FA). The first transaction is entered as an example.

	Balance Sheet			Income Statement			Statement of Cash Flows
Event No.	Assets	= Liab.	+ Stk. Equity	Rev. or Gain.	− Exp. or Loss	= Net Inc.	
1.	+	NA	+	NA	NA	NA	+ FA

b. Explain why there is or is not a difference in the way Events 8 and 9 affect the financial statements model.

TIME VALUE OF MONEY

Future Value

Suppose you recently won $10,000 cash in a local lottery. You save the money to have funds available to obtain a masters of business administration (MBA) degree. You plan to enter the program three years from today. Assuming you invest the money in an account that earns 8 percent annual interest, how much money will you have available in three years? The answer depends on whether your investment will earn *simple* or *compound* interest.

To determine the amount of funds available assuming you earn 8 percent **simple interest,** multiply the principal balance by the interest rate to determine the amount of interest earned per year ($10,000 × 0.08 = $800). Next, multiply the amount of annual interest by the number of years the funds will be invested ($800 × 3 = $2,400). Finally, add the interest earned to the principal balance to determine the total amount of funds available at the end of the three-year term ($10,000 principal + $2,400 interest = $12,400 cash available at the end of three years).

Investors can increase their returns by reinvesting the income earned from their investments. For example, at the beginning of the second year, you will have available for investment not only the original $10,000 principal balance but also $800 of interest earned during the first year. In other words, you will be able to earn interest on the interest that you previously earned. Earning interest on interest is called **compounding.** Assuming you earn 8 percent compound interest, the amount of funds available to you at the end of three years can be computed as shown in Exhibit G.1.

EXHIBIT G.1

Year	Amount Invested	×	Interest Rate	=	Interest Earned	+	Amount Invested	=	New Balance
1	$10,000.00	×	0.08	=	$ 800.00	+	$10,000.00	=	$10,800.00
2	10,800.00	×	0.08	=	864.00	+	10,800.00	=	11,664.00
3	11,664.00	×	0.08	=	933.12	+	11,664.00	=	12,597.12
Total interest earned				=	$2,597.12				

Obviously, you earn more with compound interest ($2,597.12 compound versus $2,400 simple). The computations required for **compound interest** can become cumbersome when the investment term is long. Fortunately, there are mathematical formulas, interest tables, and computer programs that reduce the computational burden. For example, a compound interest factor can be developed from the formula

$$(1 + i)^n$$

where $i = \text{interest}$

  $n = \text{number of periods}$

The value of the investment is determined by multiplying the compound interest factor by the principal balance. The compound interest factor for a three-year term and an 8 percent interest rate is 1.259712 (1.08 × 1.08 × 1.08 = 1.259712). Assuming a $10,000 original investment, the value of the investment at the end of three years is $12,597.12 ($10,000 × 1.259712). This is, of course, the same amount that was computed in the previous illustration (see the final figure in the New Balance column of Exhibit G.1).

The mathematical formulas have been used to develop tables of interest factors that can be used to determine the **future value** of an investment for a variety of interest rates and time periods. For example, Table I (shown at the end of Appendix G) contains the interest factor for an investment with a three-year term earning 8 percent compound interest. To confirm this point, move down the column marked n to the third period. Next, move across to the column marked 8 percent, where you will find the value 1.259712. This is identical to the amount computed using the mathematical formula in the preceding paragraph. Here also, the value of the investment at the end of three years can be determined by multiplying the principal balance by the compound interest factor ($10,000 × 1.259712 = $12,597.12). These same factors and amounts can be determined using computer programs in calculators and spreadsheet software.

Clearly, a variety of ways can be used to determine the future value of an investment, given a principal balance, interest rate, and term to maturity. In our case, we showed that your original investment of $10,000 would be worth $12,597 in three years, assuming an 8 percent compound interest rate. Suppose you determine this amount is insufficient to get you through the MBA program you want to complete. Assume you believe you will need $18,000 three years from today to sustain yourself while you finish the degree. Suppose your parents agree to cover the shortfall. They ask how much money you need today in order to have $18,000 three years from now.

Present Value

The mathematical formula required to convert the future value of a dollar to its **present value** equivalent is

$$(1 + i)^n$$

where i = interest

       n = number of periods

For easy conversion, the formula has been used to develop Table II, Present Value of $1 (shown at the end of Appendix G). At an 8 percent annual compound interest rate, the present value equivalent of $18,000 to be received three years from today is computed as follows: Move down the far left column to where n = 3. Next, move right to the column marked 8 percent. At this point, you should see the interest factor 0.793832. Multiplying this factor by the desired future value of $18,000 yields the present value of $14,288.98 ($18,000 × 0.793832). This means if you invest $14,288.98 (present value) today at an annual compound interest rate of 8 percent, you will have the $18,000 (future value) you need to enter the MBA program three years from now.

If you currently have $10,000, you will need an additional $4,288.98 from your parents to make the required $14,288.98 investment that will yield the future value of $18,000 you need. Having $14,288.98 today is the same as having $18,000 three years from today, assuming you can earn 8 percent compound interest. To validate this conclusion, use Table I to determine the future value of $14,288.98, given a three-year term and 8 percent annual compound interest. As previously indicated, the future value conversion factor under these conditions is 1.259712. Multiplying this factor by the $14,288.98 present value produces the expected future value of $18,000 ($14,288.98 × 1.259712 = $18,000). The factors in Table I can be used to convert present values to future values, and the corresponding factors in Table II are used to convert future values to present values.

Future Value Annuities

The previous examples described present and future values of a single lump-sum payment. Many financial transactions involve a series of payments. To illustrate, we return to the example in which you want to have $18,000 available three years from today. We continue the assumption that you can earn 8 percent compound interest. However, now we assume that you do not have $14,288.98 to invest today. Instead, you decide to save part of the money during each of the next three years. How much money must you save each year to have $18,000 at the end of three years? *The series of equal payments made over a number of periods in order to acquire a future value is called an* **annuity.** The factors in Table III, Future Value of an Annuity of $1 (shown at the end of Appendix G), can be used to determine the amount of the annuity needed to produce the desired $18,000 future value. The table is constructed so that future values can be determined by multiplying the conversion factor by the amount of the annuity. These relationships can be expressed algebraically as follows:

Amount of annuity payment × Table conversion factor = Future value

To determine the amount of the required annuity payment in our example, first locate the future value conversion factor. In Table III, move down the first column on the left-hand side until you locate period 3. Next, move to the right until you locate the 8 percent column. At this location, you will see a conversion factor of 3.2464. This factor can be used to determine the amount of the annuity payment as indicated in the following:

Amount of annuity payment × Table conversion factor = Future value
Amount of annuity payment = Future value ÷ Table conversion factor
Amount of annuity payment = $18,000.00 ÷ 3.2464
Amount of annuity payment = $5,544.60

If you deposit $5,544.60 in an investment account at the end of each of the next three years,[1] the investment account balance will be $18,000, assuming your investment earns 8 percent interest compounded annually. This conclusion is confirmed by the following schedule:

End of Year	Beg. Acct. Bal.	+	Interest Computation	+	Payment	=	End. Acct. Bal.
1	NA	+	NA	+	$5,544.60	=	$ 5,544.60
2	$ 5,544.60	+	$ 5,544.60 × 0.08 = $443.57	+	5,544.60	=	11,532.77
3	11,532.77	+	11,532.77 × 0.08 = 922.62	+	5,544.60	=	18,000.00*

*Total does not add exactly due to rounding.

PRESENT VALUE ANNUITIES

We previously demonstrated that a future value of $18,000 is equivalent to a present value of $14,288.98, given annual compound interest of 8 percent for a three-year period. If the future value of a $5,544.60 annuity for three years is equivalent to $18,000, that same annuity should have a present value of $14,288.98. We can test this conclusion by using the conversion factors in Table IV, Present Value of an Annuity of $1 (shown at the end of Appendix G). The present value annuity table is constructed so that present values can be determined by multiplying the conversion factor by the amount of the annuity. These relationships can be expressed algebraically as follows:

Amount of annuity payment × Table conversion factor = Present value

To determine the present value of the annuity payment in our example, first locate the present value conversion factor. In Table IV, move down the first column on the left-hand side until you locate period 3. Next, move to the right until you locate the column for the 8 percent

[1]A payment made at the end of a period is known as an *ordinary annuity.* A payment made at the beginning of a period is called an *annuity due.* Tables are generally set up to assume ordinary annuities. Minor adjustments must be made when dealing with an annuity due. For the purposes of this text, we consider all annuities to be ordinary.

interest rate. At this location, you will see a conversion factor of 2.577097. This factor can be used to determine the amount of the present value of the annuity payment, as indicated:

$$\text{Amount of annuity payment} \times \text{Table conversion factor} = \text{Present value}$$
$$\$5,544.60 \quad\quad \times \quad\quad 2.577097 \quad\quad = \$14,288.97^*$$

*The 1 cent difference between this value and the expected value of $14,288.98 is due to rounding.

In summary, Tables III and IV can be used to convert annuities to future or present values for a variety of different assumptions regarding interest rates and time periods.

BUSINESS APPLICATIONS

Long-Term Notes Payable

In Chapter 10, we considered a case in which Blair Company borrowed $100,000 from National Bank. We indicated that Blair agreed to repay the bank through a series of annual payments (an *annuity*) of $25,709 each. How was this amount determined? Recall that Blair agreed to pay the bank 9 percent interest over a five-year term. Under these circumstances, we are trying to find the annuity equivalent to the $100,000 present value that the bank is loaning Blair. The first step in determining the annuity (annual payment) is to locate the appropriate present value conversion factor from Table IV. At the fifth row under the 9 percent column, you will find the value 3.889651. This factor can be used to determine the amount of the annuity payment as indicated in the following:

Amount of annuity payment $\times$ Table conversion factor = Present value

Amount of annuity payment = Present value $\div$ Table conversion factor

Amount of annuity payment = $100,000 \div 3.889651$

Amount of annuity payment = $25,709

There are many applications in which debt repayment occurs through annuities. Common examples with which you are probably familiar include auto loans and home mortgages. Payment schedules for such loans may be determined from the interest tables, as demonstrated here. However, most real-world businesses have further refined the computational process through the use of sophisticated computer programs. The software program prompts the user to provide the relevant information regarding the present value of the amount borrowed, number of payments, and interest rate. Given this information and a few keystrokes, the computer program produces the amount of the amortization payment along with an amortization schedule showing the amounts of principal and interest payments over the life of the loan. Similar results can be obtained with a spreadsheet software application such as Excel. Even many handheld calculators have present and future value functions that enable users to quickly compute annuity payments for an infinite number of interest rate and time period assumptions.

Bond Liabilities: Determine Price

In Chapter 10, we discussed the use of discounts and premiums as a means of producing an effective rate of interest that is higher or lower than the stated rate of interest. For example, if the stated rate of interest is lower than the market rate of interest at the time the bonds are issued, the issuer can increase the effective interest rate by selling the bonds for a price lower than their face value. At maturity, the issuer will settle the obligation by paying the face value of the bond. The difference between the discounted bond price and the face value of the bond is additional interest. To illustrate, assume that Tower Company issues $100,000 face value bonds with a 20-year term and a 9 percent stated rate of annual interest. At the time the bonds are issued, the market rate of interest for bonds of comparable risk is 10 percent annual interest. For what amount would Tower Company be required to sell the bonds in order to move its 9 percent stated rate of interest to an effective rate of 10 percent?

Information from present value Tables II and IV is required to determine the amount of the discount required to produce a 10 percent effective rate of interest. First, we identify the future cash flows that will be generated by the bonds. Based on the stated interest rate, the bonds will pay $9,000 ($100,000 face value × 0.09 interest) interest per year. This constitutes a 20-year annuity that should be discounted back to its present value equivalent. Also, at the end of 20 years, the bonds will require a single $100,000 lump-sum payment to settle the principal obligation. This amount must also be discounted back to its present value in order to determine the bond price. The computations required to determine the discounted bond price are shown next:

Present value of principal	$100,000 × 0.148644	=	$14,864.40
	(Table II, $n = 20$, $i = 10\%$)		
Present value of interest	$9,000 × 8.513564	=	76,622.08
	(Table IV, $n = 20$, $i = 10\%$)		
Bond price (proceeds received)			$91,486.48

Tower Company bonds sell at an $8,513.52 discount ($100,000 − $91,486.48) to produce a 10 percent effective interest rate. Note that in these computations, the stated rate of interest was used to determine the amount of cash flow, and the effective rate of interest was used to determine the table conversion factors.

TABLE I — Future Value of $1

n	4%	5%	6%	7%	8%	9%	10%	12%	14%	16%	20%
1	1.040000	1.050000	1.060000	1.070000	1.080000	1.090000	1.100000	1.120000	1.140000	1.160000	1.200000
2	1.081600	1.102500	1.123600	1.144900	1.166400	1.188100	1.210000	1.254400	1.299600	1.345600	1.440000
3	1.124864	1.157625	1.191016	1.225043	1.259712	1.295029	1.331000	1.404928	1.481544	1.560896	1.728000
4	1.169859	1.215506	1.262477	1.310796	1.360489	1.411582	1.464100	1.573519	1.688960	1.810639	2.073600
5	1.216653	1.276282	1.338226	1.402552	1.469328	1.538624	1.610510	1.762342	1.925415	2.100342	2.488320
6	1.265319	1.340096	1.418519	1.500730	1.586874	1.677100	1.771561	1.973823	2.194973	2.436396	2.985984
7	1.315932	1.407100	1.503630	1.605781	1.713824	1.828039	1.948717	2.210681	2.502269	2.826220	3.583181
8	1.368569	1.477455	1.593848	1.718186	1.850930	1.992563	2.143589	2.475963	2.852586	3.278415	4.299817
9	1.423312	1.551328	1.689479	1.838459	1.999005	2.171893	2.357948	2.773079	3.251949	3.802961	5.159780
10	1.480244	1.628895	1.790848	1.967151	2.158925	2.367364	2.593742	3.105848	3.707221	4.411435	6.191736
11	1.539454	1.710339	1.898299	2.104852	2.331639	2.580426	2.853117	3.478550	4.226232	5.117265	7.430084
12	1.601032	1.795856	2.012196	2.252192	2.518170	2.812665	3.138428	3.895976	4.817905	5.936027	8.916100
13	1.665074	1.885649	2.132928	2.409845	2.719624	3.065805	3.452271	4.363493	5.492411	6.885791	10.699321
14	1.731676	1.979932	2.260904	2.578534	2.937194	3.341727	3.797498	4.887112	6.261349	7.987518	12.839185
15	1.800944	2.078928	2.396558	2.759032	3.172169	3.642562	4.177248	5.473566	7.137938	9.265521	15.407022
16	1.872981	2.182875	2.540352	2.952164	3.425943	3.970306	4.594973	6.130394	8.137249	10.748004	18.488426
17	1.947900	2.292018	2.692773	3.158815	3.700018	4.327633	5.054470	6.866041	9.276464	12.467685	22.186111
18	2.025817	2.406619	2.854339	3.379932	3.996019	4.717120	5.559917	7.689966	10.575169	14.462514	26.623333
19	2.106849	2.526950	3.025600	3.616528	4.315701	5.141661	6.115909	8.612762	12.055693	16.776517	31.948000
20	2.191123	2.653298	3.207135	3.869684	4.660957	5.604411	6.727500	9.646293	13.743490	19.460759	38.337600

TABLE II — Present Value of $1

n	4%	5%	6%	7%	8%	9%	10%	12%	14%	16%	20%
1	0.961538	0.952381	0.943396	0.934579	0.925926	0.917431	0.909091	0.892857	0.877193	0.862069	0.833333
2	0.924556	0.907029	0.889996	0.873439	0.857339	0.841680	0.826446	0.797194	0.769468	0.743163	0.694444
3	0.888996	0.863838	0.839619	0.816298	0.793832	0.772183	0.751315	0.711780	0.674972	0.640658	0.578704
4	0.854804	0.822702	0.792094	0.762895	0.735030	0.708425	0.683013	0.635518	0.592080	0.552291	0.482253
5	0.821927	0.783526	0.747258	0.712986	0.680583	0.649931	0.620921	0.567427	0.519369	0.476113	0.401878
6	0.790315	0.746215	0.704961	0.666342	0.630170	0.596267	0.564474	0.506631	0.455587	0.410442	0.334898
7	0.759918	0.710681	0.665057	0.622750	0.583490	0.547034	0.513158	0.452349	0.399637	0.353830	0.279082
8	0.730690	0.676839	0.627412	0.582009	0.540269	0.501866	0.466507	0.403883	0.350559	0.305025	0.232568
9	0.702587	0.644609	0.591898	0.543934	0.500249	0.460428	0.424098	0.360610	0.307508	0.262953	0.193807
10	0.675564	0.613913	0.558395	0.508349	0.463193	0.422411	0.385543	0.321973	0.269744	0.226684	0.161506
11	0.649581	0.584679	0.526788	0.475093	0.428883	0.387533	0.350494	0.287476	0.236617	0.195417	0.134588
12	0.624597	0.556837	0.496969	0.444012	0.397114	0.355535	0.318631	0.256675	0.207559	0.168463	0.112157
13	0.600574	0.530321	0.468839	0.414964	0.367698	0.326179	0.289664	0.229174	0.182069	0.145227	0.093464
14	0.577475	0.505068	0.442301	0.387817	0.340461	0.299246	0.263331	0.204620	0.159710	0.125195	0.077887
15	0.555265	0.481017	0.417265	0.362446	0.315242	0.274538	0.239392	0.182696	0.140096	0.107927	0.064905
16	0.533908	0.458112	0.393646	0.338735	0.291890	0.251870	0.217629	0.163122	0.122892	0.093041	0.054088
17	0.513373	0.436297	0.371364	0.316574	0.270269	0.231073	0.197845	0.145644	0.107800	0.080207	0.045073
18	0.493628	0.415521	0.350344	0.295864	0.250249	0.211994	0.179859	0.130040	0.094561	0.069144	0.037561
19	0.474642	0.395734	0.330513	0.276564	0.231712	0.194490	0.163508	0.116107	0.082948	0.059607	0.031301
20	0.456387	0.376889	0.311805	0.258419	0.214548	0.178431	0.148644	0.103667	0.072762	0.051385	0.026084

TABLE III

Future Value of an Annuity of $1

n	4%	5%	6%	7%	8%	9%	10%	12%	14%	16%	20%
1	1.000000	1.000000	1.000000	1.000000	1.000000	1.000000	1.000000	1.000000	1.000000	1.000000	1.000000
2	2.040000	2.050000	2.060000	2.070000	2.080000	2.090000	2.100000	2.120000	2.140000	2.160000	2.200000
3	3.121600	3.152500	3.183600	3.214900	3.246400	3.278100	3.310000	3.374400	3.439600	3.505600	3.640000
4	4.246464	4.310125	4.374616	4.439943	4.506112	4.573129	4.641000	4.779328	4.921144	5.066496	5.368000
5	5.416323	5.525631	5.637093	5.750739	5.866601	5.984711	6.105100	6.352847	6.610104	6.877135	7.441600
6	6.632975	6.801913	6.975319	7.153291	7.335929	7.523335	7.715610	8.115189	8.535519	8.977477	9.929920
7	7.898294	8.142008	8.393838	8.654021	8.922803	9.200435	9.487171	10.089012	10.730491	11.413873	12.915904
8	9.214226	9.549109	9.897468	10.259803	10.636628	11.028474	11.435888	12.299693	13.232760	14.240093	16.499085
9	10.582795	11.026564	11.491316	11.977989	12.487558	13.021036	13.579477	14.775656	16.085347	17.518508	20.798902
10	12.006107	12.577893	13.180795	13.816448	14.486562	15.192930	15.937425	17.548735	19.337295	21.321469	25.958682
11	13.486351	14.206787	14.971643	15.783599	16.645487	17.560293	18.531167	20.654583	23.044516	25.732904	32.150419
12	15.025805	15.917127	16.869941	17.888451	18.977126	20.140720	21.384284	24.133131	27.270749	30.850502	39.580502
13	16.626838	17.712983	18.882138	20.140643	21.495297	22.953385	24.522712	28.029109	32.088654	36.786196	48.496603
14	18.291911	19.598632	21.015066	22.550488	24.214920	26.019189	27.974983	32.392602	37.581065	43.671987	59.195923
15	20.023588	21.578564	23.275970	25.129022	27.152114	29.360916	31.772482	37.279715	43.842414	51.659505	72.035108
16	21.824531	23.657492	25.672528	27.888054	30.324283	33.003399	35.949730	42.753280	50.980352	60.925026	87.442129
17	23.697512	25.840366	28.212880	30.840217	33.750226	36.973705	40.544703	48.883674	59.117601	71.673030	105.930555
18	25.645413	28.132385	30.905653	33.999033	37.450244	41.301338	45.599173	55.749715	68.394066	84.140715	128.116666
19	27.671229	30.539004	33.759992	37.378965	41.446263	46.018458	51.159090	63.439681	78.969235	98.603230	154.740000
20	29.778079	33.065954	36.785591	40.995492	45.761964	51.160120	57.274999	72.052442	91.024928	115.379747	186.688000

TABLE IV

Present Value of an Annuity of $1

n	4%	5%	6%	7%	8%	9%	10%	12%	14%	16%	20%
1	0.961538	0.952381	0.943396	0.934579	0.925926	0.917431	0.909091	0.892857	0.877193	0.862069	0.833333
2	1.886095	1.859410	1.833393	1.808018	1.783265	1.759111	1.735537	1.690051	1.646661	1.605232	1.527778
3	2.775091	2.723248	2.673012	2.624316	2.577097	2.531295	2.486852	2.401831	2.321632	2.245890	2.106481
4	3.629895	3.545951	3.465106	3.387211	3.312127	3.239720	3.169865	3.037349	2.913712	2.798181	2.588735
5	4.451822	4.329477	4.212364	4.100197	3.992710	3.889651	3.790787	3.604776	3.433081	3.274294	2.990612
6	5.242137	5.075692	4.917324	4.766540	4.622880	4.485919	4.355261	4.111407	3.888668	3.684736	3.325510
7	6.002055	5.786373	5.582381	5.389289	5.206370	5.032953	4.868419	4.563757	4.288305	4.038565	3.604592
8	6.732745	6.463213	6.209794	5.971299	5.746639	5.534819	5.334926	4.967640	4.638864	4.343591	3.837160
9	7.435332	7.107822	6.801692	6.515232	6.246888	5.995247	5.759024	5.328250	4.946372	4.606544	4.030967
10	8.110896	7.721735	7.360087	7.023582	6.710081	6.417658	6.144567	5.650223	5.216116	4.833227	4.192472
11	8.760477	8.306414	7.886875	7.498674	7.138964	6.805191	6.495061	5.937699	5.452733	5.028644	4.327060
12	9.385074	8.863252	8.383844	7.942686	7.536078	7.160725	6.813692	6.194374	5.660292	5.197107	4.439217
13	9.985648	9.393573	8.852683	8.357651	7.903776	7.486904	7.103356	6.423548	5.842362	5.342334	4.532681
14	10.563123	9.898641	9.294984	8.745468	8.244237	7.786150	7.366687	6.628168	6.002072	5.467529	4.610567
15	11.118387	10.379658	9.712249	9.107914	8.559479	8.060688	7.606080	6.810864	6.142168	5.575456	4.675473
16	11.652296	10.837770	10.105895	9.446649	8.851369	8.312558	7.823709	6.973986	6.265060	5.668497	4.729561
17	12.165669	11.274066	10.477260	9.763223	9.121638	8.543631	8.021553	7.119630	6.372859	5.748704	4.774634
18	12.659297	11.689587	10.827603	10.059087	9.371887	8.755625	8.201412	7.249670	6.467420	5.817848	4.812195
19	13.133939	12.085321	11.158116	10.335595	9.603599	8.905115	8.364920	7.365777	6.550369	5.877455	4.843496
20	13.590326	12.462210	11.469921	10.594014	9.818147	9.128546	8.513564	7.469444	6.623131	5.928841	4.869580

KEY TERMS

Annuity 743	Compounding 741	Present value 742
Compound interest 741	Future value 742	Simple interest 741

EXERCISES

Mc Graw Hill connect   **All applicable Exercises are available in Connect.**

Exercise G1   *Future value and present value*

Required

Using Tables I, II, III, or IV in this appendix, calculate the following:

a. The future value of $30,000 invested at 8 percent for 10 years.

b. The future value of eight annual payments of $2,000 at 9 percent interest.

c. The amount that must be deposited today (present value) at 8 percent to accumulate $60,000 in five years.

d. The annual payment on a 10-year, 6 percent, $50,000 note payable.

Exercise G2   *Computing the payment amount*

Barry Rich is a business major at State U. He will be graduating this year and is planning to start a consulting business. He will need to purchase computer equipment that costs $25,000. He can borrow the money from the local bank but will have to make annual payments of principal and interest.

Required

a. Compute the annual payment Barry will be required to make on a $25,000, four-year, 8 percent loan.

b. If Barry can afford to make annual payments of $8,000, how much can he borrow?

Exercise G3   *Saving for a future value*

Billy Dan and Betty Lou were recently married and want to start saving for their dream home. They expect the house they want will cost approximately $325,000. They hope to be able to purchase the house for cash in 10 years.

Required

a. How much will Billy Dan and Betty Lou have to invest each year to purchase their dream home at the end of 10 years? Assume an interest rate of 9 percent.

b. Billy Dan's parents want to give the couple a substantial wedding gift for the purchase of their future home. How much must Billy Dan's parents give them now if they are to reach the desired amount of $325,000 in 12 years? Assume an interest rate of 9 percent.

Exercise G4   *Sale of bonds at a discount using present value*

Carr Corporation issued $50,000 of 6 percent, 10-year bonds on January 1, Year 1, for a price that reflected a 7 percent market rate of interest. Interest is payable annually on December 31.

Required

a. What was the selling price of the bonds?

b. Prepare the journal entry to record issuing the bonds.

c. Prepare the journal entry for the first interest payment on December 31, Year 1, using the effective interest rate method.

BIG DATA AND DATA VISUALIZATIONS OVERVIEW

Over the last decade, big data has fundamentally transformed the managerial decision process and provided a new insightful way for managers to gauge company performance. *Big data* is a term that describes the large volume of information primarily captured by a variety of computerized systems. As a result of the Internet and advanced computerized devices, we have created more data in the last two years than in the history of the entire human race. This data is comprised of all types of information in both quantitative and qualitative form. Companies have begun collecting data in many forms including financial information, customer demographics, and geographical information, to name a few.

While the rate at which data is being created and captured has exploded over the last decade, it is how companies utilize this data to make informed business decisions that makes the real difference in company performance. As an example, we have all seen major companies such as Google and Facebook collect large amounts of personal data from its customers in order to generate personalized ads. These ads represent the major sources of revenue for these tech giants, making big data a key element to their success. Other companies such as Salesforce.com have relied on big data to retain employees by examining wage disparities between men and women serving in the same role. Results from their analysis revealed that wages were not consistent across genders, allowing the company to make the needed corrections to retain some of their top talent. The possibilities of using big data to improve enterprises are endless; however, companies require some powerful tools to analyze and process all this data to extract meaningful information.

Clive Humby is quoted as saying "Data is the new oil. It's valuable, but if unrefined it cannot really be used. It has to be changed into gas, plastic, chemicals, etc to create a valuable entity that drives profitable activity; so must data be broken down, analyzed for it to have value."* This quote exemplifies the importance of using analytical tools to extract the information an enterprise needs to make informed business decisions. Over the last decade, many software applications have been released to the market to assist managers in making use of big data. The tools perform a variety of functions in the big data environment including data crawlers that capture all types of information from a variety of websites, tools that convert unstructured data into a structured form that can be analyzed, and software that converts data into a visual form making interpretation of the data far easier to interpret. These examples represent only a small subset of the functions these tools perform. To provide an example of how big data can assist managers in making decisions, this appendix will focus on the third function, data visualizations.

We have all heard the quote that a picture is worth a thousand words, and this is certainly true when it comes to data visualizations. Data visualizations replace columns and rows of data with statistical graphics, plots, and information graphics. Examining data in visual form allows users to gain insights into their business far more efficiently than trying to make sense of raw data. One of the leading software tools for creating and analyzing data visualizations is called Tableau. The remainder of this appendix will give you the opportunity to learn more about Tableau by teaching you how to upload data into Tableau, create data visualizations from a raw dataset, and set up user dashboards that organize multiple data elements into a summary format.

Tableau Demonstration

In order to complete the exercise outlined in this appendix, you will need to download the student version of Tableau at the following URL: https://www.tableau.com/academic/students. We have provided a dataset (Super Store) for use in this exercise that can be obtained through *Connect*. Once you have downloaded Tableau and the "Super Store" dataset

*Humby, Clive. 2006. ANA Senior marketer's summit, Kellogg School.

to your computer, we recommend watching the introduction to Tableau training video included in *Connect*. This video will walk you through the basics of Tableau and demonstrate the Tableau procedures required to complete all assignments.

Conducting Financial Statement Analysis in Tableau

This demonstration involves analyzing a dataset for Super Store, a retailer of office supplies. The company was founded by Jim Rogers, who knows a lot about office supplies, but relies on his management team to help him understand vast amount of data supplied by the company's computer systems. Super Store has performed exceptionally well over the last three years due to its rapid expansion into new markets. One of the major changes at Super Store over the last year was its expansion into the international market by opening stores in India. India's rapidly growing economy compounded by the shortage of office supply stores has provided a prosperous opportunity for Super Store. However, the expansion into international markets has come with challenges resulting in Super Store management needing additional tools and expertise to understand how this new market is affecting its business.

Assume you were recently hired by Super Store management to assist the company in preparing data visualizations for financial statement analysis using Tableau. Historically, the company has relied on companywide ratios to gauge performance but would like you to dig deeper into these ratios to provide a more detailed picture of operations at Super Store.

Super Store management has asked you to analyze two companywide ratios: accounts receivable turnover and inventory turnover. Refer to Chapter 9 for descriptions of these ratios and equations for how they are calculated. The company has provided you with a dataset containing a large variety of company data for use in your analysis. Recall that the dataset is called "Super Store" and can be found on the *Connect* course website.

Accounts Receivable Turnover

Historically, Super Store has analyzed the companywide accounts receivable ratio to gauge the quality of its collection policies and procedures. The company calculates this ratio using the following equation:

$$\frac{\text{Net Credit Sales}}{\text{Average Accounts Receivable}}$$

For purposes of this example, we assume Super Store's prior year accounts receivable balance was $4,975,830. Using this balance and the current year balance from the Super Store dataset, the AR turnover ratio for the company would be calculated as follows:

$$\frac{\$52,267,354}{(\$4,975,830 + \$5,795,254) / 2} = 9.71$$

The ratio of 9.71 tells us that the company collects its accounts receivable balances a little under 10 times a year. To make more sense of this number, the company also calculates the average number of days that accounts receivable is outstanding using the following equation:

$$\frac{365 \text{ days}}{\text{Accounts Receivable Turnover}}$$

Using this equation, the company's average days outstanding is:

$$\frac{365}{9.71} = 38 \text{ days}$$

These companywide ratios tell management that, as a whole, the company collects its receivable a little under 10 times a year or every 38 days. Overall, these ratios would indicate that the company does a good job at collecting its outstanding receivable balances, indicating that its current policies and procedures for accounts receivable are effective. Relying solely on these companywide ratios would likely result in management making no changes to its current collection processes.

While the prior ratios are useful in gauging companywide performance, Super Store management has requested more detailed information analyzing collections across geographic regions. Specifically, management wants to know how collections differ between their stores in the United States compared to the stores in India. Jim Rogers, founder of Super Store, has asked you to prepare a data visualization that he can use for presentation purposes analyzing the turnover ratios.

In order to assist Mr. Rogers, you will be using Tableau to conduct analysis on the Super Store dataset. Begin by opening the Tableau program and adding the Super Store data file to Tableau. Refer to the Introduction to Tableau video for instructions on how to add a dataset to Tableau and complete the visualization for Mr. Rogers.

The following two visualizations illustrate the accounts receivable turnover ratio and average days outstanding for the United States and India.

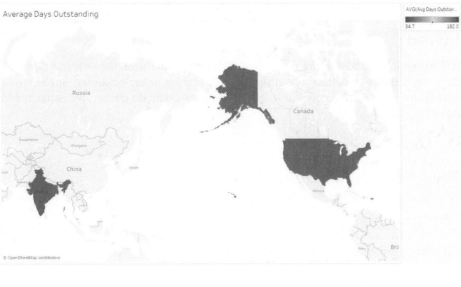

Both of these visualizations clearly show that there are large differences between the United States and India accounts receivable ratios. For the average days outstanding ratio, the color green indicates lower values and red represents higher values. Since most people associate good news with green and bad news with red, this color scheme appropriately reflects how to interpret this ratio. For the AR turnover ratio, higher numbers would be representative of good news; therefore, the color green was assigned to higher values and red to lower values. Using a common color scheme such as red for negative news and green for positive news sends a clear indicator about which country is performing better. Using the legend in the top right of the visualization gives us number information that correspond to the colors.

If you hover over each country, Tableau will display the exact numerical balance for each country.

Mr. Rogers could easily present these two visualizations to indicate to interested parties that the company is suffering collection problems in India as compared to the United States. These visualizations exemplify the importance of using visualizations to separate the ratios by country in order to better understand the differences between the two countries as compared to analyzing the ratios in total.

ASSIGNMENT

The following question pertains to the information provided in Appendix H. For additional practice using Tableau, a more detailed assignment is provided in *Connect*.

Required

Write a paragraph explaining the ratios for each country and what they mean in regards to the company's ability to collect its outstanding receivables in each country. Speculate as to the reasons for these differences and what the company could do to improve issues noted in the ratios.

APPENDIX I

CHART OF ACCOUNTS

Ch.	Balance Sheet			Income Statement
	Assets =	**Liabilities** +	**Stockholders' Equity**	
1	Cash	Note Payable	Common Stock	Advertising Expense
	Land		Retained Earnings	Interest Expense
				Operating Expense
				Rent Expense
				Revenue
				Salaries Expense
2	Accounts Receivable	Accounts Payable		Consulting Revenue
		Interest Payable		Utility Expense
		Salaries Payable		
3	Accumulated Depreciation (Contra)	Unearned Revenue		Installation Revenue
	Computer			Depreciation Expense
	Furniture			Supplies Expense
	Prepaid Insurance			
	Prepaid Rent			
	Supplies			
4	Inventory or Merchandise Inventory			Cost of Goods Sold
				Gain on the Sale of Land
				Loss on the Sale of Land
				Sales Discounts
				Sales Revenue
				Selling & Admin. Expense
				Transportation-out
5	No new accounts			
6	Petty Cash			Cash Short and Over
				Miscellaneous Expense
7	Allowance for Doubtful Accounts (Contra)			Credit Card Expense
	Interest Receivable			Uncollectible Accounts Exp.
	Note Receivable			
8	Building	Deferred Income Taxes		Amortization Expense
	Bulldozer			Depletion Expense
	Coal Mine			Impairment Loss
	Copyright			Income Tax Expense
	Equipment			Patent Expense

	Goodwill			
	Machine			
	Mineral Deposits			
	Oil and Gas Reserves			
	Patent			
	Van			
9	Marketable Securities	Contingent Liability		Federal Unemployment Tax Exp.
		Discount on Notes Payable (Contra)		FICA – Medicare Tax Expense
		Employee Income Tax Payable		FICA – Social Security Tax Exp.
		Federal Unemployment Tax Payable		Fringe Benefits Expense
		FICA – Medicare Tax Payable		Payroll Tax Expense
		FICA – Social Security Tax Payable		Sales Tax Expense
		Fringe Benefits Payable		State Unemployment Tax Exp.
		Sales Tax Payable		Warranty Expense
		State Unemployment Tax Payable		
		Warranty Payable		
10		Bonds Payable		
		Discount on Bonds Payable (Contra)		
		Installment Notes Payable		
		Line-of-Credit Payable		
		Premium on Bonds Payable		
11		Dividends Payable	Additional Paid-In Capital in Excess of Par Value	
			Additional Paid-In Capital in Excess of Stated Value	
			Additional Paid-In Capital, Treasury Stock	
			Appropriated Retained Earnings	
			Common Stock, No Par	
			Common Stock, Par Value	
			Common Stock, Stated Value	
			Partners' Capital	
			Preferred Stock	
			Proprietor's Capital	
			Treasury Stock (Contra)	
12	No new accounts			
13	No new accounts			

Other Accounts: **Dividends** (Chapter 1) are reported on the Statement of Changes in Stockholders' Equity. **Withdrawals** (Chapter 11) are reported on the Capital Statement.

KEY TERMS

Dividends 755
Withdrawals 755

GLOSSARY

absolute amounts Dollar totals reported in accounts on financial reports that can be misleading because they make no reference to the relative size of the company being analyzed.

accelerated depreciation method Depreciation method that recognizes more depreciation expense in the early stages of an asset's life than the straight-line method and less later in the asset's life.

account Record of classified and summarized transaction data; component of financial statement elements.

accounting Service-based profession developed to provide reliable and relevant financial information useful in making decisions.

accounting controls Procedures companies implement to safeguard assets and to ensure accurate and reliable accounting records and reports.

accounting equation Algebraic relationship between a company's assets and the claims on those assets, represented as Assets = Liabilities + Equity.

accounting event Economic occurrence that changes a company's assets, liabilities, or equity.

accounting period Time span covered by the financial statements; normally one year, but may be a quarter, a month, or some other time interval.

accounts payable Amounts owed but not yet paid to suppliers who have provided goods or services to the business.

accounts receivable Expected future cash receipts arising from permitting customers to *buy now and pay later;* typically relatively small balances due within a short time period.

accounts receivable turnover ratio Financial ratio that measures how fast accounts receivable are collected in cash; computed by dividing sales by accounts receivable.

accrual Accounting recognition of revenue or expense in a period before cash is exchanged.

accrual accounting Accounting system that recognizes revenues when earned and expenses when incurred, regardless of when the related cash is exchanged.

accrued expenses Expenses that are recognized before cash is paid. An example is accrued salaries expense.

accrued interest Interest revenue or expense that is recognized before cash has been exchanged.

accumulated depreciation Contra asset account that indicates the sum of all depreciation expense recognized for an asset since the date of acquisition.

acid-test ratio Measure of immediate debt-paying ability; calculated by dividing very liquid assets (cash, receivables, and marketable securities) by current liabilities.

administrative controls Procedures companies implement to evaluate performance and monitor compliance with company policies and public laws.

adverse opinion Opinion issued by a certified public accountant that means one or more departures from GAAP in a company's financial statements are so very material the auditors believe the financial statements do not fairly represent the company's status; contrast with *unqualified opinion.*

aging of accounts receivable Classifying each account receivable by the number of days it has been outstanding. The purpose of the aging schedule is to develop a more accurate estimate of the amount of uncollectible accounts.

allowance for doubtful accounts Contra asset account used to record the amount of accounts receivable estimated to be uncollectible.

allowance method of accounting for uncollectible accounts An accounting practice that recognizes an estimated rather than the actual amount of uncollectible accounts expense. Estimated expenses are used to improve matching of revenues and expenses and/or to more accurately reflect the net realizable value of accounts receivable.

American Institute of Certified Public Accountants (AICPA) National association that serves the educational and professional interests of members of the public accounting profession; membership is voluntary. See also *Code of Professional Conduct.*

amortization (1) Systematic and periodic allocation of the costs of intangible assets to expense over their useful lives; (2) periodically transferring the discount on a note or a bond to interest expense.

amortizing Systematically allocating the cost of intangible assets to expense over their useful lives; also a term for converting the discount on a note or a bond to interest expense over a designated period.

annual report Document companies publish to provide information, including financial statements, to stockholders.

annuity Series of equal cash flows received or paid over equal time intervals at a constant rate of return.

appropriated retained earnings Retained earnings restricted by the board of directors for a specific purpose (e.g., to repay debt or for future expansion); part of total retained earnings, but not available for distribution as dividends.

articles of incorporation Information about a proposed corporation, such as its name, purpose, location, expected life, proposed capital stock, and a list of the members of its board of directors, filed with a state agency when applying for the legal formation of the corporation.

articulation Characteristic of financial statements that means they are interrelated. For example, the amount of net income reported on the income statement is added to beginning retained earnings as a component in calculating the ending retained earnings balance reported on the statement of changes in stockholders' equity.

asset Economic resource used to produce revenue that is expected to provide future benefit to the business.

asset exchange transaction A transaction, such as paying cash expenses, that decreases an asset and a liability or stockholders' equity account.

asset source transaction Transaction that increases an asset and a claim on assets; three types of asset source transactions are acquisitions from owners (equity), borrowings from creditors (liabilities), or earnings from operations (revenues).

asset turnover ratio The amount of net sales divided by average total assets.

asset use transaction A transaction that decreases both an asset and a claim on assets; the three types of asset use transactions are distributions (transfers to owners), liability payments (to creditors), or expenses (costs incurred to operate the business).

audit Detailed examination of some aspect of a company's accounting records or operating procedures in order to report the results to interested parties. See also *financial statements audit.*

authority manual Written documentation outlining levels of authority and responsibility. The authority manual provides specific guidelines, such as those for a personnel officer, as well as general guidelines, such as giving all vice presidents authorization to approve up to a designated spending limit.

authorized stock   Number of shares of stock a corporation has state approval to issue.

available-for-sale securities   Classification for marketable securities that are not considered held-to-maturity or trading securities.

average days to sell inventory (average days in inventory)   Financial ratio that measures the average number of days that inventory stays in stock before it is sold.

average number of days to collect accounts receivable (average collection period)   Measure of how quickly, on average, a business collects its accounts receivable; calculated as 365 divided by the accounts receivable turnover.

bad debts expense   An expense resulting from a decrease in the amount of accounts receivable due to the inability to collect balances due from debtors. The term is a synonym for uncollectible accounts expense.

balance sheet   Financial statement that reports a company's assets and the corresponding claims (liabilities and equity) on those assets as of a specific date (usually as of the end of the accounting period).

bank reconciliation   Schedule that identifies and explains differences between the cash balance reported by the bank and the cash balance in the company's accounting records.

bank statement   Record issued by a bank (usually monthly) of all activity in the bank account for that period.

basket purchase   Acquiring several assets at once for a single purchase price; no specific cost is attributed to the individual assets.

board of directors   Group of individuals elected by the stockholders of a corporation to oversee its operations.

bond certificate   Debt security used to obtain long-term financing in which a company borrows funds from a number of lenders, called *bondholders;* usually issued in denominations of $1,000.

bond discount   Difference between the selling price and the face amount of a bond sold for less than the face amount.

bond premium   Difference between the selling price and the face amount of a bond that is sold for more than the face amount.

bondholder   The party buying a bond (the lender or creditor).

book of original entry   A journal in which a transaction is first recorded.

book value   Historical (original) cost of an asset minus accumulated depreciation to date.

book value per share   An accounting measure of a share of common stock, computed by dividing total stockholders' equity less preferred rights by the number of common shares outstanding.

call premium   Difference between the call price (the price that must be paid for a called bond) and the face amount of the bond.

call price   Specified price an issuer must pay to call bonds; usually higher than the face amount of the bonds.

callable bonds   Bonds that the issuer, at its option, may pay off prior to maturity.

capital expenditures (for an existing asset)   Substantial amounts spent to improve an asset's quality or to extend its life.

carrying value   Face amount of a bond liability less any unamortized bond discount or plus any unamortized bond premium.

cash   Coins, currency, checks, balances in checking and certain savings accounts, money orders, bank drafts, certificates of deposit, and other items that are payable on demand.

cash discount   Price reduction on merchandise sold offered by sellers to encourage prompt payment; when taken, represents a sales discount to the seller and a purchase discount to the buyer of the merchandise.

cash inflows   Sources of cash.

cash outflows   Uses of cash.

cash short and over   Account used to record the amount of cash shortages or overages; shortages represent expenses and overages represent revenues.

certified check   Check guaranteed by a bank to be drawn on an account with sufficient funds to pay the check.

certified public accountant (CPA)   Accountant who, by meeting certain educational and experiential requirements, is licensed by the state government to provide audit services to the public.

chart of accounts   List of all ledger accounts and their corresponding account numbers.

checks   Prenumbered forms, sometimes multicopy, preprinted on the face with the name of the business issuing them, authorizing the bank to disburse funds from the issuer's account. The issuer enters the transaction date, the desired payee, and the amount in the appropriate places on the check form.

claims   Owners' and creditors' interests in a business's assets.

claims exchange transaction   A transaction that decreases one claim and increases another claim; total claims remain unchanged. For example, accruing interest expense is a claims exchange transaction: liabilities increase, and the expense recognition decreases retained earnings.

classified balance sheet   Balance sheet that distinguishes between current and noncurrent items.

closely held corporation   Corporation whose stock is exchanged among a limited number of individuals.

closing entries   Entries that transfer the balances in the temporary accounts (Revenue, Expense, and Dividends accounts) to the Retained Earnings account at the end of the accounting period.

Code of Professional Conduct   Guidelines established by the American Institute of Certified Public Accountants (AICPA) to promote ethical conduct among certified public accountants; AICPA members agree to adhere to this code, which goes beyond legal requirements.

collateral   Assets pledged as security for a loan.

common size financial statements   Financial statements in which dollar amounts are converted to percentages to aid in comparing financial data among periods and among companies.

common stock   Basic class of corporate stock that has no preferential claim on assets or dividends; certificates that evidence ownership in a company.

compound interest   Interest earned on interest by reinvesting interest so that it is added to the initial principal. Contrast with *simple interest.*

compounding   Earning interest on interest.

confidentiality   Code of ethics requirement that prohibits CPAs from voluntarily disclosing information they acquire as a result of accountant–client relationships.

consistency   The generally accepted accounting principle that a company should, in most circumstances, continually use the same accounting method(s) so that its financial statements are comparable across time.

consolidated financial statements   Financial statements that represent the combined operations of a parent company and its subsidiaries.

contingent liability   Obligations with amounts due that depend on events that will be resolved in the future.

continuity   Presumption that a corporation's existence may extend well beyond the time at which any particular shareholder retires or sells his or her stock.

contra asset account   Account used to reduce the reported value of the asset to which it relates (e.g., subtracting the contra asset Allowance for Uncollectible Accounts from Accounts Receivable reduces receivables to their net realizable value).

contra liability account   Account used to reduce the reported value of the liability to which it relates (e.g., subtracting the contra liability Discount on Notes Payable from Notes Payable reduces the amount of liabilities on the balance sheet).

convertible bonds   Bonds that bondholders can convert (exchange) to ownership interests (stock) in the corporation.

copyright Legal protection of writers' works, musical compositions, and other intellectual property for the exclusive use of the creator or persons assigned the right by the creator.

corporation Legal entity separate from its owners, created by the state pursuant to an application submitted according to state laws by a group of individuals with a common purpose.

cost An amount paid to acquire a resource (asset) or to pay for a resource that has been consumed. Incurring a cost results in an asset exchange or expense recognition.

cost method of accounting for treasury stock Method of accounting for treasury stock in which treasury stock purchases are recorded in the Treasury Stock account at their cost to the company without regard to the original issue price or par value.

cost of goods available for sale Total costs paid to obtain goods and ready them for sale, including the cost of beginning inventory plus purchases and transportation-in costs, less purchase returns and allowances and purchase discounts.

cost of goods sold Total cost incurred for the goods sold during a specific accounting period.

credit Entry on the right side of an account; increases liability and equity accounts or decreases asset accounts.

credit memo Bank statement enclosure that describes an increase in the account balance.

creditor Individual or organization that has loaned goods or services to a business.

cumulative dividends Preferred dividends that accumulate from year to year until paid.

current (short-term) asset Asset that will be converted to cash or consumed within one year or an operating cycle, whichever is longer.

current (short-term) liability Obligation due within one year or an operating cycle, whichever is longer.

current ratio (working capital ratio) Measure of liquidity; calculated by dividing current assets by current liabilities.

date of record Date that establishes who will receive the dividend payment: shareholders who actually own the stock on the record date will receive the dividend even if they sell the stock before the dividend is paid.

debenture Unsecured bond backed by the general credit of the issuing company.

debit Entry on the left side of an account; increases asset accounts or decreases liability and equity accounts.

debit memo Bank statement enclosure that describes a decrease in the account balance.

debt security Type of financial instrument that represents a liability to the investee company.

debt-to-assets ratio Financial measure of a company's level of risk, calculated as total debt divided by total assets.

debt-to-equity ratio Financial ratio that compares creditor financing to owner financing; expressed as the dollar amount of liabilities for each dollar of stockholders' equity.

declaration date Date on which the board of directors declares a dividend.

deferral A revenue or expense item that is recognized in an accounting period after the period in which cash was collected or paid.

deferred tax liability Income tax payment postponed until future years because of the difference in accounting methods selected for financial reporting and methods required for tax purposes (e.g., a company may use straight-line depreciation in financial statements but use MACRS for tax reporting).

depletion The removal of natural resources from the land; the depletion costs of the natural resources are systematically transferred to expense as the resources are removed.

deposit ticket Bank form submitted along with funds that identifies the account number, account name, and a record of the checks and cash being put in the account.

deposits in transit Deposits added to a depositor's books but not received and recorded by the bank prior to the date of the bank statement.

depreciable cost Original cost minus salvage value (of a long-term depreciable asset).

depreciation Decline in value of long-term tangible assets such as buildings, furniture, or equipment. It is systematically recognized by accountants as depreciation expense over the useful lives of the affected assets.

depreciation expense Portion of the original cost of a long-term tangible asset allocated to an expense account in a given period.

direct method Method of reporting cash flows from operating activities on the statement of cash flows that shows individual categories of cash receipts from and cash payments for major activities (collections from customers, payments to suppliers, etc.).

direct write-off method Accounting practice of recognizing uncollectible accounts expense when accounts are determined to be uncollectible, regardless of the period in which the related sale occurred.

disclaimer of opinion Report on financial statements issued when the auditor is unable to obtain enough information to determine if the statements conform to GAAP; is neither positive nor negative.

discount Amount of interest included in the face of a discount note; the discount (interest) is subtracted from the face amount of the note to determine the amount of cash borrowed (principal).

discount note Note with interest included in its face value, which is also the maturity value.

discount on bonds payable Contra liability account used to record the amount of discount on a bond issue.

discount on notes payable Contra liability account subtracted from the Notes Payable account to determine the carrying value of the liability.

dividend Transfer of wealth from a business to its owners.

dividend yield Ratio for comparing stock dividends paid in relation to the market price; calculated as dividends per share divided by market price per share.

dividends in arrears Cumulative dividends on preferred stock that were not paid in prior periods; must be paid before paying any dividends to holders of common stock.

double taxation Recognition that corporate profits distributed to owners are taxed twice, once when the income is reported on the corporation's income tax return and again when the dividends are reported on the individual's return.

double-declining-balance depreciation Depreciation computations that produce larger amounts of depreciation in the early years of an asset's life and progressively smaller amounts as the asset ages.

double-entry accounting (double-entry bookkeeping) Recordkeeping system that provides checks and balances by recording two sides for every transaction.

earnings (net income) The difference between revenues and expenses. Sometimes called *profit*.

earnings per share Measure of the value of a share of common stock in terms of company earnings; calculated as net income available to common stockholders divided by the average number of outstanding common shares.

effective interest rate Yield rate of bonds, equal to the market rate of interest on the day the bonds are sold.

effective interest rate method Method of amortizing bond discounts and premiums that bases interest computations on the carrying value of the liability. As the liability increases or decreases, the amount of interest expense also increases or decreases.

elements   Key components of financials statements including assets, liabilities, stockholders' equity, common stock, retained earnings, revenue, expense, and net income.

employee   An individual whose labor is supervised, directed, and controlled by a business.

Employee's Withholding Allowance Certificate, Form W-4   A form used by an employee to report the number of withholding allowances claimed by the employee. Each withholding allowance reduces the amount of income tax withheld from the employee's pay.

Employer's Quarterly Federal Tax Return, Form 941   The form used to show the amounts due and paid to the government for federal tax withholdings.

end-of-period adjustment   Adjustment that updates account balances prior to preparing financial statements. End-of-period adjustments never affect the Cash account.

equity method   Method of accounting for investments in marketable equity securities required when the investor company owns 20 percent or more of the investee company. Under the equity method, the amount of the investment asset represents a measure of the book value of the investee rather than the cost or market value of the investment security.

equity security   Type of financial instrument that evidences an ownership interest in a company, such as a common stock certificate.

estimated useful life   Time period for which a business expects to use an asset.

ex-dividend   Stock traded after the date of record but before the payment date; does not receive the benefit of the upcoming dividend.

expenses   Economic sacrifices (decreases in assets or increases in liabilities) that are incurred in the process of generating revenue.

face value (of bond)   Amount to be paid to the bondholder at bond maturity; base for computing periodic cash interest payments.

fair value   The price at which securities or other assets sell in free markets. Also called *market value*.

Federal Unemployment Tax Act (FUTA)   The act that requires employers to pay unemployment tax for the establishment of a fund that is used to provide temporary relief to qualified unemployed persons.

fidelity bond   Insurance policy that a company buys to insure itself against loss due to employee dishonesty.

financial accounting   Branch of accounting focused on the business information needs of external users (creditors, investors, governmental agencies, financial analysts, etc.); its objective is to classify and record business events and transactions to produce external financial reports (income statement, balance sheet, statement of cash flows, and statement of changes in equity).

Financial Accounting Standards Board (FASB)   Private, independent standard-setting body established by the accounting profession that has been delegated the authority by the SEC to establish most of the accounting rules and regulations for public financial reporting.

financial leverage   Principle of increasing earnings through debt financing by investing money at a higher rate than the rate paid on the borrowed money.

financial resources   Money or credit supplied to a business by investors (owners) and creditors.

financial statements   Reports used to communicate a company's financial information to interested external parties. The four general-purpose financial statements are the income statement, statement of changes in equity, balance sheet, and statement of cash flows.

financial statements audit   Detailed examination of a company's accounting records and the documents that support the information reported in the financial statements; includes testing the reliability of the underlying accounting system used to produce the financial reports.

financing activities   Cash inflows and outflows from transactions with investors and creditors (except interest), including cash receipts from issuing stock, borrowing activities, and cash disbursements to pay dividends; one of the three categories of cash inflows and outflows reported on the statement of cash flows. This category shows the amount of cash supplied by these resource providers and the amount of cash that is returned to them.

first-in, first-out (FIFO) cost flow method   Inventory cost flow method in which cost of goods sold is computed as if the earliest items purchased are the first items sold.

fiscal year   The annual time period for which a company provides financial statements.

fixed interest rate   Interest rate (charge for borrowing money) that remains constant over the life of the loan.

FOB (free on board) destination   Shipping term that means the seller bears the freight (transportation-in) costs.

FOB (free on board) shipping point   Shipping term that means the buyer bears the freight (transportation-in) costs.

franchise   Exclusive right to sell products or perform services in certain geographic areas.

full disclosure   The accounting principle that financial statements should include all information relevant to an entity's operations and financial condition. Full disclosure frequently requires adding footnotes to the financial statements.

future value   Amount an investment will be worth at some point in the future, assuming a specified interest rate and the reinvestment of interest each period that it is earned.

gains   Increases in assets or decreases in liabilities that result from peripheral or incidental transactions.

general authority   Company guidelines that apply to various levels of a company's management, such as requiring everyone at that level to fly coach class.

general journal   Book of original entry in which any accounting transaction could be recorded, though commonly limited to adjusting and closing entries and unusual transactions.

general ledger   The set of all accounts used in an accounting system.

general uncertainties   Uncertainties such as competition and damage from storms. These uncertainties are distinguished from contingent liabilities because they arise from future rather than past events.

generally accepted accounting principles (GAAP)   Rules and practices that accountants agree to follow in financial reports prepared for public distribution.

going concern assumption   Accounting presumption that a company will continue to operate indefinitely, benefiting from its assets and paying its obligations in full; justifies reporting assets and liabilities in the financial statements.

goodwill   Intangible added value of a successful business attributable to such factors as reputation, location, and superior products that enables the business to earn above-average profits; measured by an entity acquiring the business as the excess paid over the appraised value of the net assets.

gross earnings   The total amount of employee wages or salaries before any deductions or withholdings. Gross earnings include the total of regular pay plus any bonuses, overtime, or other additions.

gross margin (gross profit)   Percentage difference between sales revenue and cost of goods sold; the amount a company makes from selling goods before subtracting operating expenses.

gross margin method   Technique for estimating the ending inventory amount without a physical count; useful when the percentage of gross margin to sales remains relatively stable from one accounting period to the next.

gross margin percentage   Expressing gross margin as a percentage of sales by dividing gross margin by net sales; the amount of each dollar of sales that is profit before deducting any operating expenses.

gross profit   See *gross margin*.

half-year convention   Tax rule that requires recognizing six months of depreciation expense on an asset both in the year of purchase and in the year of disposal regardless of the actual purchase date.

held-to-maturity securities   Classification for marketable debt securities the purchasing company intends to hold (rather than sell) until the securities mature.

historical cost concept   Accounting practice of reporting assets at the actual price paid for them when purchased regardless of estimated changes in market value.

horizontal analysis   Analysis technique that compares amounts of the same item over several time periods.

horizontal financial statements model   Concurrent representation of several financial statements horizontally across a page.

imprest basis   Maintaining an account at a specified fixed amount, such as periodically replenishing a petty cash fund to its imprest amount.

income   Increase in value created by providing goods and services through resource transformation.

income statement   Financial report of profitability; measures the difference between revenues and expenses for the accounting period (whether or not cash has been exchanged).

independent auditor   Licensed certified public accountant engaged to audit a company's financial statements; not an employee of the audited company.

independent contractor   An individual who is paid by a business but retains individual control and supervisory authority over the work performed.

indirect method   Method of reporting cash flows from operating activities on the statement of cash flows that starts with the net income from the income statement, followed by adjustments necessary to convert accrual-based net income to a cash-basis equivalent.

information overload   Situation in which the presentation of too much information confuses the user of the information.

installment notes   Obligations that require regular payments of principal and interest over the life of the loan.

intangible assets   Long-term assets having no physical substance that benefit their owners through providing rights and privileges, such as a trademark.

interest   Fee paid for the use of funds; represents expense to the borrower and revenue to the lender.

interest-bearing notes   Notes that require face value plus accrued interest to be paid at maturity.

internal controls   Policies and procedures companies establish to provide reasonable assurance of reducing fraud, providing reliable accounting records, and accomplishing organization objectives.

International Accounting Standards Board (IASB)   Private, independent body that establishes International Financial Reporting Standards (IFRS). The IASB's authority is established by various governmental institutions that require or permit companies in their jurisdiction to use IFRS. To date, over 100 countries require or permit companies to prepare their financial statements using IFRS. One notable exception is the United States of America.

International Financial Reporting Standards (IFRS)   Pronouncements established by the International Accounting Standards Board that provide guidance for the preparation of financial statements.

inventory cost flow methods   Alternative ways to allocate the cost of goods available for sale between cost of goods sold and ending inventory.

inventory turnover   A measure of sales volume relative to inventory levels; calculated as the cost of goods sold divided by average inventory; indicates how many times a year, on average, the inventory is sold (turned over).

investee   Company that receives assets or services in exchange for a debt or equity security.

investing activities   Cash inflows and outflows associated with buying or selling long-term assets and cash inflows and outflows associated with lending activities and investments in the debt and equity of other companies; one of the three categories of cash inflows and outflows reported on the statement of cash flows.

investment securities   Certificates that describe the rights and privileges that investors receive when they loan or give assets or services to investees.

investor   Company or individual who gives assets or services in exchange for security certificates representing ownership interests.

issued stock   Stock a company has sold to the public.

issuer (of a bond)   Party that issues the bond (the borrower).

journal   Book (or electronic record) of original entry in which accounting data are entered chronologically before posting to the ledger accounts.

labor resources   The intellectual and physical efforts of individuals used in the process of providing goods and services to customers.

last-in, first-out (LIFO) cost flow method   Inventory cost flow method in which cost of goods sold is computed as if the most recently purchased items are the first items sold.

legal capital   Amount of assets that should be maintained as protection for creditors; the number of shares multiplied by the par value.

liabilities   Obligations of a business to relinquish assets, provide services, or accept other obligations.

limited liability   Concept that investors in a corporation may not be held personally liable for the actions or debts of the corporation; stockholders' liability is limited to the amount they paid for their stock.

limited liability company (LLC)   Organizational form that offers many of the favorable characteristics and legal benefits of a corporation (e.g., limited liability and centralized management) but is permitted by federal law to be taxed as a partnership, thereby avoiding double taxation of profits.

line of credit   Preapproved financing arrangement with a lending institution in which a business can borrow money up to the approved limit by simply writing a check.

liquidation   Process of dividing up an organization's assets and returning them to the resource providers. In business liquidations, creditors normally have first priority; after creditor claims have been satisfied, any remaining assets are distributed to the company's owners (investors).

liquidity   Ability to convert assets to cash quickly and meet short-term obligations.

liquidity ratios   Measures of short-term debt-paying ability.

long-term operational assets   Assets used by a business, normally over multiple accounting periods, to generate revenue; contrast with assets that are sold (inventory) or held (investments) to generate revenue; also called *productive assets*.

losses   Decreases in assets or increases in liabilities that result from peripheral or incidental transactions.

lower-of-cost-or-market rule   Accounting principle of reporting inventory at its replacement cost (market) if replacement cost has declined below the inventory's original cost, regardless of the cause.

maker   The party issuing a note (the borrower).

management's discussion and analysis (MD&A)   Section of a company's annual report in which management explains many different aspects of the company's past performance and future plans.

managerial accounting   Branch of accounting focused on the information needs of managers and others working within the business; its objective is to gather and report information that adds value to the business. Managerial accounting information is not regulated or reported to the public.

manufacturing businesses   Companies that make the goods they sell customers.

market Group of people or entities organized to buy and sell resources.

market interest rate Interest rate currently available on a wide range of alternative investments with similar levels of risk.

market value The price at which securities sell in the secondary market; also called *fair value*.

marketable securities Securities that are readily traded in the secondary securities market.

matching concept Accounting principle of recognizing expenses in the same accounting period as the revenues they produce, using one of three methods: match expenses directly with revenues (e.g., cost of goods sold); match expenses to the period in which they are incurred (e.g., rent expense), and match expenses systematically with revenues (e.g., depreciation expense).

materiality The point at which knowledge of information would influence a user's decision; can be measured in absolute, percentage, quantitative, or qualitative terms. The concept allows nonmaterial matters to be handled in any convenient way, such as charging a pencil sharpener to expense rather than recording periodic depreciation over its useful life.

maturity date The date that a liability is due to be settled (the date the borrower is expected to repay a debt).

Medicare Health insurance provided by the government primarily for retired workers.

merchandise inventory Finished goods held for resale to customers.

merchandising businesses Companies that buy and resell merchandise inventory.

modified accelerated cost recovery system (MACRS) Prescribed method of depreciation for tax purposes that provides the maximum depreciation expense deduction permitted under tax law.

mortgage bond Type of secured debt that conditionally transfers title of designated property to the bondholder until the bond is paid.

multistep income statement Income statement format that matches various revenues with related expenses in order to present subtotals (steps) such as gross margin and operating income; distinguishes between routine operating items and nonoperating items such as gains, losses, and interest. Contrast with *single-step income statement*.

natural resources Wasting assets originally attached to land such as mineral deposits, oil and gas reserves, and reserves of timber, mines, and quarries; the land value declines as the resources are removed.

net income Increase in equity resulting from operating the business.

net income percentage See *return on sales*.

net loss Decrease in equity resulting from operating the business.

net margin Profitability measurement that indicates the percentage of each sales dollar resulting in profit; calculated as net income divided by net sales.

net pay Employee's gross pay less all deductions (withholdings).

net realizable value The amount of accounts receivable a company expects to actually collect in cash; the face amount of receivables less an allowance for estimated uncollectible accounts.

net sales Sales less returns from customers and allowances or cash discounts granted to customers.

non-sufficient-funds (NSF) check Customer's check deposited but returned by the bank on which it was drawn because the customer did not have enough money in its account to pay the check.

noncash investing and financing activities Certain business transactions, usually long-term, that do not involve cash, such as exchanging stock for land or purchasing property by using debt; reported separately on the statement of cash flows.

not-for-profit entities Organizations (also called *nonprofit* or *nonbusiness organizations*) established primarily for motives other than making a profit, such as providing goods and services for the social good. Examples include state-supported universities and colleges, hospitals, public libraries, and public charities.

note payable Liability represented by a legal document called a *note* that describes pertinent details such as principal amount, interest charges, maturity date, and collateral.

notes receivable Notes that evidence rights to receive cash in the future; usually specify the maturity date, rate of interest, and other credit terms.

notes to the financial statements Written explanations accompanying the financial statements that provide information about such items as estimates used and accounting methods chosen when GAAP permits alternatives.

number of times interest is earned Number of times interest is earned is calculated as the amount of earnings before interest and taxes (EBIT) divided by the amount of interest expense. Dividing EBIT by interest expense indicates how many times the company could have made its interest payments. All other things being equal, the higher the number of times interest is earned, the lower the risk of default.

operating activities Cash inflows from and outflows for routine, everyday business operations, normally resulting from revenue and expense transactions including interest; one of the three categories of cash inflows and outflows reported on the statement of cash flows.

operating cycle Process of converting cash into inventory, inventory into receivables, and receivables back to cash; its length can be measured in days using financial statement data.

operating income (or loss) Income after subtracting operating expenses from operating revenues. Gains and losses and other peripheral activities are added to or subtracted from operating income to determine net income or loss.

opportunity An element of the fraud triangle that recognizes weaknesses in internal controls that enable the occurrence of fraudulent or unethical behavior.

outstanding checks Checks the depositor company has written and deducted from its cash account balance that have not yet been presented to its bank for payment.

outstanding stock Shares of stock a corporation has issued that are still owned by outside parties (i.e., all stock that has been issued less any treasury stock the corporation has repurchased).

Paid-in Capital in Excess of Par (or Stated) Value The account in which a company records any amount received above the par or stated value of stock when stock is issued.

par value Arbitrary value assigned to stock by the board of directors; like *stated value*, designates *legal capital*.

parent company Company that holds a controlling interest (more than 50 percent ownership) in another company.

partnership Business entity owned by at least two people who share talents, capital, and the risks of the business.

partnership agreement Legal document that defines the rights and responsibilities of each partner and describes how income and losses are to be divided.

patent Legal right granted by the U.S. Patent Office ensuring a company or an individual the exclusive right to a product or process.

payee The party collecting cash.

payment date Date on which a dividend is actually paid.

percent of receivables method A method of estimating the amount of uncollectible accounts by taking a percentage of the outstanding receivables balance. The percentage is frequently based on a combination of factors such as historical experience, conditions of the economy, and the company's credit policies.

percent of revenue method A method of estimating the amount of uncollectible accounts by taking a percentage of revenue that was earned on account during the accounting period. The percentage is frequently based on a combination of factors such as historical experience, condition of the economy, and the company's credit policies.

762   Glossary

percentage analysis Analysis of relationships between two different items to draw conclusions or make decisions.

period costs Expenses recognized in the period in which they are incurred regardless of when cash payments for them are made; costs that cannot be directly traced to products.

periodic inventory system Method of accounting for inventory that requires a physical count of goods on hand at the end of the accounting period in order to determine the amount of cost of goods sold and to update the Inventory account.

permanent accounts Balance sheet accounts; contain information carried forward from one accounting period to the next (ending account balance one period becomes beginning account balance next period).

perpetual inventory system Method of accounting for inventory in which the amount of cost of goods sold is recorded for each sale of inventory; the Inventory account is increased and decreased with each purchase and sale of merchandise.

petty cash fund Small amount of currency kept on company premises to pay for minor items when writing checks is not practical.

petty cash voucher Document that verifies a petty cash disbursement, signed by the person who received the money. Supporting documents, such as an invoice, restaurant bill, or parking fee receipt, should be attached to the petty cash voucher.

physical flow of goods Physical movement of goods through a business, normally on a FIFO basis so that the first goods purchased are the first goods delivered to customers, reducing the likelihood of inventory obsolescence.

physical resources Natural resources businesses transform to create more valuable resources.

plant assets to long-term liabilities Long-lived assets should be financed with long-term liabilities, and the plant assets to long-term liabilities ratio shows the amount of assets per each dollar of long-term debt. All other things being equal, the larger the ratio, the lower the financial risk.

posting Copying transaction data from journals to ledger accounts.

preferred stock Class of stock, usually nonvoting, that has preferential claims (usually to dividends) over common stock.

Premium on Bonds Payable A liability account that represents reductions in the stated rate of interest.

prepaid items Deferred expenses. An example is prepaid insurance.

present value A measure of the value today of an amount of money expected to be exchanged on a specified future date.

pressure An element of the fraud triangle that recognizes conditions that motivate fraudulent or unethical behavior.

price-earnings (P/E) ratio Measure that reflects the values of different stocks in terms of earnings; calculated as market price per share divided by earnings (net income) per share; a higher P/E ratio generally indicates that investors are optimistic about a company's future.

primary securities market Market in which investee companies issue debt and equity securities to investors in exchange for assets; contrast with *secondary securities market*.

principal Amount of cash actually borrowed, to be repaid in the future with interest.

procedures manual Written documentation of a company's accounting policies and procedures.

proceeds The amount of cash received. An example is the principal amount borrowed on a discount note payable.

product costs All costs directly traceable to acquiring inventory and getting it ready for sale, including transportation-in. Contrast with *selling and administrative costs*.

profit Value added by transforming resources into products or services desired by customers.

profitability ratios Measurements of a firm's ability to generate earnings.

promissory note A legal document representing a credit agreement between a lender and a borrower. The note specifies technical details such as the maker, payee, interest rate, maturity date, payment terms, and any collateral.

property, plant, and equipment Assets such as machinery and equipment, buildings, and land used to produce products or to carry on the administrative and selling functions of a business; sometimes called *plant assets*.

purchase discount Reduction in the gross price of merchandise offered to a buyer if the buyer pays cash for the merchandise within a stated time (usually within 10 days of the date of the sale).

Purchase Returns and Allowances A reduction in the cost of purchases resulting from dissatisfaction with merchandise purchased.

qualified opinion Opinion issued by a certified public accountant that means the company's financial statements are, for the most part, in compliance with GAAP, but there is some circumstance (explained in the auditor's report) about which the auditor has reservations; contrast with *unqualified opinion*.

quick ratio Measure of immediate debt-paying ability; calculated by dividing very liquid assets (cash, receivables, and marketable securities) by current liabilities.

ratio analysis Analysis of relationships between two different items to draw conclusions or make decisions.

rationalization An element of the fraud triangle that recognizes a human tendency to justify fraudulent or unethical behavior.

reinstate Recording an account receivable previously written off back into the accounting records, generally when cash is collected long after the original due date.

relative market value method Method of allocating the purchase price among individual assets acquired in a basket purchase; each asset is assigned a percentage of the total price paid for all assets. The percentage assigned equals the market value of a particular asset divided by the total of the market values of all assets acquired in the basket purchase.

reporting entities Businesses or other organizations for which financial statements are prepared.

restrictive covenants Provisions specified in a loan agreement that are designed to reduce creditor risk, such as limiting additional borrowing or dividend payments.

retail companies Businesses that sell merchandise directly to consumers.

retained earnings Portion of stockholders' equity that includes all earnings retained in the business since inception (revenues minus expenses and distributions for all accounting periods).

return on investment (ROI) Measure of profitability based on the asset base of the firm; calculated as net income divided by average total assets. ROI is a product of net margin and asset turnover.

return on sales Profitability measure that reflects the percentage of net income each sales dollar generates; computed by dividing net income by net sales. Also called *net income percentage*.

return-on-assets ratio Profitability measure based on earnings a company generates relative to its asset base; calculated as net income divided by average total assets.

return-on-equity (ROE) ratio Profitability measure based on earnings a company generates relative to its stockholders' equity; calculated as net income divided by average stockholders' equity.

revenue The economic benefit (increase in assets or decrease in liabilities) gained by providing goods or services to customers.

revenue expenditures Costs incurred for repair or maintenance of long-term assets: recorded as expense and subtracted from revenue in the accounting period in which incurred.

salaries A term used to describe the amount due employees who are paid a set amount per week, month, or other earnings period regardless of how many hours they work during the period.

salaries payable   Amounts owed but not yet paid to employees for services they have already performed.

sales discount   Cash discount offered by the seller of merchandise to encourage a customer to pay promptly. When the customer takes the discount and pays less than the original selling price, the difference between the selling price and the cash collected is the sales discount.

sales returns and allowances   A reduction in sales revenue resulting from dissatisfaction with merchandise sold.

salvage value   Expected selling price of an asset at the end of its useful life.

Sarbanes–Oxley   Act of 2002 Federal legislation enacted to promote ethical corporate governance and fair financial reporting. The act requires a company's chief executive officer (CEO) and chief financial officer (CFO) to certify in writing that the financial reports being issued present fairly the company's financial status. An executive who falsely certifies the company's financial reports is subject to significant fines and imprisonment. The act also establishes the Public Company Accounting Oversight Board (PCAOB), which has the primary responsibility for developing and enforcing auditing standards for CPAs who audit SEC companies. The Sarbanes–Oxley Act also prohibits auditors from providing most types of nonaudit services to companies they audit.

schedule of cost of goods sold   Internal report used with the periodic inventory system that reflects the computation of cost of goods sold.

secondary securities market   Market in which investors exchange securities with each other; contrast with *primary securities market*.

secured bonds   Bonds secured by specific identifiable assets.

Securities Act of 1933   Federal legislation passed after the stock market crash of 1929 to regulate the issuance and subsequent trading of public company stocks and bonds; created the Securities and Exchange Commission (SEC).

Securities and Exchange Commission (SEC)   Federal agency authorized by Congress to establish financial reporting practices of public companies; requires companies that issue securities to the public to file audited financial statements with the government annually.

Securities Exchange Act of 1934   See *Securities Act of 1933.*

segregation of duties   Internal control feature of assigning the functions of authorization, recording, and custody to different individuals.

selling and administrative costs   Costs such as advertising expense and rent expense that cannot be directly traced to inventory; recognized as expenses in the period in which they are incurred. Contrast with *product costs.*

serial bonds   Bonds that mature at specified intervals throughout the life of the total issue.

service businesses   Organizations such as accounting and legal firms, dry cleaners, and insurance companies that provide services to consumers.

service charges   Fees charged by a bank for such things as services performed or penalties for overdrawn accounts or failure to maintain a specified minimum cash balance.

shrinkage   Decreases in inventory for reasons other than sales to customers.

signature card   Bank form that documents the bank account number and signatures of persons authorized to write checks on an account.

simple interest   Interest computed by multiplying the principal by the interest rate by the number of periods. Previously earned interest is not added to the principal, so no interest is earned on the interest of past periods. Contrast with *compound interest.*

single-step income statement   Income statement format that presents net income in one step, the difference between total revenues and total expenses. Contrast with *multistep income statement.*

sinking fund   Fund to which the bond issuer contributes cash annually to ensure sufficient funds will be available to pay the face amount on the maturity date.

Social Security   Insurance provided by the federal government to qualified individuals. Also called old age, survivors, and disability insurance (OASDI).

sole proprietorship   Business (usually small) owned by one person.

solvency   Ability of a business to pay liabilities in the long run.

solvency ratios   Measures of a firm's long-term debt-paying ability.

source document   Record such as a cash register tape, invoice, time card, or check stub that provides accounting information to be recorded in the accounting journals and ledgers.

special journals   Journals designed to improve recording efficiency for specific routine, high-volume transactions such as credit sales.

specific authorizations   Policies and procedures that apply to designated levels of management, such as the policy that only the plant manager can authorize overtime pay.

specific identification   Inventory costing method in which cost of goods sold and ending inventory are computed using the actual costs of the specific goods sold or those on hand at the end of the period.

spread   Difference between the rate a bank pays to obtain money (e.g., interest paid on savings accounts) and the rate the bank earns on money it lends to borrowers.

stakeholders   Parties interested in the operations of a business, including owners, lenders, employees, suppliers, customers, and government agencies.

stated interest rate   Rate of interest specified in the bond contract that is the percentage of face value used to calculate the amount of interest paid in cash at specified intervals over the life of the bond.

stated value   Arbitrary value assigned to stock by the board of directors; like *par value*, designates *legal capital.*

statement of cash flows   The financial statement that reports a company's cash inflows and outflows for an accounting period, classifying them as operating, investing, or financing activities.

statement of changes in stockholders' equity   Statement that summarizes the transactions that affected the owners' equity during the accounting period.

stewardship   Refers to a business's duty to protect and use the assets of the company for the benefit of the owners (the firm's stockholders).

stock certificate   Document showing ownership interest issued to an investor in exchange for contributing assets to a corporation; describes ownership rights and privileges.

stock dividend   Proportionate distribution of additional shares of the declaring corporation's stock.

stock split   Corporate action that proportionately reduces the par value and increases the number of outstanding shares; designed to reduce the market value of the split stock.

stockholders   Owners of a corporation.

stockholders' equity   The interest in a corporation's assets that is owned by the stockholders.

straight-line amortization   Method of amortization in which equal amounts of the account being reduced (e.g., Bond Discount, Bond Premium, Patent) are transferred to the appropriate expense account over the relevant time period.

straight-line depreciation   Depreciation computations that produce equal amounts of depreciation to allocate to expense each period over an asset's life; computed by subtracting the salvage value from the asset's cost and then dividing by the number of years of useful life.

subordinated debentures   Unsecured bonds with a lower claim on assets than general creditors; in the case of liquidation, holders are paid off after the general creditors are paid.

subsidiary company   Company controlled (more than 50 percent owned) by another company.

T-account   Simple account representation, using two bars arranged in the form of the letter "T." The account title is written across the top on the horizontal bar, debit entries are recorded on the left side of the vertical bar, and credit entries on the right side.

tangible assets   Assets that have physical form, such as equipment, machinery, natural resources, and land.

temporary accounts   Accounts used to collect retained earnings data applicable to only the current accounting period (revenues, expenses and distributions); sometimes called *nominal accounts*.

term bonds   Bonds in an issue that mature on a specified date in the future.

times-interest-earned ratio   Ratio that measures a company's ability to make its interest payments; calculated by dividing the amount of earnings available for interest payments (net income before interest and income taxes) by the amount of the interest payments.

trademark   Name or symbol that identifies a company or an individual product.

trading securities   Classification for marketable securities companies plan to buy and sell quickly to generate profits from short-term appreciation in stock and bond prices.

transaction   Business event that involves transferring something of value between two entities.

transferability   Characteristic of corporations referring to the ease of exchanging ownership interests since ownership is divided into small, readily traded ownership units (shares of stock).

transportation-in (freight-in)   Cost of freight on goods purchased under FOB shipping point terms; a product cost usually added to the cost of inventory.

transportation-out (freight-out)   Freight cost for goods delivered to customers under FOB destination terms; a period cost expensed when incurred.

treasury stock   Stock previously issued to the public that the issuing corporation has bought back. Contrast with *outstanding stock*.

trend analysis   Study of the performance of a business over a period of time.

trial balance   Schedule listing the balances of all ledger accounts; verifies mathematical accuracy of the accounting records and provides a convenient reference of current account balances.

true cash balance   Actual amount of cash owned by a company at the close of business on the date of the bank statement.

unadjusted bank balance   Depositor's cash balance reported by the bank as of the date of the bank statement.

unadjusted book balance   Cash account balance in the depositor's accounting records as of the date of the bank reconciliation before making any adjustments.

uncollectible accounts expense   Expense associated with uncollectible accounts receivable; amount recognized may be estimated using the allowance method, or actual losses may be recorded using the direct write-off method. In practice, the **uncollectible accounts expense** is frequently called **bad debts expense**.

unearned revenue   Liability arising when customers pay cash in advance for services a business will perform in the future.

units-of-production depreciation   Depreciation computations that produce varying amounts of depreciation based on the level of an asset's usage each period rather than a measure of time; for example, automobile depreciation may be based on total estimated miles to be driven rather than total estimated years to be used.

unqualified opinion   Opinion issued by a certified public accountant that means the company's financial statements are, in all material respects, in compliance with GAAP; the auditor has no reservations. Contrast with *qualified opinion*.

unrealized gains or losses   Paper gains or losses on investment securities the company still owns; not realized until the securities are sold or otherwise disposed of.

unsecured bonds (debentures)   Bonds backed by the general credit of the organization.

unsubordinated debentures   Unsecured bonds with claims on assets equal to those of general creditors.

useful life   The period of time over which an asset is expected to be used in the normal operation of a business.

users   Individuals or organizations that use financial information for decision making.

variable interest rate   Interest rate that fluctuates (changes) from period to period over the life of the loan.

vertical analysis   Analysis technique that compares items on financial statements to significant totals.

Wage and Tax Statement, Form W-2   Form used by employers to notify each employee of the amount of his or her gross earnings for the year and the amounts withheld by the employer.

wages   A term used to describe amounts due employees who are paid according to the number of hours they actually work.

warranties   Promises to correct deficiencies or dissatisfactions in quality, quantity, or performance of products or services sold.

weighted-average cost flow method   Inventory cost flow method in which the cost allocated between inventory and cost of goods sold is based on the weighted average cost per unit, which is determined by dividing the total cost of goods available for sale during the accounting period by the total units available for sale during the period. If the weighted average is recomputed with each successive purchase, the result is a moving average.

wholesale companies   Companies that sell goods to other businesses.

withdrawals   Distributions of assets to the owners of proprietorships and partnerships.

working capital   Current assets minus current liabilities.

working capital ratio   Another term for the current ratio; calculated by dividing current assets by current liabilities.

INDEX